P9-DFN-212

Consumer Behavior

Building Marketing Strategy 9/e

McGraw-Hill/Irwin Series in Marketing

Hawkins | Best | Coney

CONSUMER BEHAVIOR

ninth edition

Building **Marketing** Strategy

Consumer Behavior

Building Marketing Strategy 9/e

Del I. Hawkins
University of Oregon

Roger J. Best
University of Oregon

Kenneth A. Coney
Late of Arizona State University

Contributing Author
Eric C. Koch
Texas Tech University

 Irwin

Boston   Burr Ridge, IL   Dubuque, IA   Madison, WI   New York   San Francisco   St. Louis
Bangkok   Bogotá   Caracas   Kuala Lumpur   Lisbon   London   Madrid   Mexico City
Milan   Montreal   New Delhi   Santiago   Seoul   Singapore   Sydney   Taipei   Toronto

CONSUMER BEHAVIOR: BUILDING MARKETING STRATEGY

Published by McGraw-Hill/Irwin, a business unit of The McGraw-Hill Companies, Inc.,
1221 Avenue of the Americas, New York, NY, 10020. Copyright © 2004, 2001, 1998,
1995, 1992, 1989, 1986, 1983, 1980 by The McGraw-Hill Companies, Inc. All rights
reserved. No part of this publication may be reproduced or distributed in any form or by any
means, or stored in a database or retrieval system, without the prior written consent of
The McGraw-Hill Companies, Inc., including, but not limited to, in any network or other
electronic storage or transmission, or broadcast for distance learning.

Some ancillaries, including electronic and print components, may not be available to
customers outside the United States.

This book is printed on acid-free paper.

domestic   1 2 3 4 5 6 7 8 9 0 DOW/DOW 0 9 8 7 6 5 4 3
international 1 2 3 4 5 6 7 8 9 0 DOW/DOW 0 9 8 7 6 5 4 3

ISBN 0-07-253686-1

Publisher: *John E. Biernat*
Associate sponsoring editor: *Barrett Koger*
Editorial coordinator: *Scott Becker*
Marketing manager: *Kim Kanakes*
Media producer: *Craig Atkins*
Senior project manager: *Kari Geltemeyer*
Production supervisor: *Gina Hangos*
Coordinator freelance design: *Artemio Ortiz Jr.*
Photo research coordinator: *Jeremy Cheshareck*
Photo researcher: *Mike Hruby*
Lead supplement producer: *Cathy L. Tepper*
Senior digital content specialist: *Brian Nacik*
Cover design: *Asylum Studios*
Interior design: *Artemio Ortiz Jr.*
Typeface: *10/12 Times Roman*
Compositor: *Interactive Composition Corporation*
Printer: *R. R. Donnelley*

Library of Congress Cataloging-in-Publication Data

Hawkins, Del I.
    Consumer behavior : building market strategy / Del I. Hawkins, Roger J. Best,
Kenneth A. Coney.—9th ed.
        p. cm. — (McGraw-Hill/Irwin series in marketing)
    Includes bibliographical references and indexes.
        ISBN 0-07-253686-1 (alk. paper) — ISBN 0-07-121469-0 (international : alk. paper)
        1. Consumer behavior—United States. 2. Market surveys—United States. 3. Consumer
behavior—United States—Case studies. I. Best, Roger J. II. Coney, Kenneth A. III. Title.
IV. Series.
    HF5415.33.U6H38 2004
    658.8'342'0973—dc21
                                                                    2003041331

INTERNATIONAL EDITION ISBN 0-07-121469-0
Copyright © 2004. Exclusive rights by The McGraw-Hill Companies, Inc. for manufacture and export.
This book cannot be re-exported from the country to which it is sold by McGraw-Hill.
The International Edition is not available in North America.

www.mhhe.com

Preface

Marketing attempts to influence the way consumers behave. These attempts have implications for the organizations making the attempt, the consumers they are trying to influence, and the society in which these attempts occur. We are all consumers and we are all members of society, so consumer behavior, and attempts to influence it, are critical to all of us. This text is designed to provide an understanding of consumer behavior. This understanding can make us better consumers, better marketers, and better citizens.

MARKETING CAREERS AND CONSUMER BEHAVIOR

A primary purpose of this text is to provide the student with a usable, managerial understanding of consumer behavior. Most students in consumer behavior courses aspire to careers in marketing management, sales, or advertising. They hope to acquire knowledge and skills that will be useful to them in these careers. Unfortunately, some may be seeking the type of knowledge gained in introductory accounting classes; that is, a set of relatively invariant rules that can be applied across a variety of situations to achieve a fixed solution that is known to be correct. For these students, the uncertainty and lack of closure involved in dealing with living, breathing, changing, stubborn consumers can be very frustrating. However, if they can accept dealing with endless uncertainty, utilizing an understanding of consumer behavior in developing marketing strategy will become tremendously exciting.

It is our view that the utilization of knowledge of consumer behavior in the development of marketing strategy is an art. This is not to suggest that scientific principles and procedures are not applicable; rather, it means that the successful application of these principles to particular situations requires human judgment that we are not able to reduce to a fixed set of rules.

Let us consider the analogy with art in some detail. Suppose you want to become an expert artist. You would study known principles of the visual effects of blending various colors, of perspective, and so forth.

Then you would practice applying these principles until you developed the ability to produce acceptable paintings. If you had certain natural talents, the right teacher, and the right topic, you might even produce a masterpiece. The same approach should be taken by one wishing to become a marketing manager, a salesperson, or an advertising director. The various factors or principles that influence consumer behavior should be thoroughly studied. Then, one should practice applying these principles until acceptable marketing strategies result. However, while knowledge and practice can in general produce acceptable strategies, great marketing strategies, like masterpieces, require special talents, effort, timing, and some degree of luck (what if Mona Lisa had not wanted her portrait painted?).

The art analogy is useful for another reason. All of us, professors and students alike, tend to ask, "How can I use the concept of, say, social class to develop a successful marketing strategy?" This makes as much sense as an artist asking, "How can I use blue to create a great picture?" Obviously, blue alone will seldom be sufficient for a great work of art. Instead, to be successful, the artist must understand when and how to use blue in conjunction with other elements in the picture. Likewise, the marketing manager must understand when and how to use a knowledge of social class in conjunction with a knowledge of other factors in designing a successful marketing strategy.

This book is based on the belief that knowledge of the factors that influence consumer behavior can, with practice, be used to develop sound marketing strategy. With this in mind, we have attempted to do three things. First, we present a reasonably comprehensive description of the various behavioral concepts and theories that have been found useful for understanding consumer behavior. This is generally done at the beginning of each chapter or at the beginning of major subsections in each chapter. We believe that a person must have a thorough understanding of a concept in order to successfully apply that concept across different situations.

Second, we present examples of how these concepts have been utilized in the development of marketing strategy. We have tried to make clear that these examples are not "how you use this concept." Rather, they are presented as "how one organization facing a particular marketing situation used this concept."

Third, at the end of each chapter and each major section, we present a number of questions, activities, or cases that require the student to apply the concepts.

CONSUMING AND CONSUMER BEHAVIOR

The authors of this book are consumers, as is everyone reading this text. Most of us spend more time buying and consuming than we do working or sleeping. We consume products such as cars and fuel, services such as haircuts and home repairs, and entertainment such as television and concerts. Given the time and energy we devote to consuming, we should strive to be good at it. A knowledge of consumer behavior can be used to enhance our ability to consume wisely.

Marketers spend billions of dollars attempting to influence what, when, and how you and I consume. Marketers not only spend billions attempting to influence our behavior but also spend hundreds of millions of dollars studying our behavior. With a knowledge of consumer behavior and an understanding of how marketers use this knowledge, we can study marketers. A television commercial can be an annoying interruption of a favorite program. However, it can also be a fascinating opportunity to speculate on the commercial's objective, target audience, and the underlying behavior assumptions. Indeed, given the ubiquitous nature of commercials, an understanding of how they are attempting to influence us or others is essential to understand our environment.

Throughout the text, we present examples that illustrate the objectives of specific marketing activities. By studying these examples and the principles on which they are based, one can develop the ability to discern the underlying logic of the marketing activities encountered daily.

SOCIAL RESPONSIBILITY AND CONSUMER BEHAVIOR

Should commercial sites on the World Wide Web (Internet) that focus on children be strictly regulated, banned completely, or left alone? This issue is currently the source of a major debate. As educated citizens, we have a responsibility to take part in this debate and to

influence its outcome. Developing a sound position on this issue requires an understanding of children's information processing as it relates to advertising—an important part of our understanding of consumer behavior.

The debate described above is only one of many that require an understanding of consumer behavior. We present a number of these topics throughout the text. The objective is to develop the ability to apply consumer behavior knowledge to social and regulatory issues as well as to business and personal issues.

FEATURES OF THE NINTH EDITION

Marketing and consumer behavior, like the rest of the world, is changing at a rapid pace. Both the way consumers behave and the practices of studying that behavior continue to evolve. In order to keep up with this dynamic environment, the ninth edition includes a number of important features.

Internet and Technology Applications

The Internet and technology are rapidly changing many aspects of consumer behavior. We have integrated the latest research and practices concerning the Internet and technology throughout the text and the cases.

More Global Examples

Although previous editions have included a wealth of global material, this edition further integrates this important area. Most chapters contain multiple global examples woven into the text. In addition, Chapter 2 and several of the cases are devoted to global issues.

CHAPTER FEATURES

Each chapter contains a variety of features designed to enhance students' understanding of the material as well as to make the material more fun.

Opening Vignettes

Each chapter begins with a practical example that introduces the material in the chapter. These involve situations in which businesses, government units, or nonprofit organizations have used or misused consumer behavior principles.

Consumer Insights

These boxed discussions provide an in-depth look at a particularly interesting consumer study or marketing practice. Each has several questions with it that are designed to encourage critical thinking by the students.

Integrated Coverage Ethical/Social Issues

Marketers face numerous ethical issues as they apply their understanding of consumer behavior in the marketplace. We describe and discuss many of these issues. These discussions are highlighted in the text via ethical issues in the margin. In addition, Chapter 20 is devoted to the consumerism movement and the regulation of marketing practice. Several of the cases are also focused on ethical or regulatory issues, including all of the cases following Part Six.

Internet Exercises

The Internet is rapidly becoming both a major source of data on consumer behavior and a medium in which marketers use their knowledge of consumer behavior to influence consumers. A section at the end of each chapter has Internet assignments. These serve two purposes. One is to teach students how to use the Internet as a research tool to learn about consumers and consumer behavior. The second purpose is to enhance students' understanding of how marketers are approaching consumers using this medium.

DDB Needham Lifestyle Data Analyses

Each relevant chapter poses a series of questions that require students to analyze data from the annual DDB Needham Lifestyle survey. These data are available in spreadsheet format on the disk that accompanies this text. These exercises increase students' data analysis skills as well as their understanding of consumer behavior.

Four-Color Illustrations

Print ads, Web pages, storyboards, and photos of point-of-purchase displays and packages appear throughout the text. Each is directly linked to the text material both by text references to each illustration and by the descriptive comments that accompany each illustration.

Review Questions

The review questions at the end of each chapter allow students or the instructor to test the acquisition of the facts contained in the chapter. The questions require memorization, which we believe is an important, though insufficient, part of learning.

Discussion Questions

These questions can be used to help develop or test the students' understanding of the material in the chapter. Answering these questions requires the student to utilize the material in the chapter to reach a recommendation or solution. However, they can be answered without external activities such as customer interviews; therefore, they can be assigned as in-class activities.

Application Activities

The final learning aid at the end of each chapter is a set of application exercises. These require the students to utilize the material in the chapter in conjunction with external activities such as visiting stores to observe point-of-purchase displays, interviewing customers or managers, or evaluating television ads. They range in complexity from short evening assignments to term projects.

OTHER LEARNING AIDS IN THE TEXT

Three useful sets of learning material are presented outside the chapter format—cases, an overview of consumer research methods, and a format for a consumer behavior audit.

Cases

There are cases at the end of each major section of the text except the first. Many of the cases can be read in class and used to generate discussion of a particular topic. Students like this approach, and many instructors find it a useful way to motivate class discussion.

Other cases are more complex and data intense. They require several hours of effort to analyze. Still others can serve as the basis for a term project. We have used several cases in this manner with success (the assignment is to develop a marketing plan clearly identifying the consumer behavior constructs that underlie the plan).

Each case can be approached from a variety of angles. A number of discussion questions are provided with each case. However, many other questions can be used. In fact, while the cases are placed at the end of the major sections, most lend themselves to discussion at other points in the text as well.

Consumer Research Methods Overview

Appendix A provides a brief overview of the more commonly used research methods in consumer behavior. While not a substitute for a course or text in marketing research, it is a useful review for students who have completed a research course. It can also serve to provide students who have not had such a course with relevant terminology and a very basic understanding of the process and major techniques involved in consumer research.

Consumer Behavior Audit

Appendix B provides a format for doing a consumer behavior audit for a proposed marketing strategy. This audit is basically a list of key consumer behavior questions that should be answered for every proposed marketing strategy. Many students have found it particularly useful if a term project relating consumer behavior to a firm's actual or proposed strategy is required.

SUPPLEMENTAL LEARNING MATERIALS

We have developed a variety of learning materials to enhance the student's learning experience and to facilitate the instructor's teaching activities. Please contact your local Irwin/McGraw-Hill sales representative for assistance in obtaining ancillaries. Or contact us directly at our website, www.mhhe.com.

DDB Needham Lifestyle Data Analyses Disk

A disk accompanying the text contains data in spreadsheet format from the annual DDB Needham Lifestyle survey. It enables students to access consumer market data and draw marketing strategy recommendations based on these data.

Instructor's Manual

The Instructor's Manual contains suggestions for teaching the course, learning objectives for each chapter, additional material for presentation, lecture tips and aids, answers to the end-of-chapter questions, suggested case teaching approaches, and discussion guides for each case.

Test Bank and Computerized Test Bank

A test bank of more than 1,500 multiple-choice questions accompanies the text. These questions cover all the chapters, including the material in the opening vignettes and in the Consumer Insights. The questions are coded according to degree of difficulty. A computerized version is available in MAC, DOS, and Windows platforms.

Four-Color Acetates

A packet of 70 four-color acetates of ads, picture boards, point-of-purchase displays, and so forth is available to adopters. These acetates are keyed to specific chapters in the text. The Instructor's Manual relates the acetates to the relevant concepts in the text.

Video Cases

A set of video cases is available to adopters. These videos describe firm strategies or activities that relate to material in the text. A guide for teaching from the videos is contained in the Instructor's Manual.

Electronic Slides

Available on both the Instructor's CD-ROM and the text website, the more than 350 PowerPoint slides feature key figures from the text as well as additional images to accompany the ninth edition.

CD-ROM Presentation Manager

This instructor CD-ROM contains PowerPoint electronic slides, video clips, advertisements from the text, plus many nontext ads, the Instructor's Manual, and the test bank. This supplement is available to adopters of the text.

Website

The book-specific Online Learning center located at www.mhhe.com/hawkins09 offers comprehensive classroom support by providing resources for both instructors and students. For instructors, it gives access to downloadable teaching supplements (Instructor's Manual and PowerPoint slides), resource links, and PageOut. For students, it offers resource links and quizzes for self-testing.

ACKNOWLEDGMENTS

We enjoy studying, teaching, consulting, and writing about consumer behavior. Most of the faculty we know feel the same. As with every edition, we have tried to make this a book that students would enjoy reading and that would get them excited about a fascinating topic.

Numerous individuals and organizations helped us in the task of writing this edition. We are grateful for their assistance and would like to thank the many members of the McGraw-Hill Higher Education team, including Barrett Koger, Scott Becker, Kari Geltemeyer, Artemio Ortiz, Craig Akins, Jeremy Cheshareck, Cathy Tepper, Mike Hruby, and Dorothy Wendel. Particular thanks are also due to the many people who helped us in the development of this text. We believe that the ninth edition is improved because of your efforts: Bob Ahuja, Xavier University; Jeri Beggs, Indiana University; James Cagley, University of Tulsa; Michael Fitzmorris, Park University; Ronald Goldsmith, Florida State University; Norman Humble, Kirkwood Community College; Jane Kolodinsky, University of Vermont; Lois Mohr, Georgia State University; Peter Ochlkers, Emerson College; Kay Palan, Iowa State University; Edward Riordan, Wayne State University; Raymond Taylor, Louisiana State University—Shreveport; Janet Wagner, University of Maryland; and Michael Walsh, University of Pittsburgh.

Our colleagues at Oregon—David Boush, Marian Friestad, Dennis Howard, Lynn Kahle, Bob Madrigal, Simona Stan, and Peter Wright—generously responded to our requests for assistance. All should be held blameless for our inability to fully incorporate their ideas.

The text would have had higher quality, been more fun to read, and been much more fun to write had Ken Coney been able to write it with us. Once again, this edition is dedicated to his memory. By his life he said to us

Cherish your dreams
Guard your ideals
Enjoy life
Seek the best
Climb your mountains

Del I. Hawkins
Roger J. Best

KNOWING CONSUMER BEHAVIOR

Marketing attempts to influence the way consumers behave. These attempts have implications for the organizations making the attempt, the consumers they are trying to influence, and the society in which these attempts occur. We are all consumers: the authors of this book are consumers, as is everyone reading this text, and we are all members of society, so consumer behavior, and attempts to influence it, are critical to all of us. This text is designed to provide an understanding of consumer behavior. This understanding can make us better consumers, better marketers, and better citizens.

Throughout the text, we present examples that illustrate the objectives of specific marketing activities. By studying these examples and the principles on which they are based, one can develop the ability to discern the underlying logic of the marketing activities encountered daily. Given the time and energy we devote to consuming, we should strive to be good at it, and a knowledge of consumer behavior can be used to enhance our ability to consume wisely.

Opening Vignette

The chapter openers feature vignettes that focus on practical examples that introduce the consumer behavior concepts covered in the chapter.

420

This is not THE VERY LATEST IN VIRTUAL REALITY.

THIS IS RIDING THE RAPIDS LIVE AND IN PERSON IN ARIZONA, WHERE OUTDOOR ENTHUSIASTS CAN INDULGE IN THE GAME OF LIFE TO THE ABSOLUTE FULLEST — IN A WORLD THAT PUTS VIRTUAL REALITY TO SHAME.

FOR YOUR FREE TRAVEL PACKET, CONTACT THE ARIZONA OFFICE OF TOURISM AT 1-800-451-6056 OR VISIT ARIZONAGUIDE.COM

ARIZONA
GRAND CANYON STATE

Courtesy Arizona Office of Tourism; photo by Kerrick James.

Four-Color Illustrations

Print ads, web pages, storyboards, and photos of point-of-purchase displays and packages appear throughout the text.

ILLUSTRATION 7–1
Clothing styles originating in consumption subcultures for functional or symbolic reasons are often adopted by other groups as well. Surfers have initiated several styles that gained widespread popularity.

Rietveld

Illustrations in ad by Rick Rietveld; advertising design and layout by Rick Rietveld; © Rietveld, USA.

Part-Ending Cases

There are cases at the end of each major section of the text that can be approached from a variety of angles. They can be utilized for class discussion, more intense efforts of analysis, or as the basis for a term project.

part two

Cases

2–1 Norelco's Advantage Razor Introduction

While electric razors represent a $400 million market, less than a third of U.S. males use electric shavers, and only one in seven females use them. Norelco dominates the market, followed by Remington, Braun, and Panasonic.

In the early 1990s, electric razor marketers sharply increased their marketing efforts, but this had little impact on electric razors' share of shavers. In fact, the percentage of both men and women using electric razors declined slightly between 1991 and 1993. By 1996, Norelco had well over 50 percent of the $400 million plus electric market. In late 1996, Pat Dinley, Norelco's president, described the firm's new approach:

In 1998, Philips Electronics, Norelco's parent company, made two major moves. First, it focused Norelco strictly on men's products. Women's electric razors and other products targeting women were redesigned and introduced under the Philips Personal Care name.

Norelco then launched a new flagship razor, the Advantage. The Advantage has a Nivea for Men shaving lotion cartridge built inside the razor chamber. This unique system dispenses the lotion while shaving, offering a wet shave experience without the hassle associated with water and lather. The razor comes with five lotion cartridges, can be used wet or dry, and can be rinsed clean with tap

elf-Concept
nd Lifestyle

chapter 12

arketing study identified five ner lifestyles in relation to r activities.[1] Each of these s is described briefly below. *citement-seeking competitives* percent). Like risk, some nger, and competition, though y also like social and fitness nefits. Participate in team and ividual competitive sports. Half ong to a sports club or team. dian age of 32, two-thirds are le. Upper-middle class, and ut half are single. *away actives* (33 percent). e the opportunity to be alone experience nature. Active amping, fishing, and watch families outdo

stress. Median age of 35, equally divided between men and women.
- *Fitness-driven* (10 percent). Engage in outdoor activities strictly for fitness benefits. Walking, bicycling, and jogging are popular activities. Upscale economically. Median age of 46, over half are women.
- *Health-conscious sociables* (33 percent). Relatively inactive despite stated health concerns. Most involved with spectator activities such as sightseeing, driving for pleasure, visiting zoos, and so forth. Median age 49, two-thirds are female.

Ethical/Social Issues

The discussions regarding the numerous ethical issues facing marketers are highlighted in the margin throughout the text.

What Are the Ethical Implications of Marketing This Product in This Country?
All marketing programs should be evaluated on ethical as well as financial dimensions. As discussed at the beginning of the chapter, international marketing activities raise many ethical issues. The ethical dimension is particularly important and complex in marketing to Third World and developing countries. Consider Kellogg's attempt to introduce cold cereal as a breakfast food in Brazil. The following questions represent the type of ethical analysis that should go into such a decision:

- If we succeed, will the average nutrition level be increased or decreased?
- If we succeed, will the funds spent on cereal be diverted from other uses with more beneficial long-term impacts for the individuals or society?
- If we succeed, what impact will this have on the local producers of currently consumed breakfast products?

DDB Needham Lifestyle Data Analysis

Each relevant chapter poses a series of questions geared toward helping students increase their data analysis skills as well as their understanding of consumer behavior.

DDB NEEDHAM LIFESTYLE DATA ANALYSES

1. Use the DDB Needham data to determine the characteristics of likely innovators for the following. Why is this the case? What are the marketing implications?
   a. Foods
   b. New products in general
2. Based on the DDB Needham data, what characterizes one who is likely to be an opinion

leader for new movies? Why is this the case? What are the marketing implications?
3. What characterizes one who is likely to be a late adopter or laggard for many items (see Tables 1a, 2a, 3a, 4a, 5a, 6a, and 7a)? Why is this the case? What are the marketing implications?

Consumer Insight 4–1

Cognitive Age: As Young as You Feel?

One's age is a chronological fact but, more important, a social construct.[23] That is, the time that has passed since one's birth is directly observable and uniform. However, the meaning of age, how it is perceived, the behaviors and attitudes expected at differing ages, how one feels about aging, and so forth are constructed by cultures and within cultures by individuals.

I'm not my mother's 52. I'm not in the second half of my life. I'm in the first chapter of a whole new book.

This quote reflects the increasingly recognized fact that, in the United States at least, as consumers' chronological age increases, their subjective or cognitive age lags behind. In fact, for older consumers, cognitive age is often 10 to 15 years less than chronologi-

Respondents are asked to indicate a decade for each question (20s, 30s, 40s, etc.). The midpoint of the decade given in response to each question is used to compute an average age based on the four responses. This is one's cognitive age. Though both the adequacy of this operationalization and the validity of the concept itself have been challenged, it is gaining widespread use in marketing.

While cognitive age varies with chronological age, it is also influenced by such factors as one's health, education, income, and social support—the more of each, the lower the cognitive age. In turn, it affects a wide range of attitudes and consumption behaviors.

Cognitive age, while an artificial concept, is one with which people readily identify. Consumers have no trouble indicating how old they feel rather than how old they "are."

Consumer Insight

These boxed discussions provide an indepth look at a particularly interesting consumer study or marketing practice.

APPLICATION ACTIVITIES

27. Interview five other students and identify three consumer problems they have recognized recently. For each problem, determine
    a. The relative importance of the problem.
    b. How the problem occurred.
    c. What caused the problem (i.e., change in desired or actual states).
    d. What action they have taken.
    e. What action is planned to resolve each problem.

repeat purchases. What characteristics, if any, distinguish the brand loyal products from the repeat products?
31. Find and describe an advertisement or point-of-purchase display that attempts to influence the timing of problem recognition. Evaluate its likely effectiveness.
32. Using two consumers from a relevant market segment, conduct an activity analysis for an activity that interests you. Prepare a report on the market-

End-of-Chapter Materials

At the end of each chapter are a series of learning tools including Internet Exercises, Review Questions, Discussion Questions, and Application Activities.

DDB Needham Lifestyle Data Analyses

DDB Needham Worldwide is one of the leading advertising agencies in the world. One of the many services it provides for its clients as well as to support its own creative and strategy efforts is a major, annual lifestyle survey. This survey is conducted using a panel maintained by Consumer Mail Panel. In a panel such as this, consumers are recruited such that the panel has demographic characteristics similar to the U.S. population. Members of the panel agree to complete questions on a periodic basis.

THE DATA

The Lifestyle study involved more than 3,500 completed questionnaires. These lengthy questionnaires included approximately 200 interest and opinion items (I like to pay cash for everything I buy, I am an avid sports fan); 160 frequency of activity questions (worked in the garden, gambled in a casino), questions on preferred marital style (traditional, modern, or other), more than 200 questions on product purchase and use, approximately 75 questions on product ownership and purchase intentions, more than 100 questions on one's self-concept and ideal self-concept, and numerous questions collecting demographic and media preference data.

DDB Needham has allowed us to provide a portion of these data in spreadsheet format in the disk that accompanies this text. The data are presented in the form of cross-tabulations at an aggregate level with the cell values being percents. For example,

	Household Size			
	1	*2*	*3–5*	*> 5*
Number in sample	550	1,377	1,626	162
Rented a video	7.0%	10.7%	18.8%	20.0%
Used the Internet	6.1	5.6	5.7	1.9
Made pancakes	2.0	5.9	9.5	19.3

The previous example indicates that 7.0 percent of the 550 respondents from one-person households were heavy renters of videos, compared with 10.7 percent of the 1,377 from two-person households, 18.8 percent of those from households with three, four, or five members, and 20.0 percent of those from households with more than five members.

It is possible to combine columns within variables. That is, we can determine the percent of one- and two-person households combined that made pancakes. Because the number of respondents on which the percentages are based differs across columns, we can't simply average the cell percentage figures. Instead, we need to convert the cell percentages to numbers by multiplying each cell percentage times the number in the sample for that column. Add the numbers for the cells to be combined together and divide the result by the sum of the number in the sample for the combined cells' columns. The result is the percentage of the combined column categories that engaged in the behavior of interest.

The data available on the disk are described below.

Column Variables for the Data Tables

Tables

1 & 1A	Household size, marital status, number of children at home, age of youngest child at home, and age of oldest child at home.
2 & 2A	Male's report of female level of employment and motivation for working, female's report of female work level and motivation for working.
3 & 3A	Household income, education level of respondent.
4 & 4A	Occupation.
5 & 5A	Ethnic subculture, age.

6 & 6A   Gender, geographic region.

7 & 7A   Personality/self-concept traits (humorous, friendly, affectionate, dynamic, shy, assertive, sensitive, independent, traditional, romantic, intellectual, competitive).

Row Variables for Tables 1, 2, 3, 4, 5, 6, and 7

Activity

Heavy User   (251 times in last year)

Food delivered to home

Made pancakes

Purchased from mail catalog

Used a price-off coupon at grocery store

Attended a lecture

Went to movies

Took photographs

Used the Internet

Cooked outdoors

Jogged

Visited health club

Rented a video

Car trip over 100 miles

Attended church

Heavy User   (personal use several times a week or more)

Pain relievers

Shower gel

Dandruff shampoo

Lipstick (females)

Presweetened cereal

Cigarettes

Ownership

Personal computer

Camcorder

Microwave oven

Common stock

A handgun

Cellular phone

35mm camera

Favorite Television Shows   (personal preference, not family)

"E.R."

"Melrose Place"

"X-Files"

"Seinfeld"

"Frasier"

"Saturday Night Live"

"David Letterman"

Row Variables for Tables 1A, 2A, 3A, 4A, 5A, 6A, and 7A

Attitudes/Interests/Opinions

I am uncomfortable when the house is not completely clean.

I love to eat different food with interesting flavors.

I usually check ingredient labels when buying food.

I am confused by all the nutrition information that is available today.

I like to cook.

I have trouble getting to sleep.

I work very hard most of the time.

I have a lot of spare time.

When I have a favorite brand I buy it—no matter what else is on sale.

I always check prices even on small items.

I'm willing to pay more to shop at stores where I get better service.

I am usually among the first to try new products.

I make a special effort to buy from companies that support charitable causes.

Our family is too heavily in debt.

Most big companies are just out for themselves.

A drink or two at the end of the day is a perfect way to unwind.

Americans should always buy American products.

I make a strong effort to recycle everything I can.

Everything is changing too fast today.

My greatest achievements are still ahead of me.

Dressing well is an important part of my life.

The car I drive is a reflection of who I am.

I seek out new experiences that are a little frightening or unconventional.

I like the feeling of speed.

Children are the most important thing in a marriage.

A woman's place is in the home.

I think the women's liberation movement is a good thing.

Television is my primary form of entertainment.

I refuse to buy a brand whose advertising I dislike.

TV commercials place too much emphasis on sex.

I like to be among the first to see a new movie.

Personality   (terms that would describe me)

Interesting

Winner

Self-confident

Sexy

Life of the party

Tense

Patient

ACCESSING THE DATA

The data can be used on either a Macintosh or Windows-based machine. Once accessed, you should immediately create a backup copy of all the files either on your hard drive or on another disk.

If you have a Macintosh system 7 or later, you should be able to get an immediate translation of the disk into Macintosh format. If you have an earlier Macintosh system, you may need to run a utility program such as Apple File Exchange to translate the program. Simply follow the instructions that come with this program. Be sure to make a backup copy of the translated files before you begin to work with them.

Contents in Brief

Contents

Consumer Behavior

Building Marketing Strategy 9/e

Introduction

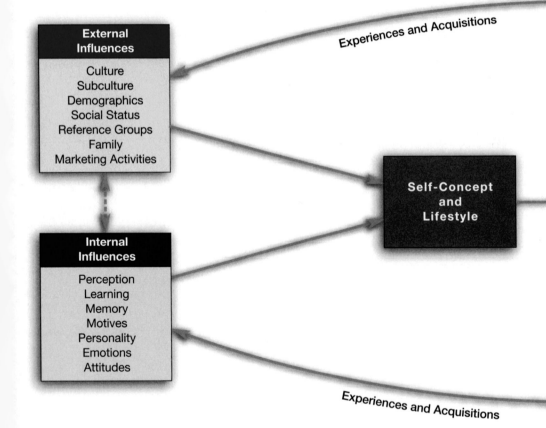

☐ What is consumer behavior? Why should we study it? Do marketing managers, regulators, and consumer advocates actually use knowledge about consumer behavior to develop marketing strategy? Will a sound knowledge of consumer behavior help you in your career? Will it enable you to be a better citizen? How does consumer behavior impact the quality of our lives and environment? How can we organize our knowledge of consumer behavior in order to understand and use it more effectively?

These and a number of other interesting questions are addressed in the first chapter of this text. This chapter describes the importance and usefulness of the material to be covered in the remainder of the text and provides an overview of this material. In addition, the logic of the model of consumer behavior shown on these pages is developed.

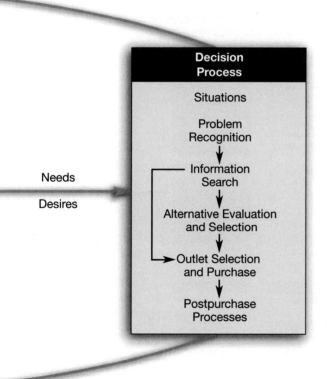

Needs

Desires

Decision Process

Situations

Problem Recognition

Information Search

Alternative Evaluation and Selection

Outlet Selection and Purchase

Postpurchase Processes

3

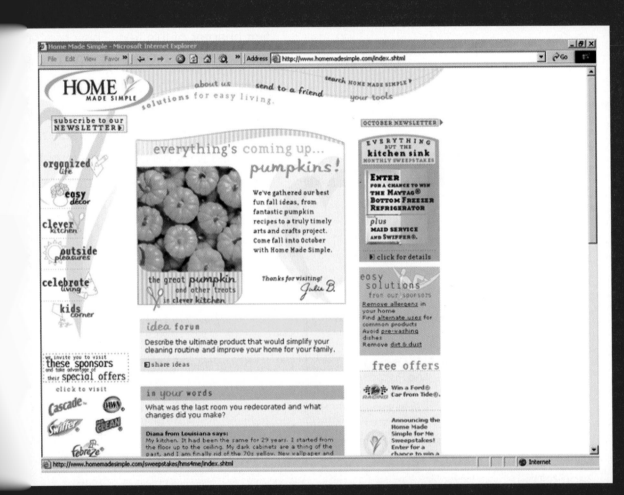

Consumer Behavior and Marketing Strategy

☐ The American Legacy Foundation (www.americanlegacy.org) is the national, independent public health foundation established by the 1998 tobacco settlement. Legacy is dedicated to reducing tobacco use in the United States with major initiatives reaching youth, women, and minority populations through grant awards, research initiatives, marketing campaigns, training programs, and collaboration with national and local partners. It faces the monumental task of convincing people to change addiction-driven behaviors and to prevent young people from consuming a product that often seems glamorous and mature to them. It spends approximately $115 million per year on marketing programs, most of which are aimed at teens.

The foundation's Truth campaign has used humor, shock tactics, and appeals to peer pressure to influence teenagers. It airs television and print ads, and sponsors a tour, a website, and activities by teenagers to call attention to facts about smoking. For example, in Miami teens put small signs next to dog poop on city streets that stated: "Ammonia is found in dog poop. Tobacco companies add it to cigarettes."

☐ The Center for Media Education released a report entitled *Web of Deception: Threats to Children from Online Marketing*. This report unleashed a barrage of calls for regulation of marketing practices on the World Wide Web. A press release from the National PTA stated in part: "The National PTA joins the Center for

Media Education and others this morning in sounding the alarm—Madison Avenue is once again 'giving kids the business,' and this time it's on the Internet and the World Wide Web. Parents and families beware!!! The wires of the next generation of telecommunications are barely warm, but the advertising targeted at children is heating up." A similar release from the Consumer Federation of America proposed that: "This emerging issue will require increased protection by the government and increased vigilance by parents. [While] our children are fearless when sitting in front of a computer, [they] are very vulnerable. They are not sophisticated consumers. . . . They have little experience or knowledge about how marketers operate."

The American Academy of Child and Adolescent Psychiatry's statement concluded: "We know that children are gullible and that advertising targeted at children can be very powerful. In the isolated world of cyberspace, where a child is interacting with a computer, a child becomes much more vulnerable to manipulation from promotional programs that promise rewards for compliance with requests for information. . . . [V]ulnerable children are unable to understand the consequences of choices made in response to computerized prompts which entice

them to advance through the program, much like the computer games with which they are familiar. Children isolated on-line are highly vulnerable to the clever manipulations of the very compelling advertising practices in cyberspace."

One result of this report, and other studies, was the passage of the Children's Online Privacy Protection Act (COPPA). ☐ Procter & Gamble created the disposable diaper market in Japan when it introduced Pampers. The product was an unmodified version of the American product and was marketed using the same rational approach used in the United States. However, Japanese competitors soon reduced P&G's share to less than 10 percent. "We really didn't understand the consumer," explained P&G's CEO.

On the basis of consumer research, P&G redesigned the diapers to be much thinner. It also introduced pink diapers for girls and blue for boys. Advertising was changed from a rational approach (a diaper is shown absorbing a cup of water) to a more indirect, emotional approach (a talking diaper promises toddlers that it won't leak or cause diaper rash). Finally, the Procter & Gamble corporate name was made prominent in both packaging and design. Unlike Americans, Japanese consider corporate identity and reputation to be critical. P&G is now very successful in Japan.

☐ Cohort management involves bundling multiple brands into a single online marketing effort aimed at a common consumer group. It represents a collective approach to marketing in contrast to the traditional individualistic brand management approach. Procter & Gamble is using cohort marketing in its new website HomeMadeSimple.com. The site offers an online guide to home and lifestyle issues while promoting five P&G brands—Cascade, Dawn, Mr. Clean, Swiffer, and Febreze. Other P&G brands are also promoted on the site. It is now the second most visited packaged goods/lifestyle magazine site on the Web (tied with MarthaStewartOnline, well behind candystand.com). Andy Walter, director of the two-year-old project, states: "The thing I've preached to my team is

HomeMadeSimple can be more successful than MarthaStewart (in terms of number of visitors). But we will end it next month if that's all we attain. We have to sell those brands."

HomeMadeSimple has regular sections on getting organized, interior decoration, cooking, outside activities, celebrating the small things in life, and kids activities. A recent "issue" also had a special feature called Open House—"Peek in the windows! Here's your chance to get a look at other people's homes. Meet real women—from all walks of life—who opened their homes and told us about their favorite things." It also features a store and special offers for P&G products. For its website to continue to attract visitors and enhance the sales and image of its products, P&G must understand much more about its customers than their cleaning requirements![1]

The field of **consumer behavior** is *the study of individuals, groups, or organizations and the processes they use to select, secure, use, and dispose of products, services, experiences, or ideas to satisfy needs and the impacts that these processes have on the consumer and society.* This view of consumer behavior is broader than the traditional one, which focused much more on the buyer and the immediate antecedents and consequences of the purchasing process. This view will lead us to examine indirect influences on consumption decisions as well as consequences that involve more than the purchaser and seller.

The opening examples summarize several attempts to apply an understanding of consumer behavior in order to develop an effective marketing strategy, to regulate a marketing practice, or to cause socially desirable behavior. The examples cited reveal four main facts about the nature of our knowledge of consumer behavior. First, successful marketing decisions by commercial firms, nonprofit organizations, and regulatory agencies require extensive information on consumer behavior. It should be obvious from these examples that *organizations are applying theories and information about consumer behavior on a daily basis*. Knowledge of consumer behavior is critical for influencing not only product purchase decisions but decisions about which college to attend, which charities to support, how much recycling to do, or whether to seek help for an addiction or behavioral problem.

The examples also indicate the need to collect information about the specific consumers involved in the marketing decision at hand. At its current state of development, *consumer behavior theory provides the manager with the proper questions to ask*. However, given the importance of the specific situation and product category in consumer behavior, it will often be necessary to conduct research to answer these questions. One executive explains the importance of consumer behavior research this way:

> Understanding and properly interpreting consumer wants is a whole lot easier said than done. Every week our marketing researchers talk to more than 4,000 consumers to find out
>
> - What they think of our products and those of our competitors.
> - What they think of possible improvements in our products.
> - How they use our products.
> - What attitudes they have about our products and our advertising.
> - What they feel about their roles in the family and society.
> - What their hopes and dreams are for themselves and their families.
>
> Today, as never before, we cannot take our business for granted. That's why understanding—and therefore learning to anticipate—consumer behavior is our key to planning and managing in this ever-changing environment.[2]

The examples also indicate that *consumer behavior is a complex, multidimensional process*. The Center for Media Education, the American Legacy Foundation, and P&G have invested millions of dollars researching consumer behavior and much more trying to influence it, yet none of them are completely successful.

Finally, the examples indicate that *marketing practice designed to influence consumer behavior influences the firm, the individual, and society*. Pampers, while providing substantial benefits to individual consumers and profits for Procter & Gamble, raises resource use and disposition issues that affect all of society. More obvious concerns arise around products such as cigarettes and alcohol. Likewise, specific marketing practices such as targeting children on the Web have implications for the family and society. We will explore these types of issues throughout the text.

Sufficient knowledge of consumer behavior currently exists to provide a usable guide to marketing practice for commercial firms, nonprofit organizations, and regulators, but the state of the art is not sufficient for us to write a cookbook with surefire recipes for success. We will illustrate how some organizations were able to combine certain ingredients for success under specific conditions. However, as conditions change, the quantities and even the ingredients required for success may change. It is up to you as a student and future marketing manager to develop the ability to apply this knowledge to specific situations. To assist you, we have included example situations and questions at the end of each chapter and a series of short cases at the end of each section that can be used to develop your application skills. Also, Appendix B at the end of the text provides a list of key questions for a consumer behavior audit for developing marketing strategy.

It is important to note that *all marketing decisions and regulations are based on assumptions about consumer behavior*. It is impossible to think of a marketing decision for which this is not the case. For example, regulations designed to protect children from

Courtesy Weider Nutrition Group—Tiger's Milk/Tiger Sport.

Courtesy PowerBar Inc.

ILLUSTRATION 1–1

These products are targeting the same consumers with very similar products, yet they use two very different approaches. Why? They are based on different assumptions about consumer behavior and how to influence it.

various marketing practices on the Web must be based on assumptions about children's ability to process information and make decisions in this environment. Likewise, a decision to match a competitor's price reduction must be based on some assumption about how consumers evaluate prices and how they would respond to a price differential between the two brands. Examine Illustration 1–1. Both these ads appeared in the same issue of *Outside* magazine and are targeted at the same consumers. *What assumptions about consumer behavior underlie each ad? Which approach is best? Why?*

APPLICATIONS OF CONSUMER BEHAVIOR

Marketing Strategy

As stated above, all marketing strategies and tactics are based on explicit or implicit beliefs about consumer behavior. Decisions based on explicit assumptions and sound theory and research are more likely to be successful than are decisions based solely on implicit intuition. Thus, knowledge of consumer behavior can be an important competitive advantage. It can greatly reduce the odds of bad decisions such as the following:

BIC Corp. introduced a small $5 bottle of perfume to be sold in supermarkets and drugstore chains where it had tremendous distribution strength. The perfume was to be easy and convenient to buy and use. However, as one expert said in examining the $11 million loss project: "Fragrance is an emotional sell, not convenience or utility. The BIC package wasn't feminine. It looked like a cigarette lighter."[3]

Nestea launched a yellowish carbonated beverage named Tea Whiz. As you might suspect, it failed as did Miller Clear Beer and Gerber adult foods.

Our primary goal is to help you obtain a usable managerial understanding of consumer behavior. The key aspect of this objective is found in the phrase *usable managerial understanding*. We want to increase your understanding of consumer behavior in order to help you become a more effective marketing manager. We will take a more in-depth look at marketing strategy and consumer behavior shortly.

Regulatory Policy

The Food and Drug Administration (FDA) ordered three manufacturers of vegetable oil to remove claims on their labels that state that the products contain no cholesterol. The FDA believes that the claims of *No Cholesterol* are misleading *even though they are true*.

The FDA staff that issued these regulations did so based on their beliefs and knowledge about how consumers process information. If they are correct, the rules will result in better (healthier or more economical) choices by consumers. However, if they are incorrect, both consumers and firms delivering a superior product are harmed. Clearly, effective regulation of many marketing practices requires an extensive knowledge of consumer behavior. We will discuss this issue throughout the text and provide a detailed treatment in Chapter 20.

Social Marketing

Some states now invest cigarette tax revenues in high-quality, prime-time antismoking television commercials. Researchers at the University of Vermont spent $2 million on a four-year television campaign that showed popular kids disdaining cigarettes or smokers being unable to get dates. Smoking rates among teenagers were 35 percent lower in communities where the campaign was shown than in similar communities without the campaign. The effect was still strong two years after the campaign quit airing.[4]

How did these researchers decide to stress negative social consequences of smoking rather than negative health consequences? The decision was based on their knowledge and assumptions about the consumer behavior of teenagers.

Social marketing is *the application of marketing strategies and tactics to alter or create behaviors that have a positive effect on the targeted individuals or society as a whole.*[5] Social marketing has been used in attempts to reduce smoking, as noted above; to increase the percentage of children receiving their vaccinations in a timely manner; to encourage environmentally sound behaviors such as recycling; to reduce behaviors potentially leading to AIDS; to enhance support of charities; to reduce drug use; and to support many other important causes.

Just as for commercial marketing strategy, successful social marketing strategy requires a sound understanding of consumer behavior. For example, the Partnership for a Drug-Free America uses a fear-based campaign in its efforts to discourage the use of crystal meth. Illustration 1–2 contains one of its milder ads. In Chapter 11, we will analyze the conditions under which such campaigns are likely to succeed.

Informed Individuals

Most economically developed societies are legitimately referred to as consumption societies. Most individuals in these societies spend more time engaged in consumption than in any other activity, including work or sleep (both of which also involve consumption). Therefore, knowledge of consumer behavior can enhance our understanding of our environment and ourselves. Such an understanding is essential for sound citizenship, effective purchasing behavior, and reasoned business ethics.

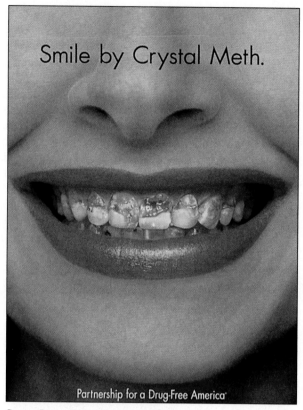

Courtesy Partnership for a Drug-Free America.

Literally thousands of firms are spending millions of dollars to influence you, your family, and your friends. These influence attempts occur in ads, packages, product features, sales pitches, and store environments. However, they also occur in the content of many television shows, in the products that are used in movies, and in the materials presented to children in schools.[6] Given the magnitude of these direct and indirect influence attempts, it is important that consumers accurately understand the strategies and tactics being used. It is equally important that all of us, as citizens, understand the consumer behavior basis of these strategies so that we can set appropriate limits on them when required.

MARKETING STRATEGY AND CONSUMER BEHAVIOR

Since all four of the applications of consumer behavior described above focus on the development, regulation, or effects of marketing strategy, we will now examine marketing strategy in more depth.

To survive in a competitive environment, an organization must provide target customers more value than is provided by its competitors. **Customer value** is *the difference between all the benefits derived from a total product and all the costs of acquiring those benefits.* For example, owning a car can provide a number of benefits, depending on the person and the type of car, including flexible transportation, image, status, pleasure, comfort, and even companionship. However, securing these benefits requires paying for the car, gasoline, insurance, maintenance, and parking fees, as well as risking injury from an accident, adding to environmental pollution, and dealing with traffic jams and other frustrations. It is the difference between the total benefits and the total costs that constitutes customer value.

The importance of understanding value *from the customer's perspective* can be seen in a product introduction by La Choy (a Hunt-Wesson Inc. brand). La Choy was a well-known brand. Frozen food sales had been growing rapidly, as had ethnic food sales. La Choy management decided to launch a line of large, meaty, frozen egg rolls to be used as a main course rather than as appetizers, as the smaller egg rolls then available were used. The logic seemed sound. Unfortunately, the large egg rolls could not be microwaved (the shells became soggy) and they took 30 minutes to heat in a regular oven. Consumers considered value in frozen foods of this type to include quick preparation. The egg rolls were a market failure and were withdrawn within two years.[7]

Providing superior customer value requires the organization to do a better job of anticipating and reacting to customer needs than the competition does. As Figure 1–1 indicates, an understanding of consumer behavior is the basis for marketing strategy formulation.

FIGURE 1–1	Marketing Strategy and Consumer Behavior

ILLUSTRATION 1–3

What do you buy when you go to a theme restaurant? The experience is the product as much or more than the actual food.

Consumers' reactions to this marketing strategy determine the organization's success or failure. However, these reactions also determine the success of the consumers in meeting their needs, and they have significant impacts on the larger society in which they occur.

Marketing strategy, as described in Figure 1–1, is conceptually very simple. It begins with an analysis of the market the organization is considering. This requires a detailed analysis of the organization's capabilities, the strengths and weaknesses of competitors, the economic and technological forces affecting the market, and the current and potential customers in the market. On the basis of the consumer analysis undertaken in this step, the organization identifies groups of individuals, households, or firms with similar needs. These market segments are described in terms of demographics, media preferences, geographic location, and so forth. Management then selects one or more of these segments as target markets based on the firm's capabilities relative to those of its competition (given current and forecast economic and technological conditions).

Next, marketing strategy is formulated. Marketing strategy seeks to provide the customer with more value than the competition while still producing a profit for the firm. Marketing strategy is formulated in terms of the marketing mix; that is, it involves determining the product features, price, communications, distribution, and services that will provide customers with superior value. This entire set of characteristics is often referred to as the **total product.** The total product is presented to the target market, which is consistently engaged in processing information and making decisions designed to maintain or enhance its lifestyle (individuals and households) or performance (businesses and other organizations).

Look at Illustration 1–3. What is the Rainforest Cafe's total product (see www. rainforestcafe.com)? Clearly, it is much more than food. The Rainforest Cafe, the Hard Rock Cafe, and similar restaurants are selling experiences as much as or perhaps more than food! As Consumer Insight 1–1 indicates, this is an increasingly important aspect of marketing.

Not too many years ago, a child's birthday cake was made at home from scratch. Then, cake mixes became the most common means of preparing a cake. Increasingly this has been replaced by cakes made (standard or customized) at bakeries or grocery stores. Now, many birthday cakes are provided as part of the birthday package arranged by Chuck E. Cheese's, the Discovery Zone, or a similar company. These companies are not selling products or services; they are selling experiences. The primary evaluation of a birthday party "conducted" by such a firm is not the taste of the cake and ice cream, the promptness of the service, or the nature of the party favors. Rather, it is the quality of the experience—Did the kids have fun? Did it have a "Wow factor"? Were the adults comfortable?

An experience occurs when a company intentionally creates a memorable event for customers. While products and services are to a large extent external to the customer, an experience is largely internal to each customer. The experience exists in the mind of an individual who has been engaged on an emotional, physical, intellectual, or even spiritual level.

Theme parks, theme restaurants, adventure travel, and similar activities are experiences that are marketed as such. Customers patronize them in order to acquire the experience. Today, many firms are wrapping experiences around their traditional products and services in order to sell them better. Niketown, the Sharper Image, Cabella's, and REI all draw customers to their outlets in part because of the experiences that are available at those outlets. The Mall of America and the Forum Shops in Las Vegas have developed shopping areas that customers visit for the experiences as much as for the merchandise.[8]

Critical Thinking Questions

1. What services could become experience-provoking events? How would they do this?

2. How can retailers, including Internet outlets, provide their customers experiences?

3. What would a store like Niketown (or a local shopping mall in your area) have to do to charge admission for customers to enter?

For the firm, the reaction of the target market to the total product produces an image of the product/brand/organization, sales (or lack thereof), and some level of customer satisfaction among those who did purchase. Sophisticated marketers seek to produce satisfied customers rather than mere sales—because satisfied customers are more profitable in the long run. For the individual, the process results in some level of need satisfaction, financial expenditure, attitude development/change, and/or behavioral changes. For society, the cumulative effect of the marketing process affects economic growth, pollution, social problems (illnesses caused by smoking and alcohol), and social benefits (improved nutrition, increased education). These individual and societal impacts are not always in the best interests of the individual or society, so the development and application of consumer behavior knowledge has many ethical implications.

Note again that an *analysis of consumers* is a key part of the foundation of marketing strategy, and *consumer reaction* to the total product determines the success or failure of the strategy. Before providing an overview of consumer behavior, we will examine marketing strategy formulation in more detail.

MARKET ANALYSIS COMPONENTS

Market analysis requires a thorough understanding of the organization's own capabilities, the capabilities of current and future competitors, the consumption process of potential customers, and the economic, physical, and technological environment in which these elements will interact.

The Consumers

It is not possible to anticipate and react to customers' needs and desires without a complete understanding of consumer behavior. Discovering customers' current needs is a complex process, but it can often be accomplished by marketing research, as the following example illustrates.

Black & Decker (B&D) had a moderately successful line of relatively inexpensive power tools with the Black & Decker brand and a successful expensive line called DeWalt for the professional market. Initial research with consumers revealed that the serious do-it-yourselfer (DIYer) wanted higher-quality tools than the inexpensive line, but few were willing to pay for the level of quality in the DeWalt line. Therefore, B&D identified 50 serious DIYers. B&D managers questioned these DIYers about the tools they used and why they had picked particular brands. They went with them on shopping trips and watched as they purchased tools and other items for projects. They observed them in their shops and questioned them as they used the tools. B&D tried to determine what these DIYers liked and disliked about particular brands and tools, how the tools felt when they used them, what problems they had while doing projects or cleaning up afterward, and so forth. They also tried to understand the emotional side of DIY projects by asking questions such as: What was your project? How did you feel when you completed it?

The color of the tools was carefully researched as well. Consumer research found that the deep green used on B&D's garden products was associated with quality and reliability. The name Quantum was also based on consumer research. It beat out such names as Excell, Caliber, and Excaliber. Consumers said it implied a product that was a step ahead of others and they could pronounce it easily. The Black & Decker name does not appear on the DeWalt products or packages because the professional contractors did not think B&D could make sophisticated tools. However, the serious DIYers had high regard for B&D, and its name appears prominently on Quantum products and packages.

The Quantum line has been very successful. As one analyst says: "Black & Decker has become very good at taking market share away from rival companies. They just know their customer."[9] Knowing the consumer requires understanding the behavioral principles that guide consumption behaviors. These principles are covered in depth in the balance of this text.

The Company

A firm must fully understand its own ability to meet customer needs. This involves evaluating all aspects of the firm, including its financial condition, general managerial skills, production capabilities, research and development capabilities, technological sophistication, reputation, and marketing skills. Marketing skills would include new-product development capabilities, channel strength, advertising abilities, service capabilities, marketing research abilities, market and consumer knowledge, and so forth.

Failure to adequately understand one's own strengths can cause serious problems. IBM's first attempt to enter the home computer market with the PC Jr. was a failure in part for this reason. Although IBM had an excellent reputation with large business customers and a very strong direct sales force for serving them, these strengths were not relevant to the household consumer market.

The Competitors

It is not possible to consistently do a better job of meeting customer needs than the competition without a thorough understanding of the competition's capabilities and strategies.

This requires the same level of knowledge of a firm's key competitors that is required of one's own firm. In addition, for any significant marketing action, the following questions must be answered:

1. If we are successful, which firms will be hurt (lose sales or sales opportunities)?
2. Of those firms that are injured, which have the capability (financial resources, marketing strengths) to respond?
3. How are they likely to respond (reduce prices, increase advertising, introduce a new product)?
4. Is our strategy (planned action) robust enough to withstand the likely actions of our competitors, or do we need additional contingency plans?

The Conditions

The state of the economy, the physical environment, government regulations, and technological developments affect consumer needs and expectations as well as company and competitor capabilities. The deterioration of the physical environment has produced not only consumer demand for environmentally sound products but also government regulations affecting product design and manufacturing.

International agreements such as NAFTA (North America Free Trade Agreement) have greatly reduced international trade barriers and increased the level of both competition and consumer expectations for many products. The development of computers has changed the way many people work and has created new industries.

Clearly, a firm cannot develop a sound marketing strategy without anticipating the conditions under which that strategy will be implemented.

MARKET SEGMENTATION

Perhaps the most important marketing decision a firm makes is the selection of one or more market segments on which to focus. A **market segment** is *a portion of a larger market whose needs differ somewhat from the larger market.* Since a market segment has unique needs, a firm that develops a total product focused solely on the needs of that segment will be able to meet the segment's desires better than a firm whose product or service attempts to meet the needs of multiple segments.

To be viable, a segment must be large enough to be served profitably. To some extent, each individual or household has unique needs for most products (a preferred color combination, for example). The smaller the segment, the closer the total product can be to that segment's desires. Historically, the smaller the segment, the more it costs to serve the segment. Thus, a tailor-made suit costs more than a mass-produced suit. However, flexible manufacturing and customized media are making it increasingly cost effective to develop products and communications for small segments or even individual consumers, as the following example shows:

Fingerhut, a catalog retailer with $2 billion in sales, has a database that stores over 500 pieces of information on each of more than 50 million potential customers. The data include not only past purchases and credit information but demographics such as age, marital status, and number of children and personal data such as hobbies and birthdays. This database enables Fingerhut to send consumers individualized catalogs at times when they are most likely to buy.[10]

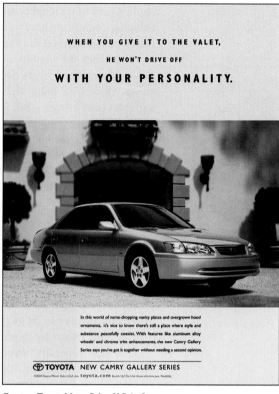

Copyright Nissan (2001). Nissan and the Nissan logo are registered trademarks of Nissan.

Courtesy Toyota Motor Sales, U.S.A., Inc.

The Nissan Xterra and the Toyota Camry are both cars. Both provide flexible, individual transportation. Yet, as these ads show, they are designed to meet a different set of needs in addition to basic transportation.

Market segmentation involves four steps:

1. Identifying product-related need sets.
2. Grouping customers with similar need sets.
3. Describing each group.
4. Selecting an attractive segment(s) to serve.

Product-Related Need Sets

Organizations approach market segmentation with a set of current and potential capabilities. These capabilities may be a reputation, an existing product, a technology, or some other skill set. The first task of the firm is to identify need sets that the organization is capable, or could become capable, of meeting. The term **need set** is used to reflect the fact that most products in developed economies satisfy more than one need. Thus, an automobile can meet more needs than just basic transportation. Some customers purchase cars to meet transportation and status needs. Others purchase them to meet transportation and fun needs. Still others purchase automobiles to meet status, fun, and transportation needs. Illustration 1–4 shows two ads for automobiles. *What needs does the Toyota ad appeal to? The Nissan ad?* These ads differ because the firms are pursuing different market segments with distinct need sets.

Customer needs are not restricted to product features. They also include types and sources of information about the product, outlets where the product is available, the price of the product, services associated with the product, the image of the product or firm, and even where and how the product is produced. For example, Nike recently lost sales as a result of publicity about child labor and abusive working conditions at some of the factories in developing countries where many of its products are made. In response, it has changed some practices and engaged in a variety of public relations activities, but the criticisms continue.[11]

Identifying the various need sets that the firm's current or potential product might satisfy typically involves consumer research, particularly focus groups and depth interviews, as well as logic and intuition. These need sets are often associated with other variables such as age, stage in the household life cycle, gender, social class, ethnic group, or lifestyle, and many firms start the segmentation process focusing first on one or more of the groups defined by one of these variables. Thus, a firm might start with various ethnic groups and attempt to discover similarities and differences in consumption-related needs across these groups. While better-defined segments will generally be discovered by focusing first on needs, then on consumer characteristics associated with those needs, both approaches are used in practice and both provide a useful basis for segmentation.

Customers with Similar Need Sets

The next step is to group consumers with similar need sets. For example, the need for moderately priced, fun, sporty automobiles appears to exist in many young single individuals, young couples with no children, and middle-aged couples whose children have left home. These consumers can be grouped into one segment as far as product features and perhaps even product image are concerned despite sharply different demographics.

This step generally involves consumer research, including focus group interviews, surveys, and product concept tests (see Appendix A). It could also involve an analysis of current consumption patterns.

Description of Each Group

Once consumers with similar need sets are identified, they should be described in terms of their demographics, lifestyles, and media usage. In order to design an effective marketing program, it is necessary to have a complete understanding of the potential customers. It is only with such a complete understanding that we can be sure we have correctly identified the need set. In addition, we cannot communicate effectively with our customers if we do not understand the context in which our product is purchased and consumed, how it is thought about by our customers, and the language they use to describe it. Thus, while many young single individuals, young couples with no children, and middle-aged couples whose children have left home may want the same features in an automobile, the media required to reach each group and the appropriate language and themes to use with each group would likely differ.

Attractive Segment(s) to Serve

Once we are sure we have a thorough understanding of each segment, we must select our **target market**—*that segment(s) of the larger market on which we will focus our marketing effort.* This decision is based on our ability to provide the selected segment(s) with superior customer value at a profit. Thus, the size and growth of the segment, the intensity of the current and anticipated competition, the cost of providing the superior value, and so forth are important considerations. Table 1–1 provides a simple worksheet for use in evaluating and comparing the attractiveness of various market segments.

It is important to remember that each market segment requires its own marketing strategy. Each element of the marketing mix should be examined to determine if changes are

Criterion	*Score**
Segment size	————
Segment growth rate	————
Competitor strength	————
Customer satisfaction with existing products	————
Fit with company image	————
Fit with company objectives	————
Fit with company resources	————
Distribution available	————
Investment required	————
Stability/predictability	————
Cost to serve	————
Sustainable advantage available	————
Communications channels available	————
Risk	————
Other (————)	————

TABLE 1–1

Market Segment
Attractiveness
Worksheet

*Score on a 1 to 10 scale, with 10 being most favorable.

required from one segment to another. Sometimes each segment will require a completely different marketing mix, including the product. At other times, only the advertising message or retail outlets may need to differ.

MARKETING STRATEGY

It is not possible to select target markets without simultaneously formulating a general marketing strategy for each segment. A decisive criterion in selecting target markets is the ability to provide superior value to those market segments. Since customer value is delivered by the marketing strategy, the firm must develop its general marketing strategy as it evaluates potential target markets.

Marketing strategy is basically the answer to the question: *How will we provide superior customer value to our target market?* The answer to this question requires the formulation of a consistent marketing mix. The **marketing mix** is *the product, price, communications, distribution, and services provided to the target market*. It is the combination of these elements that meets customer needs and provides customer value. For example, in Illustration 1–1, the Tiger Sport Energy Bar promised superior value through better taste and a lower price than its competitors.

The Product

A **product** is *anything a consumer acquires or might acquire to meet a perceived need.* Consumers are generally buying need satisfaction, not physical product attributes.[12] As the former head of Revlon said, "in the factory we make cosmetics, in the store we sell hope." Thus, consumers don't purchase quarter-inch drill bits but the ability to create quarter-inch holes. Federal Express lost much of its overnight letter delivery business not to UPS or Airborne but to fax machines and the Internet because they could meet the same consumer needs faster, cheaper, or more conveniently. Consider one analyst's description of McDonald's product:

> The source of McDonald's pre-eminence is neither hamburgers nor fast-food service. It's giving a wide range of people the experience of a reliable break from fatigue, stress, grown-up responsibility. More variety, fewer calories, even enhanced freshness are not the principal criteria for success if what those people seek is "a break today."[13]

We use the term *product* to refer to physical products and primary or core services. Thus, an automobile is a product, as is a transmission overhaul or a ride in a taxi. Over 15,000 new products and new versions of existing products are introduced to supermarkets alone each year. Obviously, many of these will not succeed. To be successful, products must meet the needs of the target market better than the competition does.

Consider the Chinese computer market. A few years ago, a state-owned company—Legend—appeared headed for oblivion as China opened its market to Western firms. Today, it dominates all competitors. How? According to its general manager, "We have much more insight into the needs of Chinese customers." These insights have been translated into bundling software products for first-time buyers (most of the market) into its computers. These include tutorials on such topics as using the computer, using the Internet, and organizing home finances.[14]

Communications

Marketing communications include *advertising, the sales force, public relations, packaging, and any other signal that the firm provides about itself and its products.* An effective communications strategy requires answers to the following questions:

1. *With whom, exactly, do we want to communicate?* While most messages are aimed at the target-market members, others are focused on channel members or those who influence the target-market members. For example, pediatric nurses are often asked for advice concerning diapers and other nonmedical infant care items. A firm marketing such items would be wise to communicate directly with these individuals.

    Often it is necessary to determine who within the target market should receive the marketing message. For a children's breakfast cereal, should the communications be aimed at the children or the parents or both? The answer depends on the target market and varies by country.

2. *What effect do we want our communications to have on the target audience?* Often a manager will state that the purpose of advertising and other marketing communications is to increase sales. While this may be the ultimate objective, the behavioral objective for most marketing communications is often much more immediate. That is, it may seek to have the audience learn something about the product, seek more information about the product, like the product, recommend the product to others, feel good about having bought the product, or a host of other communications effects.

3. *What message will achieve the desired effect on our audience?* What words, pictures, and symbols should we use to capture attention and produce the desired effect? Marketing messages can range from purely factual statements to pure symbolism. The best approach depends on the situation at hand. Developing an effective message requires a thorough understanding of the meanings the target audience attaches to words and symbols, as well as knowledge of the perception process. Consider Illustration 1–5. Many older consumers would not relate to the phrase "full time enjoyer of all that is sick." However, it communicates clearly to this target market for snowboards.

ILLUSTRATION 1–5

All aspects of the marketing mix should be designed around the needs and characteristics of the target audience. Many segments would not understand the language in this ad, but it works with the targeted segment.

4. *What means and media should we use to reach the target audience?* Should we use personal sales to provide information? Can we rely on the package to provide needed information? Should we advertise in mass media, use direct mail, or rely on consumers to find us on the Internet? If we advertise in mass media, which media (television, radio, magazines, newspapers, Internet) and which specific vehicles (television programs, specific magazines, websites, and so forth) should we use? Answering these questions requires an understanding both of the media that the target audiences use and of the effect that advertising in those media would have on the product's image.

5. *When should we communicate with the target audience?* Should we concentrate our communications near the time that purchases tend to be made or evenly throughout the week, month, or year? Do consumers seek information shortly before purchasing our product? If so, where? Answering these questions requires knowledge of the decision process used by the target market for this product.

Price

Price is *the amount of money one must pay to obtain the right to use the product.* One can buy ownership of a product or, for many products, limited usage rights (i.e., one can rent or lease the product such as a video). Economists often assume that lower prices for the same product will result in more sales than higher prices. However, price sometimes serves as a signal of quality. A product priced "too low" might be perceived as having low quality.

Owning expensive items also provides information about the owner. If nothing else, it indicates that the owner can afford the expensive item. This is a desirable feature to some consumers. Therefore, setting a price requires a thorough understanding of the symbolic role that price plays for the product and target market in question.

It is important to note that the price of a product is not the same as the cost of the product to the customer. **Consumer cost** is *everything the consumer must surrender in order to receive the benefits of owning/using the product.* As described earlier, the cost of owning/using an automobile includes insurance, gasoline, maintenance, finance charges, license fees, parking fees, time and discomfort while shopping for the car, and perhaps even discomfort about increasing pollution, in addition to the purchase price. One of the ways firms seek to provide customer value is to reduce the nonprice costs of owning or operating a product. If successful, the total cost to the customer decreases while the revenue to the marketer stays the same or even increases.

Distribution

Distribution, *having the product available where target customers can buy it,* is essential to success. Only in rare cases will customers go to much trouble to secure a particular brand. Obviously, good channel decisions require a sound knowledge of where target customers shop for the product in question, as the following example shows:

Huffy Corp., a $700 million bicycle manufacturer, did careful research before launching a new bicycle called Cross Sport. The new bike was a cross between a mountain bike and the traditional thin-framed 10-speed bicycle. Focus groups and product concept tests revealed strong consumer acceptance. Huffy quickly launched the $159 Cross Sport through its strong mass distribution channels such as Kmart and Toys "R" Us. Unfortunately, the fairly serious adult rider that these bikes targeted demands individual sales attention by knowledgeable salespeople. Such salespeople are found at specialty bike shops, not at mass retailers. As Huffy's president said: "It was a $5 million mistake."[15]

Service

Earlier, we defined *product* to include primary or core services such as haircuts, car repairs, and medical treatments. Here, **service** refers to *auxiliary or peripheral activities that are performed to enhance the primary product or service.* Thus, we would consider car repair to be a product (primary service), while free pickup and delivery of the car would be an auxiliary service. Although many texts do not treat service as a separate component of the marketing mix, we do because of the critical role it plays in determining market share and relative price in competitive markets. A firm that does not explicitly manage its auxiliary services is at a competitive disadvantage.

Auxiliary services cost money to provide. Therefore, it is essential that the firm furnish only those services that provide value to the target customers. Providing services that customers do not value can result in high costs and high prices without a corresponding increase in customer value.

CONSUMER DECISIONS

As Figure 1–1 illustrated, the consumer decision process intervenes between the marketing strategy (as implemented in the marketing mix) and the outcomes. That is, the outcomes of the firm's marketing strategy are determined by its interaction with the consumer decision process. The firm can succeed only if consumers see a need that its product can solve, become aware of the product and its capabilities, decide that it is the best available solution, proceed to buy it, and become satisfied with the results of the purchase. A significant part of this entire text is devoted to developing an understanding of the consumer decision process (Chapters 14–18).

OUTCOMES

Firm Outcomes

Product Position   The most basic outcome for a firm of a marketing strategy is its **product position**—*an image of the product or brand in the consumer's mind relative to competing products and brands.* This image consists of a set of beliefs, pictorial representations, and feelings about the product or brand. It does not require purchase or use for it to develop. It is determined by communications about the brand from the firm and other sources, as well as by direct experience with it. Most marketing firms specify the product position they want their brands to have and measure these positions on an ongoing basis. This is because a brand whose position matches the desired position of a target market is likely to be purchased when a need for that product arises.

Sauza Conmemorativo tequila attempts to build a product position as a smooth, light-hearted tequila by running a series of humorous ads all with the tag line: *"Life is harsh. Your Tequila shouldn't be"* (see Illustration 1–6). This positioning has helped the brand's sales grow at more than twice the industry average.[16]

Courtesy Domecq Importers, Inc.

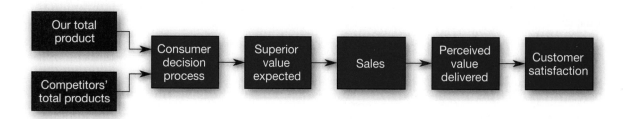

FIGURE 1–2 **Creating Satisfied Customers**

Sales Sales are a critical outcome, as they produce the revenue necessary for the firm to continue in business. Therefore, virtually all firms evaluate the success of their marketing programs in terms of sales. As we have seen, sales are likely to occur only if the initial consumer analysis was correct and if the marketing mix matches the consumer decision process.

Customer Satisfaction Marketers have discovered that it is generally more profitable to maintain existing customers than to replace them with new customers. Retaining current customers requires that they be satisfied with their purchase and use of the product. Thus, **customer satisfaction** is a major concern of marketers.

As Figure 1–2 indicates, convincing consumers that your brand offers superior value is necessary in order to make the initial sale. Obviously, one must have a thorough understanding of the potential consumers' needs and of their information acquisition processes to succeed at this task. However, *creating satisfied customers,* and thus future sales, requires that customers continue to believe that your brand meets their needs and offers superior value *after they have used it.* You must deliver as much or more value than your customers initially expected, and it must be enough to satisfy their needs. This requires an even greater understanding of consumer behavior. Honda's recent efforts in this area are described below:

Honda had the factory workers who actually assemble the cars as well as marketing managers conduct telephone interviews with over 47,000 Accord owners. The interviews sought to determine customer satisfaction levels with all aspects of the Accord as well as ideas for improvements. The interviews were conducted by those who would have to make any necessary changes.[17]

Individual Outcomes

Need Satisfaction The most obvious outcome of the consumption process for an individual, whether or not a purchase is made, is some level of satisfaction of the need that initiated the consumption process. This can range from none (or even negative if a purchase increases the need rather than reduces it) to complete. Two key processes are involved—the actual need fulfillment and the perceived need fulfillment. These two processes are closely related and are often identical. However, at times they differ. For example, people might take a food supplement because they believe it is enhancing their health while in reality it could have no direct health effects or even negative effects. One objective of government regulation and a frequent goal of consumer groups is to ensure that consumers can adequately judge the extent to which products are meeting their needs.

Injurious Consumption   While we tend to focus on the benefits of consumption, we must remain aware that consumer behavior has a dark side. **Injurious consumption** occurs *when individuals or groups make consumption decisions that have negative consequences for their long-run well-being.*

For most consumers, fulfilling one need affects their ability to fulfill others due to either financial or time constraints. For example, some estimates indicate that most Americans are not saving at a level that will allow them to maintain a lifestyle near their current one when they retire.[18] The cumulative impact of many small decisions to spend financial resources to meet needs now will limit their ability to meet what may be critically important needs after retirement. For other consumers, readily available credit, unrelenting advertising, and widespread, aggressive merchandising result in a level of expenditures that cannot be sustained by their income.[19] The result is often financial distress, delayed or bypassed medical or dental care, family stress, inadequate resources for proper child care, bankruptcy, or even homelessness.

Cigarette consumption is encouraged by hundreds of millions of dollars in marketing expenditures, as is the consumption of alcoholic beverages, snacks with high sugar or fat content, and other potentially harmful products. These expenditures cause some people to consume these products or to consume more of them. Some of these people, and their families, in turn are then harmed by this consumption.[20]

Companies are not the only entities that promote potentially harmful products. Most states in the United States now promote state-sponsored gambling, which has caused devastating financial consequences for some. The following quote indicates the magnitude of the problem:

> Every year over 10 million American consumers suffer financial losses from their addiction to gambling. . . . There are currently 10 million alcoholics and 80 million cigarette smokers in the United States. . . . Every year 25,000 people die as a result of alcohol related traffic accidents. . . . All of these disturbing and disturbed behaviors result from consumption gone wrong.[21]

While these are issues we should be concerned with and we will address throughout this text, we should also note that alcohol consumption seems to have arisen simultaneously with civilization and evidence of gambling is nearly as old. Consumers smoked and chewed tobacco long before mass media or advertising as we know it existed, and illegal drug consumption continues to grow worldwide despite the absence of large-scale marketing, or at least advertising. Thus, though marketing activities based on knowledge of consumer behavior undoubtedly exacerbate some forms of injurious consumption, they are not the sole cause and, as we will see shortly, may also be part of the cure.

Society Outcomes

Economic Outcomes   The cumulative impact of consumers' purchase decisions, including the decision to forgo consumption, is a major determinant of the state of a given country's economy. Their decisions on whether to buy or save affect economic growth, the availability and cost of capital, employment levels, and so forth. The types of products and brands purchased influence the balance of payments, industry growth rates, and wage levels. Decisions made in one society, particularly large wealthy societies like the United States, Western Europe, and Japan, have a major impact on the economic health of many other countries. A recession in the United States or a strong shift toward purchasing only

American-made products would have profound negative consequences on the economies of many other countries, both developed and developing.

Physical Environment Outcomes   Consumers make decisions that have a major impact on the physical environments of both their own and other societies. The cumulative effect of American consumers' decisions to rely on relatively large private cars rather than mass transit results in significant air pollution in American cities as well as the consumption of nonrenewable resources from other countries. The decisions of people in most developed and in many developing economies to consume meat as a primary source of protein result in the clearing of rain forests for grazing land, the pollution of many watersheds due to large-scale feedlots, and an inefficient use of grain, water, and energy to produce protein. It also appears to produce health problems for many consumers. The destruction of the rain forests and other critical habitat areas receives substantial negative publicity. However, these resources are being used because of consumer demand, and consumer demand consists of the decisions you and I and our families and our friends make!

As we will see in Chapter 3, many consumers now recognize the indirect effects of consumption on the environment and are altering their behavior to minimize environmental harm.

Social Welfare   Consumer decisions affect the general social welfare of a society. Decisions concerning how much to spend for private goods (personal purchases) rather than public goods (support for public education, parks, health care, and so forth) are generally made indirectly by consumers' elected representatives. These decisions have a major impact on the overall quality of life in a society.

Injurious consumption, as described above, affects society as well as the individuals involved. The social costs of smoking-induced illnesses, alcoholism, and drug abuse are staggering. To the extent that marketing activities increase or decrease injurious consumption, they have a major impact on the social welfare of a society. Consider the following:

According to the U.S. Public Health Service, of the 10 leading causes of death in the United States, at least 7 could be reduced substantially if people at risk would change just 5 behaviors: compliance (e.g., use of antihypertensive medication), diet, smoking, lack of exercise, and alcohol and drug abuse. Each of these behaviors is inextricably linked with marketing efforts and the reactions of consumers to marketing campaigns. The link between consumer choices and social problems is clear.[22]

However, the same authors conclude: "Although these problems appear daunting, they are all problems that are solvable through altruistic [social] marketing." Thus, marketing and consumer behavior can both aggravate and reduce serious social problems.

THE NATURE OF CONSUMER BEHAVIOR

Figure 1–3 is the model that we use to capture the general structure and process of consumer behavior and to organize this text. It is a **conceptual model.** It does not contain sufficient detail to predict particular behaviors; however, it does reflect our beliefs about the general nature of consumer behavior. Individuals develop self-concepts and subsequent lifestyles based on a variety of internal (mainly psychological and physical) and external (mainly sociological and demographic) influences. These self-concepts and lifestyles produce needs and desires, many of which require consumption decisions to satisfy. As

FIGURE 1–3   Overall Model of Consumer Behavior

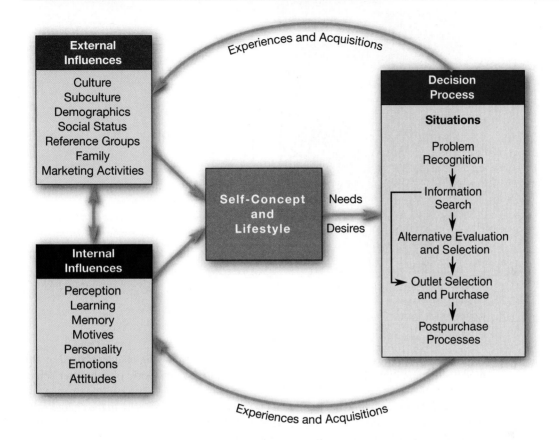

individuals encounter relevant situations, the consumer decision process is activated. This process and the experiences and acquisitions it produces in turn influence the consumers' self-concept and lifestyle by affecting their internal and external characteristics.

This model, while simple, is both conceptually sound and intuitively appealing. Each of us has a view of ourselves (self-concept), and we try to live in a particular manner given our resources (lifestyle). Our view of ourselves and the way we try to live are determined by internal factors (such as our personality, values, emotions, and memory) and external factors (such as our culture, age, friends, family, and subculture). Our view of ourselves and the way we try to live results in desires and needs that we bring to the multitude of situations we encounter daily. Many of these situations will cause us to consider a purchase. Our decision, and even the process of making it, will cause learning and may affect many other internal and external factors that will change or reinforce our current self-concept and lifestyle.

Figure 1–3 and our initial discussion of it make consumer behavior seem simple, structured, conscious, mechanical, and linear. A quick analysis of your own behavior and that of your friends will reveal the fallacy of this perception. Consumer behavior is frequently complex, disorganized, nonconscious, organic, and circular. Unfortunately, we must present it in a relatively simple, linear manner due to the limitations of written

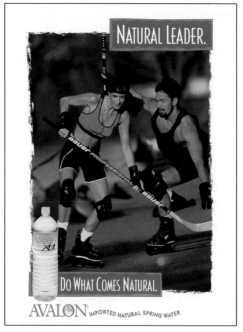

Courtesy Avalon Beverage Company.

communications. As you look at the model and read the following chapters based on this model, continually relate the descriptions in the text to the rich world of consumer behavior that is all around you.

Each of the factors shown in Figure 1–3 is given a detailed treatment in the chapters that follow. In the next sections, we will provide a brief overview so that you can see how they fit together. Our discussion and the text move through the model from left to right.

External Influences

Dividing the factors that influence consumers into categories is somewhat arbitrary. For example, we treat learning as an internal influence despite the fact that much human learning involves interaction with, or imitation of, other individuals. Thus, learning could also be considered a group process. In Figure 1–3, the two-directional arrow connecting internal and external influences is used to indicate that each set interacts with the other.

We organize our discussion of external influences from large-scale macrogroups to smaller, more microgroup influences. Culture is perhaps the most pervasive influence on consumer behavior. We begin our consideration of culture in Chapter 2 by examining differences in consumption patterns across cultures. In Chapter 3, we focus on the American culture, specifically cultural values. As we will see, while Americans share many values and consumption behaviors, there is also rich diversity and ongoing change in this society that create both marketing opportunities and unique social energy. Illustration 1–7 reflects the changing role of women in our society as well as our ethnic diversity.

Chapter 4 continues our examination of the American society by analyzing its demographics (the number, education, age, income, occupation, and location of individuals in a society) and social stratification. Chapter 5 considers ethnic, religious, and regional subcultures. While our main focus in Chapters 3, 4, and 5 is on the American culture, we continuously compare and contrast this culture with others throughout the world.

Chapter 6 analyzes families and households, including discussions of how they evolve over time, the role of families in teaching children how to consume, and household decision making. In Chapter 7, we look at the processes by which groups influence consumer behavior and group communication, including the role of groups in the acceptance of new products and technologies.

Internal Influences

Internal influences begin with perception, the process by which individuals receive and assign meaning to stimuli (Chapter 8). This is followed by learning—changes in the content or structure of long-term memory (Chapter 9). Chapter 10 covers three closely related topics: motivation—the reason for a behavior; personality—an individual's characteristic response tendencies across similar situations; and emotion—strong, relatively uncontrolled feelings that affect our behavior. We conclude our coverage of internal influences by examining attitudes in Chapter 11. An attitude is an enduring organization of motivational, emotional, perceptual, and cognitive processes with respect to some aspect of our environment. As such, our attitudes are heavily influenced by the external and internal factors that we have discussed in the preceding chapters.

Self-Concept and Lifestyle

Chapter 12 is a detailed discussion of the key concepts around which our model revolves. As a result of the interaction of all the variables described earlier, individuals develop a self-concept that is reflected in a lifestyle. The **self-concept** is *the totality of an individual's thoughts and feelings about him- or herself.* **Lifestyle** is, quite simply, *how one lives.* It includes the products one buys, how one uses them, what one thinks about them, and how one feels about them. It is the manifestation of the individual's self-concept—the total image the person has of him- or herself as a result of the culture he or she lives in and the individual situations and experiences that comprise his or her daily existence. It is the sum of the person's past decisions and future plans.

Both individuals and families exhibit distinct lifestyles. We often hear of "career-oriented individuals," "outdoor families," or "devoted parents." One's lifestyle is determined by both conscious and unconscious decisions. Often we make choices with full awareness of their impact on our lifestyle, but generally we are unaware of the extent to which our decisions are influenced by our current or desired lifestyle. Our model shows that consumers' self-concepts and lifestyles produce needs and desires that interact with the situations in which consumers find themselves to trigger the consumer decision process.

We do not mean to imply that consumers think in terms of lifestyle. None of us consciously thinks, *I'll have an Evian bottled water in order to enhance my lifestyle.* Rather, we make decisions consistent with our lifestyles without deliberately considering lifestyle. Most consumer decisions involve very little effort or thought on the part of the consumer. They are what we call *low-involvement* decisions. Feelings and emotions are as important in many consumer decisions as logical analysis or physical product attributes. Nonetheless, most consumer purchases involve at least a modest amount of decision making, and most are influenced by the purchaser's current and desired lifestyle.

Situations and Consumer Decisions

Consumer decisions result from perceived problems (*I'm thirsty*) and opportunities (*That looks like it would be fun to try*). We will use the term *problem* to refer both to problems

"I (Andre Hank) worked eight-hour shifts at one restaurant, then drove to the other one for another eight-hour shift. One day I came home and my girlfriend and our six-year-olds were gone. When she left, I fell apart. I stopped going to work, stopped sleeping. I wasn't doing anything, just going crazy . . . they took me to the hospital where I got a shot to help me sleep. I woke up in a psyche ward. After three or four months, they released me.

"When I came out of the hospital I didn't have anything. I wanted to get my old job back, but they wouldn't give me a second chance. I tried to get another job but it's hard when you don't have a phone, or an answering machine, or a pager. And I was sleeping in abandoned buildings, then on the El for a long time.

"One day more than three years ago I was hungry and didn't have any money and I saw a guy selling newspapers. I asked him what he was selling and he told me about *StreetWise* (a nonprofit, independent newspaper sold by the homeless, formerly homeless, and economically disadvantaged men and women of Chicago). So I [began to sell *StreetWise*] . . . . I don't make a lot of money but I'm good at saving it. Right now I'm saving for a coat for next winter.

"I'm no longer homeless. I've got a nice little room in a hotel . . . I can buy food . . . I even saved for [and bought] Nikes."

and to opportunities. Consumer problems arise in specific situations and the nature of the situation influences the resulting consumer behavior. Therefore, we provide a detailed discussion of situational influences on the consumer decision process in Chapter 13.

As Figure 1–3 indicates, a consumer's needs/desires may trigger one or more levels of the consumer decision process. It is important to note that for most purchases, consumers devote very little effort to this process, and emotions and feelings often have as much or more influence on the outcome as do facts and product features. Despite the limited effort that consumers often devote to this process, the results have important effects on the individual consumer, the firm, and the larger society. Therefore, we provide a detailed coverage of each stage of the process: problem recognition (Chapter 14), information search (Chapter 15), alternative evaluation and selection (Chapter 16), outlet selection and purchase (Chapter 17), and use, disposition, and purchase evaluation (Chapter 18). The increasing role of technology, particularly the Internet, in consumer decision making is highlighted throughout these chapters.

In Chapter 19, we show how our model of individual and household consumer behavior can be modified to help understand organizational consumer behavior. Chapter 20 focuses our attention on the regulation of marketing activities, especially those targeting children. We pay particular attention to the role that knowledge of consumer behavior has or could play in regulation.

THE MEANING OF CONSUMPTION

As we go through this text, we will present the results of studies of consumer behavior, theories about consumer behavior, and examples of marketing programs designed to influence consumer behavior. In reading this material, it is easy to lose sight of the fact that consumer behavior is not just a topic of study or a basis for developing marketing or regulatory strategy. Consumption frequently has deep meaning for the consumer.[23]

Consider Consumer Insight 1–2. Andre, just escaping homelessness, is clearly proud that he was able to save and buy a pair of Nikes. He could undoubtedly have purchased a

Andre is not unique among low-income consumers in wanting and buying items such as Nike shoes. As one expert says: "These people (low-income consumers) want the same products and services other consumers want." He suggests that marketing efforts reflect those desires. Another expert states: "There's this stereotype that they don't have enough money for toothpaste, and that's just not true. There has to be some significance to them being called lower-income, but they do buy things."

The working poor are forced to spend a disproportionate percent of their income on housing, utilities, and medical care (due to a lack of insurance). They generally rely on public transportation. They spend a smaller portion of their relatively small incomes on meals away from home and on all forms of entertainment such as admissions, pets, and toys. They spend very little on their own financial security. However, as Andre illustrated, they spend the same percent of their income (though a smaller dollar amount) on apparel and accessories.[24]

Critical Thinking Questions

1. What does the consumption of a product like Nikes mean to Andre?

2. What does this story say about our society and the impact and role of marketing?

different brand that would have met his physical needs as well for much less money. While he does not say why he bought the more expensive Nikes, a reasonable interpretation is that they serve as a visible symbol that Andre is back as a successful member of society. In fact, Nike is sometimes criticized for creating, through its marketing activities, symbols of success or status that are unduly expensive. *What do you think? Does Nike manipulate people like Andre into spending more than necessary for a product because of its symbolism? If ads were banned or restricted to showing only product features, would products and brands still acquire symbolic meaning?*

Perhaps some insight into the questions raised above can be found in the following description of the attitudes of several goat-herders in a narrow mountain valley in northeastern Mexico in 1964. Modern advertising was not part of their environment.

I asked Juan what were his major economic concerns. He answered very quickly, "food and clothes," he said. "How about housing?" I asked. "That is never a problem," he said, "for I can always make a house." For Juan and the others, a house is not a prestige symbol but simply a place to sleep, a place to keep dry in, a place for family privacy, and a place in which to store things. It is not a place to live, as the word is so meaningfully used in the United States.

It seems difficult to overestimate the importance of clothing. A clean set of clothes is for a pass into town or a fiesta. Clothes are the mark of a man's self-respect, and the ability of a man to clothe his family is in many ways the measure of a man. I once asked Mariano in the presence of Isidro and Juan why he wanted the new pair of trousers he had just purchased, when the pair he was wearing in the field seemed perfectly acceptable. He told me that while they were acceptable for the field, they could not be worn into town, for they were much too shabby. "They would call me a hick," he said, "if they saw me go into town this way." "Who?" I asked. "Why, everyone," he answered, adding some delightful obscenities to punctuate his feelings. Isidro thought my questions hysterically funny, for everyone knows what it is like to go into town without a good set of clothes. "Oh they would laugh; they would call him many funny things; they would call him _____. They would call anyone these things if they came into town badly dressed."[25]

Thus, as you read the chapters that follow, keep in mind that we are dealing with real people with real lives, not mere abstractions.

SUMMARY

This should be a fascinating course for you. The fact that you are enrolled in this class suggests that you are considering marketing or advertising as a possible career. If that is the case, you should be immensely curious about why people behave as they do. Such a curiosity is essential for success in a marketing-related career. That is what marketing is all about—understanding and anticipating consumer needs and developing solutions for those needs.

Even if you do not pursue a career in marketing, analyzing the purpose behind advertisements, package designs, prices, and other marketing activities is an enjoyable activity. In addition, it will make you a better consumer and a more informed citizen.

Finally, much of the material is simply interesting. For example, it is fun to read about China's attempt to market Pansy brand men's underwear in America, or Ford having to change the name of its Pinto automobile in Brazil after it learned that pinto was slang for a small male sex organ. So have fun, study hard, and expand your managerial skills as well as your understanding of the environment in which you live.

KEY TERMS

Conceptual model 26
Consumer behavior 7
Consumer cost 22
Customer satisfaction 24
Customer value 11
Distribution 22
Injurious consumption 25

Lifestyle 29
Market segment 16
Marketing communications 20
Marketing mix 19
Marketing strategy 19
Need set 17
Price 21

Product 19
Product position 23
Self-concept 29
Service 22
Social marketing 10
Target market 18
Total product 13

INTERNET EXERCISES

1. Market segmentation is one of the most important parts of developing a marketing strategy. Many commercial firms provide information and services to help define and/or describe market segments. Visit USAData's website (www.usadata.com). Select the "Tour of a Market Target Analysis." Take a tour that interests you. Prepare a report on the characteristics of that market. How valuable do you think this service would be to a marketer?

2. Visit the WorldOpinion website (www.worldopinion.com). What information can you find that is relevant to understanding consumer behavior?

3. Marketers of many products target young (under 29) single adults who live alone. How will the number of such adults change between now and 2010 (hint: visit www.census.gov)?

4. Examine magazine ads for a product category that interests you. Visit two websites identified in the ads. Which is most effective? Why? What beliefs about consumer behavior are reflected in the ads?

5. What ethical and legal issues involving the interaction of consumers and marketing are currently the concern of the following?
a. Federal Trade Commission (www.ftc.gov).
b. Better Business Bureau (www.bbb.org).

6. Evaluate several of PETA's websites (www.peta-online.org, www.circuses.com, www.nofishing.net, www.taxmeat.com, and www.furisdead.com).

7. Evaluate L'eggs' website (www.leggs.com). What assumptions about consumer behavior are reflected in this website?

DDB NEEDHAM DATA ANALYSES QUESTIONS

1. Examine the DDB Needham data in Tables 1 through 7 for differences among heavy consumers of the following. Why do you think these differences exist? How would you use these insights to develop marketing strategy?
   a. The Internet
   b. Church attendance

   c. Cellular phones
   d. Lipstick

2. Cigarettes are frequently injurious to those who consume them. Examine the DDB Needham data. What variables are most associated with smoking cigarettes? To what extent do these variables explain why people smoke?

REVIEW QUESTIONS

1. How is the field of consumer behavior defined?
2. What conclusions can be drawn from the examples at the beginning of this chapter?
3. What are the four major uses or applications of an understanding of consumer behavior?
4. What is *social marketing?*
5. What is *customer value,* and why is it important to marketers?
6. What is required to provide superior customer value?
7. What is a *total product?*
8. What is involved in the *consumer* analysis phase of market analysis in Figure 1–1?
9. What is involved in the *company* analysis phase of market analysis in Figure 1–1?
10. What is involved in the *competitor* analysis phase of market analysis in Figure 1–1?
11. What is involved in the *conditions* analysis phase of market analysis in Figure 1–1?
12. Describe the process of *market segmentation.*
13. What is *marketing strategy?*
14. What is a *marketing mix?*
15. What is a *product?*
16. What does an effective communications strategy require?
17. What is a *price?* How does the *price* of a product differ from the *cost of the product to the consumer?*
18. How is *service* defined in the text?
19. What is involved in creating satisfied customers?
20. What are the major outcomes for the firm of the marketing process and consumers' responses to it?
21. What are the major outcomes for the individual of the marketing process and consumers' responses to it?
22. What are the major outcomes for society of the marketing process and consumers' responses to it?
23. What is a *product position?*
24. What is meant by *injurious consumption?*
25. What is meant by *consumer lifestyle?*
26. Describe the consumer decision process.

DISCUSSION QUESTIONS

27. Why would someone shop on the Internet? Buy a Segway? Eat at Taco Bell frequently?
    a. Why would someone else not make those purchases?
    b. How would you choose one outlet, brand, or model over the others? Would others make the same choice in the same way?
28. Respond to the questions in Consumer Insight 1–1.
29. Of what use, if any, are models such as the one in Figure 1–3 to managers?
30. What changes would you suggest in the model in Figure 1–3? Why?
31. Describe your lifestyle. How does it differ from your parents' lifestyle?
32. Do you anticipate any changes in your lifestyle in the next five years? What will cause these

changes? What new products or brands will you consume because of these changes?

33. Describe a recent purchase you made. To what extent did you follow the consumer decision-making process described in this chapter? How would you explain any differences?

34. Describe several *total products* that are more than their direct physical features.

35. Describe the needs that the following items might satisfy and the total cost to the consumer of obtaining the benefits of the total product.
   a. Vespa motor scooter
   b. Health insurance
   c. Dog
   d. Personal digital assistant (PDA)

36. As described in the chapter, the FDA ordered three manufacturers of vegetable oil to remove claims on their labels stating that the products contain no cholesterol. The FDA believes that the claims of no cholesterol are misleading *even though they are true*. How would you explain this?

37. How would you define the product that the Hard Rock Cafe provides? What needs does it meet?

38. To what extent, if any, are marketers responsible for injurious consumption involving their products?

39. How could social marketing help alleviate some of society's problems?

40. Respond to the questions in Consumer Insight 1–2.

41. Is the criticism of Nike for creating a shoe that is symbolic of success to some groups (see Consumer Insight 1–2) valid? Why or why not?

42. Robert's American gourmet snack foods produces herbal-based snacks such as Spirulina Spirals and St. Johns Wort Tortilla Chips. According to the company president, "We're selling like crazy. We don't do research. We react as sort of a karma thing."[26] How would you explain the firm's success? What are the advantages and risks of this approach?

APPLICATION ACTIVITIES

43. Interview the manager or marketing manager of a retail firm. Determine how this individual develops the marketing strategy. Compare this person's process with the approach described in the text.

44. Interview the managers of a local charity. Determine what their assumptions about the consumer behavior of their supporters are. To what extent do they use marketing strategy to increase support for the organization or compliance with its objectives?

45. Interview five students. Have them describe the last three restaurant meals they consumed and the situations in which they were consumed. What can you conclude about the impact of the situation on consumer behavior? What can you conclude about the impact of the individual on consumer behavior?

46. Visit one or more stores that sell the following items. Report on the sales techniques used (point-of-purchase displays, store design, salesperson comments, and so forth). What beliefs concerning consumer behavior appear to underlie these strategies? It is often worthwhile for a male and a

female student to visit the same store and talk to the same salesperson at different times. The variation in salesperson behavior is sometimes quite revealing.
   a. Luxury cars
   b. Used cars
   c. Expensive jewelry
   d. Ski equipment
   e. Power tools
   f. Personal computers

47. Interview individuals who sell the following items. Try to discover their personal "models" of consumer behavior for their products.
   a. Athletic shoes
   b. Inexpensive suits
   c. Expensive suits
   d. Snowboards
   e. Flowers
   f. Life insurance

48. Interview three individuals who recently made a major purchase and three others who made a minor purchase. In what ways were their decision processes similar? How were they different?

REFERENCES

1. J. Neff, "P&G vs. Martha," *Advertising Age,* April 8, 2002, p. 24.

2. "Marketing-Oriented Lever Uses Research," *Marketing News,* February 10, 1978, p. 9.

3. C. Power, "Flops," *Business Week,* August 16, 1993, pp. 79–80.

4. "Slick TV Ads Divert Child Smoking," *Marketing News,* August 29, 1994, p. 30. See also C. Pechmann and S. Ratneshwar, "The Effects of Antismoking and Cigarette Advertising on Young Adolescents' Perceptions of Peers Who Smoke," *Journal of Consumer Research,* September 1994, pp. 236–51.

5. See A. R. Andreasen, "Social Marketing," *Journal of Public Policy & Marketing,* Spring 1994, pp. 108–14; A. R. Andreasen, *Marketing Social Chance* (San Francisco: Jossey-Bass, 1995); P. Braus, "Selling Good Behavior," *American Demographics,* November 1995, pp. 60–64; and R. E. Petty and J. T. Cacioppo, "Addressing Disturbing and Disturbed Consumer Behavior," *Journal of Marketing Research,* February 1996, pp. 1–8.

6. "The New Hucksterism," *Business Week,* July 1, 1996, pp. 76–84.

7. Power, "Flops."

8. B. J. Pine, Jr., and J. H. Gilmore, "Welcome to the Experience Economy," *Harvard Business Review,* July–August 1998, pp. 97–105.

9. S. Caminiti, "A Star Is Born," *Fortune,* Autumn 1993, pp. 44–47.

10. S. Chandler, "Data Is Power," *Business Week,* June 3, 1996, p. 69.

11. See W. McCall, "Nike Battles Backlash from Overseas Sweatshops," *Marketing News,* November 9, 1998, p. 14.

12. T. F. McMahon, "What Buyers Buy and Sellers Sell," *Journal of Professional Services Marketing,* no. 2 (1996), pp. 3–16.

13. P. Murtaugh, "Finding a Brand's Real Essence," *Advertising Age,* August 10, 1998, p. 12.

14. D. Roberts, "How Legend Lives Up to Its Name," *Business Week,* February 15, 1999, pp. 75–76.

15. Power, "Flops."

16. T. Pruzan, "Sauza Tequila Ads," *Advertising Age,* July 8, 1996, p. 29.

17. Caminiti, "A Star Is Born."

18. B. Morris, "The Future of Retirement," *Fortune,* August 19, 1996, pp. 86–94.

19. See D. N. Hassey and M. C. Smith, "Compulsive Buying," *Psychology & Marketing,* December 1996, pp. 741–52; and N. A. Mendoza and J. W. Pracejus, "Buy Now, Pay Later," *Advances in Consumer Research XXIV,* ed. M. Bruck and D. J. MacInnis (Provo, UT: Association for Consumer Research, 1997), pp. 499–503.

20. See P. Mergenhagen, "People Behaving Badly," *American Demographics,* August 1997, pp. 37–43.

21. E. C. Hirschman, "Secular Mortality and the Dark Side of Consumer Behavior," in *Advances in Consumer Research,* vol. 18, ed. R. Holman and M. R. Solomon (Provo, UT: Association for Consumer Research, 1991), pp. 1–4. See also R. J. Faber, "Two Forms of Compulsive Consumption," *Journal of Consumer Research,* December 1995, pp. 296–304.

22. See Petty and Cacioppo, "Addressing Disturbing and Disturbed Consumer Behavior," p. 1.

23. See M. L. Richins, "Special Possessions and the Expression of Material Values," *Journal of Consumer Research,* December 1994, pp. 522–33.

24. C. Miller, "The Have-Nots," *Marketing News,* August 1, 1994, pp. 1–2; P. Mergenhagen, "What Can Minimum Wage Buy?" *American Demographics,* January 1996, pp. 32–36; and A. Hank, "Hank Finds Two Families," *StreetWise,* May 16–31, 1996, p. 7.

25. J. F. Epstein, "A Shirt for Juan Navarro," in *Foundations for a Theory of Consumer Behavior,* ed. W. T. Tucker (New York: Holt, Rinehart & Winston, 1967), p. 75.

26. M. W. Fellman, "New Age Dawns for Product Niche," *Marketing News,* April 27, 1998, p. 1.

External Influences

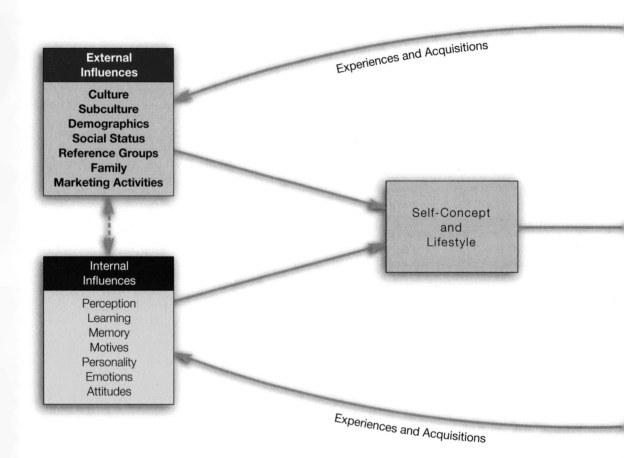

External Influences

Culture
Subculture
Demographics
Social Status
Reference Groups
Family
Marketing Activities

Internal Influences

Perception
Learning
Memory
Motives
Personality
Emotions
Attitudes

Self-Concept and Lifestyle

Experiences and Acquisitions

Experiences and Acquisitions

■ The external influence area of our model shown at the left is the focal point of this part of the text. Any division of the factors that influence consumer behavior into separate and distinct categories is somewhat arbitrary. For example, we will consider learning in Part 3 of the text, which focuses on internal influences. However, a substantial amount of learning involves interaction with, or imitation of, other individuals. Thus, learning clearly involves external influences such as family and peers. Our focus in this part is on the functioning of the various external groups, not the processes by which individuals react to these groups.

In this part, we begin with large-scale, macrogroup influences and move to smaller, more microgroup influences. As we progress, the nature of the influence exerted changes from general guidelines to explicit expectations for specific behaviors. In Chapter 2, we examine how cultures cause differing behaviors across countries and other cultural units. Chapters 3 through 6 focus primarily on the American society, examining its values, demographics, social stratification, subcultures, and family structure. Chapter 7 examines the mechanisms by which groups influence consumer behaviors. Contrasting examples from other cultures are presented throughout these chapters.

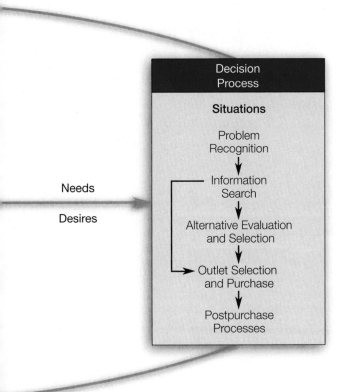

Needs

Desires

Decision
Process

Situations

Problem
Recognition

Information
Search

Alternative Evaluation
and Selection

Outlet Selection
and Purchase

Postpurchase
Processes

Cross-Cultural Variations in Consumer Behavior

☐ FedEx, while one of the top express shipping companies in the region, is not nearly as well known in Latin America and the Caribbean as it is in other parts of the world. Therefore, it decided to launch an advertising campaign to build brand awareness among small and medium-sized shippers. The ad agency was challenged to create a commercial that would work across this broad region with its differing cultures and languages. In addition, it would need to be presented in English and Portuguese in addition to Spanish without looking "dubbed." (It would cost too much to shoot three or four versions of the ad.) The ad would have to capture attention and convey the message and meaning desired.

The 30-second commercial shows a young equipment manager for a soccer team, the dominant sport in the region, worried about the delivery of five boxes of uniforms he had shipped to Madrid for a major match. An older man assures him that all will be fine as long as he had shipped them via FedEx, which he had not. The next scene is a soccer field where the opponents are about to attempt a penalty kick. As the camera reveals the defenders, the audience sees that they are defending the goal without their uniforms or any other clothing. The tagline for the ad is: "Let FedEx take the load off your shoulders."

Two versions of the last scene were shot, the nude version and a version with the men in their underwear. The underwear version was run in Mexico due to local restrictions on nudity in prime time. According to Karine Skobinsky, manager of pan-divisional advertising for FedEx Latin America and Caribbean Division: "We wanted to choose a theme that our target could relate to. And soccer is the national pastime in most Latin American markets. The script was designed to portray a realistic situation depicted from a customer's standpoint. Of course, we added a twist at the end to keep things entertaining and memorable. The tone of the advertising is in line with our brand identity, which uses humor to convey the message." Depending on the market, FedEx brand awareness increased 7 to 17 percent. "Not only did people specifically remember the ad, they could replay the message, the story, and who the sponsor was," said Skobinsky.[1]

Marketing across cultural boundaries is a difficult and challenging task. As Figure 2–1 indicates, cultures may differ in demographics, languages, nonverbal communications, and values. The success of FedEx in Latin America and elsewhere depends on how well the company understands and adapts to these differences.

FIGURE 2–1   **Cultural Factors Affect Consumer Behavior and Marketing Strategy**

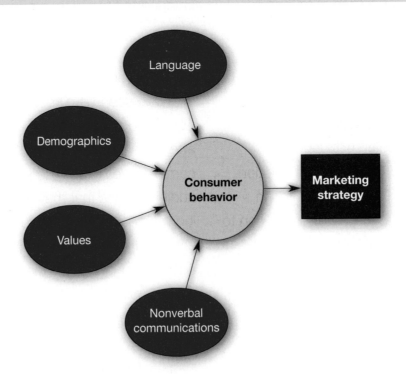

In this chapter, we focus on cultural variations in *values* and *nonverbal communications*. In addition, we briefly describe how *demographic variations* across countries and cultures influence consumption patterns.

Before we begin our discussion, we need to point out that while marketing strategy is heavily influenced by such variables as values, demographics, and languages, it also influences these variables. For example, television advertising in countries such as China and India is extensive and reflects many Western values such as individualism and youth. Over time, such advertising will influence not only how many Chinese and Indians choose to live (lifestyle) but also what they value and how they think and feel.[2]

Thus, the massive export and multinational advertising of consumer goods, particularly heavily symbolic goods such as cigarettes, soft drinks, clothing, and athletic gear, as well as experiential goods such as music, movies, and television programming, impacts the culture and desired lifestyles of the importing countries.[3] Often these products are adapted to the local culture and assume meanings and uses that greatly enrich the culture and the lives of its members. For example, many American holiday traditions are spreading through the world. Halloween originated in Ireland, Britain, and northwest France. Over time, its celebration became limited to the United States, Canada, and Ireland. Now, however, it is becoming global:

- The Abominable Giant Man Eating Zombie Tea Party is the theme for a costume bash at a Singapore nightclub.
- A radio station in Sri Lanka is hosting a competition for the weirdest Halloween recipes and the most bloodcurdling death screams.
- American-style Halloween celebrations are replacing the centuries-old festival commemorating the execution of Guy Fawkes in the Bahamas.
- Japan recently held a Hello Halloween Pumpkin Parade in Tokyo.
- In Paris, shops decorate their windows with goblins, spider webs, and skeletons; pumpkins are on sale at open-air markets; bakeries produce decorated Halloween cakes; McDonald's gives out masks with kids' meals; and some children go trick-or-treating.[4]

When such holidays do not replace local traditions and are adapted to the local culture, they can enrich the lives of the populations that adopt them. However, such imports can also be disruptive or controversial. For example, American-style celebrations of Valentine's Day are spreading throughout the world; but in countries such as India, they are being met with protests. Hindu and Indian beliefs generally restrict public displays of affection and many find Valentine cards that show young couples embracing to be offensive.[5]

In fact, many countries, both developed and developing, are concerned about the *Westernization,* and particularly the *Americanization,* of their cultures. This has led to attempts to ban or limit the importation of various American products. Europe has attempted to limit the importation of American movies, and Canada has restricted the Nashville-based Country Music Television channel. Both the French and Chinese governments have tried to restrict the use of English in brand names or advertising. American goods and services are often controversial and laced with political meaning in Islamic cultures.[6]

Despite concerns such as those described above, most categories of American products are generally prized throughout the world, as are those of Japan and Europe.[7] The American tobacco industry has taken advantage of this. American tobacco companies are aggressively marketing their products internationally where government restrictions and public attitudes are more favorable. For example, the required label on the side of a cigarette package in Japan indicates that smoking is considered as much a problem of

American tobacco companies have aggressive marketing campaigns in most developing countries. Many challenge the ethics of this practice.

© Munshi Ahmed.

politeness toward nonsmokers as it is a health hazard:

> Smoking too much can damage your health, so please be careful. Please observe good manners when smoking.

As Illustration 2–1 shows, tobacco firms have been particularly aggressive in the developing countries of Asia, Latin America, Africa, and Eastern Europe. Their advertising and promotions, frequently using Western models and alluring settings, along with the marketing activities of local tobacco firms, have been quite successful. Worldwide cigarette consumption rose by 18 percent over the past two decades, despite sharp drops in consumption in the United States, Canada, and much of Western Europe. Smoking-related deaths are now Asia's number one killer.[8] In China, one out of three men is projected to die of smoking related causes.[9] Clearly, there are both subtle (exported ads and products influencing other cultures' values) and direct (exporting harmful products) ethical issues involved in international marketing.

THE CONCEPT OF CULTURE

Culture is the *complex whole that includes knowledge, belief, art, law, morals, customs, and any other capabilities and habits acquired by humans as members of society.*

Several aspects of culture require elaboration. First, culture is a *comprehensive* concept. It includes almost everything that influences an individual's thought processes and behaviors. While culture does not determine the nature or frequency of biological drives such as hunger or sex, it does influence if, when, and how these drives will be gratified. It influences not only our preferences but how we make decisions[10] and even how we perceive the world around us. Second, culture is *acquired*. It does not include inherited responses and predispositions. However, since much of human behavior is learned rather than innate, culture does affect a wide array of behaviors.

Third, the complexity of modern societies is such that culture seldom provides detailed prescriptions for appropriate behavior. Instead, in most industrial societies, culture supplies *boundaries* within which most individuals think and act. Finally, the nature of cultural influences is such that we are *seldom aware* of them. One behaves, thinks, and feels in a manner consistent with other members of the same culture because it seems "natural" or "right" to do so.

Imagine a pizza that you and some friends are sharing. If you are an American, odds are you envisioned pepperoni on your pizza. However, in Japan, squid is the most popular topping; in England, it's tuna and corn; in Guatemala, black bean sauce; in Chile, mussels and clams; in the Bahamas, barbecued chicken; in Australia, eggs; and in India, pickled ginger.[11] Some of these toppings probably seem strange or even disgusting to you and yet are perfectly natural to members of other cultures. This is the nature of culture. We don't think about the fact that our preference for pizza topping, as well as most of our other preferences, is strongly influenced by our culture.

Culture operates primarily by setting rather loose boundaries for individual behavior and by influencing the functioning of such institutions as the family and mass media. Thus, *culture provides the framework within which individual and household lifestyles evolve.*

The boundaries that culture sets on behavior are called **norms,** which are simply *rules that specify or prohibit certain behaviors in specific situations.* Norms are derived from **cultural values,** or *widely held beliefs that affirm what is desirable.* Violation of cultural norms results in **sanctions,** or *penalties ranging from mild social disapproval to banishment from the group.* Thus, as Figure 2–2 indicates, cultural values give rise to norms and associated sanctions, which in turn influence consumption patterns.

The preceding discussion may leave the impression that people are aware of cultural values and norms and that violating any given norm carries a precise and known sanction. This is seldom the case. We tend to "obey" cultural norms without thinking because to do otherwise would seem unnatural. For example, we are seldom aware of how close we stand to other individuals while conducting business. Yet this distance is well defined and adhered to, even though it varies from culture to culture.

FIGURE 2–2   **Values, Norms, Sanctions, and Consumption Patterns**

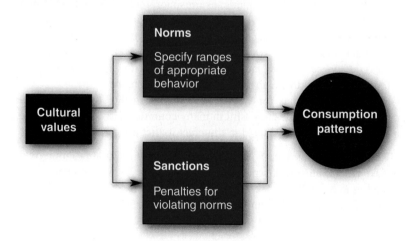

Malaysian shoppers buy American products at Makro, a Dutch-owned retail chain. The combination of low price, wide selection, and world brands is changing traditional shopping patterns around the world.

© Munshi Ahmed.

Cultures are not static. They typically evolve and change slowly over time. Marketing managers must understand both the existing cultural values and the emerging cultural values of the societies they serve. A failure to understand cultural differences can produce negative consequences such as:

- A U.S. electronics firm landed a major contract with a Japanese buyer. The U.S. firm's president flew to Tokyo for the contract-signing ceremony. Then the head of the Japanese firm began reading the contract intently. The scrutiny continued for an extraordinary length of time. At last, the U.S. executive offered an additional price discount. The Japanese executive, though surprised, did not object. The U.S. executive's mistake was assuming that the Japanese executive was attempting to reopen negotiations. Instead, he was demonstrating his personal concern and authority in the situation by closely and slowly examining the document.
- Another electronics company sent a conservative American couple to represent the firm in Sweden. They were invited for a weekend in the country where, at an isolated beach, their Swedish hosts disrobed. The Americans misinterpreted this not uncommon Swedish behavior, and their response to it destroyed a promising business relationship.
- An article in the Air Canada magazine entitled "All about Sake" focused on how to select Japanese sake and how to become a Japanese sake connoisseur. The accompanying photograph showed Chinese ceramic and bamboo steamers with Chinese writing—not a sound way to impress either their Japanese or Chinese customers.
- Procter & Gamble's commercials for Camay, in which men directly complimented women on their appearance, were successful in many countries. However, they were a failure in Japan, where men and women don't interact in that manner.

Red Wing Shoe Company put 21 executives through a three-day training program on the Middle East. As Red Wing's president explained: "We always give the customer what he wants. If we're playing in his ballpark, we'd better know his rules."[12] As Illustration 2–2 indicates, sophisticated retailers and manufacturers are able to succeed throughout the world.

VARIATIONS IN CULTURAL VALUES

Cultural values are widely held beliefs that affirm what is desirable. These values affect behavior through norms, which specify an acceptable range of responses to specific situations. A useful approach to understanding cultural variations in behavior is to understand the values embraced by different cultures.

There are numerous values that vary across cultures and affect consumption. We will present a classification scheme consisting of three broad forms of cultural values—*other-oriented, environment-oriented,* and *self-oriented.*[13] The cultural values that have the most impact on consumer behavior can be classified in one of these three general categories.

Other-oriented values reflect a society's view of the appropriate relationships *between individuals and groups* within that society. These relationships have a major influence on marketing practice. For example, if the society values collective activity, consumers will look toward others for guidance in purchase decisions and will not respond favorably to promotional appeals to "be an individual."

Environment-oriented values prescribe a society's relationship *to its economic and technical as well as its physical environment.* As a manager, you would develop a very different marketing program for a society that stressed a problem-solving, risk-taking, performance-oriented approach to its environment than you would for a fatalistic, security- and status-oriented society.

Self-oriented values reflect the objectives and approaches to life *that the individual members of society find desirable.* Again, these values have strong implications for marketing management. For instance, the acceptance and use of credit is very much determined by a society's position on the value of postponed versus immediate gratification.

Table 2–1 provides a list of 18 values that are important in most cultures. The list is not meant to be exhaustive, but it does include the major values that are relevant to consumer behavior in industrialized societies. Most of the values are shown as dichotomies (e.g., materialistic versus nonmaterialistic). However, this is not meant to represent an either/or situation. Instead, a continuum exists between the two extremes. For example, two societies can each value tradition, but one may value it more than the other and, therefore, be closer to the tradition end of the scale. For several of the values, a natural dichotomy does not seem to exist. For a society to place a low value on cleanliness does not imply that it places a high value on dirtiness. These 18 values are described in the following paragraphs.

Other-Oriented Values

Individual/Collective   Does the culture emphasize and reward individual initiative, or are cooperation with and conformity to a group more highly valued? Are individual differences appreciated or condemned? Are rewards and status given to individuals or to groups? Answers to these questions reveal the individual or collective orientation of a culture. Individualism is one of the most defining characteristics of the American culture. Australia, the United Kingdom, Canada, and New Zealand are also relatively individualistic. Taiwan, Korea, Hong Kong, Mexico, Japan, and India are more collective in their orientation.

This value is one of the core factors differentiating cultures.[14] It is so fundamental that it affects the self-concept and self-consciousness of individuals.[15] Not surprisingly, consumers from cultures that differ on this value differ in their reactions to many marketing activities such as reactions to fast-food restaurants,[16] foreign products,[17] luxury goods,[18] advertising,[19] new products,[20] and preferred sources of information.[21]

TABLE 2-1

Cultural Values of
Relevance to
Consumer Behavior

Other-Oriented Values

- *Individual/Collective.* Are individual activity and initiative valued more highly than collective activity and conformity?
- *Youth/Age.* Is family life organized to meet the needs of the children or the adults? Are younger or older people viewed as leaders and role models?
- *Extended/Limited family.* To what extent does one have a lifelong obligation to numerous family members?
- *Masculine/Feminine.* To what extent does social power automatically go to males?
- *Competitive/Cooperative.* Does one obtain success by excelling over others or by cooperating with them?
- *Diversity/Uniformity.* Does the culture embrace variation in religious belief, ethnic background, political views, and other important behaviors and attitudes?

Environment-Oriented Values

- *Cleanliness.* To what extent is cleanliness pursued beyond the minimum needed for health?
- *Performance/Status.* Is the culture's reward system based on performance or on inherited factors such as family or class?
- *Tradition/Change.* Are existing patterns of behavior considered to be inherently superior to new patterns of behavior?
- *Risk taking/Security.* Are those who risk their established positions to overcome obstacles or achieve high goals admired more than those who do not?
- *Problem solving/Fatalistic.* Are people encouraged to overcome all problems, or do they take a "what will be, will be" attitude?
- *Nature.* Is nature regarded as something to be admired or overcome?

Self-Oriented Values

- *Active/Passive.* Is a physically active approach to life valued more highly than a less active orientation?
- *Sensual gratification/Abstinence.* To what extent is it acceptable to enjoy sensual pleasures such as food, drink, and sex?
- *Material/Nonmaterial.* How much importance is attached to the acquisition of material wealth?
- *Hard work/Leisure.* Is a person who works harder than economically necessary admired more than one who does not?
- *Postponed gratification/Immediate gratification.* Are people encouraged to "save for a rainy day" or to "live for today"?
- *Religious/Secular.* To what extent are behaviors and attitudes based on the rules specified by a religious doctrine?

Thus, motivating and compensating Japanese, Indian, or Korean sales personnel using individual-based incentive systems and promotions may not be effective. Likewise, such themes as "be yourself," "stand out," and "don't be one of the crowd" are often effective in the United States but generally are not in Japan, Korea, or China. One expert describes the role that brands play in many Asian societies:

> Brands take on roles as symbols that extend well beyond the intrinsic features of the category. One is not buying a watch, or even a status brand, one is buying club membership, or an "I am just like you" (symbol). If brands are such powerful symbols it is again not surprising to find very entrenched levels of brand loyalty.[22]

However, these generalizations are less accurate today than in the recent past, at least as far as Japan is concerned. Evidence indicates that the Japanese, particularly the younger generation, are becoming more individualistic:

> Mizuho Arai knows what she likes. A 20-year-old uniformed office worker by day, at night she wears loafers, a sweater, Levi's 501s, and a black parka. Shopping with an L. L. Bean bag over her shoulder, she prefers bargain outlets to traditional department stores and designer boutiques. "I don't like to be told what's trendy. I can make up my own mind."[23]

Arai is typical of the younger generation of Japanese consumers. "They don't listen to us," complains Kenichi Mizorogi, the cosmetics manager for Shiseido Co. In the late 1980s, Shiseido launched its very successful Perky Jean makeup line with the theme: "Everyone is buying it." "That would never work now," says Mizorogi. Indeed, recent research has found that the 18–21 age group (a $33 billion market) places major emphasis on individuality.

The different values held by younger and older Japanese illustrate that few cultures are completely homogeneous. Marketers must be aware of differences both *between* cultures and *within* cultures.[24]

Youth/Age   To what extent do the primary family activities focus on the needs of the children instead of those of the adults? What role, if any, do children play in family decisions? What role do they play in decisions that primarily affect the child? Are prestige, rank, and important social roles assigned to younger or older members of society? Are the behavior, dress, and mannerisms of the younger or older members of a society imitated by the rest of the society?

While American society is clearly youth oriented, many Asian cultures have traditionally valued the wisdom that comes with age. Thus, mature spokespersons would tend to be more successful in these cultures than would younger ones. However, some Asian cultures are becoming increasingly youth oriented.[25] Consider the following description of Taiwan:

> Taiwan is very, very youth-oriented, and it is a very hip culture. . . . You have a consumer-based economy that is quite potent, and pitching to the youth is a good way of ensuring that your products are going to be bought.[26]

Variation in attitudes toward children can be seen in the percentage of the respondents from various countries who agree with the statement, Marriage without children is not complete. This percentage ranges from around 70 in France, Greece, and Portugal to 30 or less in the Netherlands, Norway, Sweden, Great Britain, and Denmark.[27] The ability of children to influence the purchase of products for their own use as well as products used by the family varies according to this value and has obvious implications for advertising.[28]

China's policy of limiting families to one child has produced a strong focus on the child. In fact, many of these children receive so much attention that they are known in Asia as "little emperors." H. J. Heinz is successfully marketing a rice cereal for Chinese babies. Its premium price (75 cents a box, where average workers earn only $40 a month) and American origin give it an image of high quality. The convenience of the instant cereal is also an advantage in a country where 70 percent of the women work outside the home.[29]

Extended/Limited Family   The family unit is the basis for virtually all societies. Nonetheless, the definition of the family and the rights and obligations of family members vary widely across cultures.[30] As we will see in Chapter 6, our families have a lifelong impact on all of us, both genetically and through our early socialization, no matter what culture we come from. However, cultures differ widely in the obligations one owes to other family members at various stages of life as well as who is considered to be a member of the family.

In the United States, the family is defined fairly narrowly and is less important than in many other cultures. In general, strong obligations are felt only to immediate family members (siblings, parents, and children), and these diminish as family members establish new families. That is, one's sense of obligation toward one's brother, sister, or even parent tends to decrease when one marries.

In many other cultures, the role of the family is much stronger. Families, and obligations, often extend to cousins, nieces, nephews, and beyond. One has responsibilities to one's parents, grandparents, and even ancestors that must be fulfilled. The following description indicates the complexity and extent of the extended Chinese family.

> The family is critically important in all aspects of Chinese life and there is a distrust of non-family members. In response to this, the Chinese have developed family-like links to a greater extent than almost any other culture. Thus the family in the Chinese context is different from the western conceptualization. It stretches to the furthest horizons, from close family, to slightly distant, to more distant, embracing people who are not really family but are connected to someone in one's family and to all their families. As such, the family is really a system of contacts, rather than purely an emotional unit as in the west.[31]

Clearly, marketers need to understand the role of families in the cultures they serve. For example, in Mexico, compared to the United States, adolescents are much more likely to seek parental advice or to respond positively to ads with parental figures in the purchase of items ranging from candy to movies to fashion clothing.[32] These differences call for related changes in the advertising of products to teenagers in these two cultures.

Masculine/Feminine   Are rank, prestige, and important social roles assigned primarily to men? Can a female's life pattern be predicted at birth with a high degree of accuracy? Does the husband, wife, or both, make important family decisions? Basically, we live in a masculine-oriented world, yet the degree of masculine orientation varies widely, even across the relatively homogeneous countries of Western Europe.

This dimension influences both obvious and subtle aspects of marketing (see Chapter 3). Obviously, the roles and manner in which one would portray women in advertisements in Muslim countries would differ from those in the United States.[33] However, suppose you were going to promote furniture in Taiwan or Japan. Would you focus on the husband, the wife, or both? Would it vary by country? Research indicates that a moderate focus on the wife would be best in both countries.[34] How would you portray a teenage Japanese girl in an ad to this audience? A more "girlish" (childlike, approval seeking) portrayal than is common in U.S. ads (a more sultry, explicitly sexual portrayal) would be appropriate.[35]

Consider the following data on participating in sports and exercise.

	Never			**Frequently**		
	Male	*Female*	*Difference*	*Male*	*Female*	*Difference*
United States	34%	44%	10%	46%	39%	−07%
United Kingdom	40	41	01	45	43	−02
South Korea	53	73	20	37	23	−14
Mexico	42	72	30	44	18	−26
Japan	66	72	06	16	16	00
Brazil	46	66	20	47	27	−20
China	45	51	06	38	32	−06
France	45	57	12	44	29	−15
Germany	30	34	04	55	48	−07
Italy	59	72	13	32	25	−07

While males are somewhat more likely to exercise across all the countries, the differences between male and female participation are quite large in traditionally masculine countries.[36] *What does this imply for marketing activities in those countries?*

The role of women is changing and expanding throughout much of the world. This is creating new opportunities as well as problems for marketers.[37] For example, the increasing

© Shiseido Cosmetics (America) Ltd.

ILLUSTRATION 2–3

The changing role of women creates new needs and products even in relatively traditional cultures such as Japan. This lipstick is targeted at Japan's new working women.

percentage of Japanese women who continue to work after marriage has led to increased demand for time-saving products as well as other products targeted at the working woman:

- Many Japanese women feel guilty preparing frozen vegetables in a microwave rather than preparing fresh vegetables. In promoting its Green Giant frozen vegetables in Japan, Pillsbury emphasized convenience and nutrition and attempted to position them as part of "modern up-to-date cooking." Sales increased 50 percent. The company has followed up with Dough Boy frozen bite-sized meat pies for busy mothers to pack in their children's school lunches.

- Lotte had dominated the caffeinated chewing gum market (used for a pick-me-up on the way to work or during working hours) by targeting men with a very masculine positioning strategy. Warner-Lambert K.K. decided that working women were under the same stresses as men and developed a brand called Sting, targeted at working women. Using fashionable advertising and sleek gold and silver packaging, Sting has been a solid success.

- Long-lasting, no-smear lipstick didn't exist in Japan until a few years ago, but it now has sales of $45 million a month (see Illustration 2–3). Targeted at working women, Shiseido's brand, Reciente Perfect Rouge, features a popular model racing through her busy day wearing the no-smear lipstick.

- Virginia Slims has grown sales by 25 percent annually with ads showing a woman wearing jeans and repairing a motorcycle or a woman with her face smeared with grease holding a wrench.[38]

Competitive/Cooperative   Is the path to success found by outdoing other individuals or groups, or is success achieved by forming alliances with other individuals and groups? Does everyone admire a winner? Variation on this value can be seen in the way different cultures react to comparative advertisements. For example, Germany and Spain ban such ads, whereas the United States encourages them.

As one would expect in a cooperative culture, the Japanese have historically found comparative ads to be distasteful. However, focus group research for Pepsi-Cola Japan found that younger consumers would appreciate advertising that mocked a rival in a frank and funny way. On the basis of this research, PepsiCo launched a TV spot in which rap singer Hammer depicted market leader Coke as the beverage that turns you into a nerd. Pepsi's sales jumped 19 percent.[39] However, in other cooperatively oriented countries, comparative ads have not fared as well.[40]

Diversity/Uniformity   Do members of the culture embrace variety in terms of religions, ethnic backgrounds, political beliefs, and other important behaviors and attitudes? A culture that values diversity not only will accept a wide array of personal behaviors and attitudes but is also likely to welcome variety in terms of food, dress, and other products and services. In contrast, a society valuing uniformity is unlikely to accept a wide array of tastes and product preferences, though such a society may be subject to fads, fashions, and other changes over time.

Japan places a strong value on uniformity, whereas Canada and Holland value diversity. While many important aspects of these cultures are affected by the differences in this value, one obvious to any tourist is the relative absence of ethnic (Mexican, Italian, Indian, and so forth) restaurants in Japan relative to Canada and Holland.

Environment-Oriented Values

Cleanliness   Is cleanliness next to godliness, or is it a rather minor matter? Are homes, offices, and public spaces expected to be clean beyond reasonable health requirements? In the United States, a high value is placed on cleanliness. In fact, people from many cultures consider Americans to be paranoid on the subject of personal hygiene.

While there are differences in the value placed on cleanliness among the economically developed cultures, the largest differences are between these cultures and many of the underdeveloped nations. In many poorer countries, cleanliness is not valued at a level sufficient to produce a healthy environment. This is true even in large parts of a rapidly developing country such as China, where a lack of basic hygiene still causes significant health problems. While often criticized for having a negative impact on local cultures, McDonald's has been credited with introducing more hygienic food preparation and toilets in several East Asian markets, including China.[41]

Performance/Status   Are opportunities, rewards, and prestige based on an individual's performance or on the status associated with the person's family, position, or class? Do all people have an equal opportunity economically, socially, and politically at the start of life, or are certain groups given special privileges? Are products and brands valued for their ability to accomplish a task or for the reputation or status of the brand?

Performance/status is closely related to the concept of **power distance,** which refers to *the degree to which people accept inequality in power, authority, status, and wealth as natural or inherent in society.* India, Brazil, France, Hong Kong, and Japan are relatively high in their acceptance of power. Austria, Denmark, New Zealand, Sweden, and the United States are relatively low. In which of these countries would an expert source have the

China evokes many images. One aspect of China's image is the consumption of tea. The ubiquitous nature of tea in China is captured in the common expression: "I wouldn't do that for all the tea in China." To visit a store or home in China is to be offered hot tea, and it comes automatically with food throughout the country.

Given the dominant position of tea in the Chinese culture, would you consider China to be a good country in which to launch a chain of coffee shops? Starbucks does! In January 1999, Starbucks, in conjunction with its Chinese partner, opened its first retail outlet in China in Beijing. While the opening ceremony was traditionally Chinese with dragons and flower wreaths, the outlet and most of its products are strictly Western.

David Sun, CEO of Starbucks' Chinese partner, states: "At Starbucks, we offer the very best of class in everything we do, from brewing the perfect cup of coffee to inspiring magical moments in the lives of our customers. This is the heart and soul of the Starbucks experience."

However, does a perfect cup of coffee provide value to a consumer who normally drinks tea? Will a Western-style coffee shop provide "inspiring magical moments" to Chinese consumers?

Not long ago, similar questions were being asked about the Starbucks concept in America. For its first 10 years, Starbucks operated a single retail outlet in Seattle. In 1983, Howard Schultz, Starbucks' director of marketing, was vacationing in Italy where he noticed the immense popularity of espresso bars. Upon his return, the firm launched a coffee bar in downtown Seattle. This experiment was successful, and the firm began its rapid expansion across the United States.[42]

Critical Thinking Questions

1. The coffee bar concept, coupled with high-quality, strongly flavored coffee, obviously transferred successfully from the Italian to the American culture. However, America has traditionally embraced coffee. Will Starbucks work in countries where tea is the dominant drink?
2. What values will affect Starbucks' success in China?
3. What ethical issues should Starbucks consider as it enters developing countries?

greatest impact in an advertisement? Research indicates that expert sources have a greater impact in a high power distance country than in a low one.[43]

A status-oriented society is more likely to prefer "quality" or established brand names and high-priced items to functionally equivalent items with unknown brand names or lower prices. This is the case in Japan, Hong Kong, Singapore, the Philippines, Malaysia, Indonesia, Thailand, and most Arabic countries, where consumers are attracted by prestigious, known brands.

One study found that almost 80 percent of the respondents in the United Kingdom agreed that a well-known brand name would have a moderate or strong influence on their purchase decisions. In contrast, less than 30 percent of the German respondents assigned that level of importance to the brand name.[44] The implications for advertising strategies, branding, and new-product development are significant. *How would your strategy change if you were exporting an established American product to Germany versus to the United Kingdom? What if it were a new product from Mexico?*

Tradition/Change Is tradition valued simply for the sake of tradition? Is change or "progress" an acceptable reason for altering established patterns? Compared to Americans, Koreans and Chinese consumers have traditionally been much less comfortable dealing with new situations or ways of thinking.[45] However, both the Korean and Chinese cultures are now enthusiastically embracing change. In China, "modernness" (often symbolized by a Western name) is an important product attribute, particularly among younger, urban Chinese. *Will this be enough for Starbucks to succeed in China* (see Consumer Insight 2–1)?

Another study found that female Irish consumers, compared to American females, had a lesser need to engage in variety-seeking behavior and achieved their optimum level of consumption variety at a lower level.[46] The marketing impact of Britain's tradition-oriented culture can be seen in the fact that three-fourths of its population claim to be generally brand loyal, compared to half in France and Germany.[47] Further, British ads, compared to those in America, are much more likely to emphasize tradition and history.[48]

Risk Taking/Security   Do the "heroes" of the culture meet and overcome obstacles? Is the person who risks established position or wealth on a new venture admired or considered foolhardy? This value relates to tolerance for ambiguity and uncertainty avoidance. It has a strong influence on entrepreneurship and economic development as well as new-product acceptance. A society that does not admire risk taking is unlikely to develop enough entrepreneurs to achieve economic change and growth. New-product introductions, new channels of distribution, and advertising themes are affected by this value.[49]

Problem Solving/Fatalistic   Do people react to obstacles and disasters as challenges to be overcome, or do they take a "what will be, will be" attitude? Is there an optimistic, "we can do it" orientation? In the Caribbean, difficult or unmanageable problems are often dismissed with the expression "no problem." This actually means: "There is a problem, but we don't know what to do about it—so don't worry!" Mexico also falls toward the fatalistic end of this continuum. As a result, Mexican customers are less likely to express formal complaints when confronted with an unsatisfactory purchase.

Nature   Is nature assigned a positive value, or is it viewed as something to be overcome, conquered, or tamed? Americans historically considered nature as something to be overcome or improved. In line with this, animals were either destroyed or romanticized and made into heroes and pets.[50] Dogs, for example, are pets in the United States, and few Americans would feel comfortable consuming them as food. However, they are a common food source in countries such as China.

Most northern European countries place a high value on the environment. Packaging and other environmental regulations are stronger in these countries than in America. In turn, Americans and Canadians appear to place a higher value on the environment than the southern European countries and most developing countries, though this may reflect variations in the financial ability to act on this value rather than in the value itself. These differences in attitudes are reflected in consumers' purchase decisions, consumption practices, and recycling efforts.[51]

As with all the values we are discussing, there are wide ranges within as well as between countries, which create market opportunities. For example, overall China does not have a strong environmental orientation. However, there are segments of the country that do have such an orientation and the means to buy products and services that reflect this focus.[52]

Self-Oriented Values

Active/Passive   Are people expected to take a physically active approach to work and play? Are physical skills and feats valued more highly than less physical performances? Is emphasis placed on doing? Americans are much more prone to engage in physical activities and to take an action-oriented approach to problems. "Don't just stand there, do something," is a common response to problems in America. Active exercise varies widely across countries, especially for women (see page 48). While this obviously limits the market for exercise equipment in these countries, it also affects advertising themes and formats. For example, the ad shown in Illustration 1–7 (page 28) would not be appropriate in a country such as Japan, where two-thirds of the men and three-fourths of the women exercise less than twice a year.

Sensual Gratification/Abstinence   Is it acceptable to pamper oneself, to satisfy one's desires for food, drink, or sex beyond the minimum requirement? Is one who forgoes such gratification considered virtuous or strange? Muslim cultures are extremely conservative on this value. Advertisements, packages, and products must carefully conform to Muslim standards. Polaroid's instant cameras gained rapid acceptance because they allowed Arab men to photograph their wives and daughters without fear that a stranger in a film laboratory would see the women unveiled.

In contrast, Brazilian and European advertisements contain nudity and blatant (by U.S. standards) appeals to sensual gratification. Consider the following billboard ad for Gossard women's underwear appearing throughout the United Kingdom:

> The picture shows the upper half of a nude woman lying on a bed with her arms above her head, her back arched. Her bra and panties are on the floor along with a man's shoe and shirt. The text says "Bring him to his knees." The tagline is *"Gossard.* Find your *G* spot." Another version has the copy line—"If he's late you can always start without him."[53]

Illustration 2–4 is an Australian ad for milk that makes use of sensuality and humor. While quite appropriate for Australia, it would not be a successful ad in a culture that did not accept sensual gratification.

Material/Nonmaterial   Is the accumulation of material wealth a positive good in its own right? Does material wealth bring more status than family ties, knowledge, or other activities? Consider the following conclusion from a study of Chinese television ownership.

> The television one owns is very much a representation of one's own self-worth. For most, the television had become almost as much a part of getting married as saying their vows. One engaged man (age 24), who was saving for his TV so he could get married, noted that he wanted a 25" or 29" Japanese model. He was willing to save for up to two years (a commonly quoted time frame) before revising his sights downward. Price was not nearly as important as projecting "a good image" to others. He was concerned about getting off to a good start. Several respondents noted that the purchase of the appropriate television set was more important than having furniture when considering marriage.[54]

There are two types of materialism. **Instrumental materialism** is *the acquisition of things to enable one to do something.* Skis can be acquired to allow one to ski. **Terminal materialism** is the *acquisition of items for the sake of owning the item itself.* Art is generally acquired for the pleasure of owning it rather than as a means to another goal. Cultures differ markedly in their relative emphasis on these two types of materialism.[55]

A further description of cultural variation in the meaning of material items is presented in the section on nonverbal communications later in this chapter.

Hard Work/Leisure   Is work valued for itself, independent of external rewards, or is work merely a means to an end? Will individuals continue to work hard even when their minimum economic needs are satisfied, or will they opt for more leisure time? In parts of Latin America, work is viewed as a necessary evil. However, in much of Europe, work is considered essential for a full life. Consequently, labor-saving products and instant food often meet with failure in countries such as Switzerland.

ILLUSTRATION 2–4

Cultures differ in their acceptance of sensual gratification. This ad works well in Australia but would not be appropriate in cultures that place a high value on abstinence.

1. Video: A young man returns from his morning jog to the apartment he shares with others. His flatmate is on his way out.
Audio: The Tex-Mex 60s hit "Wooly Bully" throughout.

2. Video (cut): In the bathroom he is stripping off his sweaty jogging gear when he spots something black and lacy hanging from the towel rack.

3. (Cut) In the shaving mirror he sees the legs of the lingerie's owner.

4. (Cut) She is dozing in a bathtub full of milk.

5. (Cut) The young man is fascinated and embarrassed at the same time.

6. (Cut) The beauty is sound asleep. He decides to steal away.

7. (Cut) But not before chancing a final look. Suddenly, he discovers ...

8. (Cut) ... a glass and a straw at the edge of the tub. This gives him an idea.

9. (Cut) He starts sucking the milk from the straw to lower the milk level and to get an even better look at the natural wonders in front of him.

10. Cut.

11. (Cut) He notices that the milk tastes quite delicious.

12. Hence he concentrates more on the tasty liquid than on the bathing beauty.

13. His enjoyment is rudely interrupted.
Audio (MVO): "Honey, I'm back."

14. Video: Quickly, he jumps into in the shower stall to hide.

15. Cut.
Audio (MVO): "Rev. It's the taste you can't resist."

Courtesy Australian Milk Marketing; agency: Clemenger Melbourne.

Postponed Gratification/Immediate Gratification   Is one encouraged to "save for a rainy day," or should one "live for today"? Is it better to secure immediate benefits and pleasures, or is it better to suffer in the short run for benefits in the future, or in the here-after or for future generations?

This value has implications for distribution strategies, efforts to encourage savings, and the use of credit. For example, in Germany and the Netherlands, buying on credit is widely viewed as living beyond one's means. In fact, the word for "debt" in German (*schuld*) is the same word used for "guilt."

Religious/Secular   To what extent are daily activities determined by religious doctrine? The United States is relatively secular. Many Islamic cultures as well as some Catholic countries are much more religiously oriented.[56] In contrast, religion plays a very small role in Chinese culture. However, even in a country such as China where few are actively involved with a formal religion, many of the culture's values were formed in part by historical religious influences. The same is true for the secular nations of the West. Understanding the extent and type of religious influences operating in a culture is essential for effectively designing all elements of the marketing mix.[57]

Clearly, the preceding discussion has not covered all of the values operating in the various cultures. However, it should suffice to provide a feel for the importance of cultural values and how cultures differ along value dimensions.

CULTURAL VARIATIONS IN NONVERBAL COMMUNICATIONS

Differences in **verbal communication systems** (languages) are immediately obvious to anyone entering a foreign culture. An American traveling in Britain or Australia will be able to communicate, but differences in pronunciation, timing, and meaning will still occur. For example, Griptight Ltd. had to change the name of its *soother* to *pacifier* when it decided to import its line of baby products from Britain to the United States.[58]

Variations in verbal language are easy to notice and accept because we realize that language is an arbitrary invention. The meaning assigned to a particular group of letters or sounds is not inherent in the letters or sounds—a word means what a group of people agree it will mean.

Attempts to translate marketing communications from one language to another can result in ineffective communications, as Ford Motor Company is painfully aware:

> Fiera (a low-cost truck designed for developing countries) faced sales problems since *fiera* means "terrible, cruel, or ugly" in Spanish. The popular Ford car *Comet* had limited sales in Mexico, where it was named Caliente. The reason—*caliente* is slang for "a streetwalker." The Pinto was briefly introduced in Brazil without a name change. Then it was discovered that *pinto* is slang for a "small male sex organ." The name was changed to Corcel, which means "horse."[59]

Coca-Cola Company avoided the problems Ford encountered by realizing that *enjoy,* which is part of its famous logo Enjoy Coca-Cola, has sensual connotations in Russian and several other languages. Coca-Cola solved this problem by changing the logo to Drink Coca-Cola where appropriate. It also altered the successful "The real thing" theme to "I feel Coke" in Japan and several other countries with great success. It is now altering its new theme, "Life tastes good," in many countries where *tastes* would not convey the same meaning it does in English.

Table 2–2 indicates that Ford is not the only company to encounter translation problems. The problems of literal translations and slang expressions are compounded by symbolic meanings associated with words, the absence of some words from various languages, and the difficulty of pronouncing certain words:[60]

• Mars addressed the problem of making the M&M's name pronounceable in France, where neither ampersands nor the apostrophe "s" plural form exists, by advertising

TABLE 2–2

Translation Problems
in International
Marketing

- An American airline operating in Brazil advertised the plush "rendezvous lounges" on its jets only to discover that *rendezvous* in Portuguese means a room hired for lovemaking.
- General Motors' "Body by Fisher" was translated as "corpse by Fisher" in Flemish.
- Colgate's Cue toothpaste had problems in France, as *cue* is a crude term for "butt" in French.
- Sunbeam attempted to enter the German market with a mist-producing curling iron named the Mist-Stick. Unfortunately, *mist* translates as "dung" or "manure" in German.
- Pet milk encounters difficulties in French-speaking countries where *pet* means, among other things, "to break wind."
- Fresca is a slang word for "lesbian" in Mexico.
- Esso found that its name pronounced phonetically meant "stalled car" in Japanese.
- Kellogg's Bran Buds translates to "burned farmer" in Swedish.
- United Airline's in-flight magazine cover for its Pacific Rim routes showed Australian actor Paul Hogan in the outback. The caption stated, "Paul Hogan Camps It Up." "Camps it up" is Australian slang for "flaunts his homosexuality."
- A car wash was translated into German as "car enema."
- China attempted to export Pansy brand men's underwear to America.
- The Dairy Association's "Got Milk?" theme was translated as "Are you lactating?" in Mexico.
- Parker Pen mistook *embarazar* (to impregnate) to mean to embarrass and ran an ad in Mexico stating "It won't leak in your pocket and make you pregnant."
- American Airlines introduced its new leather first-class seats in Mexico with the theme "Fly in Leather" which, when translated literally, read "Fly Naked."

extensively that M&M's should be pronounced "aimainaimze." Whirlpool is facing a similar problem in Spain, as its name is virtually unpronounceable in Spanish.

- To market its Ziploc food storage bags in Brazil, Dow Chemical had to use extensive advertising to create the word *zipar,* meaning to zip, since there was no such term in Portuguese.

In addition, such communication factors as humor and preferred style and pace vary across cultures, even those speaking the same basic language.[61] Nonetheless, verbal language translations generally do not present major problems as long as we are careful. What many of us fail to recognize, however, is that each culture also has nonverbal communication systems or languages that, like verbal languages, are specific to each culture. **Nonverbal communication systems** are the *arbitrary meanings a culture assigns actions, events, and things other than words.*

The following discussion examines the seven variables shown in Figure 2–3, all of which influence nonverbal communications: time, space, symbols, friendship, agreements, things, and etiquette.[62]

Time

The meaning of time varies between cultures in two major ways. First is what we call time perspective: this is a culture's overall orientation toward time.[63] The second is the interpretations assigned to specific uses of time.

Time Perspective   Most Americans, Canadians, Western Europeans, and Australians tend to view time as inescapable, linear, and fixed in nature. It is a road reaching into the future with distinct, separate sections (hours, days, weeks, and so on). Time is seen almost as a physical object: we can schedule it, waste it, lose it, and so forth. Believing that a person does one thing at a time, we have a strong orientation toward the present and the short-term future. This is known as a **monochronic time perspective.**

FIGURE 2–3	Factors Influencing Nonverbal Communications

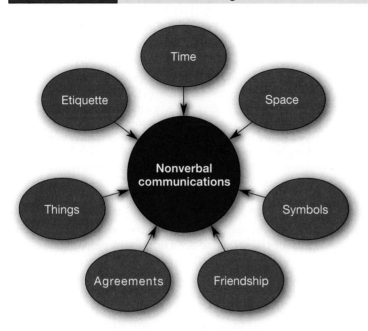

Most Latin Americans, Asians, and Indians tend to view time as being less discrete and less subject to scheduling. They view simultaneous involvement in many activities as natural. People and relationships take priority over schedules, and activities occur at their own pace rather than according to a predetermined timetable. Such cultures have an orientation toward the present and the past. This is known as a **polychronic time perspective.**

Some of the important differences between individuals with a monochronic perspective and those with a polychronic perspective are listed below.[64]

Monochronic Culture	*Polychronic Culture*
Do one thing at a time	Do many things at once
Concentrate on the job	Are highly distractible and subject to interruptions
Take deadlines and schedules seriously	Consider deadlines and schedules secondary
Committed to the job or task	Committed to people and relationships
Adhere religiously to plans	Change plans often and easily
Emphasize promptness	Base promptness on the relationship
Accustomed to short-term relationships	Prefer long-term relationships

How would marketing activities vary between monochronic and polychronic cultures? Personal selling and negotiation styles and strategies would need to differ, as would many advertising themes. Contests and sales with deadlines would generally be more effective in monochronic than in polychronic cultures. Convenience foods frequently fail when positioned in terms of timesaving and convenience in polychronic cultures where "saving time" is not part of the cultural thought processes. The following quote illustrates the impact of time perspective on the positioning strategy of fast-food outlets in polychronic cultures:

> In Argentina, McDonald's has an image of an expensive, modern restaurant where the majority of the customers are teenagers and young adults who patronize McDonald's to express their modern and liberated value systems. This is equally true in Turkey. In fact, a major reason for the popularity of fast-food restaurants in many developing countries is neither convenience nor reasonable prices. Time savings does not have the same priority in these countries as it does in the United States. What makes these restaurants popular in developing countries such as Argentina, Turkey, and many others is their "Americanness." Patronization of these restaurants enables consumers to express their "aspirational" links with developed nations.[65]

Meanings in the Use of Time   Specific uses of time have varying meanings in different cultures. In much of the world, the time required for a decision is proportional to the importance of the decision. Americans, by being well prepared with ready answers, may adversely downplay the importance of the business being discussed. Likewise, both Japanese and Middle Eastern executives are put off by Americans' insistence on coming to the point directly and quickly in business transactions.

Promptness is considered very important in America and Japan. Furthermore, promptness is defined as being on time for appointments, whether you are the person making the call or the person receiving the caller. The variation in waiting time between cultures is illustrated in this story:

> Arriving a little before the hour (the American respect pattern), he waited. The hour came and passed; 5 minutes—10 minutes—15 minutes. At this point he suggested to the secretary that perhaps the minister did not know he was waiting in the outer office—20 minutes—25 minutes—30 minutes—45 minutes (the insult period)! He jumped up and told the secretary that he had been "cooling his heels" in an outer office for 45 minutes and he was "damned sick and tired" of this type of treatment.

The principal source of misunderstanding lay in the fact that in the country in question, the five-minute delay interval was not significant. Forty-five minutes, instead of being at the tail end of the waiting scale, was just barely at the beginning. To suggest to American secretaries that perhaps their boss didn't know you were there after waiting 60 seconds would seem absurd, as would raising a storm about "cooling your heels" for five minutes. Yet this is precisely the way the minister registered the protestations of the American in his outer office.[66]

Space

The use people make of space and the meanings they assign to their use of space constitute a second form of nonverbal communication.[67] In America, "bigger is better." Thus, office space in corporations generally is allocated according to rank or prestige rather than need. The president will have the largest office, followed by the executive vice president, and so on.

Americans tend to personalize their work space and consider it their own. Few Americans would be comfortable in the following environment:

In Tokyo . . . IBM Japan provides only 4,300 desks for its 5,000 sales representatives since at least 700 are generally out on a sales call at any point in time. When sales representatives arrive at the office, they check a computer to see which desk is empty, take their personal filing cabinet from storage and roll it to the available desk where they work until they need to visit a customer. Each time they leave, they clear the desk and return their file cabinet to storage.[68]

A second major use of space is **personal space.** It is the nearest that others can come to you in various situations without your feeling uncomfortable. In the United States, normal business conversations occur at distances of 3 to 5 feet and highly personal business from 18 inches to 3 feet. In parts of northern Europe, the distances are slightly longer; in most of Latin America, they are substantially shorter.

An American businessperson in Latin America will tend to back away from a Latin American counterpart in order to maintain his or her preferred personal distance. In turn, the host will tend to advance toward the American in order to maintain his or her personal space. The resulting "chase" would be comical if it were not for the results. Both parties generally are unaware of their actions or the reasons for them. Furthermore, each assigns a meaning to the other's actions according to what the action means in his or her own culture. Thus, the North American considers the Latin American to be pushy and aggressive. The Latin American, in turn, considers the North American to be cold, aloof, and snobbish.

Symbols

An American seeing a baby wearing a pink outfit would most likely assume the child to be female. If the outfit were blue, the assumed gender would be male. These assumptions would be accurate most of the time in the United States but not in many other parts of the world, such as Holland. Colors, animals, shapes, numbers, and music have varying meanings across cultures.[69] Failure to recognize the meaning assigned to a symbol can cause serious problems:

- A leading U.S. golf ball manufacturer was disappointed in its attempts to penetrate the Japanese market. Its mistake was packaging its golf balls in sets of four. Four is a symbol of death in Japanese.
- Pepsi-Cola lost its dominant market share in Southeast Asia to Coke when it changed the color of its coolers and vending equipment from deep "regal" blue to light "ice" blue. Light blue is associated with death and mourning in parts of Southeast Asia.
- Most Chinese business travelers were shocked during the inauguration of United's concierge services for first-class passengers on its Pacific Rim routes. To mark the occasion, each concierge was proudly wearing a white carnation—an Asian symbol of death.
- AT&T had to change its "thumbs-up" ads in Russia and Poland, where showing the palm of the hand in this manner has an offensive meaning. The change was simple. The thumbs-up sign was given showing the back of the hand.

Table 2–3 presents additional illustrations of varying meanings assigned to symbols across cultures.[70] Despite frequent cultural differences in symbols, many symbols work well across a wide range of cultures. Kellogg's Tony the Tiger works in the United States, Japan (see Illustration 2–5), and many other cultures (see Case 2–4).

TABLE 2–3

The Meaning of
Numbers, Colors,
and Other Symbols

• White	Symbol for mourning or death in the Far East; happiness, purity in the United States.
• Purple	Associated with death in many Latin American countries.
• Blue	Connotation of femininity in Holland; masculinity in Sweden and the United States.
• Red	Unlucky or negative in Chad, Nigeria, and Germany; positive in Denmark, Rumania, and Argentina. Brides wear red in China, but it is a masculine color in the United Kingdom and France.
• Yellow flowers	Sign of death in Mexico; infidelity in France.
• White lilies	Suggestion of death in England.
• 7	Unlucky number in Ghana, Kenya, and Singapore; lucky in Morocco, India, Czechoslovakia, Nicaragua, and the United States.
• Triangle	Negative in Hong Kong, Korea, and Taiwan; positive in Colombia.
• Owl	Wisdom in United States; bad luck in India.
• Deer	Speed, grace in United States; homosexuality in Brazil.

ILLUSTRATION 2–5

Kellogg's tiger is an
effective symbol in
many cultures. Here
the tiger and a
contest work as well
in Japan as they do
in America.

KELLOGG'S FROSTED FLAKES® is a registered trademark of Kellogg Company. All
rights reserved. Used with permission.

Friendship

"Our intention is to drive down the cost of manufacturing to provide lower costs to the customer," McConville (CEO of Diebold China, a manufacturer of ATM machines) tells three government officials through his translator, JiLin Shi, a Diebold deputy general manager.

McConville is seated at a long table in a conference room in Diebold's manufacturing plant. He is flanked by four of his employees, all Chinese. The officials sit across the table, where cans of Coca-Cola and bottles of mineral water are offered. "The duty is paid by customer in the end," McConville says.

To get the duty lowered from 25 to 12 percent, Diebold has to prove that 60 percent of the parts it uses in manufacturing are Chinese-made. One of the officials starts speaking in Mandarin. Shi translates, "The localization looks good. We'll produce a letter for customs. We wish you prosperity."

McConville shakes hands with the officials and gives each one a gift—a shopping bag full of Tupperware. "As with most things in today's environment, team effort makes things successful, and we consider you part of our team," he says to the officials. The officials smile and the group goes to celebrate over lunch in a private, second-floor room in a nearby restaurant.

The lazy Susan in the middle of the round table groans under plates piled high with fried snake and Peking ducks and other delicacies. A waitress lifts the shell off of a cooked turtle and scoops the meat into bowls of steaming broth. As the employees and government officials chat in Mandarin and smoke Marlboros, McConville sips a Tsingtao beer and whispers to a visitor, "That meeting was only the beginning. Now we have to meet with customs to see if they even know what the process for lowering customs is." He dips his duck in plum sauce. "That'll mean dinner, some wine. In China, it doesn't matter who it is. You have to get to know them."[71]

In fact, long-run success in China involves more the just "getting to know" someone in the Western sense of that expression. Chinese relationships are complex and are described under the concept of **guanxi:**

Guanxi is literally translated as personal connections/relationships on which an individual can draw to secure resources or advantages when doing business as well as in the course of social life. Its main characteristics are (1) the notion of a continuing reciprocal relationship over an indefinite period of time, (2) favors are banked, (3) it extends beyond the relationship between two parties to include other parties within the social network (it can be transferred), (4) the relationship network is built among individuals not organizations, (5) status matters—relationships with a senior will extend to his subordinates but not vice versa, and (6) the social relationship is prior to and a prerequisite to the business relationship.[72]

Thus, the rights and obligations imposed by friendship are another nonverbal cultural variable. Americans, more so than most other cultures, make friends quickly and easily and drop them easily also. In large part, this may be due to the fact that America has always had a great deal of both social and geographic mobility. People who move every few years must be able to form friendships in a short time period and depart from them with a minimum of pain. In many other parts of the world, friendships are formed slowly and carefully because they imply deep and lasting obligations. As the following quote indicates, friendship and business are deeply intertwined in most of the world:

To most Asians and Latin Americans, good personal relationships and feelings are all that really matter in a long-term agreement. After all, the written word is less important than personal ties. Once personal trust has been established, cooperation increases. The social contacts developed between the parties are often far more significant than the technical specifications and the price.

> In many countries the heart of the matter, the major point of the negotiations, is getting to know the people involved.
>
> Americans negotiate a contract; the Japanese negotiate a relationship. In many cultures, the written word is used simply to satisfy legalities. In their eyes, emotion and personal relations are more important than cold facts.[73]

Agreements

Americans rely on an extensive and, generally, highly efficient legal system for ensuring that business obligations are honored and for resolving disagreements. Many other cultures have not developed such a system and rely instead on friendship and kinship, local moral principles, or informal customs to guide business conduct. For example, in China the business relationship is subordinate to the moralistic notion of friendship. Under the American system, we would examine a proposed contract closely. Under the Chinese system, we would examine the character of a potential trading partner closely. In the words of an American CEO based in China,

> Relationships are everything in China, more so than in the United States, which is more focused on business. The Chinese want to know and understand you before they buy from you.[74]

Americans generally assume that, in almost all instances, prices are uniform for all buyers, related to the service rendered, and reasonably close to the going rate. We order many products such as taxi rides without inquiring in advance about the cost. In many Latin American, Asian, and Middle East countries, the procedure is different. Virtually all prices are negotiated prior to the sale, including industrial products.[75] If a product such as a taxi ride is consumed without first establishing the price, the customer must pay what the seller demands. Likewise, assuming that a price list exists or has real meaning for industrial products can lead to incorrect conclusions concerning the actual price.

Things

The cultural meaning of things leads to purchase patterns that one would not otherwise predict. One observer noted a strong demand for expensive, status brands whose absolute cost was not too high among those Russians beginning to gain economically under capitalism. He concluded,

> They may stick to their locally produced toothpaste, but they want the Levi's, the Mont Blanc pens, the Moet Chandon champagne to establish their self-esteem and their class position.[76]

The differing meanings that cultures attach to things, including products, make gift-giving a particularly difficult task.[77] For example, giving a Chinese business customer or distributor a nice desk clock—a common gift in many countries—would be inappropriate. Why? In China, the word for *clock* is similar to the word for *funeral,* making clocks inappropriate gifts. When does receipt of a gift "require" a gift in return? In China this depends on the closeness of the relationship between the parties—the closer the relationship, the less a return gift is required.[78]

The business and social situations that call for a gift, and the items that are appropriate gifts, vary widely. For example, a gift of cutlery is generally inappropriate in Russia, Japan, Taiwan, and Germany. In Japan, small gifts are required in many business situations, yet in China they are less appropriate. In China, gifts should be presented privately, but in Arab countries they should be given in front of others.

Etiquette

Etiquette represents generally accepted ways of behaving in social situations. Assume that an American is preparing a commercial that shows people eating an evening meal, with one person about to take a bite of food from a fork. The person will have the fork in the right hand, and the left hand will be out of sight under the table. To an American audience this will seem natural. However, in many European cultures, a well-mannered individual would have the fork in the left hand and the right hand on the table. Likewise, portraying the American custom of patting a child on the head would be inappropriate in much of Asia, where the head is considered sacred.

Behaviors considered rude or obnoxious in one culture may be quite acceptable in another. The common and acceptable American habit, for males, of crossing one's legs while sitting, such that the sole of a shoe shows, is extremely insulting in many Eastern cultures. In these cultures, the sole of the foot or shoe should never be exposed to view. While most Americans are not hesitant to voice dissatisfaction with a service encounter, many Asians are. This can lead Western managers to misjudge customer response to their services.[79]

Normal voice tone, pitch, and speed of speech differ between cultures and languages, as do the use of gestures. Westerners often mistake the seemingly loud, volatile speech of some Asian cultures as signifying anger or emotional distress (which it would if it were being used by a Westerner) when it is normal speech for the occasion.

As American trade with Japan increases, we continue to learn more of the subtle aspects of Japanese business etiquette. For example, a Japanese executive will seldom say *no* directly during negotiations, as this would be considered impolite. Instead, he might say, "That will be very difficult," which would mean *no*. A Japanese responding *yes* to a request often means, "Yes, I understand the request," not "Yes, I agree to the request." Many Japanese find the American tendency to look straight into another's eyes when talking to be aggressive and rude. An example of another aspect of Japanese business etiquette is described below:

> "Your *meishi* is your face."
> "*Meishi* is most necessary here. It is absolutely essential."
> "A man without a *meishi* has no identity in Japan."

The exchange of *meishi* is the most basic of social rituals in a nation where social ritual matters very much. It solidifies a personal contact in a nation where personal contacts are the indispensable ingredient for success in any field. The act of exchanging *meishi* is weighted with meaning. Once the social minuet is completed, the two know where they stand in relation to each other and their respective statures within the hierarchy of corporate or government bureaucracy.

What is this mysterious "exchange of *meishi*"? It is the exchange of business cards when two people meet! A fairly common, simple activity in America, it is an essential, complex social exchange in Japan.

The importance of proper, culture-specific etiquette for sales personnel and advertising messages is obvious. Although people are apt to recognize that etiquette varies from culture to culture, there is still a strong emotional feeling that "our way is natural and right."

Conclusions on Nonverbal Communications

Can you imagine yourself becoming upset or surprised because people in a different culture spoke to you in their native language, say Spanish, French, or German, instead of English? Of course not. We all recognize that verbal languages vary around the world. Yet we generally feel that our nonverbal languages are natural or innate. Therefore, we misinterpret what is being "said" to us because we think we are hearing English when in reality it is Japanese, Italian, or Russian. It is this error that marketers can and must avoid.

GLOBAL CULTURES

An important issue facing marketers is the extent to which one or more global consumer cultures or segments are emerging. Evidence suggests that there is indeed movement in this direction.[80] Such a culture would have a shared set of consumption-related symbols with common meaning and desirability among members. One such proposed global culture is that portion of local cultures that view themselves as cosmopolitan, knowledgeable, and modern. Such individuals share many values and consumption-related behaviors with similar individuals across a range of national cultures.

Such cultures are being created by the globalization of mass media, work, education, and travel. Some product categories (cell phones, Internet) and brands (Sony, Nike) have become symbolically related to this culture. This does not imply that these brands use the same advertising globally but rather that the underlying theme and symbolism be the same. Thus, a combined shampoo/conditioner could be positioned as a time-saver for the time-pressured modern career woman. The advertisement might portray the shampoo being used in the context of a gym in the United States or Germany where many females exercise but in a home context in Japan where few women visit gyms. Philips Electronic is one firm that has developed a global positioning strategy based on such a global culture.[81]

Perhaps the closest to a global culture today are urban teenagers, which we examine next.

A Global Teenage Culture?

After classes, _____, 17, a high school junior in _____, peels off his school clothes, puts three gold and silver hoop rings in his left ear, and slips into jeans and Nikes. Then he goes to the moving company where he works after school. His job pays not only for his wardrobe but also for his record collection, which includes recordings by his favorite rappers.[82]

Can you fill in the blanks in the above story with any degree of confidence? The young man is Nasoshi Sato and he lives in Tokyo. However, his behavior differs little from that of millions of other teenagers in Europe, North and South America, and Asia. One study videotaped the bedrooms of teens from 25 countries. The conclusion:

From the gear and posters on display, it's hard to tell whether the rooms are in Los Angeles, Mexico City, or Tokyo. Basketballs sit alongside soccer balls. Closets overflow with staples from an international, unisex uniform: baggy Levi's or Diesel jeans, NBA jackets, and rugged shoes from Timberland or Doc Martens.[83]

"Teenagers—who make up a huge and growing part of the population around the world—represent the first truly international market in history," according to Larry McIntosh, Pepsi-Cola's vice president for international advertising.[84] Consider the following data on teenage clothing ownership around the world (the data for Asia exclude China).[85]

	U.S.	Europe	Asia	Latin America
Jeans	93%	94%	93%	86%
T-shirt	93	94	96	59
Running shoes	80	89	69	65
Blazer	42	43	27	30
Denim jacket	39	57	23	41

Teenagers around the world not only tend to dress alike, but are very similar in the things they find enjoyable.[86]

What is causing this movement toward uniformity? The largest single influence is worldwide mass media. Teenagers around the world watch many of the same shows, see the same movies and videos, and listen to the same music. They not only idolize the same musicians, but copy these musicians' dress styles, mannerisms, and attitudes, which provides them with many shared characteristics. This interconnectedness is rapidly increasing with the growth of the Internet.

Sports and sports figures are another unifying force. Soccer, basketball, and baseball are increasingly every country's home sports. Track, American-style football, and winter sports, particularly snowboarding, are also popular with teenagers. The Olympics have become a worldwide media event. In a school in China's rural Shaanzi province, students were asked to name the "world's greatest man," living or dead. Michael Jordan tied with the late Zhou En-lai for the title.[87] Products used or endorsed by such stars often find quick acceptance among teenagers around the world.

Marketers are using the similarities among teenagers across cultures to launch global brands or to reposition current brands to appeal to this large market. For example, Pepsi Max was introduced around the world with a single set of commercials aimed at teenagers. The ads showed a quartet of teens vying to perform the most outrageous feats, such as skydiving from Big Ben, rollerblading off the Sphinx, or surfing down the dunes of the Sahara. Likewise, 7UP recently launched similar ads targeting teenagers in Spain, Russia, Ireland, and the Netherlands. The theme is "Air conditioning for a passionate world."

It is important to note that teenagers also have a great many culturally unique behaviors, attitudes, and values. As one expert states, "European teens resent being thought of as Americans with an accent."[88] Also, the similarities described above are most noticeable among middle-class teens living in urban areas. Poorer, rural teens often conform more closely to their society's traditional culture.

GLOBAL DEMOGRAPHICS

China's economy grew rapidly throughout the 1990s, as did personal disposable income.[89] In the more prosperous regions, this has produced an explosion in the use of motorbikes as replacements for bicycles (private automobile ownership is limited by both economic and legal barriers). This sudden, large increase in motorbike usage triggered demand for gasoline in cities with no gasoline stations and few available sites. Illustration 2–6 shows how one firm dealt with this challenge by developing and deploying "mobile" service stations in the form of trucks with attached gasoline pumps.

Disposable income is one aspect of demographics. **Demographics** *describe a population in terms of its size, structure, and distribution. Size* refers to the number of individuals in the society, while *structure* describes the society in terms of age, income, education, and occupation. *Distribution* refers to the physical location of individuals in terms of geographic region and rural, suburban, and urban location.

Demographics are both a result and a cause of cultural values. Densely populated societies are likely to have more of a collective orientation than an individualistic one because a collective orientation helps such societies function smoothly. Cultures that value hard work and the acquisition of material wealth are likely to advance economically, which alters their demographics both directly (income) and indirectly (families in economically advanced countries tend to be smaller).

A critical aspect of demographics for marketers is income, particularly the distribution of income. One country with a relatively low average income can have a sizable middle-income segment, while another country with the same average income may have most of the wealth in the hands of a few individuals. As shown below, by one measure (per capita gross domestic

The rapid growth in personal income in parts of China has led to an explosion in motorbike ownership. The Chinese have responded with innovative distribution and service outlets.

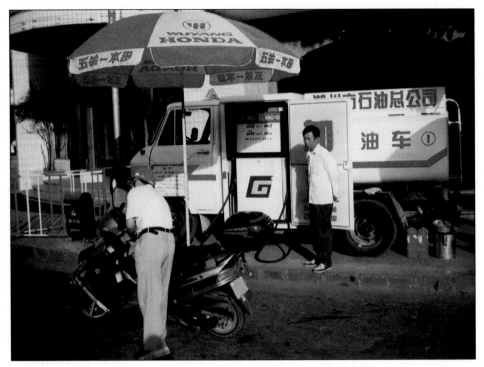

© Del Hawkins.

product expressed as purchasing power parity), Brazil's average per capita income is slightly higher than Romania's.[90] However, the distribution of that income differs sharply. Almost half of the income generated in Brazil goes to just 10 percent of the population. In contrast, the top 10 percent of households in Romania command only 20 percent of that country's income. *How will these and the other differences shown below affect consumption?*

	GDP per Capita	Percent of Total Income to Top 10%		GDP per Capita	Percent of Total Income to Top 10%
Brazil	$ 6,500	48%	Japan	$24,900	22%
Canada	24,800	24	Kenya	1,500	31
Chile	10,100	41	Korea, S.	16,100	24
China	3,600	30	Mexico	9,100	37
Egypt	3,600	25	Romania	5,900	20
France	24,400	25	United States	36,200	31

Marketers increasingly use **purchasing power parity (PPP)** rather than average or median income to evaluate markets. PPP is based on the cost in U.S. dollars of a standard market basket of products bought in each country. Suppose a product in the United States is purchased primarily by families with $20,000 annual income. A PPP analysis would show that Venezuela has 2.5 million households with incomes that allow them to consume as much as a typical U.S. household with $20,000 income. The Venezuelan household may have a lower income in U.S. dollars, but it may be able to buy more because of a lower local cost structure, government-provided health care, and so forth.[91] The World Bank now describes all countries in terms of PPP in its annual *World Bank Atlas*. The importance of considering purchasing power rather than just income can be seen in the following figures (in U.S. dollars):[92]

	Per Capita Income	Per Capita PPP		Per Capita Income	Per Capita PPP
Brazil	$4,350	$6,840	Japan	$32,030	$25,170
China	780	3,550	Russia	2,250	6,990
India	440	2,230	Switzerland	38,380	28,760
Indonesia	600	2,660	United States	31,910	31,910

The estimated age distributions of the United States, the Philippines, Japan, and Canada for the year 2000 are shown below.[93] Note that almost half the population of the Philippines is less than 20 years of age compared to less than a third for the United States, one-fourth for Canada, and about one-fifth for Japan. *What product opportunities do this and the other age differences among these countries suggest?*

Age	United States	Philippines	Japan	Canada
<10	14.3%	26.6%	9.4%	12.1%
10–19	14.4	22.6	11.1	13.4
20–29	13.3	17.5	14.0	13.6
30–39	15.5	13.4	13.2	15.8
40–49	15.3	8.9	13.2	16.3
50–59	10.8	5.5	15.3	12.1
60–69	7.6	3.3	11.9	7.8
>69	8.9	2.1	11.9	9.0

CROSS-CULTURAL MARKETING STRATEGY

There is continuing controversy over the extent to which cross-cultural marketing strategies, particularly advertising, should be standardized.[94] Standardized strategies can result in substantial cost savings. This was an important consideration in the FedEx ad strategy described in the opening example. Likewise, Maybelline's Manhattan line of cosmetics designed for the Asian market uses one ad campaign in China, Taiwan, Hong Kong, Thailand, and Singapore. The ads feature an attractive Asian model in a low-cut, short dress against the Manhattan skyline at night. This combination of appeals to youth, beauty, and sophistication could be used in many other countries, though this ad would be inappropriate, and probably banned, in most Islamic countries. Illustration 2–7 is another appeal to beauty and sensuality that would require little alteration, other than language, across most Western cultures.

In contrast, Campbell Soup is succeeding worldwide, but the particular soups range from the traditional chicken noodle in the United States to cream of chili in Mexico, split pea with ham in Argentina, peppery tripe in Poland, and watercress and duck gizzard in China. McDonald's used to strive for uniformity around the globe. Now it adapts its products as appropriate, adding fried eggs to burgers in Japan, offering Samurai Pork Burgers with a sweet barbecue sauce in Thailand, and stressing chicken and rice dishes in Indonesia. Consider its approach to India:

Eighty percent of Indians are Hindu who don't eat beef so there will be no Big Macs in India. Instead, the menu will feature the Maharaja Mac—"two all mutton patties, special sauce, lettuce, cheese, pickles, onions on a sesame-seed bun." For the strictest Hindus who eat no meat, McDonald's will offer deep-fried rice patties flavored with peas, carrots, red pepper, beans, onions, coriander, and other spices. Pork is also banned from the menu, as India's 110 million Muslims believe it is unclean.[95]

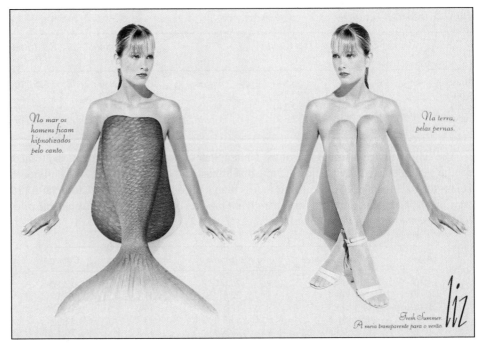

Courtesy DM9DDB, São Paulo.

The critical decision is whether utilizing a standardized marketing strategy, in any given market, will result in a greater return on investment than would an individualized campaign. Thus, the consumer response to the standardized campaign and to potential individualized campaigns must be considered in addition to the cost of each approach.

Considerations in Approaching a Foreign Market

There are seven key considerations for each geographic market that a firm is contemplating. An analysis of these seven variables provides the background necessary for deciding whether or not to enter the market and to what extent, if any, an individualized marketing strategy is required. A small sample of experts, preferably native to the market under consideration, often will be able to furnish sufficient information on each variable.

Is the Geographic Area Homogeneous or Heterogeneous with Respect to Culture?   Marketing efforts are generally directed at defined geographic areas, primarily political and economic entities. Legal requirements and existing distribution channels often encourage this approach. However, it is also supported by the implicit assumption that geographical or political boundaries coincide with cultural boundaries. This assumption is incorrect more often than not. For example, a recent study suggested that strategies in Latin America need to be designed at the metropolitan level because of major within-country differences.[96]

Likewise, China has strong regional cultures (one authority has identified eight), urban/rural cultures, as well as sharp differences associated with income, age, and education.[97] Thus, marketing campaigns must be developed for cultural groups, not just countries.

What Needs Can This Product or a Version of It Fill in This Culture?   Most firms examine a new market with an existing product or product technology in mind. The question they must answer is what needs their existing or modified product can fill in the culture involved. For example, bicycles and motorcycles serve primarily recreational needs in the United States, but they provide basic transportation in many other countries.

General Foods successfully positioned Tang as a substitute for orange juice at breakfast in the United States. However, in analyzing the French market, it found that the French drink little orange juice and almost none at breakfast. Therefore, a totally different positioning strategy was used; Tang was promoted as a new type of refreshing drink for any time of the day.

Can Enough of the People Needing the Product Afford It?
This requires an initial demographic analysis to determine the number of individuals or households that might need the product and the number that can probably afford it. For example, while China has over 1.3 billion consumers, the effective market for most Western goods is estimated to be less than 20 percent of this total.[98] In addition, the possibilities of establishing credit, obtaining a government subsidy, or making a less expensive version should be considered. For example, Levi-Strauss de Argentina launched a trade-in campaign in which consumers received a 50,000 peso "reward" (about $7) for turning in an old pair of jeans with the purchase of a new pair. A strong recession in Argentina prompted the action.

What Values or Patterns of Values Are Relevant to the Purchase and Use of This Product?
The first section of this chapter focused on values and their role in consumer behavior. The value system should be investigated for influences on purchasing the product, owning the product, using the product, and disposing of the product. Much of the marketing strategy will be based on this analysis.

What Are the Distribution, Political, and Legal Structures for the Product?
The legal structure of a country can have an impact on each aspect of a firm's marketing mix. The chapter opening example described how FedEx had to produce two endings for its Latin America/Caribbean ad because of legal restrictions in Mexico. Pepsi has been banned from running its Pepsi Challenge ads—which present the results of consumer taste tests comparing Pepsi and Coke—in Argentina. These ads are being used in many other countries, including Singapore, Malaysia, Portugal, and Mexico. Colgate encountered similar problems in India. China recently banned "superlative claims" and comparative ads. Duracell had to withdraw its famous bunny ads because of the ruling, and Budweiser was not able to launch its beer into China with its familiar tag line, "The King of Beers."[99]

Regulations also affect distribution channels. Until recently, Japan prohibited yen-based transactions on the Internet, which slowed the development of this distribution channel.[100] China recently announced a ban on direct sales to consumers, which has major consequences for Amway, Avon, Mary Kay, and other direct marketers in China.[101]

Traditional distribution patterns also differ across countries. In China, vanilla is considered a chemical and is sold in paint stores. Nutmeg, cinnamon, and some other spices are often distributed through Chinese medicine stores. Similar variations in what Americans consider normal distribution channels exist in most countries. Likewise, customers visit retail outlets with differing motives and expectations across cultures.[102]

The Internet seems a natural channel through which to sell products to developed countries. However, the percentage of adults who shop online varies sharply by country:[103]

United States	38%	South Korea	18%
United Kingdom	25	France	10
Canada	24	Italy	5
Netherlands	23	Spain	4
Germany	21	Brazil	3
Japan	20		

Whirlpool uses bright colors for its refrigerators sold in Malaysia. Refrigerators are often placed in the living room and serve as furniture as well as appliances in much of Asia.

Krapit Phanrut/Sipa.

In What Ways Can We Communicate about the Product?   This question requires an investigation into (1) available media and who attends to each type, (2) the needs the product fills, (3) values associated with the product and its use, and (4) the verbal and nonverbal communications systems in the culture(s). All aspects of the firm's promotional mix—including packaging, nonfunctional product design features, personal selling techniques, and advertising—should be based on these four factors. In Illustration 2–8, note the bright colors Whirlpool uses for the refrigerators it markets in Thailand and other Asian countries. Whirlpool does so because many consumers in these countries keep their refrigerators in their living rooms (the kitchens are too small) and want them to serve as attractive pieces of furniture, not just as appliances.

Money-back guarantees are one of the most credible advertising claims to U.S. citizens, but most Latin Americans simply do not believe them. Instead, they are influenced by claims that the brand is the "official" product of a sports group or an event, a claim that has little credibility in the United States.[104] Obviously, care must be taken to create culturally appropriate messages.

What Are the Ethical Implications of Marketing This Product in This Country?
All marketing programs should be evaluated on ethical as well as financial dimensions. As discussed at the beginning of the chapter, international marketing activities raise many ethical issues. The ethical dimension is particularly important and complex in marketing to Third World and developing countries. Consider Kellogg's attempt to introduce cold cereal as a breakfast food in Brazil. The following questions represent the type of ethical analysis that should go into such a decision:

- If we succeed, will the average nutrition level be increased or decreased?
- If we succeed, will the funds spent on cereal be diverted from other uses with more beneficial long-term impacts for the individuals or society?
- If we succeed, what impact will this have on the local producers of currently consumed breakfast products?

Understanding and acting on ethical considerations in international marketing is a difficult task. However, it is also a necessary one.

SUMMARY

Culture is defined as the complex whole that includes knowledge, beliefs, art, law, morals, customs, and any other capabilities acquired by humans as members of society. It includes almost everything that influences an individual's thought processes and behaviors.

Culture operates primarily by setting boundaries for individual behavior and by influencing the functioning of such institutions as the family and mass media. The boundaries, or *norms,* are derived from *cultural values.* Values are widely held beliefs that affirm what is desirable.

Cultural values are classified into three categories: other, environment, and self. *Other-oriented values* reflect a society's view of the appropriate relationships between individuals and groups within that society. Relevant values of this nature include *individual/collective, extended/limited family, diversity/uniformity, masculine/feminine, competitive/cooperative,* and *youth/age.*

Environment-oriented values prescribe a society's relationships with its economic, technical, and physical environments. Examples of environment values are *cleanliness, performance/status, tradition/change, risk taking/security, problem solving/fatalistic,* and *nature.*

Self-oriented values reflect the objectives and approaches to life that individual members of society find desirable. These include *active/passive, material/nonmaterial, hard work/leisure, postponed gratification/immediate gratification, sensual gratification/abstinence,* and *religious/secular.*

Differences in *verbal communication systems* are immediately obvious across cultures and must be taken into account by marketers wishing to do business in those cultures. Probably more important, however, and certainly more difficult to recognize are *nonverbal communication systems.* Major examples of nonverbal communication variables that affect marketers are *time, space, friendship, agreement, things, symbols,* and *etiquette.*

There is evidence that urban teenagers around the world share at least some aspects of a common culture. This is driven by worldwide mass media and common music and sports stars.

Demographics describe a population in terms of its size, structure, and distribution. They differ widely across cultures and influence cultural values (and are influenced by them) as well as consumption patterns.

Seven questions are relevant for developing a cross-cultural marketing strategy: (1) Is the geographic area homogeneous with respect to culture? (2) What needs can this product fill in this culture? (3) Can enough people afford the product? (4) What values are relevant to the purchase and use of the product? (5) What are the distribution, political, and legal structures concerning this product? (6) How can we communicate about the product? (7) What are the ethical implications of marketing this product in this country?

KEY TERMS

Cultural values 43
Culture 42
Demographics 65
Environment-oriented values 45
Guanxi 61
Instrumental materialism 53
Monochronic time perspective 56

Nonverbal communication systems 56
Norms 43
Other-oriented values 45
Personal space 59
Polychronic time perspective 57
Power distance 50

Purchasing power parity (PPP) 66
Sanctions 43
Self-oriented values 45
Terminal materialism 53
Verbal communication systems 55

INTERNET EXERCISES

1. Contact the Michigan State University international business resources website (globaledge.msu.edu/index.asp). Which of the resources listed is most useful for the following?
   a. Worldwide consumer data
   b. Data on consumer markets in Mexico
   c. Data on consumer markets in Japan
   d. Data on industrial markets in Germany

2. Using the Michigan State University site described in Exercise 1 above, select and describe one of the sources listed. Evaluate its usefulness for understanding international markets and other cultures.

3. Using the WWW, prepare a brief report on the following as a market for DVD players. Provide addresses for all websites used.
   a. Malaysia
   b. Italy
   c. Brazil
   d. Egypt

4. Prepare a report that describes how useful, if at all, the information available at the World Bank website (www.worldbank.org) is in terms of helping you understand the following as a market for Internet sales of CDs:
   a. Philippines
   b. China
   c. France
   d. Canada

5. Use the WWW to find an attractive country in which to introduce a small, economical, easy to repair automobile that would cost about U.S. $5,000 (PPP).

6. Visit the CIA site (www.odci.gov). Evaluate the usefulness of this site for international marketers.

REVIEW QUESTIONS

1. What are some of the ethical issues involved in cross-cultural marketing?

2. What is meant by the term *culture?*

3. What does the statement "Culture sets boundaries on behaviors" mean?

4. What is a *norm?* From what are norms derived?

5. What is a *cultural value?*

6. What is a *sanction?*

7. Cultural values can be classified as affecting one of three types of relationships—other, environment, or self. Describe each of these, and differentiate each one from the others.

8. How does the first of the following paired orientations differ from the second?
   a. Individual/Collective
   b. Performance/Status
   c. Tradition/Change
   d. Limited/Extended family
   e. Active/Passive
   f. Material/Nonmaterial
   g. Hard work/Leisure
   h. Risk taking/Security
   i. Masculine/Feminine
   j. Competitive/Cooperative
   k. Youth/Age
   l. Problem solving/Fatalistic
   m. Diversity/Uniformity
   n. Postponed gratification/Immediate gratification
   o. Sensual gratification/Abstinence
   p. Religious/Secular

9. What is meant by nonverbal communications? Why is this a difficult area to adjust to?

10. What is meant by each of the following as a form of nonverbal communication?
    a. Time
    b. Space
    c. Friendship
    d. Agreements
    e. Things
    f. Symbols
    g. Etiquette

11. What is *guanxi?*

12. What is the difference between *instrumental* and *terminal* materialism?

13. What are the differences between a *monochronic* time perspective and a *polychronic* time perspective?

14. What forces seem to be creating a global teenage culture?

15. What are demographics? Why are they important to international marketers?

16. What is *purchasing power parity?*

17. What are the seven key considerations in deciding whether or not to enter a given international market?

18. What does determining if a geographic area or political unit is homogeneous or heterogeneous with respect to culture mean? Why is this important?

DISCUSSION QUESTIONS

19. Why should we study foreign cultures if we do not plan to engage in international or export marketing?

20. Is a country's culture more likely to be reflected in its art museums or its television commercials? Why?

21. Are the cultures of the world becoming more similar or more distinct?

22. Why do values differ across cultures?

23. The text lists 18 cultural values of relevance to marketing practice. Describe and place into one of the three categories two additional cultural values that have some relevance to marketing practice.

24. Select two cultural values from each of the three categories. Describe the boundaries (norms) relevant to that value in your society and the sanctions for violating those norms.

25. What are the most relevant cultural values affecting the consumption of each of the following? Describe how and why these values are particularly important.
    a. Internet
    b. Sports participation
    c. Charity giving
    d. Dishwashers
    e. Perfume
    f. Wine

26. What variations between the United States and other societies, *other than cultural variations,* may affect the relative level of usage of the following?
    a. Internet
    b. Sports participation
    c. Charity giving
    d. Dishwashers
    e. Perfume
    f. Wine

27. Is the European Union likely to become a relatively homogeneous culture by 2025?

28. What are the marketing implications of the differences in the adult/child orientation between countries such as Greece and Portugal compared to countries such as Norway, Sweden, and the Netherlands?

29. What are the marketing implications of the differences in the *masculine/feminine orientation* across countries?

30. Respond to the questions in Consumer Insight 2–1.

31. Why do nonverbal communication systems vary across cultures?

32. What, if any, nonverbal communication factors might be relevant in the marketing of the following?
    a. Bottled water
    b. Dresses
    c. In-line skates
    d. Dish soap
    e. DVD players
    f. Charity giving

33. What are the implications of *guanxi* for a Western firm entering the Chinese market?

34. To what extent do you think teenagers are truly becoming a single, global culture?

35. Will today's teenagers still be a "global culture" when they are 40? Why or why not?

36. How do demographics affect a culture's values? How do a culture's values affect its demographics?

37. What causes the differences between purchasing power parity and income as shown in the text (page 67)?

38. The text provides a seven-step procedure for analyzing a foreign market. Using this procedure, analyze your country as a market for
    a. Automobiles from Korea
    b. Men's shoes from France
    c. Expensive watches from Brazil
    d. Wine from the Czech Republic

39. What are the major ethical issues in introducing prepared foods such as breakfast cereals to developing countries?

40. Should U.S. tobacco firms be allowed to market cigarettes in developing countries? Why or why not?

41. How can developing countries keep their cultures from being overly Westernized or Americanized?

APPLICATION ACTIVITIES

42. Interview two students from two different cultures. Determine the extent to which the following are used in those cultures and the variations in the values of those cultures that relate to the use of these products:
    a. In-line skates
    b. Cosmetics
    c. Wine
    d. Fast food
    e. Videos
    f. Internet

43. Interview two students from two different foreign cultures. Report any differences in nonverbal communications they are aware of between their culture and your culture.

44. Interview two students from two different foreign cultures. Report their perceptions of the major differences in cultural values between their culture and your culture.

45. Interview a student from China. Report on the advice that the student would give an American firm marketing consumer products in China.

46. Interview two students from EU countries. Report on the extent to which they feel the EU will be a homogeneous culture by 2025.

47. Imagine you are a consultant working with your state or province's tourism agency. You have been asked to advise the agency on the best promotional themes to use to attract foreign tourists. What would you recommend if Italy and the U.K. were the two target markets?

48. Analyze a foreign culture of your choice, and recommend a marketing program for a brand of one of the following made in your country:
    a. DVD player
    b. Fast-food outlets
    c. Wine
    d. Internet sporting good outlet
    e. Dress shoes
    f. Snowboards

REFERENCES

1. P. L. Andruss, "FedEx Kicks Up Brand," *Marketing News,* July 30, 2001, pp. 4–5.

2. See T. Srivastava and D. D. Schoenbachler, "An Examination of the Information and Thematic Content of Consumer Print Advertising in India," *Journal of International Consumer Marketing,* no. 2 (1999), pp. 63–85; and A. T. Shao, M. A. Raymond, and C. Taylor, "Shifting Advertising Appeals in Taiwan," *Journal of Advertising Research,* November 1999, pp. 61–68.

3. C. Miller, "Not Quite Global," *Marketing News,* July 3, 1995, p. 9.

4. S. Gutkin, "Spooky Fun Creeping around Globe," *Register-Guard,* October 29, 2000, p. 16A.

5. "Hindus Torch Valentines," *Register-Guard,* February 14, 2002, p. 6A.

6. J. Solomon, "Amid Anti-American Protests," *Wall Street Journal,* October 26, 2001, p. 1; and O. Sandikci and G. Ger, "Fundamental Fashions," *Advances in Consumer Research,* vol. 28, ed. M. C. Gilly and J. Meyers-Levy (Provo, UT: Association for Consumer Research, 2001), pp. 146–50.

7. See W. Bailey, "Country of Origin Attitudes in Mexico," *Journal of International Consumer Marketing,* no. 3 (1997),

pp. 25–41; and J. Marcoux, P. Filiatrault, and E. Cheron, "The Attitudes Underlying Preferences of Polish Consumers towards Products Made in Western Countries," *Journal of International Consumer Marketing,* no. 4 (1997), pp. 5–29.

8. S. Efron, "Smokers Light Up All over the World," *Register-Guard,* September 9, 1996, p. 1.

9. "Smoking-Related Deaths Almost Epidemic in China," *Register-Guard,* November 20, 1998, p. 13A.

10. See W. J. McDonald, "American versus Japanese Consumer Decision Making," *Journal of International Consumer Marketing* 7, no. 3 (1995), pp. 81–93; J. B. Ford, L. E. Pelton, and J. R. Lumpkin, "Perception of Marital Roles in Purchase Decision Processes," *Journal of the Academy of Marketing Science,* Spring 1995, pp. 120–31; J. L. Aaker and J. Sengupta, "Additivity versus Attenuation," *Journal of Consumer Psychology,* no. 2 (2000), pp. 67–82; and D. A. Briley, M. W. Morris, and I. Simonson, "Reasons as Carriers of Culture," *Journal of Consumer Research,* September 2000, pp. 157–77.

11. "And Then There's Global Pizza," *Register-Guard,* August 25, 1996, p. C1.

12. S. P. Galante, "Clash Courses," *Wall Street Journal,* European ed., July 20, 1984, p. 1.

13. For different value sets, see S. E. Beatty, L. R. Kahle, and P. Homer, "Personal Values and Gift-Giving Behaviors," *Journal of Business Research,* March 1991, pp. 149–57; and F. Hansen, "From Lifestyle to Value Systems to Simplicity," in *Advances in Consumer Research,* vol. 25, ed. J. W. Alba and J. W. Hutchinson (Provo, UT: Association for Consumer Research, 1998), pp. 181–95.

14. F. Hansen, "From Lifestyle to Value Systems to Simplicity."

15. S. Abe, R. Bagozzi, and P. Sadarangani, "An Investigation of Construct Validity and Generalizability of the Self-Concept," *Journal of International Consumer Marketing,* no. 3–4 (1996), pp. 97–123.

16. M. Lee and F. M. Ulgado, "Consumer Evaluations of Fast-Food Services," *Journal of Services Marketing,* no. 1 (1997), pp. 39–52.

17. Z. Gurhan-Canli and D. Maheswaran, "Cultural Variations in Country of Origin Effects," *Journal of Marketing Research,* August 2000, pp. 309–17.

18. N. Y. Wong and A. C. Ahuvia, "Personal Taste and Family Face," *Psychology & Marketing,* August 1998, pp. 423–41.

19. Z. Caillat and B. Mueller, "The Influence of Culture on American and British Advertising," *Journal of Advertising Research,* May–June 1996, pp. 79–88; Y. Zhang and B. D. Gelb, "Matching Advertising Appeals to Culture," *Journal of Advertising,* Fall 1996, pp. 29–46; N. D. Albers-Miller and B. D. Gelb, "Business Advertising as a Mirror of Cultural Dimensions," *Journal of Advertising,* Winter 1996, pp. 57–70; B. D. Culter, S. A. Erdem, and R. G. Javalgi, "Advertising Relative Reliance on Collectivism-Individualism Appeals," *Journal of International Consumer Marketing,* no. 3 (1997), pp. 43–55; M. P. Leach and A. H. Liu, "The Use of Culturally Relevant Stimuli in International Advertising," *Psychology & Marketing,* September 1998, pp. 523–46; L. Ha, "Advertising Appeals Used by Services Marketers," *Journal of Services Marketing,* no. 2 (1998), pp. 98–112; B. Cho et al., *Journal of Advertising,* Winter 1999, pp. 59–72; and C. Pornpitakpan and J. N. P. Francis, "The Effect of Cultural Differences, Source Expertise, and Argument Strength of Persuasion," *Journal of International Consumer Marketing,* no. 1 (2001), pp. 77–101.

20. J. E. M. Steenkamp, F. Ter Hofstede, and M. Wedel; "A Cross-National Investigation into the Individual and National Cultural Antecedents of Consumer Innovativeness," *Journal of Marketing,* April 1999, pp. 55–69.

21. G. D. Gregory and J. M. Munch, "Cultural Values in International Advertising," *Psychology & Marketing,* March 1997, pp. 99–119; and R. B. Money, M. C. Gilly, and J. L. Graham, "Explorations of National Culture and Word-of-Mouth Referral Behavior," *Journal of Marketing,* October 1998, pp. 76–87.

22. C. Robinson, "Asian Culture," *Journal of the Market Research Society,* January 1996, pp. 55–62. See also J. A. Lee, "Adapting Triandis's Model of Subjective Culture and Social Behavior Relations to Consumer Behavior," *Journal of Consumer Psychology,* no. 2 (2000), pp. 117–26.

23. K. L. Miller, "You Just Can't Talk to These Kids," *Business Week,* April 19, 1993, pp. 104–6.

24. See M. S. Roth, "The Effects of Culture and Socioeconomics on the Performance of Global Brand Image Strategies," *Journal of Marketing Research,* May 1995, pp. 163–75;

S. Ferley, T. Lea, and B. Watson, "A Comparison of U.S. and Canadian Consumers," *Journal of Advertising Research,* October 1999, pp. 55–65; and L. Y. Sin and O. H. Yau, "Female Role Orientation and Consumption Values," *Journal of International Consumer Marketing,* no. 2 (2001), pp. 49–75.

25. B. Barak et al., "Perceptions of Age-Identity," *Psychology & Marketing,* October 2001, pp. 1003–29.

26. P. L. Andruss, "Groups Make Fruits Apple of Taiwan's Eye," *Marketing News,* December 4, 2000, p. 5.

27. *Reader's Digest Eurodata—A Consumer Survey of 17 European Countries* (Pleasantville, NY: The Reader's Digest Association, Inc., 1991), p. 26.

28. J. Sherry, B. Greenberg, and H. Tokinoya, "Orientations to TV Advertising among Adolescents and Children in the U.S. and Japan," *International Journal of Advertising,* no. 2 (1999), pp. 233–50; J. Wimalasiri, "A Comparison of Children's Purchase Influence and Parental Response in Fiji and the United States," *Journal of International Consumer Marketing,* no. 4 (2000), pp. 55–73; and M. Viswanathan, T. L. Childers, and E. S. Moore, "The Measurement of Intergenerational Communication and Influence on Consumption," *Journal of the Academy of Marketing Science,* Summer 2000, pp. 406–24.

29. P. Duggan, "Feeding China's 'Little Emperors,'" *Forbes,* August 6, 1990, pp. 84–85. See also M. F. Ji and J. U. McNeal, "How Chinese Children's Commercials Differ from Those of the United States," *Journal of Advertising,* Fall 2001, pp. 79–92.

30. S. H. C. Tai and J. L. M. Tam, "A Comparative Study of Chinese Consumers in Asian Markets," *Journal of International Consumer Marketing,* no. 1 (1996), pp. 25–42; and S. H. C. Tai and J. L. M. Tam, "A Lifestyle Analysis of Female Consumers in Greater China," *Psychology & Marketing,* May 1997, pp. 287–307.

31. P. Kotler, S. W. Ang, and C. T. Tan, *Marketing Management: An Asian Perspective* (Singapore: Prentice Hall Pergamon, 1996), p. 524.

32. B. D. Keillor, R. S. Parker, and A. Schaffer, "Influences on Adolescent Brand Preferences in the United States and Mexico," *Journal of Advertising Research,* May–June 1996, pp. 47–56.

33. See F. S. Al-Olayan and K. Karande, "A Content Analysis of Magazine Advertisements from the United States and the Arab World," *Journal of Advertising,* Fall 2000, pp. 69–82.

34. C.-N. Chen, M. Lai, and D. D. C. Tarn, "Feminism Orientation, Product Attributes, and Husband-Wife Decision Dominance," *Journal of Global Marketing,* no. 3 (1999), pp. 23–39. See also A. K. Lalwani, S. C. Mehta, and T. C. Tiong, "Family Roles in the Selection for Schools in Multiracial Singapore," *Journal of Professional Services Marketing,* no. 2 (1999), pp. 73–92; and C. Webster, "Is Spousal Decision Making a Culturally Situated Phenomenon?" *Psychology & Marketing,* December 2000, pp. 1035–58.

35. M. L. Maynard and C. R. Taylor, "Girlish Images across Cultures," *Journal of Advertising,* Spring 1999, pp. 39–47.

36. From Ipsos's global consumer and civic trends reporting service, *World Monitor,* 2nd quarter, 2001. Profiled data were collected on Ipsos's *Global Express* omnibus survey in 34 countries in November–December of 2000. Never = less than twice a year; frequently = at least once a week.

37. J. Huang, "National Character and Sex Roles in Advertising," *Journal of International Consumer Marketing,* no. 4 (1995), pp. 81–96; B. D. Cutler, R. G. Javalgi, and D. Lee, "The Portrayal of People in Magazine Advertisements," *Journal of International Consumer Marketing,* no. 2 (1995), pp. 45–58; B. A. Browne, "Gender Stereotypes in Advertising on Children's Television in the 1990s" and J. B. Ford et al., "Gender Role Portrayal in Japanese Advertising," both in *Journal of Advertising,* Spring 1998, pp. 83–96 and 113–24; and L. M. Milner and J. M. Collins, "Sex-Role Portrayals and the Gender of Nations," *Journal of Advertising,* Spring 2000, pp. 67–78.

38. J. Russell, "Working Women Give Japan Culture Shock," *Advertising Age,* January 16, 1995, p. I24.

39. See Miller, "You Just Can't Talk to These Kids," p. 106; and P. Sellers, "Pepsi Opens a Second Front," *Fortune,* August 8, 1994, pp. 70–76.

40. See N. Donthu, "A Cross-Country Investigation of Recall of and Attitude toward Comparative Advertising," *Journal of Advertising,* Summer 1998, pp. 111–22.

41. J. L. Watson, *Golden Arches East* (Stanford, CA: Stanford University Press, 1997).

42. N. Madden, "Starbucks Ships Its Coffee Craze to Pacific Rim," *Advertising Age,* April 27, 1998, p. 28; and various company press releases.

43. Pornpitakpan and Francis, "The Effect of Cultural Differences, Source Expertise, and Argument Strength of Persuasion."

44. N. Giges, "Europeans Buy Outside Goods," *Advertising Age,* April 27, 1992, p. I26.

45. D. Kim, Y. Pan, and H. S. Park, "High- versus Low-Context Culture," *Psychology & Marketing,* September 1998, pp. 507–21.

46. N. M. Murray and L. A. Manrai, "Exploratory Consumption Behavior," *Journal of International Consumer Marketing,* no. 1 (1993), pp. 101–19.

47. Ibid.

48. Caillat and Mueller, "The Influence of Culture or American and British Advertising."

49. See Steenkamp, Ter Hofstede, and Wedel, "A Cross-National Investigation"; Pornpitakpan and Francis, "The Effect of Cultural Differences, Source Expertise, and Argument Strength of Persuasion" and Z. Zhou and K. Nakamoto, "Price Perceptions," *Advances in Consumer Research,* vol. 28, ed. M. C. Gilly and J. Meyers-Levy (Provo, UT: Association for Consumer Research, 2001), pp. 161–68.

50. See B. J. Phillips, "Advertising and the Cultural Meaning of Animals," *Advances in Consumer Research,* vol. 23, ed. K. P. Corfman and J. G. Lynch (Provo, UT: Association for Consumer Research, 1996), pp. 354–60.

51. T. S. Chan, "Concerns for Environmental Issues," *Journal of International Consumer Marketing,* no. 1 (1996), pp. 43–55.

52. See R. Y. K. Chan, "Environmental Attitudes and Behavior of Consumers in China," *Journal of International Consumer Marketing,* no. 4 (1999), pp. 25–74; and R. Y. K. Chan, "Determinants of Chinese Consumers' Green Purchase Behavior," *Psychology & Marketing,* April 2001, pp. 389–413.

53. "G, What Unusual Undie Ads," *Advertising Age,* October 23, 2000, p. 28. See also L. Wentz, "Absolut Goes to Movies," *Advertising Age,* October 16, 2000, p. 19.

54. K. B. Doran, "Symbolic Consumption in China," *Advances in Consumer Research,* vol. 24, ed. M. Bruck and D. J. MacInnis (Provo, UT: Association for Consumer Research, 1997), pp. 128–31.

55. C. Webster and R. C. Beatty, "Nationality, Materialism, and Possession Importance," *Advances in Consumer Research,* vol. 24, ed. M. Bruck and D. J. MacInnis (Provo, UT: Association for Consumer Research, 1997), pp. 204–10.

56. See S. S. Al-Makaty, "Attitudes toward Advertising in Islam," *Journal of Advertising Research,* May–June 1996, pp. 16–25.

57. See L. C. Huff and D. L. Alden, "An Investigation of Consumer Response to Sales Promotions in Developing Markets," *Journal of Advertising Research,* May–June 1998, pp. 47–56.

58. C. Miller, "Kiddi Just Fine in the U.K.," *Marketing News,* August 28, 1995, p. 8.

59. D. A. Ricks, *Big Business Blunders* (Burr Ridge, IL: Richard D. Irwin, 1983), p. 39.

60. See S. Zhang and B. H. Schmitt, "Creating Local Brands in Multilingual International Markets," *Journal of Marketing Research,* August 2001, pp. 313–25.

61. See M. F. Toncar, "The Use of Humor in Television Advertising," *International Journal of Advertising,* 20 (2001) pp. 521–39.

62. See E. T. Hall, *The Silent Language* (New York: Fawcett World Library, 1959), p. 39; E. T. Hall, "The Silent Language in Overseas Business," *Harvard Business Review,* May–June 1960, pp. 87–96; and E. T. Hall and M. R. Hall, *Hidden Differences* (Garden City, NY: Doubleday, 1987).

63. See N. Spears, X. Lin, and J. C. Mowen, "Time Orientation in the United States, China, and Mexico," *Journal of International Consumer Marketing,* no. 1 (2001), pp. 57–75.

64. C. J. Kaufman, P. M. Lane, and J. D. Lindquist, "Exploring More Than 24 Hours a Day," *Journal of Consumer Research,* December 1991, pp. 392–401; and L. A. Manrai and A. K. Manrai, "Effect of Cultural-Context, Gender, and Acculturation on Perceptions of Work versus Social/Leisure Time Usage," *Journal of Business Research,* February 1995, pp. 115–28.

65. Manrai and Manrai, "Effect of Cultural-Context, Gender, and Acculturation on Perceptions of Work versus Social/Leisure Time Usage." See also Lee and Ulgado, "Consumer Evaluations of Fast-Food Services"; and G. H. Brodowsky and B. B. Anderson, "A Cross-Cultural Study of Consumer Attitudes toward Time," *Journal of Global Marketing,* no. 3 (2000), pp. 93–109.

66. Adapted from E. T. Hall, *The Hidden Dimension* (Garden City, NY: Doubleday, 1966).

67. See M. Chapman and A. Jamal, "Acculturation," *Advances in Consumer Research,* vol. 24, ed. M. Bruck and D. J. MacInnis (Provo, UT: Association for Consumer Research, 1997), pp. 138–44.

68. S. Smith, "The Sales Force Plays Musical Chairs at IBM Japan," *Fortune,* July 3, 1989, p. 14.

69. N. M. Murray and S. B. Murray, "Music and Lyrics in Commercials," *Journal of Advertising,* Summer 1996, pp. 52–63.

70. See also J. Cohen, "The Search for Universal Symbols," *Journal of International Consumer Marketing,* no. 3–4 (1996), pp. 187–210.

71. Adapted from G. Brewer, "An American in Shanghai," *Sales and Marketing Management,* November 1997, pp. 39–44.

72. M. Ewing, A. Caruana, and H. Wong, "Some Consequences of *Guanzi*," *Journal of International Consumer Marketing,* no. 4 (2000), p. 77.

73. P. A. Herbig and H. E. Kramer, "Do's and Don'ts of Cross-Cultural Negotiations," *Industrial Marketing Management,* no. 4 (1992), p. 293.

74. Brewer, "An American in Shanghai," p. 42.

75. See H. McDonald, P. Darbyshire, and C. Jevons, "Shop Often, Buy Little," *Journal of Global Marketing,* no. 4 (2000), pp. 53–72; and A. G. Abdul-Muhmin, "The Effect of Perceived Seller Reservation Prices on Buyers' Bargaining Behavior in a Flexible-Price Market," *Journal of International Consumer Marketing,* no. 3 (2001), pp. 29–45.

76. Miller, "Not Quite Global."

77. S. Y. Park, "A Comparison of Korean and American Gift-Giving Behaviors," *Psychology & Marketing,* September 1998, pp. 577–93.

78. A. Joy, "Gift Giving in Hong Kong and the Continuum of Social Ties," *Journal of Consumer Research,* September 2001, pp. 239–54. See also J. Wang, F. Piron, and M. V. Xuan, "Faring One Thousand Miles to Give Goose Feathers," *Advances in Consumer Research,* vol. 28, ed. M. C. Gilly and J. Meyers-Levy (Provo, UT: Association for Consumer Research, 2001), pp. 58–63.

79. A. S. Mattila, "The Role of Culture and Purchase Motivation in Service Encounter Evaluations," *Journal of Services Marketing,* no. 4–5 (1999), pp. 376–89.

80. D. L. Alden, J. E. M. Steenkamp, and R. Batra, "Brand Positioning through Advertising in Asia, North America, and Europe," *Journal of Marketing,* January 1999, pp. 75–87; F. Ter Hofstede, J. E. M. Steenkamp, and M. Wedel, "International Market Segmentation Based on Consumer-Product Relations," *Journal of Marketing Research,* February 1999, pp. 1–17; M. T. Ewing, "Affluent Asia," *Journal of International Consumer Marketing,* no. 2 (1999), pp. 25–37; B. D. Keillor, M. D'Amico, and V. Horton, "Global Consumer Tendencies," *Psychology & Marketing,* January 2000, pp. 1–19; P. R. Dickson, "Understanding the Trade Winds," *Journal of Consumer Research,* June 2000, pp. 115–22; and D. E. Smith and H. S. Solgaard, "The Dynamics of Shifts in European Alcoholic Drinks Consumption," *Journal of International Consumer Marketing,* 12, no. 3 (2000), pp. 85–109.

81. C. Edy, "The Olympics of Marketing," *American Demographics,* June 1999, pp. 47–48.

82. S. Tully, "Teens," *Fortune,* May 1994, pp. 90–97.

83. Ibid.

84. B. G. Yovovich, "Youth Market Going Truly Global," *Advertising Age,* March 27, 1995, p. 10.

85. *The World's Teenagers* (New York: D'Arcy Masius Benton & Bowles, 1994).

86. Ibid.

87. Tully, "Teens," p. 96.

88. L. Bertagnoli, "Continental Spendthrifts," *Marketing News,* October 22, 2001, p. 15.

89. See L. Tong, "Consumerism Sweeps the Mainland," *Marketing Management,* Winter 1998, pp. 32–35.

90. *The World Fact Book* (Washington DC: Central Intelligence Agency, 2001).

91. C. Walker, "The Global Middle Class," *American Demographics,* September 1995, pp. 40–46.

92. *2001 World Population Data Sheet* (Washington, DC: Population Reference Bureau, 2001).

93. *Statistical Abstract of the United States 2001* (Washington, DC: US Census Bureau, 2001), p. 15; *2000 Philippine Statistical Yearbook* (Makati City: National Statistical Information Center, 2000), p. 1.18; *Japan Statistical Yearbook 2002* (Tokyo: Statistical Research & Training Institute, 2002), p. 46; and *Annual Demographic Statistics, 2000* (Ottawa: Canada Ministry of Industry, 2001), p. 50.

94. J. Whitelock and C. Pimblett, "The Standardization Debate," *Journal of Global Marketing,* no. 3 (1997), pp. 45–66; B. Rosenbloom, Trina Larson, and R. Mehta, "Global Marketing Channels and the Standardization Debate," *Journal of Global Marketing,* no. 1 (1997), pp. 49–64; S. Byfield and L. Caller, "Horses for Courses," *Journal of the Market Research Society,* October 1997, pp. 589–601; S. Onkvisit, and J. J. Shaw, "Standardized International Advertising," *Journal of Advertising Research,* November 1999, pp. 19–34; K. Sirisagul, "Global Advertising Practices," *Journal of Global Marketing,* no. 3 (2000), pp. 77–87; and J. Neff, "Rethinking Globalism," *Advertising Age,* October 9, 2000, p. 1.

95. D. Bryson, "Hindus Eat Mutton in Their Macs," *Register-Guard,* October 12, 1996, p. 1.

96. C. Rubel, "Survey," *Marketing News,* July 15, 1996, p. 5.

97. G. Cui, "Segmenting China's Consumer Market," *Journal of International Consumer Marketing,* no. 1 (1999), pp. 55–76.

98. P. L. Andruss, "Slow Boat to China," *Marketing News,* September 10, 2001, p. 11.

99. See M. M. A. Khan, "Indian Court Tells Lever to Clean Up Ad Claims," *Advertising Age International,* January 1998, p. 32; and C. R. Taylor, G. R. Franke, and M. L. Maynard, "Attitudes toward Direct Marketing and Its Regulation," *Journal of Public Policy and Marketing,* Fall 2000, pp. 228–37.

100. M. Haffenberg, "Report from Tokyo," *Marketing News,* May 25, 1998, p. 2.

101. N. Madden, "China's Direct Sales Ban," *Advertising Age,* May 18, 1998, p. 56.

102. M. Griffin, B. J. Babin, and D. Modianos, "Shopping Values of Russian Consumers," *Journal of Retailing,* no. 1 (2000), pp. 33–52; McDonald, Darbyshire, and Jevons, "Shop Often, Buy Little"; J. A. F. Nicholls et al., "Inter-American Perspectives from Mall Shoppers," *Journal of Global Marketing,* no. 1 (2001), pp. 87–103; and S. Kim and B. Kim, "An Evaluation of the Retail Service Quality Scale for U.S. and Korean Customers," *Advances in Consumer Research,* vol. 28, ed. M. C. Gilly and J. Meyers-Levy (Provo, UT: Association for Consumer Research, 2001), pp. 169–76.

103. R. Gardyn, "Full Speed Ahead," *American Demographics,* October 2001, p. 12.

104. I. Galceran and J. Berry, "A New World," *American Demographics,* March 1995, p. 26.

Jamie Squire/Getty Images.

The Changing American Society: Values

chapter 3

☐ What do Hyundai, Johnson & Johnson, Gillette, ERA Max, Soft & Dri, *Sports Illustrated,* Gatorade, and AFLAC have in common? They are all sponsors of the new Women's United Soccer Association (WUSA), which recently completed its first season. Attendance was higher than projected at 8,295 per game though television ratings were low. The league believes it has a great future, in part due to the huge success of the 1999 women's World Cup that was played in and won by the United States. It attracted 40 million television viewers and created several major stars. In addition, millions of girls play soccer in leagues, with some starting as young as age five. They and, more important, their parents are both learning about the game and becoming fans.

Like their Women's National Basketball Association (WNBA) counterparts, WUSA stars are becoming spokespersons for a wide array of firms. WUSA star Brandi Chastain has appeared in ads for Nike and Pringles, and Mia Hamm has represented Gatorade and Dryer's frozen yogurt. WNBA player Sheryl Swoopes has appeared for Discover Card, Rebecca Lobo has been in ads for Reebok, and Cynthia Cooper has done a commercial for Bud Light.

Two new magazines are based on the rapid increase of women as sports participants and spectators: *Conde Nast Sports for Women* and *Sports Illustrated's Women/Sport.*

Even more impressive evidence of the acceptance of women's sports is the fact that Mattel recently launched a line of WNBA Barbie dolls.

Women are not only participating in professional sports; they are also active in amateur sports. Almost two-thirds engage in some general fitness activity, compared to only a third of males. Almost a third participate in a sport of some type. Half of those women surveyed watch sports on television weekly, compared to 75 percent of males. Moreover, women do not confine their sports viewing to "women" sports. The top three "first mentions" to the question—What are the main sports you watch on TV?—were football (40 percent), baseball (19 percent), and basketball (12 percent).[1] Spending on women's sports sponsorship grew from $285 million in 1992 to $1.1 billion in 2000.[2] Clearly, sports are no longer an exclusive male domain.

In Chapter 2, we discussed how variations in values influence consumption patterns *across* cultures. In this chapter, we will describe how changes in values over time influence consumption patterns *within* cultures, particularly the U.S. culture. The changing role of women in American society reflects changes in the "masculine/feminine" value described in Chapter 2. Obviously, cultural values are not constant. Rather, they evolve over time. In the first section of this chapter, we will examine the evolution of American values in general. Next, we examine four marketing trends that have evolved in response to changing values: green marketing, cause-related marketing, marketing to gay consumers, and gender-based marketing.

CHANGES IN AMERICAN CULTURAL VALUES

Observable shifts in behavior, including consumption behavior, often reflect underlying shifts in **cultural values,** *widely held beliefs that affirm what is desirable*. Therefore, it is necessary to understand the underlying *value shifts* in order to understand current and future consumer behavior.[3] Thus, a shift away from a masculine-dominated to a more nearly balanced masculine/feminine value has produced a wide array of changes in the consumption behaviors of both men and women. Consumer Insight 3–1 describes an evolving trend in the United States: vegetarianism. Knowing which cultural values underlie it and how they are evolving enhances understanding of such a trend and its likely future course.

Although we discuss American values as though every American has the same values, in fact there is substantial variance in values across individuals and groups. In addition, changes in values tend to occur slowly and unevenly across individuals and groups. While traumatic events such as the attack on the World Trade Center and the resultant military actions can produce value shifts, a slow evolution is more common. Caution should be used in assuming that short-term behavioral or attitudinal changes in response to such events represent long-lasting value shifts.

Figure 3–1 presents our estimate of how American values are changing. These are the same values used to describe different cultures in Chapter 2 (see page 46 for definitions). It

Vegetarianism: A Fad or the Future?

Vegetarianism—ranging from avoiding only red meat to avoiding all animal products—is clearly on the rise in the United States. By the mid-1990s, 7 percent of the population classified themselves as vegetarian and 8 percent of those aged 8 to 17 did so. Sales of vegetarian foods have been increasing at almost 40 percent a year. In addition, many more people have adopted a vegetarian orientation—a preference for vegetarian meals while still consuming some meat.

Most vegetarians in the United States made a conscious decision to adopt the practice, as opposed to having been raised a vegetarian. Several studies have explored the motives for this decision. One found four primary motives: (1) moral—focused on animal welfare and suffering, (2) gustatory—relating to a negative reaction to the taste or texture of meat, (3) health—the belief that meat consumption is bad for one's health, and (4) ecological—concern that the practice of raising animals for food is not good for the environment. Another study found the first three motives listed above but identified reference group influence as a fourth motive.

Being a vegetarian now is easier than a few years ago, but it still requires considerable commitment. It is difficult and time consuming to be sure that purchased food products, particularly restaurant meals, are indeed vegetarian. Food options for vegetarians are still limited in terms of recipes, restaurant meal choices, and prepared foods. Most vegetarians face social pressures to conform to the "normal" eating practices of the majority. Sometimes these pressures can be quite strong:

> My dad was very prickly about it (my being vegetarian) because he thought this was like a value judgment against him. He thought that by disagreeing with his dietary choice I was kind of saying that his food wasn't good enough for me.

Vegetarianism is produced by a complex set of motives, which differ between males and females. For example, male vegetarians are more independent or nonconforming than are female vegetarians. This is probably due to a cultural belief that red meat is a "man's" food while vegetables and other light foods are for women. Thus, a male vegetarian is going more against social norms than is a female. There are also noticeable differences in motives between vegetarians and those with a strong vegetarian orientation. For example, vegetarians are motivated in part by a concern for the environment. This does not appear to influence those with a strong vegetarian orientation.[4]

Critical Thinking Questions

1. To what extent are vegetarianism and a vegetarian orientation influenced by values?
2. In 10 years, will vegetarianism and a vegetarian orientation be more or less common than now? Why? Will they ever become "the norm"? Why or why not?

must be emphasized that Figure 3–1 is based on the authors' *subjective* interpretation of the American society. You should feel free, indeed compelled, to challenge these judgments.

Self-Oriented Values

Traditionally, Americans have been active, materialistic, hardworking, religious people inclined toward abstinence and postponed gratification. Beginning after the end of World War II and accelerating rapidly during the 1970s and early 1980s, Americans placed increased emphasis on leisure, immediate gratification, and sensual gratification. An examination of American advertising, product features, and personal debt levels indicates that these changes have significantly affected consumers' behaviors and marketing practice. It appears that several of these trends have reversed direction and are moving back toward their traditional positions.

Religious/Secular America is basically a secular society. A religious group does not control the educational system, government, or political process and most people's daily

FIGURE 3–1   Traditional, Current, and Emerging American Values

Self-Oriented

Active	ECT*	Passive
Material	T C E	Nonmaterial
Hard work	T C E	Leisure
Postponed gratification	T EC	Immediate gratification
Sensual gratification	C E T	Abstinence
Religious	T EC	Secular

Environment-Oriented

Maximum cleanliness	TC E	Minimum cleanliness
Performance	T E C	Status
Tradition	EC T	Change
Risk taking	T E C	Security
Problem solving	T CE	Fatalistic
Admire nature	E C T	Overcome nature

Other-Oriented

Individual	T CE	Collective
Limited family	TEC	Extended family
Diversity	EC T	Uniformity
Competition	T C E	Cooperation
Youth	T C E	Age
Masculine	T C E	Feminine

*T = Traditional, E = Emerging, and C = Current.

behaviors are not guided by strict religious guidelines. Nonetheless, more than 90 percent of all Americans claim a religious affiliation, 70 percent would like religious influence on American society to grow, more than 50 percent state that religion is very important in their lives, and approximately 40 percent claim to attend a religious service almost every week (a percent that hasn't changed much since 1940). Canada has a similar pattern. However, there is strong evidence that only about half of those who claim to attend religious services actually do so (this is known in research as a positive or normative response bias—giving socially appropriate answers to survey questions). There was an upsurge in religious interest in the wake of World Trade Center tragedy, but behaviors seem to be reverting to their prior patterns.[5]

Although most Americans profess to be more religious than their behavior would suggest they are, religious-based beliefs do influence many decisions.[6] Many of the Americans for whom religion is especially important are conservative in their beliefs. They are quite active politically and as consumers. Their political activism involves attempts to regulate various marketing activities, including products (particularly "sin" products such a liquor, gambling, and pornography) and advertising. Their consumption patterns include both positive consumption (purchasing religious objects and books) and negative consumption (avoiding or boycotting products and companies).

While conservative religious groups generate substantial publicity and have considerable political power, the culture remains relatively secular. We treat religion and its impact on our society in considerable depth in Chapter 5 when we discuss subcultures.

Courtesy Norwegian Cruise Line.

Sensual Gratification/Abstinence   Closely tied to America's traditional religious orientation was a belief in the virtue of abstinence. As American society became more secular, sensual gratification became more acceptable. By the 1960s, sensual gratification was an important objective for many consumers. Now, sensual gratification is somewhat less acceptable than in the recent past. While it is still perfectly acceptable to consume products for the sensual pleasures they provide, the range of products and occasions for which this is acceptable has narrowed. This has produced some interesting marketing opportunities and challenges. For example, consumption of both frozen nonfat yogurt *and* superpremium, high-fat ice cream has increased, while consumption of regular ice cream has declined. It appears that many consumers are indulging themselves less frequently but more lavishly. Illustration 3–1 contains an ad that appeals to sensual gratification.

Postponed/Immediate Gratification   In line with the value they generally place on sensual gratification, Americans seem unwilling to delay pleasures. While concern about personal debt is high and more consumers are shopping for value and waiting for sales, personal debt, personal bankruptcies, and credit sales continue to climb. In fact, although Americans will postpone gratification to an extent during economic downturns, their willingness to consume even in these conditions has been a major force in maintaining a relatively strong economy. Virtually all major purchases in America are made on credit, and many of these involve credit card debt that is extremely expensive.

Material/Nonmaterial   Americans have also maintained a strong material orientation. An outcome of America's focus on materialism is a consumption-driven society. As we will explore later in the text, more Americans work, and they work more hours now than in the past. In part, Americans are trading time and energy for things and services such as cars and travel. Consider that the size of the average American family has dropped sharply over the past 30 years while the size of the average American home has dramatically increased. While there is some evidence that this strong value on material possessions, including the consumption of nonessential services, is moderating, it remains a central part of America's culture.

Hard Work/Leisure   As stated above, more Americans are working more now than at any time in recent history.[7] The percentage of married women who work outside the home for wages has increased by 50 percent since 1970, from 40 to 60 percent of all married women. A recent survey found that Americans work long hours for many reasons. One is clearly their material orientation. Americans work in order to have such things as a large home, two cars, and a nice vacation. Others work long hours because they lack the skills or job opportunities to provide even a moderate lifestyle without doing so. However, Americans also work long and hard because work is meaningful and valuable to them. They gain self-esteem and the respect of their peers in part by the work that they do.

Partly in response to the increase in work hours, the value placed on work relative to leisure has dropped over the past two decades. For example, a recent study found that 81 percent of employed consumers felt the need to simplify their lives and create more time for home and family. As one working wife stated,

> I want to spend more time with my family and friends, and I want time to cultivate my interests. I'm not looking for the best price anymore—I'm not looking for deals. All I'm looking for is the best service.[8]

Thus, we have a situation where hard work and leisure are both valued, often by the same people. In response, ads promoting leisure[9] *and* ads stressing hard work are common.[10]

Active/Passive   Americans continue to value an active approach to life. While less than half of all American adults exercise regularly, most Americans take an active approach to both leisure and problem-solving activities. Television viewing as a primary form of entertainment has dropped sharply from its peak in the mid-1980s. Instead, using the Internet, cooking, gardening, and a host of other activities are popular. The amount of time children spend in scheduled activities continues to increase.[11] The strength of this orientation is reflected in the tremendous acceptance of Nike's "Just Do It" theme. The following quote illustrates that Americans differ on this value, but most would agree more with the second speaker than the first.

My idea of a vacation is a nice oceanfront resort, a beach chair, and a piña colada.

Mine too. For a day or two. Then I'd go bug spit. I'd feel like I was in prison. I'd *do* something.[12]

Illustration 3–2 describes a resort designed for active leisure.

Environment-Oriented Values

Environment-oriented values prescribe a society's relationship with its economic, technical, and physical environments. Americans have traditionally admired cleanliness, change, performance, risk taking, problem solving, and the conquest of nature. While this cluster of values remains basically intact, there are some significant shifts occurring.

Courtesy Aspen Skiing Company.

Cleanliness   Americans have long valued cleanliness, particularly personal hygiene. This strong focus seems to be declining somewhat. Messier homes are more acceptable,[13] though personal hygiene remains very important to most Americans. However, these shifts are minor and do not suggest major changes. Illustration 3–3 demonstrates the emphasis Americans place on cleanliness.

Tradition/Change   Americans have always been very receptive to change. *New* has traditionally been taken to mean *improved.* While still very appreciative of change, Americans are now less receptive to change for its own sake. New-product recalls, the expense and the failure of various government programs, and the energy required to keep pace with rapid technological changes are some of the reasons for this shift. Another reason is the aging of the American population. As we will see in the next chapter, the average age of the population is increasing, and people generally become somewhat less accepting of change as they age.

Risk Taking/Security   Americans' risk-taking orientation seems to have changed somewhat over time. There was an increased emphasis on security during the period from 1930 through the mid-1980s. This attitude was a response to the tremendous upheavals and uncertainties caused by the Depression, World War II, and the Cold War. However, risk taking remains highly valued and is gaining appreciation as Americans look to entrepreneurs for economic growth and to smaller firms and self-employment to obtain desired lifestyles.

Problem Solving/Fatalistic   Americans take great pride in being problem solvers. By and large, Americans believe that virtually anything can be fixed given sufficient time and effort. For example, over two-thirds of Americans believe that they can continue to grow the economy *and* improve environmental quality.[14] Marketers introduce thousands of new products each year with the theme that they will solve a problem better than existing products will. We will examine the results of this value later in this chapter in the sections on green marketing and cause marketing.

Tilex® is a registered trademark of The Clorox Company.
Used with permission.

Admire/Overcome Nature   Traditionally, nature was viewed as an obstacle. Americans attempted to bend nature to fit their desires without realizing the negative consequences this could have for both nature and humanity. However, this attitude has shifted dramatically over the past 30 years.

Although the percentage of Americans who consider themselves to be environmentalists has dropped from 76 to 50 percent over the last decade, the statistics show that environmental concerns are still strong:

- More than 80 percent of the public are concerned about the condition of the environment.
- Ninety percent have engaged in activities to protect the environment.
- Over 70 percent purchased a product/brand because it was better for the environment.
- Forty percent contributed to an environmental agency.[15]

One firm classifies consumers into the following segments in terms of environmental activism:[16]

- *True Naturals* (11 percent): express deeply felt environmental concerns and tailor their actions and purchases to these beliefs.
- *New Green Mainstream* (17 percent): concerned about the environment but alter their actions and purchases only when it is convenient.
- *Affluent Healers* (11 percent): most concerned about environmental issues that relate to their personal health; are less inclined to consider the environment when shopping.
- *Young Recyclers* (14 percent): most concerned about environmental issues that relate to solid waste; are less inclined to consider the environment when shopping.
- *Overwhelmed* (22 percent): feel too caught up in life's demands to worry about the environment; are unlikely to favor a product for environmental reasons.
- *Unconcerned* (25 percent): do not pay attention to environmental issues, or do not feel that the environment is seriously threatened.

Firms that convince environmentally concerned consumers that their products are environmentally sound can reap huge rewards. Tom's of Maine markets environmentally sound personal care products. Its products command a 20 to 50 percent price premium and its sales have been growing rapidly. According to an executive, the firm gains additional advantages as well:

> Our environmental and social responsibility policies are a barrier to competitive advances. Even a competitor with much greater resources cannot just replicate our formula and expect to take our market share. Our corporate practices add a richness and depth to our product appeal that creates an unusually strong brand loyalty.[17]

Concerns in Canada are similar if somewhat less intense than in America.[18] We describe the marketing response to this value in the section of this chapter on green marketing.

Performance/Status   Americans are shifting back to a focus on performance rather than status. Although consumers are still willing to purchase "status" brands, these brands must provide style and functionality in addition to the prestige of the name. This has led to substantial increases in sales at stores that combine price, service, and quality, such as Wal-Mart and Target stores, and for quality retailer private-label brands such as those offered by Albertson's and Wal-Mart. In contrast, outlets with inappropriate cost structures or images, such as The Gap, Kmart, and Montgomery Ward, have struggled or failed.[19]

Other-Oriented Values

Other-oriented values reflect a society's view of the appropriate relationships between individuals and groups within that society. Historically, American society has been oriented toward individualism, competitiveness, masculinity, youth, limited families, and uniformity. However, several aspects of this orientation are undergoing change.

Individual/Collective   A strong emphasis on individualism is one of the defining characteristics of American society. Watch any American hit movie. The leading character will virtually always behave as an individual, often despite pressures to compromise to the group. Americans believe in "doing your own thing." Even the "uniforms" that each generation of teenagers invents for itself allow ample room for individual expression. This value affects incentive systems for salespeople, advertising themes, and product design.[20]

Diversity/Uniformity   While American culture has always valued individualism, it has also valued a degree of uniformity, particularly with respect to groups. America was founded in part by people seeking religious freedom or fleeing from various forms of persecution. The Constitution and many laws seek to protect diverse religions, political beliefs, and so forth. Nonetheless, Americans historically insisted that immigrants quickly adopt the language, dress, values, and many other aspects of the majority. Those who did not were often subject to various forms of discrimination. This was particularly true for racial and some religious minorities.

Since World War II, Americans have increasingly valued diversity. For example, a recent study concludes,

> [there] is an equally strong respect for religious diversity that translates into a strong tolerance of other people's beliefs. Americans seem to expect that they will encounter people of different faiths in their daily lives, and have absorbed the idea of respect into their social conduct. This recognition of the importance of both religious faith and religious diversity is underscored repeatedly in the study.[21]

ILLUSTRATION 3–4

Americans increasingly value diversity. As a result, diversity is portrayed as the norm in many ads.

for all the ways you play

moves FOR HIM **adidas**
the adidas fragrance for men

Courtesy Coty, Inc.

While far from free from racial, religious, ethnic, or class prejudice, American culture is evolving toward valuing diversity more than uniformity. The Adidas ad shown in Illustration 3–4 reflects the positive view of diversity held by most Americans.

We examine one aspect of America's increasing acceptance of diversity—marketing to gay and lesbian consumers—in the marketing strategy section of this chapter.

Limited/Extended Family   America was settled by immigrants, people who left their extended families behind. As the nation grew, the western movement produced a similar phenomenon. Even today, frequent geographic moves as well as differential rates of social mobility mean that few children grow up in close interaction with aunts, uncles, cousins, nieces, or nephews.[22] It is also common for children to leave their hometowns and parents once they begin their own careers. The physical separation of traditional family members often reduces the sense of family among those members. This, in turn, reduces the impact that the family has on the individual.

This is not to say that Americans do not love their family members or that how an American is raised does not influence the person for life. Rather, it means that a 35-year-old American is unlikely to have a cousin who would feel obligated to respond positively to a loan request (this is not the case in many other cultures). Likewise, this 35-year-old would be unlikely to have one or more cousins, aunts, or nephews live with him or her for an extended time period. The role of families in the American culture is covered in depth in Chapter 6.

Youth/Age   Traditionally, age has been highly valued in almost all cultures. Older people were considered wiser than young people and were, therefore, looked to as models and leaders. This has never been true in American culture, probably because transforming a wilderness into a new type of producing nation required characteristics such as physical strength, stamina, youthful vigor, and imagination. This value on youth continued as America became an industrial nation. Since World War II, it has increased to such an extent that products such as cars, clothing, cosmetics, and hairstyles seem designed for and sold only to the young! For example, while only about 20 percent of the population are between 16 to 30 years of age, a study found that almost 40 percent of American print ads featured models that appeared to be in this age range.[23]

But there appears to be a slow reversal of this value on youth. Because of their increasing numbers and disposable income, older citizens have developed political and economic clout and are beginning to use it. As one expert says,

> It used to be that 25-year-old women drove the fashion industry; now it's 45-year-old women. Because when you are 45, you already know what you look good in. If a designer says, "Crepe is in," this group may confidently answer that "crepe is crap."[24]

Cosmetics, medicines, and hair care products are being marketed specifically to older consumers; however, most of these products still have either a direct or indirect appeal of creating a younger appearance.

Competition/Cooperation   America has long been a competitive society, and this value remains firmly entrenched. It is reflected in our social, political, and economic systems. We reward particularly successful competitors in business, entertainment, and sports with staggering levels of financial compensation. While there is increased focus on cooperation and teamwork in schools and businesses, this is generally done so that the team or group can outperform some other team or group. It is no wonder that America was one of the first countries to allow comparative advertising.

Masculine/Feminine   American society, like most others, has reflected a masculine orientation for a long time. But as indicated by this chapter's opening story, this orientation is changing. However, while American society is becoming less masculine oriented, it still clearly leans in this direction. For example, 42 percent of parents indicate that they would prefer a boy if they could only have one child, compared to 27 percent who would opt for a girl.[25] Likewise, boys receive larger allowances than do girls.[26] The marketing implications resulting from the shift that is taking place in this value are discussed in detail in the next section of this chapter.

MARKETING STRATEGY AND VALUES

We have examined a number of marketing implications associated with values and changes in values. It is critical that all aspects of the firm's marketing mix be consistent with the value system of its target market. We will now examine four marketing responses to evolving American values: green marketing, cause-related marketing, marketing to gay and lesbian consumers, and gender-based marketing.

Green Marketing

Marketers have responded to Americans' increasing concern for the environment with an approach called **green marketing.**[27] Green marketing generally involves (1) developing products whose production, use, or disposal is less harmful to the environment than the traditional versions of the product; (2) developing products that have a positive impact on the

ILLUSTRATION 3–5

Almost 10 percent of new products introduced in America are "green" products. These crayons are made from soybeans rather than petroleum.

Courtesy Dixon Ticonderoga Company.

environment; or (3) tying the purchase of a product to an environmental organization or event. For example,

- With the cooperation of software producers, GreenDisk collects diskettes from obsolete boxes of software, reformats them, packages them in funky, low-tech packaging, and sells them. In one year, they sold 60 million disks that would have otherwise gone into landfills and saved the materials and energy it would have required to produce 60 million new disks.
- Wal-Mart has launched an "eco-store." The store carries Wal-Mart's usual merchandise mix but highlights environmentally superior products. Recycling is the theme. The store recycles much of its own waste and provides recycling services for its customers. The store itself is designed to be energy efficient and uses recycled materials both in its construction and in the shopping bags it provides for consumers.
- The Church & Dwight Company, Inc., developed sodium bicarbonate products to help purify wastewater and to restore lakes damaged by acid rain.
- Heinz changed the formula of its squeezable plastic ketchup containers to make them more readily recyclable. Church & Dwight eliminated the plastic overwrap and converted to 100 percent recycled paperboard boxes for its Arm & Hammer Carpet Deodorizer.
- Estée Lauder launched, under the Origins label, a complete line of cosmetics that are made of natural ingredients, are not tested on animals, and are packaged in recyclable containers.
- Canon USA gives the Nature Conservancy 50 cents for each laser-printer toner container that is returned for recycling. This is producing over $750,000 for the Conservancy annually.
- Prang Crayons are made from soybeans rather than petroleum-based wax (see Illustration 3–5).

As concern for the environment grew throughout the 1980s and 1990s, many firms began to improve their products and processes relative to the environment and to advertise those improvements. Unfortunately, different marketers used the same claims, such as *environmentally friendly* or *environmentally safe,* to refer to vastly differing performance levels. Further, some firms made green claims that were misleading if not completely false. For example, some firms made claims such as "Now completely phosphorous free!" when their products had contained only a trace amount of phosphorous before. While the claim is true, the elimination of trace amounts of phosphorous from the product in question had no beneficial environmental impact.

To enable consumers to receive the information they need to make environmentally sound choices and to allow marketers to benefit from their efforts to develop environmentally sound products, the Federal Trade Commission (FTC) issued a set of voluntary guidelines for green claims. The general guidelines include dozens of examples of acceptable and unacceptable practices to guide marketers, including the following:

- A "recycled" label on a soft-drink bottle made from recycled material wouldn't be considered misleading even if the cap isn't made from recycled material.
- An ad touting a package as having "50 percent more recycled content than before" could be misleading if the recycled content had only increased from 2 to 3 percent.
- An ad calling a trash bag "recyclable" without qualification would be deemed misleading because bags aren't ordinarily separated from other trash at landfills or incinerators.
- An ad touting a shampoo bottle as containing "20 percent more recycled content" would be considered misleading if it didn't say whether the product is being compared with a rival or the product's previous container.
- Labels promoting products as "environmentally safe" or "environmentally friendly" must specify what portion of the product is being referred to; otherwise, they would be deceptive.
- A shampoo advertised as "biodegradable" without qualification wouldn't be deceptive if the marketer has competent and reliable scientific support showing it will decompose in a short time.[28]

Green marketing is complex. Environmental concerns are only one criterion consumers use in making purchase decisions.[29] For example, over half those interviewed in a recent survey expressed concern about the level of pesticide residue found in food products but less than one in five looked for food grown in a pesticide-free manner.[30] Another study found that even subjects who viewed environmental problems as serious frequently used disposable products because they found them to be more convenient, hygienic, or effective than nondisposable substitutes.[31] A third study found that a consumer's concern for the environment may not translate into a willingness to pay a premium for renewable energy.[32] It appears that many environmentally concerned consumers will buy "green" if all else is equal but otherwise use other criteria for their choices. Thus, firms must balance concern for the environment with other consumer expectations and financial constraints.

Although using recycled materials generally elicits a positive response from consumers,[33] other environmentally sound actions may not work as well. For example, McDonald's and other chains were widely criticized for using polystyrene hamburger containers. However, they had originally shifted to this product in part in response to environmental concerns. Polystyrene containers actually use 30 percent less energy to produce than do those made of coated paper or paperboard, and their manufacture results in 40 percent less air pollution and 42 percent less water pollution.[34] However, the solid-waste problem they create is much more visible to consumers than the air pollution and energy depletion areas in which they create great savings. *Should a firm like McDonald's spend millions to educate a skeptical public about polystyrene or should it use coated paper?*

There is somewhat of a conflict between conservation and most business strategies. The basic thrust of environmentalism is the "three Rs"—*reduce, reuse, recycle.* Two of the three

Seventy percent of respondents to a recent survey claimed to be at least somewhat concerned that their car might be harmful to the environment (37 percent indicated extremely or very). Seventy-seven percent stated that it was extremely or very important for manufacturers to make cars that produce less carbon dioxide.

Ford's Chairman William Ford Jr. has pledged that going green will be Ford's priority in the future—"The environment will become like quality. It's a prism through which we will look when we make product decisions."

Despite Ford's environment concerns, sport-utility vehicles (SUVs), which consume significantly more gas and other resources than standard cars, are critical to the company's success, contributing nearly 20 percent of its sales and $5 billion in pretax earnings. Its most noticeable SUV, the Ford Excursion, is 230 inches long (10 inches longer than any other passenger vehicle now on the road) and weighs nearly three tons. The Sierra Club has labeled it the "Ford Valdez." The Excursion is so large that the government does not classify it as a "light vehicle," which excludes it from federal fuel economy standards. Ford sold over 50,000 Excursions the first year the model came out.

Ford did not just decide to build a giant SUV and hope it would sell. Consumer demand for its SUVs, particularly the larger models, had grown steadily. William Ford Jr. explains his dilemma:

It's a delicate balance between what the customer wants and being completely environmentally driven.

You can make a completely clean vehicle, but if it sits unsold on the dealer's lot it's not helping the environment, either. We just have to make these vehicles cleaner and cleaner every year.

Despite several attempts, electric automobiles and other superhigh mileage or low pollution cars have yet to penetrate the U.S. market. Now, however, several seemed poised to do so. The Honda Insight, a radically designed, two-seat, hybrid gas/electric car, gets 60 miles per gallon in the city and 70 on the highway. Sales were 4,000 units in 2000, with 6,500 projected for 2001.

Toyota's Prius, another $20,000 gas/electric hybrid, is a four-door, five-passenger vehicle with a 100,000-mile warranty. Much more like a traditional car in appearance and function, it is projecting sales of around 12,000 units for 2001.[35]

Critical Thinking Questions

1. Why is there so much demand for SUVs, which are not environmentally friendly, when American values strongly support environmental protection?

2. Why is demand for hybrid cars such as the Insight and the Prius so low relative to the demand for an SUV such as the Excursion?

3. How should a company such as Ford balance the ethics of providing environmentally sound products with the need to provide consumers with the products they desire in order to remain profitable?

core thrusts of the environmental movement conflict with the objective of most businesses, which is growth in sales and profits. This conflict between producing and conserving mirrors the conflict between the value Americans place on the environment and their materialistic orientation. This same conflict exists in most developed and many developing nations. How it is resolved will have major consequences for the economic and environmental health of the next generation.[36] Consumer Insight 3–2 describes some of these issues.

Cause-Related Marketing

The term *cause marketing* is sometimes used interchangeably with *social marketing* to refer to the application of marketing principles and tactics to advance a cause such as a

Courtesy Yoplait USA, Inc.

Courtesy Christian Children's Fund.

charity (United Way), an ideology (environmental protection), or an activity (breast cancer exams). Social marketing differs from traditional marketing in the intangible and abstract nature of the "product" and in the absence of a profit motive. At one extreme, such as a health-related campaign, there are potential direct benefits to the individual. However, in general, the benefits to the individual are indirect (a better society in which to live). Often, the benefit is purely or primarily emotional. Individuals are requested to change beliefs or behaviors or provide funds because it is "the right thing to do" and they will "feel good" or "be a better person" because of it.

Examine the two ads in Illustration 3–6. *What are the benefits being promised to those who respond? Why would an individual "buy" one of these "products"? Why do most individuals fail to "purchase" the "products" advertised in these ads?*

As noted in Chapter 1, social marketing is marketing done to enhance the welfare of individuals or society without direct benefit to a firm. In contrast, cause marketing or **cause-related marketing (CRM)** is *marketing that ties a company and its products to an issue or cause with the goal of improving sales or corporate image while providing benefits to the cause.*[37] Companies associate with causes to create long-term relationships with their customers, building corporate and brand equity that should eventually lead to increased sales. The Christian Children's Fund in Illustration 3–6 is an example of social marketing, as it promotes a benefit to the world community without advancing the profits or image of a commercial firm. The Yoplait ad in Illustration 3–6 is an example of cause-related marketing. It attempts to benefit a cause *and* to enhance the image and sales of a commercial firm.

The foundation of CRM is marketing to consumers' values, and it can be very effective. Consider the following results, conclusions, and recommendations from a national survey

ILLUSTRATION 3–6

The Christian Children's ad promotes a benefit to the world community without advancing the profits or image of a commercial firm. It is an example of social marketing. The Yoplait ad represents cause-related marketing as it benefits a cause *and* enhances the image and sales of a commercial firm.

of Americans:

* Sixty-one percent believe that CRM is a good way to solve social problems.
* Sixty-four percent believe it should be a standard business practice.
* Eighty-five percent believe it improves a product or firm's image.
* Sixty-two percent believe that corporate commitment to a cause should be for more than a year.
* Sixty-six percent are likely to switch brands based on CRM when price and quality are equal.
* Sixty-two percent are likely to switch stores based on CRM when price and quality are equal.
* Influentials (the 10 percent of the population who are socially active opinion and group leaders) are much more favorable toward and influenced by CRM than the general population. Upscale individuals (income, education, or occupation) are more favorable than are other groups.[38]

Another study was able to group consumers into four categories on the basis of their responses to CRM: (1) *skeptics,* who doubt the sincerity or effectiveness of CRM; (2) *balancers,* who believe in CRM but generally don't carry this over into purchase behavior; (3) *attribution-oriented,* who are concerned about the motives underlying the firm's participation; and (4) *socially concerned,* who are driven primarily by a desire to help the sponsored charity. The following quotes from a member of each group illustrate their nature.[39]

> *Skeptic:* I think those are fake, most of them. Because, what they give is so little it doesn't amount to anything.
>
> *Balancer:* I hate to say this, but, as far as grocery stores, I go to the one that is closest to me. It makes me feel better . . . about Food Lion that they were willing to do this (participate in CRM) . . . but, sometimes I don't put out that extra effort, but I guess I really should.
>
> *Attribution-oriented:* I always approach them with a skeptical eye, but I try and use good judgment and common sense based on who they are, what they're doing and try to see the end result.
>
> *Socially concerned:* I mean, as long as they're doing it, the motives can be questionable as far as I'm concerned . . . . Even if there's questionable motives, it's that much more important to support companies who do those things. Just to reinforce that good behavior.

Cause-related marketing is often effective because it is consistent with several strongly held American values.[40] A common theme in most CRM programs is the presentation of a problem such as breast cancer, AIDS, or pollution and an action that individuals can take to help solve the problem. This theme ties directly into America's strong problem-solving orientation. It is also consistent with a focus on individualism—CRM programs tend to encourage individuals to take individual actions that can contribute directly to the solution of the problem. The specific cause being promoted often taps other cultural or individually held values or concerns.

Marketing to Gay and Lesbian Consumers

As Americans in general are shifting from valuing uniformity to valuing diversity, they are increasingly embracing ethnic, religious, and racial diversity. One of the last groups to begin to gain public acceptance has been the gay and lesbian community, but acceptance is still far from complete.[41] In 1982, 51 percent of the respondents to a large survey felt that homosexuality should not be considered an acceptable lifestyle, compared to 34 percent who felt it should. In 2001, 43 percent still considered it unacceptable, while 52 percent now felt it acceptable.[42] In this section, we will follow the convention of the business press and refer to gay and lesbian consumers as the gay market.

Before we begin, we need to emphasize that gay consumers, like heterosexual consumers, are also members of ethnic groups, live in various regions of the country, and belong to occupational categories and age groups. These and a host of other factors also influence their behavior and, in most instances, play a much larger role in their consumption process than their sexual orientation.

Size estimates of the number of people in the gay market are suspect due to methodological and response bias concerns in surveys on this topic. It is generally assumed that the actual population size will be understated in sound surveys because many gays do not want to be categorized based solely on this dimension of their identity as well as concerns about social taboos, religious censure, and real or perceived risk of jeopardizing of jobs, reputations, and family situations. Several relatively large-scale surveys produced the following population estimates (percentage of the adult population):[43]

	Gay Male	Lesbian	Gay/Homosexual/Lesbian
1993, *Janus Report*	9%	5%	
1993, *Yankelovich Monitor*			5.7%
1994, *Parade* magazine survey	3	1	
1994, *Sex in America*	2.8	1.4	

The gay market is generally considered to be wealthier and in higher-status occupations than the general population. But again, measurement issues are a major concern.[44] Research firms such as MediaMark, Simmons, and Nielsen do not use sexual orientation as one of their demographic categories. Neither does the U.S. Census. Much of the data on the demographic characteristics of the gay market comes from surveys of subscribers to gay publications, who almost certainly do not represent the overall gay population. For example, a 1997 study of readers of the National Gay Newspaper Guild found them to be 12 times more likely to be in a professional job and twice as likely to own a second home or individual stocks as the average American. The $47,000 average income of the 750,000 readers represents a $35 billion market.[45] However, two 1998 studies found average gay household income to be only slightly above the U.S. average.[46]

While the exact dimensions of the gay market remain unclear and the lack of sound data reduces the willingness of many firms to target this group, many others have concluded that it represents a significantly attractive market to pursue aggressively. For example, American Express recently spent $250,000 on a study of this market before committing to additional marketing effort. Likewise, Subaru conducted a major study before deciding the market warranted a special effort.[47] This focused effort produced impressive results: subscribers to the gay magazines in which Subaru advertised were 2.6 times more likely to buy a Subaru than nonsubscribers.[48]

Any firm that desires to capture the loyalty of the gay community must have internal policies that do not discriminate against gay employees. In addition to having appropriate internal policies, firms face a number of decisions in approaching this market.

- Does the product need to be modified in any way to meet the needs of this market?
- Should the firm advertise in gay-oriented media using its standard ads?

- Should it advertise in gay media using ads with gay themes?
- To what extent should the firm be involved in gay community activities?
- Should its major media ads include ads with gay themes?

Product Issues   With the exception of a few areas, the lifestyles of gay consumers do not differ sufficiently from other consumers to require product modifications. United Airlines, Coors, Barnes & Noble, and Procter & Gamble have programs that target the gay market using their standard products. However, IBM marketed a special WorkPad palm computer loaded with gay travel information software.

One area in which standard products do frequently require alteration is financial services. As the director of segment marketing for American Express explains,

Often, gay couples are very concerned about issues like Social Security benefits and estate planning, since same-sex marriages often are not recognized under the law.[49]

The following ad content reflects one of American Express's product offerings targeting the gay market.

When you're ready to plan a future together, who can you trust to understand the financial challenges that gay men and lesbians face?

At American Express Financial Advisors we offer Domestic Partner Planning services that can help you address issues like protecting assets from unnecessary taxation and getting around restrictions placed on unmarried couples. We offer you the expertise and insight you need to make smart decisions.

Hartford Financial Services developed Diverse Household Auto Insurance that offers discounts to both heterosexual and gay couples. In a humorous ad, two blue cars are shown side-by-side with the caption, "The Hartford offers auto insurance discounts to gay couples." Beneath these cars are two side-by-side pink cars with the caption, "We also offer discounts to lesbian couples." At the bottom of the ad, a blue and a pink car are side-by-side and have the caption, "Heck, we even offer discounts to heterosexual couples. (Not that there's anything wrong with that.)"

Communication Issues   There are a large number of gay-oriented media in the United States and Canada. Rivendell Marketing Co. is a national advertising representative for 185 such publications with a combined circulation of 3.5 million. The National Gay Newspaper Guild has 12 publications with a readership of over 750,000. There are a number of gay-oriented magazines, with *Out* (circulation 110,000) being the largest.

Compared to the general population, gays are heavy Internet subscribers (52 percent), and a number of gay websites are capitalizing on this fact.[50] PlanetOut.com and Gay.com (now merged) are the most successful. They have 5 million unique visits each month and 3.6 million registered users. American Airlines, IBM, Capital One, and Bridgestone/Firestone are among the firms that advertise on them.

Since most products don't require alteration for the gay market, most firms initially approach the market by placing one of their standard ads in gay-oriented media. Anheuser-Busch, Miller Brewing, Baileys Original Irish Cream, and American Express are among the firms that first approached this market with standard ads and then developed gay-themed ads.

Firms are increasingly creating ads specifically for this market.[51] The ads may portray a gay couple instead of a heterosexual couple in a standard ad, as shown in Illustration 3–7. Or the entire ad may contain a gay theme. Baileys developed a gay-focused ad for its limited

Courtesy Brown & Company.

edition coffee cups (used to promote Baileys and coffee). The cups, which are sold in sets of two, are designed like a face with one eye winking. The ad the firm ran in *Out* showed a picture of the two cups side by side with the caption, "Our limited edition coffee cups are available nationwide, though only recognized as a set in Hawaii," a play on the fact that, at that time, Hawaii was the only state in the United States to recognize same-sex marriages.

In addition to advertising in gay media, support of gay community events such as Gay Pride week is another avenue firms use in approaching this market. Tanqueray gin has sponsored a number of events to raise funds for AIDS programs, which is an area of great concern of the gay community. Levi-Strauss cemented an already strong relationship with many gay consumers when it publicly canceled its contract to make uniforms for the Boy Scouts of America after that organization fired a scout leader for being gay.[52]

It has been estimated that slightly more than a fourth of the gay community does not use gay-oriented media. Those who do also spend considerable time using standard media. As one gay man stated, "We are not only reading *Out* and *The Advocate* all the time. If you go into any gay man's apartment you're very likely to see *Vanity Fair* and *People* as well."[53] However, very few firms have used ads with gay themes in standard mass media. The Hartford ad described earlier is being used on billboards and some local newspapers. This was unusual enough to generate an article in *Advertising Age* entitled "Insurer Places Gay-Themed Ads in Mainstream Media." Concern about backlash from the portion of the market that does not accept the gay community as well as a desire to have ads that directly appeal to the largest number of viewers are the primary reasons for the lack of gay-themed ads on mainstream media.[54]

Gender-Based Marketing

Until recently, the prevailing stereotype of an automobile purchase involved a male making the purchase alone. If accompanied by his wife or girlfriend, she only offered suggestions concerning color and interior features. Today, research indicates that women influence 80 percent of all automobile purchases, buy 26 percent of all new trucks and over half of all new cars, and are the predominant buyers of many models.[55]

Although surveys of American consumers consistently indicate that women want the same basic features in a car as males do, there are subtle differences. For example, many automobiles have radios, heaters, and other accessories that are difficult to operate with long fingernails. Likewise, women find unrealistic role portrayals in automobile advertising offensive and are frequently frustrated in their attempts to deal with auto sales personnel who don't treat them seriously. They are also more attentive to the showroom environment. Examples of the response of automobile manufacturers and others to the changing role of women include the following:

* An ad for the Pontiac Grand Am shows a young woman who brings her brother with her when she buys a car. His role is to help her pick the color.
* Four of the five introductory ads for GMC's sport-utility vehicle featured women. One illustrates the ease with which a woman executive in a suit can enter the vehicle due to its lower entry step.
* Sixty percent of the buyers of the new Mercury Mountaineer sport-utility vehicle are expected to be women. It was promoted during a women's LPGA golf tournament and in magazines such as *Mirabella* and *Vanity Fair.*
* *Good Housekeeping* is now offering a "Women's Automobile Satisfaction Award" to brands that score 5 percent or more above the average satisfaction rating among female owners.

The terms *sex* and **gender** are used interchangeably to refer to *whether a person is biologically a male or female.* **Gender identity** refers to the traits of *femininity* (expressive traits such as tenderness and compassion) and *masculinity* (instrumental traits such as aggressiveness and dominance). These traits represent the ends of a continuum, and individuals have varying levels of each trait, with biological males tending to be toward the masculine end of the continuum and biological females toward the feminine end.[56]

Gender roles are *the behaviors considered appropriate for males and females in a given society.* As the previous discussion of automobile purchasing indicates, gender roles in America have undergone massive changes over the past 25 years. The general nature of this shift has been for behaviors previously considered appropriate primarily for men to be acceptable for women too.[57]

Gender roles are ascribed roles. An **ascribed role** is based on *an attribute over which the individual has little or no control.* This can be contrasted with **achievement roles,** which are based on *performance criteria over which the individual has some degree of control.* Individuals can, within limits, select their occupational role (achievement role), but they cannot generally determine their gender (ascribed role).

Researchers find it useful to categorize women into **traditional** or **modern gender orientations** on the basis of their preference for one or the other of two contrasting lifestyles:

* *Traditional.* A marriage with the husband assuming the responsibility for providing for the family and the wife running the house and taking care of the children.
* *Modern.* A marriage where husband and wife share responsibilities. Both work, and they share homemaking and child care responsibilities.

In a 1977 survey, 65 percent of the respondents expressed a preference for a traditional lifestyle. By 1994, this figure had dropped to less than 40 percent.[58] By 1999, only 25 percent of those surveyed agreed that women should return to their tradition roles.[59]

While males and females both express strong preferences for the modern lifestyle as a general concept, most recognize that it comes with a cost, and attitudes and behaviors toward specific aspects of that lifestyle remain very conservative. For example, almost 70 percent of both women and men believe it would be best if mothers would "stay at home and just take care of the house and children."[60] Studies consistently find that many men resent and resist housework even if their spouses are employed. The following quote illustrates the struggle that this can produce:

> I told him (husband), "I don't like the example. I don't want the boys to see mommy does the housework and daddy doesn't do it." I even told him I wanted him to cook supper at least one night a week. Not only would it give me a break from cooking supper but the kids would see daddy doing it. But he cooked spaghetti every single Saturday night for months. I mean there wasn't even a salad with it, it was just a blob. (Laughs.) I think he didn't like cooking and I think he didn't like me asking him to do it, and this was his way of doing it but not doing it.[61]

Thus, we find a pattern typical of a changing value: growing acceptance of the change, but not for all aspects of it, and substantial resistance to the new behaviors from the more traditional groups or those who stand to lose as the new value is accepted.

This pattern of conflict exists not only between groups within the society but within individuals who are torn between the two orientations. Consider the following quote from a 41-year-old woman with four children who is a social worker:

> Sometimes I go through guilt trips because I work. I think women are getting out of this cycle, but I am still of the school that feels women's responsibilities are to be mothers and to be homemakers. Unfortunately, it's not changing for me. I hope it's changing for my children . . . but I'm of the generation where a lot of us still carry those guilt feelings around if your family can't come home to homemade bread and a hot meal every night. I know that's unrealistic, but, I still sort of feel like that's my responsibility.[62]

Social change is often painful for the individuals and groups involved.

As we have seen, women have a variety of role options and a range of attitudes concerning their gender. The ads in Illustration 3–8 reflect two sharply contrasting views of the female role. In the following sections, we examine some of the marketing implications of the changing role of women in American society.

Market Segmentation   Neither the women's nor the men's market is as homogeneous as it once was. At least four significant female market segments exist.[63]

1. *Traditional housewife.* Generally married. Prefers to stay at home. Very home- and family-centered. Desires to please husband and children. Seeks satisfaction and meaning from household and family maintenance as well as volunteer activities. Experiences strong pressure to work outside the home and is well aware of forgone income opportunity. Feels supported by family and is generally content with role.
2. *Trapped housewife.* Generally married. Would prefer to work, but stays at home due to young children, lack of outside opportunities, or family pressure. Seeks satisfaction and meaning outside the home. Does not enjoy most household chores. Has mixed feelings about current status and is concerned about lost opportunities.

Courtesy Giant Bicycle, Inc.

© The Procter & Gamble Company. Used by permission.

ILLUSTRATION 3–8

Women fulfill a multitude of roles today and have a wide range of attitudes about their role in society. These two ads take radically different approaches to their portrayal of women and women's attitudes.

3. *Trapped working woman.* Married or single. Would prefer to stay at home, but works for economic necessity or social/family pressure. Does not derive satisfaction or meaning from employment. Enjoys most household activities, but is frustrated by lack of time. Feels conflict about her role, particularly if younger children are home. Resents missed opportunities for family, volunteer, and social activities. Is proud of financial contribution to family.

4. *Career working woman.* Married or single. Prefers to work. Derives satisfaction and meaning from employment rather than, or in addition to, home and family. Experiences some conflict over her role if younger children are at home, but is generally content. Views home maintenance as a necessary evil. Feels pressed for time.

While the above descriptions are oversimplified, they indicate the diverse nature of the adult female population. However, it should be noted that this diversity is declining. With two-thirds of American women preferring to work and 75 percent of this group employed, the career working woman category now contains half of all adult women, compared to 30 percent in 1977.[64] Nonetheless, the other segments are still sizable, and each has somewhat different needs and communications requirements.

The male market is likewise diverse in both its attitudes and behaviors toward gender roles, work, and household chores.

Product Strategy   Many products are losing their traditional gender typing. Guns, cars, motorcycles, computer games and equipment, golf equipment, financial services, and many other once-masculine products are now designed with women in mind.[65]

ILLUSTRATION 3–9

As time pressure has mounted for women, firms have responded with new products and positioning strategies. Betty Crocker offers both products and web-based assistance to time-pressured homemakers.

While new products are being developed or altered to satisfy positive needs created by the changing role of women, others are emerging to deal with more negative consequences of the evolving roles of women. More women work more hours outside the home today than at any time in our history.[66] This has created great time pressures on most households, as the following quotes from two working wives illustrate:

> I have no time. I have absolutely no disposable time at all. I shopped at that Kroger's for probably seven or eight years, and I know where everything is and I don't have to spend any time searching for things. In fact it's real frustrating to me when Kroger's rearranges even small areas in their store, because I don't want to have to go hunt for things.
>
> The poor kids have to make do with you know, canned ravioli, or fish sticks or whatever I can round up. I run into the guilt type thing I guess. Like I should be performing what my mother did, cooking the good wholesome meal with the potatoes and the green vegetables and the meat. But if I can manage to defrost the meat and get it into the crock pot where it's doing its thing while I'm at work, then, you know, we might have a decent dinner.[67]

This time pressure has produced a wealth of time-saving products and services that these consumers use, though often with some guilt feelings.[68]

General Mills' Betty Crocker brand has responded with products and a website that make meal planning and preparation easier (see Illustration 3–9). For example, among other things, the site currently features different sets of plans for a week's worth of dinners. Likewise, EAS is positioning its AdvantEdge line of meal-on-the-run bars and drinks using Christie Brinkley and Cindy Crawford in ads as soccer moms (both have kids) who must juggle fitness and nutrition needs with the demands of busy lifestyles.

As women's roles have expanded, the consumption of potentially harmful products has become socially acceptable for women. This raises the ethical issue of targeting groups that have not historically been heavy users of products such as alcohol or tobacco. Examples include the following:

- Hiram Walker attempted to reach women while introducing its Royale Cream Liqueur by sponsoring "Melrose Place" parties at bars throughout the country. The show is very popular with women.
- Consolidated Cigar Corporation is introducing two new cigars designed for female smokers. The new cigars will be near regular size but "will be tapered at both ends to make them easier to light and more comfortable for the smaller female hand."
- A controversial but expanding product category for women is personal protection devices, particularly handguns. Smith & Wesson recently launched LadySmith, a line of guns designed specifically for women. Other manufacturers had attempted to reach the female market by "feminizing" men's guns with colored handles and engraved roses on the side plates. Smith & Wesson found through research that "if a woman is going to pull out a gun for personal protection, she doesn't want a cute gun." Smith & Wesson redesigned its guns to fit women's hands and has a very successful new line.

One female gun owner gives her reasoning for gun ownership:

> It's me or them. I have no other choice. Today right on freeways women have been killed, raped, and assaulted . . . . I feel like we are victimized. The odds of getting from birth to death without being in a life-jeopardizing situation as females is pretty dad-blamed nonexistent.[69]

While assaults against women are a major social problem, controversy surrounds the danger associated with expanding handgun ownership, independent of gender. Some evidence indicates that the odds of an accidental shooting of a family member or friend are as great as or greater than the effective use of a gun for self-defense.

Marketing Communications   Males and females respond differently to different types of marketing appeals. For example, females respond more favorably to a "help-others" type appeal for a charity, whereas males respond best to a "self-help" appeal.[70] This is caused by differing worldviews that affect a range of communications responses as well as consumption behaviors.

As gender roles evolve, it is increasingly necessary to communicate how an existing product or brand is appropriate for the gender that traditionally did not use it. Beer ads, once targeted exclusively at males, are now targeted at females as well. Miller, Budweiser, Michelob, and Coors have all launched advertising campaigns aimed at female consumers, and females now consume over 20 percent of domestic beer volume. As with developing guns for women, promoting alcoholic beverages to women raises ethical questions, given the harmful effects alcohol can have, particularly on pregnant women.

State Farm Insurance targets working mothers who have children or who are expecting a child as prospects for their life insurance products. Its ads in magazines such as *Working Mother, Working Woman,* and *American Baby* feature a picture of a woman life insurance agent with her own child. The copy from one ad reads,

> A mother's love knows no bounds. And there's no better way to show how much you love them than with State Farm life insurance. Nobody knows better than Gail Coleman—a State Farm agent and mom. When she sits down with you to talk about life insurance, she knows you need a plan designed for working moms. One that will grow as your needs grow. And she's always there to answer your questions. So when it comes to life there are two things you can always count on. A mother's love and your State Farm agent. Like a good neighbor, State Farm is there.

Fisher-Price designs the first diaper pail you can open without passing out.

Most diaper pails have a nice little fragrance tablet in the lid. But it's not *that* fragrance you usually notice first. That's why the Fisher-Price® Diaper Pail has a unique odor barrier: an inner lid that helps keep odor from sneaking out, even when you open the top.
Our exclusive design makes diaper disposal a very tidy one-way task.
And so, when you're in the nursery, surprise! All you smell is fresh air.

A second, inner lid helps keep the room fresh.

Courtesy Fisher-Price.

Advertisements portraying women must not offend any of the various segments.[71] For example, an ad that implied that housework was unimportant or that women who work outside the home are somehow superior to those who do not could insult traditional housewives. The type of role portrayal most acceptable to a wide range of women appears to be an egalitarian image in which a working woman and her husband share the household chores—images of a traditional or a superwoman were less effective across the various segments.[72]

Ads that show women primarily as decoration or as clearly inferior to males tend to produce negative responses across all female segments.[73] Despite these negative reactions, many ads still use these tactics. For example, a recent ad for Sony Handycam showed a male skier jumping from a cliff with the line—"You'll also get a great video of your girlfriend on the bunny slope." An analysis of cigarette and alcoholic beverage ads reached this conclusion:

> The world of smoke and drink is more the domain of men than women. While men balance work with smoking and drinking, women tend to occupy that world as sexual objects, interested in socializing, not working.[74]

There are relatively few ads showing men using products traditionally designed for women or performing tasks traditionally performed by women. Illustration 3–10 shows an exception.

Retail Strategy   Men are increasingly shopping for household and other products traditionally purchased by females,[75] and females are shopping for "masculine" products such as lawn mowers and hammers. In response to these changes, retailers such as Kmart are showing very masculine men shopping for household products at their stores. Campbell soup has begun advertising its Chunky Soup in *Sports Illustrated* and *Field & Stream.* In contrast, Lowe's (a home improvement store chain) is launching its first national TV campaign with a focus on women.

SUMMARY

American values have evolved and will continue to evolve. In terms of those values that influence an individual's relationship with *others,* Americans remain individualistic. We have substantially less of a masculine orientation now than in the past. We also place a greater value on older persons and diversity.

Values that affect our relationship to our *environment* have become somewhat more performance-oriented and slightly less oriented toward change. There is a strong and growing value placed on protecting the natural environment, and we increasingly value risk taking.

Self-oriented values have also undergone change. We place somewhat less emphasis on hard work as an end in itself and on sensual gratification. We are more content to delay our rewards than in the recent past. While religion is important and is perhaps becoming more so, America remains a relatively secular culture.

Americans assign a high value on the environment. Marketers have responded to this concern with *green marketing:* (1) Developing products whose production, use, or disposition is less harmful to the environment than the traditional versions of the product;

(2) developing products that have a positive impact on the environment; or (3) tying the purchase of a product to an environmental organization or event.

Cause-related marketing is marketing that ties a company and its products to an issue or cause with the goal to improve sales and corporate image while providing benefits to the cause. Companies associate with causes to create long-term relationships with their customers, building corporate and brand equity that should eventually lead to increased sales.

Roles are prescribed patterns of behavior expected of a person in a situation. *Gender roles* are *ascribed roles* based on the sex of the individual rather than on characteristics the individual can control. In contrast, an *achievement role* is acquired through performance over which an individual does have some degree of control.

Gender roles, particularly female roles, have undergone radical changes in the past 25 years. The fundamental shift has been for the female role to become more like the traditional male role. Virtually all aspects of our society, including marketing activities, have been affected by this shift.

KEY TERMS

Achievement role 98
Ascribed role 98
Cause-related marketing
  (CRM) 93

Cultural values 80
Gender 98
Gender identity 98
Gender role 98

Green marketing 89
Modern gender orientation 98
Traditional gender
  orientation 98

INTERNET EXERCISES

1. Visit a site such as the Internet Newspaper (www.trib.com/NEWS). What value does it have in helping track American values? What other sites are useful for this?
2. Search for a newsgroup that is relevant for understanding the following. Report on the insights that it can provide.
   a. American values in general
   b. Cause-related marketing

   c. Green marketing
   d. Gender roles
3. Visit www.publicagenda.org. Pick an issue that is relevant to one or more of the values discussed in this chapter and report on the data available relevant to that value.
4. Use the Internet to discover what, if any, cause-related marketing activities the following firms

are involved with

a. Nike

b. Wendy's

c. Mary Kay Cosmetics

d. A firm for which you would like to work

5. Evaluate an online green shopping mall (such as www.ecoexpo.com, environlink.org, or greenmarket.com/greenmarket). What value do these malls provide consumers? Advertisers? What types of firms advertise here? How would you characterize their ads?

6. Evaluate Ben & Jerry's website (www.benjerry.com).

7. Determine the size and average income of the gay market using the Internet (you should start with the James C. Hormel Gay and Lesbian Center at the San Francisco Public Library website).

8. Use the Internet to determine the role of women in purchasing the following:

a. Cigars

b. Mountain bikes

c. Stocks

DDB NEEDHAM DATA ANALYSES

1. What characterizes individuals with a traditional view of the female role? How do these individuals differ from those with a more modern view? (Use the DDB Needham data in Tables 1a, 2a, 3a, 4a, 5a, 6a, and 7a.)

2. Based on the data in the DDB Needham Tables 1a, 2a, 3a, 4a, 5a, 6a, and 7a, what characterizes individuals who subscribe strongly to the cleanliness value?

3. What characterizes consumers who are particularly responsive to cause-related marketing? What are the marketing strategy implications of this? (See DDB Needham data in Tables 1a, 2a, 3a, 4a, 5a, 6a, and 7a.)

4. Examine the DDB Needham data in Tables 1a, 2a, 3a, 4a, 5a, 6a, and 7a. What characterizes individuals who are active recyclers? What are the marketing strategy implications of this?

REVIEW QUESTIONS

1. What is a *cultural value?* Do all members of a culture share cultural values?

2. Describe the current American culture in terms of each of the 18 values discussed in this chapter.

3. What is *green marketing?*

4. What values underlie green marketing?

5. What problems did the questionable use of environment claims by some firms cause for consumers? For other firms? How did the Federal Trade Commission respond?

6. Describe the basic conflict between the environmental movement and many businesses.

7. What is *cause-related marketing?* Why is it often successful?

8. What are the major decisions a firm faces with respect to the gay market?

9. What is meant by *gender?*

10. What is *gender identity?*

11. What is a *gender role?*

12. How does an *ascribed role* differ from an *achievement role?*

13. What is happening to male and female gender roles?

14. What are the differences between a traditional and a modern gender role orientation?

15. Describe a segmentation system for the female market based on employment status and gender role orientation.

16. What are some of the major marketing implications of the changing role of women?

DISCUSSION QUESTIONS

17. Describe additional values you feel could, or should, be added to Figure 3–1. Describe the marketing implications of each.

18. Pick the three values you feel the authors were most inaccurate about in describing the *current* American values. Justify your answers.

19. Pick the three values you feel the authors were most inaccurate about in describing the *emerging* American values. Justify your answers.

20. Respond to the questions in Consumer Insight 3–1.

21. Which values are most relevant to the purchase or use of the following? Are they currently favorable or unfavorable for ownership/use? Are they shifting at all? If so, is the shift in a favorable or unfavorable direction?
    a. Cat
    b. Christian Children's Fund contribution
    c. Life insurance
    d. SUVs
    e. In-line skates
    f. Visa card

22. Do you believe Americans' concern for the environment is a stronger value than their materialism?

23. What are the primary ethical issues involved in green marketing?

24. Respond to the questions in Consumer Insight 3–2.

25. Cause-related marketing is done to enhance a firm's sales or image. Some consider such marketing to be unethical. What is your position?

26. Which of the four categories of responders to cause-related marketing (page 94) are you? Why?

27. Suppose AT&T showed a gay couple using its long-distance service or P&G showed a gay couple using one of its laundry products in ads on network television. Is a backlash by those who do not accept the gay community a likely response? How are such consumers likely to respond? Why?

28. Do you think housewives may be defensive or sensitive about not having employment outside of the home? If so, what implications will this have for marketing practice?

29. What is your position on targeting women as a market for the following?
    a. Handguns
    b. Alcoholic beverages
    c. Cigarettes

30. Develop an advertisement for the following for each of the four female market segments described in the chapter.
    a. Fast-food restaurant
    b. Frozen pizza
    c. Clothes detergent
    d. Breakfast cereal
    e. Visa card
    f. Cosmetics

APPLICATION ACTIVITIES

31. Find and copy or describe an advertisement for an item that reflects Americans' position on the following values.
    a. Active/Passive
    b. Material/Nonmaterial
    c. Hard work/Leisure
    d. Postponed/Immediate gratification
    e. Sensual gratification/Abstinence
    f. Religious/Secular
    g. Cleanliness
    h. Performance/Status
    i. Tradition/Change
    j. Risk taking/Security
    k. Problem solving/Fatalistic
    l. Admire/Overcome nature
    m. Individual/Collective
    n. Limited/Extended family
    o. Diversity/Uniformity
    p. Competition/Cooperation
    q. Youth/Age
    r. Masculine/Feminine

32. Interview a vegetarian and a person with a strong vegetarian orientation. What values influence their decision to adopt this eating pattern?

33. Interview a salesperson who has been selling the following for at least 10 years. See if this individual has noticed a change in the purchasing roles of women over time.
    a. Skis
    b. Furniture
    c. Hardware
    d. Wine
    e. Financial services

34. Interview a career-oriented working wife and a traditional housewife of a similar age. Report on differences in attitudes toward shopping, products, and so forth.

35. Form a team of five. Have each team member interview five married adult males. Based on these interviews, develop a typology that classifies them by their attitude toward and participation in household or child-rearing activities.

36. Find one advertisement you think is particularly appropriate for each of the female market segments (traditional housewife, trapped housewife, trapped working woman, and career working woman). Copy or describe each ad and justify its selection.

37. Interview a salesperson for each of the following. Ascertain the interest shown in the item by males and females. Determine if males and females are concerned with different characteristics of the item and if they have different purchase motivations.
    a. Wine
    b. Computers
    c. Automobiles
    d. Financial services
    e. Televisions
    f. Flowers

38. Interview 10 male and 10 female students. Ask each to describe the typical owner or consumer of the following. If they do not specify, ask for the gender of the typical owner. Then probe to find out why they think the typical owner is of the gender they indicated. Also determine the perceived marital and occupational status of the typical owner and the reasons for these beliefs.
    a. Cat
    b. Condominium
    c. Large life insurance policy
    d. Mountain bike
    e. Habitat for Humanity contributor
    f. SUV

REFERENCES

1. From Ipsos's global consumer and civic trends reporting service, *World Monitor,* 2nd quarter, 2001. Profiled data were collected on Ipsos's *Global Express* omnibus survey in 34 countries in November–December of 2000.

2. S. G. Edry, "No Longer Just Fun and Games," *American Demographics,* May 2001, p. 38.

3. See A. Jolibert and G. Baumgartner, "Values, Motivations, and Personal Goals," *Psychology & Marketing,* October 1997, pp. 675–88; and M. W. Allen and S. H. Ng, "The Direct and Indirect Influences of Human Values on Product Ownership," *Journal of Economic Psychology,* February 1999, pp. 5–39.

4. M. Grimm, "Veggie Delight," *American Demographics,* August 2000, p. 66; and S. Janda and P. J. Trocchia, "Vegetarianism," *Psychology & Marketing,* December 2001, pp. 1205–40.

5. B. A. Robinson, "How Many People Go Regularly to Weekly Religious Services?" Ontario Consultants on Religious Tolerance, www.religioustolerance.org, November 26, 2001; and *For Goodness Sakes,* New York, Public Agenda, www.publicagenda.org, 2001.

6. See P. S. La Barbera and Z. Gurhan, "The Role of Materialism, Religiosity, and Demographics in Subjective Well-Being," *Psychology & Marketing,* January 1997, pp. 71–97.

7. See "Employed Civilians and Weekly Hours," *Statistical Abstract of the United States 2001* (Washington, DC: U.S. Census Bureau, 2001), p. 372.

8. A. Miller, "The Millennial Mind-Set," *American Demographics,* January 1999, pp. 62–63.

9. C. R. Wiles, J. A. Wiles, and A. Tjernlund, "The Ideology of Advertising," *Journal of Advertising Research,* May–June 1996, pp. 57–66.

10. R. Tansey et al., "An Advertising Test of the Work Ethic in the U.K. and the U.S.," *Journal of International Consumer Marketing,* no. 3 (1997), pp. 57–77.

11. M. Slatalla, "Overscheduled?" *Time,* July 24, 2000, p. 79.

12. T. Cahill, "Exotic Places Made Me Do It," *Outside,* March 2002, p. 60.

13. See J. P. Robinson and M. Milke, "Dances with Dust Bunnies," *American Demographics,* January 1997, pp. 37–40; and Miller, "The Millennial Mind-Set."

14. "Earth in the Balance," *American Demographics,* January 2001, p. 24.

15. *Public Agenda Online,* www.publicagenda.org, February 28, 2002.

16. D. J. Lipke, "Good for Whom?" *American Demographics,* January 2001, p. 37.

17. J. Ottman, "Environmental Branding Blocks Competitors," *Marketing News,* August 17, 1998, p. 8.

18. G. H. G. McDougall, "The Green Movement in Canada," *Journal of International Consumer Marketing* 5, no. 3 (1993), pp. 69–87.

19. A. C. Cuneo, "What's in Store," *Advertising Age,* February 25, 2002, p. 1+.

20. See G. D. Gregory and J. M. Munch, "Reconceptualizing Individualism–Collectivism in Consumer Behavior," *Advances in Consumer Research,* vol. 23, ed. K. P. Corfman and J. G. Lynch (Provo, UT: Association for Consumer Research, 1996), pp. 104–10; and Miller, "The Millennial Mind-Set."

21. *For Goodness Sakes.*

22. R. Suro, "Movement at Warp Speed," *American Demographics,* August 2000, pp. 61–64.

23. Wiles, Wiles, and Tjernlurd, "The Ideology of Advertising."

24. Miller, "The Millennial Mind-Set," p. 65.

25. J. Fetto and D. J. Lipke, "Gender Bias," *American Demographics,* March 2001, p. 80.

26. J. Rosenberg, "Brand Loyalty Begins Early," *Advertising Age,* February 12, 2001, p. S2.

27. J. Ottman, "Innovative Marketers Give New Products the Green Light," *Marketing News,* March 1998, p. 10.

28. S. W. Colford, "FTC Green Guidelines May Spark Ad Efforts," *Advertising Age,* August 3, 1992, p. 11. See also D. L. Scammon and R. N. Mayer, "Agency Review of Environmental Marketing Claims," *Journal of Advertising,* Summer 1995, pp. 33–54.

29. See L. R. Stanley and K. M. Lasonde, "The Relationship between Environmental Issue Involvement and Environmentally Conscious Behavior," *Advances in Consumer Research,* vol. 23, ed. K. P. Corfman and J. G. Lynch (Provo, UT: Association for Consumer Research, 1996), pp. 183–88: T. S. Chan, "Concerns for Environmental Issues and Consumer Purchase Preferences," *Journal of International Consumer Marketing,* no. 1 (1996), pp. 43–55; J. A. Lee and S. J. S. Holden, "Understanding the Determinants of Environmentally Conscious Behavior," *Psychology & Marketing,* August 1999, pp. 373–92; and A. Biswas et al., "The Recycling Cycle," *Journal of Public Policy & Marketing,* Spring 2000, pp. 93–105.

30. T. L. Speere, "Growing the Green Market," *American Demographics,* August 1997, p. 49.

31. J. Cohen and J. Darian, "Disposable Products and the Environment," *Research in Consumer Behavior* 9 (2000), pp. 227–57.

32. H.-K. Bang et al., "Consumer Concern, Knowledge, Belief, and Attitude toward Renewable Energy," *Psychology & Marketing,* June 2000, pp. 449–68.

33. A. S. Mobley et al., "Consumer Evaluation of Recycled Products," *Psychology & Marketing,* May 1995, pp. 165–76.

34. Ibid., p. 113.

35. K. Naughton, "Ford's Green Dilemma," *Business Week,* December 21, 1998, pp. 96–97; and D. Buss, "Green Cars," *American Demographics,* January 2001, pp. 57–61.

36. See G. M. Zinkhan and L. Carlson, "Green Advertising and the Reluctant Consumer"; and W. E. Kilbourne, "Green Advertising"; both in *Journal of Advertising,* Summer 1995, pp. 1–6 and 7–19; and C. L. Hartman and E. R. Stafford, "Enviro Groups Entering Marketing Fray," *Marketing News,* July 30, 2001, p. 15.

37. For a thorough discussion see M. E. Drumwright, "Company Advertising with a Social Dimension," *Journal of Marketing,* October 1996, pp. 71–87; and P. S. Bronn and A. B. Vrioni, "Corporate Social Responsibility and Cause-Related Marketing," *International Journal of Advertising,* no. 2 (2001), pp. 207–21.

38. *The Cone/Roper Study: A Benchmark Survey of Consumer Awareness and Attitudes towards Cause-Related Marketing* (New York: Roper/Starch Worldwide, Inc., 1994), p. 1.

39. D. J. Webb and L. A. Mohr, "A Typology of Consumer Responses to Cause-Related Marketing," *Journal of Public Policy & Marketing,* Fall 1998, pp. 226–38.

40. See also M. Strahilevitz, "The Effects of Product Type and Donation Magnitude on Willingness to Pay More for a Charity-Linked Brand," *Journal of Consumer Psychology,* no. 3, 1999, pp. 215–41; M. J. Barone, A. D. Miyazaki, and K. A. Taylor, "The Influence of Cause-Related Marketing on Consumer Choice," *Journal of the Academy of Marketing Science,* Spring 2000, pp. 248–62; and S. Sen and C. B. Bhattacharya, "Does Doing Good Always Lead to Doing Better?" *Journal Marketing Research,* May 2001, pp. 225–43.

41. See M. Wilke, "Conservative Groups Ready 'Ex-Gay' TV Ads," *Advertising Age,* October 26, 1998, p. 3.

42. "Gay Rights," *Public Agenda Online,* www.publicagenda.org, February 28, 2001.

43. "How Many Lesbians and Gay Men Are There?" James C. Hormel Gay and Lesbian Center, San Francisco Public Library website 206.14.7.53/glcenter/home.htm, February 2002. See also, D. M. Smith and G. J. Gates, *Gay and Lesbian Families in the United States* (Washington, DC: Human Rights Campaign, August 22, 2001).

44. See R. Gardyn, "A Market Kept in the Closet," *American Demographics,* November 2001, pp. 37–42.

45. L. Koss-Feder, "Out and About," *Marketing News,* May 25, 1998, p. 1.

46. M. Wilke, "Fewer Gays Wealthy, Data Say," *Advertising Age,* October 19, 1998, p. 58.

47. M. Wilke, "Ads Targeting Gays Rely on Real Results," *Advertising Age,* June 22, 1998, p. 3.

48. J. Halliday, "GayRide," *Advertising Age,* February 25, 2002, p. 18.

49. Koss-Feder, "Out and About," p. 20.

50. M. Wilke, "Burgeoning Gay Web Sites Spark Advertiser Interest," *Advertising Age,* June 22, 1998; and R. X. Weissman, "Gay Market Power," *American Demographics,* June 1999, pp. 32–33.

51. For a theoretical discussion of the issues involved, see S. M. Kates, "Making the Ad Perfectly Queer," *Journal of Advertising,* Spring 1999, pp. 25–35.

52. S. M. Kates, "Out of the Closet and Out on the Street," *Psychology & Marketing,* June 2000, p. 502.

53. Gardyn, "A Market Kept in the Closet," p. 43; see also, J. J. Burnett, "Gays," *Journal of Advertising Research,* January 2000, pp. 75–83.

54. S. Bhat, T. W. Leigh, and D. L. Wardlow, "The Effect of Consumer Prejudices on Ad Processing," *Journal of Advertising,* Winter 1998, pp. 9–28; S. A. Grier and A. M. Brumbaugh, "Noticing Cultural Differences," *Journal of Advertising,* Spring 1999, pp. 79–91; and J. L. Aaker, A. M. Brumbaugh, and S. A. Grier, "Nontarget Market and Viewer Distinctiveness," *Journal of Consumer Psychology,* no. 3 (2000), pp. 127–40.

55. See T. Triplett, "Automakers Recognizing Value of Women's Market," *Marketing News,* April 11, 1994, pp. 1–2; and J. Halliday, "GM Looking to Woo Developing Clout of Females," *Advertising Age,* June 17, 1996, p. 39.

56. E. Fischer and S. J. Arnold, "Sex, Gender Identity, Gender Role Attitudes, and Consumer Behavior," *Psychology & Marketing,* March 1994, pp. 163–82; L. J. Jaffe, "The Unique Predictive

Ability of Sex-Role Identity in Explaining Women's Response to Advertising," *Psychology & Marketing,* September, 1994, pp. 467–82; and S. J. Gould, "Gender Identity and Gender Salience," *Advances in Consumer Research,* vol. 23, ed. K. P. Corfman and J. G. Lynch (Provo, UT: Association for Consumer Research, 1996), pp. 478–83.

57. See P. Ireland, *What Women Want* (New York: E. P. Dutton, 1996); D. J. Swiss, *Women Breaking Through* (Peterson's/ Pacesetter Books, 1996); and P. McCorduck and N. Ramsey, *The Futures of Women* (Reading, MA: Addison-Wesley Publishing, 1996).

58. J. S. Grigsby, "Women Change Places," *American Demographics,* November 1992, p. 48; and A. W. Fawcett, "The Consumer Mindset in the 90s," *Advertising Age,* April 18, 1994, pp. 13–14.

59. "The Family," *Public Agenda Online,* www.publicagenda.org, February 28, 2002.

60. Ibid.

61. C. J. Thompson, "Caring Consumers," *Journal of Consumer Research,* March 1996, p. 397.

62. Ibid., p. 388.

63. These segments are similar to the four categories popularized by Bartos. See C. M. Schaninger, M. C. Nelson, and W. D. Danko, "An Empirical Evaluation of the Bartos Model," *Journal of Advertising Research,* May 1993, pp. 49–63; and R. Bartos, "Bartos Responds to 'The Bartos Model,'" *Journal of Advertising Research,* January 1994, pp. 54–56.

64. R. E. Wilkes, K. M. Palan, and J. J. Burnett, "Is a Modern Feminine Orientation Synonymous with Working Status?" *Enhancing Knowledge Development in Marketing,* ed. C. Droge and R. Calantone (Chicago: American Marketing Association, 1996), pp. 244–51.

65. See G. Myers, "Selling a Man's World to Women," *American Demographics,* April 1996, pp. 36–42.

66. See J. Larson, "The New Homemakers," *American Demographics,* September 1997, pp. 45–50.

67. Thompson, "Caring Consumers," pp. 395–96.

68. See G. M. Rose, L. R. Kahle, and A. Shoham, "The Influence of Employment-Status and Personal Values on Time-Related Food Consumption Behavior and Opinion Leadership"; and J. J. Madill-Marshall, L. Heslop, and L. Duxbury, "Coping with Household Stress in the 1990s"; both in *Advances in Consumer Research,* vol. 22, ed. F. R. Kardes and M. Sujan (Provo, UT: Association for Consumer Research, 1995), pp. 367–72 and 729–34; and J. K. Maher, L. J. Marks, and P. E. Grimm, "Overload, Pressure, and Convenience," in *Advances in Consumer Research,* vol. 24, ed. M. Bruck and D. J. MacInnis (Provo, UT: Association for Consumer Research, 1997), pp. 490–98.

69. M. E. Blair and E. M. Hyatt, "The Marketing of Guns to Women," *Journal of Public Policy & Marketing,* Spring 1995, pp. 117–27. See also E. Blair and E. M. Hyatt, "Using Promises of Protection and Empowerment to Market Guns to Women," *Advances in Consumer Research,* vol. 25, ed. M. Bruck and D. J. MacInnis (Provo, UT: Association for Consumer Research, 1997), pp. 355–59.

70. F. F. Brunel and M. R. Nelson, "Explaining Gender Responses to 'Help-Self' and 'Help-Others' Charity Ad Appeals," *Journal of Advertising,* Fall 2000, pp. 15–28.

71. See L. J. Jaffe, "The Unique Predictive Ability of Sex-Role Identity in Explaining Women's Response to Advertising," *Psychology & Marketing,* September 1994, pp. 467–82; J. B. Ford and M. S. LaTour, "Contemporary Female Perspectives of Female Role Portrayals in Advertising," *Journal of Current Issues and Research in Advertising,* Spring 1996, pp. 81–95; and R. Widgery, M. G. Angur, and R. Nataraajan, "The Impact of Employment Status on Married Women's Perceptions of Advertising Message Appeals," *Journal of Advertising Research,* January 1997, pp. 54–62.

72. L. J. Jaffe and P. D. Berger, "The Effect of Modern Female Sex Role Portrayals on Advertising Effectiveness," *Journal of Advertising Research,* July 1994, pp. 32–42.

73. M. S. LaTour, T. L. Henthorne, and A. J. Williams, "Is Industrial Advertising Still Sexist," *Industrial Marketing Management,* 1998, pp. 247–55; and M. Y. Jones, A. J. S. Stanaland, and B. D. Gelb, "Beefcake and Cheesecake," *Journal of Advertising,* Summer 1998, pp. 33–51.

74. L. N. Reid, K. W. King, and H. L. Wyant, "Gender Portrayals in Cigarette and Alcohol Ads," in *Enhancing Knowledge Development in Marketing,* ed. R. Achrol and A. Mitchell (Chicago: American Marketing Association, 1994), pp. 48–56.

75. For a description and theory of male shopping behavior, see C. Otnes and M. A. McGrath, "Perceptions and Realities of Male Shopping Behavior," *Journal of Retailing,* Spring 2001, pp. 111–37.

Universal Pictures/Shooting Star.

The Changing American Society: Demographics and Social Stratification

☐ How did a movie tentatively entitled *Cheer Fever* and forecast to be a financial disaster become the remarkably successful ($17.4 million in the first week) teenage movie *Bring It On?* Initial tests showed that 62 percent of its target (teens) said they would "definitely not" see a movie about cheerleading. Universal wanted to repeat the success of *American Pie* with the movie, but it lacked its raunchy sexual jokes and edgy content. As Universal's head of marketing stated: "With that title, we are saying 'We are the cheerleading movie, and we know that 62 percent of you reject us, so now go find something else to do that weekend.'"

Universal decided to play up the overall high school experience in the movie and changed its name to *Made You Look*. The movie's one-sheet marketing poster showed the cheerleaders in a traditional cheerleading position but wearing their street clothes. "We chose to shoot them as human beings." This positioning was also a failure.

In reviewing the movie for marketing options, an executive noticed a somewhat buried subplot about a rivalry between the white cheerleading squad from the suburbs and a black squad from the inner city. A decision was made to rename the film *Bring It On* and to position it as a contest between these two squads even though it would mean substantial reshooting. This focus on the competition and the infusion of the black squad and its hip-hop culture produced huge enthusiasm among white, black, and Hispanic girls.

Next an intense marketing campaign began. The studio promoted Kirsten Dunst, the star, on the cover of *Maxim*. Over $10 million was spent on media advertising during such teen TV favorites as "Buffy the Vampire Slayer" and MTV as well as an aggressive radio campaign. Extensive grassroots marketing was done at Britney Spears and Christina Aguilera concerts.

Internet efforts were focused on Alloy.com. Alloy created a microsite for the movie, ran a sweepstakes, and sent e-zines telling teens where and when the movie's stars would appear. Ethnic sites such as 360hiphop.com, BlackVoices.com, and Hookt.com were also used. Universal also partnered with malls around the country to arrange cheerleading contests and fashion shows.

Seven days before the opening, male teens still showed no great interest in seeing the film. The studio quickly prepared a racy spot aimed at young men and aired it on a preseason "Monday Night Football" game and on ESPN2. This succeeded in generating considerable interest among teenage males.[1]

Turning the apparent disaster *Cheer Fever* into the successful *Bring It On* required substantial knowledge not only of teens' movie preferences but of how and where to communicate with them. The approach used with this age group would not succeed with older groups, since different generations have different values and ways of living. This is one aspect of demographics.

In this chapter, we will discuss the closely related concepts of demographics and social status. As we will see, several demographic variables—income, education, and occupation— serve as dimensions of social status, and they combine with others to determine social class. We will first take a broad look at the demographics of the American society, with particular attention to age and its related concept, generations. Then we will consider social status and the role that demographics play in social status.

DEMOGRAPHICS

Frito-Lay recently developed a Light product line, including Cheetos Light, Doritos Light, and Ruffles Light. Marketing research identified the primary target market for Frito-Lay's Light product line as age 35 to 54, college-educated, white-collar workers with annual incomes above $35,000. While Frito-Lay used its knowledge of the values, attitudes, and media habits of this demographically defined group to structure its communication campaign, its most creative use of demographics was in distribution.

Frito-Lay used Market Metrics, a firm with a database of 30,000 supermarkets. Market Metrics defines trading areas around each supermarket, considering distance and the presence of travel barriers such as freeways or rivers. It then uses Census Bureau data to profile the demographics of the shoppers in each store's trade area. Market Metrics took Frito-Lay's target demographics and ranked the 30,000 supermarkets in terms of how well their trading areas matched the target market. This approach allowed Frito-Lay to focus maximum sales, point-of-purchase, and promotional efforts on those specific stores with the greatest market potential based on demographics. It plans to increase its use of this approach in the future: "If we wanted to target Hispanics or Italians or married couples with children under the age of five, we could do it with this program."[2]

Frito-Lay combined a variety of demographic variables to define a primary target market. It then developed a marketing strategy to reach this segment. The benefits of such a thorough approach are obvious, and many firms use demographic data in this manner.

As defined in Chapter 2, **demographics** *describe a population in terms of its size, distribution, and structure.* Demographics influence consumption behaviors both directly and by affecting other attributes of individuals, such as their personal values and decision styles.[3]

Marketers frequently segment markets on the basis of demographics. Consider this description of the prime target market for Saturn's VUE SUV:

median age between 40 and 45; evenly split between men and women; 65 percent to 70 percent of whom are married; 60 percent to 65 percent college graduates; with a median annual household income of $75,000.[4]

Saturn will be able to select magazines and television programs whose audiences have similar demographics as well as send direct mail to households that match those domographics. The company can also design the theme and content of its communications in light of the interests and desires of these individuals.

Population Size and Distribution

The population of the United States is approximately 290 million today and is expected to surpass 310 million by 2015. The population has grown steadily since 1960 despite a declining birthrate due to longer life expectancies, the large baby boom generation moving through their child-bearing years, and significant immigration. This growth has not been even throughout the United States. For example, from 2000 to 2010, Arizona, Florida, Georgia, and Hawaii are predicted to grow by about 15 percent. In contrast, Illinois, Indiana, Michigan, Iowa, Ohio, and Pennsylvania are predicted to decrease slightly.[5] As we will discuss in detail in the next chapter, regions of the country serve as subcultures whose members (residents) have tastes, attitudes, and preferences that are unique to that region. Several examples of these differences are shown in Figure 4–1. Unique regional lifestyles create tremendous marketing opportunities for those who understand the needs of people in rapidly growing regions.[6]

Occupation

Occupation is probably the most widely applied single cue we use to initially evaluate and define individuals we meet. This should be obvious when you stop to think of the most common bit of information we seek from a new acquaintance: "What do you do?" Almost invariably we want to know someone's occupation to make inferences about his or her probable lifestyle. Occupation is strongly associated with education (which to

FIGURE 4-1   A Tale of Three Cities

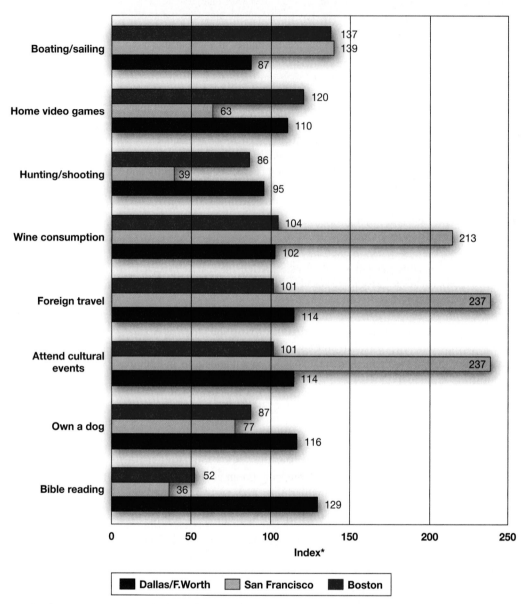

*An Index of 100 represents the average for the entire United States.

Adapted from the 2001 edition of *The Lifestyle Analyst,* published by SRDS with data supplied by Polk.

some extent determines occupation) and income (which to some extent is determined by occupation).

One's occupation provides status and income. In addition, the type of work one does and the types of individuals one works with over time also directly influence one's values, lifestyle, and all aspects of the consumption process. Differences in consumption between occupational classes have been found for products such as beer, detergents, dog food,

	Administrative/ Managerial	Technical/ Clerical/Sales	Precision/Craft
Products			
Domestic beer	104	79	183
Cigarettes	82	102	125
Diet colas	118	102	85
Laptop/notebook	223	128	72
Activities			
Sailing	192	90	97
Archery	101	90	221
Listening to music	112	110	93
Movies (frequent)	104	121	89
Shopping			
Wal-Mart	96	101	106
Ann Taylor	197	129	32
Olive Garden	133	128	80
Bonanza	82	81	164
Media			
Sports Afield	99	54	196
Outside	215	68	77
Jazz radio	191	85	65
Religious radio	91	110	80

TABLE 4–1

Occupational Influences on Consumption*

*100 = Average level of use, purchase, or consumption.

Source: *Mediamark Reporter 2002—University* (New York: Mediamark Research Inc., March 2002).

shampoo, and paper towels. Media preferences, hobbies, and shopping patterns are also influenced by occupational class (see Table 4–1).

Education

Approximately 85 percent of Americans have a high school degree, and 25 percent have completed college. Education is increasingly critical for a "family wage" job. Traditional high-paying manufacturing jobs that required relatively little education are rapidly disappearing. High-paying jobs in the manufacturing and service sectors today require technical skills, abstract reasoning, and the ability to read and learn new skills rapidly. Individuals without these skills are generally forced into minimum wage and often part-time jobs, which will rarely keep a family above the poverty level.[7] As the following data show, education clearly drives income in today's economy.

Median Income: Full-Time Workers, 25 and Older[8]

Education Level	Males	Females
9th to 12th grade	$25,094	$17,918
High school degree	34,302	24,967
Some college	40,339	28,695
Bachelor's degree	56,334	40,413
Master's degree	68,309	50,139
Professional degree	99,435	58,978

	Graduated College	Attended College	Graduated High School	Did Not Graduate High School
Product				
Champagne	148	107	82	63
Laptop/notebook	206	116	56	24
Soy sauce	124	110	91	73
Shortening (frequent)	49	81	115	164
Activities				
Mountain biking	165	135	65	30
Lottery (frequent)	84	100	115	93
Wrestling (attended)	67	108	107	117
Recycling products	137	110	89	60
Shopping				
Ames	84	82	125	102
Eddie Bauer	180	109	69	44
Ponderosa	70	104	126	83
TGI Friday's	143	114	83	55
Media				
National Enquirer	44	105	126	118
Men's Journal	154	136	74	23
Nick at Nite	77	115	110	88
CNN	133	106	90	66

*100 = Average level of use, purchase, or consumption.

Source: *Mediamark Reporter 2002—University* (New York: Mediamark Research Inc., March 2002).

Since individuals tend to have spouses with similar education levels, these differences are magnified when spousal income is considered.[9]

Education influences what one can purchase by partially determining one's income and occupation. It also influences how one thinks, makes decisions, and relates to others.[10] Those with a limited education are generally at a disadvantage not only in earning money but in spending it wisely.[11] Not surprisingly, education has a strong influence on one's tastes and preferences, as shown in Table 4–2. However, education seldom provides a complete explanation for consumption patterns. For example, a lawyer earning $30,000 per year as a public defender will have a different lifestyle from a lawyer earning $250,000 per year in private practice, despite similar educational backgrounds.

Income

A household's income level combined with its accumulated wealth determines its purchasing power. While many purchases are made on credit, one's ability to buy on credit is ultimately determined by one's current and past income (wealth).

Most of American history has been characterized by consistently increasing real per capita income. For most middle- and lower-income Americans, this increasing trend stopped in the 1980s and household incomes were stagnant or declining until they increased again in 1995.[12] For example, from 1984 to 1994, incomes of the top 5 percent of Americans grew by 37 percent while those on the bottom experienced only a 1 percent increase. Younger households and those without specialized skills suffered the most during this period.

The economic boom from 1995 through 2000 enhanced the purchasing power of most Americans. At the lower (but not lowest) and middle-income levels, this increased purchasing power was reflected in rapidly growing sales for premium products and "small luxuries" such as Gillette's Mach3 razor (35 percent more expensive than its SensorExcel) and Huggies Supreme diapers.[13]

The economic downturn at the beginning of this century reduced the wealth of many Americans, reduced the earnings of others, and, along with the attack on the World Trade Center, created economic uncertainty for most. As a result, consumers have been more cautious in their spending, and sales of many products and services are down sharply from their late 1990s highs. For example, the average number of restaurant meals consumed per person annually dropped from an all-time high of 141 in 2000 to 137 in 2001. While this seems like a small drop, it represents hundreds of millions of dollars in lost revenue for the restaurant industry.[14]

Income *enables* purchases but *does not generally cause or explain them*. For example, individuals making over $60,000 a year are almost five times more likely to read *New Yorker* magazine than individuals making less than $10,000 per year. However, relatively few low-income individuals who won a lottery paying over $60,000 per year would suddenly subscribe to the *New Yorker*. Likewise, a college professor or lawyer may have the same income as a truck driver or plumber. Nonetheless, it is likely that their consumption processes for a variety of products will differ. Occupation and education directly influence preferences for products, media, and activities; income provides the means to acquire them.[15] Thus, income is generally more effective as a segmentation variable when used in conjunction with other demographic variables.

An example of using income with other demographic variables is provided by Vons, a West Coast grocery chain. Vons analyzed the demographics and purchase patterns of consumers in the shopping area of each of its outlets. It found that the income and age distribution, along with ethnicity, of each area had a major influence on the types and amounts of items purchased at each store. As a result, it moved from a single store format to five distinct store types based on the shopping area demographics, particularly income and ethnicity.[16]

How wealthy one feels may be as important as actual income for some purchases. **Subjective discretionary income (SDI)** is *an estimate by the consumer of how much money he or she has available to spend on nonessentials*. It is measured by using the responses on a 1-to-6, agree-to-disagree scale to the following statements:

1. No matter how fast our income goes up, we never seem to get ahead.
2. We have more to spend on extras than most of our neighbors do.
3. Our family income is high enough to satisfy nearly all our important desires.

In one large-scale study, SDI was found to add considerable predictive power to total family income (TFI) measures and, for some product categories, to predict purchases when family income did not. Some of the findings include the following:

- Investments such as mutual funds, IRAs, stocks, and luxury cars require relatively high levels of both TFI and SDI.
- Loans and second mortgages are associated with relatively high TFI (necessary to qualify) but low levels of SDI (a felt need for extra cash).
- Fast-food restaurant patronage is predicted by relatively high TFI but relatively low SDI.
- Consumption of low-cost foods such as bologna and packaged spaghetti is not predicted by TFI but is associated with a low SDI.[17]

A study in Australia reached similar conclusions on the value of SDI and TFI for predicting use of various financial services.[18]

TABLE 4–3		18–24	25–34	35–44	45–54	55–64	65+
Products							
	Tequila	168	130	114	83	66	33
	Scotch	71	84	95	126	122	106
	Laptop/notebook	107	95	133	142	82	23
	Laserdisc players	127	124	115	95	98	35
Activities							
	Barbecuing	67	106	134	130	103	37
	Aerobics	140	125	115	104	64	38
	Cruise ship	61	78	88	128	139	117
	Volunteer work	80	83	116	122	100	90
Shopping							
	J.C. Penney	84	88	104	113	109	102
	Banana Republic	190	157	102	75	41	26
	Hooters	176	159	102	92	44	12
	Marie Callender's	64	80	91	129	153	96
Media							
	Reader's Digest	65	72	93	116	124	137
	Maxim	337	200	52	31	6	1
	Comedy Central	194	140	108	83	46	23
	CNN	55	80	99	119	126	121

Age Influences on Consumption*

*100 = Average level of use, purchase, or consumption.

Source: *Mediamark Reporter 2002—University* (New York: Mediamark Research Inc., March 2002).

Age

In describing the response of consumers to the initial Tiger Woods line of golf products, the manager of a major sporting store stated,

> To tell you the truth, we did not have people busting down our doors for it. The product is not grunge enough for the kids, and it's too flashy for older people. Nike is trying to market something that there is not a market for.

Proper age positioning is critical for many products. Age carries with it culturally defined behavioral and attitudinal norms.[19] It affects our self-concept and lifestyles.[20] Not surprisingly, age influences the consumption of products ranging from beer to toilet paper to vacations. Our age shapes the media we use, where we shop, how we use products, and how we think and feel about marketing activities.[21] Table 4–3 illustrates some consumption behaviors that vary with age. Illustration 4–1 shows an ad with the type of humor appreciated by many young adults.

The estimated age distributions (millions in each age category) of the U.S. population for 2005 and 2015 are[22]

Age Category	2005	2015	Percent Change
< 10	38.3	41.5	8.3
10–19	41.6	41.1	−1.2
20–29	38.5	42.5	10.4
30–39	38.6	39.9	3.3
40–49	44.9	39.4	−12.2
50–59	36.5	43.3	18.7
60–69	22.9	33.9	47.9
> 69	26.3	30.5	16.2

Courtesy Bushnell Performance Optics.

Even a quick look at these age distributions indicates that momentous changes are occurring. Some of the profound marketing implications of these changes are

- Demand for children's products such as toys, diapers, and clothes will grow moderately, as the population less than 10 years of age will grow 8 percent over this period.
- Products consumed by twentysomethings will increase moderately in demand. Since this is the prime age of household formation and childbirth, this group will have an important impact on the overall market. Demand for higher education, homes, family cars, insurance, and so forth should be strong.
- Products consumed by those aged 40 to 49 will decline as this population group grows smaller. This will have significant implications for such industries as financial services for which this is a key age group.
- The largest impact will be caused by the huge increase (11 million) in the number of individuals between 60 and 69. These will represent primarily one- or two-person households, with many retired or near retirement. Vacations, restaurants, second homes, and financial services aimed at the mature market should flourish.
- The large growth in the number of individuals over 69 will also create many opportunities for marketers ranging from beauty aids and travel and leisure to retirement homes and health care.

Age groups as defined by the census and as presented above can be useful as a means of understanding and segmenting a market. For example, P&G recently launched the Oil of Olay ProVital line targeting women over 50 years old, the fastest-growing segment of the population. The spokeswoman for the product was 51-year-old actress Anne Roberts.

One's age is a chronological fact but, more important, a social construct.[23] That is, the time that has passed since one's birth is directly observable and uniform. However, the meaning of age, how it is perceived, the behaviors and attitudes expected at differing ages, how one feels about aging, and so forth are constructed by cultures and within cultures by individuals.

> I'm not my mother's 52. I'm not in the second half of my life. I'm in the first chapter of a whole new book.

This quote reflects the increasingly recognized fact that, in the United States at least, as consumers' chronological age increases, their subjective or cognitive age lags behind. In fact, for older consumers, cognitive age is often 10 to 15 years less than chronological age. And, at least for some behaviors, it appears that you are indeed as young as you feel.

Cognitive age is defined as *one's perceived age, a part of one's self-concept.* It is most commonly measured by the following scale.

1. I *feel* like I'm in my _____.
2. I *look* like I'm in my _____.
3. My *interests* are those of a person in his/her _____.
4. I *do* the things a person does in his/her _____.

Respondents are asked to indicate a decade for each question (20s, 30s, 40s, etc.). The midpoint of the decade given in response to each question is used to compute an average age based on the four responses. This is one's cognitive age. Though both the adequacy of this operationalization and the validity of the concept itself have been challenged, it is gaining widespread use in marketing.

While cognitive age varies with chronological age, it is also influenced by such factors as one's health, education, income, and social support—the more of each, the lower the cognitive age. In turn, it affects a wide range of attitudes and consumption behaviors.

Cognitive age, while an artificial concept, is one with which people readily identify. Consumers have no trouble indicating how old they feel rather than how old they "are."

Critical Thinking Questions

1. Cognitive age is measured on four dimensions. What additional dimensions, if any, do you think should be added?
2. Do you think cognitive age is a valid concept? Why?
3. If the meaning of age is a cultural concept, how would the concept and measurement of cognitive age change across cultures?
4. How can marketers use cognitive age?

However, the product line will not be positioned as just an antiwrinkle solution:

> Age is just a number. Many women 50 and over have told us that as they age, they feel more confident, wiser, and freer than ever before. These women are redefining beauty. Our research shows that when it comes to skin, dryness and vitality are their key concerns, not just a few wrinkles.[24]

While age groups as defined by the census are often a useful way to understand and segment a market, analyzing age cohort groups or generations will often provide more meaningful segments and marketing strategies. This approach is covered in depth in the next section. In addition, as Consumer Insight 4–1 describes, age as determined by the calendar may not be the best concept of age.

UNDERSTANDING AMERICAN GENERATIONS

A **generation** or **age cohort** is *a group of persons who have experienced a common social, political, historical, and economic environment.* Age cohorts, because their shared histories produce unique shared values and behaviors, often function as unique market segments.[25]

Cohort analysis is *the process of describing and explaining the attitudes, values, and behaviors of an age group as well as predicting its future attitudes, values, and behaviors.*[26] A critical fact uncovered by cohort analysis is that each generation behaves differently from other generations as it passes through various age categories. For example, in 2010 the baby boom generation will be entering retirement. However, it would be a mistake to assume that retiring baby boomers will behave like the pre-Depression generation does today. The forces that shaped the lives of these generations were different, and their behaviors will differ throughout their life cycles. Stated another way, you won't become your parents.[27]

In the following sections, we will examine the six generations that compose the primary American market.[28] It is important to emphasize that generation is only one factor influencing behavior and the differences within generations are often larger than the differences across generations. In addition, generations do not have sharp boundaries. Those near the age breaks between generations often do not clearly belong to either generation.

The Pre-Depression Generation

The pre-Depression generation, also termed the *mature market* or *seniors,* is composed of those individuals born before 1930. More than 25 million Americans are in this generation. These individuals grew up in traumatic times. Most were children during the Depression and entered young adulthood during World War II. They have witnessed radical social, economic, and technological change. As a group, they are conservative and concerned with financial and personal security.

As with all generations, the pre-Depression generation is composed of many distinct segments, and marketing to it requires a segmented strategy.[29] In addition to variations in consumption related to differences in such variables as social class, geographic region, gender, and ethnicity, physical and mental health are major causes of consumption differences. As you would expect, health and age are closely related, with health declining over time. **Gerontographics** is *a segmentation approach to the mature market that is based on the physical health and mental outlook of older consumers* (see Consumer Insight 4–2).

This generation faces numerous consumption-related decisions. One is the disposition of valued belongings that they no longer use or that are not appropriate in nursing or retirement homes. These can be emotional decisions for both the elderly person and their family members.

The pin means a great deal to me. I would love for my granddaughter to have it. It will be strange not seeing it in my jewelry box anymore.[30]

Communications strategies need to consider media selection, message content, and message structure. For example, some aspects of information processing, memory, and cognitive performance decline with age.[31] The rapid, brief presentation of information that younger consumers respond to is generally not appropriate for older consumers.[32] Illustration 4–2 contains an ad from *Modern Maturity* magazine that uses a mature spokesperson. The copy stresses health benefits, but for an active lifestyle rather than just for staying well. The stated message, as well as the message implied by using Big John in the ad, positions this product for the "Healthy Indulger" segment described in Consumer Insight 4–2.

Products related to the unique needs of mature consumer segments range from vacations to health services to single-serving sizes of prepared foods. As this generation continues to age, assisted-living services are growing rapidly. As more members of this generation experience reduced mobility, shopping will become an increasing problem. Although Internet

Gerontographics

Gerontographics is based on the theory that people change their outlook on life when they experience major life events such as becoming a grandparent, retiring, losing a spouse, or developing chronic health conditions. Individuals who have confronted similar events are likely to have a similar outlook on life and, given similar economic resources, similar lifestyles. This approach has identified four segments in the elderly market.

Healthy Indulgers This group is physically and mentally healthy. Both spouses are generally still alive. They have prepared for retirement both financially and psychologically. They are basically content and set to enjoy life. They often sell their fairly large homes and move into apartments, townhouses, or condos. They like activities, convenience, personal service, and high-tech home appliances. They are a strong part of the market for cruises and group travel.

Ailing Outgoers These people have experienced health problems, which limits their physical abilities and frequently their financial capability. However, they maintain positive self-esteem. They accept their "old-age" status, acknowledge their limitations, and still seek to get the most out of life. They like the feeling of independence as well as the socializing that eating out provides, but they frequently have limited funds as well as dietary restrictions. International Kings Table, a restaurant chain, has responded to this by offering a moderately priced, cafeteria style meal. It also provides senior discounts, coupons, and other promotions.

Ailing outgoers are a key market for retirement communities and assisted-living housing. They need clothing that enables them to dress without assistance even with limited mobility or arthritis. However, they also want their clothes to be stylish. In response, JC Penney's

Easy Dressing catalog features fashionable clothing for older women. The clothes have Velcro fasteners rather than buttons, roomier armholes for easier access, and other features that make it easier to dress.

Healthy Hermits Members of this group retain their physical health, but life events, often the death of a spouse, have reduced their self-concept and self-worth. They have reacted by becoming psychologically and socially withdrawn. Many then resent the isolation and the feeling that they are expected to act like old people. This group does not want to stand out. They prefer clothing styles that are popular with other seniors. They will pay a premium for well-known brands. They tend to stay in the homes in which they raised their families, and they are an important part of the do-it-yourself market.

Frail Recluses Frail recluses have accepted their old-age status and have adjusted their lifestyles to reflect reduced physical capabilities and social roles. They focus on becoming spiritually stronger. Frail recluses may have been in any one of the other categories at an earlier age. They tend to stay at home, and many require home and lawn care services. They are a major market for health care products, home exercise and health testing equipment, and emergency response systems. They like high levels of personal service, particularly in the area of financial services.[33]

Critical Thinking Questions

1. The percentage of the American population that is elderly is going to increase dramatically over the next 20 years. How is this going to change the nature of American society?

2. What ethical and social responsibilities do marketers have when marketing to the elderly?

shopping would seem a good solution, relatively few members of this generation use the Internet.

Depression Generation

This is the cohort born between 1930 and 1945. These people were small children during the Depression or World War II. They matured during the prosperous years of the 1950s and early 60s. They discovered both Sinatra and Presley. They "invented" rock and roll and grew up with music and television as important parts of their lives.

Courtesy of Campbell Soup Company.

There are about 35 million individuals in this group. Most have or will soon retire. Many have accumulated substantial wealth in the form of home equity and savings. Those who still work dominate the top positions in both business and government. Here are some of the ways they describe their lives and dreams:[34]

* We have some of those Depression-type abilities our parents had—thrift, saving money for the rainy day, don't put all your eggs in one basket . . . [but] we also have that free-wheeling spirit of the younger generation.
* It's hard to find clothing that's geared to us. Somebody could make a fortune by making more clothes for our age group—something so we don't look like teenagers, but are still with it.
* I can't wait for the weekends. It's just nice to get away from your job and go to the beach. We fly kites, ride bikes—very relaxing, definitely.
* When the kids leave home and the dog dies, then you have the time and money to do something.

While still in excellent health, they are beginning to notice the physical effects of aging. Comfort as well as style is important. Levi's Action Slacks have been a major success with this generation. These slacks, which have an elastic waistband, are cut for the less lean, more mature body. This generation has given rise to many of the products low in fat, sugar, salt, or cholesterol on the market today.

Asset management is important to this group, and firms such as Merrill Lynch have developed products and services to meet these needs.[35] This generation is a major consumer of recreational vehicles, second homes, new cars, travel services, and recreational adult education.

Members of this generation are also grandparents with sufficient incomes to indulge their grandchildren, making them a major market for upscale children's furniture, toys, strollers, car seats, and clothing.

Baby Boom Generation

The baby boom generation refers to those individuals born during the dramatic increase of births between the end of World War II and 1964. There are almost 80 million baby boomers, which is substantially more than the two preceding generations combined. Most of this group grew up during the prosperous 1950s and 1960s. They were heavily influenced by the Kennedy assassination, the Vietnam War, recreational drugs, the sexual revolution, the energy crisis, the rapid growth of divorce, and the Cold War, as well as rock and roll and the Beatles. Although there are significant differences between the boomers born early in this generation and those born later, boomers are considered to be more self-centered, individualistic, economically optimistic, skeptical, suspicious of authority, and focused on the present than other generations.[36]

One reason for the focus on youth in advertising and product development has been the size of this segment and the fact that, until recently, it was young. It *is* the mass market, and as it ages, marketers will have to deal with a much more mature market.[37]

Baby boomers are characterized by high education levels, high incomes, and dual-career households. Most baby boomers are parents, and the early boomers are beginning to become grandparents. They are also characterized by time poverty as they try to manage two careers and family responsibilities. Many have recently faced economic hardships and uncertainties as companies reduced the size of their workforces, including middle management.

In 2005, the age range of this generation will be 41 to 59. This is an age range characterized by children leaving home, marrying, and producing grandchildren. The "empty nest" is rapidly becoming the norm for this generation, a circumstance that is providing them with both increased discretionary income and time. As a result, sales of adventure vacations, expensive restaurant meals, maintenance free homes, and Harley-Davidson motorcycles have grown rapidly.[38]

Retirement is no longer something in the distant future, and many have already made that step. However, surveys indicate that boomers plan to continue and expand the concept of "active retirement" begun by the Depression generation. That is, they intent not only to travel but to learn new skills, work actively both for pay and in charities, and otherwise continue to grow. Two-thirds of a recent survey of 50- to 75-year-olds selected as a definition of retirement: To begin a new, active, and involved chapter in life, starting new activities and setting new goals.[39] Or as one boomer who recently took early retirement stated: "I'm not retiring; I'm re-engineering my life."

Boomers are also facing the aging and often failing health of their parents. Becoming the caregiver rather than the care-receiver is a major challenge for this group. One result of this is the rapid growth of assisted-living centers. This type of living arrangement is a major innovation, and it arose because many baby boomers did not want their parents living with them and the healthy and active pre-Depression and Depression generations did want to be dependent on or impose on their children.[40]

As boomers age, their physical needs are changing. Weight gain has become an increasing concern, and demand for plastic surgery, baldness treatments, health clubs, cosmetics for both men and women, hair coloring, health foods, and related products is exploding.

When lotions failed to smooth the crow's feet around Cheryl Hoover's eyes and restore the firmness to her skin, the 41-year-old turned to Botox, collagen, and laser treatments. "I try to be proactive in heading off things. You want, as you get older, to appear youthful or at least look your age and not older. Our generation is looking for the fountain of youth, where it would have been more acceptable to age in previous generations."[41]

Illustration 4–3 shows an ad focused on the needs of this group. Other examples of firms focusing on the maturing needs of this generation include

- Den-Mat Corp. launched Rembrandt Age Defying mouthwash and toothpaste. The theme is "Do your teeth make you look 10 years older?" They are advertised as "revolutionary antiaging products that help restore teeth and gums to a healthier, whiter and younger look." Jaclyn Smith is the spokesperson for the line.
- Kellogg Co. dropped its Special K ads featuring young, slim, attractive women putting on tight fitting jeans or short skirts. Research revealed that boomers were alienated by these ads: "They told us they couldn't relate to advertising techniques that used unrealistic body images." One of Kellogg's new ads has men talking in a bar. "I have my mother's thighs. I have to accept that," says one. "Do these make my butt look big?" asks another. The ad uses humor to say, "Men don't obsess about these things. Why should women?"[42]
- Nestlé Drumstick has grown sales rapidly by introducing new flavors (Strawberry Swirl, Cappuccino coffee, and Coffee with Chocolate Layers) targeted at baby boomers. They are advertised in a TV commercial showing an adult couple consuming them in a horse-drawn carriage with Frank Sinatra's "The Best Is Yet to Come" playing.

Generation X

Generation X, often referred to as the baby bust generation, was born between 1965 and 1976. It is a smaller generation than its predecessor (about 45 million). This generation reached adulthood during difficult economic times. It is the first generation to be raised mainly in dual-career households, and 40 percent spent at least some time in a single-parent household before the age of 16. The divorce of their parents is often a cause of stress and other problems for the children involved.[43] However, these changes have also caused many members of Generation X to have a very broad view of a family, which may include parents, siblings, stepparents, half-siblings, close friends, live-in lovers, and others.

This is the first American generation to seriously confront the issue of "reduced expectations." These reduced expectations are based on reality for many "busters" as wages and job opportunities for young workers were limited until the economic boom that started in the mid-90s.[44] Not only has the path to success been less certain for this generation, but many Generation Xers do not believe in sacrificing time, energy, and relations to the extent the boomers did for the sake of career or economic advancement.

This generation faces a world racked by regional conflicts, terrorism, an environment that continues to deteriorate, and an AIDS epidemic that threatens their lives. Members of this group tend to blame the "me generation" and the materialism associated with the baby boom generation for the difficult future they see for themselves.

A higher percentage of Generation X attended college than any other generation, but a higher percentage also failed to obtain a degree. This generation is a more visual generation than previous generations. Although its members read less, they visit art museums and galleries more often than the general population. They watch about the same amount of television as the baby boomers (about three hours per day), and they watch the same popular shows as the mass audience. They are more avid users of the Internet than are the older generations. Likewise, they are generally very comfortable with computers and related technologies.

A noticeable change in this generation has been the decline in physical activity. Participation in virtually every form of sports or exercise from skiing to hiking to weight lifting is down from the previous generation. Surprisingly, the decline seems to be the greatest among females.

A final characteristic of this generation is the fact that they tend to leave home later and the males tend to return to live with their parents more than was common in most previous generations. A tendency to marry later as well as the difficulty of obtaining a job that would support independent living are the major reasons.

In 2005, this generation will be 29 to 40 years old. Since they tended to delay marriage, many of these consumers will be forming households and beginning families. This is one of the reasons the housing market has been strong throughout the recent economic decline. This generation will be a major force in the market for cars, appliances, and children's products. However, it is not an easy generation to reach. It is both cynical and sophisticated about products, ads, and shopping. It is materialistic and impatient. In many aspects, its tastes are "not baby boom." Thus, it created the grunge look and snowboarding. New magazines such as *Spin, Details,* and *YSP* were created for this generation as was the X Games. It responds to irreverence in advertising but not to many traditional approaches.

The ad for Jeep shown in Illustration 4–4 would appeal to this generation. They would appreciate its humor and its distinctiveness from most ads for this product category many of which focus on conquering mountains and rivers.

Busters want products and messages designed uniquely for their tastes and lifestyles. Marketers are increasingly targeting this group:

- Budweiser's talking frogs commercial represents the humorous, irrelevant advertising that this group likes. It website also uses the frogs and is designed to appeal to this generation.

Jeep is a registered trademark of DaimlerChrysler.

- Volkswagen's TV ad showing two young guys tooling around in a VW, picking up a discarded couch, discarding it (apparently because it smells bad), and continuing to drive around with the musical lyrics "da da da" playing has been very successful. It also has a website focused on Generation X that is promoted in media that the more successful members of this generation read.
- Kia Motors America recently launched it Sportage convertible targeting Generation X. It is advertised on cable TV with an ad showing the owner, "Ed," chauffeuring a couple in the convertible.

Generation Y

The traditional mass-marketing approaches that were so successful with older generations don't work well with Generation X and are even less effective with Generation Y. Pepsi is successfully appealing to the older members of Generation Y as well as the younger members of Generation X by inventing Pepsi Ball (a combination basketball, Frisbee, hockey, and team handball played on a triangle field with three goals) and promoting it on college campuses (see Illustration 4–5).

Today's 27-year-olds are the leading edge of the next generation. It is a significant one for our society because it is the next baby boom, with 71 million members. These children of the original baby boomers were born between 1977 and 1994 and are sometimes referred to as the "echo boom." While considered a single generation, it is much less a single market than the other generations. Its age range in 2005 will be from 11 to 28. Marketers typically divide the group into "tweens and teens" (11 to 18) and young adults.

Overall, it is the first generation to grow up with virtually full-employment opportunities for women, with dual-income households the standard, with a wide array of family types seen as normal, with significant respect for ethnic and cultural diversity, with

ILLUSTRATION 4–5

Attracting Generation Y requires new approaches to marketing. Traditional media and mass techniques are not as effective with this group as they were with their parents.

Courtesy of The Pepsi Cola Company.

computers in the home and schools, and with the Internet. It has also grown up with divorce as the norm,[45] AIDS, visible homelessness (including many teenagers), drug abuse, gang violence, and economic uncertainty. Columbine, the Oklahoma City bombing, the Clinton/ Lewinsky scandal, the collapse of the Soviet Union, and Kosovo were key events for this generation.[46] Global terrorism and its consequences will have an as yet unknown impact, particularly on the younger members of this generation.[47]

Generation Y is characterized by a strong sense of independence and autonomy. They are assertive, self-reliant, emotionally and intellectually expressive, innovative, and curious. They understand that advertisements exist to sell products and are unlikely to respond to "marketing hype." They prefer ads that use humor or irony and have an element of truth about them. They like the ability to customize products to their unique needs. Brand names are important to them.[48]

The older members of this generation are in the workforce or college. Those in the workforce are facing a difficult environment at this time but should encounter increased opportunities as the baby boom retires. These consumers are Internet savvy and use e-mail, cell phones, and text messaging to communicate. They are accustomed to media and TV programs designed for them (MTV, "Dawson Creek," *Maxim*), and expect this to continue as they mature.

They are becoming a major market for automobiles. Although most earn relatively low wages, many live with parents or share housing costs with one or more housemates and so have reasonable disposable income.[49] Both Toyota and Ford are trying to appeal to this market.

Abercrombie & Fitch has achieved great success by focusing on the middle- and upper-income portion of this group. Its stores blast contemporary music at corporate-specified decibel levels designed to discourage conversation. Service is provided by "brand representatives" selected to embody the brand's fraternity/sorority lifestyle and attitude positioning. It advertises in only three magazines—*Out, Rolling Stone,* and *Vanity Fair.*

The stores feature oversized posters of black and white photos of frolicking college students with sexual undertones designed to appeal to both heterosexuals and homosexuals. Its "magolog" generated significant controversy recently when it provided instructions for a variety of drinking games. (After a complaint from Mothers Against Drunk Driving, the company agreed to send postcards to students urging responsible drinking.)

The teenage segment of this generation receives the most attention. The vast majority of teenagers were raised and currently reside in dual-income or single-parent households. Therefore, they have grown up assisting in household management, including shopping. This fact, coupled with the ubiquitous presence of advertising throughout their lives, has made them cynical, smart shoppers:

> They're even more pragmatic than the baby boomers ever were, and they have a B.S. alarm that goes off quick and fast. They walk in and usually make up their minds very quickly about whether its phat or not phat, and whether they want it or don't want it. They know a lot of advertising is based on lies and hype.[50]

The teenage market is attractive to marketers for two reasons. First, preferences and tastes formed during the teenage years can influence purchases throughout life. As the Ford Focus brand manager states, "Although very few of [teenagers] are car buyers now, it is vital to create a relationship with them so they'll think of Ford when it is time to buy a car."[51] Second, it currently spends over $150 billion annually for personal consumption, three-fourths of which it earns.[52] It spends billions more while doing the household shopping and influences the purchase of many additional items:

> Kerri, age 16, hated the family's "clunky" Jeep Cherokee. She insisted on going along when her father, an attorney, went car shopping. She persuaded him to buy a Toyota Camry with a CD player and sunroof. According to Kerri: "It looks more like a hip-hoppier car."[53]

Marketers targeting teens need to use appropriate language, music, and images. Honesty, humor, and information are important to teens.[54] The ad shown in Illustration 4–6 appeals to teens through its humor and openness. Toyota recently ran a series of humorous ads in teen magazines entitled "Driver's Ed," which featured a geeky Toyota employee dispensing driving tips such as

> Attention Nose Pickers: Just because you are alone in your car—NEWS FLASH—you are not invisible.

Ads targeting this generation must be placed in appropriate magazines and on appropriate Internet sites and television and radio programs.[55] The portrayal of multiple racial and ethnic groups in ads aimed at this generation is common. This is a multiethnic generation, and single-race ads would seem unnatural to them. In addition, urban African American teenagers and Hispanic teenagers are frequently the style leaders of this generation.[56] As important as effective advertising are public relations (creating buzz) and event sponsorship.

Successful approaches to targeting this market include

- Ford is reaching teens and young adults with its new Focus. It has loaned souped-up Focus "statement-cars" to key influencers like DJs, clubbers, assistants to stars, and X-gamers. It sponsored Ricky Martin's tour and featured his dog in a commercial about cable diva Annabella Gurwich's life with her Focus.
- Cover Girl is a remarkable success among teens. It maintains a steady flow of teen-oriented products such as the seasonal Enchanted You prom collection. It is the largest

Numerous websites
compete for teens'
limited time.
Gurl.com promises
a place where
teens can focus on
their concerns and
issues.

Courtesy Prime Media.

advertiser in teen magazines. Its coverGirl.com website gets over 250,000 unique hits
a month. Teens can enter information about their skin color and other preferences and
receive free samples. It advertises heavily on teen portal Alloy.com and offers e-mail
newsletters to teens. It sponsors such events as a "Cover Girl Live Zone" mall tour that
features modeling contests, fashion shows, and cosmetics testing bars. It co-sponsors
Toejam, an on- and off-line community for teen girls. It also operates Tremor.com,
which has recruited thousands of "teen trend leaders" to aid product development.[57]

- Heinz's Bagel Bites were originally marketed only to mothers (to buy for their teens
and others). Heinz revamped its strategy to focus directly on teens. It signed on as a
sponsor of ESPN's Winter X Games and sales jumped 25 percent.[58]

Millennials

This newest generation was born after 1994. There will be over 38 million in this generation in 2005. It is too early to characterize this group as it is in its early formative years.
We will discuss marketing to children (this generation) in Chapter 6 in our discussion of
families.

SOCIAL STRATIFICATION

We are all familiar with the concept of social class, but most of us would have difficulty explaining our class system to a foreigner. The following quotes illustrate the vague nature of

social class in America and Canada:

> Like it or not, all of us are largely defined, at least in the eyes of others, according to a complex set of criteria—how much we earn, what we do for a living, who our parents are, where and how long we attended school, how we speak, what we wear, where we live, and how we react to the issues of the day. It all adds up to our socioeconomic status, our ranking in U.S. society.[59]

> I would suppose social class means where you went to school and how far. Your intelligence. Where you live. The sort of house you live in. Your general background, as far as clubs you belong to, your friends. To some degree the type of profession you're in—in fact, definitely that. Where you send your children to school. The hobbies you have. Skiing, for example, is higher than the snowmobile. The clothes you wear . . . all of that. These are the externals. It can't be (just) money, because nobody ever knows that about you for sure.[60]

The words *social class* and *social standing* are used interchangeably to mean **societal rank**—*one's position relative to others on one or more dimensions valued by society.* How do we obtain a social standing? Your social standing is a result of characteristics you possess that others in society desire and hold in high esteem. Your education, occupation, ownership of property, income level, and heritage (racial/ethnic background, parents' status) influence your social standing, as shown in Figure 4–2. Social standing ranges from the lower class, those with few or none of the socioeconomic factors desired by society, to the upper class, who possess many of the socioeconomic characteristics considered by society as desirable. Individuals with different social standings tend to have different needs and consumption patterns. Thus, a **social class system** can be defined as *a hierarchical division of a society into relatively distinct and homogeneous groups with respect to attitudes, values, and lifestyles.*

"Pure" social classes do not exist in the United States or most other industrialized societies. However, it is apparent that these same societies do have hierarchical groups of individuals and that individuals in those groups do exhibit unique behavior patterns that are different from behaviors in other groups.

What exists is *not a set of social classes* but a *series of status continua.*[61] These status continua reflect various dimensions or factors that the overall society values. In an achievement-oriented society such as the United States, *achievement-related factors* constitute the primary status dimensions. Thus, education, occupation, income, and, to a lesser extent, quality of residence and place of residence are important status dimensions in the United States. Race and gender are *ascribed* dimensions of social status that are not related to achievement but still influence status in the United States. Likewise, the status of a person's

FIGURE 4–2   Social Standing Is Derived and Influences Behavior

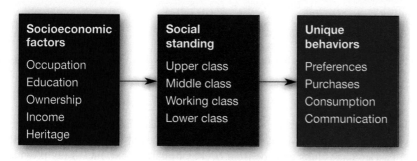

Socioeconomic factors	Social standing	Unique behaviors
Occupation	Upper class	Preferences
Education	Middle class	Purchases
Ownership	Working class	Consumption
Income	Lower class	Communication
Heritage		

parents is an ascribed status dimension that also exists in the United States. However, heritage is a more important factor in a more traditional society such as England.[62]

The various status dimensions are clearly related to each other. In a functional sense, the status of one's parents influences one's education, which in turn influences occupation that generates income, which sets limits on one's lifestyle, including one's residence. Does this mean that an individual with high status based on one dimension will have high status based on the other dimensions? This is a question of **status crystallization.** The more consistent an individual is on all status dimensions, the greater the degree of status crystallization for the individual. Status crystallization is moderate in the United States. For example, many blue-collar workers (such as plumbers and electricians) earn higher incomes than many professionals (such as public school teachers).

SOCIAL STRUCTURE IN THE UNITED STATES

The moderate level of status crystallization in the United States supports the contention that a social class system is not a perfect categorization of social position. However, this does not mean that the population cannot be subdivided into status groups whose members share similar lifestyles, at least with respect to particular product categories or activities. Furthermore, there are many people with high levels of status crystallization who exhibit many of the behaviors associated with a class system. It is useful for the marketing manager to know the characteristics of these relatively pure class types, even though the descriptions represent a simplified abstraction from reality.

A number of different sets of social classes have been proposed to describe the United States. We will use the one developed by Coleman and Rainwater.[63] In their system, shown in Table 4–4, the *upper class* (14 percent) is divided into three groups primarily on differences in occupation and social affiliations. The *middle class* (70 percent) is divided into a middle class (32 percent) of average-income white- and blue-collar workers living in better neighborhoods and a working class (38 percent) of average-income blue-collar workers who lead a "working-class lifestyle." The *lower class* (16 percent) is divided into two groups, one living just above the poverty level and the other visibly poverty-stricken. Note that the average income associated with each class, particularly the upper classes, will have increased dramatically since Table 4–4 was developed.

The percentage of the American population assigned each class in the Coleman-Rainwater system closely parallels the way Americans classify themselves. In one study, Americans were asked to classify themselves into one of five classes.[64] The results were

Poor	8%
Working	37
Middle	43
Upper-middle	8
Upper	1

The Coleman-Rainwater groups are described in more detail in the following sections.

Upper Americans

The Upper-Upper Class   Members of the upper-upper social class are aristocratic families who make up the social elite. Members with this level of social status generally are the nucleus of the best country clubs and sponsors of major charitable events. They provide

Upper Americans
- *Upper-upper* (0.3%). The "capital S society" world of inherited wealth, aristocratic names.
- *Lower-upper* (1.2%). The newer social elite, drawn from current professional, corporate leadership.
- *Upper-middle class* (12.5%). The rest of college graduate managers and professionals; lifestyle centers on careers, private clubs, causes, and the arts.

Middle Americans
- *Middle class* (32%). Average-pay white-collar workers and their blue-collar friends; live on "the better side of town"; try to "do the proper things."
- *Working class* (38%). Average-pay blue-collar workers; lead "working-class lifestyle," whatever the income, school background, and job.

Lower Americans
- *Upper-lower* (9%). "A lower group of people but not the lowest"; working, not on welfare; living standard is just above poverty.
- *Lower-lower* (7%). On welfare, visibly poverty-stricken; usually out of work, or have "the dirtiest jobs."

TABLE 4–4

The Coleman-Rainwater Social Class Hierarchy

Typical Profile				
Social Class	*Percent*	*Income*	*Education*	*Occupation*
Upper Americans				
Upper-upper	0.3%	$600,000	Master's degree	Board chairman
Lower-upper	1.2	450,000	Master's degree	Corporate president
Upper-middle	12.5	150,000	Medical degree	Physician
Middle Americans				
Middle class	32.0	28,000	College degree	High school teacher
Working class	38.0	15,000	High school	Assembly worker
Lower Americans				
Upper-lower	9.0	9,000	Some high school	Janitor
Lower-lower	7.0	5,000	Grade school	Unemployed

Source: R. P. Coleman, "The Continuing Significance of Social Class in Marketing," *Journal of Consumer Research,* December 1983, p. 267. Copyright 1983, University of Chicago. Reprinted with permission.

leadership and funds for community and civic activities and often serve as trustees for hospitals, colleges, and civic organizations.

The Kennedy family is a national example of the upper-upper class. Most communities in America have one or more families with significant "old money." These individuals live in excellent homes, drive luxury automobiles, own original art, and travel extensively. They generally stay out of the public spotlight unless it is to enter politics or support a charity or community event.

The Lower-Upper Class The lower-upper class is often referred to as "new rich—the current generation's new successful elite." These families are relatively new in terms of upper-class social status and have not yet been accepted by the upper crust of the community. In some cases, their incomes are greater than those of families in the upper-upper social strata. Bill Gates, founder of Microsoft, and Ted Turner, founder of CNN, are national examples of the lower-upper class. Most communities have one or more families who have acquired great wealth during one generation, many from the high-tech and dot-com boom of the 1990s.

Many members of this group continue to live lifestyles similar to those of the upper-middle class. Other members of the lower-upper class strive to emulate the established upper-upper class. Entrepreneurs, sports stars, and entertainers who suddenly acquire substantial wealth often engage in this type of behavior. However, they are frequently unable to join the same exclusive clubs or command the social respect accorded the true "blue bloods." Many respond by aggressively engaging in **conspicuous consumption;**

This product and ad emphasize elegance and craftsmanship as well as performance. These features appeal to the upper classes.

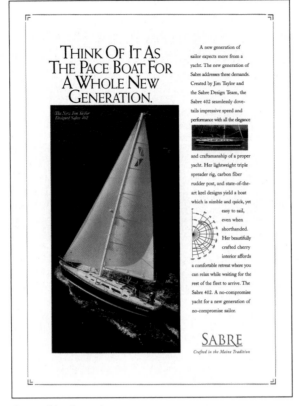

Courtesy Sabre Corporation.

that is, they purchase and use automobiles, homes, yachts, clothes, and so forth primarily to demonstrate their great wealth.[65] Thus, it is not unusual to read about a star professional athlete who owns 5 or 10 luxury cars, multiple homes, and so forth. These individuals are referred as the **nouveaux riches.** Doing the "in thing" on a grand scale is important to this group. High-status brands and activities are actively sought out by the nouveaux riches.

Although small, these groups serve as important market segments for some products and as a symbol of "the good life" to the upper-middle class. Illustration 4–7 shows a product and ad that would appeal to the upper classes.

The Upper-Middle Class   The upper-middle class consists of families who possess neither family status derived from heritage nor unusual wealth. Occupation and education are key aspects of this social stratum, as it consists of successful professionals, independent businesspeople, and corporate managers. As shown in Table 4–4, members of this social class are typically college graduates many with professional or graduate degrees.

Upper-middle-class individuals tend to be confident and forward looking. They worry about the ability of their children to have the same lifestyle they enjoy. They realize that their success depends on their careers, which in turn depend on education. As a result, having their children get a sound education from the right schools is very important to them.

This group is highly involved in the arts and charities of their local communities. They belong to private clubs where they tend to be quite active. They are a prime market for financial services that focus on retirement planning, estate planning, and college funding

Courtesy Four Seasons Hotels, Inc.

ILLUSTRATION 4–8

An ad such as this would appeal to the upper-middle class. It emphasizes celebrating a special event in an elegant and yet private way.

issues. They consume fine homes, expensive automobiles, quality furniture, good wines, and nice resorts. Illustration 4–8 contains an advertisement aimed at this group.

This segment of the U.S. population is highly visible, and many Americans would like to belong to it. Because it is aspired to by many, it is an important positioning variable for some products. Figure 4–3 describes the upward-pull strategy that many marketers use. The ad for Kahlua shown in Illustration 4–9 is an example of this approach. Kahlua, a relatively inexpensive liqueur, is shown being consumed in very elegant surroundings. Thus, a product readily affordable by the middle and working class is positioned as one that will allow its users to experience some elements of the upper-middle-class lifestyle.

FIGURE 4–3   Upward-Pull Strategy Targeted at Middle Class

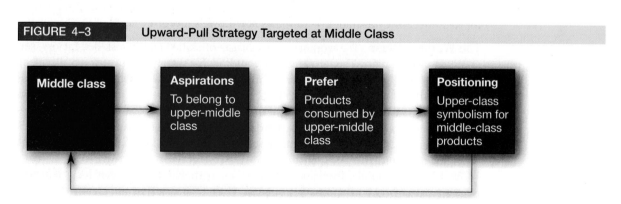

ILLUSTRATION 4–9

By positioning a moderately priced product as one that will allow its users to experience some elements of the upper-middle-class lifestyle, Kahlua is using an upward-pull strategy.

Courtesy Hiram Walker, Inc.

Middle Americans

The Middle Class   The middle class is composed of white-collar workers (office workers, schoolteachers, lower-level managers) and high-paid blue-collar workers (plumbers, factory supervisors). Thus, the middle class represents the majority of the white-collar group and the top of the blue-collar group. The middle-class core typically has some college education though not a degree, a white-collar or a factory supervisor position, and an average income. Many members of this class feel very insecure because of reductions in both government and private workforces during the recent recession.

The middle class is concerned about respectability. They care what the neighbors think. They generally live in modest suburban homes. They are deeply concerned about the quality of public schools, crime, drugs, the weakening of "traditional family values," and their family's financial security. Retirement is an increasing concern as firms reduce pension plans and health care costs escalate.

Members of the middle class are likely to get involved in do-it-yourself projects. They represent the primary target market for the goods and services of home improvement centers, garden shops, automotive parts houses, as well as mouthwashes and deodorants. With limited incomes, they must balance their desire for current consumption with aspirations for future security. Illustration 4–10 shows how Lowe's meets the needs of this segment.

The Working Class   The working class consists of skilled and semiskilled factory, service, and sales workers. Though some households in this social stratum seek advancement, members are more likely to seek security for and protection of what they already have. This segment suffered seriously during the first half of the 1990s as their average real earnings declined. Automation and the movement of manufacturing activities to developing countries also led to economic insecurity. Few of these individuals benefited from the stock market boom of the late 1990s, but many are being negatively affected by the most recent economic downturn.

Working-class families live in modest homes or apartments that are often located in marginal urban neighborhoods, decaying suburbs, or rural areas. They are greatly concerned

Courtesy Lowe's Companies.

about crime, gangs, drugs, and neighborhood deterioration. They generally cannot afford to move to a different area should their current neighborhood or school become unsafe or otherwise undesirable. With modest education and skill levels, the more marginal members of this class are in danger of falling into one of the lower classes.

The ad shown in Illustration 4–11 would appeal to those members of this class seeking advancement as well as those concerned about downward mobility due to workforce reductions.

Many **working-class aristocrats** dislike the upper-middle class and prefer products and stores positioned at their social-class level.[66] These individuals are proud of their ability to do "real work" and see themselves as the often-unappreciated backbone of America. They are heavy consumers of pickups and campers, hunting equipment, power boats, and beer. Miller Brewing Company gave up attempts to attract a broad audience for its Miller High Life beer. Instead, it is targeting working-class aristocrats with ads that feature bowling alleys, diners, and country music. The ad shown in Illustration 4–12 would appeal to this group.

Lower Americans

The Upper-Lower Class   The upper-lower class consists of individuals who are poorly educated, have very low incomes, and work as unskilled laborers.[67] Most have minimum-wage jobs. A full-time, 50-week-a-year minimum-wage job is not enough to keep a one-earner family of three above the poverty level. In fact, it keeps the family almost 30 percent below the poverty line—this is a major change from the late 1960s, when the minimum

ILLUSTRATION 4–11

This ad would appeal to members of the working class seeking advancement as well as to those concerned about downward social mobility due to the changing economy. It would also appeal to some members of the upper-lower classes as well as marginal members of the middle class.

Courtesy Olsten Corporation.

ILLUSTRATION 4–12

This product and ad would appeal to the working class, particularly the working-class aristocrats.

Courtesy Wolverine World Wide, Inc.

wage would support a family of three. Compounding the problem is that many of these jobs are part-time and few provide benefits such as health insurance or a retirement plan. Consider John Gibson, a 50-year-old part-time janitor in Nashville who makes somewhat more than minimum wage:

"I'd like to work more," John says. However, he is not qualified for many jobs. "I have to make sacrifices but I get by. When I get my check, the first thing I do is pay my rent." John lives alone in a small efficiency apartment. One of the things John sacrifices in order to get by is eating at fast-food restaurants. Although he likes the food and the convenience, a co-worker convinced him that it was much cheaper to prepare food at home.

Until recently, John drove a 1978 Pontiac Bonneville: "it started costing me a lot of money. Little things were going wrong, and it was giving me fits." His co-workers helped him buy a 1987 Ford Escort. He minimizes his expenses on clothing by shopping at thrift stores such as the one operated by the Salvation Army.

As a part-time employee, he has no company health insurance, but he is now eligible for some coverage from the state of Tennessee. A few years before he had this coverage he was hospitalized. Afterward, his wages were garnished to cover his bills, and he was forced to rely on social service agencies. Today he spends a great deal of his spare time volunteering at these same agencies. He would enjoy golf but is seldom able to play. He has no pension plan or personal insurance and wonders what his retirement years will be like.[68]

This group is 66 percent white, 18 percent black, and 12 percent Hispanic, close to the national average. Two-thirds have two adults present in the household, and 80 percent have children at home (40 percent have three or more children). Lack of education is the defining characteristic—almost 70 percent have a high school degree or less, compared to 40 percent of the nonpoor.[69]

Members of the upper-lower class live in marginal housing that is often located in depressed and decayed neighborhoods. Crime, drugs, and gangs are often close at hand and represent very real threats. They are concerned about the safety of their families and their children's future. The lack of education, role models, and opportunities often produces despair that can result in harmful consumption such as cigarettes and alcohol. It may also produce inefficient purchasing and a short-term time focus.

The marketing system has not served this group effectively. They have a particularly difficult time securing financial services, and many do not have bank accounts. This means that they generally must pay a fee for cashing pay and other checks, which is estimated to cost them $180 per year. However, research indicates substantial marketing opportunities in this group. They tend to be value-oriented rather than just cost-focused. They tend to be very brand loyal. Firms such as Wal-Mart, Dollar General, and Radio Shack have done a good and profitable job serving these consumers.[70]

The Lower-Lower Class   Members of the lower-lower social stratum have very low incomes and minimal education. This segment of society is often unemployed for long periods of time and is the major recipient of government support and services provided by nonprofit organizations. Andre Hank, as described in Consumer Insight 1–2, is an example of an individual who was in the upper-lower class and then wound up in the lower-lower class when he lost his job.

Marketing to the lower classes is frequently controversial. The rent-to-own business flourishes by renting durable goods such as televisions and refrigerators to lower-class households who frequently cannot afford to acquire them for cash and lack the credit rating to charge the purchases at regular outlets. While this service appears to meet a real need, the industry is frequently criticized for charging exorbitant interest rates on the purchases.[71]

The marketing of "sin" products is even more controversial. Malt liquors and fortified wines sell heavily in lower-class neighborhoods. However, firms that actively promote such products to this market risk significant negative publicity. When R. J. Reynolds tried to market its Uptown cigarettes to lower-class urban blacks, public protests became so strong that the product was withdrawn. Although some might applaud this outcome, the unstated assumption of the protest is that these individuals lack the ability to make sound consumption decisions and thus require protections that other social classes do not require—an assumption that is certainly controversial.

Other firms are criticized for not marketing to the lower classes. Major retail chains, particularly food chains, and financial firms seldom provide services in lower-class neighborhoods. Critics argue that such businesses have a social responsibility to locate in these areas. The businesses thus criticized respond that this is a problem for all of society and the solution should not be forced on a few firms. However, a few sophisticated chain retailers such as Dollar General Corporation have begun to meet the unique needs of this segment. As one specialist in this area said,

> People with lower household incomes are still consumers. They still have to buy food. They still wear clothing. They still have to take care of their kids.[72]

The challenge for business is to develop marketing strategies that will meet the needs of these consumers efficiently and at a reasonable profit to the firm.

THE MEASUREMENT OF SOCIAL CLASS

There are two basic approaches to measuring social status: a single-item index or a multi-item index.

Single-item indexes estimate social status on the basis of a single dimension. Since an individual's overall status is influenced by several dimensions, single-item indexes are generally less accurate at predicting an individual's social standing or position in a community than are well-developed multi-item indexes. The three most common single-item indexes are (1) education, (2) occupation, and (3) income. Each of these provides an individual with social status. However, marketers generally think of them as direct influencers of consumption behavior, not as determinants of status that then influence behavior.

The use of social class as an explanatory consumer behavior variable has been heavily influenced by two studies, each of which developed a **multi-item index** to measure social class.[73] The basic approach in each of these studies was to determine, through a detailed analysis of a relatively small community, the classes into which the community members appeared to fit. Then more objective and measurable indicators or factors related to status were selected and weighted in a manner that would reproduce the original class assignments.

Hollingshead Index of Social Position   The Hollingshead **Index of Social Position (ISP)** is a two-item index that is well developed and widely used. The item scales, weights, formulas, and social-class scores are shown in Table 4–5.

Warner's Index of Status Characteristics   Another multi-item scale of social status is Warner's **Index of Status Characteristics (ISC).** Warner's system of measurement is based on four socioeconomic factors: occupation, source of income, house type, and dwelling area. Each of these dimensions of status is defined over a range of seven categories and each carries a different weight. This system classifies individuals into one of six social

Description	Score
Occupation Scale (weight of 7)	
Higher executives of large concerns, proprietors, and major professionals	1
Business managers, proprietors of medium-sized businesses, and lesser professionals	2
Administrative personnel, owners of small businesses, and minor professionals	3
Clerical and sales workers, technicians, and owners of little businesses	4
Skilled manual employees	5
Machine operators and semiskilled employees	6
Unskilled employees	7
Education Scale (weight of 4)	
Professional (MA, MS, ME, MD, PhD, LLD, and the like)	1
Four-year college graduate (BA, BS, BM)	2
One to three years college (also business schools)	3
High school graduate	4
Ten to 11 years of school (part high school)	5
Seven to nine years of school	6
Less than seven years of school	7

ISP score = 5 (Occupation score × 7) 1 (Education score × 4)

Social Strata	Range of Scores
Classification System	
Upper	11–17
Upper-middle	18–31
Middle	32–47
Lower-middle	48–63
Lower	64–77

TABLE 4–5

Hollingshead Index of Social Position (ISP)

Source: Adapted from A. B. Hollingshead and F. C. Redlich, *Social Class and Mental Illness* (New York: John Wiley & Sons, 1958).

status groups:

Category	Percent of Population
Upper-upper	1.4%
Lower-upper	1.6
Upper-middle	10.2
Lower-middle	28.8
Upper-lower	33.0
Lower-lower	25.5

Census Bureau's Index of Socioeconomic Status   The U.S. Bureau of the Census uses a three-factor social status index based on occupation, income, and education. This scale, referred to as the **Socioeconomic Status Scale (SES),** produces four social status categories:

Category	Percent of Population
Upper	15.1%
Upper-middle	34.5
Middle	34.1
Lower-middle	16.3

It is important to note that multi-item indexes were designed to measure or reflect *an individual or family's overall social position within a community*. Because of this, it is possible for a high score on one variable to offset a low score on another. Thus, the following three individuals would all be classified as middle class on the ISP scale: (1) someone with an eighth-grade education who is a successful owner of a medium-sized firm; (2) a four-year college graduate working as a salesperson; and (3) a graduate of a junior college working in an administrative position in the civil service. All of these individuals may well have similar standing in the community. However, it seems likely that their consumption processes for at least some products will differ, pointing up the fact that overall status may mask potentially useful associations between individual status dimensions and the consumption process for particular products.

Another important aspect of these measures is that they were developed before *the rapid expansion of the role of women.* Traditionally, women acquired the status of their husbands. They had few opportunities outside the home and had limited access to education or careers. This has changed radically. Now women bring educational, financial, and occupational prestige to the household just as males do. No scale has been developed that fully accounts for the new reality of dual sources of status for a household.

Demographics or Social Status?

Social status is largely derived from demographics; that is, one's income, education, and occupation go a long way toward determining one's social class or status. Should marketers use an overall measure of social status (a multi-item index) or a demographic variable such as income? Multi-item measures of social status are clearly superior for indicating a person's or family's overall standing in a community. If this is the issue of concern, perhaps in a study of opinion leadership, a multi-item index such as the Warner's or Hollingshead's instrument would be most appropriate. However, marketers are rarely interested in social standing per se. Instead, they are more likely to focus on demographic characteristics as direct influencers on consumer behavior. Thus, research on taste and intellectually oriented activities such as magazine readership or television viewing should consider education as the most relevant dimension. Occupation might be most relevant for studies focusing on leisure-time pursuits. And as we saw earlier, marketers frequently combine demographic measures, not to produce a measure of status but to provide a more complete understanding of the target market.

SOCIAL STRATIFICATION AND MARKETING STRATEGY

While social stratification does not explain all consumption behaviors, it is certainly relevant for some product categories. For clear evidence of this, visit a furniture store in a working-class neighborhood and then an upper-class store such as Ethan Allen Galleries.

The consumption of imported wine, liqueurs, and original art varies with social class. Beer is consumed across all social classes, but Michelob is more popular at the upper end and Pabst is more popular at the lower end. A product/brand may have different meanings to members of different social strata. Blue jeans may serve as economical, functional clothing items to working-class members and as stylish, self-expressive items to upper-class individuals. Likewise, different purchase motivations for the same product may exist between social strata. Individuals in higher social classes use credit cards for convenience (they pay off the entire balance each month); whereas individuals in lower social classes use them for installment purchases (they do not pay off the entire bill at the end of each month).

Figure 4–4 illustrates how Anheuser-Busch covers more than 80 percent of the U.S. population by carefully positioning three different brands. Table 4–6 indicates that consumers perceive these brands very clearly in terms of social class.

FIGURE 4–4   Anheuser-Busch Positioning to Social Class Segments

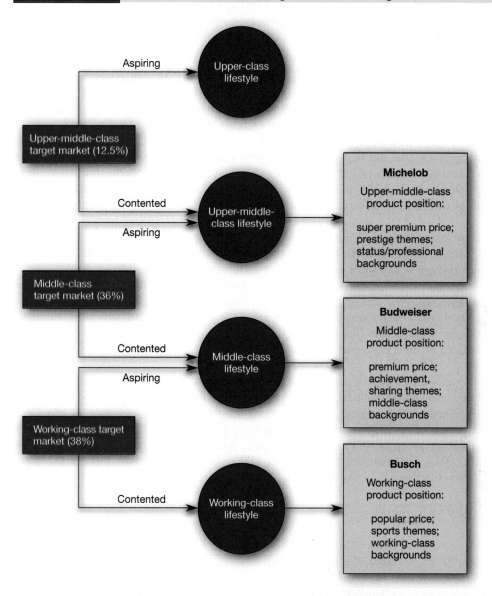

TABLE 4–6

Perceived Social Class Appeal of Various Beer Brands

	Social Class*				
Brand	Upper/Upper Middle	Middle	Lower Middle	Upper Lower/ Lower	All Classes
Coors	22	54	16	2	3
Budweiser	4	46	37	7	4
Miller	14	50	22	6	6
Michelob	67	23	4	1	2
Old Style†	3	33	36	22	1
Bud Light	22	53	14	3	5
Heineken	88	9	1	—	1

*Percentage classifying the brand as most appropriate for a particular social class.
†Local beer on tap.

Source: K. Grønhaug and P. S. Trapp, "Perceived Social Class Appeals of Branded Goods," *Journal of Consumer Marketing*, Winter 1989, p. 27.

SUMMARY

American society is described in part by its *demographics,* which include a population's size, distribution, and structure. The structure of a population refers to its age, income, education, and occupation makeup. Demographics are not static. At present, the rate of population growth is moderate, average age is increasing, southern and western regions are growing, and the workforce contains more women and white-collar workers than ever before. Marketers frequently segment markets based on a combination of two or more demographic descriptors.

In addition to actual measures of age and income, subjective measures can provide additional understanding of consumption. *Cognitive age* is how old a person feels. Many older consumers feel 10 to 15 years younger than their chronological age. *Subjective discretionary income,* which measures how much money consumers feel they have available for nonessentials, has been found to be a better predictor of some purchases than actual income.

An *age cohort* or *generation* is a group of persons who have experienced a common social, political, historical, and economic environment. *Cohort analysis* is the process of describing and explaining the attitudes, values, and behaviors of an age group as well as predicting its future attitudes, values, and behaviors. There are six major generations functioning in America today—pre-Depression, Depression, baby boom, Generation X, Generation Y, and millennials.

A *social class system* is defined as the hierarchical division of a society into relatively permanent and homogeneous groups with respect to attitudes, values, and lifestyles. A tightly defined social class system does not exist in the United States. What does seem to exist is a series of status continua that reflect various dimensions or factors that the overall society values. Education, occupation, income, and, to a lesser extent, type of residence are important status dimensions in this country. *Status crystallization* refers to the consistency of individuals and families on all relevant status dimensions (e.g., high income and high educational level).

While pure social classes do not exist in the United States, it is useful for marketing managers to know and understand the general characteristics of major social classes. Using Coleman and Rainwater's system, we described American society in terms of seven major categories—*upper-upper, lower-upper, upper-middle, middle, working class, upper-lower, and lower-lower.*

There are two basic approaches to the measurement of social classes: (1) use a combination of several dimensions, a *multi-item index;* or (2) use a single dimension, a *single-item index.* Multi-item indexes are designed to measure an individual's overall rank or social position within the community.

KEY TERMS

Age cohort 120
Cognitive age 120
Cohort analysis 121
Conspicuous consumption 133
Demographics 113
Generation 120
Gerontographics 121

Index of Social Position (ISP) 140
Index of Status Characteristics
  (ISC) 140
Multi-item indexes 140
Nouveaux riches 134
Single-item indexes 140
Social class system 131

Societal rank 131
Socioeconomic Status Scale
  (SES) 141
Status crystallization 132
Subjective discretionary income
  (SDI) 117
Working-class aristocrats 137

INTERNET EXERCISES

1. Use the Internet to describe the following characteristics of the U.S. population in 2010 (www.census.gov is a good place to start). How will this differ from the way it is today? What are the marketing strategy implications of these shifts?
   a. Total size and size by major census region
   b. Age distribution

   c. Education level
   d. Occupation structure
   e. Income level

2. Use the Internet to provide a demographic description of your community now and as forecast for 2010.

3. What is available on the Internet relevant to the role that education, occupation, and income play in the purchase of the following? What do you conclude about the usefulness of the Internet for gathering this type data at this point in time?
   a. Snowboards
   b. Internet shopping
   c. Movie attendance
   d. Cigar smoking

4. Evaluate the services and data provided at (a) www.easidemographics.com and (b) www.demographics.com.

5. Compare and evaluate two teen websites such as katrillion.com, alloy.com, teenpeople.com, gurl.com, bolt.com, goravegirl.com, and seventeen.com.

6. Tripod (www.tripod.com) is promoted as a site that Generation Xers visit and identify with. Evaluate this site. Why does it appeal to this generation?

7. Evaluate Delia's website (delias.com) and its approach to teenagers.

8. Visit AARP'S website (www.aarp.com). On the basis of what you read there, do you think AARP will appeal to baby boomers as they turn 50?

DDB NEEDHAM DATA ANALYSES

1. Which demographic variables are most closely associated with heavy consumption of the following? What would explain this association? Which contributes most to causing the consumption? (See Tables 1 through 7.)
   a. Pancakes
   b. Movie attendance
   c. Video rental
   d. Cigarettes

2. Which demographic variables are most closely associated with ownership of the following? What would explain this association? Which contributes most to causing the ownership? (See Tables 1 through 7.)
   a. 35-mm camera
   b. Personal computer
   c. Handgun
   d. Common stock

3. Examine the DDB Needham data in Tables 1 through 7. Which demographic variables are most closely associated with enjoying the following? What would explain this association? Which contributes most to causing this enjoyment?
   a. "E.R."
   b. "Melrose Place"

   c. "Seinfeld"
   d. "Saturday Night Live"

4. Which demographic variables are most closely associated with the following? What would explain this association? Which contributes most to causing the attitude or belief? (See Tables 1a, 2a, 3a, 4a, 5a, 6a, and 7a.)
   a. Liking to cook
   b. Having a lot of spare time
   c. Believing in buying American products
   d. Feeling that commercials place too much emphasis on sex
   e. Feeling like a winner
   f. Feeling sexy

5. Using the DDB Needham data in Table 5a, create age groups that approximate the generations described in the text. For which attitudes/interests/activities are there the greatest differences across the generations? Why is this the case?

6. Using the DDB Needham data in Table 5, create age groups that approximate the generations described in the text. For which products and activities are there the greatest differences in heavy consumption across the generations? Why is this the case?

REVIEW QUESTIONS

1. What are demographics?

2. Why is population growth an important concept for marketers?

3. What trend(s) characterizes the occupational structure of the United States?

4. What trend(s) characterizes the level of education in the United States?

5. What trend(s) characterizes the level of income in the United States?

6. What is meant by subjective discretionary income? How does it affect purchases?

7. What trend(s) characterizes the age distribution of the American population?

8. What is cognitive age? How is it measured?

9. What is an *age cohort?* A *cohort analysis?*

10. Describe each of the major generations in America.

11. What is a social class system?

12. What is meant by the statement, What exists is not a set of social classes but a series of status continua?

13. What underlying cultural value determines most of the status dimensions in the United States?

14. What is meant by status crystallization? Is the degree of status crystallization relatively high or low in the United States? Explain.

15. Briefly describe the primary characteristics of each of the classes described in the text (assume a high level of status crystallization).

16. What ethical issues arise in marketing to the lower social classes?

17. What are the two basic approaches used by marketers to measure social class?

18. What are the advantages of multi-item indexes? The disadvantages?

19. Describe the Hollingshead Index of Social Position.

DISCUSSION QUESTIONS

20. Which demographic shifts, if any, do you feel will have a noticeable impact on the market for the following in the next 10 years? Justify your answer.
    a. Mountain bikes
    b. Cruise ship vacations
    c. Fast-food restaurants
    d. Internet shopping
    e. Green products
    f. Magazines
    g. Charity contributions

21. Given the projected changes in America's demographics, name five products that will face increasing demand and five that will face declining demand.

22. Why do the regional differences shown in Figure 4–1 exist? What are the implications of such differences for marketers of products such as soft drinks?

23. Will the increasing median age of our population affect the general tone of our society? In what ways?

24. Respond to the questions in Consumer Insight 4–1.

25. Which demographic variable, if any, is most related to the following?
    a. Watching tennis on TV
    b. Skiing
    c. Listening to public radio
    d. SUV ownership

    e. Cat owned
    f. Deer hunting

26. Describe how each of the following firms' product managers should approach the (*i*) pre-Depression generation, (*ii*) Depression generation, (*iii*) baby boom generation, (*iv*) Generation X, and (*v*) Generation Y.
    a. Pepsi
    b. TGIFridays
    c. Monday Night Football
    d. Yahoo.com
    e. Habitat for Humanity
    f. Motorola cell phones
    g. eBay.com
    h. Colgate toothpaste

27. Respond to questions in Consumer Insight 4–2.

28. How will your lifestyle differ from your parents when you are your parents' age?

29. How could a knowledge of social stratification be used in the development of a marketing strategy for the following?
    a. A woman's clothing store
    b. A sports magazine
    c. Life insurance
    d. Toothpaste
    e. Adventure travel
    f. Habitat for Humanity

30. Do you think the United States is becoming more or less stratified over time?

31. Do your parents have a high or low level of status crystallization? Explain.

32. Based on the Hollingshead two-item index, what social class would your father be in? Your mother? What class will you be in at their age?

33. Name two products for which each of the three following demographic variables would be most influential in determining consumption. If you could combine two of the three, which would be the second demographic you would add to each? Justify your answer.
    a. Income
    b. Education
    c. Occupation

34. Name three products in addition to those described in the text for which subjective discretionary income might be a better predictor of consumption than actual income. Justify your answer.

35. How do you feel about each of the ethical issues or controversies the text described with respect to marketing to the lower classes? What other ethical issues do you see in this area?

36. Is it ethical for marketers to use the mass media to promote products that most members of the lower classes and working class cannot afford?

37. Would your answer to Question 36 change if the products were limited to children's toys?

38. Name five products for which the upward-pull strategy shown in Figure 4–3 would be appropriate. Name five for which it would be inappropriate. Justify your answers.

39. What causes the results shown in Table 4–6?

APPLICATION ACTIVITIES

40. On the basis of the demographics of the target market for the Saturn VUE (p. 113), select two magazines in which they should advertise (use Standard Rate and Data, Mediamark, or Simmons Research Bureau data). Justify your answer.

41. Interview a salesperson at the following locations and obtain a description of the average purchaser in demographic terms. Are the demographic shifts predicted in the text going to increase or decrease the size of this average-purchaser segment?
    a. Subaru dealership
    b. Ski outlet
    c. Life insurance agent (vacation travel)
    d. Wine store
    e. Harley-Davidson dealership
    f. Pizza parlor

42. Using Standard Rate and Data, Mediamark, or Simmons Research Bureau studies, pick three magazines that are oriented toward the different groups listed below. Analyze the differences in the products advertised and in the types of ads.
    a. Income groups
    b. Age groups
    c. Occupation groups
    d. Education levels

43. Interview three people over 50. Measure their cognitive age and the variables that presumably influence it. Do the variables appear to "cause" cognitive age? Try to ascertain if cognitive age or their chronological age is most influential on their consumption behavior.

44. Interview two members of the following generations. Determine the extent to which they feel the text description of their generation is accurate and how they think their generation differs from the larger society. Also determine what they think about how they are portrayed in the mass media and how well they are served by business today.
    a. Pre-Depression
    b. Depression
    c. Baby boom
    d. Generation X
    e. Generation Y

45. Interview a salesperson from an expensive, moderate, and inexpensive outlet for the following. Ascertain their perceptions of the social classes or status of their customers. Determine if their sales approach differs with differing classes.
    a. Men's clothing
    b. Women's clothing
    c. Furniture
    d. Jewelry

46. Examine a variety of magazines/newspapers and clip or copy an advertisement that positions a product as appropriate for each of the seven social classes described in the text (one ad per class). Explain how each ad appeals to that class.

47. Interview an unskilled worker, schoolteacher, retail clerk, and successful businessperson all in their 30s or 40s. Measure their social status using one of the multi-item measurement devices. Evaluate their status crystallization.

48. Visit a bowling alley and a tennis club parking lot. Analyze the differences in the types of cars, dress, and behaviors of those patronizing these two sports.

49. Volunteer to work two days or evenings at a homeless shelter, soup kitchen, or other program aimed at very low income families. Write a brief report on your experiences and reactions.

REFERENCES

1. W. Friedman, "Tinkering Turns Movie into Must-See for Teens," *Advertising Age,* October 9, 2000, p. 26.

2. J. Lawrence, "Frito's Micro Move," *Advertising Age,* February 12, 1990, p. 44.

3. J. A. McCarty and L. J. Shrum, "The Role of Personal Values and Demographics in Predicting Television Viewing Behavior," *Journal of Advertising,* December 1993, pp. 77–101; W. J. McDonald, "The Role of Demographics, Purchase Histories, and Shopper Decision-Making Styles in Predicting Consumer Catalog Loyalty," *Journal of Direct Marketing,* Summer 1993, pp. 55–65; and M. R. Stafford, "Demographic Discriminators of Service Quality in the Banking Industry," *Journal of Services Marketing,* no. 4 (1996), pp. 6–22.

4. J. Halliday, "Saturn SUV Offers 3-D VUE," *Advertising Age,* January 8, 2001, p. 29.

5. *U.S. Census Bureau,* Population Division, Population Projections Branch, March 29, 1999.

6. See S. Mitchell, "Birds of a Feather," *American Demographics,* February 1995, pp. 40–48.

7. P. Mergenhagen, "What Can Minimum Wage Buy?" *American Demographics,* January 1996, pp. 32–36; and W. O'Hare and J. Schwartz, "One Step Forward, Two Steps Back," *American Demographics,* September 1997, pp. 53–56.

8. "Median Income of People by Selected Characteristics," *Income 2000* (Washington, DC: U.S. Bureau of the Census, 2001), Table 7.

9. D. Crispell, "Dual-Earner Diversity," *American Demographics,* July 1995, p. 35.

10. Ibid; and G. E. Smith, "Framing in Advertising and the Moderating Impact of Consumer Education," *Journal of Advertising Research,* September 1996, pp. 49–64.

11. See A. D. Mathios, "Socioeconomic Factors, Nutrition, and Food Choice," *Journal of Public Policy & Marketing,* Spring 1996, pp. 45–54.

12. S. Fulwood III, "Americans Draw Fatter Paychecks," *Register-Guard,* September 27, 1996, p. 1; and E. Kacapyr, "Are You Middle Class?" *American Demographics,* October 1996, pp. 31–35.

13. See F. H. Frank, *Luxury Fever* (New York: Free Press, 1999).

14. K. MacArthur, "Overstuffed," *Advertising Age,* August 13, 2001, p. 3.

15. For an example, see F. J. Mulhern, J. D. Williams, and R. P. Leone, "Variability of Brand Price Elasticities across Retail Stores," *Journal of Retailing,* no. 3 (1998), pp. 427–45.

16. M. Johnson, "The Application of Geodemographics to Retailing," *Journal of the Market Research Society,* January 1997, p. 212.

17. T. C. O'Guinn and W. D. Wells, "Subjective Discretionary Income," *Marketing Research,* March 1989, pp. 32–41; see also P. L. Wachtel and S. J. Blatt, "Perceptions of Economic Needs and of Anticipated Future Income," *Journal of Economic Psychology,* September 1990, pp. 403–15.

18. J. R. Rossiter, "'Spending Power' and the Subjective Discretionary Income (SDI) Scale," *Advances in Consumer Research,* vol. 22, ed. F. R. Kardes and M. Sujan (Provo, UT: Association for Consumer Research, 1995), pp. 236–40.

19. P. L. Alreck, "Consumer Age Role Norms," *Psychology & Marketing,* October 2000, pp. 891–909.

20. P. Henry, "Modes of Thought That Vary Systematically with Both Social Class and Age," *Psychology & Marketing,* May 2000, pp. 421–40.

21. For example, see M. Goode and L. Moutinho, "The Effects of Consumers Age on Overall Satisfaction," *Journal of Professional Services Marketing,* no. 2 (1996), pp. 93–112.

22. "Population by Age Group," *Statistical Abstract of the United States 2001* (Washington, DC: U.S. Bureau of the Census, 2001), p. 16.

23. This section is based on K. P. Gwinner and N. Stephens, "Testing the Implied Mediational Role of Cognitive Age"; D. Guiot, "Antecedents of Subjective Age Biases among Senior Women"; E. Sherman, L. G. Schiffman, and A. Mathur, "The Influence of Gender on the New-Age Elderly's Consumption Orientation"; I. Szmigin and M. Carrigan, "Time, Consumption, and the Older Consumer"; and M. Catterall and P. Maclaran, "Body Talk," all in *Psychology & Marketing,* October 2001, pp. 1031–48, 1049–71, 1073–90, 1091–1116, and 1117–33.

24. P. Sloan and J. Neff, "With Aging Boomers in Mind, P&G, Den-Mat Plan Launches," *Advertising Age,* April 13, 1998, p. 3.

25. See A. S. Wellner, "Generational Divide," *American Demographics,* October 2000, pp. 53–58.

26. A. Rindfleisch, "Cohort Generational Influences on Consumer Socialization," in *Advances in Consumer Research,* vol. 21, ed. C. T. Allen and D. R. John (Provo, UT: Association for Consumer Research, 1994), pp. 470–76; and R. T. Rust and K. W. Y. Yeung, "Tracking the Age Wave," *Advances in Consumer Research,* vol. 22, ed. F. R. Kardes and M. Sujan (Provo, UT: Association for Consumer Research, 1995), pp. 680–85.

27. S. Mitchell, "Are Boomers Their Parents?" *American Demographics,* August 1996, pp. 40–45.

28. For a detailed treatment, see J. W. Smith and A. Clurman, *Rocking the Ages* (New York: Harper Business, 1997).

29. See N. Long, "Broken Down by Age and Sex," *Journal of the Market Research Society,* April 1998, pp. 73–91; and G. P. Moschis, "Life Stages of the Mature Market," *American Demographics,* September 1996, pp. 44–51.

30. L. L. Price, E. J. Arnould, and C. F. Curasi, "Older Consumers' Disposition of Special Possessions," *Journal of Consumer Research,* September 2000, p. 192.

31. See C. Yoon, "Age Differences in Consumers' Processing Strategies," *Journal of Consumer Research,* December 1997,

pp. 329–40; S. Law, S. A. Hawkins, and F. I. M. Craik, "Repetition-Induced Belief in the Elderly," *Journal of Consumer Research*, September 1998, pp. 91–107; G. P. Moschis, "Consumer Behavior in Later Life," *Research in Consumer Behavior* 9 (2000), pp. 103–28.

32. R. L. Johnson and C. J. Cobb-Walgren, "Aging and the Problem of Television Clutter," *Journal of Advertising Research,* July 1994, pp. 54–62; and P. Sorce, "Cognitive Competence of Older Consumers," *Psychology & Marketing,* September 1995, pp. 467–80. See also J. Perrien et al., "Exploring the Persuasive Effects of a Commercial for a Pharmaceutical Product," *Advances in Consumer Research,* vol. 25, ed. J. W. Alba and J. W. Hutchinson (Provo, UT: Association for Consumer Research, 1998), pp. 513–16.

33. G. P. Moschis, "Life Stages of the Mature Market," *American Demographics,* September 1996, pp. 44–51.

34. L. Freeman, "Completing the Span of 'Bridge' to Boomers," *Advertising Age,* November 7, 1994, p. S8; and W. Dunn, "The Eisenhower Generation," *American Demographics,* July 1994, pp. 34–40.

35. K. Parker, "Reaping What They've Sown," *American Demographics,* December 1999, pp. 34–38; and R. G. Javalgi, E. G. Thomas, and S. R. Rao, "Meeting the Needs of the Elderly in the Financial Services Market," *Journal of Professional Services Marketing* 2, no. 2 (2000), pp. 87–105.

36. C. Gibson, "The Four Baby Booms," *American Demographics,* November 1993, pp. 36–41; and P. Braus, "The Baby Boom at Mid-Decade," *American Demographics,* April 1995, pp. 40–45.

37. R. A. Lee, "The Youth Bias in Advertising," *American Demographics,* January 1997, pp. 47–50.

38. J. Raymond, "The Joy of Empty Nesting," *American Demographics,* May 2000, pp. 49–54.

39. See R. Gardyn, "Retirement Redefined," *American Demographics,* November 2000, pp. 52–57.

40. J. Raymond, "Senior Living," *American Demographics,* November 2000, pp. 58–63.

41. L. Singhania, "Boomers Spend Big on Skin," *Register-Guard,* February 27, 2002, p. E1.

42. D. Goodman, "Special K Drops Thin Models for Health Theme," *Marketing News,* March 2, 1998, p. 8.

43. N. Zill and J. Robinson, "The Generation X Difference," *American Demographics*, April 1995, pp. 24–33.

44. Ibid.

45. For a discussion of the consequences of this, see A. Rindfleisch, J. E. Burroughs, and F. Denton, "Family Structure, Materialism, and Compulsive Consumption," *Journal of Consumer Research,* March 1997, pp. 312–25.

46. P. Paul, "Getting Inside Gen Y," *American Demographics,* September 2001, pp. 43–49.

47. E. O. Lawler, "Optimistic, Empowered Kids Back to Being Kids," *Advertising Age,* February 4, 2002, p. S2.

48. J. Napoli and M. T. Ewing, "The Net Generation," *Journal of International Consumer Marketing* 13, no. 1 (2001), pp. 21–34.

49. P. Paul, "Echo Boomerang," *American Demographics,* June 2001, pp. 45–49.

50. C. Miller, "Phat Is Where It's at for Today's Teen Market," *Marketing News,* August 15, 1994, p. 6. See also D. M. Boush, M. Friestad, and G. M. Rose, "Adolescent Skepticism toward TV Advertising and Knowledge of Advertising Tactics," *Journal of Consumer Research,* June 1994, pp. 165–75; and S. Shim, "Adolescent Consumer Decision-Making Styles," *Journal of Consumer Research,* September 1996, pp. 547–69.

51. N. Shepherdson, "New Kids on the Lot," *American Demographics,* January 2000, p. 47.

52. M. Harvey, "Let's Hear IT for the Boys," *American Demographics,* August 2000, p. 30.

53. L. Zinn, "Teens," *Business Week,* April 11, 1994, p. 79.

54. D. Chaplin, "The Truth Hurts," *American Demographics,* April 1999, pp. 68–69.

55. C. La Ferle, S. M. Edwards, and W. Lee, "Teens' Use of Traditional Media and the Internet," *Journal of Advertising Research,* May 2000, pp. 55–65.

56. M. Spiegler, "Marketing Street Culture," *American Demographics,* November 1996, pp. 29–34; and J. D. Zbar, "Hispanic Teens Set Urban Beat," *Advertising Age,* June 25, 2001, p. S6.

57. J. Neff, "P7G Crawls the Malls," *Advertising Age,* February 4, 2002, p. S3.

58. K. Cleland, "Action Sports Form Fabric of Generation," *Advertising Age,* April 16, 2001, p. S22.

59. K. Labich, "Class in America," *Fortune,* February 7, 1994, p. 114.

60. R. P. Coleman and L. Rainwater, *Social Standing in America: New Dimensions of Class* (New York: Basic Books, 1978), p. 18.

61. J. E. Fisher, "Social Class and Consumer Behavior," in *Advances in Consumer Research,* vol. 14, ed. M. Wallendorf and P. Anderson (Provo, UT: Association for Consumer Research, 1987), pp. 492–96.

62. See R. P. Health, "The New Working Class," *American Demographics,* January 1998, pp. 51–55.

63. R. Coleman, "The Continuing Significance of Social Class in Marketing," *Journal of Consumer Research,* December 1983, p. 265.

64. See Heath, "The New Working Class."

65. See A. M. Kerwin, "Brands Pursue Old, New Money," *Advertising Age,* June 11, 2001, p. S1.

66. See J. P. Dickson and D. L. MacLachlan, "Social Distance and Shopping Behavior," *Journal of the Academy of Marketing Science,* Spring 1990, pp. 153–62.

67. See also D. Watson, "In Search of the Poor," *Journal of Economic Psychology* 21 (2000), pp. 495–515.

68. Mergenhagen, "What Can Minimum Wage Buy?"

69. H. Fattah, "The Rising Tide," *American Demographics,* April 2001, pp. 48–53.

70. Ibid.

71. R. H. Hill, D. L. Ramp, and L. Silver, "The Rent-to-Own Industry and Pricing Disclosure Tactics," *Journal of Public Policy & Marketing,* Spring 1998, pp. 1–10.

72. C. Miller, "The Have-Nots," *Marketing News,* August 1, 1994, p. 2.

73. See A. B. Hollingshead, *Elmstown's Youth* (New York: John Wiley & Sons, 1949); and W. L. Warner, M. Meeker, and K. Eels, *Social Class in America*: *A Manual of Procedure for the Measurement of Social Status* (Chicago: Science Research Associates, 1949).

Courtesy Girl Scouts of The United States of America.

The Changing American Society: Subcultures

☐ Slightly less than 7 percent of the Girl Scouts are Hispanic, compared to 17 percent of the girls in the appropriate age range (5 to 17). It would seem that the Girl Scouts would be very appealing to new immigrants, offering direction and building on the strong sense of community that is central to Hispanic culture.

However, attracting Hispanic youth to the Girl Scouts will require significant understanding and training. For example, although the green Girl Scout uniform may remind many non-Hispanic moms of good times and cookie sales, it may trigger memories of immigration officers in many Hispanic moms. In addition, some Hispanic parents may feel that the Girl Scouts don't teach the kids proper respect for adults by having them address troop leaders by their first names.

To address these issues and recruit more Hispanic girls, the organization recently launched a program entitled "For Every Girl, Everywhere." A spokesperson stated, "We couldn't just go in and make some ads. We had to start from within." This meant, in part, identifying the unique needs of Hispanics and the common elements between their culture and the Girl Scouts. This resulted in a major training effort for volunteers in areas with Hispanic populations.

The training focused on such basic issues as how to address a Hispanic woman (señora) and the importance of building a relationship. Hard-sell approaches and large meetings with parent groups were ruled out. Instead, soft-sell chats over coffee were encouraged.

The programming (the product) was also altered. Brothers were encouraged to attend some events. Camping, an uncommon activity for Hispanic girls, began including the entire family. Elements of Hispanic traditions are also being incorporated into Scouting. Las Posadas, a Hispanic Christmas tradition that pays homage to Mary and Joseph's search for an inn, is being conducted by Girl Scout troops in some areas.

The Girl Scouts have recognized that there is not a single best approach to this group because Hispanics are not a single culture. As the national director states, "It's a grassroots enterprise, and the grass is different in every location."[1]

In the previous chapter, we described how changes in American demographics were creating challenges and opportunities for marketers. Another extremely important aspect of the American society is its numerous subcultures such as the Hispanic subculture described above. Although American society has always contained numerous subcultures, until recently many marketers treated it as a homogeneous culture based primarily on Western European values. Though this view of America was never accurate, it is even less so today as non-European immigration, differential birthrates, and increased ethnic identification accentuate the heterogeneous nature of our society.

An array of racial, ethnic, nationality, religious, and regional groups or subcultures characterize American society. These subcultures are growing at different rates and are themselves undergoing change.

In this chapter, we describe the more important subcultures in America. We also highlight the marketing strategy implications of a heterogeneous rather than a homogeneous society.

THE NATURE OF SUBCULTURES

A **subculture** is *a segment of a larger culture whose members share distinguishing values and patterns of behavior.* The unique values and patterns of behavior shared by subculture group members are based on the social history of the group as well as on its current situation. Subculture members are also part of the larger culture in which they exist and they generally share most behaviors and beliefs with the core culture. As Figure 5–1 indicates, the degree to which an individual behaves in a manner unique to a subculture depends on the extent to which the individual identifies with that subculture.

America has traditionally been viewed as a melting pot or a soup bowl. Immigrants from various countries came to America and quickly (at least by the second generation) surrendered their old languages, values, behaviors, and even religions. In their place, they acquired American characteristics that were largely a slight adaptation of Western European, particularly British, features. The base American culture was vast enough that new immigrants did not change the flavor of the mixture to any noticeable extent. Although this is a reasonable approximation of the experience of most Western European immigrants, it isn't very accurate for African, Hispanic, Asian, or Arabic immigrants. Nor does it accurately describe the experience of Native Americans.

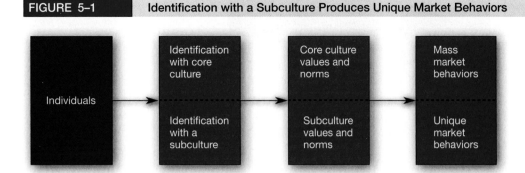

FIGURE 5–1   Identification with a Subculture Produces Unique Market Behaviors

Today, America is perhaps better described as a salad rather than a melting pot or a soup bowl.[2] When a small amount of a new ingredient is added to soup, it generally loses its identity completely and blends into the overall flavor of the soup. In a salad, each ingredient retains its own unique identity while adding to the color and flavor of the overall salad.[3] However, even in the salad bowl analogy, we should add a large serving of salad dressing, which represents the core American culture and blends the diverse groups into a cohesive society. As one expert stated,

> The future of diversity is not multiculturalism—separate and distinct ethnic enclaves—but a mixing, blurring, and blending of racial and ethnic traits.[4]

Ethnic groups are the most commonly described subcultures, but religions and geographic regions are also the bases for strong subcultures in the United States. Generations, as described in the previous chapter, also function like subcultures. Thus, *we are all members of several subcultures*. Each subculture may influence different aspects of our lifestyle. Our attitudes toward new products or imported products may be strongly influenced by our regional subculture, our taste in music by our generation subculture, our food preferences by our ethnic subculture, and our alcohol consumption by our religious subculture. The communications manager at Miller Brewing describes his firm's view of the influence of ethnicity and age on consumption:

> We used to have an ethnic marketing department up until several years ago . . . . (But now we believe) the things that young Hispanic or young African American or young white people have in common are much stronger and more important than any ethnic difference.[5]

This manager believes that age is more important than ethnicity in influencing the behaviors of the members of his target market for his product. The Mountain Dew ad shown in Illustration 5–1 reflects a modified version of this view. This ad, targeting young Hispanics, uses the same theme and style as other Mountain Dew ads, but it uses Spanish in the copy.

Identifying which subculture, if any, is an important determinant of behavior for a specific product is a key task for marketing managers. In the sections that follow, we describe the major ethnic, religious, and regional subcultures in America. While we will describe the general nature of these subcultures, it must be emphasized that *there are very large variations within each subculture*. Our focus in this chapter is on America, but all countries have a variety of subcultures that marketers must consider.

The degree to which an ad needs to be customized for an ethnic audience varies by product and strategy. This ad continues Mountain Dew's successful approach but uses the Spanish language.

© M. Hruby.

ETHNIC SUBCULTURES

Until the 2000 Census, the Bureau of the Census used the terms *black, white, Asian/Pacific Islander,* and *American Indian/Alaskan Native/Aleut* and *Other* to describe America's major racial groups. *Hispanic* was used as an ethnic term to describe individuals from Spanish-speaking cultures regardless of race. Under this system, people of Arab background were considered white and people from China, India, and Samoa were grouped together. There were obvious problems with such a system, and more than 10 million Americans refused to place themselves into one of the racial categories used in the 1990 Census. In addition, many younger Hispanics do not consider themselves to be white or black, but Hispanics or Latinos. Other individuals have parents from two different races and are proud of their mixed heritage.[6] Romona Douglas, of white, black, and American Indian descent, described her feelings thus:

> The assumption is that black people are a certain way, and white people are a particular way, and Asians are a certain way. Well, what about multi-racial families? I don't appreciate a McDonald's commercial with a street-wise black person. That is not me, that is not my upbringing. A lot of marketing campaigns are based on stereotypes of mono-racial communities.[7]

In the 2000 Census, the Hispanic question appeared before the race question. Respondents were asked if they are *Spanish/Hispanic/Latino.* To answer yes, respondents had to select a nationality group as well (*Mexican/Mexican American/Chicano, Puerto Rican, Cuban, Other*). In the race question that follows, respondents could make multiple selections from

FIGURE 5–2	Major Ethnic Subcultures in the United States: 1990–2010

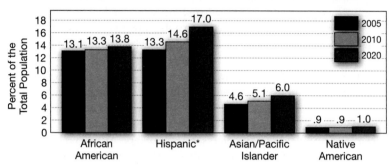

*May be of any race.

Source: "Table 10 Resident Population," *Statistical Abstract of the United States* (Washington DC: U.S. Bureau of Census, 2001), p. 13.

15 categories (*White; Black/African American/Negro; American Indian/Alaskan Native; Asian Indian; Chinese; Filipino; Japanese; Korean; Vietnamese; Native Hawaiian; Guamanian/Chamorro; Samoan; Other Pacific Islander; Other Race*). With this system, Douglas could accurately identify herself. However, Americans of Arab or Middle-Eastern descent had to choose Other Race. The new system has produced 57 race categories that render comparison of the 2000 data with prior data difficult if not impossible.[8] Despite such shortcomings, the new data provide a much richer understanding of the American society.

We define **ethnic subcultures** broadly as *those whose members' unique shared behaviors are based on a common racial, language, or nationality background*. Figure 5–2 provides the current and projected sizes of the major ethnic groups in America. As this figure makes clear, non-European ethnic groups constitute a significant and growing part of our population, from 24 percent in 1990 to 37 percent by 2020. The percentages shown in the figure understate the importance of these ethnic groups to specific geographic regions.[9] Thus, Hispanics are the largest population group in parts of Arizona, California, Florida, New Mexico, and Texas; Asian Americans are the largest group in Honolulu; and African Americans are a majority in parts of the South and urban areas in the Northeast and Midwest. In contrast, states such as Maine, Vermont, and West Virginia are more than 95 percent white.

The relatively faster growth rate of non-European groups is due to a higher birthrate among some of these groups and to greater immigration. Immigration has accounted for over a third of the U.S. population growth over the past several decades. About 800,000 legal immigrants arrive each year. In the late 1990s, the sources of these immigrants were as follows (these percentages have been relatively stable over the past decade).[10]

Asia	33.3%
Mexico	18.4
Europe	15.0
Caribbean	13.2
Central/South America	12.1
Africa	6.0

The influx of ethnic immigrants not only increases the size of ethnic subcultures, but also reinforces the unique behaviors and attitudes derived from the group's home culture. In the following sections, we describe the major ethnic subcultures. It is critical to remember that *all subcultures are very diverse, and general descriptions do not apply to all of the members*.[11]

Although one's ethnic heritage is a permanent characteristic, its influence is situational. That is, the degree to which a person's consumption is influenced by his or her ethnicity depends on such factors as who he or she is with, where he or she is, and other physical and social cues.[12] Thus, one's ethnicity might play no role in a decision to grab a quick bite for lunch during a business meeting and a large role in deciding what to prepare for family dinner.

In addition, ethnicity is only one factor that influences an individual's behavior. As we saw in the previous chapter, demographic factors also play a role. For example, a 45-year-old black doctor earning $90,000 per year and a 45-year-old white doctor with the same income would probably have more consumption behaviors in common than they would with members of their own race who were low-income service workers. As shown below, the various ethnic groups have distinct demographic profiles.[13] Thus, one must use caution in assuming that observed consumption differences between ethnic groups are caused by their ethnicity. These differences often disappear when demographic variables such as income are held constant.

	Whites	Blacks	Hispanics
Median age (2005)	38	32	27
High school or more (25 or older)	85%	79%	57%
Bachelor's degree or more (25 or older)	26%	17%	11%
Children at home	47%	55%	64%
Household income	$51,224	$31,778	$31,663

Examine Table 5–1. *Which of these differences are mainly caused by ethnicity or race and which are caused by other factors?*

TABLE 5–1		White	Black	Hispanic
Ethnic Subcultures and Consumption*	**Products**			
	Ground coffee	110	47	64
	Colas (frequent)	98	120	111
	Aftershave lotion/cologne	94	150	102
	Wok	101	64	115
	Activities			
	Barbecuing	111	35	83
	Picnic	110	17	114
	Soccer	105	48	230
	Movies (frequent)	93	141	125
	Shopping			
	TJ Maxx	90	167	92
	ShopKo	114	14	61
	Red Robin	100	68	119
	Red Lobster	95	145	86
	Media			
	Cosmopolitan	103	95	156
	GQ	78	238	108
	Jazz radio	93	163	86
	MTV	95	138	129

*100 = Average level of use, purchase, or consumption.

Source: *Mediamark Reporter 2002—University* (New York: Mediamark Research Inc., March 2002).

Astute marketers are aggressively pursuing opportunities created by increased ethnic diversity. Bank of America spent $40 million marketing to the Hispanic, Asian, and African American markets in 2002. AT&T runs broadcast and print ads in 20 different languages in the United States. EABC, a cable and satellite network, broadcasts programming in Arabic, Asian, Indian, Chinese, Filipino, Greek, Italian, Korean, Polish, and Russian. Chrysler advertises its New Yorker model by emphasizing safety features to the general market, styling to African Americans, and aspiration and achievement to Hispanics. However, marketing to ethnic groups requires a thorough understanding of the attitudes and values of each group.[14] For example, a New York Life Insurance ad designed to appeal to Koreans was a disaster because it used a Chinese model.[15]

AFRICAN AMERICANS

Debra Sandler, director of Flavor Brands (Slice, Mountain Dew, Mug Root Beer, and others) for PepsiCo, recently discussed the differences in marketing to the overall market and marketing to African Americans.

The strategy does not differ, the tactics differ. For example, if we say we want to be the beverage of choice to all teens, one of the things we have to do if we want to get to where teens are, to where they live and breathe, is to be wherever they are. We want to be available; we also want to be seen as part of their lifestyle. The difference is we may go about that differently for an 18-year-old Anglo male who lives in the suburbs than for an 18-year-old African American male who happens to live in an urban environment.

For example, we did a promotion where we gave away prizes—jet skis and convertibles. One thing we heard loud and clear from the urban teens was that they didn't participate in the promotion because they didn't think the prizes were relevant. So sometimes the tactics must change . . . . While we, African American consumers, are our own segment, we are also very much a part of the mainstream. In fact, in many cases we are driving the mainstream . . . . Again, in reaching teens, if I can produce television creative that appeals to an urban 18-year-old male, chances are that creative will appeal to all teens. It doesn't always work the other way around.

One of the challenges I think is how to get this done on a regional level where we have local application and local relevance, while taking advantage of national efficiencies . . . . How do we combine national and regional focus to make it one effort. Your overall strategy should be national, but your execution should be regional.

For example, when it comes to promotional activities like Black History month, is it better for us to develop one promotion that we execute throughout the country, or do we give the top 5 or 10 markets the budget and allow them to spend against local needs.

It's funny because I was an international business major in my undergraduate studies, and I often feel like I am doing international marketing in the domestic environment. Yes, you must take into account the cultural differences. That, in my mind is how you bring your strategy to life for that consumer.[16]

African Americans, or blacks (surveys do not indicate a clear preference for either term among African Americans[17]), constitute 13 percent of the American population. Concentrated in the South and the major metropolitan areas outside the South, African Americans represent a $575 billion market.[18] Thus, it is not surprising that marketers are very interested in this group.

On average, African Americans are younger than the white population and tend to have less education and lower household income levels. However, stereotyping African Americans as being of low income would not be accurate.[19] One-third of black households have incomes above the median level for whites:

African American Household Income	Percent
> $75,000	16%
$50,000–$74,999	16
$25,000–$49,999	29
$15,000–$24,999	16
< $15,000	24

Jaguar North America recently targeted the wealthier portion of this group with a direct-mail campaign to a list of 675,000 African Americans between the ages of 35 and 54 with annual incomes over $75,000 who do not own Jaguars. Spike Lee's agency created the mailing, which included a lifestyle-oriented brochure and an eight-minute video. The video showed a black female surgeon and her sculptor husband preparing for a jaunt to Martha's Vineyard from New York's Harlem in their Jaguar. The theme to the campaign was, "It's not luck that got you where you are."

Many of the consumption differences noted between African Americans and other groups relate as much to age, education, and economic circumstances as to race.[20] However, other differences are caused by differing values and lifestyles associated with the group's unique African American identity.

Consumer Groups

Market Segment Research conducted a major study of the African American, Hispanic, and Asian American markets in America.[21] This study identified four distinct consumer groups among African Americans.

Contented (37 percent)   This is the largest group, and it is the oldest (mean age = 44). Forty percent of the group are married; 32 percent are widowed or divorced. The average household size is 2.3. Fifty-six percent are female. Half are not employed. Three-fourths finished high school, and 13 percent completed college.

People in this segment are mature and basically contented with life. They are not concerned with social appearances or status. They are not impulsive. They prefer to stay at home and are moderately health conscious. They tend to save and are followers rather than leaders.

Upwardly Mobile (24 percent)   This group has an average age of 37. Slightly more than half are male. Sixty-two percent are married; less than 10 percent are widowed or divorced. The average household size is 3.1. More than 80 percent are employed, and 50 percent attended college.

This segment is composed of active, status-oriented professionals. They have materialistic aspirations and are quality-oriented. They are impulsive shoppers but also smart shoppers. They are financially secure, health conscious, and optimistic about the future.

Living for the Moment (21 percent)   This is the youngest group; two-thirds are less than 34. Fifty-eight percent are male; 61 percent are single. The average household size is 2.4. Almost 80 percent are employed, and 90 percent completed high school.

People in this segment are self-oriented and live for the moment. They are not concerned with social issues or responsibility. They are socially active, carefree, and image conscious.

Living Day to Day (18 percent)   This group has the lowest income and the largest average household size (5.4), although only a third are married. Its average age is 36, and

56 percent are female. Only half are employed, and more than a fourth have less than a high school education.

People in this group are typically unskilled and poor. They are not status conscious, nor are they socially active. They are most concerned with price and least concerned with quality. They are not health conscious, and they are not optimistic about their financial future.

The four-segment scheme described above is only one of many ways the African American subculture could be segmented.[22] However, the scheme has been useful to marketers and also indicates the diversity that exists within this population. Clearly, marketing strategies that target African Americans as a single market are likely to fail. It and the other ethnic groups we examine are as diverse as the white market.

Media Usage

African Americans make greater use of mass media than do whites, have different preferences, and report more influence by mass media ads than do whites.[23] In the spring of 2000, there was little overlap between the 10 most popular evening shows among black and white audiences (excluding sports specials):[24]

Blacks' Top 10	Whites' Top 10
1. *Jamie Foxx Show* (WB)	1. *Friends* (NBC)
2. *Moesha* (UPN)	2. *Frasier* (NBC)
3. *Malcolm & Eddie* (UPN)	3. *60 Minutes* (CBS)
4. *Showtime at the Apollo* (SYN)	4. *E.R.* (NBC)
5. *Law and Order* (NBC)	5. *Law and Order* (NBC)
6. *Fresh Prince of Bel Air* (SYN)	6. *Wheel of Fortune* (SYN)
7. *Walker, Texas Ranger* (CBS)	7. *Touched by an Angel* (CBS)
8. *60 Minutes* (CBS)	8. *World News Tonight* (ABC)
9. *Martin* (SYN)	9. *Drew Carey Show* (ABC)
10. *The Simpsons* (FOX)	10. *Walker, Texas Ranger* (CBS)

Clearly, African Americans prefer shows with African American themes or performers. Likewise, radio stations that play music popular with African Americans and magazines like *Essence* and *Ebony* focused on African American concerns receive most of the attention from this segment. Areas with large black populations will also often have a black-owned and -focused newspaper with substantial black readership.

African Americans have not been heavy users of the Internet, and less than half had a computer at home in 2001, compared to two-thirds of whites. However, this gap is rapidly narrowing.[25] Black-focused sites such as NetNoir (www.netnoir.com) and BlackVoices (www.blackvoices.com) are attracting advertisers such as IBM, Hewlett-Packard, Wells Fargo, and Walt Disney. General Motors recently entered a three-year partnership with BlackVoices.[26] GM will post its job openings on the site's Career Center area and offer scholarships and off-line events.

As emphasized earlier, subcultures are not homogeneous. The data above indicate limited overlap between the television shows watched by adult blacks and whites. However, 11 programs appeared on both black and white teenagers' top 20 lists.[27] Thus, the television preferences of black and white teenagers are more similar than are those of their parents.

Marketing to African Americans

Marketing to African Americans should be based on the same principles as marketing to any other group. That is, the market should be carefully analyzed, relevant needs should be identified among one or more segments of the market, and the entire marketing mix

© The Procter & Gamble Company. Used by permission.

Courtesy of Alberto-Culver Company.

should be designed to meet the needs of the target segments. At times, the relevant segment of the African American market will require a unique product. At other times, it will require a unique package, advertising medium, or message. Or no change may be required from the marketing mix used to reach a broader market. However, it is critical that the decision on how to appeal to this market be based on a sound understanding of the needs of the selected segments.

Products   African Americans have different skin tones and hair from white Americans. Cosmetics and similar products developed for white consumers are often inappropriate for black consumers. Recognition of this fact by major firms has created aggressive competition for the $750 million that African American women spend each year on cosmetics, hair care, and skin care.

Estée Lauder's subsidiary, Prescriptives, recently launched a product line called All Skins with 115 different shades designed to reach this market. Maybelline introduced Shades of You to meet the unique needs of this market. Illustration 5–2 shows a print advertisement for a product designed specifically for the unique needs of this market and another for a product designed to meet the needs of all ethnic groups but that is being promoted to African Americans.

Other manufacturers have found it worthwhile to alter their products to meet unique social needs of African Americans. Hallmark has a Mahogany line of greeting cards that features black characters and sayings. Mattel had considerable success with *Shani,* a Barbie-type doll with broader facial features and dark skin. Tyco Toys and others now offer a variety of African American dolls. Bank of America offers Kente checks with Kente cloth borders and the option of several symbols of relevance to the black community in the center of the check.

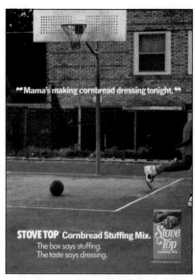

Used with permission of Kraft Foods, Inc.

ILLUSTRATION 5–3

This product is widely used by African Americans and white Americans. However, this ad was designed to reflect the fact that African Americans generally refer to this product category as *dressing* while whites term it *stuffing*.

Blacks often use the same products as whites but in different ways. For example, African Americans tend to prefer their coffee sweeter and with more cream or nondairy creamer than the general population. Coffee-Mate used this fact to develop a marketing campaign with ads in *Ebony* and *Essence,* spots on black-oriented radio shows, billboards in black neighborhoods, and a sweepstakes promotion featured in black-oriented local newspapers. It was rewarded with significant sales and market share gains.

Communications   A common mistake when communicating with any ethnic group is to assume that its members are the same as the larger culture except for superficial differences. However, as one expert says, "Black people are not dark-skinned white people."[28] Failure to recognize this often results in commercials targeted at African Americans that simply place the firm's standard ad in black media or that replace white actors with black actors, without changing the script, language, or setting. For example, Greyhound Bus targeted blacks by placing its standard commercials on black radio stations. Unfortunately, the soundtrack for the commercials was country and western, which is not popular with most black audiences.

Not all messages targeted at African Americans need to differ significantly from those targeted at other groups, though the use of black actors and spokespersons is important.[29] This is particularly the case for ethnically relevant products such as cosmetics and for those with strong ethnic identities.[30] The appeal of the Motions ad in Illustration 5–2 is to the desire for attractiveness that is the same for whites and blacks, though the product is designed to meet the unique grooming needs of black women. In other instances, advertisers can simply change the race of the models in the ads and perhaps the consumption setting to help indicate that the product is appropriate for the needs of African Americans. This works when the product, the appeal, and the appropriate language are the same for the black target market and the other groups being targeted. The Head & Shoulders ad in Illustration 5–2 is a good example of this approach. Such ads can be effectively run in both black and general media.

In contrast, the ad for Stove Top Stuffing shown in Illustration 5–3 is used specifically to target African Americans. Research revealed that many African Americans refer to foods of this type as dressing rather than stuffing. Thus, in ads targeting this segment the word *dressing* is used. Note also the use of the term *Mama* and the outdoor basketball court setting.

Another means of communicating with the African American and other ethnic communities is **event marketing,** which involves *creating or sponsoring an event that has a particular appeal to a market segment.* For example,

* Coors Light sponsored the Roots of Rhythm concert tour along with a nationwide sweepstakes in conjunction with Black Music Month. The brand also helped sponsor such events as the Indianapolis Black Expo and Harlem Day in New York.
* Honey Nut Cheerios sponsors the Soul Fest music event that travels to 30 urban markets each year.

Retailing   JCPenney Co. has had great success with its Authentic African boutiques in stores located near significant African American populations. These small shops, located inside JCPenney stores, feature clothing, handbags, hats, and other accessories imported from Africa.

KFC has launched a "neighborhood program" to tie its outlets to the character of the neighborhood in which they operate. In African American neighborhoods, employees wear traditional African-style uniforms, up-tempo R&B music is played in the outlets, and the menu features additional items that reflect local tastes, such as red beans and rice, sweet potato pie, Honey BBQ Wings, and Mean Greens.

Surveys reveal that a major difference between white and black shoppers' store selection criteria is respect. More than 60 percent of African American shoppers say that one of their most important reasons for choosing a store is that it treats its customers with respect.[31] This focus on respect is caused by the sad fact that many black shoppers still encounter obviously disrespectful acts such as being closely watched while shopping as well as more subtle discrimination such as slower service.[32] Another study showed that middle-class African Americans felt unwelcome at a variety of leisure activities.[33] The need for cultural sensitivity training for retail and service employees is clear.[34]

African Americans also use shopping as a form of recreation more than whites.[35] This suggests that stores with black customers should pay particular attention to providing a pleasant and fun shopping environment. Blacks also respond to sales differently than whites and have differing desires with respect to credit card, cash, and check payments.[36] Thus, all aspects of the shopping experience need to be carefully aligned to the needs of the target shoppers.

HISPANICS

The Bureau of the Census defines **Hispanic** as *a person of Cuban, Mexican, Puerto Rican, South or Central American, or other Spanish culture or origin regardless of race.* It is measured by a person's response to the question: Are you Spanish/Hispanic/Latino?

A dominant characteristic of Hispanics is the extensive use of the Spanish language. Although more than 90 percent of the people in this group are bilingual (87 percent) or speak only English (4 percent), more than half speak Spanish primarily or exclusive when at home. More than 60 percent of those who are bilingual prefer marketing messages in Spanish.[37] The use of Spanish among Hispanic Americans is increasing rather than decreasing. Extensive immigration is one reason for the increased use of Spanish. It is estimated that 35 percent of Hispanic Americans were born outside the United States.[38] Another reason is the growth of self-contained Spanish-speaking communities, coupled with the rapid expansion of national Spanish-language magazines and television channels.

However, one must be cautious in generalizing about this, or any, subculture. Hispanic teenagers exhibit different behaviors with respect to language than do their parents.

Hispanic teens constitute about 15 percent of all teenagers but are far more important to marketers than that percentage suggests.[39] First, they spend more than other teenagers. Hispanic teens spend an average of $375 per month. Hispanic teenage girls spend 60 percent more on makeup and twice as much on hair products as other teenagers. More important, these teens are joining black teenagers as fashion and style leaders for the overall teenage market.

Hispanic teens differ sharply from their parents, who felt strong pressures to blend in and "be American" (i.e., act and speak like white Americans). These teens don't. As three experts describe it,

I'm always amazed by the "Hispanicness" of Hispanic teens. They're speaking Spanish at home, both with friends, English for college and the Internet, but they're very much into the Hispanic culture. Even when they're born here. It's downright breathtaking.

It's not about being bilingual. It's about being bicultural. They are engrossed in the American culture, but they take an incredible amount of pride in being Latino.

It's very cool to be Hispanic at this age. It almost makes them more attractive, exotic. Hispanic teens are brushing up on their Spanish and celebrating their culture.

These bilingual teens read the same English language magazines and watch the same television programs as their non-Hispanic counterparts. In fact, they are much more likely to read such teen magazines as *Seventeen* and *YM*. One of the magazines targeting

the female Hispanic teenager, *Latina,* is mostly English, though most of the ads are in Spanish. However, they also utilize Spanish language magazines, television, and radio. They grew up listening not only to hip-hop and other popular music but to Hispanic-based rhythms as well—mariachi, banda, and norteño in California; tejano in Texas; salsa in Florida; and meringue in New York. Now they are helping popularize these sounds and variations of them throughout the larger teen population.

One of the core values that differentiates Hispanic teens is *familismo,* or a strong family orientation. This influences many aspects of their behavior. Family activities and events play a larger role in their lives than for non-Hispanics. Family means an extended family, not just the nuclear family. Children, including teenagers, are encouraged to be dependent longer. The Office of National Drug Control Policy attempts to capitalize on this value in an antidrug campaign targeting this group. It uses the theme, "If you do drugs, you are letting down your family."

Inspired by stars such as Jennifer Lopez and Ricky Martin, teenagers throughout America are adopting styles long popular with Hispanic youth. "Spanglish" is "in" in many areas. Hispanic youth are also in the vanguard of the movement away from colas toward sweeter, flavored drinks.

Critical Thinking Questions

1. To what extent are Hispanic teenagers leading the teenage market? Justify your response.

2. Many Hispanic teenagers are truly bicultural. What challenges does this present marketers?

3. Why are Hispanic teenage girls heavier readers of magazines such as *Cosmopolitan* and heavier users of cosmetics than white teenagers?

For example, these teens generally watch Spanish language television with their parents but watch English language programs with siblings and friends.[40] See Consumer Insight 5–1 for additional information on the Hispanic teenage market.

Like the other ethnic groups in America, Hispanics are diverse. Many marketers feel that the Hispanic subculture is not a single ethnic subculture but instead is three main and several minor nationality subcultures: Mexican Americans (66 percent), Puerto Ricans (9 percent), Cubans (4 percent), and other Latinos, mainly from Central America (14 percent). Each group speaks a slightly different version of Spanish and has somewhat distinct values and lifestyles. Further, each group tends to live in distinct regions of the country: Mexican Americans in the Southwest and California, Puerto Ricans in New York and New Jersey, Cubans in Florida, and other Latinos in California, New York, and Florida. Income levels also vary across the groups, with Cuban Americans having incomes well above the others.

Others argue that while one must be sensitive to nationality-based differences, the common language, common religion (Roman Catholic for most Hispanics), and the emergence of national Spanish-language media and entertainment figures create sufficient cultural homogeneity for most products and advertising campaigns. Thus, the decision to treat Hispanics as a single ethnic subculture or several nationality subcultures depends on the product and the nature of the intended communication.

Identification with Traditional Hispanic Culture

Acculturation is *the degree to which an immigrant has adapted to his or her new culture.*[41] Using level of identification with the traditional Hispanic culture as a measure of acculturation, the Market Segment Research study mentioned earlier found three Hispanic groups:

- *Strong Hispanic identification.* Members of this group are almost entirely Spanish speaking. They tend to live in areas populated exclusively by Hispanics. They are recent arrivals and retain close ties to family and friends "at home." They are generally low on all measures of social status. Their media usage is heavily Spanish language. About 60 percent of all Hispanic nationality groups, except Puerto Ricans (38 percent), are in this group.
- *Moderate Hispanic identification.* Members of this group speak both Spanish and English but are most comfortable with Spanish. They live in areas of moderate Hispanic density. Most have been in the United States for 12 years or more. They have average levels of income and social status. Their ties to the "old country" are moderate. They use both Spanish-language and English media. About 25 percent of all Hispanic nationality groups, except Puerto Ricans (35 percent), are in this group.
- *Limited Hispanic identification.* Members of this group speak both Spanish and English. They are very comfortable with English and live in areas dominated by non-Hispanics. They have lived in the United States for a long time and many are second- or third-generation Americans. Their ties to their country of origin are limited. They tend to use English-language media. Their income and social status are relatively high. About 18 percent of all Hispanic nationality groups, except Puerto Ricans (27 percent), are in this group.[42]

As the above discussion indicates, most Hispanics identify more or less strongly with a Hispanic culture.[43] This culture is heavily influenced by the Roman Catholic religion. It is family oriented, with the extended family playing an important role. It is also a masculine culture, and sports are very important to Hispanics, particularly boxing, baseball, and soccer. This masculine orientation manifests itself in many ways, including "macho" rules for interaction between males and male-dominant relationships between males and females. Although it varies with the product category, a strong Hispanic identification is associated with husband-dominant household decision making.[44]

Examine Illustration 5–4 (the voiceover was in Spanish only). Note the family focus and the strong presence of the male.

The Hispanic culture generally has a fairly traditional view of the appropriate role of women. For example, the wife is expected to prepare the food for the family. This produces

Courtesy of Bank of America.

ILLUSTRATION 5–4

The family is very important to the Hispanic subculture, and the male plays a major role. This television ad is in Spanish and has a strong family theme with a strong male presence. It also emphasizes the dominant American cultural values of achievement and material success.

challenges and opportunities for marketers.

- Church's Chicken encounters resistance to its restaurant and takeout foods among Hispanic consumers. Church's vice president of marketing stated, "In the Latino community, there are a number of cultural barriers to not cooking." A result of these barriers is a social stigma against women who do not prepare meals for their families. To counter this, Church's has launched an advertising campaign to make eating out more acceptable. The new campaign will try to position the chain as a place that provides a value-price dinner that frees up consumers to engage in more pressing activities.[45]
- The California Milk Processor Board targets Mexican Americans in California with ads that position milk as a vehicle through which families come together. Its research found that in this culture, cooking not only is the wife's responsibility but is central to her role. It is a way of expressing love for her family and a source of great pleasure. Commercials focus on women preparing food for the family with milk as a key ingredient. One of the most successful ads shows a grandmother teaching her six-year-old granddaughter how to cook using milk.[46]

Marketing to Hispanics

Although average Hispanic household income is relatively low ($31,663 versus $51,524 for non-Hispanic whites), the Hispanic market is estimated to be worth more than $450 billion, and it is the most rapidly growing segment of our population.[47] Thus, many marketers are targeting it with a variety of approaches:

- "It's tough to get Hispanics to switch brands. And while the general buyer looks at price first, Hispanics are willing to pay extra to purchase quality products for their family. So handing out coupons or reducing price is not an effective way to get them to try our products. A far better approach is to do in-store promotions to get Hispanics to sample our product." [Martin Serna, president of the firm that does Borden's promotions in the Hispanic community.]
- Anheuser-Busch, Campbell Soup, and Coca-Cola sponsor the nine-day Carnival Miami, one of the largest Hispanic festivals in America. Adolph Coors sponsors a variety of events, including community cook-offs and Cinco de Mayo celebrations. American Honda Motor Company helped fund the U.S. tour of Mexico City's Ballet Folklorico. Ford has helped fund soccer teams in Hispanic communities.
- See's Candies shows ads on Spanish television that feature a tour of its manufacturing plant. The fact that 70 percent of its workforce is Hispanic is apparent and shows the company's support of the Hispanic community.
- Pepsi developed an advertisement that appealed to all the Hispanic nationality groups. It produced a Spanish version of its Pepsi-generation campaign that focuses on a "sweet 15" party, the *quinceañera,* which celebrates the coming of age for Hispanic girls. In contrast, Nestlé had to depart from its normal one-ad approach for Butterfinger candy. It found that peanut butter was *mantequilla de man* for Hispanics from the Caribbean and *crema de cacahuate* for those from Mexico. Therefore, it created two different sets of copy for its Spanish-language ads.[48]

Communications   As we saw earlier, most Hispanics speak Spanish most of the time and prefer Spanish-language media. Therefore, although it is possible to reach part of this market using mass media, any serious attempt to target Hispanics must use Spanish-language media as well.

There are two Spanish-language television networks in the United States—Telemundo and Univision. Spanish language radio is widespread, with both local and network stations. Heavy radio advertisers include American Airlines, Sears, AT&T, McDonald's, and other major consumer goods marketers.

There are numerous Spanish-language magazines, including Spanish versions of *Cosmopolitan, National Geographic, Maxim, Men's Health, People,* and *Reader's Digest.* One company represents 18 such magazines, with a paid circulation of more than 750,000 and an estimated 4.9 million readers. *Latina* targets younger, affluent Hispanic women. Its readers have an average household income of almost $50,000. There are also many Spanish-language newspapers.

Until recently, Hispanics have not been heavy users of the Internet. However, approximately 55 percent now have a computer at home and 40 percent have Internet access, and both these percentages are growing rapidly.[49] In response, new sites focused on Hispanics are rapidly coming online. The most successful is Univision.com with 7 million unique visits per month (see Illustration 5–5). Gateway, Colgate-Palmolive, Coca-Cola, MasterCard, and GM are some of the firms that advertise on it. Pregunta.com is a Spanish language version of AskJeeves.com. Cadamujer.com is a woman's site sponsored by L'Oréal. Mattel recently launched BarbieLatina.com, a Spanish version of its extremely successful

ILLUSTRATION 5–5

Use of the Internet by Hispanics is exploding. Sites such as this one by Univision are being developed to appeal to the unique needs of this market.

Barbie.com. Although it is very similar to the English version, it is not merely a translation. For example, while both Hispanic and non-Hispanic girls aged three to eight have a passion for fantasy and nurturing behavior, the Hispanic girls had less interest in games and more interest in activity-based play. The content of the two sites reflects these differences.[50]

Successfully communicating to Hispanic consumers involves more than directly translating ad copy from English to Spanish. Tang introduced itself in its Spanish ads as *jugo de chino,* which worked well with Puerto Ricans who knew it meant orange juice. However, the phrase had no meaning to most other Hispanics. Other examples of translation difficulties include the following:

- Frank Perdue's chicken slogan, "It Takes a Tough Man to Make a Tender Chicken," was translated as "It Takes a Sexually Excited Man to Make a Chick Affectionate."
- Budweiser's slogan ended up being "The Queen of Beers," and Miller's was "Filling; Less Delicious."
- A candy marketer wanted to print a statement on its package, bragging about its 50 years in the business. When a tilde did not appear over the appropriate *n*, the package claimed it contained 50 anuses.
- One food company's burrito became *burrada,* a colloquialism for "big mistake."
- Coors' beer slogan "Get loose with Coors" came out as "Get the runs with Coors."[51]

Successful marketing to Hispanics moves beyond accurate translations into unique appeals and symbols. It requires marketers to be "in-culture," that is, to understand the value system and the overall cultural context of the various Hispanic groups.[52]

- Sears recognized the importance of the extended family in a successful ad for baby furniture. In the English ad, a husband and wife are shown selecting the furniture. In the Spanish ad, a teenage daughter and the grandparents join the expectant couple.

- Prego spaghetti sauce recognized the traditional Hispanic family role structure in its advertising. In its English ad, a father and son are shown alone in the kitchen preparing dinner. In the Spanish language ad, the entire family—mother, father, and child—are shown in the kitchen. Showing men cooking would not appeal to many traditional Hispanics.

- A car ad for Honda showed a young man enthusiastically washing a new car and admiring its features. The commercial ends with the man handing the keys to his brother who is the owner of the car. This humorous approach reflected the importance of the family in the Hispanic culture. When someone in the family buys a car, it belongs to the entire family.[53]

- Hispanic teens are particularly difficult to target with effective communications. Frito-Lay's successful campaign for Doritos was themed *Sabor a todo volumen* (roughly, "The loudest taste on earth"). TV ads featured loud Hispanic music and Hispanic teens with an emphasis on Doritos' bold and spicy taste. Research revealed that the music was key to the success of the campaign. According to a spokesperson, "Music is one of the major attributes of Hispanic teens that bind them together. The styles differ from salsa to Latin pop, but all are based on Latin roots."[54]

Products   Other than specialty food products, few marketers have developed unique products or services for the Hispanic market. And some that have made the attempt have failed. For example, many Hispanics find repugnant the current trend in houses of having the kitchen open onto the family room. One Hispanic who recently purchased a home described it thus:

I'm still terrified that when I have my non-Latino friends in my home, everyone will come into the kitchen. It's not so well received in Latino culture, that strangers come into the kitchen to help cook. It's embarrassing. (Many homes built for Hispanic buyers) . . . go for something that is too stereotypical—very bright Mexican tiles, the burro-and-sombrero look. This is like someone telling you that since you're American, you want a cowboy in your living room, standing there.[55]

In contrast, Frito-Lay was very successful in extending its Doritos line with versions targeting Hispanics. It launched zesty flavors such as Salsa Verde and Flamin' Hot Sabrositos. The packages included a Mexican happy face icon and pictures of chilies and onions.

An emerging trend is for marketers with food and household products developed for the Central and South American markets to distribute them in areas of the United States with large Hispanic populations. Examples include,

- Colgate-Palmolive distributes its Mexican household cleaner Fabuloso in Los Angeles and Miami.
- Nestlé sells Nido, its Mexican powdered milk brand, and Nestum, one of its cereals from Venezuela, in the United States.
- PepsiCo is marketing its Gamesa brand cookies from Mexico in Hispanic areas in the United States.
- Hormel imports a full line of Mexican sauces and ingredients under the Herdez, Maria, and Buffalo brands, all well established in Mexico.

Retailing   The primary retailing responses to this market have been increasing the number of bilingual salespeople; the use of Spanish language signs, directions, and point-of-purchase displays; and merchandise assortments that reflect the needs of the local Hispanic community. The following examples describe more focused responses:

- Tiangus, a grocery chain aimed at the Mexican American market in southern California, was launched with a fiesta atmosphere. Stands served a wide variety of Mexican foods, the walls were splashed with bright colors, and shoppers were serenaded with mariachi bands. The shelves were stocked with empanadas, handmade tortillas, and other items typically found only in specialty stores.

The stores are not just standard stores with a Latin flair and a few specialty items. The chain is based on extensive research. For example, it was found that the Hispanic shopper "is fussier about freshness, so she shops more frequently and uses less refrigeration. She may have less disposable income but she'll spend a higher share of it on food." On the basis of these findings, Tiangus stores emphasize fresh food. Half the selling space is devoted to fresh food with reduced space for packaged items and freezer foods.[56]

- Warehouse Entertainment recently launched a chain of Tu Música (Your Music) stores catering to Hispanic consumers. The stores carry music ranging from Hispanic rock to pop crossover to Mexican favorites. The logic of starting the stores was simple according to the firm's president: "The market in which we operated was changing and we needed to change with it." Tu Música targets first- to third-generation Hispanics who speak Spanish and seek Latino music. It advertises on Spanish-language TV, radio, and newspapers. It uses Spanish-speaking sales personnel. About one-third of its titles (more than 10,000) are in Spanish, compared to 2 percent in a typical outlet.[57]

- Bank of America converted its 5,000 ATM machines into a bilingual format. In regions of the country with large Hispanic populations, its branches have a Spanish language service line, first-time homebuyer education programs in Spanish, and a Spanish language loan-by-phone program. Its brochures are available in a bilingual format. These and other activities are tied together in an image campaign called *Cerca de ti,* or "Close to you."

ASIAN AMERICANS

Asian Americans are a rapidly growing subculture, due primarily to immigration. Asian Americans have the highest average household income of any ethnic group—$56,316, compared to $51,224 for non-Hispanic whites. This produces a market with more than $250 billion in buying power. However, Asian Americans are also the most diverse group, with numerous nationalities, languages, and religions. The U.S. Census includes Asian-Indians in their summary figures for this group. However, we will discuss them separately in the next section.

Asian Americans are not a single subculture. Consider the website in Illustration 5–6. Ads on this site are probably quite effective with many of the Chinese members of this subculture. However, as Figure 5–3 shows, Chinese represent only a little over a fourth of all Asian Americans and they share neither a common language nor culture with most of the other groups.

As shown below, the percentage of each nationality group that primarily uses its native language is high, except for Filipinos.[58]

Country	Percentage Using Native Language Primarily
Vietnam	85%
Hong Kong	82
China	64
Korea	64
Taiwan	64
Japan	46
Philippines	27

More than languages differ between the groups. In fact, the concept and term *Asian American* was developed and used by marketers and others who study these groups rather

than the members themselves. Members of the various nationalities involved generally refer to themselves by their nationality without the term *American,* that is, Vietnamese not Vietnamese American. An exception are the Japanese Americans.[59]

While each nationality group is a distinct culture with its own language and traditions, there are some commonalities across most of these groups. All have experienced the need to adjust to the American culture while being physically distinct from the larger population. Most come from home cultures influenced by Confucianism. Confucianism emphasizes subordination of the son to the father, the younger to the elder, and the wife to the husband. It values conservatism and prescribes strict manners. Their base cultures have also typically placed a very strong value on traditional, extended families. Education, collective effort, and advancement are also highly valued.[60]

Consumer Groups

The Market Segment Research study identified three groups of Asian Americans on the basis of their demographics and attitudes that cut across nationality groups: traditionalist, established, and live for the moment.

FIGURE 5–3   National Background of Asian Americans

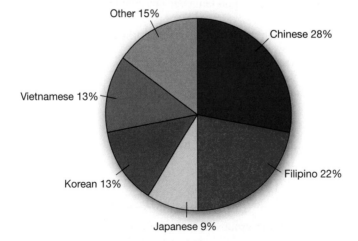

Traditionalist (49 percent)   This group has an average age of 41, but almost 40 percent are over 50. Seventy percent are married. Almost half are unemployed, but a large number of these are retired. They have relatively limited educations, with 50 percent having a high school diploma or less. Their average household size is small, with 3.1 members.

Traditionalists have a strong identification with their original culture. Almost half speak their native language exclusively, and three-fourths speak only their native language at home. They are not status conscious. They are not highly concerned with price or quality when shopping. While not concerned with financial security, they are also not optimistic about their financial future.

Established (27 percent)   This group's average age of 40 is almost the same as for the traditionalists, but only 22 percent are over 50. Eighty percent are married, and 60 percent are employed full-time. Seventy-three percent have at least some college, and over half have a college degree. Their average household has 4.1 members.

Individuals in this group have relatively weak identification with their native cultures. Only a fourth speak their native language exclusively, and less than half prefer native-language television programming.

This is a conservative, professional group. They are financially secure and optimistic about their financial futures. They are quality oriented and are willing to pay a premium for high quality.

Live for the Moment (24 percent)   This is the youngest of the three segments (average age = 35). Most (70 percent) are married, and half are employed full-time. Almost half have at least some college. Their average household size is 4.0.

This group has a moderate level of identification with their traditional cultures. About 30 percent speak their native language exclusively, though two-thirds do so at home. This is a spontaneous, materialistic group. They are impulsive shoppers and are concerned about status and quality. They are spenders rather than savers.

Marketing to Asian Americans

Rather than one culture and market, there are several Asian American markets, based primarily on nationality and language. Each of these in turn can be further segmented on degree of acculturation,[61] social class, generation, lifestyle, and other variables. Thus, while the number and average income of Asian Americans make them attractive to marketers, the diversity of languages and cultures has precluded major marketing efforts focused on them as a group.

There are, however, opportunities to market effectively to the nationality subgroups. These groups tend to be clustered in limited geographic regions (half of all Asian Americans live in just three states—California, New York, and Hawaii). Where there is a concentration of any of the nationality groups, there are native-language television and radio stations as well as newspapers.[62] Thus, targeted nationalities can be efficiently reached with native-language ads. For example, in San Francisco, KTSF presents a live one-hour newscast in Cantonese every weeknight. It covers both mainstream news and news of particular interest to the Chinese community. Many KTSF advertisers, such as McDonald's, dub their existing ads in Cantonese. Others, such as Colgate-Palmolive, run the ads they are using for the same products in Asia.

An important new communications channel has recently become available for these markets—direct broadcast satellite (DBS). While just under way, DBS providers have the potential to provide a means of reaching virtually all of the native-language speakers of

Marketing to Asian Americans involves more than translating ads into the appropriate languages. This promotion is based on the Lunar New Year, which is special to many Asian cultures.

Courtesy of Bank of America.

any of nationality nationwide. For example, EchoStar's Dish network offers a "Chinese Package" with three channels, and DirecTV has a Mandarin-language channel.

More than three-fourths of Asian American households are estimated to have personal computers in their homes, and most are connected to the Internet. Internet-based marketing to the Asian community is growing rapidly. Firms can reach Chinese consumers in their native language on Sinanet.com (see Illustration 5–6). Similar sites are gaining popularity among other Asian nationality groups, and firms such as Charles Schwab are using them as communications channels.

Marketing to the various Asian nationality groups should follow the same basic guidelines discussed earlier for Hispanics. Examine Illustration 5–7. It is bilingual and can communicate to Vietnamese with differing language preferences. More important, it is a special promotion based on the Lunar New Year that is meaningful to this group. It shows that Bank of America is doing more than just translating an ad used for the broader market but is focusing special attention on the Vietnamese market.

Other examples of successful marketing to Asian Americans include,

- A Los Angeles chain selected four outlets with large numbers of Chinese and Vietnamese customers. At the time of the Moon Festival (an important holiday in many Asian cultures), the store ran ads and distributed coupons for free moon cakes and lanterns. Sales increased by 30 percent in these stores during the promotion. Likewise, Sears advertises the Moon Festival in Mandarin, Cantonese, Vietnamese, or Korean, depending on the population near each outlet. It provides nationality-relevant gifts and entertainment such as traditional dances.

• The Filipino Channel mainly broadcasts time-shifted programs from Manila. Geffin Records recently tested the channel by advertising a single by Kia on "Flames," a program that appeals to young American Filipinos. It resulted in an instant and sharp sales increase.

NATIVE AMERICANS

The number of Native Americans (American Indians and Alaska Natives in U.S. Census terms) depends on the measurement used. The census reports three numbers for Native Americans: (1) one tribe only, (2) one tribe only or in combination with another tribe, and (3) number 2 plus in combination with any other race. The first definition produces an estimate of 2.5 million Native Americans; the total jumps to 4.1 million when the third definition is used. Nearly half live in the West, and 30 percent reside in the South. While many Native Americans live on or near reservations, others are dispersed throughout the country.

There are approximately 550 Native American tribes, each with its own language and traditions. Many of the tribes have reservations and quasi-independent political status. In general, Native Americans have limited incomes, but this varies widely by tribe. The overall buying power of this group is estimated to be more than $35 billion.[63] The larger tribes are

Tribes	One Tribe Only	Multiracial
Cherokee	281,000	730,000
Navajo	269,000	298,000
Sioux	109,000	153,000
Chippewa	106,000	150,000
Choctaw	87,000	159,000
Pueblo	60,000	74,000
Apache	57,000	97,000
Eskimo	46,000	55,000

In recent years, Native Americans have taken increased pride in their heritage and are less tolerant of inaccurate stereotypes of either their history or their current status. Thus, marketers using Native American names or portrayals must ensure accurate and appropriate use.

The larger tribes all have their own newspapers and radio stations. In addition, there are two national Indian-oriented newspapers and several national radio shows and magazines.[64]

Although each tribe is small relative to the total population, the geographic concentration of each tribe provides easy access for marketers. Sponsorship of tribal events and support for tribal colleges, training centers, and community centers can produce good results for firms that do so over time.

ASIAN-INDIAN AMERICANS

There are approximately 1.7 million Americans of Indian heritage (from India). This segment of the population is growing rapidly due to immigration. Asian-Indian Americans are concentrated in New York and California, with significant numbers in New Jersey, Illinois, and Texas as well. As a group, they are well educated, affluent, and fluent in English; yet most retain cultural ties to their Indian background.

Those unfamiliar with India often assume that it is a homogeneous country. However, in some ways it is more like Europe than America. It has 25 states, 7 union territories, 15 official languages, and dozens of other languages and dialects. Thus, while those who immigrate to America have much in common, they also have many differences based on their background in India.

While diverse in many ways, most share a number of important cultural traits:

- They place great value on education, particularly their children's education.
- They are concerned with financial security and save at a rate much higher than the average American.
- They do not have a "throw-away" mentality. They shop for value and look for quality and durability.
- Husbands tend to have a dominant role in family decisions.

Asian-Indian Americans attend to the general mass media. They can also be targeted via specialty magazines such as *Masal, Onwars, Hum,* and *India Abroad* and cable TV, radio stations, and newspapers in regions with significant populations. For example, Western Union advertises to this segment on Eye on Asia, a cable channel focused on this group. National reach is now possible through EchoStar's Dish Network's South Asia Package with five channels from India.

Long-term involvement in the Indian community is an effective way to gain support from this segment:

> Metropolitan Life was a major sponsor of a Navaratri, a religious festival that attracted 100,000 participants from around New York and New Jersey. As one participant said, "One of the chief executives of the company attended the festival, and the company took out a series of ads in the souvenir program. Now we feel we should reward the company for taking an interest in us."[65]

The Internet is also an effective way to market to these consumers. However, such an effort requires a sound knowledge of the community:

> It's December but Namaste.com's holiday rush has been over for two months. Christmas is not the big season for its customers. "To suggest gifting to Indians around Christmas time doesn't make sense. It's the wrong marketing message. Diwali [a festival of lights that happens in late October] is the Indian 'Christmas.'"[66]

ARAB AMERICANS

There are about 1 million Arab Americans in the United States. Perhaps no group in America has a more inaccurate stereotype. For example: What is the most common religion of Arab Americans? About half identify themselves as Christians, about half are Muslim, and a few are Jewish.

Arab Americans come from a variety of countries, including Morocco, Algeria, Egypt, Lebanon, Jordan, Saudi Arabia, and Kuwait. They share a common Arabic heritage and the Arabic language. Since World War II, many Arab immigrants have been business proprietors, landowners, or influential families fleeing political turmoil in their home countries. Many of these individuals attended Western or Westernized schools and were fluent in English before arriving.

Eighty-two percent of Arab Americans are U.S. citizens, and 63 percent were born in the United States. They are somewhat younger than the general population, better educated, and have a higher than average income. They are also much more likely to be entrepreneurs. A third of all Arab Americans live in California, New York, and Michigan.

Most Arab Americans are tired of negative stereotyping and misrepresentations about their culture. Even the film *Aladdin* contained insults and mistakes. Aladdin sings about the "barbaric" country from which he came. A guard threatened to cut off a young girl's hand for stealing food for a hungry child. Such an action would be contrary to Islamic law. The storefront signs in the mythical Arabic land had symbols that made no sense in Arabic or any other language. The aftermath of the attack on the World Trade Center has aroused some prejudice against these citizens as well as some enhanced knowledge of their backgrounds and beliefs.

The first rule in reaching this market is to treat its members with respect and accuracy. There are specialized newspapers, magazines, and radio and television stations focused on this market. EchoStar's Dish Network offers an Arabic-language package with six channels. Attention to the unique traditions of this community can pay large dividends.[67]

RELIGIOUS SUBCULTURES

As discussed in Chapter 3, America is basically a **secular society.** That is, the educational system, government, and political process are not controlled by a religious group, and most people's daily behaviors are not guided by strict religious guidelines. Nonetheless, more than 90 percent of all Americans claim a religious affiliation, 70 percent would like religious influence on American society to grow, more than 50 percent state that religion is very important in their lives, and approximately 40 percent claim to attend a religious service almost every week, a percent that hasn't changed much since 1940. Canada has a similar pattern. However, there is strong evidence that only about half of those who claim to attend religious services actually do so (this is known in research as a positive or normative response bias—giving socially appropriate answers to survey questions).[68]

The fact that the American culture is largely secular is not viewed as optimal by all of society. Many conservative Christians would prefer a society and legal system more in line with their faith. The intense debates over abortion, prayer in schools, the teaching of evolution versus creationism, homosexual rights, and a host of other issues are evidence of this division in American society.

Religion is important to, and directly influences the behaviors of, many Americans. This includes consuming religiously themed products[69] such as those sold by Deerlake (see Illustration 5–8) and avoiding the consumption of other products such as alcohol. The different religions in America prescribe differing values and behaviors. Thus, a number of **religious subcultures** exist in America.

Christian Subcultures

Much of the American value system and the resultant political and social institutions are derived from the Christian, and largely Protestant, beliefs of the early settlers. Although American culture is basically secular, many of its traditions and values are derived from the Judeo–Christian heritage of the majority of Americans. Most of the major American holidays, including Christmas, Easter, and Thanksgiving, have a religious base. However, except for Easter, the pure religious base of these holidays is no longer the central theme that it once was.

Although the United States is 90 percent Christian, Christianity takes many forms in this country, each with some unique beliefs and behaviors. Table 5–2 lists the major Christian

ILLUSTRATION 5–8

Because many Americans are religious, religiously themed products appeal to many.

TABLE 5–2

Demographic Differences across the Major Religious Subcultures in America

Religion	Percentage of U.S.	Employed Full-Time	College Graduates	Median Income ($000)	Own Home
Christian					
Roman Catholic	26.2%	54.3%	20.0%	$27.7	69.3%
Baptist	19.4	52.3	10.4	20.6	66.6
Methodist	8.0	49.6	21.1	25.1	75.2
Lutheran	5.2	50.0	18.0	25.9	76.5
"Christian"	4.5	51.8	16.0	20.7	63.7
Presbyterian	2.8	48.8	33.8	29.0	76.9
Pentecostal	1.8	52.8	06.9	19.4	60.8
Episcopalian	1.7	52.6	39.2	33.0	70.6
Mormon	1.4	49.9	19.2	25.7	74.0
Non-Christian					
Jewish	1.8	50.1	46.7	36.7	61.7
Muslim	0.5	62.5	30.4	24.7	43.3
Buddhist	0.4	59.4	33.4	28.5	50.6
Agnostic	0.7	63.5	36.3	33.3	59.7
No religion	7.5	60.5	23.6	27.3	60.6

Source: Seymour P. Lachman and Barry A. Kosmin, *One Nation Under God*. Copyright © 1993 by Seymour P. Lachman and Barry A. Kosmin. Reprinted by permission of Harmony Books, a division of Crown Publishers, Inc.

faiths as well as the other major religions in America. As the table shows, there are significant demographic differences across the various religions.

Roman Catholic Subculture   The Catholic church is highly structured and hierarchical. The pope is the central religious authority, and individual interpretation of scripture and events is minimal. A controversial tenet of the Catholic church is that the sole purpose of sex is for procreation. Therefore, the use of birth control devices is prohibited, though many Catholics deviate from this tenet. A result of this is a larger average family size for Catholics than for Protestants or Jews. The larger family size makes economic gains and upward social mobility more difficult. It also has a major influence on the types of products consumed by Catholics relative to many other religions.

More than 20 percent of Catholics are ethnic minorities—15 percent are Hispanic, 5 percent are African American, and 2 percent are Asian. Catholics are concentrated in the Northeast and in areas with large Hispanic populations.

Like Protestants, Catholics vary in their commitment and conservatism. The more conservative members share many values and behaviors with Protestant religious conservatives.

Catholics have few consumption restrictions or requirements associated with their religion. Marketers targeting this group can reach the more committed members through specialized magazines and radio programs. It is important for marketers to recognize that since one in four Americans is a Roman Catholic, they are part of almost all market segments. Marketing activities, particularly advertising, should be reviewed to avoid being disrespectful to Catholic ideas and practices. For example,

> The print ad shows a grinning man in a communion line with a bowl of onion dip that he intends to use with a communion wafer. This sparked an outcry from the Catholic League. "The blessed sacrament is something that Catholics believe is actually the body of Christ. To use it in an advertisement in and of itself is offensive and to use it in the way they were makes the insult even worse."[70]

Protestant Subcultures   Approximately 60 percent of all Americans identify themselves as Protestant. While there are many types of Protestant faiths with significant differences between them, most emphasize direct individual experience with God as a core tenet. In general, Protestant faiths emphasize individual responsibility and control. This focus has been credited with creating a strong work ethic, desire for scientific knowledge, a willingness to sacrifice for the future, and relatively small families. These characteristics in turn have created upward social mobility and produced the majority of the ruling elite in America.

Since almost two-thirds of Americans are Protestants, they are not generally considered a subculture. Rather, Protestant values and attitudes tend to define the core American culture. This is particularly true for white Protestants of Western European heritage—WASPs (white Anglo-Saxon Protestants). This group has historically dominated America in terms of numbers, wealth, and power, with power historically belonging to the male members of this group.

Although Protestants constitute the basic core culture of America, the diversity across and within denominations creates numerous subcultures within the larger group. Many of these religious groups have unique beliefs of direct relevance to marketers. These generally involve the consumption of products containing stimulates such as caffeine (prohibited by the Mormon Church) or alcohol (prohibited by the Southern Baptist church, among others). However, the basic distinction among Protestants, like the Catholics, is degree of conservatism in their religious beliefs. The majority of Protestants are middle of the road in terms of conservatism. This is consistent with America's dominant cultural values. However, a sizable minority are very conservative and, along with conservative Catholics, represent a significant subculture.

The Born-Again Christian Subculture   Born-again Christians have been referred to as the Christian Right, Religious Right, Conservative Christians, Evangelical Christians, and Fundamentalist Christians. **Born-again Christians** are *characterized by a strong belief in the literal truth of the Bible, a very strong commitment to their religious beliefs, having had a "born-again" experience, and encouraging others to believe in Jesus Christ.*

Born-again Christians tend to have somewhat lower education and income levels than the general population. They tend to have a more traditional gender role orientation. Born-again Christians are best known for their political stands on issues such as abortion, homosexual rights, and prayer in the schools.

Their beliefs also influence their consumption patterns. They generally oppose the use of alcohol and drugs. They do not consume movies or television programs that are overly focused on sex or other activities that they consider to be immoral. In fact, various groups of born-again Christians have organized boycotts against advertisers that sponsor shows they find inappropriate.

In contrast, they are very receptive to programs, books, and movies that depict traditional (i.e., Protestant) family (husband, wife, children) values. Firms with a reputation for supporting similar values would be well received by this segment. In contrast, Disney products have faced boycotts because of Disney's personnel policies, which extend some benefits to same-sex couples.

Non-Christian Subcultures

Jewish Subculture   Judaism is unique in that historically it has been an inseparable combination of ethnic and religious identity. Until recently, Jews in America tended to marry other Jews. Today, about 30 percent of all married Jews in America are married to a member of another faith.[71] Jews are heavily concentrated in the Northeast (44 percent, down from 63 percent in 1971) but are increasingly dispersing throughout the United States, particularly into the Sunbelt.[72] American Jews tend to have higher-than-average incomes and education levels. In most ways, Jewish consumption patterns are similar to those of other Americans with similar education and income levels.

Like other religious groups, the committed, conservative Jews represent a distinct subculture from mainstream Jews. Orthodox Jews have strict dietary rules that prohibit some foods such as pork and specify strict preparation requirements for other foods (see Illustration 5–9). They also strictly observe Jewish holidays, and many do not participate in even the secular aspects of the major Christian holiday, Christmas. Reformed Jews and Jews less committed to the strict interpretations of Judaism are less influenced by these practices.[73]

Muslim Subculture   It is important to recall from our earlier discussion that Muslims in America are not necessarily Arabs. Although the core of the 3 to 4 million Muslims in America are of Arabic heritage, many others are African Americans (about 25 percent) or are from Asian, Hispanic, or European backgrounds. Like the Protestants, there are a variety of Muslim sects with varying belief patterns, though all are based on the Koran. Like Protestants, Catholics, and Jews, the most obvious division among Muslims is the degree of conservatism and the importance attached to the literal teachings of the religion. As with the other religious groups in America, most Muslims' lives are centered on work, family, school, and the pursuit of success and happiness.

In general, Muslims tend to be conservative with respect to drug and alcohol use and sexual permissiveness. In fact, many oppose dating. They also place considerable emphasis on the family, with the eldest male as the head of the family, and on respect for elders. The more devout Muslims avoid not only pork products but also any foods that have not been prepared in accordance with the strict rules of Islam. The following quote from a devout Pakistani Muslim on why he does not eat in Western restaurants illustrates the stress this can cause:

Well, how can I be sure that the cook who has cooked pork or bacon in a pan did not cook my vegetables in the same pan? How can I be sure that even if he used different pans he washed his hands in between cooking bacon and a vegetable? I do not think there is any way I can get a pure food out there.[74]

Courtesy of Empire Kosher.

These beliefs conflict with the practices in the larger society and the images portrayed on television and in the movies and are also a source of conflict between older Muslims who immigrated to America and their children who were raised here.[75] Muslims in America have their own magazines, schools, social clubs, marriage services, and bookstores. There are more than 1,100 Muslim mosques and sanctuaries in America. In general, this subculture has not attracted the attention of marketers except as it overlaps with the Arab American subculture.

Buddhist Subculture   There are nearly as many Buddhists in America as there are Muslims. They are primarily Asian American or white. It is important to note that only about 5 percent of Asian Americans are Buddhists. Buddhists tend to be slightly above average in income and education, and they are concentrated in the West.

There are a variety of Buddhist sects in America. All emphasize the basic idea that all beings are caught in *samsara,* a cycle of suffering and rebirth that is basically caused by desire and actions that produce unfavorable *karma.* Samsara can be escaped and a state of *nirvana* reached by following the noble *Eightfold Path.* This combines ethical and disciplinary practices, training in concentration and meditation, and the development of enlightened wisdom.

Thus far, marketers have largely ignored this market. Its small size and diverse ethnic composition make it difficult to target. However, as specialized media evolve to serve Buddhists, opportunities will exist for astute marketers.

REGIONAL SUBCULTURES

Distinct **regional subcultures** arise as a result of climatic conditions, the natural environment and resources, the characteristics of the various immigrant groups that have settled in each region, and significant social and political events. These distinct subcultures present numerous opportunities and challenges for marketers. Examples include,

- Anheuser-Busch divided Texas into several regions and developed unique marketing programs for Budweiser in each. In the northern part of the state, it used a cowboy image; in the southern region, a Hispanic identity was stressed. Market share rose from 23 to 37 percent.
- Campbell Soup's original pork and beans did not sell well in the Southwest. In response, Campbell's removed the pork and added chili pepper and ranchero beans. Sales increased dramatically. A Campbell's subsidiary developed Zesty Pickles for the Northeast because consumers there prefer sourer pickles than do other Americans.
- Mercedes-Benz has half of its total advertising budget controlled by its four regional divisions. Chevrolet allocates 20 percent of its advertising budget to regional ads, some of which are targeted at the state level (Suburbans are advertised in Texas as the "national car of Texas"). Coca-Cola has developed specific ad campaigns for Texas and Minnesota. In addition, Coca-Cola bottlers conduct extensive local advertising campaigns.
- Frito-Lay potato chips are darker and oilier in the Northeast, lighter tasting and heavier textured in the Southeast. Its Pizza Hut unit allocates half its ad budget for local advertising.

TABLE 5–3		Northeast	North Central	South	West
Regional Consumption Differences*	**Media**				
	Elle	99	65	86	164
	Outdoor Life	69	126	115	71
	Ebony	88	81	155	42
	Gourmet	121	87	86	118
	Classic rock radio	103	129	85	91
	Country radio	55	110	131	80
	Hobbies/Activities				
	Hunting (with rifle)	80	118	118	69
	Tennis	116	91	78	130
	In-line skating	124	117	67	115
	Auto racing (attending)	82	115	103	94
	Product Use				
	Imported wine	144	88	96	80
	Domestic wine	118	91	86	116
	Candy (frequent)	83	105	107	99
	Laptop/notebook	92	88	92	134
	Restaurants/Shopping				
	Dominos	81	85	119	103
	Wal-Mart	74	106	119	86
	Eddie Bauer	94	155	67	101
	Banana Republic	145	55	77	144

*Note: 100 = Average consumption or usage.

Source: *Mediamark Reporter 2002—University* (New York: Mediamark Research Inc., March 2002).

- McDonald's Egg McMuffin was an instant success in most of the country but a disaster in the Southeast, where most people had never heard of eggs Benedict and English muffins were not commonly consumed. Only after the southeastern McDonald's franchisees developed a customized regional marketing strategy to explain the new product in a humorous way did the Egg McMuffin become a nationwide success.[76]

Although the most effective regional marketing strategies are often based on small geographic areas, we can observe significant consumption differences across much larger regions. Table 5–3 illustrates some of the consumption differences across the four U.S. census regions. Given such clear differences in consumption patterns, marketers are beginning to realize that, for at least some product categories, the United States is no more a single market than is the European Union (see Chapter 2). Since specialized (regional) marketing programs generally cost more than standardized (national) programs, marketers must balance potential sales increases against increased costs. This decision process is exactly the same as described in the section on multinational marketing decisions in Chapter 2.

SUMMARY

The United States is becoming increasingly diverse. Much of this diversity is fueled by immigration and an increase in ethnic pride and by identification with non-European heritages among numerous Americans. Most members of a culture share most of the core values, beliefs, and behaviors of that culture. However, most individuals also belong to several subcultures. A *subculture* is a segment of a larger culture whose members share distinguishing patterns of behavior. An array of ethnic, nationality, religious, and regional subcultures characterizes American society. The existence of these subcultures provides marketers with the opportunity to develop unique marketing programs to match the unique needs of each.

Ethnic subcultures are defined broadly as those whose members' unique shared behaviors are based on a common racial, language, or nationality background. Non-European ethnic groups constitute a significant and growing part of the U.S. population, from 24 percent in 1990 to 37 percent by 2020.

African Americans are tied with Hispanics as the largest non-European ethnic group, 13 percent of the U.S. population. While African Americans are, on average, younger and poorer than the general population, they are a large, diverse group with many segments.

Hispanics are predicted to surpass African Americans in numbers by 2010. While Hispanics have a variety of national backgrounds (Mexico, 66 percent; Puerto Rico, 9 percent; Cuba, 4 percent), the Spanish language, a common religion (Roman Catholic), and national Spanish-language media and entertainment figures have created a somewhat homogeneous Hispanic subculture.

Asian Americans are the most diverse of the major ethnic subcultures. They are characterized by a variety of nationalities, languages, and religions. From a marketing perspective, it is not appropriate to consider Asian Americans as a single group. Instead, Asian Americans are best approached as a number of nationality subcultures.

Native Americans, Asian-Indian Americans, and *Arab Americans* are smaller but important subcultures. Each is diverse yet shares enough common values and behaviors to be approached as a single segment for at least some products. Geographic concentration and specialized media allow targeted marketing campaigns.

Although the United States is a relatively secular society, 90 percent of all Americans claim a religious affiliation, and 40 percent claim to attend church regularly. Ninety-five percent of those with a religious affiliation are Christian; however, a variety of *religious subcultures* exist within both the Christian faiths and the Jewish, Muslim, and Buddhist faiths that several million other Americans embrace. Within each faith, the largest difference is the degree of conservatism between the members. Conservatism in this case refers to the extent to which the initial teachings of the faith are taken in their literal context as the only truth. The born-again

Christian movement is the most visible example of a subculture based on religion.

Regional subcultures arise as a result of climatic conditions, the natural environment and resources, the characteristics of the various immigrant groups that have settled in each region, and significant social and political events. Regional subcultures affect all aspects of consumption behavior, and sophisticated marketers recognize that the United States is composed of numerous regional markets.

KEY TERMS

Acculturation 164
Born-again Christians 177
Ethnic subcultures 155

Event marketing 162
Hispanic 162
Regional subcultures 180

Religious subcultures 175
Secular society 175
Subculture 152

INTERNET EXERCISES

1. Visit the U.S. Census website (www.census.gov). What data are available there on the following? Which of this is most useful to marketers? Why?
   a. Native Americans
   b. African Americans
   c. Hispanics
2. Use the Internet to determine the cities in the United States that have the largest population of the following. Why is this useful to marketers?
   a. Native Americans
   b. African Americans
   c. Hispanics
   d. Asian-Indian Americans
   e. Arab Americans
3. Identify and describe a website that provides useful information on the following.
   a. Roman Catholic subculture
   b. Protestant subcultures

   c. Jewish subculture
   d. Muslim subculture
   e. Buddhist subculture
4. Evaluate the Namaste.com site. Could this be adapted to the Native American market?
5. Find and evaluate a website targeting
   a. Roman Catholics
   b. Conservative Christians
   c. Jews
   d. Muslims
   e. Buddhists
6. Find and evaluate a website targeting
   a. Native Americans
   b. African Americans
   c. Hispanics
   d. Asian-Indian Americans
   e. Arab Americans

DDB NEEDHAM LIFESTYLE DATA ANALYSES

1. Which heavy-user consumption categories have the greatest differences across the ethnic subcultures? Why is this the case?
2. For which products does ownership differ the most across ethnic groups? Why is this the case?

3. For which television shows do preferences differ the most across the ethnic subcultures? Why is this the case?
4. Based on the DDB Needham data in Table 5a, which attitudes/interests/activities vary the most across the ethnic subcultures? Why is this the case?

REVIEW QUESTIONS

1. What is a *subculture?*
2. What determines the degree to which a subculture will influence an individual's behavior?
3. Is the American culture more like a soup or a salad?
4. What is an *ethnic subculture?*
5. How large are the major ethnic subcultures in America? Which are growing most rapidly?
6. What countries/regions are the major sources of America's immigrants?
7. Are the various ethnic subcultures homogeneous or heterogeneous?
8. Describe the income distribution of African Americans. What are the marketing implications of this distribution?
9. Describe the four African American consumer groups found by the Market Segment Research study.
10. What are the basic principles that should be followed in marketing to an African American market segment?
11. To what extent is the Spanish language used by American Hispanics?
12. Can Hispanics be treated as a single market?
13. How homogeneous are Asian Americans?
14. To what extent do Asian Americans use their native language?
15. Describe the three Asian American consumer groups identified by the Market Segment Research study.
16. Why is the United States considered to be a *secular society?*
17. Describe the *Roman Catholic subculture.*
18. Describe the *born-again Christian subculture.*
19. Describe the *Jewish subculture.*
20. Describe the *Muslim subculture.*
21. Describe the *Buddhist subculture.*
22. What is a regional subculture?

DISCUSSION QUESTIONS

23. Examine Table 5–1. Which of these differences are mainly caused by ethnicity or race and which are caused by other factors?
24. Do you agree that America is becoming more like a salad than a soup in terms of the integration of ethnic groups? Is this good or bad?
25. Do you agree with Miller Brewing that "the things that young Hispanic or young African American or young white people have in common are much stronger and more important than any ethnic difference"? For what types of products is this view most correct? Least correct?
26. Most new immigrants to America are non-European and have limited English-language skills. What opportunities does this present to marketers? Does this raise any ethical issues for marketers?
27. A significant number of African Americans live in inner cities or rural areas and have household incomes below the poverty level. What are the marketing implications of this fact? Does a firm's social responsibility play a role here? If so, what?
28. Respond to the questions in Consumer Insight 5–1.
29. Although many of the following have very limited incomes, others are quite prosperous. Does marketing to prosperous members of these groups require a marketing mix different from the one used to reach other prosperous consumers?
    a. African American
    b. Hispanic
    c. Asian American
30. Describe how each of the following firms' product managers should approach (*i*) the African American, (*ii*) the Hispanic, (*iii*) the Asian American, (*iv*) the Asian-Indian American, (*v*) the Arab American, or (*vi*) the Native American markets.
    a. Pepsi
    b. McDonald's
    c. NFL

d. *Maxim* magazine

e. Habitat for Humanity

f. Motorola cell phones

g. Amazon.com

h. Gillette razors

31. Describe how each of the following firms' product managers should approach each of the (*i*) African American or (*ii*) Asian American consumer groups identified by the Market Segment Research study.
    a. Pepsi
    b. McDonald's
    c. NFL
    d. *Maxim* magazine
    e. Habitat for Humanity
    f. Motorola cell phones
    g. Amazon.com
    h. Gillette razors

32. What, if any, unique ethical responsibilities exist when marketing to ethnic subcultures?

33. Do you agree that the United States is a secular society? Why or why not?

34. Describe how each of the following firms' product managers should approach the (*i*) Catholic,

(*ii*) Christian, (*iii*) born-again Christian, (*iv*) Jewish, (*v*) Muslim, and (*vi*) Buddhist subcultures.

a. Pepsi

b. McDonald's

c. NFL

d. *Maxim* magazine

e. Habitat for Humanity

f. Motorola cell phones

g. Amazon.com

h. Gillette razors

35. Will regional subcultures become more or less distinct over the next 20 years? Why?

36. Select one product, service, or activity from each category in Table 5–3 and explain the differences in consumption for the item across the regions shown.

37. Why does the consumption of laptop/notebook computers differ across regions? Are regions a better explanation for laptop/notebook use than the demographic factors identified in Chapter 4 (see Tables 4–1, 4–2, and 4–3)?

APPLICATION ACTIVITIES

38. Watch two hours of prime-time major network (ABC, CBS, FOX, or NBC) television. What subculture groups are portrayed in the programs? Describe how they are portrayed. Do these portrayals match the descriptions in this text? How would you explain the differences? Repeat these tasks for the ads shown during the programs.

39. Pick a product of interest and examine the Simmons Market Research Bureau or MediaMark studies on the product in your library (these are often in the journalism library on CD-ROM). Determine the extent to which its consumption varies by ethnic group and region. Does consumption also vary by age, income, or other variables? Are the differences in ethnic and regional consumption due primarily to ethnicity and region or to the fact that the ethnic group or region is older, richer, or otherwise different from the larger culture?

40. Examine several magazines or newspapers aimed at a non-European ethnic or nationality group. What types of products are advertised? Why?

41. Interview three members of the following subcultures and ascertain their opinions of how their ethnic or nationality group is portrayed on network television shows and in national ads.
    a. African Americans
    b. Asian Americans
    c. Hispanics
    d. Arab Americans
    e. Asian-Indian Americans
    f. Native Americans

42. Interview three members of the following subcultures and ascertain the extent to which they identify with the core American culture, their ethnic subculture within America, or their nationality subculture. Also determine the extent

to which they feel others of their ethnic/race group feel as they do and the reasons for any differences.
a. African Americans
b. Asian Americans
c. Hispanics
d. Arab Americans
e. Asian-Indian Americans
f. Native Americans

43. Interview three members of the following subcultures and determine the extent to which their consumption patterns are influenced by their religion.

a. Catholics
b. Mainstream or moderate Christians
c. Born-again Christians
d. Jews
e. Muslims
f. Buddhists

44. Interview two students from other regions of the United States and determine the behavior and attitudinal differences they have noticed between their home and your present location. Try to determine the causes of these differences.

REFERENCES

1. C. P. Taylor, "Girl Scouts Extend Multicultural Reach," *Advertising Age,* January 28, 2002, p. 18.
2. See R. Suro, "Recasting the Melting Pot," *American Demographics,* March 1999, pp. 30–32.
3. For conflicting data, see S. Reese, "When Whites Aren't a Mass Market," *American Demographics,* March 1997, pp. 51–54.
4. L. Wentz, "Reverse English," *Advertising Age,* November 19, 2001, p. S1. See also R. Suro, "Recasting the Melting Pot," *American Demographics,* March 1999, pp. 30–33.
5. M. G. Briones, "Coors Turns Up the Heat," *Marketing News,* June 22, 1998, p. 15.
6. See R. Suro, "Mixed Doubles," *American Demographics,* November 1999, pp. 57–62.
7. C. Fisher, "It's All in the Details," *American Demographics,* April 1998, p. 45.
8. A. S. Wellner and J. Fette, "Technical Difficulties," *American Demographics,* May 2001, pp. 24–25.
9. W. H. Frey, "Micro Melting Pots," *American Demographics,* June 2001, pp. 20–23.
10. *Legal Immigration, Fiscal 1997* (Washington DC: U.S. Department of Justice, January 1999), p. 9.
11. See L. R. Oswald, "Culture Swapping," *Journal of Consumer Research,* March 1999, pp. 303–18.
12. M. R. Forehand and R. Deshpande, "What We See Makes Us Who We Are," *Journal of Marketing Research,* August 2001, pp. 336–48.
13. *Statistical Abstract of the United States 2001* (Washington, DC: U.S. Census Bureau, 2001).
14. J. Holland and J. W. Gentry, "Ethnic Consumer Reaction to Targeted Marketing," *Journal of Advertising,* Spring 1999, pp. 65–76.
15. T. McCarroll, "It's a Mass Market No More," *Time,* Fall 1993, p. 80.
16. M. L. Rossman, *Multicultural Marketing* (New York: American Management Association, 1994), pp. 153–57.
17. E. Morris, "The Difference in Black and White," *American Demographics,* January 1993, p. 46.
18. J. M. Humphreys, "Minority Buying Power," *Marketing News,* July 2, 2001, p. 17.
19. J. Raymond, "The Multicultural Report," *American Demographics,* November 2001, pp. 53–54.
20. For example, see B. E. Bryant and J. Cha, "Crossing the Threshold," *Marketing Research,* Winter 1996, pp. 21–28.
21. *The 1993 Minority Market Report* (Coral Gables, FL: Market Segment Research, Inc., 1993).
22. See A. S. Wellner, "The Forgotten Baby Boom," *American Demographics,* February 2001, pp. 47–51.
23. Y. K. Kim and J. Kang, "The Effects of Ethnicity and Product on Purchase Decision Making," *Journal of Advertising Research,* March 2001, pp. 39–48.
24. *Mediamark Reporter 2002—University* (New York: Mediamark Research Inc., March 2002).
25. G. Berman, *Portrait of the New America* (Coral Gables, FL: The Market Segment Group, 2002), p. 13.
26. J. Halliday, "General Motors Links with BlackVoices.com," *Advertising Age,* October 9, 2000, p. 50.
27. J. Hodges, "Black, White Teens Show Similarity in TV Tastes," *Advertising Age,* May 13, 1996, p. 24.
28. H. Schlossberg, "Many Marketers Still Consider Blacks 'Dark-Skinned' Whites," *Marketing News,* January 19, 1993, p. 1.
29. E. M. Simpson et al., "Race, Homophily, and Purchase Intentions and the Black Consumer," *Psychology & Marketing,* October 2000, pp. 877–99. See also L. A. Perkins, K. M. Thomas, and G. A. Taylor, "Advertising and Recruitment," *Psychology & Marketing,* March 2000, pp. 235–55.

30. C. L. Green, "Ethnic Evaluations of Advertising," *Journal of Advertising,* Spring 1999, pp. 49–63; and O. Appiah, "Ethnic Identification on Adolescents' Evaluations of Advertisements," *Journal of Advertising Research,* September 2001, pp. 7–21.

31. C. Fisher, "Black, Hip and Primed to Shop," *American Demographics,* September 1996, p. 56. See also K. P. Marshall and J. R. Smith, "Race-Ethnic Variations in the Importance of Service Quality Issues," *Journal of Professional Services Marketing* 18, no. 2 (1999), pp. 119–31.

32. T. L. Ainscough and C. M. Motley, "Will You Help Me Please?" *Marketing Letters,* May 2000, pp. 129–36.

33. S. F. Philipp, "Are We Welcome," *Journal of Leisure Research* 31, no. 4 (1999), pp. 385–403.

34. See V. D. Bush et al., "Managing Culturally Diverse Buyer–Seller Relationships," *Journal of the Academy of Marketing Science,* Fall 2001, pp. 391–404.

35. M. F. Floyd and K. J. Shinew, "Convergence in Leisure Style and Whites and African Americans," *Journal of Leisure Research* 31, no. 4 (1999), pp. 359–84.

36. N. Delener, "Consumer Payment System Attribute Perceptions and Preferences," *Journal of Professional Services Marketing,* no. 1 (1995), pp. 53–71; and F. J. Mulhern, J. D. Williams, and R. P. Leone, "Variability of Brand Price Eslasticities across Retail Stores," *Journal of Retailing,* no. 3 (1998), pp. 427–45.

37. See Wentz, "Reverse English," p. 1.

38. "No 43. Native and Foreign-Born Populations," *Statistical Abstract of the United States: 2001* (Washington, DC: U.S. Census Bureau, 2001), p. 44.

39. Based on R. X. Weissman, "Los Ninos Go Shopping," *American Demographics,* May 1999, pp. 37–39; H. Stapinski, "Generacion Latino," *American Demographics,* July 1999, pp. 63–68; R. Gardyn, "Habla English," *American Demographics,* April 2001, pp. 54–57; J. D. Zbar, "Hispanic Teens Set Urban Beat," *Advertising Age,* p. S6; and H. Chura, "Sweet Spot," *Advertising Age,* November 12, 2001, p. 1.

40. R. Gardyn, "Habla English," *American Demographics,* April 2001, p. 57.

41. An excellent description of this process for Mexican immigrants appears in L. Penaloza, "*Atravesando Fronteras*/Border Crossings," *Journal of Consumer Research,* June 1994, pp. 32–54.

42. *The 1993 Minority Market Report,* pp. 41–43.

43. Berman, *Portrait of the New America,* p. 21.

44. C. Webster, "The Effects of Hispanic Identification on Marital Roles in the Purchase Decision Process," *Journal of Consumer Research,* September 1994, pp. 319–31.

45. L. Kramer, "Church's Chicken Chain Courts Latino Audience," *Advertising Age,* October 19, 1998, p. 12.

46. R. Maso-Fleischman, "Archetype Research for Advertising," *Journal of Advertising Research,* October 1997, pp. 81–84.

47. Humphreys, "Minority Buying Power."

48. S. Livingston, "Marketing to the Hispanic-American Community," *Journal of Business Strategy,* March 1992, pp. 54–57.

49. C. P. Taylor, "BarbieLatina Says 'Hola' to Net," *Advertising Age,* October 1, 2001, p. 54.

50. Ibid.

51. "Marketing to Hispanics," *Advertising Age,* February 8, 1987, p. S23; and M. Westerman, "Death of the Frito Bandito," March 1989, pp. 28–32.

52. See Gardyn, "Habla English."

53. K. Morral, "Connecting with the Hispanic Market," *Bank Marketing,* June 1996, pp. 43–48.

54. L. Giegoldt, "Brand Loyalty Opportunities Abound," *Advertising Age,* August 24, 1998, p. S10. See also S. Shim and K. C. Gehrt, "Hispanic and Native American Adolescents," *Journal of Retailing,* no. 3 (1996), pp. 307–24.

55. A. S. Wellner, "Gen X Homes In," *American Demographics,* August 1999, p. 61.

56. M. Johnson, "The Application of Geodemographics to Retailing," *Journal of the Market Research Society,* January 1997, p. 213.

57. J. D. Zbar, "Latinization Catches Retailers' Ears," *Advertising Age,* November 16, 1998, p. S22.

58. See B. Edmundson, "Asian Americans in 2001," *American Demographics,* February 1997, pp. 16–17.

59. M. C. Tharp, *Marketing and Consumer Identity in Multicultural America* (Thousand Oaks, CA: Sage Publications, 2001), p. 259.

60. Ibid., pp. 253–57.

61. S. F. Ownby and P. E. Horridge, "Acculturation Level and Shopping Orientations of Asian American Consumers," *Psychology & Marketing,* January 1997, pp. 1–18; D. D'Rozario and S. P. Douglas, "Effects of Assimilation on Prepurchase External Information-Search Tendencies," *Journal of Consumer Psychology* 8, no. 2 (1999), pp. 187–209; and Y.-K. Kim and J. Kang, "Effects of Asian-Americans' Ethnicity and Acculturation on Personal Influences," *Journal of Current Issues and Research in Advertising,* Spring 2001, pp. 43–53.

62. See P. Paul, "Mediachannels," *American Demographics,* November 2001, pp. 26–31.

63. See Humphreys, "Minority Buying Power."

64. See A. S. Wellner, "Discovering Native America," *American Demographics,* August 2001, p. 21.

65. This section was based on M. Mogelonsky, "Asian Indian Americans," *American Demographics,* August 1995, pp. 32–39.

66. A. S. Wellner, "Every Day's a Holliday," *American Demographics,* December 2000, p. 63.

67. This section was based on S. El-Badry, "The Arab-American Market," *American Demographics,* January 1994, pp. 22–30.

68. B. A. Robinson, "How Many People Go Regularly to Weekly Religious Services?" Ontario Consultants on Religious Tolerance, www.religioustolerance.org, November 26, 2001; and *For Goodness Sakes,* Public Agenda,

www.publicagenda.org, 2001. See also B. A. Kosmin and
S. P. Lachman, *One Nation Under God* (New York: Harmony
Books, 1993), pp. 88–93; G. E. Witt, "Women Show Their
Spiritual Side," *American Demographics,* April 1999, p. 23;
R. Gardyn and J. Fetto, "Somebody Say Amen," *American
Demographics,* April 2000, p. 72; A. S. Wellner, "Oh Come
All Ye Faithful," *American Demographics,* June 2001,
pp. 50–55; and P. Paul, "A Holier Holier Holiday Season,"
American Demographics, pp. 41–45.

69. See R. Cimino and D. Lattin, "Choosing My Religion,"
American Demographics, April 1999, pp. 6–65.

70. J. Neff, "Dip Ad Stirs Church Ire," *Advertising Age,* July 2,
2001, p. 8.

71. Kosmin and Lachman, *One Nation Under God,* p. 245.

72. R. Thau, "The New Jewish Exodus," *American Demographics,*
June 1994, p. 11.

73. Kosmin and Lachman, *One Nation Under God,* p. 12.

74. M. Chapman and A. Jamal, "The Floodgates Open," *Enhancing
Knowledge Development in Marketing* (Chicago: American
Marketing Association, 1996), p. 198.

75. See S. El-Badry, "Understanding Islam in America," *American
Demographics,* January 1994, p. 10.

76. S. L. Hapoienu, "The Rise of Micromarketing," *Journal of
Business Strategy,* November–December 1990, p. 3.

The American Society: Families and Households

☐ Americans spend approximately $150 billion a year on babies and children. For infants, the marketing task is relatively clear: parents and grandparents are the key decision makers and buyers. One study reached the following conclusions:

- Gifts are a significant part of the market.
- New mothers look to other mothers in deciding what to buy.
- Mothers want a special look for their baby that is different from other kids.
- Collections and coordination are not critical.
- Comfort is important, durability less so.
- Practical features such as ease of dressing are very important.
- Price/value is important, as the baby quickly outgrows the clothing.

However, by age two, children begin to influence the purchase of items bought for them. By six, many are insisting on "cool" clothes, foods, and other items. By their early teens, they may play the dominant role in purchasing electronics and computers for the household.

☐ Marketers are increasingly pursuing this market. However, it is not easy. Both children and parents must be satisfied. Eddie Bauer tested a line of children's clothes in its catalogs and stores. The clothes were basically downsized versions of its adult lines. Several years after this experiment failed, Eddie Bauer reentered the market with "cooler" styles for kids and an eddiebauer.com Internet site. The site was marketed in the *Disney* magazine, *Family PC, Family Fun,* and *Working Mother* as well as in Eddie Bauer stores and catalogs. However, a visit to that site today connects you to Eddie Bauer's main home page. It is difficult to become cool with kids.

☐ In contrast, the Nautica Kids line is doing well as are many others that target this group. Limited Too targets 7- to 14-year-old girls. It sells through both an Internet site and a rapidly expanding set of retail stores. Rave Girl, targeting

tweens, is also growing rapidly. Abercrombie & Fitch is quickly expanding its line of stores focused on 7- to 16-year-olds. Wal-Mart recently launched a line of fashionable clothing for 6- to 14-year-old girls under the Mary-Kate and Ashley Olsen brands.

☐ Jell-O has shifted focus from marketing primarily to mothers to reaching kids directly. It launched X-treme Jell-O in flavors such as Green Apple, Watermelon, Blue Raspberry, and Tangerine to appeal to this market. A spokesperson said, "X-treme Jell-O gelatin is a logical next step for us—particularly when kids are so interested in dialed up tastes, flavors, and colors."[1]

How do eight-year-olds acquire X-treme Jell-O? They might buy it at a store with their own money, they may request a parent to buy it for them, or a parent might buy it without a request. Most of the time, such a purchase will involve more than just the child. Even if the child has the money for the purchase, the parent might prohibit it. Such purchases are made in the context of a family or household.

The household is the basic consumption unit for most consumer goods. Major items such as housing, automobiles, and appliances are consumed more by household units than by individuals. Furthermore, the consumption patterns of individual household members seldom are independent from those of other household members. For example, deciding to grant a child's request for a bicycle may mean spending discretionary funds that could have been used to purchase a weekend away for the parents, new clothing for a sister or brother, or otherwise used by another member of the household. Therefore, it is essential that marketers understand the household as a consumption unit, as shown in Figure 6–1.

Households are important not only for their direct role in the consumption process but also for the critical role they perform in socializing children. The family household is the primary mechanism whereby cultural and subcultural values and behavior patterns are passed on to the next generation. Purchasing and consumption patterns are among those attitudes and skills strongly influenced by the family household unit.

This chapter examines (1) the nature and importance of families and households in contemporary American society, (2) the household life cycle, (3) the nature of the family decision process, and (4) consumer socialization.

| FIGURE 6–1 | The Household Influences Most Consumption Decisions |

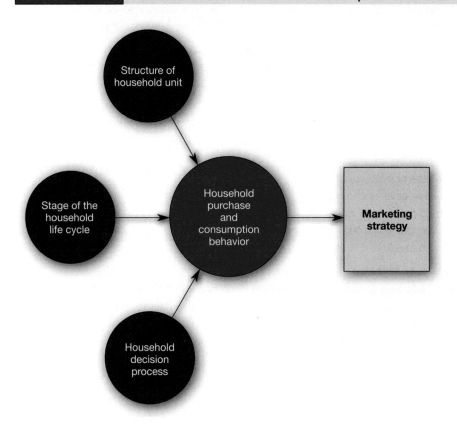

THE NATURE OF AMERICAN HOUSEHOLDS

Types of Households

There are a variety of types of households. The Census Bureau defines a **household** as *all the people who occupy a housing unit* (a house, apartment, group of rooms, or single room designed to be occupied as a separate living quarters). It defines a **family** as *a group of two people or more (one of whom is the householder) related by birth, marriage, or adoption and residing together.* A **family household** is defined as a *household consisting of a family and any unrelated people residing in the same housing unit.* A **nonfamily household** is a *householder living alone or exclusively with others to whom he or she is not related.* Table 6–1 indicates the current distribution of household types in the United States.

These definitions are important because the Census Bureau, which provides most of the available data on households, uses them. Unfortunately, these terms do not cover the richness of the American family structure. The **blended family**—*a family consisting of a couple, one or both of whom were previously married, their children, and the children from the previous marriage of one or both parents*—is one missing form.[2] While more than 40% of first marriages end in divorce, most of these divorced individuals remarry.[3] Thus, a significant percentage of American children grow up with stepparents and stepsiblings. Many

There are 8.5 million unmarried, opposite-sex households in the United States.[4] This number is forecast to grow rapidly. For some, cohabitation is a temporary arrangement before marriage; for others, it represents a long-term relationship:

> Our relationship has lasted longer than those of any of our friends near our own age—married or not. We are actually looked up to as a model couple. I don't want to mess with what works.

Unmarried couples increasingly resemble the general population. Forty-five percent are 35 or older, and less than 20 percent are under 25. A third have one or more children under the age of 15 living with them. As one real estate agent that serves this market said,

> It used to be that unmarrieds were on the fringe— they were hippies, poor, or gay—and they didn't accumulate a lot of property. Now my clients are anything from 70-year-olds who choose not to remarry because they don't want to lose Medicare benefits, to young, highly successful professionals

who want to keep their independence and yet own a business and two homes with their partner.

In many ways, the needs of unmarried couples are the same as those of married couples with similar demographics. However, there are exceptions, such as finding knowledgeable assistance with legal and financial issues concerning joint home ownership, estate planning, and so forth.

When Dorain and Marshall—both twentysomething and cohabiting for eight years—applied for joint tenants insurance, they were told by a local agent that their only choice was to apply for individual policies at almost twice the cost. They eventually found an agency catering to the gay and lesbian community that signed them up for joint tenants and auto insurance with no problem. In fact, many heterosexual couples turn to gay professionals who are better equipped to navigate the complex legal and financial issues that unmarried couples often face.

of these children spend significant time in two such families, one formed by their mother and the other by their father.

The term **traditional family** refers to *a married couple and their own or adopted children living at home*. Much publicity has been given to its demise and this type of family has clearly declined over time. This is particularly true if one were to consider a traditional

TABLE 6–1	2000		
	Type of Household	*Number (000)*	*Percentage*
Family and Nonfamily Households	**All households**	104,705	100.0%
	Family households	72,025	68.8
	Married couples	55,311	52.8
	Children under 18 at home	26,392	25.2
	No children under 18 at home	28,919	27.6
	Single father	2,202	2.1
	Single mothers	8,762	8.4
	Other families	5,750	5.5
	Nonfamily households	32,680	31.2
	Male householder	14,641	14.0
	Female householder	16,278	15.5

Source: *America's Families and Living Arrangements* (Washington, DC: U.S. Census Bureau, June 2001), p. 2.

One reason marketers rarely target unmarried couples is that they are not easy to identify or reach. There are no media dedicated to this audience, and they are not demographically unique. Another reason is that cohabitation is not fully accepted:

Companies that might benefit from targeting this group—banks, lawyers, and so forth—don't want to be viewed as doing anything that undermines marriage because they could be viewed as promoting an uncommitted lifestyle.

Most unmarried couples realize and deal with the difficulties and prejudices associated with their status. However, they would also like some recognition that they matter:

It would be so refreshing to see an ad occasionally that feels like it represents my life. I'd love to hear companies say they realize "It's not the ring that matters," or "We know that families today come in all shapes and sizes."

Hallmark Cards is one firm that has responded. It recently launched a "Ties That Bind" line of greeting cards aimed at nontraditional families, including unmarried partnerships:

Our cards reflect the times. Relationships today are so nebulous that they are hard to pin down, but in creating products, we have to be aware that they are there. Companies need to respect and be sensitive to how people are truly living their lives now, and not how they might wish or hope for them to live.

Critical Thinking Questions
1. Do you agree that unmarried couples will become increasingly more common?
2. What needs do unmarried couples have that demographically similar married couples do not have?
3. Should firms such as banks develop and advertise products to meet the unique needs of this group?

family to be one headed by a never-divorced couple. However, most households (53%) are headed by married couples (this has declined from 71% in 1970) and more than 70% of households with children are headed by a married couple. The decline in traditional families is due in part to an increase in single parent households as a result of divorce. A larger cause is a significant increase in single individuals. This increase has been largely a result of the overall delay in the median age of marriage—from 23.2 and 20.8 years for males and females in 1970 to 26.8 and 25.1 in 2000—and by an increase in sole survivors as the percent of the population over 65 has grown significantly.

Other common household structures are also not adequately captured by Census reports or other major data sources such as Mediamark, Simmons, or Nielsen. Unmarried couples, both same sex and opposite sex, have consumption patterns similar to married couples but are not counted as families by the Census. Consumer Insight 6–1 describes some of the marketing issues and opportunities these consumers create.

Kraft recognizes the diversity and importance of families in its campaign featuring brief, unscripted videos of actual families interacting around food. One spot features an apparently single mother shopping with her teenage sons, another features a traditional family of seven, while a third portrays an extended family get-together. At the end of the family get-together commercial, the grandmother says: "Everyone needs to connect as a family. Just a simple thing such as making dinner. Everybody gets a little bit of attention—which I don't mind giving. I like that." Illustration 6–1 contains a television ad that shows how Merita bread can be used to create the favorite sandwiches of various family members.

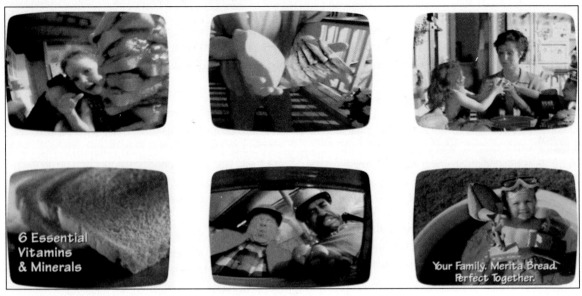

Courtesy Interstate Bakeries Corporation.

THE HOUSEHOLD LIFE CYCLE

The traditional view of the American household life cycle was quite simple. People married by their early 20s (in 1960, the median age was 20.3 for women and 22.8 for men); they had several children; these children grew up and started their own families; the original couple retired; and the male would eventually die, followed after a few years by the female. This was known as the *family life cycle,* and it was a useful tool for segmenting markets and developing marketing strategy. The basic assumption underlying the family life cycle approach is that most families pass through an orderly progression of stages, each with its own characteristics, financial situation, and purchasing patterns.

However, as described earlier, American households follow much more complex and varied cycles today. Therefore, researchers have developed several models of the **household life cycle (HLC).**[5] All are based on the age and marital status of the adult members of the household and the presence and age of children. A useful version is shown in Figure 6–2.

The HLC assumes that households move into a variety of relatively distinct and well-defined categories over time. There are a variety of routes into most of the categories shown in Figure 6–2, and movement from one category into another frequently occurs. For example, it is common for singles to marry and then divorce within a few years without having children (move from single to young married back to young single). Or one can become a single parent through divorce or through birth or adoption without a cohabiting partner.

Each category in the household life cycle poses a set of problems that household decision makers must solve. The solution to these problems is bound intimately to the selection and maintenance of a lifestyle and, thus, to consumption. For example, all young couples with no children face a need for relaxation or recreation. Solutions to this common problem differ. Some couples opt for an outdoors-oriented lifestyle and consume camping equipment and related products. Others choose a sophisticated urban lifestyle and consume

FIGURE 6–2	Stages of the Household Life Cycle

Stage	Marital Status		Children at Home		
	Single	Married	None	< 6 years	> 6 years
Younger (< 35)					
Single I	×		×		
Young married		×	×		
Full nest I		×		×	
Single parent I	×			×	
Middle-aged (35–64)					
Single II	×		×		
Delayed full nest I		×		×	
Full nest II		×			×
Single parent II	×				×
Empty nest I		×	×		
Older (> 64)					
Empty nest II		×	×		
Single III	×		×		

tickets to the theater and opera, restaurant meals, and so forth. As these families move into another stage in the HLC such as the "full nest I" stage, the problems they face change. The amount of time and resources available for recreation usually diminishes. New problems related to raising a child become more urgent.

Each stage presents unique needs and wants as well as financial conditions and experiences. Thus, the HLC provides marketers with relatively homogeneous household segments that share similar needs with respect to household-related problems and purchases.

While Figure 6–2 categorizes households into married and unmarried, it is "coupleness" rather than the legal status of the relationship that drives most of the behavior of the household. Committed couples, same sex or opposite sex, tend to exhibit most of the category specific behaviors described below whether or not they are married.

Single I   This group consists of young (under 35), unmarried individuals. It is basically the unmarried members of Generation X, as described in Chapter 4. During this time, individuals generally leave home and establish their own distinct identities. It is a time of growth and change, both exciting and positive and frightening and painful. As one thirty-something said,

> I wouldn't go through my 20s again for all the money in the world. You are out of undergraduate school and it's like, "What's expected of me?" You still haven't come to know yourself, and it's like that there is this gigantic world out there and you must somehow get all the experiences you can under your belt before you can get to know yourself. So you try on a lot of labels and I guess that somehow you think that that assemblage is you, when it isn't.[6]

This group can be subdivided into those who live with one or both parents and those who live alone or with other individuals. The 40.4 million single individuals in this age

Ad courtesy of Club Med a Publicis US.

range live as follows:

	Males	*Females*	*Total*
Live alone	13%	11%	12%
Live with parent(s)	46	35	41
Live with others	41	54	47

Those who live with parents tend to be younger; 80 percent are less than 25. A significant number are in school or have recently graduated from high school or college and are beginning their working careers. Though people in this group have low incomes, they also have few fixed expenses. They lead active, social lifes. They go to bars, movies, and concerts, and purchase sports equipment, clothes, and personal care items.

Although some of those who live with others are involved with a partner, most share quarters with one or more housemates. This arrangement is more common with females than males and is slightly more common among older members. These individuals have more fixed living expenses than do those who live with their parents, but they generally have ample disposable income as they share rent and other fixed housing costs.

These singles are a good market for the same types of products as those who live at home as well as for convenience-oriented household products. They are also a prime market for nice apartments, sports cars, Club Med vacations, and similar activities. They are beginning to develop financial portfolios such as life insurance, savings, and stocks or mutual funds. The ad shown in Illustration 6–2 would appeal to both groups.

haven't thought about work at all today.
haven't made the bed once this week.
haven't felt this close in years.

who are they sleeping with?

WESTIN
HOTELS & RESORTS®

Realign your priorities at a Westin resort.
Make time for doing nothing.
Make twilight an official holiday.
Make love often.

Choose your travel partner wisely.®

For reservations at over 100 hotels and resorts worldwide
call your travel agent or
1-800-WESTIN-1
www.westin.com

Courtesy Starwood Hotels & Resorts.

ILLUSTRATION 6–3

This ad positions Westin Hotels and Resorts as an ideal place for couples to escape the pressures of a hectic work schedule for relaxation and romance.

Singles who live alone are older; 75 percent are over 25. In general they have higher incomes than the others but also have much higher expenses as they have no one with whom to share the fixed cost of a house or apartment. They are a good market for most of the same products and services as the other singles.

Young Couples: No Children   The decision to marry, or to live together, brings about a new stage in the household life cycle. The lifestyles of two young singles are greatly altered as they develop a shared lifestyle. Joint decisions and shared roles in household responsibilities are in many instances new experiences.[7] Savings, household furnishings, major appliances, and more comprehensive insurance coverage are among the new areas of problem recognition and decision making to which a young married couple must give serious consideration.

Like the young single stage, the time spent by a young couple in this stage of the HLC has grown as couples either delay their start in having children or choose to remain childless.

Most households in this group have dual incomes and thus are relatively affluent. Compared to full nest I families, this group spends heavily on theater tickets, expensive clothes, luxury vacations, restaurant meals (more than half their food expenditures are for restaurant and takeout meals), and alcoholic beverages. They can afford nice cars, stylish apartments, and high-quality home appliances.

Illustration 6–3 contains an ad that would appeal to this group as well as to some members of the single I and full nest I segments. Note that romance plays a major role in the ad. It also plays on the desire to escape worries and everyday responsibilities.

Full Nest I: Young Married with Children   Slightly more than 7 percent of households are young married couples with children. The addition of the first child to a family creates many changes in lifestyle and consumption. Naturally, new purchases in the areas of baby clothes, furniture, food, and health care products occur in this stage. Lifestyles are also greatly altered. The wife typically withdraws fully or partly from the labor force (in less than 60 percent of married couples with a child under three does the wife work outside the home) for several months to several years, with a resulting decline in household income. The couple may have to move to another place of residence since their current apartment may not be appropriate for children. Likewise, choices of vacations, restaurants, and automobiles must be changed to accommodate young children.

Some of the changes in income and annual expenditures that occur as a household moves from childless to the young child stage include the following (based on no child versus one child for 25- to 35-year-old couples):[8]

Expenditure	Percentage Change
Income	−9.3%
Food at home	11.8
Meals out	−34.7
Alcoholic beverages	−43.4
Adult apparel	−28.4
Health care	7.9
Pets, toys	23.0
Education	−48.1
Personal care products	−8.5

As shown above, discretionary and adult expenditures are reduced by the need to spend on child-related products such as food, health care, and toys as well as to offset the decline in income.

Obtaining competent child care becomes an issue at this or the single parent I stage. It remains a major concern of parents at all stages of the household life cycle. Households with a stay-at-home spouse confront this issue mainly for evenings out or weekends away. Single-parent and dual-earner households generally require daily child care. This often requires stressful trade-offs:

> Sure, like everyone I wanted a place that was reasonable, convenient, stimulating, full of warmth and caring, and also safe. I wanted care provided by trained, competent, and loving caregivers, just like I would, but finding such care is impossible. So what do I do? I get realistic, have fewer expectations, and become extra vigilant. I know I can't have it all.[9]

Illustration 6–4 contains an ad aimed at this market segment. It shows how the choice of recreational activities may change with the addition of young children. Another example of marketing to this group is done by Cox Direct, which mails packets of discount coupons to parents of new babies (a program called "Just Delivered") and to parents of toddlers (a program called "See Them Grow). The latter program sends coupons to 750,000 families quarterly. McDonald's attempts to attract this segment by providing recreational equipment at its outlets that cater heavily to families with young children.

Single Parent I: Young Single Parents   Birth or adoption by singles is increasingly common. Although the rate has declined over the past several years, around 25 percent of children are born to unmarried mothers.[10] However, as many as 40 percent of these may

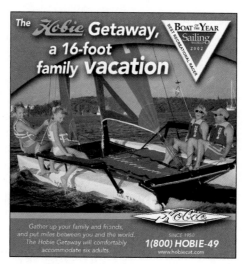

Courtesy The Hobie Cat Company.

actually be born to cohabiting unmarried parents.[11] Divorce also continues to be a significant part of American society, with 40 percent of first marriages ending in divorce. Although most divorced individuals remarry and most women who bear children out of wedlock eventually get married, more than 4 percent of American households are single-parent households, and 85 percent of these are headed by women.

The younger members of this group, particularly those who have never been married, tend to have a limited education and a very low income. These individuals are often members of one of the lower social classes, as described in Chapter 4. The older members of this segment and the divorced members receiving support from their ex-spouses are somewhat better off financially, but most are still under significant stress as they raise their young children without the support of a partner who is physically present:

> I feel like I have no time for anything. It's just a day-in and day-out grind of things you have to take care of, while trying to have a little fun. Right now it's 9:30 at night and I have dirty dishes in the sink. I'll probably just wait until tomorrow to do them. So you're constantly living in an environment that is not completely chaotic, but not completely together.[12]

This type of family situation creates many unique needs in the areas of child care, easy-to-prepare foods, and recreation. The need to work and raise younger children creates enormous time pressures and places tremendous demands on the energy of these parents. Most are renters and so are not a major market for home appliances and improvements. Their purchases focus on getting by and time- and energy-saving products and services that are not overly expensive.

Few firms have developed marketing campaigns that explicitly focus on this group. An exception is John Hancock Financial Services, which targeted divorced mothers with this ad:

> In a dimly lit suburban kitchen, a divorced couple is quarreling bitterly. The thirtysomething woman tells her ex-husband that he's not doing enough for their son. He retaliates that he's never missed a payment. She responds that he just doesn't get it. And then, almost as if he's trying to prove her point, the man says that his girlfriend wants him to move to California. "You tell Joey that, you tell him," she replies.[13]

Middle-Aged Single   The middle-aged single category is made up of people who have never married and those who are divorced and have no child-rearing responsibilities. These individuals are in the 35 to 64 age category.

Middle-aged singles generally live alone. They have higher incomes than young singles. However, all live-alone singles suffer from a lack of scale economies. That is, a couple or family needs only one dishwasher, clothes dryer, and so forth for everyone in the household; but the single-person household needs the same basic household infrastructure even though only one person uses it. Likewise, many foods and other items come in sizes inappropriate for singles, or the small sizes are disproportionately expensive.

The needs of middle-aged singles in many ways reflect those of young singles. But middle-aged singles are likely to have more money to spend on their lifestyles. Thus, they may live in nice condominiums, frequent expensive restaurants, own a luxury automobile, and travel often. They are a major market for gifts, and the males buy significant amounts of jewelry as gifts.

Empty Nest I: Middle-Aged Married with No Children   The lifestyle changes in the 1980s and 1990s influenced many young couples to not have children.[14] In other cases, these households represent second marriages in which children from a first marriage are not living with the parent. This group also includes married couples whose children have left home. These three forces have produced a huge market consisting of middle-aged couples without children at home. The size of this segment will grow rapidly over the next 10 years as the baby boomers enter this stage.

Both adults typically will have jobs, so they are very busy. However, the absence of responsibilities for children creates more free time than they have enjoyed since their youth. They also have money to spend on dining out, expensive vacations, second homes, luxury cars, and time-saving services such as house-cleaning, laundry, and shopping. They are a prime market for financial services. Less obviously, they are also heavy purchasers of upscale children's products, as gifts for nieces, nephews, grandchildren, and friends' children. The ad and product in Illustration 6–5 would appeal to this group, as well as the full nest II and empty nest II segments.

Delayed Full Nest I: Older Married with Young Children   Many members of the baby boom generation delayed having their first child until they were in their mid-30s. This produced the new phenomenon of a large number of middle-aged, established families entering into parenthood for the first time.

A major difference between this group and younger new parents is income. Older new parents' incomes are significantly larger than those of younger new parents. They have had this income flow longer and so have acquired more capital and possessions. They spend heavily on child care, mortgage payments, home maintenance, lawn care, and household furnishings. They can also spend more on nonchild expenditures such as food, alcohol, entertainment, savings, and contributions than can younger new parents.

Full Nest II: Middle-Aged Married with Children at Home   The children of this group are generally over six years old and are less dependent than the children of the younger couples. However, the fact that the children are older creates another set of unique consumption needs. Families with children six and older are the primary consumers of lessons of all types (piano, dance, gymnastics, and so on), dental care, soft drinks, presweetened cereals, and a wide variety of snack foods. Greater demands for space create a need for larger homes and cars. Transporting children to multiple events places time demands on the parents and increases transportation-related expenditures. These factors, coupled with heavy demand for clothing and an increased need to save for college, create

Ad created by Tinsley Advertising for Super Clubs Resorts.

a considerable financial burden on households in this stage of the HLC. This is offset somewhat by the tendency of the wife to return to work as the children enter school.

As we saw in Chapter 4, the teenage members of this segment, as well as those in the single parent II segment (described next), are important consumers in their own right as well as important influencers on household consumption decisions.

Single Parent II: Middle-Aged Single with Children at Home   Single individuals in the 35 to 64 age group who have children are often faced with serious financial pressures. The same demands that are placed on the middle-aged married couple with children are present in the life of a middle-aged single with children. However, the single parent often lacks some or all of the financial, emotional, and time support that the presence of a spouse generally provides. Many individuals in this position are thus inclined to use time-saving alternatives such as ready-to-eat food, and they are likely to eat at fast-food restaurants. The children of this segment are given extensive household responsibilities.

Empty Nest II: Older Married Couples   There are about 10 million households in this segment, and it is expected to grow rapidly over the next 10 years. For the most part, couples in the over-64 age group are either fully or partially retired. The younger members of this group are healthy, active, and often financially well-off. They have ample time. They are a big market for travel trailers, cruises, and second homes. They also spend considerable time and income on grandchildren. Increasingly, they take their grandchildren and occasionally their children on vacations. As described in Chapter 4, as they advance in age, health care and assisted living become more important. Illustration 6–6 shows an ad for a product designed to meet one of this segment's needs.

Courtesy McDonald's Corporation.

Older Single   There are more than 15 million older singles in the United States, and this group is growing rapidly. Almost three-fourths are female and two-thirds live alone. The conditions of being older, single, and generally retired create many unique needs for housing, socialization, travel, and recreation. Many financial firms have set up special programs to work with these individuals. They often have experienced a spouse's death and now are taking on many of the financial responsibilities once handled by the other person.

MARKETING STRATEGY BASED ON THE HOUSEHOLD LIFE CYCLE

The preceding sections have illustrated the power of the HLC as a segmentation variable. The purchase and consumption of many products are driven by the HLC. The reason for this is that each stage in the HLC poses unique problems or opportunities to the household members; and the resolution of these problems often requires the consumption of products or services. Our earlier discussion and illustrations indicated how marketers are responding to the unique needs of each stage in the HLC.

While stage in the HLC causes many of the problems or opportunities individuals confront as they mature, it does not provide solutions. For example, while all full nest I families face similar needs and restrictions with respect to recreation, such factors as their income, occupation, and education heavily influence how they will meet those needs. Thus, it makes sense to combine stage in the HLC with one of these variables to aid in market segmentation and strategy formulation.

TABLE 6–2 HLC/Occupational Category Matrix

	Occupational Category				
HLC Stage	*Executive/ Elite Professional*	*Administrative/ Professional*	*Technical/ Sales/Clerical*	*Crafts*	*Unskilled/ Manual*
Single I					
Young married					
Full nest I					
Single parent I					
Single II					
Delayed full nest I					
Full nest II					
Single parent II					
Empty nest I					
Empty nest II					
Single III					

For example, think of how the need for vacations differs as one moves across the stages of the household life cycle. Young singles often desire vacations focused on activities, adventure, and the chance for romance. Young married couples without children would have similar needs but without the desire to meet potential romantic partners. Full nest I and single parent I families need vacations that allow both parents and young children to enjoy themselves. The manner in which these needs will be met will vary sharply across occupational, income, and educational categories. For example, a young professional couple may vacation in Paris or at a resort in the tropics. A white-collar couple may visit a domestic ski resort or visit Hawaii on a package deal. A young blue-collar couple may visit family or go camping.

Table 6–2 presents the **HLC/occupational category matrix.** The vertical axis is the particular stage in the HLC, which determines the problems the household will likely encounter; the horizontal axis is a set of occupational categories, which provide a range of acceptable solutions. While this version has been found to be useful across a range of products, using income, education, or social class instead of occupation should be considered for some product categories.

This matrix can be used to segment the market for many products and to develop appropriate marketing strategies for the targeted segments. An effective use of the matrix is to isolate an activity or problem of interest to the firm, such as preparing the evening meal, snacks, weekend recreation, vacations, and so forth. Research, often in the form of focus group interviews, is used to determine the following information for each relevant cell in the matrix:

1. What products or services are now being used to meet the need or perform the activity?
2. What, if any, symbolic or social meaning is associated with meeting the need or using the current products?
3. Exactly how are the current products or services being used?
4. How satisfied are the segment members with the current solutions, and what improvements are desired?

Attractive segments are those that are large enough to meet the firm's objectives and that have needs that current products are not fully satisfying. This approach has been used successfully for movies, regional bakeries, and financial services.[15] *What type automobile would be best suited for each cell and what type of ad should promote it?*

FAMILY DECISION MAKING

Family decision making is *the process by which decisions that directly or indirectly involve two or more family members are made.* Decision making by a group such as a family differs in many ways from decisions made by an individual. Consider the purchase of a breakfast cereal that children, and perhaps the adults, will consume. Who recognizes the need for the product? How is a type and brand selected? Does everyone consider the same attributes? A parent typically makes the actual *purchase;* does that mean that the parent also makes the *choice?* Or is the choice made by the children, the other parent, or some combination? Which parents are involved, and how does this change across products and over time? How does it differ by stage in the household lifecycle?

Family purchases are often compared to organizational buying decisions. Although this can produce useful insights, it fails to capture the essence of family decision making. Organizations have relatively objective criteria, such as profit maximization, that guide purchases. Families generally lack such explicit, overarching goals. Most industrial purchases are made by strangers or have little impact on those not involved in the purchase. Most family purchases directly affect the other members of the family.

Most important, *many family purchases are inherently emotional and affect the relationships between the family members.*[16] The decision to buy a child a requested toy or new school clothes is more than simply an acquisition. It is a symbol of love and commitment to the child. The decision to take the family to a restaurant for a meal or to purchase a new television has emotional meaning to the other family members. Disagreements about how to spend money are a major cause of marital discord. The processes families use to make purchase decisions and the outcomes of those processes have important effects on the well-being of the individual family members and the family itself. Thus, while family decision making has some things in common with organizational decision making, it is not the same.

The Nature of Family Purchase Roles

Figure 6–3 illustrates the six roles that frequently occur in family decision making, using a cereal purchase as an example.[17] It is important to note that individuals will play various roles for different decisions.

- *Initiator(s).* The family member who first recognizes a need or starts the purchase process.
- *Information gatherer(s).* The individual who has expertise and interest in a particular purchase. Different individuals may seek information at different times or on different aspects of the purchase.
- *Influencer(s).* The person who influences the alternatives evaluated, the criteria considered, and the final choice.
- *Decision maker(s).* The individual who makes the final decision. Of course, joint decisions also are likely to occur.
- *Purchaser(s).* The family member who actually purchases the product. This is typically an adult or teenager.
- *User(s).* The user of the product. For many products there are multiple users.

FIGURE 6-3	The Household Decision-Making Process for Children's Products

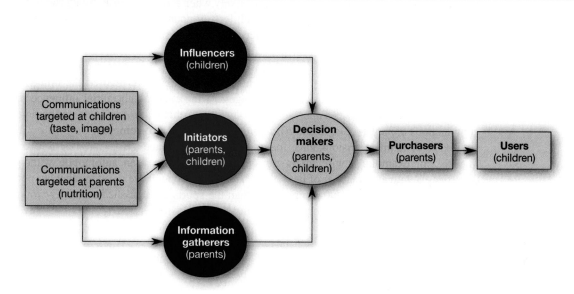

Courtesy The Dannon Company, Inc.

ILLUSTRATION 6-7

Children often determine the products and brands they use. At other times, they influence these choices but the parents play the dominant role. In such cases, the marketer must meet the needs of both the child and the parents.

Marketers must determine who in the family plays which role before they can affect the family decision process. After thorough study, Crayola shifted its advertising budget from children's television to women's magazines. Its research revealed that mothers rather than children were more likely to recognize the problem, evaluate alternatives, and make the purchase. Illustration 6–7 shows a product designed for use by children that is selected by both the children and the parents and purchased by parents.

Family decision making has been categorized as *husband-dominant, wife-dominant, joint,* or *individualized.* Husband-dominant decisions have traditionally occurred with the purchase of such products as automobiles, liquor, and life insurance. Wife-dominant decisions were more common in the purchase of household maintenance items, food, and kitchen appliances. Joint decisions were most likely when buying a house, living room furniture, and vacations. These patterns are much less pronounced today. As women's occupational roles have expanded, so has the range of family decisions in which they participate or dominate.[18]

A moment's reflection will reveal that the above four categories omit critical participants in many family decisions. Until recently, most studies have ignored the influence of children.[19] Yet children, particularly teenagers, often exert a substantial influence on family purchase decisions.[20] Thus, we need to recognize that *child-dominant,* and various combinations of *husband, wife,* and *child joint decisions* are also common.

Studies of family decisions have focused on direct influence and ignored indirect influence. For example, a wife might report that she purchased an automobile without discussing it with any member of her family. Yet she might purchase a van to meet her perceptions of the desires of the family rather than the sports car that she personally would prefer. Most research studies would classify the above decision as strictly wife-dominated. Clearly, however, other family members influenced the decision.

Different family members often become involved at different stages of the decision process. Figure 6–4 shows the influence of wives and husbands at each stage of the decision process for a variety of services. As can be seen, roles vary across services and across stages in the decision process.

Family decisions also allow different members to make specific subdecisions of the overall decision. When an individual makes a decision, he or she evaluates all the relevant attributes of each alternative and combines these evaluations into a single decision. In a family decision, different members often focus on specific attributes. For example, a child

FIGURE 6–4	Husband/Wife Decision Roles for Services

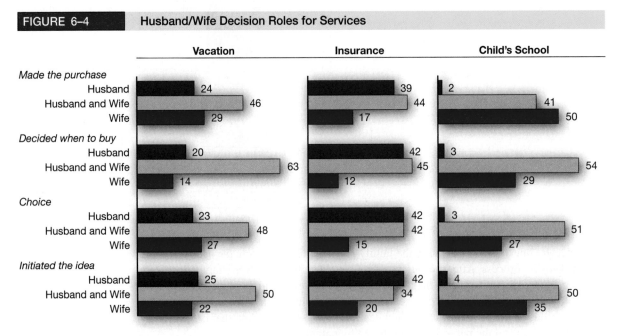

Note: Totals do not add to 100 because other individuals were involved in some decisions.

Source: M. R. Stafford, G. K. Ganesh, and B. C. Garland, "Marital Influence in the Decision-Making Process for Services," *Journal of Services Marketing* 10, no. 1 (1996), p. 15.

may evaluate the color and style of a bicycle while one or both parents evaluate price, warranty, and safety features.

Determinants of Family Purchase Roles

How family members interact in a purchase decision is largely dependent on the *culture and subculture* in which the family exists, the *role specialization* of different family members, the degree of *involvement* each has in the product area of concern, and the *personal characteristics* of the family members.[21]

America has less of a masculine orientation than many other cultures. As one would expect, wives are more involved in a wider range of decisions in the United States than they are in cultures with a more masculine focus.[22] However, subcultures and other groups in the United States vary on this value. As we saw in Chapter 5, the Hispanic subculture has more of a masculine orientation than the broader culture. Research indicates that Hispanics who identify strongly with the Hispanic culture tend to make more husband-dominant decisions than do others.

Over time, each spouse develops more specialized roles as a part of the family lifestyle and family responsibilities. Husbands traditionally specialized in mechanical and technical areas, while wives specialized in home care and child rearing. Although particular roles are no longer automatically assigned to one gender in the marriage, they still tend to evolve over time. It is simply much more efficient for one person to specialize in some decisions than it is to have to reach a joint decision for every purchase.

Involvement or expertise in a product area is another major factor that affects how a family purchase decision will be made. Naturally, the more involved a spouse is with a product area, the more likely he or she will be to exert influence over other family members during a purchase in that product area. For example, teenagers who are involved with computers might dominate the decision for a family computer or the choice of an Internet access service. The following reveals how even preteens can influence adult purchases:

> Occasionally I will ask her to go along with me when I need to select a new cologne or a new tie or a new shirt and get some feedback from her as to her opinion of how it looks and how it would fit into today's goings-on. . . . Whether we agree on it or not is two different things; you know, I value her opinion. (Father with daughter, age 12)[23]

Several personal characteristics have an effect on the influence individuals will have on purchase decisions.[24] Education is one such personal characteristic. The higher a wife's education, the more she will participate in major decisions. For example, 70 percent of married women with a college degree claim to have equal say with their husband in the brand of a new car to buy, compared to 35 percent of those with less than a high school degree and 56 percent of those with only a high school degree.[25]

Personality is an important determinant of family decision roles. Traits such as aggressiveness, locus of control (belief in controlling one's own situation), detachment, and compliance influence family decision power.[26] The age and capabilities of the various family members, including the children, are also important determinants.

Conflict Resolution

Given the number of decisions families make daily, disagreements are inevitable. How they are resolved is important to marketers as well as to the health of the family unit. A recent study revealed six basic approaches that individuals use to resolve purchase conflicts after they have arisen (most couples generally seek to avoid open conflicts):[27]

- *Bargaining.* Trying to reach a compromise.
- *Impression management.* Misrepresenting the facts in order to win.
- *Use of authority.* Claiming superior expertise or role appropriateness (the husband/wife should make such decisions).
- *Reasoning.* Using logical argument to win.
- *Playing on emotion.* Using the silent treatment or withdrawing from the discussion.
- *Additional information.* Getting additional data or a third-party opinion.

Although this study did not include children, a study focused on how children and parents attempt to influence each other found a similar though more complex set of influence strategies.[28]

Conclusions on Family Decision Making

Much remains to be learned about family decision making. But we can offer five general conclusions:

1. Different family members are often involved at different stages of the decision process.
2. Different family members often evaluate different attributes of a product or brand.
3. The direct involvement of family members in each stage of the decision process represents only a small part of the picture. Taking into account the desires of other family members is also important, though seldom studied.
4. Who participates at each stage of the decision process and the method by which conflicts are resolved are primarily a function of the product category and secondarily a function of the characteristics of the individual family members and the characteristics of the family. The product category is important because it is closely related to who uses the product.
5. Overt conflicts in decision making are less common than agreement.

MARKETING STRATEGY AND FAMILY DECISION MAKING

Formulating an effective marketing strategy for most consumer products requires a thorough understanding of the family decision-making process in the selected target markets with respect to that product. Table 6–3 provides a framework for such an analysis.

The family decision-making process often varies across market segments such as stages in the family life cycle or subculture. Therefore, a marketer must analyze family decision making *within* each of the firm's defined target markets. Within each target market, the marketer needs to,

- Discover which family members are involved at each stage of the decision process.
- Determine what their motivations and interests are.
- Develop a marketing strategy that will meet the needs of each participant.

For example, younger children are often involved in the problem recognition stage related to breakfast. They may note a new cartoon-character-based cereal or discover that their friends are eating a new cereal. They are interested in identifying with the cartoon

Segment: _____			
Stage in the Decision Process	Family Members Involved	Family Members' Motivation and Interests	Marketing Strategy and Tactics
Problem recognition			
Information search			
Alternative evaluation			
Purchase			
Use/consumption			
Disposition			
Evaluation			

TABLE 6–3

Marketing Strategy Based on the Family Decision-Making Process

Courtesy of Polaris Industries.

ILLUSTRATION 6–8

This product is positioned as one that the kids and father will use. It indicates that most of the pleasure will go to the kids. However, the ad is targeted at the father, who is likely to be the primary participant in the decision process for this type of product.

character or being like their friends. When they request the new cereal, the parents, generally the mother, may become interested. However, she is more likely to focus on nutrition and price. Thus, a marketer needs to communicate fun, taste, and excitement to children and nutrition, value, and taste to the parents. The children can be reached on Saturday cartoons, appropriate Internet sites, and similar media, while the mother may be more effectively communicated with through magazine ads and package information.

Consider Illustration 6–8. This product is being positioned as one that will be used by the father and the children. The ad is targeted at the father and emphasizes the pleasure he will bring to the children if he buys the Polaris. It also implies that it will increase the popularity of his children. The last line says "mother approved." This suggests the potential for some conflict over such a purchase.

CONSUMER SOCIALIZATION

The family provides the basic framework in which consumer socialization occurs. **Consumer socialization** is *the process by which young people acquire skills, knowledge, and attitudes relevant to their functioning as consumers in the marketplace.*[29] We are concerned with understanding both the content of consumer socialization and the process of consumer socialization. The *content* of consumer socialization refers to what children learn with respect to consumption; *process* refers to how they learn it. Before we address these two issues, we need to consider the ability of children of various ages to learn consumption-related skills.

The Ability of Children to Learn

Younger children have limited abilities to process certain types of information. **Piaget's stages of cognitive development** are a widely accepted set of stages of cognitive development:

Stage 1 *The period of sensorimotor intelligence (0 to 2 years).* During this period, behavior is primarily motor. The child does not yet "think" conceptually, though cognitive development is seen.

Stage 2 *The period of preoperational thoughts (3 to 7 years).* This period is characterized by the development of language and rapid conceptual development.

Stage 3 *The period of concrete operations (8 to 11 years).* During these years, the child develops the ability to apply logical thought to concrete problems.

Stage 4 *The period of formal operations (12 to 15 years).* During this period, the child's cognitive structures reach their greatest level of development, and the child becomes able to apply logic to all classes of problems.

Other researchers have proposed other stages, with learning rather than aging as the underlying cause of observed differences. However, the general pattern of less ability to deal with abstract, generalized, unfamiliar, or large amounts of information by younger children is common to all approaches.[30]

The changing capabilities of children to process information as they age present challenges to parents who are attempting to teach their children appropriate consumption behaviors.[31] As we will discuss shortly, this also poses ethical and practical issues for marketers.[32] This limited learning capacity is the basis for substantial regulation of advertising to children. We describe existing and proposed regulations of marketing to children in depth in Chapter 20.

The Content of Consumer Socialization

The content of consumer learning can be broken down into three categories: consumer skills, consumption-related preferences, and consumption-related attitudes.[33] **Consumer skills** are *those capabilities necessary for purchases to occur such as understanding money, budgeting, product evaluation, and so forth.* A child has to learn how to shop, how to compare similar brands, how to budget available income, and so forth. The following are examples of attempts to teach adolescents appropriate, from the parent's perspective, shopping rules:

> Son, look at this. This is just going to wash nicer, it will come through the laundry nicer, and you do a lot of the laundry yourself, and I just would rather that it's something that would wash easy, that doesn't have to be ironed, that isn't 100 percent cotton. (Mother with son, age 13)

> Well, I usually try to get her to shop a little bit more and see if she can't find the same item for a little less, so I always suggest, "Look around, just because you found this one, maybe you can find another one that's a better buy." Or I get her to try to think about sales, maybe it's not exactly what she wanted, but I try to get her to go that route. (Mother with daughter, age 14)[34]

Consumption-related preferences are *the knowledge, attitudes, and values that cause people to attach differential evaluations to products, brands, and retail outlets*. For example, some parents through their comments and purchases may "teach" their children that Calvin Klein is a prestigious brand name and that prestigious brands are desirable. This information about Calvin Klein's prestige is not necessary to carry out the actual purchase (consumer skills), but it is extremely important in deciding *to* purchase and *what* to purchase (consumption-related preferences).

Consumption-related attitudes are *cognitive and affective orientations toward marketplace stimuli such as advertisements, salespeople, warranties, and so forth*.[35] For example, children may learn from their parents or other family members that "you get what you pay for." This would lead them to assume a strong price–quality relationship. Or they may be taught that salespeople are not trustworthy. These attitudes will influence how they react to the various activities undertaken by marketers. *What type of attitude is being formed in the following interaction?*

> I'm always trying to get her to learn the relative value of things and particularly the impact of advertising and its effect on driving purchases and desires. So we try to talk about that. I point out manipulative or deceptive advertising, and give her a sense of being a critical consumer. (Father with daughter, age 13)[36]

The Process of Consumer Socialization

Although advertising and other marketing activities have a strong influence, the family is the primary source of consumer socialization. Parents teach their children consumer skills, consumption-related preferences, and consumption-related attitudes. They do so both deliberately and casually through instrumental training, modeling, and mediation.

Instrumental training *occurs when a parent or sibling specifically and directly attempts to bring about certain responses through reasoning or reinforcement*. In other words, a parent may try directly to teach a child which snack foods should be consumed by explicitly discussing nutrition. Or a parent may establish rules that limit the consumption of some snack foods and encourage the consumption of others.

Parents use many venues to teach consumption skills and related values. Consumer Insight 6–2 describes how some mothers of three- to five-year-olds use birthday parties for instrumental training. The following example shows an approach used with older children:

> One thing that we always talk about when we're looking at something is the price of it. "For what you're buying, is the price worth the quality of what you're buying?" (Mother with son, age 13)[37]

Consumer Socialization and Birthday Parties

A study of birthday parties for children aged three to five revealed that the mothers used the situation to (1) teach children how to plan a party, (2) indicate approval or disapproval of certain themes (e.g., Barbie, Ninja Turtles), (3) teach sharing and other positive values, and (4) instill social skills.[38] The following examples indicate the instrumental nature of the process.

Planning Skills

- She was involved in choosing some of the little prizes and the cake. We took her with us when we went to the store . . . that has a bakery and they make these birthday cakes on various themes . . . . [She] was allowed to choose which one.
- He was pretty involved . . . he knew what he wanted on his cake . . . . I knew that if I just went and got something and he knew how he wanted it, it just did not work. So we did a lot together.

Theme Approval

- [Explaining why she would not let her son have a commercial theme at his party.] It is not so much the money but the values I have about it . . . but I have to explain to Carl that we decided to do it this way because we think birthdays are very special, but we celebrate them differently than other people . . . that's what we think is important that is the lesson we try to show.
- We don't encourage [Jake] to be into Ninja Turtles . . . in fact we discourage him. [When he requested a Ninja Turtle theme for his party] I was fighting it all the way . . . . I think I gave

him some other options. I think they are too aggressive.

Positive Values

- [I use] outdoor games . . . something where everybody wins. [In a treasure hunt] they all got in like one big cohort, and they all helped each other . . . . It was really nice, they really liked it, and everyone got a prize in the end.
- [My daughter] has a class with 9 or 10 girls and I made it very clear that if it was a big group, we'd invite all of the girls even if we had to sacrifice. Rather than exclude three or four. It has been very hurtful to her in the last year where, you know, the majority is invited and a few are excluded.

Social Skills

- I am petrified they are going to say something like, "Hey, I already have this." My eight-year-old would never do this because he knows I'll take all his toys and give them to the Salvation Army if I find out . . . . With the four-year-old, I worry.
- I think [birthday parties] should teach them to be good . . . . I've always emphasized the importance of thank-you notes.

Critical Thinking Questions

1. Parents need to teach their children appropriate consumption skills. However, parents are not taught how to do this. How should parents learn what and how to teach their children about consumption?
2. Should consumption skills be taught in school? If so what should be taught and in which grades?

Illustration 6–9 illustrates how easy it is to inadvertently teach children dysfunctional behavior. The Chef Boyardee ad (one of a series of such ads) provides a valuable service by alerting parents to the danger of using food as a reward for positive behavior.

Modeling *occurs when a child learns appropriate, or inappropriate, consumption behaviors by observing others.* Modeling generally, though not always, occurs without direct instruction from the role model and frequently without conscious thought or effort on the part of the child. Modeling is an extremely important way for children to learn relevant skills, knowledge, and attitudes. Children learn both positive and negative consumption

Courtesy of International Home Foods.

patterns through modeling. For example, children whose parents smoke are more likely to start smoking than are children whose parents do not smoke.

Mediation *occurs when a parent alters a child's initial interpretation of, or response to, a marketing or other stimulus.* This can easily be seen in the following example.

CHILD: Can I have one of those? See, it can walk!

PARENT: No. That's just an advertisement. It won't really walk. They just make it look like it will so kids will buy them.

The advertisement illustrated a product attribute and triggered a desire, but the parent altered the belief in the attribute and in the believability of advertising in general. This is not to suggest that family members mediate all commercials. However, children often learn about the purchase and use of products during interactions with other family members. Thus, a firm wishing to influence children must do so in a manner consistent with the values of the rest of the family.

The Supermarket as a Classroom

Professor James McNeal developed a five-stage model of how children learn to shop by visiting supermarkets and other retail outlets with a parent.[39]

Stage I: Observing   Parents begin taking children to the store with them at a median age of two months. During this stage, children make sensory contact with the marketplace and begin forming mental images of marketplace objects and symbols. In the early months, only sights and sounds are being processed. However, by 12 to 15 months, most children can begin to recall some of these items. This stage ends when children understand that a visit to the market may produce rewards beyond the stimulation caused by the environment.

Stage II: Making Requests   At this stage (median age is two years), children begin requesting items in the store from their parents. They use pointing and gesturing as well as statements to indicate that they want an item. Throughout most of this stage, children make requests only when the item is physically present, as they do not yet carry mental images of the products in their minds. In the latter months of stage II, they begin to make requests for items at home, particularly when they are seen on television.

Stage III: Making Selections   Actually getting an item off the shelf without assistance is the first act of an independent consumer (median age is three and a half years). At its simplest level, a child's desire is triggered by an item in his or her immediate presence and this item is selected. Soon, however, children begin to remember the store location of desirable items, and they are allowed to go to those areas independently or to lead the parent there.

Stage IV: Making Assisted Purchases   Most children learn by observing (modeling) that money needs to be given in order to get things from a store. They learn to value money given to them by their parents and others as a means to acquire things. Soon they are allowed to select and pay for items with their own money. They are now primary consumers (median age is five and a half years).

Stage V: Making Independent Purchases   Making a purchase without a parent to oversee it requires a fairly sophisticated understanding of value as well as the ability to visit a store, or a section of a store, safely without a parent. Most children remain in stage IV a long time before their parents allow them to move into stage V (median age is eight years).

McNeal's research indicates that children learn to shop, at least in part, by going shopping. Retailers are developing programs based on these learning patterns. A&P has installed child-sized shopping carts in 100 of its outlets. The objectives are to occupy the children and make their visit to the store fun, which will also increase the parents' pleasure, and to get the children involved in the shopping process. Piggly Wiggly is starting Piggly Wiggly Pals Clubs in many of its outlets. Children can get their membership cards stamped at the store and receive such items as the Earth Pals kit, which includes tree seedlings.

MARKETING TO CHILDREN

Children are a very large market. Spending by children aged 5 to 14 is estimated to be $35 billion, and they influence about $200 billion of their parents' purchases.[40] Brand loyalties developed at this age may produce returns for many years. Thus, it is no surprise that marketers are aggressively pursuing these young consumers.

However, marketing to children is fraught with ethical concerns. The major source of these concerns is the limited ability of younger children to process information and to make informed purchase decisions. There are also concerns that marketing activities, particularly advertising, produce undesirable values in children, result in inappropriate diets, and cause unhealthy levels of family conflict. The opening vignette for Chapter 1 describes concerns that using the Internet to market to younger consumers has raised. We will examine questionable marketing practices focused on children and the regulations designed to control them in detail in Chapter 20.

Although marketers need to be very sensitive to the limited information-processing skills of younger consumers, ethical and effective marketing campaigns can be designed to meet the needs of children and their parents. All aspects of the marketing mix must consider the capabilities of the child. Consider these responses to an ad:

The ad reads "Inhale a lethal dose of carbon monoxide and it's called suicide. Inhale a smaller amount and it's called smoking. Believe it or not, cigarette smoke contains the same poisonous gas as automobile exhaust. So if you wouldn't consider sucking on a tailpipe, why would you want to smoke?" A picture of a smoking exhaust pipe was below the copy.

Seven- and eight-year-old responses:
"Never stand behind a bus because you could get poisonous in your face."
"People sometimes get sick from exhaust."

Nine- and ten-year-old responses:
"The person who is driving is smoking."
"No matter what kind of smoking it is, it can always make you sick."

Eleven-year-old responses:
"You could hurt yourself with that stuff. The same stuff in car exhaust is in cigarettes."
"The tailpipe of a car is like the same as smoking and smoking could kill you . . . both of them could kill you."

Only the older children could fully engage in the analogical reasoning required to completely understand this ad. In contrast, a simpler ad that showed a dirty, grimy sock next to an ashtray full of cigarette butts with the word *gross* under the sock and *really gross* under the ashtray was understood by children of all ages (7 through 11).[41]

Reaching children used to mean advertising on Saturday morning cartoons. Now there are many more options, even for the very young. *Barbie, Outside Kids,* and *Sports Illustrated for Kids* have wide circulation among children who can read. CD-ROMs with interactive capabilities and titles such as "The Magic School Bus" are becoming big sellers. They provide the opportunity to offer entertainment, education, and commercial messages to children and their parents. Children as young as three are active Internet users. Sites such as Foxkids.com, Cartoonnetwork.com, Nick.com, Pokemon.com, and Barbie.com are visited by millions of children aged 2 to 11. Radio is popular with older children who are very much into pop music and stars such as Britney Spears.

Direct mail can be an effective means to reach even very young children. Many firms target children or families with young children by forming "kid's clubs." Unfortunately, many of these clubs engage in sales techniques that are controversial if not clearly unethical (see Chapter 20). However, if done properly, they can be fun and educational for the children while delivering responsible commercial messages. Consider the Burger King Kids Club:

Kids (or their parents) can pick up a membership form at any Burger King for free. After it is sent in, they receive a kit containing a membership certificate, stickers, a membership card and iron-on transfers for T-shirts. On their birthdays, they receive a card good for a free meal at their local Burger King. Bimonthly Kids Club newsletters are distributed through the restaurants. A quarterly

32-page, full-color magazine is sent to the members' homes. There are three different versions of the magazine geared to the age of the member. Each issue has six pages of outside advertising. Burger King does not sell its membership list.[42]

If the content is sound and the ads are constructed in a manner appropriate for the age groups, this program appears to be one that children would benefit from and enjoy.

SUMMARY

The household is the basic purchasing and consuming unit and is, therefore, of great importance to marketing managers of most products. Family households also are the primary mechanism whereby cultural and social-class values and behavior patterns are passed on to the next generation.

The *family household* consists of two or more related persons living together in a dwelling unit. *Nonfamily households* are dwelling units occupied by one or more unrelated individuals.

The *household life cycle* is the classification of the household into stages through which it passes over time based on the age and marital status of the adults and the presence and age of children. The household life cycle is a valuable marketing tool because members within each stage or category face similar consumption problems. Thus, they represent potential market segments.

The *household life cycle/occupational category matrix* is a useful way to use the HLC to develop marketing strategy. One axis is the stages in the HLC, which determine the problems the household will likely encounter; the other is a set of social strata, which provide a range of acceptable solutions. Each cell represents a market segment.

Family decision making involves consideration of questions such as who buys, who decides, and who uses. Family decision making is complex and involves emotion and interpersonal relations as well as product evaluation and acquisition.

Marketing managers must analyze the household decision process separately for each product category within each target market. Household member participation in the decision process varies by *involvement with the specific product, role specialization, personal characteristics,* and one's *culture and subculture.* Participation also varies by stage in the decision process. Most decisions are reached by consensus. If not, a variety of conflict resolution strategies may be employed.

Consumer socialization deals with the processes by which young people (from birth until 18 years of age) learn how to become consumers. Children's learning abilities are limited at birth, then slowly evolve with experience over time. Consumer socialization deals with the learning of consumer skills, consumption-related preferences, and consumption-related attitudes. Families influence consumer socialization through direct *instrumental training, modeling,* and *mediation.* Young consumers appear to go through five stages of learning how to shop. This learning takes place primarily in retail outlets in interaction with the parents.

Marketing to children is fraught with ethical issues. The main source of ethical concern is the limited ability of children to process information and make sound purchase decisions or requests. There are also concerns about the role of advertising in forming children's values, influencing their diets, and causing family conflict. However, ethical and effective marketing programs can be developed for children.

KEY TERMS

Blended family 191
Consumer skills 210
Consumer socialization 210
Consumption-related
  attitudes 211
Consumption-related
  preferences 211

Family 191
Family decision making 204
Family household 191
HLC/occupational category
  matrix 203
Household 191
Household life cycle (HLC) 194

Instrumental training 211
Mediation 213
Modeling 212
Nonfamily household 191
Piaget's stages of cognitive
  development 210
Traditional family 192

INTERNET EXERCISES

1. Prepare a report on the information available on the Internet concerning the percentage of the U.S. population that is in each stage of the household life cycle. Provide the addresses for all sites used.

2. Visit the Federal Trade Commission (www.ftc.gov) and Better Business Bureau (www.bbb.org) sites. What ethical and legal issues involving marketing to children appear?

3. Visit one of the sites listed below. Evaluate the effectiveness of the site in terms of marketing to children and the degree to which it represents an ethically sound approach to marketing to children.
   a. www.kelloggs.com
   b. www.fritolay.com
   c. www.warnerbros.com
   d. www.crayola.com
   e. www.nabisco.com
   f. www.barbie.com

4. Visit one of the sites listed below. Evaluate the effectiveness of the site in terms of marketing to children and the degree to which it represents an ethically sound approach to marketing to children. What ages is it best suited for?
   a. www.surfmonkey.com
   b. www.foxkids.com
   c. www.nick.com
   d. www.cartoonnetwork.com
   e. www.mtv.com
   f. www.disney.com

5. Find and describe two sites targeting children under six. What is your evaluation of these sites?

DDB NEEDHAM LIFESTYLE DATA ANALYSES

1. For which products, activities, or programs does consumption, participation, or viewing vary the most by household size (see Table 1)? Why is this the case?

2. Based on Table 1, consumption, participation, or viewing of which products, activities, or programs varies the most by marital status? Why is this the case?

3. Examine the data in Table 1. For which products, activities, or programs does consumption, participation, or viewing vary the most by number of children at home? Why is this the case?

4. For which attitudes/interests/activities in Table 1a are there the greatest differences across various size households? Why is this the case?

REVIEW QUESTIONS

1. The household is described as "the basic consumption unit for consumer goods." Why?

2. What is a *traditional family?* Can a single-parent family be a nuclear family?

3. How does a *nonfamily household* differ from a *family household?*

4. What is a *family* according to the Census Bureau?

5. How has the distribution of household types in the United States been changing? What are the implications of these shifts?

6. What is meant by the *household life cycle?*

7. What is meant by the following statement? "Each stage in the household life cycle poses a series of problems that household decision makers must solve."

8. Describe the general characteristics of each of the stages in the household life cycle.

9. Describe the *HLC/occupational category matrix.* What is the logic for this matrix?

10. What is meant by *family decision making?* How can different members of the household be involved with different stages of the decision process?

11. How does family decision making differ from most organizational decision making?

12. The text states that the marketing manager must analyze the family decision-making process separately within each target market and for each product. Why?

13. What factors influence involvement of a household member in a purchase decision?

14. How do family members attempt to resolve conflict over purchase decisions?

15. What is *consumer socialization?* How is knowledge of it useful to marketing managers?

16. What are Piaget's stages of cognitive development?

17. What do we mean when we say that children learn consumer skills, consumption-related attitudes, and consumption-related preferences?

18. What processes do parents use to teach children to be consumers?

19. According to the text, what types of consumer socialization occur at young children's birthday parties?

20. Describe each of the five stages children go through as they learn to shop at stores.

21. What ethical issues arise in marketing to children?

DISCUSSION QUESTIONS

22. Respond to the questions in Consumer Insight 6–1.

23. Canada defines a family as "a married or common-law [defined as any cohabiting nonmarried couple] living together . . . with or without children." How does this differ from the definition used by the U.S. Census Bureau? What are the implications of this difference?

24. Canada has legislation giving cohabiting couples who have been living together for one year or more the same federal rights and responsibilities as married couples. Should the United States have similar legislation?

25. Rate the stages of the household life cycle in terms of their probable purchase of the following. Justify your answers.
    a. Cruise
    b. Trip to Hawaii
    c. Cell phone
    d. Breakfast cereal
    e. Contribution to United Way
    f. Snowmobile

26. Pick two stages in the household life cycle. Describe how your marketing strategy for the following would differ depending on which group was your primary target market.
    a. Sports car
    b. Mouthwash
    c. Italian restaurant
    d. Resort

27. Do you think the trend toward nonfamily households will continue? Justify your response.

28. What are the primary marketing implications of Table 6–1?

29. How would the marketing strategies for the following differ by stage of the HLC? (Assume each stage is the target market.)
    a. Health club (gym)
    b. Life insurance
    c. Energy drink
    d. Deodorant
    e. Detergent
    f. SUV

30. What are the marketing implications of Figure 6–4?

31. What type of the following would be best suited for each cell in Table 6–2?
    a. Resort
    b. Television program
    c. Restaurant for the entire household
    d. Automobile

32. Name two products for which the horizontal axis in Table 6–2 should be the following. Justify your response.
    a. Occupational category
    b. Income
    c. Education
    d. Social class

33. How can a marketer use knowledge of how family members seek to resolve conflicts?

34. Describe a recent family purchase in which you were involved. Use this as a basis for completing Table 6–3 for a marketer attempting to influence that decision.

35. Describe four types of activities or situations in which direct *instrumental training* is likely to occur.

36. Describe four types of activities or situations in which *modeling* is likely to occur.

37. Describe four types of activities or situations in which *mediation* is likely to occur.

38. Respond to the questions in Consumer Insight 6–2.

39. Are Piaget's stages of cognitive development consistent with the five stages of learning to shop that McNeal identified?

APPLICATION ACTIVITIES

40. Interview a middle school student and determine and describe the household decision process involved in the purchase of his or her (*a*) clothes, (*b*) breakfast foods, (*c*) bedroom furniture, and (*d*) expensive hobby items such as a snowboard or computer.

41. Interview two furniture salespersons from different price-level outlets. Try to ascertain which stages in the household life cycle constitute their primary markets and why this is so.

42. Interview one individual from each stage in the household life cycle. Determine and report the extent to which these individuals conform to the descriptions provided in the text.

43. Interview a family with a child under 13 at home. Interview both the parents and the child, but interview the child separately. Try to determine the influence of each family member on the following products *for the child's use*. In addition, ascertain what method(s) of conflict resolution are used.
    a. Toothpaste
    b. Shoes
    c. Snacks
    d. Major toys, such as a bicycle
    e. Television viewing
    f. Restaurant meals

44. Interview a couple who have been married for the following periods. Ascertain and report the degree and nature of role specialization that has developed with respect to their purchase decisions. Also determine how conflicts are resolved.
    a. Less than 1 year
    b. 1–5 years
    c. 6–10 years
    d. More than 10 years

45. Pick a product and market segment of interest and interview three households. Collect sufficient data to complete Table 6–3.

46. Pick a product of interest and with several fellow students complete enough interviews to fill the relevant cells in Table 6–2 using the four questions in the text (p. 203). Develop an appropriate marketing strategy based on this information.

47. Interview several parents of preschool children. Determine the extent to which they agree with Piaget's four stages and McNeal's five stages.

48. Watch several hours of Saturday morning cartoons. What ethical concerns, if any, did they cause?

REFERENCES

1. S. Chandler, "Kids' Wear Is Not Child's Play," *Business Week,* June 19, 1995, p. 118; M. M. Cardona and A. Z. Cuneo, "Retailers Reaching Out to Capture Kids' Clout," *Advertising Age,* October 9, 2000, p. 16; and S. Thompson, "Jell-O Taken to 'X-tremes,'" *Advertising Age,* November 19, 2001, p. 4.

2. See P. Kiecker and N. R. McClure, "Redefining the Extended Family in Recognition of Blended Family Structures," *Enhancing Knowledge Development in Marketing* (Chicago: American Marketing Association, 1996), pp. 242–43.

3. See F. F. Furstenberg, Jr., "The Future of Families," *American Demographics,* June 1996, pp. 34–40; R. Gardyn, "Happily Unmarried," *American Demographics,* December 2000, pp. 56–61; S. Raymond, "The Ex-Files," *American Demographics,* February 2001, pp. 60–64; and P. Paul, "Millennial Myths," *American Demographics,* December 2001, p. 20.

4. This Consumer Insight is based on Gardyn, "Happily Unmarried."

5. See C. M. Schaninger and W. D. Danko, "A Conceptual and Empirical Comparison of Alternative Household Life Cycle Models," *Journal of Consumer Research,* March 1993, pp. 580–94; and R. E. Wilkes, "Household Life-Cycle Stages, Transitions, and Product Expenditures," *Journal of Consumer Research,* June 1995, pp. 27–42.

6. G. J. Thompson, "Interpreting Consumers," *Journal Marketing Research,* November 1997, p. 448.

7. See J. Raymond, "For Richer or Poorer," *American Demographics,* July 2000, pp. 59–64.

8. Estimated from *Consumer Expenditure Survey* (Washington, DC: U.S. Bureau of Labor Statistics, 2000).

9. J. Mukherui, "Consumption of Child Care," *Advances in Consumer Research,* vol. 24, eds. M. Bruck and D. J. MacInnis (Provo, UT: Association for Consumer Research, 1997), p. 77.

10. Furstenberg, "The Future of Families," p. 36.

11. Gardyn, "Happily Unmarried, " p. 61.

12. S. Eckel, "Single Mothers," *American Demographics,* May 1999, p. 66.

13. Raymond, "The Ex-Files," p. 60.

14. P. Paul, "Childless by Choice," *American Demographics,* November 2001, pp. 45–50.

15. For a different approach, see L. G. Pol and S. Pak, "Consumer Unit Types and Expenditures on Food Away from Home," *Journal of Consumer Affairs,* Winter 1995, pp. 403–28.

16. See J. Park, P. Tansuhaj, E. R. Spangenberg, "An Emotion-Based Perspective of Family Purchase Decisions," *Advances in Consumer Research,* vol. 22, eds. F. R. Kardes and M. Sujan (Provo, UT: Association for Consumer Research, 1995), pp. 723–28.

17. C. Lackman and J. M. Lanasa, "Family Decision-Making Theory," *Psychology & Marketing,* March–April 1993, pp. 81–113.

18. For an expanded view of this in an international context, see J. Ruth and S. R. Commuri, "Shifting Roles in Family Decision Making," *Advances in Consumer Research,* vol. 25, eds. J. W. Alba and J. W. Hutchinson (Provo, UT: Association for Consumer Research, 1998), pp. 400–6. See also W. Na, Y. Son, and R. Marshall, "An Empirical Study of the Purchase Role Structure in Korean Families," *Psychology & Marketing,* September 1998, pp. 563–76.

19. An exception is S. E. Beatty and S. Talpade, "Adolescent Influence in Family Decision Making," *Journal of Consumer Research,* September 1994, pp. 332–41.

20. See F. Holbert and G. Antonides, "Family Type Effects on Household Members' Decision Making," *Advances in Consumer Research,* vol. 24, eds. M. Bruck and D. J. MacInnis (Provo, UT: Association for Consumer Research, 1997), pp. 48–54; C. Kim and H. Lee, "Development of Family Triadic Measures for Children's Purchase Influence," *Journal Marketing Research,* August 1997, pp. 307–21; B. Dellaert, M. Prodigalidad, and J. Louviere, "Family Members' Projections of Each Other's Preference and Influence," *Marketing Letters,* no. 2 (1998), pp. 135–45; K. M. Palan, "Relationships between Family Communication and Consumer Activities of Adolescents," *Journal of the Academy of Marketing Science,* Fall 1998, pp. 338–49; and L. A. Williams and A. C. Burns,

"Exploring the Dimensionality of Children's Direct Influence Attempts," *Advances in Consumer Research,* vol. 27, eds. S. J. Hoch and R. J. Meyer (Provo, UT: Association for Consumer Research, 2000), pp. 64–71.

21. See C. Webster, "Determinants of Marital Power in Decision Making," *Advances in Consumer Research,* vol. 22, eds. F. R. Kardes and M. Sujan (Provo, UT: Association for Consumer Research, 1995), pp. 717–22; R. Madrigal and C. M. Miller, "Construct Validity of Spouses' Relative Influence Measures," *Journal of the Academy of Marketing Science,* Spring 1996, pp. 157–70; and C.-N. Chen, M. Lai, and D. D. C. Tarn, "Feminism Orientation, Product Attributes and Husband-Wife Decision Dominance," *Journal of Global Marketing,* 12, no. 3 (1999), pp. 23–39.

22. J. B. Ford, L. E. Pelton, and J. R. Lumpkin, "Perception of Marital Roles in Purchase Decision Processes," *Journal of the Academy of Marketing Science,* Spring 1995, pp. 120–31.

23. K. M. Palan and R. E. Wilkes, "Adolescent–Parent Interaction in Family Decision Making," *Journal of Consumer Research,* September 1997, pp. 159–69.

24. See C. Webster and S. Rice, "Equity Theory and the Power Structure in a Marital Relationship," *Advances in Consumer Research,* vol. 23, eds. K. P. Corfman and J. G. Lynch (Provo, UT: Association for Consumer Research, 1996), pp. 491–97; M. C. Reiss and C. Webster, "Relative Influence in Purchase Decision Making," *Advances in Consumer Research,* vol. 24, eds. M. Bruck and D. J. MacInnis (Provo, UT: Association for Consumer Research, 1997), pp. 42–47; and C. Webster, "The Meaning and Measurement of Marital Power," *Advances in Consumer Research,* vol. 25, eds. J. W. Alba and J. W. Hutchinson (Provo, UT: Association for Consumer Research, 1998), pp. 395–99.

25. D. Crispell, "Dual-Earner Diversity," *American Demographics,* July 1995, pp. 32–37.

26. C. Webster, "Is Spousal Decision Making a Culturally Situated Phenomenon?" *Psychology & Marketing,* December 2000, pp. 1035–58.

27. C. Kim and H. Lee, "A Taxonomy of Couples Based on Influence Strategies," *Journal of Business Research,* June 1996, pp. 157–68. See also L. Mallalieu and C. Faure, "Toward an Understanding of the Choice of Influence Tactics," *Advances in Consumer Research,* vol. 25, eds. J. W. Alba and J. W. Hutchinson (Provo, UT: Association for Consumer Research, 1998), pp. 407–14.

28. Palan and Wilkes, "Adolescent–Parent Interaction in Family Decision Making."

29. For a thorough review, see D. R. John, "Consumer Socialization of Children," *Journal of Consumer Research,* December 1999, pp. 183–209.

30. See J. Gregan-Paxton and D. R. John, "The Emergence of Adaptive Decision Making in Children," *Journal of Consumer Research,* June 1997, pp. 43–56; T. Davis, "What Children Understand about Consumption Constellations," *Advances in Consumer Research,* vol. 27, eds. S. J. Hoch and R. J. Meyer (Provo, UT: Association for Consumer Research, 2000), pp. 72–78; and E. S. Moore and R. J. Lutz, "Children, Advertising, and Product Experiences," *Journal of Consumer Research,* June 2000, pp. 31–47.

31. Parental responses differ across cultures; see G. M. Rose, "Consumer Socialization, Parental Style, and Developmental Timetables in the United States and Japan," *Journal of Marketing,* July 1999, pp. 105–19.

32. For example, see M. C. Macklin, "Preschoolers' Learning of Brand Names from Visual Cues," *Journal of Consumer Research,* December 1996, pp. 251–61; D. R. Pawlowski, D. M. Badzinski, and N. Mitchell, "Effects of Metaphors on Children's Comprehension and Perception of Print Advertisements," *Journal of Advertising,* Summer 1998, pp. 83–98.

33. M. Viswanathan, T. L. Childers, and E. S. Moore, "The Measurement of Intergenerational Communication and Influence on Consumption," *Journal of the Academy of Marketing Science,* Summer 2000, pp. 406–24.

34. Palan and Wilkes, "Adolescent–Parent Interaction in Family Decision Making."

35. See G. M. Rose, V. D. Bush, and L. R. Kahle, "The Influence of Family Communication Patterns on Parental Reactions toward Advertising," *Journal of Advertising,* Winter 1998, pp. 71–85; T. F. Mangleburg and T. Bristol, "Socialization and Adolescents' Skepticism toward Advertising," *Journal of Advertising,* Fall 1998, pp. 11–20; and L. Carlson, R. N. Laczniak, and J. E. Keith, "Socializing Children about Television," *Journal of the Academy of Marketing Science,* Summer 2001, pp. 276–88.

36. Palan and Wilkes, "Adolescent–Parent Interaction in Family Decision Making."

37. Ibid.

38. C. Otnes, M. Nelson, and M. A. McGrath, "The Children's Birthday Party," in *Advances in Consumer Research,* vol. 22, eds. F. R. Kardes and M. Sujan (Provo, UT: Association for Consumer Research, 1995), pp. 622–27.

39. J. U. McNeal, *Kids as Consumers* (New York, Lexington Books, 1992); and J. U. McNeal and C. Yeh, "Born to Shop," *American Demographics,* June 1993, pp. 34–39.

40. J. Rosenberg, "Brand Loyalty Begins Early," *Advertising Age,* February 12, 2001, p. S2.

41. L. A. Peracchio and D. Luna, "The Development of an Advertising Campaign to Discourage Smoking Initiation among Children and Youth," *Journal of Advertising,* Fall 1998, pp. 49–56.

42. C. Miller, "Marketers Hoping Kids Will Join Club," *Marketing News,* January 31, 1994, pp. 1–2.

Courtesy Jeep Jamboree USA.

Group Influences on Consumer Behavior

☐ For most products and brands, a consumer or family makes a purchase decision, acquires the item, and consumes it. The basic purchase motivation relates to the ability of the product or service itself to meet a need of the consumer.

Other purchases are fundamentally different. The consumer buys more than the product or brand. Membership in a group is also being purchased. A prime example of this is the purchase of a Harley-Davidson motorcycle. Most purchasers of a Harley-Davidson acquire not only the bike and some aspect of the image that comes with it; they also join a group or subculture. While there are a number of distinct Harley-Davidson groups, most share a core ethos or value system.

An important part of the biker identity involves product consumption. Obviously, one must own a Harley; however, just owning a Harley isn't enough. People, both other bikers and the general public, have expectations about the dress and behaviors of Harley bikers. As one study found: "The newcomer becomes acutely aware of another aspect of Harley ownership, performance before an audience. Much of what guides the newcomer's purchases of protective clothing, footwear, helmets, and accessories can be explained as tasks of impression management driven by perceptions of audience expectation."[1]

☐ Likewise, some Jeep owners elect to become members of a "Jeep community." These owners attend "brandfests" such as Jeep Jamborees, Jeep 101, and Camp Jeep. At these events, they meet and form relationships with other, geographically dispersed owners, deepen their involvement with their Jeeps and with the manufacturer (DaimlerChrysler), and become acculturated into the rituals and traditions of the community. The following quote illustrates how Susan, a first-time Jeep owner, began to become a member of this community.

I've been very happy. I get a lot of communications from Jeep, which I've been so impressed with. Usually you buy a car and you're a forgotten soul. It's kinda like they want you to be part of the family. As soon as I got the invitation for Jeep 101, I registered. I was very excited. But I was also nervous. I didn't think I would end up driving. I was very relieved to see someone in the car with you, 'cause it gave you the confidence to do what you're supposed to. Otherwise, I had visions of abandoning the truck on the hill and saying, "I can't do it!" I thought I might wimp out, but I didn't (smiles).[2]

Of course, other Jeep owners elect not to join this community and may even remain unaware that it exists.

Purchasing a Harley and "becoming a biker" or joining the Jeep "family" is clearly a group-based process. Even in an individualistic society like America, group memberships and identity are very important to all of us. And while we don't like to think of ourselves as conformists, most of us conform to group expectations most of the time.

When you decided what to wear to the last party you attended, you probably based your decision in part on the anticipated responses of the other individuals at the party. Likewise, your behavior at an anniversary celebration for your grandparents probably would differ from your behavior at a graduation party for a close friend. These behaviors are responses to group influences and expectations.

TYPES OF GROUPS

The terms *group* and *reference group* need to be distinguished. A **group** is defined as *two or more individuals who share a set of norms, values, or beliefs and have certain implicitly or explicitly defined relationships to one another such that their behaviors are interdependent*. A **reference group** is *a group whose presumed perspectives or values are being used by an individual as the basis for his or her current behavior*. Thus, a reference group is simply a group that an individual uses as a guide for behavior in a specific situation.

Most of us belong to a number of different groups and perhaps would like to belong to several others. When we are actively involved with a particular group, it generally functions as a reference group. As the situation changes, we may base our behavior on an entirely different group, which then becomes our reference group. We may belong to many groups simultaneously, but we generally use only one group as our primary point of reference in any given situation. This is illustrated in Figure 7–1.

FIGURE 7–1	Reference Groups Change as the Situation Changes

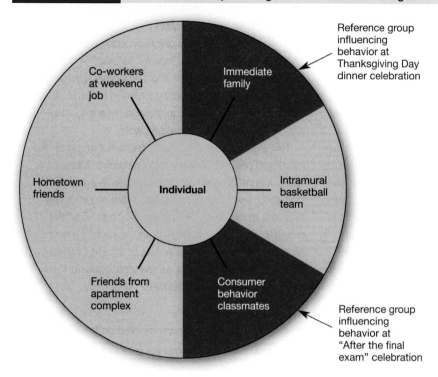

Groups may be classified according to a number of variables. Marketers have found three classification criteria to be particularly useful: (1) membership, (2) type of contact, and (3) attraction.

The *membership* criterion is dichotomous: Either one is a member of a particular group or one is not a member of that group. Of course, some members are more secure in their membership than others are; that is, some members feel they really belong to a group, while others lack this confidence.

Type of contact refers to how much interpersonal contact the group members have with each other. As group size increases, interpersonal contact tends to decrease. Type of contact is generally treated as having two categories. *Groups characterized by frequent interpersonal contact* are called **primary groups.** *Groups characterized by limited interpersonal contact* are referred to as **secondary groups.** Consumer Insight 7–1 discusses the unique nature of groups formed when contact is based solely on the Internet.

Attraction refers to the desirability that membership in a given group has for the individual. This can range from negative to positive. Groups with negative desirability— **dissociative reference groups**—can influence behavior just as do those with positive desirability. For example, teenagers tend to avoid clothing styles associated with older consumers.

Nonmembership groups with a positive attraction—**aspiration reference groups**—also exert a strong influence. Individuals frequently purchase products thought to be used by a desired group in order to achieve actual or symbolic membership in the group.

A recent study identified an aspiration and a dissociative reference group for junior- and senior-level undergraduate business majors.[3] The students were asked to rate various lifestyle groups listed in the PRIZM lifestyle clusters (a set of 62 types of American

The terms *virtual community* and *cybercommunity* are increasingly used to describe groups of people who interact over time around a topic of interest on the Internet.[4] These interactions generally take place in the Usenet portion of the Internet or on sites maintained by firms, media, or professional and nonprofit groups. Examples would include Saturn owners, scuba divers, *Star Wars* fans, and Planned Parenthood.

While it is easy to imagine that true communities are evolving on the Internet, the evidence is less clear. Such groups lack the wide range of functions and interactions that characterize "real" communities. Many participants in virtual communities lack any ongoing commitment to the group. The lack of face-to-face or even voice-to-voice interaction removes much of the symbolic and emotional meaning conveyed in real communities. The anonymity of participants removes responsibility for the consequences of their communications. Finally, there is seldom the explicit or implicit quid pro quo that characterizes most ongoing social relations.

Despite these distinctions from real communities or traditional groups, research indicates that Usenet and similar groups are indeed virtual communities for many participants. Studies have found ongoing communications among subsets of these interest groups. In addition, the patterns of communication indicate a group structure, with the more experienced members serving as experts and leaders and the newer members seeking advice and information.

These groups develop unique vocabularies such as "WTB" (want to buy) and "walks and talks" (a knife whose blade cleanly opens then smoothly springs back into place when slightly pushed toward closure). They also evolve their own netiquette and means for dealing with behaviors deemed inappropriate.

Not everyone involved with an interest group on the Internet is part of the community or group. Many "participants" are "lurkers" who peruse the group discussions without participating. Others participate at a very limited level. Still others are "drop-ins." For example, one of the authors of this text visits a scuba diving interest group once a year or so. He inquires about dive sites and other recreational opportunities in the area of his planned vacation.

Critical Thinking Questions

1. Can meaningful communities exist on the Internet?
2. What are the implications for society of the emergence of Internet-based communities?
3. What are the ethics of marketers monitoring Internet interest groups for product and advertising insights?
4. What are the ethics of marketers participating in Internet interest groups without revealing their identity or purpose?

lifestyles—see Chapter 12) in terms of "These people are very similar to how I would like to be" (aspiration group) and "These people are very similar to how I would not like to be" (dissociative group). The students were provided descriptions of some of the consumption patterns of each of the groups on which to base their ratings. The consumption descriptions of two groups are

	Money & Brains	Smalltown Downtown	Money & Brains	Smalltown Downtown
Heavy Users of			**Light Users of**	
	Travel/entertainment cards	Saltwater fishing gear	Hunting	Money market funds
	Aperitif/specialty wines	Pro wrestling	Pickup trucks	Racquetball
	Classical music	Gospel music	CB radios	Travel/entertainment cards
	Valid passports	Cafeterias	Roller derby	Chewing tobacco
	Natural cold cereal	Canned meat spreads	Presweetened cereal	Natural cold cereal
	Whole wheat bread	Instant mashed potatoes	Canned stews	Mexican foods
	TV movies	"The Today Show"	"As the World Turns"	"David Letterman"

Thirty-eight other groups were evaluated, but these two were the groups most and least aspired to. To which would you like to belong? Would you want to avoid belonging to the other group? (The students in this study aspired to be like the Money & Brains group and to avoid the Smalltown Downtown group.) Based on these consumption patterns, what kinds of jobs, attitudes, and hobbies do you think each group has? What other products do they use?

The business students in this study thought, with a good degree of accuracy, that the Money & Brains group would drive BMWs and Mercedes; read travel magazines, *Vogue,* and *Business Week;* drink Heineken, expensive wine and Scotch; and use Polo and Obsession. In contrast, the students described the Smalltown Downtown group as driving Fords and Chevrolets; reading *People, Sports Illustrated,* and *TV Guide;* drinking Budweiser and Miller; and using Brut and Old Spice. Since people tend to consume products associated with aspiration groups and avoid products associated with dissociative groups, this study suggests that Ford and Chevrolet are not well positioned to capture the next generation of upper-middle-class consumers. *What other marketing implications do you see? What should the various brands mentioned above do?*

Consumption Subcultures

A consumption-based group, often termed a **consumption subculture** is *a distinctive subgroup of society that self-selects on the basis of a shared commitment to a particular product class, brand, or consumption activity.* These groups have (1) an identifiable, hierarchical social structure; (2) a set of shared beliefs or values; and (3) unique jargon, rituals, and modes of symbolic expression.[5] Thus, they are reference groups for their members as well as those who aspire to join or avoid them.

A number of such subcultures have been studied in some detail, including those focused on a style/attitude (the "punk" culture[6]), an organization (an art museum[7]), a product (sports cards[8]), a television program/movie ("Star Trek"[9]), and activities (bodybuilding,[10] judo,[11] and skydiving[12]).

Activity-based subcultures are the most common type. Snowboarding, golfing, home brewing (beer), and gardening all have consumption subcultures built around them. Each has a set of self-selecting members. They have hierarchies at the local and national levels. For example, home brewing status is determined by whether or not one is a serious brewer, one's skill, length of time as a brewer, awards won, amount and type of equipment, role in the local club, and so forth. Each also has shared beliefs and unique jargon and rituals. Most hobbies and participation sports have consumption-based group subcultures built around them.

Consumption need not be shared physically to be a shared ritual that creates and sustains a group.[13] Serious fans of professional football, "Dawson's Creek," or "Star Trek" form consumption subcultures. For example, following a team gives a fan something in common with other fans of the same team, and enthusiasm for the sport itself provides a common ground for all members of the group.[14]

Note that not all, or even most, product owners or participants in an activity become members of the consumption subculture associated with it. For example, one can enjoy the "Star Trek" TV shows without becoming a member of the associated subculture. Self-selecting into a consumption subculture involves more than merely participating in the activity or owning the product. Commitment is required, as are the acquisition of the group's beliefs and values, participation in its indirect activities, and use of its jargon and rituals.

> It is a feeling of family. When I visit other dojos for a judo competition, I feel like I came back home. No other sports that I know do this and have the community judo has.[15]

> I once heard someone describe going to their first Star Trek convention as feeling like coming home. My first reaction was "Yes. THESE are my kind of people."[16]

As with other types of groups, members of subcultures vary in their commitment to and interpretation of the group's values and norms. Members of the Star Trek consumption subculture tend to vary along a continuum from fandom to Trekkers to Trekkies (varying in part by when and how much Star Trek symbols, such as clothing, are worn). Members are quite cognizant of these gradients:

> Still, propeller beanies and Trekkies do exist, and fandom does tolerate them. We don't emulate them, and they are nowhere near as typical as the media portrays, but they're there.

> You have to learn to be yourself, to feel secure at expressing what you're really all about. When I tell people that the uniform symbolizes my devotion to the series, to Gene's vision, and I tell them the philosophy behind the show . . . they want to know more.

> To me, a "Trekkie" is someone who is pretty much lost in the fantasy world of "Star Trek," someone who has taken an escapist approach to the show and almost literally "escaped" into it. I like to think I am a fan with a more appropriate detachment to the show.[17]

Marketing and Consumption Subcultures   Consumption subcultures based on activities obviously are markets for the requirements of the activity itself, such as golf clubs for golfers. However, these groups develop rituals and modes of symbolic communication that often involve other products or services. Golf is renowned for the "uniform" that many of its adherents wear. Clothes, hats, and other items designed for golfers are based as much on providing symbolic meaning as they are for functional benefits.

While these subcultures adopt consumption patterns in large part to affirm their unique identity, the larger market often appropriates all or parts of their symbols, at least for a time. Thus, clothing initially worn by a consumption subculture such as snowboarders or surfers for functional or symbolic reasons may emerge as a style for a much larger group (see Illustration 7–1). Marketers such as Nike observe such groups closely for clues to new trends.

Participating in a shared consumption experience is a means of developing and maintaining social relationships among individuals. When two or more individuals share a consumption event such as attending a performance, the consumption experience is not just the direct effect of seeing the performance. It includes the social interactions with the other individuals, the fact of sharing, and the meanings attached to these interactions. Thus, organizations marketing the arts, as well as sports marketers and others, should focus on providing and promoting the social, group aspects of the experience as well as the artistic and entertaining features. Illustration 7–2 shows how *Runner's World* promotes the formation of consumption groups and social experiences around the often solitary act of running.

Brand Communities

Consumption subcultures focus on the interactions of individuals around an activity, product category, or occasionally a brand. A **brand community** is *a nongeographically bound community, based on a structured set of social relationships among owners of a brand and the psychological relationship they have with the brand itself, the product in use, and the firm.*[18] A **community** is *characterized by consciousness of kind, shared rituals and traditions, and a sense of moral responsibility.*[19]

Illustrations in ad by Rick Rietveld; advertising design and layout by Rick Rietveld; © Rietveld, USA.

ILLUSTRATION 7–1

Clothing styles originating in consumption subcultures for functional or symbolic reasons are often adopted by other groups as well. Surfers have initiated several styles that gained widespread popularity.

Both Jeep and Harley-Davidson have created brand communities as described at the beginning of this chapter, as have Saab, Ford Bronco, and Macintosh. The following examples illustrate the nature of brand communities:

Consciousness of Kind

Who else drives Broncos? Guys like myself and guys who like engines.

A lot of people actually purchased the cars [Saabs] who I feel shouldn't have purchased them. There's a certain type of owner who is proper for the car.

To get down to task, there are several new classes of riders fouling the wind with the misapprehension that merely owning a Harley will transform them into a biker. This is the same type of dangerous ignorance that suggests that giving a dog an artichoke turns him into a gourmet.

Rituals and Traditions

If you drove a Saab, whenever you passed someone else driving a Saab, you beeped or flashed your headlights.

You can find out more about the history of Apple, but arguably its greatest contribution to the world was introduced on January 24, 1984, under the leadership of founder and chairman Steve Jobs. Apple introduced Macintosh, the machine that would change the world (from an individual's Macintosh website).

Courtesy *Runner's World.*

Moral Responsibility

Yeah, we see another Saab on the side of the road; we pull over to help, no matter what it is.

In Colorado, a longtime Jeep owner spent time at an intimidating stream crossing, loudly guiding drivers along the correct route through the rough water. He encouraged inexperienced drivers and reassured them about the capabilities of their vehicles.

Marketing and Brand Communities   Brand communities can add value to the ownership of the product and build intense loyalty. A "mere" Jeep owner derives the functional and symbolic benefits associated with owning a Jeep. A member of the Jeep community derives these benefits plus increases in self-esteem from gaining skill in the off-road operation of a Jeep, the ability and confidence to use the Jeep in a wider range of situations, new friendships and social interactions, a feeling of belongingness, a positive association with DaimlerChrysler, and a deeper relationship with their Jeep.

If a consumer anticipates these benefits in advance and values them, he or she is much more likely to buy the brand. Once a consumer becomes a member of a brand community, remaining in the community generally requires continuing to own and use the brand. This can create a very intense brand loyalty. Thus, a "mere" Jeep owner who needed to replace his Jeep might compare a new Jeep with other competing brands by comparing attributes across the brands. However, a Jeep community member would also consider the social and psychological costs of leaving the Jeep community.

A number of firms work diligently to foster brand communities. An initial question a manager must ask is, Does a brand community makes sense for this product and brand? Brand communities seem most relevant for high-involvement, activity-based products.

A second condition for a strong brand community appears to be a degree of uniqueness to the brand itself. Harley-Davidson has its historical association with "outlaw bikers." Jeep conjures up images from endless World War II movies. Saab has its unique design and foreign origin. It would certainly be more difficult to build a strong brand community around a mundane brand.

Given that a brand community is feasible, what is required to foster one? Saturn faced that question when it was launched as a new brand with a unique approach to the market. It works to create a community through the image it portrays of its customers in its advertising; the barbecues, workshops, and other events local dealers sponsor for owners; and the annual "vacation get-together at the factory" program. It also sponsors CarClubs through its dealers, as described on its website:

> Buy a Saturn and chances are you'll suddenly start noticing all the other Saturns already out on the road. Even if you think of yourself as being pretty restrained behind the wheel, you might find that every Saturn driver you see sparks a nearly uncontrollable impulse to wave hello. That feeling of being connected to other Saturn owners was the inspiration behind the CarClub.
>
> You're probably wondering, "What exactly do CarClub chapters do?" Hard to say exactly, since no two are alike. But in the past year, club chapters have held community fund-raisers for animal shelters, cancer research, and Habitat for Humanity; gone on short road trips to local vineyards and longer ones to Spring Hill; organized barbecues and road rallies; and learned more about their cars at special Saturn Customer Clinics.

Fostering a community requires the firm to establish a relationship with the owner. Saturn attempts this through portraying itself as a customer-focused firm, by direct mail sent to owners, and by dealer-organized events. It helps owners understand and value their cars through its Customer Clinics. It encourages the formation of social relationships among owners through its sponsorship of CarClubs, the annual vacation get-together, and dealership-sponsored activities.

One important tool for community building that Saturn does not utilize is the brandfest. A **brandfest** is *a gathering of owners and others for the purposes of interacting with one another in the context of learning about and using the brand.* Jeep makes extensive use of its brandfests with its Jeep Jamborees and Camp Jeep. It encourages Jeep owners to attend these events and to bring friends and family. Part of its website promotion for Camp Jeep reads,

> If you enjoy outdoor activities, this is your event. There'll be four-wheeling, mountain biking, free outdoor concerts, kids activities, vehicle displays, engineering roundtables, and much more. And this year, you could win a two-year lease on a new Jeep vehicle and other great prizes.

REFERENCE GROUP INFLUENCES ON THE CONSUMPTION PROCESS

We all conform in a variety of ways to numerous groups. Look around your classroom. The odds are that, except for gender differences, most of you will be dressed in a similar manner. In fact, a student who comes to class dressed in a suit will generally be asked about the job interview that others will assume is the cause of the more formal clothing. Note that we, as individuals, do not generally consider these behaviors to constitute conformity.

Group members often use other members as a source of information for their purchase decisions. This is known as informational influence. This ad shows how this works.

Courtesy Galderma Laboratories, L.P.; Agency: J. Walter Thompson.

Normally, we conform without even being aware of doing so, though we also frequently face conscious decisions on whether or not to go along with the group.

Reference groups have been found to influence a wide range of consumption behaviors. Before examining the marketing implications of these findings, we need to examine the nature of reference group influence more closely.

The Nature of Reference Group Influence

Reference group influence can take three forms: *informational, normative,* and *identification*. It is important to distinguish among these types since the marketing strategy required depends on the type of influence involved.

Informational influence *occurs when an individual uses the behaviors and opinions of reference group members as potentially useful bits of information.* This influence is based on either the similarity of the group's members to the individual or the expertise of the influencing group member.[20] Thus, a person may notice several members of a given group using a specific brand of nutrition bar. He or she may then decide to try that brand simply because there is evidence (its use by friends) that it may be a good brand.

Illustration 7–3 shows the nature of informational influence. Notice that the text of the ad indicates that one of the friends engaged in a fairly extensive search process and sought information from an expert before using Cetaphil. Then she told her friends about the recommendation and how well the product worked for her.

Normative influence, sometimes referred to as *utilitarian* influence, *occurs when an individual fulfills group expectations to gain a direct reward or to avoid a sanction.*[21] You may purchase a particular brand of wine to win approval from a colleague. Or you may refrain from wearing the latest fashion for fear of teasing by friends or to fit in with or be accepted by them. As you might expect, normative influence is strongest when individuals have strong ties to the group and the product involved is socially conspicuous.[22] This type of influence appears particularly important to younger consumers:

> Some of my friends would be unbelievably mad at me if I ever did start to smoke.

> I wanted to fit in with older people and everyone else was smoking.[23]

> Girls can like the Spice Girls and not get called lesbian or anything but if boys like boy bands they get called gay.[24]

Ads that promise social acceptance or approval if a product is used are relying on normative influence. Likewise, ads that suggest group disapproval if a product is not used, such as a mouthwash or deodorant, are based on normative influence.

Identification influence, also called *value-expressive* influence, *occurs when individuals have internalized the group's values and norms.* These then guide the individuals' behaviors without any thought of reference group sanctions or rewards. The individual has accepted the group's values as his or her own. The individual behaves in a manner consistent with the group's values because his or her values and the group's values are the same.

Figure 7–2 illustrates a series of consumption situations and the type of reference group influence that is operating in each case.

Degree of Reference Group Influence

Reference groups may have no influence in a given situation, or they may influence usage of the product category, the type of product used, or the brand used. Brand influence is most likely to be a category influence rather than a specific brand; that is, a group is likely to approve, or disapprove, a range of brands such as imported beers or luxury automobiles.

Table 7–1 shows how two consumption situation characteristics—necessity/nonnecessity and visible/private consumption—combine to affect the degree of reference group influence likely to operate in a specific situation. In the following paragraphs, we will discuss these two characteristics and three additional determinants of reference group influences.

1. Group influence is strongest *when the use of product or brand is visible to the group.* For a product such as running shoes, the product category (shoes), product type (running), and brand (Reebok) are all visible. The consumption of other products, such as vitamins, is generally private. Reference group influence typically affects only those aspects of the product (category, type, or brand) that are visible to the group.[25]
2. Reference group influence is higher *the less of a necessity an item is.* Thus, reference groups have strong influence on the ownership of products such as snowboards and designer clothes, but much less influence on necessities such as refrigerators.
3. In general, *the more commitment an individual feels to a group, the more the individual will conform to the group norms.* People are much more likely to consider group expectations when dressing for a dinner with a group they would like to join (stay with) than for dinner with a group that is unimportant to them.
4. The *more relevant a particular activity is to the group's functioning, the stronger the pressure to conform to the group norms concerning that activity.* Thus, style of dress may be important to a social group that frequently eats dinner together at nice restaurants and unimportant to a group that meets for basketball on Thursday nights.
5. The final factor that affects the degree of reference group influence is *the individual's confidence in the purchase situation.* One study found the purchase of color

FIGURE 7–2   Consumption Situations and Reference Group Influence

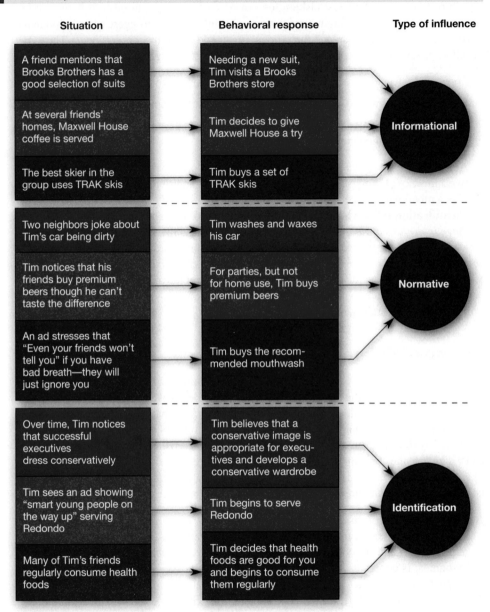

Situation	Behavioral response	Type of influence
A friend mentions that Brooks Brothers has a good selection of suits	Needing a new suit, Tim visits a Brooks Brothers store	Informational
At several friends' homes, Maxwell House coffee is served	Tim decides to give Maxwell House a try	
The best skier in the group uses TRAK skis	Tim buys a set of TRAK skis	
Two neighbors joke about Tim's car being dirty	Tim washes and waxes his car	Normative
Tim notices that his friends buy premium beers though he can't taste the difference	For parties, but not for home use, Tim buys premium beers	
An ad stresses that "Even your friends won't tell you" if you have bad breath—they will just ignore you	Tim buys the recommended mouthwash	
Over time, Tim notices that successful executives dress conservatively	Tim believes that a conservative image is appropriate for executives and develops a conservative wardrobe	Identification
Tim sees an ad showing "smart young people on the way up" serving Redondo	Tim begins to serve Redondo	
Many of Tim's friends regularly consume health foods	Tim decides that health foods are good for you and begins to consume them regularly	

televisions, automobiles, home air conditioners, insurance, refrigerators, medical services, magazines or books, clothing, and furniture to be particularly susceptible to reference group influence. Several of these products such as insurance and medical services are neither visible nor important to group functioning. Yet they are important to the individual and are products about which most individuals have limited information. Thus, group influence is strong because of the individual's lack of confidence in purchasing these products. In addition to confidence in the purchase situation, there is evidence that individuals differ in their tendency to be influenced by reference groups.[26]

	Degree Needed	
Consumption	Necessity	Nonnecessity
	Weak reference group influence on product	Strong reference group influence on product

Visible
Strong reference group influence on brand
	Public Necessities
	Influence: Weak product and strong brand
	Examples:
	  Shoes
	  Automobile
		Public Luxuries
		Influence: Strong product and brand
		
		Examples:
		  Snow board
		  Health club

Private
Weak reference group influence on brand
	Private Necessities
	Influence: Weak product and brand
	Examples:
	  Clothes washer
	  Insurance
		Private Luxuries
		Influence: Strong product and weak brand
		Examples:
		  Hot tub
		  Cell phone

TABLE 7–1

Two Consumption Situation Characteristics and Product/Brand Choice

Figure 7–3 summarizes the major determinants of the degree to which a reference group is likely to influence product and brand usage. Marketing managers can use this structure to determine the likely degree of group influence on the consumption of their brand.

MARKETING STRATEGIES BASED ON REFERENCE GROUP INFLUENCES

The first task a manager faces in using reference group influence is to determine the degree and nature of the influence that exists, *or can be created,* for the product in question. Figure 7–3 provides the starting point for this analysis.

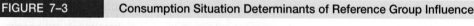

FIGURE 7–3   Consumption Situation Determinants of Reference Group Influence

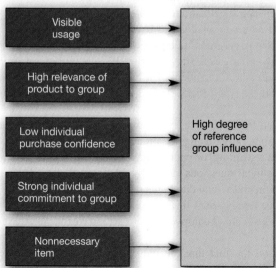

Personal Sales Strategies

The power of groups was initially demonstrated in a classic series of studies. Eight subjects are shown four straight lines on a board—three unequal lines are grouped close together, and another appears some distance from them. The subjects are asked to determine which one of the three unequal lines is closest to the length of the fourth line shown some distance away. The subjects are to announce their judgments publicly. Seven of the subjects are working for the experimenter, and they announce incorrect matches. The order of announcement is arranged so that the naive subject responds last. The naive subject almost always agrees with the incorrect judgment of the others. This is known as the **Asch phenomenon.**

This study has been repeated in a variety of formats and has generally achieved the same results. For example, student evaluations of the nutritional value of a new diet food were strongly affected by the stated opinions of other students even when they did not know the other students.[27] Imagine how much stronger the pressures to conform are among friends or when the task is less well defined, such as preferring one brand or style to another.

Consider this direct application of the Asch phenomenon in personal selling. A group of potential customers are brought together for a sales presentation. As each design is presented, the salesperson scans the expressions of the people in the group, looking for the one who shows approval (e.g., head nodding) of the design. The salesperson then asks that person for an opinion, since the opinion is certain to be favorable. The person is asked to elaborate. Meanwhile, the salesperson scans the faces of the other people, looking for more support, and then asks for an opinion of the person now showing most approval. The salesperson continues until the person who initially showed the most disapproval is reached. In this way, by using the first person as a model, and by social group pressure on the last person, the salesperson gets all or most of the people in the group to make a positive public statement about the design. *Do you see any ethical issues in using group influences in this way?*

Advertising Strategies

Marketers often position products as appropriate for group activities. French wines gained an image of being somewhat expensive and snobbish. Many consumers viewed them as appropriate only for very special occasions. A trade group, Food and Wines from France, launched a campaign to broaden their appeal. Illustration 7–4 shows an ad that positions French champagne as appropriate for casual group parties.

Marketers use all three types of reference group influence when developing advertisements. Informational influence in advertising was shown earlier in Illustration 7–3. Ads using informational influence typically show members of a group using a product. The message, generally unstated, is that "these types of people find this brand to be the best; if you are like them, you will too."

Normative group influence is not portrayed in ads as much as it once was. It involves the explicit or implicit suggestion that using, or not using, the brand will result in members of a group you belong to or wish to join rewarding, or punishing, you. One reason for the reduced use of this technique is the ethical questions raised by implying that a person's friends would base their reactions to the individual due to his or her purchases. Ads showing a person's friends saying negative things about them behind their back because their coffee was not great (yes, there was such an ad campaign) were criticized for playing on people's insecurities and fears.

Identification influence is based on the fact that the individual has internalized the group's values and attitudes. The advertising task is to demonstrate that the product is

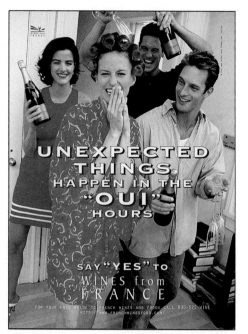

Courtesy of Food and Wines from France, Inc.

consistent with the group's and therefore the individual's beliefs. This often involves show-ing the brand being used by a particular type of group such as socially active young singles or parents of young children.

Teenagers and preteenagers are strongly influenced by peer pressure, or normative and identification group influences.[28] Unfortunately, these influences sometimes lead to injuri-ous consumption involving cigarettes, alcohol, drugs, sexual activities, and so forth. Orga-nizations working to combat these behaviors are up against a powerful foe. It is difficult to "just say no to drugs" if your friends are doing them and you face teasing and being ostra-cized if you don't join them.

One way to succeed in such a situation is to alter the group norms; that is, engaging in the injurious behavior needs to become a violation of the group norms. The text below is from a 30-second Partnership for a Drug-Free America commercial targeted at preteens. The visual showed a teenage boy smoking a joint and looking at two nearby girls. It clearly defines smoking pot as inappropriate group behavior subject to group sanctions (girls won't like you). Similar antismoking ads targeting teenagers have been very effective (one said, "Your friends won't come near you").[29]

TOMMY: Whoa, look at . . .

GIRLS: Tommy. He's so stoned.

TOMMY: This is totally . . .

GIRLS: Look what's happened to him.

TOMMY: You know I look like . . .

GIRLS: . . . such a mess. What a loser.

TOMMY: Yeah, this weed is definitely . . .

GIRLS: Gross. Ever since he started smoking pot, he's gross.

TOMMY: Like everybody's doing it.

GIRLS: And it's so uncool.

TOMMY: They're really into me. They think I'm so . . .

GIRLS: Out of it.

GIRLS: He's really out of it.

COMMUNICATIONS WITHIN GROUPS AND OPINION LEADERSHIP

Delores Sotto, a longtime resident of a large apartment building on Manhattan's West End Avenue, is explaining the problem with dry cleaning in her neighborhood. "If you ask me," she says, "none of the dry cleaners in this area is any good. They all should have gone out of business long ago." Over the course of the next 10 minutes, Delores relays horror stories about ruined Armani ("Collezin, for God's sake!"), shrunken custom-made shirts now suitable for only a pre-teen nephew, and stains mysteriously appearing on garments days after they have been cleaned.

It turns out that Delores's information comes not from direct experience but from the collective wisdom of her apartment building. In the laundry room, hallways, and elevators of her building, Delores's neighbors pass on the negative experiences they have with neighborhood vendors.[30]

As Delores illustrates, consumers are particularly likely to tell others about negative experiences in the marketplace. Do they also share positive experiences? An analyst with Morgan Stanley & Company characterizes Wal-Mart as "a company built on word-of-mouth reputation." What does this mean? By providing "everyday low prices" before they were popular, along with a broad selection of merchandise, fully stocked shelves, and superior customer services, Wal-Mart was able to generate excitement among its customers, who in turn told their friends about the store. Based on this, Wal-Mart has become America's largest retailer. However, it spends just 0.5 percent of its sales on advertising, compared to 2.5 percent for Kmart and 3.8 percent for Sears. This translates into a *billion dollars more profit* per year compared to Sears' performance.[31] Clearly, positive word-of-mouth communications are worth a great deal to a firm.

Word-of-mouth (WOM) communications, *individuals sharing information with other individuals,* are a critical influence on consumer decisions and business success. We learn about new products, restaurants, and retail outlets from our friends and other reference groups (1) by observing or participating with them as they use product and services or (2) by seeking or receiving advice and information from them. About half of Americans agree that they "often seek the advice of others before making a decision to buy products or services," and 40 percent feel that people often come to them for purchase advice.[32] Below are the percentages of men and women who rely on the advice of others before purchasing various products and services:

Product	Men	Women	Product	Men	Women
New doctor	45%	47%	Movie	26%	28%
Legal advice	41	42	Personal loan	17	20
Car mechanic	40	49	Automobile purchase	15	22
Restaurant	39	38	Haircut	10	24

FIGURE 7–4   Mass Communication Information Flows

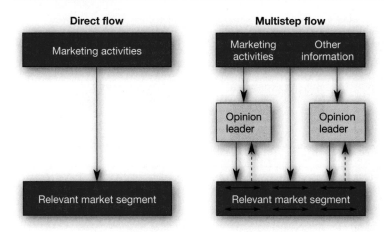

The Internet has and continues to change the nature of interpersonal communications. Sometimes referred to as *word-of-mouse,* market-related Internet communications between individuals who have no traditional interpersonal ties are rapidly increasing in importance, as are Internet communications that replace and often expand communications previously conducted by phone or mail or face to face. Thus, one can seek and receive advice from strangers about brands and activities through chat rooms and Usenet groups. In fact, these weak-tie communications, whether by Internet or other means, may have more total impact on behavior than strong-tie (between close acquaintances) communications.[33]

It is common for some individuals to actively filter, interpret, or provide product and brand relevant information to their family, friends, and colleagues. An individual who does this is known as an **opinion leader.** The process of one person receiving information from the mass media or other sources and passing it on to others is known as the **two-step flow of communication.** The two-step flow explains some aspects of communication within groups, but it is too simplistic to account for most communication flows. What usually happens is a multistep flow of communication. Figure 7–4 contrasts the direct flow of information from a firm to customers with the more realistic multistep flow of mass communications.

The **multistep flow of communication** involves opinion leaders for a particular product area who actively seek relevant information from the mass media as well as other sources. These opinion leaders process this information and transmit their interpretations of it to some members of their groups. These group members also receive information from the mass media as well as from group members who are not opinion leaders. Figure 7–4 also indicates that these non–opinion leaders often initiate requests for information and supply feedback to the opinion leaders. Likewise, opinion leaders receive information from their followers as well as from other opinion leaders.

Situations in Which Opinion Leadership Occurs

The exchange of advice and information between group members can occur (1) when one individual seeks information from another, (2) when one individual volunteers information, and (3) as a by-product of normal group interaction.[34]

Imagine that you are about to make a purchase in a product category with which you are not very familiar. Further imagine that the purchase is important to you—perhaps a new

FIGURE 7–5	Likelihood of Seeking an Opinion Leader

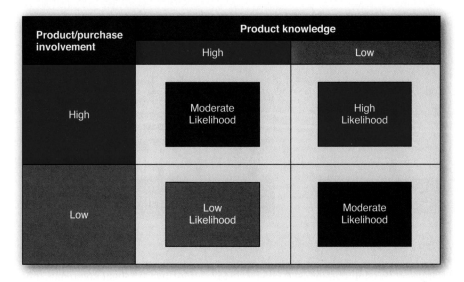

Product/purchase involvement	Product knowledge	
	High	Low
High	Moderate Likelihood	High Likelihood
Low	Low Likelihood	Moderate Likelihood

sound system, skis, or a bicycle. How would you go about deciding what type and brand to buy? Chances are you would, among other things, consult someone you know who you believe to be knowledgeable about the product category. This person would be an opinion leader for you. Notice that we have described a *high-involvement* purchase situation in which the purchaser had limited product knowledge about an important decision. Figure 7–5 illustrates how these factors lead to varying levels of opinion leadership.[35]

In addition to *explicitly* seeking or volunteering information, group members provide information to each other through observable behaviors. For example, suppose you visit a friend's house, a digital camera is used to take pictures, and these are then shown on the television screen. You have learned that your friend likes this product, and you have gained personal experience with it.

> Dinah Mohajer, a student at the University of Southern California, made some funky-colored nail polish to match a pair of sandals. Other students saw her and wanted similar polishes. Soon she and her boyfriend were making nail polish in her bathtub. Next she obtained distribution for the polish, now named Hard Candy, in trendy local salons. News photos showing Quentin Tarantino and Drew Barrymore wearing it generated more interest. The actress Alicia Silverstone wore and praised the product on David Letterman. In three years sales grew to $30 million.[36]

Hard Candy succeeded mainly through observation. Stylish individuals were seen wearing it on campus (Dinah and her friends). Then other individual style leaders used it (by being distributed through trendy salons it was seen and purchased by style-conscious individuals). Finally, celebrities were seen in mass media wearing Hard Candy.

Opinion Leader Characteristics

What characterizes opinion leaders? The most salient characteristic is greater long-term involvement with the product category than the non–opinion leaders in the group. This is referred to as **enduring involvement,** and it leads to enhanced knowledge about and experience with the product category or activity.[37] This knowledge and experience make opinion leadership possible.[38] Thus, an individual tends to be an opinion leader only for specific product or activity clusters.

Opinion leadership functions primarily through interpersonal communications and observation. These activities occur most frequently among individuals with similar demographic characteristics. Thus, it is not surprising that opinion leaders are found within all demographic segments of the population and seldom differ significantly on demographic variables from the people they influence.

Opinion leaders tend to be more gregarious than others are. They also have higher levels of exposure to relevant media than do non–opinion leaders.

The findings described above are based primarily on studies conducted in the United States. A study of opinion leadership for personal computers among undergraduate business students in eight countries (Australia, Germany, Hong Kong, India, Indonesia, Korea, New Zealand, and the United States) reached similar conclusions while noting some differences across countries. Expertise (a function of involvement) and sociability were important in all eight countries. In three of the Asian countries (Korea, Indonesia, and India), the opinion leaders tended to be older than those they influenced (in all three countries, a greater value is placed on maturity than in most Western countries).[39]

In addition to the previous individual characteristics associated with opinion leadership, a very important situational characteristic has been identified: the product, service, or store experience.[40] Substantial research evidence indicates that dissatisfied consumers are highly motivated to tell others about the reasons for their dissatisfaction, and these negative messages influence the recipients' attitudes and behaviors. Likewise, satisfied customers, particularly those with a positive affective response to a service, frequently provide positive recommendations to others (see Chapter 18).[41] This phenomenon makes imperative both consistent product and service quality and quick, positive responses to consumer complaints.

Market Mavens   Opinion leaders are generally product or activity specific. However, some individuals have information about many kinds of products, places to shop, and other aspects of markets. They both initiate discussions with others about products and shopping and respond to requests for market information. They are referred to as **market mavens.**

Market mavens provide significant amounts of information to others across a wide array of products, including durables and nondurables, services, and store types. They provide information on product quality, sales, usual prices, product availability, store personnel characteristics, and other features of relevance to consumers. Like opinion leaders, market mavens do not differ demographically from those they provide information to except they are more likely to be female.

Market mavens are extensive users of media.[42] They are also more extroverted and conscientious than others.[43]

Market Helping Behavior and Purchase Pals   Consumers do more than respond to requests for information or volunteer advice. Many consumers engage in **market helping behavior**—*actively helping others acquire goods and services.* Individuals clip coupons, collect information from a variety of sources, visit stores, and buy and return products for others. They teach others how to shop and connect them with helpful salespeople.

Marketplace involvement and altruism are the key defining characteristics of those actively engaged in market helping behaviors. This suggests a marketing strategy that appeals to the altruism of those highly involved in the marketplace. One approach would be a promotion such as "Bring a senior citizen shopping to the Bon Marche and receive a 10 percent discount on your purchases."[44]

Consumers use personal sources as their primary opinion leaders. However, experts whom they don't know personally can also fill this role. Survey results indicating that the brand is recommended by experts or typical users are also effective.

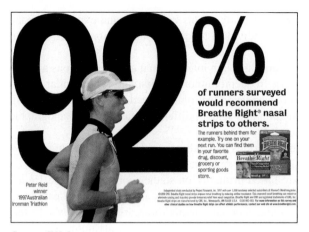

Courtesy CNS, Inc.

A **purchase pal** is a *person who accompanies another on a shopping trip primarily to aid in the purchase process.* Two types of aid are generally sought or provided: symbolic/social and functional/technical. Buyers seeking symbolic or social support (Does this look good on me? Should I really buy this?) tend to request help from close personal sources such as family members or close friends. The purchase pal must know and understand the buyer's personal needs and use situations. Buyers seeking functional or technical support (Is this a good price? Is this superior quality?) tend to seek help from experts who are colleagues or acquaintances.[45]

Marketing Strategy and Opinion Leadership

The importance of opinion leadership varies from product to product and from target market to target market. Therefore, the initial step in using opinion leaders is to determine—through research, experience, or logic—the role opinion leadership has in the situation at hand. Once this is done, marketing strategies can be devised to make use of opinion leadership.

Advertising   Advertising attempts to both *stimulate* and *simulate* opinion leadership. Stimulation involves themes designed to encourage current owners to talk about the product/brand (tell a friend about) or prospective owners to ask current owners (ask someone who owns one) for their impressions. Before such a campaign is used, the firm needs to be certain that there is a high degree of satisfaction among existing owners.

Simulating opinion leadership involves having an acknowledged opinion leader—such as Shaquille O'Neal or Sheryl Swoopes for basketball equipment—endorse a brand. Illustration 7–5 is an example of this approach. Or it can involve having an apparent opinion leader recommend the product in a "slice of life" commercial. These commercials involve an "overheard" conversation between two individuals in which one person provides brand advice to the other. Finally, advertising can present the results of surveys showing that a high percentage of either knowledgeable individuals (9 out of 10 dentists surveyed recommend . . .) or typical users (see Illustration 7–5) recommend the brand.[46]

Negative WOM   An obvious fact that has been confirmed by research is that consumers talk to other consumers about their experiences with products, stores, and services. Therefore, it is absolutely essential that marketers meet or exceed customer expectations concerning their products. When customer expectations are not met, the firm must respond quickly and fairly to customer complaints. Unhappy customers tell an average of nine others about their dissatisfaction.[47] Such negative word of mouth can more than offset millions in positive media advertising.[48] This issue is discussed in detail in Chapter 18.

Marketing Research Since opinion leaders often receive, interpret, and relay marketing messages to others, marketing research should focus on them rather than "representative" samples in those product categories and groups in which opinion leaders play a critical role. Thus, product-use tests, pretests of advertising copy, and media preference studies should be conducted on samples of individuals likely to be opinion leaders. It is essential that these individuals be exposed to, and respond favorably to, the firm's marketing mix. Of course, for those product categories or groups in which opinion leadership is not important, such a strategy would be unwise.

Product Sampling *Sampling*—sending a sample of a product to a group of potential consumers—is an effective means of generating interpersonal communications concerning the product. However, instead of using a random sample, marketers should attempt to send the samples to individuals likely to be opinion leaders.

Chrysler introduced its LH cars by offering the use of a new car to 6,000 presumed opinion leaders for a weekend. These included executives and community leaders. However, it also included less obvious people who often offer advice—for example, barbers. Follow-up research found that more than 32,000 people drove or rode in the car, and positive WOM reached many more.[49]

Clairol wanted to get ahead of its competition by creating WOM for its Herbal Essences True Intense Color line before the product was available in stores. Therefore, it ran an online promotional campaign that allowed consumers to receive free samples. Note that consumers visiting Clairol's website are likely to be more interested in this product category than others and are therefore potential opinion leaders.

Retailing/Personal Selling Numerous opportunities exist for retailers and sales personnel to use opinion leadership. Clothing stores can create "fashion advisory boards" composed of likely style leaders from their target market. An example would be cheerleaders and class officers for a store catering to teenagers. Restaurant managers can send special invitations, 2-for-1 meal coupons, and menus to likely leaders in their target markets, such as officers in the Junior League, League of Women Voters, and Rotary.

Retailers and sales personnel can encourage their current customers to pass along information to potential new customers. For example, an automobile salesperson, or the dealership, might provide a free car wash or oil change to current customers who send friends in to look at a new car. Real estate agents might send a coupon good for a meal for two at a nice restaurant to customers or other contacts who send them new clients.[50] Illustration 7–6 illustrates one firm's efforts in this area.

Identifying Opinion Leaders Opinion leaders can be identified by using self-designating questionnaires such as the one shown in Table 7–2. While the instrument in the table allows you to identify opinion leaders through direct research, what if you want to know who the opinion leaders are for a product on a national scale? Opinion leaders are hard to identify a priori because they tend to be demographically similar to those they influence.

The fact that opinion leaders are heavily involved with the mass media, particularly media that focus on their area of leadership, provides a partial solution to the identification problem. For example, Nike could assume that many subscribers to *Runner's World* serve as opinion leaders for jogging and running shoes. Likewise, the fact that opinion leaders tend to be gregarious and tend to belong to clubs and associations suggests that Nike could also consider members, and particularly leaders, of local running clubs to be opinion leaders.

SAGE ADVANCE CORPORATION
"JUST REWARDS" PROGRAM

We at Sage Advance Corporation have discovered that our satisfied customers have been giving very positive testimonials for our product and referring new customers to us. Our "Just Rewards" Program acknowledges the value of your word-of-mouth referrals. The program also offers you another means to recoup the cost of your Copper Cricket solar water heating system.

WHAT IS THE "JUST REWARDS" PROGRAM?

Sage Advance Corporation will pay a $100 reward to any owner of a Copper Cricket system who introduces the Copper Cricket to another person IF that introduction results in the sale of a new system to that person.

HOW DOES THE PROGRAM WORK?

1. You must be a Copper Cricket owner.
2. The new purchaser of a Copper Cricket system must identify you as the person who introduced them to the system. The only way to do this is to have the new purchaser fill out the "Just Rewards" card which they then present to the Sage Advance representative at time of purchase. If there is no Sage Advance representative in their area, call Sage Advance direct (503) 485-1947, and we will record your claim in the customer file.
3. You are eligible for the "Just Rewards" Program for two (2) years from the date of your purchase of the Copper Cricket system.
4. The new purchaser can reside in any state of the U.S.A.
5. This $100 reward per system sale is not a rebate or otherwise a part of the sales price of the system.

Sage Advance Corporation is committed to establishing a sustainable energy future. We welcome your assistance in reaching this goal. The rewards for us and you are many. Not only can you help reduce our national dependency on fossil fuels and nuclear energy, you can also reduce your living expenses and make a personal statement about your concern for the future. Pure, safe, renewable solar energy has been, and will continue to be, the public's choice. So, call a friend and share the rewards.

Courtesy Sage Advance Corporation.

Some product categories have professional opinion leaders. For products related to livestock, county extension agents are generally very influential. Barbers and hair stylists serve as opinion leaders for hair care products. Pharmacists are important opinion leaders for a wide range of health care products.

Levi Strauss has taken a unique and productive approach to identifying and influencing opinion leaders. In an attempt to increase the preference for Dockers among the key 24- to 35-year-old urban market, it has created the position of "urban networker" for such key cities as San Francisco, Chicago, Los Angeles, New York, and Boston. The job of the urban networker is to identify emerging trendsetters in their cities and tie them to Dockers. This could involve noticing a new band that is beginning to catch on and providing Dockers to the members. Or the networker might sponsor the band or a performance at which it will perform. Emerging artists, entertainment promoters, athletes, and other potential opinion leaders are contacted and encouraged to wear Dockers and are provided various types of assistance. The objective is not to cause events or create stars (which Nike tends to do) but to be associated with emerging urban "happenings" and young influentials as they evolve.[51]

Teen People takes a different tack. It has a group of 4,000 young "trend spotters" on call. The magazine encourages them to submit story ideas and respond to published

TABLE 7–2

Opinion Leadership
and Opinion Seeking
Scales*

Instructions: This short questionnaire is about _____ (product category).
Please read each statement carefully. For each statement, please circle the number that most closely matches
your view of the opinions stated. The items are scaled from 1 to 7, with a higher number meaning stronger
agreement.

1. My opinion on _____ seems not to count with other people.

2. When I consider buying a _____, I ask other people for advice.

3. When they choose a _____, other people do not turn to me for advice.

4. I don't need to talk to others before I buy _____.

5. Other people come to me for advice about choosing _____.

6. I rarely ask other people what _____ to buy.

7. People that I know pick _____ based on what I have told them.

8. I like to get others' opinions before I buy a _____.

9. I often persuade other people to buy the _____ that I like.

10. I feel more comfortable buying a _____ when I have gotten other
people's opinions on it.

*Even-numbered items measure opinion seeking and odd-numbered items measure opinion leadership. Scoring needs to be
reversed on some items for consistency.

Source: L. A. Flynn, R. E. Goldsmith, and J. K. Eastman, "Opinion Leaders and Opinion Seekers," *Journal of the Academy of
Marketing Science,* Spring 1996, p. 146. © Academy of Marketing Science.

articles. It invites them to monthly meetings at regional offices to discuss what's cool and
what is not.

Creating Buzz   Buzz can be defined as *the exponential expansion of WOM.* It happens
when "word spreads like wildfire" with no or limited mass media advertising supporting
it. Buzz drove demand for Hard Candy nail polish as described earlier. It also made massive successes of Pokemon, Beanie Babies, the original *Blair Witch Project,* and the Harry
Potter books. Buzz was largely responsible for the creation of such product categories as
the Internet, snowboards, and in-line skates. It is estimated that 13 percent of the U.S.
economy is largely driven by buzz (toys, sporting goods, movies, and similar products).
Another 54 percent is partially driven by buzz, including investment products, beverages,
and electronics.[52]

Buzz is not supported by large advertising budgets, but it is often created by marketing activities. In fact, creating buzz is a key aspect of *guerrilla marketing*—marketing
with a limited budget using nonconventional communications strategies. In addition,
creating buzz is often part of a larger strategy that includes significant mass media
advertising.

Earlier we described how Clairol attempted to create WOM for its True Intense Color
line via an online sampling program. It also launched a sweepstakes, "Be the Attraction,"
with a grand prize of an all-expenses-paid trip for four to the premiere of *Legally Blond.* As
the product moved into stores, ads promoting the product and the sweepstakes were placed
in movie theater lobbies. Models with hair colored by the product appeared on street cor-
ners, college campuses, and high-profile public venues in major cities to demonstrate the
line. All this was done to create buzz. However, these efforts were soon supplemented with
a major mass media advertising campaign.[53]

Marketers create buzz by providing opinion leaders advance information and product
samples, having celebrities use the product, placing the product in movies, sponsoring "in"

events tied to the product, restricting supply, courting publicity, and otherwise generating excitement and mystic about the brand. Consider the following:

> When Julia Roberts won the Academy Award for best actress, she waved to the audience with a snowflake-designed Van Cleef & Arpels diamond bracelet on her right wrist. That image was not only broadcast worldwide via television but also appeared in numerous magazine photos of the event. It generated widespread interest and was mentioned by brand in many newspaper and magazine articles.
>
> A lucky break for Van Cleef & Arpels? No. Van Cleef's PR agent brought Ms. Roberts to a suite in the exclusive hotel L'Ermitage where he had representatives for several of his clients, including Van Cleef, Diane Furstenberg fashions, Helena Rubinstein beauty products, and Adrienne cashmere shawls. Ms. Roberts, after some persuasion and a gift or two, chose the bracelet and matching earrings to complement her Valentino dress.[54]

DIFFUSION OF INNOVATIONS

An **innovation** is *an idea, practice, or product perceived to be new by the relevant individual or group.* Whether or not a given product *is* an innovation is determined by the perceptions of the potential market, not by an objective measure of technological change. The manner by which a new product is accepted or spreads through a market is basically a group phenomenon. In this section, we will examine this process in some detail.[55]

Categories of Innovations

Try to recall new products that you have encountered in the past two or three years. As you reflect on these, it may occur to you that there are degrees of innovation. For example, the Internet is more of an innovation than a new fat-free snack. The changes required in one's behavior, including attitudes and beliefs, or lifestyle if a person adopts the new product or service determine the degree of innovation, not the technical or functional changes in the product.

We can place any new product somewhere on a continuum ranging from no change to radical change, depending on the target market's perception of the item. This continuum is often divided into three categories or types of innovations.

Continuous Innovation   Adoption of this type of innovation requires relatively minor changes in behavior or changes in behaviors that are unimportant to the consumer. Examples include Crest Dual Action Whitening toothpaste, Wheaties Energy Crunch cereal, Pria (an afternoon snack bar), and DVD players. Note that several of these products are complex technological breakthroughs. However, their use requires little change in the owner's behavior or attitude. Illustration 7–7 is another example of a continuous innovation.

Dynamically Continuous Innovation   Adoption of this type of innovation requires a moderate change in an important behavior or a major change in a behavior of low or moderate importance to the individual. Examples include digital cameras, personal navigators, and Jergens' Naturally Smooth (a moisturizer designed to also make the hair on a woman's legs finer and less noticeable, reducing the need for shaving). Illustration 7–8 shows a product that is a dynamically continuous innovation for most consumer groups.

Discontinuous Innovation   Adoption of this type of innovation requires major changes in behavior of significant importance to the individual or group. Examples would include Norplant contraceptive, becoming vegetarian, and the Segway Human Transporter (see Illustration 7–9).

Reprinted with permission and courtesy of Bayer Corporation.

Courtesy of Light Years Ahead; Den-Mat Corporation.

Buying and using the Segway for transportation would involve a major change in an important activity. Most consumers will react to this as a discontinuous innovation.

Ric Feld/AP Wide World Photos.

Most of the more than 20,000 new products or alterations introduced each year tend toward the no-change end of the continuum. Much of the theoretical and empirical research, however, has been based on discontinuous innovations. For example, individual consumers presumably go through a series of distinct steps or stages known as the **adoption process** when purchasing an innovation. These stages are shown in Figure 7–6.

Figure 7–6 also shows the steps in extended decision making described in Chapter 1. As can be seen, the *adoption process* is basically a term used to describe extended decision making when a new product is involved. As we will discuss in detail in Chapter 14, extended decision making occurs when the consumer is *highly involved* in the purchase. High purchase involvement is likely for discontinuous innovations such as the decision to purchase an electric car, and most studies of innovations of this nature have found that consumers use extended decision making.

However, it would be a mistake to assume that all innovations are evaluated using extended decision making (the adoption process). In fact, most continuous innovations probably trigger limited decision making. As consumers, we generally don't put a great deal of effort into deciding to purchase such innovations as Hershey Food's new Marabou Milk chocolate rolls or the new Scotch-Brite Never Rust soap pad.

Diffusion Process

The **diffusion process** is *the manner in which innovations spread throughout a market.* The term *spread* refers to purchase behavior in which the product is purchased with some degree of regularity.[56] The market can range from virtually the entire society (for a new soft

| FIGURE 7–6 | Adoption Process and Extended Decision Making |

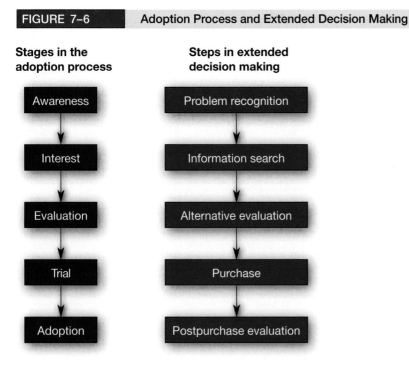

Stages in the adoption process

Steps in extended decision making

Awareness	Problem recognition
Interest	Information search
Evaluation	Alternative evaluation
Trial	Purchase
Adoption	Postpurchase evaluation

drink, perhaps) to the students at a particular high school (for an automated fast-food and snack outlet).

For most innovations, the diffusion process appears to follow a similar pattern over time: a period of relatively slow growth, followed by a period of rapid growth, followed by a final period of slower growth. This pattern is shown in Figure 7–7. However, there are exceptions to this pattern. In particular, it appears that for continuous innovations such as new ready-to-eat cereals, the initial slow-growth stage may be skipped.

An overview of innovation studies reveals that the time involved from introduction until a given market segment is saturated (i.e., sales growth has slowed or stopped) varies from a few days or weeks to years. This leads to two interesting questions: (1) What determines how rapidly a particular innovation will spread through a given market segment? and (2) In what ways do those who purchase innovations relatively early differ from those who purchase them later?

Factors Affecting the Spread of Innovations   The rate at which an innovation is diffused is a function of the following 10 factors.

1. *Type of group.* Some groups are more accepting of change than others. In general, young, affluent, and highly educated groups accept change, including new products, readily. Thus, the target market for the innovation is an important determinant of the rate of diffusion.
2. *Type of decision.* The type of decision refers to an individual versus a group decision. The fewer individuals involved in the purchase decision, the more rapidly an innovation will spread.
3. *Marketing effort.* The rate of diffusion is heavily influenced by the extent of marketing effort involved. Thus, the rate of diffusion is not completely beyond the control of the firm.

| FIGURE 7–7 | Diffusion Rate of an Innovation over Time |

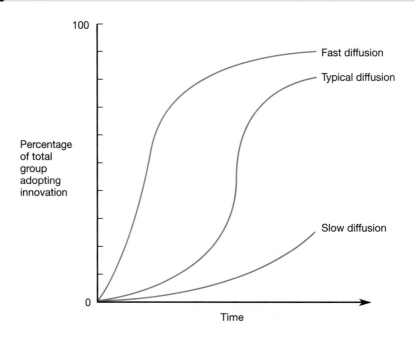

4. *Fulfillment of felt need.* The more manifest or obvious the need that the innovation satisfies, the faster the diffusion. Rogaine, a cure for some types of hair loss, gained rapid trial among those uncomfortable with thin hair or baldness.

5. *Compatibility.* The more the purchase and use of the innovation is consistent with the individual's and group's values or beliefs, the more rapid the diffusion.[57]

6. *Relative advantage.* The better the innovation is perceived to meet the relevant need compared to existing methods, the more rapid the diffusion. Both the performance and the cost of the product are included in relative advantage. Thus, some innovations offering noticeable performance advantages, such as CD players for automobiles, are accepted slowly or not at all because of a high price. *To succeed, an innovation must have either a performance advantage or a cost advantage.* It is the combination of these two that we call *relative advantage.*

7. *Complexity.* The more difficult the innovation is to understand and use, the slower the diffusion. The key to this dimension is ease of use, *not* complexity of product. For example, Panasonic's portable videodisc player, while a very complex product, is very simple for most consumers to use.

8. *Observability.* The more easily consumers can observe the positive effects of adopting an innovation, the more rapid its diffusion will be. Cellular telephones are relatively visible. Laser eye surgery, while less visible, may be a frequent topic of conversation. On the other hand, new headache remedies, such as naproxen sodium (Aleve), are less obvious and generally less likely to be discussed.

9. *Trialability.* The easier it is to have a low-cost or low-risk trial of the innovation, the more rapid its diffusion. The diffusion of products like laser eye surgery has been hampered by the difficulty of trying out the product in a realistic manner. This is much less of a problem with low-cost items such as headache remedies, or such items as videodisc players that can be rented, borrowed, or tried at a retail outlet.

FIGURE 7–8	Diffusion Rates for Popular Consumer Electronics

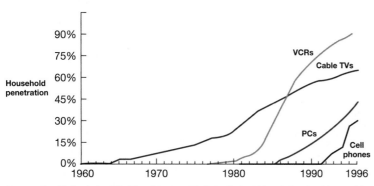

Source: "New Technologies Take Time," *Business Week,* April 19, 1999, p. 8. Reprinted by special permission. © 1999 McGraw-Hill and Companies, Inc.

10. *Perceived risk.* The more risk associated with trying an innovation, the slower the diffusion. Risk can be financial, physical, or social. **Perceived risk** is a function of three dimensions: (1) *the probability that the innovation will not perform as desired;* (2) *the consequences of its not performing as desired;* and (3) *the ability to reverse, and the cost of reversing, any negative consequences.*[58] Thus, many consumers feel a need for the benefits offered by laser eye surgery and view the probability of its working successfully as being quite high. However, they perceive the consequences of failure as being extreme and irreversible and therefore do not adopt this innovation.

Figure 7–8 shows the diffusion curves for four popular consumer electronic products. *How would you explain the differences in the rate and level of penetration of U.S. households?*

Characteristics of Individuals Who Adopt an Innovation at Varying Points in Time The curves shown in Figures 7–7 and 7–8 are cumulative curves that illustrate the increase in the percentage of adopters over time. If we change those curves from a cumulative format to one that shows the percentage of a market that adopts the innovation at any given point in time, we will have the familiar bell-shaped curves shown in Figure 7–9.

Figure 7–9 reemphasizes the fact that a few individuals adopt an innovation very quickly, another limited group is reluctant to adopt the innovation, and the majority of the group adopts at some time in between the two extremes.

Researchers have found it useful to divide the adopters of any given innovation into five groups based on the relative time at which they adopt. These groups, called **adopter categories,** are shown in Figure 7–9 and defined below:

Innovators	The first 2.5 percent to adopt an innovation
Early adopters	The next 13.5 percent to adopt
Early majority	The next 34 percent to adopt
Late majority	The next 34 percent to adopt
Laggards	The final 16 percent to adopt

How do these five groups differ? The first answer is: It depends on the product category being considered. Table 7–3 illustrates the rather dramatic differences between early

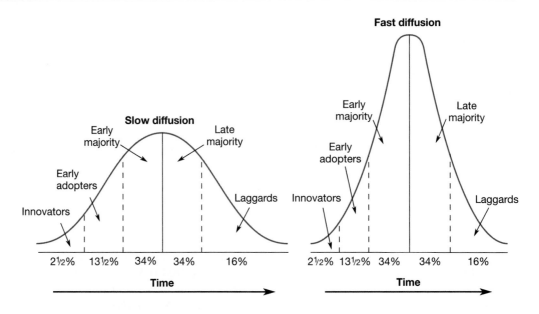

FIGURE 7-9	Adoptions of an Innovation over Time

Slow diffusion

Innovators — 2½%
Early adopters — 13½%
Early majority — 34%
Late majority — 34%
Laggards — 16%
Time

Fast diffusion

Innovators — 2½%
Early adopters — 13½%
Early majority — 34%
Late majority — 34%
Laggards — 16%
Time

TABLE 7-3		*Home Computer*	*VCR*
Early Purchasers of Home Computers and VCRs	**Age***		
	18–24	103	163
	25–34	113	91
	35+	94	84
	Education*		
	College graduate	179	152
	Attended college	125	86
	High school	77	92
	Marital status*		
	Married	209	92
	Single	107	136
	Products owned†		
	Tennis clothing	0	+
	Squash racquet	0	−
	Water skis	−	+
	Target gun	−	+
	Bowling ball	−	+
	Ski boots	−	0
	Luxury car	−	0
	Men's diamond ring	−	+
	Classical folk records/tapes	0	−
	Contemporary jazz records/tapes	−	0
	Book club	0	−
	Solar heating	+	−
	Food dehydrator	+	−
	Electric ice cream maker	−	+

*Results are index numbers where 100 equals average consumption.

†+ = Heavy consumption; 0 = Moderate consumption; and − = Light consumption.

Source: A. J. Kover, "Somebody Buys New Products Early—But Who?" Unpublished paper prepared for Cunningham & Walsh, Inc.

purchasers of home computers and VCRs. Thus, although we propose some broad generalizations, they may not hold true for a particular product category.

Innovators are venturesome risk takers. They are capable of absorbing the financial and social costs of adopting an unsuccessful product. They are cosmopolitan in outlook and use other innovators rather than local peers as a reference group. They tend to be younger, better educated, and more socially mobile than their peers. Innovators make extensive use of commercial media, sales personnel, and professional sources in learning of new products.

Early adopters tend to be opinion leaders in local reference groups. They are successful, well educated, and somewhat younger than their peers. They are willing to take a calculated risk on an innovation but are concerned with failure. Early adopters also use commercial, professional, and interpersonal information sources, and they provide information to others.

Early majority consumers tend to be cautious about innovations. They adopt sooner than most of their social group but also after the innovation has proven successful with others. They are socially active but seldom leaders. They tend to be somewhat older, less well educated, and less socially mobile than the early adopters. The early majority relies heavily on interpersonal sources of information.

Late majority members are skeptical about innovations. They often adopt more in response to social pressures or a decreased availability of the previous product than because of a positive evaluation of the innovation. They tend to be older and have less social status and mobility than those who adopt earlier.

Laggards are locally oriented and engage in limited social interaction. They tend to be relatively dogmatic and oriented toward the past. Laggards adopt innovations only with reluctance.

Marketing Strategies and the Diffusion Process

Market Segmentation   Since earlier purchasers of an innovation differ from later purchasers, firms should consider a "moving target market" approach. That is, after selecting a general target market, the firm should initially focus on those individuals within the target market most likely to be innovators and early adopters.[59]

Messages to this group can often emphasize the newness and innovative characteristics of the product as well as its functional features. Since this group is frequently very involved with, and knowledgeable about, the product category, marketing communications may be able to focus on the new technical features of the product and rely on the audience to understand the benefits these features will provide.

As the innovation gains acceptance, the focus of attention should shift to the early and late majority. This will frequently require different media. In addition, message themes should generally move away from a focus on radical newness. Instead, they should emphasize the acceptance the product has gained and its proven performance record.

Diffusion Enhancement Strategies   Table 7–4 provides a framework for developing strategies to enhance the market acceptance of an innovation. The critical aspect of this process is to analyze the innovation *from the target market's perspective*. This analysis will indicate potential obstacles—*diffusion inhibitors*—to rapid market acceptance. The manager's task is then to overcome these inhibitors with *diffusion enhancement strategies*. Table 7–4 lists a number of potential enhancement strategies, but many others are possible.

Consider the innovation shown in Illustration 7–10. Which factors will inhibit its diffusion, and what strategies can be used to overcome them?

TABLE 7–4

Innovation Analysis
and Diffusion
Enhancement
Strategies

Diffusion Determinant	*Diffusion Inhibitor*	*Diffusion Enhancement Strategies*
1. Nature of group	Conservative	Search for other markets Target innovators within group
2. Type of decision	Group	Choose media to reach all deciders Provide conflict reduction themes
3. Marketing effort	Limited	Target innovators within group Use regional rollout
4. Felt need	Weak	Use extensive advertising to show importance of benefits
5. Compatibility	Conflict	Emphasize attributes consistent with normative values
6. Relative advantage	Low	Lower price Redesign product
7. Complexity	High	Distribute through high-service outlets Use skilled sales force Use product demonstrations Undertake extensive marketing efforts
8. Observability	Low	Use extensive advertising
9. Trialability	Difficult	Use free samples to early adopter types Offer special prices to rental agencies Use high-service outlets
10. Perceived risk	High	Document success Highlight endorsement by credible sources Provide guarantees

ILLUSTRATION 7–10

Ten factors
determine the suc-
cess of innovations.
How do you think
this innovation will
fare based on these
10 factors?

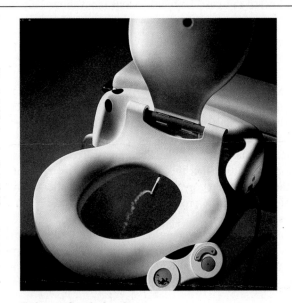

Toto U.S.A.

SUMMARY

A *group* in its broadest sense includes two or more individuals who share a set of norms, values, or beliefs and have certain implicit or explicit relationships such that their behaviors are interdependent. Some groups require membership; others (e.g., aspiration groups) do not. Groups that have frequent personal contact are called *primary groups;* those with limited interpersonal contact are called *secondary groups. Attraction* refers to the degree of positive or negative desirability the group has to the individual.

The degree of *conformity* to a group is a function of (1) the visibility of the usage situation, (2) the level of commitment the individual feels to the group, (3) the relevance of the behavior to the functioning of the group, (4) the individual's confidence in his or her own judgment in the area, and (5) the necessity/nonnecessity nature of the product.

A *consumption subculture* is a group that self-selects on the basis of a shared commitment to a particular product or consumption activity. These subcultures also have (1) an identifiable, hierarchical social structure; (2) a set of shared beliefs or values; and (3) unique jargon, rituals, and modes of symbolic expression.

A *brand community* is a nongeographically bound community, based on a structured set of social relationships among owners of a brand and the psychological relationship they have with the brand itself, the product in use, and the firm. A community is characterized by consciousness of kind, shared rituals and traditions, and a sense of moral responsibility. Brand communities can add value to the ownership of the product and build intense loyalty. They seem most relevant for high-involvement, activity-based products and for brands with a degree of uniqueness. Both Jeep and Harley-Davidson have benefited from strong brand communities.

Group influence varies across situations. *Informational influence* occurs when individuals simply acquire information shared by group members. *Normative influence* happens when an individual conforms to group expectations to gain approval or avoid disapproval. *Identification influence* exists when an individual identifies with the group norms as a part of his or her self-concept and identity.

Communication within groups is a major source of information about certain products. It is a particularly important source when an individual has a high level of *purchase involvement* and a low level of *product*

knowledge. In such cases, the consumer is likely to seek information from a more knowledgeable group member. This person is known as an *opinion leader.* Opinion leaders are sought out for information, and they also volunteer information. Of course, substantial product information is exchanged during normal group interactions.

Opinion leaders are product-category or activity-group specific. They tend to have greater product knowledge, more exposure to relevant media, and more gregarious personalities than their followers. They tend to have demographics similar to their followers. A situational variable, *product dissatisfaction,* motivates many individuals to become temporary opinion leaders. The term *market maven* is used to describe individuals who are opinion leaders about the shopping process in general.

Many consumers engage in *market helping behavior*—actively helping others acquire goods or services. Others serve as *purchase pals*—people who accompany others on shopping trips primarily to aid in the purchase process.

Marketers attempt to identify opinion leaders primarily through their media habits and social activities. Identified opinion leaders then can be used in marketing research, product sampling, retailing/personal selling, advertising, and creating buzz.

Groups greatly affect the diffusion of innovations. *Innovations* vary in degree of behavioral change required and the rate at which they are diffused. The first purchasers of an innovative product or service are termed *innovators;* those who follow over time are known as *early adopters, early majority, late majority,* and *laggards.* Each of these groups differs in personality, age, education, and reference group membership. These characteristics help marketers identify and appeal to different classes of adopters at different stages of an innovation's diffusion.

The time it takes for an innovation to spread from innovators to laggards is affected by several factors: (1) nature of the group involved, (2) type of innovation decision required, (3) extent of marketing effort, (4) strength of felt need, (5) compatibility of the innovation with existing values, (6) relative advantage, (7) complexity of the innovation, (8) ease in observing usage of the innovation, (9) ease in trying the innovation, and (10) perceived risk in trying the innovation.

KEY TERMS

Adopter categories 251
Adoption process 248
Asch phenomenon 236
Aspiration reference
  groups 225
Brand community 228
Brandfest 231
Buzz 245
Community 228
Consumption subculture 227
Diffusion process 248
Dissociative reference groups 225
Early adopters 253

Early majority 253
Enduring involvement 240
Group 224
Identification influence 233
Informational influence 232
Innovation 246
Innovators 253
Laggards 253
Late majority 253
Market helping behavior 241
Market mavens 241
Multistep flow of
  communication 239

Normative influence 232
Opinion leader 239
Perceived risk 251
Primary group 225
Purchase pal 242
Reference group 224
Secondary group 225
Two-step flow of
  communication 239
Word-of-mouth (WOM)
  communications 238

INTERNET EXERCISES

1. Monitor a chat group or bulletin board on a topic that interests you for a week. Are the participants in this activity a group? A reference group? A virtual community?
2. Find a consumption-based group or subculture that uses the Internet as one means of communication. What can you learn about this group by monitoring the Internet?
3. Find and describe an example of a marketer using the Internet to encourage the formation or communications of a brand community.
4. Visit the websites for the following and describe the firms' efforts to foster brand communities.
   a. Ford Bronco
   b. Harley-Davidson

c. Jeep
d. Saab
e. Macintosh
f. K2 skies
g. Specialized bicycles
h. Tabasco sauce

5. Find and describe evidence of market maven or everyday market helping behavior on the Internet.
6. Find and describe two examples of opinion leadership and two examples of seeking an opinion leader on the Internet.
7. Pick a recent innovation of interest. Prepare a report on the information available about this innovation on the Internet.

DDB NEEDHAM LIFESTYLE DATA ANALYSES

1. Use the DDB Needham data to determine the characteristics of likely innovators for the following. Why is this the case? What are the marketing implications?
   a. Foods
   b. New products in general
2. Based on the DDB Needham data, what characterizes one who is likely to be an opinion

leader for new movies? Why is this the case? What are the marketing implications?
3. What characterizes one who is likely to be a late adopter or laggard for many items (see Tables 1a, 2a, 3a, 4a, 5a, 6a, and 7a)? Why is this the case? What are the marketing implications?

REVIEW QUESTIONS

1. How does a *group* differ from a *reference group?*
2. What criteria are used by marketers to classify groups?
3. What is a *dissociative reference group?* In what way can dissociative reference groups influence consumer behavior?
4. What is an *aspiration reference group?* How can an aspiration reference group influence behavior?
5. What factors determine the degree of influence a reference group will have on a given consumer decision?
6. What is a *consumption-based group* or a *consumption subculture?* What are the characteristics of such a group?
7. How can marketers develop strategy based on consumption subcultures?
8. What is a *brand community?* What are the characteristics of such a group?
9. For what products are brand communities most appropriate? How can a marketer foster a brand community?
10. What types of group influence exist? Why must a marketing manager be aware of these separate types of group influence?
11. What five factors determine the strength of reference group influence in a situation?
12. What is the *Asch phenomenon* and how do marketers utilize it?
13. How can a marketer use knowledge of reference group influences to develop advertising strategies?
14. What is an *opinion leader?* How does an opinion leader relate to the *multistep flow of communication?*
15. What characterizes an opinion leader?
16. What determines the likelihood that a consumer will seek information from an opinion leader?
17. How does a *market maven* differ from an *opinion leader?*
18. What is a *purchase pal?* What are the marketing implications of purchase pals?
19. What is *market helping behavior?* Why is it important to marketers?
20. How can marketing managers identify opinion leaders?
21. How can marketers utilize opinion leaders?
22. What is *buzz?* How can marketers create it?
23. What is an *innovation?* Who determines whether a given product is an innovation?
24. What are the various categories of innovations? How do they differ?
25. What is the *diffusion process?* What pattern does the diffusion process appear to follow over time?
26. Describe the factors that affect the diffusion rate for an innovation. How can these factors be utilized in developing marketing strategy?
27. What are *adopter* categories? Describe each of the adopter categories.
28. How can a marketer use knowledge of adopter categories to develop marketing strategy?

DISCUSSION QUESTIONS

29. Respond to the questions in Consumer Insight 7–1.
30. Using college students as the market segment, describe the most relevant reference group(s) and indicate the probable degree of influence on decisions for each of the following:
    a. Brand of mouthwash
    b. Purchase of a Segway
    c. Novel to read
    d. Becoming a vegetarian
    e. Choice of movie

Answer Questions 31–34 using (a) sports drinks, (b) DVD players, (c) dentists, (d) an Internet connection, (e) Segway HT, and (f) volunteering with a nonprofit organization.

31. How important are reference groups to the purchase of the above-mentioned products or activities? Would their influence also affect the brand or model? Would their influence be informational, normative, or identification? Justify your answers.

32. What reference groups would be relevant to the decision to purchase the product or activity (based on students on your campus)?

33. What are the norms of the social groups of which you are a member concerning the product or activity?

34. Could an Asch-type situation be used to sell the product or activity?

35. Describe two groups that serve as aspiration reference groups for you. In what ways, if any, have they influenced your consumption patterns? Do they resemble the Money & Brains group described in this chapter?

36. Describe two groups to which you belong. For each, give two examples of instances when the group has exerted (*a*) informational, (*b*) normative, and (*c*) identification influence on you.

37. Develop two approaches using reference group theory to reduce drug, alcohol, or cigarette consumption among teenagers.

38. What ethical concerns arise in using reference group theory to sell products?

39. Describe a consumption subculture to which you belong. How does it affect your consumption behavior? How do marketers attempt to influence your behavior with respect to this subculture?

40. Do you belong to a brand community? If so, describe the benefits you derive from this group and how it affects your consumption.

41. Answer the following questions for: (*i*) DVD players, (*ii*) Segway HT, (*iii*) wireless Internet connection, and (*iv*) naturopathic medicines.
    a. Is the product an innovation? Justify your answer.
    b. Assume the product becomes widely used on your campus. Speculate on the characteristics of the adopter categories.
    c. Using the student body on your campus as a market segment, evaluate the perceived attributes of the product.
    d. Who on your campus would serve as opinion leaders for the product?
    e. Will the early adopters of the product use the adoption process (extended decision making), or is a simpler decision process likely?

42. Describe two situations in which you have served as or sought information from an opinion leader. Are these situations consistent with the text?

43. Are you aware of market mavens on your campus? Describe their characteristics, behaviors, and motivation.

44. Have you used or served as a purchase pal recently? Why? How did it work? What marketing implications does this suggest?

45. Have you received or provided market helping behavior recently? Why? How did it work? What marketing implications does this suggest?

46. Identify a recent (*a*) continuous innovation, (*b*) dynamically continuous innovation, and (*c*) discontinuous innovation. Justify your selections.

47. Analyze the Segway HT in terms of the determinants in Table 7–4 and suggest appropriate marketing strategies.

48. Conduct a diffusion analysis and recommend appropriate strategies for the innovation shown in Illustration 7–10.

49. Assume that you are a consultant to firms with new products. You have members of the appropriate market segments rate the innovation on the 10 characteristics described in Table 7–4. Based on these ratings, you develop marketing strategies. Assume that a rating of 9 is extremely favorable (e.g., strong relative advantage or a lack of complexity), and 1 is extremely unfavorable. Suggest appropriate strategies for each of the following consumer electronic products (see table below).

Attribute	Product
	A	B	C	D	E	F	G	H	I

Attribute	A	B	C	D	E	F	G	H	I
Fulfillment of felt need	9	7	3	8	8	5	7	8	9
Compatibility	8	8	8	8	9	2	8	9	8
Relative advantage	9	2	8	9	7	8	9	8	8
Complexity	9	9	9	9	9	3	8	8	7
Observability	8	8	9	1	9	4	8	8	8
Trialability	8	9	8	9	9	2	9	2	9
Nature of group	3	8	7	8	9	9	7	7	3
Type of decision	3	7	8	8	6	7	7	3	7
Marketing effort	6	7	8	7	8	6	3	8	7
Perceived risk	3	8	7	7	3	7	8	8	5

APPLICATION ACTIVITIES

50. Find two advertisements that use reference groups in an attempt to gain patronage. Describe the advertisement, the type of reference group being used, and the type of influence being used.

51. Develop an advertisement for (*i*) toothpaste, (*ii*) energy drink, (*iii*) nice Italian restaurant, (*iv*) Habitat for Humanity, (*v*) in-line skates, or (*vi*) facial skin moisturizer using the following.
    a. An informational reference group influence
    b. A normative reference group influence
    c. An identification reference group influence

52. Interview two individuals who are strongly involved in a consumption subculture. Determine how it affects their consumption patterns and what actions marketers take toward them.

53. Interview an individual who is involved in a brand community. Describe the role the firm plays in maintaining the community, the benefits the person gets from the community, and how it affects his or her consumption behavior.

54. Identify and interview several opinion leaders on your campus for the following. To what extent do they match the profile of an opinion leader as described in the text?
    a. Clothing styles
    b. Recreation equipment
    c. Entertainment
    d. Computer equipment

55. Interview two salespersons for the following products. Determine the role that (*i*) opinion leaders and (*ii*) purchase pals play in the purchase of their product and how they adjust their sales process in light of these influences.
    a. Pets
    b. Fashion clothing
    c. Computers
    d. Art
    e. Snowboards
    f. Musical instruments

REFERENCES

1. J. W. Schouten and J. H. McAlexander, "Subcultures of Consumption," *Journal of Consumer Research,* June 1995, pp. 43–61.

2. J. H. McAlexander, J. W. Schouten, and H. F. Koenig, "Building Brand Community," *Journal of Marketing,* January 2002, pp. 38–54.

3. B. G. Englis and M. R. Solomon, "To Be *and* Not to Be," *Journal of Advertising,* Spring 1995, pp. 13–28.

4. N. A. Granitz and J. C. Ward, "Virtual Community," *Advances in Consumer Research,* vol. 23, eds. K. P. Corfman and J. G. Lynch (Provo, UT: Association for Consumer Research, 1996), pp. 161–66; C. Okleshen and S. Grossbart, "Usenet Groups, Virtual Community and Consumer Behaviors," S. Dann and S. Dann, "Cybercommuning," both in *Advances in Consumer Research,* vol. 25, eds. J. W. Alba and J. W. Hutchinson (Provo, UT: Association for Consumer Research, 1998), pp. 276–82 and 379–85; C. Okleshen and C. Witte, "Social Norms and Mental Accounting Processes," in S. P. Brown and D. Subharshan, *Enhancing Knowledge Development in Marketing 1999* (Chicago: American Marketing Association, 1999), pp. 262–69; and C. L. Beav, "Cracking the Niche," *American Demographics,* June 2000, pp. 38–40.

5. Schouten and McAlexander, "Subcultures of Consumption," p. 43.

6. K. J. Fox, "Real Punks and Pretenders," *Journal of Contemporary Ethnology,* October 1987, pp. 344–70.

7. C. B. Bhattacharya, H. Rao, and M. A. Glynn, "Understanding the Bond of Identification," *Journal of Marketing Research,* October 1995, pp. 46–57.

8. S. M. Baker and M. C. Martin, "The Meaning of Exchange in a Sports Card Subculture of Consumption," *Research in Consumer Behavior* 9 (2000), pp. 173–96.

9. R. V. Kozinets, "Utopian Enterprise," *Journal of Consumer Research,* June 2001, pp. 67–87.

10. A. M. Klein, "Pumping Iron," *Sociology of Sport Journal,* June 1986, pp. 68–75.

11. J. H. McAlexander, K. Fushimi, and J. W. Schouten, "A Cross-Cultural Examination of a Subculture of Consumption," *Research in Consumer Behavior* 9 (2000), pp. 47–69.

12. R. L. Celsi, R. L. Rose, and T. W. Leigh, "An Exploration of High Risk Consumption," *Journal of Consumer Research,* June 1993, pp. 1–23.

13. B. Gainer, "Ritual and Relationships," *Journal of Business Research,* March 1995, pp. 253–60. See also E. J. Arnould and P. L. Price, "River Magic," *Journal of Consumer Research,* June 1993, pp. 24–45.

14. See R. J. Fisher, "Group-Derived Consumption," *Advances in Consumer Research,* vol. 25, eds. J. W. Alba and J. W. Hutchinson (Provo, UT: Association for Consumer Research, 1998), pp. 283–88; and R. J. Fisher and K. Wakefield, "Factors Leading to Group Identification," *Psychology & Marketing,* January 1998, pp. 23–40.

15. McAlexander, Fushini, and Schouten, "A Cross-Cultural Examination of a Subculture of Consumption," p. 66.

16. Kozinets, "Utopian Enterprise," p. 72.

17. Ibid.

18. Based on J. H. McAlexander, J. W. Schouten, and H. F. Koenig, "Building Brand Community," *Journal of Marketing,* January 2002, pp. 38–54.

19. A. M. Muniz Jr. and T. C. O'Guinn, "Brand Community," *Journal of Consumer Research,* March 2001, p. 413. See also R. P. Bagozzi, "On the Concept of Intentional Social Action in Consumer Behavior," *Journal of Consumer Research,* December 2000, pp. 388–96.

20. See T. F. Mangleburg and T. Bristol, "Socialization and Adolescents' Skepticism toward Advertising," *Journal of Advertising,* Fall 1998, pp. 11–20.

21. See R. J. Fisher and D. Ackerman, "The Effects of Recognition and Group Need on Volunteerism," *Journal of Consumer Research,* December 1998, pp. 262–77.

22. See K. R. Lord, M.-S. Lee, and P. Choong, "Differences in Normative and Informational Social Influence," *Advances in Consumer Research,* vol. 28, eds. M. C. Gilly and J. Meyers-Levy (Provo, UT: Association for Consumer Research, 2001), pp. 280–85.

23. L. A. Peracchio and D. Luna, "The Development of an Advertising Campaign to Discourage Smoking Initiation among Children and Youth," *Journal of Advertising,* Fall 1998, pp. 49–56.

24. M. K. Hogg and E. N. Banister, "The Structure and Transfer of Cultural Meaning," *Advances in Consumer Research,* vol. 27, eds. S. J. Itoch and R. J. Meyer (Provo, UT: Association for Consumer Research, 2000), pp. 19–23.

25. See E. Day and M. R. Stafford, "Age-Related Cues in Retail Services Advertising." *Journal of Retailing,* no. 2, 1997, pp. 211–33.

26. B. D. Keillor, R. S. Parker, and A. Schaefer, "Influences on Adolescent Brand Preferences," *Journal of Advertising Research,* May 1996, pp. 47–56; C. S. Areni, M. E. Ferrell, and J. B. Wilcox, "The Persuasive Impact of Reported Group Opinions," *Psychology & Marketing,* October 2000, pp. 855–75; Y.-K. Kim and J. Kang, "Effects of Asian-Americans' Ethnicity and Acculturation on Personal Influences," *Journal of Current Issues and Research in Advertising,* Spring 2001, pp. 44–52; and D. D'Rozario, "The Structure and Properties of the Consumer Susceptibility to Interpersonal Influence Scale," *Journal of International Consumer Marketing* 13, no. 2 (2001), pp. 77–101.

27. D. N. Lascu, W. O. Bearden, and R. L. Rose, "Norm Extreme and Interpersonal Influences on Consumer Conformity," *Journal of Business Research,* March 1995, pp. 201–13. See also P. F. Bone, "Word-of-Mouth Effects on Short-Term and Long-Term Product Judgments," *Journal of Business Research,* March 1995, pp. 213–23.

28. See S. Auty and R. Elliot, "Being Like or Being Liked," *Advances in Consumer Research,* vol. 28, eds. M. C. Gilly and J. Meyers-Lcvy (Provo, UT: Association for Consumer Research, 2001), pp. 235–41.

29. C. Pechmann, "The Effects of Antismoking and Cigarette Advertising on Young Adolescents' Perceptions of Peers Who Smoke," *Journal of Consumer Research,* September 1994, pp. 236–51. See also D. D. Schoenbachler and T. E. Whittler, "Adolescent Processing of Social and Physical Threat Communications," *Journal of Advertising,* Winter 1996, pp. 37–54.

30. C. Walker, "Word of Mouth," *American Demographics,* July 1995, p. 38.

31. C. Fisher, "Wal-Mart's Way," *Advertising Age,* February 18, 1991, p. 3.

32. Walkes, "Word of Mouth," p. 40.

33. A. Goldenberg, B. Libai, and E. Muller, "Talk of the Net," *Marketing Letters,* August 2001, pp. 211–23.

34. See W. G. Mangold, F. Miller, and G. R. Brockway, "Word-of-Mouth Communication in the Service Marketplace," *Journal of Services Marketing* 13, no. 1 (1999), pp. 73–89.

35. For a thorough discussion, see D. F. Duhan, S. D. Johnson, J. B. Wilcox, and G. D. Harrell, "Influences on Consumer Use of Word-of-Mouth Recommendation Sources," *Journal of the Academy of Marketing Science,* Fall 1997, pp. 283–95.

36. R. Dye, "The Buzz on Buzz," *Harvard Business Review,* November 2000, p. 145.

37. G. M. Rose, L. R. Kahle, and A. Shoham, "The Influence of Employment-Status and Personal Values on Time-Related Food Consumption Behavior and Opinion Leadership," in *Advances in Consumer Research,* vol. 22, eds. F. R. Kardes and M. Sujan (Provo, UT: Association for Consumer Research, 1995), pp. 367–72; and U. M. Dholakia, "Involvement-Response Models of Joint Effects," *Advances in Consumer Research,* vol. 25, eds. J. W. Alba and J. W. Hutchinson (Provo, UT: Association for Consumer Research, 1998), pp. 499–506.

38. See M. C. Gilly, J. L. Graham, M. F. Wolfinbarger, and L. J. Yale, "A Dyadic Study of Interpersonal Information Search," *Journal of the Academy of Marketing Science,* Spring 1998, pp. 83–100.

39. R. Marshall and I. Gitosudarmo, "Variation in the Characteristics of Opinion Leaders across Borders," *Journal of International Consumer Marketing* 8, no. 1 (1995), pp. 5–22.

40. See D. S. Sundaram, K. Mitra, and C. Webster, "Word-of-Mouth Communications," *Advances in Consumer Research,* vol. 25, eds. J. W. Alba and J. W. Hutchinson (Provo, UT: Association for Consumer Research, 1998), pp. 527–31.

41. M. Johnson, G. M. Zinkhan, and G. S. Ayala, "The Impact of Outcome, Competency, and Affect on Service Referral," *Journal of Services Marketing,* no. 5 (1998), pp. 397–415.

42. L. F. Feick and L. L. Price, "The Market Maven," *Journal of Marketing,* January 1987, pp. 83-97. See also R. A. Higie, L. F. Feick, and L. L. Price, "Types and Amount of Word-of-Mouth Communications about Retailers," *Journal of Retailing,* Fall 1987, pp. 260–78; M. E. Slama and T. G. Williams, "Generalization of the Market Maven's Information Tendency across Product Categories," in *Advances in Consumer Research,* vol. 27, eds. M. E. Goldberg, G. Gorn, and R. W.

Pollay (Provo, UT: Association for Consumer Research, 1990), pp. 48–52; K. C. Schneider and W. C. Rodgers, "Generalized Marketplace Influencers' Attitudes toward Direct Mail as a Source of Information," *Journal of Direct Marketing,* Autumn 1993, pp. 20–28; and J. E. Urbany, P. R. Dickson, and R. Kalapurakal, "Price Search in the Retail Grocery Market," *Journal of Marketing,* April 1996, pp. 91–104.

43. T. A. Mooradian, "The Five Factor Model and Market Mavenism," *Advances in Consumer Research,* vol. 23, eds. K. P. Corfman and J. G. Lynch (Provo, UT: Association for Consumer Research, 1996), pp. 260–63.

44. L. L. Price, L. F. Feick, and A. Guskey, "Everyday Market Helping Behavior," *Journal of Public Policy & Marketing,* Fall 1995, pp. 255–66.

45. C. L. Hartman and P. Kiecker, "Buyers and Their Purchase Pals," in *Enhancing Knowledge Development in Marketing,* eds. R. Achrol and A. Mitchell (Chicago: American Marketing Association, 1994), pp. 138–44; and P. Kiecker and C. L. Hartman, "Predicting Buyers' Selection of Interpersonal Sources," in *Advances in Consumer Research,* vol. 21, eds. C. T. Allen and D. R. John (Provo, UT: Association for Consumer Research, 1994), pp. 464–69.

46. See C. S. Areni, M. E. Ferrell, and J. B. Wilcox, "The Persuasive Impact of Reported Group Opinions on Individuals Low vs. High in Need for Cognition," *Psychology & Marketing,* October 2000, pp. 855–75.

47. Walker, "Word of Mouth," p. 40.

48. See R. N. Laczniak, T. E. DeCarlo, and S. N. Ramaswami, "Consumers' Responses to Negative Word-of-Mouth Communication," *Journal of Consumer Psychology* 11, no. 1 (2001), pp. 57–73.

49. Walker, "Word of Mouth," p. 44.

50. See E. Biyalogorsky, E. Gerstner, and B. Libai, "Customer Referral Management," *Marketing Science,* Winter 2001, pp. 82–95.

51. A. Z. Cuneo, "Dockers Strives for Urban Credibility," *Advertising Age,* May 25, 1998, p. 6.

52. Dye, "The Buzz on Buzz," p. 140.

53. K. Fitzgerald, "Bristol-Meyers Builds Buzz," *Advertising Age,* April 23, 2001, p. 18.

54. B. S. Bulik, "Well-Heeled Heed the Need for PR," *Advertising Age,* June 11, 2001, p. S2.

55. See also E. M. Rogers, *Diffusion of Innovations* (New York: Free Press, 1983); H. Gatignon and T. S. Robertson, "A Propositional Inventory for New Diffusion Research," *Journal of Consumer Research,* March 1985, pp. 849–67; and V. Mahajan, E. Muller, and F. M. Bass, "New Product Diffusion Models in Marketing," *Journal of Marketing,* January 1990, pp. 1–26.

56. See M. I. Nabith, S. G. Bloem, and T. B. C. Poiesz, "Conceptual Issues in the Study of Innovation Adoption Behavior," *Advances in Consumer Research,* vol. 24, eds. M. Bruck and D. J. MacInnis (Provo, UT: Association for Consumer Research, 1997), pp. 190–96.

57. See N. Y.-M. Siu and M. M.-S. Cheng, "A Study of the Expected Adoption of Online Shopping," *Journal of International Consumer Marketing* 13, no. 3 (2001), pp. 87–106.

58. For a more complete analysis, see U. M. Dholakia, "An Investigation of the Relationship between Perceived Risk and Product Involvement," *Advances in Consumer Research,* vol. 24, eds. M. Bruck and D. J. MacInnis (Provo, UT: Association for Consumer Research, 1997), pp. 159–67.

59. For a discussion of when this is not appropriate, see V. Mahajan and E. Muller, "When Is It Worthwhile Targeting the Majority Instead of the Innovators in a New Product Launch," *Journal Marketing Research,* November 1998, pp. 488–95.

Cases

While electric razors represent a $400 million market, less than a third of U.S. males use electric shavers, and only one in seven females use them. Norelco dominates the men's segment, followed by Remington, Braun, and Panasonic.

In the early 1990s, electric razor marketers sharply increased their marketing efforts, but this had little impact on electric razors' share of shavers. In fact, the percentage of both men and women using electric razors declined slightly between 1991 and 1993. By 1996, Norelco had well over 50 percent of the $400 million plus electric market. In late 1996, Pat Dinley, Norelco's president, described the firm's new approach:

> Over the years, we've fought the market share battle with other electric shavers. Long term, the big opportunity is in converting people who use blades to electric.

Norelco used a two-pronged approach to gain share in the overall shaving market, focusing on younger shavers and directly targeting blade users. According to Dinley,

> Traditionally, our target market has been 35-plus. We believe we've got a real opportunity to bring some new people into the category, so we're going after 18- to 54-year-olds.

Targeting younger consumers has involved using different media and themes. Some of the media used include ESPN sports, "Monday Night Football," and "Friends," as well as select men's magazines.

The creative theme focused heavily on the irritation that can be associated with blade shaving. One television ad featured sneering blade razors that turn into dragons and snakes. The comfort of a Norelco shave was emphasized with the tagline "Anything closer would be too close for comfort."

In 1998, Philips Electronics, Norelco's parent company, made two major moves. First, it focused Norelco strictly on men's products. Women's electric razors and other products targeting women were redesigned and introduced under the Philips Personal Care name.

Norelco then launched a new flagship razor, the Advantage. The Advantage has a Nivea for Men shaving lotion cartridge built inside the razor chamber. This unique system dispenses the lotion while shaving, offering a wet shave experience without the hassle associated with water and lather. The razor comes with five lotion cartridges, can be used wet or dry, and can be rinsed clean with tap water.

The product was launched with an estimated $35 million campaign. The ads take a humorous approach that challenges consumers to put the razor "to the test." One ad makes this offer, "If you don't make it part of your routine after 21 days, we'll give you your money back, guaranteed." According to VP–marketing Rich Sorota, "The advertising is part of our holistic approach to get consumers to put it to the test. [The objective] is to get really dissatisfied blade users to trade up to electrics. [Marketing research has found] over 10 million dissatisfied blade users out there."

A spokesperson for the ad agency says the ads also try to eliminate the perception that electric razors are "some old razor your grandmother gave you in high school" and instead position them as the "high-tech way to shave." Advantage commercials will run on network, cable, and syndicated TV and in such magazines as *Rolling Stone, Details, Spin,* and *Sports Illustrated.*

Table A provides demographic data on the users of electric razors, disposable razors, and replaceable-blade razors and on the users of Remington and Norelco electric shavers.

	Type			Brand		
Variable	Electric	Disposable	Blades	Norelco	Remington	Braun
Percent Adults Using	29.8%	54.4%	44.9%	16.0%	5.3%	4.6%
Age						
18–24 years	92	97	120	66	95	107
25–34	93	103	111	81	89	125
35–44	88	108	101	86	86	89
45–54	90	105	96	93	91	89
55–64	109	93	94	121	111	89
> 64	143	86	75	173	146	100
Education						
College graduate	105	95	107	109	90	141
Some college	102	96	107	100	109	98
High school graduate	94	104	97	96	102	85
No degree	101	105	87	95	97	75
Occupation						
Professional	99	96	113	95	88	141
Managerial/administrative	95	100	107	100	78	133
Technical/clerical/sales	92	102	113	94	71	107
Precision/craft	95	106	105	94	92	93
Race/Ethnic Group						
White	103	100	102	108	101	103
Black	77	102	85	41	103	67
Spanish speaking	86	106	101	78	56	114
Region						
Northeast	89	99	103	86	102	90
North Central	115	98	101	108	130	125
South	95	104	101	97	92	77
West	103	97	95	109	81	118
Household Income						
< $10,000	97	111	76	105	62	49
$10,000–19,999	98	102	85	90	108	47
$20,000–29,999	104	103	84	99	98	99
$30,000–39,999	99	101	98	108	122	75
$40,000–49,999	110	100	99	108	143	74
$50,000–59,999	93	97	108	99	91	109
$60,000–74,999	105	99	107	93	105	152
$75,000 +	96	97	113	100	77	127
Household Structure						
Single	92	99	110	70	97	111
Married	103	100	98	111	103	99

TABLE A

Demographics and Razor Use*

*100 = Average use or consumption unless a percent is indicated. Base = All males.

Source: *Mediamark Reporter 2002—University* (New York: Mediamark Research Inc., March 2002).

Discussion Questions

1. Prepare a two-page summary, accompanied by no more than four graphs, that conveys the key information in Table A to a manager.
2. Describe the typical user of an electric razor, a disposable razor, and a blade razor, in one paragraph each.
3. Conduct an innovation analysis of the Advantage using Table 7–4 as the basis. What insights does the innovation analysis provide into its probable sales growth?
4. Which of the demographic factors are most relevant for developing marketing strategy for the Advantage? Why?

5. Using demographics, describe the best target market for the Advantage.

6. What additional demographic data would you like to have in order to develop marketing strategy for the Advantage? Justify your answer.

7. Why would "10 million dissatisfied blade users" continue to use blades?

8. Evaluate Norelco's objective to, and strategy for, switching dissatisfied blade users to electric razors.

9. Using the available data, develop a marketing strategy for the Advantage.

Source: R. A. Davis, "Electric Razors Plan Aggressive Fourth-Quarter," *Advertising Age,* October 12, 1992, p. 20; L. Petrecca, "Norelco Courts Younger Crowd," *Advertising Age,* September 1996, p. 64; L. Petrecca, "Norelco Puts New Shaver to the Test," *Advertising Age,* August 31, 1998, p. 10; and "Electric Razors Retain Strong Category Position," *MMR,* January 1999, p. 30.

2–2   Crest Rejuvenating Effects

Procter & Gamble is spending $50 million this fall to launch a cosmetic-style toothpaste called Crest Rejuvenating Effects. Targeting women aged 30 to 44, it will be the first attempt to position a toothpaste for a relatively narrow adult market. The effort is headed by three women executives who refer to themselves as "chicks in charge."

The new sub-brand provides multibenefit whitening, a glimmering "pearlescent" box, and sparkly, teal-toned toothpaste with vanilla and cinnamon notes. It also leaves a slight tingling sensation that Crest hopes will serve as a "sensory signal" of gum health and fresh breath. However, it will not provide any functional benefits not available in other toothpastes. It will be priced similarly to other multifunctional toothpastes.

One of the "chicks in charge" stated,

> This is one of the few categories [in personal care] where there are no products specifically marketed to women. I think times are changing and women want products specifically for themselves.

The introductory campaign will feature actress/singer Vanessa Williams. The general market campaign will differ from the one targeting African American consumers. The general market ads will position Rejuvenating Effects as a natural extension of the many other things women do for beauty care. Thus, it will be part of a beauty routine, not just a dental hygiene activity. However, P&G's research indicates that, compared to white women, black women don't

age as noticeably, don't have as involved beauty-care routines, and are more likely to see aging as desirable and conferring respect. Ads specifically targeting this audience will show scenes from various times in Ms. Williams life, noting that she hasn't aged much and praising a toothpaste "that cares for her mouth and allows it to look as good as her face."

Discussion Questions

1. Will Rejuvenating Effects succeed? Why or why not?

2. Is Rejuvenating Effects an innovation? If so, what type?

3. What values are relevant to the success or failure of Rejuvenating Effects?

4. Why would women want "their own" toothpaste?

5. How would you market Rejuvenating Effects to Hispanic consumers?

6. Why do you think the age range of 30 to 44 was selected as the primary target market?

7. What social classes are most likely to purchase this product? Why?

8. How would you market this product and how likely would it be to succeed in the following countries?

   a. Germany

   b. Japan

   c. France

   d. Brazil

Source: J. Neff, "Crest Spinoff Targets Women," *Advertising Age,* June 3, 2002, p. 1; and "Crest Dresses Up for Women Users," *Advertising Age,* June 10, 2002, p. 28.

2–3   Tony the Tiger Goes Global

Kellogg Company has distribution in more than 150 countries and yet is still "unknown to half the world's population," according to Arnold Langbo, Kellogg's CEO. Langbo plans to change that.

Kellogg recently built a company-owned cereal plant in Latvia and currently has sales in Poland, Hungary, and Czechoslovakia. It has also started construction on a plant in India and is entering China.

However, international expansion and the development of global brands will not be easy.

To become more international, the firm recently reorganized into four divisions: North America, Latin America, Europe, and Australasia. According to Langbo:

> The way we used to be organized, we were a U.S.-based multinational—a company with a big domestic business and, by the way, some international business. That was the way we were thinking; that's the way the organization was structured.
>
> Today, if you talk to customers in the U.K., Canada, or Australia, they think of Kellogg as being based in the U.K. or Canada or Australia. We're global in organizational structure and business but also multidomestic.
>
> We now have a number of truly global brands (Frosted Flakes and Corn Flakes, with Froot Loops and Rice Krispies close, and Frosted Mini-Wheats and Honey Nut Loops moving rapidly). There used to be slight variations in our food around the world, but now you'll recognize the product wherever you go.

Expanding into many markets will involve more than trying to gain share from other cereal marketers. It will require altering long-held traditions:

> In Eastern Europe it's going to be pretty slow because we're going to have to go in there and literally create the habit—much as we did in Germany 25 years ago or France 20 years ago. Cereal is a whole new breakfast concept for these people. However, they do eat breakfast in those countries, and they eat fairly substantial breakfasts.
>
> In Asia, consumers are used to eating something warm, soft, and savory for breakfast—and we're going to sell them something that's cold, crisp, and sweet or bran tasting. That's quite a difference.

The challenge is made greater by the presence of aggressive competition in many developed or developing markets. Competition is particularly intense in Europe where Nestlé and General Mills formed a joint venture called Cereal Partners Worldwide. Langbo characterizes the new competitor this way:

> They are a very formidable competitor with Nestlé's distribution strength and knowledge of the European market and General Mills' technology and cereal marketing expertise.

The result of the entry of the new competitor, which spent an estimated $35 to $50 million in advertising in the top six European markets, and the response of existing firms such as Kellogg was an increase in the growth rate of total cereal sales as well as share erosion among the weaker brands.

Competition is strong even in some countries where consumption is low. For example, in Japan, with consumption at four bowls per year per person, compared to 10 pounds in the United States, there are more than 100 products fighting for shelf space.

According to Langbo, a global brand requires a core position strategy or product benefit that will work in multiple countries and local execution of that idea to reflect local attitudes. The key ideas for three of Kellogg's global or near-global brands are described by Langbo in the following paragraphs.

Frosted Flakes

Frosted Flakes is based on the concept of vitality. This idea originated in the United States but is a universal idea that both translates and travels well. Because the product has a special appeal to children, the cultural differences are not so pronounced. Tony the Tiger illustrates the vitality theme in a universally understandable manner. Tony is loved throughout the world, symbolizing appeals that are truly global. We use Tony and the vitality message everywhere from the United States to Taiwan to Argentina.

Corn Flakes

The basic positioning concept for Corn Flakes is simple, unadulterated food that tastes surprisingly good. This concept also has universal appeal. It is typically the first product we introduce in a new market. It is the foundation of our line, and it is the world's most popular cereal.

All-Bran

The value proposition for All-Bran is the health benefits of fiber in the diet. This proposition does not have universal appeal without development. The concept of the value of fiber in the diet is new to many countries and is often resisted.

In 1984, we began a massive campaign to countries where the benefits of fiber were not widely accepted. The campaign varied across countries due to differences in the attitudes of local medical and nutritional professionals, specific diseases that were most on the minds of the local population, and local restrictions on health claims. However, the basic approach was to educate and support the medical and nutritional community in each country. We would sponsor symposia on dietary fiber. As a country's experts became convinced of the value of fiber, they told their story in their academic press, the general press, and in public service announcements. Today, despite competition from many other high-fiber cereals, All-Bran is one of the top 15 cereals worldwide.

Discussion Questions

1. What type of innovation would cold cereal be to a country not accustomed to this type of food?
2. Conduct an innovation analysis based on Table 7–4 for cold cereal in China.
3. What values are involved in the consumption of a product such as breakfast cereal?
4. What values would support and what values would harm the chances of Kellogg succeeding with cold cereal in the following countries? What other factors would be important?

   a. China

   b. Mexico

   c. Japan

   d. France

5. What nonverbal communications factors would be important in developing an advertising campaign for a cold cereal?
6. Develop a marketing program to market one of Kellogg's cold cereals in the following countries.

   a. China

   b. Mexico

   c. Japan

   d. France

7. Why does Tony the Tiger "travel" so well?
8. Evaluate the communications process Kellogg used to gain acceptance for All-Bran. Could a version of this work for gaining acceptance of cold cereals in China?

Source: J. Liesse, "Kellogg Chief to Push Harder for Int'l Growth," *Advertising Age,* August 24, 1992, p. 4; A. G. Langbo, "Building a Global Company," in *Marketing's New Strategic Direction* (New York: The Conference Board, 1995), pp. 14–16; A. G. Langbo, "Touring the World with Tony the Tiger," *Across the Board,* July 1995, p. 56; and P. Galarza, "Snap, Crackle, Flop?" *Financial World,* March 25, 1996, p. 26.

2–4   Wal-Mart Enters China

In 1991, Wal-Mart opened its first store outside the United States in Mexico City. In 1997, Wal-Mart had 2,744 stores in the United States, 145 in Mexico, 136 in Canada, 11 in Puerto Rico, 6 in Argentina, 5 in Brazil, and 2 in Indonesia. By 2002, it had more than 1,200 outlets in nine countries outside the United States (Argentina, Brazil, Canada, China, Germany, Korea, Mexico, Puerto Rico, and the United Kingdom).

U.S. firms are not the only ones expanding across the globe. Makro, a Dutch wholesale club, is Southeast Asia's leading store group, with sales of more than $2 billion. Carrefour of France is the leading retailer in Brazil and Argentina and recently opened an outlet in Shanghai. Yaohan, a Japanese retail chain with headquarters in Hong Kong, has plans to open 1,000 stores in China. The chain is also expanding into Europe and the United States. In fact, four non-U.S. retailers operate in more countries and have significantly more foreign sales than Wal-Mart, America's largest retailer.

Some analysts feel that internationalization is essential for retailers to prosper in the future. One expert predicts the rise of four or five dominant global

retailers that will enjoy substantial advantages in pricing, sourcing, and logistics. Another states: "We're really moving to boundaryless retailing."

Retail firms that succeed internationally find a way to bring value to local markets that local competitors cannot match. This value may be in the form of low price, selection, service, image, unique products, or other features desired in multiple cultures. Toys "R" Us has found unmatched selection a feature that offers it a strong brand image and a competitive advantage in Europe and Japan despite prices higher than in the United States. Michael Goldstein, the CEO, noted,

> I remember talking to customers who were leaving one of our stores in Wales. When I asked what they liked about the store, every one of them said selection. No one paid attention to pricing, which was one of our big concerns.

In Hong Kong, as elsewhere, it is Disney's products and image that draw customers. There was a near riot when a Disney store opened in Hong Kong in 1994. The outlet can hold only 150 people at a time, and 5,000 people routinely show up each day. The store has giant screens continually showing clips from Disney films and clerks dressed in 1950s collegiate gear.

The Hong Kong Market

Hong Kong shoppers are very price sensitive. Many appear to treat shopping almost as a competitive sport in which the person who gains the lowest price wins. However, despite the desire for low price, convenience often plays a dominant role in store choice. Few Hong Kong Chinese have access to a private car. Instead, they rely on buses and taxis. Carrying large items or bulk purchases home by bus is difficult or impossible. Using a taxi is expensive. Thus, most Hong Kong residents shop within a few kilometers of their residence.

Even if transportation were not an issue, house size would be. Most residents live in very small apartments. Many of these apartments are only 300 square feet. Given small refrigerators and limited storage space, Hong Kong consumers shop for food and other items virtually daily. They cannot easily buy in large quantities or sizes and store the product no matter what savings they might obtain by doing so. Frequent shopping is made easier by the fact that most of the large apartment buildings contain a number of retail outlets such as a small grocery store, pharmacy, laundry, and restaurant.

Hong Kong has thousands of small businesses. However, most face the same purchasing constraints that households do. They do not have access to private transportation and lack storage space. The small business often doubles as the family residence, and potential storage space is required for family activities.

Wal-Mart's Approach

Wal-Mart is entering the market with a small chain of Value Clubs that are similar to small Sam's Clubs; that is, they will be small-scale retail/wholesale, cash and carry, membership warehouse operations. Wal-Mart's traditional approach is to offer customers the goods and services they desire at a price well below the

competition. However, it also relies on relatively large, bulk purchases for much of its sales.

One opportunity for Wal-Mart is to open outlets near the many new apartment houses being constructed in the New Territories. The enormous building boom in this region will house many less sophisticated new residents from China who may be particularly appreciative of the low price and selection Value Clubs will offer.

Wal-Mart has learned how to make its U.S. customers feel like they are shopping at their own personal store. It will continue this approach in Hong Kong. For example, it will accept returned goods with a smile. This policy basically does not exist in Hong Kong, even if the items are defective. However, it remains to be seen if low price and unique service will be enough. As one shopper commented while visiting the store and looking at a four-pound jar of Skippy peanut butter: "The price is right, but where would I put it?"

Discussion Questions

1. Will Wal-Mart succeed? What would you recommend to help it succeed?

2. What values are relevant to the success of retail stores such as Wal-Mart? How should Wal-Mart adjust its strategies to be consistent with the prevailing value system in Hong Kong?

3. How will Wal-Mart need to alter its approach as it opens stores in the following countries?

   a. Japan

   b. Egypt

   c. Germany

   d. South Africa

4. How can Wal-Mart use reference group influences to its advantage in Hong Kong?

Source: N. Herndon, "Wal-Mart Goes to Hong Kong," *Marketing News*, November 21, 1994, p. 2; C. Rapoport, "Retailers Go Global," *Fortune*, February 20, 1995, pp. 102–8; W. Zellner, "Wal-Mart Spoken Here," *Business Week*, June 23, 1997, pp. 138–43; and www.walmart.com.

2–5   Skoda's U.K. Turnaround Attempt

In December 1998, Chris Hawken took over Skoda, U.K. The Czech Republic–made car had a terrible image—98 percent of the public viewed it as a low-quality, low-end car, and 60 percent would not consider buying it. While the Skoda was viewed as a prestigious, luxury car prior to WWII, its years under

Communist management after the war completely eroded this image. Volkswagen acquired Skoda in 1991 and quickly improved its quality, winning automotive awards and the praise of motor journalists. Its image improved sharply in much of Europe, but the British continued to regard it as a joke. In fact, there were several websites dedicated to Skoda jokes:

- How do you double the value of a Skoda? Fill it with gas.
- Why are a Skoda's rear windows heated? To keep your hands warm while you push it.

Faced with the demand for strong sales increases in the United Kingdom, Hawken concluded that he would have to change the entire country's perception of the car. The image campaign began in March 2000 with the launch of a new hatchback, the Fabia, and the reintroduction of its midsized Octavia.

Given a very small budget (about $7 million), Hawken avoided several common campaign elements such as event marketing and sponsorships and focused primarily on television ads, public relations, and direct mail.

He decided to confront the Skoda's negative image, particularly among "rejecters" (those who would not even consider a Skoda), head-on with self-deprecating humor. The five television ads for the two models were shot documentary-style and featured people in situations where they assumed a car could not be a Skoda because it looks so good:

A distraught parking attendant tells a man returning to his car "I'm afraid some little vandal has stuck a Skoda badge on the front of your car."

A pompous English dignitary on a tour of a Skoda heaps praise on the new plant and the car. At the end of the tour, he whispers to the guide: "I hear you make those funny little Skoda cars, too."

Each of the ads ends with the tagline "It's a Skoda. Honest." Hawken put about 75 percent of his budget in these ads. Summarizing the objective of the ads, Hawken said, "What we wanted the viewer to take away from the ads is the fact that these are just beautiful-looking cars."

For public relations, his team focused on influential journalists from major consumer publications rather than the traditional automotive journalists. The latter had been writing favorably about Skoda for some time. However, according to an ad agency executive working with Skoda, automotive journalists "are not brand influencers."

A few weeks before the March campaign broke, these consumer journalists were provided new Skodas to drive and a preview of the commercial. As a result, the car received headlines like this one from the *Mirror*: "History's biggest comeback since Bobby Ewing stepped out of the shower. Skoda is hip and sexy—yes, sexy." The press was given extensive information on Skoda's pre-Communist heritage and its many awards and technical features.

The final element of the campaign was direct marketing to current owners and those who resemble them. Research revealed that

One of the key things determining whether someone is likely to drive a Skoda is not their age or where they live, but their attitude. Our strategy was to talk to people who are more rational in making decisions—as Skoda owners are.

Discussion Questions

1. Is this strategy likely to succeed?
2. What values will influence the success of this campaign?
3. Would this campaign be more or less likely to succeed in America?
4. Why would the image of the Skoda be so much lower in Britain than in the rest of Europe?
5. How would you identify people "who are more rational in making decisions" in order to reach them via direct marketing.
6. Why wouldn't automotive journalists be "brand influencers" for Skoda? Why would general consumer journalists be brand influencers?

Source: A. B. Ellick, "Nothing to Pity," *AutoWeek,* November 12, 2001, p. 1; "Creative Review," *Ad Age Global,* February 2002, p. 1; and D. Jones, "Skoda Is Taken from Trash to Treasure," *Marketing News,* February 18, 2002, p. 4.

2–6   McDonald's Social Responsibility Report

McDonald's issued it first Social Responsibility Report on April 15, 2002. It covered the firm's activities and issues in four broad areas—community, environment, people, and the marketplace. A few findings from the "highlights" version of the report follow.

Community

- Ronald McDonald House Charities (RMHC) have provided more than $300 million for children's programs since 1984.

- RMHC operates more the 200 houses in 21 countries where families can stay in a homelike environment while a child undergoes care at a nearby medical facility.
- RMHC awarded $4 million in grants to fund 40 medical missions in developing countries providing facial reconstruction surgery to children who otherwise would not have access to such treatments.
- The Ronald McDonald Mobile Care program brings high-quality medical and dental care to underserved communities throughout the world.
- McDonald's outlets purchase 80 percent of their supplies and services from within the countries in which they operate.
- McDonald's provides free food and water to victims and volunteers at disasters throughout the world, including 750,000 free meals to rescue workers at the World Trade Center tragedy.

Environment

- Since 1990, McDonald's has purchased more than $4 billion worth of products made from recycled materials, thus helping create and sustain a market for such materials.
- The firm recycles its own by-products to the extent practical given the local recycling infrastructure.
- It has worked with the Environmental Defense Fund to minimize the environmental impact of its packaging.
- It is working with Conservation International to implement sustainable agricultural standards.
- It eliminated growth-promoting antibiotics for poultry in Europe and fluoroquinolones for poultry in the United States.

People

- Pay rates are at or above the local rates in the marketplace with a benefits package.
- Employees are provided opportunities for growth and development.
- Workplace safety committees in seven countries champion safe practices and systems.

Marketplace

- McDonald's is implementing improvements in farm animal welfare.

- It has established the McDonald's Animal Welfare Council, an independent board of academic and animal protection experts.
- It works with independent third-party labs to develop state-of-the-art toy safety research.
- It develops and provides to the U.S. Consumer Product Safety Commission the McBaby—a "virtual" child for use in testing toy safety.
- It uses external monitors to conduct "social compliance verification audits" of suppliers' operations to ensure that these operations are run in accordance with McDonald's Code of Conduct for suppliers.

Discussion Questions

1. Review the *Highlights from Social Responsibility Report* (www.mcdonalds.com). Evaluate the firm's social responsibility? Are any important issues missing?

2. Review the *Highlights from Social Responsibility Report* (www.mcdonalds.com). Are your friends aware of the positive things McDonald's does? If not, should McDonald's promote its positive activities more? If it decided to do so, how should it go about it?

3. Read the "Community" section of *McDonald's Social Responsibility Report* (www.mcdonalds.com). Evaluate the firm's social responsibility in this area. Are any important issues missing?

4. Read the "Environment" section of *McDonald's Social Responsibility Report* (www.mcdonalds.com). Evaluate the firm's social responsibility in this area. Are any important issues missing?

5. Read the "People" section of *McDonald's Social Responsibility Report* (www.mcdonalds.com). Evaluate the firm's social responsibility in this area. Are any important issues missing?

6. Read the "Marketplace" section of *McDonald's Social Responsibility Report* (www.mcdonalds.com). Evaluate the firm's social responsibility in this area. Are any important issues missing?

Source: www.mcdonalds.com.

2-7   Dixon Ticonderoga's Prang Soybean Crayon

In a contest held by Purdue University to develop new uses for soybeans, one entrant used them to make crayons. As a result, Dixon Ticonderoga entered into an agreement to develop and market the new crayon. After years of research, the product was launched as the "first new crayon in 100 years."

Named Prang Fun Pro Soybean Crayons, they promise a number of advantages over traditional crayons:

- They are made from soybeans, a renewable resource. Most crayons are made from paraffin, a petroleum product.
- They don't flake like petroleum-based crayons.
- They don't create a waxy build-up.
- Prang crayons allow users to blend or layer colors, which is not possible with traditional crayons.

While Prang crayons have a number of desirable features, they also face a serious obstacle. Crayola is virtually synonymous with crayons. It dominates the market in terms of sales, distribution, and advertising. Crayola features many products in addition to traditional crayons, including Crayola Construction Paper crayons that provide consistent, true color across all types of paper, including black construction paper, brown paper bags, and colored poster board; Crayola Washable highlighters and Crayola Erasable highlighters; Crayola Poster markers; Crayola School glue; Crayola Student scissors; Crayola Metallic colored pencils; Crayola Computer & Craft Paper; Crayola Color WipeOffs Whiteboard Combo sets; and Crayola Color WipeOffs washable dry erase markers.

Crayola Kids' Katchalls designed for organizing kids' crayons, markers, and supplies are durable plastic boxes with a snap-close top and handle that makes them easy for kids to grip and carry. Crayola backpacks come in a variety of colors and sizes, and some styles include a matching lunch bag. Crayola shoes are available in infant size 1 through children's size 12.

Discussion Questions

1. What type innovation is the new Prang crayon? Evaluate it as an innovation using Table 7–4 as a structure.
2. How can the firm use opinion leaders to help the Prang Crayon succeed?
3. How can the firm use reference group influence to help the Prang Crayon succeed?
4. What values will help this product succeed?
5. Would you target children or adults? How would your approach differ between the two groups?
6. What demographic groups would you target?
7. How would you compete against Crayola?
8. How would you market the Prang Crayon in these countries?
   a. Japan
   b. European Union
   c. Mexico
   d. Egypt

Source: www.prang.com; D. Gardner, "Soy-Based Crayons Color the Countryside," *Agri Marketing*, February 1998, pp. 18–19; and "Soybean Crayons Add Color," *PR Newswire*, August 31, 1999.

2-8   The Mosquito Magnet

Female mosquitoes bite humans and other creatures to acquire blood for the protein they need to lay eggs. They are attracted to humans by the carbon dioxide and other compounds in their breath as well as body heat, moisture, and organic compounds on the skin. Mosquitoes typically do not fly more than a few hundred yards from where they are hatched (unless wind-blown) during their short (several weeks) lives. Thus, if most females are continuously killed in an area, the population should collapse in six to eight weeks.

American Biophysics recently introduced the Mosquito Magnet on the basis of these facts. It looks a bit like a small gas barbecue grill, complete with

propane tank. It mimics a large mammal by emitting a plume of carbon dioxide, heat and moisture, and octenol (a chemical in human breath). This plume attracts female mosquitoes, no-see-ums, biting midges, black flies, and sand flies. It only attracts blood-sucking insects. As the insects approach the Magnet, they are vacuumed into a net where they dehydrate and die. A variety of tests indicate that this system does indeed work and is the most effective available (see www.mosquitomagnet.com).

The system needs to operate 24 hours a day as it works by creating a mosquito-free (or low-density) area. It takes about two weeks for there to be a noticeable decrease in the mosquito population. The company claims that the population will typically collapse in four to six weeks, leaving only occasional, wind-blown mosquitoes in the area.

The 20-gallon propane tank will need to be refilled approximately every three weeks (approximately $10). The octenol cartridge (which is not essential but improves the attraction power of the system) also needs to be replaced every three weeks (about $6 each). The net needs to be emptied when half full (frequency depends on the mosquito density in the area).

There are three models of the Mosquito Magnet as described below (prices do not include the propane tank, which costs less than $50).

- *Liberty:* covers three-quarters of an acre; needs a 110-volt plug to operate the vacuum fan; $495.
- *Freedom:* covers three-quarters of an acre; generates its own electricity; $795.
- *Pro:* covers one acre; generates its own electricity; $1,295.

Discussion Questions

1. Is the Mosquito Magnet an innovation? If so, what type?
2. Conduct an innovation analysis on the Mosquito Magnet, and develop appropriate marketing strategies based on this analysis.
3. How can the firm use the test results in marketing the Mosquito Magnet?
4. How can the firm encourage word-of-mouth communications about the Mosquito Magnet?
5. Who do you think the opinion leaders will be for this product, and how can the firm use them?
6. What, if any, values are relevant to marketing this product?
7. List the top five countries outside the United States in order of their attractiveness as an export market for this product. Justify your selection.
8. Which family members will be involved in the purchase decision? What roles will they play?

Source: www.mosquitomagnet.com; J. E. Guyette, "Easing Summer's Sting," *LP/Gas,* August 2001, p. 1; F. Antowiewicz, "Mosquitoes Help Save Firm from Bankruptcy," *Plastics News,* June 24, 2002, p. 1; and S. O'Neill, "Skeeter Snuffers," *Kiplinger's Personal Finance,* June 2002, p. 3.

2–9   Marketing Seasoning Sauces to African Americans and Hispanics

As Table A indicates, African Americans are relatively heavy users of bottled barbecue and seasoning sauces. Spanish-speaking consumers are relatively light consumers of these products compared to non-Spanish-speaking whites. Both of these groups are growing faster than the overall population and represent attractive segments to marketers of bottled sauces.

However, an examination of Table A reveals that there is considerable variation in the success that various firms have with each segment.

Discussion Questions

1. Why do African Americans consume relatively more bottled sauces than whites or Hispanics?
2. How would you explain the variation in the relative consumption of various brands of hot sauce across the three groups?
3. How would you explain the variation in consumption across the various brands of steak sauce among Hispanic consumers?
4. Which of the African American segments described in Chapter 5 would be the best target market(s) for Heinz 57 Sauce? Why?
5. Does it make sense to treat African Americans as a separate segment for these products? Why?
6. Develop a complete marketing strategy for the following to use to gain sales among African American consumers. What additional data would you like to have to develop your strategy?

   a. Bull's Eye Barbecue Sauce

   b. Tabasco Sauce
7. Which of the Hispanic market segments described in Chapter 5 would be the best target market(s) for Kraft BBQ Sauce? Why?
8. Would it make more sense to treat Hispanics as several nationality groups or as a single Hispanic group, perhaps with demographic submarkets, with respect to bottled sauces? Why?
9. Develop a complete marketing strategy for the following to use to gain sales among Hispanic consumers.

   a. Heinz 57

   b. Louisiana Hot Sauce

   c. Kraft BBQ Sauce

TABLE A		White	Black	Spanish Speaking
Ethnic Group Bottled Sauce Consumption*	Heavy sauce users	93	150	85
	Heavy beef consumers	107	64	111
	Barbecue frequently	111	35	83
	A-1 Original	104	77	94
	A-1 Bold	98	120	111
	Heinz 57	99	112	67
	Lea & Perrins Steak Sauce	103	91	108
	Bull's Eye Barbecue Sauce	104	88	104
	Open Pit Barbecue Sauce	96	149	56
	Hunts BBQ Sauce	96	126	102
	Kraft BBQ Sauce	95	147	76
	Kraft Thick 'N Spicy	92	164	81
	Tabasco Sauce	100	105	88
	Frank's Red Hot Sauce	78	254	62
	Louisiana Hot Sauce	81	243	74
	Worcestershire Sauce	108	58	69

*100 = Average use or consumption. Base = female homemakers.

Source: *Mediamark Reporter 2002—University* (New York: Mediamark Research Inc., March 2002).

2–10 Fighting Obesity in Kids

In the mid-60s, less than 5 percent of children aged 6 to 11 or 12 to 19 were significantly overweight. By the end of the century, the percentage for both groups was approaching 15 percent. A diet rich in high-fat, high-calorie foods coupled with limited physical activity is acknowledged as the cause.

In July, the Centers for Disease Control (CDC) launched a $125 million campaign, including $50 million for media purchases and $43 million for various marketing and public relations activities; funding for subsequent years will be substantial but less. The funding legislation from Congress directed the CDC to target childhood obesity but left it wide latitude as to how. It did require that the CDC "communicate messages that help foster good health over a lifetime, including diet, physical activity, and avoidance of illicit drugs, tobacco and alcohol."

The CDC opted to narrow the approach to increased physical activity, particularly among 9- to 13-year-olds. Mike Greenwell, communications director for the CDC, stated, "What we want is behavior change. That would be success for us."

The barriers to physical activity for kids are substantial. First, nonphysical entertainment options have exploded in recent years. Not only has cable television greatly expanded the number of television channels targeting kids, but magazines focusing on

them have also expanded. Videos and video games are now a major recreational choice for children. Of course, the time spent online has grown from none to several hours per week in just a few years.

Coupled with the vast growth in nonphysical exercise options, there has been a radical decline in required physical education in school. CDC estimates that the number of kids getting physical education in schools has dropped from 50 percent to 21 percent in the past decade.

An initial 15-second spot launched in July shows computer animation of action words turning into an image of a boy running. The theme is "Verb: It's what you do." This and similar teaser spots will run on kid-targeted network and cable TV shows. In September, the full campaign will begin. The ads will all promote the fun of a physically active lifestyle rather than warning about the dangers of not exercising or of excess weight.

The CDC campaign will be the exclusive sponsor of a weekly live-action Nickelodeon show called "WACK" (Wild & Crazy Kids), a related nine-city tour, Nick.com's WACK website, and a "Nick News" special program. Customized advertorials will appear in *Nick Magazine*. It will also be a sponsor of MTV's Rock & Jock programming. Public service announcements will appear on Westwood One. Simon &

Schuster will custom-print a fitness book. Blockbuster Video will run the spots on its in-store monitors in nine markets.

There is controversy about the positive-lifestyle approach of the campaign. Antidrug ads targeting the same age were not successful. In explaining why, the Partnership for a Drug-Free America argued that the positive-lifestyle approach does not motivate nearly as well as ads warning about drug dangers.

Discussion Questions

1. The campaign focuses primarily on children, with limited attention to parents. Teachers and other potential influencers are not directly targeted. What do you think is the appropriate balance among these groups? Why?

2. Is the positive approach better than the negative approach in this situation? Why?

3. Describe a series of three positive-lifestyle ads you would use to encourage physical activity among 9- to 13-year-olds.

4. Describe a series of three warning ads you would use to encourage physical activity among 9- to 13-year-olds.

5. Describe a series of three positive-lifestyle ads targeting parents that you would use to encourage physical activity among their 9- to 13-year-old children.

6. Describe a series of three warning ads targeting parents that you would use to encourage physical activity among their 9- to 13-year-old children.

Source: I. Teinowitz and W. Friedman, "U.S. Launches $125 Mil Push to Combat Obesity," *Advertising Age,* July 17, 2002, p. 4; and www.cdc.gov.

Internal Influences

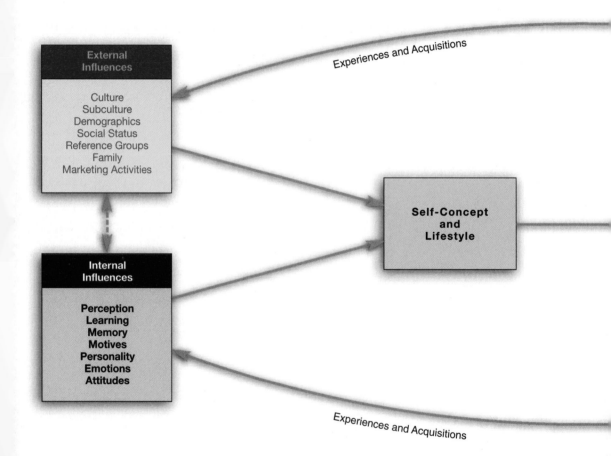

The highlighted areas of our model, internal influences and self-concept and lifestyle, are the focal point of this part of the text. Our attention shifts from forces that are basically outside the individual to processes that occur primarily within the individual.

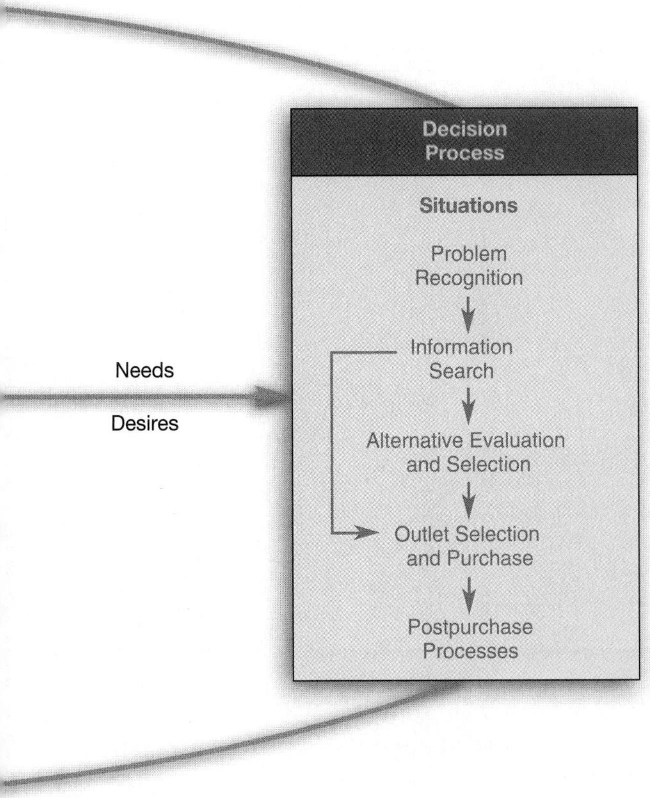

This part begins with a discussion of perception, the process by which individuals access and assign meaning to environmental stimuli. In Chapter 9, we consider learning and memory. Chapter 10 covers motivation, personality, and emotions. Chapter 11 focuses on the critical concept of attitudes and the various ways attitudes are formed and changed.

As a result of the interaction of the external influences described in the previous part of the text and the internal processes examined in this part, individuals form self-concepts and desired lifestyles, as discussed in Chapter 12. These are the hub of our model of consumer behavior. Self-concept refers to the way individuals think and feel about themselves as well as how they would like to think and feel about themselves. Their actual and desired lifestyles are the way they translate their self-concepts into daily behaviors, including consumption behaviors.

Needs

Desires

Decision Process

Situations

Problem Recognition
↓
Information Search
↓
Alternative Evaluation and Selection
↓
Outlet Selection and Purchase
↓
Postpurchase Processes

Perception

☐ Marketers often use intriguing headlines or attractive models to attract attention to their advertisements. How effective is this tactic?

An eye-tracking device is a combination of computer and video technology that allows one to record eye movements in relation to a stimulus such as a website, package, or commercial. The respondent sits in a chair at a table and reads a magazine, watches television commercials, views a website, or observes slides of print advertisements, billboards, shelf facings, point-of-purchase displays, and so forth. Respondents control how long they view each scene. The eye-tracking device sends an unnoticeable beam of filtered light that is reflected off the respondent's eyes. This reflected beam represents the focal point and can be superimposed on whatever is being viewed. It allows the researcher to determine how long an ad or other marketing stimulus is viewed, the sequence in which it was examined, which elements were examined, and how much time was devoted to looking at each element.

RCA used an attractive model in a television ad for its Colortrack television sets. The model wore a conservative dress. Eye tracking revealed that the audience focused substantial attention on the product. Seventy-two hours later, brand name recall was 36 percent. In contrast, a similar commercial used an attractive female in a revealing dress. Eye tracking showed that the ad attracted considerable attention but most of it was focused on the attractive model. Seventy-two hours later, brand name recall was only 9 percent![1]

Marketers do not want their target audience to look only at the models in their ads. They want to communicate something about their product as well. However, since there are many more commercials than consumers can possibly look at, marketers often use attractive models, humor, or other factors to attract the target market's interest. The opening example illustrates that if not well done, these factors may attract attention only to themselves, not to the advertising message. *Will the chapter opening ad effectively communicate its message to its target audience?*

THE NATURE OF PERCEPTION

Information processing is *a series of activities by which stimuli are perceived, transformed into information, and stored.* Figure 8–1 illustrates a useful information-processing model

FIGURE 8–1	Information Processing for Consumer Decision Making

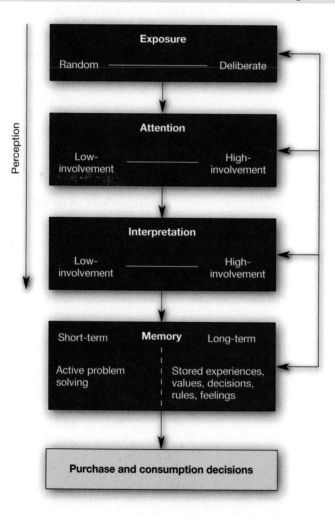

having four major steps or stages: exposure, attention, interpretation, and memory. The first three of these constitute **perception.**

Exposure occurs when a stimulus such as a banner ad comes within range of a person's sensory receptor nerves—vision, in this example. *Attention* occurs when stimulus (banner ad) is "seen" (the receptor nerves pass the sensations on to the brain for processing). *Interpretation* is the assignment of meaning to the received sensations. *Memory* is the short-term use of the meaning for immediate decision making or the longer-term retention of the meaning.

Figure 8–1 and the above discussion suggest a linear flow from exposure to memory. However, *these processes occur virtually simultaneously and are clearly interactive.* For example, a person's memory influences the information he or she is exposed to and attends to and the interpretations the person assigns to that information. At the same time, memory itself is being shaped by the information it is receiving.

Both perception and memory are extremely selective. Of the massive amount of information available, an individual can be exposed to only a limited amount. Of the information to which the individual is exposed, only a relatively small percentage is attended to and passed on to the central processing part of the brain for interpretation. The meaning assigned to a stimulus is as much or more a function of the individual as it is the stimulus itself. Further, much of the interpreted information will not be available to active memory when the individual needs to make a purchase decision.

This selectivity, sometimes referred to as **perceptual defenses,** means that *individuals are not passive recipients of marketing messages.* Rather, consumers largely determine the messages they will encounter and notice as well as the meaning they will assign them. Clearly, the marketing manager faces a challenging task when communicating with consumers.

EXPOSURE

Exposure *occurs when a stimulus comes within range of our sensory receptor nerves.* For an individual to be exposed to a stimulus requires only that the stimulus be placed within the person's relevant environment. That is, you have been exposed to a television commercial if it aired while you were in the room, even if you were "not paying attention" and did not notice the commercial.

An individual can be exposed to only a minuscule fraction of the available stimuli. There are now hundreds of television channels, thousands of radio stations, innumerable magazines, and an exponentially increasing number of websites. Yet, one normally watches only one television station at a time, reads one magazine, newspaper, or book at a time, and so forth. What determines which stimuli an individual will be exposed to? Is it a random process or purposeful?

Why are you reading this text? Clearly, you are doing so for a reason. Most of the stimuli to which individuals are exposed are "self-selected." That is, people deliberately seek out exposure to certain stimuli and avoid others.

Generally, people seek *information that they think will help them achieve their goals.* These goals may be immediate or long range. Immediate goals could involve seeking stimuli such as a television program for amusement or a website to assist in a purchase decision. Long-range goals might involve studying this text in hopes of passing the next exam, obtaining a degree, becoming a better marketing manager, or all three. An individual's goals and the types of information needed to achieve those goals are a function of that person's existing and desired lifestyle and such short-term motives as hunger or curiosity.

Of course, people are also exposed to a large number of stimuli on a more or less random basis during their daily activities. While driving, they may hear commercials, see billboards and display ads, and so on that they did not purposefully seek out.

The impact of the active, self-selecting nature of exposure can be seen in the zipping, zapping, and muting of television commercials. **Zipping** occurs when one fast-forwards through a commercial on a prerecorded program. **Zapping** involves switching channels when a commercial appears. **Muting** is turning the sound off during commercial breaks. The nearly universal presence of remote controls makes zipping, zapping, and muting very simple. And yes, males do use the remote more than women for zapping, changing channels during the show, and channel surfing.[2]

Most television commercials appear to be avoided, though there is high variance among consumers. Avoidance is increased by the situation itself (presence of a remote control, a VCR time shifter, cable TV), the amount of clutter (number of ads during a time period), placement of the ad (at the end of a program rather than in the middle), and the type of household (multiple-person, higher income, with males present, with children under 18 increase zapping).[3]

These findings are valid only for the American market. A study of commercial viewing in New Zealand (with basically only three channels) found very little viewing drop-off during commercials.[4] However, a large-scale study in the Netherlands (with five main channels) found significant zapping during commercial breaks,[5] as did a study in Hong Kong.[6]

Avoidance of commercials is not limited to television. Automobile drivers avoid about half of the radio commercials broadcast by switching stations.[7] Newspaper readers now read only about half the daily paper.[8] People frequently avoid ads in magazines, and many remove all advertising inserts before reading a magazine.[9] Forty percent of Internet users claim they never look at banner ads while using the Internet.[10]

In response to consumers' tendency to avoid ads, marketers increasingly seek to gain exposure by placing their messages in unique media such as on the side of trucks and taxis (see Illustration 8–1), on street pole banners, in television programs and movies, in bus stop shelters, at events, and inside taxis. For example, CabTV places interactive touch-screen TVs in cabs. These TVs hold 75 minutes of video, much of which is a tour guide to the city. If the screen isn't touched, it runs a 12-minute loop of 30-second commercials. As an executive explained,

Most travelers know where they are going to stay, but they don't know where they're going to eat, shop, gamble, etc. So it's very compelling. It's a 10-inch screen less than two feet from your face.[11]

Months before the Segway HT was available for retail purchase, it was the focal point on "Frasier," with Niles riding one throughout the show. Did the show's writers think this up and seek out a Segway to use? The opposite is more likely. Firms expend tremendous effort into placing their products within entertainment. This provides exposure that consumers don't try to avoid as well as showing how and when to use the product and enhancing its image (see Consumer Insight 8–1).

An area of significant social concern about product placement is the extensive, frequently positive portrayal of smoking in movies. While smoking may be crucial to some storylines and for certain characters, it appears that smoking is shown more often and more favorably in movies than in real life. One study found that 57 percent of movie characters of high socioeconomic status smoked, compared with 19 percent in reality. Why is this a concern? A recent study concluded that "smoking scenes positively aroused young viewers (14- to 15-year-olds), enhanced their perceptions of smokers' social stature, and increased their intent to smoke."[12]

Although consumers often avoid commercials, sometimes they actively seek them out. Many viewers look forward to the commercials developed for the Super Bowl. More

Courtesy mobileoutdoor.com advertising.

ILLUSTRATION 8–1

Marketers increasingly use nontraditional media to gain exposure for their messages.

impressive is the positive response consumers have to **infomercials**—program-length commercials (often 30 minutes), generally with an 800 number and/or Web address through which to order the product or request additional written information. They have been found to positively affect brand recall, attitudes, and purchase intentions.[13] One study found that early adopters, opinion leaders, and active shoppers are more likely to view infomercials than are other consumers.[14] This suggests that they may have significant indirect effects through their impact on word-of-mouth communications.

Exposure to ads and other marketing messages on the Internet can be voluntary or involuntary. **Banner ads** are *distinct areas of a website that are linked to a sponsor's website.* The sponsor's website, referred to as the *target site,* could be the sponsor's home page or, more typically, a specialized site promoting a particular product. Banner ads are the dominant form of advertising on the Internet. Exposure to these ads is generally *involuntary,* as consumers encounter them while seeking other information or entertainment.

A consumer who notices a banner ad and then clicks on it, referred to as *clickthrough,* is now *voluntarily* being exposed to the target site and its marketing message. Consumers also voluntarily expose themselves to marketing messages by deliberately visiting firms' home pages and other marketer sites. Thus, if you were considering buying in-line skates, you might decide to visit Rollerblade's site (www.rollerblade.com). In one survey, 75 percent of recent Internet users had visited a company's home page, primarily to obtain product information. Eighty-five percent of these sought out a website because they saw or heard about it in a mass media ad. The study also found that half of those using the Internet sometimes click on banner ads for additional information.[15]

Product placement involves incorporating brands into movies, television programs, and other entertainment venues in exchange for payment or promotional or other consideration.[16] Product placement agents read scripts and meet with set designers to find scenes where their clients' brand names and products can be placed or written into the dialogue. The goal is to add realism to the scene, give subtle exposure to the brand, and influence consumers in an unobtrusive manner. In general, product placement in movies is unrestricted, but in television, sponsor identification rules may apply (the Federal Communications Commission is the regulatory authority).

While product placements have probably been used since the advent of movies, they really caught marketers' attention when sales of Reese's Pieces candy jumped 6 percent in the three months following the release of *E.T.* in which they were featured. However, merely obtaining presence in a movie or program does not guarantee success. In fact, the effective use of product placement is difficult and not fully understood. How prominent should the brand be? How should it be used? Who, if anyone, should use it? How do consumers feel about seeing brands in movies and programs?

Most consumers understand and even appreciate the use of branded products in movies and TV shows. The use of brands can make scenes more realistic, set the time, provoke feelings of nostalgia, and help establish the personality/lifestyle of the characters. Consumers tend to be aware that the brands used are often placed there as subtle, and not so subtle, ads. However, overemphasis of brands can have negative effects.

Placements appear to work best when the principal actor is present and the placement is manifest and well integrated into the scene. Other factors have ambivalent effects. Prominence enhances the visibility of the brand but may well detract from its evaluation. Smoothly integrating the product into the scene enhances its acceptability and liking but has a negative impact on its being remembered. Ideally, it seems that one would want to have the principal character use the product in a noticeable but positive, natural way. Recall in *E.T.* that the hero used the Reese's Pieces in a key scene to lure *E.T.* to his house. This was a noticeable use of the candy yet a natural strategy for a child to try, and *E.T.*'s liking the candy provided the positive evaluation.

An additional consideration for marketers is that many American movies and television programs are seen by as many people outside the United States as inside. Generally, the English language is dubbed over to the local language. Since only one version of the movie is made, marketers with multinational or global brands must be certain the portrayal of the brand in the movie is appropriate across the countries in which they operate.

Critical Thinking Questions

1. What ethical questions, if any, do you see in using product placement as a marketing tool? Are your feelings the same across all product categories?

2. Are there unique issues and perhaps rules that should govern product placements in movies targeting children?

3. How could a marketer determine how much to pay for a brand placement in a particular movie or television program episode?

ATTENTION

Attention *occurs when the stimulus activates one or more sensory receptor nerves, and the resulting sensations go to the brain for processing.* People are constantly exposed to thousands of times more stimuli than they can process. The average supermarket has 30,000 individual items. It would take hours to attend to each of them. Each television network shows 6,000 commercials per week, and radio stations air many more. Therefore, consumers have to be selective in attending to marketing as well as to other messages.

This selectivity has major implications for marketing managers and others concerned with communicating with consumers. For example, a Federal Trade Commission report

ILLUSTRATION 8–2

This ad uses stimulus factors to capture attention. The stimulus factors used and the headline tie directly to the main message of the ad, which will increase ad comprehension.

Courtesy Overture Services.

indicates that fewer than 3 percent of those reading cigarette ads ever notice the health warning.[17] Less than half of the direct-mail ads received are read.[18] As the following example illustrates, anyone wishing to communicate effectively with consumers must understand how to obtain attention after obtaining exposure.

The Federal Crop Insurance Corporation (FCIC) spent $13.5 million over a four-year period on an advertising campaign to increase awareness and knowledge among farmers of the federal crop insurance program. The campaign included "direct mailings to millions of producers of crops covered by the farmers' disaster program and to FCIC policyholders; national and local news releases; feature stories in national magazines, a radio campaign; publication of several brochures. . . ."

However, "farmers ended up knowing no more about this program after the ad campaign than they did before." A spokesperson described the problem with the program thusly: "It was very good and very effective advertising. The trouble is that we had a hard time getting people to read it."[19]

"Very good and very effective advertising" that no one reads is neither good nor effective. People must attend to the messages. As one advertising agency director stated,

Every year it gets more and more important to stand out and be noticed, to be loud but simple, and to say something relevant and compelling because there is less and less opportunity to talk to consumers and you can't waste any chances.[20]

The ad in Illustration 8–2 is very likely to attract attention. What determines or influences attention? At this moment, you are attending to these words. If you shift your concentration to your feet, you will most likely become aware of the pressure being exerted by your shoes. A second shift in concentration to sounds will probably produce awareness of a number of background noises. These stimuli are available all the time but are not processed until a deliberate effort is made to do so. However, no matter how hard you are concentrating on this text, a loud scream or a sudden hand on your shoulder would probably get your attention. Of course, attention always occurs within the context of a situation. The *same individual* may devote different levels of attention to the *same stimulus* in *different situations*. Attention is determined by these three factors: the *stimulus,* the *individual,* and the *situation*.

Stimulus Factors

Stimulus factors are physical characteristics of the stimulus itself. A number of stimulus characteristics tend to attract our attention independently of individual or situational characteristics.

Size and Intensity   Larger stimuli are more likely to be noticed than smaller ones. Thus, a large banner ad is more likely to be noticed than a small one.[21] In one study, consumers seeking a business from the Yellow Pages attended to more than 90 percent of the quarter-page ads but only a quarter of the small listings.[22] Figure 8–2 indicates the relative attention-attracting ability of various sizes of magazine ads. Another analysis of 86,000 ads found the following average number of inquiries for additional information in relation to ad size:[23]

Size	Number of Responses
Spread	107
One page	76
Two-thirds page	68
One-half page	56
One-third page	47

Insertion frequency, the number of times the same ad appears in the same issue of a magazine, has an impact similar to ad size. Multiple insertions were found to increase recall by 20 percent in one study and by 200 percent in another.[24] However, the amount of attention to multiple inserts has been found to drop by 50 percent from the first to the third exposure.[25] Thus, the subsequent exposures, while generating much less attention, appear to reinforce the learning that occurred on the first exposure.

Like the other stimulus factors, the insertion or exposure frequency interacts with individual characteristics. For example, banner ads for familiar brands appear to capture attention and generate clickthrough with only one exposure. The clickthrough rate drops sharply after the first exposure. In contrast, the clickthrough rate for unfamiliar brands is very low on the first exposure but increases dramatically on the fifth exposure.[26] Thus, the frequency and duration which a banner ad should be run depend in part on the familiarity of the brand to the target audience.

The *intensity* (e.g., loudness, brightness, length) of a stimulus operates in the same manner as size. For instance, the longer a scene in an advertisement is held on-screen, the more likely it is to be noticed and recalled.[27] Intensity for banner ads is the degree to which one is forced to see the banner ad in order to see the desired content (the banner's intrusive-

FIGURE 8-2	The Impact of Size on Advertising Readership*

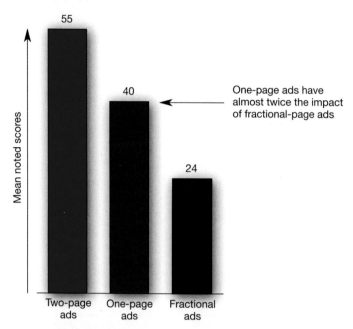

One-page ads have almost twice the impact of fractional-page ads

*Based on an analysis of 85,000 ads.

Source: *Cahners Advertising Research Report 110.1B* (Boston: Cahners Publishing, undated).

ness). Intrusiveness can range from low when the banner is small and at the top or bottom of the site, to high when one must click on or otherwise interact with the banner to get to some or all of the site's content. A study in which the banner ad was the only thing on the screen for a brief period before the consumer was connected to the sought-after site produced over three times the level of noticing the ad compared with a standard banner format, and almost 25 times the clickthrough rate.[28]

Color and Movement   Both *color* and *movement* serve to attract attention, with brightly colored and moving items being more noticeable. Thus, banner ads with dynamic animation attract more attention than similar ads without dynamic animation.[29] A brightly colored package is more apt to receive attention than a dull package. In an eye-tracking study of Yellow Page usage, it was found that color ads were attended to before noncolor ads, more frequently than noncolor ads, and for longer time periods than noncolor ads.[30] Figure 8–3 shows the relative attention-attracting ability of black-and-white and of four-color magazine ads of different sizes.

Illustration 8–3 shows two ads that are identical except for the use of color. The ad with the color was noticed by significantly more readers than the black-and-white ad. However, while color can increase attention and readership, if not used properly, it can also distract from the message and the ability of the audience to effectively process it.[31]

Position   *Position* refers to the placement of an object in a person's visual field. Objects placed near the center of the visual field are more likely to be noticed than those near the edge of the field. This is a primary reason why consumer goods manufacturers compete fiercely for eye-level space in grocery stores. Likewise, advertisements on the right-hand page receive more attention than those on the left. The position of text and illustrations

FIGURE 8–3	Color and Size Impact on Attention*

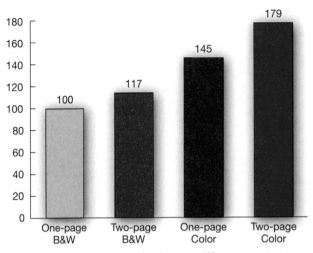

*Readership of a 1-page black and white ad was set at 100.

Source: "How Important Is Color to an Ad?" *Starch Tested Copy,* February 1989, p. 1, Roper Starch Worldwide, Inc.

ILLUSTRATION 8–3

Color can attract attention to an ad. In this case, the color ad had a noted score of 62 percent, compared with 44 percent for the identical black-and-white ad.

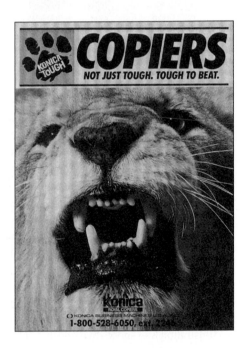

Courtesy of Konica Business Machines, U.S.A.

within a print ad has a significant influence on which will be attended to first and how much attention each will receive.[32] The probability of a television commercial being viewed drops sharply as it moves from being the first to air during a break to the last to air.[33]

Isolation   *Isolation* is separating a stimulus object from other objects. The use of "white space" (placing a brief message in the center of an otherwise blank or white advertisement) is based on this principle, as is surrounding a key part of a radio commercial with a brief moment of silence.[34] Illustration 8–4 shows an effective television ad that uses isolation

Courtesy Mendelsohn/Zien.

and contrast (discussed shortly). This ad for the Green Burrito fast-food chain contains only the green smiley face set on a black background. The mouth moves as the face speaks or sings the ad message in a "calming but off-key" male voice.

Format   Catalog merchants wishing to display multiple items per page often create an environment in which the competition for attention across items reduces attention to all of the items. However, with proper arrangement and formatting, this competition for attention can be reduced and sales improved.[35] *Format* refers to the manner in which the message is presented. In general, simple, straightforward presentations receive more attention than complex presentations. Elements in the message that increase the effort required to process the message tend to decrease attention. Advertisements that lack a clear visual point of reference or have inappropriate movement (too fast, slow, or "jumpy") increase the processing effort and decrease attention. Likewise, audio messages that are difficult to understand due to foreign accents, inadequate volume, deliberate distortions (computer voices), loud background noises, and so forth also reduce attention.[36]

Contrast/Expectations   Consumers pay more attention to stimuli that *contrast* with their background than to stimuli that blend with it. Ads that differ from the type of ad consumers *expect* for a product category often motivate more attention than ads that are more typical for the product category.[37] Likewise, ads that contain unexpected information receive more attention than those that do not.[38] The headline, colors, and design of the ad in Illustration 8–5 contrast with expectations and will cause many to attend to it.

Over time, people adjust to the level and type of stimuli to which they are exposed. Thus, an advertisement that stands out when new will eventually lose its contrast effect and its ability to capture or hold attention.[39] There is a body of knowledge called **adaptation level theory** that deals with this phenomenon.

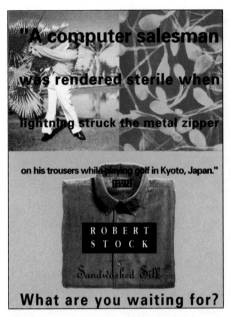

Courtesy Robert Stock.

Interestingness   What one is interested in is generally an individual characteristic. Snowboarders would be likely to attend to ads related to that activity, whereas nonboarders would not. However, there are characteristics of the message itself that cause ads to interest a large percentage of the population. For example, Folgers' series of ads concerning the evolving relationship between a man and woman (virtually a soap opera) attracted a great deal of attention even among people not at all interested in coffee. Factors that increase curiosity such as a plot, the possibility of a surprise ending, uncertainty as to the point of the message till the end, and so forth can increase interest and the attention paid to the ad. In fact, a recent survey of users of personal video recorders (PVRs), which make skipping commercials very easy, found that more than 90 percent watched certain ads because they found them interesting.[40]

Information Quantity   A final stimulus factor, *information quantity,* relates more to the total stimulus field than to any particular item in that field. Although there is substantial variation among individuals, all consumers have limited capacities to process information. **Information overload** occurs when consumers are confronted with so much information that they cannot or will not attend to all of it. Instead, they become frustrated and either postpone or give up the decision, make a random choice, or utilize a suboptimal portion of the total information available.

One study found that consumers purchased more items as the number of catalogs they received increased, and then at a certain point the number of items purchased decreased as additional catalogs were received. The explanation was that information overload had been reached and consumers had stopped reading any of the catalogs.[41]

Individual Factors

Individual factors are characteristics of the individual. *Interest* and *need* are the primary individual characteristics that influence attention. Interest is a reflection of overall lifestyle as well as a result of long-term goals and plans (e.g., becoming a sales manager) and short-term needs (e.g., hunger). Short-term goals and plans are, of course, heavily influenced by the situation. In addition, individuals differ in their *ability* to attend to information.[42]

Individuals seek out (exposure) and examine (attend to) information relevant to their current needs and interests.[43] Thus, an individual contemplating a vacation is likely to attend to vacation-related advertisements. Individuals attending to a specialized medium such as *Runner's World* or *Vogue* are particularly receptive to advertisements for related products. Not surprisingly, products are generally advertised in magazines with editorial copy related to the product or product usage.

Interest or involvement with a brand, product category, or activity can be relatively enduring or very temporary. An in-line skater may be interested in and attentive to information about that activity and related products across a range of situations over an extended time period. In contrast, that same individual may have virtually no interest in dishwashers until faced with one that needs to be replaced. Then, interest may be quite high until a new dishwasher is purchased and installed, at which time interest reverts to a very low level.[44]

One way marketers have responded to temporary interests is by developing smart banners for the Internet. **Smart banners** are *banner ads that are activated based on terms used in search engines.*[45] In our previous example, the consumer with the broken dishwasher might go to Askjeeves.com seeking information about energy-efficient dishwashers. When dishwasher is keyed into the search engine, it would then produce banner ads from sponsoring advertisers for their dishwashers. Related products such as homeowner's insurance might also appear.

Situational Factors

Situational factors include stimuli in the environment other than the focal stimulus (i.e., the ad or package) and temporary characteristics of the individual that are induced by the environment, such as time pressures or a crowded store. For example, consumers pay less attention to a commercial in a large cluster of commercials than they do to one in a smaller set.[46]

Obviously, individuals in a hurry are less likely to attend to available stimuli than are those with extra time (if you have ever been on a long flight without a book, you may recall reading even the ads in the airline magazine). Individuals in an unpleasant environment, such as an overcrowded store, will not attend to many of the available stimuli as they attempt to minimize their time in such an environment.

Program Involvement Print, radio, Internet, and television ads occur in the context of a program, magazine, site, or newspaper. In general, the audience is attending to the medium because of the program or editorial content, not the advertisement. In fact, as we saw earlier, many individuals actively avoid commercials by zapping them. Does the nature of the program or editorial content in which an ad appears influence the attention that the ad will receive? The answer to this question is clearly *yes*.[47] Figure 8–4 demonstrates the positive impact that involvement with a magazine has on attention to print ads. Below we see that a high level of involvement with a television program greatly increases the percentage of viewers who (1) recall the ads aired during the commercial, (2) find them to be credible, and (3) form positive purchase intentions:[48]

	Program Involvement		
	Low	*Medium*	*High*
Unaided recall	18%	21%	22%
Aided recall	34	48	54
Copy credibility	24	37	41
Purchase interest	13	16	18

| FIGURE 8–4 | Involvement with a Magazine and Advertising Effectiveness |

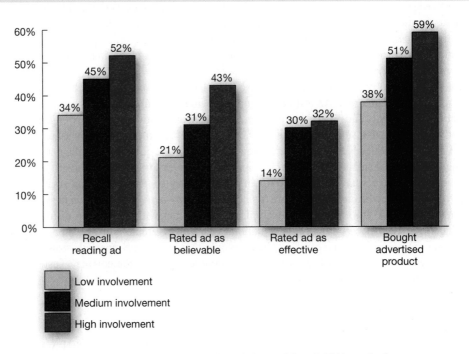

Source: *Cahners Advertising Research Report 120.1 and 120.12* (Boston: Cahners Publishing, undated).

Nonfocused Attention

Thus far we have been discussing a fairly high involvement attention process in which the consumer focuses attention on some aspect of the environment due to stimulus, individual, or situational factors. However, stimuli may be attended to without deliberate or conscious focusing of attention. For example, brands contained in ads to which subjects are exposed but pay little or no attention (incidental exposure) nonetheless have an enhanced probability of being considered for purchase.[49]

Hemispheric Lateralization   **Hemispheric lateralization** is a term applied to activities that take place on each side of the brain. The left side of the brain is primarily responsible for verbal information, symbolic representation, sequential analysis, and the ability to be conscious and report what is happening. It controls those activities we typically call *rational thought*. The right side of the brain deals with pictorial, geometric, timeless, and nonverbal information without the individual being able to verbally report it. It works with images and impressions.

The left brain needs fairly frequent rest. However, the right brain can easily scan large amounts of information over an extended time period. This had led Krugman to suggest that "it is the right brain's picture-taking ability that permits the rapid screening of the environment—to select what it is the left brain should focus on."[50] This indicates that advertising, particularly advertising repeated over time, may have substantial effects that traditional measures of advertising effectiveness cannot detect. The nature of these effects is discussed in more detail in the next chapter.

Subliminal Stimuli   A message presented so fast or so softly or so masked by other messages that one is not aware of seeing or hearing it is called a **subliminal stimulus.** Subliminal stimuli have been the focus of intense study as well as public concern.

Two books triggered public interest in masked subliminal stimuli.[51] The author "documents" numerous advertisements that, once you are told where to look and what to look for, appear to contain the word *sex* in ice cubes, phalli in mixed drinks, and nude bodies in the shadows. Most, if not all, of these symbols are the chance result of preparing thousands of print ads each year; a diligent search could no doubt produce large numbers of religious symbols, animals, or whatever. Such masked symbols, deliberate or accidental, do not appear to affect standard measures of advertising effectiveness or influence consumption behavior.[52] Research on messages presented too rapidly to elicit awareness indicates that such messages have little or no effect.[53] In addition, there is no evidence marketers are using subliminal messages.[54]

INTERPRETATION

Interpretation is *the assignment of meaning to sensations*. It is a function of the *gestalt,* or pattern, formed by the characteristics of the stimulus, the individual, and the situation. Thus, the entire message, including the context in which it occurs, influences our interpretation, as does the situation in which we find ourselves. For example, our beliefs about a product are influenced by our beliefs about the capabilities and social responsibility of the company that produces it as well as its price, country of origin, and the store in which it is sold.[55] Likewise, consumers may interpret advertising or promotions for some products as meaning that the products are of low quality.[56] The interpretation of a "sale" sign on a brand depends on how many other brands are on sale[57] as well as the past history of sales for the brand.[58]

People assign meaning to the tone and feel of the message as well as the actual words and symbols. In a television ad, one actor can say "Thanks a lot" to another. Is this an expression of gratitude? It depends. Sometimes it is, and sometimes it means just the opposite. Members of the same culture or subculture easily and accurately assign the correct meaning based on voice tone or context.[59]

Cognitive interpretation is *a process whereby stimuli are placed into existing categories of meaning*.[60] This is an interactive process. The addition of new information to existing categories also alters those categories and their relationships with other categories. When DVD players were first introduced, most consumers probably grouped them in the general category of video players in order to be able to evaluate them. With further experience and information, many consumers have gained detailed knowledge about the product and have formed several subcategories for classifying the various brands and types. Further, as a result of this process, their category structure for VCRs is also altered.

The more radically "new" a new product is (a discontinuous innovation), the more difficult it is to place into an existing category or knowledge structure.[61] How does one categorize the Segway when first being exposed to it? It does not easily fit into the bicycle, skateboard, scooter, or motorbike category. Instead, consumers may be required to develop a new category borrowed from several others. Unless provided explicit help by marketers, this may slow understanding and acceptance of the product.[62]

It is the individual's interpretation, not objective reality, that influences behavior. A firm may introduce a high-quality new brand at a lower price than existing brands because the firm has a more efficient production or marketing process. However, if consumers interpret this lower price to mean lower quality, the new brand will not be successful regardless of the objective reality.[63]

Courtesy Pepsi; Agency: Jager di Paola Kemp Design.

The previous example indicates the critical importance of distinguishing between *semantic meaning,* the conventional meaning assigned to a word such as found in the dictionary, and *psychological meaning,* the specific meaning assigned a word by a given individual or group of individuals based on their experiences and the context or situation in which the term is used.

Marketers must be concerned with psychological meaning. The semantic meaning of the expression *on sale* is "a price reduction from the normal level." However, when applied to fashion clothes, the psychological meaning that some consumers would derive is "these clothes are, or soon will be, out of style."

Affective interpretation is *the emotional or feeling response triggered by a stimulus such as an ad.* Like cognitive interpretation, there are "normal" (within-culture) emotional responses to many stimuli (e.g., most Americans experience a feeling of warmth when seeing pictures of young children with kittens). Likewise, there are also individual variations to this response (a person allergic to cats might have a negative emotional response to such a picture). Consumers confronting new products or brands often assign them to emotional as well as cognitive categories.[64] The ad shown in Illustration 8–6 is likely to trigger an emotional interpretation as well as a cognitive one.

Individual Characteristics

Marketing stimuli have meaning *only* as individuals interpret them.[65] Individuals are not passive interpreters of marketing and other messages but actively assign meaning based on their needs, desires, expectations, and experiences. Thus, consumers' interpretations of negative publicity depend on their prior commitment to the brand involved.[66] Likewise, consumers interpret movie critics' reviews in light of their knowledge about the critic and his or her biases and preferences.[67] The fairness of a price increase is interpreted on the basis of the consumer's inferred motive for the increase.[68] Information about competing brands is often inaccurately interpreted to favor a preferred brand.[69]

A number of individual characteristics influence interpretation. Two particularly important personal variables are *learning* and *expectations.*

Learning   We saw in Chapter 2 that the meanings attached to such "natural" things as time, space, friendship, and colors are learned and vary widely across cultures. Even within the same culture, different subcultures assign different meanings to similar stimuli. For example, *dinner* refers to the noon meal in some geographic regions of the United States and to the evening meal in other geographic regions.

Likewise, many consumers have a warm emotional response when presented with pictures of fried chicken or people frying chicken. They learned this response because of fried chicken's role in picnics and family gatherings when they were young. Thus, we are referring to learning in this context not as formal learning such as one encounters in an academic setting but as the accumulation of life experiences. Consider how Kim, a young woman who values control, responded to several beer ads:

INTERVIEWER (referring to beer party ad): What evidence did the advertiser provide for conveying the theme that beer makes the party?

KIM: They wanted you to see the party. Everyone looks like they're having fun. When you go to a party, someone is out of control or doing something stupid. Everything here is under control. That was trying to portray a positive image of a party.

KIM (responding to a question about a bar scene beer ad): Beer makes you smile laugh, get along. Everyone's attractive, younger, having a good time. They don't look like they'd been drinking. No one looked like they've been drinking numerous beers.

INTERVIEWER: You've said that several times. Do you expect to see the downside of drinking?

KIM: Yeah, I guess I'm used to it. I wouldn't expect them to show that to a customer. I compare it to what I see. In college and high school, people don't really have control over it. They go too far. It's difficult for me to see leisurely drinking.[70]

Clearly consumers base their interpretations of marketing messages and activities on their own experiences and needs.

Expectations   Individuals' interpretations of stimuli tend to be consistent with their *expectations*. Most consumers expect dark brown pudding to taste like chocolate, not vanilla, because dark pudding is generally chocolate flavored and vanilla pudding is generally cream colored. In a taste test, 100 percent of a sample of college students accepted dark brown *vanilla* pudding as chocolate. Further, in comparing three versions of the vanilla pudding that differed only in degree of darkness, the students rated the darkest as having the best chocolate flavor.[71] Thus, their expectations, cued by color, led to an interpretation that was inconsistent with objective reality. The ad in Illustration 8–7 uses color to reinforce an interpretation that Godiva truffles are "rich" and "luscious." This works because we have learned, through our culture, to assign this type of meaning to the color gold.

Consumers will frequently evaluate the performance of a well-known brand or a more expensive brand as higher than that of an identical product with an unknown brand name or a lower price. Consumers also frequently attribute advertisements for new or unknown brands to well-known brands. Brands with promotional signs on them in retail stores are interpreted as having reduced prices even when the sign does not indicate that prices have been reduced and when, in fact, prices have *not* been reduced.[72]

The old saying "First impressions matter" is borne out by research. One's first impression of a salesperson, a product, or a customer provides a set of expectations. Subsequent experiences with the individual or product tend to be interpreted consistently with the expectations established by the initial encounter.[73]

Situational Characteristics

A variety of situational characteristics influence interpretation. Temporary characteristics of the individual, such as hunger or loneliness, influence the interpretation of a given stimulus, as do moods.[74] The amount of time available affects the meaning assigned to marketing messages. Likewise, physical characteristics of the situation such as temperature, the

Colors are often used to convey product characteristics and meanings. The use of gold in this ad conveys a meaning of richness.

SAY IT LIKE YOU MEAN IT.

Nothing expresses your gratitude more eloquently than our indulgent assortments of rich, luscious truffles. Wrapped with true beauty and grace, they speak all the words you can't. Stop in or call 1-800-643-1579.

GODIVA
Chocolatier

Courtesy Godiva Chocolatier, Inc.

number and characteristics of other individuals present, the nature of the material surrounding the message in question, external distractions, and the reason the message is being processed affect how the message is interpreted.

Will consumers interpret the price of a product offered in a sale ad or display that asks them to compare it with the price offered at another store versus one that asks them to compare the price with the store's regular price, as offering the most value (given identical savings)? The answer depends in large part on *where* the consumer is when attending to the ad. If at home, the "compare to another store" tends to be evaluated as offering the best value while the opposite is true if the ad is read in the store.[75]

Both Coca-Cola and General Foods have refused to advertise some products during news broadcasts because they believe that "bad" news might affect the interpretation of their products. According to a Coca-Cola spokesperson,

It's a Coca-Cola corporate policy not to advertise on TV news because there's going to be some bad news in there, and Coke is an upbeat, fun product.[76]

The above example expresses a concern about context effects, or what researchers refer to as **contextual priming effects.** This refers to the impact that the content of the material surrounding an ad will have on the interpretation of the ad. The immediate contexts in which ads appear are generally the television/radio program in which they are embedded or the magazine/newspaper/website in which they appear. As Coca-Cola suspects, it appears that ads are evaluated in a more positive light when surrounded with positive programming.[77]

Consider the following actual scenario.

> An episode of QVC Network's *Extreme Shopping* program offers Muhammad Ali's boxing robe (priced at over $12,000), followed by Jane Mansfield's former mansion (almost $3.5 million), and a Volkswagen Beetle painted by Peter Max ($100,000). Then, signed and personalized Peter Max prints were offered for about $200.

Will the prints be interpreted as less expensive in this scenario than they would be if presented first or with lower-priced items. Consumers tended to interpret the print price as lower when it followed the higher priced items. This is another example of priming effects.[78] *Is it ethical?*

Stimulus Characteristics

> Pontiac's Aztek did sell as well as projected during its introductory period. "The prospects who went to the showrooms were surprised the minivan is as big as it is. Somewhere in the advertising, its true size doesn't come across well."[79]

The problem for Pontiac is not only that consumers who visit a showroom expecting a small car are finding one larger than they want, but that consumers desiring a larger car are unlikely to consider the Aztek since the advertising leads them to expect a smaller vehicle. Obviously, it is critical that marketers provide a stimulus set that will lead to the desired interpretation.

The stimulus is the basic structure to which an individual responds. The product, package, advertisement, or sales presentation have a major impact on the nature of the mental processes that are activated and on the final meaning assigned to the message.[80]

However, the meanings of most, if not all, stimuli are learned. Earlier in this chapter, we saw how color influenced taste perceptions of pudding. When Barrelhead Sugar-Free Root Beer changed the background color on its cans from blue to beige, consumers rated it as *tasting* more like old-fashioned root beer. Canada Dry's sugar-free ginger ale sales increased dramatically when the can was changed to green and white from red. Red is interpreted as a cola color and thus conflicted with the taste of ginger ale.[81]

Other aspects of how stimuli are interpreted appear to be more innate. For example, people tend to interpret tall or elongated packages as containing more than an equal-volume, shorter package. This in turn appears to affect both consumption and subsequent satisfaction with the brand.[82]

All aspects of the message itself influence interpretation. This can include the reaction to the overall style, visual and auditory background, and other nonverbal and verbal aspects of the message, as well as its explicit content. For instance, the type of background music played during an ad has been found to influence the interpretation of and response to the ad.[83] The other brands displayed with a brand in a retail outlet affect its perceived value.[84] Similarly, promoting a new product in conjunction with an existing product influences the perceived quality of the new product.[85]

In Illustration 8–8, the attention-attracting device, the mannequin being pulled into the billboard by the vacuum cleaner, reinforces the verbal content of the message ("The incredible suction power of the AEG Vampyr Rosso"). This billboard is likely to attract attention and communicate the key message that the AEG vacuum cleaner is powerful.

Sensory Discrimination   The ability of an individual to distinguish between similar stimuli is called **sensory discrimination.** This involves such variables as the sound of stereo systems, the taste of food products, or the clarity of display screens. The minimum

This billboard uses a unique attention-attracting device, ample white space, and a brief message. All the elements are consistent. It is likely to both capture attention and be interpreted as intended.

Courtesy HVR/FCB Advertising/The Netherlands.

amount that one brand can differ from another with the difference still being noticed is referred to as the **just noticeable difference (j.n.d.).** Marketers seeking to find a promotable difference between their brand and a competitor's must surpass the j.n.d. in order for the improvement or change to be noticed by consumers.

The higher the initial level of the attribute, the greater the amount that attribute must be changed before the change will be noticed. Thus, a small addition of salt to a pretzel would not distinguish the product from a competitor's unless the competitor's pretzel contained only a small amount of salt. As a generalization, *individuals typically do not notice relatively small differences between brands or changes in brand attributes.*

Makers of candy bars have utilized this principle for years. Since the price of cocoa fluctuates widely, they simply make small adjustments in the size of the candy bar rather than altering price. Marketers want some product changes, such as reductions in the size of the candy bars, to go unnoticed. These changes must be below the j.n.d. Charmin reduced the size of its tissue roll from 500 to 380 sheets and then to 350 without changing the price. The sheets were fluffed up to reduce the visible effect of the downsizing and the package communication focused on "fluffiness." It appears that consumers did not notice the change as sales did not decrease.[86] *What is your evaluation of the ethics of this practice?*

Interpreting Images

Clinique ran an ad that pictured a tall, clear glass of mineral water and ice cubes. A large slice of lime was positioned on the lip of the glass. In the glass with the ice cubes and mineral water were a tube of Clinique lipstick and a container of cheek base. Nothing else appeared in the ad. *What does this mean?*

Until recently, actual pictures in marketing messages were thought to convey reality. Since they duplicated a part of the visual world, it was assumed that they carried no cultural or individual meaning beyond the meaning attached to the objects they portrayed. If this is indeed the case, the Clinique ad is irrelevant or nonsensical:

> The [ad] would be utterly unintelligible for a theory in which advertising pictures illustrate tangible product attributes or represent the consumption experience in a relevant way. No one stores open lipsticks in glasses of soda water and the ability of makeup to withstand such icy submersion would be an improbable benefit at best. It is not a common consumption practice to garnish mineral water with lipstick, cheek base, and a slice of lime.[87]

Courtesy Pfizer, Inc.

ILLUSTRATION 8–9

Pictures and imagery do more than merely represent reality. They convey feelings and meanings that often cannot be expressed in words.

Is Clinique guilty of ineffective or even foolish advertising in this case? No. All of us intuitively recognize that pictures do more than represent reality; they supply meaning. Thus, one interpretation of the Clinique ad is "Clinique's new summer line of makeup is as refreshing as a tall glass of soda with a twist." The verbal translation of the meaning conveyed by images is generally incomplete and inadequate. A picture is worth a thousand words not just because it may convey reality more efficiently than words but because it may convey meanings that words cannot adequately express. Words and pictures have differing communications capabilities.

Marketers must understand the meanings their audiences assign various images and words and use them in combination to construct messages that will convey the desired meaning.[88] One well-established principle for organizing ad elements is proximity. The *proximity principle* refers to a tendency to perceive objects or events that are close to one another as being related or as sharing attributes. Thus, Hershey's introduced its new Kisses With Almonds by placing them next to its well-known Kisses in an ad with the expression "Kissin' cousins."

Illustration 8–9 is an example of an ad based heavily on imagery. *What does this ad mean to you? Would it mean the same to older consumers? Consumers from other cultures?*

Consumer Inferences

When it comes to advertising, "what you see is not what you get." Consumers use available data and their own ideas to make inferences about information not contained in the ad. A **consumer inference** is *the process by which consumers assign a value to an attribute or item not contained in an ad on the basis of other data in the ad.* When data about an attribute are missing, consumers may assign it a value based on a presumed relationship between that attribute and one for which data are available; they may assign it the average of their assessments of the available attributes; they may assume it to be weaker than the attributes for which data are supplied; or any of a large number of other strategies may be used.[89]

We are just beginning to study consumer inferences; however, it is clear that certain types of information portrayal may lead to incorrect inferences and suboptimal consumer decisions. For example, an ad stating that a product contains no cholesterol may induce consumers to infer that the product is also low in fat.[90]

Consider the following hypothetical ad copy:

- The Subaru Outback gets better gas mileage than the Pontiac Aztek.
- It has more cargo space than the Saturn VUE.
- It has more power than the Toyota RAV4.

Some consumers would infer from this that the Subaru gets better gas mileage than the VUE and the RAV4; has more cargo space than the Aztek and the RAV4; and has more power than the Aztek and the VUE.[91] These claims are not stated in the ad. Thus, a factually correct ad could still mislead some consumers. *Are such ads ethical?*

PERCEPTION AND MARKETING STRATEGY

Information is the primary raw material the marketer works with in influencing consumers. Therefore, an understanding of the perception process is an essential guide to marketing strategy. In the following sections, we briefly discuss a number of areas for which such an understanding is particularly useful. The role of theories of perception in the regulation of advertising is discussed in Chapter 20.

Retail Strategy

In recent years, many retailers have felt a need to reduce the number of SKUs (stockkeeping units—individual items such as brands, sizes, and versions) within product categories in order to reduce operating costs. However, they have been reluctant to do so for fear that consumers would perceive this as a reduction in choice and shop elsewhere. What should they do? Research shows that eliminating low-preference items while holding total product category shelf space constant does not have a negative impact on consumer perceptions.[92]

Retailers often use exposure very effectively. Store interiors are designed with frequently purchased items (canned goods, fresh fruits/vegetables, meats) separated so that the average consumer will travel through more of the store. This increases total exposure. High-margin items are often placed in high-traffic areas to capitalize on increased exposure.

Shelf position and amount of shelf space influence which items and brands are allocated attention. Point-of-purchase displays also attract attention to sale and high-margin items. Stores are designed with highly visible shelves and overhead signs to make locating items (an information-processing task) as easy as possible. Stores provide reference prices to increase consumers' abilities to accurately interpret price information. Unit price information by brand may be displayed on a separate sign in ascending or descending order to facilitate price comparisons. Nutritional information provided in a similar manner enhances consumers' abilities to choose nutritious brands.

Brand Name and Logo Development

Shakespeare notwithstanding, marketers do not believe that "a rose by any other name would smell as sweet." *Would you rather have a soft drink sweetened with NutraSweet or with aspartame?* Mountain Dew's marketing director ascribes part of the success of Code Red to its name: "Had it been called 'Mountain Dew Cherry' it would've done very differently."[93] In fact, research indicates that brand names can influence how food products taste to consumers.[94] Given the tendency toward global brands, it is easy to imagine how complex creating an appropriate name can be.[95]

Did you see the movie *3,000?* You probably did, but with the name *Pretty Woman.* Consumer research showed that *3,000,* the planned title, had no meaning to consumers (it referred to the number of dollars to spend an evening with Julia Roberts' character). *Teenie Weenies* became *Honey, I Shrunk the Kids* for a similar reason.

Companies such as NameLab use linguists and computers to create names that convey the appropriate meaning for products. For example, NameLab created the *Compaq* computer name. The focus of NameLab is the total meaning conveyed by the interaction of the meanings of the name's parts. For Compaq, *com* means computer and communications while *paq* means small. The unique spelling attracts attention and gives a "scientific" impression. In general, concrete terms with relevant, established visual images such as Mustang, Apple, or Cup-a-Soup are easier to recognize and recall than are more abstract terms. However, alphanumeric names (word and letter combinations such as Z210) are very effective for some product categories (generally technical or chemical) and target markets.[96]

Marketers are increasingly using the strategy of **co-branding,** also referred to as *co-marketing, brand alliances,* and *joint marketing,* in which two brand names are given to a single product. Examples include "Intel Inside" Compaq computers, Breyer's ice cream containing Reese's Pieces candies, and the vast array of Visa cards affiliated with airlines and other organizations. Co-branding has been shown to modify attitudes toward the participating brands. However, the effects can be positive or negative and can differ for the two brands involved. Thus, a firm considering co-branding should be sure that its target market views the potential partner positively and that the two brands fit together in a way that adds value.[97]

How a product or service's name is presented—its *logo*—is also important.[98] Figure 8–5 shows the additional positive or negative impact the graphic part of a logo can have on the image associated with a name. The scores shown in the figure are the percentage of respondents who rated the company very high on such attributes as "trustworthy," "high

FIGURE 8–5   Logos Influence the Image Consumers Have of Firms

Name Only	Rated Very High	Name and Logo	Rated Very High	Percent Change
UPS	68%	UPS	58%	−15%
FedEx	67	FedEx	50	−25
Federal Express	62	FEDERAL EXPRESS	68	+10
United States Postal Service	53	UNITED STATES POSTAL SERVICE	54	+2

Note: The percentage shown on the Name and Logo columns is average top-box ratings ("agree strongly") within a 5-point rating scale on the image contribution attributes, based only on respondents who are aware of the company or brand.

quality," "relevant for today's lifestyles," and "I would use." One rating was obtained from consumers who saw only the company name; the second was in response to the full logo including the name.[99] *What advice would you offer these firms?*

Media Strategy

The fact that the exposure process is selective rather than random is the underlying basis for effective media strategies. Since exposure is not random, the proper approach is to determine to which media the consumers in the target market are most frequently exposed and then place the advertising messages in those media. As one executive stated,

> We must look increasingly for matching media that will enable us best to reach carefully targeted, emerging markets. The rifle approach rather than the old shotgun.[100]

For some products and target markets, consumers are highly involved with the product category itself and will go to considerable trouble to secure product-relevant information. This occurs most frequently among heavy users of hobby items such as skis and stereo equipment or for fashion items.

For other products and target markets, consumers have limited involvement with the product category. Products such as gasoline or detergents are examples. In a situation such as this, the marketer must find media that the target market is interested in and place the advertising message in those media. As we learned earlier, potential target markets as defined by age, ethnic group, social class, or stage in the family life cycle have differing media preferences. Table 8–1 illustrates selective exposure to several magazines based on demographic characteristics.

Preliminary research on Internet advertising suggests that banner ads for high-involvement products should be placed on websites with content relevant to the product. Thus, a banner ad for a product such as specialized mountain bikes should be placed on a site such as the one maintained by *Outside* magazine. In contrast, it appears that the best placement for a banner for a low-involvement product would be on a well-established

TABLE 8–1

Selective Exposure to Magazines Based on Demographic Characteristics*

Demographic Characteristics	Better Homes & Gardens	Cosmopolitan	Maxim	National Geographic	Family Circle
Gender					
Male	45	34	172	114	19
Female	151	161	34	87	175
Age					
18–24	56	217	337	98	38
25–34	91	151	200	80	77
35–44	112	99	52	106	105
45–54	119	77	31	124	124
55–64	117	32	6	101	123
65+	96	21	1	90	127
Education					
Graduated college	108	100	111	154	80
Graduated high school	101	92	61	74	111
Household Income					
$75,000+	119	119	147	128	94
$40,000–$49,999	96	105	82	103	109
$20,000–$29,999	89	78	66	82	111

*100 represents an average level of usage.

Source: *Mediamark Reporter 2002—University* (New York: Mediamark Research Inc., March 2002).

website with good reputation independent of content, as long as it is frequented by the target market.[101]

Many marketers want consumers to visit their websites. These sites are often like magazines published by the marketing firm. And, like magazines, many of them offer content ranging from entertainment to education to attract consumers to the sites. For example, P&G's "S" online magazine (www.s-mag.com) provides a wide array of advice for simplifying life and dealing with the stresses of modern living as well as conveying product information. Its "Ask Iris," a girl's health advice feature of its BeingGirl.com site, gets 30,000 e-mail queries each week.[102]

Technology is radically altering the media choices available to marketers beyond the Internet. One of the earliest advertising media was the sandwich board—a wooden sign promoting a product, store, or event attached front and back by shoulder straps and carried by a person standing outside a store or walking through town. Consider its modern reincarnation.

> While a cab travels from one end of a city to the other, an electronic billboard on top changes according to location and time of day. Thanks to a satellite feed and Global Positioning System, the bright, attention-getting ads on the taxi roof keep changing. As the cab passes by a college, an ad for a bookstore appears. While the cab moves through the business district at noon, an ad for a local deli fills the screen. As the cab travels through a Hispanic neighbor, a Spanish-language ad for a snack food is shown.[103]

Advertisements and Package Design

Advertisements and packages must perform two critical tasks—capture attention and convey meaning. Unfortunately, the techniques appropriate for accomplishing one task are often counterproductive for the remaining task.

What should a manager do to attract attention to a package or advertisement? As with most aspects of the marketing process, it depends on the target market, the product, and the situation. If the target market is interested in the product category, or in the firm or brand, attention will not constitute much of a problem. Once consumers are exposed to the message, they will most likely attend to it. Unfortunately, most of the time consumers are not actively interested in a particular product. Interest in a product tends to arise only when the need for the product arises. Since it is difficult to reach consumers at exactly this point, marketers have the difficult task of trying to communicate with them at times when their interest is low or nonexistent.

Assume that you are responsible for developing a campaign designed to increase the number of users for your firm's toilet bowl freshener. Research indicates that the group you wish to reach has very little interest in the product. What do you do? Two strategies seem reasonable. One is to *utilize stimulus characteristics* such as full-page ads, bright colors, animated cartoons, or surrealism to attract attention to the advertisement. The second is to *tie the message to a topic in which the target market is interested.* Celebrities are often used in advertisements in part for this reason, as is humor. Sex appeal, in the form of attractive models, is also frequently used.

Using either stimulus characteristics or consumer interests unrelated to the product category to attract attention presents two dangers. The first is that the strategy will be so successful in attracting attention to the stimulus object that it will reduce the attention devoted to the sales message. The reader may observe an attractive member of the opposite sex in an advertisement and not attend to the sales message or copy. This occurred with the ad for RCA Colortrack described in this chapter's opening example.

The second risk associated with using stimulus characteristics or unrelated consumer interests to attract attention is that the *interpretation* of the message will be negatively

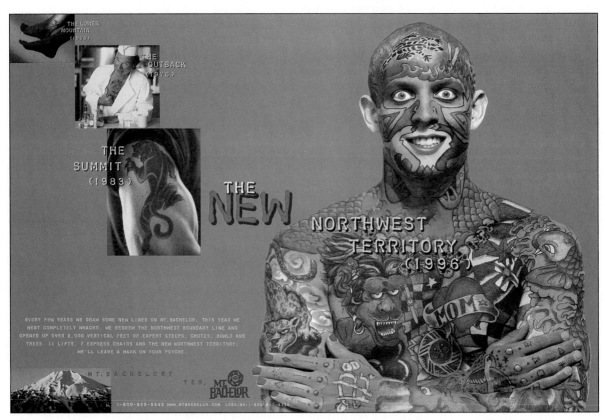

Courtesy Mt. Bachelor.

affected. For example, the use of humor to attract attention to a commercial for insurance may result in the brand being interpreted as flighty or not worthy of serious consideration. Thus, caution must be used to ensure that attention-attracting devices do not have a negative impact on attention to, or interpretation of, the main message.

The ad shown in Illustration 8–10 appeared in *Outside* magazine. It uses color, contrast, and size (two full pages) to attract attention. However, the connection between these attention-attracting devices and the brand's features or image is not clear. Ads that rely on stimulus factors not directly related to the product should be thoroughly pretested to determine how the target market interprets them. *Does this ad inspire you to want to ski Mt. Bachelor?* (Management states that the ad was designed to attract snowboarders who it believes relate to the ad.)

Developing Warning Labels and Disclaimers

A recent U.S. Court of Appeals decision in *Pearson* v. *Shalala* allows sellers of dietary supplements to make health claims on less than "significant scientific agreement" when these claims are accompanied by a disclaimer (such as "this claim is not approved by the FDA"). The court held that the FDA must demonstrate with empirical evidence that a disclaimer would "bewilder consumers and fail to correct for deceptiveness" before it can prohibit a health claim. One researcher in this area concluded,

The tragic result of the *Pearson* court's misstep is that consumers will again be exploited by health claims riddled with half-truths and will be duped into taking products that jeopardize their health.[104]

Clearly being able to develop effective disclosures and warning labels is critically important. Both ethical and legal considerations require marketers to place warning labels on a wide array of products (cigarettes, alcoholic beverages, many over-the-counter drugs, tampons, lawn mowers, power tools, and so forth). These can range from general warnings such as those on cigarette packages to warnings that apply to only a small portion of the population such as "Don't take this drug if you have diabetes."

The government, consumer groups, and ethical marketers want the warnings to accomplish their primary task—that is, they should effectively alert the potential user to the risk associated with using the product in a manner that allows the consumer to make an informed decision concerning the product. In addition, marketers do not want warnings to detract unduly from the image of the product or cause inappropriately negative assessments of its risk-to-benefit ratio.

Unfortunately, it appears that some marketers err on the side of protecting their brand's image and sales. For instance, in television ads, most warnings or disclosures are presented via only one mode (oral or visual) rather than two, and visual disclosures tend to be low contrast (i.e., white lettering on medium or light backgrounds).[105] For these and other reasons, many warning labels are not noticed or are not effectively processed.[106]

Despite the fact that many warnings and disclosures are ignored, there is substantial evidence that well-designed warnings are attended to and do influence knowledge, beliefs, and, to a lesser extent, behaviors.[107] The challenge, then, is to design warnings with a maximum likelihood of being successful. The first step is to understand the needs and vocabulary of the target audience. As one expert concluded,

> Warnings designed with input from consumers about what they wish to know and how and when they wish to know it would not only provide a greater number of options for warning content, it is also likely to increase the probability that a given warning will have its intended effect.[108]

Advertising Evaluation

A successful advertisement, or any other marketing message, must accomplish four tasks:

1. *Exposure.* It must physically reach the consumer.
2. *Attention.* The consumer must attend it to.
3. *Interpretation.* It must be properly interpreted.
4. *Memory.* It must be stored in memory in a manner that will allow retrieval under the proper circumstances.

Advertising evaluation covers all of these tasks. However, most of the effort is focused on attention and, to a lesser extent, memory.

Measures of Exposure   Exposure to print media is most frequently measured in terms of circulation. Data on circulation are provided by a variety of commercial firms. However, frequently these data are not broken down in a manner consistent with the firm's target market. Thus, a firm may be targeting the lower-middle social class, but circulation data may be broken down by income rather than social class.

Diary reports, in which respondents record their daily listening patterns, and telephone interviews are the two methods used to measure radio listening. Television viewing is measured primarily by **people meters,** which are electronic devices that automatically determine if a television is turned on and, if so, to which channel. They allow each household member to log on when viewing by punching an identifying button. The demographics of each potential viewer are stored in the central computer so viewer profiles can be developed.

Websites can automatically record the number of total and unique (from distinct computers) visits per time period.[109] Banner ads and the sites on which they appear are often evaluated on the *clickthrough rate*—the percentage of site visitors or total number of people who click on the banner ad. However, evidence indicates that banner ads also can have a positive impact on consumers who do not click on them.[110]

Measures of Attention   The attention-attracting powers of commercials, packages, and websites can be partially measured in a direct manner using **eye tracking,** or eye fixations. While a consumer looks at images of print ads, billboards, store shelves, packages, or websites, a camera underneath the screen sends an invisible beam of light off the consumer's pupil. The camera indicates exactly what the consumer is attending to. This technology allows marketers to determine (1) what parts of the message were attended to, (2) what sequence was used in viewing the message, and (3) how much time was spent on each part.[111]

Indirect measures of attention, which also tap at least some aspects of memory, include theater tests, day-after recall, recognition tests, and Starch scores. *Theater tests* involve showing commercials along with television programs in a theater. Viewers complete questionnaires designed to measure which commercials, and what aspects of those commercials, attracted their attention. **Day-after recall (DAR)** is the most popular method of measuring the attention-getting power of television commercials. Individuals are interviewed the day after a commercial is aired on a program they watched. Recall of the commercial and recall of specific aspects of the commercial are interpreted as a reflection of the amount of attention.

DAR measures of television commercials have been criticized as favoring rational, factual, hard-sell ads and high-involvement products while discriminating against feeling, emotional, soft-sell ads. However, for many product/target market combinations, the latter approach may be superior. In response, substantial work has been done to develop recognition measures for television commercials. In **recognition tests,** the commercial of interest, or key parts of it, along with other commercials are shown to target-market members. Recognition of the commercial, or key parts of it, is the measure. This technique appears to work better than standard recall measures.[112]

Starch scores are the most popular technique for evaluating the attention-attracting power of print ads. The respondents are shown advertisements from magazine issues they have recently read. For each advertisement, they indicate which parts (headlines, illustrations, copy blocks) they recall reading. Three main scores are computed:

1. *Noted.* The percentage of people who recall seeing the ad in that issue.
2. *Seen-associated.* The percentage of those who recall reading a part of the ad that clearly identifies the brand or advertiser.
3. *Read most.* The percentage of those who recall reading 50 percent or more of the copy.

Starch scores allow an indirect measure of attention to the overall ad and to key components of the ad.

Measures of Interpretation   Marketers investigate *interpretation* primarily through the use of focus groups, theater tests, and day-after recall. *Focus groups* involve a group of 5 to 15 members of the target audience who have a relatively free-form discussion of the meaning conveyed by the advertisement.

Marketers are just beginning to measure the emotional or feeling reactions or meanings that consumers assign to ads. Although standard methods do not yet exist, this is clearly an important area for development (more details are provided in Chapter 11).

Commercial sponsorship of events, particularly sporting events, has become a major marketing activity and a major source of revenue for the events. Sponsors derive a variety of benefits from sponsorship ranging from exposure of their brand name to image enhancement by association with the event.

Ambush marketing involves *any communication or activity that implies, or from which one could reasonably infer, that an organization is associated with an event, when in fact it is not.* Such communications seek to achieve some or all of the benefits of being associated with the event without incurring the cost of sponsorship fees or to overcome exclusive sponsorship rights awarded to a rival.

Ambush marketing can take many forms. One is to sponsor media coverage of the event rather than the event itself. Another is to sponsor a small part of the larger event and then to promote that sponsorship heavily; that is, rather than sponsoring the Olympics, a firm might sponsor the U.S. swim team and advertise that sponsorship heavily throughout the Olympics.

A common form of ambush marketing is to advertise heavily during the event. Such advertising can be either a firm's regular advertisements or ads related to the event. A firm such as Coca-Cola or Pepsi Cola could purchase extensive advertising time during the Olympics on the network carrying the games. Viewers watching the games would then see numerous Coke or Pepsi ads and might conclude that that firm is a sponsor of the Olympics. This conclusion would be more likely if the ads contained Olympic athletes as spokespersons, offered a "salute" to the Olympic athletes, or otherwise used symbols that related directly or indirectly to the Olympics. For example, Wendy's ran ads featuring Olympic gold medalist Kristi Yamaguchi as a spokesperson during the 1992 Olympics while McDonald's was the official sponsor of the U.S. skating team.[113]

Critical Thinking Questions
1. How does ambush marketing work?
2. Ambush marketing does what harm, if any?
3. What ethical issues, if any, arise in ambush marketing?

Ethical Concerns

A host of ethical concerns arise as marketers apply their understanding of the perceptual process. We addressed a number of these issues such as subliminal messages and incorrect consumer inferences earlier in this chapter. In Chapter 20, we will examine some of the regulations that have been created to protect consumers from misuse of perceptual cues.

Most of the ethical concerns in this area relate to the conflict between presenting a brand in a favorable light and presenting it completely accurately. Consider the following situations:

- An ad shows a plate with a large helping (9 ounces or so) of a food product such as pork. While the helping shown is no larger than that commonly consumed, the calorie count supplied in the ad is for 3 ounces (a recommended serving size).
- Television ads consistently show a particular sports utility vehicle in extremely rugged terrain. Although it is possible that the vehicle could be driven in such terrain, it is designed primarily for on-road operation. Extensive off-road use would likely damage the vehicle.
- A car is advertised as having better acceleration than brand X, better fuel economy than brand Y, and a larger interior than brand Z. These are all true claims, but the advertised brand is worse than each competitor on two dimensions that are not mentioned for that competitor (i.e., it has worse fuel economy and a smaller interior than brand X).

Are these practices ethical? Part of the answer resides with consumer expectations and knowledge; that is, to some extent it depends on how consumers interpret the ads.

Consumer Insight 8–2 describes *ambush marketing,* in which firms attempt to associate their companies with an event such as the Olympics without becoming an official sponsor. Is this ethical?

SUMMARY

Perception consists of those activities by which an individual acquires and assigns meaning to stimuli. Perception begins with *exposure*. This occurs when a stimulus comes within range of one of an individual's primary sensory receptors. People are exposed to only a small fraction of the available stimuli, and this is usually the result of self-selection.

Attention occurs when the stimulus activates one or more of the sensory receptors and the resulting sensations go into the brain for processing. Because of the amount of stimuli they are exposed to, people selectively attend to those stimuli that physically attract (stimulus factors) or personally interest them (individual factors). *Stimulus factors* are physical characteristics of the stimulus itself, such as contrast, size, intensity, color, movement, position, isolation, format, and information quantity. *Individual factors* are characteristics of the individual, such as interests and needs. Both these factors are moderated by the *situation* in which they occur. *Program involvement,* the degree of interest the consumer has in the program or magazine in which the advertisement is embedded, is a situational factor of particular interest to marketers.

Nonfocused attention occurs when a person takes in information without deliberate effort. *Hemispheric lateralization* is a term applied to activities that take place on each side of the brain. The left side of the brain is concerned primarily with those activities typically called rational thought and the ability to be conscious and report what is happening. The right side of the brain deals with pictorial, geometric, timeless, and nonverbal information without the individual being able to verbally report it.

A message presented so fast or so softly or so masked by other messages that one is not aware of seeing or hearing it is called a *subliminal message*. Subliminal messages have generated a great deal of interest but do not affect brand choice or other aspects of consumer behavior in a meaningful way.

Interpretation is the assignment of meaning to stimuli that have been attended to. Interpretation is a function of individual as well as stimulus and situation characteristics. *Cognitive interpretation* appears to involve a process whereby new stimuli are placed into existing categories of meaning. *Affective interpretation* is the emotional or feeling response triggered by the stimulus. Interpretation is largely a function of individual learning and expectations that are triggered by the stimulus and moderated by the situation.

Marketers are particularly interested in how consumers *differentiate between brands,* how they *interpret images,* and how they *form inferences* about missing information. Both marketing managers and regulators are concerned with the amount of information that is misinterpreted.

Marketing managers use their knowledge of information processing in a variety of ways. The fact that media exposure is selective is the basis for *media strategy. Retailers* can enhance their operations by viewing their outlets as information environments. Both stimulus and personal interest factors are used to attract attention to *advertisements* and *packages.* Characteristics of the target market and the message are studied to ensure that accurate interpretation occurs. The meaning that consumers assign to words and parts of words is the basis for selecting *brand names.* Information processing theory guides a wide range of *advertising evaluation techniques.* Likewise, information processing theory is a basis for *developing warning labels and posters.* Finally, marketers need to be sensitive to the host of ethical issues that arise when developing marketing messages.

KEY TERMS

Adaptation level theory 287
Affective interpretation 292
Ambush marketing 305
Attention 282
Banner ads 281
Co-branding 299
Cognitive interpretation 291
Consumer inference 297
Contextual priming effects 294
Day-after recall (DAR) 304

Exposure 279
Eye tracking 304
Hemispheric lateralization 290
Information overload 288
Information processing 278
Infomercials 281
Interpretation 291
Just noticeable
    difference (j.n.d.) 296
Muting 280

People meters 303
Perception 279
Perceptual defenses 279
Recognition tests 304
Sensory discrimination 295
Smart banners 289
Starch scores 304
Subliminal stimulus 291
Zapping 280
Zipping 280

INTERNET EXERCISES

1. Examine several magazines. Copy two ads that do a good job of encouraging the reader to visit a website. Justify your selection using the principles of perception described in this chapter.

2. Visit one of the following websites. Evaluate the site on the principles of perception covered in this chapter.
   a. www.hollywood.com
   b. www.absolutvodka.com
   c. www.nj.com/yucky
   d. www.elle.com
   e. www.purina.com

3. Visit several company websites until you find one that you feel makes effective use of the principles of perception that we have covered and one that violates these principles. Provide the URL of each and justify your selections.

4. Use the Internet to determine the following. What do you conclude from this?
   a. Who is advertising on the Internet?
   b. Who is using the Internet?
   c. Who is reading the ads on the Internet?

DDB NEEDHAM LIFESTYLE DATA ANALYSES

1. Examine the DDB Needham data in Tables 1a, 2a, 3a, 4a, 5a, 6a, and 7a. What characterizes a person who is unlikely to buy products whose advertising he or she dislikes? Why is this the case? What are marketing implications?

REVIEW QUESTIONS

1. What is *information processing?* How does it differ from *perception?*

2. What is meant by *exposure?* What determines which stimuli an individual will be exposed to? How do marketers utilize this knowledge?

3. What are *zipping, zapping,* and *muting?* Why are they a concern to marketers?

4. What are *infomercials?* How effective are they?

5. Do consumers seek or avoid commercial information on the Internet?

6. What is meant by *attention?* What determines which stimuli an individual will attend to? How do marketers utilize this?

7. What stimulus factors can be used to attract attention? What problems can arise when stimulus factors are used to attract attention?

8. What is *adaptation level theory?*

9. What is *information overload?* How should marketers deal with information overload?

10. What impact does *program involvement* have on the attention paid to commercials embedded in the program?

11. What is *contextual priming?* Why is it of interest to marketers?

12. What are the six major reasons people watch television?

13. What is meant by *nonfocused attention?*

14. What is meant by *hemispheric lateralization?*

15. What is meant by *subliminal perception?* Is it a real phenomenon? Is it effective?

16. What is meant by *interpretation?*

17. What determines how an individual will interpret a given stimulus?

18. What is the difference between *cognitive* and *affective* interpretation?

19. What is the difference between *semantic* and *psychological* meaning?

20. What is *sensory discrimination?* A *just noticeable difference* (j.n.d.)?

21. What is a *consumer inference?* Why is this of interest to marketers?

22. How does a knowledge of information processing assist the manager in the following?
    a. Formulating retail strategy
    b. Developing brand names and logos

c. Formulating media strategy

d. Designing advertisements and packages

e. Developing warning labels and posters

f. Evaluating advertising

23. What is *co-branding?* Is it effective?

24. How is exposure measured? What problems are encountered in this process?

25. What is *eye tracking?*

26. What is a *Starch score?*

27. What is meant by *day-after recall?*

28. What is meant by *recognition tests?*

29. What is a *people meter?*

30. What ethical concerns arise in applying knowledge of the perceptual process?

31. What is *ambush marketing?*

DISCUSSION QUESTIONS

32. Given that smoking scenes in movies increase the positive image and intention to smoke among youth, what regulations, if any, should apply to this?

33. How could a marketing manager for (*a*) the Habitat for Humanity, (*b*) Rollerblade, (*c*) TGIFridays, (*d*) Tide detergent, or (*e*) Mennen deodorant use the material in this chapter to guide the development of a national advertising campaign? To assist local retailers or organizations in developing their promotional activities? Would the usefulness of this material be limited to advertising decisions?

34. Respond to the questions in Consumer Insight 8–1.
    a. Question 1
    b. Question 2
    c. Question 3

35. Anheuser-Busch test-marketed a new soft drink for adults called Chelsea. The product was advertised as a "not-so-soft drink" that Anheuser-Busch hoped would become socially acceptable for adults. The advertisements featured no one under 25 years of age, and the product contained 0.5 percent alcohol (not enough to classify the product as an alcoholic beverage). The reaction in the test market was not what the firm expected or hoped for. The Virginia Nurses Association decided to boycott Chelsea, claiming that it "is packaged like a beer and looks, pours, and foams like beer, and the children are pretending the soft drink is beer." The Nurses Association claimed the product was an attempt to encourage children to become beer drinkers later on. The secretary of health, education and welfare urged the firm to "rethink their marketing strategy." Others made similar protests. Although Anheuser-Busch reformulated the product and altered the marketing mix substantially, the product could not regain momentum and was withdrawn. Assuming Anheuser-Busch was in fact attempting to position Chelsea as an adult soft drink, which appears to have been its objective, why do you think it failed?

36. Honda uses only alphanumeric names for its cars, and Toyota uses letter names for virtually all of its models. Why do the two companies have differing strategies? Which is superior?

37. Develop a brand name for (*a*) a competitor for the Segway, (*b*) a vegetarian fast-food chain, (*c*) an Internet grocery shopping service, (*d*) a national magazine for high school students, or (*e*) a "fun" restaurant targeting students on your campus. Justify your name.

38. Develop a logo for (*a*) a competitor for the Segway, (*b*) a vegetarian fast-food chain, (*c*) an Internet grocery shopping service, (*d*) a national magazine for high school students, or (*e*) a "fun" restaurant targeting students on your campus. Justify your design.

39. Evaluate the ad in the following in-text illustrations. Analyze the attention-attracting characteristics and the meaning they convey. Are they good ads? What risks are associated with each?
    a. 8–1
    b. 8–2
    c. 8–3
    d. 8–4
    e. 8–5
    f. 8–6
    g. 8–7
    h. 8–8
    i. 8–9
    j. 8–10

40. Develop three co-branded products: one that would be beneficial to both individual brands, one that would benefit one brand but not the other, and one that would benefit neither brand. Explain your logic.

41. Respond to the questions in Consumer Insight 8–2.
    a. Question 1
    b. Question 2
    c. Question 3

42. What problems do you see with people meters?

APPLICATION ACTIVITIES

43. Find and copy or describe examples of advertisements that specifically use stimulus factors to attract attention. Look for examples of each of the various factors discussed earlier in the chapter and try to find their use in a variety of promotions. For each example, evaluate the effectiveness of the stimulus factors used.

44. Repeat Question 43, but this time look for advertisements using individual factors.

45. Complete Question 37 and test your names on a sample of students. Justify your testing procedure and report your results.

46. Complete Question 38 and test your logos on a sample of students. Justify your testing procedure and report your results.

47. Find two brand names that you feel are particularly appropriate and two that you feel are not very appropriate. Explain your reasoning for each name.

48. Find and describe a logo that you feel is particularly appropriate and one that you feel is not very appropriate. Explain your reasoning.

49. Interview three students about their behavior during television and radio commercial breaks. What do you conclude?

50. Interview three students who use the Internet. Determine how they respond to banner ads and the extent to which they attend to various commercial messages on the Internet.

51. Go to a health food or alternative medicines store or section of a store. Find three products that make health claims. Evaluate the likely effectiveness of any disclaimers that they contain.

52. Find and copy or describe an ad or other marketing message that you think makes unethical use of the perceptual process. Justify your selection.

53. Develop an ad but omit information about some key product attributes. Show the ad to five students. After they have looked at the ad, give them a questionnaire that asks about the attributes featured in the ad and about the missing attributes. If they provide answers concerning the missing attributes, ask them how they arrived at these answers. What do you conclude?

REFERENCES

1. *What the Eye Does Not See, the Mind Does Not Remember,* Telecom Research, Inc., undated. See also S. M. Smith, C. P. Haugtvedt, J. M. Jadrich, and M. R. Anton, "Understanding Responses to Sex Appeals in Advertising," in *Advances in Consumer Research,* vol. 22, eds. F. R. Kardes and M. Sujan (Provo, UT: Association for Consumer Research, 1995), pp. 735–39; and P. M. Simpson, S. Horton, and G. Brown, "Male Nudity in Advertisements," *Journal of the Academy of Marketing Science,* Summer 1996, pp. 257–62.

2. C. M. Frisby, "Building Theoretical Insights to Explain Differences in Remote Control Use between Males and Females," *Journal of Current Issues and Research in Advertising,* Fall 1999, pp. 59–75.

3. F. S. Zufryden, J. H. Pedrick, and A. Sankaralingam, "Zapping and Its Impact on Brand Purchase Behavior," *Journal of Advertising Research,* January–February 1993, pp. 58–66; L. van

Meurs, "Zapp!" *Journal of Advertising Research,* February 1998, pp. 43–53; and S. Siddarth and A. Chattopadhyay, "To Zap or Not to Zap," *Marketing Science,* no. 2 (1998), pp. 124–38.

4. P. J. Danaher, "What Happens to Television Ratings during Commercial Breaks?" *Journal of Advertising Research,* January 1995, pp. 37–47.

5. Van Meurs, "Zapp!"

6. A. C. B. Tse and R. P. W. Lee, "Zapping Behavior during Commercial Breaks," *Journal of Advertising Research,* May 2001, pp. 25–28.

7. A. M. Abernethy, "Differences between Advertising and Program Exposure for Car Radio Listening," *Journal of Advertising Research,* April–May 1991, pp. 33–42.

8. C. Fisher, "Newspaper Readers Get Choosier," *Advertising Age,* July 26, 1993, p. 22.

9. P. S. Speck and M. T. Elliot, "Predictors of Advertising Avoidance in Print and Broadcast Media," *Journal of Advertising,* Fall 1997, pp. 61–76.

10. *TeleNation* (New York: Market Facts, Inc, October 2, 1998), p. 43.

11. K. Strauss, "Pedestrian Cab Reborn as Ad Star," *Advertising Age,* July 9, 2001, p. S6.

12. C. Pechmann and D.-F. Shih, "Smoking Scenes in Movies and Antismoking Advertisements before Movies," *Journal of Marketing,* July 1999, pp. 1–13.

13. M. Singh, S. K. Balasubramanian, and G. Chakraborty, "A Comparative Analysis of Three Communication Formats," *Journal of Advertising,* Winter 2000, pp. 59–75.

14. M. T. Elliot and P. S. Speck, "Antecedents and Consequences of Informercials," *Journal of Direct Marketing,* Spring 1995, pp. 39–51.

15. K. Maddox, "Survey Shows Increase in Online Usage, Shopping," *Advertising Age,* October 26, 1998, p. S6.

16. This insight is based on D. E. DeLorme and L. N. Reid, "Moviegoers' Experiences and Interpretations of Brands in Films Revisited," *Journal of Advertising,* Summer 1999, pp. 71–95; S. J. Gould, P. B. Gupta, and S. Grabner-Krauter, "Product Placements in Movies," *Journal of Advertising,* Winter 2000, pp. 42–56; R. Ferraro and R. J. Avery, "Brand Appearances on Prime-Time Television"; A. d'Astous and F. Chartiere, "A Study of Factors Affecting Consumer Evaluations and Memory of Product Placements in Movies"; and P. B. Gupta, S. K. Balasubramanian, and M. L. Klassen, "Viewers' Evaluations of Product Placements in Movies," all in *Journal of Current Issues and Research in Advertising,* Fall 2000, pp. 1–25, 31–40, and 41–52; and S. Law and K. A. Braum, "I'll Have What She's Having," *Psychology & Marketing,* December 2000, pp. 1059–75.

17. See E. T. Popper and K. B. Murray, "Format Effects on an In-Ad Disclosure," in *Advances in Consumer Research,* vol. 16, eds. T. K. Srull (Provo, UT: Association for Consumer Research, 1989), pp. 221–30; and D. M. Krugman et al., "Do Adolescents Attend to Warnings in Cigarette Advertising?" *Journal of Advertising Research,* November 1994, pp. 39–52.

18. J. L. Rogers, "Consumer Response to Advertising Mail," *Journal of Advertising Research,* January 1990, p. 22.

19. "Farm Ads Win Golden Fleece," *Stars and Stripes,* July 10, 1984, p. 6.

20. S. Thompson, "Media Recipe," *Advertising Age,* October 23, 2000, p. 42.

21. C.-H. Cho, "How Advertising Works on the WWW," *Journal of Current Issues and Research in Advertising,* Spring 1999, pp. 33–49.

22. G. L. Lohse, "Consumer Eye Movement Patterns on Yellow Pages Advertising," *Journal of Advertising,* Spring 1997, pp. 61–73.

23. *CARR Report No. 250.1A* (Boston: Cahners Publishing Co., undated).

24. *CARR Report No. 120.3* (Boston: Cahners Publishing Co., undated); and P. H. Chook, "A Continuing Study of Magazine Environment, Frequency, and Advertising Performance," *Journal of Advertising Research,* August–September 1985, pp. 23–33. See also S. N. Singh et al., "Does Your Ad Have Too Many Pictures," *Journal of Advertising Research,* January 2000, pp. 11–27.

25. R. Pieters, E. Rosbergen, and M. Wedel, "Visual Attention to Repeated Print Advertising," *Journal of Marketing Research,* November 1999, pp. 424–38.

26. M. Dahlen, *Journal of Advertising Research,* July 2001, pp. 23–30.

27. J. R. Rossiter and R. B. Silberstein, "Brain-Imaging Detection of Visual Scene Encoding in Long-Term Memory for TV Commercials," *Journal of Advertising Research,* March 2001, pp. 13–21. See also S. L. Crites, Jr., and S. N. Aikman-Eckenrode, "Making Inferences Concerning Physiological Responses, *Journal of Advertising Research,* March 2001, p. 25; and J. R. Rossiter et al., "So What?" *Journal of Advertising Research,* May 2001, pp. 59–61.

28. C.-H. Cho, J.-G. Lee, and M. Tharp, "Different Forced-Exposure Levels to Banner Ads," *Journal of Advertising Research,* July 2001, pp. 45–54.

29. Cho, "How Advertising Works on the WWW."

30. Lohse, "Consumer Eye Movement Patterns." See also K. V. Fernandez and D. L. Rosen, "The Effectiveness of Information and Color in Yellow Pages Advertising," *Journal of Advertising,* Summer 2000, pp. 62–73.

31. J. Meyers-Levy and L. A. Peracchio, "Understanding the Effects of Color," *Journal of Consumer Research,* September 1995, pp. 121–38.

32. C. Garcia, V. Ponsoda, and H. Estebaranz, "Scanning Ads," *Advances in Consumer Research,* vol. 27, eds. S. J. Hoch and R. J. Meyer (Provo, UT: Association for Consumer Research, 2000), pp. 104–9.

33. J. C. Cronin, "In-Home Observations of Commercial Zapping Behavior," *Journal of Current Issues and Research in Advertising,* Fall 1995, pp. 69–75.

34. See G. D. Olsen, "Creating the Contrast," *Journal of Advertising,* Winter 1995, pp. 29–44.

35. C. Janiszewski, "The Influence of Display Characteristics on Visual Exploratory Search Behavior," *Journal of Consumer Research,* December 1998, pp. 290–301.

36. D. Walker and M. F. von Gonten, "Explaining Related Recall Outcomes," *Journal of Advertising Research,* July 1989, pp. 11–21.

37. R. C. Goodstein, "Category-Based Applications and Extensions in Advertising," *Journal of Consumer Research,* June 1993, pp. 87–99.

38. Y. H. Lee, "Manipulating Ad Message," *Journal of Advertising,* Summer 2000, pp. 29–43.

39. R. Pieters, E. Rosbergen, and M. Hartog, "Visual Attention to Advertising," *Advances in Consumer Research,* vol. 23, eds. K. P. Corfman and J. G. Lynch (Provo, UT: Association for Consumer Research, 1996), pp. 242–48.

40. T. Elkin, "PVR Not Yet a Big Threat," *Advertising Age,* May 6, 2002, p. 55. See also L. F. Allwitt, "Effects of Interestingness on Evaluations of TV Commercials," *Journal of Current Issues and Research in Advertising,* Spring 2000, pp. 41–53; and W. Friedman, "72.3% of PVR Viewers Skip Commercials," *AdAge.com,* July 02, 2002.

41. M. A. Eastlick, R. Feinberg, and C. Trappey, "Information Overload in Mail Catalog Shopping," *Journal of Direct*

Marketing, Autumn 1993, pp. 14–19. For a different explanation, see Y. Ganzach and P. Ben-Or, "Information Overload, Decreasing Marginal Responsiveness, and the Estimation of Nonmonotonic Relationships in Direct Marketing," *Journal of Direct Marketing,* Spring 1996, pp. 7–12.

42. See D. Maheswaran and B. Sternthal, "The Effects of Knowledge, Motivation, and Type of Message on Ad Processing and Product Judgments," *Journal of Consumer Research,* June 1990, pp. 66–73; and D. J. MacInnis, C. Moorman, and B. J. Jaworski, "Enhancing and Measuring Consumers' Motivation, Opportunity, and Ability to Process Brand Information from Ads," *Journal of Marketing,* October 1991, pp. 32–53.

43. E. Rosbergen, R. Pieters, and M. Wedel, "Visual Attention to Advertising," *Journal of Consumer Research,* December 1997, pp. 305–15.

44. For a discussion of advertising message involvement, see R. N. Laczniak, D. S. Kempf, and D. D. Muehling, "Advertising Message Involvement," *Journal of Current Issues and Research in Advertising,* Spring 1999, pp. 51–61.

45. See W. Dou, R. Linn, and S. Yang, "How Smart Are 'Smart Banners'?" *Journal of Advertising Research,* July 2001, pp. 31–43.

46. R. G. M. Pieters and T. H. A. Bijmolt, "Consumer Memory for Television Advertising," *Journal of Consumer Research,* March 1997, pp. 362–72.

47. See D. L. Hoffman and R. Batra, "Viewer Response to Programs," *Journal of Advertising Research,* August–September 1991, pp. 46–56; K. G. Celuch and M. Slama, "Program Content and Advertising Effectiveness," *Psychology & Marketing,* July–August 1993, pp. 285–99; and K. R. Lord and R. E. Burnkrant, "Attention versus Distraction," *Journal of Advertising,* March 1993, pp. 47–60.

48. K. J. Clancy, "CPMs Must Bow to Involvement Measurement," *Advertising Age,* January 20, 1992, p. 7.

49. S. Shapiro, D. J. MacInnis, S. E. Heckler, "The Effects of Incidental Ad Exposure on the Formation of Consideration Sets," *Journal of Consumer Research,* June 1997, pp. 94–104; and S. Shapiro, "When an Ad's Influence Is beyond Our Conscious Control," *Journal of Consumer Research,* June 1999, pp. 16–36.

50. H. E. Krugman, "Sustained Viewing of Television," *Journal of Advertising Research,* June 1980, p. 65; and H. E. Krugman, "Low Recall and High Recognition of Advertising," *Journal of Advertising Research,* February–March 1986, pp. 79–86.

51. W. B. Key, *Subliminal Seduction* (Englewood Cliffs, NJ: Pretice Hall, 1973); and W. B. Key, *Media Sexploitation* (Englewood Cliffs, NJ: Prentice Hall, 1976).

52. D. L. Rosen and S. N. Singh, "An Investigation of Subliminal Embed Effect on Multiple Measures of Advertising Effectiveness," *Psychology & Marketing,* March–April 1992, pp. 157–73; and K. T. Theus "Subliminal Advertising and the Psychology of Processing Unconscious Stimuli," *Psychology & Marketing,* May 1994, pp. 271–90. In contrast, see A. B. Aylesworth, R. C. Goodstein, and A. Kalra, "Effect of Archetypical Embeds on Feelings," *Journal of Advertising,* Fall 1999, pp. 73–81.

53. C. L. Witte, M. Parthasarathy, and J. W. Gentry, "Subliminal Perception versus Subliminal Persuasion," in *Enhancing Knowledge Development in Marketing,* eds. B. B. Stern and G. M. Zinkhan (Chicago: American Marketing Association, 1995), pp. 133–38; and C. Trappey, "A Meta-Analysis of Consumer Choice and Subliminal Advertising," *Psychology & Marketing,* August 1996, pp. 517–30.

54. M. Rogers and C. A. Seiler, "The Answer Is No," *Journal of Advertising Research,* March 1994, pp. 36–45.

55. T. J. Brown and P. A. Dacin, "The Company and the Product," *Journal of Marketing,* January 1997, pp. 68–84; and A. C. B. Tse, "Factors Affecting Consumer Perceptions on Product Safety," *Journal of International Consumer Marketing,* 12 (1999), pp. 39–55. See also L. A. Manrai, A. K. Manrai, D. Lascu, and, J. K. Ryans, Jr., "How Green-Claim Strength and Country Disposition Affect Product Evaluation and Company Image," *Psychology & Marketing,* August 1997, pp. 511–37.

56. H. R. Moser and H. E. Johns, "An Empirical Analysis of Consumers' Attitudes toward Attorney Advertising," *Journal of Professional Services Marketing,* no. 1 (1996), pp. 85–104; A. Kirmani, "Advertising Repetition as a Signal of Quality, *Journal of Advertising,* Fall 1997, pp. 77–86; P. Raghubir and K. Corfman, "When Do Price Promotions Affect Pretrail Brand Evaluations," *Journal of Marketing Research,* May 1999, pp. 211–22; and J. A. Garretson and K. E. Clow, "The Influence of Coupon Face Value on Service Quality Expectations," *Journal of Services Marketing* 13, no. 1 (1999), pp. 59–72.

57. E. T. Anderson and D. I. Simester, "Are Sale Signs Less Effective When More Products Have Them?" *Marketing Science,* Spring 2001, pp. 121–42.

58. J. W. Alba et al., "The Effect of Discount Frequency and Depth on Consumer Price Judgments," *Journal of Consumer Research,* September 1999, pp. 99–114.

59. See L. M. Scott, "The Bridge from Text to Mind," *Journal of Consumer Research,* December 1994, pp. 461–80.

60. S. S. Liu, "When the Irrelevant Becomes Relevant," *Journal of Current Issues and Research in Advertising,* Fall 1999, pp. 31–47; and M. Viswanathan and T. L. Childers, "Understanding How Product Attributes Influence Product Categorization," *Journal of Marketing Research,* February 1999, pp. 75–94.

61. G. P. Moreau, D. R. Lehmann, and A. B. Markman, "Entrenched Knowledge Structures and Consumer Responses to New Products," *Journal of Marketing Research,* February 2001, pp. 14–29.

62. G. Page Moreau, A. B. Markham, and D. R. Lehmann, "'What Is It?' Categorization Flexibility and Consumers' Responses to Really New Products," *Journal of Consumer Research,* March 2001, pp. 489–498.

63. See D. Grewal, K. B. Monroe, and R. Krishnan, "The Effects of Price-Comparison Advertising," *Journal of Marketing,* April 1998, pp. 46–59; and D. Grewal, R. Krishnan, J. Baker, and N. Borin, "The Effects of Store Name, Brand Name, and Price Discounts," *Journal of Retailing,* no. 3 (1998), pp. 331–52.

64. J. Z. Sojka and J. L. Giese, "Thinking and/or Feeling," *Advances in Consumer Research,* vol. 24, eds. M. Bruck and D. J. MacInnis (Provo, UT: Association for Consumer Research, 1997), pp. 438–42; and J. A. Ruth, "Promoting a Brand's Emotional Benefits," *Journal of Consumer Psychology* 11, no. 2 (2001), pp. 99–113.

65. See S. Ratneshwar, "Goal-Derived Categories," *Journal of Consumer Psychology* 10, no. 3 (2001), pp. 147–57.

66. R. Ahluwalia, R. E. Burnkrant, and H. R. Unnava, "Consumer Response to Negative Publicity," *Journal of Marketing Research,* May 2000, pp. 203–14.

67. A. d'Astous and N. Touiol, "Consumer Evaluations of Movies on the Basis of Critics' Judgments," *Psychology & Marketing,* December 1999, pp. 677–94.

68. M. C. Campbell, "Perceptions of Price Unfairness," *Journal of Marketing Research,* May 1999, pp. 187–99.

69. J. E. Russo, M. G. Meloy, and V. H. Medvec, "Predecisional Distortion of Product Information," *Journal of Marketing Research,* November 1998, pp. 438–52.

70. B. J. Parker, "Exploring Life Themes and Myths in Alcohol Advertisements through a Meaning-Based Model," *Journal of Advertising,* Spring 1998, pp. 97–111.

71. G. Tom et al., "Cueing the Consumer," *Journal of Consumer Marketing,* Spring 1987, pp. 23–27. See also D. S. Kempf and R. N. Laczniak, "Advertising's Influence on Subsequent Product Trial Processing," *Journal of Advertising,* Fall 2001, pp. 27–40.

72. J. J. Inman, L. McAlister, and W. D. Hoyer, "Promotion Signal," *Journal of Consumer Research,* June 1990, pp. 74–81.

73. See K. R. Evans et al., "How First Impressions of a Customer Impact Effectiveness in an Initial Sales Encounter," *Journal of the Academy of Marketing Science,* Fall 2000, pp. 512–26.

74. See M. G. Meloy, "Mood-Driven Distortion of Product Information," *Journal of Consumer Research,* December 2000, pp. 345–58.

75. D. Grewal, H. Marmorstein, and A. Sharma, "Communicating Price Information through Semantic Cues," *Journal of Consumer Research,* September 1996, pp. 148–55.

76. "GF, Coke Tell Why They Shun TV News," *Advertising Age,* January 28, 1980, p. 39.

77. K. R. France and C. W. Park, "The Impact of Program Affective Valence and Level of Cognitive Appraisal on Advertisement Processing and Effectiveness," *Journal of Current Issues and Research in Advertising,* Fall 1997, pp. 1–21; J. H. Watt et al., "The Effects of Program Involvement and Commercial Position on Reactions to Embedded Commercials," *Advances in Consumer Research,* vol. 25, eds. J. W. Alba and J. W. Hutchinson (Provo, UT: Association for Consumer Research, 1998), pp. 492–98; A. B. Aylesworth and S. B. MacKenzie, "Context Is Key," *Journal of Advertising,* Summer 1998, pp. 17–31; Q. Chen and W. D. Wells, "Attitude toward the Site," *Journal of Advertising Research,* September 1999, pp. 27–37; and B. M. Tennis and A. B. Bakker, "Stay Tuned—We Will Be Right Back after These Messages," *Journal of Advertising,* Fall 2001, pp. 15–25.

78. T. F. Stafford, "Alert or Oblivious?" *Psychology & Marketing,* September 2000, pp. 745–60.

79. J. Halliday, "Pontiac's Aztek Launch Isn't So Pretty," *Advertising Age,* November 6, 2000, p. 61.

80. See D. E. Sprott, D. M. Hardesty, and A. D. Miyazaki, "Disclosure of Odds Information," *Journal of Public Policy & Marketing,* Spring 1998, pp. 11–23.

81. R. Alsop, "Color Grows More Important in Catching Consumers' Eyes," *Wall Street Journal,* November 29, 1989, p. B1.

82. P. Raghubir and A. Krishna, "Vital Dimensions in Volume Perception," *Journal of Marketing Research,* August 1999, pp. 313–26.

83. J. J. Kellaris, A. D. Cox, and D. Cox, "The Effect of Background Music on Ad Processing," *Journal of Marketing,* October 1993, pp. 100–14; and G. Brooker and J. J. Wheatley, "Music and Radio Advertising," *Advances in Consumer Research,* vol. 21, eds. C. T. Allen and D. R. John (Provo, UT: Association for Consumer Research, 1994), pp. 286–91.

84. See C. K. Hsee and F. Leclerc, "Will Products Look More Attractive When Presented Separately or Together?" *Journal of Consumer Research,* September 1998, pp. 175–86; J. R. Doyle et al., "The Robustness of the Asymmetrically Dominated Effect," *Psychology & Marketing,* May 1999, pp. 225–43; L. Buchanan, C. J. Simmons, and B. A. Bickart, "Brand Equity Dilution," *Journal of Marketing Research,* August 1999, pp. 345–55; and R. Dhar, S. M. Nowlis, and S. J. Sherman, "Trying Hard or Hardly Trying," *Journal of Consumer Psychology* 9, no. 4 (2000), pp. 189–200.

85. J. Harris, "The Effects of Promotional Bundling," *Advances in Consumer Research,* vol. 24, eds. M. Bruck and D. J. MacInnis (Provo, UT: Association for Consumer Research, 1997), pp. 168–72; and A. R. Rao, L. Qu, and R. W. Ruekert, "Signaling Unobservable Product Quality through a Brand Ally," *Journal of Marketing Research,* May 1999, pp. 258–68.

86. A. Adams, C. A. di Denedetto, and R. Chandran, "Can You Reduce Your Package Size without Damaging Sales?" *Long Range Planning* 24, no. 4 (1991), pp. 86–96.

87. L. M. Scott, "Images in Advertising," *Journal of Consumer Research,* September 1994, p. 254. See also K. Bremer and M. Lee, "Metaphors in Marketing," *Advances in Consumer Research,* vol. 24, eds. M. Bruck and D. J. MacInnis (Provo, UT: Association for Consumer Research, 1997), pp. 419–24.

88. B. J. Phillips, "The Impact of Verbal Anchoring on Consumer Response to Image Ads," *Journal of Advertising,* Spring 2000, pp. 15–24; and E. F. McQuarrie and D. G. Mick, "Visual Rhetoric in Advertising," *Journal of Consumer Research,* June 1999, pp. 37–54.

89. See R. Kivetz and I. Simonson, "The Effects of Incomplete Information on Consumer Choice," *Journal of Marketing Research,* November 2000, pp. 427–48.

90. J. C. Andrews, R. G. Netemeyer, and S. Burton, "Consumer Generalization of Nutrient Content Claims in Advertising," *Journal of Marketing,* October 1998, pp. 62–75; and B. Roe, A. S. Levy, and B. M. Derby, "The Impact of Health Claims on Consumer Search and Product Evolution Outcomes," *Journal of Public Policy & Marketing,* Spring 1999, pp. 89–105.

91. G. V. Johar, "Consumer Involvement and Deception from Implied Advertising Claims," *Journal of Marketing Research,* August 1995, pp. 267–79; C. Pechmann, "Do Consumers Overgeneralize One-Sided Comparative Price Claims?" *Journal of Marketing Research,* May 1996, pp. 150–62; M. J. Barone and P. J. Miniard, "How and When Factual Ad Claims Mislead Consumers," *Journal of Marketing Research,* February 1999, pp. 58–74; and M. J. Barone et al., "Enhancing the Detection of Misleading Comparative Advertising," *Journal of Advertising Research,* September 1999, pp. 43–50.

92. S. M. Broniarcyzk, W. D. Hoyer, and L. McAlister, "Consumers' Perceptions of the Assortment Offered in a Grocery Category," *Journal Marketing Research,* May 1998, pp. 166–76.

93. H. Chura, "Pepsi-Cola's Code Red Is White Hot," *Advertising Age,* August 27, 2001, p. 24.

94. F. Leclerc, B. H. Schmitt, and L. Dube, "Foreign Branding and Its Effects on Product Perceptions and Attitudes," *Journal of Marketing Research,* May 1994, pp. 263–70.

95. S. Zhang and B. H. Schmitt, "Creating Local Brands in Multilingual International Markets," *Journal of Marketing Research,* August 2001, pp. 313–25.

96. T. Pavia and J. A. Costa, "The Winning Number," *Journal of Marketing,* July 1993, pp. 85–98; T. Pavia, "Brand Names and Consumer Inference," in *Advances in Consumer Research,* vol. 21, eds. C. T. Allen and D. R. John (Provo, UT: Association for Consumer Research, 1994), pp. 195–200; and K. L. Keller, S. E. Heckler, and M. J. Houston, "The Effects of Brand Name Suggestiveness on Advertising Recall," *Journal of Marketing,* January 1998, pp. 48–57.

97. B. L. Simonin and J. A. Ruth, "Is a Brand Known by the Company It Keeps?" *Journal Marketing Research,* February 1998, pp. 30–42; I. P. Levin and A. M. Levin, "Modeling the Role of Brand Alliances in the Assimilation of Product Evaluations," *Journal of Consumer Psychology* 9, no. 1 (2000), pp. 43–52; and K. K. Desai and K. I. Keller, "The Effects of Ingredient Branding Strategies on Host Brand Extendibility," *Journal of Marketing,* January 2002, pp. 73–93.

98. See J. Tantillo, J. D. Lorenzo-Aiss, and R. E. Mathisen, "Quantifying Perceived Differences in Type Styles," *Psychology & Marketing,* August 1995, pp. 447–57; and C. Janiszewski and T. Meyvis, "Effects of Brand Logo Complexity, Repetition, and Spacing on Processing Fluency and Judgment," *Journal of Marketing Research,* June 2001, pp. 18–32.

99. A. H. Schechter, "Measuring the Value of Corporate and Brand Logos," *Design Management Journal,* Winter 1993, pp. 33–39.

100. "Ford Boss Outlines Shift to 'Rifle' Media," *Advertising Age,* October 26, 1981, p. 89. See also P. J. Danaher, "Wearout Effects in Target Marketing," *Marketing Letters,* no. 3 (1996), pp. 275–87.

101. P. N. Shamdasani, A. J. S. Stanaland, and J. Tan, "Location, Location, Location," *Journal of Advertising Research,* July 2001, pp. 7–20.

102. J. Neff, "P&G Reins in Its Domains," *Advertising Age,* October 29, 2001, p. 32.

103. J. Guterman, "Outdoor Interactive," *American Demographics,* August 2001, p. 32.

104. D. C. Vladeck, "Truth and Consequences," *Journal of Public Policy & Marketing,* Spring 2000, p. 133. See also M. J. Mason and D. L. Scammon, "Health Claims and Disclaimers," *Journal of Public Policy & Marketing,* Spring 2000, pp. 144–50; and J. C. Andrews, S. Burton, and R. G. Netemeyer, "Are Some Comparative Nutrition Claims Misleading?" *Journal of Advertising,* Fall 2000, p. 42.

105. M. G. Hoy and M. J. Stankey, "Structural Characteristics of Televised Advertising Disclosures," *Journal of Advertising,* June 1993, pp. 47–58.

106. R. J. Fox et al., "Adolescents' Attention to Beer and Cigarette Print Ads and Associated Product Warnings," *Journal of Advertising,* Fall 1998, pp. 57–68.

107. See E. P. Cox et al., "Do Product Warnings Increase Safe Behavior?" *Journal of Public Policy & Marketing*, Fall 1997, pp. 195–204; J. A. Garretson and S. Burton, "Alcoholic Beverage Sales Promotion"; M. D. Slater et al., "Developing and Assessing Alcohol Warning Content"; J. R. Hankin, J. J. Sloan, and R. J. Sokol, "The Modest Impact of the Alcohol Beverage Warning Label"; and P. S. Ellen, P. F. Bone, and E. W. Stuart, "How Well Do Young People Follow the Label?" all in *Journal of Public Policy & Marketing,* Spring 1998, pp. 35–47, 48–60, 61–69, and 70–85; P. Raghubar and G. Menon, "AIDS and Me," *Journal of Consumer Research,* June 1998, pp. 52–63; A. Zuckerman and S. Chaiken, "A Heuristic-Systematic Processing Analysis of the Effectiveness of Product Warning Labels"; G. K. Rousseau, N. Lamson, and W. A. Rogers, "Designing Warnings to Compensate for Age-Related Changes"; and B. Fischhoff et al., "What Information Belongs in a Warning?" all in *Psychology & Marketing,* October 1998, pp. 621–42, 643–62, and 663–86; and L. Nohre et al., "The Association between Adolescents' Receiver Characteristics and Exposure to the Alcohol Warning Label"; and T. K. Greenfield, K. L. Graves, and L. A. Kaskutas, "Long-Term Effects of Alcohol Warning Labels," both in *Psychology & Marketing,* May 1999, pp. 245–59 and 261–82.

108. See D. W. Stewart and I. M. Martin, *Journal of Public Policy & Marketing,* Spring 1994, pp. 1–19.

109. For a thorough discussion of the issues, see S. Lee and J. D. Leckenby, "Impact of Measurement Periods on Website Rankings and Traffic Estimation," *Journal of Current Issues and Research in Advertising,* Fall 1999, pp. 1–10.

110. R. Briggs and N. Hollis, "Advertising on the Web," *Journal of Advertising Research,* March 1997, pp. 33–46; and T. Elkin, "What's Next on the Net," *Advertising Age,* January 14, 2002, p. 54.

111. M. Wedel and R. Pieters, "Eye Fixations on Advertisements and Memory for Brands," *Marketing Science,* Fall 2000, pp. 297–312; and N. Shachtman, "What Users See," *Advertising Age,* June 18, 2001, p. T18.

112. C. R. Duke and L. Carlson, "A Conceptual Approach to Alternative Memory Measures for Advertising Effectiveness," *Journal of Current Issues and Research in Advertising,* Fall 1993, pp. 1–14; E. duPlessis, "Recognition versus Recall"; J. S. Dubow, "Recall Revisited"; L. D. Gibson, "Recall Revisited"; and H. J. Ross, Jr., "Recall Revisited," all in *Journal of Advertising Research,* May 1994, pp. 75–91, 92–106, 107–108, and 109–11; J. S. Dubow, "Rejoinder to Larry Gibson's Response to 'Recall'"; and J. S. Dubow, "'Revisited' Rejoinder to Hal Ross' Response to 'Recall Revisited'", both in *Journal of Advertising Research,* July 1994, pp. 70–73 and 74–76; and J. Stapel, "Recall and Recognition," *Journal of Advertising Research,* July 1998, pp. 41–45. For a different approach, see S. Shapiro and H. S. Krishnan, "Memory-Based Measures for Assessing Advertising Effects," *Journal of Advertising,* Fall 2001, pp. 1–13.

113. T. Meenaghan, ed., special issue, "Ambush Marketing," *Psychology & Marketing,* July 1998.

Learning, Memory, and Product Positioning

☐ Imagine a company buying a brand whose sales had declined 90 percent over the past 15 years in large part because its use was linked with a deadly disease. Further imagine that for all of its 110-year history it has been marketed exclusively as a children's product, and you are going to market it to baby boomers and older adults. A foolish idea? Johnson & Johnson doesn't think so.

Johnson & Johnson recently acquired St. Joseph Aspirin, which, since its beginning in the late 1800s, had been sold strictly as a children's aspirin. It is sold only in orange-flavored, 81-milligram doses, compared with 325 milligrams in standard aspirin. It was quite successful until the 1980s, when using aspirin to treat viral infections in children was linked to Reye's syndrome (a disease that affects all organs of the body, but most lethally the liver and the brain).

Johnson & Johnson hopes to reposition St. Joseph as the best source for a low-dosage aspirin regime to reduce the risk of heart attacks and strokes in adults. The firm hopes to capture the positive memories many adults have of St. Joseph while teaching them that it is the optimal source for low-dosage aspirins. Thus, the firm faces the dual challenge of reviving old memories and positive feelings while teaching consumers that the product is uniquely appropriate for this use by adults.

The marketing team asked itself, How would baby boomers remember St. Joseph? They went on eBay and bought old St. Joseph packages and posters; they redesigned the package using elements from its old packages, when the brand was at its strongest. Of course, any reference to children was removed and adult usage was emphasized. Evidence indicated that most adults had heard the message that aspirin is good for one's heart. The challenge was to teach consumers that St. Joseph was the best aspirin to use.

The first commercial in a $10 million campaign featured a caring, middle-aged couple, with the man much taller than the woman. The background music was the old tune "Mr. Sandman." The wife states, "We both take St. Joseph because its low dose is safe for every size adult." The commercial ends with the tagline: "Trust it with all your heart."[1]

Johnson & Johnson is spending more than $10 million in an advertising campaign designed to teach consumers that St. Joseph is the best aspirin for adults to use in a low-dosage aspirin regime. Since most adults think of St. Joseph as a children's aspirin, this will require what is called *product repositioning*. Its success will depend on how well the marketing team understands and uses learning principles.

Nonprofit organizations such as EarthSave are interested in teaching consumers about the consequences of their consumption choices. Firms and business associations such as Old Navy and the Milk Producers Council want consumers to learn about the positive features of their products and services. In this chapter, we discuss the nature of learning and memory, conditioning and cognitive theories of learning, and general characteristics of learning. Implications for marketing managers also are examined within each section. The outcome of consumer learning about a brand and product category—product position and the resultant brand equity—is discussed in the final section.

NATURE OF LEARNING

In the previous chapter, we described information processing as *a series of activities by which stimuli are perceived, transformed into information, and stored*. The four activities in the series are exposure, attention, interpretation, and memory. *Learning* is the term used to describe the processes by which memory and behavior are changed as a result of conscious and nonconscious information processing.

Learning is essential to the consumption process. In fact, consumer behavior is largely *learned* behavior. As illustrated in Figure 9–1, people acquire most of their attitudes, values, tastes, behaviors, preferences, symbolic meanings, and feelings through learning. Culture and social class, through such institutions as schools and religious organizations, as well as family, friends, mass media, and advertising, provide learning experiences that greatly influence the type of lifestyle people seek and the products they consume.

A wide array of social organizations attempt to help consumers learn "appropriate" attitudes and behaviors about issues such as racial discrimination, environmental protection, proper nutrition, drinking and driving, and date rape. Marketers expend considerable effort to ensure that consumers learn of the existence and nature of their products. Firms that help consumers learn about their products in an efficient manner often obtain a long-term competitive advantage.[2]

FIGURE 9–1	Learning Is a Key to Consumer Behavior

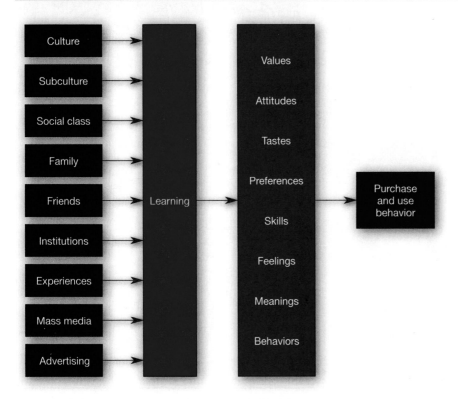

Learning is *any change in the content or organization of long-term memory or behavior*.[3] Thus, learning is the result of information processing, as described in the last chapter. Recall from Chapter 9 that information processing may be conscious and deliberate in high-involvement situations. Or it may be nonfocused and even nonconscious in low-involvement situations.

LEARNING UNDER CONDITIONS OF HIGH AND LOW INVOLVEMENT

A moment's reflection will reveal that people learn things in different ways.[4] Preparing for an exam generally involves intense, focused attention. The outcome of these efforts is rewarded with a grade. However, most learning is of a much different nature. Most people know who is playing in the World Series each year even if they don't care for baseball because they hear about it frequently. People can identify clothes that are stylish even though they never really think much about clothing styles.

As just described, learning may occur in either a high-involvement or a low-involvement situation. A **high-involvement learning** situation is one in which *the consumer is motivated to process or learn the material*. For example, an individual reading *Laptop Buyer's Guide* prior to purchasing a computer is probably highly motivated to learn relevant material dealing with the various computer brands. A **low-involvement learning** situation is one in which *the consumer has little or no motivation to process or learn the material*. A consumer whose television program is interrupted by a commercial for a product he or

Courtesy GlaxoSmithKline.

Courtesy Unilever United States, Inc.

she doesn't currently use or feel a desire for generally has little motivation to learn the material presented in the commercial. Much, if not most, consumer learning occurs in relatively low involvement contexts.[5]

Consider a person reading a newspaper. Often the reader is focused on the articles in the paper and does not consciously or deliberately read the ads near the articles. However, the reader is exposed to these ads. This is termed **incidental exposure,** which has been shown to increase the reader's liking of the brands in these ads despite not being able to recall having seen the ads themselves. Incidental exposure has also been shown to increase the likelihood that a brand will be included in a consumer's consideration set (the set of brands a consumer would consider purchasing to achieve a purchase goal) across a variety of conditions and product classes.[6] Clearly the low-involvement learning that occurs with incidental exposure is important for marketers and consumers alike.

Involvement is a function of the interaction between the individual, the stimulus, and the situation. For example, an individual not interested in clothing may merely glance at most ads for clothes. However, a clothing ad featuring a celebrity who the consumer greatly admires may cause the individual to examine that ad in some detail (high involvement) and to pay significant attention to the celebrity's clothing. Likewise, consumers who ignore most clothing ads may become much more involved with this type of information if they face a need to buy new clothes soon.

As we will see in the following sections, the way a communication should be structured differs depending on the level of involvement the audience is expected to have.[7] Illustration 9–1 shows one ad that assumes high-involvement learning and another based on

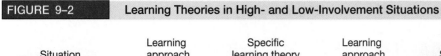

FIGURE 9–2   Learning Theories in High- and Low-Involvement Situations

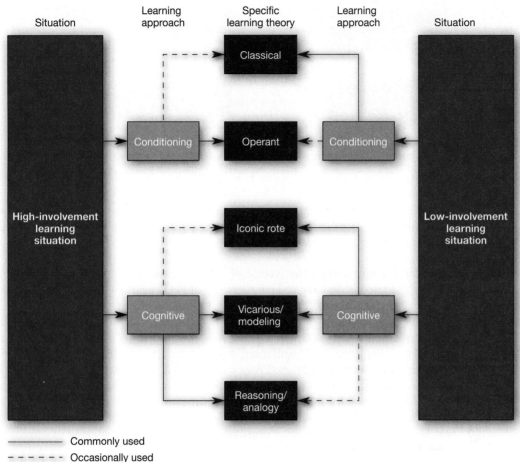

low-involvement learning. *Why does one ad assume a highly involved audience and the other a low-involvement audience? What differences do you notice between these two ads? Do those differences make sense?*

Figure 9–2 shows the two general situations and the five specific learning theories that we are going to consider. The level of involvement is the primary determinant of how material is learned. The solid lines in the figure indicate that operant conditioning, vicarious learning/modeling, and reasoning/analogy are commonly used learning processes in high-involvement situations. Classical conditioning, iconic rote learning, and vicarious learning/ modeling tend to occur in low-involvement situations. Each of these specific theories is described in the following pages.

Conditioning

Conditioning refers to learning based on *association of a stimulus (information) and response (behavior or feeling)*. The word *conditioning* has a negative connotation to many of people and brings forth images of robotlike humans. However, conditioned learning

| FIGURE 9–3 | Consumer Learning through Classical Conditioning |

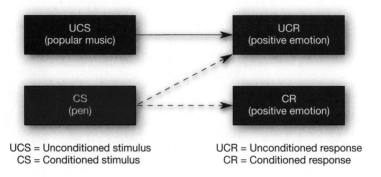

UCS = Unconditioned stimulus   UCR = Unconditioned response
CS = Conditioned stimulus   CR = Conditioned response

simply means that through exposure to some stimulus and a corresponding response, one learns that they go together (or do not go together). There are two basic forms of conditioned learning—classical and operant.

Classical Conditioning   The process of using an established relationship between a stimulus and response to bring about the learning of the same response to a different stimulus is called **classical conditioning.** Figure 9–3 illustrates this type of learning.

Hearing popular music (unconditioned stimulus) elicits a positive emotion (unconditioned response) in many individuals. If this music is consistently paired with a particular brand of pen or other product (conditioned stimulus), the brand itself may come to elicit the same positive emotion (conditioned response).[8] In addition, some features, such as the masculine/feminine qualities of the unconditioned stimulus, may also become associated with the conditioned stimulus. That is, using a scene showing males or females in an activity that elicits positive emotions may not only cause a positive emotional response to a brand consistently paired with it, but also cause the brand to have a masculine or a feminine image.[9]

For example, Marlboro cigarettes are presented on billboards and, in countries where it is legal, in media ads showing the brand name or package and a beautiful outdoor scene. Part of the objective of such ads is to associate the positive emotional response to the outdoor scene with the brand. This in turn will increase the likelihood that the individual will like the brand. Other marketing applications include,

- Consistently advertising a product on exciting sports programs may result in the product itself generating an excitement response.
- An unknown political candidate may elicit patriotic feelings by consistently playing patriotic background music in his or her commercials and appearances.
- Christmas music played in stores may elicit emotional responses associated with giving and sharing, which in turn may increase the propensity to purchase.

Classical conditioning is most common in low-involvement situations. In the Marlboro example described above, it is likely that many consumers devote little or no focused attention to the advertisement, since cigarette ads are low-involvement messages even for most smokers. However, after a sufficient number of low-involvement "scannings" or "glances at" the advertisement, the association may be formed. It is important to note that what is learned is generally not information but emotion, or an affective response. If this affective response leads to learning about the product or leads to a product trial, we have this situation:

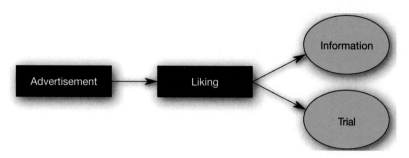

Operant Conditioning   *Instrumental learning,* or **operant conditioning,** differs from classical conditioning primarily in the role and timing of reinforcement. Suppose you are the product manager for Pacific Snax's Rice Popcorn snack. You believe your product has a light, crisp taste that consumers will like. How can you influence them to learn to consume your brand? One approach would be to distribute a large number of free samples through the mail, at shopping malls, or in stores. Many consumers would try the free sample (desired response). To the extent that the taste of Rice Popcorn is indeed pleasant (reinforcement), the probability of continued consumption is increased. This is shown graphically in Figure 9–4.

Notice that reinforcement plays a much larger role in operant conditioning than it does in classical conditioning. Since no automatic stimulus–response relationship is involved, the subject must first be induced to engage in the desired behavior. Then this behavior must be reinforced.

Operant conditioning often involves the actual usage of the product. Thus, a great deal of marketing strategy is aimed at securing an initial trial. Free samples (at home or in the store), special price discounts on new products, and contests all represent rewards offered to consumers to try a particular product or brand. If they try the brand under these conditions and like it (reinforcement), they are likely to take the next step and purchase it in the future. This process of encouraging partial responses leading to the final desired response (consume a free sample, buy at a discount, buy at full price) is known as **shaping.** This process is illustrated in Figure 9–5.

In one study, 84 percent of those given a free sample of a chocolate while in a candy store made a purchase, whereas only 59 percent of those not provided a sample made a

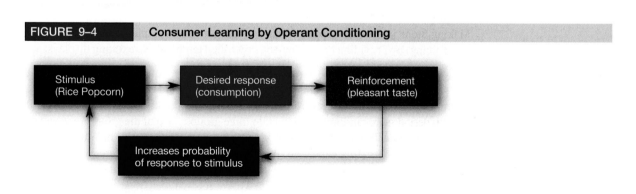

FIGURE 9–4   **Consumer Learning by Operant Conditioning**

| FIGURE 9–5 | The Process of Shaping in Purchase Behavior |

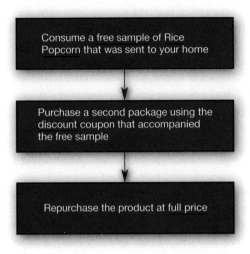

purchase. Thus, shaping can be very effective. Illustration 9–2 shows an ad designed to induce trial, the first step in shaping.

While reinforcement increases the likelihood of behavior such as a purchase being repeated, a negative consequence (punishment) has exactly the opposite effect. Thus, the purchase of a brand that does not function properly greatly reduces the chances of future purchases of that brand. This underscores the critical importance of consistent product quality.

Operant conditioning is used widely by marketers. The most common application is to offer consistent quality products so that the use of the product to meet a consumer need is reinforcing. Other applications include,

- Direct-mail or personal contact after a sale that congratulates the purchaser for making a wise purchase.
- Giving extra reinforcement for shopping at a store, such as trading stamps, rebates, or prizes.
- Giving extra reinforcement for purchasing a particular brand, such as rebates, toys in cereal boxes, or discount coupons.
- Giving free product samples or introductory coupons to encourage product trial (shaping).
- Making store interiors, shopping malls, or downtown areas pleasant places to shop (reinforcing) by providing entertainment, controlled temperature, exciting displays, and so forth.

The power of operant conditioning was demonstrated by an experiment conducted by an insurance company. More than 2,000 consumers who purchased life insurance over a one-month period were randomly divided into three groups. Two of the groups received reinforcement after each monthly payment in the form of a nice "thank-you" letter or telephone call. The third group received no such reinforcement. Six months later, 10 percent of the members of the two groups that received reinforcement had terminated their policies, while 23 percent of those who had not received reinforcement had done so! Reinforcement (being thanked) led to continued behavior (sending in the monthly premium).[10]

Courtesy Johnson & Johnson.

Cognitive Learning

Cognitive learning encompasses all the mental activities of humans as they work to solve problems or cope with situations. It involves learning ideas, concepts, attitudes, and facts that contribute to our ability to reason, solve problems, and learn relationships without direct experience or reinforcement. Cognitive learning can range from very simple information acquisition to complex, creative problem solving. Three types of cognitive learning are important to marketers.

Iconic Rote Learning   Learning the *association between two or more concepts in the absence of conditioning* is known as **iconic rote learning.** For example, one may see an ad that states "Ketoprofin is a headache remedy" and associate the new concept "ketoprofin" with the existing concept "headache remedy." There is neither an unconditioned stimulus nor a direct reward involved.

A substantial amount of low-involvement learning involves iconic rote learning. Numerous repetitions of a simple message that occur as the consumer scans the environment may result in the essence of the message being learned. Through iconic rote learning, consumers may form beliefs about the characteristics or attributes of products without being aware of the source of the information. When the need arises, a purchase may be made based on those beliefs.[11]

Vicarious Learning/Modeling   It is not necessary for consumers to directly experience a reward or punishment to learn. Instead, they can observe the outcomes of others'

Ads not only convey information and elicit feelings; they can challenge existing assumptions and cause readers to think and reexamine their beliefs.

What does an outdoor clothing company know about genetic engineering?

Not enough, and neither do you.

Even the scientists working on genetic engineering admit they don't know the full story. But despite the fact that we know so little about the impacts, a salmon has already been engineered that grows at twice the rate of normal salmon, a strain of corn has been created with pesticide in every cell, and trees have been engineered with less lignin to break down more easily in the pulping process. What will be the impact on our health, and the health of the ecosystem, once these new species make it out into the wild or into our food supply? No one knows.

Let's not repeat the mistakes we've made in the past with such inadequately tested technologies as DDT and nuclear energy. We don't know enough about the dangers of genetic engineering. Let's find out all the risks before we turn genetically modified organisms loose on the world, or continue to eat them in our food.

Find out more at
www.patagonia.com/enviroaction

patagonia

Photo: Topher Donahue © 2001 Patagonia, Inc.

© 2002 Patagonia, Inc.

behaviors and adjust their own accordingly. Similarly, they can use imagery to anticipate the outcome of various courses of action. This is known as **vicarious learning** or **modeling.**

This type of learning is common in both low- and high-involvement situations. In a high-involvement situation, such as purchasing a new suit shortly after taking a job, a consumer may deliberately observe the styles worn by others at work or by role models from other environments, including advertisements. Many ads encourage consumers to imagine the feelings and experience of using a product.[12] Such images not only enhance learning about the product, but may even influence how the product is evaluated after an actual trial.

A substantial amount of modeling also occurs in low-involvement situations. Throughout the course of their lives, people observe others using products and behaving in a great variety of situations. Most of the time they pay little attention to these behaviors. However, over time they learn that certain behaviors, and products, are appropriate in some situations and others are not.

Reasoning/Analogy   The most complex form of cognitive learning is **reasoning,** including **analogical reasoning.** In reasoning, individuals engage in creative thinking to restructure and recombine existing information as well as new information to form new associations and concepts. Information from a credible source that contradicts one's existing beliefs will often trigger reasoning.[13] The ad in Illustration 9–3 encourages the reader to think about the risk involved in genetically engineered foods.

Analogical learning occurs when a consumer uses an existing knowledge base to understand a new situation or object. Suppose you hear about new software programs called off-line Web readers that are designed to download Web pages to PCs. You might learn about this new software by analogical reasoning such as,

> relating it to something you understand better such as VCRs. You notice that the Web readers and VCRs are designed to retrieve media content. Given this similarity of purpose, you may logically expect them to share other characteristics. Since VCRs record TV programs onto a disk that allows them to be replayed on other VCR players at any desired time, you may conclude that the Web readers will record Web pages onto a disk that can then be accessed from other computers as desired. You may also believe that VCR players are difficult to program and assume that the new Web readers will also be difficult to use properly. At the end of this process, you may have a fairly complete set of beliefs about the new Web reader without having seen or used the product or read or viewed any information about its characteristics.[14]

Summary of Learning Theories

Theories of learning help us understand how consumers learn across a variety of situations. We have examined five specific learning theories: operant conditioning, classical conditioning, iconic rote learning, vicarious learning/modeling, and reasoning. Each of these learning theories can operate in a high- or a low-involvement situation. Table 9–1 summarizes these theories and provides examples from both high- and low-involvement contexts.

TABLE 9–1   Summary of Learning Theories with Examples of Involvement Level

Theory	Description	High-Involvement Example	Low-Involvement Example
Classical Conditioning	A response elicited by one object will be elicited by the second object if both objects frequently occur together.	The favorable emotional response elicited by the word *America* comes to be elicited by the brand Chrysler after a consumer reads that Chrysler plans to use only American-made parts.	The favorable emotional response elicited by a song comes to be elicited by a brand name that is consistently paired with that song even though the consumer does not pay attention to the advertising.
Operant Conditioning	A response that is given reinforcement is more likely to be repeated when the same situation arises in the future.	A suit is purchased and the purchaser finds that it does not wrinkle and generates several compliments. A sport coat made by the same firm is then purchased.	A familiar brand of peas is purchased without much thought. They taste "all right." The consumer continues to purchase this brand.
Iconic Rote Learning	Two or more concepts become associated without conditioning.	A jogger learns about various brands of running shoes as a result of closely reading many shoe advertisements that he or she finds enjoyable.	A consumer learns that Apple makes home computers, without ever really thinking about Apple advertisements or products.
Vicarious Learning or Modeling	Behaviors are learned by watching the outcomes of others' behaviors or by imagining the outcome of a potential behavior.	A consumer watches the reactions people have to her friend's new short skirt before deciding to buy one.	A child learns that men don't wear dresses without ever really thinking about it.
Reasoning/Analogy	Individuals use thinking to restructure and recombine existing information to form new associations and concepts.	A consumer believes that baking soda removes odors from the refrigerator. Noticing an unpleasant aroma in the carpet, the consumer decides to sweep some baking soda into the carpet.	Finding that the store is out of black pepper, a consumer decides to substitute white pepper.

GENERAL CHARACTERISTICS OF LEARNING

Regardless of which approach to learning is applicable in a given situation, several general characteristics of learning are relevant and of interest to marketing managers. Five of the most important are strength of learning, extinction (or forgetting), stimulus generalization, stimulus discrimination, and the response environment.

Strength of Learning

What is required to bring about a strong and long-lasting learned response? How can the HIV Alliance teach you to eliminate or minimize your risk of AIDS such that you will not forget? How can Revlon teach you about its new line of vitamins and how they differ from other vitamins? The *strength of learning* is heavily influenced by six factors: *importance, message involvement, mood, reinforcement, repetition,* and *imagery.* Generally, learning comes about more rapidly and lasts longer (1) the more important the material to be learned, (2) the more involved the consumer is with the message, (3) the more positive the consumer's mood, (4) the more reinforcement (or punishment) received during the process, (5) the greater the number of stimulus repetitions (or practice) that occurs, and (6) the more imagery contained in the material.

Importance   Importance refers to the value that the consumer places on the information to be learned. The more important it is for the individual to learn a particular behavior or piece of information, the more effective and efficient he or she becomes in the learning process. This is largely due to the effort expended to fully process and categorize the material.

Importance is one dimension that separates high-involvement learning situations from low-involvement situations. Therefore, high-involvement learning tends to be more complete than low-involvement learning.[15] Unfortunately, marketers are most often confronted with consumers in low-involvement learning situations.

Message Involvement   When a consumer is not motivated to learn the material, the depth of processing can be increased by causing the person to become involved *with the message itself.* Playing an instrumental version of a popular song with lyrics related to product attributes ("Like a rock" in Chevrolet pickup ads) may cause people to "sing along," either out loud or mentally. This deepened involvement with the message, relative to merely listening to the lyrics being sung, increases the depth of processing of the message and memory of the associated features or theme.[16]

Marketers use a variety of techniques to increase message involvement, including interesting ads that involve factors such as a plot, the possibility of a surprise ending, uncertainty on the point of the message until the end, and so forth.[17]

Mood   Get happy, learn more? Research indicates that this is indeed true. A positive mood during the presentation of information such as brand names enhances learning. A positive mood during the reception of information appears to enhance its relational elaboration—it is compared with and evaluated against more categories. This produces a more complete and stronger set of linkages among a variety of other brands and concepts, which in turn enhances retrieval (access to the information).[18]

Learning enhancement caused by a positive mood suggests the types of programs that marketers attempting to encourage consumer learning should advertise on. Likewise, it suggests that those commercials that enhance one's mood would also increase learning.[19]

Reinforcement   Anything that increases the likelihood that a given response will be repeated in the future is considered **reinforcement.** While learning frequently occurs in the

Courtesy Head USA.

ILLUSTRATION 9–4

Reinforcement is anything that increases the probability that a response will be repeated in the future. It can involve a positive outcome such as providing pleasure or the removal or avoidance of a negative outcome such as sore feet.

absence of reinforcement, reinforcement has a significant impact on the speed at which learning occurs and the duration of its effect.

A *positive reinforcement* is a pleasant or desired consequence. A couple who likes Italian food and dining out sees an ad for a new Olive Garden restaurant in their area and decides to try it. They enjoy the food, service, and ambience. They are now more likely to select the Olive Garden the next time they dine out.

A *negative reinforcement* involves the removal or the avoidance of an unpleasant consequence. In Illustration 9–4, Head promises to provide high performance and the avoidance of foot pain. If the ad convinces a consumer to try Head boots, and they perform well and feel comfortable, this consumer is likely to purchase and use the boots and, based on stimulus generalization (discussed shortly), to try other Head products as well.

Punishment is the opposite of reinforcement. It is any consequence that decreases the likelihood that a given response will be repeated in the future. If the couple who tried the Olive Garden restaurant described earlier thought that the service was bad or that the food was poorly prepared, they would be unlikely to patronize it in the future.

From the above discussion, we can see that there are two important reasons for marketers to determine precisely what reinforces specific consumer purchases: (1) *to obtain repeat purchases, the product must satisfy the goals sought by the consumer;* and (2) *to induce the consumer to make the first purchase, the promotional messages must promise the appropriate type of reinforcement*—that is, satisfaction of the consumer's goals.

Repetition   Repetition increases the strength and speed of learning.[20] Quite simply, the more times people are exposed to information or practice a behavior, the more likely they are to learn it. For example, advertisements in sports arenas have a greater effect on those who attend the games regularly than on those who attend infrequently.[21]

The effects of repetition are of course directly related to the importance of the information and the reinforcement given. Less repetition of an advertising message is necessary for someone to learn the message if the subject matter is important or if there is a great deal of relevant reinforcement. Since many advertisements do not contain information of current

| FIGURE 9–6 | Impact of Repetition on Brand Awareness for High- and Low-Awareness Brands |

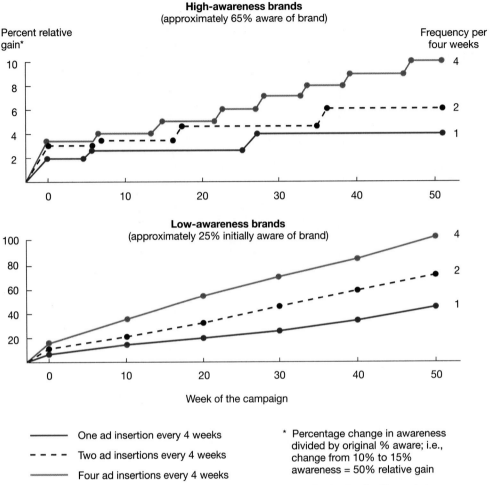

Source: *A Study of the Effectiveness of Advertising Frequency in Magazines,* © 1993 Time Inc. Reprinted by permission.

importance to consumers or direct rewards for learning, repetition plays a critical role in the promotion process for many products.[22]

Figure 9–6, based on a study of 16,500 respondents, shows the impact of various levels of advertising repetition over a 48-week period on brands that had either high or low levels of initial awareness. Several features stand out. First, the initial exposure has the largest impact.[23] Second, frequent repetition (once a week) outperforms limited repetition (once every other week or every four weeks). This advantage grows the longer the campaign lasts. Finally, relative gains are much greater for unknown brands.

Both the number of times a message is repeated and the timing of those repetitions affect the extent and duration of learning.[24] Figure 9–7 illustrates the relationship between repetition timing and product recall for a food product. One group of homemakers, represented by the curved line in the figure, was exposed to a food product advertisement once a week for 13 consecutive weeks. For this group, product recall (learning) increased rapidly and reached its highest level during the thirteenth week, forgetting occurred rapidly, and recall was virtually zero by the end of the year.

FIGURE 9–7   Repetition Timing and Advertising Recall

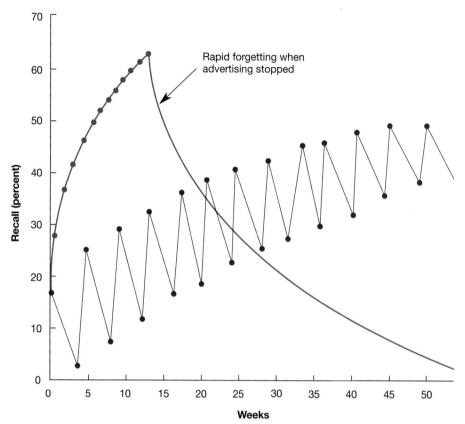

Source: Reprinted from H. J. Zielski, "The Remembering and Forgetting of Advertising," *Journal of Marketing,* January 1959, p. 240, with permission from The American Marketing Association. The actual data and a refined analysis were presented in J. L. Simon, "What Do Zielski's Data Really Show about Pulsing?" *Journal of Marketing Research,* August 1979, pp. 415–20.

A second group of homemakers was exposed to the same 13 direct-mail advertisements. However, they received one ad every four weeks. The zigzag line in the figure shows the recall pattern for this group. In this case, learning increased throughout the year, but substantial forgetting occurred between message exposures.

Concentrating ad messages during a single television broadcast has a similar effect. Compared with one showing of a Miller Lite beer commercial, three showings during a championship baseball game produced two and one-third times the recall.[25] The results below are based on the number of times another commercial appeared during an NFC championship game:

Number of Times Commercial Shown	*Average Recall (percent)*
1	28%
2	32
3	41
4	45

Given a finite budget, how should a firm allocate its advertising across a budget cycle? The answer depends on the task. Any time it is important to produce widespread knowledge of the product rapidly, such as during a new-product introduction, frequent (close together) repetitions should be used. This is referred to as **pulsing.** Thus, political candidates frequently hold back a significant proportion of their media budgets until shortly before the election and then use a media blitz to ensure widespread knowledge of their desirable attributes. More long-range programs, such as store or brand image development, should use more widely spaced repetitions.

Consumers frequently complain about repetition in advertising, and because of excess repetition, some even vow to never buy that brand. Thus, the marketer must walk a fine line in terms of repetition. Too much repetition can cause people to actively shut out the message, evaluate it negatively, or disregard it.[26]

Imagery   Words, whether a brand name or a corporate slogan, create certain images. For example, brand names such as Camel and Mustang evoke sensory images or well-defined mental pictures. This aids learning, as words high in imagery are substantially easier to learn and remember than low-imagery words. The theory behind the imagery effect is that high-imagery words leave a dual code, because they can be stored in memory on both verbal and pictorial dimensions, whereas low-imagery words can only be coded verbally.

In addition, advertising claims consistent with the image evoked by the brand name are easy to recall. Thus, a television brand with a name such as PicturePerfect would be learned more quickly than one named Emporium. Similarly, advertising claims related to picture quality would be associated with the PicturePerfect brand more readily than with the Emporium brand. However, marketers need to be careful when selecting brand names that reflect a single attribute of a product. While claims associated with the attribute in the name are easily associated with the brand, advertised benefits unrelated to the brand (such as sound quality in our PicturePerfect example) are more difficult for consumers to recall compared with the same benefits claimed for a neutral or nonsuggestive brand name.[27]

Pictures *are* images and thus, by definition, have a high level of imagery. Pictures enhance the consumer's visual imagery, which is a particularly effective learning device.[28] They also appear to assist consumers in encoding the information into relevant chunks. Thus, the key communication points of an ad should be reflected in the images elicited by its pictorial component and reinforced in the headline or major text.[29]

There is also evidence that echoic memory—memory of sounds, including words—has characteristics distinct from visual memory.[30] Background music that conveys meanings congruent with the meaning being conveyed by the verbal message has been found to increase learning.[31]

Extinction

Liggett & Myers' share of the cigarette market slid from 20 percent to less than 4 percent. Much of this decline appears to have resulted from sharply reduced advertising. As one executive stated,

> Some time after the company moved away from advertising and marketing, it became clear that people would quickly forget about our products if we didn't support them in the marketplace.[32]

The above example emphasizes that marketers want consumers to learn *and* remember positive features, feelings, and behaviors associated with their brands. However, **extinction,** or *forgetting* as it is more commonly termed, occurs when the reinforcement for the learned response is withdrawn, the learned response is no longer used, or the individual is no longer reminded of the response.

FIGURE 9–8	Forgetting over Time: Magazine Advertisement

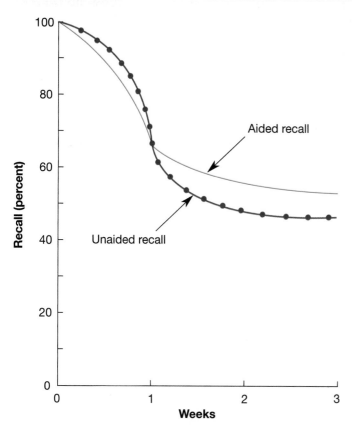

Source: LAP Report #5260.1 (New York: Weeks McGraw-Hill, undated). Reprinted with permission from McGraw-Hill Companies, Inc.

Figure 9–8 illustrates a commonly found rate of forgetting for advertising—the **decay curve.** In this study, aided and unaided recall of four advertisements from *American Machinist* magazine was measured. As can be seen, recall dropped rapidly after five days, then stabilized.

The rate at which extinction occurs is inversely related to the strength of the original learning. That is, the more important the material, the more reinforcement, the more repetition, and the greater the imagery, the more resistant the learning is to extinction.

At times, marketers or regulatory groups desire to accelerate extinction. For example, the American Cancer Society and other organizations offer programs designed to help individuals "unlearn" smoking behavior. Manufacturers want consumers to forget unfavorable publicity or outdated product images.

Corrective advertising, a government requirement that firms remove inaccurate learning caused by past advertising, is described in Chapter 21.

Stimulus Generalization

Stimulus generalization, often referred to as the *rub-off effect, occurs when a response to one stimulus is elicited by a similar but distinct stimulus.*[33] Thus, a consumer who learns that Nabisco's Oreo Cookies taste good and therefore assumes that the company's new Oreo Chocolate Cones will also taste good has engaged in stimulus generalization.

Stimulus generalization is common and provides a major source of brand equity and brand extensions based on brand equity. This area is so important that we devote the last major section of this chapter to it.

Stimulus Discrimination

Stimulus discrimination refers to the *process of learning to respond differently to similar but distinct stimuli*. At some point, stimulus generalization becomes dysfunctional because less and less similar stimuli are still being grouped together. Then, consumers must begin to be able to differentiate among the stimuli. For example, the management of Bayer aspirin feels that consumers should not see its aspirin as being the same as other brands. In order to obtain a premium price or a large market share, Bayer must teach consumers that its aspirin is distinct from other brands.

Marketers have a number of ways to do this, the most obvious of which is advertising that specifically points out brand differences, real or symbolic. The product itself is frequently altered in shape or design to help increase product differentiation.[34] For example, Nuprin did not gain market share with ads showing research indicating that two Nuprins gave more headache relief than Extra Strength Tylenol. The campaign was changed to focus on the color of Nuprin ("Little—Yellow—Different—Better") with a picture of the yellow Nuprin capsules. The campaign made Nuprin the segment's fastest-growing brand. According to the advertising director,

That Nuprin is yellow is superficial to the superiority, yet it opens people's minds that this product is different.[35]

Response Environment

Consumers generally learn more information than they can readily retrieve. That is, they frequently have relevant information stored in memory that they cannot access when needed. One factor that influences the ability to retrieve stored information is the strength of the original learning. The stronger the original learning, the more likely relevant information will be retrieved when required.

A second factor affecting retrieval is the similarity of the retrieval environment to the original learning environment and type of learning.[36] Thus, the more the retrieval situation offers cues similar to the cues present during learning, the more likely effective retrieval is to occur. (This suggests that studying at a desk in a quiet environment rather than on a sofa with music playing might enhance exam performance.) To the extent practical, marketers should do one of two things: (1) configure the learning environment to resemble the most likely retrieval environment, or (2) configure the retrieval environment to resemble the original learning environment.

Matching the retrieval and learning environments requires an understanding of when and where consumers make brand or store decisions. Decisions on brand or store made at home do not have the same set of cues that are available at a retail outlet or in a shopping mall.

Suppose a firm teaches consumers to have a positive feeling toward its brand of gum by consistently pairing the pronouncement of its brand name with a very pleasant, fun scene in a television ad (classical conditioning). However, it does not show the package, and the name is presented visually only briefly. In the purchase situation, the consumer faces a shelf with many packages but no auditory presentation of brand names. Thus, the retrieval environment is not conducive to triggering the learned response. A better strategy would have been to associate the response with the package, which is what the consumer will encounter in the purchase situation.

Suppose someone asked how much you last paid for a product you purchase periodically such as a six-pack of Coke. Could you remember? Many consumers will not remember this information. Yet many of these same consumers will judge the advertised or actual price of a six-pack of Coke to be "too expensive," "a great deal," or "about average." When asked how they reached such a conclusion, some would reply that they "know a bargain when they see one." We all "know" things for which we cannot recall the source or even the exact nature of our knowledge.

Traditionally, we have thought of remembering, and thus memory, as the ability to recall specific items or events. If you read this chapter and then try to answer the review questions at the end without referring back to the chapter, you are engaging in traditional memory recall. This is referred to as **explicit memory,** which is characterized by *the conscious recollection of an exposure event*.

In contrast to remembering, knowing utilizes implicit memory. **Implicit memory** involves *the nonconscious retrieval of previously encountered stimuli*. It is a sense of familiarity, a feeling, or a set of beliefs about an item without conscious awareness of when and how they were acquired.[37]

The distinction between explicit memory (remembering) and implicit memory (knowing) is important for marketing research, pricing, and advertising strategy. For example, it suggests that measuring the effectiveness of ads using advertising recall (explicit memory) may not work for ads aimed at establishing a brand image. Much of a brand image will take the form of an implicit memory. A consumer will "know" Mountain Dew is cool, that Levi's are old-fashioned, and that Volkswagen is fun without being able to explain how he or she acquired this knowledge. Thus, recall of the ad or any of its features is not as relevant as its long-term impact on what consumers "know" about the brand.

It is also important for marketers to understand and monitor what their target consumers "know" relative to their firm and brand. This is because consumers' knowledge about a product, brand, or process frequently does not correspond with reality. For example, a consumer may "know" that Bayer aspirin provides superior inflammation reduction, compared with less expensive store brands. If that is not the actual case, Bayer benefits, but other brands and the consumer lose.

Critical Thinking Questions

1. What is the relationship between explicit and implicit memory?

2. Why do marketers rely so much on measuring of advertising recall?

Quaker Oats applied this concept in a very direct manner. It developed and ran an extremely popular advertising campaign for Life cereal. As the popularity of the campaign became evident, Quaker placed a photo of a scene from the commercial on the front of the Life cereal package. This enhanced the ability of consumers to recall both affect and information from the commercial and was very successful.

Thus far, we have examined specific theories and approaches to learning. Knowledge of learning theories can be used to structure communications that will assist consumers in learning relevant facts, behaviors, and feelings about products. We will now turn our attention to an outcome of learning—memory.

MEMORY

Memory is the total accumulation of prior learning experiences. It consists of two interrelated components: short-term and long-term memory.[38] These are *not* distinct physiological entities. Instead, *short-term memory* is that portion of total memory that is currently activated or in use. In fact, it is often referred to as *working memory*. As Consumer Insight 9–1 indicates, people also have explicit memory (memory of specific events or objects) and implicit memory (generalized memory about events or objects).

Short-Term Memory

Short-term memory has a limited capacity to store information and sensations. In fact, it is not used for storage in the usual sense of that term. It is more like a file in a computer system that is currently in use. Active files are used to hold information while it is being analyzed, augmented, or altered. After the processing is complete, the reconfigured information is transferred to another system (printed, for example) or returned to a more permanent storage facility such as the hard drive. A similar process occurs with short-term memory. Individuals use short-term memory to hold information while they analyze and interpret it. They may then transfer it to another system (write or type it), place it in long-term memory, or both. Thus, short-term memory is closely analogous to what we normally call thinking. *It is an active, dynamic process, not a static structure.*

Two basic types of information processing activities occur in short-term memory—elaborative activities and maintenance rehearsal. **Elaborative activities** are *the use of previously stored experiences, values, attitudes, beliefs, and feelings to interpret and evaluate information in working memory as well as to add relevant previously stored information.* Elaborative activities serve to redefine or add new elements to memory.

Suppose your firm has developed a new product targeted initially at bike riders. The product is a water bottle that one wears strapped to the back with a tube from which the rider can drink without using hands. How will this product be categorized or assigned meaning by the market? The answer depends in large part on *how* it is presented. How it is presented will influence the nature of the elaborative activities that will occur, which in turn will determine how the product is remembered.

Illustration 9–5 shows how CamelBak introduced such a product. First, it used an image-rich name that conveys much of the product's function. Camels are known for their ability to store water, and this system is worn on one's back. The visual in the ad clearly, if symbolically, shows the product's primary benefit. The text expands on this theme. Thus, this ad should help trigger elaborative activities that will allow consumers to define this as a new and useful product for providing fluids on bike trips. The high-imagery name should help retention and recall of the key benefits of the product.

Maintenance rehearsal is *the continual repetition of a piece of information in order to hold it in current memory for use in problem solving or transferal to long-term memory.* Repeating the same formula or definition several times before taking an exam is an example. Marketers frequently simulate this by repeating the brand name or a key benefit in a prominent manner several times in an ad.

Short-term memory activities involve both concept and imagery manipulation. **Concepts** are *abstractions of reality that capture the meaning of an item in terms of other concepts.* They are similar to a dictionary definition of a word. Thus, a consumer might bring forth concepts such as water bottle and backpack when first processing the new concept CamelBak.

Imagery involves *concrete sensory representations of ideas, feelings, and objects.* It permits a direct recovery of aspects of past experiences. Thus, imagery processing involves the recall and mental manipulation of sensory images, including sight, smell, taste, and tactile sensations. The CamelBak ad might induce some consumers to experience the thirst they felt on their last ride and to feel cool water quenching that thirst. The two tasks below will help clarify the distinctions between concepts and imagery in working memory:

- Write down the first 10 *words* that come to mind in response to the phrase "romantic evening."
- Imagine a "romantic evening."

© Fasttrack Systems, Inc. 1996. Created by Mizuno & Associates, Westlake Village, CA.

ILLUSTRATION 9-5

Successful new products and brands must enter into memory in a favorable manner, and they must be recalled when required. In this case, the brand name, the visual in the ad, and the ad text will enhance the elaborative activities appropriate for the product.

Obviously, marketers often want to elicit imagery responses rather than or in addition to verbal ones. We are just beginning to study imagery responses; however, they are a significant part of consumers' mental activities.[39]

Long-Term Memory

Long-term memory is viewed as *an unlimited, permanent storage.* It can store numerous types of information such as concepts, decision rules, processes, affective (emotional) states, and so forth. Marketers are particularly interested in **semantic memory,** which is *the basic knowledge and feelings an individual has about a concept.* It represents the person's understanding of an object or event at its simplest level. At this level, a brand such as Acura might be categorized as "a luxury car."

Another type of memory of interest to marketers is **episodic memory.** This is *the memory of a sequence of events in which a person participated.* These personal memories of events such as a first date, graduation, or learning to drive can be quite strong. They often elicit imagery and feelings. Marketers frequently attempt to evoke episodic memories either because their brand was involved in them or to associate the positive feelings they generate with the brand.

Recalling from long-term memory is not a completely objective or mechanical task. If asked to recall the sponsor of the last summer Olympics, some consumers will not remember instantly and certainly. These individuals may *construct* a memory based on limited

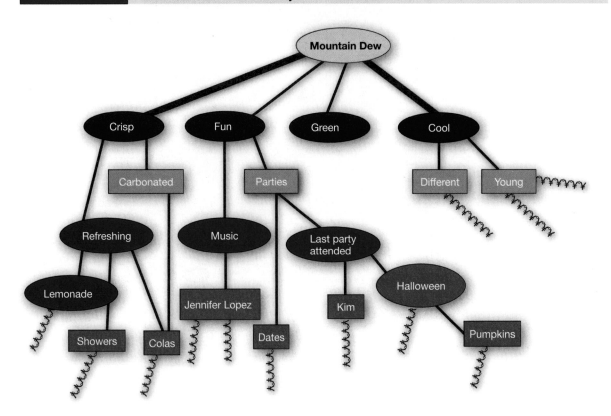

FIGURE 9-9   A Partial Schematic Memory for Mountain Dew

recall and a series of judgments. For example, many might "recall" Nike because it is a dominant firm in sports equipment and apparel; thus, it would "make sense" for Nike to be the sponsor. This may occur at a level well below conscious guessing such that the respondent believes that Nike was indeed a sponsor of the event.[40] Therefore, memory is sometimes shaped and changed as it is accessed. Likewise, memory of an actual event may be altered as new or additional information about that event is received.[41]

Schema   Both concepts and episodes acquire a depth of meaning by becoming associated with other concepts and episodes. A pattern of such associations around a particular concept is termed a **schema** or *schematic memory,* sometimes called a *knowledge structure.* Schematic memory is a complex web of associations. Figure 9–9 provides a simplified example of a schema by showing how one might associate various concepts with Mountain Dew to form a network of meaning for that brand. Notice that our hypothetical schema contains *product characteristics, usage situations, episodes,* and *affective reactions.* The source of some of the schema is personal experience, but other aspects may be completely or partially based on marketing activities.[42] The schematic memory of a brand is the same as the brand image (discussed in the next section). It is what the consumer thinks of *and* feels when the brand name is mentioned.

In the partial schema shown in Figure 9–9, concepts, events, and feelings are stored in *nodes* within memory. Thus, the concept "cool" is stored in a node, as are "music," "fun," and "parties." Each of these is associated either directly or indirectly with Mountain Dew. *Associative links* connect various concepts to form the complete meaning assigned to an item.

Associative links vary in terms of how strongly and how directly they are associated with a node. In our example, crisp, fun, green, and cool are directly associated with Mountain Dew. However, one or two of these may be strongly associated with the brand, as crisp and cool are shown to be by the bold lines in our example. Other nodes may have weaker links, such as fun and green. Without reinforcement, the weaker links may disappear over time (over the longer run, so will the stronger ones). Marketers spent enormous effort attempting to develop strong, easily activated links between their brands and desirable product benefits.[43]

Some aspects of a schema are relatively permanent; others are transitory. In our example, crisp and fun are likely to remain associated with the brand for quite some time. However, the Halloween party linkage will probably fade fairly quickly.

The memory activation shown in Figure 9–9 originated with the name of a particular brand. If the activation had begun with the concept "cool," would Mountain Dew arise as a node directly linked to cool? It would depend on the total context in which the memory was being activated. In general, multiple memory nodes are activated simultaneously. Thus, a question like "What is a cool soft drink?" might quickly activate a memory schema that links Mountain Dew directly to cool. However, a more abstract question like "What is cool?" might not. And a request for the name of a cool brand would be unlikely to trigger a memory of cool soft drinks.[44]

Marketers expend substantial effort to influence the schema consumers have for their brands. We will discuss this process in detail in the next section of this chapter. Marketers also strive to influence the schema consumers have for consumption situations.

What do you think of when you see the word *thirst?* The various things, including brands, that come to mind constitute the schema for thirst. PepsiCo exerts substantial marketing efforts in an attempt to have its brands, including Mountain Dew, become part of the schema associated with thirst. Brands in the schematic memory for a consumer problem such as thirst are known as the *evoked set.* We will discuss the way consumers and marketers use the evoked set in Chapter 15.

Scripts   *Memory of how an action sequence should occur,* such as purchasing and drinking a soft drink in order to relieve thirst, is a special type of schema known as a **script.** Scripts are necessary for consumers to shop effectively. One of the difficulties new forms of retailing have is teaching consumers the appropriate script for acquiring items in a new manner. This is the problem facing firms wanting to sell products via the Internet. Before these firms can succeed, their target markets must learn appropriate scripts for Internet shopping.

Marketers and public policy officials want consumers to develop scripts for appropriate product acquisition, use, and disposal behavior. For example, using a product or service requires one to learn a process. This process often includes the disposition of the package or some part of the product.[45] Unfortunately, many consumers have learned consumption scripts that do not include appropriate disposition activities such as recycling. Thus, both government agencies and environment groups spend substantial effort attempting to teach consumers consumption scripts that include recycling.

BRAND IMAGE AND PRODUCT POSITIONING

Brand image refers to *the schematic memory of a brand.* It contains the target market's interpretation of the product's attributes, benefits, usage situations, users, and manufacturer/marketer characteristics. It is what people think of and feel when they hear or see a brand name.[46] It is, in essence, what consumers have *learned* about the brand.[47] *Company image* and *store image* are similar except they apply to companies and stores rather than brands.

ILLUSTRATION 9-6

Brand names provide an anchor to which consumers can attach meaning. This allows marketers to invest in product improvements and communications with a reasonable possibility of benefiting from those investments.

Suppose you were the marketing manager for IBP, the leading beef processor in the United States. You know that beef has steadily lost share to "white meat" such as chicken and pork. Many consumers have mixed beliefs about the nutritional value of beef—it is good for you with lots of protein but may also be bad for your heart. Perhaps more important, many see it as difficult and time-consuming to prepare. As one industry expert said,

> A lot of consumers don't have the time and expertise to take a raw roast and cook it for six to eight hours, so what we have to do in this industry is understand that and do something about it.[48]

What would you do? The image of beef is mixed at best. One approach would be to follow the lead of the Milk Producers Council and run ads designed to enhance the image of beef, which is being done. However, several firms, such as IBP, are moving beyond this. These firms are precooking beef (and pork), *branding* it, and promoting it. IBP has launched the Thomas E. Wilson brand of precooked meats with an initial $12 million campaign that could grow to $120 million. The brand name is essential so that consumers can learn (form an image) of IBP's precooked beef that allows them to distinguish it from regular beef as well as other brands of precooked beef that are also being launched. The brand allows IBP to invest in product improvements and communications (see Illustration 9–6) with some assurance that it can benefit from its investment. The ability to benefit from a brand image is called *brand equity,* which we discuss in the next section.

Brand image is a major concern of both industrial and consumer good marketers. Consider the following headlines from recent marketing publications:

- Volvo Plans Ad Campaign to Clarify Automaker's Image.
- Samsung's Marketing Chief Outlines $400 Million Brand Challenge.
- Meat Gets Branded.
- Calgon Ads Refresh Brand Image.

How powerful are brand images? Think of Nike, McDonald's, Delia's, Calvin Klein, Coke, Oil of Olay, Amazon.com, and Midas. For many consumers, each of these names conjures up a rich pattern of meanings and feelings. Brand images can be important in any product category.[49]

Over the past few years, Volvo has introduced a number of new models targeting younger and less affluent consumers than it had in the past. As a Volvo representative stated,

> Consumers still think of the brand primarily in terms of safety but are unclear whether the cars are luxury vehicles, what their average prices are, and who the brand's target is. There is less clarity about Volvo now than when we had one car and one wagon. We are going to explain to people what we are.[50]

Brand images can hinder as well as help products. What do you think of when you hear the word *Teflon?* That will depend in part on how successful a current $40 million advertising campaign for Teflon-treated clothes is. At present, most people have a strong image of Teflon as a slick, hard, nonsticky cookware surface. Would you want your slacks to have these features? Probably not. However, you probably would like them to be stain-repellent. Thus, Dupont is spending a large sum of money to change the image of Teflon to make it compatible for use on clothing. A theme being tested for the campaign is "Cotton feels like cotton, wool feels like wool, red wine doesn't stain like red wine."

Product Positioning

Product positioning is a *decision by a marketer to try to achieve a defined brand image relative to competition within a market segment.* That is, marketers decide that they want the members of a market segment to think and feel in a certain way about a brand relative to competing brands. The term *product positioning* is most commonly applied to decisions concerning brands, but it is also used to describe the same decisions for stores, companies, and product categories.

Product positioning has a major impact on the long-term success of the brand, presuming the firm can create the desired position. Consider Saturn's positioning strategy. Saturn emphasizes value, made in America by caring workers, and dealers who care about and respect customers and who do not haggle over price. Saturn wants to be viewed as superior to its competitors on each of these attributes. If it achieves this desired positioning, it will succeed *to the extent that this position is desired by the target market.*[51] If the target market does not value this image or values the image portrayed by competitors more, Saturn will not succeed.

An important component of brand image is the appropriate usage situations for the product or brand. Often marketers have the opportunity to influence the usage situations for which a product or brand is seen as appropriate. What do you think of when you think of cranberry sauce? Odds are that Thanksgiving and perhaps Christmas are part of your image of cranberry sauce. In fact, these are probably the only usage situations that came to mind. However, in one study, sales for cranberry sauce increased almost 150 percent over a three-month period after consumers saw advertisements promoting nontraditional uses. Thus, expanding the usage situation component of cranberry sauce's product position could dramatically increase its sales.[52]

The terms *product position* and *brand image* are often used interchangeably. In general, however, product position involves an explicit reference to a brand's image relative to another brand or the overall industry. It is characterized by statements such as "HP printers are the most reliable printers available." Brand image generally considers the firm's image without a direct comparison to a competitor. It is characterized by statements such as "HP printers are extremely reliable."

Once a marketer decides on an appropriate product position, the marketing mix is manipulated in a manner designed to achieve that position in the target market. The stimuli that marketing managers employ to influence a product's interpretation and thus its position can be quite subtle. Sunkist Growers offers a pectin-based candy, Sunkist Fruit Gems, available in various fruit flavors (pectin is a carbohydrate obtained from orange and lemon peels). The candy contains no preservatives and less sugar than most fruit jelly candies.

Sunkist is positioning the candy as a "healthful, natural" snack. The company hopes to attract adults as well as children. As part of the overall marketing strategy, Sunkist is attempting to distribute the candy through the produce departments of supermarkets. Notice how the distribution plan supports the desired product position or image. A consumer receiving a message that this is a healthful, natural product may agree when the product is found near other healthful, natural products such as apples and oranges.

Marketing managers frequently fail to achieve the type of product image or position they desire because they fail to anticipate or test for consumer reactions. Toro's initial lightweight snow thrower was not successful. Why? It was named the Snowpup, and consumers interpreted this to mean that it was a toy or lacked sufficient power. Sales success came only after a more macho, power-based name was utilized—first Snowmaster and later Toro.

Perceptual mapping offers marketing managers a useful technique for measuring and developing a product's position. Perceptual mapping takes consumers' perceptions of how similar various brands or products are to each other and relates these perceptions to product attributes. Figure 9–10 is a perceptual map for several automobile models.

This perceptual map also provides the ideal points for three market segments—TM1, TM2, and TM3. These ideal points represent the image/characteristics each segment desires in an automobile. If the models in this map were all that existed, it would indicate that TM1 consumers are not being offered the products they want. At present, they have to spend more than they want and buy a Saturn SC2 or a less sporty car than they desire such as the Honda Accord or the Kia Spectra. If this segment is large enough, one or more firms should consider developing a fun, sporty, but low-cost, economical car and target this group. If TM1 and TM2 were the only ideal points in the lower portion of the perceptual map, both the Ford Focus and the Kia Spectra would be in trouble. *Why?*

Product Repositioning   The images consumers have of brands change over time. Thus, HP may maintain a reputation for having reliable printers while losing its position as having the most reliable printers in the industry if a superior competitor evolves. Likewise, HP's image and position could evolve over time depending on changes in the company's marketing mix.

The evolution of images and product positions over time is natural and to an extent inevitable. **Product repositioning,** on the other hand, refers to *a deliberate decision to significantly alter the way the market views a product.* This could involve its level of performance, the feelings it evokes, the situations in which it should be used, or even who uses it.[53]

Mug Root Beer was repositioned to be more appropriate to Generation X and to older teens (its primary target market is 15- to 29-year-olds). This is noticeably younger than its prior target. To accomplish this repositioning, it was advertised on television shows that appeal to young adults as well as on MTV. In one ad, a young man drinks Mug while flipping the city's master light switch on and off to the beat of a rock song. In another ad, a young man drinks Mug while talking to a prairie dog in a pet store about freeing him from his "jail." In addition to advertising and promotion changes, the package was redesigned to

FIGURE 9–10   **Perceptual Map for Automobiles**

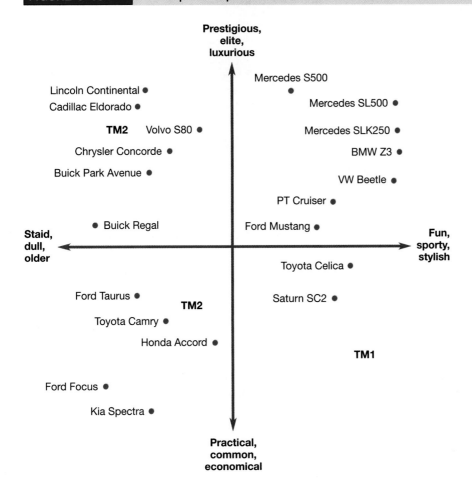

a brighter red from its original brown in order to appeal more to this market segment (see Illustration 9–7).

PepsiCo is attempting to reposition Mug primarily in terms of its user group. What do you think of when you hear Midas? If you still think only of mufflers, Midas will not have succeeded in its attempt to expand its image. It wants to be seen as an expert in auto systems and plans to spend $23 million in advertising to reposition itself (it feels it already has the service capabilities to support the image). One ad compares auto repairs to math:

"Repairing a car is like math. Once you master the basics, then you can build on them. Same as Midas. They excelled in mufflers, and expanded into other systems on your car." The tagline: "Midas Auto Systems Experts. What can we do for you today?"

Other recent repositioning efforts include,

- H&R Block is moving from being a tax preparation specialist to "the accessible provider of financial services to Middle America."[54]
- Infiniti is attempting to move from a diffuse luxury car image to a "new brand image that is about performance."[55]

© M. Hruby.

* Marks & Spencer, once the U.K.'s standard for good quality at reasonable prices, had come to be viewed as staid. It is trying to add currency, excitement, and emotion to its image. Its use of Rubenesque nudes in its ads for larger-sized clothes has generated extensive publicity and controversy. It is too soon to tell how it is affecting its product position.[56]

BRAND EQUITY AND BRAND LEVERAGE

Brand equity is *the value consumers assign to a brand above and beyond the functional characteristics of the product.*[57] For example, many people pay a significant premium for Bayer aspirin relative to store brands of aspirin although they are chemically identical.

Brand equity is nearly synonymous with the reputation of the brand.[58] However, the term *equity* implies economic value. Thus, brands with "good" reputations have the potential for high levels of brand equity, whereas unknown brands or brands with weak or negative reputations do not.

Brand equity is based on the product position of the brand. A consumer who believes that a brand delivers superior performance, is exciting to use, and is produced by a company with appropriate social values is likely to be willing to pay a premium for the brand, to go to extra trouble to locate and buy it, to recommend it to others, to forgive a mistake or product flaw, or to otherwise engage in behaviors that benefit the firm that markets the brand. Thus, one source of economic value from a positive brand image results from consumers' behaviors toward existing items with that brand name.[59]

Another source of value for a brand image is that consumers may assume that the favorable aspects of the image associated with an existing product will apply to a new product with the same brand name. This is based on the principle of stimulus generalization described earlier in this chapter.

Brand leverage, often termed *family branding, brand extensions, or umbrella branding,* refers to *marketers capitalizing on brand equity by using an existing brand name for new products.*[60] If done correctly, consumers will assign some of the characteristics of the existing brand to the new brand. Recent brand extensions include Bounty paper napkins (previously, only paper towels), Tartar Control Listerine, and Toyota ski boats.

However, stimulus generalization does not occur just because two products have the same brand name. There must be a connection between the products. Bacardi is particularly conservative in using its name for fear of adversely affecting sales of Bacardi rum, the world's largest-selling distilled spirit. However, it successfully launched Bacardi Tropical Fruit Mixers (frozen nonalcoholic drinks) on the basis of the following rationale:

> Our research found that tropical drinks—piña coladas and frozen daiquiris—are highly associated with Bacardi rum. We already have credibility in that area, which made this new venture right. Bacardi has a lot of equity in its name; it means quality in areas related to rum . . . . But we feel the name wouldn't have that equity in another area. Bacardi wine, for example, wouldn't mean a lot because rum has nothing to do with wine.[61]

In contrast, Campbell's was not able to introduce a spaghetti sauce under the Campbell's name (it used Prego instead). Consumer research found that,

> Campbell's, to consumers, says it isn't authentic Italian. Consumers figured it would be orangy and runny like our tomato soup.[62]

Successful brand leverage generally requires that the original brand have a strong positive image and that the new product fit with the original product on at least one of four dimensions:[63]

1. *Complement.* The two products are used together.
2. *Substitute.* The new product can be used instead of the original.
3. *Transfer.* Consumers see the new product as requiring the same manufacturing skills as the original.
4. *Image.* The new product shares a key image component with the original.

Porsche has a high-quality, sporty image among many consumers. It could logically extend its name to tires (complement), motorcycles (substitute), ski boats (transfer), or sunglasses (image). In fact, it recently introduced a Porsche mountain bike—for $4,500!

What do cosmetics and vitamins have in common? On the surface, very little. However, think about Revlon's image. It is known for skin care and beauty enhancement products. It launched Revlon Vitamins with the expression "Now, Revlon beauty begins from the inside-out." The vitamins are positioned in terms of the specific health benefits associated with each that relate directly to beauty such as nail strength. *Will consumers accept this new line because of Revlon's image in beauty and skin care?* If they do, Revlon will have successfully used brand leverage to take advantage of its brand equity.

Neutrogena has successfully extended its brand from a bar "soap" to shampoos, cleansing clothes, make-ups, and lipsticks. The extensions to shampoos and acne cleansing cloths were very consistent with the base product and image. Lipsticks are further removed, but their introduction has been very successful (see Illustration 9–8).

Other examples of successful and unsuccessful brand extensions include the following:

- Gillette was unsuccessful with a facial moisturizer line under the Silkience brand name. Silkience's excellent reputation in hair care simply did not translate to face creams.
- Harley-Davidson has applied its name successfully to a wide variety of products, but its Harley-Davidson wine coolers were not successful.
- Levi Strauss failed in its attempt to market Levi's tailored suits for men.
- Country Time could not expand from lemonade to apple cider.
- LifeSavers gum did not succeed.
- Coleman successfully expanded from camping stoves and lanterns into a complete line of camping equipment.
- Oil of Olay bar soap is successful in large part due to the equity of the Oil of Olay lotion.

Courtesy Neutrogena Corporation.

When marketers want to offer a version of a popular brand to distinct market segments with a distinct image from the original brand, they generally need to create a new brand rather than extend the existing one. AT&T did this by creating the Lucky Dog Phone Co. to offer low-cost dial-around phone service to cost-focused customers. Similarly, The Gap created Old Navy to target value-oriented students and young families. Miller Brewing uses the Plank Road Brewery to market specialty beers such as Red Dog, Southpaw, and Icehouse. These new brands have images that are distinct from the original brand. Using unique brand names for this purpose avoids diluting or confusing the original brand image.

Brand extensions are sometimes done to bolster the image of the brand rather than to capitalize on its current equity. Mercedes, like Porsche and BMW, has launched a mountain bike with its name attached. However, much of the reason is because mountain bikes have a hip, active image. A marketer for Mercedes says the firm wants to "appeal to a larger, wider, younger audience."[64] In these cases, the new product is designed to enhance the base brand image and increase its equity.

Brand extensions involve several risks for marketers. One is that a failure of any product with a brand name can hurt all the products with the same brand name (consumers generalize bad outcomes as well as good ones).

Another risk is diluting or unfavorably altering the original brand image.[65] A strong image is generally focused on a fairly narrow set of characteristics. Each additional product added to that product name alters the image somewhat. If too many or too dissimilar products are added to the brand name, the brand image may become diffuse or confused. For example, if Porsche launched skis, backpacks, tennis equipment, fashion clothes for both genders, stereos, and so forth, it would eventually lose its unique meaning. Many feel that Nike is in danger of such a brand dilution as it attaches its name to an ever-wider array of products.

Likewise, brand extensions of prestige products to models or products of less prestige can harm brand equity, particularly among existing owners.[66] Thus, if Porsche were to launch a ski boat, it should be a high-performance stylish one, not one that competes on price.

Federal law has recently recognized the danger of brand equity dilution by other firms. Until 1996, a firm in a noncompeting industry could use a famous brand name such as Apple if there were no danger of consumer confusion. However, the Federal Trademark Dilution Act of 1995 allows a firm to take action if another uses its brand name or trademark in a way that lessens

the capacity of a famous mark to identify and distinguish goods and services, regardless of the presence or absence of (1) competition between the owner of the famous mark and other parties, or (2) likelihood of confusion, mistake, or deception.[67]

SUMMARY

Consumers must learn almost everything related to being a consumer—product existence, performance, availability, values, preference, and so forth. Marketing managers, therefore, are very interested in the nature of consumer learning.

High-involvement learning occurs when an individual is motivated to acquire the information. *Low-involvement learning* occurs when an individual is paying only limited or indirect attention to an advertisement or other message. Low-involvement learning tends to be limited due to a lack of elaborative activities.

Learning is defined as any change in the content or organization of long-term memory or behavior. Two basic types of learning, *conditioning* and *cognition,* are used by consumers.

There are two forms of conditioned learning—classical and operant. *Classical conditioning* refers to the process of using an existing relationship between a stimulus and response to bring about the learning of the same response to a different stimulus. In *operant conditioning,* reinforcement plays a much larger role than it does in classical conditioning. No automatic stimulus–response relationship is involved, so the subject must first be induced to engage in the desired behavior and then this behavior must be reinforced.

The *cognitive* approach to learning encompasses the mental activities of humans as they work to solve problems, cope with complex situations, or function effectively in their environment. It includes *iconic rote learning* (forming associations between unconditioned stimuli without rewards), *vicarious learning/modeling*

(learning by imagining outcomes or observing others), and *reasoning*.

The strength of learning depends on six basic factors: importance, reinforcement, mood, message involvement, repetition, and imagery. *Importance* refers to the value that the consumer places on the information to be learned—the greater the importance, the greater the learning. *Reinforcement* is anything that increases the likelihood that a response will be repeated in the future—the greater the reinforcement, the greater the learning. *Mood* is the temporary mental state or feeling of the consumer. Learning appears to be greater in positive mood conditions. *Message involvement* is the degree to which the consumer is interested in the message itself—the greater the message involvement, the greater the learning. *Repetition* or practice refers to the number of times that we are exposed to the information or that we practice a behavior. Repetition increases the strength and speed of learning. *Imagery* is the degree to which concepts evoke well-defined mental images. High-image concepts are easier to learn.

Remembering a fact or specific event is known as *explicit memory*. Knowing something without awareness of the source or exact nature of the knowledge is referred to as *implicit memory*. Both forms of memory are important to marketers but implicit memory is particularly important for understanding how consumers form and use brand images.

Stimulus generalization is one way of transferring learning by generalizing from one stimulus situation to other, similar ones. *Stimulus discrimination* refers to the opposite process of learning—responding differently to somewhat similar stimuli.

Extinction, or forgetting, is also of interest to marketing managers. Extinction is directly related to the strength of original learning, modified by continued repetition.

Memory is the result of learning. Most commonly, information goes directly into *short-term memory* for problem solving or elaboration where two basic activities occur—elaborative activities and maintenance rehearsal. *Elaborative activities* are the use of stored experiences, values, attitudes, and feelings to interpret and evaluate information in current memory. *Maintenance rehearsal* is the continual repetition of a piece of information in order to hold it in current memory.

Long-term memory is information from previous information processing that has been stored for future use. It undergoes continual restructuring as new information is acquired. Information is retrieved from retention for problem solving, and the success of the retrieval process depends on how well the material was learned and the match between the retrieval and learning environment.

Brand image, a market segment or individual consumer's schematic memory of a brand, is a major focus of marketing activity. *Product positioning* is a decision by a marketer to attempt to attain a defined brand image, generally in relation to specific competitors. A brand image that matches a target market's needs and desires will be valued by that market segment. Such a brand is said to have *brand equity* because consumers respond favorably toward it in the market. In addition, these consumers may be willing to assume that other products with the same brand name will have some of the same features. Introducing new products with the same name as an existing product is referred to as *brand leverage* or *brand extension.*

KEY TERMS

Analogical reasoning 324
Brand equity 342
Brand image 337
Brand leverage 342
Classical conditioning 320
Cognitive learning 323
Concept 334
Conditioning 319
Decay curve 331
Elaborative activities 334
Episodic memory 335
Explicit memory 333
Extinction 330

High-involvement learning 317
Iconic rote learning 323
Imagery 334
Implicit memory 333
Incidental exposure 318
Learning 317
Long-term memory 335
Low-involvement learning 317
Maintenance rehearsal 334
Modeling 324
Operant conditioning 321
Perceptual mapping 340
Product positioning 339

Product repositioning 340
Pulsing 330
Punishment 327
Reasoning 324
Reinforcement 326
Schema 336
Scripts 337
Semantic memory 335
Shaping 321
Short-term memory 334
Stimulus discrimination 332
Stimulus generalization 331
Vicarious learning 324

INTERNET EXERCISES

1. Visit one of the following websites. Evaluate the site in terms of its application of learning principles.
   a. www.airwalk.com
   b. www.fogdog.com
   c. www.revlon.com
   d. www.mountaindew.com

2. Visit several company websites until you find one that you feel makes particularly effective use of one or more of the learning theories we have covered and one that makes very little use of these principles. Describe each and justify your selections.

3. Evaluate the following three websites in terms of their ability to create/support a good brand image and product position.
   a. www.volvo.com
   b. www.bmw.com
   c. www.mercedes.com

REVIEW QUESTIONS

1. What is *learning?*
2. Describe *low-involvement learning.* How does it differ from *high-involvement learning?*
3. What is *incidental exposure?*
4. What do we mean by *cognitive learning,* and how does it differ from the *conditioning theory* approach to learning?
5. Distinguish between learning via classical conditioning and learning that occurs via operant conditioning.
6. What is *iconic rote learning?* How does it differ from *classical conditioning? Operant conditioning?*
7. Define *modeling.*
8. What is meant by *learning by reasoning?*
9. Describe *analogical reasoning.*
10. What factors affect the *strength of learning?*
11. What is *imagery?*
12. What is meant by *stimulus generalization?* When do marketers use it?
13. Define *stimulus discrimination.* Why is it important?
14. Explain *extinction* and tell why marketing managers are interested in it.
15. Why is it useful to match the retrieval and learning environments?
16. What is *memory?*
17. Define *short-term memory* and *long-term memory.*
18. What is *maintenance rehearsal?*
19. What is meant by *elaborative activities?*
20. What is meant by *imagery* in working memory?
21. What is *semantic memory?*
22. How does a *schema* differ from a *script?*
23. What is *episodic memory?*
24. What is the difference between *knowing* and *remembering?*
25. What is the difference between *implicit memory* and *explicit memory?*
26. What is a *brand image?* Why is it important?
27. What is *product positioning?*
28. What is *perceptual mapping?*
29. What is *brand equity?*
30. What does *leveraging brand equity* mean?

DISCUSSION QUESTIONS

31. How would you determine the best product position for the following?
    a. A candidate student body president at your university
    b. A sports drink targeting children
    c. A nonprofit organization focused on preventing AIDS
    d. A line of clothing targeting Hispanic females
    e. A brand of tofu
32. Is low-involvement learning really widespread? Which products are most affected by low-involvement learning?
33. Almex and Company introduced a new coffee-flavored liqueur in direct competition with Hiram Walker's tremendously successful Kahlua brand. Almex named its new entry Kamora and packaged it in a bottle similar to that of Kahlua, using a pre-Columbian label design. The ad copy for Kamora reads, "If you like coffee—you'll love Kamora."

Explain Almex's marketing strategy in terms of learning theory.
34. Describe the brand images the following "brands" have among students on your campus.
    a. Fraternities
    b. Your student government
    c. Code Red
    d. Chrysler PT
    e. The Marines
    f. Prunes
35. In what ways, if any, would the brand images you described in response to the previous question differ with different groups, such as (*a*) middle-aged professionals, (*b*) young blue-collar workers, (*c*) high school students, and (*d*) retired couples?
36. What is the relationship between imagery and schema?
37. Respond to the questions in Consumer Insight 9–1.

38. Evaluate the following illustrations in light of their apparent objectives and target market.
    a. 9–1
    b. 9–2
    c. 9–3
    d. 9–4
    e. 9–5
    f. 9–6
39. How would you teach teenagers an eating script that involved consistently washing one's hands first? use of seat belts?

APPLICATION ACTIVITIES

40. Fulfill the requirements of Question 34 by interviewing three male and three female students.
41. Answer Question 35 based on interviews with five individuals from each group.
42. Pick a consumer convenience product, perhaps a personal care product such as deodorant or mouthwash, and create advertising copy stressing (*a*) a positive reinforcement, (*b*) a negative reinforcement, and (*c*) a punishment.
43. Find and describe three advertisements, one based on cognitive learning, another based on operant conditioning, and the third based on classical conditioning. Discuss the nature of each advertisement and how it utilizes that type of learning.
44. Find and describe three advertisements that you believe are based on low-involvement learning and three that are based on high-involvement learning. Justify your selection.
45. Select a product and develop an advertisement based on low-involvement learning and one on high-involvement learning. When should each be used (be specific)?

46. Select a product that you feel has a good product position and one that has a weak position. Justify your selection. Describe an ad or package for each product and indicate how it affects the product's position.
47. Select a product, store, or service of relevance to students on your campus. Using a sample of students, measure its brand image. Develop a marketing strategy to improve its image.
48. Develop a campaign to reduce the risk of AIDS for students on your campus by teaching them the value of
    a. Abstinence from sex outside of marriage
    b. Safe sex
49. Find a recent brand extension that you feel will be successful and one that you feel will fail. Explain each of your choices.

REFERENCES

1. A. Klaassen, "St. Joseph," *Advertising Age,* July 9, 2001, p. 1.
2. B. Wernerfelt, "Efficient Marketing Communication," *Journal of Marketing Research,* May 1996, pp. 239–46.
3. A. A. Mitchell, "Cognitive Processes Initiated by Exposure to Advertising," in *Information Processing Research in Advertising,* ed. R. Harris (New York: Lawrence Erlbaum Associates, 1983), pp. 13–42.
4. See W. E. Baker and R. J. Lutz, "An Empirical Test of an Updated Relevance–Accessibility Model of Advertising Effectiveness," *Journal of Advertising,* Spring 2000, pp. 1–13; and S. M. J. Van Osselaer and C. Janiszewski, "Two Ways of Learning Brand Associations," *Journal of Consumer Research,* September 2001, pp. 202–23.
5. S. A. Hawkins, S. J. Hoch, and J. Meyers-Levy, "Low-Involvement Learning," *Journal of Consumer Psychology* 11, no. 1 (2001), pp. 1–11.
6. S. Shapiro, S. J. MacInnis, and S. E. Heckler, "The Effects of Incidental Ad Exposure on the Formation of Consideration Sets," *Journal of Consumer Research,* June 1997, pp. 94–104. See also S.-W. Chung and K. Szymanski, "Effects of Brand Name Exposure on Brand Choice," in *Advances in Consumer Research,* vol. 24, eds. M. Bruck and D. J. MacInnis (Provo, UT: Association for Consumer Research, 1997), pp. 288–94; and S. Shapiro, "When an Ad's Influence Is Beyond Our Conscious Control," *Journal of Consumer Research,* June 1999, pp. 16–36.
7. See G. D. Olsen, "The Impact of Interstimulus Interval and Background Silence on Recall"; and J. Sengupta, R. C. Goodstein, and D. S. Boninger, "All Cues Are Not Created Equal," both in *Journal of Consumer Research,* March 1997, pp. 295–303 and 351–61.
8. See G. Tom, "Classical Conditioning of Unattended Stimuli," *Psychology & Marketing,* January 1995, pp. 79–87; J. Kin,

C. T. Allen, and F. R. Kardes, "An Investigation into the Mediational Mechanisms Underlying Attitudinal Conditioning," *Journal of Marketing Research,* August 1996, pp. 318–28; R. P. Grossman and B. D. Till, "The Persistence of Classically Conditioned Brand Attitudes," *Journal of Advertising,* Spring 1998; J. Kim, J.-S. Lim, and M. Bhargava, "The Role of Affect in Attitude Formation," *Journal of the Academy of Marketing Science,* Spring 1998, pp. 143–52; W. E. Baker, "When Can Affective Conditioning and Mere Exposure Directly Influence Brand Choice," *Journal of Advertising,* Winter 1999, pp. 31–46; and B. D. Till and R. L. Priluck, "Stimulus Generalization in Classical Conditioning," *Psychology & Marketing,* January 2000, pp. 55–72.

9. B. D. Till and R. L. Priluck, "Conditioning of Meaning in Advertising," *Journal of Current Issues and Research in Advertising,* Fall 2001, pp. 1–8.

10. B. J. Bergiel and C. Trosclair, "Instrumental Learning," *Journal of Consumer Marketing,* Fall 1985, pp. 23–28. See also W. Gaidis and J. Cross, "Behavior Modification as a Framework for Sales Promotion Management," *Journal of Consumer Marketing,* Spring 1987, pp. 65–74.

11. See J. W. Pracejus, "Is More Always Better," in *Advances in Consumer Research,* vol. 22, eds. F. R. Kardes and M. Sujan (Provo, UT: Association for Consumer Research, 1995), pp. 319–22; and K. P. Gwinner and J. Eaton, "Building Brand Image through Event Sponsorship," *Journal of Advertising,* Winter 1999, pp. 47–57.

12. For a way to measure such images, see L. A. Babin and A. C. Burns, *Psychology & Marketing,* no. 3 (1998), pp. 261–78.

13. S. P. Jain and D. Maheswaran, "Motivated Reasoning," *Journal of Consumer Research,* March 2000, pp. 358–71.

14. J. Gregan-Paxton and D. R. John, "Consumer Learning by Analogy," *Journal of Consumer Research,* December 1997, pp. 266–85. See also J. Gregan-Paxton, "The Role of Abstract and Specific Knowledge in the Formation of Product Judgments," *Journal of Consumer Psychology* 11, no. 3 (2001), pp. 141–58.

15. See R. G. M. Pieters, E. Rosbergen, and M. Hartog, "Visual Attention to Advertising," *Advances in Consumer Research,* vol. 23, eds. K. P. Corfman and J. G. Lynch (Provo, UT: Association for Consumer Research, 1996), pp. 242–48; and S. M. Leong, S. H. Ang, and L. L. Tham, "Increasing Brand Name Recall in Print Advertising among Asian Consumers," *Journal of Advertising,* Summer 1996, pp. 65–81.

16. M. L. Roehm, "Instrumental vs. Vocal Versions of Popular Music in Advertising," *Journal of Advertising Research,* May 2001, pp. 49–58. See also Baker and Lutz, "An Empirical Test of an Updated Relevance–Accessibility Model."

17. L. F. Allwitt, "Effects of Interestingness on Evaluations of TV Commercials," *Journal of Current Issues and Research in Advertising,* Spring 2000, pp. 41–53.

18. A. Y. Lee and B. Sternthal, "The Effects of Positive Mood on Memory," *Journal of Consumer Research,* September 1999, pp. 115–27; M. J. Barone, P. W. Miniard, and J. B. Romeo, "The Influence of Positive Mood on Brand Extension Evaluations," *Journal of Consumer Research,* March 2000, pp. 386–400; K. R. Lord, R. E. Burnkrant, and H. R. Unnava, "The Effects of Program-Induced Mood States on Memory for Commercial Information," *Journal of Current Issues and Research in Advertising,* Spring 2001, pp. 1–14; and S. J. Newell, K. V. Henderson, and B. T. Wu, "The Effects of Pleasure and Arousal on Recall of Advertisements during the Super Bowl," *Psychology & Marketing,* November 2001, pp. 1135–53.

19. T. Ambler and T. Burne, "The Impact of Affect on Memory of Advertising," *Journal of Advertising Research,* March 1999, pp. 25–39; and S. Youn et al., "Commercial Liking and Memory," *Journal of Advertising Research,* May 2001, pp. 7–13.

20. See P. Malaviya, J. Meyers-Levy, and B. Sternthal, "Ad Repetition in a Cluttered Environment," *Psychology & Marketing,* March 1999, pp. 99–118.

21. L. W. Turley and J. R. Shannon, "The Impact and Effectiveness of Advertisements in a Sports Arena," *Journal of Services Marketing* 14, no. 4 (2000), pp. 323–36.

22. See Hawkins, Scott, and Meyers-Levy, "Low-Involvement Learning."

23. See also J. P. Jones, "Single-Source Research Begins to Fulfill Its Promise," *Journal of Advertising Research,* May 1995, pp. 9–16.

24. See S. N. Singh and C. A. Cole, "The Effects of Length, Content, and Repetition on Television Commercial Effectiveness," *Journal of Marketing Research,* February 1993, pp. 91–104; C. P. Haugtveld, D. W. Schumann, W. L. Schneier, and W. L. Warren, "Advertising Repetition and Variation Strategies," *Journal of Consumer Research,* June 1994, pp. 176–89; S. N. Singh, S. Mishra, N. Bendapudi, and D. Linville, "Enhancing Memory of Television Commercials through Message Spacing," *Journal of Marketing Research,* August 1994, pp. 384–92; E. Ephron, "More Weeks, Less Weight," *Journal of Advertising Research,* May 1995, pp. 18–23; Pieters, Rosbergen, and Hartog, "Visual Attention to Advertising"; and Leong, Ang, and Tham, "Increasing Brand Name Recall."

25. J. O. Eastlack, Jr., "How to Get More Bang from Your Television Bucks," *Journal of Consumer Marketing,* Third Quarter 1984, pp. 25–34.

26. See M. H. Blair and M. J. Rabuck, "Advertising Wearin and Wearout," *Journal of Advertising Research,* September 1998, pp. 7–25; D. Vakratsas and T. Ambler, "How Advertising Works," *Journal of Marketing,* January 1999, pp. 26–43; and D. W. Stewart, "Advertising Wearout," *Journal of Advertising Research,* September 1999, pp. 39–42.

27. K. L. Keller, S. E. Heckler, and M. J. Houston, "The Effects of Brand Name Suggestiveness on Advertising Recall," *Journal of Marketing,* January 1998, pp. 48–57. See also Sengupta, Goodstein, and Boninger, "All Cues Are Not Created Equal."

28. See Leong, Ang, and Tham, "Increasing Brand Name Recall"; M. C. Macklin, "Preschoolers' Learning of Brand Names from Visual Cues," *Journal of Consumer Research,* December 1996, pp. 251–61; and J. C. McCracken and M. C. Macklin, "The Role of Brand Names and Visual Cues in Enhancing Memory for Consumer Packaged Goods," *Marketing Letters,* no. 2 (1998), pp. 209–26.

29. W. J. Bryce and R. F. Yalch, "Hearing versus Seeing," *Journal of Current Issues and Research in Advertising,* Spring 1993, pp. 1–20; A. C. Burns, A. Biswas, and L. A. Babin, "The Operation of Visual Imagery as a Mediator of Advertising Effects,"

Journal of Advertising, June 1993, pp. 71–85; K. R. Lord and S. Putrevu, "Communicating in Print," *Journal of Current Issues and Research in Advertising,* Fall 1998, pp. 1–18; A. Kumar, "Interference Effects of Contextual Cues in Advertisements," *Journal of Consumer Psychology* 9, no. 3 (2000), pp. 155–66; and M. Wedel and R. Pieters, "Eye Fixations on Advertisements and Memory for Brands," *Marketing Science,* Fall 2000, pp. 297–312.

30. T. Clark, "Echoic Memory Explored and Applied," *Journal of Consumer Marketing,* Winter 1987, pp. 39–46. See also C. E. Young and M. Robinson, "Video Rhythms and Recall," *Journal of Advertising Research,* July 1989, pp. 22–25.

31. J. J. Kellaris, A. D. Cox, and D. Cox, "The Effect of Background Music on Ad Processing," *Journal of Marketing,* October 1993, pp. 114–25. See also M. Hahn and I. Hwang, "Effects of Temps and Familiarity of Background Music on Message Processing in TV Advertising," *Psychology & Marketing,* December 1999, pp. 659–75.

32. "L&M Lights Up Again," *Marketing & Media Decisions,* February 1984, p. 69.

33. See Till and Priluck, "Stimulus Generalization in Classical Conditioning."

34. G. S. Carpenter, R. Glazer, and K. Nakamoto, "Meaningful Brands from Meaningless Differences," *Journal of Marketing Research,* August 1994, pp. 339–50.

35. P. Winters, "Color Nuprin's Success Yellow," *Advertising Age,* October 31, 1988, p. 28.

36. See M. C. Macklin, "The Effects of an Advertising Retrieval Cue on Young Children's Memory and Brand Evaluations," *Psychology & Marketing,* May 1994, pp. 291–311; J. W. Park, "Memory-Based Product Judgments"; and E. J. Cowley, "Altering Retrieval Sets," both in *Advances in Consumer Research,* vol. 22, eds. F. R. Kardes and M. Sujan (Provo, UT: Association for Consumer Research, 1995), pp. 159–64 and 323–27; and M. E. Hill and M. King, "Comparative vs. Noncomparative Advertising," *Journal of Current Issues and Research in Advertising,* Fall 2001, pp. 33–52.

37. This discussion is based on K. B. Monroe and A. Y. Lee, "Remembering versus Knowing," *Journal of the Academy of Marketing Science,* Spring 1999, pp. 207–225. See also H. S. Krishnan and C. V. Trappey, "Nonconscious Memory Processes in Marketing"; and S. J. S. Holden and M. Vanhuele, "Know the Name, Forget the Exposure," both in *Psychology & Marketing,* September 1999, pp. 451–57 and 479–96; J. W. Alba and J. W. Hutchinson, "Knowledge Calibration," *Journal of Consumer Research,* September 2000, pp. 123–48; and S. Shapiro and H. S. Krishnan, "Memory-Based Measures for Assessing Advertising Effects," *Journal of Advertising,* Fall 2001, pp. 1–13.

38. For differing views see A. J. Malter, "An Introduction to Embodied Cognition," *Advances in Consumer Research,* vol. 23, eds. K. P. Corfman and J. G. Lynch (Provo, UT: Association for Consumer Research, 1996), pp. 272–76; and M. E. Hill, R. Radtke, and M. King, "A Transfer Appropriate Processing View of Consumer Memory," *Journal of Current Issues and Research in Advertising,* Spring 1997, pp. 1–21.

39. See L. M. Scott, "Images in Advertising," *Journal of Consumer Research,* September 1994, p. 254.

40. G. Venkataramani and M. T. Pham, "Relatedness, Prominence, and Constructive Sponsor Identification," *Journal of Marketing Research,* August 1999, pp. 299–312.

41. E. Cowley and M. Caldwell, "Truth, Lies, and Videotape," *Advances in Consumer Research,* vol. 28, eds. M. C. Gilly and J. Meyers-Levy (Provo, UT: Association for Consumer Research, 2001), pp. 20–25.

42. K. A. Braun, "Postexperience Advertising Effects on Consumer Memory," *Journal of Consumer Research,* March 1999, pp. 319–34.

43. See M. T. Pham and G. V. Johar, "Contingent Processes of Source Identification," *Journal of Consumer Research,* December 1997, pp. 249–66.

44. See E. J. Cowley, "Recovering Forgotten Information," in *Advances in Consumer Research,* vol. 21, eds. C. T. Allen and D. R. John (Provo, UT: Association for Consumer Research, 1994), pp. 58–63.

45. See S. E. Heckler, "The Role of Memory in Understanding and Encouraging Recycling Behavior," *Psychology & Marketing,* July 1994, pp. 375–92.

46. See D. Padgett and D. Allen, "Communicating Experiences," *Journal of Advertising,* Winter 1997, pp. 49–62; and W. R. Dillon et al., "Understanding What's in a Brand Rating," *Journal of Marketing Research,* November 2001, pp. 415–29.

47. S. M. J. Van Osselaer and J. W. Alba, "Consumer Learning and Brand Equity," *Journal of Consumer Research,* June 2000, pp. 1–16.

48. S. Thompson, "Meat Gets Branded," *Advertising Age,* September 24, 2001, p. 6.

49. See S. Ward, L. Light, and J. Goldstine, "What High-Tech Managers Need to Know about Brands," *Harvard Business Review,* July 1999, pp. 85–95.

50. J. Halliday, "Volvo Plans Ad Campaign to Clarify Automaker's Image," *Advertising Age,* October 9, 2000, p. 4.

51. For a differing view, see G. S. Carpenter, R. Glazer, and K. Nakamoto, "Meaningful Brands from Meaningless Differences," *Journal of Marketing Research,* August 1995, pp. 339–50.

52. B. Wansink, "Making Old Brands New," *American Demographics,* December 1998, pp. 53–58.

53. See V. Gerson, "Showing Customers Your Best Face," *Bank Marketing,* January 1999, pp. 26–30; and D. James, "Image Makeovers Require Gentle Touch," *Marketing News,* July 2, 2001, p. 4.

54. M. Cardona, "Block's Less Taxing Future," *Advertising Age,* January 15, 2001, p. 6.

55. J. Halliday, "New Q45 Effort," *Advertising Age,* March 2001, p. 8.

56. E. Bowes, "Faltering U.K. Retailer," *Advertising Age,* October 9, 200, p. 12.

57. See P. Feldwick, "What Is Brand Equity Anyway, and How Do You Measure It?" *Journal of the Market Research Society,* April 1996, pp. 85–104; P. K. Teas and T. H. Grapentine, "Demystifying Brand Equity," *Marketing Research,* Summer 1996, pp. 25–29; M. Supphellen, "Understanding Core Brand Equity," *International Journal of Marketing Research* 42, no. 3

(2000), pp. 319–38; M. M. Mackay, "Application of Brand Equity Service Measures in Service Markets," *Journal of Services Marketing* 15, no. 3 (2001), pp. 21–29; B. J. Krishnan and M. D. Hartline, "Brand Equity," *Journal of Services Marketing* 15, no. 5 (2001), pp. 328–42; M. Littman, "To Your Brand's Health," *American Demographics,* July 2001, pp. 37–39; and D. A. Aaker and R. Jacobson, "The Value of Brand Attitude in High-Technology Markets," *Journal of Marketing Research,* November 2001, pp. 485–93.

58. See P. Herbig, J. Milewicz, and J. Golden, "A Model of Reputation Building and Destruction," *Journal of Business Research,* September 1994, pp. 23–31.

59. C. J. Cobb-Walgren, C. A. Ruble, and N. Donthu, "Brand Equity, Brand Preference, and Purchase Intent," *Journal of Advertising,* Fall 1995, pp. 25–40; J. A. Quelch and D. Harding, "Brands versus Private Labels," *Harvard Business Review,* January 1996, pp. 99–109; S. J. Agres and T. M. Dubitsky, "Changing Needs for Brands," *Journal of Advertising Research,* January 1996, p. 30; M. K. Agarwal and V. R. Rao, "An Empirical Comparison of Consumer-Based Measures of Brand Equity," *Marketing Letters,* no. 3 (1996), pp. 237–47; E. Crowly and J. Zajas, "Evidence Supporting the Importance of Brands in Marketing Computer Products," *Journal of Professional Services Marketing,* no. 2 (1996), pp. 121–37; M. S. Sullivan, "How Brand Names Affect the Demand of Twin Automobiles," *Journal of Marketing Research,* May 1998, pp. 154–65; and N. Dawar and M. M. Pillutla, "Impact of Product-Harm Crises on Brand Equity," *Journal of Marketing Research,* May 2000, pp. 215–26.

60. See T. Erdem, "An Empirical Analysis of Umbrella Branding," *Journal of Marketing Research,* August 1998, pp. 339–51.

61. L. Freeman and P. Winters, "Franchise Players," *Advertising Age,* August 18, 1986, pp. 3, 61.

62. H. Schlossberg, "Slashing through Market Clutter," *Marketing News,* March 5, 1990, p. 6.

63. D. M. Boush, "Brand Name Effects on Interproduct Similarity Judgments," *Marketing Letters,* no. 4 (1997), pp. 419–27; B.-D. Kim and M. S. Sullivan, "The Effect of Parent Brand Experience on Line Extension Trial and Repeat Purchase," *Marketing Letters,* no. 2 (1998), pp. 181–93; S. Bridges, K. L. Keller, and S. Sood, "Communication Strategies for Brand Extensions," *Journal of Advertising,* Winter 2000, pp. 1–12; V. R. Lane, "The Impact of Ad Repetition and Ad Content on Consumer Perceptions of Incongruent Extensions," *Journal of Marketing,* April 2000, pp. 80–91; K. de Ruyter and M. Wetzels, "The Role of Corporate Image and Extension Similarity in Service Brand Extensions," *Journal of Economic Psychology* 21 (2000), pp. 639–59; G. Oakenfull et al., "Measuring Brand Meaning," *Journal of Advertising Research,* September 2000, pp. 43–53; and I. M. Martin and D. W. Stewart, "The Differential Impact of Goal Congruency on Attitiudes, Intentions, and the Transfer of Brand Equity"; and P. A. Bottomley and S. J. S. Holden, "Do We Really Know How Consumers Evaluate Brand Extensions?" both in *Journal of Marketing Research,* November 2001, pp. 471–84 and 494–500.

64. B. Forrest, "Two-Wheel Drives," *Men's Journal,* November 1996, p. 34.

65. See V. Lane and R. Jacobson, "The Reciprocal Impact of Brand Leveraging," *Marketing Letters,* no. 3 (1997), pp. 261–71; D. R. John, B. Loken, and C. Joiner, "The Negative Impact of Extensions," *Journal of Marketing,* January 1998, pp. 19–32; Z. Gurhan-Canli and D. Maheswaran, "The Effects of Extensions on Brand Name Dilution and Enhancement," *Journal of Marketing Research,* November 1998, pp. 464–73; M. Morrin, "The Impact of Brand Extensions on Parent Brand Memory Structures and Retrieval Processes," *Journal of Marketing Research,* November 1999, pp. 517–25; C. Janiszewski and S. M. J. van Osselaer, "A Connectionist Model of Brand-Quality Associations," *Journal of Marketing Research,* August 2000, pp. 331–50; and R. Ahluwalia and Z. Gurhan-Canli, "The Effects of Extensions on the Family Brand Name," *Journal of Consumer Research,* December 2000, pp. 371–81.

66. A. Kirmani, S. Sood, and S. Bridges, "The Ownership Effect in Consumer Response to Brand Line Stretches," *Journal of Marketing,* January 1999, pp. 88–101.

67. R. A. Peterson, K. H. Smith, and P. C. Zerrillo, "Trademark Dilution and the Practice of Marketing," *Journal of the Academy of Marketing Science,* Spring 1999, pp. 255–68. See also M. Morrin and J. Jacoby, "Trademark Dilution," *Journal of Public Policy & Marketing,* Fall 2000, pp. 265–76.

silver meshstream - Swiss made - www.swatch.com

swatch+
SKIN

THE ULTRAFLAT FROM SWATCH

Courtesy Swatch/SMH.

Motivation, Personality, and Emotion

☐ Nicolas Hayek performed what some consider to be a business miracle by changing SMH, today called the Swatch Group, the Swiss firm best known for its Swatch watch, from a $1.1 billion firm losing $124 million a year to a $2.7 billion firm making $336 million a year. His success was surprising because he ignored the conventional wisdom that firms must seek the countries with the lowest labor cost in which to produce products subject to global price competition. The Swatch Group is committed to its Swiss home base. The bulk of its technology, people, and production are centered in the Jura Mountains of Switzerland. As Hayek said, "We are all global companies competing in global markets. But that does not mean we owe no allegiance to our own societies and cultures." Parts of an interview with Hayek follow. The comments focus on the success of the Swatch watch line he created.

What did you see that others didn't?

I understood that we were not just selling a consumer product, or even a branded product. We were selling an emotional product. You wear a watch on your wrist, right against your skin. You have it there for 12 hours a day, maybe 24 hours a day. It can be an important part of your self-image. It doesn't have to be a commodity. It shouldn't be a commodity. I knew that if we could add genuine emotion to the product, and attack the low end with a strong message, we could succeed.

How do you "emotionalize" a watch? Do you mean to say that Swatch turned something that was mundane and functional into a fashion statement?

That is how most people describe what we did. But it's not quite right.

Fashion is important . . . . But take a trip to Hong Kong and look at the styles, the designs, the colors. They make pretty watches over there too.

We are not offering people a style. We are offering them a message. This is an absolutely critical point. Fashion is about image. Emotional products are about message—a strong, exciting, distinct, authentic message that tells people who you are and why you do what you do. There are many elements that make up the Swatch message. High quality. Low cost. Provocative. Joy of life. But the most important element of the Swatch message is the hardest for others to copy. Ultimately, we are not just offering watches. We are offering our personal culture.[1]

As Swatch illustrates, emotion can play an important role in consumer decisions and marketing strategies. This chapter focuses on emotion and two closely related concepts: motivation and personality. *Motivation* is the energizing force that activates behavior and provides purpose and direction to that behavior. *Personality* reflects the common responses (behaviors) that individuals make to a variety of recurring situations. *Emotions* are strong, relatively uncontrollable feelings that affect our behavior. The three concepts are closely interrelated and are frequently difficult to separate.

THE NATURE OF MOTIVATION

Water is inexpensive from municipal agencies, yet millions of consumers now pay 1,000 times the price of municipal water to purchase bottled water. While heavily advertised brands such as Perrier are well known, bulk water delivered to homes and offices in 5-gallon containers makes up half the market.

Why do consumers pay to purchase a nearly free item? There appear to be three major purchase motives. Health concerns focusing on nutrition and fitness motivate some users. These individuals want natural, untreated, "pure" water. Safety motivates other purchases. Many consumers are concerned with groundwater contamination and reports of deteriorating water quality. The third motivating factor is snob appeal or status. Ordering or serving Perrier is more chic and higher status than plain water. The marketing strategy implications of these differing motivations are

- *Safety*. Show danger of municipal water. Emphasize filtration, safe source, low price, and home/office delivery.
- *Health*. Emphasize purity and taste, no additives or treatments, moderate price, home/office delivery.
- *Status*. Emphasize quality, usage situations, exclusive taste, high price; retail, restaurant, and bar outlets.

Motivation is *the reason for behavior.* A **motive** is *a construct representing an unobservable inner force that stimulates and compels a behavioral response and provides specific direction to that response.* A motive is why an individual does something. As the example above illustrates, the motivations underlying the consumption of even a simple product like water can be quite complex.

There are numerous theories of motivation, and many of them offer useful insights for the marketing manager. This section describes two particularly useful approaches to understanding consumer motivation. The first approach, Maslow's need hierarchy, is a macro theory designed to account for most human behavior in general terms. The second approach, based on McGuire's work, uses a fairly detailed set of motives to account for specific aspects of consumer behavior.

Maslow's Hierarchy of Needs

Maslow's hierarchy of needs is based on four premises:[2]

1. All humans acquire a similar set of motives through genetic endowment and social interaction.
2. Some motives are more basic or critical than others.
3. The more basic motives must be satisfied to a minimum level before other motives are activated.
4. As the basic motives become satisfied, more advanced motives come into play.

Thus, Maslow proposed a need hierarchy shared by all. Table 10–1 illustrates this hierarchy, briefly describes each level, and provides marketing examples.

Maslow's theory is a good guide to general behavior. It is not an ironclad rule, however. Numerous examples exist of individuals who sacrificed their lives for friends or ideas, or who gave up food and shelter to seek self-actualization. However, we do tend to regard such behavior as exceptional, which indicates the general validity of Maslow's overall approach.[3] It is important to remember that any given consumption behavior can satisfy more than one need. Likewise, the same consumption behavior can satisfy different needs at different times. For example, a number of motives could cause one to join the National Guard. The ad in Illustration 10–1 appeals to self-actualization.

McGuire's Psychological Motives

Maslow presented a hierarchical set of five basic motives, and other researchers have proposed hundreds of additional, very specific motives. McGuire developed a classification system that organizes these various theories into 16 categories.[4] This system helps marketers isolate motives likely to be involved in various consumption situations. McGuire first divides motivation into four main categories using two criteria:

1. Is the mode of motivation cognitive or affective?
2. Is the motive focused on preservation of the status quo or on growth?

Cognitive motives focus on the person's need for being adaptively oriented toward the environment and achieving a sense of meaning. Affective motives deal with the need to reach satisfying feeling states and to obtain personal goals. Preservation-oriented motives emphasize the individual as striving to maintain equilibrium, while growth motives emphasize development.

TABLE 10-1	Marketing Strategies and Maslow's Need Hierarchy

I. Physiological: Food, water, sleep, and, to an extent, sex are physiological motives.

Products   Health foods, medicines, sports drinks, low-cholesterol foods, and exercise equipment.

Themes   Band-Aid—"Blister-proof your feet."
Quaker Oats—"Eating oatmeal is good for your heart."
NordicTrack—"Only NordicTrack gives you a total-body workout."

II. Safety: Seeking physical safety and security, stability, familiar surroundings, and so forth are manifestations of safety needs.

Products   Smoke detectors, preventive medicines, insurance, retirement investments, seat belts, burglar alarms, and sunscreen.

Themes   Sleep Safe—"We've designed a travel alarm that just might wake you in the middle of the night—because a fire is sending smoke into your room. You see, ours is a smoke alarm as well as an alarm clock."
Partnership for a Drug-Free America—"Heroin: Dying's the Easy Part."
Revo cycling glasses—"Should've worn Revo" under a picture of a wrecked bike.

III. Belongingness: Belongingness motives are reflected in a desire for love, friendship, affiliation, and group acceptance.

Products   Personal grooming, foods, entertainment, clothing, and many others.

Themes   Olive Garden Restaurants—"Italians didn't invent sharing. They just made it impossible to resist."
Tums—"You are important. You are loved. You should take your calcium."
JC Penney—"Wherever teens gather, you'll hear it. It's the language of terrific fit and fashion."

IV. Esteem: Desires for status, superiority, self-respect, and prestige are examples of esteem needs. These needs relate to the individual's feelings of usefulness and accomplishment.

Products   Clothing, furniture, liquors, hobbies, stores, cars, and many others.

Themes   Sheaffer—"Your hand should look as contemporary as the rest of you."
New Balance—"One more woman chasing a sunset. One more woman going a little farther. One more woman simply feeling alive. One less woman relying on someone else."
Cadillac—"Those long hours have paid off. In recognition, financial success, and in the way you reward yourself. Isn't it time you owned a Cadillac?"

V. Self-actualization: This involves the desire for self-fulfillment, to become all that one is capable of becoming.

Products   Education, hobbies, sports, some vacations, gourmet foods, and museums.

Themes   U.S. Army—"Be all you can be."
Avia—"She wasn't just training her body, she was training her mind."
Outward Bound School—"Challenges, adventure, growth."

These four main categories are then further subdivided on the bases of source and objective of the motive:

3. Is this behavior actively initiated or in response to the environment?
4. Does this behavior help the individual achieve a new internal state or a new external relationship to the environment?

The third criterion distinguishes between motives that are actively or internally aroused versus those that are a more passive response to circumstances. The final criterion is used to categorize outcomes that are internal to the individual and those focused on a relationship with the environment.

Each of McGuire's 16 motives and their implications for marketing are briefly described in the following sections.

Cognitive Preservation Motives

Need for Consistency (active, internal)   A basic desire is to have all facets or parts of oneself consistent with each other.[5] These facets include attitudes, behaviors, opinions,

ILLUSTRATION 10–1

Appeals to self-actualization focus on individuals challenging themselves and reaching their full potential.

self-images, views of others, and so forth. *Cognitive dissonance* is a common motive of this type. Often making a major purchase is not consistent with the need to save money, to make other purchases, or to purchase a different brand with desirable features not in the purchased brand. This inconsistency motivates the individual to reduce it. How this is done is covered in depth in Chapter 18.

Understanding the need for consistency is also important for structuring advertising messages and developing attitude change strategies. Consumers have a need for internal consistency, so they are reluctant to accept information that disagrees with existing beliefs. Thus, marketers wishing to change attitudes must use highly credible sources or other techniques to overcome this (see Chapter 11).

Need for Attribution (active, external)   This set of motives deals with our need to determine who or what causes the things that happen to us. Do we attribute the cause of a favorable or unfavorable outcome to ourselves or to some outside force?

The fact that consumers need to attribute cause underlies an area of research known as **attribution theory.**[6] This approach to understanding the reasons consumers assign particular meanings to the behaviors of others has been used primarily for analyzing consumer reactions to promotional messages (in terms of credibility). When consumers attribute a sales motive to advice given by a salesperson or advertising message, they tend to discount the advice. In contrast, similar advice given by a friend would likely be attributed to a desire to be helpful and might therefore be accepted.

Courtesy Timex Corporation; Photo by: Platon.

Because consumers do not passively receive messages but rather attribute sales motives and tactics to ads and the advice of sales personnel, they do not believe or they discount many of these messages.[7] Marketers use a variety of means to overcome this. One approach is to use a credible spokesperson in the ads, such as in Illustration 10–2. This technique is discussed in depth in Chapter 11.

Need to Categorize (passive, internal)   People have a need to categorize and organize the vast array of information and experiences they encounter in a meaningful yet manageable way.[8] So they establish categories or mental partitions that allow them to process large quantities of information. Prices are often categorized such that different prices connote different categories of goods. Automobiles over $20,000 and automobiles under $20,000 may elicit two different meanings because of information categorized on the basis of price level. Many firms price items at $9.95, $19.95, $49.95, and so forth. One reason is to avoid being categorized in the over $10, $20, or $50 group.

Need for Objectification (passive, external)   These motives reflect needs for observable cues or symbols that enable people to infer what they feel and know. Impressions, feelings, and attitudes are subtly established by viewing one's own behavior and that of others and drawing inferences as to what one feels and thinks. In many instances, clothing plays an important role in presenting the subtle meaning of a desired image and consumer lifestyle. This is so critical that companies such as Anheuser-Busch use clothing consulting firms to tailor clothes for executives that are consistent with the firm's desired image.

Courtesy Windsor Fashion.

ILLUSTRATION 10–3

Americans respond positively to ads and products that encourage uniqueness and individuality.

Cognitive Growth Motives

Need for Autonomy (active, internal)   The need for independence and individuality is a characteristic of the American culture, as described in Chapter 2. All individuals in all cultures have this need at some level. Americans are taught that it is proper and even essential to express and fulfill this need. In contrast, in countries such as Japan, fulfillment of this need is discouraged, while fulfillment of the need for affiliation is more socially acceptable.

Owning or using products and services that are unique is one way consumers express their autonomy.[9] The increasing popularity of handmade craft goods, original art, antiques, and other unique products reflects this need. Marketers have responded to this motive by developing limited editions of products and providing wide variety and customization options. In addition, many products are advertised and positioned with independence, uniqueness, or individuality themes, as shown in Illustration 10–3.

Need for Stimulation (active, external)   People often seek variety and difference out of a need for stimulation.[10] Such variety-seeking behavior may be a prime reason for brand switching and some so-called impulse purchasing.[11] The need for stimulation is curvilinear and changes over time.[12] That is, individuals experiencing rapid change generally become satiated and desire stability, whereas individuals in stable environments become bored and desire change.

Today's hurried lifestyles often produce uncomfortable levels of tension. Products that relieve this stress fulfill a fundamental need.

Courtesy Rosemary Beach.

Teleological Need (passive, internal)   Consumers are pattern matchers who have images of desired outcomes or end states to which they compare their current situation. Behaviors are changed and the results are monitored in terms of movement toward the desired end state. This motive propels people to prefer mass media such as movies, television programs, and books with outcomes that match their view of how the world should work (the good guys win, the hero and heroine get together, and so forth). This has obvious implications for advertising messages.

Utilitarian Need (passive, external)   These theories view the consumer as a problem solver who approaches situations as opportunities to acquire useful information or new skills. Thus, a consumer watching a situation comedy on television not only is being entertained but is learning clothing styles, etiquette, lifestyle options, and so forth. Likewise, consumers may approach ads, salespeople, and other marketing stimuli as a source of learning for future decisions as well as for the current one.

Affective Preservation Motives

Need for Tension Reduction (active, internal)   People encounter situations in their daily lives that create uncomfortable levels of stress. In order to effectively manage tension and stress, people are motivated to seek ways to reduce arousal. Recreational products and activities are often promoted in terms of tension relief. Illustration 10-4 contains a product and appeal focused on this need.

Need for Expression (active, external)   This motive deals with the need to express one's identity to others. People feel the need to let others know who and what they are by their actions, which include the purchase and use of goods. The purchase of many products such as clothing and automobiles allows consumers to express an identity to others, because

Weider Nutrition International, Inc.

these products have symbolic or expressive meanings. Thus, the purchase of the latest in skiwear may reflect much more than a desire to remain warm while skiing. The Swatch example in the chapter-opening vignette relates directly to this need.

Need for Ego Defense (passive, internal)   The need to defend one's identity or ego is another important motive. When one's identity is threatened, the person is motivated to protect his or her self-concept and utilize defensive behaviors and attitudes. Many products can provide ego defense. A consumer who feels insecure may rely on well-known brands for socially visible products to avoid any chance of making a socially incorrect purchase.

Need for Reinforcement (passive, external)   People are often motivated to act in certain ways because they were rewarded for behaving that way in similar situations in the past. This is the basis for operant learning as described in the previous chapter. Products designed to be used in public situations (clothing, furniture, and artwork) are frequently sold on the basis of the amount and type of reinforcement that will be received. Keepsake Diamonds exploits this motive with an advertisement that states, "Enter a room and you are immediately surrounded by friends sharing your excitement."

Affective Growth Motives

Need for Assertion (active, internal)   Many people are competitive achievers who seek success, admiration, and dominance. Important to them are power, accomplishment, and esteem. As Illustration 10–5 shows, the need for assertion underlies numerous ads.

Need for Affiliation (active, external)   Affiliation is the need to develop mutually helpful and satisfying relationships with others. It relates to altruism and seeking acceptance and affection in interpersonal relations. As we saw in Chapter 6, group membership is a critical part of most consumers' lives, and many consumer decisions are based on the need to maintain satisfying relationships with others. Marketers frequently use such affiliation-based themes as "Your kids will love you for it" in advertisements.[13]

Need for Identification (passive, internal)   The need for identification results in the consumer playing various roles. A person may play the role of college student, sorority member, bookstore employee, fiancée, and many others. One gains pleasure from adding new, satisfying roles and by increasing the significance of roles already adopted. Marketers encourage consumers to assume new roles (become a skateboarder) and position products as critical for certain roles ("No working mother should be without one").

Need for Modeling (passive, external)   The need for modeling reflects a tendency to base behavior on that of others. Modeling is a major means by which children learn to become consumers. The tendency to model explains some of the conformity that occurs within reference groups. Marketers utilize this motive by showing desirable types of individuals using their brands. For example, some Rolex ads devote most of their copy to a description of very successful people such as Picabo Street or Monica Kristensen. They then state that this person owns a Rolex.

MOTIVATION THEORY AND MARKETING STRATEGY

Beck's and Heineken are imported beers that are consumed primarily by confident, upscale, professional men. However, BBDO (a major advertising agency) found through its motivation research that Heineken consumption is driven by a desire for status, whereas Beck's is associated with a desire for individuality. Likewise, both Classico and Newman's Own spaghetti sauces are consumed by upscale, sophisticated adults. However, Classico buyers are motivated by indulgence and romance while Newman's Own buyers are showing ambition and individuality. Since the purchase of each of these brands is caused by a different motive, each requires a distinct marketing and advertising program.[14]

Consumers do not buy products; instead, they buy motive satisfaction or problem solutions. Thus, consumers do not buy perfume or cologne (or a chemical compound with certain odoriferous characteristics). Instead, they buy romance, sex appeal, sensual pleasure, sophistication, or a host of other emotional and psychological benefits. Managers must discover the motives that their products and brands can satisfy and develop marketing mixes around these motives.

As an example, consumers often buy products and services as gifts for themselves, though they may feel some guilt at being self-indulgent. Motivation research has found that people make such purchases for a variety of motives, including rewarding themselves for an accomplishment.[15] Consistent with this research, Keepsake has run advertising campaigns emphasizing the appropriateness of self-gifts of diamond jewelry as a reward.

The preceding section provided a number of examples of firms appealing to specific consumer motives. We often find that multiple motives are involved in consumption behavior. In the following sections, we examine (1) how to discover which motives are likely to affect the purchase of a product category or brand, (2) how to develop strategy based on the total array of motives that are operating, and (3) how to reduce conflict between motives.

Discovering Purchase Motives

Suppose a marketing researcher asked a consumer why he wears Gap clothes (or owns a mountain bike, or uses cologne, or whatever). Odds are the consumer would offer several

FIGURE 10–1	Latent and Manifest Motives in a Purchase Situation

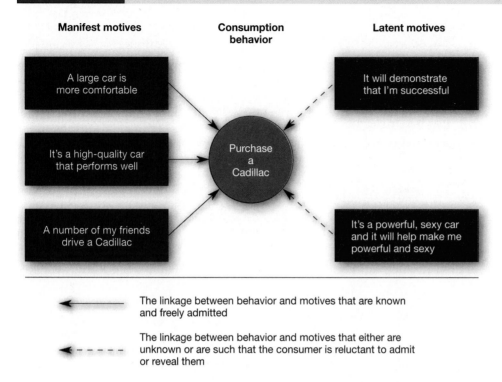

Manifest motives

A large car is more comfortable

It's a high-quality car that performs well

A number of my friends drive a Cadillac

Consumption behavior

Purchase a Cadillac

Latent motives

It will demonstrate that I'm successful

It's a powerful, sexy car and it will help make me powerful and sexy

⬅——— The linkage between behavior and motives that are known and freely admitted

⬅- - - - - The linkage between behavior and motives that either are unknown or are such that the consumer is reluctant to admit or reveal them

reasons, such as "They're in style," "My friends wear them," "I like the way they fit," or "They look good on me." However, there may be other reasons that the consumer is reluctant to admit or perhaps is not even aware of: "They show that I have money," "They make me sexually desirable," or "They show I'm still young." All or any combination of the above motives could influence the purchase of clothes or many other items.

The first group of motives mentioned above were known to the consumer and admitted to the researcher. Motives that are known and freely admitted are called **manifest motives.** Any of the motives we have discussed can be manifest; however, motives that conform to a society's prevailing value system are more likely to be manifest than are those in conflict with such values.

The second group of motives described above either were unknown to the consumer or were such that he was reluctant to admit them. Such motives are **latent motives.** Figure 10–1 illustrates how the two types of motives might influence a purchase.

Given that a variety of manifest and latent motives may be operative in a particular purchase such as that shown in Figure 10–1, the first task of the marketing manager is to determine the combination of motives influencing the target market. Manifest motives are relatively easy to determine. Direct questions (Why did you buy a Cadillac?) will generally produce reasonably accurate assessments of manifest motives.[16]

Determining latent motives is substantially more complex. Sophisticated analytical techniques such as multidimensional scaling can sometimes provide insights into latent motives. Motivation research or **projective techniques** are designed to provide information on latent motives. Table 10–2 describes some of the more common projective techniques.

These techniques are used to enhance and enrich the insights that can be gained from more empirical sources. For example, Oreo used projective techniques in a focus group setting to gain a fuller understanding of the brand: "We had always known that Oreo

TABLE 10–2		
I. Association Techniques		
Word association	Consumers respond to a list of words with the first word that comes to mind.	
Successive word association	Consumers give the series of words that come to mind after hearing each word on the list.	
Analysis and use	Responses are analyzed to see if negative associations exist. When the time to respond (response latency) is also measured, the emotionality of the word can be estimated. These techniques tap semantic memory more than motives and are used for brand name and advertising copy tests.	
II. Completion Techniques		
Sentence completion	Consumers complete a sentence such as "People who buy a Cadillac _____ _____."	
Story completion	Consumers complete a partial story.	
Analysis and use	Responses are analyzed to determine what themes are expressed. Content analysis—examining responses for themes and key concepts—is used.	
III. Construction Techniques		
Cartoon techniques	Consumers fill in the words or thoughts of one of the characters in a cartoon drawing.	
Third-person techniques	Consumers tell why "an average woman," "most doctors," or "people in general" purchase or use a certain product. Shopping lists (describe a person who would go shopping with this list) and lost wallets (describe a person with these items in his wallet) are also third-person techniques.	
Picture response	Consumers tell a story about a person shown buying or using a product in a picture or line drawing.	
Analysis and use	Same as for completion techniques.	

Motivation Research Techniques

evoked strong emotions but what surprised us in these focus groups was that many regarded Oreo as almost 'magical.'" As a result, "Unlocking the Magic of Oreo" became a campaign theme.[17]

Not only are the traditional projective techniques being used at an increasing rate, but new approaches are being developed.[18] One popular approach is **laddering,** or constructing a **means-end** or **benefit chain.**[19] A product or brand is shown to a consumer who names all the benefits that possession or use of that product might provide. Then for each benefit mentioned, the respondent is asked to identify further benefits that the named benefit provides. This is repeated for each round of benefits until the consumer can no longer identify additional benefits.

For example, a respondent might mention "fewer colds" as a benefit of taking a daily vitamin. When asked the benefit of fewer colds, one respondent might identify "more efficient at work" and "more energy." Another might name "more skiing" and "looking better." Both use the vitamin to reduce colds but as a means to different ultimate benefits. *How should vitamin ads aimed at each of these two consumers differ?*

Marketing Strategies Based on Multiple Motives

Once a manager has isolated the combination of motives influencing the target market, the next task is to design the marketing strategy around the appropriate set of motives. This involves everything from product design to marketing communications. The nature of

Courtesy Toyota Motor Sales U.S.A., Inc.

these decisions is most apparent in the communications area. Suppose the motives shown in Figure 10–1 are an accurate reflection of a desired target market. *What communications strategy should the manager use?*

First, to the extent that more than one motive is important, the product must provide more than one benefit and the advertising for the product must communicate these multiple benefits. Communicating manifest benefits is relatively easy. For example, an advertisement for Cadillac states, "From the triple-sanded finish (once with water and twice with oil) to that superbly refined Cadillac ride, the quality comes standard on Cadillac." This is a direct appeal to a manifest motive for product quality. Direct appeals are generally effective for manifest motives, since these are motives that consumers are aware of and will discuss.

However, since latent motives often are less than completely socially desirable, indirect appeals frequently are used. The bulk of the copy of the Cadillac ad referred to above focuses on the quality of the product. However, the artwork (about 60 percent of the ad) shows the car being driven by an apparently wealthy individual in front of a luxurious club. This is a dual appeal. The direct appeal in the copy focuses on quality, while the indirect appeal in the artwork focuses on status.

While any given advertisement for a product may focus on only one or a few purchasing motives, the campaign needs to cover all the important purchase motives of the target market. In essence, the overall campaign attempts to position the product in the schematic memory of the target market in a manner that corresponds with the target market's manifest and latent motives for purchasing the product. *To what motives does the ad shown in Illustration 10–6 appeal?*

Marketing Strategies Based on Motivation Conflict

With the many motives consumers have and the many situations in which these motives are activated, there are frequent conflicts between motives. The resolution of a motivational conflict often affects consumption patterns. In many instances, the marketer can analyze situations that are likely to result in a motivational conflict, provide a solution to the conflict, and attract the patronage of those consumers facing the motivational conflict. There are three types of motivational conflict of importance to marketing managers: approach–approach conflict, approach–avoidance conflict, and avoidance–avoidance conflict.

Approach–Approach Motivational Conflict   A consumer who must choose between two attractive alternatives faces **approach–approach conflict.** The more equal this attraction, the greater the conflict. A consumer who recently received a large cash gift for graduation (situational variable) might be torn between a trip to Hawaii (perhaps powered by a need for stimulation) and a new mountain bike (perhaps driven by the need for assertion). This conflict could be resolved by a timely advertisement designed to encourage one or the other action. Or a price modification, such as "buy now, pay later," could result in a resolution whereby both alternatives are selected.

Approach–Avoidance Motivational Conflict   A consumer facing a purchase choice with both positive and negative consequences confronts **approach–avoidance conflict.** A person who is concerned about gaining weight yet likes snack foods faces this type of problem. He or she may want the taste and emotional satisfaction associated with the snacks (approach) but does not want to gain weight (avoidance). The development of lower-calorie snack foods reduces this conflict and allows the weight-sensitive consumer to enjoy snacks and also control calorie intake. Similarly, many consumers want a tan but don't want to risk the skin damage and health risks associated with extended sun exposure. Neutrogena's Instant Bronze sunless tanner resolves this problem.

Avoidance–Avoidance Motivational Conflict   A choice involving only undesirable outcomes produces **avoidance–avoidance conflict.** When a consumer's old washing machine fails, this conflict may occur. The person may not want to spend money on a new washing machine, or pay to have the old one repaired, or go without one. The availability of credit is one way of reducing this motivational conflict. Advertisements emphasizing the importance of regular maintenance for cars, such as oil filter changes, also use this type of motive conflict: "Pay me now, or pay me (more) later."

Do Marketers Create Needs?

Marketers are often accused of creating a need for a product that would not exist except for marketing activities, particularly advertising. Mouthwash, deodorant, and jet skis are used as examples of products for which there would be no need had not advertising created one.

Do marketers create needs? The answer depends in part on what is meant by the term *need.* If it is used to refer to a basic motive such as those described earlier in this chapter, it is clear that marketers seldom if ever create a need. Human genetics and the general experiences all humans encounter as they mature basically determine human motives. An analysis of literature and myths across cultures and centuries reveals a remarkably consistent set of human motives.

These common motives involve much more than the first two levels of Maslow's need hierarchy. Long before marketing or advertising appeared, individuals used perfumes, clothing, and other items to gain acceptance, display status, and so forth. Marketing and advertising are not the cause of these basic human motives.

However, marketers do create **demand.** Demand is *the willingness to buy a particular product or service.* It is caused by a need or motive, but it is not the motive. For example, advertising has helped create a demand for mouthwash. One way some firms did this was to indicate that without mouthwash, one would have bad breath, and if you had bad breath, people would not like you. This message ties mouthwash to the need for affiliation or belongingness. It does not create the need for affiliation but suggests that using a certain brand of mouthwash is essential for satisfying this need. In so doing, the marketer hopes to create demand for the brand.

Given the definitions above, marketers do not create needs. This does not mean that there are not ethical issues involved in how marketers create demand as well as in the consequences of the demand that is created. Critics feel that creating demand by emphasizing threats to consumers' esteem or affiliation needs is unethical. For example, the headline in an ad for Retin-A states, "My mom thought I was beautiful (pimples and all) but you can't date your mom." Critics would argue that such ads unduly play on the insecurities of young women in order to generate demand for the brand.

PERSONALITY

While motivations are the energizing and directing force that makes consumer behavior purposeful and goal directed, the personality of the consumer guides and directs the behavior chosen to accomplish goals in different situations. **Personality** is *an individual's characteristic response tendencies across similar situations.*

If someone asked you, "What is your dad like?" it is unlikely that you would describe him in terms of demographics. Instead, you would probably use a combination of physical features and personality characteristics. We can easily describe the personalities of our family members and friends. For example, you might say that one of your friends is fairly aggressive, competitive, outgoing, and witty. What you have described are the behaviors your friend has exhibited over time across a variety of situations. These characteristic ways of responding to a wide range of situations should, of course, also include responses to marketing strategies.

While there are many personality theories, all have two common assumptions: (1) all individuals have internal characteristics or traits, and (2) there are consistent and measurable differences between individuals on those characteristics. Most of these theories state that the traits or characteristics are inherited or formed at an early age and are relatively unchanging over the years. Differences between personality theories center on the definition of which traits or characteristics are the most important.

Single-trait theories emphasize one personality trait as being particularly relevant to understanding a particular set of behaviors. They do not suggest that other traits do not exist or are not important; rather, they study a single trait for its relevance to a set of behaviors, in our case, consumption-related behaviors. Some examples of single-trait theories that have been shown to be relevant to marketing are those that deal with neuroticism,[20] consumer conformity,[21] vanity,[22] affect intensity,[23] trait anxiety,[24] locus of control, sensation seeking,[25] self-monitoring,[26] and the need for cognitive closure.[27]

The most widely studied single-trait theory is described in Consumer Insight 10–1. Two others are described next.

Individuals differ in their tendency to engage in and enjoy thinking.[28] Some have a stronger need to understand and make sense out of the world they experience than do others. This is known as the *need for cognition (NFC)*. High-NFC individuals intrinsically enjoy thinking, whereas low-NFC individuals tend to avoid effortful cognitive work. Low-NFC consumers are fully able to process information and differentiate cogent from specious arguments, but they typically prefer to avoid the effortful cognitive work required to derive their attitudes on the merits of the arguments presented.

Because the NFC varies across consumers, it is considered to be a personality trait. Cacioppo and Petty have developed a widely used scale to measure the NFC. The instrument consists of 18 statements that respondents use to characterize themselves. Some of the statements used are "I really enjoy a task that involves coming up with new solutions to problems" and "I like tasks that require little thought once I've learned them."

Research has found that, compared to low-NFC individuals, those high in NFC (1) search for more information when making decisions, (2) engage in more effortful processing of persuasive communications, (3) are more open-minded, (4) enjoy more effortful cognitive tasks, (5) develop more complex causal explanations for the behaviors of others, (6) hold attitudes that are more persistent over time, (7) devote more topic-relevant thought to persuasive communications, (8) consider a wider range of prices in purchase decisions, (9) prefer verbal to visual information, and (10) are less swayed by the opinions of others and expert sources.

Critical Thinking Questions

1. What problems and issues would arise in segmenting a market into high- and low-NFC segments?

2. What implications does each of the 10 research findings described above have for marketing practice?

3. How do you think media preferences would vary between high- and low-NFC consumers?

Romanticism/classicism is a personality variable that offers useful potential to marketers. Romantics are characterized by being inspirational, imaginative, creative, and intuitive. Feelings rather than facts predominate. Classics tend to be straightforward, unadorned, unemotional, economical, and carefully proportional. One study using MBA students as respondents found that those classified as romantics preferred vacations involving warm weather destinations and risky activities such as hang gliding, compared with those categorized as classics.[29] *For what other product categories do you think these two groups would have differing preferences?*

Another single-trait theory of use to marketers is termed *consumers' need for uniqueness*. It is defined as an individual's pursuit of differentness relative to others that is achieved through the acquisition, utilization, and disposition of consumer goods for the purpose of developing and enhancing one's personal and social identity.[30] It affects what consumers own and value, why they own it, and how they use it. The concept fits with the increasingly common marketing practice of deliberate scarcity—producing less of an item than the predicted demand. Such a strategy helps preserve the uniqueness of the product and enhances the distinctiveness and status of those who own it.

In contrast to a single-trait theory, a *multitrait personality theory* specifies several traits that in combination capture a substantial portion of the personality of the individual. The multitrait theory used most commonly by marketers is the **Five-Factor Model** of personality.[31] This theory identifies five basic traits that are formed by genetics and early

Core Trait	Manifestation
Extroversion	Prefer to be in a large group rather than alone Talkative when with others Bold
Instability	Moody Temperamental Touchy
Agreeableness	Sympathetic Kind to others Polite with others
Openness to experience	Imaginative Appreciative of art Find novel solutions
Conscientiousness	Careful Precise Efficient

TABLE 10–3

The Five-Factor
Model of Personality

learning. These core traits interact and manifest themselves in behaviors triggered by situations. Table 10–3 lists the five traits and some of their manifestations.

The Five-Factor Model has proven useful in such areas as understanding bargaining and complaining behavior[32] and compulsive shopping.[33] There is evidence that it may have validity across cultures.[34] The advantage of a multitrait approach such as this is the fuller picture it allows of the determinants of behavior. For example, suppose research focused on the single dimension of extroversion and found that those who complained about a dissatisfactory purchase tended to be extroverts. *What insights does this provide for training those who deal with consumer complaints? What training insights are added if we also learn such people are conscientious?* Clearly, the more we know, the better we can satisfy these customers.

THE USE OF PERSONALITY IN MARKETING PRACTICE

Often consumers use products to bolster an area of their personality. Thus, a timid person might drive a powerful car. While driving the car, this person might feel less timid and more powerful. However, another timid person might forgo a powerful or flashy car because "it's just not me." Consider one consumer's explanation of why she did not purchase the conservative clothing she felt was most suitable for her work:

> ELLA: You still have your personality when you're shopping. And I think a part of my personality is something like, "Wow, get the Carole Little" (a colorful line of clothing).
>
> INTERVIEWER: So you think your clothes are an expression of yourself?
>
> ELLA: Oh sure, yeah. It tells a lot about your personality.[35]

In the previous chapter, we described brand image as what people think of and feel when they hear or see a brand name. A particular type of image that some brands acquire

FIGURE 10–2   Dimensions of Brand Personality

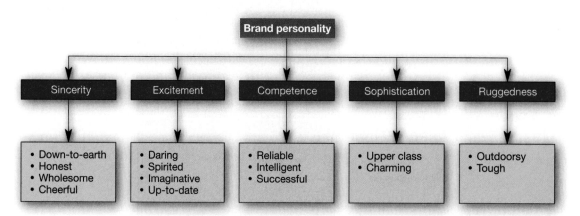

Source: J. L. Aaker, "Dimensions of Brand Personality," *Journal of Marketing Research,* August 1997, p. 352. Published by the American Marketing Association; reprinted with permission.

is a **brand personality.** Brand personality is *a set of human characteristics that become associated with a brand.* Consumers perceive brand personalities in terms of five basic dimensions, each with several facets as shown in Figure 10–2. A 42-item Likert scale has been developed to measure brand personality on these dimensions.[36] Stores, malls, websites, and geographic areas such as cities and regions can also acquire personalities.[37]

Brands acquire personalities whether marketers want them to or not, and these personalities influence purchases. Therefore, marketers need to manage the personalities of their brands. Here is how the head of the Swatch Group (maker of Swatch, Omega, and numerous other brands) views it:

> My job is to sit in the bunker with a machine gun defending the distinct messages of all my brands. I am the custodian of our messages. I review every new communications campaign for every single brand.[38]

Marketers are paying increasing attention to brand personalities. For example, Chrysler began trying to establish unique personalities for each of its car brands with the 1997 models, and Ford began enhancing the personalities of its products in 1999.[39]

Researchers at Whirlpool Corp. reached the following conclusions concerning brand personalities:[40]

* Consumers readily assign human characteristics to brands even if the brands are not managed or the characteristics are not wanted by the marketers.
* Brand personalities create expectations about key characteristics, performance and benefits, and related services.
* Brand personalities are often the basis for a long-term relationship with the brand.

This research found the following brand personality profiles, including a description of what type of person the brand would be if it were human and what it would do and like, for a Whirlpool and a KitchenAid appliance (the larger the score, the more that trait is

ILLUSTRATION 10–7

People assign personalities to brands whether marketers want them to or not. Therefore, marketing managers increasingly try to manage the brand personalities of their products.

associated with the brand):

Whirlpool	KitchenAid
Gentle (146)	Sophisticated (206)
Sensitive (128)	Glamorous (186)
Quiet (117)	Wealthy (180)
Good natured (114)	Elegant (178)
30 years old (125)	30 years old (135)
1970s (140)	1990s (167)
Cosmo (132)	Cosmo (136)
Sailing (125)	Theater (124)
Jazz (118)	Classical (126)

The difference in the personality consumers assign to these brands is obvious. *What type of target market will each appeal to?*

Research conducted by Kraft Foods revealed that consumers assign distinct personalities to the various flavors of LifeSavers candies.[41] The firm decided to reinforce these brand/flavor personalities with a major advertising campaign. The ad copy for cherry and for a new sour and sweet version targeting teens is:

ms. popularity
always the first one picked,
cherry has taste and beauty.
and she knows it. tends to
act innocent. she isn't.

the troublemaker
he likes it sour. sun in your eye sour.
monster wedgie sour. and THEN,
all of a sudden, he goes
sweet on you. what gives?

What type of brand personality is being created by the ad in Illustration 10–7?

EMOTION

Earlier, we defined **emotion** as *strong, relatively uncontrolled feelings that affect behavior.*[42] All of us experience a wide array of emotions. Think for a moment about a recent emotional experience. What characterized this experience? All emotional experiences tend to have several elements in common. Emotions are generally triggered by *environmental events.* Anger, joy, and sadness are most frequently a response to a set of external events. However, we can also initiate emotional reactions by *internal processes* such as imagery. Athletes frequently use imagery to "psych" themselves into a desired emotional state.

Emotions are accompanied by *physiological changes.* Some characteristic changes are (1) eye pupil dilation, (2) increased perspiration, (3) more rapid breathing, (4) increased heart rate and blood pressure, and (5) enhanced blood sugar level.

Another characteristic feature of an emotional experience is *cognitive thought.* Emotions generally, though not necessarily, are accompanied by thinking.[43] The types of thoughts and our ability to think rationally vary with the type and degree of emotion.[44] Extreme emotional responses are frequently used as an explanation for inappropriate thoughts or actions: "I was so mad I couldn't think straight."

Emotions also have associated *behaviors.* While the behaviors vary across individuals and within individuals across time and situations, there are unique behaviors characteristically associated with different emotions: fear triggers fleeing responses, anger triggers striking out, grief triggers crying, and so forth.

Finally, emotions involve *subjective feelings.* In fact, it is the feeling component we generally refer to when we think of emotions. Grief, joy, anger, jealousy, and fear feel very different to us. These subjectively determined feelings are the essence of emotion.

These feelings have a specific component that we label as the emotion, such as sad or happy. In addition, emotions carry an evaluative or a like/dislike component. We use *emotion* to refer to the identifiable, specific feeling, and *affect* to refer to the liking/disliking aspect of the specific feeling. Emotions are generally evaluated (liked and disliked) in a consistent manner across individuals and within individuals over time, but there are cultural, individual, and situational variations.[45] For example, few of us generally want to be sad or afraid, yet we occasionally enjoy a movie or book that scares or saddens us.

Figure 10–3 reflects current thinking on the nature of emotions.

FIGURE 10–3	Nature of Emotions

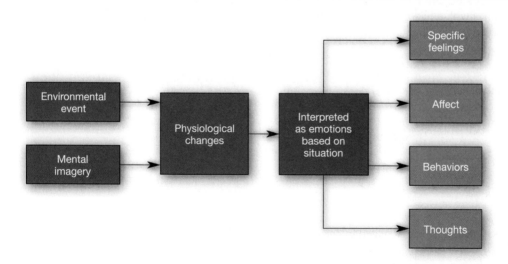

Dimension	Emotion	Indicator/Feeling
Pleasure	Duty	Moral, virtuous, dutiful
	Faith	Reverent, worshipful, spiritual
	Pride	Proud, superior, worthy
	Affection	Loving, affectionate, friendly
	Innocence	Innocent, pure, blameless
	Gratitude	Grateful, thankful, appreciative
	Serenity	Restful, serene, comfortable, soothed
	Desire	Desirous, wishful, craving, hopeful
	Joy	Joyful, happy, delighted, pleased
	Competence	Confident, in control, competent
Arousal	Interest	Attentive, curious
	Hypoactivation	Bored, drowsy, sluggish
	Activation	Aroused, active, excited
	Surprise	Surprised, annoyed, astonished
	Déjà vu	Unimpressed, uninformed, unexcited
	Involvement	Involved, informed, enlightened, benefited
	Distraction	Distracted, preoccupied, inattentive
	Surgency	Playful, entertained, lighthearted
	Contempt	Scornful, contemptuous, disdainful
Dominance	Conflict	Tense, frustrated, conflictful
	Guilt	Guilty, remorseful, regretful
	Helplessness	Powerless, helpless, dominated
	Sadness	Sad, distressed, sorrowful, dejected
	Fear	Fearful, afraid, anxious
	Shame	Ashamed, embarrassed, humiliated
	Anger	Angry, agitated, enraged, mad
	Hyperactivation	Panicked, confused, overstimulated
	Disgust	Disgusted, revolted, annoyed, full of loathing
	Skepticism	Skeptical, suspicious, distrustful

TABLE 10–4

Emotional Dimensions, Emotions, and Emotional Indicators

Source: Adapted with permission from M. B. Holbrook and R. Batra, "Assessing the Role of Emotions on Consumer Responses to Advertising," *Journal of Consumer Research,* December 1987, pp. 404–20. Copyright © 1987 by the University of Chicago.

Types of Emotion

If asked, you could doubtless name numerous emotions and your friends could name others that did not appear on your list. Thus, it is not surprising that researchers have attempted to categorize emotions into manageable clusters. Some researchers have suggested that three basic dimensions—pleasure, arousal, and dominance (PAD)—underlie all emotions. Specific emotions reflect various combinations and levels of these three dimensions. Table 10–4 lists the three primary PAD dimensions, a variety of emotions or emotional categories associated with each dimension, and indicators or items that can be used to measure each emotion.

EMOTIONS AND MARKETING STRATEGY

This chapter's opening vignette illustrates how Swatch achieved substantial success in part by positioning the brand in emotional terms. Although marketers have always used emotions to guide product positioning, sales presentations, and advertising on an intuitive level, the deliberate, systematic study of the relevance of emotions in marketing strategy is relatively new. For example, salespeople and other service providers frequently must deal with consumers displaying an array of emotions. Only recently have marketers developed sufficient understanding to create systematic training programs related to responding to emotional consumers.[46]

In this section, we will briefly describe strategies focused on emotion arousal as a product benefit, emotion reduction as a product benefit, emotion arousal in the context of advertising, and measuring emotional responses.

Emotion Arousal as a Product Benefit

Emotions are characterized by positive or negative evaluations. Consumers actively seek products whose primary or secondary benefit is emotion arousal.[47] Although consumers seek positive emotions the majority of the time, this is not always the case. ("The movie was so sad, I cried and cried. I loved it. You should see it.")

Many products feature emotion arousal as a primary benefit. Movies, books, and music are the most obvious examples.[48] Las Vegas, Atlantic City, and Disney World are positioned as emotion-arousing destinations, as are various types of adventure travel programs. Long-distance telephone calls have been positioned as emotion-arousing products ("Reach out and touch someone"). Several brands of soft drinks emphasize excitement and fun as primary benefits. Even automobiles are sometimes positioned as emotion-arousing products: Toyota—"Oh What a Feeling"; and Pontiac—"We Build Excitement." Stores feature events and environments that arouse emotions such as excitement.[49]

Products often arouse emotions in ways unintended by marketers. Most of us have experienced emotions such as frustration and anger as we have tried to assemble toys and other products or program VCRs and similar devices.

Emotion Reduction as a Product Benefit

As a glance at Table 10–4 indicates, many emotional states are unpleasant to most individuals most of the time. Few people like to feel sad, powerless, humiliated, or disgusted. Responding to this, marketers design or position many products to prevent or reduce the arousal of unpleasant emotions.

The most obvious of these products are the various over-the-counter medications designed to deal with anxiety or depression. Shopping malls, department stores, and other retail outlets are often visited to alleviate boredom or loneliness. Food and alcohol are consumed, often harmfully, to reduce stress. Flowers are heavily promoted as an antidote to sadness. Weight-loss products and other self-improvement products are frequently positioned primarily in terms of guilt-, helplessness-, shame-, or disgust-reduction benefits. Personal grooming products often emphasize anxiety reduction as a major benefit. Charities frequently stress guilt reduction or avoidance as a reason for contributing.[50]

Emotion in Advertising

Emotion arousal is often used in advertising even when emotion arousal or reduction is not a product benefit. Consider the following recent headlines from *Advertising Age:*

* Lee takes emotional path to reach women for Riders.
* Discover's new ads bank on emotion.
* Marketers play heartstrings for ordinary products.
* Emotional appeal of laundry to replace performance claims in ads.

Illustration 10–8 provides an example of the effective use of emotion to attract attention to an ad and to position a line of products. In this ad, the young girl is being introduced to her new foster mother. After a shy start, the girl tries some soup. As the girl tastes the soup she says, "My mother used to make me that soup." "So did mine," says the foster mother. "Why don't I tell you about my mom and then you can tell me about yours." The tag line for the campaign is "Good for the body. Good for the soul."

ILLUSTRATION 10–8

Emotional appeals can play a powerful role in developing a brand image.

© Campbell Soup Company.

We are just beginning to develop a sound understanding of how emotional responses to advertising influence consumer behavior,[51] as well as what causes an ad to elicit particular emotions.[52] Therefore, the general conclusions discussed below must be regarded as tentative.[53]

Emotional content in advertisements *enhances their attention attraction and maintenance capabilities.* Advertising messages that trigger the emotional reactions of joy, warmth, or even disgust are more likely to be attended to than are more neutral ads. As we saw in Chapter 9, attention is a critical step in the perception process.

Emotions are characterized by a state of heightened physiological arousal. Individuals become more alert and active when aroused. Given this enhanced level of arousal, *emotional messages may be processed more thoroughly* than neutral messages. More effort and increased elaboration activities may occur in response to the emotional state.[54]

Emotional advertisements that *trigger a positively evaluated emotion enhance liking of the ad itself.*[55] For example, warmth is a positively valued emotion that is triggered by experiencing directly or vicariously a love, family, or friendship relationship. Ads high in warmth, such as the Campbell's ad in Illustration 10–8, are liked more than neutral ads. Liking an ad has a positive impact on liking the product. As you might suspect, ads that irritate consumers can create negative reactions to the advertised brand.[56]

Emotional ads *may be remembered better than neutral ads.*[57] As discussed in Chapter 8, recognition measures, rather than recall measures, may be required to measure this enhanced memory.

Repeated exposure to positive-emotion-eliciting ads *may increase brand preference through classical conditioning.*[58] Repeated pairings of the unconditioned response (positive emotion) with the conditioned stimulus (brand name) may result in the positive effect occurring when the brand name is presented.

Emotional appeals can capture attention and enhance the retention of advertising messages. They can also help humanize the brand and associate feelings with it.

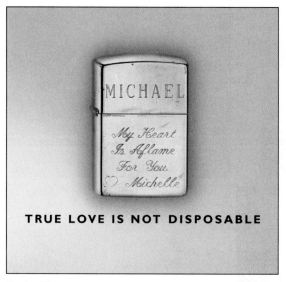

TRUE LOVE IS NOT DISPOSABLE

Courtesy Zippo.com.

Brand liking may also occur in a direct, high-involvement manner. A person having a single or few exposures to an emotional ad may simply decide that the product is a good, or likable, product. This is a much more conscious process than implied by classical conditioning. For example, the "lizard" ads for Budweiser beer are enjoyed by many. Some who enjoy the ads may simply decide that they would enjoy a beer made by a firm with that type of humor.

Advertising using emotion-based appeals is gaining popularity. For example, Zippo recently launched an emotion-based campaign for its lighters. It has eight print ads, each with a picture of an engraved lighter and a simple headline (see Illustration 10–9). A spokesperson said of the campaign, "We wanted to make a human, emotional attachment."[59]

Measuring Emotional Responses

A variety of approaches for measuring the emotional response to advertisements, packages, products, and so forth exist.[60] BBDO, a major ad agency, has a list of 26 emotions it believes can be triggered by advertising. To measure the emotions triggered by an ad, it developed the Emotional Measurement System—a set of 53 pictures of actors portraying the 26 emotions.

To test a commercial, respondents quickly sort through the 53 pictures and set aside those that reflect how they felt while watching the commercial. The percentage of respondents selecting particular pictures provides a profile of the emotional response to the commercial. The system has been used for such companies as Gillette, Pepsi-Cola, Polaroid, and Wrigley.

The **galvanic skin response (GSR)** has been used to measure emotional arousal. GSR involves fitting the respondent with small electrodes that monitor the electrical resistance of the skin. This resistance changes with the slight changes in perspiration that accompany emotional arousal. The most well-known application of GSR is the lie detector test.

The validity of the GSR for marketing applications is controversial, but evidence is beginning to suggest that it can be a useful measure.[61] Consider the results shown in Table 10–5. This study was conducted for *Better Homes and Gardens* and shows that, in this case, the GSR results were a better predictor of market response than were verbal evaluations of the ads.

Promotional Claim/Offer	GSR Score*	GSR Ranking†	Verbal Ranking†	Market Results	
1-cent sale	.300	1	4	1	**TABLE 10–5**
Special saving	.284	2	3	2	Emotional Arousal
Sampler	.248	3	1	3	and Mail Response
Macramé	.231	4	2	4	Rates

*The higher the score, the higher the arousal.

†Predicted market response.

Source: P. L. LaBarbera and J. D. Tucciarone, "GSR Reconsidered," *Journal of Advertising Research,* September 1995, p. 45.

SUMMARY

Consumer motivations are energizing forces that activate behavior and provide purpose and direction to that behavior. There are numerous motivation theories. Maslow's need hierarchy states that basic motives must be minimally satisfied before more advanced motives are activated. It proposes five levels of motivation: physiological, safety, belongingness, esteem, and self-actualization.

McGuire developed a more detailed set of motives—the needs for consistency, attribution, categorization, objectification, autonomy, stimulation, desired outcomes (teleological), utility, tension reduction, expressive, ego defense, reinforcement, assertion, affiliation, identification, and modeling.

Consumers are often aware of and will admit to the motives causing their behavior. These are *manifest motives.* They can be discovered by standard marketing research techniques such as direct questioning. Direct advertising appeals can be made to these motives. At other times, consumers are unable or are unwilling to admit to the motives that are influencing them. These are *latent motives.* They can be determined by motivation research techniques such as word association, sentence completion, and picture response. Although direct advertising appeals can be used, indirect appeals are often necessary. Both manifest and latent motives are operative in many purchase situations.

Because of the large number of motives and the many different situations that consumers face, motivational conflict can occur. In an *approach–approach conflict,* the consumer faces a choice between two attractive alternatives. In an *approach–avoidance conflict,* the consumer faces both positive and negative consequences in the purchase of a particular product. And finally, in the *avoidance–avoidance conflict,* the consumer faces two undesirable alternatives.

The *personality* of a consumer guides and directs the behavior chosen to accomplish goals in different situations. There are many personality theories, but all have two common assumptions: (1) individuals have internal characteristics or traits, and (2) there are consistent differences between individuals on these characteristics or traits that can be measured. Most of these theories assume that traits are formed at an early age and are relatively unchanging over the years.

Single-trait theories focus on one aspect of personality in an attempt to understand a limited part of consumer behavior. The need for cognition is the most widely used theory by consumer researchers. Multitrait theories attempt to capture a significant portion of a consumer's total personality using a set of personality attributes. The Five-Factor Model of personality is the most widely used multitrait approach.

Brands, like individuals, have personalities, and consumers tend to prefer products with brand personalities that are pleasing to them. Consumers also prefer advertising messages that portray their own or a desired personality.

Emotions are strong, relatively uncontrollable feelings that affect our behavior. Emotions occur when environmental events or our mental processes trigger physiological changes, including increased perspiration, eye pupil dilation, increased heart and breathing rate, and elevated blood sugar level. These changes are interpreted as specific emotions resulting from the situation. They affect consumers' thoughts and behaviors. Marketers design and position products to both arouse and reduce emotions. Advertisements include emotion-arousing material to increase attention, degree of processing, remembering, and brand preference through classical conditioning or direct evaluation.

KEY TERMS

Approach–approach conflict 366
Approach–avoidance
  conflict 366
Avoidance–avoidance
  conflict 366
Attribution theory 357
Benefit chain 364

Brand personality 370
Demand 367
Emotion 372
Five-Factor Model 368
Galvanic skin response (GSR) 376
Laddering 364
Latent motives 363

Manifest motives 363
Maslow's hierarchy of needs 355
Means-end chain 364
Motivation 355
Motive 355
Personality 367
Projective techniques 363

INTERNET EXERCISES

1. Visit several company websites. Find and describe one that makes effective use of an appeal or theme based on the following:
   a. One of Maslow's need hierarchy levels
   b. One of McGuire's motives
   c. An emotional appeal
2. Visit several general interest or entertainment sites on the Internet that contain ads. Find and describe an ad that uses the following:
   a. One of Maslow's need hierarchy levels
   b. One of McGuire's motives
   c. An emotional appeal

3. Monitor a hobby- or product-based interest group for a week. What types of motives and emotions are involved with the activity or product? What are the marketing implications of this?
4. Search for "emotional intelligence" on Google or another search engine. What do the results of this search indicate?

DDB NEEDHAM LIFESTYLE DATA ANALYSES

1. The DDB Needham questionnaire measures personality by asking people to list characteristics that describe themselves. Use Table 7a to answer the following:
   a. Do any of these personality characteristics seem to be associated with heavy consumption of any of the products or activities? Why do you think this is?
   b. Is product ownership associated with any of these personality characteristics? How would you explain this?

   c. Do any of these personality characteristics appear to influence television show preferences? Why do you think this is?
   d. Do any of these personality characteristics seem to be associated with any of the attitude, interest, or opinion items? Why do you think this is?

REVIEW QUESTIONS

1. What is a *motive?*
2. What is meant by a *motive hierarchy?* How does Maslow's hierarchy of needs function?
3. Describe each level of Maslow's hierarchy of needs.
4. Describe each of McGuire's motives.

5. What is meant by *motivational conflict,* and what relevance does it have for marketing managers?
6. What is a *manifest motive?* A *latent motive?*
7. How do you measure manifest motives? Latent motives?

8. How do you appeal to manifest motives? Latent motives?
9. Describe the following motivation research techniques:
   a. Association
   b. Completion
   c. Construction
10. What is *personality?*
11. How can knowledge of personality be used to develop marketing strategy?
12. What is an *emotion?*
13. What physiological changes accompany emotional arousal?
14. What factors characterize emotions?
15. How can we type or categorize emotions?
16. How do marketers use emotions in product design and positioning?
17. What is the role of emotional content in advertising?
18. Describe BBDO's Emotional Measurement System.
19. What is the GSR? How do marketers use it?

DISCUSSION QUESTIONS

20. How could Maslow's motive hierarchy be used to develop marketing strategy for the following?
    a. Habitat for Humanity
    b. Neutrogena's lipsticks
    c. Code Red soft drink
    d. McDonald's
    e. Segway HT
    f. Listerine mouthwash
21. Which of McGuire's motives would be useful in developing a promotional campaign for the following? Why?
    a. Ford Explorer
    b. Precision Cuts (hair salon chain)
    c. Nokia cell phones
    d. Just for Men hair coloring
    e. Amazon.com
    f. Sierra Club
22. Describe how motivational conflict might arise in purchasing, or giving to, the following:
    a. EarthSave
    b. BMW convertible
    c. Target (chain store)
    d. Coke Light
    e. Taco Bell restaurant
    f. Life insurance
23. Describe the manifest and latent motives that might arise in purchasing, shopping at, or giving to the following:
    a. Greenpeace
    b. Swimsuit
    c. Bose sound system
    d. Puppy
    e. BMW convertible
    f. Segway HT
24. Do marketers create needs? Do they create demand? What ethical issues are relevant?
25. Respond to the questions in Consumer Insight 10–1.
26. How might knowledge of personality be used to develop an advertising campaign for the following?
    a. Rainforest Action Network (an environmental group)
    b. Specialized mountain bikes
    c. H&R Block financial services
    d. Pizza Hut
    e. Reebok athletic shoes
    f. Tiger's Milk energy bars
27. Using Table 10–3, discuss how you would use one of the core personality source traits in developing a package design for an organic, shade-grown coffee.
28. How would the media preferences of those on each end of the consumer need for unique continuum differ?
29. How would the media preferences of those on each end of the romanticism/classicism continuum differ?
30. How would you use emotion to develop marketing strategy for each of the following?
    a. Visa card use
    b. Crest toothpaste
    c. Whirlpool energy saving appliances
    d. Silk (soy milk)
    e. Ford SVT Focus
    f. Telluride, Colorado
31. List all the emotions you can think of. Place each in one of the core traits in Table 10–3.

APPLICATION ACTIVITIES

32. Develop an advertisement for one of the items in Question 20 based on relevant motives from McGuire's set.

33. Repeat Question 31 using Maslow's need hierarchy.

34. Repeat Question 31 using emotions.

35. Find and copy or describe two advertisements that appeal to each level of Maslow's hierarchy. Explain why the ads appeal to the particular levels, and speculate on why the firm decided to appeal to these levels.

36. Find and copy or describe an ad that contains direct appeals to manifest motives and indirect appeals to latent motives. Explain how and why the ad is using each approach.

37. Select a product of interest and use motivation research techniques to determine the latent purchase motives for five consumers.

38. Have five students describe the personality of the following. To what extent are the descriptions similar? Why are there differences?
    a. New Orleans
    b. Pepsi
    c. Mercedes-Benz
    d. Macintosh computer
    e. Taco Bell
    f. The university bookstore

39. Find and copy an ad with strong emotional appeals and another ad from the same product category with limited emotional appeals. Why do the companies use different appeals?
    a. Have 10 students rank or rate the ads in terms of their preferences and then explain their rankings or ratings.
    b. Have 10 different students talk about their reactions to each ad as they view it. What do you conclude?

REFERENCES

1. W. Taylor, "Message and Muscle," *Harvard Business Review,* March 1993, pp. 99–110.
2. A. H. Maslow, *Motivation and Personality,* 2nd ed. (New York: Harper & Row, 1970).
3. See R. Yalch and F. Brunel, "Need Hierarchies in Consumer Judgments of Product Designs," *Advances in Consumer Research,* vol. 23, eds. K. P. Corfman and J. G. Lynch (Provo, UT: Association for Consumer Research, 1996), pp. 405–10.
4. W. J. McGuire, "Psychological Motives and Communication Gratification," in *The Uses of Mass Communications,* eds. J. G. Blumler and C. Katz (Newbury Park, CA: Sage Publications, 1974), pp. 167–96; and W. J. McGuire, "Some Internal Psychological Factors Influencing Consumer Choice," *Journal of Consumer Research,* March 1976, pp. 302–19.
5. See A. G. Woodside and J.-C. Chebat, "Updating Heider's Balance Theory in Consumer Behavior," *Psychology & Marketing,* May 2001, pp. 475–95.
6. M. C. Campbell, "Perceptions of Price Unfairness," *Journal of Marketing Research,* May 1999, pp. 187–99; A. d'Astous and N. Touil, "Consumer Evaluations of Movies on the Basis of Critics' Judgments," *Psychology & Marketing,* December 1999, pp. 677–94; M. C. Campbell and A. Kirmani, "Consumers' Use of Persuasion Knowledge," *Journal of Consumer Research,* June 2000, pp. 69–83; and R. N. Laczniak, T. E. DeCarlo, and S. N. Ramaswami, "Consumers' Responses to Negative Word-of-Mouth Communication," *Journal of Consumer Psychology* 11, no. 31 (2001), pp. 57–73.
7. See D. M. Boush, M. Friestad, and G. M. Rose, "Adolescent Skepticism toward TV Advertising and Knowledge of Advertiser Tactics"; and M. Friestad and P. Wright, "The Persuasion Knowledge Model," both in *Journal of Consumer Research,* June 1994, pp. 1–31 and 165–75; and M. Friestad and P. Wright, "Persuasion Knowledge," *Journal of Consumer Research,* June 1995, pp. 62–74.
8. See B. H. Schmit and S. Zhang, "Language Structure and Categorization," *Journal of Consumer Research,* September 1998, pp. 108–22.
9. M. Lynn and J. Harris, "The Desire for Unique Consumer Products," *Psychology & Marketing,* September 1997, pp. 601–16.
10. See R. K. Ratner, B. E. Kahn, and D. Kahneman, "Choosing Less-Preferred Experiences for the Sake of Variety," *Journal of Consumer Research,* June 1999, pp. 1–15.
11. S. Menon and B. E. Kahn, "The Impact of Context on Variety Seeking in Product Choice," *Journal of Consumer Research,* December 1995, pp. 285–95; T. H. Dodd, B. E. Pinkleton, and Q. W. Gustafson, "External Information Sources of Product Enthusiasts," *Psychology & Marketing,* May 1996, pp. 291–304; H. C. M. Van Trijp, W. D. Hoyer, and J. J. Inman, "Why Switch?" *Journal of Marketing Research,* August 1996, pp. 281–92; K. L. Wakefield and J. H. Barnes, "Retailing Hedonic Consumption," *Journal of Retailing,* no. 4 (1996), pp. 409–27; B. E. Kahn, R. K. Ratner, and D. Kahneman, "Patterns of Hedonic Consumption over Time," *Marketing Letters,* no. 1 (1997), pp. 85–96; P. Leszczyc and

H. Timmermans, "Store-Switching Behavior," *Marketing Letters,* no. 2 (1997), pp. 193–204; and M. Trivedi, "Using Variety-Seeking-Based Segmentation to Study Promotional Response," *Journal of the Academy of Marketing Science,* Winter 1999, pp. 37–49.

12. See D. Goldman, "Pain? It's a Pleasure," *American Demographics,* January 2000, pp. 60–61; and J. J. Inman, "The Role of Sensory-Specific Satiety in Attribute-Level Variety Seeking," *Journal of Consumer Research,* June 2001, pp. 105–19.

13. See G. M. Zinkhan, J. W. Hong, and R. Lawson, "Achievement and Affiliation Motivation," *Journal of Business Research,* March 1990, pp. 135–43.

14. C. Miller, "Spaghetti Sauce Preference," *Marketing News,* August 31, 1992, p. 5.

15. G. D. Mick, M. DeMoss, and R. J. Faber, "A Projective Study of Motivations and Meanings of Self-Gifts," *Journal of Retailing,* Summer 1992, pp. 122–44.

16. For an excellent approach, see G. Berstell and D. Nitterhouse, "Looking 'Outside the Box,'" *Marketing Research,* Summer 1997, pp. 5–13.

17. C. Rubel, "Three Firms Show That Good Research Makes Good Ads," *Marketing News,* March 13, 1995, p. 18.

18. See T. Collier, "Dynamic Reenactment," *Marketing Research,* Spring 1993, pp. 35–37; G. Zaltman, "Metaphorically Speaking," *Marketing Research,* Summer 1996, pp. 13–20; and C. B. Raffel, "Vague Notions," *Marketing Research,* Summer 1996, pp. 21–23.

19. See J. F. Durgee, G. C. O'Connor, and R. W. Veryzer, "Translating Values into Product Wants," *Journal of Advertising Research,* November 1996, pp. 90–99; J. Gutman, "Means-End Chains as Goal Hierarchies," *Psychology & Marketing,* September 1997, pp. 545–60; B. Wansink, "Making Old Brands New," *American Demographics,* December 1997, pp. 53–58; F. T. Hofstede, J.-B. E. M. Steenkamp, and M. Wedel, "International Market Segmentation Based on Consumer-Product Relations," *Journal of Marketing Research,* February 1999, pp. 1–17; C. E. Gengler, M. S. Mulvey, and J. E. Oglethorpe, "A Means-End Analysis of Mothers' Infant Feeding Choices," *Journal of Public Policy & Marketing,* Fall 1999, pp. 172–88; and T. J. Reynolds and J. C. Olson, *Understanding Consumer Decision Making* (Mahwah, NJ: Lawrence Erlbaum Associates, 2001).

20. See T. A. Mooradian, "Personality and Ad-Evoked Feelings," *Journal of the Academy of Marketing Science,* Spring 1996, pp. 99–109; and "I Can't Get No Satisfaction," *Psychology & Marketing,* July 1997, pp. 379–93.

21. D. M. Boush, C. H. Kim, L. R. Kahle, and R. Batra, "Cynicism and Conformity as Correlates of Trust in Product Information Sources," *Journal of Current Issues and Research in Advertising,* Fall 1993, pp. 71–79.

22. R. G. Netemeyer, S. Burton, and D. R. Lichtenstein, "Trait Aspects of Vanity," *Journal of Consumer Research,* March 1995, pp. 612–26.

23. M. Geuens and P. D. Pelsmacker, "Affect Intensity Revisited," *Psychology & Marketing,* May 1999, pp. 195–209; and D. J.

Moore and P. M. Homer, "Dimensions of Temperament," *Journal of Consumer Psychology* 9, no. 4 (2000), pp. 231–42.

24. R. Suri and K. B. Monroe, "The Effects of Need for Cognition and Trait Anxiety on Price Acceptability," *Psychology & Marketing,* January 2001, pp. 21–42.

25. C. Boone, B. D. Brabander, and A. van Witteloostuijn, "The Impact of Personality in Five Prisoner's Dilemma Games," *Journal of Economic Psychology* 20 (1999), pp. 344–76.

26. Ibid.; J. L. Aaker, "The Malleable Self," *Journal of Marketing Research,* February 1999, pp. 45–57; and M. J. Dutta and B. Vanacker, "Effects of Personality on Persuasive Appeals," *Advances in Consumer Research,* vol. 27, eds. S. J. Hoch and R. J. Meyers (Provo, UT: Association for Consumer Research, 2000), pp. 119–24.

27. D. C. Houghton and R. Grewal, "Please, Let's Get an Answer—Any Answer," *Psychology & Marketing,* November 2000, pp. 911–34.

28. This insight is based on S. P. Mantel and F. R. Kardes, "The Role of Direction of Comparison, Attribute-Based Processing, and Attitude-Based Processing in Consumer Preference," *Journal of Consumer Research,* March 1999, pp. 335–51; Y. Zhang and R. Buda, "Moderating Effects of Need for Cognition on Responses to Positively versus Negatively Framed Messages," *Journal of Advertising,* Summer 1999, pp. 1–15; C. S. Areni, M. E. Ferrell, and J. B. Wilcox, "The Persuasive Impact of Reported Group Opinions on Individuals Low vs. High in Need for Cognition," *Psychology & Marketing,* October 2000, pp. 855–75; R. Suri and K. B. Monroe, "The Effects of Need for Cognition on Price Acceptability," *Psychology & Marketing,* January 2001, pp. 21–41; and J. Z. Sojka and J. L. Giese, "The Influence of Personality Traits on the Processing of Visual and Verbal Information," *Marketing Letters,* February 2001, pp. 91–106.

29. M. B. Holbrook and T. J. Olney, "Romanticism and Wanderlust," *Psychology & Marketing,* May 1995, pp. 207–22.

30. K. T. Tian, W. O. Bearden, and G. L. Hunter, "Consumers' Need for Uniqueness," *Journal of Consumer Research,* June 2001, pp. 50–66. See also K. T. Tian and K. McKenzie, "The Long-Term Predictive Validity of the Consumers' Need for Uniqueness Scale," *Journal of Consumer Psychology* 10, no. 3 (2001), pp. 171–93.

31. See J. S. Wiggins, *The Five-Factor Model of Personality* (New York: Guilford Press, 1996).

32. E. G. Harris and J. C. Mowen, "The Influence of Cardinal-, Central-, and Surface-Level Personality Traits on Consumers' Bargaining and Complaint Behaviors," *Psychology & Marketing,* November 2001, pp. 1155–85.

33. J. C. Mowen and N. Spears, "Understanding Compulsive Buying among College Students," *Journal of Consumer Psychology* 8, no. 4 (1999), pp. 407–30.

34. W. Na and R. Marshall, "Validation of the 'Big Five' Personality Traits in Korea," *Journal of International Consumer Marketing* 12, no. 1 (1999), pp. 5–19.

35. V. Larsen and N. D. Wright, "The Mirror and the Lamp, the Mask and the Elephant," in *Advances in Consumer Research,*

vol. 25, eds. J. W. Alba and J. W. Hutchinson (Provo, UT: Association for Consumer Research, 1998), p. 101.

36. J. L. Aaker, "Dimensions of Brand Personality," *Journal of Marketing Research,* August 1997, pp. 347–56.

37. K. D. Aiken, E. C. Koch, and R. Madrigal, "What's in a Name? Explorations in Geographic Equity and Geographic Personality," *AMA 2000 Winter Educators Conference Proceedings* 11 (2000), pp. 301–8.

38. Taylor, "Message and Muscle," p. 105.

39. J. Halliday, "Chrysler Brings Out Brand Personalities with '97 Ads," *Advertising Age,* September 30, 1996, p. 3; and J. Halliday, "Ford Extends Story-Telling Ads," *Advertising Age,* August 24, 1998, p. 3.

40. B. F. Roberson, "Brand Personality and the Brand-Consumer Relationship," Whirlpool Corporation, April 5, 1994. Also see T. Triplett, "Brand Personality Must Be Managed or It Will Assume a Life of Its Own," *Marketing News,* May 9, 1994, p. 9.

41. S. Thompson, "LifeSavers Effort Gets Personality," *Advertising Age,* January 21, 2002, p. 40.

42. For a thorough discussion, see R. P. Bagozzi, M. Gopinath, and P. U. Nyer, "The Role of Emotions in Marketing," *Journal of the Academy of Marketing Science,* Spring 1999, pp. 184–207. Also see M. E. Hill et al., "The Conjoining Influences of Affect and Arousal on Attitude Formation," *Research in Consumer Behavior* 9 (2000), pp. 129–46.

43. See P. U. Nyer, "A Study of the Relationships between Cognitive Appraisals and Consumption Emotions," *Journal of the Academy of Marketing Science,* Fall 1997, pp. 296–305.

44. See B. J. Babin, J. S. Boles, and W. R. Darden, "Salesperson Stereotypes, Consumer Emotions, and Their Impact on Information Processing," *Journal of the Academy of Marketing Science,* Spring 1995, pp. 94–105.

45. See D. J. Moore and W. D. Harris, "Affect Intensity and the Consumer's Attitude toward High Impact Emotional Advertising Appeals," *Journal of Advertising,* Summer 1996, pp. 37–50; L. Dube and M. S. Morgan, "Trend Effects and Gender Differences in Retrospective Judgments of Consumption Emotions," *Journal of Consumer Research,* September 1996, pp. 156–62; M.-H. Huang, "Exploring a New Typology of Emotional Appeals," *Journal of Current Issues and Research in Advertising,* Fall 1997, pp. 24–37; J. L. Aaker and P. Williams, "Empathy versus Pride," *Journal of Consumer Research,* December 1998, pp. 241–61; and M. Geuens and P. D. Pelsmacker, "Affect Intensity Revisited," *Psychology & Marketing,* May 1999, pp. 195–209.

46. K. Menon and L. Dube, "Ensuring Greater Satisfaction by Engineering Salesperson Response to Customer Emotions," *Journal of Retailing* 76, no. 3 (2000), pp. 285–307; and W. van Dolen et al., "Affective Consumer Responses in Service Encounters," *Journal of Economic Psychology* 22 (2001), pp. 359–76.

47. See N. V. Raman, P. Chattopadhyay, and W. D. Hoyer, "Do Consumers Seek Emotional Situations?" *Advances in Consumer Research,* vol. 22, eds. F. R. Kardes and M. Sujan (Provo, UT: Association for Consumer Research, 1995), pp. 537–42; and J. A. Ruth, "Promoting a Brand's Emotion

Benefits," *Journal of Consumer Psychology* 11, no. 2 (2001), pp. 99–113.

48. See K. T. Lacher and R. Mizerski, "An Exploratory Study of the Responses and Relationships Involved in the Evaluation of, and in the Intention to Purchase New Rock Music," *Journal of Consumer Research,* September 1994, pp. 366–80.

49. See E. Sherman, A. Mathur, and R. B. Smith, "Store Environment and Consumer Purchase Behavior," *Psychology & Marketing,* July 1997, pp. 361–78.

50. B. A. Huhmann and T. P. Brotherton, "A Content Analysis of Guilt Appeals in Popular Magazine Advertisements," *Journal of Advertising,* Summer 1997, pp. 35–45.

51. M.-H. Huang, "Is Negative Affect in Advertising General or Specific?" *Psychology & Marketing,* May 1997, pp. 223–40; and G. Gorn, M. T. Pham, and L. Y. Sin, "When Arousal Influences Ad Evaluation and Valence Does Not (and Vice Versa)," *Journal of Consumer Psychology* 11, no. 1 (2001), pp. 43–55.

52. E. Kamp and D. J. MacInnis, "Characteristics of Portrayed Emotions in Commercials," *Journal of Advertising Research,* November 1995, pp. 19–28; H. Baumgartner, M. Sujan, and D. Padgett, "Patterns of Affective Reactions to Advertisements," *Journal of Marketing Research,* May 1997, pp. 219–32; D. W. Miller and L. J. Marks, "The Effects of Imagery-Evoking Radio Advertising Strategies on Affective Responses," *Psychology & Marketing,* July 1997, pp. 337–60; J. D. Morris and M. A. Boone, "The Effects of Music on Emotional Response," *Advances in Consumer Research,* vol. 25, eds. J. W. Alba and J. W. Hutchinson (Provo, UT: Association for Consumer Research, 1998), pp. 518–26; and D. J. Howard and C. Gengler, "Emotional Contagion Effects on Product Attitudes," *Journal of Consumer Research,* September 2001, pp. 189–201.

53. See S. P. Brown, P. M. Homer, and J. J. Inman, "A Meta-Analysis of Relationships between Ad-Evoked Feelings and Advertising Responses," *Journal of Marketing Research,* February 1998, pp. 114–26.

54. H. Mano, "Affect and Persuasion," *Psychology & Marketing,* July 1997, pp. 315–35; and A. M. Isen, "An Influence of Positive Affect on Decision Making in Complex Situations," *Journal of Consumer Psychology* 11, no. 2 (2001), pp. 75–85.

55. See J. P. Murry, Jr., and P. A. Dacin, "Cognitive Moderators of Negative-Emotion Effects," *Journal of Consumer Research,* March 1996, pp. 439–47; and K. S. Coulter, "The Effects of Affective Responses to Media Context on Advertising Evaluations," *Journal of Advertising,* Winter 1998, pp. 41–51.

56. B. M. Fennis and A. B. Bakker, "Stay Tuned—We Will Be Right Back after These Messages," *Journal of Advertising,* Fall 2001, pp. 15–25.

57. A. Y. Lee and B. Sternthal, "The Effects of Positive Mood on Memory," *Journal of Consumer Research,* September 1999, pp. 115–27; M. J. Barone, P. W. Miniard, and J. B. Romeo, "The Influence of Positive Mood on Brand Extension Evaluations," *Journal of Consumer Research,* March 2000, pp. 386–400; K. R. Lord, R. E. Burnkrant, and H. R. Unnava, "The Effects of Program-Induced Mood States on Memory for Commercial Information," *Journal of Current Issues and*

Research in Advertising, Spring 2001, pp. 1–14; and S. J. Newell, K. V. Henderson, and B. T. Wu, "The Effects of Pleasure and Arousal on Recall of Advertisements during the Super Bowl," *Psychology & Marketing,* November 2001, pp. 1135–53.

58. See E. A. Groenland and J. P. L. Schoormans, "Comparing Mood-Induction and Affective Conditioning as Mechanisms Influencing Product Evaluation and Product Choice," *Psychology & Marketing,* March 1994, pp. 183–97.

59. C. Beardi, "Zippo's Eternal Flame," *Advertising Age,* August 13, 2001, p. 4.

60. See J. D. Morris and J. S. McMullen, "Measuring Multiple Emotional Responses to a Single Television Commercial," in *Advances in Consumer Research,* vol. 21, eds. C. T. Allen and D. R. John (Provo, UT: Association for Consumer Research, 1994), pp. 175–80; P. M. A. Desmet, P. Hekkert, and J. J. Jacobs, "When a Car Makes You Smile," *Advances in Consumer Research,* vol. 27, eds. S. J. Hoch and R. J. Meyers

(Provo, UT: Association for Consumer Research, 2000), pp. 111–17; and M.-H. Huang, "Measuring Ad-Evoked Love," *Advances in Consumer Research,* vol. 28, eds. M. C. Gilly and J. Meyers-Levy (Provo, UT: Association for Consumer Research, 2001), pp. 295–300.

61. P. L. LaBarbera and J. D. Tucciarone, "GSR Reconsidered," *Journal of Advertising Research,* September 1995, pp. 33–53. See also P. V. Abeele and D. L. MacLachlan, "Process Tracing of Emotional Responses to TV Ads," *Journal of Consumer Research,* March 1994, pp. 586–600; and P. V. Abeele and D. L. MacLachlan, "Process Tracing of Physiological Responses to Dynamic Commercial Stimuli," in *Advances in Consumer Research,* vol. 21, eds. C. T. Allen and D. R. John (Provo, UT: Association for Consumer Research, 1994), pp. 226–32. For a similar methodology see R. L. Hazlett and S. Y. Hazlett, "Emotional Response to Television Commercials," *Journal of Advertising Research,* March 1999, pp. 7–20.

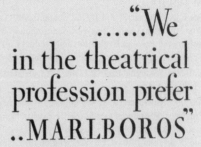

384

Nawrocki Stock Photo, Inc.

Attitudes and Influencing Attitudes

☐ Close your eyes and think of Marlboro cigarettes. What comes to mind? Is it an effeminate, sissy cigarette with an ivory tip or a red beauty tip? Certainly not when one thinks of the Marlboro man!

Philip Morris began marketing Marlboro in 1924 as an extremely mild filter cigarette. In fact, "Mild as May" was its slogan. Early campaigns featured decidedly unmasculine historical characters using the product. By the 1940s, it was promoted as an elegant cigarette primarily for women, though some ads showed men in tuxedos with Marlboros. At this time it came with either an ivory tip or a red beauty tip! It was advertised in a very plush atmosphere and was widely used by women. By the 1950s, the image described here was firmly established. In addition, at that time all filter cigarettes were viewed as somewhat effeminate.

By the mid-1950s, it was becoming increasingly apparent that filter cigarettes would eventually take over the market. Philip Morris decided to make Marlboro acceptable to the heavy user market segment—males. To accomplish this, everything but the name was changed. A more flavorful blend of tobaccos was selected along with a new filter. The package design was changed to red and white with an angular design (more masculine than a curved or circular design). One version of the package was the crushproof box—again, a very rugged, masculine option.

The advertising used "regular guys," not professional models, who typified masculine confidence. The Marlboro cowboy (a real cowboy) was introduced as "the most generally accepted symbol of masculinity in America." To lend credence to the new brand, it was tied to the well-known Philip Morris name with "new from Philip Morris" in the introductory advertising.

How successful was it? What did you think of a few minutes ago when asked to think about Marlboro? This image shift resulted in Marlboro becoming the largest-selling brand of cigarettes in the world.

☐ In the 1960s, most adult American males smoked cigarettes and more women were beginning to smoke. However, the health hazards of smoking were becoming increasingly well

documented. Various groups, particularly the American Cancer Society, began promotional campaigns to reduce smoking. These campaigns used a variety of techniques, including rational arguments, fact sheets, celebrity spokespersons, fear appeals, and humorous appeals.

The results of these attempts to change attitudes and behaviors about smoking have been as impressive as Marlboro's image change. Smoking among adult males in America is lower than it has been in decades. The growth in adult female smoking has stopped. While there has been a recent increase in teenage smoking, there is strong evidence that antismoking advertisements targeting teenagers can change the attitudes of many and noticeably reduce smoking among this group.

As the chapter's opening indicates, businesses and social agencies alike frequently succeed in altering behavior by changing attitudes toward a product, service, or activity. And, as also indicated above, these changes can result in injurious or beneficial consumption decisions.

An **attitude** is *an enduring organization of motivational, emotional, perceptual, and cognitive processes with respect to some aspect of our environment.* It is a learned predisposition to respond in a consistently favorable or unfavorable manner with respect to a given object. Thus, an attitude is the way one thinks, feels, and acts toward some aspect of his or her environment such as a retail store, television program, or product.[1]

Attitudes serve four key functions for individuals:[2]

* *Knowledge function.* Some attitudes serve primarily as a means of organizing beliefs about objects or activities such as brands and shopping. These attitudes may be accurate or inaccurate with respect to objective reality, but the attitude will often determine subsequent behaviors rather than that reality. For example, a consumer's attitude toward cola drinks may be "they all taste the same." This consumer would be likely to purchase

the least expensive or most convenient brand. This would be true even if in a taste test the consumer could tell the brands apart and would prefer one over the others. Obviously, firms like Pepsi spend considerable effort to influence consumers' beliefs about colas.

- *Value-expressive function*. Other attitudes are formed and serve to express an individual's central values and self-concept. Thus, consumers who value nature and the environment are likely to develop attitudes about products and activities that are consistent with that value. These consumers are likely to express support for environment protection initiatives, to recycle, and to purchase and use "green" products.
- *Utilitarian function.* This function is based on operant conditioning, as described in Chapter 9. People tend to form favorable attitudes toward objects and activities that are rewarding and negative attitudes toward those that are not. Marketers frequently promise rewards in advertising and conduct extensive product testing to be sure the products are indeed rewarding.
- *Ego-defensive function*. People form and use attitudes to defend their egos and self-images against threats and shortcomings. Products promoted as very macho may be viewed favorably by men who are insecure in their masculinity. Or individuals who feel threatened in social situations may form favorable attitudes toward products and brands that promise success or at least safety in such situations. These individuals would be likely to have favorable attitudes toward popular brands and styles of clothes and use personal care products such as deodorants, dandruff shampoo, and mouthwash.

Any given attitude can perform multiple functions, though one may predominate. Marketers need to be aware of the function that attitudes relevant to the purchase and use of their brands fulfill or could fulfill for their target markets.

Attitudes are formed as the result of all the influences we have been describing in the previous chapters, and they represent an important influence on an individual's lifestyle. In this chapter, we will examine attitude components, the general strategies that can be used to change attitudes, and the effect of marketing communications on attitudes.

ATTITUDE COMPONENTS

As Figure 11–1 illustrates, it is useful to consider attitudes as having three components: cognitive (beliefs), affective (feelings), and behavioral (response tendencies). Each of these attitude components is discussed in more detail below.

Cognitive Component

The **cognitive component** consists of *a consumer's beliefs about an object.* For most attitude objects, people have a number of beliefs. For example, an individual may believe that Mountain Dew

- Is popular with younger consumers.
- Contains a lot of caffeine.
- Is competitively priced.
- Is made by a large company.

The total configuration of beliefs about this brand of soda represents the cognitive component of an attitude toward Mountain Dew. Beliefs can be about the emotional benefits of owning or using a product (one can believe it would be exciting to own or drive a convertible) as well as about objective features.[3]

FIGURE 11–1   Attitude Components and Manifestations

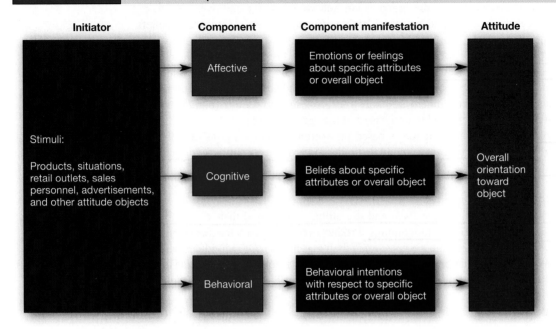

Many beliefs about attributes are evaluative in nature; for example, high gas mileage, attractive styling, and reliable performance are generally viewed as positive beliefs. The more positive beliefs associated with a brand, the more positive each belief is, and the easier it is for the individual to recall the beliefs, the more favorable the overall cognitive component is presumed to be.[4] And because all of the components of an attitude are generally consistent, the more favorable the overall attitude is. This logic underlies what is known as the **multiattribute attitude model.**

There are several versions of this model. The simplest is

$$A_b = \sum_{i=1}^{n} X_{ib}$$

where

A_b = Consumer's attitude toward a particular brand b.

X_{ib} = Consumer's belief about brand b's performance on attribute i.

n = Number of attributes considered.

This version assumes that all attributes are equally important in determining our overall evaluation. However, a moment's reflection suggests that frequently a few attributes such as price, quality, or style are more important than others. Thus, it is often necessary to add an importance weight for each attribute:

$$A_b = \sum_{i=1}^{n} W_i X_{ib}$$

where

W_i = The importance the consumer attaches to attribute i.

This version of the model is useful in a variety of situations. However, it assumes that more (or less) is always better. This is frequently the case. More miles to the gallon is always better than fewer miles to the gallon, all other things being equal. This version is completely adequate for such situations.

For some attributes, more (or less) is good up to a point, but then further increases (decreases) become bad. For example, adding salt to a saltless pretzel will generally improve the consumer's attitude toward the pretzel up to a point. After that point, additional amounts of salt will decrease the attitude. Thus, we need to introduce an *ideal point* into the multiattribute attitude model:

$$A_b = \sum_{i=1}^{n} W_i \, |I_i - X_{ib}|$$

where

I_i = Consumer's ideal level of performance on attribute i.

Because multiattribute attitude models are widely used by marketing researchers and managers, we will work through an example using the weighted, ideal point model. The simpler models would work in a similar manner.

Assume that a segment of consumers perceive Diet Coke to have the following levels of performance (the *X*s) and desired performance (the *I*s) on four attributes:

Low price	—	—	*I*	*X*	—	—	—	High price
Sweet taste	—	*I*	—	—	—	*X*	—	Bitter taste
High status	—	—	*I*	—	*X*	—	—	Low status
Low calories	*IX*	—	—	—	—	—	—	High calories
	(1)	(2)	(3)	(4)	(5)	(6)	(7)	

This segment of consumers believes (the *X*s) that Diet Coke is average priced, very bitter in taste, somewhat low in status, and extremely low in calories. Their ideal soda (the *I*s) would be slightly low priced, very sweet in taste, somewhat high in status, and extremely low in calories. Since these attributes are not equally important to consumers, they are assigned weights based on the relative importance a segment of consumers attaches to each.

A popular way of measuring importance weights is with a 100-point **constant-sum scale.** For example, the importance weights shown below express the relative importance of the four soft-drink attributes such that the total adds up to 100 points.

Attribute	Importance
Price	10
Taste	30
Status	20
Calories	40
	100 points

In this case, calories are considered the most important attribute, with taste slightly less important. Price is given little importance.

From this information, we can index this segment's attitude toward Diet Coke as follows:

$$A_{Diet\ Coke} = (10)(|3 - 4|) + (30)(|2 - 6|) + (20)(|3 - 5|) + (40)(|1 - 1|)$$
$$= (10)(1) + (30)(4) + (20)(2) + (40)(0)$$
$$= 170$$

This involves taking the absolute difference between the consumer's ideal soft-drink attributes and beliefs about Diet Coke's attributes and multiplying these differences times the importance attached to each attribute. In this case, the attitude index is computed as 170. Is this good or bad?

An attitude index is a relative measure, so in order to fully evaluate it, we must compare it to the segment's attitudes toward competing products or brands. However, if these consumers perceived Diet Coke to be the ideal soft drink, then all their beliefs and ideals would be equal and an attitude index of zero would be computed. Thus, the closer an attitude index calculated in this manner is to zero, the better.

We have been discussing the multiattribute view of the cognitive component as though consumers explicitly and consciously went through a series of deliberate evaluations and summed them to form an overall impression. However, this level of effort would occur only in very high involvement purchase situations. In general, the multiattribute attitude model merely *represents* a nonconscious process that is much less precise and structured than implied by the model.

Affective Component

Feelings or emotional reactions to an object represent the **affective component** of an attitude. A consumer who states "I like Diet Coke" or "Diet Coke is a terrible soda" is expressing the results of an emotional or affective evaluation of the product. This overall evaluation may be simply a vague, general feeling developed without cognitive information or beliefs about the product. Or it may be the result of several evaluations of the product's performance on each of several attributes. Thus, the statements "Diet Coke tastes bad" and "Diet Coke is not good for your health" imply a negative affective reaction to specific aspects of the product that, in combination with feelings about other attributes, will determine the overall reaction to the brand.

Because products are evaluated in the context of a specific situation, one's affective reaction to a product may change as the situation changes. For example, a consumer may believe that (1) Diet Coke has caffeine and (2) caffeine will keep you awake. These beliefs may cause a positive affective response when a consumer needs to stay awake to study for an exam and a negative response when he wants to drink something late in the evening that won't keep him awake later.

Due to unique motivations and personalities, past experiences, reference groups, and physical conditions, individuals may evaluate the same belief differently. Some individuals may have a positive feeling toward the belief that "Diet Coke is made by a large multinational firm," whereas others could respond negatively. Would you enjoy an experience that induced the following? "Muscles screaming. Heart pounding. Lungs feeling as if they could burst." This is the "benefit" the ad shown in Illustration 11–1 promises. Some individuals in some situations do evaluate these outcomes positively.

Behavioral Component

The **behavioral component** of an attitude is *one's tendency to respond in a certain manner toward an object or activity.* A series of decisions to purchase or not purchase Diet Coke

Courtesy Cycle-Ops Products.

or to recommend it or other brands to friends would reflect the behavioral component of an attitude. As we will see in the next section, the behavioral component provides response tendencies or behavioral intentions. *Actual behaviors reflect these intentions as they are modified by the situation in which the behavior will occur.*

Since behavior is generally directed toward an entire object, it is less likely to be attribute specific than are either beliefs or affect. However, this is not always the case, particularly with respect to retail outlets. For example, many consumers buy canned goods at discount or warehouse-type grocery outlets but purchase meats and fresh vegetables at regular supermarkets. Thus, for retail outlets, it is possible and common to react behaviorally to specific beliefs about the outlet. This is generally difficult to do with products because consumers have to either buy or not buy the complete product.

Component Consistency

Figure 11–2 illustrates a critical aspect of attitudes: *All three attitude components tend to be consistent.*[5] This means that a change in one attitude component tends to produce related changes in the other components. This tendency is the basis for a substantial amount of marketing strategy.

Marketing managers are ultimately concerned with influencing behavior. But it is often difficult to influence behavior directly. Marketers generally are unable to directly cause consumers to buy, use, or recommend their products. However, consumers will often listen to sales personnel, attend to advertisements, or examine packages. Marketers can, therefore, indirectly influence behavior by providing information, music, or other stimuli that

FIGURE 11–2   Attitude Component Consistency

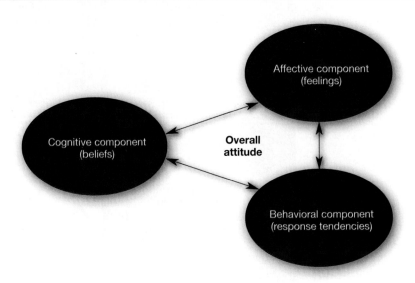

influence a belief or feeling about the product if the three components are indeed consistent with each other.

A number of research studies have found only a limited relationship among the three components.[6] Let's examine the sources of this inconsistency by considering an example. Suppose an individual has a set of positive beliefs toward the Palm m500 and also has a positive affective response to this brand and model. Further, suppose that these beliefs and affect are more favorable toward the Palm m500 than any other product of this nature. This customer responds to a questionnaire and indicates these positive beliefs and feelings. However, the consumer does not own a Palm m500, or purchases another brand or model. Thus, a researcher might conclude that the three components are not consistent.

At least seven factors can operate to reduce the consistency between *measures* of beliefs and feelings and *observations* of behavior.

1. A favorable attitude requires a need or motive before it can be translated into action. Thus, the consumer may not feel a need for a handheld or might already own an acceptable, though less preferred, brand.
2. Translating favorable beliefs and feelings into ownership requires ability. The consumer might not have sufficient funds to purchase a Palm m500, thus she might purchase a less expensive model.
3. Only attitudes toward handhelds were measured above. Purchases often involve trade-offs not only within but also between product categories. Thus, the consumer might purchase a less expensive handheld in order to save resources to buy skis, a DVD player, or a weekend trip.
4. If the cognitive and affective components are weakly held, and if the consumer obtains additional information while shopping, then the initial attitudes may give way to new ones.
5. An individual's attitudes were measured above. However, as we saw in Chapter 6, many purchase decisions involve other household members either directly or indirectly. Thus, the shopper may purchase something other than a Palm m500 in order to better meet the needs of the entire family.

6. Brand attitudes are generally measured independent of the purchase situation. However, items are purchased for, or in, specific situations. The consumer might purchase an inexpensive handheld now if she anticipates access to more sophisticated equipment in the near future.

   The **theory of reasoned action** is based in part on this concept.[7] It holds that behavioral intentions are based on a combination of the attitude toward a specific behavior, such as purchasing a brand; the social or normative beliefs about the appropriateness of the behavior; and the motivation to comply with the normative beliefs. Thus, a consumer might have a favorable attitude toward having a drink before dinner at a restaurant. However, the intention to actually order the drink will be influenced by the consumer's beliefs about the appropriateness of the action in the current situation (with friends for a fun meal, or on a job interview) and her motivation to comply with those normative beliefs.

7. It is difficult to measure all of the relevant aspects of an attitude. Consumers may be unwilling or unable to articulate all of their feelings and beliefs about various products or brands. Therefore, attitude components are sometimes more consistent than measures suggest them to be.

In summary, attitude components—cognitive, affective, and behavioral—tend to be consistent. However, the degree of apparent consistency between measures of cognitions and affect and observations of behavior may be reduced by a variety of factors, as mentioned above. Further, it is critical to remember that the behavioral component is a *response tendency,* not an actual behavior. Response tendencies are manifest in many ways short of purchase, such as being receptive to new information about the brand, complimenting others who purchase it, and so forth.

Measurement of Attitude Components

Purchase and use behavior at the brand level is predicted most accurately by overall measures of brand liking or affect. However, because components of attitudes are often an integral part of a marketing strategy, it is important that marketers be able to measure each component. Common approaches to measuring the components are shown in Table 11–1 and discussed briefly below. Additional details are provided in Appendix A.

Measuring Beliefs In Table 11–1, beliefs about Diet Coke are measured using a **semantic differential scale.** This scale lists the various attributes and characteristics of a brand that might be part of the target market's attitude toward the brand. These characteristics can be discovered through focus group interviews (in-depth discussions with 6 to 12 consumers at a time—see Appendix A), projective techniques, and logical analysis. Each characteristic is presented in terms of the opposite extremes that it might have, such as large/small, light/dark, or fast/slow.

These extremes are separated by five to seven spaces. Consumers are asked to indicate how closely one or the other extreme describes the item being evaluated by placing an X in the appropriate space, with the end positions indicating "extremely," the next pair in from either end representing "very," the next pair in indicating "somewhat," and the middle position meaning "neither-nor."

Consumers' beliefs about the ideal brand are also frequently measured using semantic differential scales. The process is the same as described above, except the ideal brand is generally indicated by placing an *I* in the appropriate space rather than an *X.*

The Likert scale described next can also be used to measure beliefs about existing brands and the ideal brand.

TABLE 11–1

Measuring Attitude
Components

Cognitive Component—Measuring Beliefs about Specific Attributes Using the Semantic Differential Scale							
Diet Coke							
Strong taste	—	—	—	—	—	—	—	Mild taste
Low priced	—	—	—	—	—	—	—	High priced
Caffeine free	—	—	—	—	—	—	—	High in caffeine
Distinctive in taste	—	—	—	—	—	—	—	Similar in taste to most

Affective Component—Measuring Feelings about Specific Attributes or the Overall Brand Using Likert Scales					
	Strongly Agree	*Agree*	*Neither Agree nor Disagree*	*Disagree*	*Strongly Disagree*
I like the taste of Diet Coke.	——	——	——	——	——
Diet Coke is overpriced.	——	——	——	——	——
Caffeine is bad for your health.	——	——	——	——	——
I like Diet Coke.	——	——	——	——	——

Behavioral Component—Measuring Actions or Intended Actions

The last soft drink I consumed was a _____.

I usually drink _____ soft drinks.

What is the likelihood you will buy Diet Coke the
next time you purchase a soft drink?

_____ Definitely will buy
_____ Probably will buy
_____ Might buy
_____ Probably will not buy
_____ Definitely will not buy

Measuring Feelings   The Likert scale shown in Table 11–1 also requires a list of the
various attributes and characteristics of a brand that might be part of the target market's attitude toward the brand. The list can be generated in the same manner described above for
the semantic differential scale.

A **Likert scale** presents statements claiming that the brand has a certain characteristic or
that the consumer has a specific affective response to the overall brand or an aspect of it.
An example is "Going to McDonald's makes me feel happy." Consumers are then asked to
state a degree of agreement or disagreement with the statement. As shown in Table 11–1,
five levels of agreement are usually used.

In Chapter 10 (page 376), several sophisticated approaches to measuring affective reactions to advertisements were described. These approaches can also be used to measure the
feeling or emotional reactions to a brand or activity.

Measuring Response Tendencies   Response tendencies are most often measured by
fairly direct questioning, as shown in Table 11–1. For many products, this works quite well.
However, for products for which there are strong social norms, such as alcohol or pornography consumption, eating patterns, and media usage, it works less well. People tend to
understate the consumption or the intention to consume negative products such as alcohol
and to overstate their consumption of positive products such as educational television.

In such cases, carefully worded questions and indirect questions can sometimes help. For example, rather than asking a person about his or her consumption of such products, some researchers ask them to estimate the consumption of other people similar to themselves such as their neighbors or people with similar jobs.

ATTITUDE CHANGE STRATEGIES

The attitude change induced by manipulating the marketing mix for Marlboro as described in the opening vignette is a classic in marketing history. As this example illustrates, managers can form and change attitudes toward products and brands. It also raises ethical questions concerning how firms use this knowledge. In addition to ethical issues, it poses difficult challenges to regulators who want to limit the ability of firms to develop favorable attitudes toward products whose consumption may prove harmful to some portion of the population.

Marketers and others ultimately want to change behaviors or response tendencies. A challenge organizations face when attempting to reduce smoking is that many smokers know the habit is harmful to their health but postpone quitting or are unable to quit. Thus, the belief component appears to be in place but the behavior component is not. Consumer Insight 11–1 describes how one organization is dealing with this.

Change the Cognitive Component

A common and effective approach to changing attitudes is to focus on the cognitive component.[8] Thus, to change attitudes toward cigarette smoking, the American Cancer Society has presented information on the negative health consequences of smoking. The theory is that by influencing this belief, affect and behavior will then change.

Four basic marketing strategies are used for altering the cognitive structure of a consumer's attitude.

Change Beliefs   This strategy involves shifting beliefs about the performance of the brand on one or more attributes. There is some evidence that beliefs tend to be consistent with each other.[9] Thus, changing one belief about a brand may result in other beliefs changing to remain consistent with the changed belief. For example, causing consumers to believe that the Kia Sportage has a smooth ride rather than a rough ride may result in them having enhanced beliefs about its handling and safety.

Attempts to change beliefs generally provide facts or statements about performance. Illustration 11–2 shows an ad for plastics that is designed to change the belief held by many consumers that plastics are harmful for the environment. *Does the ad change any of your beliefs about plastic?*

Shift Importance   Most consumers consider some product attributes to be more important than others. Marketers often try to convince consumers that those attributes on which their brands are relatively strong are the most important. For example, Quaker Oatmeal currently emphasizes that consumption of its ingredients has been shown to reduce the risks of heart disease. It uses themes such as "Thinking about a heart-healthy breakfast?" to make this attribute more important to consumers.

Add Beliefs   Another approach to changing the cognitive component of an attitude is to add new beliefs to the consumer's belief structure. Budweiser now promotes freshness in the form of its "born on date" as an important attribute for a beer. Before this campaign, few considered the age of a beer to be a relevant attribute.

As a result of Minnesota's settlement with the tobacco industry, the Minnesota Partnership for Action Against Tobacco (MPAAT) acquired funds to launch an antismoking campaign. It began with focus groups conducted throughout the state with both smokers and nonsmokers. In addition to other topics, the MPAAT showed participants antismoking commercials used elsewhere and asked them to rate the commercials' impact.

One finding was that just another warning about health risks would not be effective. "The overwhelming sentiment was, 'We know smoking is bad. Now we need something to move us from that understanding to action.'" As a result MPAAT decided to emphasize the devastating effects of smoking (secondhand smoke) on children and families. Many smokers still did not fully realize this, and it was felt that this knowledge would provide a fresh, strong incentive for action.

Another key finding from the focus groups was that "smokers are regular people who don't deserve to be chastised. Smoking is very tough to kick, and we didn't want to be demeaning or just tell them things they already knew." Therefore two categories of ads were created. One illustrated in hard-hitting terms the deadly impact of secondhand smoke. After this campaign ran for three months and then alternating with it, the second series of ads promoted MPAAT's 24-hour help-line. Smokers can call this line anytime for encouragement and information on quitting smoking.

A spokesperson explained the logic: "We knew we needed to be firm but also offer hope, and that's where the help-line ads came in."

The ads in both categories were brutally frank. A television commercial showed secondhand smoke becoming a ghostly hand that reaches out to choke an infant (see Illustration 11–6). A restroom poster pictured a pet bird lying dead on the floor of its cage as a result of secondhand smoke. A radio spot featured the croaky, distressed voice of a smoker who had to have her larynx and vocal cords removed because of throat cancer.

A spokesperson explained the reason for the ads' somber nature:

> We are dealing with an addiction and I think you have to be harsh about the realities of tobacco use. Quitting smoking is a task most smokers prefer to put off. MPAAT's guiding principle was to get their attention and make them see that quitting needs to happen today. You need to do that forcefully.

Critical Thinking Questions

1. What attitude component is MPAAT focusing on? What theory or assumption makes this reasonable?

2. What type of appeals is MPAAT using? Is this an appropriate use of this type appeal?

3. How successful do you think this campaign will be? Why?

4. Does this campaign raise any ethical concerns?

Change Ideal The final strategy for changing the cognitive component is to change the perceptions of the ideal brand or situation. Thus, many conservation organizations strive to influence our beliefs about the ideal product in terms of minimal packaging, nonpolluting manufacturing, extensive use of recycled materials, and nonpolluting disposition after its useful life.

Change the Affective Component

It is increasingly common for a firm to attempt to influence consumers' liking of its brand without directly influencing either beliefs or behavior. If the firm is successful, increased liking will tend to lead to increased positive beliefs, which could lead to purchase behavior should a need for the product category arise. Or, perhaps more common, increased liking will lead to a tendency to purchase the brand should a need arise,[10] with purchase and use leading to increased positive beliefs. Marketers use three basic approaches to directly increase affect: classical conditioning, affect toward the ad itself, and mere exposure.

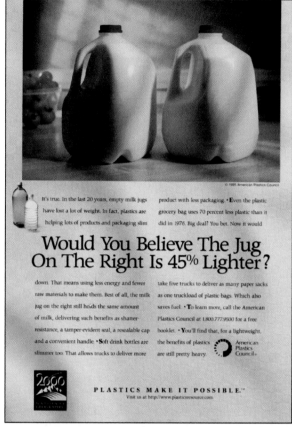

Courtesy American Plastics Council.

ILLUSTRATION 11–2

The cognitive component of an attitude can be altered by changing current beliefs, adding new beliefs, shifting the importance of beliefs, or changing the beliefs about the ideal product. This ad focuses primarily on changing beliefs.

Classical Conditioning   One way of directly influencing the affective component is through classical conditioning (see Chapter 9). In this approach, a stimulus the audience likes, such as music, is consistently paired with the brand name. Over time, some of the positive affect associated with the music will transfer to the brand.[11] Other liked stimuli, such as pictures, are frequently used for this reason.

Affect toward the Ad or Website   As we saw in Chapter 10, liking the advertisement generally increases the tendency to like the product.[12] Somewhat similar results are associated with liking the website on which an ad appears.[13] Positive affect toward the ad or website may increase liking of the brand through classical conditioning, or it may be a more high-involvement, conscious process. Using humor, celebrities, or emotional appeals increases affect toward the ad. Vivid websites with rich sensory content that appeals to multiple senses produce more positive attitudes toward the site than do less vivid sites.[14] Illustration 11–3 contains an ad that relies on positive affect.

Ads that arouse negative affect or emotions such as fear, guilt, or sorrow can also enhance attitude change. For example, an ad for a charity assisting refugees could show pictures that would elicit a variety of unpleasant emotions such as disgust or anger and still be effective.[15]

Mere Exposure   While controversial, there is evidence that affect or brand preference may also be increased by **mere exposure.**[16] That is, simply presenting a brand to an

Courtesy Lancaster Group; Agency: Deloge/Paris.

individual on a large number of occasions might make the individual's attitude toward the brand more positive. Thus, the repetition of advertisements for low-involvement products may well increase liking and subsequent purchase of the advertised brands without altering the initial belief structure.

Classical conditioning, affect toward the ad itself, and mere exposure can alter affect directly and, by altering affect, alter purchase behavior without first changing beliefs. This has a number of important implications:

- Ads designed to alter affect need not contain any cognitive (factual or attribute) information.
- Classical conditioning principles should guide such campaigns.
- Attitudes (liking) toward the ad itself are critical for this type of campaign (unless mere exposure is being used).
- Repetition is critical for affect-based campaigns.
- Traditional measures of advertising effectiveness focus on the cognitive component and are inappropriate for affect-based campaigns.

Change the Behavioral Component

Behavior, specifically purchase or use behavior, may precede the development of cognition and affect. Or it may occur in contrast to the cognitive and affective components. For example, a consumer may dislike the taste of diet soft drinks and believe that artificial sweeteners are unhealthy. However, rather than appear rude, the same consumer may accept a diet drink when offered one by a friend (see the discussion of reasoned action above, page 393). Drinking the beverage may alter her perceptions of its taste and lead to liking; this in turn may lead to increased learning, which changes the cognitive component.

Behavior can lead directly to affect, to cognitions, or to both simultaneously.[17] Consumers frequently try new brands or types of low-cost items in the absence of prior knowledge or affect. Such purchases are as much for information (Will I like this brand?) as for satisfaction of some underlying need such as hunger.

Changing behavior prior to changing affect or cognition is based primarily on operant conditioning (see Chapter 10). Thus, the key marketing task is to induce people to purchase or consume the product while ensuring that the purchase or consumption will indeed be rewarding.[18] Coupons, free samples, point-of-purchase displays, tie-in purchases, and price reductions are common techniques for inducing trial behavior. Since behavior often leads to strong positive attitudes toward the consumed brand, a sound distribution system (limited stockouts) is important to prevent current customers from trying competing brands.

INDIVIDUAL AND SITUATIONAL CHARACTERISTICS THAT INFLUENCE ATTITUDE CHANGE

Attitude change is determined by the individual and the situation as well as the activities of the firm or social agency. There are individual differences in how easily individuals will shift attitudes. Some people are more stubborn or closed-minded or less subject to social influence than are others.[19]

Attitudes that are strongly held are more difficult to change than are those that are weakly held. Think of something you feel strongly about—perhaps your school, your favorite sports team or band, or a disliked behavior such as chewing tobacco. What would be required to change your attitude about this item or activity? Clearly, it would be difficult. Consumers tend to avoid messages that are counter to their attitude. For instance, few committed smokers read articles on the harmful effects of smoking. And if they do encounter such messages, they tend to discount them.[20] Thus, most marketers do not try to capture sales from consumers who are committed to competing brands. Rather, they focus on those who are less committed, as these consumers are more willing to attend and respond to their messages.

Consumers are not passive when marketers attempt to change their attitudes.[21] Instead, they frequently infer the advertiser's intent and respond to the communications in light of a presumed selling intent. For example, a consumer could respond to the American Plastics Council ad in Illustration 11–2 as follows: "They only want to avoid regulation, so they are trying to fool people. They don't really care about the environment." To avoid such an interpretation, the Council put factual evidence about plastics in the ad. Another approach would have been to use a highly credible source such as a well-known environmentalist or scientist.

The consumer reaction described above presumed a highly involved consumer. Indeed, the ad itself attempts to generate involvement by the use of the question in the headline and the picture of the two apparently identical jugs. If the headline does not generate a fairly high level of involvement and processing, it will fail. An alternative would be to presume limited involvement. Such an ad might feature a pleasant aspect of the environment, a simple headline such as "Plastics make a difference," and limited text. A consumer might glance at this ad and make a connection, perhaps without even thinking about it, between a healthy environment and plastics.

The **elaboration likelihood model (ELM)** is a theory about how attitudes are formed and changed under varying conditions of involvement as described earlier.[22] The ELM suggests that brand involvement (the degree of personal relevance of the brand, which may change with the situation) and decision motivation are key determinants of how information is processed and attitudes are changed. High involvement results in a *central route* to attitude change by which consumers deliberately and consciously examine and process those message elements that they believe are relevant to a meaningful and logical evaluation of the brand (see Figure 11–3). These elements are elaborated on (combined with other bits of information, related to past experiences and potential outcomes, and so forth), compared with existing knowledge, and combined into an overall evaluation. The multiattribute attitude model represents a high-involvement view of attitude change.

In contrast, low involvement results in a *peripheral route* to attitude change in which consumers form impressions of the brand based on exposure to the readily available cues in the message regardless of the relevance of those cues to the brand itself. Thus, consumers may attend to only such aspects as the consumption environment portrayed, the characteristics of the people in the ad, the package, and similar cues.

FIGURE 11–3   The Elaboration Likelihood Model

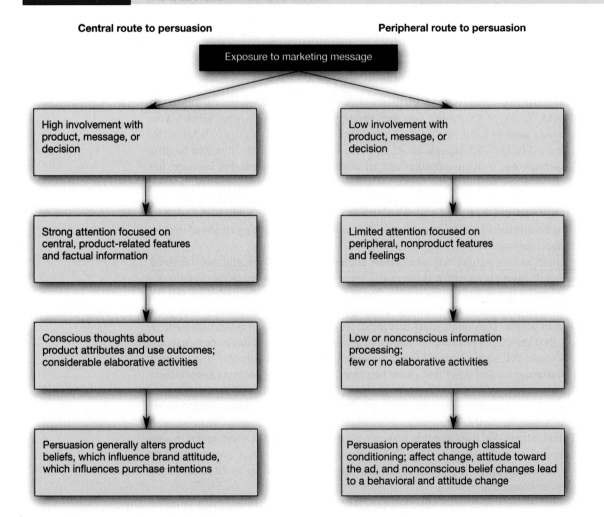

The ELM suggests that vastly different communications strategies are required to communicate effectively with consumers highly involved with the product compared with consumers with little product involvement. In general, more detailed, factual, and logical information can be used in high-involvement, central route situations. Low-involvement, peripheral route situations generally require limited information, such as pictorial ads that allow quick association to the key attribute with the brand. Or techniques such as the question headline shown in Illustration 11–2 can be used to increase involvement and processing level. While this model has been found to explain advertising effects across a variety of situations, it may not be completely valid for Internet advertising where peripheral clues seem to have little effect regardless of involvement level.[23]

COMMUNICATION CHARACTERISTICS THAT INFLUENCE ATTITUDE FORMATION AND CHANGE

In this section, we describe communication techniques that enhance attitude change. It must be emphasized that, as with all aspects of consumer behavior, individual and situational characteristics interact with the communication features to determine effectiveness.[24] For example, individuals with negative attitudes toward a product category respond favorably to ads employing absurdity, whereas those with positive initial attitudes toward the product category respond unfavorably.[25]

Source Characteristics

The source of a communication can be an identifiable person, an unidentifiable person (a "typical" homemaker), a company or organization, or an inanimate figure such as a cartoon character. The source of a message is important because consumers respond differently to the same message delivered by different sources.

Source Credibility   Influencing attitudes is easier when the target market views the source of the message as highly credible. This is referred to as **source credibility.** Source credibility appears to be composed of two basic dimensions: *trustworthiness* and *expertise.* A source that has no apparent reason other than to provide complete, objective, and accurate information would generally be considered trustworthy. Most of us would consider our good friends trustworthy on most matters. However, our friends might not have the knowledge necessary to be credible in a certain area. Although sales personnel and advertisers often have ample knowledge, many consumers doubt their trustworthiness because it might be to their advantage to mislead the consumer.

Individuals who are recognized experts and who have no apparent motive to mislead can be influential sources.[26] However, when consumers believe that the firm is paying the source for his or her endorsement, this effectiveness is diminished.[27] Likewise, relatively unknown individuals similar to the target market can be effective spokespersons. In a **testimonial ad,** *a person, generally a typical member of the target market, recounts his or her successful use of the product, service, or idea.* Such ads can be quite effective.[28]

Organizations that are widely viewed as both trustworthy and expert, such as the American Dental Association (ADA), can have a tremendous influence on attitudes.[29] The remarkable success of Crest toothpaste is largely attributable to the ADA endorsement. Underwriters' Laboratories, *Good Housekeeping,* and other trustworthy and expert sources are widely sought for their endorsements. These endorsements are most effective when consumers lack the ability to form direct judgments of the product's performance or the value of engaging in the promoted behavior and have faith in the endorsing organization.[30]

Celebrity sources and humor can attract attention and help shift attitudes when properly employed. This ad uses both, as well as an element of shock.

Courtesy PETA; photographer: Robert Serbee; model: Sandra Bernhard.

Of course, the company itself is the most obvious source of most marketing messages. This means developing a corporate reputation or image for trustworthiness can greatly enhance the impact of the firm's marketing messages.[31] The following examples illustrate this point:

> I don't like insurance companies. Insurance is such a pain; it's confusing on purpose. You pay all this money in premiums, then when you have to use it; they raise your premiums like you haven't already paid for the service. So if an insurance company was trying to tell me something about AIDS or drinking and driving, I wouldn't believe one word.
>
> "Just say no?" Those people saying that don't live in the projects like I do. They're sitting up in their big offices saying, "all those people got to do is say no." How do they know what my kid's life is like? I've got drug dealers on my corner everyday telling my kids they can get rich and have things if they sell. I have to tell my kids that they have to wait, be patient, go to school, make good grades then they might get a job. So don't try to talk to me if you don't know what my life is like.
>
> If Ronald McDonald or McDonald's speaks, kids and parents will stop and listen because the kids know all the characters and kids like the food. And they have a good history of service in children's charities. It seems like they genuinely care about more than just selling junk food to kids.[32]

Celebrity Sources   Celebrities are widely used in advertising, and evidence indicates that their use may increase a firm's value.[33] A visible use of celebrity endorsers in recent years has been the mustache campaign for milk. People for the Ethical Treatment of Animals (PETA) used comedian Sandra Bernhard in a takeoff on the mustache campaign to increase consumer concern about the way horses are used in the preparation of Premarin (see Illustration 11–4). Marketers such as McDonald's, KFC, Blockbuster, and Ford are

FIGURE 11–4   Matching Endorser with Product and Target Audience

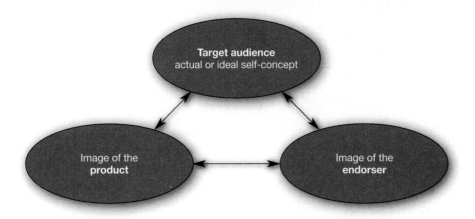

using celebrities such as Daisy Fuentes, Fernando Arau, John Leguizamo, and Salma Hayek to reach Hispanic consumers.

Celebrity sources may enhance attitude change for a variety of reasons.[34] First, they may attract more attention to the advertisement than would noncelebrities. Second, they may be viewed as more credible than noncelebrities. Third, consumers may identify with or desire to emulate the celebrity. Finally, consumers may associate known characteristics of the celebrity with attributes of the product that coincide with their own needs or desires.

The effectiveness of using a celebrity to endorse a firm's product can generally be improved by matching the image of the celebrity with the personality of the product and the actual or desired self-concept of the target market. For example, skier Picabo Street is leading Nike's attempt to enhance its image and sales among young girls. Her image of reckless enthusiasm and a disregard for the status quo fits with both Nike's image and the desired image of many young women. According to a Nike executive, "Her energy and personality appeal strongly to young girls and we will be using her to support our girls' sports initiatives."[35]

When the three components shown in Figure 11–4 are well matched, effective attitude formation or change can result.[36] For example, celebrity endorsements by Jimmy Connors and Joe Montana are credited with increasing Nuprin's sales almost 25 percent. Their images as maturing athletes now subject to aches and pains matched well with the target market and the product.

Using a celebrity as a company spokesperson creates special risks for the sponsoring organization. Few well-known personalities are admired by everyone. In addition, while attractive models generally have a positive impact, using highly attractive female models as spokespersons can cause negative reactions toward the ad and product in some women.[37] Thus, it is important to be certain that most of the members of the relevant target markets will respond favorably to the spokesperson.

Another risk involves overexposure. If one celebrity endorses many products, consumers' reactions to that person and the ads containing his or her endorsement may become less positive. Thus, marketers need to limit the number of products "their" celebrities endorse.[38]

An additional risk is that some behavior involving the spokesperson will affect the individual's credibility after he or she is associated with the firm. For example, while serving as spokespersons for the Beef Industry Council, Cybill Shepherd admitted in a magazine interview that she avoided red meat and James Garner had heart surgery. PepsiCo has

ILLUSTRATION 11–5

Spokes-characters
are gaining
popularity. They can
add credibility to a
message as well as
attract attention.
Some come to
serve as a symbol
of the product.

Courtesy Church & Dwight Co., Inc.

had problems with commercials featuring Madonna (after a controversial video), Mike Tyson (after his conviction for rape), Magic Johnson (after acquiring AIDS through an admittedly extensive series of affairs), and Michael Jackson (after child molestation charges). Campbell Soup distanced itself from Reggie White after he made controversial remarks concerning homosexuality. Such events can detract from the image and value of the brand.[39]

Rather than use celebrity spokespersons, many firms are creating **spokes-characters.**[40] Tony the Tiger and the Green Giant are perhaps the most famous such characters. Dole's Bobby Banana and Chiquita's Miss Chiquita are used aggressively to promote bananas to young consumers. Spokes-characters can be animated animals, people, products, or other objects. Betty Crocker is an example of a realistic, fictitious human spokesperson, and Count Chocula is a caricature of a fictitious person.

A major advantage of spokes-characters is the ability to have complete control over the character. This eliminates or reduces many of the problems associated with real celebrities. Such characters can come to symbolize the brand and give it an identity that competitors cannot easily duplicate. Illustration 11–5 shows Boxman, who serves as a spokes-character for Arm & Hammer's baking soda.

Sponsorship   **Sponsorship,** *a company providing financial support for an event* such as the Olympics or a concert, is one of the most rapidly growing marketing activities.[41] It often works in much the same manner as using a celebrity endorser. That is, the characteristics of the sponsored event may become associated with the sponsoring organization. Such an association is most likely and most effective when the match-up described in Figure 11–4 occurs, with the event taking the place of the endorser.[42] Thus, a financial institution sponsoring a sophisticated art show may enhance its image as being discriminating, sophisticated, elite, and serious. Or fans seeing a new, upcoming band wearing Airwalk gear may come to see Airwalk as cool and "with it."

However, sponsorship can have effects beyond enhancing the image of the brand.[43] It can also augment the company's image as a good corporate citizen, as the following example indicates:[44]

> I think also that it [Texaco Children's Art Competition] is genuinely doing good as a result of its [sponsorship]. It is putting it [funds] into something that wouldn't be done otherwise and it is promoting and it has been promoting children's art around the country and it gets a lot of entries and all that.[45]

It can also generate goodwill toward the brand or company, particularly among the more involved fans.[46] These fans may react along the lines of "Reebok supports my team, I'm going to support them." This type of reaction seems particularly common and powerful when companies support events tied to subcultural groups such as Native American celebrations (see Chapter 5).

In addition, an event serves as an advertising medium, with attendees being exposed to the sponsor's name and perhaps additional information. This can increase awareness of the sponsor just as would an ad in a traditional media.[47]

The evidence is clear that firms should do more than just sponsor the event. They should also promote the fact that they are doing so.[48] This can greatly increase the impact of event sponsorship and is an option not available with celebrities.

Appeal Characteristics

As you would expect, the nature of the appeal used affects attitude formation and change. As with all aspects of attitude change, appeal characteristics interact with the consumer and the situation to influence attitudes. For example, argument-based and negatively framed appeals have been found to be particularly effective in new markets, whereas emotion-based and positively framed appeals work better in more established markets.[49]

Fear Appeals

> The picture at the top of an ad is a snapshot of a young couple sitting together on their back deck. The headline reads: "I woke up in the hospital. Patti never woke up." The copy describes how carbon monoxide poisoning caused the tragedy. The ad, one of a series of similar ads, is for First Alert carbon monoxide detector.

Fear appeals use *the threat of negative (unpleasant) consequences if attitudes or behaviors are not altered*. Fear appeals have been studied primarily in terms of physical fear (physical harm from smoking, unsafe driving, and so forth), but social fears (disapproval of one's peers for incorrect clothing, bad breath, or inadequate coffee) are also used in advertising.[50]

There is some evidence that individuals avoid or distort extremely threatening messages. At the same time, fear appeals tend to be more effective as higher levels of fear are aroused. Thus, those using fear appeals want to maximize the level of fear aroused while not presenting a threat so intense as to cause the consumer to distort, reject, or avoid the message. This task is difficult because individuals respond differently to threats. Thus, the same "threatening" advertisement may arouse no fear in one individual or group and a high level of fear in another.[51]

Using a fear appeal as a way to gain attention and emphasize the dangers of second-hand smoke, the MPAAT sponsors the ad shown in Illustration 11–6 (see Consumer Insight 11–1). *Is this an effective use of a fear appeal?*

Courtesy of Minnesota Partnership for Action Against Tobacco.

Fear appeals are frequently criticized as unethical. Frequent targets of such criticisms are fear appeals based on social anxieties about bad breath, body odor, dandruff, or soiled clothes. The thrust of these complaints is that these appeals raise anxieties unnecessarily; that is, the injury or harm that they suggest will occur is unlikely to occur or is not really harmful. Fear appeals used to produce socially desirable behaviors such as avoiding drug use or avoiding acknowledged physical risks such as carbon monoxide poisoning are subject to much less criticism even though they often use more intense fear-arousing stimuli.[52]

Humorous Appeals   At almost the opposite end of the spectrum from fear appeals are **humorous appeals.**[53] Ads built around humor appear to increase attention to and liking of the ad. Their overall effectiveness is generally increased when the humor relates to the product or brand in a meaningful way and is viewed as appropriate for the product by the target audience.

Illustration 11–7 contains an ad from New Zealand that makes effective use of humor. Note that the humor ties very directly to the product. Other firms that have used humorous advertising closely tied to their product include

- A Sunsweet Growers' commercial shows an attractive young woman in a swimsuit with the heading "This is an ad for prunes." As the camera zooms in on her attractive face, the message changes to "You expected something old and wrinkled?"
- Mitsubishi's Montero Sport television commercial shows the faces of several men applying mascara, eye shadow, and lipstick as another man drives on a country road. The point is made that the drive is smooth enough to allow the makeup to be applied accurately. At the end of the commercial, the men leave the vehicle as rodeo clowns.
- The FedEx ad for its Latin America region described in the opening for Chapter 2 showed the humorous consequences (having to play a soccer match nude) of using another delivery service.

It is generally recommended that the humor be tied directly to the product or brand; however, Budweiser has had success with its lizard campaign even though the commercials are only loosely associated with beer.

Using humorous ads also involves risk. Humor varies across individuals and groups.[54] Humor viewed as demeaning or insulting can cost a company image and sales. For example, Toyota issued a public apology to the African American community after it placed an ad in *Jet* with the headline "Unlike your last boyfriend, it goes to work in the morning," which many viewed as insulting.

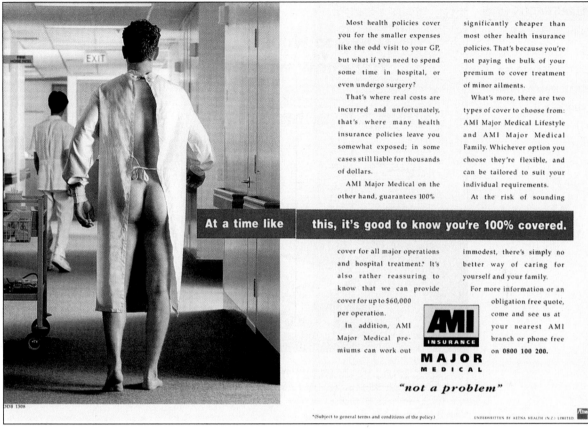

Most health policies cover you for the smaller expenses like the odd visit to your GP, but what if you need to spend some time in hospital, or even undergo surgery?

That's where real costs are incurred and unfortunately, that's where many health insurance policies leave you somewhat exposed; in some cases still liable for thousands of dollars.

AMI Major Medical on the other hand, guarantees 100%

significantly cheaper than most other health insurance policies. That's because you're not paying the bulk of your premium to cover treatment of minor ailments.

What's more, there are two types of cover to choose from: AMI Major Medical Lifestyle and AMI Major Medical Family. Whichever option you choose they're flexible, and can be tailored to suit your individual requirements.

At the risk of sounding

At a time like this, it's good to know you're 100% covered.

cover for all major operations and hospital treatment.* It's also rather reassuring to know that we can provide cover for up to $60,000 per operation.

In addition, AMI Major Medical premiums can work out

immodest, there's simply no better way of caring for yourself and your family.

For more information or an obligation free quote, come and see us at your nearest AMI branch or phone free on 0800 100 200.

AMI INSURANCE

MAJOR MEDICAL

"not a problem"

*(Subject to general terms and conditions of the policy.)   UNDERWRITTEN BY AETNA HEALTH (N.Z.) LIMITED.

© 1996 Aetna Health (N.Z.) Limited. Agency: DDB Needham New Zealand, L.T.D.

Comparative Ads   **Comparative ads** *directly compare the features or benefits of two or more brands* (see Illustration 11–8). Comparative ads are often more effective than non-comparative ads in generating attention, message and brand awareness, levels of message processing, favorable sponsor brand attitudes, and increased purchase intentions and behaviors. They also evoke a lower level of source believability and a less favorable attitude toward the ad.[55] In addition, they do not always produce the positive benefits described above. At times, the results of such ads may be negative for the sponsoring brand; they may even be positive for the brand with which it is being compared. Available evidence suggests that comparative ads should follow these guidelines:[56]

- Comparative advertising may be particularly effective for promoting new or little-known brands with strong product attributes.
- Comparative advertising is likely to be more effective if its claims are substantiated by credible sources.
- Comparative advertising may be used effectively to establish a brand's position or to upgrade its image by association.
- Audience characteristics, especially the extent of brand loyalty associated with the sponsoring brand, are important. Users or owners of the named competitor brands appear to resist comparative claims.
- Since people consider comparative advertisements to be more interesting than non-comparative advertisements (as well as being more offensive), these commercials may

Comparison ads can be effective at changing attitudes about lesser-known brands.

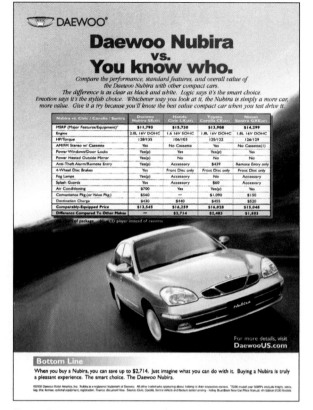

Courtesy Daewoo.

be effective if the product category is relatively static and noncomparative advertising has ceased to be effective.
- Appropriate theme construction can significantly increase the overall effectiveness of comparative advertising.
- It is important to ascertain how many product attributes to mention in a comparative advertisement.
- Print media appear to be better vehicles for comparative advertisements, because print lends itself to more thorough comparisons.

Emotional Appeals   Emotional or feeling ads are being used with increasing frequency. **Emotional ads** are *designed primarily to elicit a positive affective response rather than provide information or arguments*. As we saw in Chapter 10, emotional ads such as those that arouse feelings of warmth trigger a physiological reaction. They are also liked more than neutral ads and produce more positive attitudes toward the product. Emotional advertisements may enhance attitude formation or change by increasing[57]

- The ad's ability to attract and maintain attention.
- The level of mental processing given the ad.
- Ad memorability.
- Liking of the ad.
- Product liking through classical conditioning.
- Product liking through high-involvement processes.

Illustrations 11–9 and 10–8 (page 375) are designed to elicit emotional responses.

Courtesy Cease Fire, Inc.

Value-Expressive versus Utilitarian Appeals **Value-expressive appeals** *attempt to build a personality for the product or create an image of the product user.* **Utilitarian appeals** *involve informing the consumer of one or more functional benefits that are important to the target market.* Which is best under what conditions?

Both theory and some empirical evidence indicate that utilitarian appeals are most effective for functional products and that value-expressive appeals are most effective for products designed to enhance self-image or provide other intangible benefits.[58] For example, marketers generally should not use image (value-expressive) advertising for lawn fertilizers or factual (utilitarian) advertising for perfumes. However, many products such as automobiles, some cosmetics, and clothes serve both utilitarian and value-expressive purposes. Which approach is best for these products? There is no simple answer. Some marketers opt to present both types of appeals, others focus on one or the other, and still others vary their approach across market segments. Illustration 11–10 contains an example of each approach.

Research also indicates that banner ads should differ for the two types of products. For utilitarian products, banner ads serve primarily to transport consumers to the more detailed target ads or sites. For value-expressive products, banner ads should influence attitudes on the basis of exposure to the banner ad itself, not on clickthrough to the target ad.[59]

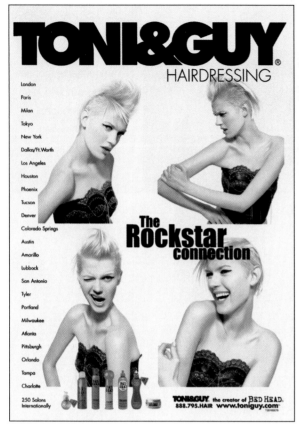

Courtesy Toni & Guy/TIGI Linea USA, Inc.

Courtesy Merck; Agency: Prime Access, Inc.

Message Structure Characteristics

One-Sided versus Two-Sided Messages   In advertisements and sales presentations, marketers generally present only the benefits of their product without mentioning any negative characteristics it might possess or any advantages a competitor might have. These are **one-sided messages,** since only one point of view is expressed. The idea of a **two-sided message,** presenting both good and bad points, is counterintuitive, and most marketers are reluctant to try such an approach. However, two-sided messages are generally more effective than one-sided messages in changing a strongly held attitude. They are particularly effective with highly educated consumers. One-sided messages are most effective at reinforcing existing attitudes. However, product type, situational variables, and advertisement format influence the relative effectiveness of the two approaches.[60]

Positive versus Negative Framing   **Message framing** refers to *presenting one of two equivalent value outcomes either in positive or gain terms (positive framing) or in negative or loss terms (negative framing).* Describing (framing) ground beef as "98 percent fat free" would be positive framing, whereas describing it as "2 percent fat" would be negative framing.

Studies, particularly those dealing with health messages, tend to show negative framing as superior. However, there is significant variation across product categories, consumers, and situations. Thus, the decision to use positive or negative framing must be based on research for the specific product and target market.[61]

Nonverbal Components   In Chapter 9, we discussed how pictures enhance imagery and facilitate learning. Pictures, music, surrealism, and other nonverbal cues are also effective in attitude change.[62] Emotional ads, described earlier, often rely primarily or exclusively on nonverbal content to arouse an emotional response. Nonverbal ad content can also affect cognitions about a product. For example, an ad showing a person drinking a new beverage after exercise provides information about appropriate usage situations without stating "good to use after exercise."

Although the impact of nonverbal ad elements is not yet completely understood, it is clear that they can have significant influence.[63] Therefore, the nonverbal portion of advertising messages should be designed and tested with as much care as the verbal portion.

MARKET SEGMENTATION AND PRODUCT DEVELOPMENT STRATEGIES BASED ON ATTITUDES

Market Segmentation

The identification of market segments is a key aspect of marketing. Properly designed marketing programs should be built around the unique needs of each market segment. The importance of various attributes is one way of defining customer needs for a given product. *Segmenting consumers on the basis of their most important attribute or attributes* is called **benefit segmentation.**[64]

To define benefit segments, a marketer needs to know the importance attached to the respective features of a particular product or service. This allows the marketer to group consumers seeking the same benefits into segments.

The marketer then can obtain additional information about consumers within each segment to develop a more complete picture of each segment. Knowing the primary benefit sought by each segment and the descriptive characteristics of each segment, separate marketing programs can be developed for each of the segments to be served by a particular organization.

Product Development

While the importance consumers attach to key attributes provides a meaningful way to understand needs and form benefit segments, the ideal levels of performance indicate the consumers' desired level of performance in satisfying those needs. These ideal levels of performance can provide valuable guidelines in developing a new product or reformulating an existing one.

Table 11–2 describes how Coca-Cola used this approach in developing a new soft drink.[65] The first step is to construct a profile of a segment of consumers' ideal level of performance with respect to key attributes of a soft drink. As shown in Table 11–2, four attributes were identified for a particular type of soft drink, and the ideal level of performance was obtained from consumer ratings.

A second step involves creation of a product concept that closely matches the ideal profile. The concept could be a written description, picture, or actual prototype of the product to be developed. As section B in Table 11–2 shows, consumers evaluated the product concept developed by Coca-Cola as being fairly close to their ideal level of performance on each of the four attributes. It appears that only their concept of color was off target by being a little too dark.

TABLE 11-2

Using the Multiattribute Attitude Model in the Product Development Process

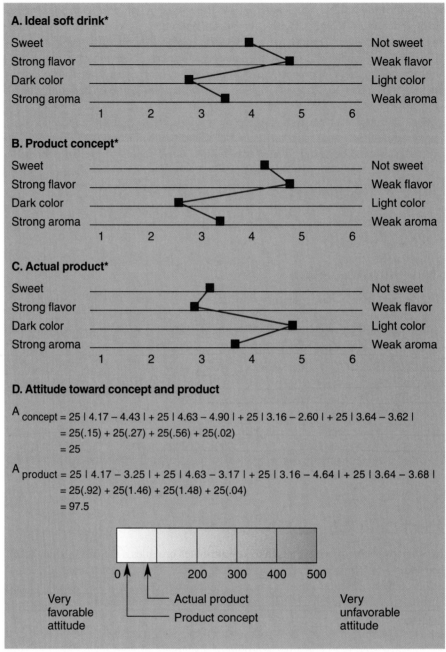

A. Ideal soft drink*

	1	2	3	4	5	6	
Sweet				■			Not sweet
Strong flavor					■		Weak flavor
Dark color			■				Light color
Strong aroma				■			Weak aroma

B. Product concept*

	1	2	3	4	5	6	
Sweet				■			Not sweet
Strong flavor					■		Weak flavor
Dark color		■					Light color
Strong aroma				■			Weak aroma

C. Actual product*

	1	2	3	4	5	6	
Sweet			■				Not sweet
Strong flavor			■				Weak flavor
Dark color					■		Light color
Strong aroma			■				Weak aroma

D. Attitude toward concept and product

$$A_{concept} = 25 \mid 4.17 - 4.43 \mid + 25 \mid 4.63 - 4.90 \mid + 25 \mid 3.16 - 2.60 \mid + 25 \mid 3.64 - 3.62 \mid$$
$$= 25(.15) + 25(.27) + 25(.56) + 25(.02)$$
$$= 25$$

$$A_{product} = 25 \mid 4.17 - 3.25 \mid + 25 \mid 4.63 - 3.17 \mid + 25 \mid 3.16 - 4.64 \mid + 25 \mid 3.64 - 3.68 \mid$$
$$= 25(.92) + 25(1.46) + 25(1.48) + 25(.04)$$
$$= 97.5$$

0 — 200 — 300 — 400 — 500

Very favorable attitude   Actual product   Very unfavorable attitude
                                 Product concept

*Measured on a six-point schematic differential scale.

The next step is to translate the concept into an actual product. When Coca-Cola did this and presented the product to the consumers, they did not perceive it to be similar to either the product concept or their ideal levels of performance (see section C in Table 11–2). While the actual product achieved a reasonable attitude rating, the product concept scored higher (section D, Table 11–2). Thus, the product could benefit from further improvement.

On the basis of this information, management would attempt to further improve the actual product to better align it with ideal levels of performance prior to market introduction. This same type of procedure can be used to help design ads, packages, or retail outlets.

SUMMARY

Attitudes can be defined as the way people think, feel, and act toward some aspect of their environment. A result of all the factors discussed so far in the text, attitudes influence, as well as reflect, the lifestyle individuals pursue.

Attitudes have three component parts: cognitive, affective, and behavioral. The *cognitive component* consists of the individual's beliefs or knowledge about the object. It is generally assessed by using a version of the multiattribute attitude model. Feelings or emotional reactions to an object represent the *affective component* of the attitude. The *behavioral component* reflects overt actions and statements of behavioral intentions with respect to specific attributes of the object or the overall object. In general, all three components of an attitude tend to be consistent with each other.

Attitude change strategies can focus on affect, behavior, cognition, or some combination. Attempts to change affect generally rely on classical conditioning. Change strategies focusing on behavior rely more on operant conditioning. Changing cognitions usually involves information processing and cognitive learning.

Source credibility is composed of two basic dimensions: trustworthiness and expertise. Influencing attitudes is much easier when the source of the message is viewed as highly credible by the target market. Celebrities are widely used as product or company spokespersons. They are most effective when their image matches the personality of the product and the actual or desired self-concept of the target market.

The appeals used to change attitudes are important and are varied. *Fear appeals* use threat of negative consequences if attitudes or behaviors are not altered. *Humorous appeals* can also be effective in influencing attitudes. However, the humorous message must remain focused on the brand or main selling point to be effective.

Comparative ads produce mixed results. They are most effective for unknown brands having a strong functional advantage. The decision to use a *value-expressive* or *utilitarian appeal* depends on whether the brand fills value-expressive or utilitarian needs. However, this is complicated when the brand fills both types of needs. *Emotional appeals* have been found to have a strong effect on attitudes toward both the ad and the product.

Three aspects of the structure of the message affect its effectiveness. The effectiveness of *one-* versus *two-sided messages* depends largely on the situation and characteristics of the target audience. The same is true for *message framing*—presenting one of two equivalent value outcomes either in positive or gain terms (positive framing) or in negative or loss terms (negative framing). Nonverbal aspects of the ad, such as pictures, surrealism, and music, also affect attitudes.

Attitudes, particularly the cognitive component, are the basis for market segmentation strategies, such as *benefit segmentation,* and for new-product development strategies.

KEY TERMS

Affective component 390
Attitude 386
Behavioral component 390
Benefit segmentation 411
Cognitive component 387
Comparative ads 407
Constant-sum scale 389
Elaboration likelihood
  model (ELM) 400
Emotional ads 408
Fear appeals 405
Humorous appeals 406
Likert scale 394
Mere exposure 397
Message framing 410
Multiattribute attitude model 388
One-sided message 410
Semantic differential scale 393
Source credibility 401
Spokes-characters 404
Sponsorship 404
Testimonial ads 401
Theory of reasoned action 393
Two-sided message 410
Utilitarian appeals 409
Value-expressive appeals 409

INTERNET EXERCISES

1. Visit several general interest or entertainment sites on the Internet that contain ads. Find and describe an ad that attempts to change the following to help form or change attitudes:
   a. Affective component
   b. Cognitive component
   c. Behavioral component

2. Visit several company websites. Find and describe one that attempts to change the following to help form or change attitudes:
   a. Affective component
   b. Cognitive component
   c. Behavioral component

3. Visit several interest or entertainment sites on the Internet that contain ads. Find and describe an ad that uses one of the following to help form or change attitudes:
   a. Credible source
   b. Celebrity source
   c. Humorous appeal
   d. Fear appeal
   e. Comparative appeal
   f. Emotional appeal

4. Visit several company websites. Find and describe one that uses one of the following to help form or change attitudes:
   a. Credible source
   b. Celebrity source
   c. Humorous appeal
   d. Fear appeal
   e. Comparative appeal
   f. Emotional appeal

5. Visit the American Plastics Council website (www.plasticsresource.com). What attitude change techniques does it use? Are they effective?

REVIEW QUESTIONS

1. What is an *attitude?*
2. What are the functions of attitudes?
3. What are the components of an attitude?
4. Are the components of an attitude consistent? What factors reduce the apparent consistency between attitude components?
5. What is a *multiattribute attitude model?*
6. What strategies can be used to change the following components of an attitude?
   a. Affective
   b. Behavioral
   c. Cognitive
7. What is meant by *mere exposure?*
8. What is the *elaboration likelihood model?*
9. Describe the *theory of reasoned action.*
10. What are the two characteristics of the source of a message that influence its ability to change attitudes? Describe each.
11. What is *source credibility?* What causes it?
12. Why are celebrity sources sometimes effective? What risks are associated with using a celebrity source?
13. Name five possible characteristics of an appeal that would influence or change attitudes. Describe each.
14. Are *fear appeals* always effective in changing attitudes? Why?
15. What characteristics should *humorous ads* have?
16. Are *emotional appeals* effective? Why?
17. Are *comparative appeals* effective? Why?
18. What is a *value-expressive appeal?* A *utilitarian appeal?* When should each be used?
19. What are the three characteristics of the message structure that influence its ability to change attitudes? Describe each.
20. What is meant by *positive message framing* and *negative message framing?*
21. What are the nonverbal components of an ad? What impact do they have on attitudes?
22. When is a *two-sided message* likely to be more effective than a *one-sided message?*
23. How can attitudes guide new-product development?
24. What is a *benefit segment?*

DISCUSSION QUESTIONS

25. Which version of the multiattribute attitude model and which attributes would you use to assess student attitudes toward the following? Justify your answer.
    a. Your university
    b. Listerine mouthwash
    c. Paper grocery bags
    d. Dogs as pets
    e. Code Red
    f. Segway HT

26. Respond to the questions in Consumer Insight 11–1.

27. Assume you wanted to improve or create favorable attitudes among college students toward the following. Would you focus primarily on the affective, cognitive, or behavioral component? Why?
    a. Habitat for Humanity
    b. Kia automobiles
    c. Pork consumption
    d. In-line skating
    e. Not driving after drinking
    f. Using the bus for most local trips
    g. McDonald's
    h. Career with the FBI

28. Suppose you used the multiattribute attitude model and developed a fruit-based carbonated drink that was successful in the United States. Could you use the same model in the following countries? If not, how would it have to change?
    a. Japan
    b. Brazil
    c. Germany

29. Suppose you wanted to form highly negative attitudes toward smoking among college students.
    a. Which attitude component would you focus on? Why?
    b. Which message characteristic would you use? Why?
    c. What type of appeal would you use? Why?

30. What communications characteristics would you use in an attempt to improve college students' attitudes toward the following?
    a. Taco Bell
    b. Harley-Davidson motorcycles
    c. Daily exercise
    d. Vitamin supplements
    e. Habitat for Humanity
    f. Diet Pepsi

31. Is it ethical to use fear appeals to increase demand for the following?
    a. Complexion medication among teenagers
    b. Deodorant among adults
    c. Smoke alarms among elderly consumers
    d. Handguns among women

32. Name two appropriate and two inappropriate celebrity spokespersons for each of the products or causes in Question 30. Justify your selection.

33. What benefit segments do you think exist for attendance at the following?
    a. High school football games
    b. Broadway theater presentations
    c. Major art museums
    d. Professional wrestling matches

APPLICATION ACTIVITIES

34. Find and copy two magazine or newspaper advertisements, one based on the affective component and the other on the cognitive component. Discuss the approach of each ad in terms of its copy and illustration and what effect it creates in terms of attitude. Also, discuss why the marketer might have taken that approach in each advertisement.

35. Repeat Question 34 for utilitarian and value-expressive appeals.

36. Identify a television commercial that uses a humorous appeal. Then interview five individuals not enrolled in your class and measure their
    a. Awareness of this commercial
    b. Recall of the brand advertised
    c. Recall of relevant information
    d. Liking of the commercial
    e. Preference for the brand advertised

Evaluate your results and assess the level of communication that has taken place in terms of these five consumers' exposure, attention, interpretation, and preferences for this product and commercial.

37. Describe a magazine, Internet, or television advertisement, or a package that uses the following. Evaluate the effectiveness of the ad or package.
    a. Source credibility
    b. Celebrity source
    c. Testimonial
    d. Fear appeal
    e. Humorous appeal
    f. Emotional appeal
    g. Comparative approach
    h. Extensive nonverbal elements
    i. A two-sided appeal
    j. Positive message framing
    k. Negative message framing

38. Measure another student's ideal beliefs and belief importance for the following. Examine these ideal beliefs and importance weights and then develop a verbal description (i.e., concept) of a new brand of these items that would satisfy this student's needs. Next, measure that student's attitude toward the concept you have developed in your verbal description.
    a. Sports drink
    b. Nice restaurant
    c. Automobile
    d. Mouthwash
    e. Movie
    f. Charity

39. Use the multiattribute attitude model to assess 10 students' attitudes toward several brands in the following product categories. Measure the students' behavior with respect to these brands. Are they consistent? Explain any inconsistencies.
    a. Television programs
    b. Sports drinks
    c. Cereals
    d. Fast-food restaurants
    e. Exercise
    f. Fruits

40. Develop two advertisements for the following with college students as the target. One ad should focus on the cognitive component and the other on the affective component.
    a. Listerine toothpaste
    b. Kia automobiles
    c. Pepsi One
    d. Reducing smoking
    e. Increasing exercise
    f. McDonald's

41. Repeat Question 40 using utilitarian and value-expressive appeals.

42. Develop a positively framed and an equivalent negatively framed message about a product attribute. Have five students react to these messages. What do you conclude?

REFERENCES

1. See R. E. Petty, D. T. Wegener, and L. R. Fabriger, "Attitudes and Attitude Change," *Annual Review of Psychology* 48 (1997), pp. 609–38.

2. D. Katz, "The Functional Approach to the Study of Attitudes," *Public Opinion Quarterly,* Summer 1960, pp. 163–204. For discussion of a fifth function, social identity, see R. Grewal, R. Mehta, and F. R. Kardes, "The Role of Social-Identity Function of Attitudes in Consumer Innovativeness and Opinion Leadership," *Journal of Economic Psychology* 21 (2000), pp. 233–52.

3. J. A. Ruth, "Promoting a Brand's Emotional Benefits," *Journal of Consumer Psychology* 11, no. 2 (2001), pp. 99–113.

4. See M. Wanke, G. Bohner, and A. Jurkowitsch, "There Are Many Reasons to Drive a BMW," *Journal of Consumer Research,* September 1997, pp. 170–77.

5. For an excellent review, see P. A. Dabholkar, "Incorporating Choice into an Attitudinal Framework," *Journal of Consumer Research,* June 1994, pp. 100–18. See also A. Ehrenberg, "In Search of Holy Grails"; and A. L. Baldinger and J. Rubinson, "In Search of the Holy Grail," both in *Journal of Advertising Research,* January 1997, pp. 9–12 and 18–20; and J.-F. Aurifeille, F. Clerfeuille, and P. Quester, "Consumers' Attitude Profiles," *Advances in Consumer Research,* vol. 28, eds. M. C. Gilly and J. Meyers-Levy (Provo, UT: Association for Consumer Research, 2001), pp. 301–08.

6. R. E. Petty and J. A. Krosnick, *Attitude Strength* (Mahwah, NJ: Erlbaum, 1995); S. J. Kraus, "Attitudes and the Prediction of Behavior," *Personality and Social Psychology Bulletin* 21 (1995), pp. 58–75; R. Madrigal, "Social Identity Effects in a Belief-Attitude-Intentions Hierarchy," *Psychology & Marketing,* February 2001, pp. 145–65; and W. E. Baker, "The Diagnosticity of Advertising Generated Brand Attitudes in Brand Choice Contexts," *Journal of Consumer Psychology* 11, no. 2 (2001), pp. 129–39.

7. See R. P. Bagozzi et al., "Cultural and Situational Contingencies and the Theory of Reasoned Action," *Journal of Consumer Psychology* 9, no. 2 (2000), pp. 97–106.

8. See S. A. Hawkins, S. J. Hoch, and J. Meyers-Levy, "Low-Involvement Learning," *Journal of Consumer Psychology* 11, no. 31 (2001), pp. 1–11.

9. F. R. Kardes, "Down the Garden Path," *Journal of Consumer Psychology* 11, no. 3 (2001), pp. 159–68.

10. See M. J. J. M. Candel and J. M. E. Pennings, "Attitude-Based Models for Binary Choices," *Journal of Economic Psychology* 20 (1999), pp. 547–69.

11. R. P. Grossman and B. D. Till, "The Persistence of Classically Conditioned Brand Attitudes," *Journal of Advertising,* Spring 1998, pp. 23–31; J. Kim, J.-S. Lim, and M. Bhargava, "The Role of Affect in Attitude Formation," *Journal of the Academy of Marketing Science,* Spring 1998, pp. 143–52; and W. E. Baker, "When Can Affective Conditioning and Mere Exposure Directly Influence Brand Choice?" *Journal of Advertising,* Winter 1999, pp. 31–46.

12. See K. G. Celuch and M. Slama, "Cognitive and Affective Components of A_{ab} in a Low Motivation Processing Set," *Psychology & Marketing,* March 1995, pp. 123–33; N. S. Hollis, "Like It or Not, Liking Is Not Enough," *Journal of Advertising Research,* September 1995, pp. 7–16; C. M. Derbaix, "The Impact of Affective Reactions on Attitudes toward the Advertisement and the Brand," *Journal of Marketing Research,* November 1995, pp. 47–79; J. E. Phelps and M. G. Hoy, "The A_{ab}–A_b–PI Relationship in Children," *Psychology & Marketing,* January 1996, pp. 77–105; D. J. Moore and W. D. Harris, "Affect Intensity and the Consumer's Attitude toward High Impact Emotional Advertising Appeals," *Journal of Advertising,* Summer 1996, pp. 37–50; H. Mano, "Affect and Persuasion," *Psychology & Marketing,* July 1997, pp. 315–35; E. Curlo and R. Chamblee, "Ad Processing and Persuasion," *Psychology & Marketing,* May 1998, pp. 279–99; E. Curlo and R. Ducoffe, "Product Use Goals and Attitudinal Response to Ads," *Journal of Current Issues and Research in Advertising,* Spring 1998, pp. 19–32; and M. Geuens and P. D. Pelsmacker, "Affect Intensity Revisited," *Psychology & Marketing,* May 1999, pp. 195–209.

13. J. S. Stevenson, G. C. Bruner II, and A. Kumard, "Webpage Background and Viewer Attitudes"; and G. C. Bruner II and A. Kumard, "Web Commercials and Advertising Hierarchy-of-Effects," both in *Journal of Advertising Research,* January 2000, pp. 29–34 and 35–43.

14. J. R. Coyle and E. Thorson, "The Effects of Progressive Levels of Interactivity and Vividness in Web Marketing Sites," *Journal of Advertising,* Fall 2001, pp. 65–77.

15. See M.-H. Huang, "Is Negative Affect in Advertising General or Specific?" *Psychology & Marketing,* May 1997, pp. 223–40. See also P. S. Ellen and P. F. Bone, "Does It Matter If It Smells?" *Journal of Advertising,* Winter 1998, pp. 29–39.

16. S.-W. Chang, "Effects of Brand Name Exposure on Brand Choice," *Advances in Consumer Research,* vol. 24, eds. M. Bruck and D. J. MacInnis (Provo, UT: Association for Consumer Research, 1997), pp. 288–94; A. Rindfleisch and J. J. Inman, "Explaining the Familiarity-Liking Relationship," *Marketing Letters,* no. 1 (1998), pp. 5–19; Baker, "When Can Affective Conditioning and Mere Exposure Directly Influence Brand Choice"; and C. Janiszewski and T. Meyvis, "Effects of Brand Logo Complexity, Repetition, and Spacing on Processing Fluency and Judgment," *Journal of Consumer Research,* June 2001, pp. 18–32.

17. See D. S. Kempf, "Attitude Formation from Product Trial," *Psychology & Marketing,* January 1999, pp. 35–50.

18. See G. J. Gaeth et al., "Consumers' Attitude Change across Sequences of Successful and Unsuccessful Product Usage," *Marketing Letters,* no. 1 (1997), pp. 41–53; and L. A. Brannon and T. C. Brock, "Limiting Time for Response Enhances Behavior Corresponding to the Merits of Compliance Appeals," *Journal of Consumer Psychology* 10, no. 3 (2001), pp. 135–46.

19. See D. M. Boush, C. H. Kim, L. R. Kahle, and R. Batra, "Cynicism and Conformity as Correlates of Trust in Product Information Sources," *Journal of Current Issues and Research in Advertising,* Fall 1993, pp. 71–79; and J. L. Aaker and D. Maheswaran, "The Effect of Cultural Orientation on Persuasion," *Journal of Consumer Research,* December 1997, pp. 315–28.

20. See R. Ahluwalia, "Examination of Psychological Processes Underlying Resistance to Persuasion," *Journal of Consumer Research,* September 2000, pp. 217–32.

21. See D. M. Boush, M. Friestad, and G. M. Rose, "Adolescent Skepticism toward TV Advertising and Knowledge of Advertiser Tactics"; and M. Friestad and P. Wright, "The Persuasion Knowledge Model"; both in *Journal of Consumer Research,* June 1994; pp. 1–31 and 165–75; M. Friestad and P. Wright, "Persuasion Knowledge," *Journal of Consumer Research,* June 1995, pp. 62–74; and M. Friestad and P. Wright, "Everyday Persuasion Knowledge," *Psychology & Marketing,* March 1999, pp. 185–94.

22. See R. E. Petty, J. T. Cacioppo, and D. Schumann, "Central and Peripheral Routes to Advertising Effectiveness," *Journal of Consumer Research,* September 1993, pp. 135–46; K. R. Lord, M.-S. Lee, and P. L. Sauer, "The Combined Influence Hypothesis," *Journal of Advertising,* Spring 1995, pp. 73–85; K. Yoon, R. N. Laczniak, D. D. Muehling, and B. B. Reece, "A Revised Model of Advertising Processing," *Journal of Current Issues and Research in Advertising,* Fall 1995, pp. 53–67; M. T. Pham, "Cue Representation and Selection Effects of Arousal on Persuasion," *Journal of Consumer Research,* March 1996, pp. 373–87; and F. Kokkinaki and P. Lunt, "The Effect of Advertising Message Involvement on Brand Attitude Accessibility," *Journal of Economic Psychology* 20 (1999), pp. 41–51.

23. C.-H. Cho, "How Advertising Works on the WWW," *Journal of Current Issues and Research in Advertising,* Spring 1999, pp. 33–50; and E. J. Karson and P. K. Korgaonkar, "An Experimental Investigation of Internet Advertising and the Elaboration Likelihood Model," *Journal of Current Issues and Research in Advertising,* Fall 2001, pp. 52–72.

24. Se P. M. West and S. M. Broniarczyk, "Integrating Multiple Opinions," *Journal of Consumer Research,* June 1998, pp. 38–51.

25. L. Arias-Bolzmann, "Effects of Absurdity in Advertising," *Journal of Advertising,* Spring 2000, pp. 35–49.

26. See A. C. B. Tse, "Factors Affecting Consumer Perceptions on Product Safety," *Journal of International Consumer Marketing* 12, no. 1 (1999), pp. 39–55.

27. D. J. Moore, J. C. Mowen, and R. Reardon, "Multiple Sources in Advertising Appeals," *Journal of the Academy of Marketing Science,* Summer 1994, pp. 234–43. See also N. Artz and A. M. Tybout, "The Moderating Impact of Quantitative Information on the Relationship between Source Credibility and Persuasion," *Marketing Letters* 10, no. 1 (1999), pp. 51–62.

28. R. D. Reinartz, "Testimonial Ads," *Bank Marketing,* March 1996, pp. 25–30.

29. D. H. Dean, "Brand Endorsement, Popularity, and Event Sponsorship as Advertising Cues Affecting Pre-Purchase Attitudes," *Journal of Advertising,* Fall 1999, pp. 1–11.

30. E. Haley, "Exploring the Construct of Organization as Source," *Journal of Advertising,* Summer 1996, pp. 19–35; and S. P. Jain and S. S. Posavac, "Prepurchase Attribute Verifiability, Source Credibility, and Persuasion," *Journal of Consumer Psychology* 11, no. 3 (2001), pp. 169–80.

31. R. E. Goldsmith, B. A. Lafferty, and S. J. Newell, "The Impact of Corporate Credibility and Celebrity Credibility on Consumer Reaction to Advertisements and Brands," *Journal of Advertising,* Fall 2000, pp. 43–54.

32. Ibid., p. 28.

33. J. Agrawal and W. A. Kamakura, "The Economic Worth of Celebrity Endorsers," *Journal of Marketing,* July 1995, pp. 56–62.

34. J. Sengupta, R. C. Goodstein, and D. S. Boninger, "All Cues Are Not Created Equal," *Journal of Consumer Research,* March 1997, pp. 351–61; and R. Nataraajan and S. K. Chawla, "Fitness Marketing," *Journal of Professional Services Marketing,* no. 2 (1997), pp. 119–29.

35. J. Jenson, "Picabo Street Wins Starring Role in Nike Game Plan," *Advertising Age,* November 11, 1996, p. 3.

36. M. A. Kamins and K. Gupta, "Congruence between Spokesperson and Product Type," *Psychology & Marketing,* November 1994, pp. 569–86; J. D. Mittelstaedt, P. C. Riesz, and W. J. Burns, "Why Are Endorsements Effective?" *Journal of Current Issues and Research in Advertising,* Spring 2000, pp. 55–65; B. D. Till and M. Busler, "The Match-Up Hypothesis," *Journal of Advertising,* Fall 2000, pp. 1–13; and B. Z. Erdogan, M. J. Baker, and S. Tagg, "Selecting Celebrity Endorsers," *Journal of Advertising Research,* May 2001, pp. 39–48.

37. A. B. Bower, "Highly Attractive Models in Advertising and the Women Who Loathe Them," *Journal of Advertising,* Fall 2001, pp. 51–63.

38. C. Tripp, T. D. Jensen, and L. Carlson, "The Effects of Multiple Product Endorsements by Celebrities on Consumers' Attitudes and Intentions," *Journal of Consumer Research,* March 1994, pp. 535–47.

39. B. D. Till and T. A. Shimp, "Endorsers in Advertising," *Journal of Advertising,* Spring 1998, pp. 67–82; and T. A. Louie, R. L. Kulik, and R. Jacobson, "When Bad Things Happen to the Endorsers of Good Products," *Marketing Letters,* February 2001, pp. 13–23.

40. M. F. Callcott and W.-N. Lee, "Establishing the Spokes-Character in Academic Inquiry," *Advances in Consumer Research,* vol. 22, eds. F. R. Kardes and M. Sujan (Provo, UT: Association for Consumer Research, 1995), pp. 144–51; and M. F. Callcott and B. J. Phillips, "Elves Make Good Cookies," *Journal of Advertising Research,* September 1996, pp. 73–79.

41. For an excellent overview, see T. Meenaghan, "Understanding Sponsorship Effects," *Psychology & Marketing,* February 2001, pp. 95–122.

42. S. R. McDaniel, "An Investigation of Match-Up Effects in Sport Sponsorship Advertising," *Psychology & Marketing,* March 1999, pp. 163–84; and T. B. Cornwell, S. W. Pruitt, and R. V. Ness, "The Value of Winning in Motorsports," *Journal of Advertising Research,* January 2001, pp. 17–31.

43. B. Harvey, "Measuring the Effects of Sponsorship," *Journal of Advertising Research,* January 2001, pp. 59–65.

44. Dean, "Brand Endorsement, Popularity, and Event Sponsorship."

45. T. Meenaghan, "Sponsorship and Advertising," *Psychology & Marketing,* February 2001, pp. 191–215.

46. R. Madrigal, "The Influence of Social Alliances with Sports Teams on Intentions to Purchase Corporate Sponsors' Products," *Journal of Advertising,* Winter 2000, pp. 13–24.

47. T. Lardinoit and C. Derbaix, "Sponsorship and Recall of Sponsors," *Psychology & Marketing,* February 2001, pp. 167–90.

48. P. G. Quester and B. Thompson, "Advertising and Promotion Leverage on Arts Sponsorship Effectiveness," *Journal of Advertising Research,* January 2001, pp. 33–47; and A. M. Levin, C. Joiner, and G. Cameron, "The Impact of Sports Sponsorship on Consumers' Brand Attitudes and Recall," *Journal of Current Issues and Research in Advertising,* Fall 2001, pp. 23–31. Conflicting evidence is in T. Lardinoit and P. G. Quester. "Attitudinal Effects of Combined Sponsorship and Sponsor's Prominence on Basketball in Europe," *Journal of Advertising Research,* January 2001, pp. 48–58.

49. R. K. Chandy et al., "What to Say When," *Journal Marketing Research,* November 2001, pp. 399–414.

50. D. D. Schoenbachler and T. E. Whittler, "Adolescent Processing of Social and Physical Threat Communications," *Journal of Advertising,* Winter 1996, pp. 37–54.

51. P. A. Keller and L. G. Block, "Increasing the Persuasiveness of Fear Appeals," *Journal of Consumer Research,* March 1996, pp. 448–60; M. S. LaTour and H. J. Rotfeld, "There Are Threats and (Maybe) Fear-Caused Arousal," *Journal of Advertising,* Fall 1997, pp. 45–59; and M. Laroche et al., "A Cross-Cultural Study of the Persuasive Effect of Fear Appeal Messages in Cigarette Advertising," *International Journal of Advertising* 3 (2001), pp. 297–317.

52. See M. S. LaTour, R. L. Snipes, and S. J. Bliss, "Don't Be Afraid to Use Fear Appeals," *Journal of Advertising Research,* March 1996, pp. 59–66.

53. M. C. Weinberger, H. Spotts, L. Campbell, and A. L. Parsons, "The Use and Effect of Humor in Different Advertising Media," *Journal of Advertising Research,* May 1995, pp. 44–56; Y. Zhang, "Responses to Humorous Advertising," *Journal of Advertising,* Spring 1996, pp. 15–32; Y. Zhang, "The Effect of Humor in Advertising," *Psychology & Marketing,* September 1996, pp. 531–45; H. E. Sparks, M. G. Weinberger, and A. L. Parsons, "Assessing the Use and Impact of Humor on Advertising Effectiveness," *Journal of Advertising,* Fall 1997, pp. 17–32; T. W. Cline and J. J. Kellaris, "The Joint Impact of Humor and Argument Strength in a Print Advertising Context," *Psychology & Marketing,* January 1999, pp. 69–86; and D. L. Alden, A. Mukherjee, and W. D. Hoyer, "The Effects of Incongruity, Surprise and Positive Moderators and Perceived Humor in Television Advertising," *Journal of Advertising,* Summer 2000, pp. 1–14.

54. D. L. Fugate, J. B. Gotlieb, and D. Bolton, "Humorous Services Advertising," *Journal of Professional Services Marketing* 21, no. 1 (2000), pp. 9–22.

55. D. Grewal et al., "Comparative versus Noncomparative Advertising," *Journal of Marketing,* October 1998, pp. 1–15; and M. E. Hill and M. King, "Comparative vs. Noncomparative Advertising," *Journal of Current Issues and Research in Advertising,* Fall 2001, pp. 33–52.

56. S. Putrevu and K. R. Lord, "Comparative and Noncomparative Advertising," *Journal of Advertising,* June 1995, pp. 77–91; T. H. Stevenson and L. E. Swayne, "The Use of Comparative Advertising in Business-to-Business Direct Marketing," *Industrial Marketing Management,* January 1995, pp. 53–59; H. Yi, J. E. Phelps, and D. R. Roskos-Ewoldsen, "Examining the Effectiveness of Comparative Advertising," *Journal of Current Issues and Research in Advertising,* Spring 1998, pp. 61–74; N. Donthu, "A Cross-Country Investigation of Recall of and Attitude toward Comparative Advertising," *Journal of Advertising,* Summer 1998, p. 22; A. Chattopadhyay, "When Does Comparative Advertising Influence Brand Attitude?" *Psychology & Marketing,* August 1998, pp. 461–75; S. V. Auken and A. J. Adams, "Across- versus Within-Class Comparative Advertising," *Psychology & Marketing,* August 1999, pp. 429–50; A. B. Sorescu and B. D. Gelb, "Negative Comparative Advertising," *Journal of Advertising,* Winter 2000, pp. 25–40; S. P. Jain, B. Buchanan, and D. Maheswaran, "Comparative versus Noncomparative Advertising," *Journal of Consumer Psychology* 9, no. 4 (2000), pp. 201–11; and A. V. Muthukrishnan, L. Warlop, and J. W. Alba, "The Piecemeal Approach to Comparative Advertising," *Marketing Letters* 12, no. 1 (2001), pp. 63–73.

57. See those cited in note 13; and M. E. Hill et al., "The Conjoining Influences of Affect and Arousal on Attitude Formation," *Research in Consumer Behavior* 9 (2000), pp. 129–46.

58. J. S. Johar and M. J. Sirgy, "Value-Expressive versus Utilitarian Advertising Appeals," *Journal of Advertising,* September 1991, pp. 23–33; S. Sharitt, "Evidence for Predicting the Effectiveness of Value-Expressive versus Utilitarian Appeals," *Journal of Advertising,* June 1992, pp. 47–51; M. R. Stafford and E. Day, "Retail Services Advertising," *Journal of Advertising,* Spring 1995, pp. 57–71; M. E. Slama and R. B. Singley, "Self-Monitoring and Value-Expressive vs. Utilitarian Ad Effectiveness," *Journal of Current Issues and Research in Advertising,* Fall 1996, pp. 39–49; L. Dube, A. Chattopadhyay, and A. Letarte, "Should Advertising Appeals Match the Basis of Consumers' Attitudes?" *Journal of Advertising Research,* November 1996, pp. 82–89; and A. M. Fiore and H. Yu, "Effects of Imagery Copy and Product Samples on Responses Toward the Product," *Journal of Interactive Marketing,* Spring 2001, pp. 36–46.

59. M. Dahlen and J. Bergendahl, "Informing and Transforming on the Web," *International Journal of Advertising* 20, no. 2 (2001), pp. 189–205.

60. C. Pechmann, "Predicting When Two-Sided Ads Will Be More Effective Than One-Sided Ads," *Journal of Marketing Research,* November 1992, pp. 441–53; and A. E. Crowley and W. D. Hoyer, "An Integrative Framework for Understanding Two-Sided Persuasion," *Journal of Consumer Research,* March 1994, pp. 561–74.

61. Y. Zhang and R. Buda, "Moderating Effects of Need for Cognition on Responses to Positively versus Negatively Framed Advertising Messages," *Journal of Advertising,* Summer 1999, pp. 1–15; and R. J. Donovan and G. Jalleh, "Positively versus Negatively Framed Product Attributes," *Psychology & Marketing,* October 1999, pp. 613–30.

62. A. C. Burns, A. Biswas, and L. A. Babin, "The Operation of Visual Imagery as a Mediator of Advertising Effects," *Journal of Advertising,* June 1993, pp. 71–85.

63. See P. W. Miniard, D. Sirdeshmukh, and D. E. Innis, "Peripheral Persuasion and Brand Choice," *Journal of Consumer Research,* September 1992, pp. 226–39.

64. J. W. Harvey, "Benefit Segmentation for Fund Raisers," *Journal of the Academy of Marketing Science,* Winter 1990, pp. 77–86. D. S. P. Cermak, K. M. File, and R. A. Prince, "A Benefit Segmentation of the Major Donor Market," *Journal of Business Research,* February 1994, pp. 121–30; P. J. O'Connor and G. L. Sullivan, "Market Segmentation," *Psychology & Marketing,* October 1995, pp. 613–35; T.-Z. Chang and S.-J. Chen, "Benefit Segmentation," *Journal of Professional Services Marketing,* no. 2 (1995), pp. 69–80; and J. W. Peltier and J. A. Schribrowsky, "The Use of Need-Based Segmentation for Developing Segment-Specific Direct Marketing Strategies," *Journal of Direct Marketing,* Fall 1997, pp. 53–62.

65. H. E. Bloom, "Match the Concept and the Product," *Journal of Advertising Research,* October 1977, pp. 25–27.

This is not THE VERY LATEST IN VIRTUAL REALITY.

THIS IS RIDING THE RAPIDS LIVE AND IN PERSON IN ARIZONA, WHERE OUTDOOR ENTHUSIASTS CAN INDULGE IN THE GAME OF LIFE TO THE ABSOLUTE FULLEST — IN A WORLD THAT PUTS VIRTUAL REALITY TO SHAME.

FOR YOUR FREE TRAVEL PACKET, CONTACT THE ARIZONA OFFICE OF TOURISM AT 1-800-451-6066 OR VISIT ARIZONAGUIDE.COM

ARIZONA
GRAND CANYON STATE

Courtesy Arizona Office of Tourism; photo by Kerrick James.

Self-Concept and Lifestyle

A marketing study identified five consumer lifestyles in relation to outdoor activities.[1] Each of these lifestyles is described briefly below.

- *Excitement-seeking competitives* (16 percent). Like risk, some danger, and competition, though they also like social and fitness benefits. Participate in team and individual competitive sports. Half belong to a sports club or team. Median age of 32, two-thirds are male. Upper-middle class, and about half are single.

- *Getaway actives* (33 percent). Like the opportunity to be alone or experience nature. Active in camping, fishing, and birdwatching. Not loners; focus on families or close friends. Half use outdoor recreation to reduce stress. Median age of 35, equally divided between men and women.

- *Fitness-driven* (10 percent). Engage in outdoor activities strictly for fitness benefits. Walking, bicycling, and jogging are popular activities. Upscale economically. Median age of 46, over half are women.

- *Health-conscious sociables* (33 percent). Relatively inactive despite stated health concerns. Most involved with spectator activities such as sightseeing, driving for pleasure, visiting zoos, and so forth. Median age 49, two-thirds are female.

- *Unstressed and unmotivated* (8 percent). Not interested in outdoor recreation except as an opportunity for the family to be together. Median age of 49, equally divided between males and females.

What are the marketing implications of this study for Aspen, Schwinn bicycles, Jazzercise Inc., and Old Town canoes?

In this chapter, we will discuss the meaning of lifestyle and the role it plays in developing marketing strategies. Lifestyle is, in many ways, an outward expression of one's self-concept. That is, the way an individual chooses to live, given the constraints of income and ability, is heavily influenced by that person's current and desired self-concept. Therefore, we begin the chapter with an analysis of the self-concept. We then describe lifestyles, the ways in which lifestyle is measured, and examples of how lifestyle is being used to develop marketing programs.

SELF-CONCEPT

Self-concept is defined as *the totality of the individual's thoughts and feelings having reference to him- or herself as an object*. It is an individual's perception of and feelings toward him- or herself. In other words, your self-concept is composed of the attitudes you hold toward yourself.

The self-concept can be divided into four basic parts, as shown in Table 12–1: actual versus ideal, and private versus social. The actual/ideal distinction refers to the individual's perception of *who I am now* (**actual self-concept**) and *who I would like to be* (**ideal self-concept**). The private self refers to *how I am or would like to be to myself* (**private self-concept**), and the social self is *how I am seen by others or how I would like to be seen by others* (**social self-concept**).

Interdependent/Independent Self-Concepts   The self-concept is important in all cultures. However, those aspects of the self that are most valued and most influence consumption and other behaviors vary across cultures. Researchers have found it useful to categorize self-concepts into two types—independent and interdependent, also referred to as separateness and connectedness.[2]

An independent construal of the self is based on the predominant Western cultural belief that individuals are inherently separate. The **independent self-concept** *emphasizes personal goals, characteristics, achievements, and desires*. Individuals with an independent self-concept tend to be individualistic, egocentric, autonomous, self-reliant, and self-contained. They define themselves in terms of what they have done, what they have, and their personal characteristics.

An interdependent construal of the self is based more on the common Asian cultural belief in the fundamental connectedness of human beings. The **interdependent self-concept** *emphasizes family, cultural, professional, and social relationships*. Individuals with an interdependent self-concept tend to be obedient, sociocentric, holistic, connected, and

TABLE 12–1	Dimensions of Self-Concept	Actual Self-Concept	Ideal Self-Concept
Dimensions of a Consumer's Self-Concept	*Private self*	How I actually see myself	How I would like to see myself
	Social self	How others actually see me	How I would like others to see me

Courtesy Bonne Bell.

relation oriented. They define themselves in terms of social roles, family relationships, and commonalities with other members of their groups.

Independent and interdependent self-concepts are not discreet categories; rather, they are constructs used to describe the opposite ends of a continuum along which most cultures lie. However, as we emphasized in Chapter 2, most cultures are heterogeneous. Therefore, within a given culture, subcultures and other groups will vary on this dimension, as will individuals.[3] For example, women across cultures tend to have more of an interdependent self-concept than do males.[4]

Variation in the degree to which an individual or culture is characterized by an independent versus an interdependent self-concept has been found to influence message preferences, consumption of luxury goods, and the types of products preferred. For example, ads emphasizing acting alone and autonomy tend to be effective with consumers with independent self-concepts, whereas ads emphasizing group membership work better with consumers with interdependent self-concepts.[5] The ad in Illustration 12–1 should be effective with individuals whose independent self-concept is dominant.

Possessions and the Extended Self

Some products acquire substantial meaning to an individual or are used to signal particularly important aspects of that person's self to others. Belk developed a theory called the *extended self* to explain this.[6] The **extended self** consists of *the self plus possessions;* that is, people tend to define themselves in part by their possessions. Thus, some possessions are not just a manifestation of one's self-concept; they are an integral part of the person's self-identity. People are, to some extent, what they possess. If one lost key possessions, he or she would be a somewhat different individual.[7]

While these key possessions might be major items, such as one's home or automobile, they are equally likely to be smaller items with unique meanings, such as a souvenir, a photograph, a pet, or a favorite cooking pan. These objects have meaning to the individual beyond their market value. Consider these examples from consumers who lost their positions in natural disasters and who had ample insurance to replace them:

Yea, we got better stuff, but it doesn't mean anything to us. It's just stuff.

I had so much love tied up in my things. I can't go through that kind of loss again. What I'm buying now won't be as important to me.

You can't put back or replace what you had. It was too personal—it was customized.

I wanted a different house so that the missing items wouldn't seem gone. I couldn't look in a room and see something was not there anymore.[8]

Products become part of one's extended self for a variety of reasons. Souvenirs often become part of the extended self as representations of memories and feelings:

You can't really tell what Paris is like . . . you know, a lot of it is just feelings; feelings you can't put into words, or [that] pictures cannot capture . . . . They [a hat and blouse] are just reminders.

I had a really wonderful trip and really sort of discovered myself, you know, I learned to be independent on my own. I really didn't have the money to buy this [necklace and boomerang charm], but I decided I wanted something really permanent . . . . The boomerang is a symbol of going back there sometime. [9]

Gifts often take on important meanings as representations of relationships:

That gift was my grandfather's ring . . . . Even now when I look at it, I think about its past with him and the journeys it took around the world in the Navy back in World War II.

The key chain is special because every so often, when I think about who gave it to me, it brings back old thoughts and feelings. It is a symbol of friendship between us, and it keeps us in touch.

There stood Daddy . . . holding a beautiful old violin . . . . As proud as I was of the gift at the time, it means more to me today as I raise my first child. My violin is old and dusty now, but I will always treasure it and keep its meaning alive.[10]

Some products become embedded with meaning and value as they are used over time. Use over time allows a product to become associated with an array of memories. One of the products in the author's extended self is the old, cheap briefcase he purchased to take to his first academic conference many years ago. To his surprise, the briefcase has lasted 30 years and has been on trips through much of the world. Although well worn, it is now "part of" the author, and he plans to continue to use it as long as possible.

At other times a single peak experience with a product such as a mountain bike can propel the product into the extended self. A **peak experience** is *an experience that surpasses the usual level of intensity, meaningfulness, and richness and produces feelings of joy and self-fulfillment.*[11] Products that are acquired or used to help consumers with major life transitions (leaving home, first job, marriage, children, and so forth) are also likely to be or become part of the extended self.[12]

Consumer Insight 12–1 describes a product that is likely to become part of one's extended self as well as one's physical self.

Tattoos and the Extended Self

Most products and services associated with the extended self are distinct from the physical self.[13] Until recently, exceptions were limited primarily to hairstyles, hair coloring, and cosmetics. One could also alter the physical self through exercise, diet, weight training, and plastic surgery. In recent years, body piercing and tattooing have become additional ways to alter both the extended self and the physical self. Tattooing is unique (except for plastic surgery) in that it is a relatively unalterable change to the physical self. It can be done primarily for adornment or beauty enhancement reasons. Or it can serve primarily as a public or private symbol.

For most of this century, tattooing was not socially acceptable among most groups in the United States. The most noticeable exception was enlisted men in the Navy, and even then alcohol consumption was frequently involved in the decision to secure a tattoo. This has changed sharply in recent years. Why has this become socially acceptable, and what does it mean to the self-concept of those who secure tattoos?

A *tattoo renaissance* began in the 1960s with the hippie movement and the evolution of skilled tattoo artists in the San Francisco area. Interest also began to grow in the historical and ethnographic aspects of the tattoo medium. The commercial art world and academic art historians began to pay attention to tattooing as an art form. This, in turn, attracted better tattoo artists. By the early 1990s, public figures, particularly athletes, began to wear visible tattoos, which increased their acceptability among the more venturesome members of mainstream society.

Tattoos have meanings on at least three levels. First, there is the meaning associated with *having a tattoo*. While increasingly common, having a tattoo is still far from the norm. Thus, having a tattoo in and of itself makes a statement about the person. A person with a tattoo is still viewed as somewhat of a risk taker or nonconformist. The location of the tattoo also contains meaning. The more visible the tattoo, the more rebellious or nonconforming the individual appears to be. The tattoo itself is a major source of meaning, both private and symbolic. Tattoos may symbolize group membership, interests, activities, relationships, life transitions, accomplishments, or values. Tattoos may be unique and filled primarily with personal meaning or their meaning may be rooted in cultural practice and myths.

Acquiring a tattoo is risky. It is very expensive to remove or alter a tattoo. Thus, if a person doesn't like his or her tattoo or his or her tastes change over time, that individual is at financial risk. There is also the social risk that one's current or future friends, colleagues, or employers will have a negative reaction to the tattoo. Finally, there is still physiological risk associated with acquiring a tattoo.

Critical Thinking Questions

1. How does a tattoo affect one's self-concept and become part of one's extended self?

2. Will one or multiple visible tattoos become the norm for younger consumers over the next 10 years?

3. How is the renaissance in tattooing similar to the revival of cigar smoking? How is it different?

A scale has been developed to measure the extent to which an item has been incorporated into the extended self.[14] It is a Likert scale (see Appendix A) in which consumers express agreement (from strongly agree to strongly disagree on a seven-point scale) to the following statements:

1. My _____ helps me achieve the identity I want to have.

2. My _____ helps me narrow the gap between what I am and what I try to be.

3. My _____ is central to my identity.

4. My _____ is part of who I am.

5. If my _____ is stolen from me I will feel as if my identity has been snatched from me.

6. I derive some of my identity from my _____.

TABLE 12–2									
1. Rugged	—	—	—	—	—	—	—	Delicate
2. Excitable	—	—	—	—	—	—	—	Calm
3. Uncomfortable	—	—	—	—	—	—	—	Comfortable
4. Dominating	—	—	—	—	—	—	—	Submissive
5. Thrifty	—	—	—	—	—	—	—	Indulgent
6. Pleasant	—	—	—	—	—	—	—	Unpleasant
7. Contemporary	—	—	—	—	—	—	—	Noncontemporary
8. Organized	—	—	—	—	—	—	—	Unorganized
9. Rational	—	—	—	—	—	—	—	Emotional
10. Youthful	—	—	—	—	—	—	—	Mature
11. Formal	—	—	—	—	—	—	—	Informal
12. Orthodox	—	—	—	—	—	—	—	Liberal
13. Complex	—	—	—	—	—	—	—	Simple
14. Colorless	—	—	—	—	—	—	—	Colorful
15. Modest	—	—	—	—	—	—	—	Vain

Measurement Scales for Self-Concepts, Person Concepts, and Product Concepts

Source: N. K. Malhotra, " A Scale to Measure Self-Concepts, Person Concepts, and Product Concepts," *Journal of Marketing Research,* Published by the American Marketing Association; reprinted with permission. November 1981, p. 462.

Owning a product affects a person even if it does not become an important part of the person's extended self. The **mere ownership effect,** or the *endowment effect,* is *the tendency of an owner to evaluate an object more favorably than a nonowner.* This occurs almost immediately upon acquiring an object and increases with time of ownership. Thus, people tend to value an object more after acquiring it than before. People also tend to value objects they own more highly than they value similar objects owned by others.[15]

The concept of the extended self and the mere ownership effect have numerous implications for marketing strategy. One is that communications that cause potential consumers to visualize product ownership might result in enhanced product evaluations. Product sampling or other trial programs may have similar results.

Measuring Self-Concept

Utilizing the self-concept in marketing requires that it be measurable. The most common measurement approach is the semantic differential (see Appendix A). Malhotra has developed a set of 15 pairs of adjectives shown in Table 12–2. These have proven effective in describing the ideal, actual, and social self-concepts of individuals as well as the images of automobiles and celebrities. *Using this scale, determine your actual and desired private and social self-concepts.*

This instrument can be used to ensure a match between the self-concept (actual or ideal) of a target market, the image of a brand, and the characteristics of an advertising spokesperson. For example, Nike undoubtedly studied the desired self-concept of young girls and the image of Picabo Street before selecting her as a primary company spokesperson to that segment.[16]

Using Self-Concept to Position Products

People's attempts to obtain their ideal self-concept, or maintain their actual self-concept, often involve the purchase and consumption of products, services, and media.[17] This

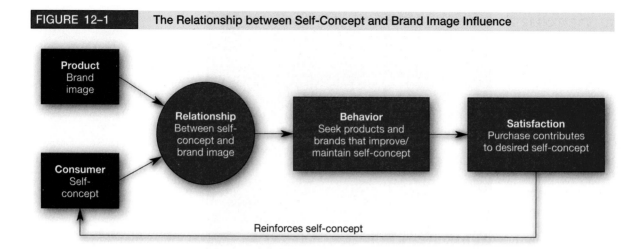

FIGURE 12–1   The Relationship between Self-Concept and Brand Image Influence

process is described in Figure 12–1. This figure implies a rather conscious, deliberate process by which consumers determine their actual and desired self-concept and proceed to purchase products consistent with these concepts. Although something like this may occasionally occur, most of the time the process is not deliberate, at least at the conscious level. For example, a person may drink diet colas because his desired self-concept includes a trim figure, but he is unlikely to think about the purchase in these terms. However, as the following statement illustrates, on occasion people do.

> And I feel if you present yourself in the right way, people will start to notice. But this leads back to image and self-worth, which can be achieved through having the right clothes and a good haircut . . . having a good portrait of yourself on the outside can eventually lead to an emotionally stable inside.[18]

This suggests that marketers should strive to develop product images that are consistent with the self-concepts of their target markets.[19] While everyone's self-concept is unique, there is also significant overlap across individuals. For example, many consumers see themselves as environmentalists. Companies and products that create an image as being concerned about or good for the environment are likely to be supported by these consumers.

Consumers maintain and enhance their self-concepts not only by what they consume, but by what they avoid.[20] Some consumers make a point of avoiding certain product categories such as red meat or brands such as Nike as part of maintaining "who they are."

Consumers prefer brands that are similar to their self-concepts; however, the degree to which they would be attracted to such a brand varies with the *symbolism* and *conspicuousness* of that product class. Furthermore, the interaction between self-concept and product image is situation specific. This suggests the need to measure ideal self-concepts in a situational context.[21]

Look at Illustration 12–2. *What type of self-concept does this ad appeal to?*

Marketing Ethics and the Self-Concept

The self-concept contains many dimensions. Marketers have been criticized for focusing too much attention on the importance of being beautiful, with *beautiful* being defined as young and slim with a fairly narrow range of facial features. Virtually all societies appear to define and desire beauty, but the intense exposure to products and advertisements

© 2002 Wyeth Consumer Healthcare.

focused on beauty in America today is unique. Critics argue that this concern leads individuals to develop self-concepts that are heavily dependent on their physical appearance
rather than other equally or more important attributes.

Consider the following statements from two young women:

- I never felt that I looked right. The styles that I always want to wear, I always feel like
I look fat. I always have to wear like a long skirt or sweater or at least baggy pants and
a tight shirt. Like I can see outfits that I'd love to wear, but I know that I could never
wear them. I probably could wear them and get away with it, but I'd be so self-
conscious walking around that I'd be like, "oh, my God." Like I always try to look thinner and I guess everybody does.

- I am pretty content with my hair because I have good hair. I have good eyesight (laughs)
so I don't have to wear glasses or anything that would make my face look different from
what it is. In terms of bad points, well there is a lot. I got a lot of my father's features. I
wish I had more of my mother's. My hands are pretty square. I have a kind of a big butt.
Then, I don't have that great of a stomach. I like my arms. They're not flabby arms. I
like my ankles. It sounds really stupid, but a lot of people have like these trunks and it's
very unattractive. So, I don't have huge, fat ankles. One thing I really hate is that I have
large calves, which I don't like.[22]

These young women have self-concepts that are partly negative as a result of their
perceptions of their beauty relative to the standard portrayed in the media. Critics of advertising claim that most individuals, but particularly young women, acquire negative components to their self-concepts because very few can achieve the standards of beauty presented
in advertising. Recent research indicates that similar negative self-evaluations occur in
males as a result of idealized images of both physical attractiveness and financial success.[23]

The ethical question is complex. No one ad or company has this type of impact. It is the cumulative effect of many ads across many companies reinforced by the content of the mass media that presumably causes some to be overly focused on their physical beauty. And, as stated earlier, concern with beauty existed long before advertising.

THE NATURE OF LIFESTYLE

As Figure 12–2 indicates, **lifestyle** is basically *how a person lives.* It is how one enacts his or her self-concept. It is determined by the person's past experiences, innate characteristics, and current situation. It influences all aspects of one's consumption behavior. One's lifestyle is a function of inherent individual characteristics that have been shaped and formed through social interaction as the person evolves through the life cycle.

Individuals and households both have lifestyles. Although household lifestyles are in part determined by the individual lifestyles of the household members, the reverse is also true.

An individual's desired lifestyle influences his or her needs and desires and thus purchase and use behavior. It determines many of the person's consumption decisions, which in turn reinforce or alter that individual's lifestyle.

Marketers can use lifestyle analysis with respect to specific areas of consumers' lives, such as outdoor recreation. Many firms have conducted lifestyle studies focused on those aspects of individual or household lifestyles most relevant to their product or service. For example, the lifestyle study described at the beginning of this chapter focused on outdoor activities. The ad shown in Illustration 12–3 would appeal to individuals classified as "getaway actives" and "health-conscious sociables" in this study. A second approach, also widely used in practice, is to study the general lifestyle patterns of a population. Both approaches are described in detail in the next section.

Consumers are seldom explicitly aware of the role lifestyle plays in their purchase decisions. For example, few consumers would think, "I'll have a Starbucks coffee at a

FIGURE 12–2   Lifestyle and the Consumption Process

Lifestyle determinants	Lifestyle	Impact on behavior
• Demographics	How we live	Purchases
• Subculture		• How
• Social class	• Activities	• When
• Motives	• Interests	• Where
• Personality	• Likes/dislikes	• What
• Emotions	• Attitudes	• With whom
• Values	• Consumption	Consumption
• Household life cycle	• Expectations	• Where
• Culture	• Feelings	• With whom
• Past experiences		• How
		• When
		• What

Courtesy Marc Resorts.

Starbucks outlet to maintain my lifestyle." However, individuals pursuing an active, social lifestyle might purchase Starbucks in part because of its convenience, "in" status, and the presence of others at Starbucks' outlets. Thus, lifestyle frequently provides the basic motivation and guidelines for purchases, although it generally does so in an indirect, subtle manner.

Measurement of Lifestyle

Attempts to develop quantitative measures of lifestyle were initially referred to as **psychographics.**[24] In fact, the terms *psychographics* and *lifestyle* are frequently used interchangeably. Psychographics or lifestyle studies typically include the following:

- *Attitudes*—evaluative statements about other people, places, ideas, products, and so forth.
- *Values*—widely held beliefs about what is acceptable or desirable.
- *Activities and interests*—nonoccupational behaviors to which consumers devote time and effort, such as hobbies, sports, public service, and church.
- *Demographics*—age, education, income, occupation, family structure, ethnic background, gender, and geographic location.
- *Media patterns*—the specific media the consumers utilize.
- *Usage rates*—measurements of consumption within a specified product category; often consumers are categorized as heavy, medium, light, or nonusers.

A large number of individuals, often 500 or more, provide the above information. Statistical techniques are used to place them into groups whose members have similar response patterns. Most studies use the first two or three dimensions described above to group individuals. The other dimensions are used to provide fuller descriptions of each group. Other studies include demographics as part of the grouping process.[25]

Lifestyle measurements can be constructed with varying degrees of specificity. At one extreme are broad measurements dealing with general ways of living. Examples of these are provided in the next sections. More common measurements are product or activity specific, such as the study of outdoor activities described earlier. For example, a study of lifestyles related to fashion clothing included 40 statements such as the following (respondents stated their degree of agreement with each):[26]

I like parties with music and chatting.
I like clothes with a touch of sensuality.
I choose clothes that match my age.
No matter where I go, I dress the way I want to.
I think I spend more time than I should on fashion.

This study also included measures of relevant activities and demographics. The value of such lifestyle information on a particular target market is easy to understand.

Table 12–3 presents a small portion of a lifestyle analysis of British women between the ages of 15 and 44. This was an activity/product–specific analysis focused on appearance, fashions, exercise, and health. Six groups were formed solely on the basis of their attitudes and values with respect to the four areas mentioned. *After* the groups were formed, significant differences were found in terms of product usage, shopping behaviors, media patterns, and demographics. Attempts to segment the market using demographics alone produced much less useful results.

TABLE 12-3

Lifestyle Analysis of the British Cosmetics Market

Cosmetic Lifestyle Segments
1. *Self-aware:* concerned about appearance, fashion, and exercise.
2. *Fashion-directed:* concerned about fashion and appearance, not about exercise and sport.
3. *Green goddesses:* concerned about sport and fitness, less about appearance.
4. *Unconcerned:* neutral attitudes to health and appearance.
5. *Conscience-stricken:* no time for self-realization, busy with family responsibilities.
6. *Dowdies:* indifferent to fashion, cool on exercise, and dress for comfort.

Behaviors and Descriptors

	Cosmetic Use Index*	Blush Use Index*	Retail Outlets*				Age† (15–44)	Social Class‡
			Wallis	Miss Selfridge	Etam	C&A		
Self-aware	162	188	228	189	151	102	51%	60%
Fashion-directed	147	166	153	165	118	112	43	56
Green goddesses	95	76	74	86	119	103	32	52
Unconcerned	82	81	70	89	74	95	44	64
Conscience-stricken	68	59	53	40	82	99	24	59
Dowdies	37	19	17	22	52	85	20	62

*100 = Average usage.
†Read as "_____ percent of this group is between 15 and 44."
‡Read as "_____ percent of this group is in the working and lower middle class."

Source: T. Bowles, "Does Classifying People by Lifestyle Really Help the Advertiser?" *European Research*, February 1988, pp. 17–24.

Courtesy Connectix.

The value of this type of data is obvious. For example, *how would you develop a marketing strategy to reach the conscience-stricken segment shown in Table 12–3?*

The Arbitron Company discovered eight lifestyles of relevance to media usage. Three are briefly described below. *How would you advertise Internet services or direct digital television to each?*

- *Fast laners* (14 percent of population). Younger, overrepresenting Generation X and teenagers. Social and busy, they are impulse shoppers despite slightly below average income. They are heavy users of late-night television, MTV, HBO, contemporary comedies, premium cable services, and pay-per-view. They are open to technology and innovation and are optimistic about the future.
- *Savvy sophisticates* (11 percent of population). Overrepresents high-income and highly educated baby boomers. They describe themselves as confident, innovative, and curious. They are optimistic about the future but somewhat skeptical about new media possibilities. They own and use more computer, telephone, and communications equipment than any other segment. They read *Newsweek* magazine and watch "60 Minutes" and PBS.
- *The settled set* (17 percent of population). Older than the general population with a thrifty, conservative, family values orientation. They watch "Wheel of Fortune" and read *Reader's Digest.* They are not comfortable with technology and change.[27]

To which of these three groups will the ad in Illustration 12–4 appeal? How should ads for the other two groups differ from this one?

Lifestyle analysis has been used to develop a successful lottery in Britain,[28] to predict sales at a new department store location,[29] to understand service expectations with respect to health care,[30] to study subcultures in Canada,[31] to compare Hong Kong and Singapore consumers,[32] to analyze complaint behavior by elderly patients dissatisfied with their health care,[33] and to develop dining menus at U.S. college campuses.[34]

While product- or activity-specific lifestyle studies are useful, many firms have found general lifestyle studies to be of great value also. Three popular general systems are described next.[35]

THE VALS SYSTEM

By far the most popular application of psychographic research by marketing managers is SRI Consulting Business Intelligence's (SRIC-BI) VALS program. Introduced in 1978 and significantly revised in 1989, **VALS** provides a systematic classification of American adults into eight distinct consumer segments.[36] The updated VALS has more of a psychological base than the original, which was more activity and interest based. The psychological base attempts to tap relatively enduring attitudes and values. It is measured by 42 statements with which respondents state a degree of agreement or disagreement. The following are examples:

- I am often interested in theories.
- I often crave excitement.
- I consider myself an intellectual.
- I like to make things with my hands.
- I must admit that I like to show off.
- I would like to spend a year or more in a foreign country.
- I like being in charge of a group.
- I like my life to be pretty much the same from week to week.

The questions are designed to classify respondents according to their *self-orientation* (similar in many ways to the self-concept), which serves as one of VALS's two dimensions. SRIC-BI has identified three primary self-orientations:

- *Principle oriented.* These individuals are guided in their choices by their beliefs and principles rather than by feelings, events, or desire for approval.
- *Status oriented.* The actions, approval, and opinions of others heavily influence these individuals.
- *Action oriented.* These individuals desire social or physical activity, variety, and risk taking.

These three orientations determine the types of goals and behaviors that individuals will pursue.

The second dimension, termed *resources,* reflects the ability of individuals to pursue their dominant self-orientation. It refers to the full range of psychological, physical, demographic, and material means on which consumers can draw. Resources generally increase from adolescence through middle age and then remain relatively stable until they begin to decline with older age.

On the basis of these two concepts, SRIC-BI has identified eight general psychographic segments, as shown in Figure 12–3. Table 12–4 provides a demographic description of each segment. Table 12–5 provides information on product ownership and activities for each segment. Each of these segments is described briefly next.

FIGURE 12–3   VALS™ Lifestyle System

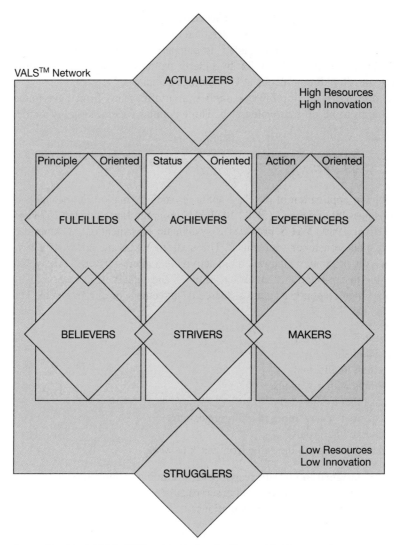

TABLE 12–4   Demographics of the VALS Segments

	Actualizer (%)	Fulfilled (%)	Believer (%)	Achiever (%)	Striver (%)	Experiencer (%)	Maker (%)	Struggler (%)	Total (%)
U.S. Distribution	10.0	11.3	16.5	14.2	11.5	12.7	11.8	12.0	100
Median Age	*43 Yrs*	*54 Yrs*	*50 Yrs*	*40 Yrs*	*28 Yrs*	*25 Yrs*	*45 Yrs*	*70 Yrs*	*43 Yrs*
Female	46	49	69	56	41	42	43	63	52
Married	66	80	65	71	36	27	67	46	57
Education:									
College Degree or Higher	91	69	1	30	2	11	0	2	23
Median Income	*$104K*	*$76K*	*$34K*	*$67K*	*$22K*	*$47K*	*$39K*	*$15K*	*$41K*
Occupation:									
White Collar Professions	78	60	24	58	23	33	23	6	37

TABLE 12–5   VALS Segment Ownership and Activities

	All 100	Actualizer 100	Fulfilled 100	Believer 100	Achiever 100	Striver 100	Experiencer 100	Maker 100	Struggler 100
Own a truck	100	54	99	106	121	78	83	158	89
Drink herb tea	100	219	152	71	97	47	92	92	61
Mountain bicycle $100+	100	145	36	14	141	146	221	122	0
Golf clubs $100+	100	148	120	89	209	54	134	28	7
Own a fishing rod	100	105	125	77	105	93	80	168	58
Attend country music performances	100	59	95	107	116	87	92	159	74
Play chess	100	210	91	48	93	106	161	114	12
Do crossword puzzles	100	120	141	112	94	68	77	91	100
Go to live theater	100	255	177	74	102	48	91	51	40
Do woodworking	100	113	159	43	90	41	55	236	93
See movies on opening weekend	100	94	44	73	99	156	245	51	37
Go hunting	100	43	83	79	117	101	89	228	56
Do gardening	100	131	141	110	100	53	50	110	109
Go to bars/night clubs	100	161	70	56	117	116	180	96	24
Play bingo	100	32	74	151	84	94	115	96	123

Source: SRI Consulting Business Intelligence.

The VALS Segments

Actualizers *Actualizers* are successful, sophisticated, active, take-charge people with high self-esteem and abundant resources. They are interested in growth and seek to develop, explore, and express themselves in a variety of ways—sometimes guided by principle and sometimes by a desire to have an effect, to make a change. Image is important to Actualizers, not as evidence of status or power but as an expression of their taste, independence, and character.

Actualizers are among the established and emerging leaders in business and government, yet they continue to seek challenges. They have a wide range of interests, are concerned with social issues, and are open to change. Their possessions and recreation reflect a cultivated taste for the finer things in life. The ad in Illustration 12–5 would appeal to Actualizers.

Fulfilleds and Believers: Principle Oriented Principle-oriented consumers seek to make their behavior consistent with their views of how the world is or should be.

Fulfilleds are mature, satisfied, comfortable, reflective people who value order, knowledge, and responsibility. Most are well educated, and in or recently retired from professional occupations. They are well informed about world and national events and are alert to opportunities to broaden their knowledge. Content with their careers, families, and station in life, they tend to center their leisure activities on the home.

Fulfilleds have a moderate respect for the status quo institutions of authority and social decorum but are open-minded about new ideas and social change. They tend to base their decisions on strongly held principles and consequently appear calm and self-assured. Fulfilleds are conservative, practical consumers; they look for functionality, value, and durability in the products they buy.

Believers are conservative, conventional people with concrete beliefs based on traditional, established codes: family, church, community, and the nation. Many Believers express moral codes that are deeply rooted and literally interpreted. They follow established

Courtesy Ford Plantation.

routines, organized in large part around their homes, families, and the social or religious organizations to which they belong. As consumers, they are conservative and predictable, favoring American products and established brands.

The ad in Illustration 12–6 would appeal to both the Fulfilleds and the Believers.

Achievers and Strivers: Status Oriented   Status-oriented consumers have or seek a secure place in a valued social setting. They make choices to enhance their position or to facilitate their move to another, more desirable group. Strivers look to others to indicate what they should be and do, whereas Achievers, more resourceful and active, seek recognition and self-definition through achievements at work and in their families.

Achievers are successful career- and work-oriented people who like to, and generally do, feel in control of their lives. They value consensus, predictability, and stability over risk, intimacy, and self-discovery. They are deeply committed to work and family. Work provides them with a sense of duty, material rewards, and prestige. Their social lives reflect this focus and are structured around family, church, and career. Achievers live conventional lives, are politically conservative, and respect authority and the status quo. Image is important to them; they favor established, prestige products and services that demonstrate success to their peers.

The ad in Illustration 12–7 would appeal to Achievers.

Strivers seek motivation, self-definition, and approval from the world around them. They are striving to find a secure place in life. Unsure of themselves and low on economic, social, and psychological resources, Strivers are concerned about the opinions and approval of others. Money defines success for Strivers, who don't have enough of it and often feel that life has given them a raw deal. Strivers are easily bored and impulsive. Many of

Courtesy Landau Boats II, LLC.

ILLUSTRATION 12–6

Both Believers and Fulfilleds have a strong family orientation. This ad would appeal to both groups.

Courtesy Casio, Inc..

ILLUSTRATION 12–7

This ad would appeal to the Achievers' family focus, appreciation of prestige products, and comfort with technology.

ILLUSTRATION 12–8

Experiencers are
impulsive and
social. They like
new and offbeat
things.

Courtesy Plano Molding.

them seek to be stylish. They emulate those who own more impressive possessions, but
what they wish to obtain is generally beyond their reach.

Experiencers and Makers: Action Oriented   Action-oriented consumers like to
affect their environment in tangible ways. Makers do so primarily at home and with constructive activity, whereas Experiencers do so in the wider world through adventure and
vivid experiences.

Experiencers are young, vital, enthusiastic, impulsive, and rebellious. They seek variety
and excitement, savoring the new, the offbeat, and the risky. Still in the process of formulating life values and patterns of behavior, they quickly become enthusiastic about new
possibilities but are equally quick to cool. At this stage of their lives, they are politically
uncommitted, uninformed, and highly ambivalent about what they believe.

Experiencers combine an abstract disdain for conformity with an outsider's awe of others' wealth, prestige, and power. Their energy finds an outlet in exercise, sports, outdoor
recreation, and social activities. Experiencers are avid consumers and spend much of their
income on clothing, fast food, music, movies, and video. The ad in Illustration 12–8 would
be particularly appealing to this segment.

Makers are practical people who have constructive skills and value self-sufficiency.
They live within a traditional context of family, practical work, and physical recreation
and have little interest in what lies outside that context. Makers experience the world by
working on it—building a house, raising children, fixing a car, or canning vegetables—and
have sufficient skill, income, and energy to carry out their projects successfully. Makers are
politically conservative, suspicious of new ideas, respectful of government authority and

organized labor, but resentful of government intrusion on individual rights. They are unimpressed by material possessions other than those with a practical or functional purpose (e.g., tools, pickup trucks, washing machines, or fishing equipment). The product shown in Illustration 12–9 would appeal to this group.

Strugglers   *Strugglers'* lives are constricted. Chronically poor, with limited educations and skills, without strong social bonds, frequently elderly and concerned about their health, they are often resigned and passive. Because they must struggle to meet the urgent needs of the present moment, they do not show a strong self-orientation. Their chief concerns are for security and safety. Strugglers are cautious consumers. They represent a modest market for most products and services, and they are loyal to favorite brands. As described in Chapter 4, meeting the needs of these consumers is a challenge for both marketers and public policy makers.

> **ILLUSTRATION 12–9**
>
> Makers focus on their families and homes. They are practical and value functional products.

Issues and Uses of VALS

More than 100,000 U.S. consumers complete the VALS questionnaire every year as part of Mediamark Research's syndicated studies, SRIC-BI's company studies, and proprietary client studies. There are separate VALS systems for the United Kingdom and Japan.

Despite its widespread use, there are some concerns about VALS, including:

- VALS are *individual* measures, but most consumption decisions are *household* decisions or are heavily influenced by other household members.
- Few individuals are pure in terms of self-orientation. Although one of the three themes SRIC-BI has identified may be dominant for most individuals, the degree of dominance will vary, as will the orientation that is second in importance.

- The types of values and demographics measured by VALS may be inappropriate for particular products or situations. Product- or activity-specific lifestyles may provide more useful information. For example, VALS seems most useful for important or ego-involving purchases. Will it work well for laundry detergent?

Despite these concerns, VALS is the most complete general segmentation system available. It is widely used by marketing managers. A recent study examined Internet usage by the VALS groups. Which groups would you guess to be heavy users? Actualizers are 10 percent of the population but represent more than 30 percent of those using the Internet for five or more years. Experiencers and Strivers are the people most likely to visit Internet chat sites. Believers are those most leery of providing their credit numbers online.

YANKELOVICH'S MONITOR MINDBASE

Since 1971, Yankelovich has conducted 2,500, 2.5-hour interviews with American households.[37] Using data from interviews over the last 10 years, the company has developed a system based on values, lifestyles, and motivations. Called the **MONITOR MindBase,** this system is designed to go beyond describing a group's behaviors into explaining why they behave that way. A company spokesperson explains the importance of this by contrasting the underlying reason two of the segments identified in this system save for their children's college education:

> While saving for college is considered an obligation for the Family Limited segment, it's more of a pleasurable reward for having successful kids for those in the New Traditionalist segment. This would obviously affect how you should market an educational investment product.

MONITOR MindBase combines an individual's position on a set of core values with his or her life cycle stage. Some of the key core values identified include

- *Materialism*—value possessions more than experience; driven by material measures of success.
- *Technology orientation*—technology as friend or foe, enabler or barrier.
- *Family values*—getting most of satisfaction from children, family, and home.
- *Conservatism*—traditional values in government, family, and society.
- *Cynicism versus optimism*—questioning the motives and integrity of institutions and government.
- *Social interaction*—joining groups; getting involved with others.
- *Activity level*—couch potato or active; involved in sports.

Measures of these values are then combined with stage in the life cycle, producing a large number of potential segments, which are then aggregated into 32 target segments according to similar behavioral, motivational, and attitudinal patterns. These 32 target segments are then grouped into eight high-level segments. Table 12–6 indicates some of the consumption differences between the eight high-level segments. Each segment is briefly described below.

- *Up and Comers* (16 percent) are young singles and couples without children who have positive, upwardly mobile perspectives and expect to benefit from their own skills and abilities. They are gregarious, socially conscious, and lead active lifestyles. They are interested in fun and adventure and are enthusiastic about technology and information. They do not worry about finances but are concerned about health and staying in shape.
- *Aspiring Achievers* (8 percent) are younger, self-driven individuals who are skeptical about institutions and feel the need to look out for themselves. They believe that money

| TABLE 12–6 | Consumption Differences across MindBase Segments* | | | | |

	Consumption Activity				
Segment	*Use Internet*	*Take Overnight Trips*	*Have Car Loan*	*Make Stock Transactions*	*Make 401k Contributions*
Up and Comers	126	131	89	106	78
Aspiring Achievers	109	92	61	236	26
Realists	84	91	100	77	72
New Traditionalist	129	100	145	91	194
Family Centereds	112	81	137	140	133
Individualists	123	97	108	140	117
Renaissance Masters	95	121	89	70	94
Maintainers	40	68	54	66	45

*100 = an average level of use, ownership, or activity.

is the measure of success and the key to control. Style is important, as are brands. They tend not to be socially concerned or strongly rooted in religion, family, or community. They are ethnically diverse, receptive to technology, and materialistic.

- *Realists* (12 percent) are resource constrained and strive to balance their needs with the needs of their families as most have children under 18 at home. They feel a need for stress reduction and time management. They like to be entertained via television, movies, and interacting with family and friends. They don't try to live within their limited means and enjoy shopping. They want to keep up with the latest styles. It is an ethnically diverse group concentrated in urban areas.
- *New Traditionalists* (14 percent) are upscale, involved in community, and family oriented. Success comes from a good marriage and healthy, happy children. They are involved in their communities and religions. They pursue an array of home-related activities such as gardening. They like technology and use it effectively. They tend to be well-educated, successful baby boomers with children under 18 at home.
- *Family Centereds* (14 percent) are not interested in social issues or self-exploration. They have few interests or activities outside the family. They are skeptical about institutions. They do not spend much time shopping, traveling, or going to the movies. Technology and computers are of interest as a means for family activities.
- *Individualists* (6 percent) are childless and driven by technology and success at work. They have little time for social interests and prefer to focus on climbing the career ladder. They do not actively seek out extra fun or novelty. They are receptive to technology and spend a lot of time on the Internet. They are highly educated and enjoy saving, investing, and planning for the future.
- *Renaissance Masters* (13 percent) are family and community oriented. They are religious and are avid readers and television viewers. They are concerned about their health and diet. They are comfortable financially and like to manage their own funds. Most are empty nesters.
- *Maintainers* (17 percent) use the past as their point of reference. Resource constrained, they lead traditional, content lives. They view themselves as neighborly, personal, and old-fashioned. Change is not appealing to them. They are conservative with their funds and do not like technology. They enjoy home-based activities such as yard and garden work. They like to keep up with current events. Many are empty nesters.

A recent application of MONITOR MindBase involved a bank with 750,000 clients. It wanted to cross-sell high-potential value customers a new product that would increase bank revenue and length of client tenure. All of the bank's customers were classified into one of the 32 MindBase target segments. Analysis revealed the best prospects for the product were concentrated in 11 of these segments. Based on the unique attitudes and motivations of each segment, 11 distinct direct mail offers were constructed. They differed in terms of envelope text, letter headline, benefits emphasized, call to action, and response channel. A standard generic appeal was also developed. A mailing to almost 50,000 clients produced a 47 percent improvement in revenue generated by the customized compared to the generic appeal.

GEO-DEMOGRAPHIC ANALYSIS (PRIZM)

Claritas, a leading firm in this industry, describes the logic of **geo-demographic analysis:**

People with similar cultural backgrounds, means, and perspectives naturally gravitate toward one another. They choose to live amongst their peers in neighborhoods offering affordable advantages and compatible lifestyles.

Once settled in, people naturally emulate their neighbors. They adopt similar social values, tastes, and expectations. They exhibit shared patterns of consumer behavior toward products, services, media, and promotions.[38]

Geo-demographic analyses are based on the premise that lifestyle, and thus consumption, is largely driven by demographic factors, as described above.[39] The geographic regions analyzed can be quite small, ranging from standard metropolitan statistical areas, through five-digit ZIP codes, census tracts, and down to census blocks (averaging only 340 households). Such data are used for target market selection, promotional emphasis, and so forth by numerous consumer goods marketers.

Claritas has taken geo-demographic analysis one step further and incorporated extensive data on consumption patterns. The output is a set of 62 lifestyle clusters organized into 12 broad social groups. This is called the **PRIZM** system. Every neighborhood in the United States can be profiled in terms of these lifestyle groups. Eight of the 62 lifestyle clusters are described as follows:

- *Furs and Station Wagons* is typified by "new money." People in this cluster live in expensive neighborhoods in the suburbs. They are well-educated, mobile professionals and managers. They are winners—big producers and big spenders.
- *Pools and Patios* once resembled Furs and Station Wagons. Today, the children in these families are grown, leaving aging couples in homes too expensive for younger homemakers. Good educations, high white-collar employment levels, and double incomes ensure the "good life."
- *Young Suburbia* is one of the largest clusters, found coast to coast in most major markets. It is composed of large, young families and ranks second in incidence of married couples with children. Their relative affluence and high white-collar employment levels distinguish these neighborhoods. As a result, they are strong consumers of most family products.
- *Blue Chip Blues* is similar to Young Suburbia on most dimensions except social rank. The cluster is characterized by high school educations and blue-collar occupations with fewer high-end incomes and lower home values. However, high employment and double incomes yield similar discretionary spending patterns as for Young Suburbia.
- *Blue-Collar Nursery* leads the nation in craftsmen, the elite of the blue-collar world. The cluster is also number one in married couples with children and households of three

or more. These are low-density satellite towns and suburbs of smaller industrial cities. They are well paid and very stable.

- *Middle America* is at the center of the socioeconomic scale and is close to the U.S. average on most measures such as age, ethnicity, household composition, and lifecycle. It is concentrated in the geographic center of the United States.
- *Emergent Minorities* is almost 80 percent black, the remainder largely Hispanic. The cluster has above-average concentrations of children, almost half of them with single parents. It also shows below-average levels of education and white-collar employment.
- *Shotguns and Pickups* are common in outlying areas and rural communities. The cluster is characterized by large families, headed by blue-collar craftsmen with high school educations. Many are dedicated outdoorsmen.

Unlike the VALS typology, PRIZM does not measure values or attitudes (though the distribution of VALS types within each geographic area covered by PRIZM is available). It is primarily driven by demographics, with substantial support from consumption and media usage data. Claritas and its competitors are widely used by consumer marketing firms such as General Motors and Hertz.

An illustration of PRIZM lifestyle clusters can be seen in their use to redesign two bowling alleys.

Charlie Boyd operated two similar bowling alleys in the Kansas City suburb of Olathe—Olathe Lanes East (OL East) and Olathe Lanes West (OL West). The two facilities were less than three miles apart and drew most of their patronage from a six-square-mile area split by a major highway.

When the owner decided to redesign the facilities, the firm that was called in to rebuild noticed that the cars of the patrons of OL East were BMWs, sports vans, and other upscale vehicles. In contrast, the cars in the lot at OL West were Fords, Chevrolets, and pickups. This led to questioning that revealed that the patrons of the two similar bowling alleys differed in income, education, and food and beverage preferences. Research based on the PRIZM clusters revealed that customers at OL East were primarily Young Suburbia (38 percent), Pools and Patios (30 percent), and Furs and Station Wagons (23 percent). In contrast, OL West's bowlers were Middle America (39 percent), Blue Collar Nursery (17 percent), Blue Chip Blues (13 percent), and Shotguns and Pickups (9 percent).

Not surprisingly, the reasons the two groups bowled and their desires and expectations differed sharply. The upscale clusters that patronized OL East came for relaxation and exercise. Women in particular came for exercise. Socialization was also important, but these women belonged to other groups and their socialization needs were met elsewhere. Men came to escape the tensions of their professional careers and to relax. They were not interested in bowling as a competitive activity. In fact, they weren't very interested in bowling at all. It was a way to unwind.

The blue-collar clusters that patronized OL West were much more focused on socializing and bowling. Many of the women's groups bowled several times per week, and it served as a major source of socializing. For the men, it was both a place to socialize and to compete with their peers and excel.

These results and the wealth of data on the lifestyles and preferences led to a complete redesign of both facilities. The designers identified 82 key surfaces in the facilities and created each one to be consistent with the tastes and needs of the key lifestyle groups. For example, the upscale groups preferred a quiet environment, so all aspects of the new facility were designed to dampen noise. Floor-to-ceiling windows were used, and the ultimate overall effect was a modern, stylish, open environment. The OL West facility was done in a folksy, outdoors style.

Within a year, food and beverage sales had increased by 2.5 times the prior level and the profits of both facilities were up sharply. The president of the design firm described the impact of the project on his business as follows: "The development of the Olathe lanes facilities changed our business from one driven by traditional interior design into one driven by marketing. Today, we begin every project by looking at customers' lifestyles rather than design trends."[40]

INTERNATIONAL LIFESTYLES: GLOBAL SCAN

Both VALS, MONITOR MindBase, and PRIZM are oriented to the United States. In addition, VALS is now available for Japan and the United Kingdom. As we saw in Chapter 2, marketing is increasingly a global activity. If there are discernible lifestyle segments that cut across cultures, marketers can develop cross-cultural strategies around these segments. Although language and other differences would exist, individuals pursuing similar lifestyles in different cultures should be responsive to similar product features and communication themes.

Not surprisingly, a number of attempts have been made to develop such systems.[41] Large, international advertising agencies have provided much of the impetus behind these efforts. One such system was developed by Backer Spielvogel Bates Worldwide (BSBW), called GLOBAL SCAN.

GLOBAL SCAN is based on surveys of 15,000 consumers in 14 countries (Australia, Canada, Colombia, Finland, France, Germany, Hong Kong, Indonesia, Japan, Mexico, Spain, the United Kingdom, the United States, and Venezuela). It measures more than 250 value and attitude components in addition to demographics, media usage, and buying preferences.

Combining lifestyle and purchasing data, BSBW found five global lifestyle segments, as described in Table 12–7. While these segments exist in all 14 countries studied, the percentage of the population in each group varies by country, as shown in Figure 12–4.

Suppose you were developing an international strategy for Whirlpool Appliances. You would notice that Strivers are the largest global segment, although this is not true in all countries. A product line targeted at this group would need to be relatively inexpensive and readily available, would require access to credit, and should have a maximum number of convenience features (perhaps at the expense of durability, if this is necessary to keep costs low). The communications theme would emphasize convenience, gratification, and value. Promotional efforts would be allocated disproportionately to those countries with large concentrations of Strivers. Illustration 12–10 shows an international ad that would appeal to Strivers and Achievers.

TABLE 12–7
Global Lifestyle Segments Identified by GLOBAL SCAN

Strivers (26 percent). These are young people on the run. Their median age is 31, and their average day is hectic. They push hard to achieve success, but they're hard-pressed to meet all their goals. They're materialistic, they look for pleasure, and they insist on instant gratification. Short of time, energy, and money, they seek out convenience in every corner of their lives.

Achievers (22 percent). These people are slightly older and several giant steps ahead of the Strivers—affluent, assertive, and on the way up. Opinion leaders and style setters, Achievers shape mainstream values. They led the way to the fitness craze and still set the standard for what many eat, drink, and wear today. Achievers are hooked on status and fixated on quality, and together with Strivers, they create the youth-oriented values that drive most societies today.

Pressured (13 percent). These are downtrodden people with more than their share of problems. Largely women from every age group, the Pressured face economic and family concerns that drain their resources and rob much of the joy from their lives.

Adapters (18 percent). They may be an older crowd, but these folks are hardly shocked by the new. Content with themselves and their lives, they respect new ideas without rejecting their own standards. And they are all ready to take up whatever activities will enrich their golden years.

Traditionals (16 percent). These people embody the oldest values of their countries and cultures. Conservative, rooted in the heartland, and tied to the past, Traditionals prefer the tried and true, the good old ways of thinking, eating, and living their lives.

ILLUSTRATION 12–10

This Brazilian ad would have strong appeal to the GLOBAL SCAN Achiever segment as well as the Strivers.

FIGURE 12–4   GLOBAL SCAN Segment Sizes across Countries

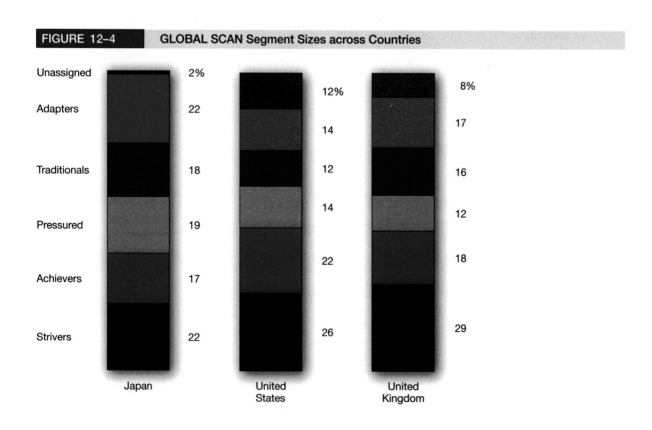

	Japan	United States	United Kingdom
Unassigned	2%	12%	8%
Adapters	22	14	17
Traditionals	18	12	16
Pressured	19	14	12
Achievers	17	22	18
Strivers	22	26	29

SUMMARY

The *self-concept* is one's beliefs and feelings about oneself. There are four types of self-concept: *actual self-concept, social self-concept, private self-concept,* and *ideal self-concept.* The self-concept is important to marketers because consumers purchase and use products to express, maintain, and enhance their self-concepts. Marketers, particularly those in international marketing, have found it useful to characterize individuals and cultures by whether they have a predominantly *independent self-concept* (the individual is the critical component) or an *interdependent self-concept* (relationships are of primary importance).

An individual's self-concept, the way one defines his- or herself, typically includes some of the person's possessions. The self-concept, including the possessions one uses to define oneself, is termed the *extended self.*

Lifestyle can be defined simply as how one lives. It is a function of one's inherent individual characteristics that have been shaped through social interaction as the person moves through his or her life cycle. It is how an individual expresses his or her self-concept in actions.

Psychographics is the primary way that lifestyle is made operationally useful to marketing managers. This is a way of describing the psychological makeup or lifestyle of consumers by assessing such lifestyle dimensions as activities, interests, opinions, values, and demographics. Lifestyle measures can be macro and reflect how individuals live in general, or micro and describe their attitudes and behaviors with respect to a specific product category or activity.

The *VALS* system, developed by SRIC-BI, divides the United States into eight groups—Actualizers, Fulfilleds, Believers, Achievers, Strivers, Experiencers, Makers, and Strugglers. These groups were derived on the basis of two dimensions. The first, self-orientation, has three categories: *principle oriented* (those guided by their basic beliefs and values); *status oriented* (those influenced by the actions, approval, and opinions of others); and *action oriented* (those who seek social or physical activity, variety, and risks). The second dimension is the physical, mental, and material resources to pursue one's dominant self-orientation.

The *MONITOR MindBase* combines an individual's position on a set of core values with his or her life-cycle stage to produce 32 target segments based on similar behavioral, motivational, and attitudinal patterns. These 32 target segments are then grouped into eight high-level segments—Up and Comers, Aspiring Achievers, Realists, New Traditionalists, Family Centereds, Individualists, Renaissance Masters, and Maintainers.

Geo-demographic analysis is based on the premise that individuals with similar lifestyles tend to live near each other. PRIZM is one system that has analyzed demographic and consumption data down to the census block. It has developed profiles of each block in terms of 62 lifestyle clusters.

In response to the rapid expansion of international marketing, a number of attempts have been made to develop lifestyle measures applicable across cultures. *GLOBAL SCAN* is the largest of these. It has found five segments that exist across the 14 countries it has analyzed to date.

KEY TERMS

Actual self-concept 422
Extended self 423
Geo-demographic
   analysis 442
GLOBAL SCAN 444
Ideal self-concept 422

Independent self-concept 422
Interdependent self-concept 422
Lifestyle 429
Mere ownership effect 426
MONITOR MindBase 440
Peak experience 424

Private self-concept 422
PRIZM 442
Psychographics 430
Self-concept 422
Social self-concept 422
VALS 433

INTERNET EXERCISES

1. Visit SRIC-BI's VALS site (www.sric-bi.com/VALS). Complete the survey for yourself and your parents. Are you and your parents' classifications and the behaviors associated with them accurate?

2. Visit Claritas's website (www.claritas.com). Report on its approach to lifestyle segmentation.

3. Visit Yankelovich's website (www.yankelovich.com) and take the Monitor MindBase survey. Do you agree with the results?

DDB NEEDHAM LIFESTYLE DATA ANALYSES

1. The DDB Needham questionnaire measures personality by asking people to list characteristics that describe themselves. These measures could also be interpreted as measures of self-concept.
   a. Based on Table 7a, do any of these self-concept characteristics seem to be associated with heavy consumption of any of the products or activities? Why do you think this is?
   b. Based on Table 7a, do any of these self-concept characteristics seem to be associated with product ownership? Why do you think this is?
   c. Based on Table 7a, do any of these self-concept characteristics seem to be associated with television show preferences? Why do you think this is?
   d. Based on Table 7a, do any of these self-concept characteristics seem to be associated with any of the attitude, interest, or opinion items? Why do you think this is?

2. Identify attitude, interest, or opinion statements that match those that the text says are associated with one of the VALS lifestyle groups. Do the demographics of those who agree with those statements match the demographics associated with the VALS groups?

3. Examine the DDB Needham data in Tables 1a, 2a, 3a, 4a, 5a, 6a, and 7a. What characterizes one who is likely to have his or her (*a*) car or (*b*) clothing become part of his or her extended self?

REVIEW QUESTIONS

1. What is a *self-concept?* What are the four types of self-concept?
2. How do marketers use insights about the self-concept?
3. How can one measure the self-concept?
4. How does an *interdependent self-concept* differ from an *independent self-concept?*
5. What is the *extended self?*
6. What is a *peak experience?*
7. What ethical issues arise in using the self-concept in marketing?
8. What do we mean by *lifestyle?* What factors determine and influence that lifestyle?
9. What is *psychographics?*
10. When is a product- or activity-specific psychographic instrument superior to a general one?
11. What are the dimensions on which VALS is based? Describe each.
12. Describe the VALS system and each segment in it.
13. Describe the MONITOR MindBase system and each segment in it.
14. What is *geo-demographic analysis?*
15. Describe the PRIZM system.
16. Describe the GLOBAL SCAN system.

DISCUSSION QUESTIONS

17. Use Table 12–1 to measure your four self-concepts. To what extent are they similar? What causes the differences? To what extent do you think they influence your purchase behavior?

18. Use Table 12–1 to measure your self-concept (you choose which self-concept and justify your choice). Also measure the image of three celebrities you admire. What do you conclude?

19. Respond to the questions in Consumer Insight 12–1.

20. What possessions are part of your extended self? Why?

21. Is your self-concept predominantly independent or interdependent? Why?

22. For each of the following products, develop one ad that would appeal to a target market characterized by predominantly independent self-concepts and another for a target market characterized by predominantly interdependent self-concepts.
    a. Coldwater Creek's Internet store
    b. Grape-Nuts breakfast cereal
    c. Specialized mountain bike
    d. Domino's pizza

23. Use the self-concept theory to develop marketing strategies for the following products:
    a. Habitat for Humanity contributions
    b. Amazon.com
    c. Coast Guard recruitment
    d. Dr. Pepper
    e. Cheer detergent
    f. Club Med

24. Does VALS make sense to you? What do you like or dislike about it?

25. How would one use VALS to develop a marketing strategy?

26. Develop a marketing strategy based on VALS for
    a. Banana Republic
    b. Vail ski resort
    c. NBC television
    d. Silk soy milk
    e. Harley-Davidson motorcycles
    f. Women's United Soccer Association (WUSA)

27. Develop a marketing strategy for each of the eight VALS segments for
    a. Electric razor (for men)
    b. Vacation package
    c. Spice Islands spices

    d. TV series
    e. Crest toothpaste
    f. Taco Bell

28. Does the MONITOR MindBase system make sense to you? What do you like or dislike about it?

29. How would one use the MONITOR MindBase to develop a marketing strategy?

30. Develop a marketing strategy based on the MONITOR MindBase for
    a. Banana Republic
    b. Vail ski resort
    c. NBC television
    d. Silk soy milk
    e. Harley-Davidson motorcycles
    f. Women's United Soccer Association (WUSA)

31. Develop a marketing strategy for each of the eight MONITOR MindBase segments for
    a. Electric razor (for men)
    b. Vacation package
    c. Spice Islands spices
    d. TV series
    e. Crest toothpaste
    f. Taco Bell

32. Does PRIZM make sense to you? What do you like or dislike about it? Is it really a measure of lifestyle?

33. How would one use PRIZM to develop a marketing strategy?

34. Does GLOBAL SCAN make sense to you?

35. How would you use GLOBAL SCAN to develop marketing strategy?

36. Develop a marketing strategy for each of the GLOBAL SCAN segments for the products in Question 26.

37. The following quote is from Paul Casi, president of Glenmore distilleries: "Selling cordials is a lot different from selling liquor. Cordials are like the perfume of our industry. You're really talking high fashion and you're talking generally to a different audience—I don't mean male versus female—I'm talking about lifestyle."
    a. In what ways do you think the lifestyle of cordial drinkers would differ from those who drink liquor but not cordials?
    b. How would you determine the nature of any such differences?

c. Of what use would knowledge of such lifestyle differences be to a marketing manager introducing a new cordial?

38. How is one likely to change his or her lifestyle at different stages of the household life cycle? Over one's life, is one likely to assume more than one of the VALS lifestyle profiles described? GLOBAL SCAN's?

39. To which VALS category do you belong? To which do your parents belong? Which will you belong to when you are your parents' age?

40. Based on the outdoor activity lifestyles described in the chapter opening example, develop a marketing strategy for
a. A beach resort
b. A fitness club

c. In-line skates
d. Schwinn bicycles
e. Snowboards
f. Old Town canoes

41. Using Table 12–3, develop a cosmetics line and marketing program targeting the following segments.
a. Self-aware
b. Fashion-directed
c. Green goddesses
d. Unconcerned
e. Conscience-stricken
f. Dowdies

APPLICATION ACTIVITIES

42. Develop an instrument to measure the interdependent versus dependent self-concept.

43. Use the instrument you developed in Question 42 to measure the self-concepts of 10 male and 10 female students, all of the same nationality. What do you conclude?

44. Develop your own psychographic instrument (set of relevant questions) that measures the lifestyles of college students.

45. Using the psychographic instrument developed in Question 44, interview 10 students (using the questionnaire instrument). On the basis of their responses, categorize them into lifestyle segments.

46. Find and copy or describe ads that would appeal to each of the eight VALS segments.

47. Find and copy or describe ads that would appeal to each of the eight MONITOR MindBase segments.

48. Repeat Question 47 for the five GLOBAL SCAN segments.

49. Identify and describe a male and a female TV personality or role played on television that fits each of the eight VALS profiles outlined.

50. Repeat Question 49 for the eight MONITOR MindBase segments.

51. Repeat Question 49 for the five GLOBAL SCAN segments.

REFERENCES

1. B. E. Bryant, "Built for Excitement," *American Demographics,* March 1987, pp. 39–42.

2. S Abe, R. P. Bagozzi, and P. Sadarangani, "An Investigation of Construct Validity and Generalizability of the Self-Concept," *Journal of International Consumer Marketing,* no. 3/4 (1996), pp. 97–123; and N. Y. Wong and A. C. Ahuvia, "Personal Taste and Family Face," *Psychology & Marketing,* August 1998, pp. 423–41.

3. C. L. Wang and J. C. Mowen, "The Separateness-Connectedness Self-Schema," *Psychology & Marketing,* March 1997, pp. 185–207.

4. C. L. Wang et al., "Alternative Modes of Self-Construal," *Journal of Consumer Psychology* 9, no. 2 (2000), pp. 107–15.

5. See Abe, Bagozzi, and Sadarangani, "An Investigation of Construct Validity and Generalizability of the Self-Concept"; Wong and Ahuvia, "Personal Taste and Family Face"; Wang and Mowen, "The Separateness-Connectedness Self-Schema"; Wang et al., "Alternative Modes of Self-Construal"; and C. Webster and R. C. Beatty, "Nationality, Materialism, and Possession Importance," in *Advances in Consumer Research,* vol. 24, eds. M. Bruck and D. J. MacInnis (Provo, UT: Association for Consumer Research, 1997), pp. 204–10.

6. R. W. Belk, "Possessions and the Extended Self," *Journal of Consumer Research,* September 1988, pp. 139–68; R. Belk, "Extended Self and Extending Paradigmatic Perspective," *Journal of Consumer Research,* June 1989, pp. 129–32.

See also M. L. Richins, "Valuing Things"; and M. L. Richins, "Special Possessions and the Expression of Material Values," both in *Journal of Consumer Research,* December 1994, pp. 504–21 and 522–31; E. Sivadas and R. Venkatesh, "An Examination of Individual and Object-Specific Influences on the Extended Self and Its Relation to Attachment and Satisfaction"; and J. Gentry, S. M. Baker, and F. B. Kraft, "The Role of Possessions in Creating, Maintaining, and Preserving One's Identity," both in *Advances in Consumer Research,* vol. 22, eds. F. R. Kardes and M. Sujan (Provo, UT: Association for Consumer Research, 1995), pp. 406–11 and 412–18.

7. See S. S. Kleine, R. E. Kleine, Jr., and C. T. Allen, "How Is a Possession 'Me' or 'Not Me'?" *Journal of Consumer Research,* December 1995, pp. 327–43.

8. S. Sayre and D. Horne, "I Shop, Therefore I Am," *Advances in Consumer Research,* vol. 23, eds. K. P. Corfman and J. G. Lynch (Provo, UT: Association for Consumer Research, 1996), pp. 323–28.

9. See L. L. Love and P. S. Sheldon, "Souvenirs," *Advances in Consumer Research,* vol. 25, eds. J. W. Alba and J. W. Hutchinson (Provo, UT: Association for Consumer Research, 1998), pp. 170–74.

10. C. S.Areni, P. Kiecker, and K. M. Palan, "Is It Better to Give Than to Receive?" *Psychology & Marketing,* January 1998, pp. 81–109.

11. K. J. Dodson, "Peak Experiences and Mountain Biking," *Advances in Consumer Research,* vol. 23, eds. K. P. Corfman and J. G. Lynch (Provo, UT: Association for Consumer Research, 1996), pp. 317–22.

12. C. H. Noble and B. A. Walker, "Exploring the Relationships among Liminal Transitions, Symbolic Consumption, and the Extended Self," *Psychology & Marketing,* January 1997, pp. 29–47.

13. Based on J. Watson, "Why Did You Put That There"; and A. M. Velliquette, J. B. Murray, and E. H. Creyer, "The Tattoo Renaissance," both in *Advances in Consumer Research,* vol. 25, eds. J. W. Alba and J. W. Hutchinson (Provo, UT: Association for Consumer Research, 1998), pp. 453–60 and 461–67; and R. P. Libbon, "Why Do So Many Kids Sport Tattoos?" *American Demographics,* September 2000, p. 26.

14. E. Sivadas and K. A. Machleit, "A Scale to Determine the Extent of Object Incorporation in the Extended Self," in *Marketing Theory and Applications,* vol. 5, eds. C. W. Park and D. C. Smith (Chicago: American Marketing Association, 1994).

15. S. Sen and E. J. Johnson, "Mere-Possession Effects without Possession in Consumer Choice," *Journal of Consumer Research,* June 1997, pp. 105–17; M. A. Strahilevitz and G. Loewenstein, "The Effect of Ownership History of the Valuation of Objects," *Journal of Consumer Research,* December 1998, pp. 276–89; and K. P. Nesselroade, Jr., J. K. Beggan, and S. T. Allison, "Possession Enhancement in an Interpersonal Context," *Psychology & Marketing,* January 1999, pp. 21–34.

16. J. Jenson, "Picabo Street Wins Starring Role in Nike Game Plan," *Advertising Age,* November 11, 1996, p. 3.

17. T. R. Graeff, "Image Congruence Effects on Product Evaluations," *Psychology & Marketing,* August 1996, pp. 481–99; J. E. Burroughs, "Product Symbolism, Self Meaning, and Holistic Matching," *Advances in Consumer Research,* vol. 23, eds. K. P. Corfman and J. G. Lynch (Provo, UT: Association for Consumer Research, 1996), pp. 463–69; N. Y. C. Wong, "Suppose You Own the World and No One Knows?" *Advances in Consumer Research,* vol. 24, eds. M. Bruck and D. J. MacInnis (Provo, UT: Association for Consumer Research, 1997), pp. 197–203; G. Lantz and S. Loeb, "An Examination of the Community Identity and Purchase Preferences Using the Social Identity Approach," *Advances in Consumer Research,* vol. 25, eds. J. W. Alba and J. W. Hutchinson (Provo, UT: Association for Consumer Research, 1998), pp. 486–91; and R. E. Kleine and S. S. Kleine, "Consumption and Self-Schema Changes throughout the Identity Project Life Cycle," *Advances in Consumer Research,* vol. 27, eds. S. J. Hoch and R. J. Meyer (Provo, UT: Association for Consumer Research, 2000), pp. 279–85.

18. S. J. Gould, "An Interpretive Study or Purposeful, Mood Self-Regulating Consumption," *Psychology & Marketing,* July 1997, pp. 395–426.

19. See J. W. Hong and G. M. Zinkham, "Self-Concept and Advertising Effectiveness," *Psychology & Marketing,* January 1995, pp. 53–77; A. Mehta, "Using Self-Concept to Assess Advertising Effectiveness, *Journal of Advertising Research,* January 1999, pp. 81–89; and M. J. Barone, T. A. Shimp, and D. E. Sprott, "Product Ownership as a Moderator of Self-Congruity Effects," *Marketing Letters,* February 1999, pp. 75–85.

20. E. N. Banister and M. K. Hogg, "Mapping the Negative Self"; and A. M. Muniz and L. O. Hamer, "Us versus Them," both in *Advances in Consumer Research,* vol. 28, eds. M. C. Gilly and J. Meyers-Levy (Provo, UT: Association for Consumer Research, 2001), pp. 242–48 and 355–61.

21. T. R. Graeff, "Consumption Situations and the Effects of Brand Image on Consumers' Brand Evaluations," *Psychology & Marketing,* January 1999, pp. 49–70.

22. J. Meyers-Levy and L. A. Peracchio, "Understanding the Socialized Body," *Journal of Consumer Research,* September 1995, p. 147.

23. C. S. Gulas and K. McKeage, "Extending Social Comparison," *Journal of Advertising,* Summer 2000, pp. 17–28.

24. See E. H. Demby, "Psychographics Revisited," *Marketing Research,* Spring 1994, pp. 26–30.

25. See F. W. Gilbert and W. E. Warren, "Psychographic Constructs and Demographic Segments," *Psychology & Marketing,* May 1995, pp. 223–37.

26. W. A. Kamakura and M. Wedel, "Life-Style Segmentation with Tailored Interviewing," *Journal of Marketing Research,* August 1995, pp. 308–17.

27. Publicity release from the Arbitron Company, New York, March 5, 1995. See also K. Shermach, "Study Identifies Types of Interactive Shoppers," *Marketing News,* September 1995, p. 22.

28. E. Kent-Smith and S. Thomas, "Luck Had Nothing to Do with It," *Journal of the Market Research Society,* April 1995, pp. 127–41.

29. P. Leblang, "A Theoretical Approach for Predicting Sales at a New Department Store Location via Lifestyles," *Journal of Direct Marketing,* Autumn 1993, pp. 70–74.

30. A. M. Thompson and P. F. Kaminski, "Psychographic and Lifestyle Antecedents of Service Quality Expectations," *Journal of Services Marketing* 7, no. 4 (1993), pp. 53–61.

31. M. Hui, A. Joy, C. Kim, and M. Laroche, "Equivalence of Lifestyle Dimensions across Four Major Subcultures in Canada," *Journal of International Consumer Marketing,* no. 3 (1993), pp. 15–35.

32. S. H. C. Tai and J. L. M. Tam, "A Comparative Study of Chinese Consumers in Asian Markets," *Journal of International Consumer Marketing,* no. 1 (1996), pp. 25–42.

33. A. L. Dolinsky et al., "The Role of Psychographic Characteristics as Determinants of Complaint Behavior by Elderly Consumers," *Journal of Hospital Marketing,* no. 2 (1998), pp. 27–51.

34. D. J. Lipke, "You Are What You Eat," *American Demographics,* October 2000, pp. 42–46.

35. For a critical review and alternative approach, see D. B. Holt, "Poststructuralist Lifestyle Analysis," *Journal of Consumer Research,* March 1997, pp. 326–50. Alternative lifestyle systems are also described in C. Walker and E. Moses, "The Age of Self-Navigation," *American Demographics,* September 1996, pp. 36–42; and P. H. Ray, "The Emerging Culture," *American Demographics,* February 1997, pp. 29–56.

36. Based on material provided by SRI Consulting Business Intelligence.

37. This section is based on D. J. Lipke, "Head Trips," *American Demographics,* October 2000, pp. 38–40; and material supplied by MONITOR MindBase.

38. *How to Use PRIZM* (Alexandria, VA: Claritas, 1986), p. 1.

39. See S. Mitchell, "Birds of a Feather," *American Demographics,* February 1995, pp. 40–48.

40. B. J. Eichhorn, "Selling by Design," *American Demographics,* October 1996, pp. 45–48.

41. For example, see M. T. Ewing, "Affluent Asia," *Journal of International Consumer Marketing* 12, no. 2 (1999), pp. 25–37.

Cases

Levi's sales in 1996 were $7.1 billion. In 2001, they were down to $4.25 billion. The second quarter of 2002 produced sales 12 percent below 2001's low level. Levi's U.S. jeans market share has dropped by a third from 18.7 percent to 12.1 percent in the past five years. Many teenagers and tweens view Levi's jeans as being for middle-aged consumers. One 19-year-old consumer said, "They're too plain. There's just not enough style to them."

How did this happen? Super success in the 1980s led to complacency and a lack of focus on evolving customer needs. Levi's created women's jeans from men's patterns, resulting in a poor fit. It treated teenage girls and women as one segment, producing jeans too tight for many moms and too high-waisted for the teens. It ignored emerging style competitors such as Calvin Klein, Old Navy, Seven, and Blue Asphalt.

Three years ago, Philip Marineau was brought in from PepsiCo to turn the company around. He quickly revamped advertising and created some memorable ads such as "Crazy Legs," which showed a guy ambling through traffic with his legs moving at impossible angles. Another was "Odyssey," in which a couple crashes through walls and sprints up trees. Currently, its "Dangerously Low" print campaign is drawing attention.

He has also brought in designers from Levi's more fashion-oriented European division, but the new designs won't hit the market till next year.

Marineau is trying hard to get Levi's into specialty chains that are economically healthier and more popular with younger consumers than Levi's traditional department store outlets. However, success has been limited. Some chain buyers don't think the brand passes the "cool test." Others find the waistband too high even on the "low rise" jeans. The VP of marketing for Wet Seal, Inc., said the chain will not carry the Levi's because "it's not on the radar screen of young women now."

Marineau is having some success getting Levi's into upscale chains such as Neiman Marcus, Saks Fifth Avenue, and Bloomingdale's. According to a buyer from Neiman Marcus, "Many customers want an all-American jean and Levi's is a name associated with that."

Marineau is also considering creating a new brand to sell through such discounters as Wal-Mart and Target. If it does, it will still likely use the Levi's name somewhere on it. This poses some risks. The reaction of the Wet Seal marketing VP was "The brand's not cool when you're at Target for detergent and you see a rack of Levi's."

Marineau, however, is upbeat: "People are predisposed to the brand. So, if we get the product right, they'll buy."

Discussion Questions

1. If Levi's decided to create a brand for discounters such as Target, should it also carry the Levi's brand name? Present both sides of the case. Take and justify a position.

2. Are consumers predisposed to Levi's? Is this equally true for all segments? What are the marketing implications of your response?

3. Will consumers really think less of a Levi sub-brand if they see it in Target or Wal-Mart?

4. Should Levi's consider a special brand for the specialty chains that cater to younger, hip consumers?

5. What is Levi's image among the following?
   a. Tween girls (aged 10 to 12)
   b. Tween boys (aged 10 to 12)
   c. Teenage girls
   d. Teenage boys
   e. Women aged 21 to 35
   f. Men aged 21 to 35
   g. Women aged 36 to 55
   h. Men aged 36 to 55

6. How can Levi's use each of the following to enhance its brand image?

a. Emotion

b. Humor

c. Maslow's needs

d. McGuire's needs

e. Brand personality

f. Self-concept

7. How should Levi's market to teen consumers in each of the following ethnic groups?

a. African American

b. Arab American

c. Asian American

d. Asian-Indian American

e. Native American

f. White

Source: A. Z. Cuneo, "Ailing Levi Strauss Refits U.S. Strategy," *Advertising Age,* July 15, 2002, p. 12; and L. Lee, "Why Levi's Still Looks Faded," *Business Week,* July 22, 2002, p. 54.

3–2 Marketing the California Avocado

In 1999, Integrated Marketing Works and the California Avocado Commission conducted a set of minifocus groups (five to seven participants) in an ongoing research program designed to increase their understanding of the consumption of avocados in general and California avocados in particular. This set of interviews focused on light to moderate users in geographic regions with heavy consumption (three in California and three in Colorado) and on nonusers in the light-use areas (three with nonusers and one with light/moderate users in Atlanta). All of the groups were composed of 35- to 49-year-old females who were the primary grocery shoppers for their households. On the basis of these and previous research studies, users and nonusers are described as follows.

Users derive pleasure both from the taste of avocados and from the emotional and usage situations associated with avocado consumption. The following represents the agency's view of how avocados trigger emotional or sensual responses in consumers.

Characteristic	*Emotional Response*
Flavor/texture	Delicious, creamy, pizzazz, special
Green	Natural, good for me, friendly
Implied occasions	Festive, feeling good, fun, upbeat, carefree, happy
Implied usage	Pizzazz, healthy, satisfying, delicious
Unique	Special, different, fun
California "aspirational"	Healthy, natural, fun, outdoors, active, feeling good

Barriers to the consumption of avocados by users are price, the fat content, and the view that they are only for special occasions.

Nonusers are actually nonretail purchasers. Many of them have had avocados in restaurants, and many are attached to the avocados. Thus, they have some of the same emotional responses to avocados as do users. They also feel the same barriers. However, in addition, they are unsure of how to purchase one (How do you select a ripe one for use today or one that will ripen for use in three or four days?) and how to peel and use them in recipes.

Until recently, California avocados have had virtually no direct competition except in the Northeast where avocados from Mexico have been imported and the South where Florida avocados are available. However, with the ongoing removal of trade barriers, it is likely that competition will spread throughout the country and will involve additional countries. Therefore, the California Avocado Commission wants to develop a strong brand image and brand equity for its product. In addition, avocados compete for share of stomach with 240 other items in a typical produce department.

In light of the research and the changing competitive situation, two campaigns were prepared—one targeting light/moderate users in core market areas and one targeting nonusers in light-usage areas. A description of each campaign and wording for one of the commercials for each follow. Table A contains demographic data relevant to avocado consumption.

Core Market Campaign

Objective   Convince current users to buy California avocados more often.

TABLE A	Variable	Avocados	Bananas	Apples	Kiwis
Demographics and Avocado Consumption*	**Percent of Adults****	15%	72%	69%	17%
	Age				
	18–24 years	82	86	89	115
	25–34	100	95	94	92
	35–44	109	100	106	111
	45–54	108	105	104	117
	55–64	119	104	102	98
	> 64	77	105	98	74
	Education				
	College graduate	136	106	108	130
	Some college	114	101	103	115
	High school graduate	72	100	97	88
	No degree	88	91	92	63
	Occupation				
	Professional	135	109	109	150
	Managerial/administrative	122	101	102	113
	Technical/clerical/sales	90	99	102	96
	Precision/craft	113	102	97	104
	Race/Ethnic Group				
	White	105	104	102	101
	Black	48	76	84	84
	Spanish speaking	185	93	97	100
	Region				
	Northeast	57	99	101	96
	North Central	52	106	104	111
	South	79	93	93	89
	West	235	105	106	111
	Household Income				
	< $10,000	69	87	88	73
	$10,000–19,999	75	91	88	71
	$20,000–29,999	81	97	96	80
	$30,000–39,999	101	102	101	100
	$40,000–49,999	105	103	99	106
	$50,000–59,999	97	102	106	113
	$60,000–74,999	107	102	109	112
	$75,000+	137	110	109	131
	Household Structure				
	Single	101	86	89	96
	Married	106	105	105	109
	Any child in household	102	99	103	113

*100 = Average use or consumption unless a percent is indicated. Base = female homemakers.

**Purchased in the past 30 days.

Source: *Mediamark Reporter 2002—University* (New York: Mediamark Research Inc., March 2002).

Target Market The target market is moderate to light users, women, 25 to 54, middle and upper income, families and single households. These individuals are always on the go. They are rushed in shopping and have little time for elaborate food preparation. They like the produce department and feel good about incorporating fresh and natural foods into their diets. They have rich feelings about avocados. Beyond the physical experience of eating the avocado, there is a rich experiential association that stems from usage—happy, fun festive, outdoors, natural, upbeat, satisfying, delicious, creamy, special, feeling good, carefree.

The Campaign It will leverage attachment to the product through the physical and emotional attributes to inspire cravings for California avocados that will cause consumers to eat them more often. It will emphasize the California origin, where the best produce comes from. This will also provide an image of natural, fresh, healthy, and tasty. The unique taste will be emphasized. The tone will be evocative, natural, fun. After seeing the ad, consumers should think, "I love California avocados and I need to satisfy my cravings for them more often."

Radio Ad Copy

SOUND EFFECTS: Music under, throughout.

ANNOUNCER: In a world where love and good taste are misunderstood . . .

MAN: To hide your love is . . . not . . . good.

ANNOUNCER: In a house where love is hard to find . . .

ANNOUNCER: In a kitchen where one woman can love despite looks . . .

WOMAN: Oh avocado, dark and slightly soft when ripe. You may have bumpy skin . . . but I . . . I love you!

ANNOUNCER: In a mouth that craves great taste, there is, the Genuine California Avocado.

WOMAN: Did you ever think a burger could be like this?

MAN: (Mouth full) Hang on . . . (chewing swallows) . . . there . . . what was your question, Love?

ANNOUNCER: The Genuine California Avocado (fast, like legal disclosure). Opening in markets everywhere today. This fruit is not yet rated.

Underdeveloped Market Campaign

Objective   Convince nonpurchasers of California Avocados to buy them at retail supermarkets.

Target Market   Basically the same as for the core market. The difference is that avocados are not part of their consideration set when shopping. Since displays for avocados in these regions tend to be small, these consumers may remain unaware of them at retail. While many of them may have had and enjoyed avocados as part of a dish or salad at a restaurant, they may not be aware of its physical appearance and may not recognize it at retail.

The Campaign   It is important to differentiate the California avocado from the Florida one (there are noticeable physical differences) in order to avoid building sales for the competition. The campaign will focus on "I know I like California Avocados (guacamole) and now it's easy to enjoy them at home." Why? They aren't hard to pick, purchase, or use, and they have a taste unlike anything else. The tone will be fun, sophisticated, and natural. After seeing the ad, people should think, "I've never considered buying a California Avocado before. I know I like them and they're much easier to use than I previously thought. I should buy one next time I'm at the supermarket."

Radio Ad Copy

NARRATOR: It has come to my attention that, due to not knowing exactly what they are, some people out there are using Genuine California Avocados for things other than what they are intended. I have been instructed to tell you that California Avocados are NOT for use as fishing line weights;

SOUND EFFECTS: Buzzer.

NARRATOR: A drain plug;

SOUND EFFECTS: Buzzer.

NARRATOR: A doggie chew-toy;

SOUND EFFECTS: Buzzer.

NARRATOR: A dish scrubber;

SOUND EFFECTS: Buzzer.

NARRATOR: A go-kart wheel;

SOUND EFFECTS: Buzzer.

NARRATOR: Or a videotape machine head-cleaner.

SOUND EFFECTS: Buzzer.

NARRATOR: California Avocados ARE intended for use in guacamole;

SOUND EFFECTS: Ding.

NARRATOR: Sliced on a sandwich;

SOUND EFFECTS: Ding.

NARRATOR: Or chopped up in salad, and other delicious uses;

SOUND EFFECTS: Ding.

NARRATOR: So whatever you do, when you see a California Avocado, think, "Man, I'm really in the mood for a Turkey Avocado Sandwich";

SOUND EFFECTS: Ding.

NARRATOR: Not, "Say, that thing is just about the same size as the hole in my heating duct?"

SOUND EFFECTS: Ding.

ANNOUNCER: This has been a word from Genuine California Avocados.

Discussion Questions

1. Evaluate these ads in terms of their ability to capture attention. How will they be interpreted?

2. How can nonusers be taught the proper way to select avocados at retail?

3. In light of increasing competition, for what product position should California Avocados strive?

4. What role does emotion play in the consumption of avocados?

5. Is there any motivational conflict in avocado consumption? If so, what should the California Avocado Commission do about it?

6. Evaluate the attitude change strategy being used.

7. Evaluate the use of humor in these ads. Propose and defend two other approaches.

8. Develop a lifestyle-based television ad to increase avocado consumption.

9. What insights, if any, are provided by the demographic data?

10. Develop a marketing campaign to increase avocado use among nonusers.

11. Visit the California Avocado Commission website (www.avocado.org). Evaluate its effectiveness in promoting the consumption of avocados. What behavioral principles and assumptions does it rely on?

Source: Based on materials supplied by Integrated Marketing Works. Used with permission.

3–3 Dairy Queen Sells Irradiated Burgers

Food irradiation was developed in the 1950s. It involves exposing food to ionizing energy such as gamma rays that kill all bacteria, parasites, mold, and fungus in or on agricultural products, including red meat, poultry, fresh fruits, vegetables, herbs, and spices. The U.S. Food and Drug Administration (FDA) began approving irradiation applications in 1963. By 2000, most foods could be treated with irradiation, but they had to carry a prominent "Radura" symbol (a stylized flower) along with the phrase "treated with irradiation." This scared many consumers, and few retailers carried irradiated meats.

While it sounds exotic, irradiation is similar to X-rays. As the dean of the Yale University School of Medicine and former FDA commissioner stated, "The process of irradiating food does not make food radioactive. Food that is being irradiated never comes in direct contact with radioactive material and the gamma rays or X-rays or electrons used do not have the potential to make the food radioactive."

Forbes magazine ran an article in 1999 entitled "These People Didn't Have to Die." The article described how nine adult deaths and three stillborn births were caused by tainted hot dogs sold by Sara Lee Corp. In addition to the immeasurable grief caused by the deaths, Sara Lee faced a $60 million product recall. According to the article, people have been eating irradiated fruit, vegetables, and spices for years (although other sources indicate that irradiated foods rarely appear in American supermarkets), but the pork and chicken industry still make virtually no use of it and it was not allowed on red meats until 2000. The article quotes a university scientist as saying, "It [irradiation] could have prevented this outbreak. These people didn't need to die."

Irradiation has been widely used as a food safety measure in Europe for years. Groups such as the World Health Organization and the American Medical Association endorse its use. However, it has yet to catch on in the United States. As the CEO of ConAgra stated, "ConAgra stands ready to use irradiation technology once public acceptance of irradiation becomes stronger." The primary reason that is advanced for the lack of public acceptance is a phobia about radiation and the absence of a coordinated industry effort to address this concern.

Others suggest that the public is largely indifferent but that a vocal, if small, opposition has prevented widespread acceptance. According to the *Forbes* article,

> A group called Food & Water, Inc., has instilled in a fair number of consumers a visceral fear of the process, as if eating irradiated meat were the equivalent of swallowing radium capsules. Hoping to stop technology in the supermarket if they can't stop it in Washington, D.C., the irradiation opponents have run fear-mongering ad campaigns. Irradiation-bashers also say the meat should carry warning labels suggestive of what you see on hazardous materials cargo.

Despite the efforts of opponents and the lack of aggressive industry promotion, recent surveys show fairly high level of public acceptance of irradiated foods. Among the findings,

- 48 percent favor the use of irradiation to increase the safety of foods such as meat, poultry, and fish; 26 percent oppose it and 26 percent are undecided.
- Shoppers who have confidence in the safety of nationally branded products are much more favorably inclined toward irradiation than are those who doubt the safety of these brands.
- Males and frequent users of microwaves are particularly supportive of irradiation.

Another survey found that 31 percent would certainly try and 41 percent would probably try irradiated meat if it were available even if it cost more than regular meat.

One thing the food industry does agree on: Greater acceptance will require changing the name of the process from *irradiation*. As one industry spokesperson stated, "This is a word that has 'radiation' in it, and for many people, that raises [concerns]." In late 1999, at industry's urging, the FDA began consideration of changing the required use of the Radura symbol and the "treated with irradiation" label to alternatives such as "cold pasteurized" and "electronic pasteurization." In May 2002, legislation was passed and signed into law that allowed irradiated foods to be labeled as pasteurized. However, many consumers appear to find the term and concept *irradiated* much more acceptable when applied to meat

than *pasteurized*. As one consumer stated, "Pasteurized steak, yuk."

Dairy Queen (DQ) did not wait for the new law to take effect. Early in 2002, it began a trial in one outlet that has subsequently expanded to a dozen. DQ ran internal tests to be certain its employees could not tell the difference between burgers made with regular meat versus irradiated meat. When they could not, the test with consumers began.

The test outlets use menu board messages, tray liners, posters, crew uniform stickers, and numerous other means to let consumers know they are being served irradiated meat and the advantages this has.

Discussion Questions

1. How will consumers respond to the irradiated meat in the Dairy Queen test?

2. What type of innovation is irradiated meat? Conduct a diffusion analysis on irradiated meat, using Table 7–4 as a guide.

3. What meaning will the new label *pasteurized* convey to the average consumer? How would you determine if this is misleading?

4. How will consumers respond to *pasteurized* steak? Is this a better term than *irradiated* steak, or *protected by irradiation?*

5. What product position should the industry try to obtain for irradiated foods?

6. How could the industry teach consumers about the benefits of irradiated foods?

7. How could the industry change the attitudes of those consumers opposed to irradiated foods?

8. How could the Food & Water, Inc., organization change the attitudes of those in favor of irradiated foods?

Source: L. Rothstein, "An Idea Whose Time Has Come—and Gone," *Bulletin of the Atomic Scientists,* July 1998, pp. 7–11; L. Freeman, " 'Irradiation' Designation May Finally Become a Sales Pitch," *Marketing News,* September 14, 1998, p. 1; M. Conlin, "These People Didn't Have to Die," *Forbes,* February 8, 1999, p. 54; A. Allen, "Ready for Irradiation," *Food Processing,* August 1999, p. 68; "Radiation Scandal," *The Ecologist,* August 1999, p. 304; "Most Await Irradiated Meat," *The Shopper Report,* April 2000, p. 1; and A. J. Liddle, "DQ Field Tests Irradiated Burgers," *Nation's Restaurant News,* May 5, 2002, p. 1.

3–4   Kraft's Umbrella Campaign

The following is part of an interview *Advertising Age* conducted with Robert Eckert, president and CEO of Kraft Foods.

AA: Last year Kraft assigned a major corporate branding effort to J. Walter Thompson USA. When is that coming?

ECKERT: It will be later this year. We are working on the next evolution of using our scale and competing at a higher level. And that is to tie some of these great brand names together.

AA: How specifically?

ECKERT: First, let me tell you where we're trying to go as a company . . . . Part of the reason (for success) is that we've started to act less like a holding company and more like an operating company.

AA: How has that worked?

ECKERT: It's been particularly effective for us in sales. When we go to call on a retail customer, there is one person who represents all Kraft and that person has several experts working for him or her who are specialists in a category. We speak with one voice.

    We go in and talk about meal solutions broadly, and the fact that consumers are spending 21 minutes in a supermarket, down 25 percent in the last five years—the number one question in America is "What's for dinner?"

    Another advantage we have is that we're the only company that covers breakfast, lunch, and dinner, as well as snacks.

AA: So how does the new corporate campaign fit in?

ECKERT: We have four $1 billion brands—Kraft (cheeses), Maxwell House, Post, and Oscar Mayer. We have 26 other brands with sales between $100 million and $1 billion—household names: Miracle Whip, Philadelphia, Cool Whip, Country Time, Digiorno. We've been very effective in going into the supermarket and talking about the collection of brands—how you can put these things together to satisfy what busy moms are going through in trying to put together meal solutions.

    The next logical step is to do this with consumers as well. So we are working on a marketing program that does recognize what's going on in households today and does bring together our brands to address it. Yes we are working on a campaign. It's more than advertising but advertising is an important component.

AA: This isn't like the ill-fated 1980s "We're Beatrice" branding effort, is it?

ECKERT: My recollection of "We're Beatrice" is that of a brand name on top of things—Stiffel lamps, Samsonite luggage, Fisher nuts, County Line cheese—and it was billed as "a company that makes all these." This, you'll see when we finalize it, it's about what's going on with consumers today and how our products happen to fit into that. It's not about us. That's the absolutely wrong way to do this.

As the $50 million corporate campaign began, Eckert stated that its goal wasn't "to hawk our products," but "to show consumers how Kraft understands their food needs and the connections that it brings to them whether it's lunch, dinner or snacks." The campaign is to involve all corporate communications—TV and print ads, direct mail and comarketing, consumer promotion, and the Internet.

The ad agency filmed hours of real families interacting around food to be edited into commercials. According to Eckert, "There's no acting, no scripts. It's very human. It captures how they live . . . how these people work through obstacles." Busy families have essentially changed the way people related to eating: "There are no more fancy meals like we grew up with. Today, your son could be eating a Lunchable, you could be eating something else . . . (but even) if you're only together for 5 or 10 minutes there is a food-based connection."

The first three spots were described by a reviewer as "understated, yet extraordinarily powerful iterations of the family ethic." One portrays a single mom shopping with her teenage sons, another a nuclear family of seven, and the third an extended family get-together. There is no narration, just interview bites and New Age Irish fiddle music in the background. The only "sales" message follows a brief sequence of stylized logo cards of familiar Kraft Labels. The message is "Kraft Foods. We make it taste good, but you make it feel good. Food brings us together. Let's make something good."

Discussion Questions

1. Evaluate Kraft's decision to use this umbrella campaign. What are the benefits and risks?

2. For what product position is Kraft striving? Is this the optimal position for them?

3. Evaluate Kraft's use of emotional appeals in its strategy.

4. How can Kraft effectively teach consumers about the range of products it makes and how these products fit into consumers' lives?

5. Visit Kraft's website (www.kraftfoods.com). Does it advance the "one image" theme? How? How would you improve it?

6. Assume you are a representative of VALS. Prepare a proposal for Kraft indicating how your database can help them achieve their goals.

Source: J. Pollack, "Eckert Positions Kraft as Microsoft of Food Industry," *Advertising Age,* March 23, 1998, p. 1.

3–5   Revlon for Men?

Males have three reasons for trying to look good (which, in American society, also implies looking young). First, one's career may be enhanced by looking good, which includes being attractive, fit appearing, and energetic (young). One businesswoman stated,

> Any guy who goes into consulting has to be attractive. It struck me one day: Every time I met a good-looking guy and asked him "So, little boy, what do you do?" he was a consultant. The ugly ones are all accountants.

A second reason for men's concern about looks is to be attractive to women. Many middle-aged men who go through divorce engage in a wide variety of "beauty" enhancement activities. Most women no longer need to rely on men for financial support, which allows them to focus more on the physical and personal characteristics of potential partners.

A final reason is a combination of ego and competitiveness. If looks matter, then competitive men will compete to look good. Knowing that one looks good or receiving compliments or "admiring glances" is also gratifying to a person's ego.

In 1995, the men's grooming market was approximately $3.3 billion (figures below in millions of dollars):

Fragrances	$1,600
Shaving	632
Deodorant	537
Hair care	362
Hair color	100
Skin care	100

While growing, the explosion that many expected in the mid-90s still has not occurred as the new century begins. Sales data are not available except for an estimate that skin care sales had grown to $122 million in the four years following the survey shown before. This represents a sound but not overwhelming growth rate of 5 percent a year. In the spring of 2000, men were using the following facial care products (see Table A for details):

Complexion care (all)	25%
Cleansers	10.5
Lotion	5.6
Cream	5.3
Scrub	3.6
Mask	2.5
Toner	2.5

Research and observation have led those in the industry to reach several conclusions. One is that men are willing to buy and experiment with all kinds and types of new fragrances and colognes, but they almost uniformly do not want anything that smells too strong or in any way draws attention to themselves. According to one expert, the challenge is

> How to entice more men to smell good, put gooey things in their hair, and oily lotions on their faces without feeling somehow unmanly?

While this market has yet to explode as predicted, numerous firms are entering with a variety of beauty-enhancing products that are generally positioned as skin care products. Nivea's product line and approach are described in the opening vignette for Chapter 14 (page 499). There are numerous small niche marketers serving this market through online sales (use a search engine for "men's skin care products"). Some of the

TABLE A	Hair Coloring Products	Complexion Care Products	Cleansers	Lotion	Cream
Demographics and Male Cosmetic Use* Variable					
Percent of Males	9.8%	25%	10.5%	5.6%	5.3%
Age					
18–24 years	115	140	179	150	172
25–34	96	105	121	87	110
35–44	107	98	89	94	94
45–54	109	91	85	88	64
55–64	86	68	57	71	65
> 64	79	95	66	120	100
Education					
College graduate	78	85	88	89	80
Some college	93	100	100	90	103
High school graduate	109	104	105	99	105
No degree	123	113	107	130	114
Occupation					
Professional	98	96	102	96	90
Managerial/administrative	76	90	94	102	105
Technical/clerical/sales	108	102	117	92	100
Precision/craft	105	98	107	93	91
Race/Ethnic Group					
White	90	94	92	90	92
Black	170	140	149	160	141
Spanish speaking	108	111	114	116	149
Region					
Northeast	81	88	80	63	63
North Central	82	92	80	76	81
South	119	113	128	127	117
West	104	98	94	114	126
Household Income					
< $10,000	SS**	117	SS**	SS**	SS**
$10,000–19,999	118	111	117	SS**	SS**
$20,000–29,999	120	115	112	131	145
$30,000–39,999	99	103	97	98	137
$40,000–49,999	128	97	100	101	106
$50,000–59,999	88	90	99	89	77
$60,000–74,999	73	95	89	71	86
$75,000+	85	91	98	89	75
Household Structure					
Single	112	117	134	116	126
Married	93	95	90	94	95
Any child in household	113	105	117	92	107

*100 = Average use or consumption unless a percent is indicated.

**SS = sample size too small for a reliable index.

Source: *Mediamark Reporter 2002—University* (New York: Mediamark Research Inc., March 2002).

major participants in this emerging market are described below.

- *Clinique* promotes a three-step skin care process for men featuring Clinique Facial Soap, Clinique Scruffing Lotion (a facial cleanser), and Clinque M Lotion (a moisturizing lotion). It also offers a complete line of shaving-related products, including

Cream Shave and M Shave Aloe Gel (shaving gels), Face Scrub (a facial cleaner), Post-Shave Healer, Happy for Men After Shave Balm, and Turnaround Lotion. It addition, it markets Eye Treatment Formula, Surge Extra Oil-Free Gel (a moisturizer), Non-Streak Bronzer, and deodorants.

- *Mënaji* focuses exclusively on men's cosmetic products. Its slogan is "Men don't wear makeup, they use

Mënaji." Its products include the following. CAMO Concealer, in four shades, is designed to hide dark circles, age spots, and razor burn. 911 Eye Jell reduces puffiness or darkness around the eye area in about 30 minutes. Glycolic Skin Toner reduces the appearance of fine lines and wrinkles. Mënaji Mask is used once a week to thoroughly deep clean one's face. H.D.P.V. Dual Active Powder is used to eliminate oily shine without looking like pancake makeup. Mënaji Polishing Scrub is designed to be used twice a week to deep clean one's face.

- *Neutrogena Men* offers nine products for men, several of which are versions of traditional shaving products: Skin Clearing Face Bar, Skin Clearing Face Wash, Razor Defense Daily Face Scrub, Skin Clearing Shave Cream, Razor Defense Shave Gel, Skin Clearing Astringent After Shave, Skin Clearing Targeted Acne Treatment, and Razor Defense Daily Face Lotion.

Table A contains material related to the use of beauty items by men.

Discussion Questions

1. Develop a marketing strategy for Revlon to enter the men's cosmetics market with a complete product line.
2. Develop a marketing strategy for Gillette to enter the men's cosmetics market with a complete product line.
3. Evaluate Clinique's men's product line and branding strategy. Suggest changes where appropriate.
4. Visit one of the websites listed below. Is it effective at promoting its products to men? What behavior principles and assumptions does it rely on?
   a. Clinique (www.clinique.com)
   b. Neutrogena (www.neutrogena.com)
   c. Mënaji (www.menaji.com)
5. If Revlon were to enter the men's cosmetics market, what branding strategy should it use?
6. How, if at all, could Gillette use the following as the basis for its appeal for a men's cosmetic line?

a. Personality
b. Emotion
c. Self-concept

7. What motives should Clinique appeal to in promoting its men's line?
8. Persuading many men to use skin care products will require a significant attitude change. Which attitude change techniques would be most appropriate? Which would be least appropriate?
9. What type of brand image and product position would you want a line of skin care products by Gillette to have?
10. Design an ad for a line of men's skin care products by Gillette. Explain how it will work at each stage of the perception process.
11. What learning theories would you use to teach your target market to take proper care of their skin?
12. Which of the following would be the best target market?
   a. Demographic groups
   b. Occupational categories
   c. VALS segments
   d. MONITOR MindBase segments
   e. PRIZM segments
13. Develop a strategy for Revlon to use to introduce a complete line of men's cosmetics to the following countries.
   a. Japan
   b. Germany
   c. France
   d. Mexico
14. How would you explain the differences in usage across the demographic groups in Table A?

Source: A. Wallenstein, "Boomers Put New Life in Hair Dye for Men," *Advertising Age,* September 1995, p. 1; A. Farnham, "You're So Vain," *Fortune,* September 9, 1996, pp. 66–82; G. Boulard, "Men's Personal Care Market," *I,* January 1999, pp. 50–54; and K. Yamanouchi, "Men Wake Up to Makeup," *Hartford Courant,* May 24, 2002, p. 3.

3–6   Made in Mexico*

The passage of NAFTA greatly lowered the trade barriers among Canada, the United States, and Mexico. Many manufacturers in each country are actively evaluating opportunities to export to the other two countries, as well as facing increased competition from imports from those countries.

Productos Superior, Inc., is a leading manufacturer of appliances in Mexico. The firm is considering a major effort to market its brand in the United States. Product testing indicates that its appliances are slightly above average in terms of quality, design, and reliability compared to the brands currently sold in the United States. Productos Superior's cost structure is such that its products will cost 10 to 20 percent less than products with similar quality currently selling in the United States.

Productos Superior's management is very concerned about the image that products made in Mexico have in the United States. Because Productos Superior is virtually unknown in the United States, management is concerned that consumers will generalize any image they have of products made in Mexico onto Productos Superior's products. Although it has yet to conduct research on the image that appliances made in Mexico have in the United States, it did find a study on the general image U.S. consumers had of products made in other countries.

Table A contains the results of this study. Respondents were asked to rate "the typical product made in" on a 1 to 10 scale, with 1 being "very poor" and 10 being "excellent."

Discussion Questions

1. Should Productos Superior's management be concerned that the relatively weak image of products made in Mexico will be attached to their line of products? Why?

2. How can Productos Superior introduce its appliances and avoid consumers attaching the negative aspects of "Made in Mexico" to their brand?

3. Develop a marketing strategy, including specific ads, to introduce Productos Superior appliances into the U.S. market.

4. What product position would you try to establish for Productos Superior appliances? Why?

5. What learning approach and principles would you use to teach consumers about Productos Superior appliances?

6. How would you establish a favorable attitude for Productos Superior appliances?

7. What name and logo or tag line would you use for Productos Superior's appliance line in the United States? Why?

8. Develop an ad or marketing approach to create a positive attitude toward Productos Superior appliances, focusing on the following components:
   a. Cognitive
   b. Affective
   c. Behavioral

9. Develop an ad or marketing approach to create a positive attitude toward Productos Superior appliances, using the following:
   a. Humor
   b. Emotion
   c. Utilitarian appeal
   d. Value-expressive appeal
   e. Celebrity endorser
   f. Self-concept

10. What VALS lifestyle segment(s) would be the best target market(s) for Productos Superior appliances? Why?

11. To what motive(s) would you appeal to induce consumers to purchase Productos Superior appliances?

12. Develop an ad for Productos Superior appliances that would attract the attention of consumers not interested in appliances. Explain how your ad will attract attention and why it will also convey the desired message or image.

*The company name and data in this case are fictitious. See B. E. Richey, P. B. Rose, and L. Dominquez, "Perceived Value of Mexican vs. U.S. Products," *Journal of Global Marketing* 13, no. 2 (1999), pp. 49–65.

TABLE A		United				
U.S. Consumer Perceptions of Products Made in Other Countries	Attribute	States	Japan	Germany	Taiwan	Mexico
	Quality	7.3	8.7	9.1	6.9	5.2
	Style	8.2	8.5	8.7	7.1	6.7
	Reliability	7.8	8.2	8.9	7.4	5.4
	Price	8.3	7.9	6.2	9.1	9.0
	Design	8.5	8.2	9.3	7.6	6.2
	Prestige	7.4	7.3	8.2	6.9	4.3

3–7   ThirstyDog! and ThirstyCat!

The Original Pet Drink Co., Inc., recently launched its first product—a line of purified bottled beverages for cats and dogs. The beverages are slightly carbonated, flavored ("crispy beef" for dogs, or "tangy fish" for cats), and contain a number of nutritional supplements. They are intended to replace tap water for pets and to supplement, but not replace, normal pet food.

Relevant facts about the product include the following: All ingredients have FDA approval for human consumption, and the product is approved for human consumption as bottled; no refrigeration is required; the product is Kosher; and its shelf life is six to eight months. Patent protection is not practical. There have been over 15,000 palatability tests conducted on dogs and cats. Most animals, about 70 percent, like the current versions more than tap water. Some need to acquire a taste (it is recommended that the product be the pet's only source of water until it prefers the taste). Others never develop a preference for the product.

Reaction from veterinarians has been mixed. Some praise the product; others refer to it as "frivolous. It does no harm but don't rely on it to do any good." Research has shown that 42 percent of homeowners with a pet are concerned about giving their pet tap water, 32 percent stated they would try this product after hearing a description of it, and 14 percent are currently giving their cat or dog an alternative to tap water (generally plain bottled water that retails from $.89 per gallon to $2.98 per gallon).

The firm is excited about the product because it has the potential to create an entirely new product category. Furthermore, the potential market appears huge. An average cat consumes a liter of water a week, and a relatively small dog consumes two to three liters a week.

The firm has named the product ThirstyDog! and ThirstyCat! It is expected to retail at $1.79 to $1.99 per liter bottle. Point-of-purchase displays, brochures, and the package itself will emphasize the nutritional and health benefits associated with using the product.

Table A contains demographic data relevant to the ownership of dogs and cats and the purchase of products for them.

Discussion Questions

1. Conduct an innovation analysis (see Table 7–4) and recommend specific diffusion enhancement strategies for ThirstyDog!/ThirstyCat!
2. What product position would you try to establish for ThirstyDog!/ThirstyCat!? Why?
3. What learning approach and principles would you use to teach consumers about ThirstyDog!/ThirstyCat!?
4. How would you establish a favorable attitude for ThirstyDog!/ThirstyCat!?
5. What name and logo or tag line would you use for the product? Why?
6. Develop an ad or marketing approach to create a positive attitude toward ThirstyDog!/ThirstyCat!, focusing on the following components:
   a. Cognitive
   b. Affective
   c. Behavioral
7. Develop an ad or marketing approach to create a positive attitude toward ThirstyDog!/ThirstyCat!, using the following:
   a. Humor
   b. Emotion
   c. Utilitarian appeal
   d. Value-expressive appeal
   e. Celebrity endorser
   f. Self-concept
   g. Fear
8. Evaluate the ThirstyDog!/ThirstyCat! brand name.
9. What VALS lifestyle segment(s) would be the best target market(s) for ThirstyDog!/ThirstyCat!? Why?
10. Based on the demographic data in Table A, what would be the best target(s) market for ThirstyDog!/ThirstyCat!?

TABLE A	Variable	Cat Owners	Cat Treats	Dog Owners	Dog Treats
Demographics and Pet Ownership*	**Percent of Adults**	22%	10%	30%	22%
	Age				
	18–24 years	93	111	63	62
	25–34	103	102	111	105
	35–44	119	111	124	122
	45–54	125	126	127	124
	55–64	99	94	93	104
	> 64	52	57	54	59
	Education				
	College graduate	117	116	118	119
	Some college	114	109	115	119
	High school graduate	99	104	95	94
	No degree	59	55	64	59
	Occupation				
	Professional	123	119	123	121
	Managerial/Administrative	123	135	121	121
	Technical/clerical/sales	120	115	118	119
	Precision/craft	117	105	129	128
	Race/Ethnic Group				
	White	114	112	110	112
	Black	20	26	43	36
	Spanish speaking	80	75	76	79
	Region				
	Northeast	98	139	79	89
	North Central	100	98	110	110
	South	91	78	100	95
	West	119	105	109	107
	Household Income				
	< $10,000	67	75	56	63
	$10,000–19,999	65	81	54	49
	$20,000–29,999	87	86	76	76
	$30,000–39,999	93	88	102	99
	$40,000–49,999	104	85	116	111
	$50,000–59,999	126	118	123	122
	$60,000–74,999	121	125	133	124
	$75,000+	128	129	133	142
	Household Structure				
	Single	93	107	70	74
	Married	113	107	119	118
	Child < 2	87	62	94	82
	Child 2–5	90	64	93	73
	Child 6–11	103	100	114	104
	Child 12–17	128	125	134	127

*100 = Average use or consumption unless a percent is indicated. Base = female homemakers.

Source: *Mediamark Reporter 2002—University* (New York: Mediamark Research Inc., March 2002).

3–8 Hardiplank's Pull Strategy

In 1989, James Hardie Siding Products launched a line of fiber cement home siding products. The product was guaranteed against rotting or cracking for 50 years and had a warm, textured look that vinyl siding could not match. For most of the next decade, Hardie tried the traditional "push" approach of selling the product to builders, remodelers, and home improvement centers with ads and product demonstrations.

Unfortunately, builders did not like the siding. It was heavy, was hard on saw blades, and showed any flaws in a poor frame job. In addition, there were other fiber cement sidings available so a builder or home improvement center that decided to use or carry the product would frequently buy on price.

In the late 1990s, Hardie's USA President Lewis Gries decided to build a brand image for the siding, which was named Hardiplank. The project began with a very small budget of $500,000. The head of the ad agency chosen for the project stated,

> The first step was to do some research to find out what homeowners thought about the building materials used in their homes. Our assumption was that siding was a low-interest category but that turned out to be incorrect.

The research revealed that people are very emotional about their homes. When one focuses on what building materials provide, such as safety, security, beauty, warmth, and so forth, rather than what they actually are, home buyers and remodelers care a lot. This led the team to shift from a pure push (selling to builders and retailers who would then sell to home buyers) to more of a pull strategy (selling to home buyers who would then demand the product from builders and retailers).

Advertising was shifted from homebuilding trade publications to lifestyle magazines such as *Southern Living, Sunset,* and *Coastal Living.* The ads emphasized the emotional appeal of houses made with strong, weather-resistant materials. Trade ads were used to explain this positioning and emphasized the interest that would be generated on behalf of builders and remodelers.

Hardie's sales force also had to be trained. Historically, they had called on purchasing agents and talked price and delivery schedules. Now they needed to reach the marketing directors of major homebuilders and communicate the value this product and its emerging reputation could provide to their sales programs.

Another major effort was to put Hardiplank on model homes, in "dream homes" promoted by the lifestyle magazines, and in builder design centers.

While Hardiplank had to compete against wood siding and other fiber cement brands, vinyl was perhaps its strongest competitor. It lasted longer than wood, and builders liked it because it was easy to install. However, it did not look or feel like wood. So Hardie built displays that placed vinyl and Hardiplank side by side and encouraged consumers not only to do a visual comparison but to do a "tap test." Unlike Hardiplank, vinyl is thin and rattles when tapped. According to Louis Sawyer, CEO of Hardie's advertising agency,

> Vinyl siding met the functional requirements, but not the emotional ones. Our ads and displays spoke directly to the affluent baby boomer audience, and they appreciated the difference immediately.

Discussion Questions

1. Will Hardie's pull strategy work? Why or why not?
2. What product position is Hardie trying to establish for Hardiplank?
3. What learning approach and principals would you use to teach consumers about Hardiplank?
4. How would you develop a favorable attitude toward Hardiplank?
5. Evaluate the name Hardiplank. Suggest and justify two others.
6. Conduct a diffusion analysis from the perspective of the home buyer, and develop appropriate strategies based on this analysis.
7. Conduct a diffusion analysis from the perspective of the builder, and develop appropriate strategies based on this analysis.
8. Develop two ads to create a positive attitude toward Hardiplank, one using a cognitive approach and one using an affective approach. Which is best? Why?
9. How can Hardie use emotion in marketing Hardiplank?

Source: B. Lamons, "Another Story about an Unlikely Brand," *Marketing News,* May 27, 2002, p. 8. Lamons is president of Robert Lamons & Associates in Houston, Texas.

3–9   National Campaign to Prevent Teen Pregnancy

Pregnancy among teenagers is a major problem in the United States, much more so than in other developed nations (twice that of Canada or England, 10 times that of Japan). Almost 40 percent of girls become pregnant before they are 20. Eighty percent of these pregnancies are unplanned, and 80 percent of the girls are unwed.

About half end in birth, a third in abortion, and the rest in miscarriage.

The consequences of these pregnancies, particularly the unplanned out-of-wedlock ones, are severe for the mother and often the father, the child, and society.

- Teen mothers are less likely to complete high school (only one-third receive a high school diploma) and more likely to end up on welfare (nearly 80 percent of unmarried teen mothers end up on welfare).
- The children of teenage mothers have lower birth weights, are more likely to perform poorly in school, and are at greater risk of abuse and neglect.
- The sons of teen mothers are 13 percent more likely to end up in prison, and teen daughters are 22 percent more likely to become teen mothers themselves.
- It has been estimated that U.S. taxpayers spent about $30 billion to support families started by teenage mothers.

Given the high cost of teenage pregnancies, why is the rate so high in the United States? Unfortunately, there is no solid evidence to answer this question. Proposed explanations include,

- Less social stigma attached to pregnancy or childbearing by unmarried teenage girls.
- Few consequences for the boys and men who father out-of-wedlock teenage pregnancies.
- The absence of clear, forceful messages from all social sectors and leaders that teenagers are too young for pregnancy and childbearing—that "parenthood is for adulthood."
- A media environment that glorifies sexuality generally, and high-risk, nonmarital sexual behavior in particular, which typically is portrayed with no serious consequences.
- Continuing arguments about whether and when sexual activity by unmarried teenagers is acceptable and about whether abstinence or contraception is the best remedy for teenage pregnancy—arguments that are often divisive and hamper the ability of communities to take action to reduce teenage pregnancy.
- Sexual abuse of young girls, which results, among other things, in an increased vulnerability to teenage pregnancy later.
- Sexual exploitation of teenage girls by men who are older, sometimes by five years or more.
- A failure of parents and communities to nurture and supervise adolescent children—to monitor and support them adequately in order to teach and enforce moral standards of behavior; to talk about and model respectful male/female relationships; and to engage them in constructive after-school activities.
- Earlier puberty combined with a later average age of marriage—a gap that has led to increasing levels of premarital intercourse and a greater number of premarital sexual partners among teenagers.
- A judgment by poor teenage girls that there is little to be gained in postponing pregnancy and parenthood.
- The failure to develop a highly accessible system of family planning services and information for teenagers or to develop contraceptive methods more suited to them.
- Insufficient information provided to children and teenagers about human sexuality, how to avoid pregnancy and sexually transmitted diseases (STDs), and related topics in reproductive health.

Several factors appear to reduce the likelihood of a teen becoming pregnant:

- The primary reason that teenage girls who have never had intercourse give for abstaining is that having sex would be against their religious or moral values. Other reasons cited include desire to avoid pregnancy, fear of contracting an STD, and not having met the appropriate partner. Three of four girls and more than half of boys report that girls who have sex do so because their boyfriends want them to.
- Teenagers who have strong emotional attachments to their parents are much less likely to become sexually active at an early age.
- Contraceptive use among sexually active teens has increased but remains inconsistent. A sexually active teen who does not use contraception has a 90 percent chance of pregnancy within one year.
- Parents rate high among many teens as trustworthy and preferred information sources on birth control. One in two teens say they trust their parents most for reliable and complete information about birth control; only 12 percent say a friend.
- Teens who have been raised by both parents (biological or adoptive) from birth have lower probabilities of having sex than teens who grew up in any other family situation. At age 16, 22 percent of girls from intact families and 44 percent of other girls have had sex at least once.
- A majority of both girls and boys who are sexually active wish they had waited. Eight in ten girls and six in ten boys say they wish they had waited until they were older to have sex.

Courtesy The National Campaign to Prevent Teen Pregnancy.

In response to this issue, The National Campaign to Prevent Teen Pregnancy was founded as a nonpartisan, nonprofit organization with a primary mission to sharply reduce teen pregnancy in the United States. One of the principles that will guide its actions is,

> The Campaign will focus on boys as well as girls, and emphasize the importance of mutual respect between the sexes; shared responsibility for children; the need for pregnancy to be undertaken with deep commitment by both partners; further, the Campaign should send a message that becoming pregnant and bringing a child into the world is an enormous responsibility, and that couples should not have a child until they are able to support, nurture, and care for that child.

The campaign has taken a multifaceted approach to achieve its goal. One component of its approach is the development of a series of public service announcements (PSAs) such as posters, magazine ads, and television commercials that are distributed widely over a long period of time.

Its current series of PSAs targeting teens focuses on the theme "Sex has consequences." It attempts to show teens that there is a downside to sex. Each of the six poster/magazine ads features a picture of a teen (four feature girls, two feature boys) with small text running up the left side and one large, negative term that goes horizontally across the picture of the teen (see Illustration A). Across the bottom of each is "sex has consequences / www.teenpregnancy.org." The text for each ad follows (the four ads featuring a girl are described first):

> Condoms are CHEAP. If we'd used one, I wouldn't have to tell my parents I'm pregnant.
>
> I want to be with my friends. Instead, I'm changing DIRTY diapers at home.
>
> Now that I'm home with a baby, NOBODY calls me anymore.
>
> I had sex so my boyfriend wouldn't REJECT me. Now I have a baby. And no boyfriends.
>
> My scholarship is USELESS. Now I need a job to support my baby.
>
> All it took was one PRICK to get my girlfriend pregnant. At least that's what her friends say.

Discussion Questions

1. How effective are the current PSAs likely to be?

2. Is there any risk that these ads could make teen sex "cool" rather than dangerous?

3. What theme or message would you use to reduce teen pregnancy? How would you convey that message?

4. Design a poster to discourage teenage girls from becoming sexually active. Justify your design in terms of the relevant concept from the text and the information in this case.

5. Design a poster to discourage teenage boys from becoming sexually active. Justify your design in terms of the relevant concept from the text and the information in this case.

6. Design a poster to encourage sexually active teenage girls to use birth control. Justify your design in terms of the relevant concept from the text and the information in this case. What is the risk that your poster will encourage nonsexually active girls to become sexually active?

7. Design a poster to encourage sexually active teenage boys to use birth control. Justify your design in terms of the relevant concept from the text and the information in this case. What is the risk that your poster will encourage nonsexually active boys to become sexually active?

8. Evaluate www.teenpregnancy.org from the perspective of a 15-year-old who is under pressure to become sexually active. Does it provide the needed information? Will it reduce the likelihood of the person becoming sexually active? Should the PSAs targeting teens list a separate site designed just for them?

9. Evaluate www.teenpregnancy.org from the perspective of a 15-year-old who is sexually active and is concerned about becoming pregnant or fathering a child. Does it provide the needed information? Will it reduce the likelihood of pregnancy? Should the PSAs targeting teens list a separate site designed just for them?

Source: Teenpregnancy.org.

3–10 Bayer Ibuprofen?

For many years, aspirin dominated the market for nonprescription pain relief, and Bayer aspirin dominated the aspirin market. However, in recent years, acetaminophen- and ibuprofen-based pain relievers have taken over much of the market. By 1989, aspirin-based products held only 40 percent of the total analgesics market. This dropped to 35 percent by 1992. At that time, Bayer had a 6.6 percent share of the total analgesics market and 19 percent of the aspirin market. By 1995, Bayer had less than 5 percent of the analgesics market.

Competition in the analgesics market is intense. There are three main types of analgesics—aspirin, acetaminophen, and ibuprofen. There are several advertised brands within each type of analgesic as well as private-label and store brands. Product differences within analgesic categories are limited.

The intense competition has given rise to product proliferation and niche strategies. Advil is the leader in the ibuprofen category with a 50 percent share. Motrin, with a 15 percent share, has used three different commercials to target backache, arthritis, and headache pain. It attempts to "maintain the brand's appeal as a general analgesic while reaching out to specific groups of pain sufferers through advertising." The strategy appears to be working, as its share is growing. Nuprin (13 percent share) has attempted to compete with a focus on muscle aches, using celebrities such as Jimmy Connors, Michael Chang, and Joe Montana.

Similar niche strategies are appearing in the acetaminophen and aspirin categories. Acetaminophen-based Midol is attempting to position itself as "the menstrual relief specialist." It further focuses with such line extensions as Midol PM Nighttime Formula and Midol IB Cramp Relief Formula. Tylenol is increasingly positioned in terms of arthritis pain relief, though it is also widely used for headache relief.

The private-label and store brands compete on price. They may sell for a third the price of the national brands.

Recent medical findings indicate that the regular use of aspirin helps certain heart and colon conditions. Bayer introduced Therapy Bayer for this application, but aspirin sales in general and Bayer aspirin sales both continue their relative decline.

In 1995, Bayer launched a $40 million campaign to increase its overall market share. Television ads target the aging baby boomers. One features an older father painlessly horsing around with his younger son after taking Extra Strength Bayer. These ads emphasize effectiveness. A print campaign for the new Aspirin Regimen Bayer focuses on aspirin's ability to prevent heart attacks and strokes.

Excedrin was historically behind Bayer in the aspirin category. However, it now has a greater total market share in the overall analgesics market. It has managed to grow its market share by aggressively adding line extensions: ibuprofen-based Excedrin IB and acetaminophen-based Excedrin AF and Excedrin PM.

Bayer management is considering introducing nonaspirin-based analgesics using the Bayer name.

Discussion Questions

1. What is Bayer aspirin's current product position?

2. What are the benefits and risks of introducing an acetaminophen- or ibuprofen-based analgesic, or both, with the Bayer name? Should Bayer do this?

3. If it proceeds, what would it want consumers to learn about the new brands? What learning principles should it use?

4. Develop an ad or series of ads to introduce a Bayer acetaminophen- or ibuprofen-based analgesic.

a. Explain the perception principles that you used to design the ad(s).

b. Explain the learning principles you used to design the ad(s).

c. Explain the attitude influence principles you used to design the ad(s).

5. Develop an ad or series of ads to introduce a Bayer acetaminophen- or ibuprofen-based analgesic using the following:

a. Lifestyle-based theme

b. Self-concept-based theme

c. Personality-based theme

6. Develop an ad or series of ads to introduce a Bayer acetaminophen- or ibuprofen-based analgesic focusing on the following:

a. Cognitive component of an attitude

b. Affective component of an attitude

c. Behavioral component of an attitude

Source: Adapted from P. Sloan, "Bayer to Offer Non-Aspirin Pain Reliever," *Advertising Age,* July 13, 1992, p. 12; and M. Kuntz, "Extra-Strength Aspiration," *Business Week,* May 1, 1995, p. 46.

Consumer Decision Process

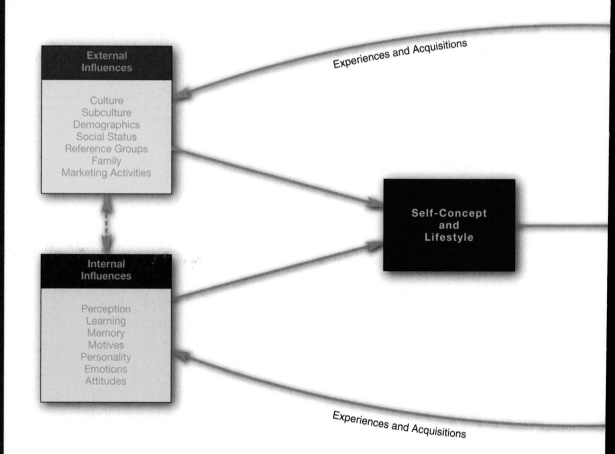

External
Influences

Culture
Subculture
Demographics
Social Status
Reference Groups
Family
Marketing Activities

Internal
Influences

Perception
Learning
Memory
Motives
Personality
Emotions
Attitudes

Experiences and Acquisitions

Self-Concept
and
Lifestyle

Experiences and Acquisitions

Up to now, we have focused on various sociological and psychological factors that contribute to different patterns of consumer behavior. Though these various influences play a significant role in behavior, all behavior takes place within the context of a situation. Chapter 13 provides a discussion of the impact situational variables have on consumer behavior.

Of particular importance to marketers is how situations and internal and external sources of influence affect the purchase decision process. The extended consumer decision process, shown on this page, is composed of a sequence of activities: problem recognition, information search, brand evaluation and selection, outlet choice and purchase, and postpurchase processes. However, extended decision making occurs only in those relatively rare situations when the consumer is highly involved in the purchase. Lower levels of purchase involvement produce limited or nominal decision making.

Chapter 14 describes those various types of decisions and their relationship to involvement. It also analyzes the first stage of the process—problem recognition.

Information search constitutes the second stage of the consumer decision process and is discussed in Chapter 15. Chapter 16 examines the alternative evaluation and selection process. Chapter 17 deals with outlet selection and the in-store and "in-site" influences that often determine final brand choice. The final stage of the consumer decision process, presented in Chapter 18, involves behaviors after the purchase. These include postpurchase dissonance and regret, product use, satisfaction, disposition, and repurchase motivation. Both cognitive (thinking) and emotional (feeling) processes are important at each stage of the decision process.

Needs

Desires

Decision Process

Situations

Problem Recognition

↓

Information Search

↓

Alternative Evaluation and Selection

↓

Outlet Selection and Purchase

↓

Postpurchase Processes

Situational Influences

☐ Weddings are a joyous moment in the lives of those involved. The 2.4 million weddings each year in the United States are also big business ($35 billion). Weddings are not only social, legal, and religious rituals; they are also *consumption rituals*. Bridal gowns, tuxedo rentals, bridal showers, wedding gifts, dinners and receptions, rings, honeymoons, and other consumption activities are now an integral part of a wedding. While details differ, ritualized consumption patterns surround this event in most cultures.

☐ Freixenet, marketers of Cordon Negro sparkling wine, advertises heavily to this market, "not only for the cases bought, but for exposure of the product" to the many guests. Freixenet offers a free Wedding Beverage Guide, which includes toasts, graces, and paper tuxedos to wrap around the wine bottles. It also provides a coupon good for a $1 refund per bottle.

☐ Bridal registries, once limited to department stores, now appear at retailers ranging from hardware stores to sporting goods outlets to the Metropolitan Museum of Art. Marshall Field's emphasizes customer service in its approach to gaining bridal registries. After the wedding, Field's sends a coupon offering discounts on merchandise the couple may not have received from their list. It also hosts an annual "Marriage of Style" show, featuring a fashion show, a vendor exhibit area, and a speaker's panel covering topics such as etiquette and finance. Almost 900 people attended a recent show.

☐ The Internet is quickly becoming a major part of the marriage market. The WeddingChannel.com currently makes it easy for couples to create personal wedding Web pages on which they can post directions and pictures, notify guests of last-minute changes, recount how they met, and so forth. The goal is to have a constantly updated gift registry available. This would allow guests to learn what gifts the couple desires that they have not yet received and to order those gifts online from participating retailers.

☐ Walt Disney World capitalizes on this consumption ritual by serving as a wedding site through its Fairytale Weddings department. In the Cinderella wedding, the bride arrives in a glass coach drawn by six white horses complete with a costumed driver and footman. A fairy godmother and stepsisters mix with the guests at the reception, where dessert is served in a white chocolate slipper. Almost 2,000 couples are married at Walt Disney World each year.[1]

A wedding is a type of situation known as a *ritual situation*. As the model we have used to organize this text indicates, the purchase decision and consumption process always occur in the context of a specific situation. Therefore, before examining the decision process, we must first develop an understanding of situations. In this chapter, we will examine the situations in which consumption occurs, the way situations influence consumption behaviors, key characteristics of situations, the nature of ritual situations, and situation-based marketing strategies.

THE NATURE OF SITUATIONAL INFLUENCE

We define **situational influence** as *all those factors particular to a time and place that do not follow from a knowledge of personal and stimulus (choice alternative) attributes and that have an effect on current behavior.*[2] That is, a situation is a set of factors outside of and removed from the individual consumer as well as removed from the characteristics of the primary stimulus object (e.g., a product, a television advertisement) to which the consumer is reacting (e.g., purchasing a product, viewing a commercial).

Consumers do not respond to stimuli such as advertisements and products presented by marketers in isolation; instead, they respond to marketing influences and the situation simultaneously. To understand a consumer's behavior, we must know about the consumer, about the object such as a product that the consumer is responding to, and about the situation in which the response is occurring.[3] This is shown in Figure 13–1.

The consumption process occurs within four broad categories or types of situations: the communications situation, the purchase situation, the usage situation, and the disposition situation.

The Communications Situation

The situation in which consumers receive information has an impact on their behavior. Whether one is alone or in a group, in a good mood or bad, in a hurry or not influences the

FIGURE 13–1	The Situation Interacts with the Marketing Activity and the Individual to Determine Behavior

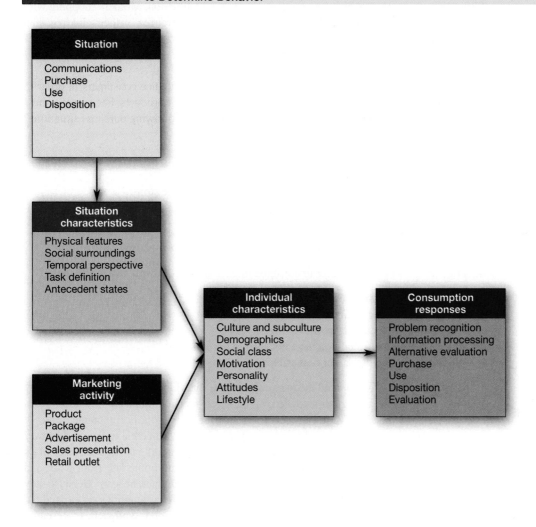

degree to which he or she sees and listens to marketing communications. Is it better to advertise on a happy or sad television program? A calm or exciting program? These are some of the questions managers must answer with respect to the **communications situation.**[4]

A marketer is able to deliver an effective message to consumers who are interested in the product and are in a receptive communications situation. However, finding high-interest potential buyers in receptive communications situations is a difficult challenge. For example, consider the difficulty a marketer would have in communicating to you in the following communications situations:

- Your favorite team just lost the most important game of the year.
- Final exams begin tomorrow.
- Your roommates only watch comedy programs.
- You have the flu.
- You are driving home on a cold night, and your car heater doesn't work.

The Purchase Situation

Situations can also affect product selection in a purchase situation. Mothers shopping with children are more apt to be influenced by the product preferences of their children than when shopping without them. A shortage of time, such as trying to make a purchase between classes, can affect the store-choice decision, the number of brands considered, and the price the shopper is willing to pay.

Marketers must understand how **purchase situations** influence consumers in order to develop marketing strategies that enhance the purchase of their products. For example, how would you alter your decision to purchase a beverage in the following purchase situations?

- You are in a very bad mood.
- A good friend says "That stuff is bad for you!"
- You have an upset stomach.
- There is a long line at the checkout counter as you enter the store.
- You are with someone you want to impress.

The Usage Situation

What beverage would you prefer to consume in each of the following usage situations?

- Friday afternoon after your last final exam.
- With your parents for lunch.
- After dinner on a cold, stormy evening.
- At a dinner with a friend you have not seen in several years.
- When you are feeling sad or homesick.

Marketers need to understand the **usage situations** for which their products are, or may become, appropriate. Using this knowledge, marketers can communicate how their products create consumer satisfaction in each relevant usage situation. For example, a recent study found that consuming two, 1.5-cup servings of oat-based cereal a day could lower cholesterol. How could General Mills take advantage of this finding to increase sales of its oat-based cereal, Cheerios? A recent ad depicts a dad coming home late from work and having Cheerios for dinner. When asked why by his young daughter, he says "Because they taste just as good at night." Illustration 13–1 shows how Kraft has attempted to expand the appropriate usage situations for Grey Poupon mustard beyond sandwiches. Research indicates that such expanded usage situation strategies can produce major sales gains for established products.[5]

The Disposition Situation

Consumers must frequently dispose of products or product packages after or before product use. As we will examine in detail in Chapter 18, decisions made by consumers regarding the **disposition situation** can create significant social problems as well as opportunities for marketers.

Some consumers consider ease of disposition an important product attribute. These people may purchase only items that can be easily recycled. Often disposition of an existing product must occur before or simultaneously with the acquisition of the new product. For example, most consumers must remove their existing bed before using a new one. Marketers need to understand how situational influences affect disposition decisions in order to develop more effective and ethical products and marketing programs. Government

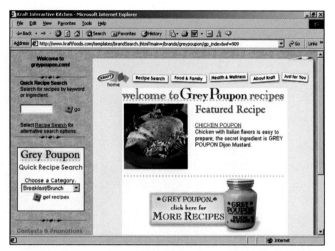

ILLUSTRATION 13–1
Many products become defined for particular usage situations. Firms that are able to expand the range of usage situations deemed appropriate for their brands can capture significant sales gains.

and environmental organizations need the same knowledge in order to encourage socially responsible disposition decisions.

How would your disposition decision differ in these situations?

- You have finished a soft drink in a can at a mall. There is a trash can nearby, but there is no sign of a recycling container.
- You have finished reading the newspaper after class, and you note that you are running late for a basketball game.
- You and two friends have finished soft drinks. Both your friends toss the recyclable cans into a nearby garbage container.
- A local charity will accept old refrigerators if they are delivered to the charity. Your garbage service will haul one to the dump for $15. You just bought a new refrigerator. You don't (do) know anyone with a pickup or van.

SITUATIONAL CHARACTERISTICS AND CONSUMPTION BEHAVIOR

A number of features or characteristics of situations influence behaviors across the various types of situations described above. We will describe five key characteristics of situations that help determine the situation's impact on behavior—physical features, social surroundings, temporal perspectives, task objectives, and antecedent states.[6] These factors have been studied primarily in the United States. While the same characteristics of the situation exist across cultures, a marketer should not assume that the response to those characteristics would be the same. For example, a crowded store might cause a different emotional reaction among American consumers than among Indian consumers.[7]

Physical Features

Information Professionals, Inc., offers a service called "advertiming." The service relies on an extensive computer database that compares consumption patterns with the current weather. Based on observed relationships between weather and product category sales, the firm uses weather forecasts to advise its clients on spot advertising buys, sales, point-of-purchase displays, and related issues.

Retail store interiors
should provide a
physical environment
consistent with the
nature of the target
market, the product
line, and the desired
image of the outlet.

Courtesy J. T. Nakaoka Associates Architects.

Tannen Maury/Image Works.

A number of firms have used simpler versions of this approach for some time. For example, Blistex, Inc., and Campbell Soup have based spot radio advertising on weather forecasts for several years. However, Information Professionals provides data on less obvious relationships and products. For example, does hot cocoa sell better on a warm but dark winter day or on a frigid but bright day? The answer is dark and warm. Therefore, cocoa advertisers would be better off timing spot buys and special promotions to coincide with dark, cloudy days as opposed to average days, or cold, clear days.[8]

Physical surroundings include decor, sounds, aromas, lighting, weather, and configurations of merchandise or other material surrounding the stimulus object. Physical surroundings are a widely used type of situational influence, particularly for retail applications.

For example, store interiors are often designed to create specific feelings in shoppers that can have an important cuing or reinforcing effect on purchase. All physical aspects of the store, including lighting, layout, presentation of merchandise, fixtures, floor coverings, colors, sounds, odors, and dress and behavior of sales personnel, combine to produce these feelings, which in turn influence purchase tendencies.[9] A retail clothing store specializing in extremely stylish, modern clothing would want its fixtures, furnishings, and colors to reflect an overall mood of style, flair, and newness. In addition, the store personnel should carry this theme in terms of their own appearance and apparel. Illustration 13–2 shows the interior of the Bergdorf Goodman men's store in New York City. Its target market is males with upscale incomes and taste levels. Its fixtures, design, and layout present an environment appropriate for this group. Compare this interior with that of the men's clothing section of Wal-Mart that is also shown in the illustration. It is important to note that one is not superior to the other. Each attempts to create an appropriate atmosphere for its target audience.

FIGURE 13–2	Typology of Service Environments

Consumption Purpose

Time Spent in Facility: Utilitarian -- Hedonic

Time Spent in Facility	Utilitarian		Hedonic
Short [minutes]	Dry cleaner / Bank	Fast food / Hair salon	Facial / Coffee at Starbucks
Moderate [hour(s)]	Medical appointment / Legal consultation	Business dinner / Exercise class	Theater / Sporting event
Extended [day(s)]	Hospital / Trade show	Conference hotel / Training center	Cruise / Resort

Note: The darker the shading, the more important the physical features of the servicescape are.

Source: Adapted from K. L. Wakefield and J. G. Blodgett, "Customer Response to Intangible and Tangible Service Factors," *Psychology & Marketing,* January 1999, p. 54. Copyright © 1999 John Wiley & Sons. Reprinted by permission of John Wiley & Sons, Inc.

The sum of all the physical features of a retail environment is referred to as the **store atmosphere** or environment (see Chapter 17). A store's atmosphere influences the consumers' judgments of the quality of the store and the store's image.[10] It also has been shown to influence shoppers' moods and their willingness to visit and linger.[11] **Atmospherics** is *the process managers use to manipulate the physical retail environment to create specific mood responses in shoppers.*

Atmosphere is referred to as **servicescape** when describing a service business such as a hospital, bank, or restaurant.[12] Figure 13–2 classifies services according to the reason the customer is using the service and the length of time the service will be used. The consumption purpose is categorized along a continuum from strictly utilitarian, such as dry cleaning, to completely hedonic, such as a massage. The time can range from a few minutes to days or weeks. Physical characteristics and the feelings and image they create become increasingly important as hedonic motives and the time involved with the service increase. Thus, the physical characteristics of a vacation resort may be as or more important than the intangible services provided.

It is important that Figure 13–2 be interpreted correctly. It indicates that the physical environment at Starbucks is more important to the service experience than the physical features of dry cleaners are. *This does not mean that the physical aspects of dry cleaners are not important.* Indeed, an organized, professional-appearing dry cleaning establishment is likely to produce more satisfied customers than one with the opposite characteristics. What the figure does indicate is that the relative importance of tangible physical features increases as one moves to extended, hedonic consumption experiences.

Having established the importance of the physical environment, we will now examine some of its components.

Colors   The color *red* is effective at attracting consumers' attention and interest. However, while physically arousing, red is also perceived as tense and negative. Softer colors such as *blue* are less attention-attracting and arousing. They are perceived as calm, cool, and positive. Which color would be best for store interiors? Research indicates that blue is

TABLE 13–1	*Variables*	*Slow Music*	*Fast Music*
The Impact of Background Music on Restaurant Patrons	Service time	29 min.	27 min.
	Customer time at table	56 min.	45 min.
	Customer groups leaving before seated	10.5%	12.0%
	Amount of food purchased	$55.81	$55.12
	Amount of bar purchases	$30.47	$21.62
	Estimated gross margin	$55.82	$48.62

Source: Reprinted with permission of R. E. Milliman, "The Influence of Background Music on the Behavior of Restaurant Patrons," *Journal of Consumer Research,* September 1986, p. 289. Copyright © 1986 by the University of Chicago.

superior to red in terms of generating positive outcomes for both the retailer (sales) and the consumer (satisfaction).[13]

As we saw in Chapter 2, the meaning of colors varies across cultures. Therefore, this and all other aspects of the physical environment should be designed specifically for the cultures involved.

Aromas   Research is just beginning, but there is increasing evidence that odors can affect consumer shopping behaviors.[14] One study found that a scented environment produced a greater intent to revisit the store, higher purchase intention for some items, and a reduced sense of time spent shopping.[15] Another study found that one aroma, but not another, increased slot machine usage in a Las Vegas casino.[16] A third study reported that a floral-scented environment increased sales of Nike shoes.[17]

Despite these results, it is far from clear if, when, and how scents can be used effectively in a retail environment.[18] In addition, scent preferences are highly individualized such that a pleasant scent to one individual may be repulsive to another. In addition, some shoppers object to anything being deliberately added to the air they breathe, and others worry about allergic reactions.[19]

Music   Music influences consumers' moods, which influence a variety of consumption behaviors.[20] Is slow-tempo or fast-tempo background music better for a restaurant? Table 13–1 indicates that slow music increased gross margin for one restaurant by almost 15 percent per customer group compared with fast music! However, before concluding that all restaurants should play slow music, examine the table carefully. Slow music appears to have relaxed and slowed down the customers, resulting in more time in the restaurant and substantially more purchases from the bar. Restaurants that rely on rapid customer turnover may be better off with fast-tempo music.

A study of the impact of music in a supermarket environment found that the match between the music being played and the customer's music preference affected purchasing behavior.[21] Another study found that music, particularly music that the audience liked, increased their perception of how long a wait for a service was. However, it also increased their positive emotional response to the service environment and to the wait itself. And it increased the consumers' positive behavioral intentions (continue using and recommending the service provider).[22]

Because of the impact that music can have on shopping behavior, firms now exist to develop music programs to meet the unique needs of specific retailers. This music is not like the stereotypical "elevator" or background music such as that generally supplied by Muzak. Background music is designed to mask general noises and to go unnoticed. The new approach is to have foreground music that shoppers will hear and respond to. The music becomes part of the shopping experience.

AEI, a major supplier of foreground music, does intense research on the demographics and psychographics of each client store's customers. The age mix, buying patterns, and traffic flows of each part of the day are analyzed. An AEI spokesperson characterized the company's approach as follows:

> Our retailers are passionate about their environment. We call our clients "passion retailers" because their success is tied directly to how you and I view them. Fashion apparel companies like the Limited or The Gap are passionate about their image. They control the factors within their stores that shape the behavior of their buyers. From store fixtures to color schemes, everything is planned to communicate that image, including the music. Besides heat and light, music is the only thing that impacts you 100 percent of the time you are in the store.[23]

Firms such as the Banana Republic, Bath & Body Works, Eddie Bauer, and County Seat use services such as those offered by AEI to help create an appropriate and consistent shopping environment throughout their chains.

Crowding   Crowding generally produces negative outcomes for both the retail outlet and the consumer.[24] As more people enter a store or as more of the space of the store is filled with merchandise, an increasing percentage of the shoppers will experience a feeling of being crowded, confined, or claustrophobic. Most consumers find these feelings to be unpleasant and will take steps to change them. The primary means of doing so is to spend less time in the store by buying less, making faster decisions, and using less of the available information. This in turn tends to produce less satisfactory purchases, an unpleasant shopping trip, and a reduced likelihood of returning to the store.

Marketers need to design their outlets in ways that will help reduce consumers' perceptions of crowding. This is difficult because retail shopping tends to occur at specific times, such as holiday weekends. Retailers must balance the expense of having a larger store than required most of the time against the cost of dissatisfied customers during key shopping periods. Using extra personnel, adding additional checkout lines, and similar measures can enhance the flow of consumers through a store during peak periods and reduce the crowding sensation.

Marketing Strategy and Physical Surroundings   Individuals visit retail outlets for reasons other than or in addition to making a purchase. Physical activity, social contacts, and sensory stimulation are three such motives. Enclosed shopping malls offer clear advantages in providing a safe, comfortable area for walking. The sights and sounds of a variety of stores, events, and individuals also provide a high degree of sensory stimulation and opportunities for social contacts. These factors play an important role in the overall success of shopping centers and other shopping areas.[25] If there are physical aspects that the retailer can influence or control, then it should do so in a manner that will make the physical situation compatible with the lifestyle of its target market.

Often the marketer can neither control nor influence the physical situation the consumer will encounter, such as winter versus summer for beverage consumption. In these cases, it is appropriate to alter the various elements of the marketing mix to match the needs and expectations of the target market. Both Dr. Pepper and Lipton tea have varied their advertising between summer and winter. Coca-Cola's CEO caused a minor furor when he described a new vending machine that would automatically increase prices in hot weather. While perhaps a rational strategy, consumers worldwide felt it to be unfair and inappropriate.

Products are also designed to help consumers deal with the physical situations they will encounter. Illustration 13–3 is an ad for a product designed to enhance consumers' enjoyment of outdoor summer activities.

This product is designed to help consumers cope with a potential, unpleasant physical situation—allergy symptoms when engaging in outdoor activities.

Courtesy The Quantum Group.

Social Surroundings

Social surroundings are *the other individuals present during the consumption process.* People's actions are frequently influenced by those around them. What would you wear in each of the following situations?

* Studying alone for a final.
* Meeting at the library with a date to study for a final.
* Going to a nice restaurant with a date.
* Meeting a prospective employer for lunch.

Most people would change their apparel for at least some of these situations. Illustration 13–4 shows how Allen Edmonds designs shoes for different types of social situations.

Social influence is a significant force acting on our behavior, since individuals tend to comply with group expectations, particularly when the behavior is visible (see Chapter 7). Thus, shopping, a highly visible activity, and the use of many publicly consumed brands are subject to social influences.[26]

Shopping can provide a social experience outside the home for making new acquaintances, meeting existing friends, or just being near other people. Some people seek status and authority in shopping since the salesperson's job is to wait on the customer. This allows these individuals a measure of respect or prestige that may otherwise be lacking in their lives. Thus, consumers, on occasion, shop *for* social situations rather than, or in addition to, products.

Frequently, marketing managers will not have any control over social characteristics of a situation. For example, when a television advertisement is sent into the home, the advertising manager cannot control whom the viewer is with at the time of the reception. However, the manager can utilize the knowledge that some programs are generally viewed alone (weekday, daytime programs), some are viewed by the entire family (prime-time family comedies), and others by groups of friends (Super Bowl). The message presented can be structured to these viewing situations.

Courtesy Allen Edmonds.

There are a number of occasions where marketing managers can influence the social aspects of a situation. For instance, the advertiser can encourage you to "ask a friend" or, better yet, "bring a friend along." Some firms, such as Tupperware, have been ingenious in structuring social situations that encourage sales. Salespersons know that frequently they can use the shopper's companion as an effective sales aid by soliciting his or her opinion and advice.[27]

Temporal Perspectives

Temporal perspectives are *situational characteristics that deal with the effect of time on consumer behavior.* Time as a situational factor can manifest itself in a number of ways.[28] The amount of time available for the purchase has a substantial impact on the consumer decision process. In general, the less time there is available (i.e., increased time pressure), the shorter will be the information search, the less available information will be used, and the more suboptimal purchases will be made.[29]

Limited purchase time can also result in a smaller number of product alternatives being considered. The increased time pressure experienced by many dual-career couples and single parents tends to increase the incidence of brand loyalty, particularly for nationally branded products. The obvious implication is that these consumers feel safer with nationally branded or "known" products, particularly when they do not have the time to engage in extensive comparison shopping.

Time as a situational influence affects consumers' choice of stores and behaviors in those stores.[30] A number of retail firms have taken advantage of the temporal perspective factor. Perhaps the most successful of these is the 7-Eleven chain, which caters almost

ILLUSTRATION 13–5

In the United States and other countries, dual-career and single-parent families have caused consumers to feel time starved. Internet shopping provides many such consumers both time savings and control over when they shop.

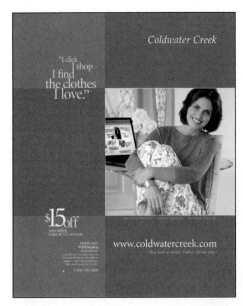

Used by permission of Coldwater Creek.

exclusively to individuals either who are in a hurry or who want to make a purchase after regular shopping hours.

Internet shopping is growing rapidly in part as a result of the time pressures felt by many dual-career and single-parent households. Shopping on the Internet has two important time-related dimensions. First, it has the potential to reduce the amount of time required to make a specific purchase. Second, it provides the consumer with almost total control over *when* the purchase is made (see Chapter 17). These features are among the major reasons for the rapid growth in Internet outlets and sales (see Illustration 13–5).

Task Definition

Task definition is *the reason the consumption activity is occurring*. The major task dichotomy used by marketers is between purchases for self-use versus gift giving.

Gift Giving   Consumers use different shopping strategies and purchase criteria when shopping for gifts versus shopping for the same item for self-use.[31] Consumers give gifts for many reasons.[32] Social expectations and ritualized consumption situations such as birthdays often require gift giving independent of the giver's actual desires. Gifts are also given to elicit return favors in the form of either gifts or actions. And, of course, gifts are given as an expression of love and caring.[33]

The type of gift given and desired varies by occasion and gender.[34] One study found that wedding gifts tend to be *utilitarian* (the top four attributes are durability, usefulness, receiver's need, and high performance); while birthday gifts tend to be *fun* (the top four attributes are enjoyability, uniqueness, durability, and high performance). Thus, both the general task definition (gift giving) and the specific task definition (gift-giving occasion) influence purchase behavior as does the relationship between the giver and the recipient.

Gift giving produces anxieties on the part of both givers and receivers.[35] Gifts communicate symbolic meaning on several levels. The gift item itself generally has a known, or knowable, price that can be interpreted as a measure of the esteem the giver has for the receiver. The image and functionality of the gift implies the giver's impression of the image and personality of the receiver. It also reflects on the image and thoughtfulness of the giver.

The nature of a gift can signify the type of relationship the giver has or desires with the receiver.[36] A gift of stationery implies a very different desired relationship between two individuals than does a gift of cologne. Consider these statements from two different women:

> He actually gave Ann an electric frying pan for Christmas. That's not a gift, it's a chore . . . . I tried to control my dismay when I asked Ann how the frying pan made her feel. She said, "I got the feeling he had visions of me barefoot and pregnant." She quit dating him shortly after.

> The biggest moment of revelation, the moment I knew he was "serious" about me was when he showed up with a gift for my daughter. Other men had shown the typical false affection for her in order to get on my good side, but he was only civil and polite to her, never gushy. One day, however, he showed up with a very nice skateboard for my daughter . . . . The gift marked a turning point in our relationship. I think for him it marked the time that he decided it would be OK to get serious about a woman with a child.[37]

As the examples above indicate, the act of giving/receiving a gift can alter the relationship between the giver and receiver. Items received as gifts often take on meaning associated with the relationship or the giver:

> To me, the roses and vase mark the time we became more than friends. I will always keep the vase to symbolize my friendship with him before the relationship, because, like the vase, I will always have his friendship.

> I was given a diamond ring from an old lady that was a very special friend of the family. We were friends, although there was an age difference of 60 years. It reminds me of her—a very nice and very strong personality.[38]

Of course, the meaning and nature of gift giving is culture specific (see Chapter 2, page 62).[39]

Antecedent States

Features of the individual person that are not lasting characteristics, such as momentary moods or conditions, are called **antecedent states.** For example, most people experience states of depression or excitement from time to time that are not normally part of their individual makeup.

Moods   **Moods** are *transient feeling states that are generally not tied to a specific event or object.*[40] They tend to be less intense than emotions and may operate without the individual's awareness. Although moods may affect all aspects of a person's behavior, they generally do not completely interrupt ongoing behavior as an emotion might. Individuals use such terms as *happy, cheerful, peaceful, sad, blue,* and *depressed* to describe their moods.

Moods both affect and are affected by the consumption process.[41] For example, television, radio, and magazine program content can influence consumers' moods and arousal levels, which, in turn, influence their information-processing activities.[42] Moods also influence perceptions of service and waiting time.[43]

Moods influence decision processes and the purchase and consumption of various products.[44] Positive moods appear to be associated with increased browsing and impulse purchasing. Negative moods also increase impulse and compulsive purchasing in some consumers.[45]

Consumers actively manage their mood states (see Illustration 13–6).[46] That is, consumers often seek situations, activities, or objects that will alleviate negative moods or

Courtesy Advance Research Laboratories.

enhance positive ones. Products and services are one means consumers use to manage their mood states. Thus, a person feeling bored, sad, or down might view a situation comedy on television, go to a cheerful movie, visit a fun store, eat at an upbeat restaurant, or purchase a new compact disc, shirt, or other fun product.[47] Consumers engage in such mood-regulating behavior at a nonconscious level and also at a deliberate, conscious level:

> [T]here are certain products that I purchase specifically to make me feel better. For instance, occasionally, I enjoy smoking a cigar. Certainly the cigar serves no other purpose than to make me feel good.
>
> While other cosmetics, perfumes and nice clothes can make me feel good, they seldom have the same power to transform my temperament like a manicure and pedicure can.
>
> What do freshness, softness, and sensuality have in common? Me, and that's why I use these products that enhance my spirit because using the products is much more than just physical, it's a spiritual voyage as well. One goes from feeling bored, dull, and tired to feeling sexy, beautiful, and confident.[48]

Marketers attempt to influence moods and to time marketing activities with positive mood-inducing events.[49] Many companies prefer to advertise during light television programs because viewers tend to be in a good mood while watching these shows. Restaurants, bars, shopping malls, and many other retail outlets are designed to induce positive moods in patrons. As discussed earlier, music is often played for this reason.

Since consumers actively manage their moods, marketers can position products and services with mood enhancement as one of the benefits. Such positioning can involve direct claims like "Give yourself a treat" or "You deserve a break today." It can also be done more subtly through the usage situations shown in advertisements for the product or service.

Momentary Conditions   Whereas moods reflect states of mind, *momentary conditions reflect temporary states of being* such as being tired, being ill, having extra money, being broke, and so forth. However, for conditions, as for moods, to fit under the definition of antecedent states, they must be momentary and not constantly with the individual. Hence, an individual who is short of cash only momentarily will act differently than someone who is always short of cash.[50]

As with moods, individuals attempt to manage their momentary conditions, often through the purchase or consumption of products and services. For example, individuals feeling tired or sleepy during the day may drink a cup of coffee or a soft drink or eat a candy bar. Massages are consumed to relieve sore muscles. A variety of medications are sold to relieve physical discomfort associated with overexertion, colds, allergies, and so forth. Pawnshops provide cash for individuals temporarily needing funds, as do banks and other financial institutions. Thus, a great deal of marketing activity is directed toward momentary conditions.

RITUAL SITUATIONS

Rituals are receiving increasing attention by marketing scholars and practitioners. A **ritual situation** can be described as *a socially defined occasion that triggers a set of interrelated behaviors that occur in a structured format and that have symbolic meaning.*[51] Ritual situations can range from completely private to completely public. A completely private ritual situation would be an individual's decision to drink a private toast or say a private prayer on the anniversary of an event with special meaning to the individual. A couple that celebrates their first date by returning to the same restaurant every year is involved in a more public ritual. Weddings, as described in the opening vignette, tend to be even more public. Finally, national and global holidays present very public ritual situations.

Ritual situations are of major importance to marketers because they often involve prescribed consumption behaviors. Every major American holiday (ritual situation) has *consumption rituals* associated with it. For example, more than 60 percent of the toy industry's sales occur at Christmas.

While there is significant variation across individuals and households, there is enough shared behavior that marketers can develop products and promotions around the common ritual situations that arise each year. For example, candy marketers produce and promote a wide array of candies for Valentine's Day and Halloween. Illustration 13–7 shows how an Internet firm is capitalizing on the consumption rituals associated with high school proms.

Marketers also attempt to change or create consumption patterns associated with ritual situations.[52] For instance, Halloween cards are being promoted, as are Halloween lights.[53] As we saw in the opening example, a wide array of firms seek to make their products and services part of the consumption pattern associated with weddings. The same is true for most other rites of passage in America such as graduation.

Ritual situations can also result in injurious consumption. Binge or excessive drinking is a serious health and social problem on many college campuses. Recent research suggests that this can be understood as a ritual behavior (see Consumer Insight 13–1). When approached from this perspective, more effective strategies for minimizing such behaviors may result.

Binge Drinking among College Students as Ritual Behavior

Binge drinking has been described as one of the most significant health and social issues on college campuses.[54] It is associated with deaths due to alcohol poisoning and traffic accidents, unplanned and unsafe sex, physical and sexual assaults, crime, nontraffic accidents, interpersonal problems, cognitive impairment, and poor academic performance. Despite widespread publicity about its dangers and efforts by university officials to curb it, binge drinking continues to be a problem. One explanation for its persistence is that it has become an important ritual of college life on many campuses.

The social occasions that trigger binge drinking can range from private ones, such as birthdays, to shared ones, such as sports events on campus, traditional "drinking nights," and bar specials.

> We have our routine. We go to one bar because they have a special. When that's ended, we go next door to a dance place because ladies get in free until 12. We stay until 11:30 and we go next door and get in free there.

> If it is a day game like at 1:00 P.M., we usually start drinking around 11:00 A.M. and just drink throughout the game . . . . If it was a 7:00 P.M. game, it [drinking] would start around 4:00 P.M.

> We are creatures of habit. I tend to go out on Thursdays. It's apparently a tradition. There used to not be classes on Fridays—it's tradition that Fridays are pretty relaxed days so that's why Thursdays are big.

Binge drinking also has as set of interrelated behaviors that participants follow, with variations across groups and campuses. As can be seen, some of these behaviors place the participants at serious risk.

> I and the other girls don't eat much on the day we go drinking because if you have a full stomach, you really can't get drunk. If we're going drinking at night, we eat lunch around noon and won't eat for the rest of the day.

> People tend to go where they know their friends are going versus places where they don't know anyone. It is very much a pattern.

You don't take dates to "those" places [where you drink heavily]. You go somewhere else where you can eat and have a few drinks and go somewhere afterward.

Sometimes we do put ourselves into risky situations as far as driving under the influence. But, when the situation arises, how else are we going to get home?

There have been several times when I blacked out I don't remember a whole lot. There were days when I asked someone how I got home.

As with all ritual behaviors, binge drinking has meaning and rewards for its participants.

> It was fun feeling drunk . . . laughing, have fun and being in a social situation where a lot of people are the same way. Everyone decided to collectively go there for that reason and have a good time.

> I've tried several times not to drink, but it's really hard with the social crowd not to. I mean if you're out on a Friday night, I guess I'm going to drink. I mean, you're surrounded by it; it's just the thing to do.

> You don't want the guys to go "Oh, she's not the type of person that likes to have fun." The guys we hang around with think it is cool to have a couple of beers.

> The joke is that once you turn 21, it's not exciting anymore. The thrill of getting through that door and trying to get served is gone because you are legal.

Critical Thinking Questions

1. Do you agree that binge drinking by college students is a form of ritual behavior?
2. Utilizing the "fact" that binge drinking among college students is a ritual behavior, develop a commercial to minimize this type behavior.

BestPromDresses.com; Art Direction: Merrill Singer Design.

ILLUSTRATION 13–7

Ritual situations generally have consumption patterns associated with them. This Internet firm makes a wide selection of prom dresses available to girls no matter where they live.

SITUATIONAL INFLUENCES AND MARKETING STRATEGY

In the previous sections, we described a variety of marketing strategies based on situational influences. Here we will focus more specifically on the process by which such strategies can be developed.

It is important to note that individuals do not encounter situations randomly. Instead, most people "create" many of the situations they face. Thus, individuals who choose to engage in physically demanding sports such as jogging, tennis, or racquetball are indirectly choosing to expose themselves to the situation of "being tired" or "being thirsty." This allows marketers to develop products, advertising, and segmentation strategies based on the situations that individuals selecting various lifestyles are likely to encounter.

After identifying the different situations that might involve the consumption of a product, marketers must determine which products or brands are most likely to be purchased or consumed across those situations. One method of dealing with this question is to jointly scale situations and products. An example is shown in Figure 13–3. Here, *use situations* that ranged from "private consumption at home" to "consumption away from home where there is a concern for other people's reaction to you" were scaled in terms of their similarity and relationship to products appropriate for that situation.

For use situation I, "to clean my mouth upon rising in the morning," toothpaste and mouthwash are viewed as most appropriate (see Figure 13–3). However, use situation II, "before an important business meeting late in the afternoon," involves both consumption away from home and a concern for the response from others. As a result, mint-flavored gums or candies are preferred.

Determining how products are *currently used* across situations can help the marketer develop appropriate advertising and positioning strategies. In our example, Wrigley's might advertise its Spearmint Gum as having breath-freshening capabilities that make it appropriate for use in social situations away from home. Or a marketer may try to change the situations for which a product is used. In Figure 13–3, mouthwash is not seen as

FIGURE 13–3   **Use Situations and Product Positioning**

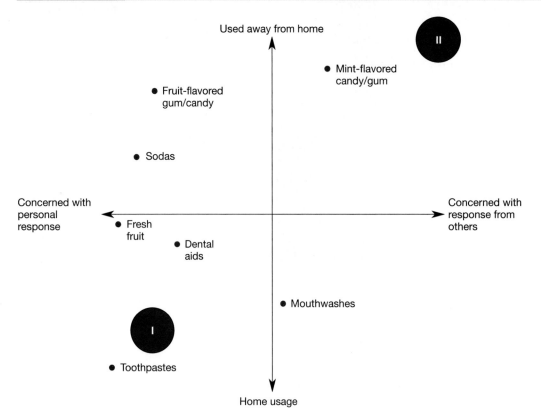

I = Use situation: "To clean my mouth upon rising in the morning."
II = Use situation: "Before an important business meeting late in the afternoon."

appropriate for consumption away from home. What if a version of Scope was developed that one swallowed after use? Could it successfully be promoted for use away from home? Illustration 13–8 shows one of a series of ads designed to convince consumers that French champagne is appropriate for casual social situations, not just very special celebrations (the primary current use situation).

Another approach for developing situation-based marketing strategies is to follow these five steps:[55]

1. Use observational studies, focus group discussions, depth interviews, and secondary data to discover the various usage situations that influence the consumption of the product.
2. Survey a larger sample of consumers to better understand and quantify how the product is used and the benefits sought in the usage situation by the market segment.
3. Construct a person–situation segmentation matrix. The rows are the major usage situations and the columns are groups of users with unique needs or desires. Each cell contains the key benefits sought. Table 13–2 illustrates such a matrix for suntan lotion.
4. Evaluate each cell in terms of potential (sales volume, price level, cost to serve, competitor strength, and so forth).
5. Develop and implement a marketing strategy for those cells that offer sufficient profit potential given your capabilities.

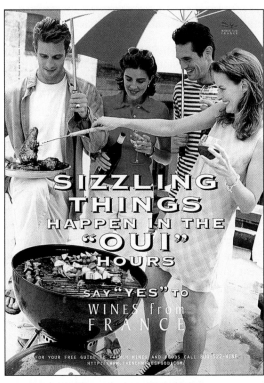

ILLUSTRATION 13–8

This ad attempts to position French wine as appropriate for casual, fun social situations.

Courtesy Food and Wines from France/Sopexa U.S.A.

TABLE 13–2   Person–Situation Segments for Suntan Lotions

Suntan Lotion Use Situation	Potential Users of Suntan Lotion				
	Young Children	Teenagers	Adult Women	Adult Men	Situation Benefits
Beach/boat activities	Prevent sunburn/skin damage	Prevent sunburn while tanning	Prevent sunburn/skin change/dry skin	Prevent sunburn	Container floats
Home/pools sunbathing	Prevent sunburn/skin damage	Tanning without sunburn	Tanning without skin damage or dry skin	Tanning without sunburn/skin damage	Lotion won't stain clothes or furniture
Tanning booth		Tanning	Tanning with moisturizer	Tanning	Designed for sunlamps
Snow skiing		Prevent sunburn	Prevent sunburn/skin damage/dry skin	Prevent sunburn	Antifreeze formula
Person benefits	Protection	Tanning	Protection and tanning with soft skin	Protection and tanning	

Source: Adapted from P. Dickson, "Person–Situation: Segmentation's Missing Link," *Journal of Marketing,* Fall 1982, pp. 56–64. Published by the American Marketing Association. Reprinted with permission.

SUMMARY

Marketing managers should view the consumer and marketing activities designed to affect and influence that consumer in light of the situations that the consumer faces. A *consumer situation* is a set of factors outside of and removed from the individual consumer, as well as removed from the characteristics or attributes of the product.

Situations have been classified into a scheme of five objectively measured variables. *Physical surroundings* include geographical and institutional location, decor, sound, aromas, lighting, weather, and displays of merchandise or other material surrounding the product. Retailers are particularly concerned with the effects of physical surroundings. The sum of all the physical features of a retail environment is referred to as the *store atmosphere* or environment. *Atmospherics* is the process managers use to manipulate the physical retail environment to create specific mood responses in shoppers. Atmosphere is referred to as *servicescape* when describing a service business such as a hospital, bank, or restaurant.

Social surroundings deal with other persons present who could have an impact on the individual consumer's behavior. The characteristics of the other persons present, their roles, and their interpersonal interactions are potentially important social situational influences.

Temporal perspectives deal with the effect of time on consumer behavior. It includes such concepts as time of day, time since last purchase, time since or until meals or payday, and time constraints imposed by commitments. Convenience stores have evolved and been successful by taking advantage of the temporal perspective factor.

Task definition reflects the purpose or reason for engaging in the consumption behavior. The task may reflect different buyer and user roles anticipated by the individual. For example, a person shopping for dishes to be given as a wedding present is in a different situation than if the dishes were for personal use.

Antecedent states are features of the individual person that are not lasting or relatively enduring characteristics. *Moods* are such things as temporary states of depression or high excitement, which all people experience. *Momentary conditions* are such things as being tired, ill, having a great deal of money (or none at all), and so forth.

A *ritual situation* can be described as a set of interrelated behaviors that occur in a structured format, that have symbolic meaning, and that occur in response to socially defined occasions. Ritual situations can range from completely private to completely public. They are of major importance to marketers because they often involve prescribed consumption behaviors.

Situational influences may have direct influences, but they also interact with product and individual characteristics to influence behavior. In some cases, the situation will have no influence whatsoever, because the individual's characteristics or choices are so intense that they override everything else. But the situation is always potentially important and therefore is of concern to marketing managers.

KEY TERMS

Antecedent states 485	Physical surroundings 478	Social surroundings 482
Atmospherics 479	Purchase situation 476	Store atmosphere 479
Communications situation 475	Ritual situation 487	Task definition 484
Disposition situation 476	Servicescape 479	Temporal perspective 483
Moods 485	Situational influence 474	Usage situation 476

INTERNET EXERCISES

1. Visit several online malls. How would you characterize this shopping situation relative to shopping at an actual mall?

2. What type of store environment does Amazon.com have?

3. Prepare a report listing and describing several useful sites for gathering current information about ritual situations such as marriages, high school graduation, Thanksgiving, or proms.

4. Evaluate the WeddingChannel.com.

REVIEW QUESTIONS

1. What is meant by the term *situation?* Why is it important for a marketing manager to understand situation influences on purchasing behavior?

2. What are *physical surroundings* (as a situational variable)? Give an example of how they can influence the consumption process.

3. How does crowding affect shopping behavior?

4. What is *store atmosphere?*

5. What is *atmospherics?*

6. What is a *servicescape?*

7. What are *social surroundings* (as a situational variable)? Give an example of how they can influence the consumption process.

8. What is *temporal perspective* (as a situational variable)? Give an example of how it can influence the consumption process.

9. What is *task definition* (as a situational variable)? Give an example of how it can influence the consumption process.

10. Why do people give gifts?

11. How might the receipt of a gift affect the relationship between the giver and the receiver?

12. What are *antecedent conditions* (as a situational variable)? Give an example of how they can influence the consumption process.

13. What is a *mood?* How does it differ from an *emotion?* How do moods influence consumption behavior?

14. How do people manage their moods?

15. How do *moods* differ from *momentary conditions?*

16. What is meant by the statement, "Situational variables may interact with object or personal characteristics"?

17. Are individuals randomly exposed to situational influences? Why?

18. What is a *ritual situation?* Why are they important?

19. Describe a process for developing a situation-based marketing strategy.

DISCUSSION QUESTIONS

20. Discuss the potential importance of each type of situational influence in developing a marketing strategy to promote the purchase of (gifts to/shopping at):
    a. Habitat for Humanity
    b. Taco Bell
    c. Rollerblade in-line skates
    d. Diet Pepsi
    e. Life insurance
    f. Banana Republic

21. What product categories seem most susceptible to situational influences? Why?

22. Flowers are appropriate gifts for women for many situations but seem to be appropriate for men only when they are ill. Why is this so? How might FTD change this?

23. How could the store atmosphere at the following be improved?
    a. The main bookstore near campus
    b. A bank near campus
    c. A pizza restaurant near campus

    d. A grocery store near campus
    e. The student advising office

24. Speculate on what a matrix like the one shown in Table 13–2 would look like for the following:
    a. Soft drinks
    b. Mouthwash
    c. Milk
    d. Fast-food restaurants
    e. Bicycles
    f. Coffee

25. Does Table 13–1 have implications for outlets other than restaurants? If yes, which ones and why?

26. Does your shopping behavior and purchase criteria differ between purchases made for yourself and purchases made as gifts? How?

27. Describe a situation in which a mood (good or bad) caused you to make an unusual purchase.

28. Describe a relatively private ritual that you or someone you know has. What, if any, consumption pattern is associated with it?

29. Describe the consumption rituals your family has associated with the following ritual situations:
    a. Fourth of July
    b. Christmas
    c. Memorial Day
    d. Valentine's Day
    e. Mother's Day
    f. Father's Day
    g. Your birthday

30. Respond to the questions in Consumer Insight 13–1.

APPLICATION ACTIVITIES

31. Interview five people who have recently purchased the following. Determine the role, if any, played by situational factors.
    a. A magazine
    b. Dress shoes
    c. Candy
    d. A fast-food restaurant meal
    e. A cup of coffee
    f. Life insurance

32. Interview a salesperson for the following. Determine the role, if any, this individual feels situational variables play in his or her sales.
    a. Life insurance
    b. Mountain bikes
    c. Flowers
    d. Jewelry

33. Conduct a study using a small (five or so) sample of your friends in which you attempt to isolate the situational factors that influence the type, brand, or amount of the following purchased or used.
    a. Nice restaurant meals
    b. Perfume
    c. Movie attendance
    d. Charity donations
    e. Candy bars
    f. Paperback books

34. Create a list of 10 to 20 use situations relevant to campus area restaurants. Then interview 10 students and have them indicate which of these situations they have encountered, and ask them to rank order these situations in terms of how likely they are to occur. Discuss how a restaurant could use this information in trying to appeal to the student market.

35. Visit three stores selling the same product line. Describe how the atmosphere differs across the stores. Why do you think these differences exist?

36. Visit three pizza restaurants. Describe how the servicescape differs across the restaurants. Why do you think these differences exist?

37. What kind of site atmosphere does each of the following have? How would you improve it?
    a. Kia.com
    b. Harley-davidson.com
    c. Gap.com
    d. Christianchildrensfund.org
    e. Rei.com
    f. Mountaindew.com

38. Copy or describe an advertisement that is clearly based on a situational appeal. Indicate
    a. Which situational variable is involved
    b. Why the company would use this variable
    c. Your evaluation of the effectiveness of this approach

39. Create a wedding gift, birthday gift, and self-use ad for the following. Explain the differences across the ads:
    a. DVD player
    b. Microwave oven
    c. Power drill
    d. Set of kitchen knives
    e. Blender
    f. Clock/radio/alarms

40. Interview five students and determine instances where their mood affected their purchases. What do you conclude?

41. Interview five students and determine the consumption rituals they have with respect to the following. What do you conclude?
    a. Fourth of July
    b. Christmas
    c. Memorial Day
    d. Valentine's Day
    e. Mother's Day
    f. Father's Day

REFERENCES

1. C. Miller, "Til Death Do They Part," *Marketing News,* May 27, 1995, pp. 1–2.

2. R. W. Belk, "Situational Variables and Consumer Behavior," *Journal of Consumer Research,* December 1975, p. 158.

3. See K. S. Lim and M. A. Razzaque, "Brand Loyalty and Situational Effects," *Journal of International Consumer Marketing,* no. 4 (1997), pp. 95–115.

4. See K. R. France and C. W. Park, "The Impact of Program Affective Valence and Level of Cognitive Appraisal on Advertising Processing and Effectiveness," *Journal of Current Issues and Research in Advertising,* Fall 1997, pp. 1–21; and A. B. Aylesworth and S. B. MacKenzie, "Context Is Key," *Journal of Advertising,* Summer 1998, pp. 17–31.

5. B. Wansink, "Making Old Brands New," *American Demographics,* December 1997, pp. 53–58.

6. Ibid.; and I. Sinha, "A Conceptual Model of Situation Type on Consumer Choice Behavior and Consideration Sets," in *Advances in Consumer Research,* vol. 21, eds. C. T. Allen and D. R. John (Provo, UT: Association for Consumer Research, 1994), pp. 477–82.

7. See J. A. F. Nicholls et al., "Situational Influences on Shoppers," *Journal of International Consumer Marketing* 9, no. 2 (1996), pp. 21–39; and J. A. F. Nicholls, T. Li, and S. Roslow, "Oceans Apart," *Journal of International Consumer Marketing* 12, no. 1 (1999), pp. 57–72.

8. D. A. Michals, "Pitching Products by the Barometer," *Business Week,* July 8, 1985, p. 45.

9. See E. Sherman, A. Mathur, and R. B. Smith, "Store Environment and Consumer Purchase Behavior," *Psychology & Marketing,* July 1997, pp. 361–78; and J. Baker et al., "The Influence of Multiple Design Cues on Perceived Merchandise Value and Patronage Intentions," *Journal of Marketing,* April 2002, pp. 120–41.

10. See J. Baker, D. Grewal, and A. Parasuraman, "The Influence of Store Environment on Quality Inferences and Store Image," *Journal of the Academy of Marketing Science,* Fall 1994, pp. 328–39; W. R. Darden and B. J. Badin, "Exploring the Concept of Affective Quality," *Journal of Business Research* 29 (1994), pp. 101–09; and C. S. Areni, J. R. Sparks, and P. Dunne, "Assessing Consumers' Affective Responses to Retail Environments," *Advances in Consumer Research,* vol. 23, eds. K. P. Corfman and J. G. Lynch (Provo, UT: Association for Consumer Research, 1996), pp. 504–9.

11. B. Babin and W. R. Darden, "Good and Bad Shopping Vibes," *Journal of Business Research,* March 1996, pp. 210–60.

12. M. J. Bitner, "Servicescapes," *Journal of Marketing,* April 1992, pp. 57–71. See also J. Podel, "Bank Design," *Bank Marketing,* May 1994, pp. 10–14; K. L. Wakefield and J. G. Blodgett, "The Importance of Servicescapes in Leisure Service Settings," *Journal of Services Marketing* 8, no. 3 (1994), pp. 66–76; and K. L. Wakefield and J. G. Blodgett, "The Effect of the Servicescape on Customers' Behavioral Intentions in Leisure Service Settings," *Journal of Services Marketing,* no. 6 (1996), pp. 45–61.

13. See J. A. Bellizzi and R. E. Hite, "Environmental Color, Consumer Feelings, and Purchase Likelihood," *Psychology & Marketing,* September 1992, pp. 347–63.

14. D. J. Mitchell, B. E. Kahn, and S. C. Knasko, "There's Something in the Air," *Journal of Consumer Research,* September 1995, pp. 229–38.

15. E. R. Spangenberg, A. E. Crowley, and P. W. Henderson, "Improving the Store Environment," *Journal of Marketing,* April 1996, pp. 67–80.

16. A. R. Hirsch, "Effects of Ambient Odors on Slot-Machine Usage in a Las Vegas Casino," *Psychology & Marketing,* October 1995, pp. 585–94.

17. M. Wilkie, "Scent of a Market," *American Demographics,* August 1995, pp. 40–49.

18. P. F. Bone and P. S. Ellen, "Scents in the Marketplace," *Journal of Retailing* 75, no. 2 (1999), pp. 243–62.

19. P. Sloan, "Smelling Trouble," *Advertising Age,* September 11, 1995, p. 1.

20. See S. Oakes, "The Influence of the Musicscape within Service Environments," *Journal of Services Marketing* 4, no. 7 (2000), pp. 539–56.

21. J. D. Herrington and L. M. Capella, "Effect of Music in Service Environments," *Journal of Services Marketing* 10, no. 2 (1996), pp. 26–41.

22. M. K. Hui, L. Dube, and J.-C. Chebat, "The Impact of Music on Consumers' Reactions to Waiting for Services," *Journal of Retailing,* Spring 1997, pp. 87–104.

23. C. Rudel, "Marketing with Music," *Marketing News,* August 12, 1996, p. 21.

24. See K. A. Machleit, S. A. Eroglu, and S. P. Mantel, "Perceived Retail Crowding and Shopping Satisfaction," *Journal of Consumer Psychology* 9, no. 1 (2000), pp. 29–42.

25. See K. L. Wakefield and J. Baker, "Excitement at the Mall," *Journal of Retailing* 74, no. 4 (1998), pp. 515–39; and B. Jin and J.-O. Kim, "Discount Store Retailing in Korea," *Journal of Global Marketing* 15, no. 2 (2001), pp. 81–107.

26. See B. Dubois and G. Laurent, "The Functions of Luxury," *Advances in Consumer Research,* vol. 23, eds. K. P. Corfman and J. G. Lynch (Provo, UT: Association for Consumer Research, 1996), pp. 470–77; Y. Zhang and B. Gelb, "Matching Advertising Appeals to Culture," *Journal of Advertising,* Fall 1996, pp. 29–46; and T. R. Graeth, "Consumption Situations and the Effects of Brand Image on Consumers' Brand Evaluations," *Psychology & Marketing,* January 1997, pp. 49–70.

27. See C. L. Hartman and P. Kiecker, "Buyers and Their Purchase Pals," in *Enhancing Knowledge Development in Marketing,* eds. R. Achrol and A. Mitchell (Chicago: American Marketing Association, 1994), pp. 138–44; and P. Kiecker and C. L. Hartman, "Predicting Buyers' Selection of Interpersonal Sources," in *Advances in Consumer Research,* vol. 21, eds. C. T. Allen and D. R. John (Provo, UT: Association for Consumer Research, 1994), pp. 464–69; and L. L. Price,

L. F. Feick, and A. Guskey, "Everyday Market Helping Behavior," *Journal of Public Policy & Marketing,* Fall 1995, pp. 255–66.

28. See B. L. Gross, "Consumer Response to Time Pressure"; L. K. Anglin, J. K. Stuenkel, and L. R. Lepisto, "The Effect of Stress on Price Sensitivity and Comparison Shopping"; and F. Denton, "The Dynamism of Personal Timestyle," all in *Advances in Consumer Research,* vol. 21, eds. C. T. Allen and D. R. John (Provo, UT: Association for Consumer Research, 1994), pp. 120–24, 125–31, and 131–36; and L. A. Brannon and T. C. Brock, "Limiting Time for Responding Enhances Behavior Corresponding to the Merits of Compliance Appeals," *Journal of Consumer Psychology* 10, no. 3 (2001), pp. 135–46.

29. S. M. Nowlis, "The Effect of Time Pressure on the Choice of Brands That Differ in Quality, Price, and Product Features," *Marketing Letters,* October 1995, pp. 287–96; R. Dhar and S. M. Nowlis, "The Effect of Time Pressure on Consumer Choice Deferral," *Journal of Consumer Research,* March 1999, pp. 369–84; and R. Pieters and L. Warlop, "Visual Attention during Brand Choice," *International Journal of Research in Marketing,* February 1999, pp. 1–16.

30. P. Van Kenhove, K. De Wulf, and W. Van Waterschoot, "The Impact of Task Definition on Store-Attribute Saliences and Store Choice," *Journal of Retailing* 75, no. 1 (1999), pp. 125–37; P. Van Kenhove and K. De Wulf, "Income and Time Pressure," *International Review of Retail, Distribution and Consumer Research,* April 2000, pp. 149–66.

31. See B. H. Schmitt and C. J. Shultz II, "Situational Effects on Brand Preferences for Image Products," *Psychology & Marketing,* August 1995, pp. 433–46.

32. M. A. McGrath, "Gender Differences in Gift Exchanges," *Psychology & Marketing,* August 1995, pp. 371–93.

33. R. W. Belk, "The Perfect Gift," in C. Otnes and R. F. Beltramini, eds., *Gift-Giving* (Bowling Green: Bowling Green University Press, 1996), pp. 59–84; D. R. Horne, S. Sayre, and D. A. Horne, "Gifts," *Advances in Consumer Research,* vol. 23, eds. K. P. Corfman and J. G. Lynch (Provo, UT: Association for Consumer Research, 1996), pp. 30–34; and R. F. Beltramini, "Exploring the Effectiveness of Business Gifts," *Journal of Advertising,* Summer 2000, pp. 75–78.

34. S. Athay, "Giving and Getting," *American Demographics,* December 1993, pp. 46–54; C. Otnes, J. A. Ruth, and C. C. Milbourne, "The Pleasure and Pain of Being Close"; M. Rucker, A. Freitas, and J. Dolstra, "A Toast for the Host," both in *Advances in Consumer Research,* vol. 21, eds. C. T. Allen and D. R. John (Provo, UT: Association for Consumer Research, 1994), pp. 159–62 and 163–68; and K. M. Palan, C. S. Areni, and P. Kiecker, "Gender Role Incongruency and Memorable Gift Exchange Experiences"; and J. F. Durgee and T. Sego, "Gift-Giving as a Metaphor for Understanding New Products That Delight," both in *Advances in Consumer Research,* vol. 28, eds. M. C. Gilly and J. Meyers-Levy (Provo, UT: Association for Consumer Research, 2001), pp. 51–57 and 64–69.

35. D. B. Wooten, "Qualitative Steps toward an Expanded Model of Anxiety in Gift-Giving," *Journal of Consumer Research,* June 2000, pp. 84–95.

36. See M. F. Wolfinbarger and M. C. Gilly, "An Experimental Investigation of Self-Symbolism in Gifts," *Advances in Consumer Research,* vol. 23, eds. K. P. Corfman and J. G. Lynch (Provo, UT: Association for Consumer Research, 1996), pp. 458–62; R. G. M. Pieters and H. S. J. Robben, "Beyond the Horses Mouth," *Advances in Consumer Research,* vol. 25, eds. J. W. Alba and J. W. Hutchinson (Provo, UT: Association for Consumer Research, 1998), pp. 163–69; and J. A. Ruth, C. C. Otnes, and F. F. Brunel, "Gift Receipt and the Reformulation of Interpersonal Relationships," *Journal of Consumer Research,* March 1999, pp. 385–402.

37. R. W. Belk and G. S. Coon, "Gift Giving as Agapic Love," *Journal of Consumer Research,* December 1993, pp. 404–5.

38. C. S. Areni, P. Kiecker, and K. M. Palan, "Is It Better to Give Than to Receive?" *Psychology & Marketing,* January 1998, pp. 81–109.

39. S.-Y. Park, "A Comparison of Korean and American Gift-Giving Behaviors," *Psychology & Marketing,* September 1998, pp. 577–93; and A. Joy, "Gift Giving in Hong Kong and the Continuum of Social Ties," *Journal of Consumer Research,* September 2001, pp. 239–55.

40. See R. P. Bagozzi, M. Gopinath, and P. U. Nyer, "The Role of Emotion in Marketing," *Journal of the Academy of Marketing Science,* Spring 1999, pp. 184–206; and H. T. Luomala and M. Laaksonen, "Contributions from Mood Research," *Psychology & Marketing,* March 2000, pp. 195–233.

41. M. B. Holbrook and M. P. Gardner, "Illustrating a Dynamic Model of the Mood-Updating Process in Consumer Behavior," *Psychology & Marketing,* March 2000, pp. 165–94.

42. K. R. France and C. W. Park, "The Impact of Program Affective Valence and Level of Cognitive Appraisal on Advertisement Processing and Effectiveness," *Journal of Current Issues and Research in Advertising,* Fall 1997, pp. 1–21; A. B. Aylesworth and C. B. MacKenzie, "Context Is Key," *Journal of Advertising,* Summer 1998, pp. 17–31; A. J. Lee and B. Sternthal, "The Effects of Positive Mood on Memory," *Journal of Consumer Research,* September 1999, pp. 115–27; K. R. Lord, R. E. Burnkrant, and H. R. Unnava, "The Effects of Program-Induced Mood States on Memory for Commercial Information," *Journal of Current Issues and Research in Advertising,* Spring 2001, pp. 1–14; R. Adaval, "Sometimes It Just Feels Right," *Journal of Consumer Research,* June 2001, pp. 1–17; and A. M. Isen, "An Influence of Positive Affect on Decision Making in Complex Situations," *Journal of Consumer Psychology* 11, no. 2 (2001), pp. 75–85.

43. J.-C. Chebat et al., "Impact of Waiting Attribution and Consumer's Mood on Perceived Quality," *Journal of Business Research,* November 1995, pp. 191–96.

44. See M. T. Curren and K. R. Harich, "Consumers' Mood States," *Psychology & Marketing,* March 1994, pp. 91–107; J. Hadjimarcou, J. W. Barnes, and R. S. Jacobs, "The Effects of Contest-Induced Mood States on Initial and Repeat Product Evaluations," *Advances in Consumer Research,* vol. 23, eds. K. P. Corfman and J. G. Lynch (Provo, UT: Association for Consumer Research, 1996), pp. 337–41; and J. P. Forgas and J. Ciarrochi, "On Being Happy and Possessive," *Psychology & Marketing,* March 2001, pp. 239–60.

45. D. W. Rook and M. P. Gardner, "In the Mood," *Research in Consumer Behavior* 6 (1993), pp. 1–28; W. R. Swinyard, "The Effects of Mood, Involvement, and Quality of Store Experience on Shopping Intentions," *Journal of Consumer Research,* September 1993, pp. 271–80; and R. J. Faber and G. A. Christenson, "In the Mood to Buy," *Psychology & Marketing,* December 1996, pp. 803–19.

46. H. T. Luomala and M. Laaksonen, "A Qualitative Exploration of Mood-Regulatory Self-Gift Behaviors," *Journal of Economic Psychology* 20 (1999), pp. 147–82.

47. H. Mano, "The Influence of Pre-Existing Negative Affect on Store Purchase Intentions," *Journal of Retailing* 75, no. 2 (1999), pp. 149–73.

48. S. J. Gould, "An Interpretive Study of Purposeful, Mood Self-Regulating Consumption," *Psychology & Marketing,* July 1997, pp. 395–426.

49. See M. G. Meloy, "Mood-Driven Distortion of Product Information," *Journal of Consumer Research,* December 2000, pp. 345–58.

50. See P. A. Walsh and S. Spiggle, "Consumer Spending Patterns," in *Advances in Consumer Research,* vol. 21,

eds. C. T. Allen and D. R. John (Provo, UT: Association for Consumer Research, 1994), pp. 35–40; and N. Karlsson, T. Garling, and M. Selart, "Explanations of Prior Income Changes on Buying Decisions," *Journal of Economic Psychology* 20 (1999), pp. 449–63.

51. See B. Gainer, "Ritual and Relationships," *Journal of Business Research,* March 1995, pp. 253–60.

52. See C. C. Otnes and L. M. Scott, "Something Old, Something New," *Journal of Advertising,* Spring 1996, pp. 33–50.

53. A. Z. Cuneo, "Using Halloween to Scare Up Sales," *Advertising Age,* October 8, 2001, p. 4.

54. D. Treise, J. M. Wolburg, and C. C. Otnes, "Understanding the 'Social Gifts' of Drinking Rituals," *Journal of Advertising,* Summer 1999, pp. 17–30.

55. For a similar approach see R. Brodie, "Segmentation and Market Structure When Both Consumer and Situational Characteristics Are Explanatory," *Psychology & Marketing,* September 1992, pp. 395–408.

498

Consumer Decision Process and Problem Recognition

☐ Beiersdorf, marketers of the Nivea brand, recently introduced its Nivea for Men line in the United States.[1] Nivea for Men has been very popular in Europe for the past 10 years. However, according to the director of marketing for Beiersdorf Inc. USA,

American men are the most powerful men in the world in finance and the Internet. However, in terms of styling, they lag 15–20 years behind their European counterparts.

Nivea for Men currently consists of seven products and a four-step facial care system:

Step One: Cleanse Face

Wash your face twice a day with Double Action Face Wash. Soap free, it clears away everyday dirt and excess oils without drying out your skin.

Wash your face three or four times a week with Exfoliating Face Scrub. It deeply cleanses and purifies to help clear away dry, rough skin, built-up dirt and helps prevent clogged pores.

Step Two: Shave

Use Mild Shaving Gel every time you shave. It gives you an extra thick lather for a closer, smoother shave. Enriched with unique moisturizers, it improves the condition of your skin while shaving and helps to protect against razor burn and skin dryness.

For sensitive skin use Sensitive Shaving Gel. Enriched with soothing Aloe and moisturizing agents, it protects your skin while shaving. Unscented and free of dyes, it minimizes the risk of irritation.

Step Three: Apply After Shave

Use After Shave Balm every time you shave to help calm the irritations that are caused by shaving. It soothes and moisturizes the skin after shaving, and noticeably improves the condition of your skin.

For sensitive skin use Sensitive After Shave Balm. This light, unscented, easily absorbed balm moisturizes the skin without burning it.

Step Four: Moisturize

Use Moisturizing Lotion every day to provide valuable moisture to the skin. It leaves skin smooth and protected.

Currently, 98 percent of American men wash their faces with bar soap despite the fact that many have dry skin, which soap can exacerbate. Beiersdorf is betting millions that they can change that pattern.

The time is right—American men are ready. Because of tough competition in the workplace, the changing dynamics between men and women, and the increased societal value placed upon youth, American men of all ages are now realizing that looking good can give them a significant advantage, both in professional and personal areas.

Problem recognition is the first stage of the consumer decision process. For Nivea for Men to succeed in America, Beiersdorf must cause significant numbers of American men to recognize a problem with their current methods of facial care. If Beiersdorf can trigger problem recognition, consumers may then proceed to evaluate, purchase, and use the new product line.

This chapter examines the nature of the consumer decision process and analyzes the first step in that process, problem recognition. Within problem recognition, we focus on (1) the process of problem recognition, (2) the uncontrollable determinants of problem recognition, and (3) marketing strategies based on the problem recognition process.

TYPES OF CONSUMER DECISIONS

The term *consumer decision* produces an image of an individual carefully evaluating the attributes of a set of products, brands, or services and rationally selecting the one that solves a clearly recognized need for the least cost. It has a rational, functional connotation. Consumers do make many decisions in this manner; however, many other decisions involve little conscious effort. Further, many consumer decisions focus not on brand attributes but rather on the feelings or emotions associated with acquiring or using the brand or with the environment in which the product is purchased or used. Thus, a brand may be selected not because of an attribute (price, style, functional characteristics) but because "It makes me feel good" or "My friends will like it."[2]

Although purchases and related consumption behavior driven by emotional or environmental needs have characteristics distinct from the traditional attribute-based model, the decision process model provides useful insights into all types of consumer purchases. As we describe consumer decision making in this and the next four chapters, we will indicate how it helps us understand emotion-, environment-, and attribute-based decisions.

Consumer decisions are frequently the result of a single problem, for example, running low on gasoline. At other times, they result from the convergence of several problems, such as an aging automobile and a growing feeling of inadequacy or low self-esteem. Furthermore, once the decision process begins, it may evolve and become more complex with multiple goals. A consumer noticing a simple need for gas may want to minimize the price paid, avoid one or more brands because of their environmental record, and decide to find a station with food service attached. This consumer may wind up choosing between a station with a lower price and its own food service, or another station with a higher price but with a preferred food outlet such as Taco Bell attached, or perhaps spending the extra time to buy gas at one and food at the other.[3]

As Figure 14–1 indicates, there are various types of consumer decision processes.[4] As the consumer moves from a very low level of involvement *with the purchase* to a high level of involvement, decision making becomes increasingly complex. While purchase involvement is a continuum, it is useful to consider nominal, limited, and extended decision making as general descriptions of the types of processes that occur along various points on the continuum. Keep in mind that the types of decision processes are not distinct but rather blend into each other.

Before describing each type of decision process, the concept of purchase involvement must be clarified. We define **purchase involvement** as *the level of concern for, or interest in, the purchase process triggered by the need to consider a particular purchase*. Thus, purchase involvement is a *temporary state* of an individual or household. It is influenced by the interaction of individual, product, and situational characteristics.

Note that purchase involvement is *not* the same as **product involvement** or enduring involvement. A consumer may be very involved with a brand (Starbucks or Saturn) or a product category (coffee or cars) and yet have a very low level of involvement with a particular purchase of that product because of brand loyalty, time pressures, or other reasons. For example, think of your favorite brand of soft drink or other beverage. You may be quite loyal to that brand, think it is superior to other brands, and have strong, favorable feelings about it. However, when you want a soft drink, you probably just buy your preferred brand without much thought.

Or a consumer may have a rather low level of involvement with a product (school supplies or automobile tires) but have a high level of purchase involvement because he or she desires to set an example for a child, impress a friend who is on the shopping trip, or save money.

The following sections provide a brief description of how the purchasing process changes as purchase involvement increases.

Nominal Decision Making

Nominal decision making, sometimes referred to as *habitual decision making,* in effect *involves no decision per se*. As Figure 14–1 indicates, a problem is recognized, internal search (long-term memory) provides a single preferred solution (brand), that brand is purchased, and an evaluation occurs only if the brand fails to perform as expected. Nominal decisions occur when there is very low involvement *with the purchase.*

A completely nominal decision does not even include consideration of the "do not purchase" alternative. For example, you might notice that you are nearly out of Aim toothpaste

| FIGURE 14–1 | Involvement and Types of Decision Making |

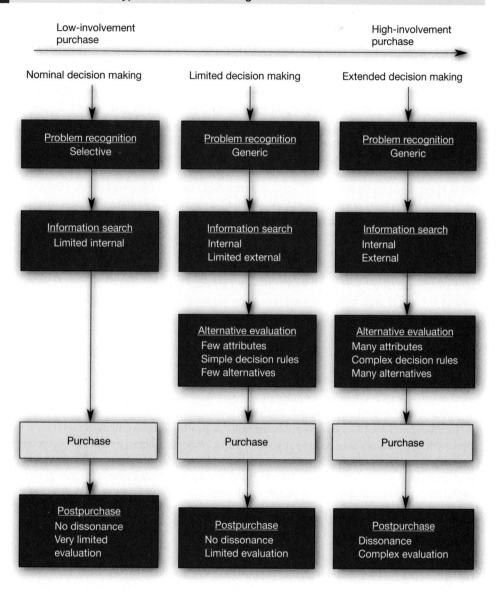

and resolve to purchase some the next time you are at the store. You don't even consider not replacing the toothpaste or purchasing another brand. At the store, you scan the shelf for Aim and pick it up without considering alternative brands, its price, or other potentially relevant factors.

Nominal decisions can be broken into two distinct categories: brand loyal decisions and repeat purchase decisions. These two categories are described briefly below and examined in detail in Chapter 19.

Brand Loyal Purchases   At one time, you may have been highly involved in selecting a brand of toothpaste and, in response, used an extensive decision-making process. Having selected Aim as a result of this process, you may now purchase it without further consideration, even though using the best available toothpaste is still important to you. Thus, you are committed to Aim because you believe it best meets your overall needs and you have formed an emotional attachment to it (you like it). You are brand loyal. It will be very difficult for a competitor to gain your patronage.

In this example, you have a fairly high degree of product involvement but a low degree of purchase involvement because of your brand loyalty. Should you encounter a challenge to the superiority of Aim, perhaps through a news article, you would most likely engage in a high-involvement decision process before changing brands.

Repeat Purchases   In contrast, you may believe that all catsup is about the same and you may not attach much importance to the product category or purchase. Having tried Del Monte and found it satisfactory, you now purchase it whenever you need catsup. Thus, you are a repeat purchaser of Del Monte catsup, but you are not committed to it.

Should you encounter a challenge to the wisdom of buying Del Monte the next time you need catsup, perhaps because of a point-of-sale price discount, you would probably engage in only a limited decision process before deciding on which brand to purchase.

Limited Decision Making

Limited decision making involves *internal and limited external search, few alternatives, simple decision rules on a few attributes, and little postpurchase evaluation.* It covers the middle ground between nominal decision making and extended decision making. In its simplest form (lowest level of purchase involvement), limited decision making is similar to nominal decision making. For example, while in a store you may notice a point-of-purchase display for Jell-O and pick up two boxes without seeking information beyond your memory that "Jell-O tastes good," or "Gee, I haven't had Jell-O in a long time." In addition, you may have considered no other alternative except possibly a very limited examination of a "do not buy" option. Or you may have a decision rule that you buy the cheapest brand of instant coffee available. When you run low on coffee (problem recognition), you simply examine coffee prices the next time you are in the store and select the cheapest brand.

Limited decision making also occurs in response to some emotional or environmental needs. For example, you may decide to purchase a new brand or product because you are bored with the current, otherwise satisfactory, brand. This decision might involve evaluating only the newness or novelty of the available alternatives.[5] Or you might evaluate a purchase in terms of the actual or anticipated behavior of others. For example, you might order or refrain from ordering wine with a meal depending on the observed or expected orders of your dinner companions.

In general, limited decision making involves recognizing a problem for which there are several possible solutions. There is internal and a limited amount of external search. A few alternatives are evaluated on a few dimensions using simple selection rules. The purchase and use of the product are given very little evaluation afterward, unless there is a service problem or product failure.

Extended Decision Making

As Figure 14–1 indicates, **extended decision making** involves *an extensive internal and external information search followed by a complex evaluation of multiple alternatives and significant postpurchase evaluation.* It is the response to a high level of purchase involvement. After the purchase, doubt about its correctness is likely and a thorough evaluation of the purchase takes place. Relatively few consumer decisions reach this level of complexity. However, products such as homes, personal computers, and complex recreational items such as backpacks and stereo systems are frequently purchased via extended decision making.

Even decisions that are heavily emotional may involve substantial cognitive efforts. For example, a consumer may agonize over a decision to take a ski trip or visit parents even though the needs being met and the criteria being evaluated are largely emotions or feelings rather than attributes per se, and are therefore typically fewer in number with less external information available.

As Figure 14–1 illustrates, problem recognition is the first stage of the decision process. We will describe this stage and discuss the marketing applications associated with it in the balance of this chapter. We devote the next four chapters to the remaining four stages of the consumer decision process and discuss the relevant marketing applications in those chapters.

Our discussion of the decision process is based primarily on studies conducted in America. Although the evidence is very limited, it appears that consumers in other cultures use similar processes.[6]

THE PROCESS OF PROBLEM RECOGNITION

A day rarely passes in which a person does not face multiple problems that are resolved by consuming products and services. Routine problems of depletion, such as the need to get gasoline as the gauge approaches empty, or the need to replace a frequently used food item, are readily recognized, defined, and resolved. The unexpected breakdown of a major appliance such as a refrigerator creates an unplanned problem that is also easily recognized but is often more difficult to resolve. Recognition of other problems, such as the need for a palm-sized electronic organizer, may take longer, as they may be subtle and evolve slowly over time.

Feelings, such as boredom, anxiety, or the "blues," may arise quickly or slowly over time. Such feelings are often recognized as problems subject to solution by purchasing behavior (I'm sad, I think I'll go shopping/to a movie/to a restaurant). At other times, such feelings may trigger consumption behaviors without deliberate decision making. A person feeling restless may eat snack food without really thinking about it. In this case, the problem remains unrecognized (at the conscious level) and the solutions tried are often inappropriate (eating may not reduce restlessness).

Marketers develop products to help consumers solve problems. They also attempt to help consumers recognize problems, sometimes well in advance of their occurrence (see Illustration 14–1).

The Nature of Problem Recognition

Problem recognition is the first stage in the consumer decision process. **Problem recognition** is *the result of a discrepancy between a desired state and an actual state that is sufficient to arouse and activate the decision process.*[7] An **actual state** is *the way an individual perceives his or her feelings and situation to be at the present time.* A **desired state** is *the way an individual wants to feel or be at the present time.* For example, you probably don't want to be bored on Friday night. If you find yourself alone and becoming bored, you would treat this as a problem because your actual state (being bored) and your desired state (being pleasantly occupied) were different. You could then choose to consume a television program, rent a video, call a friend, go out, or take a wide array of other actions.

Reprinted with permission of Kemper Distributors Inc.

The kind of action taken by consumers in response to recognized problems relates directly to its importance to the consumer, the situation, and the dissatisfaction or inconvenience created by the problem.

Without recognition of a problem, there is no need for a decision. This condition is shown in Figure 14–2, when there is no discrepancy between the consumer's desired state (what the consumer would like) and the actual state (what the consumer perceives as already existing). Thus, if Friday night arrives and you find yourself engrossed in a novel, your desire to be pleasantly occupied (desired state) and your condition of enjoying a novel would be consistent, and you would have no reason to search for other activities.

On the other hand, when there is a discrepancy between a consumer desire and the perceived actual state, recognition of a problem occurs. Figure 14–2 indicates that any time the desired state is perceived as being greater than or less than the actual state, a problem exists. For example, being pleasantly occupied (desired state) would generally exceed being bored (actual state) and result in problem recognition. However, if your roommate suddenly showed up with a rowdy party, you might find yourself with more stimulation (actual state) than the medium level you actually desire. This too would result in problem recognition.

In Figure 14–2, consumer desires are shown to be the result of the desired lifestyle of the consumer (as described in Chapter 12) and the current situation (time pressures, physical surroundings, and so forth, as described in Chapter 13). Thus, a consumer whose self-concept and desired lifestyle focus on outdoor activities will desire frequent participation

FIGURE 14–2   The Process of Problem Recognition

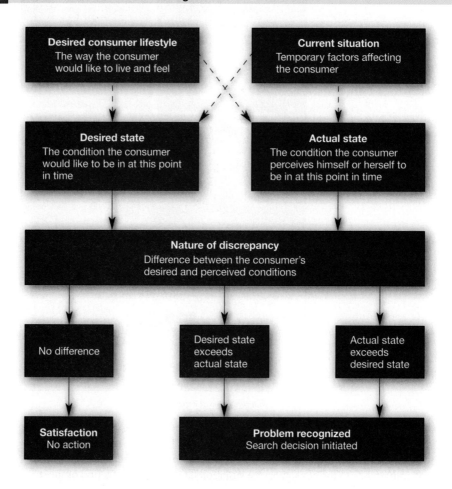

in such activities. A current situation of new snow in the mountains or warm weather at the beach would tend to increase that person's desire to be engaged in outdoor sports.

Perceptions of the actual state are also determined by a consumer's lifestyle and current situation. Consumers' lifestyles are a major determinant of their actual state because that is how they choose to live given the constraints imposed by their resources. Thus, a consumer who has chosen to raise a family, have significant material possessions, and pursue a demanding career is likely to have little free time for outdoor activities (actual state). The current situation—a day off work, a big project due, or a sick child—also has a major impact on how consumers perceive the actual situation.

It is important to note that it is the consumer's perception of the actual state that drives problem recognition, not some objective reality. Consumers who smoke cigars may believe that this activity is not harming their health because they do not inhale. These consumers do not recognize a problem with this behavior despite the reality that it is harmful.

The Desire to Resolve Recognized Problems   The level of one's desire to resolve a particular problem depends on two factors: (1) *the magnitude of the discrepancy between the desired and actual states,* and (2) *the relative importance of the problem.* An individual could desire to have a car that averages at least 25 miles per gallon while still meeting certain size and power desires. If the current car obtains an average of 22 miles per gallon, a discrepancy exists, but it may not be large enough to motivate the consumer to proceed to the next step in the decision process.

On the other hand, a large discrepancy may exist and the consumer may not proceed to information search because the *relative importance* of the problem is small. A consumer may desire a new Volkswagen and own a 15-year-old Toyota. The discrepancy is large. However, the relative importance of this particular discrepancy may be small compared to other consumption problems such as those related to housing, utilities, and food. Relative importance is a critical concept because all consumers have budget constraints, time constraints, or both. Only the relatively more important problems are likely to be solved. In general, importance is determined by how critical the problem is to the maintenance of the consumer's desired lifestyle.

Types of Consumer Problems

Consumer problems may be either active or inactive. An **active problem** is *one the consumer is aware of or will become aware of in the normal course of events*. An **inactive problem** is *one of which the consumer is not aware*. This concept is very similar to the concept of felt need discussed in the Diffusion of Innovations section of Chapter 7 (page 250). The following example should clarify the distinction between active and inactive problems.

Timberlane Lumber Co. acquired a source of supply of Honduran pitch pine. This natural product lights at the touch of a match even when damp and burns for 15 to 20 minutes. It will not flare up and is therefore relatively safe. It can be procured in sticks 15 to 18 inches long and 1 inch in diameter. These sticks can be used to ignite fireplace fires, or they can be shredded and used to ignite charcoal grills.

Prior to marketing the product, Timberlane commissioned a marketing study to estimate demand and guide in developing marketing strategy. Two large samples of potential consumers were interviewed. The first sample was asked how they lit their fireplace fires and what problems they had with this procedure. Almost all of the respondents used newspaper, kindling, or both, and very few experienced any problems. The new product was then described, and the respondents were asked to express the likelihood that they would purchase such a product. Only a small percentage expressed any interest. However, a sample of consumers that were paid to use the new product for several weeks felt it was a substantial improvement over existing methods and expressed a strong desire to continue using the product. Thus, the problem was there (because the new product was strongly preferred over the old by those who tried it), but most consumers were not aware of it. This is an *inactive problem*. Before the product can be successfully sold, the firm must activate problem recognition.

In contrast, a substantial percentage of those interviewed about lighting charcoal fires expressed a strong concern about the safety of liquid charcoal lighter. These individuals expressed great interest in purchasing a safer product. This is an *active problem*. Timberlane need not worry about problem recognition in this case. Instead, it can concentrate on illustrating how its product solves the problem that the consumers already know exists.

As this example indicates, active and inactive problems require different marketing strategies. Active problems only require the marketer to convince consumers that its brand is the superior solution. Consumers are already aware of the problem. In contrast, inactive problems require the marketer to convince consumers that they have the problem *and* that the marketer's brand is a superior solution to the problem. This is a much more difficult task.

Courtesy Nestle Purina Pet Care.

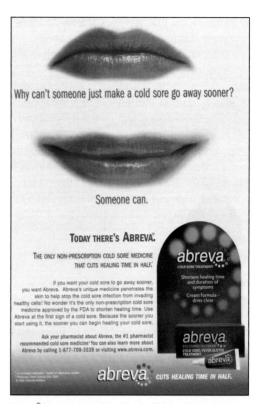

Abreva® is a trademark of the GlaxoSmithKline Group of Companies.

ILLUSTRATION 14–2

Often, marketers need to trigger problem recognition in market segments. However, at other times the market is well aware of the problem and the communication can focus on the brand's ability to solve the problem.

Illustration 14–2 contains an ad that is designed to activate a problem that is inactive for many pet owners. Note that an important component of the ad is to alert pet owners that the appearance of their young dog may not reveal an unhealthy level of body fat. Thus, it attempts to cause a change in their perception of the actual state and trigger the recognition of an inactive problem. In contrast, the Abreva ad assumes that these consumers are aware of the problem. It focuses on its unique ability to solve the problem.

UNCONTROLLABLE DETERMINANTS OF PROBLEM RECOGNITION

A discrepancy between what is desired by a consumer and what the consumer has is the necessary condition for problem recognition. A discrepancy can be the result of a variety of factors that influence consumer desires, perceptions of the existing state, or both. These factors are often beyond the direct influence of the marketing manager, such as a change in family composition. Figure 14–3 summarizes the major nonmarketing factors that influence problem recognition. The marketing factors influencing problem recognition are discussed in the next section of this chapter.

Most of the nonmarketing factors that affect problem recognition are fairly obvious and logical. Most were described in some detail in prior chapters. For example, as we discussed in Chapter 2, a person's culture affects almost all aspects of his or her desired state. Thus, the desire to be recognized as an independent, unique person with distinctive behaviors and possessions differs sharply between American and Japanese consumers because of cultural influences.

FIGURE 14–3	Nonmarketing Factors Affecting Problem Recognition

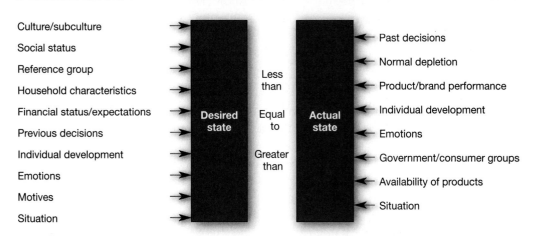

Culture/subculture →

Social status →

Reference group →

Household characteristics →

Financial status/expectations →   **Desired**

Previous decisions →   **state**

Individual development →

Emotions →

Motives →

Situation →

Less than

Equal to

Greater than

Actual state

← Past decisions

← Normal depletion

← Product/brand performance

← Individual development

← Emotions

← Government/consumer groups

← Availability of products

← Situation

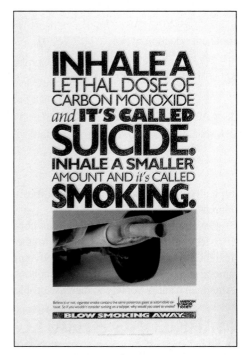

Courtesy The American Cancer Society.

Previous decisions and individual development were not discussed in earlier chapters. A previous decision to buy a bike or skis could lead to a current desire to have a car rack to carry them. A decision to become a home owner may trigger desires for numerous home and garden items. Past decisions may also deplete purchasing power with the result that fewer problems are recognized or are assigned sufficient importance to trigger action.[8]

Individual development causes many changes in the desired state. As people age, their needs and desires evolve noticeably. An ad for Scotch appearing in men's magazines recognizes this—its headline, "When you were young, you didn't like girls either," appears over a picture of an attractive woman and a bottle of Scotch. As individuals gain skills, their desires related to those skills change. Beginning skiers, musicians, and gardeners

Consumer groups and government officials have been concerned that many consumers do not recognize the danger to health and other problems associated with alcohol use. As a result of these concerns, since November 1989, all alcoholic beverage containers must carry the following warning:

GOVERNMENT WARNING: (1) ACCORDING TO THE SURGEON GENERAL, WOMEN SHOULD NOT DRINK ALCOHOLIC BEVERAGES DURING PREG-NANCY BECAUSE OF THE RISK OF BIRTH DEFECTS, (2) CONSUMPTION OF ALCOHOLIC BEVERAGES IMPAIRS YOUR ABILITY TO DRIVE A CAR OR OPERATE MACHINERY, AND MAY CAUSE HEALTH PROBLEMS.

In addition to the label warnings, some groups want all advertising of alcoholic beverages to carry warnings. Additional legislation has been introduced but not passed that would require every print and broadcast ad to carry one of five rotated health warnings. Two of the five warnings are

SURGEON GENERAL'S WARNING: DRINKING DURING PREGNANCY MAY CAUSE MENTAL RETARDATION AND OTHER BIRTH DEFECTS. AVOID ALCOHOL DURING PREGNANCY.

WARNING: ALCOHOL MAY BE HAZARDOUS IF YOU ARE USING ANY OTHER DRUGS, SUCH AS OVER-THE-COUNTER, PRESCRIPTION, OR ILLICIT DRUGS.

Research has shown that the current warning is not as effective as other warnings. However, marketers of alcoholic beverages do not want warnings that would unnecessarily alarm consumers or tarnish the overall image of the product. Thus, the task is to develop warnings that clearly communicate the risks and trigger problem recognition in the appropriate audiences without unduly raising concerns among other consumers.

Critical Thinking Questions

1. What responsibilities do marketers have in terms of warning consumers of potential harmful effects of using their products?
2. Is it possible to effectively warn consumers of the health dangers of alcohol consumption without tarnishing the image of the product category?

typically desire products and capabilities that will no longer be appropriate as their skills increase.

Government agencies and various consumer groups actively attempt to trigger problem recognition, often in relation to the consumption of various products. Consumer Insight 14–1 is an example of the government attempting to trigger problem recognition among some consumers who drink alcoholic beverages. Illustration 14–3 is an ad used by the American Cancer Society to increase problem recognition related to the dangers of smoking.

MARKETING STRATEGY AND PROBLEM RECOGNITION

Marketing managers have four concerns related to problem recognition. First, they need to know the problems consumers are facing. Second, managers must know how to develop the marketing mix to solve consumer problems. Third, they occasionally want to cause consumers to recognize problems. Finally, there are times when managers desire to suppress problem recognition among consumers. The remainder of this chapter discusses these issues.

Discovering Consumer Problems

A wide variety of approaches are used to determine the problems consumers face. The most common approach undoubtedly is *intuition;* that is, a manager can analyze a given product category and logically determine where improvements could be made. Thus, soundless vacuum cleaners or lawnmowers are logical solutions to potential consumer problems. The difficulty with this approach is that the problem identified may be of low importance to most consumers. Therefore, several research techniques are also employed.

A common research technique is the *survey,* which asks relatively large numbers of individuals about the problems they are facing. This was the technique used by Timberlane, as described earlier. A second common technique is *focus groups.* Focus groups are composed of 8 to 12 similar individuals—such as male college students, lawyers, or teenage girls—brought together to discuss a particular topic. A moderator is present to keep the discussion moving and focused on the topic, but otherwise the sessions are free flowing.

Both surveys and focus groups tend to take one of three approaches to problem identification: *activity analysis, product analysis,* or *problem analysis.* A fourth approach, *human factors research,* does not rely on surveys or focus groups. *Emotion research,* a fifth effort, attempts to discover the role emotions play in problem recognition.

Activity Analysis   Activity analysis focuses on a particular activity such as preparing dinner, maintaining the lawn, or eating out. The survey or focus group attempts to determine what problems consumers encounter during the performance of the activity. For example, Johnson Wax had a national panel of women report on how they cared for their hair and the problems they encountered. Their responses revealed a perceived problem with oiliness that existing brands could not resolve. As a result, Johnson Wax developed Agree Shampoo and Agree Crème Rinse, both of which became very successful.

In another case, a survey of kitchen problems among homemakers showed a lack of organization to be the most commonly expressed problem. Food storage was not seen as a problem by very many, and dealing with leftovers was a very minor concern.[9]

Product Analysis   Product analysis is similar to activity analysis but examines the purchase or use of a particular product or brand. Thus, consumers may be asked about problems associated with using their mountain bikes or laptop computers. Curlee Clothing used focus groups to analyze the purchase and use of men's clothing. The results indicated a high level of insecurity in purchasing men's clothing. This insecurity was combined with a distrust of both the motivations and competence of retail sales personnel. As a result, Curlee initiated a major effort to train retail sales personnel through specially prepared films and training sessions.

Problem Analysis   Problem analysis takes the opposite approach from the previous techniques. It starts with a list of problems and asks the respondent to indicate which activities, products, or brands are associated with those problems. Such a study dealing with packaging could include questions such as,

- _____ packages are hard to open.
- Packages of _____ are hard to reseal.
- _____ doesn't pour well.
- Packages of _____ don't fit on the shelf.
- Packages of _____ waste too many resources.

Human Factors Research   Human factors research attempts to determine human capabilities in areas such as vision, strength, response time, flexibility, and fatigue and the effect on these capabilities of lighting, temperature, and sound. While many methods can be employed in human factors research, observational techniques such as slow-motion and time-lapse photography, video recording, and event recorders are particularly useful to marketers.

This type of research can sometimes identify functional problems that consumers are unaware of. For example, it can be used in the design of such products as vacuum cleaners,

A key task of marketers is to identify consumer problems and to position their brands as solutions for them.

Campbell Soup Company; Agency: Young & Rubicam.

lawnmowers, kitchen utensils, and computers to minimize user fatigue. The growth in carpal tunnel syndrome (injury resulting from repeating the same movements such as inputting data into a computer over time) has resulted in substantial interest in this area.

Emotion Research   Marketers are just beginning to conduct research on the role of emotions in the decision process. Common approaches are focus group research and one-on-one personal interviews that focus on either (1) the emotions associated with a certain product or (2) the products associated with reducing or arousing certain emotions. For more subtle or sensitive emotions or products, projective techniques (see Table 10–2, page 364) can provide useful insights.[10] Likewise, the various techniques used to measure emotions and emotional responses to advertising (see Chapter 10, page 376) can also be used to measure emotional responses to decision situations.

Responding to Consumer Problems

Once a consumer problem is identified, the manager may structure the marketing mix to solve the problem. This can involve developing a new product or altering an existing one, modifying channels of distribution, changing pricing policy, or revising advertising strategy. For example, in Illustration 14–4 V8 is being positioned as the solution to the need for a balanced diet in the face of hectic schedules.

As you approach graduation, you will be presented with opportunities to purchase insurance, acquire credit cards, and solve other problems associated with the onset of financial independence and a major change in lifestyle. These opportunities reflect various firms' knowledge that many individuals in your situation face problems that their products will help solve.

Weekend and night store hours and, in part, the rapid growth of Internet stores are a response of retailers to the consumer problem of limited weekday shopping opportunities. Solving this problem has become particularly important to families with both spouses employed.

The examples described above represent only a small sample of the ways in which marketers react to consumer problem recognition. Each firm must be aware of the consumer problems it can solve, which consumers have these problems, and the situations in which the problems arise.

Helping Consumers Recognize Problems

There are occasions when the manager will want to cause problem recognition rather than react to it. In the earlier example, Timberlane faced having to activate problem recognition in order to sell its product as a fireplace starter. Toy marketers are attempting to reduce their dependence on the Christmas season by activating problem recognition at other times of the year. For example, Fisher-Price has had "rainy day" and "sunny day" promotions in the spring and summer months. Illustrations 14–1 and 14–2, presented earlier, show attempts to activate problem recognition.

Generic versus Selective Problem Recognition   Two basic approaches to causing problem recognition are *generic problem recognition* and *selective problem recognition*. These are analogous to the economic concepts of generic and selective demand.

Generic problem recognition involves a *discrepancy that a variety of brands within a product category can reduce.* Generally, a firm will attempt to influence generic problem recognition when the problem is latent or of low importance and one of the following conditions exists:

* It is early in the product life cycle.
* The firm has a high percentage of the market.
* External search after problem recognition is apt to be limited.
* It is an industrywide cooperative effort.

Telephone sales programs often attempt to arouse problem recognition, in part because the salesperson can then limit external search to one brand. Cooperative advertising frequently focuses on generic problem recognition. Illustration 14–5 is an example of one of the most notable ongoing campaigns of this type. Note that the copy attempts to make individuals aware of the need for calcium that milk provides but does not promote any particular brand of milk.

Firms with large market shares in a product category often focus on generic problem recognition because any sales increase will probably come to their brands. However, a smaller firm that generates generic problem recognition for its product category may be generating more sales for its competitors than for itself. But even firms with large market share can lose share if generic problem recognition campaigns are not done carefully. Borden's Creamette is the largest brand of pasta in the United States. It increased its marketing efforts substantially and promoted recipes using pasta. Its sales increased only 1.6 percent,

Courtesy National Fluid Milk Processor Promotion Board; Agency: Bozell
Worldwide, Inc.

compared with the industry's growth of 5.5 percent.[11] Its efforts apparently helped the sales
of its competitors more than its own sales.

Selective problem recognition involves *a discrepancy that only one brand can solve.*
The ad shown in Illustration 14–6 is focused on creating selective problem recognition.
Firms attempt to cause selective problem recognition to gain or maintain market share,
whereas increasing generic problem recognition generally results in an expansion of the
total market.

Approaches to Activating Problem Recognition   How can a firm influence problem
recognition? Recall that problem recognition is a function of the (1) *importance* and
(2) *magnitude* of a discrepancy between the desired state and an existing state. Thus, the
firm can attempt to influence the size of the discrepancy by altering the desired state or
the perceptions of the existing state. Or the firm can attempt to influence the perception of
the importance of an existing discrepancy.

Many marketing efforts attempt to *influence the desired state;* that is, marketers often
advertise the benefits their products will provide, hoping that these benefits will become
desired by consumers. The ad in Illustration 14–7 attempts to influence the desired state by
showing how white and bright teeth can be.

It is also possible to *influence perceptions of the existing state* through advertisements.
Many personal care and social products take this approach. "Even your best friend won't

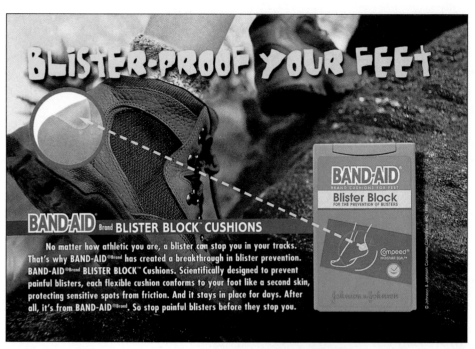

Courtesy Johnson & Johnson.

© The Procter & Gamble Company. Used by permission.

Many adults may not be aware that two kids riding on one ATV is unsafe. This ad triggers problem recognition by altering perceptions of the safety of the existing state.

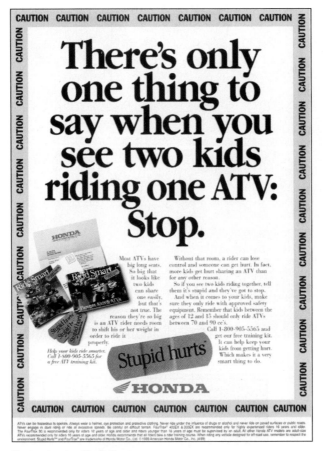

Courtesy American Honda Co.

tell you . . ." or "Kim is a great worker but this coffee . . ." are examples of messages designed to generate concern about an existing state. The desired state is assumed to be fresh breath and good coffee. These messages are designed to cause individuals to question if their existing state coincides with this desired state.

The Honda ad in Illustration 14–8 attempts to make parents and other adults aware that the common practice (actual state) of two children riding one ATV is not as safe as it may appear. This would trigger problem recognition that would hopefully result in parents restricting such behaviors.

Critics frequently question the ethics of activating problem recognition. This is particularly true for problems related to status or social acceptance. This debate is generally discussed in terms of "creating needs," which we discussed in some depth in Chapter 10 (page 366).

The Timing of Problem Recognition   Consumers often recognize problems at times when purchasing a solution is difficult or impossible, as the following examples demonstrate:

* We decide we need snow chains when caught in a blizzard.
* We become aware of a need for insurance *after* an accident.

- We desire a flower bed full of tulips in the spring but forgot to plant bulbs in the fall.
- We want cold medicine when we are sick but don't feel like driving to the store.

In some instances, marketers attempt to help consumers solve such problems after they arise. For example, some pharmacies will make home deliveries. However, the more common strategy is to trigger problem recognition in advance of the actual problem (see Illustration 14–1). That is, it is often to the consumer's and marketer's advantage for the consumer to recognize and solve potential problems *before* they become actual problems.

Some companies, particularly insurance companies, attempt to initiate problem recognition through mass media advertising; others rely more on point-of-purchase displays and other in-store influences (see Chapter 17). Retailers, as well as manufacturers, are involved in this activity. For example, prior to snow season, the following sign was placed on a large rack of snow shovels in the main aisle of a large hardware store:

REMEMBER LAST WINTER
WHEN YOU *NEEDED*
A SNOW SHOVEL?
THIS YEAR
BE PREPARED!

Suppressing Problem Recognition

As we have seen, competition, consumer organizations, and governmental agencies occasionally introduce information in the marketplace that triggers problem recognition that particular marketers would prefer to avoid. The American tobacco industry has made strenuous attempts to minimize consumer recognition of the health problems associated with cigarette smoking. For example, a Newport cigarette advertisement showed a happy, laughing couple under the headline, "Alive with pleasure." This could easily be interpreted as an attempt to minimize any problem recognition caused by the mandatory warning at the bottom of the advertisement, "Warning: The Surgeon General has determined that cigarette smoking is dangerous to your health."

Obviously marketers do not want their current customers to recognize problems with their brands. Effective quality control and distribution (limited out-of-stock situations) are important in this effort. Packages and package inserts that assure the consumer of the wisdom of their purchase are also common.

SUMMARY

Consumer decision making becomes more extensive and complex as *purchase involvement* increases. The lowest level of purchase involvement is represented by *nominal decisions:* a problem is recognized, long-term memory provides a single preferred brand, that brand is purchased, and only limited postpurchase evaluation occurs. As one moves from *limited decision making* toward *extended decision making,* information search increases, alternative evaluation becomes more extensive and complex, and postpurchase evaluation becomes more thorough.

Problem recognition involves the existence of a discrepancy between the consumer's desired state (what the consumer would like) and the actual state (what the consumer perceives as already existing). Both the desired state and the actual state are influenced by the consumer's lifestyle and current situation. If the discrepancy between these two states is sufficiently large and important, the consumer will begin to search for a solution to the problem.

A number of factors beyond the control of the marketing manager can affect problem recognition. The desired state is commonly influenced by (1) culture/subculture, (2) social status, (3) reference groups, (4) household characteristics, (5) financial status/expectations, (6) previous decisions, (7) individual development, (8) motives, (9) emotions, and the (10) current situation.

The actual state is influenced by (1) past decisions, (2) normal depletion, (3) product/brand performance, (4) individual development, (5) emotions, (6) government/consumer groups, (7) availability of products, and the (8) current situation.

Before marketing managers can respond to problem recognition generated by outside factors, they must be able to *measure* consumer problems. Surveys and focus groups using *activity, product,* or *problem analysis* are commonly used to measure problem recognition. *Human factors research* approaches the same task from an observational perspective. *Emotion research* focuses on the emotional causes of and responses to product purchase and use.

Once managers are aware of problem recognition patterns among their target market, they can react by designing the marketing mix to solve the recognized problem. This may involve product development or repositioning, a change in store hours, a different price, or a host of other marketing strategies.

Marketing managers often want to influence problem recognition rather than react to it. They may desire to generate *generic problem recognition,* a discrepancy that a variety of brands within a product category can reduce, or to induce *selective problem recognition,* a discrepancy that only one brand in the product category can solve.

Attempts to *activate problem recognition* generally do so by focusing on the desired state. However, attempts to make consumers aware of negative aspects of the existing state are also common. In addition, marketers attempt to influence the timing of problem recognition by making consumers aware of potential problems before they arise.

Finally, managers may attempt to minimize or suppress problem recognition by current users of their brands.

KEY TERMS

Active problem 507
Actual state 504
Desired state 504
Extended decision making 503

Generic problem recognition 513
Inactive problem 507
Limited decision making 503
Nominal decision making 501

Problem recognition 504
Product involvement 501
Purchase involvement 501
Selective problem recognition 514

INTERNET EXERCISES

1. Visit several general interest or entertainment websites that contain ads. Find and describe an ad that attempts to trigger problem recognition. How does it do this?

2. Visit several company websites. Find and describe one that attempts to trigger problem recognition. How does it do this?

3. Monitor several chat sites or interest groups for a week. Prepare a report on how a marketer could learn about the consumption problems of consumers by doing this.

REVIEW QUESTIONS

1. What is meant by *purchase involvement?* How does it differ from product involvement?

2. How does consumer decision making change as purchase involvement increases?

3. What is the role of *emotion* in the consumer decision process?

4. How do *nominal, limited,* and *extended decision making* differ? How do the two types of nominal decision making differ?

5. What is *problem recognition?*

6. What influences the motivation to resolve a recognized problem?

7. What is the difference between an *active* and an *inactive problem?* Why is this distinction important?

8. How does lifestyle relate to problem recognition?

9. What are the main uncontrollable factors that influence the *desired* state?

10. What are the main uncontrollable factors that influence the *existing* state?

11. How can you measure problem recognition?

12. In what ways can marketers react to problem recognition? Give several examples.

13. How does *generic problem recognition* differ from *selective problem recognition?* Under what conditions would a firm attempt to influence generic problem recognition? Why?

14. How can a firm cause problem recognition? Give examples.

15. How can a firm suppress problem recognition?

DISCUSSION QUESTIONS

16. What products do you think *generally* are associated with nominal, limited, and extended decision making? Under what conditions, if any, would these products be associated with a different form of decision making?

17. What products do you think *generally* are purchased or used for emotional reasons? How would the decision process differ for an emotion-driven purchase compared to a more functional purchase?

18. What products do you think *generally* are associated with brand loyal decision making and which with repeat purchase decision making? Justify your response.

19. Describe a purchase you made using nominal decision making, one using limited decision making, and one using extended decision making. What caused you to use each type of decision process?

20. Describe two recent purchases you have made. What uncontrollable factors, if any, triggered problem recognition? Did they affect the desired state, the actual state, or both?

21. How would you measure consumer problems among the following?
    a. College students
    b. Children aged 2 to 4

    c. Internet shoppers
    d. New residents in a town
    e. Vegans
    f. Newly married couples

22. How would you determine the existence of consumer problems of relevance to a marketer of the following?
    a. Men's facial care products
    b. Internet retail outlets
    c. Lipstick
    d. Pizza restaurants
    e. Compact cars
    f. Mountain bikes

23. Discuss the types of products that resolve specific problems that occur for most consumers at different stages of their household life cycle.

24. How would you activate problem recognition among college students for the following?
    a. Christian Childrens' Fund sponsorships
    b. Frequent exercise
    c. A vegan diet
    d. A gourmet pizza restaurant
    e. Using a designated driver if drinking
    f. In-line skates

25. How would you influence the time of problem recognition for the following?
    a. Car tire replacement
    b. Candy as a gift
    c. Health checkups
    d. Flashlight batteries
    e. Athletic shoes
    f. Allergy medication

26. Respond to the questions in Consumer Insight 14–1.

APPLICATION ACTIVITIES

27. Interview five other students and identify three consumer problems they have recognized recently. For each problem, determine
    a. The relative importance of the problem.
    b. How the problem occurred.
    c. What caused the problem (i.e., change in desired or actual states).
    d. What action they have taken.
    e. What action is planned to resolve each problem.

28. Find and describe an advertisement that is attempting to activate problem recognition. Analyze the advertisement in terms of the type of problem and the action the ad is suggesting. Also, discuss any changes you would recommend to improve the effectiveness of the ad in terms of activating problem recognition.

29. Interview three other students and identify three recent instances when they engaged in nominal, limited, and extended decision making (a total of nine decisions). What specific factors appear to be associated with each type of decision?

30. Interview three other students and identify five products that each buys using a nominal decision process. Also, identify those that are based on brand loyalty and those that are merely repeat purchases. What characteristics, if any, distinguish the brand loyal products from the repeat products?

31. Find and describe an advertisement or point-of-purchase display that attempts to influence the timing of problem recognition. Evaluate its likely effectiveness.

32. Using two consumers from a relevant market segment, conduct an activity analysis for an activity that interests you. Prepare a report on the marketing opportunities suggested by your analysis.

33. Using two consumers from a relevant market segment, conduct a product analysis for a product that interests you. Prepare a report on the marketing opportunities suggested by your analysis.

34. Conduct a problem analysis, using a sample of five college freshmen. Prepare a report on the marketing opportunities suggested by your analysis.

35. Interview five smokers and ascertain what problems they see associated with smoking.

36. Interview someone from the local office of the American Cancer Society concerning their attempts to generate problem recognition among smokers.

REFERENCES

1. Based on V. MacDonald, "Nivea for Men Debuts in U.S.," *Happi-Household & Personal Products Industry,* April 2001, p. 50; and "A More Sophisticated Male Shopper Emerges," *MMR,* May 13, 2002, p. 34.

2. See B. Shiv and J. Huber, "The Impact of Anticipating Satisfaction on Consumer Choice," *Journal of Consumer Research,* September 2000, pp. 202–16; and M. T. Pham et al., "Affect Monitoring and the Primacy of Feelings in Judgment," *Journal of Consumer Research,* September 2001, pp. 167–88.

3. See J. R. Bettman, M. F. Luce, and J. W. Payne, "Constructive Consumer Choice," *Journal of Consumer Research,* December 1998, pp. 187–217.

4. For more complex but valuable approaches, see Bettman, Luce, and Payne, "Constructive Consumer Choice"; and R. Lawson, "Consumer Decision Making within a Goal-Driven Framework," *Psychology & Marketing,* August 1997, pp. 427–49.

5. M. Trivedi, F. M. Bass, and R. C. Rao, "A Model of Stochastic Variety-Seeking," *Marketing Science,* Summer 1994,

pp. 274–97; S. Menon and B. E. Kahn, "The Impact of Context on Variety Seeking in Product Choice," *Journal of Consumer Research,* December 1995, pp. 285–95; T. H. Dodd, B. E. Pinkleton, and Q. W. Gustafson, "External Information Sources of Product Enthusiasts," *Psychology & Marketing,* May 1996, pp. 291–304; and H. C. M. Van Trijp, W. D. Hoyer, and J. J. Inman, "Why Switch? Product Category-Level Explanations for True Variety-Seeking Behavior," *Journal of Marketing Research,* August 1996, pp. 281–92.

6. See W. J. McDonald, "Developing International Direct Marketing Strategies with a Consumer Decision-Making Content Analysis," *Journal of Direct Marketing,* Autumn 1994, pp. 18–27; and W. J. McDonald, "American versus Japanese Consumer Decision Making," *Journal of International Consumer Marketing* 7, no. 3 (1995), pp. 81–93.

7. See C. J. Hill, "The Nature of Problem Recognition and Search in the Extended Health Care Decision," *Journal of Services Marketing* 15, no. 6 (2001), pp. 454–79.

8. D. Soman, "Effects of Payment Mechanism on Spending Behavior," *Journal of Consumer Research,* March 2001, pp. 460–74.

9. J. Parks, "Weary of Kitchen Clutter," *Advertising Age,* September 12, 1994, p. 12.

10. See T. Collier, "Dynamic Reenactment," *Marketing Research,* Spring 1993, pp. 35–37; G. Zaltman, "Metaphorically Speaking," *Marketing Research,* Summer 1996, pp. 13–20; and C. B. Raffel, "Vague Notions," *Marketing Research,* Summer 1996, pp. 21–23.

11. E. Lesly, "Why Things Are So Sour at Borden," *Business Week,* November 22, 1993, p. 84.

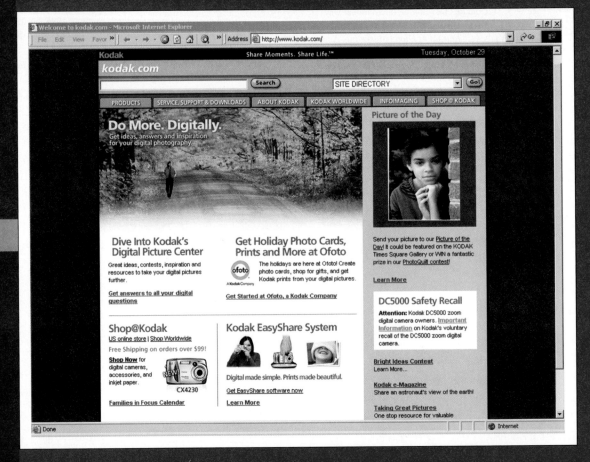

Information Search

☐ The ability of consumers to search for information has increased radically since the advent of the Internet. The Internet allows easy access to manufacturers' websites, to other consumers, and to third parties such as consumer groups and government agencies. It also greatly expands the ability of marketers to provide information to consumers. Marketers can provide information to consumers who are directly seeking information about the firm's products, typically through the company or brand's home page or website. Marketers can also provide consumers information that they are not explicitly seeking by placing ads in other sites on the Web.

Company websites can do more than merely provide company and product information to consumers:

- Revlon's website includes extensive corporate, product, and beauty information. It also has a "magazine" and, at the time of this writing, featured the movie trailer for an upcoming James Bond film. Neutrogena's site features extensive skin care information and an interactive adviser that makes recommendations based on individual beauty needs.

- Kraft Foods' site, the Kraft Interactive Kitchen, provides quick and easy help with food planning, shopping, and preparation chores. It has a searchable cookbook, a recipe box, a shop-ping list customized to generate a list of ingredients by grocery aisle for selected recipes, a party planner, a meal planner, and recipes by e-mail (recipes delivered to the consumer's e-mail address on a regular schedule). It also featured a contest at the time of this writing.

- Pepsi's Pepsi World/Pepsi Pop Culture site provides updates of new movies, games, and music. It provides free downloads of screensavers and wallpaper and contains contests. A unique feature is the Pepsi Live Webcast Concert series. Pepsi explains its approach as: "Simply put, the goal was to reach our core young consumer where they're hanging out (online), and give them an innovative, interactive experience."

- Eastman Kodak's site has more than 35,000 pages of information, images, and digital imaging applications. Among the noteworthy features are PictureThis postcards that enable site users to create and send photo-realistic multimedia postcards; rotating feature articles on the individual and emotional aspects of photography; PhotoNet online, which allows members to store and upload photos online; and PhotoQuilt, an application that weaves personal stories and pictures into a huge collection arranged into a virtual patchwork quilt.[1]

Note that each of these websites provides basic product information similar to that which a consumer could get from a brochure or catalog. However, each site goes much further than this. They provide application and usage suggestions often personalized for each consumer. They add value for the consumer both in terms of providing easily accessible product information and by adding other information, activities, and applications of relevance to the consumer. These firms want consumers to use their sites not only when explicitly seeking product specific information but on a regular basis for a variety of purposes. This is one way a firm can build a relationship with the consumer.

Consumers continually recognize problems and opportunities, so internal and external searches for information to solve these problems are ongoing processes. Searching for information is not free. Information search involves mental as well as physical activities that consumers must perform. It takes time, energy, and money and can often require giving up more desirable activities.

The benefits of information search, however, often outweigh the cost of search. For example, a search may produce a lower price, a preferred style of merchandise, a higher-quality product, or greater confidence in the choice. In addition, the physical and mental processes involved in information search are, on occasion, rewarding in themselves.

Finally, marketers must keep in mind that consumers acquire a substantial amount of relevant information without deliberate search—through low-involvement learning (see Chapter 9).

NATURE OF INFORMATION SEARCH

Suppose your television quit working, or you noticed that you were low on gas, or you felt particularly restless, or you decided you needed a bicycle. What would you do in response to each of these recognized problems? The odds are you would first remember how you usually solve this type of problem. This might produce a satisfactory solution (I'd better stop at the next Texaco and fill up), which you proceed to implement. Or you might decide that you need to get additional information (I'll check the Yellow Pages to see who repairs my brand of television).

Once a problem is recognized, relevant information from long-term memory is used to determine if a satisfactory solution is known, what the characteristics of potential solutions are, what are appropriate ways to compare solutions, and so forth. This is **internal search.** If a resolution is not reached through internal search, then the search process is focused on external information relevant to solving the problem. This is **external search.**

It is important to note that even in extended decision making with extensive external search, the initial internal search generally produces a set of guides or decision constraints that limit and guide external search. Such constraints might be a price range, a set of manufacturers, "must have" performance criteria, and so forth.[2]

Many problems are resolved by the consumer using only previously stored information. If, in response to a problem, a consumer recalls a single, satisfactory solution (brand or store), no further information search or evaluation may occur. The consumer purchases the recalled brand and *nominal decision making* has occurred. For example, a consumer who catches a cold may recall that Dristan nasal spray provided relief in the past. He or she then purchases Dristan at the nearest store without further information search or evaluation.

Likewise, a consumer may notice a new product in a store because of the attention-attracting power of a point-of-purchase display. He or she reads about the attributes of the product and recalls an unresolved problem that these attributes would resolve. The purchase is made without seeking additional information. This represents *limited decision making,* involving mainly internal information.

Had the consumer in the example above looked for other brands that would perform the same task or looked at another store for a lower price, we would have an example of limited decision making using both internal and external information. As we move into *extended decision making,* the relative importance of external information search tends to increase.[3]

External information can include,

- The opinions, attitudes, behaviors, and feelings of friends, neighbors, relatives, and, increasingly, strangers contacted on the Internet.
- Professional information that is provided in pamphlets, articles, books, websites, and personal contacts.
- Direct experiences with the product through inspection, trial, or observation.
- Marketer-generated information presented in advertisements, websites, and displays and by sales personnel.

Deliberate external search also occurs in the absence of problem recognition. **Ongoing search** is done both *to acquire information for possible later use and because the process* *itself is pleasurable.* For example, individuals highly involved with an activity such as tennis are apt to seek information about tennis-related products on an ongoing basis without a recognized problem with their existing tennis equipment. This search could involve reading ads in tennis magazines, visiting tennis equipment shops, observing professionals on television, or talking with and observing fellow players and local professionals. These activities would provide the individual both pleasure and information for future use.

TYPES OF INFORMATION SOUGHT

A consumer decision requires information on the following:[4]

1. The appropriate evaluative criteria for the solution of a problem.
2. The existence of various alternative solutions.
3. The performance level or characteristic of each alternative solution on each evaluative criterion.

Information search, then, seeks each of these three types of information, as shown in Figure 15–1.

Evaluative Criteria

Suppose you are provided with money to purchase a notebook computer, perhaps as a graduation present. Assuming you have not been in the market for a computer recently, your first thought would probably be, "What features do I want in a computer?" You would then engage in internal search to determine the features or characteristics required to meet your needs. These desired characteristics are your *evaluative criteria.* If you have had limited experience with computers, you might also engage in external search to learn which characteristics a good computer should have. You could check with friends, read reviews in *PC Magazine,* talk with sales personnel, visit computer company websites, or personally inspect several computers.

Thus, one potential objective of both internal and external search is *the determination of appropriate evaluative criteria.* Government agencies and consumer organizations want consumers to use sound evaluative criteria such as the nutrition content of foods. Marketers want consumers to use evaluative criteria that match their brand's strengths. Thus, both marketers and government agencies provide information designed to influence

FIGURE 15–1	Information Search in Consumer Decisions

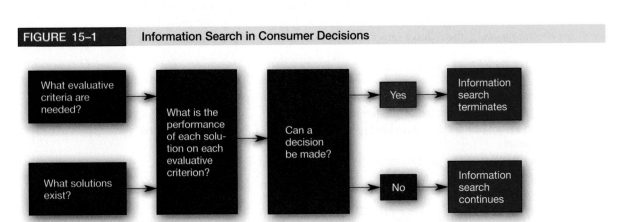

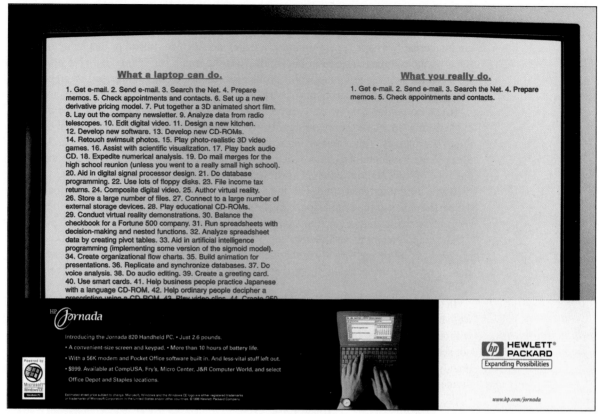

What a laptop can do.

1. Get e-mail. 2. Send e-mail. 3. Search the Net. 4. Prepare memos. 5. Check appointments and contacts. 6. Set up a new derivative pricing model. 7. Put together a 3D animated short film. 8. Lay out the company newsletter. 9. Analyze data from radio telescopes. 10. Edit digital video. 11. Design a new kitchen. 12. Develop new software. 13. Develop new CD-ROMs. 14. Retouch swimsuit photos. 15. Play photo-realistic 3D video games. 16. Assist with scientific visualization. 17. Play back audio CD. 18. Expedite numerical analysis. 19. Do mail merges for the high school reunion (unless you went to a really small high school). 20. Aid in digital signal processor design. 21. Do database programming. 22. Use lots of floppy disks. 23. File income tax returns. 24. Composite digital video. 25. Author virtual reality. 26. Store a large number of files. 27. Connect to a large number of external storage devices. 28. Play educational CD-ROMs. 29. Conduct virtual reality demonstrations. 30. Balance the checkbook for a Fortune 500 company. 31. Run spreadsheets with decision-making and nested functions. 32. Analyze spreadsheet data by creating pivot tables. 33. Aid in artificial intelligence programming (implementing some version of the sigmoid model). 34. Create organizational flow charts. 35. Build animation for presentations. 36. Replicate and synchronize databases. 37. Do voice analysis. 38. Do audio editing. 39. Create a greeting card. 40. Use smart cards. 41. Help business people practice Japanese with a language CD-ROM. 42. Help ordinary people decipher a prescription using a CD-ROM. 43. Play video clips. 44. Create 250

What you really do.

1. Get e-mail. 2. Send e-mail. 3. Search the Net. 4. Prepare memos. 5. Check appointments and contacts.

HP *Jornada*

Introducing the Jornada 820 Handheld PC. • Just 2.6 pounds.
• A convenient-size screen and keypad. • More than 10 hours of battery life.
• With a 56K modem and Pocket Office software built in. And less-vital stuff left out.
• $999. Available at CompUSA, Fry's, Micro Center, J&R Computer World, and select Office Depot and Staples locations.

Estimated street price subject to change. Microsoft, Windows and the Windows CE logo are either registered trademarks or trademarks of Microsoft Corporation in the United States and/or other countries. ©1998 Hewlett-Packard Company.

Powered by Microsoft Windows CE

HEWLETT® PACKARD
Expanding Possibilities

www.hp.com/jornada

Courtesy Hewlett-Packard Company.

the evaluative criteria used by consumers. The ad in Illustration 15–1 encourages consumers to use five primary evaluative criteria when choosing a portable computer. Implied in the ad is that using too many evaluative criteria produces unneeded capabilities and an unnecessarily high price.

A detailed discussion of evaluative criteria appears in Chapter 17.

Appropriate Alternatives

After, and while, searching for appropriate evaluative criteria, you would probably seek *appropriate alternatives*—in this case brands or, possibly, stores. Again, you would start with an internal search. You might say to yourself,

> IBM, Compaq, Toshiba, Apple, NEC, Sony, Fujitsu, and HP all make notebook computers. After my brother's experience, I'd never buy Fujitsu. I've heard good things about IBM, Apple, and Compaq. I think I'll check them out.

The eight brands you thought of as potential solutions are known as the **awareness set.** The awareness set is composed of three subcategories of considerable importance to marketers.[5] The three brands that you have decided to investigate are known as the **evoked set,** or the **consideration set.** An evoked set *is those brands or products one will evaluate for* *the solution of a particular consumer problem.* It is important to note that the consideration set will vary depending on the usage situation. For example, a person might choose from among cereal (perhaps several brands), a bagel, an Egg McMuffin, or just a cup of coffee for a weekday breakfast option but might consider eggs, waffles, or leftover pizza for a weekend breakfast.[6] Note that while evoked sets are frequently composed of brands from a single product category (brands of cereals or computers), this need not be the case.[7]

If you do not have an evoked set for notebook computers, or lack confidence that your evoked set is adequate, you would probably engage in external search to learn about additional alternatives. You may also learn about additional acceptable brands such as Acer and Sharp as an incidental aspect of moving through the decision process. Thus, an important outcome of information search is the development of a complete evoked set.

If you are initially satisfied with the evoked set, information search will be focused on the performance of the brands in the evoked set on the evaluative criteria. Thus, the evoked set is of particular importance in structuring subsequent information search and purchase.

The brand you found completely unworthy of further consideration is a member of what is called the **inept set.** Brands in the inept set are *actively disliked or avoided by the consumer.* Positive information about these brands is not likely to be processed even if it is readily available.

In our example, Sony, Toshiba, NEC, and HP were brands of which you were aware but were basically indifferent toward. They compose what is known as an **inert set.** Consumers will generally accept favorable information about brands in the inert set, although they do not seek out such information. Brands in this set are generally acceptable when preferred brands are not available. Thus, the eight brands in the initial awareness set can be subdivided as follows:

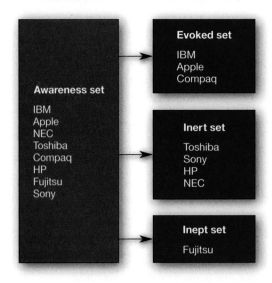

Figure 15–2 illustrates the general relationships among these classes of alternatives.

Figure 15–3 illustrates the results of several studies comparing the size of the awareness and evoked sets for a variety of products. Notice that in all cases, the evoked set is substantially smaller than the awareness set. Because the evoked set generally is the one from which consumers make final evaluations and decisions, *marketing strategy that focuses only on creating awareness may be inadequate.* Thus, marketers must strive to have

FIGURE 15–2	**Categories of Decision Alternatives**

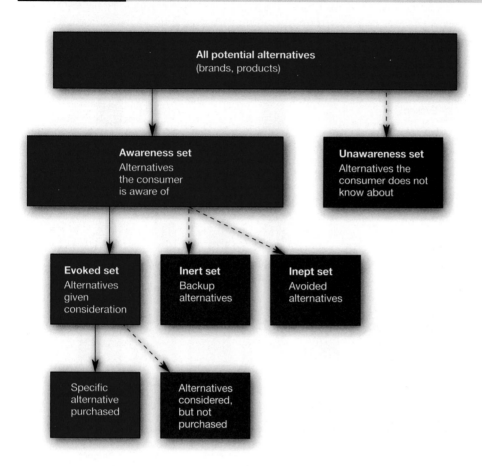

consumers recall their brand in response to a recognized problem *and* consider the brand a worthy potential solution.

A similar process operates with respect to retail outlet selection.[8]

Alternative Characteristics

To choose among the brands in the evoked set, the consumer compares them on the relevant evaluative criteria. This process requires the consumer to gather information about *each brand on each pertinent evaluative criterion.*[9] In our example of a computer purchase, you might collect information on the price, memory, processor, weight, screen clarity, and software package for each brand you are considering.

In summary, consumers engage in internal and external search for (1) appropriate evaluative criteria, (2) the existence of potential solutions, and (3) the characteristics of potential solutions. However, extensive search generally occurs for only a few consumption decisions. Nominal and limited decisions that involve little or no active external search are the rule. In addition, consumers acquire substantial information without deliberate search through low-involvement learning. Finally, while our discussion has focused on searching for functional information, emotions and feelings are more important in many purchases.

| FIGURE 15–3 | Awareness and Evoked Sets for Various Products |

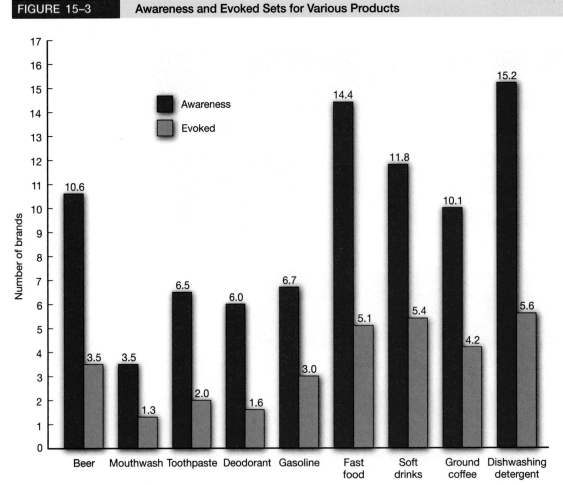

Source: J. Roberts, "A Grounded Model of Consideration Set Size and Composition," in *Advances in Consumer Research,* vol. 26, ed. T. K. Skrull (Provo, UT: Association for Consumer Research, 1989), p. 750.

SOURCES OF INFORMATION

Refer again to our rather pleasant example of receiving cash with which to purchase a computer. We suggested that you might recall what you know about computers, check with friends and an online users group, consult *Consumer Reports* and read reviews in *PC Magazine,* talk with sales personnel, or personally inspect several computers to collect relevant information. These represent the five primary sources of information available to consumers:

- *Memory* of past searches, personal experiences, and low-involvement learning.
- *Personal sources,* such as friends, family, and others.
- *Independent sources,* such as magazines, consumer groups, and government agencies.
- *Marketing sources,* such as sales personnel, websites, and advertising.
- *Experiential sources,* such as inspection or product trial.[10]

These sources are shown in Figure 15–4. Consumers decide how many and which sources of information to use at both the macro (personal sources) and micro (specific individuals) levels. Thus, a purchase decision requires a subset of decisions concerning information seeking.[11]

FIGURE 15-4   Information Sources for a Purchase Decision

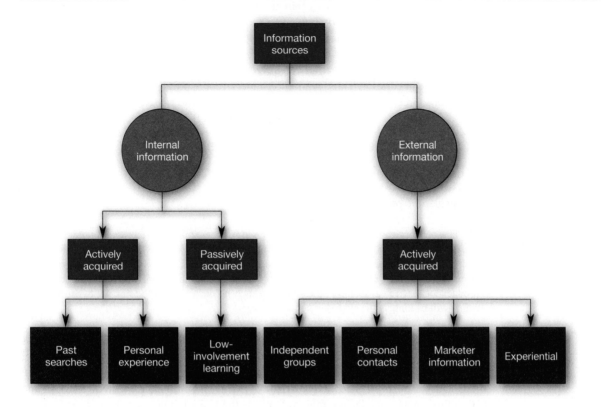

Internal information is the primary source used by most consumers most of the time (nominal and limited decision making). However, note that information in long-term memory was *initially* obtained from external sources. Thus, a consumer may resolve a consumption problem using only or mainly stored information. At some point, however, the individual acquired that information from an external source, such as direct product experience, friends, or low-involvement learning.

Marketing-originated messages are only one of five potential information sources, and they are frequently reported to be of limited *direct* value in consumer decisions.[12] However, marketing activities influence all five sources. Thus, the characteristics of the product, the distribution of the product, and the promotional messages about the product provide the underlying or basic information available in the market. An independent source such as *Consumer Reports* bases its evaluation on the functional characteristics of the product. Personal sources such as friends also must base their information on experience with the product or its promotion, or on other sources that have had contact with the product or its promotion.

A substantial amount of marketing activity is designed to influence the information that consumers will receive from nonmarketing sources. For example, when Johnson & Johnson introduced a new-formula baby bath,

Product information, demonstrations, monographs, journal ads, and direct-mail programs were targeted at pediatricians and nurses to capitalize on health care professionals' direct contact with new mothers. Print ads and coupons appeared in baby care publications, and a film exploring the parent–infant bonding process was distributed to teaching centers, hospitals, and medical schools.

In addition, although consumers may not use advertising or other marketer-provided data as immediate input into many purchase decisions, there is no doubt that continual exposure to advertising frequently influences the perceived need for the product, the composition of the consideration and evoked sets, the evaluative criteria used, and the beliefs about the performance levels of each brand.[13] There is also substantial evidence that advertising for consumer nondurables can have a significant impact on sales for some but not all product categories.[14] Thus, while consumers report only limited direct influence by marketing sources, other types of evidence indicate that the effect may be stronger.

Information Search on the Internet

The Internet is altering consumer information search in ways that are not yet fully understood.[15]

Consider the prediction of one expert:

> The news is very good for consumers, not so good for companies and investors. Within the near future, simple, yet extraordinarily powerful price-and-quality search engines and services are likely to have a significant impact on consumer behavior. For a modest annual membership fee, Internet price-search services will be able to identify the cheapest *delivered* large-dollar-ticket products or services available in the world. In such product markets the readily informed consumer will be king, at the click of a button.[16]

One study estimated that 183 million people in the United States and Canada had access to the Internet at home in early 2002,[17] and another projected 143 million active Internet users in the United States at that time.[18] It is forecast that there will be 236 million active Internet users in the United States by 2007 (with 290 million in Western Europe, and 610 million in the Asia/Pacific region).[19] While the United States currently has the largest number of Internet users, several European countries have a higher percentage of users, and China is forecast to surpass the United States in total number of users in a few years.

As Figure 15–5 shows, the Internet is not used equally by all segments of the population (one difference the figure does not show is that Internet use drops sharply among those older than 55). The differences shown in this table are rapidly decreasing. For example, the annual growth rate in Internet use from 1998 through 2001 was 19 percent for whites, 26 percent for Hispanics, and 31 percent for blacks. Likewise, usage among low-income groups is growing more rapidly than among upper-income groups.

Individuals who use the Internet use it for

Accessing e-mail	84%
Searching for product or service information	67
Reading news, weather, or sports information	62
Playing games	42
Purchasing products or service	39
Searching for health services or practices information	35
Searching for government services	31
Viewing TV/movies; listening to radio	19
Online banking	18
Visiting chat rooms	17
Trading stocks	9

More than half the population now uses the Internet, and more than a third of all consumers report using it for product/service information searches. Surveys support this by

FIGURE 15–5	Demographics of Internet Users

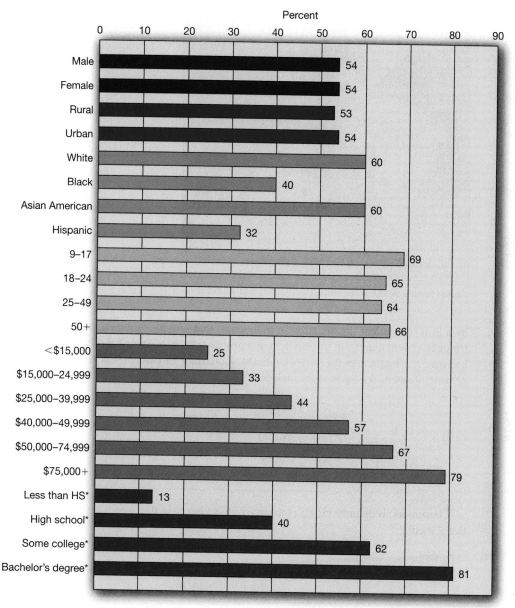

*Age 25 or older

Source: *A Nation Online* (Washington DC: U.S. Department of Commerce, February 2002), p. 26.

indicating that the Internet is a preferred source of product-related information among Internet users.[20] Clearly, it has become an important information source for purchase decisions.

Note that the Internet contains marketer-supplied data in the form of ads associated with search, entertainment, and general information sites and home pages or Internet presence sites. A **home page** or **Internet presence site** (IPS) is a website developed and maintained

The Internet is becoming an important source of information as well as a place to purchase products and services. Marketers often use traditional mass media ads to encourage consumers to visit their websites.

Courtesy Lavalife, Inc.; Illustrator: Marcus Chin; Agency: Zig/Toronto, Canada.

by a firm (or another organization or individual) that provides product and company data (or independent data from government and private sources). Among those consumers who had used the Internet in the past six months, more than 75 percent had visited a company website. Reasons for these visits included[21]

Seeking product information	90%
Seeking company information	88
Getting coupons, discounts	30
Buying products	23
Entering contests	15

Consumers frequently visit a company website because they see it mentioned in traditional media:[22]

Percentage visiting a website because they saw it mentioned in	
Magazine/newspaper ad	71%
TV ad	57
Product packaging	49
Radio ad	36
Direct mail	32
Billboard	22

The above data indicate that ads such as the one shown in Illustration 15–2 can be effective at guiding consumers' information search activities to company websites. For instance, Mars saw unique visits to its M&M site jump 145 percent in response to an advertising campaign inviting consumers to visit and to vote for a new color M&M (purple won).

The presence of a website address in an advertisement appears to enhance various aspects of the firm's image, including being customer-oriented, responsive, sophisticated, and successful.[23] As website addresses become the norm, it is possible that their presence will no longer generate positive image benefits but their absence might produce negative connotations.

Consumers also encounter ads on the Internet while visiting general information, search, and entertainment sites. These are generally **banner ads** that, when clicked, will take the consumer to the company or product's home page or to a special advertisement (see Chapter 8, page 281). The Internet also contains personal sources of information in bulletin boards and chat rooms as well as in the brand review features associated with some shopping services.[24]

The Internet is undergoing rapid expansion in terms of usage, capabilities, and characteristics. For example, there are a number of shopping services on the Internet that can search all or most of the retail sites and identify the site with the lowest price for a particular product. The services use **bots,** which are software "robots" that do the searching for users. For example, consumers using the Excite shopping service type in the name of a specific product. Excite's bot then goes to 500 online merchants' sites and reports back current data and prices. These services, which are rapidly evolving, are likely to substantially alter the way many consumers search for information.[25]

One of the steps you might take in your quest for a new notebook computer would be to type in "notebook, computer" in Google.com (a search engine). The top listing in the search (at the time of this writing) is DealTime.com. Clicking on this link and choosing notebook computer allow you to search for computers by price range or brand. If you were to select "under $700" for a price range, the computer would identify 31 available models/brands many with consumer reviews attached. If you looked at the IBM ThinkPad 600, you would find five for sale at three different stores, with prices ranging from $475 to $625 depending on the store and other features. You could then purchase the computer online or use this information as you shopped at other websites or stores in your area (buying at a store is the norm for those who research products online).[26]

Some Internet sites are proactive at providing information. For example, Amazon.com will provide a list of other books purchased by people who also purchased the book you are considering. If you make a series of book or movie purchases at Amazon.com (or similar sites), it will recommend additional books or movies based on assumed preferences it derives from your past purchases.[27]

Marketing Strategy and Information Search on the Internet   Marketers have four major decisions with respect to marketing on the Internet:

1. Should they have a company/brand website?
2. If they have a website, should it be active or passive?
3. Should they advertise on the Internet?
4. Should they sell their products directly to consumers via the Internet?

We will discuss the first three of these issues now. The fourth will be covered in Chapter 17 on outlet selection.

A website is increasingly essential for consumer product companies. As we saw earlier, most Internet users visit these sites and they tend to be younger, upscale consumers. A firm without a website is likely to be viewed as unresponsive and out of date. Therefore, the real decision is whether the site itself should focus strictly on providing product and company information and services (a passive site) or contain additional features and activities

ILLUSTRATION 15–3

Websites differ in the extent to which they offer non-product-related inducements to visit the site. This site is heavily product focused.

designed to draw consumers to the site (an active site).[28] The sites described in the chapter-opening example were all active sites.

An active site allows the firm to develop a relationship with consumers over time and provide them product information as well as other relevant information and entertainment. However, it is also expensive and often appeals to a relatively small percentage of the market. Active sites should generally have a natural tie to the activities they are providing. In the opening example, Revlon's activities focused on beauty, whereas Kraft's focused on food preparation and shopping. Firms such as Disney would be a natural for an active site, whereas Amana (refrigerators, microwaves, and so forth) would be less so. The Kodak site shown at the beginning of the chapter is an active site; the Leatherman site in Illustration 15–3 is passive. Note that the Leatherman site has many useful features for those who have or are considering acquiring a Leatherman product. It is considered a passive site because it does not provide non-product-related inducements to visit the site.

Whether a site is active or passive, it needs to be quick to load (appear on the screen), easy to access and negotiate, up to date, logical, and focused on the customers' needs.[29] The more complex the purchase decision or use of the product, the more complete and interactive the website should be. A site for a backpack manufacturer might have a series of questions concerning the consumer's intended product uses, physical characteristics, and other desires. Using the responses to these questions, the program would then recommend one or more products from the firm's line, giving the advantages of each. Such an approach would make little sense for simpler products such as breath mints.

As consumers increasingly visit company websites, it is likely that consumer expectations for easily accessed, useful information presented in an entertaining format will become the norm. Firms that do not live up to these expectations will see their image and sales decline.

While the use of home pages by marketers is now common, Internet advertising is still quite limited though growing rapidly. It is estimated that between $4 and $7 billion was spent on Internet advertising in 2002, a tiny percentage of total advertising expenditures ($240 billion).[30] However, as marketers learn more about Internet marketing in general and advertising in particular, both the total and relative amount of advertising done on the Internet will increase. In the meantime, marketers are "learning by doing" on the Web. As the CEO of Unilever, a firm with more than 40 branded websites, stated,

I don't know what's going to happen, but I'm convinced we've got to play and we've got to engage our consumers. This is truly experimental. For me, it's the same as investing in having scientists play with molecules in order to come up with a new product.[31]

AMOUNT OF EXTERNAL INFORMATION SEARCH

Marketing managers are particularly interested in external information search, as this provides them with direct access to the consumer. How much external information search do consumers actually undertake? Most purchases are a result of nominal or limited decision making and therefore involve limited external search immediately prior to purchase. This is particularly true for relatively low priced convenience goods such as soft drinks, canned foods, and detergents. Therefore, the discussion in this section focuses on major purchases such as appliances, professional services, and automobiles. Intuitively, we would expect substantial amounts of direct external search prior to such purchases.

Different measures of external information search have been used: (1) number of stores visited, (2) number of alternatives considered, (3) number of personal sources used, and (4) overall or combination measures. Each of these measures of search effort assesses a different aspect of behavior, yet each measure supports one observation: *external information search is skewed toward limited search, with the greatest proportion of consumers performing little external search immediately prior to purchase.*

Surveys of *shopping behavior* have shown a significant percentage of all durable purchases are made after the consumer has visited only one store.[32] The *number of alternatives* considered also shows a limited amount of prepurchase search. Although the number of alternative brands or models considered tends to increase as the price of the product increases, for some product categories, such as watches, almost half of the purchasers considered only one brand *and* one model. Another study found that 27 percent of the purchasers of major appliances considered only one brand.[33]

Measures of the use of *personal* and other *nonmarket* sources also show somewhat limited levels of search. Approximately 40 percent of the purchasers of a new appliance consulted others, and one-fourth consulted *Consumer Reports.*[34]

Seven separate studies that span 40 years, two product categories, four services, and two countries found remarkable consistency in terms of the total external information search undertaken. These studies classified consumers in terms of their total external information search as (1) nonsearchers, (2) limited information searchers, and (3) extended information searchers.[35] As shown in the following table, approximately half of the purchases were preceded by virtually no external information search, about one-third were associated with limited information search, and only 12 percent involved extensive information seeking immediately prior to the purchase.

Country/Product/ Year	Nonsearchers	Limited Searchers	Extended Searchers
America/appliances/1955	65%	25%	10%
America/appliances/1972	49	38	13
America/appliances/1974	65	27	8
Australia/automobiles/1981	24	58	18
America/appliances/1989	24	45	11
America/professional services/1989	55	38	7
Australia/professional services/1995	53	35	12

Most consumers engage in minimal external information search *immediately* prior to the purchase of consumer durables. The level of search for less important items is even lower. However, limited information search does not necessarily mean that the consumer is not following a sound purchasing strategy. Nor does it mean that substantial amounts of internal information are not being used.

COSTS VERSUS BENEFITS OF EXTERNAL SEARCH

Why do 50 percent of the buyers of major appliances described above do little or no external search, while 12 percent engage in extensive external search? Part of the answer lies in the differences between the buyers' perceptions of the benefits and costs of search associated with a particular purchase situation.[36] The ability to make such cost–benefit trade-offs appears to be limited in preschool children but to develop rapidly at about the time they enter school.[37] Thus, most active consumers appear to be able to make search decisions based on their estimates of the costs and benefits involved.

The benefits of external information search can be tangible, such as a lower price, a preferred style, or a higher-quality product. Or the benefits can be intangible—reduced risk, greater confidence in the purchase, or even providing enjoyment.[38] Perceptions of these benefits are likely to vary with the consumer's experience in the market, media habits, and the extent to which the consumer interacts with others or belongs to differing reference groups. Therefore, one reason 50 percent of major appliance buyers do little or no external search is that they do not perceive significant benefits resulting from such an effort.

Furthermore, acquisition of external information is not free, and consumers may engage in limited search because the costs of search exceed the perceived benefits. The costs of search can be both monetary and nonmonetary. Monetary costs include the cost of transportation, parking, lost wages, charges for child care, and so forth. Nonmonetary costs of search are less obvious but may have an even greater impact than monetary costs. Almost every external search effort involves time and physical and psychological effort. Frustration and conflict between the search task and other more desirable activities, as well as fatigue, may shorten or otherwise alter the search effort.

As we saw in the previous section, the Internet has the potential to greatly lower search costs. When it does, it has been shown to increase search and result in better consumer decisions and a more enjoyable shopping experience.[39]

In this section, we are going to examine four basic types of factors that influence the expected benefits and perceived costs of search: *market characteristics, product characteristics, consumer characteristics,* and *situation characteristics.*[40] These four factors and their components are shown in Table 15–1.

Influencing Factor	Increasing the Influencing Factor Causes the Search to
I. Market Characteristics	
A. Number of alternatives	Increase
B. Price range	Increase
C. Store concentration	Increase
D. Information availability	Increase
1. Advertising	
2. Point-of-purchase	
3. Sales personnel	
4. Packaging	
5. Experienced consumers	
6. Independent sources	
II. Product Characteristics	
A. Price	Increase
B. Differentiation	Increase
C. Positive products	Increase
III. Consumer Characteristics	
A. Learning and experience	Decrease
B. Shopping orientation	Mixed
C. Social status	Increase
D. Age and household life cycle	Mixed
E. Product involvement	Mixed
F. Perceived risk	Increase
IV. Situation Characteristics	
A. Time availability	Increase
B. Purchase for self	Decrease
C. Pleasant surroundings	Increase
D. Social surroundings	Mixed
E. Physical/mental energy	Increase

TABLE 15–1

Factors Affecting External Search Immediately Prior to Purchase

Market Characteristics

Market characteristics include the number of alternatives, price range, store distribution, and information availability. It is important to keep in mind that it is the consumer's perception of, or beliefs about, the market characteristics that influence shopping behavior, *not* the actual characteristics.[41] While beliefs and reality are usually related, often they are not identical.

Obviously, the greater the *number of alternatives* (products, stores, brands) available to resolve a particular problem, the more external search there is likely to be. At the extreme, there is no need to search for information in the face of a complete monopoly such as utilities or driver's licenses.

However, if too many models and brands are available, information overload (see Chapter 8) may cause consumers to shop less. In particular, a wide range of models or brands may make the search process virtually impossible if the models vary across stores. That is, if one store has two brands with five models each and a second store has the same two brands but with five different models each, the consumer must compare 20 distinct brands/models. In response, many consumers will limit their shopping to a single retail outlet. This leads some marketers to develop a large number of models so that key accounts can have exclusive models and avoid direct price competition with other retailers on those exact models.[42]

The *perceived range of prices* among equivalent brands in a product class is a major factor in stimulating external search. For example, shopping 36 retail stores in Tucson for five popular branded toys produced a total low cost of $51.27 and a total high cost of $105.95.

Clearly, efficient shopping for these products in this market would provide a significant financial gain.

It appears that the percentage savings available from shopping may be as important as the dollar amount. Consumers who perceive the chance to save $50 when purchasing a $200 item may be motivated to engage in search but not if the same savings were available for a $5,000 item.[43]

Store distribution—the number, location, and distances between retail stores in the market—affects the number of store visits a consumer will make before purchase. Because store visits take time, energy, and in many cases money, a close proximity of stores will often increase this aspect of external search.[44]

In general, *information availability,* including format, is directly related to information use.[45] However, too much information can cause information overload and the use of less information. In addition, readily available information tends to produce learning over time, which may reduce the need for additional external information immediately prior to a purchase.[46] *Advertising, point-of-purchase displays, websites, sales personnel, packages, other consumers,* and *independent sources* such as *Consumer Reports* are major sources of consumer information.

Product Characteristics

Product *differentiation*—feature and quality variation across brands—is associated with increased external search.

In addition, consumers appear to enjoy shopping for *positive products*—those whose acquisition results in positive reinforcement. Thus, shopping for flowers and plants, dress clothing, sports equipment, and cameras is viewed as a positive experience by most consumers. In contrast, shopping for *negative products*—those whose primary benefit is negative reinforcement (removal of an unpleasant condition)—is viewed as less pleasant. Shopping for groceries, extermination services, and auto repairs is not enjoyed by most individuals. Other things being equal, consumers are more likely to engage in external search for positive products.[47]

Consumer Characteristics

A variety of consumer characteristics affect perceptions of expected benefits, search costs, and the need to carry out a particular level of external information search.[48] As described earlier, the first step a consumer normally takes in response to a problem or opportunity is a search of memory for an appropriate solution. If the consumer finds a solution that he or she is confident is satisfactory, external search is unlikely. Thus, confidence in one's knowledge of existing solutions is an important determinant of search. However, as Consumer Insight 15–1 illustrates, consumers often do not know what they think they know!

A satisfying *experience* with a particular brand is a positively reinforcing process. It increases the probability of a repeat purchase of that brand and decreases the likelihood of external search. As a result, external search is generally greater for consumers who have limited purchase experience with brands in a particular product category.[49]

However, there is evidence that at least some familiarity with a product class is necessary for external search to occur. For example, external search prior to purchasing a new automobile is high for consumers who have a high level of *general knowledge about cars* and low for those who have a substantial level of *knowledge* about existing brands.[50] Thus, consumers facing a completely unfamiliar product category may feel threatened by the

Do You Know What You Think You Know?

A recent study concluded that "consumers are overconfident—they think they know more than they actually do."[51] Consumers who are motivated to purchase the lowest-priced groceries available and who "know" that store A has the lowest prices are likely to shop at store A. If, instead, store B is equally accessible and has the same items at a lower price, both the consumers and the more efficient store suffer from this lack of accurate knowledge.

Two aspects of consumer knowledge are important. One is the knowledge, memory, or belief itself and its correspondence to objective reality (accuracy). The other is the consumer's confidence that his or her belief is accurate. The more confident an individual is in his or her belief, the more likely he or she is to act accordingly without seeking additional information. Unfortunately, research reveals that the correspondence (calibration) between confidence and accuracy is sometimes quite low.

There are a variety of types of knowledge where a low level of calibration frequently occurs to the detriment of consumers and firms. Some of these include

Memory of facts—"Saturn scores highest of all small cars on most customer satisfaction ratings." Consumers tend to be more confident in this type of knowledge than accuracy levels justify.

Memory of events—"John had to have his Saturn repaired three times the first year he owned it." Again, individuals tend to be more confident in their memories than is justified.

Belief polarization—"I like the looks of the new Saturn. The new Saturn handles well." Research shows that consumers who form a preference for a brand on one dimension tend to form positive, sometimes inaccurate, beliefs about other attributes.

Belief validity—"The Saturn costs more than the Kia so it is a higher quality car." Both general (higher price equals higher quality) and specific beliefs (Volvo is the safest car in a crash) are often unexamined for accuracy when consumers make decisions.

Personal forecasts—"I can afford a new Saturn because I'll earn a bonus next year." Research indicates that consumers are often very confident in overly optimistic assessments of the occurrence of desirable personal events.

A large variety of complex factors account for the low levels of calibration that frequently occur between the accuracy of one's knowledge and one's confidence in that knowledge. For example, memory is often not just inaccurate but distorted. People tend to remember things in a manner consistent with a prior judgment; that is, they make a decision, then "remember" facts or events in a manner consistent with the decision. Or as individuals become predisposed toward a choice, they remember mainly those aspects of the past that are consistent with the predisposition.

Critical Thinking Questions

1. What, if any, implications does the above have for our educational system?

2. What are the primary marketing implications of the above?

---

amount of new information or may simply lack sufficient knowledge to conduct an external search.

External search tends to increase with various measures of *social status* (education, occupation, and income), though middle-income individuals search more than those at higher or lower levels. *Age* of the shopper is inversely related to information search. External search appears to decrease as the age of the shopper increases. This may be explained in part by increased learning and product familiarity gained with age. New households and individuals moving into new stages of the *household life cycle* have a greater need for external information than established households.

Consumers tend to form general approaches or patterns of external search. These general approaches are termed *shopping orientations*.[52] While individuals will exhibit substantial variation from the general pattern across situations and product categories, many do take a stable shopping approach to most products across a wide range of situations. Other individuals engage in extensive ongoing information search because they are market mavens, as described in Chapter 7.

Consumers who are *highly involved with a product category* generally seek information relevant to the product category on an ongoing basis.[53] This ongoing search and the knowledge base it produces may reduce their need for external search immediately before a purchase. However, this may vary with the nature of their involvement with the product category. One study found that wine enthusiasts who desired variety engaged in significantly more external search than those who were less interested in variety.[54]

Perceived Risk   The **perceived risk** associated with unsatisfactory product performance, either instrumental or symbolic, increases information search prior to purchase.[55] Higher perceived risk is associated with increased search and greater reliance on personal sources of information and personal experiences.

Perceived risk is a function of the individual, the product, and the situation. It varies from one consumer to another and for the same consumer from one product to another and from one situation to another. For example, the purchase of a bottle of wine may not involve much perceived risk when buying for one's own consumption. However, the choice of wine may involve considerable perceived risk when buying wine for a dinner party for one's boss. Likewise, it might be perceived as risky if the individual has little knowledge and is buying an expensive bottle for personal consumption.

While perceived risk varies across consumers and situations, some products and services are generally seen as riskier than others (see Table 17–2, page 604).[56] Likewise, perceived risk is high for products whose failure to perform as expected would result in a high

- *Social cost* (e.g., a new suit that is not appreciated by one's peers).
- *Financial cost* (e.g., an expensive vacation during which it rained all the time).
- *Time cost* (e.g., an automobile repair that required the car to be taken to the garage, left, and then picked up later).
- *Effort cost* (e.g., a computer that is loaded with important software before the hard drive crashes).
- *Physical cost* (e.g., a new medicine produces a harmful side effect).

Situation Characteristics

As indicated in Chapter 13, situational variables can have a major impact on search behavior. For example, recall that one of the primary reactions of consumers to crowded store conditions is to minimize external information search. *Temporal perspective* is probably the most important situational variable with respect to search behavior. As the time available to solve a particular consumer problem decreases, so does the amount of external information search.[57]

Gift-giving situations (*task definition*) tend to increase perceived risk, which, as we have seen, increases external search. Likewise, multiple-item purchase tasks such as buying a bike and a bike rack or several items for a meal produce increased levels of information search.[58] Shoppers with limited physical or emotional energy (*antecedent state*) will search for less information than others. Pleasant *physical surroundings* increase the tendency to search for information, at least *within* that outlet. *Social surroundings* can increase or decrease search, depending on the nature of the social setting (see Chapter 13 for a more complete discussion of these issues).

MARKETING STRATEGIES BASED ON INFORMATION SEARCH PATTERNS

Sound marketing strategies take into account the nature of information search engaged in by the target market prior to purchase. Two dimensions of search are particularly appropriate: the type of decision influences the level of search, and the nature of the evoked set influences the direction of the search. Table 15–2 illustrates a strategy matrix based on these two dimensions. This matrix suggests the six marketing strategies discussed in the following sections. As you will see, while there is considerable overlap between the strategies, each has a unique thrust.

Maintenance Strategy

If the brand is purchased habitually by the target market, the marketer's strategy is to maintain that behavior. This requires consistent attention to product quality, distribution (avoiding out-of-stock situations), and a reinforcement advertising strategy. In addition, the marketer must defend against the disruptive tactics of competitors. Thus, it needs to maintain product development and improvements and to counter short-term competitive strategies such as coupons, point-of-purchase displays, or rebates.

Morton salt and Del Monte canned vegetables have large repeat purchaser segments that they have successfully maintained. Budweiser, Marlboro, and Crest have large brand-loyal purchaser segments. They have successfully defended their market positions against assaults by major competitors in recent years. In contrast, Liggett & Myers lost 80 percent of its market share when it failed to engage in maintenance advertising.[59] Quality control problems caused Schlitz to lose substantial market share.

Illustration 15–4 shows part of Masterfoods USA's maintenance strategy for its 3 MUS-KETEERS® BAR against the challenge of multiple competitors. Note that the ad stresses the improvements that Masterfoods USA has made in the candy.

Disrupt Strategy

If the brand is not part of the evoked set and the target market engages in nominal decision making, the marketer's first task is to *disrupt* the existing decision pattern. This is a difficult task since the consumer does not seek external information or even consider alternative brands before a purchase. Low-involvement learning over time could generate a positive product position for our brand, but this alone would be unlikely to shift behavior.

In the long run, a major product improvement accompanied by attention-attracting advertising could shift the target market into a more extensive form of decision making. In the short run, attention-attracting advertising aimed specifically at breaking habitual decision

	Target Market Decision-Making Pattern		
Position	*Nominal Decision Making (no search)*	*Limited Decision Making (limited search)*	*Extended Decision Making (extensive search)*
Brand in Evoked Set	Maintenance strategy	Capture strategy	Preference strategy
Brand Not in Evoked Set	Disrupt strategy	Intercept strategy	Acceptance strategy

TABLE 15–2

Marketing Strategies Based on Information Search Patterns

Whipped-up. Fluffy. Now with better-tasting chocolate.

(It could only be better if it were free.)

FREE one(1) 3 MUSKETEERS® full-size single bar

MANUFACTURER COUPON   EXPIRATION DATE 4/30/02

140265

5 40000 31101 5 (8101)0 14026 0402

Introducing the new 3MUSKETEERS® Bar. It's what you've always loved, but now with even better-tasting chocolate inside and out. So go ahead. Have one on us.

NEW Better Chocolate Taste
3 Musketeers
You deserve it!

3 Musketeers

TM® 3 Musketeers is a registered trademark of Mars, Incorporated and its affiliates. They are used with permission. Mars, Incorporated is not associated with McGraw-Hill Companies or Michael J. Hruby & Associates. Advertisement printed with permission of Mars, Incorporated. © Mars, Inc., 2002.

ILLUSTRATION 15–4

Firms with a significant group of loyal or repeat purchasers must continually improve their products and communicate their advantages to their consumers.

making can be successful. Free samples, coupons, rebates, and tie-in sales are common approaches to disrupting nominal decision making. Likewise, striking package designs and point-of-purchase displays may disrupt a habitual purchase sequence.[60] Comparative advertising is also often used for this purpose.

Illustration 15–5 is an example of a disrupt strategy. Silk has found that once consumers try its various soymilk products, many prefer them. However, most consumers drink either cow's milk or no milk at all. Therefore, Silk has tried a number of ways to disrupt these behaviors and induce trial. In this attention-attracting ad, Silk uses humor and a direct challenge.

Capture Strategy

Limited decision making generally involves a few brands that are evaluated on only a few criteria such as price or availability. Much of the information search occurs at the point-of-purchase or in readily available media prior to purchase. If the brand is one given this type of consideration by the target market, the marketer's objective is to capture as large a share of their purchases as practical.

Because these consumers engage in limited search, the marketer needs to know where they search and what information they are looking for. In general, the marketer will want to supply information, often on price and availability, in local media through cooperative advertising and at the point-of-purchase through displays and adequate shelf space. If appropriate for the product category, an active website might be beneficial. The marketer will also be concerned with maintaining consistent product quality and adequate distribution.

Our marketing experts
have advised us to use the
triple double dog dare.

All natural, lactose free, high in protein, with a surprisingly good taste. *Don't be so stubborn.*

Courtesy White Wave.

ILLUSTRATION 15–5

Firms trying to disrupt the habitual purchase or consumption patterns of consumers who do not even consider their brand need attention-attracting ads and a strong benefit or other inducement to try the brand.

Intercept Strategy

If the target market engages in limited decision making and the brand is not part of their evoked set, the objective will be to intercept the consumer during the search for information on the brands in the evoked set. Again, the emphasis will be on local media with cooperative advertising and at the point-of-purchase with displays, shelf space, package design, and so forth. Coupons can also be effective. The marketer will have to place considerable emphasis on attracting the consumers' attention as they will not be seeking information on the brand. If appropriate for the product category, an active website could be particularly useful. The promotion shown in Illustration 15–6 was distributed in the newspaper. It would be effective as part of a capture or intercept strategy.

In addition to the strategies mentioned above, low-involvement learning, product improvements, and free samples can be used to move the brand into the target market's evoked set.

Preference Strategy

Extended decision making with the brand in the evoked set requires a preference strategy. Because extended decision making generally involves several brands, many attributes, and a number of information sources, a simple capture strategy may not be adequate. Instead, the marketer needs to structure an information campaign that will result in the brand being preferred by members of the target market.

Courtesy Pietro's Pizza.

The first step is a strong position on those attributes important to the target market. This is discussed in considerable detail in Chapter 16. Next, information must be provided in all the appropriate sources. This may require extensive advertising to groups that do not purchase the item but recommend it to others (e.g., druggists for over-the-counter drugs, veterinarians and county agents for agricultural products). Independent groups should be encouraged to test the brand, and sales personnel should be provided detailed information on the brand's attributes. In addition, it may be wise to provide the sales personnel with extra motivation (e.g., extra commissions paid by the manufacturer) to recommend the product. Point-of-purchase displays and pamphlets should also be available. A well-designed website is essential.

The WinBook J^4 ad shown in Illustration 15–7 is part of an effective preference strategy. It assumes an involved search and provides detailed information relative to multiple product attributes.

Acceptance Strategy

Acceptance strategy is similar to preference strategy. However, it is complicated by the fact that the target market is not seeking information about the brand. Therefore, in addition to the activities involved in the preference strategy described above, the marketer must attract the consumers' attention or otherwise motivate them to learn about the brand. Consider the following quote by Lee Iaccoca while he was head of Chrysler:

> Our biggest long-term job is to get people in [the showroom] to see how great these cars are—to get some traffic—and let them compare, so we're going head to head on price and value.[61]

Courtesy WinBook Corporation.

Because of this situation, Chrysler implemented an acceptance strategy. In addition to product improvements and heavy advertising, Chrysler literally paid consumers to seek information about their cars! They did this by offering cash to individuals who would test drive a Chrysler product prior to purchasing a new car.

Long-term advertising designed to enhance low-involvement learning is another useful technique for gaining acceptance. Extensive advertising with strong emphasis on attracting attention can also be effective. The primary objective of these two approaches is not to sell the brand; rather, they seek to move the brand into the evoked set. Then, when a purchase situation arises, the consumer will seek additional information on this brand.

SUMMARY

Following problem recognition, consumers may engage in extensive internal and external search, limited internal and external search, or only internal search. Information may be sought on (1) the appropriate *evaluative criteria* for the solution of the problem, (2) the existence of various *alternative solutions,* and (3) the *performance* of each alternative solution on each evaluative criterion.

Most consumers, when faced with a problem, can recall a limited number of brands that they feel are probably acceptable solutions. These acceptable brands, the *evoked set,* are the initial ones that the consumer seeks additional information on during the remaining internal and external search process. Therefore, marketers are very concerned that their brands fall within the evoked set of most members of their target market.

Consumer internal information (information stored in memory) may have been actively acquired in previous searches and personal experiences or it may have been passively acquired through low-involvement learning. In addition to their own *memory,* consumers can seek information from four major types of external sources: (1) *personal sources,* such as friends and family; (2) *independent sources,* such as consumer groups, paid professionals, and government agencies; (3) *marketing sources,* such as sales personnel and advertising; and (4) *experiential sources,* such as direct product inspection or trial.

The Internet is changing consumer information search in ways that are not yet fully understood. However, millions of households use the Internet to seek information about companies and products. Marketers must maintain well-designed websites referred to as *home pages* or *Internet presence sites.* In addition, firms are increasingly using the Internet as an advertising medium.

Explicit external information search *after* problem recognition is limited. This emphasizes the need to communicate effectively with consumers prior to problem recognition. Characteristics of the market, the product, the consumer, and the situation interact to influence the level of search.

It is often suggested that consumers generally should engage in relatively extensive external search prior to purchasing an item. However, this view ignores the fact that information search is not free. It takes time, energy, money, and can often require giving up more desirable activities. Therefore, consumers should engage in external search only to the extent that the expected benefits such as a lower price or a more satisfactory purchase outweigh the expected costs.

Sound marketing strategy takes into account the nature of information search engaged in by the target market. The level of search and the brand's position in or out of the evoked set are two key dimensions. Based on these two dimensions, six potential information strategies are suggested: (1) *maintenance,* (2) *disrupt,* (3) *capture,* (4) *intercept,* (5) *preference,* and (6) *acceptance.*

KEY TERMS

Awareness set 527
Banner ads 535
Bots 535
Consideration set 527
Evoked set 527

External search 525
Home page 533
Inept set 528
Inert set 528
Internal search 525

Internet presence
  site (IPS) 533
Ongoing search 525
Perceived risk 542

INTERNET EXERCISES

1. Find and describe a magazine ad that is particularly effective at causing readers to consult a website. Why is it effective?

2. Use the Internet to find information on (*i*) the appropriate evaluative criteria, (*ii*) the available alternatives, and (*iii*) the performance characteristics of the products listed below. Describe your results. What do you conclude?
   a. Cosmetics
   b. Vitamins
   c. Digital cameras
   d. Dogs

3. Visit the websites of three firms in each of the product categories listed below. Report on the quality of the information provided at each site. What general suggestions do you have?
   a. Hiking shoes
   b. Lipstick

   c. Notebook computers
   d. DVD players
   e. Sunglasses
   f. Charities focused on poverty relief

4. Describe three Internet shopping services.

5. Use an Internet shopping service such as mysimon.com to determine the "best buy" for a product that interests you. Evaluate this process. How could it be improved? If you were actually going to make the purchase, would you buy this one or would you purchase elsewhere? Why?

6. Visit Amazon.com, epionions.com, or a similar site. Examine the product reviews provided by other customers. How useful do you think these are? What could make them more useful?

7. Compare the PepsiWorld.com site with the MountainDew.com site. How are they similar?

Different? How would you explain the differences?

8. Click on two banner ads for similar products. Describe where you encountered the banner ads and evaluate each banner ad and the target site.

9. Visit an Internet store. Compare the information available at that store with the information available at a similar outlet in a mall.

10. Visit the sites listed below and classify each as an active or a passive site. Justify your classification.
  a. Hardrock.com
  b. Freshlookcontacts.com
  c. Specialized.com
  d. Rollerblade.com
  e. Fossil.com
  f. Kia.com

DDB NEEDHAM LIFESTYLE DATA ANALYSES

1. Based on the DDB Needham data, what characterizes one who is likely to read ingredient labels carefully? What are the marketing implications of this? What are the regulatory implications?

2. Examine the DDB Needham data in Tables 1 through 7. What characterizes one who is likely to be confused by nutrition labeling? What are the marketing implications of this?

REVIEW QUESTIONS

1. When does *information search* occur? What is the difference between internal and external information search?

2. What kind of information is sought in an external search for information?

3. What are *evaluative criteria* and how do they relate to information search?

4. How does a consumer's *awareness set* influence information search?

5. What roles do the *evoked set, inert set,* and *inept set* play in a consumer's information search?

6. What are the primary sources of information available to consumers?

7. What is the *Internet?*

8. What is an *Internet presence site?*

9. What is the difference between an active and a passive website?

10. When should company or brand websites be extensive and, if applicable, interactive?

11. How do *nonsearchers, information searchers,* and *extended information searchers* differ in their search for information?

12. What factors might influence the search effort of consumers who are essentially one-stop shoppers? How do these factors differ in terms of how they

influence information searchers and extended information searchers?

13. What factors have to be considered in the total cost of the information search? How might these factors be different for different consumers?

14. Explain how different *market characteristics* affect information search.

15. How do different *consumer characteristics* influence a consumer's information search effort?

16. How do *product characteristics* influence a consumer's information search effort?

17. How do *situational characteristics* influence a consumer's information search effort?

18. Describe the information search characteristics that should lead to each of the following strategies:
  a. Maintenance
  b. Disrupt
  c. Capture
  d. Intercept
  e. Preference
  f. Acceptance

19. Describe each of the strategies listed in Question 18.

DISCUSSION QUESTIONS

20. Pick a product/brand that you believe would require each strategy in Table 15–2 (six products in total). Justify your selection. Develop a specific marketing strategy for each (six strategies in total).

21. Of the products shown in Figure 15–3, which product class is most likely to exhibit the most brand switching? Explain your answer in terms of the information provided in Figure 15–3.

22. Describe a product and brand that you believe should have an extensive website (not necessarily active). Justify your choice and indicate in detail what the site should contain.

23. Have you used an Internet shopping service such as mysimon.com? If so, what is your evaluation of it? If no, why not?

24. How should a firm determine if it should have an active website?

25. What information sources do you think students on your campus use when acquiring the items listed below? Consider the various sources listed in Figure 15–4 in developing your answer. Do you think there will be individual differences? Why?
    a. Movies
    b. Dentist
    c. Apartment
    d. Vitamins
    e. Bicycle
    f. A charity contribution
    g. Dress clothes
    h. Mother's Day gifts

26. What factors contribute to the size of the awareness set, evoked set, inert set, and inept set?

27. Discuss factors that may contribute to external information search and factors that act to reduce

external search for information before purchase or adoption of the following:
    a. Bicycle repairs
    b. Health insurance
    c. Exercise club
    d. Clothes for a big party
    e. Vegetarianism
    f. Counseling services

28. Is it ever in the best interest of a marketer to encourage potential customers to carry out an extended prepurchase search? Why or why not?

29. What implications for marketing strategy does Figure 15–2 suggest?

30. What role, if any, should the government play in ensuring that consumers have easy access to relevant product information? How should it accomplish this?

31. Respond to the questions in Consumer Insight 15–1.

32. Describe a recent purchase in which you engaged in extensive search and one in which you did little prepurchase search. What factors caused the difference?

33. What is your awareness set, evoked set, inert set, and inept set for the following? In what ways, if any, do you think your sets will differ from the average member of your class? Why?
    a. Notebook computers
    b. Cereals
    c. Sports drinks
    d. Clothing stores
    e. Book stores
    f. Internet shopping services
    g. Restaurants

APPLICATION ACTIVITIES

34. Develop an appropriate questionnaire and complete Question 25 using information from five students not in your class. Prepare a report discussing the marketing implications of your findings.

35. For the same products listed in Question 33, ask five students to list all the brands they are aware of in each product category. Then have them indicate

which ones they might buy (evoked set), which ones they are indifferent toward (inert set), and which brands they strongly dislike and would not purchase (inept set). What are the marketing implications of your results?

36. Develop a short questionnaire designed to measure the information search consumers engage in prior to purchasing an expensive recreational or

entertainment item or service. Your questionnaire should include measures of types of information sought, as well as sources that provide this information. Also include measures of the relevant consumer characteristics that might influence information search, as well as some measure of past experience with the products. Then interview two recent purchasers of each product, using the questionnaire you have developed. Analyze each consumer's response and classify each consumer

in terms of information search. What are the marketing implications of your results?

37. For each strategy in Table 15–2, find one brand that appears to be following that strategy. Describe in detail how it is implementing the strategy.

38. Develop a questionnaire to determine which products college students view as positive and which they view as negative. Measure the shopping effort associated with each type. Explain your overall results and any individual differences you find.

REFERENCES

1. "The 1998 CASIE Awards Finalists," *Advertising Age,* October 12, 1998, special section.
2. G. Punji and R. Brookes, "Decision Constraints and Consideration-Set Formation in Consumer Durables," *Psychology & Marketing,* August 2001, pp. 843–63.
3. An outstanding discussion of the trade-off consumers make between memory-based decisions (internal search) and external search is in J. R. Bettman, M. F. Luce, and J. W. Payne, "Constructive Consumer Choice Processes," *Journal of Consumer Research,* December 1998, pp. 187–217.
4. For a more comprehensive view, see R. Lawson, "Consumer Decision Making within a Goal-Driven Framework," *Psychology & Marketing,* August 1997, pp. 427–49.
5. See D. R. Lehmann and Y. Pan, "Context Effects, New Brand Entry, and Consideration Sets," *Journal of Marketing Research,* August 1994, pp. 364–74; I. Sinha, "A Conceptual Model of Situation Type on Consumer Choice Behavior and Consideration Sets," in *Advances in Consumer Research,* vol. 21, eds. C. T. Allen and D. R. John (Provo, UT: Association for Consumer Research, 1994), pp. 477–82; K. Jedidi, R. Kohli, and W. S. DeSarbo, "Consideration Sets in Conjoint Analysis," *Journal of Marketing Research,* August 1996, pp. 364–72; M. D. Johnson and D. R. Lehmann, "Consumer Experience and Consideration Sets for Brands and Product Categories," *Advances in Consumer Research,* vol. 24, eds. M. Bruck and D. J. MacInnis (Provo, UT: Association for Consumer Research, 1997), pp. 295–300; and S. Shapiro, D. J. MacInnis, and S. E. Heckler, "The Effects of Incidental Ad Exposure on the Formation of Consideration Sets," *Journal of Consumer Research,* June 1997, pp. 94–104.
6. P. Aurier, S. Jean, and J. L. Zaichkowsky, "Consideration Set Size and Familiarity with Usage Context," *Advances in Consumer Research,* vol. 27, eds. S. J. Hoch and R. J. Meyer (Provo, UT: Association for Consumer Research, 2000), pp. 307–13; and K. K. Desai and W. D. Hoyer, "Descriptive Characteristics of Memory-Based Consideration Sets," *Journal of Consumer Research,* December 2000, pp. 309–23.
7. E. M. Felcher, P. Malaviya, and A. L. McGill, "The Role of Taxonomic and Goal-Derived Product Categorization in, within, and across Category Judgments," *Psychology & Marketing,* August 2001, pp. 865–87.

8. R. R. Brand and J. J. Cronin, "Consumer-Specific Determinants of the Size of Retail Choice Sets," *Journal of Services Marketing* 11, no. 1 (1997), pp. 19–38.
9. D. Butler and A. M. Abernethy, "Information Consumers Seek from Advertisements," *Journal of Professional Services Marketing* 10, no. 2 (1994), pp. 75–92.
10. See S. C. Mooy and H. S. J. Robben, "How Consumers Learn from and about Products," *Advances in Consumer Research,* vol. 25, eds. J. W. Alba and J. W. Hutchinson (Provo, UT: Association for Consumer Research, 1998), pp. 318–23.
11. C. B. Jarvis, "An Exploratory Investigation of Consumers' Evaluations of External Information Sources in Prepurchase Search," *Advances in Consumer Research,* vol. 25, eds. J. W. Alba and J. W. Hutchinson (Provo, UT: Association for Consumer Research, 1998), pp. 446–51.
12. For a review and conflicting evidence, see A. A. Wright and J. G. Lynch, Jr., "Communications Effects of Advertising versus Direct Experience When Both Search and Experience Attributes Are Present," *Journal of Consumer Research,* March 1995, pp. 108–18.
13. See C. F. Mela, S. Gupta, and D. R. Lehmann, "The Long-Term Impact of Promotion and Advertising on Consumer Brand Choice," *Journal Marketing Research,* May 1997, pp. 248–61; and M. J. Sirgy et al., "Does Television Viewership Play a Role in the Perception of Quality of Life," *Journal of Advertising,* Spring 1998, pp. 125–42.
14. See L. M. Lodish et al., "How TV Advertising Works," *Journal Marketing Research,* May 1995, pp. 125–39; L. D. Gibson, "What Can One TV Exposure Do?" *Journal of Advertising Research,* March 1996, pp. 9–18; and D. R. Riskey, "How TV Advertising Works," *Journal Marketing Research,* May 1997, pp. 292–93; A. G. Woodside, "Advertising and Consumption of Alcoholic Beverages," *Journal of Consumer Psychology* 8, no. 2 (1999), pp. 167–86; M. Duffy, "The Influence of Advertising on the Pattern of Food Consumption in the UK," *International Journal of Advertising* 18, no. 2 (1999), pp. 131–68; S. Burton, D. R. Lichtenstein, and R. G. Netemeyer, "Exposure to Sales Flyers and Increased Purchases in Retail Supermarkets," *Journal of Advertising Research,* September 2000, pp. 7–14; S. Findlay, "Prescription Drugs and Mass Media Advertising," NICHM Foundation, September 2000,

pp. 1–8; F. F. Gonul et al., "Promotion of Prescription Drugs and Its Impact on Physician's Choice Behavior," *Journal of Marketing,* July 2001, pp. 79–90; and J. P. Nelson and D. J. Young, "Do Advertising Bans Work?" *International Journal of Advertising* 20, no. 3 (2001), pp. 273–96.

15. See D. L. Hoffman and T. P. Novak, "Marketing in Hypermedia Computer-Mediated Environments," *Journal of Marketing,* July 1996, pp. 50–68; J. Alba et al., "Interactive Home Shopping," *Journal of Marketing,* July 1997, pp. 38–53; A. Peterson, S. Balasubramanian, and B. J. Bronnenberg, "Exploring the Implications of the Internet for Consumer Marketing"; J. Deighton, "Commentary"; and R. A. Burke, "Do You See What I See?" all in *Journal of the Academy of Marketing Science,* Fall 1997, pp. 329–46, 347–51, and 352–60.

16. P. R. Dickson, "Understanding the Global Trade Winds," *Journal of Consumer Research,* June 2000, pp. 115–22. See also M. S. Nadel, "The Consumer Product Selection Process in an Internet Age," *Harvard Journal of Law and Technology,* Fall 2000, pp. 181–263.

17. *Nielsen/NetRatings Global Internet Trends,* Q1 2002.

18. *A Nation Online* (Washington DC: U.S. Department of Commerce, February 2002), p. 1.

19. *Internet Users Will Top 1 Billion in 2005* (Buffalo Grove, IL: Computer Industry Almanac Inc., March 21, 2002).

20. S. Hays, "Has Online Advertising Finally Grown Up?" *Advertising Age,* April 1, 2002, p. C1.

21. *Interactive Media Study* (Arlington Heights, IL: Market Facts' TeleNation, October 1998).

22. Ibid. See also J. A. Bellizzi, "Drawing Prospects to E-Commerce Websites," *Journal of Advertising Research,* January 2000, pp. 43–53; and S. Edwards and C. LaFerle, *Journal of Current Issues and Research in Advertising,* Spring 2000, pp. 1–12.

23. L. M. Maddox and D. Mehta, "The Role and Effect of Web Addresses in Advertising," *Journal of Advertising Research,* March 1997, pp. 47–59; and X. Fang and D. L. Rosen, "Source-Contact Cue Influence on Attitude Formation and Attitude Persistence," *Advances in Consumer Research,* vol. 27, eds. S. J. Hoch and R. J. Meyer (Provo, UT: Association for Consumer Research, 2000), pp. 196–201.

24. B. Bickart and R. M. Schindler, *Journal of Interactive Marketing,* Summer 2001, pp. 31–40; and P. Chatterjee, "Online Reviews," *Advances in Consumer Research,* vol. 28, eds. M. C. Gilly and J. Meyers-Levy (Provo, UT: Association for Consumer Research, 2001), pp. 129–33.

25. H. Green, "A Cybershopper's Best Friend." *Business Week,* May 4, 1998, p. 84.

26. "Click First, Buy Later," *Marketing News,* May 21, 2001, p. 5; and S. Shim et al., "An Online Prepurchase Intentions Model," *Journal of Retailing* 77 (2001), pp. 377–416.

27. A. Ansari, S. Essegaier, and R. Kohli, "Internet Recommendation Systems," *Journal of Marketing Research,* August 2000, pp. 363–75; and D. Lacobucci, P. Arabie, and A. Bodapati, "Recommendation Agents on the Internet," *Journal of Interactive Marketing,* Summer 2000, pp. 2–11.

28. See D. Kenny and J. F. Marshall, "Contextual Marketing," *Harvard Business Review,* November 2000, pp. 119–25.

29. J. Eighmey, "Profiling User Responses to Commercial Web Sites," *Journal of Advertising Research,* May 1997, pp. 59–66; R. A. Oliva, "Help Them Find It—Fast," *Marketing Management,* Winter 1998, pp. 36–39; S. Ghose and W. Dou, "Interactive Functions and Their Impacts on the Appeal of Internet Presence Sites," *Journal of Advertising Research,* March 1998, pp. 29–43; A. Y. Hogue and G. L. Lohse, "An Information Search Cost Perspective for Designating Interfaces for Electronic Commerce," *Journal of Marketing Research,* August 1999, pp. 387–94; and B. D. Weinberg, "Don't Keep Your Internet Customers Waiting Too Long," *Journal of Interactive Marketing,* Winter 2000, pp. 30–39.

30. M. M. Cardona, "Industry Comes to Terms with a New Economy," *Advertising Age,* December 10, 2001, p. 6.

31. B. Synder, "Unilever Speaks Up about Internet Strategy," *Advertising Age,* August 17, 1998, p. 30.

32. R. A. Westbrook and C. Farnell, "Patterns of Information Source Usage among Durable Goods Buyers," *Journal of Marketing Research,* August 1979, pp. 303–12; and J. E. Urbany, P. R. Dickson, and W. L. Wilkie, "Buyer Uncertainty and Information Search," *Journal of Consumer Research,* September 1989, pp. 208–15.

33. Urbany, Dickson, and Wilkie, "Buyer Uncertainty and Information Search"; and *Warranties Rule Consumer Follow-Up* (Washington DC: Federal Trade Commission, 1984), p. 26.

34. Ibid.

35. G. Katona and E. Mueller, "A Study of Purchase Decisions," in *Consumer Behavior: The Dynamics of Consumer Reaction,* ed. L. Clark (University Press, 1955), pp. 30–87; J. Newman and R. Staelin, "Prepurchase Information Seeking for New Cars and Major Household Appliances," *Journal of Marketing Research,* August 1972, pp. 249–57; J. Claxton, J. Fry, and B. Portis, "A Taxonomy of Prepurchase Information Gathering Patterns," *Journal of Consumer Research,* December 1974, pp. 35–42; G. C. Kiel and R. A. Layton, "Dimensions of Consumer Information Seeking Behavior," *Journal of Marketing Research,* May 1981, pp. 233–39; J. B. Freiden and R. E. Goldsmith, "Prepurchase Information-Seeking for Professional Services," *Journal of Services Marketing,* Winter 1989, pp. 45–55; G. N. Souter and M. M. McNeil, *Journal of Professional Services Marketing* 11, no. 2 (1995), pp. 45–60; and Urbany, Dickson, and Wilkie, "Buyer Uncertainty and Information Search"; See also B. L. Bagus, "The Consumer Durable Replacement Buyer," *Journal of Marketing,* January 1991, pp. 42–51.

36. For more elaborate models, see P. A. Titus and P. B. Everett, "The Consumer Retail Search Process," *Journal of the Academy of Marketing Science,* Spring 1995, pp. 106–19; S. Moorthy, B. T. Ratchford, and D. Talukdar, "Consumer Information Search Revisited," *Journal of Consumer Research,* March 1997, pp. 263–77; and S. Putrevu and B. T. Ratchford, "A Model of Search Behavior with an Application to Grocery Shopping," *Journal of Retailing,* no. 4 (1997), pp. 463–86.

37. J. Gregan-Paxton and D. R. John, "Are Young Children Adaptive Decision Makers?" *Journal of Consumer Research,* March 1995, pp. 567–80.

38. See W. K. Darley, "The Relationship of Antecedents of Search and Self-Esteem to Adolescent Search Effort," *Psychology & Marketing,* August 1999, pp. 409–27.

39. J. G. Lynch, Jr., and D. Ariely, "Wine Online," *Marketing Science,* Winter 2000, pp. 83–103; and D. Ariely, "Controlling the Information Flow," *Journal of Consumer Research,* September 2000, pp. 233–48.

40. For a different model, see J. G. Blodgett, D. J. Hill, and G. Stone, "A Model of the Determinants of Retail Search," in *Advances in Consumer Research,* vol. 22, eds. F. R. Kardes and M. Sujan (Provo, UT: Association for Consumer Research, 1995), pp. 518–23.

41. D. R. Lichtenstein, N. M. Ridgway, and R. G. Netemeyer, "Price Perceptions and Consumer Shopping Behavior," *Journal of Marketing Research,* May 1993, pp. 234–45.

42. M. N. Bergen, S. Dutta, and S. M. Shugan, "Branded Variants," *Journal of Marketing Research,* February 1996, pp. 9–19.

43. D. Grewal and H. Marmorstein, "Market Price Variation, Perceived Price Variation, and Consumers' Price Search Decisions for Durable Goods," *Journal of Consumer Research,* December 1994, pp. 453–60.

44. See B. G. C. Dellaert, "Investigating Consumers' Tendency to Combine Multiple Shopping Purposes and Destinations," *Journal Marketing Research,* May 1998, pp. 177–89.

45. See C. Moorman, "Market-Level Effects of Information," *Journal Marketing Research,* February 1998, pp. 82–98; and A. D. Miyazaki, D. E. Sprott, and K. C. Manning, "Unit Prices on Retail Shelf Labels," *Journal of Retailing* 76, no. 1 (2000), pp. 93–112.

46. See C. M. Fisher and C. J. Anderson, "The Relationship between Consumer Attitudes and Frequency of Advertising in Newspapers for Hospitals," *Journal of Hospital Marketing* 7, no. 2 (1993), pp. 139–56.

47. S. Widrick and E. Fram, "Identifying Negative Products," *Journal of Consumer Marketing,* no. 2 (1983), pp. 59–66.

48. See D. D'Rozario and S. P. Douglas, "Effect of Assimilation on Prepurchase Information-Search Tendencies," *Journal of Consumer Psychology* 8, no. 2 (1999), pp. 187–209; and C. Merrill, "Where the Cars Are Caliente," *American Demographics,* January 2000, pp. 56–59.

49. C. M. Heilman, D. Bowman, and G. P. Wright, "The Evolution of Brand Preferences and Choice Behaviors of Consumers New to a Market," *Journal of Marketing Research,* May 2000, pp. 139–55.

50. See C. A. Fiske et al., "The Relationship between Knowledge and Search," in *Advances in Consumer Research,* vol. 21, eds. C. T. Allen and D. R. John (Provo, UT: Association for Consumer Research, 1994), pp. 43–50; L.-T. Bei and R. Heslin, "The *Consumer Reports* Mindset," *Advances in Consumer Research,* vol. 24, eds. M. Bruck and D. J. MacInnis (Provo, UT: Association for Consumer Research, 1997), pp. 151–58; G. E. Smith, M. P. Venkatraman, and R. R. Dholakia, "Diagnosing the Search Cost Effort," *Journal of Economic Psychology* 20 (1999), pp. 285–314; and B. T. Ratchford, "The Economics of Consumer Knowledge," *Journal of Consumer Research,* March 2001, pp. 397–411.

51. This insight is based on J. W. Alba and J. W. Hutchinson, "Knowledge Calibration," *Journal of Consumer Research,* September 2000, pp. 123–49.

52. See J. R. Lumpkin; "Shopping Orientation Segmentation of the Elderly Consumer," *Journal of the Academy of Marketing Science,* Spring 1985, pp. 271–89; T. Williams, M. Slama, and J. Rogers, "Behavioral Characteristics of the Recreational Shopper," *Journal of Academy of Marketing Science,* Summer 1985, pp. 307–16; and J. R. Lumpkin, J. M. Hawes, and W. R. Darden, "Shopping Patterns of the Rural Consumer," *Journal of Business Research,* February 1986, pp. 63–81.

53. See G. Wang, S. M. Fletcher, and D. H. Carley, "Consumer Factors Influencing the Use of Nutrition Information Sources," in *Advances in Consumer Research,* vol. 22, eds. F. R. Kardes and M. Sujan (Provo, UT: Association for Consumer Research, 1995), pp. 573–81; and U. M. Dholakia, "Involvement-Response Models of Joint Effects," *Advances in Consumer Research,* vol. 25, eds. J. W. Alba and J. W. Hutchinson (Provo, UT: Association for Consumer Research, 1998), pp. 499–506.

54. T. H. Dodd, B. E. Pinkleton, and A. W. Gustafson, *Psychology & Marketing,* May 1996, pp. 291–304. See also J. R. McColl-Kennedy and R. E. Fetter, Jr., "An Empirical Examination of the Involvement to External Search Relationship," *Journal of Services Marketing* 15, no. 2 (2001), pp. 82–98.

55. G. R. Dowling and R. Staelin, "A Model of Perceived Risk and Intended Risk-Handling Activity," *Journal of Consumer Research,* June 1994, pp. 119–34. See also J. B. Smith and J. M. Bristor, "Uncertainty Orientation," *Psychology & Marketing,* November 1994, pp. 587–607.

56. A. Chaudhuri, "Product Class Effects on Perceived Risk," *International Journal of Research in Marketing,* May 1998, pp. 157–68; and K. Mitra, M. C. Reiss, and L. M. Capella, "An Examination of Perceived Risk, Informational Search, and Behavioral Intentions," *Journal of Services Marketing* 13, no. 3 (1999), pp. 208–28.

57. See D. S. Sundaram and R. D. Taylor, "An Investigation of External Search Effort," *Advances in Consumer Research,* vol. 25, eds. J. W. Alba and J. W. Hutchinson (Provo, UT: Association for Consumer Research, 1998), pp. 440–45. For an exception, see C. J. Hill, "The Nature of Problem Recognition and Search in the Extended Health Care Decision," *Journal of Services Marketing* 15, no. 6 (2001), pp. 454–79.

58. A. G. Abdul-Muhmin, "Contingent Decision Behavior," *Journal of Consumer Psychology* 8, no. 1 (1999), pp. 91–111.

59. "L&M Lights Up Again," *Marketing and Media Decisions,* February 1984, p. 69.

60. L. L. Garber, "The Package Appearance in Choice," in *Advances in Consumer Research,* vol. 22, eds. F. R. Kardes and M. Sujan (Provo, UT: Association for Consumer Research, 1995), pp. 653–60.

61. R. Gray, "Chrysler Hinges Price on Popularity," *Advertising Age,* October 5, 1981, p. 7.

Sunbeam®
Easy Clean Blenders

1.50
1.25
5

Sunbeam®

WHIP — MIX — BLEND
PURÉE — — FRAPPÉ
OFF — — LIQUIFY

Ice the Competition

Courtesy Hill, Knowlton, Sancor.

554

Alternative Evaluation and Selection

☐ Sunbeam Appliance Company successfully redesigned its many lines of small kitchen appliances. The redesign of its food processor line illustrates the four-stage process used:

1. A *consumer usage and attitude survey* was used to determine how and for what purpose products in the product category are used, frequency of use, brand ownership, brand awareness, and attitudes toward the product.

2. A *consumer attribute and benefit survey* was used to provide importance ratings of product attributes and benefits desired from the product category, along with perceptions of the degree to which each brand provides the various attributes and benefits.

3. A *conjoint analysis study* (a technique described in this chapter) was used to provide data on the structure of consumers' preferences for product features and their willingness to trade one feature for more of another feature. Conjoint analysis provides the relative importance *each* consumer attaches to various levels of each potential product feature. This allows individuals with similar preference structures to be grouped into market segments.

4. *Product line sales and market share simulations* were used to determine the best set of food processors to bring to the market. Based on the preference struc- tures and sizes of the market seg- ments discovered in step 3 and

the perceived characteristics of competing brands, the market share of various Sunbeam product sets was estimated using computer simulations.

The above process involved interviewing hundreds of product category users. Twelve different product attributes were tested and four distinct market segments were uncovered. The existing product line was replaced with four new models (down from six) targeted at three of the four segments. The results were increased market share, reduced costs, and increased profitability.[1]

The opening example describes Sunbeam's successful analysis of consumers' desired product benefits (evaluative criteria) and the manner in which they choose between products with differing combinations of benefits. The process by which consumers evaluate and choose among alternatives is illustrated in Figure 16–1.

We will organize our discussion around four basic areas. First, we will provide an overview of the processes consumers use to select among alternatives. Then, the nature and characteristics of evaluative criteria (the benefits the product should provide) will be described. After examining evaluative criteria, we will focus on the ability of consumers to judge the performance of products on the evaluative criteria. Finally, we will examine the decision rules that consumers use in selecting one alternative from those considered.

It is important to remember that many purchases involve little or no evaluation of alternatives. Nominal decisions do not require the evaluation of any alternatives. The last purchase is repeated without considering other information. Limited decisions may involve comparing a few brands (small evoked set) on one or two dimensions (I'll buy Heinz or Del Monte catsup, depending on which is cheaper at Safeway).

HOW CONSUMERS MAKE CHOICES

Any attempt to describe a complex, nonlinear process such as consumer choice necessarily simplifies it and removes much of its richness. Thus, our discussion will make consumer choice seem more logical, structured, rational, and deliberate than it often is. Fortunately,

FIGURE 16–1   **Alternative Evaluation and Selection Process**

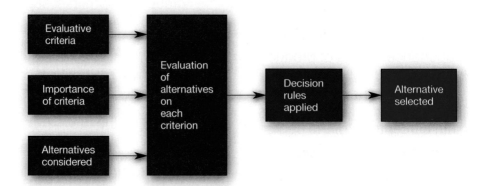

we have all made numerous consumer choices and we know that they are frequently circular, emotional, incomplete, and based on expediency rather than optimality. We also know that the situation plays an important role in the processes we use to make consumer choices. For example, when we are tired or hurried, we are very likely to use different choice processes than we would if we had more energy or time.

A substantial amount of research and marketing strategy has assumed a rational consumer decision maker with well-defined, stable preferences. The consumer is also assumed to have sufficient skills to calculate which option will maximize his or her value, and will choose on this basis. This approach is referred to as *rational choice theory*. The task in rational choice theory is to *identify* or discover the one optimal choice for the decision confronting the decision maker. The decision maker simply collects information on the levels of the attributes of the alternatives, applies preexisting values to those levels, applies the appropriate choice rule, and the superior option is revealed.

In reality, all consumers have **bounded rationality**—*a limited capacity for processing information*. Moreover, consumers often have goals that are different from, or in addition to, selecting the optimal alternative (see Consumer Insight 16–1). Further, recent research indicates that preferences are not stable. That is, if an individual is comparing brands A and B, he or she might prefer brand A. However, if brand C is added to the evoked set, the consumer's preference might shift to brand B.[2] Therefore, for many decisions consumers do not engage in a strictly rational choice; instead, they construct a decision process that is appropriate for the situation at hand.

In addition, many consumer decisions do not involve the comparison of brands on their features at all. Instead, they are based on emotional responses to the brand or overall impressions of the brand. In this section, we will examine three types of consumer choice processes: affective choice, attitude-based choice, and attribute-based choice. Keep in mind that these are not mutually exclusive and combinations may be used in a single decision.

Affective Choice

Consider a consumer buying an alarm clock. She inspects several models, noticing many differences among them. Some models have a snooze-alarm feature, some don't. Some have a battery backup, others don't. The models also vary on wake-to-music or -to-alarm feature, top-mounted versus side controls, push-button versus rotary or sliding switches, lighted alarm-set indicator, automatic FM frequency control, the type of finish, and the price. She reviews her relative preference for these diverse features and chooses the model that gives her the best combination of the desired features.

Now consider her buying a dress for an upcoming big social event. Scanning a rack full of dresses in a store, she pulls out a few that seemed nice. One of them particularly caught her eye: she tries it on, and thinks she looks great in it. She tries another one which she thought made her look too conservative. A third one made her look too sexy. Somehow, the first one looked so right for her: a few more minutes of contemplation about what a great impression she would make donning that dress in the party, and she has made up her mind about that dress.[3]

The purchase of the alarm clock is an example of an attribute-based choice, discussed in the following section. It was based on a conscious evaluation of the various features of the clocks considered. The purchase of the dress is primarily an **affective choice.** Affective choices tend to be more holistic in nature. The brand is not decomposed into distinct components, each of which is evaluated separately from the whole. The evaluation of such products is generally focused on the way they will make the user *feel* as they are used.

Consumer choice goals are usually described in terms such as "getting the least expensive calculator with the functions I need" or "selecting a dress that makes me feel great." These are the specific purchase goals or outcomes the consumer wants to obtain. A **metagoal** refers to *the general nature of the outcome being sought*.[4] The purchase goals just described are examples of a metagoal of *maximizing the accuracy of the decision*. This is the only goal assumed in many studies of consumer decision making. However, other metagoals exist.

Consumers often seek to *minimize the cognitive effort required for the decision*. This is often the goal in nominal and limited decision making. However, it can also play an important role in extended decision making as well. Consumers seeking to minimize effort tend to use simple choice rules, consider fewer alternatives, place more importance on the dominant attribute, and evaluate fewer attributes of each alternative.[5] Consumers may also delay or avoid the decision.[6]

Choices that involve conflicts between valued goals such as an attractive, low-effort lawn versus the use of pesticides and herbicides can generate significant negative emotions.[7] Thus, another consumer metagoal is to *minimize the experience of negative emotion while making the decision*. One strategy consumers use for this purpose is to avoid or delay the decision and stay with the status quo.

A fourth metagoal is to *maximize the ease with which a decision can be justified*. Consumers are social beings and often feel compelled to justify a decision to others or to themselves.[8] This is particularly true for luxury items and items that are different or more extravagant than those used by one's reference groups. Anticipating the need for such justifications can affect how a consumer makes the initial decision.

These metagoals are not mutually exclusive. In fact, many decisions are characterized by multiple goals with differing levels of importance. Further, the relative importance of the goals may change as the consumer moves through the decision process. For example, a consumer deciding to purchase a lawnmower may begin with maximizing the accuracy of the decision as the primary goal. However, as the consumer learns of the vast number of brands, models, and features, minimizing effort may become increasingly important. As the consumer learns of incompatible features (the model that pollutes the least costs the most and does not perform as well) minimizing negative emotion may become more salient.

Critical Thinking Questions

1. Do you agree with the four metagoals described above? What others do you think are common?

2. What are the marketing implications of each of the metagoals described above (assume all four are widely used by consumers)?

The evaluation itself is often based exclusively or primarily on the immediate emotional response to the product or service:

> I'm getting married, and we were looking for a place to have the wedding and we had been to about five or six places . . . this (place) was not quite right . . . and this other place was not quite right . . . but then we went to a place called The Highlander in Glens Falls. I went in the lobby and I knew immediately that this was right. It was immaculately clean, the floor was not just marble but inlaid different types of patterns on the floor . . . its restaurant, the doors were lead and glass and you just knew that this was right . . . . You go in there and sure enough they had a wedding coordinator.[9]

Decisions based on affect use the "How do I feel about it" heuristic or decision rule.[10] Consumers imagine or picture using the product or service and evaluate the feeling that this

Courtesy Häagen-Dazs.

Courtesy FreshLook Cosmetic Contact Lenses.

use will produce.[11] For example, a consumer choosing between a weekend at a bed-and-breakfast on a beach and a weekend in a nice hotel in a city might imagine each episode to see how he or she feels. The decision would then be made largely or completely on these expected feelings.

Affective choice is most likely when the underlying motive is consummatory rather than instrumental. **Consummatory motives** *underlie behaviors that are intrinsically rewarding to the individual involved*. **Instrumental motives** *activate behaviors designed to achieve a second goal*. For example, one person might read a best-seller for the pleasure of reading the book (consummatory motive), whereas another might read the same book to be able to appear "with it" to his or her friends (instrumental motive).[12] Illustration 16–1 contains ads appealing to each of these motives.

Marketers are just beginning to study affect-based decisions.[13] However, it is clear that such decisions require different strategies than the more cognitive decisions generally considered in marketing. For those decisions that are likely to be affective in nature (largely triggered by consummatory motives), marketers should design products and services that will provide the appropriate emotional responses.[14] They also should help consumers visualize how they will feel during and after the consumption experience.[15] This is particularly important for new brands or products and services. Consumers who have experience with a product or brand have a basis for imagining the affective response it will produce. Those who do not may incorrectly predict the feelings the experience will produce. For example,

ILLUSTRATION 16–1

The Häagen-Dazs ad appeals to the consummatory motive associated with the pleasure of consuming the product. The FreshLook ad appeals to an instrumental motive by positioning the contact lenses as a means to the end of being attractive.

Courtesy of Samsung Electronics America, Inc. Reprinted by permission.

individuals imagining a whitewater rafting trip may conclude that it would produce feelings of terror rather than exhilaration. Illustration 16–2 contains an ad that helps consumers envision the positive experiences and accompanying feelings they would have if they owned a Samsung DigitAll.

Attribute-Based versus Attitude-Based Choice Processes

Consider the following two processes a consumer might use to purchase an answering machine:

Process 1: The consumer remembers that the Casio his last roommate had worked well and looked "good," his parents had a Toshiba that also worked well but was rather large and bulky, and his old Samsung had not performed as well as he had expected. He goes to a store and gathers information on price, recording time, and ease of remote access for each of these brands. He mentally ranks each brand on these three attributes and his general impression of their quality. On the basis of these evaluations, he makes a choice.

Process 2: The consumer remembers that the Casio his last roommate had seemed to work well and looked "good," his parents had a Toshiba that also worked well but was rather large and bulky, and his old Samsung had not performed as well as he had expected. At the store, he sees that the Casio and Toshiba are about the same price and decides to buy the Casio.

The first example above is attribute-based choice. **Attribute-based choice** *requires the knowledge of specific attributes at the time the choice is made, and it involves attribute-by-attribute comparisons across brands.* The second example above is attitude-based choice. **Attitude-based choice** *involves the use of general attitudes, summary impressions, intuitions, or heuristics; no attribute-by-attribute comparisons are made at the time of choice.*[16] There can also be combinations of these forms. A common combination would be for a consideration set to be formed using attitude-based processing, with the final choice being made on the basis of a brand-by-brand comparison on a few important attributes such as price and color.

Attribute-based choices require the comparison of each specific attribute across all the brands considered. This is a much more effortful and time-consuming process than the global comparisons made when attitude-based choice is involved. It also tends to produce a more nearly optimal decision.

Motivation, information availability, and situational factors interact to determine which choice process will be used. As one would suspect, the greater the motivation to make an optimal decision, the more likely an attribute-based choice will be made. In general, the importance of making an optimal decision increases with the value of the item being considered and consequences of a nonoptimal decision. Thus, attribute-based processing is more likely for a laptop computer or an athletic shoe for a marathoner than it is for an inexpensive calculator or an athletic shoe to wear around campus.

The easier it is to access complete attribute-by-brand information, the more likely attribute-based processing will be used. This can be used by marketers of brands that have important attribute-based advantages but that lack strong reputations or images in the target market. The approach would be to provide attribute-based comparisons in an easy-to-process format such as a brand-by-attribute matrix. Such a matrix could be presented in ads, on packages, in point-of-purchase displays, in brochures, or on the brand's website. A firm using such a strategy should use an appropriate comparison format and structure the information so that its brand will be the focal point of comparison.[17] This could be done by listing it first, perhaps in bold or colored type.

A variety of situations influence which choice approach is most likely. As we saw in Chapter 13, task definition influences the importance assigned to purchases, with gift purchases often being assigned more importance than similar purchases for oneself. Thus, gift purchases would be more likely to produce attribute-based decision processes. Time pressure is a major determinant of choice process used, with increasing time pressures producing more use of attitude-based decisions.

It is important to note that many decisions, even for important products, appear to be attitude-based. Recall from the previous chapter that most individuals collect very little product information from external sources immediately before a purchase. They are most likely making attitude-based decisions.

The ads in Illustration 16–3 illustrate the differences between attribute-based and attitude-based choice strategies. The Chem ad focuses on features and emphasizes its built-in wireless LAN card and antenna. In contrast, the ASICS ad focuses on the brand and an overall impression of the product and its users.

Marketers for most products and services, even expensive, important ones, have a dual task. They must provide information and experiences that produce a strong attitude-based position (for those consumers making an attitude-based choice) *and* they must provide

Courtesy ChemUSA.

Courtesy ASICS Tiger, Inc.

performance levels and supporting information that will result in preference among those consumers making attribute-based choices.

EVALUATIVE CRITERIA

As the prior discussion described, consumers often make decisions based on affect or on overall attitude toward the brand or to minimize effort or negative emotion. Many of these types of decisions involve very little consideration of specific product features. However, most decisions involve an evaluation of the likely performance of the product or service on one or more dimensions. **Evaluative criteria** are *the various dimensions, features, or benefits a consumer looks for in response to a specific problem.* Before purchasing a computer, you might be concerned with cost, speed, memory, operating system, display, and warranty. These would be your evaluative criteria. Someone else could approach the same purchase with an entirely different set of evaluative criteria.

Nature of Evaluative Criteria

Evaluative criteria are typically product features or attributes associated with either benefits desired by customers or the costs they must incur. Thus, many consumers who want to avoid cavities use toothpaste that contains fluoride. For these consumers, fluoride is an evaluative criterion associated with the benefit cavity prevention. In this case, the

Tamron USA, Inc. 2002.

ILLUSTRATION 16–4

Consumers are generally interested in product features only in relation to the benefits those features provide. This ad emphasizes the ability of the lens to capture memories rather than its technical characteristics.

evaluative criterion and the desired benefit are not identical, and fluoride is important as a feature only to the extent that it helps prevent cavities. In such cases, marketers should emphasize the benefit the feature will provide the consumer, not just the feature itself. The ad in Illustration 16–4 focuses on the ability of the Tamron zoom lens to capture memories not on its technical specifications.

In other situations, the product feature and the benefit or cost are the same. For example, price is often an evaluative criterion that is identical to one aspect of cost (as we will see, price can have many meanings).

As we saw earlier, products and services purchased primarily for emotional reasons may involve anticipating the effect of purchase or use on feelings rather than on analysis of product attributes per se. Likewise, a product purchased for use in a social situation often involves anticipation of the reaction of others to the product instead of an analysis of its attributes. In these cases, the anticipated feelings or reactions would be the evaluative criteria.

Evaluative criteria can differ in type, number, and importance. The *type of evaluative criteria* a consumer uses in a decision varies from *tangible* cost and performance features to *intangible* factors such as style, taste, prestige, feelings generated, and brand image.[18] Illustration 16–5 shows how two similar products stress very different types of evaluative criteria. The Jergens ad stresses tangible attributes and technical performance. The Nivea ad focuses on intangible attributes and feelings.

Evaluative criteria may exist in terms of extremes (lower price or more miles per gallon is better), limits (it must not cost more than $100; it must get more than 25 miles per gallon), or ranges (any price between $85 and $99 is acceptable).[19] For new product categories, consumers must often determine which levels of a various criteria are desirable. For example, a consumer who buys a barbecue grill for the first time and has very limited

Reprinted by permission of the Andrew Jergen Company.   Courtesy Beiersdorf, Inc.

experience with such grills may have to determine if he prefers gas to charcoal, domed or traditional shape, appropriate size, and so forth. After purchase and use, these preference levels are likely to become more firmly established and stable.[20]

For fairly simple products such as toothpaste, soap, or facial tissue, consumers use relatively few evaluative criteria. On the other hand, the purchase of an automobile, stereo system, or house may involve numerous criteria. Characteristics of the individual (such as product familiarity and age) and characteristics of the purchase situation (such as time pressure) also influence the number of evaluative criteria considered.[21]

The *importance* that consumers assign to each evaluative criterion is of great interest to marketers. Three consumers could use the same six evaluative criteria shown in the following table when considering a notebook computer. However, if the importance rank they assigned each criterion varied as shown, they would likely purchase different brands.

	Importance Rank for		
Criterion	*Consumer A*	*Consumer B*	*Consumer C*
Price	**1**	6	3
Processor	5	**1**	4
Display quality	3	3	**1**
Memory	6	**2**	5
Weight	4	4	**2**
After-sale support	**2**	5	6

Consumer A is concerned primarily with cost and support services. Consumer B wants computing speed and power. Consumer C is concerned primarily with ease of use. If each of these three consumers represented a larger group of consumers, we would have three distinct market segments based on the importance assigned the same criteria.

The importance of evaluative criteria varies among individuals and also within the same individual across situations. For example, a consumer might consider the price of food items to be the most important attribute most of the time. However, when in a hurry, speed of service and convenient location may be more important.[22]

The importance of a particular criterion depends in part on the level of the criterion. For example, you might not assign the weight of a notebook computer much importance if all the ones under consideration weighed between 3.5 and 5 pounds. However, weight might become quite important if you examined an additional brand that weighed 10 pounds.[23]

Evaluative criteria, and the importance that individuals assign them, influence not only the brands selected but if and when a problem will be recognized. For example, consumers who attach more importance to automobile styling and product image relative to comfort and cost buy new cars more frequently than do those with the opposite importance rankings.[24]

Marketers must understand the criteria consumers use to evaluate their brands for two reasons. First, as we saw in the opening example, understanding these criteria is essential for developing or communicating appropriate brand features to the target market. In addition, marketers frequently want to influence the evaluative criteria used by consumers.[25]

Measurement of Evaluative Criteria

Before a marketing manager or a public policy decision maker can develop a sound strategy to affect consumer decisions, he or she must determine

- Which evaluative criteria are used by the consumer.
- How the consumer perceives the various alternatives on each criterion.
- The relative importance of each criterion.

Consumers sometimes will not or cannot verbalize their evaluative criteria for a product. Therefore, it is often difficult to determine which criteria they are using in a particular brand-choice decision, particularly if emotions or feelings are involved. This is even more of a problem when trying to determine the relative importance they attach to each evaluative criterion.

Determination of Which Evaluative Criteria Are Used   To determine which criteria are used by consumers in a specific product decision, the marketing researcher can utilize either *direct* or *indirect* methods of measurement. *Direct* methods include asking consumers what criteria they use in a particular purchase or, in a focus group setting, noting what consumers say about products and their attributes. Of course, direct measurement techniques assume that consumers can and will provide data on the desired attributes.

In the research that led to the development of Sunbeam's new food processor line, consumers readily described their desired product features and benefits. However, direct questioning is not always as successful. For example, Hanes Corporation suffered substantial losses ($30 million) on its L'erin cosmetics line when, *in response to consumer interviews,* it positioned it as a functional rather than a romantic or emotional product. Eventually, the brand was successfully repositioned as glamorous and exotic, although consumers did not *express* these as desired attributes.[26]

Indirect measurement techniques differ from direct in that they assume consumers will not or cannot state their evaluative criteria. Hence, frequent use is made of indirect methods such as **projective techniques** (see Table 10–2, page 364), which allow the respondent to indicate the criteria someone else might use. The "someone else" will likely be a projection of the respondent, of course—thus, the marketer can indirectly determine the evaluative criteria that would be used.

Perceptual mapping is another useful indirect technique for determining evaluative criteria. First, consumers judge the similarity of alternative brands. This generally involves the consumer looking at possible pairs of brands and indicating which pair is most similar, which is second most similar, and so forth until all pairs are ranked. These similarity judgments are processed via a computer to derive a perceptual map of the brands. No evaluative criteria are specified by the consumer. The consumer simply ranks the similarity between all pairs of alternatives, and a perceptual configuration is derived in which the consumer's still unnamed evaluative criteria are the dimensions of the configuration.

For example, consider the perceptual map of beers shown in Figure 16–2. This configuration was derived from a consumer's evaluation of the relative similarity of these brands of beer. The horizontal axis is characterized by physical characteristics such as taste, calories, and fullness. The vertical axis is characterized by price, quality, and status. Naming each axis, and thus each evaluative criterion, is done using judgment. This procedure allows marketers to understand consumers' perceptions and the evaluative criteria they use to differentiate brands.

FIGURE 16–2   **Perceptual Mapping of Beer Brand Perceptions**

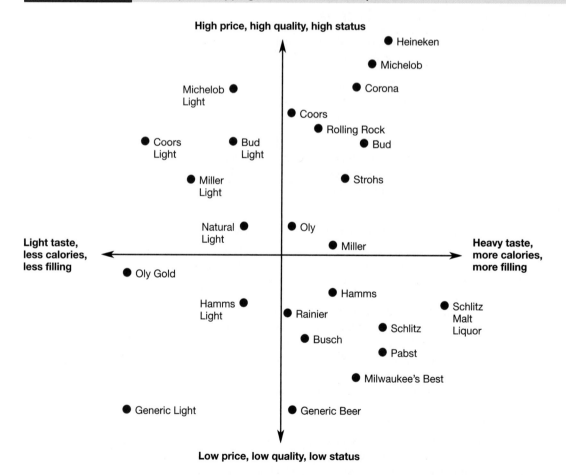

There may be attributes that consumers consider important but that they do not use in choosing among brands.[27] Such attributes will generally not be discovered in the techniques we have described. This situation would occur when consumers consider all brands either to be equivalent on the attribute or to be above their desired level. Thus, a consumer might consider all brands of bottled water to be safe to drink (not contaminated). Therefore, they do not use this as a criterion when comparing brands.

Determination of Consumers' Judgments of Brand Performance on Specific Evaluative Criteria   A variety of methods are available for measuring consumers' judgments of brand performance on specific attributes. These include *rank ordering scales, semantic differential scales,* and *Likert scales* (see Appendix A). The semantic differential scale is probably the most widely used technique (see Table 11–1).

None of these techniques are very effective at measuring emotional responses to products or brands. Projective techniques can provide some insights. However, BBDO's Emotional Measurement System and the other approaches designed to measure emotional responses to ads (see Chapter 10) can be adapted to measure responses to products as well.

Determination of the Relative Importance of Evaluative Criteria   The importance assigned to evaluative criteria can be measured either by direct or by indirect methods. No matter which technique is used, the usage situation should be specified as attribute importance varies with the situation. The **constant sum scale** is the most common method of direct measurement (see Chapter 11, page 389).

The most popular indirect measurement approach is **conjoint analysis.** In conjoint analysis, the consumer is presented with a set of products or product descriptions in which the evaluative criteria vary. For example, the consumer may be presented with the description of 24 different notebook computers that vary on four criteria. Two might be

Pentium 4 2.0 GHz	Pentium 4 1.6 GHz
Integrated modem	No modem
5.1 pounds	3.0 pounds
$2,500	$2,000

The consumer ranks all 24 such descriptions in terms of his or her preference for those combinations of features. Using these preference ranks, sophisticated computer programs derive the relative importance consumers assign to each level of each attribute tested (see Appendix B for details).

Conjoint analysis was used in the Sunbeam example that opened this chapter. Sunbeam tested 12 different attributes, such as price, motor power, number of blades, bowl shape, and so forth. As stated earlier, four segments emerged *based on the relative importance of these attributes.* In order of importance, the key attributes for two segments were

Cheap/Large Segment	*Multispeed/Multiuse Segment*
$49.99 price	$99.99 price
4-quart bowl	2-quart bowl
Two speeds	Seven speeds
Seven blades	Functions as blender and mixer
Heavy-duty motor	Cylindrical bowl
Cylindrical bowl	Pouring spout

INDIVIDUAL JUDGMENT AND EVALUATIVE CRITERIA

If you were buying a notebook computer, you would probably make direct comparisons across brands on features such as price, weight, and display clarity. These comparative judgments may not be completely accurate. For example, the display that is the easiest to read in a five-minute trial may not be the easiest to read over a two-hour work session. For other attributes, such as quality, you might not be able to make direct comparisons. Instead, you might rely on brand name or price to indicate quality. The accuracy of direct judgments and the use of one attribute to indicate performance on another (surrogate indicator) are critical issues for marketers.

Accuracy of Individual Judgments

The average consumer is not adequately trained to judge the performance of competing brands on complex evaluative criteria such as quality or durability. For more straightforward criteria, however, most consumers can and do make such judgments. Prices generally can be judged and compared directly. However, even this can be complex. Is a six-pack of 12-ounce cans of Coca-Cola selling for $2.49 a better buy than two liters priced at 99 cents each? Consumer groups have pushed for unit pricing (pricing by common measurements such as cost per ounce) to make such comparisons simpler. The federal truth-in-lending law was passed to facilitate direct price comparisons among alternative lenders.

The ability of an individual to distinguish between similar stimuli is called **sensory discrimination** (see Chapter 8, page 295). This could involve such variables as the sound of stereo systems, the taste of food products, or the clarity of display screens. The minimum amount that one brand can differ from another with the difference still being noticed is referred to as the *just noticeable difference (j.n.d.)*. As we saw in Chapter 8, this ability is not well developed in most consumers. In general, research indicates that *individuals typically do not notice relatively small differences between brands or changes in brand attributes.* In addition, the complexity of many products and services as well as the fact that some aspects of performance can be judged only after extensive use makes accurate brand comparisons difficult.[28]

The inability of consumers to accurately evaluate many products can result in inappropriate purchases (buying a lower-quality product at a higher price than necessary).[29] This is a major concern of regulatory agencies and consumer groups as well as for marketers of high-value brands.

Use of Surrogate Indicators

Consumers frequently use an observable attribute of a product to indicate the performance of the product on a less observable attribute.[30] For example, most consumers use price as a guide to the quality of at least some products. *An attribute used to stand for or indicate another attribute* is known as a **surrogate indicator.**

Consumers' reliance on an attribute as a surrogate indicator of another attribute is a function of its predictive value and confidence value.[31] *Predictive value* refers to the consumer's perception that one attribute is an accurate predictor of the other. *Confidence value* refers to the consumer's ability to distinguish between brands on the surrogate indicator. Thus, a consumer might believe that ingredients accurately indicate (high predictive value)

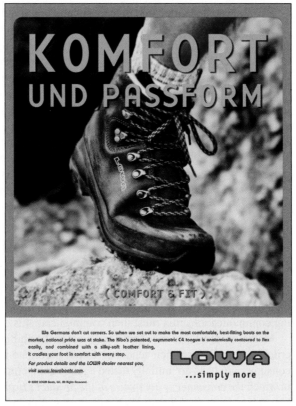

Lowa Boots LLC.

the nutritional value of foods but not use them as indicators because of an inability to make the complex between-brand comparisons (low confidence value).

Perhaps the most widely used surrogate indicator, due in part to its high confidence value, is *price*. Price has been found to influence the perceived quality of shirts, radios, and aftershave lotion, appliances, carpeting, automobiles, and numerous other product categories.[32] These influences have been large, but as might be expected, they decline with increases in visible product differences, prior product use, and additional product information. Unfortunately, for many products the relationship between price and functional measures of quality is low.[33] Thus, consumers using price as a surrogate for quality frequently make suboptimal purchases.

Brand name often is used as a surrogate indicator of quality. It has been found to be very important when it is the only information the consumer has available and to interact with or, on occasion, replace the impact of price.[34] Firms with a limited reputation can sometimes form brand alliances with a reputable firm and gain from the quality associated with the known brand. Thus, New Brand Ice Cream with M&Ms would gain from M&Ms quality image.[35]

Country of manufacture is another widely used indicator of quality.[36] Would you prefer a stereo made in Japan or in Russia? Most consumers would assume the stereo from Japan to be superior. Since many consumers cannot directly judge the quality of products such as stereos, country of manufacture can be an important quality cue. Illustration 16–6 shows how Lowa takes advantage of Germany's reputation for engineering and manufacturing excellence.

Warranties are another cue that consumers use to indicate quality. The longer and more inclusive the warranty, the better the quality of the product is assumed to be.[37] *Advertised brands and services* are often assumed to be superior to unadvertised brands.[38] Likewise, *national brands* are frequently considered to be superior to store brands.[39] Packaging, color, and style have also been found to affect perceptions of quality.

Surrogate indicators are based on consumers' beliefs that two features such as price level and quality level generally go together. Consumers also form beliefs that certain variables do not go together—such as *lightweight* and *strong, rich taste* and *low calories,* and *high fiber* and *high protein.*[40] Marketers attempting to promote the presence of two or more variables that many consumers believe to be mutually exclusive have a high risk of failure unless very convincing messages are used. Thus, it is important for marketers to fully understand consumers' beliefs about the feasible relationships of attributes related to their products.

Evaluative Criteria, Individual Judgments, and Marketing Strategy

Obviously, marketers must understand the evaluative criteria consumers use relative to their products and develop products that excel on these features. All aspects of the marketing communications mix must then communicate this excellence.

Marketers must also recognize and react to the ability of individuals to judge evaluative criteria, as well as to their tendency to use surrogate indicators. For example, most new consumer products are initially tested against competitors in **blind tests.** A blind test is one in which *the consumer is not aware of the product's brand name.* Such tests enable the marketer to evaluate the functional characteristics of the product and to determine if an advantage over a particular competitor has been obtained without the contaminating, or halo, effects of the brand name or the firm's reputation.

Marketers also make direct use of surrogate indicators. Andecker is advertised as "the most expensive taste in beer." This is an obvious attempt to utilize the price–quality relationship that many consumers believe exists for beer. On occasion, prices are raised to increase sales because of the presumed price–quality relationship. For example, a new mustard packaged in a crockery jar did not achieve significant sales priced at 49 cents, but it did at $1.[41]

Marketers frequently use brand names as an indicator of quality. Elmer's glue emphasized the well-established reputation of its brand in promoting a new super glue (ads for Elmer's Wonder Bond said "Stick with a name you can trust"). "Intel Inside" is found on many brands of personal computers. Other firms stress "Made in America," "Italian Styling," or "German Engineering."

Other types of surrogate indicators are also used. A marketer stressing the rich taste of a milk product, for example, would likely want to make it cream colored rather than white, and a hot, spicy sauce would be colored red. A high-quality package signals product quality to many consumers.

DECISION RULES FOR ATTRIBUTE-BASED CHOICES

As we describe some of the choice rules consumers use to select among alternatives, remember that these rules are representations of imprecise and often nonconscious or low-effort mental processes. The following example is a good representation of a consumer using a complex choice rule (compensatory with one attribute weighted heavily):

> I really liked the Ford [minivan] a lot, but it had the back tailgate that lifted up instead of the doors that opened. I suspect that if that had been available we might have gone with the Ford instead because it was real close between the Ford and the GM. The lift gate in the back was the main difference, and we went with the General Motors because we liked the doors opening the way they did. I loved the way the Ford was designed on the inside. I loved the way it drove. I loved the way it felt and everything, but you are there manipulating all these kids and groceries and things and you have got to lift this thing, and it was very awkward. It was hard to lift, and if you are holding something you have got to steer all the kids back, or whack them in the head. So that was a big thing. You know it was a lot cheaper than the GM. It was between $1,000 and $2,000 less than General Motors, and because money was a factor, we did go ahead and actually at one point talk money with a [Ford] dealer. But we couldn't get the price difference down to where I was willing to deal with that tailgate is what it comes down to.[42]

Despite the fact that the choice rules we describe are not precise representations of consumer decisions, they do enhance our understanding of how consumers make decisions and provide guidance for marketing strategy.

Suppose you have six notebook computers in your evoked set and that you have assessed them on six evaluative criteria: price, weight, processor, battery life, after-sale support, and display quality. Further, suppose that each brand excels on one attribute but falls short on one or more of the remaining attributes, as shown in Table 16–1.

Which brand would you select? The answer would depend on the decision rule you utilize. Consumers commonly use five decision rules: conjunctive, disjunctive, elimination-by-aspects, lexicographic, and compensatory. More than one rule may be used in any given decision. The most common instance of this is using a relatively simple rule to reduce the number of alternatives considered and then to apply a more complex rule to choose among the remaining options.[43] An example would be eliminating from consideration all those apartments that are too far from campus or that rent for more than $700 per month (conjunctive decision rule). The choice from among the remaining apartments might involve carefully trading off among features such as convenience of location, price, presence of a pool, size of rooms, and so forth (compensatory rule).

The first four rules we will describe are *noncompensatory* rules. This means that a high level of one attribute cannot offset a low level of another. In the apartment example, the consumer would not consider an apartment that was right next to campus if it cost more than $700 per month. An excellent location could not compensate for an inappropriate price. In contrast, the last rule we will describe is a *compensatory* rule in which consumers average across attribute levels. This allows a high level of one value to offset a low value of another.

Evaluative Criteria	Consumer Perceptions*					
	WinBook	HP	Compaq	Dell	IBM	Toshiba
Price	5	3	3	4	2	1
Weight	3	4	5	4	3	4
Processor	5	5	5	2	5	5
Battery life	1	3	1	3	1	5
After-sale support	3	3	4	3	5	3
Display quality	3	3	3	5	3	3

TABLE 16–1

Performance Levels on the Evaluative Criteria for Six Notebook Computers

*1 = Very poor; 5 = Very good.

Finally, note that the conjunctive and disjunctive decision rules may produce a set of acceptable alternatives, whereas the remaining rules generally produce a single "best" alternative.

Conjunctive Decision Rule

The **conjunctive decision rule** *establishes minimum required performance standards for each evaluative criterion and selects the first or all brands that surpass these minimum standards.* Thus, in making the decision on the computer, you would say, "I'll consider all (or I'll buy the first) brands that are all right on the attributes I think are important." For example, assume that the following represent your minimum standards:

Price	3
Weight	4
Processor	3
Battery life	1
After-sale support	2
Display quality	3

Any brand of computer falling below *any* of these minimum standards (cutoff points) would be eliminated from further consideration. Referring to Table 16–1, we can see that four computers are eliminated—IBM, WinBook, Dell, and Toshiba. These are the computers that failed to meet *all* the minimum standards. Under these circumstances, the two remaining brands may be equally satisfying. Or you might use another decision rule to select a single brand from these two alternatives.

Because individuals have limited ability to process information, the conjunctive rule is frequently used to reduce the size of the information processing task to some manageable level. This is often done in the purchase of such products as homes, computers, and bicycles; in the rental of apartments; or in the selection of vacation options. A conjunctive rule is used to eliminate alternatives that are out of a consumer's price range, are outside the location preferred, or do not offer other desired features. After eliminating those alternatives not providing these features, the consumer may use another decision rule to make a brand choice among those remaining alternatives that satisfy these minimum standards.

The conjunctive decision rule is commonly used in many low-involvement purchases as well. In such a purchase, the consumer generally evaluates a set of brands one at a time and selects the first brand that meets all the minimum requirements.

If the conjunctive decision rule is used by a target market, it is critical to surpass the consumers' minimum requirement on each criterion. For low-involvement purchases, consumers often purchase the first brand that does so. For such products, extensive distribution and dominant shelf space are important. It is also necessary to understand how consumers "break ties" if the first satisfactory option is not chosen. The ad in Illustration 16–7 assures consumers that the Motorola Talkabout has every feature they might need.

Disjunctive Decision Rule

The **disjunctive decision rule** *establishes a minimum level of performance for each important attribute* (often a fairly high level). All brands that surpass the performance level for *any* key attribute are considered acceptable. Using this rule, you would say, "I'll consider all (or buy the first) brands that perform really well on any attribute I consider to be

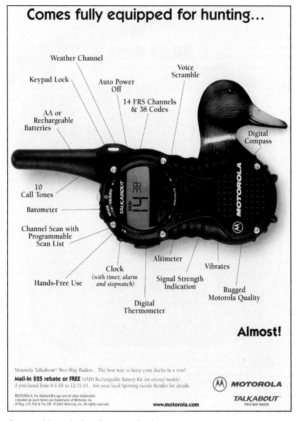

Courtesy Motorola, Inc. Consumer Products.

ILLUSTRATION 16–7

This ad assures consumers that the Talkabout has every feature they might need. This is consistent with consumers using a conjunctive decision rule.

important." Assume that you are using a disjunctive decision rule and the attribute cutoff points shown below:

Price	5
Weight	5
Processor	Not critical
Battery life	Not critical
After-sale support	Not critical
Display quality	5

You would find WinBook (price), Compaq (weight), and Dell (display quality) to warrant further consideration (see Table 16–1). As with the conjunctive decision rule, you might purchase the first brand you find acceptable, use another decision rule to choose among the three, or add additional criteria to your list.

When the disjunctive decision rule is used by a target market, it is critical to surpass the consumers' requirements on at least one of the key criteria. This should be emphasized in advertising messages and on the product package. Because consumers often purchase the first brand that exceeds one of the requirements, extensive distribution and dominant shelf space are important. Again, it is also necessary to understand how consumers break ties if the first satisfactory option is not chosen. Illustration 16–8 stresses one important attribute of the Eureka Mountain Pass tent—speed of setting up.

Printed with permission of the Eureka!® Tent Brand, Johnson Outdoors, Inc.

Elimination-by-Aspects Decision Rule

The **elimination-by-aspects decision rule** *requires the consumer to rank the evaluative criteria in terms of their importance and to establish a cutoff point for each criterion.* All brands are first considered on the most important criterion. Those that do not surpass the cutoff point are dropped from consideration. If more than one brand passes the cutoff point, the process is repeated on those brands for the second most important criterion. This continues until only one brand remains. Thus, the consumer's logic is, "I want to buy the brand that has a high level of an important attribute that other brands do not have."

Consider the rank order and cutoff points shown below. What would you choose using the elimination-by-aspects rule?

	Rank	Cutoff Point
Price	1	3
Weight	2	4
Display quality	3	4
Processor	4	3
After-sale support	5	3
Battery life	6	3

Price would eliminate IBM and Toshiba (see Table 16–1). Of those remaining, Compaq, HP, and Dell surpass the weight hurdle (WinBook is eliminated). Notice that Toshiba also exceeds the minimum weight requirement but would not be considered because it had been

Finally, a maximum strength anti-perspirant that helps prevent shaving irritation.

Introducing Ban Beautifully Smooth.

Courtesy The Andrew Jergens Company.

eliminated in the initial consideration of price. Only Dell exceeds the third requirement, display quality.

Using the elimination-by-aspects rule, you end up with a choice that has all the desired features of all the other alternatives, plus one more.

For a target market using the elimination-by-aspects rule, it is critical to surpass the consumers' requirements on one more (in order) of the criteria used than the competition. This competitive superiority should be emphasized in advertising messages and on the product package. Firms can also attempt to alter the relative importance that consumers assign to the evaluative criteria. The ad in Illustration 16–9 is consistent with this rule. It indicates that Ban Beautifully Soft has maximum strength (as do competitors) but also prevents shaving irritation (which other maximum-strength antiperspirants do not).

Lexicographic Decision Rule

The **lexicographic decision rule** *requires the consumer to rank the criteria in order of importance*. The consumer then selects the brand that performs *best* on the most important attribute. If two or more brands tie on this attribute, they are evaluated on the second most important attribute. This continues through the attributes until one brand outperforms the others. The consumer's thinking is something like this: "I want to get the brand that does best on the attribute of most importance to me. If there is a tie, I'll break it by choosing the one that does best on my second most important criterion."

Courtesy Orbitz.

The lexicographic decision rule is similar to the elimination-by-aspects rule. The difference is that the lexicographic rule seeks maximum performance at each stage, whereas the elimination-by-aspects seeks satisfactory performance at each stage. Thus, using the lexicographic rule and the data from the elimination-by-aspects example above would result in the selection of WinBook, because it has the best performance on the most important attribute. Had WinBook been rated a 4 on price, it would be tied with Dell. Then, Dell would be chosen based on its superior weight rating.

When this rule is being used by a target market, the firm should try to be superior to the competition on *the* key attribute. This competitive superiority should be emphasized in advertising. It is essential that the product at least equal the performance of all other competitors on the most important criterion. Outstanding performance on lesser criteria will not matter if a competitor is superior on the most important attribute. If a competitive advantage is not possible on the most important feature, attention should be shifted to the second most important (assuming equal importance on the most important one). If it is not possible to meet or beat the competition on the key attribute, the firm must attempt to make another attribute more important.

The ad shown in Illustration 16–10 emphasizes that Orbitz has more low fares than any other travel site. This ad would be particularly effective for consumers who use a lexicographic rule and consider low fares as the most important attribute.

Compensatory Decision Rule

The four previous rules are *noncompensatory* decision rules, because very good performance on one evaluative criterion cannot compensate for poor performance on another evaluative criterion. On occasion, consumers may wish to average out some very good features with some less attractive features of a product in determining overall brand preference. Consider the following example:

> PepsiCo's Frito-Lay will introduce a new single-serve canister line called Go Snacks this January backed by $60 million in marketing in hopes that consumers' desire for convenience outweighs their concern for price.[44]

The new snacks will be in a single-serving size container with resealable cup lids designed to fit easily into car beverage-holders as well as backpacks and lunch boxes. However, it will be priced at $1.29 per serving, which is more than many large bags of chips cost. Frito-Lay knows that price is important to customers but believes that the added convenience of the new packaging will more than offset the higher price. That is, it assumes its target market will use a compensatory decision rule for this product.

The **compensatory decision rule** states that *the brand that rates highest on the sum of the consumer's judgments of the relevant evaluative criteria will be chosen.* This can be illustrated as

$$R_b = \sum_{i=1}^{n} W_i B_{ib}$$

where

R_b = Overall rating of brand b

W_i = Importance or weight attached to evaluative criterion i

B_{ib} = Evaluation of brand b on evaluative criterion i

n = Number of evaluative criteria considered relevant

This is the same as the multiattribute attitude model described in Chapter 11. If you used the relative importance scores shown below, which brand would you choose using the compensatory rule?

	Importance Score
Price	30
Weight	25
Processor	10
Battery life	05
After-sale support	10
Display quality	20
Total	100

Using this rule, Dell has the highest preference (see Table 16–1). The calculations for Dell are as follows:

$$R_{\text{Dell}} = 30(4) + 25(4) + 10(2) + 5(3) + 10(3) + 20(5)$$
$$= 120 + 100 + 20 + 15 + 30 + 100$$
$$= 385$$

Products and services targeting consumers likely to use a compensatory rule can offset low performance on some features with relatively high performance on others. However, it is important to have a performance level at or near the competition on the more important features because they receive more weight in the decision than do other attributes. Recall the description of the minivan purchase from the beginning of this section. This customer preferred most of the features of the Ford but bought the GM because Ford was very weak on one key attribute. However, the consumer did express a willingness to change the decision had the price differential been greater. Thus, for compensatory decisions, the total mix of the relevant attributes must be considered to be superior to those of the competition.

Summary of Decision Rules

As shown below, each decision rule yields a somewhat different choice. Therefore, marketers must understand which decision rules are being used by target consumers in order to position a product within this decision framework.

Decision Rule	Brand Choice
Conjunctive	HP, Compaq
Disjunctive	Dell, Compaq, WinBook
Elimination-by-aspects	Dell
Lexicographic	WinBook
Compensatory	Dell

Research clearly indicates that people do use these decision rules.[45] Low-involvement purchases generally involve relatively simple decision rules (conjunctive, disjunctive, elimination-by-aspects, or lexicographic), because consumers will attempt to minimize the mental cost of such decisions.[46] High-involvement decisions and purchases involving considerable perceived risk tend to increase evaluation efforts and often may involve not only more complex rules (compensatory) but stages of decision making, with different attributes being evaluated using different rules at each stage.[47] Of course, individual, product, and situational characteristics also influence the type of decision rule used.[48]

A marketing manager must first determine which rule or combination of rules the target consumers will most likely use in a particular purchase situation; then develop the appropriate marketing strategy.

SUMMARY

During and after the time that consumers gather information about various alternative solutions to a recognized problem, they evaluate the alternatives and select the course of action that seems most likely to solve the problem. Consumer choices are sometimes based on extremely simple decision rules such as "buy the cheapest brand available." At other times, they are extremely complex, involving multiple stages and processes.

There are a number of ways consumers make choices. *Affective choice* is most likely when the underlying motive is consummatory rather than instrumental. *Consummatory motives* underlie behaviors that are intrinsically rewarding to the individual involved. *Instrumental motives* activate behaviors designed to achieve a second goal.

Affective choice tends to be holistic in nature. The brand is not decomposed into distinct components, each of which is evaluated separately from the whole. The evaluation of such products is generally focused on the way they will make the user *feel* as they are used.

Decisions based on affect are said to use the "How do I feel about it" heuristic or decision rule. Consumers imagine or picture using the product or service and evaluate the feeling that this use will produce.

Attribute-based choice requires the knowledge of the specific attributes of the alternatives at the time the choice is made, and it involves attribute-by-attribute comparisons across brands. *Attitude-based choice* involves the use of general attitudes, summary impressions, intuitions, or heuristics; no attribute-by-attribute comparisons are made at the time of choice. There can also be combinations of these forms. A common combination would be for overall preferences to be formed using attitude-based processing, with the final choice being made on the basis of a brand-by-brand comparison on the price attribute.

Rational choice theory assumes a rational decision maker with well-defined preferences that do not depend on how the options are presented. Each option or alternative in a choice set is assumed to have a value to the consumer that depends only on the characteristics of that option. The consumer is also assumed to have sufficient skill to calculate which option will maximize his or her value and will choose on this basis.

Although useful, rational choice theory is incomplete. An emerging view is that many choices are constructed by the consumer as the decision is made. All consumers have *bounded rationality*—a limited capacity for processing information. In addition, consumers often have goals that are different from, or in addition to, selecting the optimal alternative. A *metagoal* refers to the general nature of the outcome being sought in a decision. Four metagoals characterize many consumer choices—maximizing the accuracy of the decision, minimizing the cognitive effort required for the decision, minimizing the experience of negative emotion while making the decision, and maximizing the ease with which a decision can be justified. These goals may shift in importance as the consumer moves through the decision process.

Evaluative criteria are the various features or benefits a consumer looks for in response to a specific problem. They are the performance levels or characteristics consumers use to compare different brands in light of their particular consumption problem. The number, type, and importance of evaluative criteria used differ from consumer to consumer and across product categories.

The measurement of (1) which evaluative criteria are used by the consumer, (2) how the consumer perceives the various alternatives on each criterion, and (3) the relative importance of each criterion is a critical first step in utilizing evaluative criteria to develop marketing strategy. The measurement task is not easy; however, a number of techniques ranging from direct questioning to projective techniques and multidimensional scaling are available.

Evaluative criteria such as price, size, and color can be judged easily and accurately by consumers. Other criteria, such as quality, durability, and health benefits, are much more difficult to judge. In such cases, consumers often use price, brand name, or some other variable as a *surrogate indicator* of quality.

When consumers judge alternative brands on several evaluative criteria, they must have some method to select one brand from the various choices. Decision rules serve this function. A decision rule specifies how a consumer compares two or more brands. Five commonly used decision rules are *disjunctive, conjunctive, lexicographic, elimination-by-aspects,* and *compensatory.* The decision rules work best with functional products and cognitive decisions. Marketing managers must be aware of the decision rule(s) used by the target market, because different decision rules require different marketing strategies.

KEY TERMS

Affective choice 557
Attitude-based choice 561
Attribute-based choice 561
Blind tests 570
Bounded rationality 557
Compensatory decision rule 577
Conjoint analysis 567

Conjunctive decision rule 572
Constant sum scale 567
Consummatory motives 559
Disjunctive decision rule 572
Elimination-by-aspects
  decision rule 574
Evaluative criteria 562

Instrumental motives 559
Lexicographic decision rule 575
Metagoal 558
Perceptual mapping 566
Projective techniques 565
Sensory discrimination 568
Surrogate indicator 568

INTERNET EXERCISES

1. Monitor several chat sites or interest groups for a week. Prepare a report on how a marketer could learn about the following used by consumers by doing this.
   a. Evaluative criteria
   b. Decision rules

2. Visit Ski-Europe.com. Use the "Where should I go?" feature to select a ski area for vacation. On what decision rule does this feature appear to be based?

3. Visit K2skis.com. Use the "Ski Selector?" feature to select a ski for your personal use or for a friend. On what decision rule does this feature appear to be based?

4. Visit three websites for brands in the same product category. Using the brand information provided and the manner in which it is provided, determine what decision rule each brand appears to assume its market uses. If there are differences, how would you explain them?

DDB NEEDHAM LIFESTYLE DATA ANALYSES

1. Based on the DDB Needham Tables 1a, 2a, 3a, 4a, 5a, 6a, and 7a, what characterizes individuals who place considerable emphasis on store service as an evaluative criterion? What are the marketing implications of this?

REVIEW QUESTIONS

1. What is *rational choice* theory?
2. What is meant by *bounded rationality?*
3. What is a *metagoal?*
4. What are four common metagoals for consumer decisions?
5. What is *affective choice* and when is it most likely to occur?
6. What is the difference between *consummatory motives* and *instrumental motives?*
7. How does *attribute-based choice* differ from *attitude-based choice?* When is each most likely?
8. What are *evaluative criteria* and on what characteristics can they vary?
9. How can you determine which evaluative criteria consumers use?
10. What methods are available for measuring consumers' judgments of brand performance on specific attributes?

11. How can the importance assigned to evaluative criteria be assessed?
12. What is *sensory discrimination,* and what role does it play in the evaluation of products? What is meant by a *just noticeable difference?*
13. What are *surrogate indicators?* How are they used in the consumer evaluation process?
14. What is the *conjunctive decision rule?*
15. What is the *disjunctive decision rule?*
16. What is the *elimination-by-aspects decision rule?*
17. What is the *lexicographic decision rule?*
18. What is the *compensatory decision rule?*
19. How can knowledge of consumers' evaluative criteria and criteria importance be used in developing marketing strategy?
20. How can knowledge of the decision rules consumers might use in a certain purchase assist a firm in developing marketing strategy?

DISCUSSION QUESTIONS

21. Respond to the questions in Consumer Insight 16–1.

22. Would you use an attribute-based or an attitude-based decision approach to purchasing (or renting or giving to) the following? Which, if any, situational factors would change your approach?

    a. A present for your romantic partner
    b. A movie
    c. A bicycle
    d. A dog
    e. A hairdresser
    f. Athletic shoes
    g. A new facial moisturizer
    h. A weekend pleasure trip
    i. A notebook computer
    j. Habitat for Humanity

23. Repeat Question 22, but speculate on how your instructor would answer. In what ways might his or her answer differ from yours? Why?

27. Repeat Question 26, but speculate on how your instructor would answer. In what ways might his or her answer differ from yours? Why?

28. Describe a purchase decision for which you used affective choice, one for which you used attitude-based choice, and one for which you used attribute-based choice. Why did the type of decision process you used vary?

29. Identify five products for which surrogate indicators may be used as evaluative criteria in a brand choice decision. Why are the indictors used, and how might a firm enhance their use (i.e., strengthen their importance)?

30. The table below represents a particular consumer's evaluative criteria, criteria importance, acceptable level of performance, and judgments of performance with respect to several brands of mopeds. Discuss the brand choice this consumer would make when using the lexicographic, compensatory, and conjunctive decision rules.

Evaluative Criteria	Criteria Importance	Minimum Acceptable Performance	Alternative Brands					
			Motron	Vespa	Cimatti	Garelli	Puch	Motobecane
Price	30	4	2	4	2	4	2	4
Horsepower	15	3	4	2	5	5	4	5
Weight	5	2	3	3	3	3	3	3
Gas economy	35	3	4	4	3	2	4	5
Color selection	10	3	4	4	3	2	5	2
Frame	5	2	4	2	3	3	3	3

Note: 1 = Very poor; 2 = Poor; 3 = Fair; 4 = Good; and 5 = Very good.

24. For which, if any, of the options in Question 22 would you make an affective decision? What role would situational factors play?

25. What metagoals might you have, and what would be their relative importance to you, in purchasing (or renting or giving to) the options in Questions 22?

26. List the evaluative criteria and the importance of each that you would use in purchasing (or renting or giving to) the options in Question 22. Would situational factors change the criteria? The importance weights? Why?

31. Describe the decision rule(s) you used or would use in buying, renting, or giving to the options listed for Question 22. Would you use different rules in different situations? Which ones? Why? Would any of these involve an affective choice?

32. Describe your last two major and your last two minor purchases. What role did emotions or feelings play? How did they differ? What evaluative criteria and decision rules did you use for each? Why?

33. Discuss surrogate indicators that could be used to evaluate the perceived quality of the products or activities listed in Question 22.

APPLICATION ACTIVITIES

34. Interview five students and determine if they use mental budgeting and how it affects their purchase decisions. Do your results support Consumer Insight 16–1? How would you explain any differences?

35. Conduct an extensive interview with two students who recently made a major purchase. Have them describe the process they went through. Report your results. If each represented a market segment, what are the strategy implications?

36. Develop a list of evaluative criteria that students might use in evaluating alternative apartments they might rent. After listing these criteria, go to the local newspaper or student newspaper, select several apartments, and list them in a table similar to the one in Question 30. Then have five other students evaluate this information and have each indicate the apartment they would rent if given only those alternatives. Next, ask them to express the importance they attach to each evaluative criterion, using a 100-point constant sum scale. Finally, provide them with a series of statements that describe different decision rules and ask them to indicate the one that best describes the way they made their choice. Calculate the choice they should have made given their importance ratings and stated decision rules. Have them explain any inconsistent choices. Report your results.

37. Develop a short questionnaire to elicit the evaluative criteria consumers might use in selecting the following. Also, have each respondent indicate the relative importance he or she attaches to each of the evaluative criteria. Then, working with several other students, combine your information and develop a segmentation strategy based on consumer evaluative criteria and criteria importance. Finally, develop an advertisement for each market segment to indicate that their needs would be served by your brand.
    a. Bicycle
    b. Jeans
    c. Movie
    d. Nice restaurant
    e. Notebook computer
    f. Charity
    g. Pet
    h. Health club

38. Set up a taste-test experiment to determine if volunteer taste testers can perceive a just noticeable difference between three different brands of the following. To set up the experiment, store each test brand in a separate but identical container and label the containers L, M, and N. Provide volunteer taste testers with an adequate opportunity to evaluate each brand before asking them to state their identification of the actual brands represented as L, M, and N. Evaluate the results and discuss the marketing implications of these results.
    a. Colas
    b. Diet colas
    c. Lemon-lime drinks
    d. Carbonated waters
    e. Chips
    f. Orange juices

39. For a product considered high in social status, develop a questionnaire that measures the evaluative criteria of that product, using both a *direct* and an *indirect* method of measurement. Compare the results and discuss their similarities and differences and which evaluative criteria are most likely to be utilized in brand choice.

40. Find and copy or describe an ad that uses a surrogate indicator. Is it effective? Why? Why do you think the firm uses this approach?

41. Find and copy or describe an ad that attempts to change the importance consumers assign to product class evaluative criteria. Is it effective? Why? Why do you think the firm uses this approach?

42. Find and copy or describe two ads that are based on affective choice. Why do you think the firm uses this approach? Are the ads effective? Why?

43. Interview a salesperson for one of the following products. Ascertain the evaluative criteria, importance weights, decision rules, and surrogate indicators that he or she believes consumers use when purchasing this product. What marketing implications are suggested if their beliefs are accurate for large segments?
    a. Inexpensive new cars
    b. Kitchen furniture
    c. Notebook computers
    d. Cosmetics
    e. Ski clothes
    f. Fine art

REFERENCES

1. A. L. Page and H. F. Rosenbaum, "Redesigning Product Lines with Conjoint Analysis," *Journal of Product Innovation Management,* no. 4 (1987), pp. 120–37.

2. J. R. Doyle et al., "The Robustness of the Asymmetrically Dominated Effect," *Psychology & Marketing,* May 1999, pp. 225–43; M. Bhargava, J. Kim, and R. K. Srivastava, "Explaining Context Effects on Choice Using a Model of Comparative Judgment," *Journal of Consumer Psychology* 9, no. 3 (2000), pp. 167–77; and R. Dhar, S. M. Nowlis, and S. J. Sherman, "Trying Hard or Hardly Trying," *Journal of Consumer Psychology* 9, no. 4 (2000), pp. 189–200.

3. B. Mittal, "A Study of the Concept of Affective Choice Mode for Consumer Decisions," in *Advances in Consumer Research,* vol. 21, eds. C. T. Allen and D. R. John (Provo, UT: Association for Consumer Research, 1994), p. 256.

4. J. R. Bettman, M. F. Luce, and J. W. Payne, "Constructive Consumer Choice Processes," *Journal of Consumer Research,* December 1998, pp. 187–217.

5. See C. A. Mandrik, "Consumer Heuristics," *Advances in Consumer Research,* vol. 23, eds. K. P. Corfman and J. G. Lynch (Provo, UT: Association for Consumer Research, 1996), pp. 301–07; and J. Swait and W. Adamowicz, "The Influence of Task Complexity on Consumer Choice," *Journal of Consumer Research,* June 2001, pp. 135–48.

6. See R. Dhar and S. M. Nowlis, "The Effects of Time Pressure on Consumer Choice Deferral," *Journal of Consumer Research,* March 1999, pp. 369–84.

7. See E. C. Garbarino and J. A. Edell, "Cognitive Effort, Affect, and Choice," *Journal of Consumer Research,* September 1997, pp. 147–58; M. F. Luce, "Choosing to Avoid," *Journal of Consumer Research,* March 1998, pp. 409–33; and M. F. Luce, J. W. Payne, and J. R. Bettman, "Emotional Trade-Off Difficulty and Choice," *Journal of Marketing Research,* May 1999, pp. 143–59.

8. See C. L. Brown and G. S. Carpenter, "Why Is the Trivial Important?" *Journal of Consumer Research,* March 2000, pp. 372–85.

9. J. F. Durgee and G. C. O'Connor, "Why Some Products 'Just Feel Right'" in *Advances in Consumer Research,* vol. 22, eds. F. R. Kardes and M. Sujan (Provo, UT: Association for Consumer Research, 1995), p. 652.

10. See M. T. Pham et al., "Affect Monitoring and the Primacy of Feelings in Judgment," *Journal of Consumer Research,* September 2001, pp. 167–87.

11. M. T. Pham, "Representativeness, Relevance, and the Use of Feelings in Decision Making," *Journal of Consumer Research,* September 1998, pp. 144–59.

12. See also R. Dhar and K. Wertenbroch, "Consumer Choice between Hedonic and Utilitarian Goods," *Journal of Marketing Research,* February 2000, pp. 60–71.

13. See B. Shiv and A. Fedorikhin, "Heart and Mind in Conflict," *Journal of Consumer Research,* December 1999, pp. 278–91.

14. J. A. Ruth, "Promoting a Brand's Emotional Benefits," *Journal of Consumer Psychology* 11, no. 2 (2001), pp. 99–113.

15. See P. Krishnamurthy and M. Sujan, "Retrospection versus Anticipation," *Journal of Consumer Research,* June 1999, pp. 55–69. See also B. Shiv and J. Huber, "The Impact of Anticipating Satisfaction on Consumer Choice," *Journal of Consumer Research,* September 2000, pp. 202–16.

16. This section is based on S. P. Mantell and F. R. Kardes, "The Role of Direction of Comparison, Attribute-Based Processing, an Attitude-Based Processing in Consumer Preference," *Journal of Consumer Research,* March 1999, pp. 335–52.

17. See R. Dhar, S. M. Nowlis, and S. J. Sherman, "Comparison Effects on Preference Construction," *Journal of Consumer Research,* December 1999, pp. 293–306.

18. P. H. Bloch, "Seeking the Ideal Form," *Journal of Marketing,* July 1995, pp. 16–29; and Dhar and Wertenbroch, "Consumer Choice."

19. G. Kalyanaram and J. D. C. Little, "An Empirical Analysis of Latitude of Price Acceptance in Consumer Package Goods," *Journal of Consumer Research,* December 1994, pp. 408–18.

20. See S. Hoeffler and D. Ariely, "Constructing Stable Preferences," *Journal of Consumer Psychology* 8, no. 2 (1999), pp. 113–39; and A. V. Muthukrishnan and F. R. Kardes, "Persistent Preferences for Product Attributes," *Journal of Consumer Research,* June 2001, pp. 89–102.

21. D. J. Mitchell, B. E. Kahn, and S. C. Knasko, "There's Something in the Air," *Journal of Consumer Research,* September 1995, pp. 229–38; D. R. Lichtenstein, R. G. Netemeyer, and S. Burton, "Assessing the Domain Specificity of Deal Proneness," *Journal of Consumer Research,* December 1995, pp. 314–26; D. R. Lichtenstein, S. Burton, and R. G. Netemeyer, "An Examination of Deal Proneness across Sales Promotion Types," *Journal of Retailing,* no. 2 (1997), pp. 283–97; and V. Ramaswamy and S. S. Srinivasan, "Coupon Characteristics and Redemption Intentions," *Psychology & Marketing,* January 1998, pp. 50–80.

22. See A. Ostrom and D. Iacobucci, "Consumer Trade-Offs and the Evaluation of Services," *Journal of Marketing,* January 1995, pp. 17–28; R. Dhar and I. Simonson, "Making Complementary Choices in Consumption Episodes," *Journal of Marketing Research,* February 1999, pp. 29–44; and J. K. H. Lee and J. H. Steckel, "Consumer Strategies for Purchasing Assortments within a Single Product Class," *Journal of Retailing* 75, no. 3 (1999), pp. 387–403.

23. See M. Abe, "Measuring Consumer, Nonlinear Brand Choice Response to Price," *Journal of Retailing* 74, no. 4 (1998), pp. 541–68.

24. B. L. Bagus, "The Consumer Durable Replacement Buyer," *Journal of Marketing,* January 1991, pp. 42–51.

25. A. Kirmani and P. Wright, "Procedural Learning, Consumer Decision Making, and Marketing Choice," *Marketing Letters* 4, no. 1 (1993), pp. 39–48; G. S. Carpenter, R. Glazer, and K. Nakamoto, "Meaningful Brands from Meaningless Differentiation," *Journal of Marketing Research,* August 1994, pp. 339–50; and S. M. Broniarczyk and A. D. Gershoff, "Meaningless Differentiation Revisited," *Advances in Consumer Research,* vol. 24, eds. M. Bruck and D. J. MacInnis

(Provo, UT: Association for Consumer Research, 1997), pp. 223–28.

26.   B. Abrams, "Hanes Finds L'eggs Methods Don't Work with Cosmetics," *The Wall Street Journal,* February 3, 1983, p. 33.

27.   See R. Dhar and S. J. Sherman, "The Effect of Common and Unique Features in Consumer Choice," *Journal of Consumer Research,* December 1996, pp. 193–203; and A. Chernev, "The Effect of Common Features on Brand Choice," *Journal of Consumer Research,* March 1997, pp. 304–11.

28.   See S. H. Ang, G. J. Gorn, and C. B. Weinberg, "The Evaluation of Time-Dependent Attributes," *Psychology & Marketing,* January 1996, pp. 19–35.

29.   P. M. Parker, "Sweet Lemons," *Journal of Marketing Research,* August 1995, pp. 291–307.

30.   See A. Kirmani and A. R. Rao, "No Pain, No Gain," *Journal of Marketing,* April 2000, pp. 66–79.

31.   See N. Dawar and P. Parker, "Marketing Universals," *Journal of Marketing,* April 1994, pp. 81–95.

32.   D. R. Lichtenstein, N. M. Ridgway, and R. G. Netemeyer, "Price Perceptions and Consumer Shopping Behavior," *Journal of Marketing Research,* May 1993, pp. 234–45; T.-Z. Chang and A. R. Wildt, "Impact of Product Information on the Use of Price as a Quality Cue," *Psychology & Marketing,* January 1996, pp. 55–75; and G. S. Bobinski, Jr., D. Cox, and A. Cox, "Retail 'Sale' Advertising, Perceived Retailer Credibility, and Price Rationale," *Journal of Retailing,* no. 3 (1996), pp. 391–406.

33.   S. Burton and D. R. Lichtenstein, "Assessing the Relationship between Perceived and Objective Price-Quality," in *Advances in Consumer Research,* vol. 27, eds. M. E. Goldberg, G. Gorn, and R. W. Pollay (Provo, UT: Association for Consumer Research, 1990), pp. 715–22; and D. J. Faulds, O. Grunewald, and D. Johnson, "A Cross-National Investigation of the Relationship between the Price and Quality of Consumer Products," *Journal of Global Marketing* 8, no. 1 (1994), pp. 7–25.

34.   See P. S. Richardson, A. S. Dick, and A. K. Jain, "Extrinsic and Intrinsic Cue Effects on Perceptions of Store Brand Quality," *Journal of Marketing,* October 1994, pp. 28–36.

35.   A. R. Rao, L. Qu, and R. W. Ruekert, "Signaling Unobservable Product Quality through a Brand Ally," *Journal of Marketing Research,* May 1999, pp. 258–68; and C. Janiszewski and S. M. J. van Osselaer, "A Connectionist Model of Brand-Quality Associations," *Journal of Marketing Research,* August 2000, pp. 331–50.

36.   G. R. Iyer and J. K. Kalita, "The Impact of Country-of-Origin and Country-of-Manufacture Cues on Consumer Perceptions of Quality and Value," *Journal of Global Marketing,* no. 1 (1997), pp. 7–28; L. A. Manrai et al., "How Green-Claim Strength and Country Disposition Affect Product Evaluation and Company Image," *Psychology & Marketing,* August 1997, pp. 511–37; S. Janda and C. P. Rao, "The Effect of Country-of-Origin Related Stereotypes and Personal Beliefs on Product Evaluation," *Psychology & Marketing,* October 1997, pp. 689–702; F. M. Ulgado and M. Lee, "The Korean versus American Marketplace," *Psychology & Marketing,* September 1998, pp. 595–614; B. E. Richey, P. B. Rose, L. Dominguez,

"Perceived Value of Mexican vs. U.S. Products," *Journal of Global Marketing* 13, no. 2 (1999), pp. 49–65; G. Haubl and T. Elrod, "The Impact of Congruity between Brand Name and Country of Production," *International Journal of Research in Marketing,* September 1999, pp. 199–215; P. W. J. Verlegh and J.-B. E. M. Steenkamp, "A Review and Meta-Analysis of Country-of-Origin Research," *Journal of Economic Psychology* 20 (1999), pp. 521–46; R. Batra et al., "Effects of Brand and Nonlocal Origin," *Journal of Consumer Psychology* 9, no. 2 (2000), pp. 83–95; Z. Gurhan-Canli and D. Maheswaran, "Determinants of Country-of-Origin Evaluations," *Journal of Consumer Research,* June 2000, pp. 96–108; and C. W. Lee, Y. Suh, and B.-J. Moon, "Product-Country Images," *Journal of International Consumer Marketing* 13, no. 3 (2001), pp. 47–62.

37.   See W. Boulding and A. Kirmani, "A Consumer-Side Experimental Examination of Signaling Theory," *Journal of Consumer Research,* June 1993, pp. 11–23; and D. Purohit and J. Srivastava, "Effect of Manufacturer Reputation, Retailer Reputation, and Product Warranty on Consumer Judgments of Product Quality," *Journal of Consumer Psychology* 10, no. 3 (2001), pp. 123–34.

38.   J. E. Urbany et al., "Do Buyers Believe That Advertised Brands Are Better Buys?" in *Enhancing Knowledge Development in Marketing,* eds. D. W. Cravens and P. R. Dickson (Chicago: American Marketing Association, 1993), pp. 434–41.

39.   J. Scattone, "Factors Influencing Consumer Perceptions, Attitudes, and Consideration of Store Brands," in *Enhancing Knowledge Development in Marketing,* eds. B. B. Stern and G. M. Zinkhan (Chicago: American Marketing Association, 1995), pp. 27–33; and Richardson, Dick, and Jain, "Extrinsic and Intrinsic Cue Effects."

40.   K. M. Elliott and D. W. Roach, "Are Consumers Evaluating Your Products the Way You Think and Hope They Are," *Journal of Consumer Marketing,* Spring 1991, pp. 5–14; and J. Baumgartner, "On the Utility of Consumers' Theories in Judgments of Covariation," *Journal of Consumer Research,* March 1995, pp. 634–43.

41.   K. B. Monroe, *Pricing* (New York: McGraw-Hill, 1979), p. 38.

42.   C. J. Thompson, "Interpreting Consumers," *Journal Marketing Research,* November 1997, p. 443.

43.   See G. Haubl and V. Trifts, "Consumer Decision Making in Online Shopping Environments," *Marketing Science,* Winter 2000, pp. 2–21.

44.   S. Thompson, "Snacks to Go," *Advertising Age,* October 1, 2001, p. 4.

45.   M. L. Ursic and J. G. Helgeson "The Impact of Choice and Task Complexity on Consumer Decision Making," *Journal of Business Research,* August 1990, pp. 69–86; and P. L. A. Dabholkar, "Incorporating Choice into an Attitudinal Framework," *Journal of Consumer Research,* June 1994, pp. 100–18.

46.   See E. Coupey, "Restructuring," *Journal of Consumer Research,* June 1994, pp. 83–99.

47.   See D. L. Alden, D. M. Stayman, and W. D. Hoyer, "Evaluation Strategies of American and Thai Consumers," *Psychology & Marketing,* March 1994, pp. 145–61; and J. E. Russo and F. Lecleric, "An Eye-Fixation Analysis of Choice Processes for

Consumer Nondurables," *Journal of Consumer Research,* September 1994, pp. 274–90.

48. See J. G. Helgeson and M. L. Ursic, "Information Load, Cost/Benefit Assessment and Decision Strategy Variability," *Journal of the Academy of Marketing Science,* Winter 1993, pp. 13–20; W. J. McDonald, "The Roles of Demographics, Purchase Histories, and Shopper Decision-Making Styles in Predicting Consumer Catalog Loyalty," *Journal of Direct Marketing,* Summer 1993, pp. 55–65; M. S. Yadav, "How Buyers Evaluate Product Bundles," *Journal of Consumer Research,* September 1994, pp. 342–53; A. V. Muthukrishnan, "Decision Ambiguity and Incumbent Brand Advantage," *Journal of Consumer Research,* June 1995, pp. 98–109; and D. E. Hansen and J. G. Helgeson, "Consumer Response to Decision Conflict from Negatively Correlated Attributes," *Journal of Consumer Psychology* 10, no. 3 (2001), pp. 150–69.

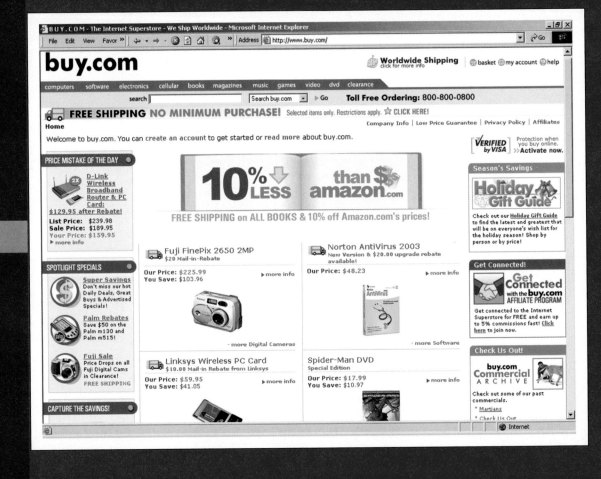

Outlet Selection
and Purchase

chapter 7

◻ Can a retailer make money selling many of its items at or below the price it pays for them? Scot Blum, CEO of Buy.com, is betting that his company can. The secret—sell online, minimize operating costs, generate very large volumes, and make profits selling advertising space on the site. Will it work? At this time it is not yet clear. However, Buy.com is now the seventh-largest online retailer, with sales over $400 million and growing rapidly, as are advertising revenues.

Buy.com opened its Internet business in November 1997 as Buycomp.com. It sold computers and related items with a commitment to have the lowest price on the Web for every one of its 30,000 items. To do so, it uses a technology that allows it to search through other online sellers' sites and determine their prices. The most straightforward way to determine the lowest price is to use a search program on a single high-speed connection from one address. However, competitors could easily identify this and block its access to their sites. Therefore, Buy.com set up hundreds of accounts with Internet service providers using low-speed modem connections. Each one visits a rival's site no more than seven times making it virtually impossible to distinguish from a curious customer. Prices are searched daily. Once the lowest price is determined, Buy.com undercuts it and sends it off to price-comparison search engines, which make it available to comparison shoppers.

To keep costs low, Buy.com does not provide amenities. It does not score well on customer service, ease of use, or overall customer experience. This does not appear to have been a problem for computer-related products. However, Buy.com has recently gone into the book, movie, and video game businesses using the same formula. This puts it in direct competition with Amazon.com, Barnesandnoble.com, and Reel.com. Will the lowest price–limited service concept work here?

Blum plans to stick with the strategy:

We're going for someone who knows what they want and wants it for the best price. We're trying to keep our site simple, effective, and easy to use—not cluttered with a lot of links and long reviews and stuff.

Since Amazon.com and others offer these features, some customers may use those sites to determine what they want and then buy it from Buy.com (this is known as free-riding). However, the CEO of Amazon.com isn't worried. According to him,

with books and music, there's a different dynamic. Customers want selection, ease of use, and a low price—in that order.

Buy.com has locked up 3,000 website addresses that start with "Buy," including BuyCars.com, BuyInsurance.com, and even BuyCheeseburgers.com.[1]

Selecting a retail outlet involves the same process as selecting a brand, as described in the previous chapters.[2] That is, the consumer recognizes a problem that requires an outlet to be selected, engages in internal and possibly external search, evaluates the relevant alternatives, and applies a decision rule to make a selection. We are not going to repeat our discussion of these steps. Instead we will describe the evaluative criteria that consumers frequently use in choosing retail outlets, consumer characteristics that influence the criteria used, and in-store characteristics that affect the amounts and brands purchased.

OUTLET CHOICE VERSUS PRODUCT CHOICE

Outlet selection is obviously important to managers of retail firms such as Amazon.com, Sears, and L. L. Bean. However, it is equally important to consumer goods marketers. There are three basic sequences a consumer can follow when making a purchase decision: (1) brand (or item) first, outlet second; (2) outlet first, brand second; or (3) brand and outlet simultaneously.

Our model and discussion in the previous two chapters suggest that brands are selected first and outlets second. This situation may arise frequently. For example, a consumer considering buying a notebook computer may look in relevant consumer publications and talk with knowledgeable individuals. On the basis of this information, the consumer may select a brand and purchase it from the outlet with the lowest price (or easiest access, best image,

Decision Sequence	Level in the Channel	
	Retailer	*Manufacturer*
1. Outlet first, brand second	Image advertising Margin management on shelf space, displays Location analysis Appropriate pricing	Distribution in key outlets Point-of-purchase, shelf space, and position Programs to strengthen existing outlets
2. Brand first, outlet second	Many brands or key brands Co-op ads featuring brands Price specials on brands Yellow Pages listings under brands	More exclusive distribution Brand availability advertising (Yellow Pages) Brand image management
3. Simultaneous	Margin training for sales personnel Multiple brands/key brands High-service or low-price structure	Programs targeted at retail sales personnel Distribution in key outlets Co-op advertising

TABLE 17–1

Marketing Strategy Based on the Consumer Decision Sequence

service, or other relevant attributes). This has been the process assumed in the discussion in this text thus far.

However, for many individuals and product categories, stores rather than brands form the evoked set.[3] In our notebook computer example, the consumer might be familiar with one store—Campus Computers—that sells personal computers. He or she may decide to visit that store and select a computer from the brands available there.

A third strategy is to compare the brands in one's evoked set at the stores in the evoked set. The decision would involve a simultaneous evaluation of both store and product attributes. Thus, a consumer might choose between a second preferred computer at a store with friendly personnel and excellent service facilities versus a favorite computer at an impersonal outlet with no service facilities.

The appropriate marketing strategies for both retailers and manufacturers differ depending on the decision sequence generally used by the target market. How would a manufacturer's strategy differ depending on whether the brand or store was selected first? A brand-first decision sequence would suggest brand image and feature advertising, Yellow Pages listings by brand, and possibly a limited distribution strategy. An outlet-first choice would tend to produce a focus on point-of-purchase materials, distribution through key outlets, and programs to encourage good shelf space and support from store personnel. Table 17–1 highlights additional strategic implications.

Manufacturers often provide advertising dollars to retailers in exchange for featuring their products in the retailers' ads. At other times, the manufacturer lists one or more retailers as a source for its products. This both creates product demand and directs consumers to the appropriate retail outlet (see Illustration 17–1). Retailers often share in the cost of such ads. In other cases, firms use retailers' names in the ads as an inducement for the retailer to carry or display the brand.

THE RETAIL SCENE

We use *retail outlet* to refer to any source of products or services for consumers. In earlier editions of this text, we used the term *store*. However, increasingly consumers see or hear descriptions of products in catalogs, direct-mail pieces, or various print media; on television or radio; or on the Internet; they then acquire the products through mail, telephone, or computer orders. Generally referred to as **in-home shopping,** these sources

ILLUSTRATION 17–1

Marketers often use advertising to create brand demand and to direct consumers to appropriate outlets.

Courtesy Posner.

represent a small but rapidly growing percentage of total retail sales. Consider this view of the future of retailing:

> You're watching "Seinfeld" on TV, and you like the jacket he's wearing. You click on it with your remote control. The show pauses and a Windows-style dropdown menu appears at the top of the screen, asking if you want to buy it. You click "yes." The next menu offers you a choice of colors; you click on black. Another menu lists your credit cards asking which one you'll use for this purchase. Click on MasterCard or whatever. Which address should the jacket go to, your office or your home or your cabin? Click on one address and you're done—the menus disappear and "Seinfeld" picks up where it left off.
>
> Just as you'll already have taught the computer about your credit cards and addresses, you will have had your body measured by a 3-D version of supermarket scanners, so the system will know your exact size. And it will send the data electronically to a factory, where robots will custom tailor the jacket to your measurements. An overnight courier service will deliver it to your door the next morning.[4]

Far-fetched? The quote is from Bill Gates, founder of Microsoft! While "Seinfeld" is now seen only in reruns and we are not yet near this level of sophistication in retailing, parts of the scenario are possible. Skiers can have their feet scanned into a computer along with data on their skiing style, and the computer will provide a list of the brands and sizes of ski boots that will fit best and meet their performance needs. A consumer can also have a "mass-produced" bicycle designed for his or her body size and produced in an automated factory in a matter of days. So while Gates's vision may still be a bit futuristic, at least some aspects of it will be commonplace in a few years. Clearly, retailing is one of the most exciting areas of business in most developed economies.

We will briefly describe Internet and store, often referred to as *bricks-and-mortar,* retailing in the next sections. We focus on Internet retailing rather than other forms of nonstore retailing because online sales are now slightly larger than either catalog sales or direct marketing sales (telemarketing, direct mail, television, and so forth). And Internet sales are growing much more rapidly than other nonstore or traditional store sales.

Internet Retailing

As shown below,[5] Internet retailing is a booming and increasingly competitive business (see Chapter 15 for a discussion of the use of the Internet as a source of information for purchases):

	Year	
	2000	*2005*
U.S. consumers 14 and older online (millions)	105	169
Buying online in past year (millions)	64	130
Average annual online expenditures	$597	$1,200
Total U.S. retail expenditures online (billions)	$38	$156

Forrester Research categorizes products and services into three categories based on their purchase characteristics relative to Internet shopping:

- *Convenience items:* low-risk discretionary items. Internet sales will be most successful for those where huge selection and deep discounts are important and easy shipping is available. Examples are books, CDs, flowers, and event tickets.
- *Researched items:* high-information, big-ticket planned purchases. Internet sales will be led by items with low style content and those for which "touch" is not important. Examples are leisure travel, computer hardware, and consumer electronics.
- *Replenishment goods:* moderate cost, high-frequency purchases. Items that are relatively expensive and easy to ship will be most successful. Examples include health care items such as vitamins, beauty aids, and gourmet foods.[6]

Figure 17–1 reveals that touch is not as critical as Forrester Research predicted. Apparel is one of the largest sales categories on the Internet and one of the fastest growing. Part of the reason for this is the rapid growth in Internet shopping by women, traditionally heavy purchaser of clothing from catalogs.

Internet sales are currently almost 2.5 percent of total retail sales, and this percentage is growing rapidly. Internet sales are particularly important in several product categories such as computer and computer software (25 percent) and books (12.5 percent).

Consumers shop online for the reasons similar to those for shopping from catalogs:[7]

Reason	*Online Shopping*	*Catalog Shopping*
Convenience	67%	62%
Price was right	41	40
Unique merchandise	33	40
Past experience with company	28	39
Wanted product delivered	16	31
No time to go to store	13	17
Recommendation from a friend	7	7
Impulse	4	5

However, for many consumers online shopping outperforms catalogs on these key reasons. Thus, online shopping is not only growing more rapidly than catalog shopping but appears to be taking substantial business from traditional catalogs.[8]

FIGURE 17-1   **Online Sales by Categories in Billions**

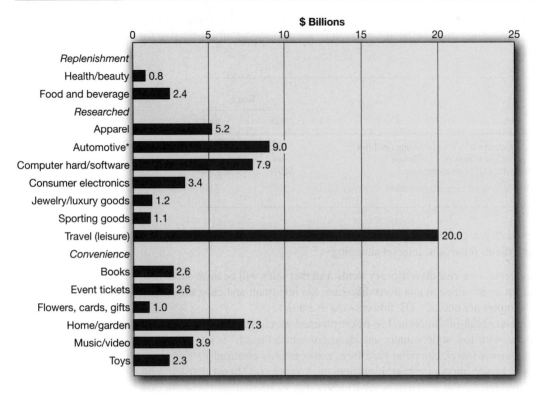

*Includes Web-referred sales as well as parts.

Source: eMarketer, Inc. subscription services, June 12, 2002.

In Illustration 17–2, BestBuy.com promotes selection and the availability of the newest products as a primary advantage of its outlet.

Barriers to Internet Shopping   For some products, people, and situations, the Internet outlets offer a better combination of selection, convenience, price, and other attributes than do catalogs, traditional stores, or other outlets. However, for most purchases most consumers prefer traditional retail outlets. In one survey, consumers provided the following reasons for not buying online in the past year:[9]

	Percent
All Consumers	
No Internet access	47%
Among Those with Internet Access	
Don't trust ordering online	43%
Lack of touch	34
Don't see what I want	9
Don't want to wait for delivery	4
Too expensive	3
Other	26

ILLUSTRATION 17–2

Some online outlets such as Buy.com focus primarily on price; others stress selection, convenience, information, or unique merchandise.

Courtesy Best Buy Co., Inc.

Sending a credit card number via the Internet remains an issue despite programs designed to provide secure transmissions. Almost half of Americans consider this a major concern and more than 40 percent say that it reduces their online shopping.[10] Other barriers to Internet purchases include shipping charges and the hassle of returning items.

Buying a product online generally requires the consumer to provide the firm at least a shipping address in addition to a credit card number. Often firms request more information than a shipping address when a purchase is made or even for access to all or parts of a website. Of course, the same is true of many other purchase environments such as catalog purchases and "club card" purchases at traditional stores.[11]

Consumers are concerned anytime they must provide personal information to strangers, but these concerns appear to be multiplied when the information is provided over the Internet. In part, this increased concern reflects doubt about the security of Internet transmissions. It also reflects a fear of "big brother" and interlinked databases where information about individual consumers might be compiled from various sources and used to manipulate or otherwise take advantage of them.

These online **privacy concerns** represent a major challenge to the continued growth of Internet commerce.[12] In fact, it is estimated that privacy concerns cost Internet retailers $5.5 billion in sales in 2001, with a forecast loss of $24.5 billion in 2006![13] The number one privacy concern among consumers is that information collected online will be used to unfairly target children (see Chapter 20). However, a recent survey revealed the following additional areas where consumers are extremely or very concerned:[14]

I'll be bombarded with advertisements	64%
My private information will be used against me	58
I'll be robbed or cheated	55
Someone will steal my identity	54

While there is a high level of concern with privacy among all demographic groups, it tends to be higher among women, married people, older people, and people with higher incomes and education levels.[15]

On the surface, a solution seems simple. Firms could collect no more information than necessary to complete the sale and then not use it again. Unfortunately, this removes many of the benefits of the Internet for both consumers and companies:

> On the one hand, consumers want companies to read their minds and give them what they want. On the other hand, that means companies have to collect information, data mine, and create profiles, which makes consumers feel like they're being tracked and exploited.[16]

In fact, many consumers are quite willing to provide substantial personal data online if they are assured that its use will be limited to prespecified purposes and that they will receive some benefit from providing it.[17] For example, a consumer might be quite willing to receive a weekly e-mail from Amazon.com describing any new blues CDs released that week.

Firms can take an "opt in" approach where the consumer chooses how the firm can use any information provided.[18] This would deny some firms valuable marketing tactics as many consumers would fail to "opt in" for information uses that might benefit them and the company. For example, most Internet consumers don't mind receiving e-mails describing special offers related to their previous purchase. However, as we saw above, they are fearful of being bombarded by such offers and thus many would not opt to receive them.

In addition, Internet shopping, like other forms of in-home shopping, is not viewed as being as satisfying as store shopping by many consumers. This is caused by the inability to physically exam the products, the lack of social interaction involved in the process, and the lack of activity, stimulation, and "getting out of the house or office" provided by store visits.

Consider the following statements about making substantial purchases such as cars:

> Part of the enjoyment of it [bargaining] is winning the game. Part of the enjoyment is the pleasure it gives . . . . There is the thrill of victory.
>
> My attitude toward buying a car is more like a fight . . . . A one-price policy would mean that I automatically lose the fight.
>
> I was able to play "Big Man Daddy" in front of my daughters. And they were impressed. In a way I was putting on a show.[19]

These examples indicate some of the noneconomic value that some consumers obtain from bargaining. Others value different types of interactions that are common in store-based shopping but are not easily duplicated on the Internet.

Characteristics of Online Shoppers   Obviously, online shoppers must first be Internet users. As we saw in Chapter 15, Internet users tend to have higher income and education levels than the general population and to be white or Asian American. Chapter 15 also indicated that these differences are diminishing as Internet usage becomes more universal. Currently, online shoppers tend to be younger and more affluent than the average Internet user. However, as online shopping grows, online shoppers increasingly resemble the typical Internet user in terms of demographics.

Scott and Swinyard identified eight online shopper segments based on their recent shopping behavior (a purchase during the most recent Christmas season) and their attitudes and behaviors with respect to the Internet and online shopping.[20] These segments and recommended marketing strategies for each are as follows:

- *Shopping Lovers* (11.1 percent of online households [HHs], 24 percent of online spending) enjoy buying online and do so frequently. They are competent computer users and will likely continue their shopping habits. They also spread the word to others about joys of online shopping whenever they have the opportunity. They represent an ideal target for retailers.
- *Adventurous Explorers* (9 percent of online HHs, 30 percent of online spending) are a small segment that presents a large opportunity. They require little special attention by Internet vendors because they believe online shopping is fun. They are likely the opinion leaders for all things online. Retailers should nurture and cultivate them to be online community builders and shopping advocates.
- *Suspicious Learners* (10 percent of online HHs, 15 percent of online spending) constitute another small segment with growth potential. Their reluctance to purchase online more often hinges on their lack of computer training, but they are open to new ways of doing things. In contrast to more fearful segments, they don't have a problem giving a computer their credit card number. Further guidance and training would help coax them into online buying.
- *Business Users* (12 percent of online HHs, 19 percent of online spending) are among the most computer literate. They use the Internet primarily for business purposes. They take a serious interest in what it can do for their professional life. They don't view online shopping as novel and aren't usually champions of the practice.
- *Fearful Browsers* (11 percent of online HHs, 5 percent of online spending) are on the cusp of buying online. They are capable Internet and computer users, spending a good deal of time "window shopping." They could become a significant buying group if their fears about credit card security, shipping charges, and buying products sight unseen were overcome.
- *Shopping Avoiders* (16 percent of online HHs, 3 percent of online spending) have an appealing income level, but their values make them a poor target for online retailers. They don't like to wait for products to be shipped to them, and they like seeing merchandise in person before buying. They have online shopping issues that retailers will not easily be able to overcome.
- *Technology Muddlers* (20 percent of online HHs, 3 percent of online spending) face large computer literacy hurdles. They spend less time than any other segment online and show little excitement about increasing their online comfort level. They are not an attractive market for online retailers.
- *Fun Seekers* (12 percent of online HHs, 2 percent of online spending) are the least wealthy and least educated market segment. They see entertainment value in the Internet, but buying things online frightens them. Although security and privacy issues might be overcome, the spending power of the segment suggests that only a marginal long-term payback would be possible.

Store-Based Retailing

There is a tendency to think of Internet retailers as distinct from store-based retailers and other forms of in-home shopping such as catalogs. Internet retailers bring to mind start-up firms such as Amazon.com, Priceline, and eBay. However, most large store-based retailers and catalog firms also have Internet sales sites. In fact, such multichannel retail strategies are increasingly essential.[21] Thus, firms such as Eddie Bauer and The Gap actively market through retail outlets, catalogs, and the Internet. J. Crew now generates almost 20 percent of its revenue from Internet sales. In fact, 8 of the 10 largest online retailers are multi-channel retailers:[22]

Retailer	Online Sales (billions)
1. Amazon.com	$3.12
2. Office Depot	1.60
3. Staples	.95
4. Costco Wholesale	.45
5. Barnesandnoble.com	.41
6. Buy.com	.40
7. QVC.com	.35
8. Spiegel Group	.33
9. JCPenney	.32

Kmart, like many other retailers, now has Internet shopping kiosks in all its traditional outlets. This allows consumers to purchase items not carried at that store or that are out of stock. In addition, consumers can use this service to purchase items for delivery to their homes or to be delivered as gifts.

The Internet allows region retailers such as Eastern Mountain Sports to instantly become national and international in scope (see Illustration 17–3). It also allows traditional retailers such as Toys "R" Us and Macy's to reach smaller communities where they could not economically operate before.

Consumer goods manufacturers such as Levi Strauss and Nike are increasingly offering their products directly to consumers via the Internet. A deterrent to manufacturers selling directly to consumers is concern about alienating their traditional distribution channels. In fact, less than a third of consumer package goods manufacturers' sites sell products online that they also sell through off-line retailers. Instead, they are likely to have links to online retailers that sell these products as well as a guide to traditional retail outlets.

As we have seen, nonstore retailing is growing rapidly. However, the vast majority of retail sales take place in stores, and this will remain true for the foreseeable future. In fact, today there is an explosion in store-based retailing activities.[23] Brand stores are emerging as major sales volume outlets as well as promotional devices for brands such as Levi's, Nike, Reebok, and OshKosh B'Gosh. The Sharper Image and similar outlets function as adult toy stores where one can play with the latest fun items for adults. Category killers or superstores provide a huge range of brands and variety of items within one product category at low prices. Toys "R" Us and Home Depot are well-known examples.

Giant outlets are not the only way to succeed. McDonald's has found that 75 percent of its customers decide where to eat just five minutes before they make the purchase. Thus, it and its fast-food competitors are building thousands of small outlets inside other outlets such as Wal-Mart, Home Depot, and gas stations.

Other firms are pursuing excellence in narrow niches. Sunglass Hut operates small kiosks in malls, airports, and other high-traffic areas. The kiosks carry 1,000 different kinds of sunglasses at very low prices. Byerly's is an upscale supermarket chain that offers a large selection of prepared foods, carpeting to deaden the noise and add to the ambience, and candy that is kept well out of the reach of children.[24] Giant superstores such as Staples, Home Depot, Costco, and Blockbuster are opening ministores in small towns, tiny shopping centers, and downtown areas.[25]

Traditional department stores such as J.C. Penney are successfully fighting back with renovations (planning to spend $1 billion over the next few years) and new product lines ("Neiman Marcus fashion at Penney prices"). At the same time, it is aggressively developing its catalog and online sales.

Courtesy Eastern Mountain Sports.

ILLUSTRATION 17–3

An Internet sales site instantly converts a local or regional firm into a national and even international one.

Target has "reinvented the whole discount store concept." It has "been able to carve out the ultimate retail positioning with both a perception of having the highest-quality products and, at the same time, a perception of being a low-price leader." It is predicted that soon Target will be the second-largest retailer in the United States (Wal-Mart is the largest).[26]

Malls are becoming giant entertainment centers. For example, the Mall of America near Minneapolis is built around an amusement park. It also has a miniature golf course, 9 nightclubs, 45 restaurants, a 14-screen movie complex, and a wedding chapel (see Illustration 17–4).[27] Retailing is clearly an exciting, competitive area. Those retailers who best understand their consumers will be the ones to prosper in the future.

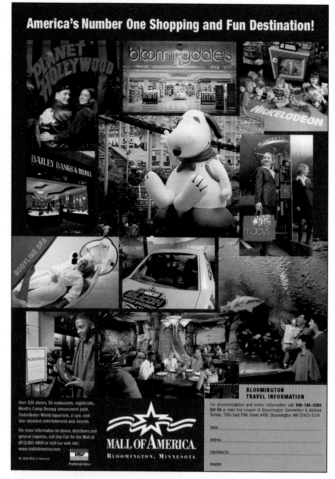

Courtesy Mall of America.

ATTRIBUTES AFFECTING RETAIL OUTLET SELECTION

The selection of a specific retail outlet, whether online or traditional, involves a comparison of the alternative outlets on the consumer's evaluative criteria. This may involve selecting an outlet type such as the Internet, a catalog, or a store and then a specific outlet within an outlet type such as Buybooks.com versus Amazon.com. This section considers a number of evaluative criteria commonly used by consumers to select retail outlets. Unfortunately, virtually all of this material relates most directly to choosing from among stores, as little research is available on how consumers select online outlets.

Outlet Image

A given consumer's or target market's perception of all the attributes associated with a retail outlet is generally referred to as the **store image.** This is the same as the concept of *brand image* discussed in Chapter 9. One study found the following nine dimensions and 23 components of these nine dimensions of store image.[28] Notice that the store atmosphere component is primarily affective or feeling in nature.

Dimension	Components
Merchandise	Quality, selection, style, and price
Service	Layaway plan, sales personnel, easy return, credit, and delivery
Clientele	Customers
Physical facilities	Cleanliness, store layout, shopping ease, and attractiveness
Convenience	Location and parking
Promotion	Advertising
Store atmosphere	Congeniality, fun, excitement, and comfort
Institutional	Store reputation
Post-transaction	Satisfaction

This study focused on stores; the components and probably the dimensions will require adjusting for use with other types of retail outlets. For example, 800 numbers, 24-hour operations, and ample in-bound phone lines (no busy signals) are relevant to the convenience of a catalog merchant such as L. L. Bean, not location and parking as listed in the table. *What determines convenience for an Internet site?*

A study that focused on the affective component of store image or personality found the following differences across stores (the higher the number, the more the component fits the outlet):[29]

	Affective Component			
Store	Pleasant	Unpleasant	Active	Sleepy
JCPenney	18.5	12.8	13.7	14.3
Kmart	15.2	12.6	14.8	12.9
Macy's	25.2	7.2	19.0	6.7
The Sharper Image	23.5	7.8	22.4	6.9
Victoria's Secret	25.5	9.5	16.0	12.7

Notice that JCPenney and Kmart are about as strong on the unpleasant component as on the pleasant component, and they are viewed as being neither active nor sleepy. This suggests that shopping motives will have to come from price, selection, or other functional features. In contrast, Macy's is a pleasant, active place to shop. Consumers will shop at stores such as Macy's because they are pleasant and active rather than, or in addition to, their functional characteristics. Victoria's Secret and The Sharper Image are both pleasant places to shop, but the former is a less active experience than the latter. *What do these affective results suggest for JCPenney's marketing strategy?*

Marketers make extensive use of image data in formulating retail strategies.[30] First, marketers control many of the elements that determine an outlet's image. Second, differing groups of consumers desire different things from various types of retail outlets. Thus, a focused, managed image that matches the target market's desires is essential for most retailers.

Courtesy Target Corporation.

This stylish swimsuit was designed by artist Stephen Sprouse. It was available for a limited time at Target stores and Target.com for $29.99.

Target has been able to develop an image as a source of high-quality, stylish products for very low prices. One of the ways it does this is by developing and promoting its own exclusive, stylish merchandise that it then sells at a low price (see Illustration 17–5).

Other outlets concentrate on one or more attributes that are important to a segment of consumers or that are important to most consumers in certain situations. As we saw earlier, Buy.com emphasizes price as its main competitive advantage. 7-Eleven has followed the second approach, which is to provide customers "what they want, when they want it, where they want it." Thus, it focuses on providing convenience (easy access, extended hours, and quick service) for consumers in those situations where convenience is the key attribute.

Retailer Brands

Closely related to store image are **store brands.** At the extreme, the store or outlet is the brand. The Gap, Victoria's Secret, and Body Shop International are examples. All the items carried in the store are the store's own brand. Traditionally, retailers carried only manufacturers' brands, and only a few, such as Sears and Wards, developed their own house or store brands. In the 1970s, many stores began to develop store brands as low-price alternatives to national brands, and many continue with this approach.[31]

Increasingly, however, retailers such as Wal-Mart and Target are developing and promoting high-quality brands with either the store's name or an independent name. Sears has been very active and effective in this area. Such brands not only provide attractive margins for these outlets; if they are developed appropriately, they become an important attribute of the outlet. That is, they are another reason for the consumer to shop that store.[32] And importantly, no other outlet can carry this brand. Thus, the Kenmore and Craftsman brands are important features of a Sears store.

The key to success of store brands seems clear—high quality at a reasonable price. The traditional pattern of providing reasonable quality at a low price is no longer necessarily optimal.[33] In fact, emphasizing quality over price may be particularly beneficial if the brand carries the store's name or will become associated with the store.

Retail Advertising

Retailers use advertising to communicate their attributes, particularly sale prices, to consumers. It is clear that price advertising can attract people to stores. Revealing results were obtained in a major study involving newspaper ads in seven cities for a range of product categories (motor oil, sheets, digital watches, pants, suits, coffee makers, dresses, and mattresses). The impact of the retail advertisements varied widely by product category. For example, 88 percent of those who came to the store in response to the advertisement for motor oil purchased the advertised item, compared with only 16 percent of those responding to the dress ad. Approximately 50 percent of the shoppers overall purchased the advertised item that attracted them to the store.

As Figure 17–2 illustrates, purchases of the advertised item understate the total impact of the ad. *Sales of additional items to customers who came to purchase an advertised item are referred to as* **spillover sales.** Spillover sales in this study equaled sales of the advertised items; that is, for every $1 spent on the sale item by people who came to the store in response to the advertising, another $1 was spent on some other item(s) in the store.[34]

Another study produced the results shown below:[35]

	Reason for Visiting Store	
Action	Purchase Promoted Item	Other Reason
Dollars spent on promoted items	$11.30	$ 3.27
Dollars spent on regular items	18.48	21.90
Total	$29.78	$25.17
Store profit	$ 5.64	$ 5.77

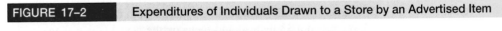

FIGURE 17–2   Expenditures of Individuals Drawn to a Store by an Advertised Item

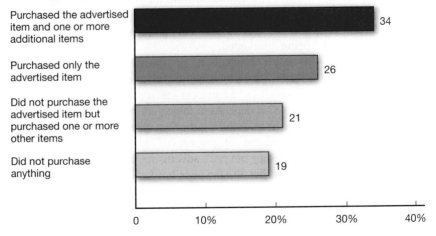

Purchased the advertised item and one or more additional items — 34

Purchased only the advertised item — 26

Did not purchase the advertised item but purchased one or more other items — 21

Did not purchase anything — 19

0   10%   20%   30%   40%

Retailers evaluating the benefits of price or other promotions must consider the impact on overall store sales and profits, not just those of the advertised item.

Although a large percentage of retail advertising stresses price, particularly sales price, studies continue to show that price is frequently not the prime reason consumers select a retail outlet. This suggests that many retailers could benefit by emphasizing service, selection, or the affective benefits of their outlets.[36]

As the ads in Illustrations 17–2 and 17–3 show, online retailers advertise in mass media both to attract consumers to their sites and to build an image. Catalog merchants use both mass media and mail to persuade consumers to use their catalogs.

Price Advertising Decisions   Retailers face three decisions when they consider using price advertising:

1. How large a price discount should be used?
2. Should comparison or reference prices be used?
3. What verbal statements should accompany the price information?

Consumers tend to assume that any advertised price represents a price reduction or sale price. Showing a comparison price increases the perceived savings significantly. However, the strength of the perception varies with the manner in which the comparison or reference price is presented. A **reference price** is *a price with which other prices are compared.* In the claim, "Regularly $9.95, now only $6.95," $9.95 is the reference price. An **external reference price** is *a price presented by a marketer for the consumer to use to compare with the current price.* An **internal reference price** is *a price or price range*[37] *that a consumer retrieves from memory to compare with a price in the market.*[38]

Although there are situational influences and individual differences,[39] most consumers understand external reference prices and are influenced by them but do not completely believe them.[40] The reason for the lack of belief is the practice of some retailers of using inflated reference prices. These inflated prices could be "suggested list prices" in markets where virtually all sales are at a lower level. Or they may reflect prices that the store set for the merchandise originally that were too high and produced few sales. The price reduction being shown then merely corrects an earlier pricing error but does not provide meaningful benefit to the consumer. Since price and sale advertising have a strong impact on consumer purchases, the FTC and many states have special guidelines and regulations controlling their use.[41]

The best approach for retailers seems to be to present the sale price and (1) the dollar amount saved if it is large, (2) the percentage saved when it is large, and (3) both if both are large. Thus, $10 savings on a $200 item should show the dollar savings but not the percentage savings. A $10 saving on a $20 item could emphasize both the dollar and the percentage savings. A $1 saving on a $3 item should focus on the percentage savings.[42] The regular price could be shown in any of these conditions.[43] The regular price (the price on which the savings are calculated) should be the price at which the store normally sells a reasonable volume of the brand being discounted.

Such words or phrases as "now only," "compare at," or "special" appear to enhance the perceived value of a sale. However, this varies by situation, initial price level and discount size, consumer group, and retail outlet.[44] Is "50 percent off" or "buy one, get one free" likely to be perceived as a better value? It depends in large part on the nature of the item being promoted. For stock-up items such as detergent, they are viewed as equivalent. However, for perishable items such as bread, the "50 percent off" is seen as a better value.[45]

Retailers need to use caution in how they use price advertising. Such advertising signals not only the price of the advertised items but also the price level of the store.[46] And because price level, quality, service, and other important attributes are often linked in the consumer's mind, inappropriate price advertising can have a negative effect on the store's image.[47]

Courtesy The Sharper Image.

ILLUSTRATION 17–6

This sale ad focuses primarily on the dollar savings. Should the percentage savings also be stressed?

The ad in Illustration 17–6 places primary emphasis on the dollar savings but also shows the reference price and the sale price. Since the dollar savings are relatively large, the research we have reviewed suggests that this is a sound strategy.

Outlet Location and Size

The location of a retail outlet plays an important role in consumer store choice. If all other things are approximately equal, the consumer generally will select the closest store. Likewise, the size of an outlet is an important factor in store choice. Unless the customer is particularly interested in fast service or convenience, he or she would tend to prefer larger outlets over smaller outlets, all other things being equal.[48]

The **retail attraction model,** also called the **retail gravitation model,** is used to calculate the level of store attraction based on store size and distance from the consumer. In the retail gravitation model, store size is measured in square footage and assumed to be a measure of breadth of merchandise. The distance or travel time to a store is assumed to be a measure of the effort, both physical and psychological, to reach a given retail area.

The effect of distance or travel time varies by product.[49] For a convenience item or minor shopping good, distance is important, since shoppers are unwilling to travel very far for such items. However, major high-involvement purchases such as automobiles or specialty items such as wedding dresses generate greater willingness to travel.

Willingness to travel also varies with the size of the shopping list for that trip.[50] Thus, a consumer who would not be willing to travel very far to purchase three or four convenience items may willingly go much farther if 20 or 30 such items are to be purchased on the same trip.

Consumers often combine shopping trips and purposes.[51] Thus, a consumer may visit a health club, have lunch with a friend, pick up the laundry, shop for food for the next few days, and pick up a prescription on one trip. Thus, retail patronage is in part a function of an outlet's location in relation to other outlets and consumers' travel patterns. Combining outlets or adding departments in response to such shopping patterns can produce value for customers and increased revenue for the firm.[52] For example, supermarkets such as Safeway and Albertson's have added pharmacies to their outlets.

CONSUMER CHARACTERISTICS AND OUTLET CHOICE

The preceding discussion by and large has focused on store attributes independently of the specific characteristics of the consumers in the target market. However, different consumers have vastly differing desires and reasons for shopping. This section of the chapter examines two consumer characteristics that are particularly relevant to store choice: perceived risk and shopper orientation.

Perceived Risk

The purchase of products involves the risk that they may not perform as expected. As described in Chapter 15, such a failure may result in a high

- *Social cost* (e.g., a hairstyle that is not appreciated by one's peers).
- *Financial cost* (e.g., an expensive pair of shoes that become too uncomfortable to wear).
- *Time cost* (e.g., a television repair that required the set to be taken to the shop, left, and then picked up later).
- *Effort cost* (e.g., a computer disk that is loaded with several hours of work before it fails).
- *Physical cost* (e.g., a new medicine that produced a harmful side effect).

The first of these is generally termed *social risk;* the next three are often considered to be *economic risk.* Product categories vary in the level and type of risk generally associated with them.[53] Table 17–2 shows that socks and gasoline are low in economic and social risk, while hairstyles and small gifts are low in economic risk but high in social risk. Other products, such as personal computers and auto repairs, are low in social risk but high in economic risk. Finally, automobiles and living room furniture are high in both economic and social risk.[54] Table 17–2 also indicates the role of the situation in perceived risk. Wine is shown as low in both social and economic risk when used for personal consumption but high in social risk when served while entertaining.

The perception of these risks *differs* among consumers, depending in part on their past experiences and lifestyles. For this reason, **perceived risk** is considered a consumer

TABLE 17–2		
The Economic and Social Risk of Various Types of Products	**Economic Risk**	
Social Risk	*Low*	*High*
Low	Wine (personal use) Stocks Kitchen supplies Pens/pencils Gasoline	Personal computer Auto repairs Clothes washer Insurance Doctor/lawyer
High	Fashion accessories Hairstyles Gifts (inexpensive) Wine (entertaining) Deodorant	Business suits Living room furniture Automobile Snowboard Ski suit

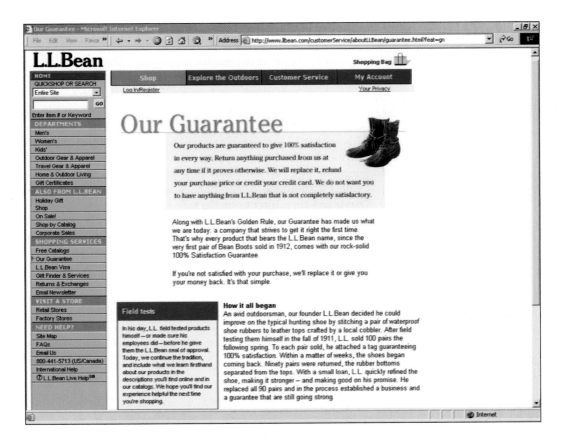

characteristic as well as a product characteristic.[55] For example, while many individuals would feel no social risk associated with the brand of car owned, others would.

Like product categories, retail outlets are perceived as having varying degrees of risk. Traditional outlets are perceived as low in risk, whereas more innovative outlets such as online stores are viewed as higher risk.[56]

The above findings lead to a number of insights into retailing strategy,[57] including the following:

- Nontraditional outlets need to minimize the perceived risk of shopping particularly if they sell items with either high economic or social risk. Lands' End attempts to reduce perceived risk by emphasizing toll-free ordering, 24-hour toll-free customer service telephones with trained assistants, and a 100 percent satisfaction guarantee. Word of mouth from satisfied customers reinforces these advertised policies.
- Nontraditional outlets need brand-name merchandise in those product categories with high perceived risk. Most Internet retailers feature such items.
- Traditional outlets and websites of well-known retailers have a major advantage with high-perceived-risk product lines. These lines should generally be their primary strategy focus. Low-risk items can be used to round out the overall assortment.
- Economic risks can be reduced through warranties and similar policies. Social risk is harder to reduce. A skilled sales force, known brands, and satisfaction guarantees can help reduce this type of risk.

Illustration 17–7 shows how L.L. Bean reduces perceived risk by guaranteeing complete satisfaction no matter how long you own their clothing.

ILLUSTRATION 17–7

Guaranteeing complete satisfaction no matter what can greatly reduce the perceived risk of a purchase, particularly one made via catalog or online.

Shopping Orientation

Individuals go shopping for more complex reasons than simply acquiring a product or set of products. Diversion from routine activities, exercise, sensory stimulation, social interactions, learning about new trends, and even acquiring interpersonal power ("bossing" clerks) are nonpurchase reasons for shopping.[58] Of course, the relative importance of these motives varies both across individuals and within individuals over time as the situation changes.[59] Illustration 17–4 (page 598) shows how malls can provide an inviting environment for activities in addition to shopping.

A shopping style that puts particular emphasis on certain activities or shopping motivations is called a **shopping orientation.** Shopping orientations are closely related to general lifestyle and are subject to similar influences. A recent study used projective techniques to ascertain the ways college students approach shopping.[60] It had consumers "Think about an animal that best describes you as a shopper . . . [and] explain what it is about your behavior that makes this animal an appropriate metaphor." One response was, in part,

> The reason I chose a hawk is basically the speed and grace in which my shopping is done. I glide through the mall and when I see what I want I dive in and "attack" it. To extend this metaphor, the trip to the mall is short and to the point. Just as a hawk swoops down and kills its prey, I see the item and grab it.

Using this projective research, the study uncovered six shopping orientations:

1. *Chameleons* indicated that their shopping styles are situation-specific or constantly changing. Their shopping approach is based on product type, shopping impetus, and purchase task.
2. *Collectors/Gatherers* are characterized by their propensity to stockpile items and to purchase large quantities to either save money or alleviate the need for shopping. They attempt to get the best price and take advantage of retailer guarantees.
3. *Foragers* are particular and are motivated to purchase only the desired items. They are willing to search extensively and have little store loyalty. They like to shop alone.
4. *Hibernants* are indifferent toward shopping. Their shopping patterns are opportunistic rather than need driven and they will often postpone even required purchases.
5. *Predators* are purposive and speed oriented in their shopping. They plan before shopping and like to shop alone. They don't enjoy shopping and tend to shop outlets where they are assured of getting the items they need quickly.
6. *Scavengers* enjoy shopping both to make purchases and as an activity. They like to go to sales and consider shopping to be entertainment. They make numerous unplanned purchases.

The opportunities for developing segment-specific marketing strategies are clearly evident.[61] For example, Predators might respond to home delivery. Scavengers would respond well to entertainment-focused malls and outlets. However, as a single store attempts to target more of the segments, the risk of failure with all groups increases, as many of their desires are, if not mutually exclusive, difficult to meet within the same outlet. *Which of these groups would shop at Wal-Mart? Banana Republic? Sears? Which are the best targets for Internet outlets?*

IN-STORE INFLUENCES THAT AFFECT BRAND CHOICES

It is not uncommon to enter a retail outlet with the intention of purchasing a particular brand but to leave with a different brand or additional items. Influences operating within the store induce additional information processing and subsequently affect the final purchase decision. This portion of the chapter examines six variables that singularly and in combination influence brand decisions inside a retail outlet: *point-of-purchase displays, price reductions, outlet atmosphere, stockout situations, website design*, and *sales personnel*. First, however, we need to fully understand the extent and nature of unplanned purchases.

The Nature of Unplanned Purchases

The fact that consumers often purchase brands different from or in addition to those planned has led to an interest in unplanned purchases. **Unplanned purchases** are defined as *purchases made in a store that are different from those the consumer planned to make prior to entering the store*. The term *unplanned purchase* implies a lack of rationality or alternative evaluation. However, this is not necessarily true. The decision to purchase Del Monte rather than Green Giant peas because Del Monte is on sale is certainly not illogical. Nor is an unplanned decision to take advantage of the unexpected availability of fresh strawberries.

Considering most in-store purchase decisions as the result of additional information processing within the store leads to more useful marketing strategies than does considering these purchases to be random or illogical.[62] This approach allows the marketer to utilize knowledge of the target market, its motives, and the perception process to increase sales of specific items. The Point-of-Purchase Advertising Institute uses the following definitions:

- *Specifically planned.* A specific brand or item decided on before visiting the store and purchased as planned.
- *Generally planned.* A prestore decision to purchase a product category such as vegetables but not the specific item.
- *Substitute.* A change from a specifically or generally planned item to a functional substitute.
- *Unplanned.* An item bought that the shopper did not have in mind on entering the store.
- *In-store decisions.* The sum of generally planned, substitute, and unplanned purchases.

Unplanned purchases as defined above can be further subdivided into two categories— reminder purchases and impulse purchases. A *reminder purchase* would occur when a consumer notices Band-Aids in a store and remembers that she is almost out at home.[63] An **impulse purchase** would occur when a consumer sees a candy bar in the store and purchases it with little or no deliberation as the result of a sudden, powerful urge to have it.[64]

Figure 17–3 and Table 17–3 illustrate the extent of purchasing (in the United States and Canada) that is not specifically planned. It reveals that consumers make most item or brand decisions *after* entering the store. Thus, marketing managers not only must strive to position their brand in the target market's evoked set but also must attempt to influence the in-store decisions of their potential consumers. Retailers not only must attract consumers to their outlets but should structure the purchasing environment in a manner that provides maximum encouragement for unplanned purchases, particularly of high-margin items.[65] The appropriate way to do this would depend on the type of unplanned purchase associated with the product category.

We now turn our attention to some of the strategies that manufacturers and retailers can use to influence in-store decisions.

FIGURE 17–3 Supermarket Decisions: Two-Thirds Are Made In-Store

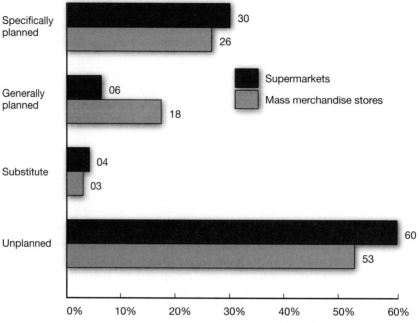

Source: *The 1995 POPAI Consumer Buying Habits Study* (Washington, DC, Point-of-Purchase Institute, www.popai.com, 1995 ©), p. 18.

TABLE 17–3

In-Store Purchase Behavior

Product	Specifically Planned	Generally Planned +	Substituted +	Unplanned =	In-Store Decisions
Total study average*	30%	61%	4%	60%	70%
Hair care*	23	4	5	68	77
Magazines/newspapers*	11	3	1	84	89
Oral hygiene products*	30	5	5	61	71
Automotive oil*	21	—	—	79	79
Tobacco products*	32	6	—	61	68
Coffee*	42	5	6	47	58
First aid products*	7	10	—	83	93
Cereal*	33	9	6	52	67
Soft drinks*	40	3	5	51	60
Mixers	23	6	4	68	77
Fresh fruits, vegetables*	67	7	1	25	33
Cold remedies[†]	28	35	19	18	72
Toothpaste/toothbrushes[†]	38	31	16	15	62
Antacids/laxatives[†]	39	37	12	12	61
Facial cosmetics[†]	40	34	11	15	60

Sources: *1995 POPAI Consumer Buying Habits Study* (Englewood, NJ: Point-of-Purchase Advertising Institute, 1995); [†]*1992 POPAI/Horner Canadian Drug Store Study* (Englewood, NJ: Point-of-Purchase Advertising Institute, 1992).

FIGURE 17–4   **The Sales Impact of Point-of-Purchase Displays**

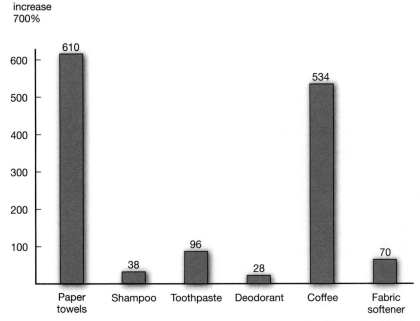

Source: *The POPAI/Kmart/Procter & Gamble Study of P-O-P Effectiveness in Mass Merchandizing Stores
Study* (Washington, DC, Point-of-Purchase Institute, www.popai.com, 1993 ©).

Point-of-Purchase Displays

Point-of-purchase (P-O-P) displays are common in the retailing of many products, and the impact these displays have on brand sales is often tremendous. Figure 17–4 provides a visual representation of this impact for six product categories. Notice the impact that product type has on the effectiveness of P-O-P material. The effect of P-O-P materials also varies with the location of the material, as shown below:

Location	*Percent Sales Increase*
On the shelf	11%
Rear endcap	141
Front endcap	162

Although the sales impact of displays varies widely by product type and location and between brands within a product category, there is generally a strong increase in sales.[66]

Illustration 17–8 shows two successful point-of-purchase displays from different cultures.

Price Reductions and Promotional Deals

Price reductions and promotional deals (coupons, multiple-item discounts, and gifts) are generally accompanied by the use of some point-of-purchase materials. Therefore, the relative impact of each is sometimes not clear.[67] Nonetheless, there is ample evidence that in-store price reductions affect brand decisions. The general pattern, observed in the United States, the United Kingdom, Japan, and Germany, is a sharp increase in sales when the

Courtesy Federation of Swiss Milk Producers.

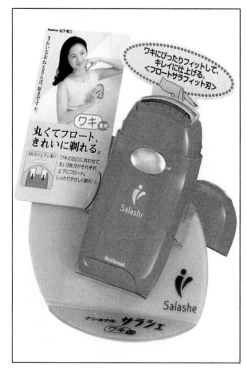

Courtesy Matsushita Electric Works, Ltd.

ILLUSTRATION 17–8

Point-of-purchase displays are effective across cultures.

price is first reduced, followed by a return to near-normal sales over time or after the price reduction ends.[68]

Sales increases in response to price reductions come from four sources:[69]

1. Current brand users may buy ahead of their anticipated needs (stockpiling). Stockpiling often leads to increased consumption of the brand, since it is readily available.
2. Users of competing brands may switch to the reduced price brand. These new brand buyers may or may not become repeat buyers of the brand.
3. Nonproduct category buyers may buy the brand because it is now a superior value to the substitute product or to "doing without."
4. Consumers who do not normally shop at the store may come to the store to buy the brand.

High-quality brands tend to benefit more than brands from lower quality tiers when prices are reduced, and they suffer less when prices are raised.[70]

As discussed earlier under price advertising, consumers judge store quality and image in part on the basis of the number and nature of reduced price items in the store.[71] Therefore, retailers need to carefully consider their sale price policies in light of both the sales of the discounted items and the impact these discounts will have on the store image. In addition, shoppers who purchase a large number of items at one time prefer stores with "everyday low prices"—all items in the store have relatively low prices but few are reduced beyond that level ("on sale")—to stores with somewhat higher standard prices but many sale items.[72]

Is a shirt from an Internet retailer priced at $24.95 plus $5.00 shipping and handling a better or worse deal than the same shirt priced at $29.95 with shipping and handling free? Consumers tend to perceive the former to be a better deal than the latter. Research has shown that *partitioned prices* (the first scenario above) produced greater demand and a lower recalled total cost than the combined price (the second scenario).[73]

Retail prices typically end just below a round number (a number ending in one or more zeros), such as $24.95 rather than $25.00 or $2.49 rather than $2.50.[74] Having the last two digits (the rightmost digits) be 99 is particularly popular for lower-priced goods, with 95 being more common for higher-priced items. Why? Even numbers are probably easier to remember and compare, and adding the cost of several items together is certainly simpler with round numbers.

Two theoretical explanations have been advanced, and both have received support in empirical studies. Both are probably valid but for different consumers or situations. The first and most supported explanation is the "left-to-right" theory. Multidigit numbers are processed left-to-right. As we saw in Chapters 9, 15, and 16, consumers frequently seek to minimize or at least reduce their information processing efforts. Therefore, they may ignore or pay little attention to the rightmost digits in a price. The number of digits receiving limited attention depends on the total number present. Thus, a price of $.99 may be interpreted as $.90, but one of $119.99 may be viewed as $110. To the extent that such a mechanism operates, marketers using 99 or 95 rightmost digits are receiving the highest possible price relative to the price consumers will perceive.

Another explanation is the sale-association theory. While many prices end in 99 normally, it is even more common for reduced-price items. Therefore, consumers may associate (low-involvement learning) a 99 ending price as a sale or bargain price.

Critical Thinking Questions

1. Is it ethical for retailers to set prices with 99 rightmost digits knowing that consumers will interpret the price to be lower than it is?
2. Why don't consumers simply round up to the next larger number? Wouldn't it be easier to think of $9.99 as $10.00 rather than as $9.90 or even $9.00?

Consumer Insight 17–1 explores an additional retailing pricing phenomenon, the tendency to end prices in 99.

Outlet Atmosphere

Store atmosphere is influenced by such attributes as lighting, layout, presentation of merchandise, fixtures, floor coverings, colors, sounds, odors, and the dress and behavior of sales and service personnel (see Chapter 13, page 479).

Atmosphere is referred to as **servicescape** when describing a service business such as a hospital, bank, or restaurant.[75] **Atmospherics** is the process managers use to manipulate the physical retail or service environment to create specific mood responses in shoppers. Internet retailers also have atmospheres that are determined by graphics, colors, layout, content, entertainment features, interactivity, tone, and so forth.[76] *What type of atmosphere is portrayed in Macy's site as shown in Illustration 17–9?*

A store's atmosphere affects the shopper's mood and willingness to visit and linger. It also influences the consumer's judgments of the quality of the store and the store's image.[77] Perhaps more important, a positive mood induced while in the store increases satisfaction with the store, which can produce repeat visits and store loyalty.[78]

A major component of atmosphere is the *number, characteristics, and behavior of customers.*[79] Entertainment parks spend substantial time, effort, and resources training their staff. However, as the following examples indicate, they cannot train their customers, who sometimes have a negative and sometimes a positive impact on the overall atmosphere.

> While standing in line at the Magic Kingdom at Disney some man in front of me continually blew cigar smoke in our faces.

> While standing in line at Universal Studios, these people . . . were using foul language and yelling to get the line moving. It made Universal less enjoyable than it could have been.

ILLUSTRATION 17–9

Retail website designs should create an appropriate atmosphere or feelings as well as provide content and functionality.

At Busch Gardens we always seemed to be in the same place as this elderly couple and they made sure our two kids could see the animals or dancers.

I met these really nice people from Canada who talked to me in line waiting for the ET ride.[80]

Music can have a major impact on the store environment (see Chapter 13, page 480). It has been shown to influence the time spent in the store or restaurant, the mood of the consumer, and the overall impression of the outlet.[81] It also enhances perceptions of waiting time for services.[82] However, it is important to match the music to the target audience. As shown below, baby boomers responded positively to classic rock music in a supermarket setting, but older adults did not:[83]

	Baby Boomers			Older Adults		
	Classic Rock	*Big Band*	*Top 40*	*Classic Rock*	*Big Band*	*Top 40*
Items purchased	31	11	15	4	12	14
Dollars spent	34	21	21	16	17	24
Shopping minutes	27	16	29	21	30	28

Findings such as these suggest the possibility of using different music styles during different times of the day, week, or month if customers with specific music preferences shop at distinct times.

Marketers are also beginning to investigate the impact of *odors* on shopping behaviors (see page 480).[84] Early studies suggest that odors can have a positive effect on the shopping experience, particularly if they are consistent with other aspects of the atmosphere such as the music being played.[85] However, like music, odor preference varies across customers, so caution must be used to ensure that the aroma is not offensive to target customers.[86] In addition, many consumers don't want anything artificial or unnecessary added to the air they breathe. A firm "spiking" the air with artificial aromas could irritate some consumers as well as risk adverse publicity.

Figure 17–5 illustrates the way store atmosphere influences shopper behavior. Several things in this figure are noteworthy. First, the physical environment interacts with the characteristics of individuals to determine response. Thus, an atmosphere that would produce a favorable response in teenagers might produce a negative response in older shoppers. Second, the store atmosphere influences *both* the sales personnel and the customers, whose interactions then influence each other.

FIGURE 17–5   **Store Atmosphere and Shopper Behavior**

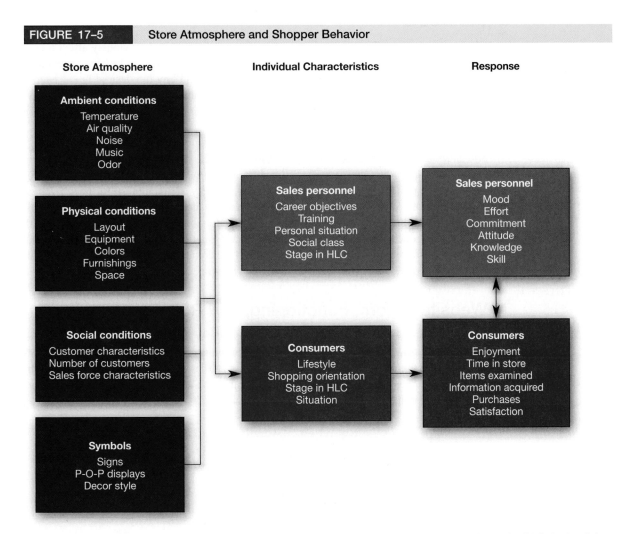

Source: Adapted from M. J. Bitner, "Servicescapes," *Journal of Marketing,* April 1, 1992, pp. 57–71. Published by the American Marketing Association; reprinted with permission.

TABLE 17–4

Impact of a Stockout
Situation

I. **Purchase behavior**
   A. Purchase a substitute size, brand, or product at the original store. The substitute brand/product may or may not replace the regular brand in future purchases.
   B. Delay the purchase until the brand is available at the original store.
   C. Forgo the purchase entirely.
   D. Purchase the desired brand at a second store. All of the items initially desired may be purchased at the second store or only the stockout items. The second store may or may not replace the original store on future shopping trips.
II. **Verbal behavior**
   A. The consumer may make negative comments to peers about the original store.
   B. The consumer may make positive comments to peers about the substitute store.
   C. The consumer may make positive comments to peers about the substitute brand/product.
III. **Attitude shifts**
   A. The consumer may develop a less favorable attitude toward the original store.
   B. The consumer may develop a more favorable attitude toward the substitute store.
   C. The consumer may develop a more favorable attitude toward the substitute brand/product.

Stockouts

Stockouts, *the store being temporarily out of a particular brand,* obviously affect a consumer's purchase decision. The customer then must decide whether to buy the same brand but at another store, switch brands, delay the purchase and buy the desired brand later at the same store, or forgo the purchase altogether. In addition, the consumer's verbal behaviors and attitudes may change. Table 17–4 summarizes the impacts that a stockout situation may have.

Three types of perceived costs affect the likely response of a consumer to a stockout.[87] *Substitution costs* refer to the reduction in satisfaction the consumer believes a replacement size, brand, or product will provide. This is a function of the consumer's commitment or loyalty to the preferred brand and the perceived similarity of potential substitutes.[88] *Transaction costs* refer to the mental, physical, time, and financial costs of purchasing a substitute product or brand. *Opportunity costs* are the reduction in satisfaction associated with forgoing or reducing consumption of the product. How these costs will be perceived and thus which of the outcomes, or combinations of outcomes, in Table 17–4 will occur depends on the particular consumer, product, and situation.

Website Layout, Functioning, and Requirements

Less than 4 percent of those who visit an online outlet make a purchase.[89] A major reason for this, as we saw in Chapter 15, is the practice of many consumers to look at products online then buy them in traditional stores. However, studies estimate that only 18 to 35 percent of online customers intending to make a purchase actually do so. This loss of purchases costs online retailers an estimated $3.8 billion.[90] One study[91] found the following causes:

Too much information required	52%
Did not want to give credit card number	46
Website malfunction	42
Could not find product	40
Had to make a phone call	16
Did not like return policy	16

Another study[92] found that consumers had the following problems shopping for gifts online during the Christmas season:

Gift out of stock	24%
Shipping and handling costs	21
Slow site performance	18
Long shipping time	15
Slow e-mail response	10
Credit card security	9
Return issues	8

Recall from the previous section that stockout situations generally produce negative consequences for the retailer. Clearly, there are many areas in which the design and functioning of retail websites can be improved to increase online sales among those customers who start the purchase process online.[93]

Sales Personnel

For most low-involvement purchases in the United States, self-service is predominant. As purchase involvement increases, the likelihood of interaction with a salesperson also increases. Thus, most studies of effectiveness in sales interactions have focused on high-involvement purchases such as insurance, automobiles, or industrial products. There is no simple explanation for effective sales interactions. Instead, the effectiveness of sales efforts is influenced by the interactions of

- The salesperson's knowledge, skill, and authority.
- The nature of the customer's buying task.
- The customer–salesperson relationship.

Thus, specific research is required for each target market and product category to determine the optimal personnel selling strategy.

Consider the following shopping experience:

I also had lousy service in the store. The sales guy seemed to be trying to sell me the cheaper shoe to get me out the door . . . . The thing that irritated me was that I thought I was a fairly knowledgeable shopper and I thought that they should understand some of these things . . . . They weren't very knowledgeable . . . . I got the impression they didn't like their jobs.[94]

Is this consumer likely to return to this outlet? Will he recommend it to his friends? It is clear that knowledgeable, helpful salespeople enhance the shopping experience, while those who are not have the opposite effect.

PURCHASE

Once the consumer has selected the brand and store, he or she must complete the transaction. This involves what is normally called *purchasing* or *renting* the product. In traditional retail environments, this was straightforward and did not generally stop or delay purchases. An exception is a major purchase such as a home or car for which financing must be secured, insurance arranged, and so forth.

However, as we saw earlier, most consumers starting to make a purchase in an Internet store quit without making one. This may be due to uncertainty as to how to "check out," a decision against providing a credit card number online, or a negative reaction to shipping charges. Increasing the percentage of potential purchasers who actually purchase is a major challenge for most online retailers.

Until recently, purchasing or renting an item or service involved giving cash to acquire the rights to the product. However, credit now plays a major role in consumer purchases. The use of bank credit cards (e.g., Visa, MasterCard, Discover, and American Express) and store charge cards (e.g., Sears and JCPenney) is the major way consumers finance all but major items such as cars or homes. Research indicates that the ability to pay by credit card rather than cash substantially increases consumers' willingness to pay and the amount they purchase.[95] Thus, it may be to the retailer's advantage to encourage credit card use even though it must pay a percentage of these sales to the credit card companies.

Of course, credit not only is a means to purchase a product; it is a product itself. Thus, the decision to purchase a relatively expensive item may trigger problem recognition for credit. Because various forms of credit are available, the decision process then may be repeated for this problem.

Businesses need to simplify the actual purchase as much as possible. This involves strategies as simple as managing the time spent in line at the checkout register to more complex operations such as computerized credit checks to minimize credit authorization time. Many businesses appear to overlook the fact that the actual purchase act is generally the last contact the consumer will have with the store on that trip. Although first impressions are important, so are final ones. Store personnel need to be not only efficient at this activity but also helpful and personable. Their behaviors and attitudes should reflect the image the store wants the customer to leave with.

SUMMARY

Consumers generally must select outlets as well as products. There are three general ways these decisions can be made: (1) *simultaneously;* (2) *item first, outlet second;* or (3) *outlet first, item second.* Both the manufacturer and the retailer must be aware of the decision sequence used by their target market, as it will have a major impact on their marketing strategy.

The decision process used by consumers to select a retail outlet is the same as the process described for selecting a brand. The only difference is in the nature of the evaluative criteria used. The store's *image* is an important evaluative criterion. The major dimensions of store image are merchandise, service, clientele, physical facilities, convenience, promotion, store atmosphere, institutional, and post-transaction factors. *Store brands* can both capitalize on a store's image and enhance, or detract from, it. Outlet location is an important attribute for many consumers, with closer outlets being preferred over more distant ones. Larger outlets generally are preferred over smaller outlets. These variables have been used to develop *retail attraction,* or *gravitation, models.* These models can predict the market share of competing shopping areas with reasonable accuracy.

Consumers visit retail shops and shopper areas for a variety of reasons. *Shopping orientation* refers to the general approach one takes to acquiring both brands and nonpurchase satisfactions from various types of retail outlets. Knowledge of a target market's shopping orientations for a product category is extremely useful in structuring retailing strategy.

While in a store, consumers often purchase a brand or product that differs from their plans before entering the store. Such purchases are referred to as *unplanned purchases.* Most of these decisions are the result of additional information processing induced by in-store stimuli. However, some are impulse purchases made with little or no deliberation in response to a sudden, powerful urge to buy or consume the product. Such variables as *point-of-purchase displays, price reductions, store atmosphere, website design, sales personnel,* and brand or product *stockouts* can have a major impact on sales patterns.

Once the outlet and brand have been selected, the consumer must acquire the rights to the item. Increasingly, this involves the use of credit—particularly the use of credit cards. Use of such cards appears to increase the amount purchased. However, major purchases often require the consumer to make a second purchase decision: "What type of credit shall I buy to finance this purchase?" Financial institutions increasingly recognize the opportunities in the consumer credit field and are beginning to utilize standard consumer goods marketing techniques. Online retailers lose substantial sales because consumers intending to make a purchase do not, due to frustration with the site, fear of providing a credit number over the Internet, concern over shipping charges, or other reasons.

KEY TERMS

Atmospherics 611
External reference price 602
Impulse purchase 607
In-home shopping 590
Internal reference price 602
Perceived risk 604

Privacy concerns 593
Reference price 602
Retail attraction (gravitation) model 603
Servicescape 611
Shopping orientation 606

Spillover sales 601
Stockouts 614
Store atmosphere 611
Store brands 600
Store image 598
Unplanned purchases 607

INTERNET EXERCISES

1. Visit three Internet retail outlets. Which is the best? Why? Which is the worst? Why?
2. Visit two Internet retailers for the same product category. Evaluate the outlet atmosphere of each. What, if anything, in the atmosphere provides the following?
   a. Encouragement for impulse purchases
   b. Nonpurchase reasons for visiting
   c. Risk reduction
   d. Service
   e. Fun
3. Visit two online retailers and select an item of interest. Go through the checkout process up to the last step (don't buy it unless you want it!). What aspects of the process at each store might cause a user to stop before completing the purchase?

DDB NEEDHAM LIFESTYLE DATA ANALYSES

1. Examine the DDB Needham data in Tables 1a, 2a, 3a, 4a, 5a, 6a, and 7a. What characterizes individuals who place considerable emphasis on price as an evaluative criterion? What are the marketing implications of this for store-based retailers? For Internet retailers?

REVIEW QUESTIONS

1. The consumer faces the problems of both what to buy and where to buy it. How do these two types of decisions differ?
2. How does the sequence in which the brand/outlet decision is made affect the brand strategy? The retailer strategy?
3. How is the retail environment changing?
4. Describe Internet retailing.
5. What is meant by *privacy concern?* Why is it a particularly important issue for online shoppers?
6. Describe the eight segments of online shoppers.
7. What is a *store image,* and what are its dimensions and components?
8. What is a *store brand?* How do retailers use store brands?
9. What key decisions do retailers make with respect to retail price advertising?
10. What is meant by the term *spillover sales?* Why is it important?

11. How does the size of and distance to a retail outlet affect store selection and purchase behavior?

12. Describe the model of *retail gravitation* presented in the chapter.

13. How is store choice affected by the *perceived risk* of a purchase?

14. What is meant by *social risk?* How does it differ from *economic risk?*

15. What is a *shopping orientation?*

16. Describe six motivation-based shopping orientations of college students.

17. What is meant by an *in-store purchase decision?* Why is it important?

18. What is meant by an *impulse purchase?* Why is it important?

19. Once in a particular store, what in-store characteristics can influence brand and product choice? Give an example of each.

20. Describe the impact of point-of-purchase displays on retail sales.

21. Describe the impact of price reductions and deals on retail sales.

22. What is meant by *store atmosphere?* How does it affect consumer behavior?

23. What is a *servicescape?*

24. Why do consumers planning to make a purchase at an online outlet frequently fail to do so?

25. What are frequent problems consumers encounter while shopping online?

26. What can happen in response to a *stockout?*

DISCUSSION QUESTIONS

27. Name two product categories for which the brand is generally selected first and the outlet second, two for which the reverse is true, and two for which these decisions are generally made simultaneously. Justify your selections. How should marketing strategy differ across these products?

28. How would you measure the image of a retail outlet? How would your measurement differ between a traditional store and an online store?

29. Does the image of a retail outlet affect the image of the brands it carries? Do the brands carried affect the image of the retail outlet?

30. The discussion of outlet image lists nine dimensions and 23 components of these nine dimensions of store images. How would this change for the following types of outlets?
    a. Internet stores
    b. Catalog merchants

31. Respond to the questions in Consumer Insight 17–1.

32. How are social and economic risks associated with the following products likely to affect the outlet choice behavior of consumers? How would the perception of these risks differ by consumer? Situation?
    a. Nice sweaters
    b. Athletic shoes (for running)
    c. Wine (as a gift)
    d. Hairdresser

    e. Mountain bike
    f. Mouthwash
    g. DVD player
    h. Movie for a date

33. Describe an appropriate strategy for an online store such as Target for each of the motivation-based shopping orientations described in the text (page 606).

34. Describe an appropriate strategy for an online store such as J. Crew for each of the eight online shopper types described in the text (page 595).

35. The motivation-based shopping orientations described in the text were developed using a small sample of students. Do you think these are accurate descriptions of the shopping orientations of students on your campus? How should they be modified?

36. How should retailer strategies to encourage unplanned purchases differ depending on the type of unplanned purchase generally associated with the product category?

37. What in-store characteristics could traditional retailers use to enhance the probability of purchase among individuals who visit a store? Describe each factor in terms of how it should be used, and describe its intended effect on the consumer for the following products:
    a. Perfume
    b. Underwear
    c. Coffee after a meal

d. Flowers from a supermarket
e. Vitamins
f. Batteries

38. What site characteristics could online retailers use to enhance the probability of purchase among individuals who visit their sites? Describe each factor in terms of how it should be used, and describe its intended effect on the consumer for the following products:
    a. Jewelry from Target.com
    b. Books from Amazon.com
    c. Digital camera from Buy.com
    d. Backpack from REI.com
    e. Music CD from JCPenney.com
    f. Cosmetics from Macys.com
    g. Tools from Sears

39. What type of store atmosphere is most appropriate for each of the following store types? Why?
    a. Bank serving college students
    b. Cosmetic section of Sears
    c. Dentist

d. Consumer electronics
e. Kia automobiles
f. JCPenney (Neiman Marcus clothes at JCPenney's prices)
g. Inexpensive furniture
h. Thai food restaurant

40. Repeat Question 40 (except for *c*, *e*, and *h*) for online retailers.

41. Retailers often engage in "loss leader" advertising, in which a popular item is advertised at or below cost. Does this make sense? Why?

42. How would you respond to a stockout of your preferred brand of the following? What factors other than product category would influence your response?
    a. Toothpaste
    b. Cereal
    c. Deodorant
    d. Coffee
    e. Perfume/aftershave lotion
    f. Soft drink

APPLICATION ACTIVITIES

43. Describe the current state of Internet retailing.

44. Pick a residential area in your town and develop a gravitational model for (*a*) nearby supermarkets or (*b*) shopping malls. Conduct telephone surveys to test the accuracy of your model.

45. Develop a questionnaire to measure the image of the following. Have 10 other students complete these questionnaires. Discuss the marketing implications of your results.
    a. Target
    b. Amazon.com
    c. Domino's Pizza
    d. Campus bookstore
    e. eBay
    f. Sears
    g. The Gap
    h. Banana Republic

46. Have 10 students on your campus describe their shopping orientations in terms of animals as discussed in the section of the text on motivation-based shopping orientations. Combine your descriptions with those of two other students. Do any patterns emerge? Do they match those described in the text? How would you explain the differences?

47. For several of the products listed in Table 17–3, interview several students not enrolled in your class and ask them to classify their last purchase as specially planned, generally planned, substitute, or unplanned. Then combine your results with those of your classmates to obtain an estimate of student behavior. Compare student behavior with the behavior shown in Table 17–3 and discuss any similarities or differences.

48. Arrange with a local retailer (convenience store, drugstore, or whatever) to temporarily install a point-of-purchase display. Then set up a procedure to unobtrusively observe the frequency of evaluation and selection of the brand before and while the display is up. Describe your finding.

49. Visit two retail stores selling the same type of merchandise and prepare a report on their use of P-O-P displays. Explain any differences.

50. Interview the manager of a drug, department, or grocery store on their views of P-O-P displays and price advertising.

51. Answer Question 43 using a sample of 10 students. What are the marketing implications of your results?

52. Develop an appropriate questionnaire and construct a new version of Table 17–2, using products relevant to college students. What are the marketing implications of this table?

53. Determine, through interviews, the general shopping orientations of students on your campus. What are the marketing implications of your findings?

54. Interview 10 students on your campus and determine their attitudes toward and use of the Internet and online shopping. Place each into one of the eight online shopper segments described in the text. Do they fit into these segments? Combine your results with those of four other students. What do you conclude?

REFERENCES

1. L. Armstrong, "Anything You Sell, I Can Sell Cheaper," *Business Week,* December 14, 1998, pp. 130–31; and J. W. Gurley, "Buy.com May Fail," *Fortune,* January 11, 1999, pp. 150–51.

2. The most thorough coverage of this topic is M. Laaksonen, "Retail Patronage Dynamics," *Journal of Business Research,* September 1993, pp. 3–174.

3. R. R. Brand and J. J. Cronin, "Consumer-Specific Determinants of the Size of Retail Choice Sets," *Journal of Services Marketing,* no. 1 (1997), pp. 19–38.

4. S. Sherman, "Will the Information Superhighway Be the Death of Retailing," *Fortune,* April 18, 1994, p. 17. For a successful approach, see A. Taylor III, "How to Buy a Car on the Internet," *Fortune,* March 4, 1996, pp. 164–68.

5. From eMarketer, Inc. subscription services, September 10, 2001.

6. J. L. McQuivey et al., "On-Line Retail Strategies," *The Forrester Report,* November 1998, p. 5.

7. S. Chiger, "Consumer Shopping Survey: Part III," *Catalog Age,* November 1, 2001, pp. 1–4.

8. "Catalog Buyers Shifting to Web," www.internetnews.com, December 10, 2001.

9. Chiger, "Consumer Shopping Survey: Part III."

10. R. Gardyn, "Full Speed Ahead?" *American Demographics,* October 2001, p. 13.

11. See S. Sayre and D. Horne, "Trading Secrets for Savings," *Advances in Consumer Research,* vol. 27, eds. S. J. Hoch and R. J. Meyer. (Provo, UT: Association for Consumer Research, 2000), pp. 151–55.

12. See K. B. Sheehan and M. G. Hoy, "Flaming, Complaining, and Abstaining," *Journal of Advertising,* Fall 1999, pp. 37–51; J. E. Phelps, G. D'Souza, and G. J. Nowak, "Antecedents and Consequences of Consumer Privacy Concerns," *Journal of Interactive Marketing,* Autumn 2001, pp. 2–17.

13. Jupiter Media Metrix, Inc., June 2002.

14. P. Paul, "Mixed Signals," *American Demographics,* July 2001, p. 47.

15. Ibid; and K. B. Sheehan, "An Investigation of Gender Differences in On-Line Privacy Concerns," *Journal of Interactive Marketing,* Autumn 1999, pp. 24–38.

16. Paul, "Mixed Signals," p. 46.

17. See R. Gardyn, "Swap Meet," *American Demographics,* July 2001, pp. 51–55.

18. For a description of the FTC's approach in this area and its fit with consumer concerns, see K. B. Sheehan and M. G. Hoy, "Dimensions of Privacy Concern among Online Consumers," *Journal of Public Policy & Marketing,* Spring 2000, pp. 62–73. See also J. Phelps, G. Nowak, and E. Ferrell, "Privacy Concerns and Consumer Willingness to Provide Personal Information," *Journal of Public Policy & Marketing,* Spring 2000, pp. 27–41; and K. B. Sheehan and T. W. Gleason, "Online Privacy," *Journal of Current Issues and Research in Advertising,* Spring 2001, pp. 31–41.

19. M. A. Jones, P. J. Trocchia, and D. L. Mothersbaugh, "Noneconomic Motivations for Price Haggling," *Advances in Consumer Research,* vol. 24, eds. M. Bruck and D. J. MacInnis (Provo, UT: Association for Consumer Research, 1997), pp. 388–91.

20. www.byu.edu/news/releases/archive01/Jul/Internet.htm.

21. R. Gulati and J. Garino, "Getting the Right Mix of Bricks & Clicks," *Harvard Business Review,* May 2000, pp. 107–14.

22. "Top 10 US E-Retailers," *Retail Forward,* July 2002.

23. See A. Z. Cuneo, "What's in Store?" *Advertising Age,* February 25, 2002, pp. 1+.

24. See C. Talmadge, "Retailers Injecting More Fun into Stores," *Advertising Age,* October 30, 1996, p. 38; S. Chandler, "Reinventing the Store," *Business Week,* November 27, 1995, pp. 84–96; and K. Naughton, "Revolution in Retailing," *Business Week,* February 19, 1996, pp. 7–76.

25. S. A. Forest, "Look Who's Thinking Small," *Business Week,* May 17, 1999, pp. 67–70.

26. A. Z. Cuneo, "On Target," *Advertising Age,* December 11, 2000, p. 1.

27. K. Labich, "What It Will Take to Keep People Hanging Out at the Mall," *Fortune,* May 1995, pp. 102–6.

28. J. D. Lindquist, "Meaning of Image," *Journal of Retailing,* Winter 1974, pp. 29–38; see also M. R. Zimmer and L. L. Golden, "Impressions of Retail Stores," *Journal of Retailing,* Fall 1988, pp. 265–93.

29. W. R. Darden and B. J. Badin, "Exploring the Concept of Affective Quality," *Journal of Business Research,* February 1994, p. 106.

30. See N. Sirohi, E. W. McLaughlin, and D. R. Witink, "A Model of Consumer Perceptions and Store Loyalty Intentions for a Supermarket Retailer," *Journal of Retailing,* no. 2 (1998), pp. 223–45.

31. See S. Burton, D. R. Lichtenstein, R. G. Netemeyer, and J. A. Garretson, "A Scale for Measuring Attitude toward Private Label Products," *Journal of the Academy of Marketing Science,* Fall 1998, pp. 293–306.

32. See M. Corstjens and R. Lal, "Building Store Loyalty through Store Brands," *Journal of Marketing Research,* August 2000, pp. 281–91.

33. P. S. Richardson, A. K. Jain, and A. Dick, "Household Store Brand Proneness," *Journal of Retailing,* no. 2 (1996), pp. 159–85. For a conflicting view, see K. L. Ailawadi, S. A. Neslin, and K. Gegdenk, "Pursuing the Value-Conscious Consumer," *Journal of Marketing,* January 2001, pp. 71–89.

34. *The Double Dividend* (New York: Newspaper Advertising Bureau Inc., February 1977).

35. F. J. Mulhern and D. T. Padgett, "The Relationship between Retail Price Promotions and Regular Price Purchases," *Journal of Marketing,* October 1995, pp. 83–90. For similar results, see S. Burton, D. R. Lichtenstein, and R. G. Netemeyer, "Exposure to Sales Flyers and Increased Purchases in Retail Supermarkets," *Journal of Advertising Research,* September 1999, pp. 7–14.

36. See M. R. Stafford and E. Day, "Retail Services Advertising," *Journal of Advertising,* Spring 1995, pp. 57–71.

37. See C. Janiszewski and D. R. Lichtenstein, "A Range Theory of Price Perception," *Journal of Consumer Research,* March 1999, pp. 353–68.

38. See R. A. Briesch, L. Krishnamurthi, and T. Mazumdar, "A Comparative Analysis of Reference Price Models," *Journal of Consumer Research,* September 1997, pp. 202–14; T. Mazumdar and P. Papatla, "An Investigation of Reference Price Segments," *Journal of Marketing Research,* May 2000, pp. 246–58; and T. Erdem, G. Mayhew, and B. Sun, "Understanding Reference-Price Shoppers," *Journal of Marketing Research,* November 2001, pp. 445–57. For a different approach, see K. B. Monroe and A. Y. Lee, "Remembering versus Knowing," *Journal of the Academy of Marketing Science,* Spring 1999, pp. 207–25.

39. See V. Kumar, K. Karande, and W. J. Reinartz, "The Impact of Internal and External Reference Prices on Brand Choice," *Journal of Retailing,* no. 3 (1998), pp. 401–26.

40. T. Mazumdar and P. Papatla, "Loyalty Differences in the Use of Internal and External Reference Prices," *Marketing Letters* 6, no. 2 (1995), pp. 111–22; T. A. Suter and S. Burton, "Reliability and Consumer Perceptions of Implausible Reference Prices in Retail Prices," *Psychology & Marketing,* January 1996, pp. 37–54; M. S. Yadav and K. Seiders, "Is the Price Right?" *Journal of Retailing,* no. 3 (1998), pp. 311–29; and L. D. Compeau and D. Grewal, "Comparative Price Advertising," *Journal of Public Policy & Marketing,* Fall 1998, pp. 257–73.

41. See A. Biswas et al., "Consumer Evaluation of Reference Price Advertisements," *Journal of Public Policy & Marketing,* Spring 1999, pp. 52–65.

42. T. B. Geath, S. Chatterjee, and K. R. France, "Mental Accounting and Changes in Price," *Journal of Consumer Research,* June 1995, pp. 90–97.

43. See S.-F. S. Chen, K. B. Monroe, and Y.-C. Lou, "The Effects of Framing Price Promotion Messages on Consumers' Perceptions and Purchase Intentions," *Journal of Retailing,* no. 3 (1998), pp. 353–72; and M. R. Stafford and T. F. Stafford, "The Effectiveness of Tensile Pricing Tactics in the Advertising of Services," *Journal of Advertising,* Summer 2000, pp. 45–60.

44. See A. Biswas and S. Burton, "Consumer Perceptions of Tensile Price Claims in Advertisements," *Journal of the*

Academy of Marketing Science, Summer 1993, pp. 217–30; K. N. Rajendran and G.-J. Tellis, "Contextual and Temporal Components of Reference Price," *Journal of Marketing,* January 1994, pp. 22–39; and D. Grewal, H. Marmorstein, and A. Sharma, "Communicating Price Information through Semantic Cues," *Journal of Consumer Research,* September 1996, pp. 148–55.

45. I. Sinha and M. F. Smith, "Consumers' Perceptions of Promotional Framing of Price," *Psychology & Marketing,* March 2000, pp. 257–75.

46. See D. Simester, "Signaling Price Image Using Advertised Prices," *Marketing Science* 14, no. 2 (1995), pp. 166–88; and J. Srivastave and N. Lurie, "A Consumer Perspective on Price-Matching Refund Policies," *Journal of Consumer Research,* September 2001, pp. 296–307.

47. G. S. Bobinski, Jr., D. Cox, and A. Cox, "Retail 'Sale' Advertising, Perceived Retailer Credibility, and Price Rationale," *Journal of Retailing,* no. 3 (1996), pp. 291–306.

48. See I. Simonson, "The Effect of Product Assortment on Buyer Preferences"; and R. E. Stassen, J. D. Mittelstaedt, and R. A. Mittelstaedt, "Assortment Overlap," both in *Journal of Retailing* 75, no. 3 (1999), pp. 347–70 and 371–86.

49. C. S. Craig, A. Ghosh, and S. McLafferty, "Models of the Retail Location Process: A Review," *Journal of Retailing,* Spring 1984, pp. 5–33.

50. See D. R. Bell, T.-H. Ho, and C. S. Tang, "Determining Where to Shop," *Journal Marketing Research,* August 1998, pp. 352–69.

51. See B. G. C. Dellaert et al., "Investigating Consumers' Tendency to Combine Multiple Shopping Purposes and Destinations," *Journal Marketing Research,* May 1998, pp. 177–88.

52. See P. R. Messinger and C. Narasimhan, "A Model of Retail Formats Based on Consumers' Economizing on Shopping Time," *Marketing Science,* no. 1 (1997), pp. 1–23.

53. A. Chaudhuri, "Product Class Effects on Perceived Risk," *International Journal of Research in Marketing,* May 1998, pp. 157–68; and R. Batra and I. Sinha, "Consumer-Level Factors Moderating the Success of Private Label Brands," *Journal of Retailing* 76, no. 2 (2000), pp. 175–91.

54. Based on V. Prasad, "Socioeconomic Product Risk and Patronage Preferences of Retail Shoppers," *Journal of Marketing,* July 1975, p. 44.

55. G. R. Dowling and R. Staelin, "A Model of Perceived Risk and Intended Risk-Handling Activity," *Journal of Consumer Research,* June 1994, pp. 119–34; L. W. Turley and R. P. LeBlanc, "An Exploratory Investigation of Consumer Decision Making in the Service Sector," *Journal of Services Marketing* 7, no. 4 (1993), pp. 11–18; and J. B. Smith and J. M. Bristor, "Uncertainty Orientation," *Psychology & Marketing,* November 1994, pp. 587–607.

56. Settle, Alreck, and McCorkle, "Consumer Perceptions of Mail/Phone Order Shopping Media"; and C. R. Jasper and S. J. Ouellette, "Consumers' Perception of Risk and the Purchase of Apparel from Catalogs," *Journal of Direct Marketing,* Spring 1994, pp. 23–36.

57. See also J. C. Sweeney, G. N. Soutar, and L. W. Johnson, "The Role of Perceived Risk in the Quality-Value Relationship," *Journal of Retailing* 75, no. 1 (1999), pp. 75–105.

58. See K. L. Wakefield and J. Baker, "Excitement at the Mall," *Journal of Retailing* 74, no. 4 (1998), pp. 515–39; H. McDonald, P. Darbyshire, and C. Jevons, "Shop Often, Buy Little," *Journal of Global Marketing* 13, no. 4 (2000), pp. 53–71; J. A. F. Nicholls et al., "Inter-American Perspectives from Mall Shoppers," *Journal of Global Marketing* 15, no. 1 (2001), pp. 87–103; and B. Jin and J.-O. Kim, "Discount Store Retailing in Korea," *Journal of Global Marketing* 15, no. 2 (2001), pp. 81–107.

59. See M. A. Eastlick and R. A. Feinberg, "Gender Differences in Mail-Catalog Patronage Motives," *Journal of Direct Marketing,* Spring 1994, pp. 37–44; "The Call of the Mall," *EDK Forecast,* October 1994, pp. 1–3; and "Black, Hip, and Primed to Shop," *American Demographics,* September 1996, pp. 52–58.

60. D. N. Hassay and M. C. Smith, "Fauna, Foraging and Shopping Motives," *Advances in Consumer Research,* vol. 23, eds. K. P. Corfman and J. G. Lynch (Provo, UT: Association for Consumer Research, 1996), pp. 510–15.

61. See N. Paden and R. Stell, "Using Consumer Shopping Orientations to Improve Retail Web Site Design," *Journal of Professional Services Marketing* 20, no. 2 (2000), pp. 73–85; and K. E. Reynolds and S. E. Beatty, "A Relationship Customer Typology," *Journal of Retailing* 75, no. 4 (1999), pp. 509–23.

62. See J. E. Russo and F. Lecleric, "An Eye Fixation Analysis of Choice Processes for Consumer Nondurables," *Journal of Consumer Research,* September 1994, pp. 274–90.

63. See L. G. Block and V. G. Morwitz, "Shopping Lists as an External Memory Aid for Grocery Shopping," *Journal of Consumer Psychology* 8, no. 4 (1999), pp. 343–75.

64. See D. W. Rook and R. J. Fisher, "Normative Influences on Impulsive Buying Behaviors," *Journal of Consumer Research,* December 1995, pp. 305–13; R. Puri, "Measuring and Modifying Consumer Impulsive Buying Behavior," *Journal of Consumer Psychology* 5, no. 2 (1996), pp. 87–113; S. Youn and R. J. Faber, "Impulse Buying," *Advances in Consumer Research,* vol. 27, eds. S. J. Hoch and R. J. Meyer (Provo, UT: Association for Consumer Research, 2000), pp. 179–85; and U. M. Dholakia, "Temptation and Resistance," *Psychology & Marketing,* November 2000, pp. 955–82.

65. See S. E. Beatty and M. E. Ferrell, "Impulse Buying," *Journal of Retailing,* no. 2 (1998), pp. 169–91.

66. See *POPAI/Horner Drug Store Study* (Englewood, NJ: Point-of-Purchase Advertising Institute, 1992); A. J. Greco and L. E. Swayne, "Sales Response of Elderly Consumers to P-O-P Advertising," *Journal of Advertising Research,* September 1992, pp. 43–53; and *POPAI/Kmart/Procter & Gamble Study of P-O-P Effectiveness* (Englewood, NJ: Point-of-Purchase Advertising Institute, 1993). For an exception, see C. S. Areni, D. F. Duhan, and P. Kiekeer, "Point-of-Purchase Displays, Product Organization, and Brand Purchase Likelihoods," *Journal of the Academy of Marketing Science,* Fall 1999, pp. 428–41.

67. See E. T. Anderson and D. I. Simester, "The Role of Sale Signs," *Marketing Science,* no. 2 (1998), pp. 139–55.

68. A. S. C. Ehrenberg, K. Hammond, and G. J. Goodhardt, "The After-Effects of Price-Related Consumer Promotions," *Journal of Advertising Research,* July 1994, pp. 11–21; and P. Papatla

and L. Krishnamurthi, "*Journal of Marketing Research,* February 1996, pp. 20–36.

69. See C. F. Mela, K. Jedidi, and D. Bowman, "The Long-Term Impact of Promotions on Consumer Stockpiling Behavior," *Journal of Marketing Research,* May 1998, pp. 250–62; and J. E. Urbany, P. R. Dickson, and A. G. Sawyer, "Insights into Cross- and Within-Store Price Search," *Journal of Retailing* 76, no. 2 (2000), pp. 243–58.

70. K. Sivakumar and S. P. Raj, "Quality Tier Competition," *Journal of Marketing,* July 1997, pp. 71–84; and S. M. Nowlis and I. Simonson, "Sales Promotions and the Choice Context as Competing Influences on Consumer Decision Making," *Journal of Consumer Psychology* 9, no. 1 (2000), pp. 1–16.

71. D. Grewal, R. Krishnan, J. Baker, and N. Borin, "The Effect of Store Name, Brand Name, and Price Discounts on Consumers' Evaluations and Purchase Intentions," *Journal of Retailing,* no. 3 (1998), pp. 331–52.

72. D. R. Bell and J. M. Lattin, "Shopping Behavior and Consumer Preference for Store Price Format," *Marketing Science,* no. 1 (1998), pp. 66–88. See also R. Lal and R. Rao, "Supermarket Competition," *Marketing Science,* no. 1 (1997), pp. 60–80.

73. V. G. Morwitz, E. A. Greenleaf, and E. J. Johnson, "Divide and Prosper," *Journal of Consumer Research,* November 1998, pp. 453–63.

74. Based on R. M. Schindler and T. M. Kibarian, "Increased Consumer Sales Response through Use of 99-Ending Prices," *Journal of Retailing,* no. 2 (1996), pp. 187–99; M. Stiving and R. S. Winer, "An Empirical Analysis of Price Endings with Scanner Data," *Journal of Consumer Research,* June 1997, pp. 57–67; R. M. Schindler and P. N. Kiby, "Patterns of Rightmost Digits Used in Advertised Prices," September 1997, pp. 192–201; and R. M. Schindler, "Relative Price Level of 99-Ending Prices," *Marketing Letters,* August 2001, pp. 239–47.

75. K. L. Wakefield and J. G. Blodgett, "The Importance of Servicescapes in Leisure Service Settings," *Journal of Services Marketing* 8, no. 3 (1994), pp. 66–76; K. L. Wakefield and J. G. Blodgett, "The Effect of the Servicescape on Customers' Behavioral Intentions in Leisure Service Settings," *Journal of Services Marketing,* no. 6 (1996), pp. 45–61; and K. L. Wakefield and J. G. Blodgett, "Customer Response to Intangible and Tangible Service Factors," *Psychology & Marketing,* January 1999, pp. 51–68.

76. See C. Mathwick, N. Malhotra, and E. Rigdon, "Experiential Value," *Journal of Retailing* 77 (2001), pp. 39–56; and P. D. Lynch, R. J. Kent, and S. S. Srinivasan, "The Global Internet Shopper," *Journal of Advertising Research,* May 2001, pp. 15–23.

77. J. Baker, D. Grewal, and A. Parasuraman, "The Influence of Store Environment on Quality Inferences and Store Image," *Journal of the Academy of Marketing Science,* Fall 1994, pp. 328–39; and E. Sherman, A. Mathur, and R. B. Smith, "Store Environment and Consumer Purchase Behavior," *Psychology & Marketing,* July 1997, pp. 361–78.

78. B. Babin and W. R. Darden, "Good and Bad Shopping Vibes," *Journal of Business Research,* March 1996, pp. 210–60; and K. Chang, "The Impact of Perceived Physical Environments on Customers' Satisfaction and Return Intentions," *Journal of Professional Services Marketing* 21, no. 2 (2000), pp. 75–85.

79. See K. A. Machleit, S. A. Eroglu, and S. P. Mantel, "Perceived Retail Crowding and Shopping Satisfaction," *Journal of Consumer Psychology* 9, no. 1 (2000), pp. 29–42.

80. S. J. Grove and R. P. Fisk, "The Impact of Other Customers on Service Experiences," *Journal of Retailing,* no. 1 (1997), pp. 63–85.

81. J. D. Herrington and L. M. Capella, "Practical Applications of Music in Service Settings," *Journal of Services Marketing* 8, no. 3 (1994), pp. 50–65; L. Dube, J.-C. Chebat, and S. Morin, "The Effects of Background Music on Consumers' Desire to Affiliate in Buyer–Seller Interactions," *Psychology & Marketing,* July 1995, pp. 305–19; J. D. Herrington and L. M. Capella, "Effect of Music in Service Environments," *Journal of Services Marketing* 10, no. 2 (1996), pp. 26–41; C. Rudel, "Marketing with Music," *Marketing News,* August 12, 1996, p. 21; C. S. Areni, J. R. Sparks, and P. Dunne, "Assessing Consumers' Affective Responses to Retail Environments," *Advances in Consumer Research,* vol. 23, eds. K. P. Corfman and J. G. Lynch (Provo, UT: Association for Consumer Research, 1996), pp. 504–09; and S. Oakes, "The Influence of Musicscape within Service Environments," *Journal of Services Marketing* 4, no. 7 (2000), pp. 539–56.

82. M. K. Hui, L. Dube, and J.-C. Chebat, "The Impact of Music on Consumers' Reactions to Waiting for Services," *Journal of Retailing,* no. 1 (1997), pp. 87–104.

83. C. S. Gulas and C. D. Schewe, "Atmospheric Segmentation," in *Enhancing Knowledge Development in Marketing,* eds. R. Achrol and A. Mitchell (Chicago: American Marketing Association, 1994), pp. 325–30. Similar results are in J. D. Herrington and L. M. Capella, "Effects of Music in Service Environments," *Journal of Services Marketing,* no. 2 (1996), pp. 26–41.

84. D. J. Mitchell, B. E. Kahn, and S. C. Knasko, "There's Something in the Air," *Journal of Consumer Research,* September 1995, pp. 229–38; A. R. Hirsch, "Effects of Ambient Odors on Slot-Machine Usage in a Las Vegas Casino," *Psychology & Marketing,* October 1995, pp. 585–94; M. Wilkie, "Scent of a Market," *American Demographics,* August 1995, pp. 40–49; and P. Sloan, "Smelling Trouble," *Advertising Age,* September 11, 1995, p. 1; E. R. Spangenberg, A. E. Crowley, and P. W. Henderson, "Improving the Store Environment," *Journal of Marketing,* April 1996, pp. 67–80; and P. F. Bone and P. S. Ellen, "Scents in the Marketplace," *Journal of Retailing* 75, no. 2 (1999), pp. 243–62.

85. A. S. Mattila and J. Wirtz, "Congruency of Scent and Music as a Driver of In-Store Evaluations and Behavior," *Journal of Retailing* 77, no. 2 (2001), pp. 273–89.

86. See A. M. Fiore, X. Yah, and E. Yoh, "Effects of Product Display and Environmental Fragrancing on Approach Responses and Pleasurable Experiences," *Psychology & Marketing,* January 2000, pp. 27–54.

87. K. Campo, E. Gijsbrechts, and P. Nisol, "Towards Understanding Consumer Response to Stock-Outs," *Journal of Retailing,* vol. 76, no. 2, 2000, pp. 219–42.

88. G. J. Fitzsimons, "Consumer Response to Stockouts," *Journal of Consumer Research,* September 2000, pp. 249–67.

89. From eMarketer, Inc., subscription services, September 10, 2001. See also J. Raymond, "No More Shoppus Interruptus," *American Demographics,* May 2001, pp. 39–40.

90. Reported by Pacific Online, Inc., www.pon.net/service/ecommerce/etailors, July 30, 2002.

91. Ibid.

92. From eMarketer, Inc., subscription services, September 10, 2001.

93. See L. Vincent, "Small Banks, Big Bytes," *Bank Marketing,* June 2000, pp. 25–29.

94. B. B. Stern, G. J. Thompson, and E. J. Arnould, "Narrative Analysis of a Marketing Relationship," *Psychology & Marketing,* no. 3 (1998), pp. 195–214.

95. D. Prelec and D. Simester, "Always Leave Home without It," *Marketing Letters,* February 2001, pp. 5–12; and D. Soman, "Effects of Payment Mechanism on Spending Behavior," *Journal of Consumer Research,* March 2001, pp. 460–74.

Powered by **SportsLine.com**

NFL INTERNET NETWORK
OFFICIAL SITE OF THE NATIONAL FOOTBALL LEAGUE

NFL .com

NEWS | SCORES | STATS | SCHEDULES | STANDINGS | TEAMS | PLAYERS

- ►FANTASY
- ►TV & RADIO
- ►ROSTERS
- ►DEPTH CHARTS
- ►NFL FILMS
- ►NFL INSIDER
- ►TICKETS
- ►AUCTIONS
- ►YOUTH FOOTBALL
- ►NFL SHOP

Click Here for Player Sideline Caps

Team Sites

Redskins:
Set for key battle with Colts
Chiefs:
The Vermeil Way
Dolphins:
Behind the scenes with Jamie Nails

Customize
[Select Team ▾]

Register for a FREE NFL.com Newsletter

NFL NETWORK
- ►KIDS
- ►GAMES
- ►NFLPLAYERS.COM
- ►UNDER THE HELMET
- ►SUPER BOWL
- ►PRO BOWL
- ►NFL EUROPE
- ►HALL OF FAME
- ►NFL ALUMNI

MORE FROM NFL.COM
- ►ESPANOL
- ►IN THE COMMUNITY
- ►NFL SUNDAY TICKET
- ►BASICS
- ►HISTORY
- ►INTERNATIONAL
- ►WIRELESS
- ►COACHES CLUB

 MOTOROLA

Dominating win

The Eagles won their third consecutive game over New York as they defeated the Giants 17-3 on Monday night. Donovan McNabb led the offensive attack, accounting for 248 total yards and scoring the game's lone touchdown. The Eagles own a two-game lead in the NFC East with the victory.

- Vote: Pepsi Rookie of the Week
- Recaps | Scores | Leaders | Photos
- Video: Carucci reviews NYG-PHI

Donovan McNabb ran for 111 yards and a TD against the Giants on Monday night.

Headlines
- Cowboys' Smith runs past Payton into record book
- Bucs' DT McFarland sidelined 6-8 weeks
- Falcons' Vick says he will play against Baltimore
- Ravens LB Lewis could be out for season
- Seahawks QB Dilfer out with torn Achilles
- Vote now: 2003 Pro Bowl balloting under way
- More headlines

NFL on SportsLine.com
- Week 8 review: Emmitt's good to be the king
- Dodd: Rice proves even great ones make mistakes
- Prisco: Griese on fast track as Brady crashes

Around the NFL

NFL GameDay 2003 Game Before the Game
Who will claim superiority as Super Bowl contenders battle it out in the NFL GameDay 2003 Game Before the Game at Super Bowl XXXVII?

NFL Tuesdays: Players in the community
Tuesday is the traditional day off for NFL players during the season. Find out how the players are helping their communities.

NFL Shop Weekly Feature - Shop By Team

New Fall Sideline Jackets
- Wear your team Reversible Jacket
- ON SALE: Hats, Tees & More

- Holiday Gift Ideas - Watches, Ornaments and more
- Beat the Clock: Personalized Gift deadline 12/14

Analysis & Opinion

Gil Brandt
- A Brandt's eye view of Emmitt

Pat Kirwan
- Favre tops midseason awards

McInally: What to eat pre-game
David Letterman: Scrapbook
Brandt: Midseason All-2002

More Analysis and Opinion

Featured Sites

NFL in the Community
- Apply for Junior Community QB award
- Players reach out
- Find out about NFL youth programs

CAST YOUR VOTE FOR NFL ROOKIE OF THE WEEK
BROUGHT TO YOU BY

Rookie of the Year

Features

Today in the NFL:
Carucci, Emmitt, Broncos among Week 8's top performers

- Marv Lew's Week 8 snapshot
- Smith NFL's new rushing king
  More Features

Fantasy:
- Fantasy index
- Week 8 Wrapup: Proving their worth
- Brandt: Special-teams impact

NFL FILMS tv
Donovan McNabb explains to NFL Insider's Vic Carucci why the Eagles beat the Giants 17-3.
56k | 100k | 300k
- NFL Fantasy 2002 LIVE!
- Vote for the Play of the Week
- Bears-Vikings: 56k | 100k | 300k
- Texans-Jaguars: 56k | 100k | 300k
More: Video | Radio
Visit the NFL Films Library

NFL POLL

Who is the most exciting quarterback in the NFL?
- ○ Aaron Brooks
- ○ Brett Favre
- ○ Donovan McNabb
- ○ Michael Vick

[Submit Vote]

Postpurchase Processes, Customer Satisfaction, and Customer Commitment

☐ Many firms now send consumers e-mail newsletters on a regular basis. The purpose of these letters is less to generate immediate sales than it is to build a relationship with customers. For example, Procter & Gamble sponsors a website called HomeMadeSimple.com that sends subscribers a monthly e-mail newsletter designed to help consumers achieve "easy living." According to a P&G spokesperson, "The ultimate goal is to build strong relationships with our customers."

The NFL has launched a similar program to supplement its website. It hopes to build a more personal relationship with its fans through a weekly e-mail newsletter. The newsletters provide a preview of the team's next game, information on trades, cuts, injuries, and so forth. There are also links to various NFL and team sites.

The program currently has 1.5 million subscribers. According to the NFL, "the e-mail newsletters are the most direct, most customized and the most critical to fan development." The NFL.com newsletter is customized by team and then further tailored to match the individual fan's specific interests.

The newsletter is not interactive: "We haven't gone to the full community model where fans can interact through message boards. But we are able to communicate with them by watching what they are interested in. We know what pieces of the newsletter they're clicking on. It allows us to better tailor the merchandising to the individual fan." Subscribers are informed when they register that they will be monitored to allow for customized information. They are invited to visit and update their profiles.[1]

Rare only a few years ago, customer relationship programs are now common in American firms. The objective of such programs is to increase the satisfaction, commitment, and retention of key customers. In this chapter, we will examine the postpurchase processes that produce customer satisfaction and commitment and the marketing strategies these processes suggest.

Figure 18–1 illustrates the relationships among the postpurchase processes. As the figure indicates, some purchases are followed by a phenomenon called *postpurchase dissonance*. This occurs when a consumer doubts the wisdom of a purchase he or she has made. Other purchases are followed by nonuse. The consumer keeps or returns the product without using it. Most purchases are followed by product use, even if postpurchase dissonance is present. Product use often requires the disposition of the product package or the product itself. During and after use, the purchase process and the product are evaluated by the consumer. Unsatisfactory evaluations may produce complaints by those consumers. Appropriate responses by the firm may reverse the initial dissatisfaction among those who complained. The result of all these processes is a final level of satisfaction, which in turn can result in a loyal, committed customer, one who is willing to repurchase, or a customer who switches brands or discontinues using the product category.

FIGURE 18–1	Postpurchase Consumer Behavior

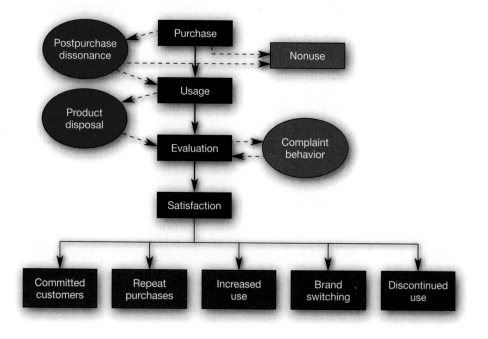

POSTPURCHASE DISSONANCE

I still like it [a dining room set] a whole lot better than what we used to have. But I think if we had taken longer we would have gotten more precisely what we wanted. I mean we got a great deal. You couldn't get that for that price, so I am happy with the money part of it, but some days I wish we had spent more and gotten something a bit different.[2]

This is a common consumer reaction after making a difficult, relatively permanent decision. Doubt or anxiety of this type is referred to as **postpurchase dissonance.**[3] Figure 18–1 indicates that some, but not all, consumer purchase decisions are followed by postpurchase dissonance. The probability of a consumer experiencing postpurchase dissonance, as well as the magnitude of such dissonance, is a function of

- *The degree of commitment or irrevocability of the decision.* The easier it is to alter the decision, the less likely the consumer is to experience dissonance.
- *The importance of the decision to the consumer.* The more important the decision, the more likely dissonance will result.
- *The difficulty of choosing among the alternatives.* The more difficult it is to select from among the alternatives, the more likely the experience and magnitude of dissonance. Decision difficulty is a function of the number of alternatives considered, the number of relevant attributes associated with each alternative, and the extent to which each alternative offers attributes not available with the other alternatives.
- *The individual's tendency to experience anxiety.* Some individuals have a higher tendency to experience anxiety than do others. The higher the tendency to experience anxiety, the more likely the individual will experience postpurchase dissonance.

Dissonance occurs because making a relatively permanent commitment to a chosen alternative requires one to give up the attractive features of the unchosen alternatives. This is inconsistent with the desire for those features. Thus, nominal and most limited decision making will not produce postpurchase dissonance, because these decisions do not consider attractive features in an unchosen brand that do not also exist in the chosen brand. For example, a consumer who has an evoked set of three brands of detergent could consider them to be equivalent on all relevant attributes except price and, therefore, always purchases the least expensive brand. Such a purchase would not produce postpurchase dissonance.

Because most high-involvement purchase decisions involve one or more of the factors that lead to postpurchase dissonance, these decisions often are accompanied by dissonance. And, since dissonance is unpleasant, consumers generally attempt to avoid or reduce it.

Decisions that involve giving up some or all of a desirable feature to obtain a slightly more desirable feature often generate negative emotions while the decision is being made. These negative emotions may be sufficient to cause the consumer to avoid or delay the decision (I'll just keep this car a while longer).[4] This suggests that firms marketing products such as automobiles, vacation homes, expensive vacation packages, and similar products train their salespeople to help minimize these negative emotions. Advertising that emphasizes the fun and positive emotions of the decision outcome and incentive programs that encourage consumers to continue with the purchase process could also be effective.

Consumers may also use decision rules designed to minimize the experience of postpurchase doubt. Such a rule or tactic would focus on minimizing the regret or doubt that a decision might produce rather than maximizing the value or benefits of the decisions.[5] The following choice exemplifies this rule:

> And I think that fear was one reason that we bought the General Motors van because we were afraid that if we bought the Ford . . . . Well, there is a feeling that if something is too much less, then you start asking yourself why is it that much less . . . . We had read how Ford uses more automatization in their manufacturing and we knew that it cost them less to make a car than GM. So we knew that there was a real reason for why theirs is so much cheaper, but you keep asking yourself, "Am I going to kick myself for this? Am I going to wish that I spent more and gotten the other one?"[6]

After the purchase is made, the consumer may utilize one or more of the following approaches to reduce dissonance:

* Increase the desirability of the brand purchased.
* Decrease the desirability of rejected alternatives.
* Decrease the importance of the purchase decision.
* Reverse the purchase decision (return the product before use).

Although postpurchase dissonance may be reduced by internal reevaluations, searching for additional external information that serves to confirm the wisdom of a particular choice is also a common strategy. Naturally, information that supports the consumer's choice acts to bolster confidence in the correctness of the purchase decision.

The consumer's search for, or heightened receptiveness to, information *after* the purchase greatly enhances the role that advertising and follow-up sales efforts can have. To build customer confidence in choosing their brand, many marketers of consumer durables such as major appliances and automobiles send recent purchasers direct-mail materials designed in large part to confirm the wisdom of the purchase. Local retailers can place follow-up calls to make sure the customer is not experiencing any problems with the car or appliance and to reduce any dissonance. Even a simple message such as "Thanks for buying a new Saturn from us. We know you'll be happy with your decision. Is there anything we can do to help you enjoy your new car more?" can reduce dissonance and increase satisfaction.

Many advertisements help recent purchasers confirm the wisdom of their purchase as well as attract new purchasers. Imagine that you have just purchased a new Compaq computer after agonizing between it and several other options. Now you are wondering if you made the best choice. At this point, you are likely to be very receptive to positive information about Compaq. So if you encounter the ad shown in Illustration 18–1, you are apt to read it.

A concept very similar to postpurchase dissonance is **consumption guilt.** Consumption guilt occurs when *negative emotions or guilt feelings are aroused by the use of a product or a service.* A person driving a large car may experience some negative feelings due to concern over resource utilization and pollution. The example below illustrates consumption guilt quite clearly:

> I have to count calories much more than I did before. I still buy a sundae once in a while but the joy of eating ice cream will probably forever be connected with guilt over eating something so unhealthy. When I think about it, I realize that most products make me feel good and bad at the same time.[7]

Marketers of products whose target markets might experience consumption guilt need to focus on validating the consumption of the product. They need to find ways to give the consumer permission or a rationale for indulging in that consumption act.

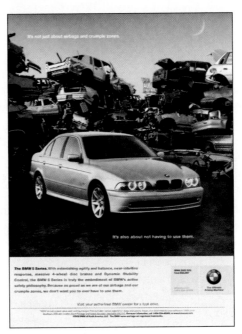

ILLUSTRATION 18–1

Advertisements for high-involvement purchase items can serve to confirm the wisdom of a purchase as well as influence new purchasers.

As Consumer Insight 18–1 indicates, consumers also engage in "what if" thinking after and sometimes before purchases.

PRODUCT USE AND NONUSE

Product Use

Most consumer purchases involve nominal or limited decision making and therefore arouse little or no postpurchase dissonance. Instead, the purchaser or some other member of the household uses the product without first worrying about the wisdom of the purchase. And, as Figure 18–1 shows, even when postpurchase dissonance occurs, it is still generally followed by product use.

Marketers need to understand how consumers use their products for a variety of reasons. Understanding both the functional and symbolic ways in which a product is used can lead to more effective product designs. For example, Nike uses observation of basketball players at inner-city courts to gain insights into desired functional and style features. One insight gained through these observations is that the process of putting on and tying/buckling basketball shoes before a match is full of meaning and symbolism. In many ways, it is the equivalent of a knight putting on armor before a jousting match or combat. Nike has used this insight in several aspects of its shoe designs.

Use innovativeness refers to *a consumer using a product in a new way*.[8] Marketers who discover new uses for their products can greatly expand sales. Two products famous for this are Arm & Hammer's baking soda and WD-40. Arm & Hammer discovered that consumers were using its baking soda for a variety of noncooking uses such as deodorizing refrigerators. It now advertises such uses. WD-40, a lubricant, is renowned for the wide array of applications that consumers suggest for it, including as an additive to fish bait and for removing gum from a carpet.

Counterfactual thinking refers to imagining the outcome if a different decision had been made in the past.[9] These thoughts are generally in the form of a conditional proposition such as "If I had a convertible instead of this sedan, I would be a lot happier now." Typically the antecedent (*if*) refers to an action or decision by an individual. The consequence (*then*) generally describes a state of being in evaluative terms (*happy*). Counterfactual thinking can be negative (I'd be better off had I made a different choice) or positive (I'd be worse off had I made a different choice). Such thoughts are different from cognitive dissonance in that the antecedent—a convertible in this case—might not have been considered at the time of the original decision.

Prefactual thinking is the same as counterfactual except it occurs before a decision is made. A common form of such thinking is "If I buy this notebook computer today and it goes on sale somewhere else next week, I'll really regret it." Research shows that this particular type of purchase barrier can be removed by price guarantees. These guarantees not only reduce the negative effect such thinking produces but tend to increase long-term satisfaction even if they were not exercised.

Marketers often encourage counterfactual and prefactual thinking (see Illustration 18–2). State lotteries are one industry that frequently uses ads that directly encourage people to imagine what they would do with the money had they won (counterfactual) or if they win (prefactual) the lottery. Likewise, resorts and cruise lines encourage prefactual thinking about the pleasures of using their services. Firms seek to reassure purchasers of major items that they did indeed make an optimal decision, which decreases negative counterfactual thinking.

Critical Thinking Questions

1. What ethical issues, if any, are there with state lotteries encouraging counterfactual and prefactual thinking about winning the lottery?

2. Why is counterfactual thinking so common among consumers (it is common)?

ILLUSTRATION 18–2

Marketers frequently try to encourage prefactual thinking by encouraging consumers to imagine a positive outcome for a decision not yet made.

Think of the possibilities.

Remodeling with Marvin windows and doors can change your whole outlook. Take the Marvin clad or all-wood Ultimate Double Hung, for example. Not only is it easier to open, close and clean than other double hungs, but it's available in enough size and lite pattern options to make a truly impressive statement. On the other hand, if you're satisfied with the view but not with the windows framing it, Marvin Tilt-Pac replacement sash are an ideal solution. Either way, you'll find things much more to your liking.

For a free brochure, call 1-800-268-7644.

MARVIN
Windows and Doors
Made for you.

(In Canada, 1-800-263-6161) www.marvin.com

Courtesy of Marvin Windows & Doors.

Many firms attempt to obtain relevant information on product usage via surveys using standard questionnaires. Such surveys can lead to new-product development, indicate new uses or markets for existing products, or indicate appropriate communications themes. For example, *what marketing strategies are suggested by the following uses of a microwave oven?*[10]

Use	Times per Month
Reheat food	11.4
Cook food	2.6
Cook frozen food (TV dinner)	2.3
Boil water (for coffee)	2.1
Defrost food	1.6

Surveys can provide useful information, but observation, depth interviews, and case studies often produce deeper insights:

* During the summer, several Chicago organizations offer "architectural boat cruises" on the Chicago River. They compete on the architectural credentials of their guides, the sites shown, and the boats used. One company did a standard survey and virtually all the respondents checked "interest in architecture" as a "very important" or "extremely important" reason for taking the cruise. However, depth research with 50 passengers showed that architecture was a relatively minor reason for their being there. Most of the Chicago residents were there as a means to entertain out-of-town guests on a nice day. This finding resulted in very different positioning and advertising themes for the sponsoring firm.
* A few years back, a number of upscale frozen gourmet dinner entrées were introduced with great expectations—which none achieved. Researchers observed the frozen food cases that still sold the product and found that, while most consumers ignored it, a few bought substantial quantities. Interviews with these consumers revealed that they were not using them for home meals but rather were preparing them in the office microwave for lunch. They stated that good restaurants were too slow, inconvenient, and expensive for lunch and fast-food places lacked quality and nutrition. This led to opportunities to reposition a line for office-based lunch consumption.[11]

Retailers can frequently take advantage of the fact that the use of one product may require or suggest the use of other products. Consider the following product sets: houseplants and fertilizer, bikes and helmets, cameras and carrying cases, sport coats and ties, and dresses and shoes. In each case, the use of the first product is made easier, more enjoyable, or safer by the use of the related product. Retailers can promote such items jointly, display them together, or train their sales personnel to make relevant complementary sales.

Stringent product liability laws and aggressive civil suits also are forcing marketing managers to examine how consumers use their products. These laws have made firms responsible for harm caused by products *not only when the product is used as specified by the manufacturer but in any reasonably foreseeable use of the product*. Thus, the manufacturer must design products with both the primary purpose *and* other potential uses in mind. This requires substantial research into how consumers actually use products.

When marketers discover confusion about the proper way to use a product, it is often to their advantage to teach consumers how to use it. At other times, a firm can gain a competitive advantage by redesigning the product so that it is easier to use properly (see Illustration 18–3).

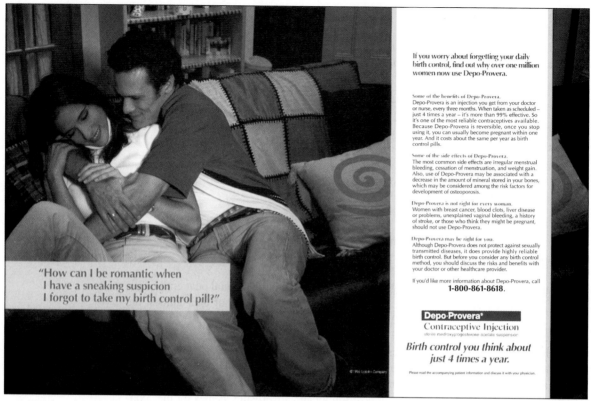

If you worry about forgetting your daily birth control, find out why over one million women now use Depo-Provera.

Some of the benefits of Depo-Provera.
Depo-Provera is an injection you get from your doctor or nurse, every three months. When taken as scheduled – just 4 times a year – it's more than 99% effective. So it's one of the most reliable contraceptives available. Because Depo-Provera is reversible, once you stop using it, you can usually become pregnant within one year. And it costs about the same per year as birth control pills.

Some of the side effects of Depo-Provera.
The most common side effects are irregular menstrual bleeding, cessation of menstruation, and weight gain. Also, use of Depo-Provera may be associated with a decrease in the amount of mineral stored in your bones, which may be considered among the risk factors for development of osteoporosis.

Depo-Provera is not right for every woman.
Women with breast cancer, blood clots, liver disease or problems, unexplained vaginal bleeding, a history of stroke, or those who think they might be pregnant, should not use Depo-Provera.

Depo-Provera may be right for you.
Although Depo-Provera does not protect against sexually transmitted diseases, it does provide highly reliable birth control. But before you consider any birth control method, you should discuss the risks and benefits with your doctor or other healthcare provider.

If you'd like more information about Depo-Provera, call **1-800-861-8618**.

Depo·Provera®
Contraceptive Injection
depo medroxyprogesterone acetate suspension

Birth control you think about just 4 times a year.

Please read the accompanying patient information and discuss it with your physician.

"How can I be romantic when I have a sneaking suspicion I forgot to take my birth control pill?"

Courtesy Pharm & Upjohn, Inc.

ILLUSTRATION 18–3	

Consumers frequently discontinue using, or use improperly, products that require consistent daily behaviors over long periods of time or that are otherwise difficult to use correctly. Firms that are able to redesign such products in a manner that makes them easier to use can gain a competitive advantage.

Product Nonuse

As Figure 18–1 indicates, not all purchases are followed by product use. **Product nonuse** occurs when *a consumer actively acquires a product that is not used or used only sparingly relative to its potential use.*[12]

For many products and most services, the decisions to purchase and to consume are made simultaneously. A person who orders a meal in a restaurant is also deciding to eat the meal at that time. However, a decision to purchase food at a supermarket requires a second decision to prepare and consume the food. The second decision occurs at a different point in time and in a different environment from the first. Thus, nonuse can occur because the situation or the purchaser changes between the purchase and the potential usage occasion. For example, a point-of-purchase display featuring a new food item shown as part of an appealing entrée might cause a consumer to imagine an appropriate usage situation and to purchase the product. However, without the stimulus of the display, the consumer may not remember the intended use or may just never get around to it. Nonuse situations such as the following are common:[13]

Wok—"I wanted to try and cook stirfry, but I didn't take time out to use it."

Skirt—"My ingenious idea was that I'd lose a few pounds and fit into the size 4 rather than gain a few and fit into the size 6. Obviously, I never lost the weight, so the skirt was snug."

Gym membership—"Couldn't get in the groove to lift."

Courtesy Campbell Soup Company.

In such cases, the consumer has wasted money and the marketer is unlikely to get repeat sales or positive referrals. Many such purchases are difficult for the marketer to correct after the purchase. In other cases, consumers would have used the product if reminded or motivated at the proper time. In the last example above, good records would indicate that this member was not using the gym. A personal letter, e-mail, or telephone invitation to come in might be enough to get this person started.

Campbell Soup Company has conducted research that shows that most homes have several cans of Campbell's soup on hand. Therefore, a major goal of its ads is to encourage people to consume soup at the next appropriate meal through such tactics as radio commercials aired prior to mealtime. Since consumers have the product available, the task is not to encourage purchase but to motivate near-term consumption.

The ad in Illustration 18–4 would serve to encourage both the purchase of Campbell's soup and the near-term consumption of soup already on hand.

The division between the initial purchase decision and the decision to consume is particularly strong with catalog and online purchases. In effect, two decisions are involved in these purchases—the initial decision to order the product, and a second decision to keep or return the item when it is received. Not only is it likely that several days will have passed between the two decisions, but substantially different information is available at the "keep or return" decision point. In particular, consumers can physically touch, try on, or otherwise experience the item.

Obviously, online and catalog retailers want to maximize the percentage of items kept rather than returned. Intuitively, one might think that a strict return policy would accomplish this. However, such a policy might also reduce the number of initial orders. In fact, a liberal return policy appears to maximize initial orders *and* may also minimize returns.

Such a policy reduces perceived risk and signals higher quality (surrogate indicator), which increases initial orders. Consumers also tend to perceive items ordered under liberal return policies as having higher quality after receiving them, which reduces returns.[14]

DISPOSITION

Disposition of the product or the product's container may occur before, during, or after product use. Or for products that are completely consumed, such as an ice cream cone, no disposition may be involved.

The United States produces several hundred million tons of household and commercial refuse a year, more than 1,500 pounds per person, not including industrial waste. Many landfills are rapidly being filled. Collection and dumping costs for most urban and suburban areas continue to climb. Environmental concerns involving dioxins, lead, and mercury are growing. Clearly, disposition is a major concern for marketers.

Millions of pounds of product packages are disposed of every day. These containers are thrown away as garbage or litter, used in some capacity by the consumer, or recycled. Creating packages that utilize a minimal amount of resources is important for economic reasons as well as being a matter of social responsibility. Many firms are responding to this issue, as the examples below illustrate:

- Rubbermaid repositioned its trash barrel line to a recycling container line. The new line has four models designed to store newspapers, cans, bottles, and yard waste.
- Procter & Gamble uses recycled paper in 80 percent of its product packaging and is packaging liquid Spic and Span, Tide, Cheer, and Downy in containers made from recycled packages.
- Mobil Chemical Co. recently introduced Hefty degradable trash bags. Poly-Tech Inc. sells Ruggies and Sure-Sac degradable bags (however, the bags require exposure to sunlight to degrade).
- The plastics industry has introduced a coding system that identifies a container's plastic resin composition and indicates whether it can be recycled.

For many product categories, a physical product continues to exist even though it may no longer meet a consumer's needs. A product may no longer function physically (instrumental function) in a manner desired by a consumer. Or it may no longer provide the symbolic meaning desired by the consumer. An automobile that no longer runs is an example of a product ceasing to function instrumentally. An automobile whose owner decides it is out of style no longer functions symbolically, for that particular consumer. In either case, once a replacement purchase is made, or even before the purchase, a disposition decision must be made.

Figure 18–2 illustrates the various alternatives for disposing of a product or package. Unfortunately, while "throw it away" is only one of many disposition alternatives, it is by far the most widely used by consumers. Environmental groups work hard to change these behaviors, as do some firms (see Illustration 18–5). Other firms, however, continue to use unnecessary or hard to recycle packaging and product components. Some of these same firms also spend millions of dollars campaigning against stricter laws on recycling and product/package disposition.

Product Disposition and Marketing Strategy

Why should a marketing manager be concerned about the disposition of a used product? Perhaps the best reason is the cumulative effect that these decisions have on the quality of the environment and the lives of current and future generations. However, there are also

FIGURE 18–2	**Disposition Alternatives**

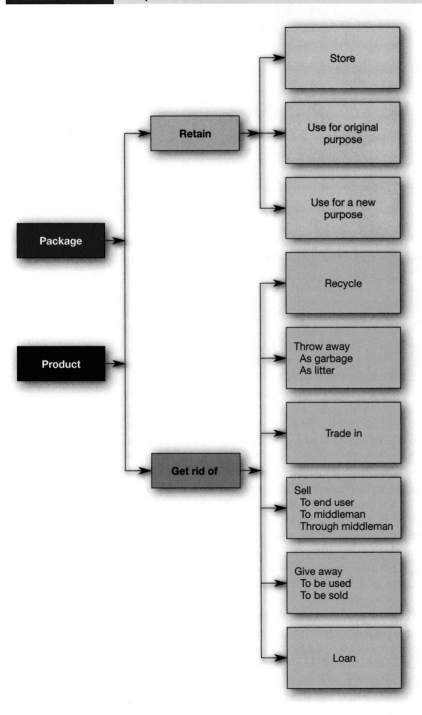

Proper product dis-
position is important
to many consumers
and therefore to
many firms and
industries.

© 2002 Rechargeable Battery Recycling Corporation.

short-term economic reasons for concern. Disposition decisions affect the purchase decisions of both the individual making the disposition and other individuals in the market for
that product category.

There are five major ways in which disposition decisions can affect a firm's marketing
strategy. First, for most durable goods consumers are reluctant to purchase a new item until
they have "gotten their money's worth" from the old one. These consumers mentally de-
preciate the value of a durable item over time. If the item is not fully mentally depreciated,
they are reluctant to write it off by disposing of it to acquire a new one. Allowing old items
to be traded in is one way to overcome this reluctance.[15]

Second, disposition sometimes must occur before acquisition of a replacement because
of space or financial limitations. For example, because of a lack of storage space, a family
living in an apartment may find it necessary to dispose of an existing bedroom set before
acquiring a new one. Or someone may need to sell his current bicycle to raise supplemen-
tal funds to pay for a new bicycle. Thus, it is to the manufacturer's and retailer's advantage
to assist the consumer in the disposition process.

Third, frequent decisions by consumers to sell, trade, or give away used products may
result in a large used-product market that can reduce the market for new products. A
consumer-to-consumer sale occurs when *one consumer sells a product directly to another with or without the assistance of a commercial intermediary.* Garage sales, swap
meets, flea markets, classified ads, and postings on electronic bulletin boards are growing
rapidly. And eBay has created a huge online market that consumers use to sell used items
(see Illustration 18–6).

In addition to consumer-to-consumer sales, consumers may give or sell their used items
to resellers. Thrift stores, featuring used clothing, appliances, and furniture, run by both

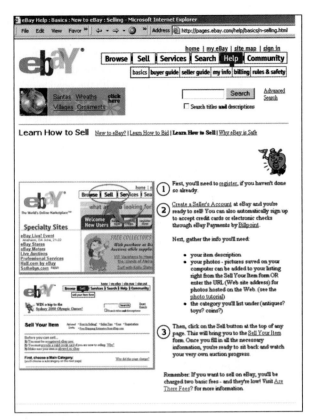

ILLUSTRATION 18–6

Consumer-to-consumer sales are an important way to dispose of products. The eBay auction site has built a substantial business by facilitating this process.

commercial and nonprofit groups, are an important part of the economy. Low-income consumers are the primary shoppers at thrift stores, but most economic groups engage in consumer-to-consumer sales, and eBay is currently used by relatively upscale customers.

A fourth reason for concern with product disposition is that the United States is not completely a throwaway society. Many Americans continue to be very concerned with waste and how their purchase decisions affect waste.[16] Such individuals might be willing to purchase, for example, a new vacuum cleaner if they were confident that the old one would be rebuilt and resold. However, they might be reluctant to throw their old vacuums away or to go to the effort of reselling the machines themselves. Thus, manufacturers and retailers could take steps to ensure that products are reused.

The fifth reason is that environmentally sound disposition decisions benefit society as a whole and thus the firms that are part of that society. Firms' owners and employees live and work in the same society and environment as many of their consumers. Their environment and lives are affected by the disposition decisions of consumers. Therefore, it is in their best interest to develop products, packages, and programs that encourage proper disposition decisions.

PURCHASE EVALUATION AND CUSTOMER SATISFACTION

As we saw in Figure 18–1, a consumer's evaluation of a purchase can be influenced by the purchase process itself, postpurchase dissonance, product use, and product/package disposition. Further, the outlet or the product or both may be involved in the evaluation.[17] Consumers may evaluate each aspect of the purchase, ranging from information availability to price to retail service to product performance.[18] For many products, this is a dynamic process, with the factors that drive satisfaction evolving over time.[19]

Overall satisfaction with a purchase could include satisfaction with the purchase process, including the information available for the decision and the experience of actually making the purchase, as well as satisfaction with the service or product purchased.[20] In addition, satisfaction with one component, such as the product itself, may be influenced by the level of satisfaction with other components, such as the salesperson.[21] However, keep in mind that nominal decisions and many limited decisions are actively evaluated only if some factor, such as an obvious product malfunction, directs attention to the purchase.

The Evaluation Process

A particular alternative such as a product, brand, or retail outlet is selected because it is thought to be a better overall choice than other alternatives considered in the purchase process. Whether that particular item is selected because of its presumed superior functional performance or because of some other reason, such as a generalized liking of the item or outlet, the consumer has a level of expected performance for it. The expected level of performance can range from quite low (this brand or outlet isn't very good, but it's the only one available and I'm in a hurry) to quite high.[22] As you might suspect, expectations and perceived performance are not independent. Up to a point, consumers tend to perceive performance to be in line with their expectations.[23]

While and after using the product, service, or outlet, the consumer will perceive some level of performance. This perceived performance level could be noticeably above the expected level, noticeably below the expected level, or at the expected level. As Table 18–1 indicates, satisfaction with the purchase is primarily a function of the initial performance expectations and perceived performance relative to those expectations.[24]

Table 18–1 shows that an outlet or brand whose performance confirms a low-performance expectation generally will result in neither satisfaction nor dissatisfaction but rather with what can be termed *nonsatisfaction*. That is, the consumer is not likely to feel disappointment or engage in complaint behavior. However, this purchase will not reduce the likelihood that the consumer will search for a better alternative the next time the problem arises.

A brand whose perceived performance fails to confirm expectations generally produces dissatisfaction. If the discrepancy between performance and expectation is sufficiently large, or if initial expectations were low, the consumer may restart the entire decision process. Most likely, he or she will place an item performing below expectations in the inept set (see Chapter 15) and no longer consider it. In addition, the consumer may complain or initiate negative word-of-mouth communications.

When perceptions of product performance match expectations that are at or above the minimum desired performance level, satisfaction generally results. Likewise, performance

TABLE 18–1

Expectations, Performance, and Satisfaction

Perceived Performance Relative to Expectation	Expectation Level	
	Below Minimum Desired Performance	Above Minimum Desired Performance
Better	Satisfaction*	Satisfaction/commitment
Same	Nonsatisfaction	Satisfaction
Worse	Dissatisfaction	Dissatisfaction

*Assuming the perceived performance surpasses the minimum desired level.

above the minimum desired level that exceeds a lower expectation tends to produce satisfaction. Satisfaction reduces the level of decision making the next time the problem is recognized; that is, a satisfactory purchase is rewarding and encourages one to repeat the same behavior in the future (nominal decision making). Satisfied customers are also likely to engage in positive word-of-mouth communications about the brand.

Product performance that exceeds expected performance will generally result in satisfaction and sometimes in commitment. Commitment, discussed in depth in the next section, means that the consumer is enthusiastic about a particular brand and is somewhat immune to actions by competitors.

Table 18–1 focuses on only the chosen alternative. However, the evaluation of the chosen alternative is somewhat dependent on the quality of the set of alternatives from which it was selected. A clearly superior choice may be held to lower standards than one that was nearly equal to one or more unchosen alternatives.[25] Other situational factors such as mood also affect how individuals evaluate products and services,[26] as do individual characteristics[27] and the general shopping environment.[28]

The need to develop realistic consumer expectations poses a difficult problem for the marketing manager.[29] For a brand or outlet to be selected, the consumer must view it as superior on the relevant combination of attributes. Therefore, the marketing manager naturally wants to emphasize its positive aspects. If such an emphasis creates expectations in the consumer that the item cannot fulfill, a negative evaluation may occur. Negative evaluations can produce brand switching, unfavorable word-of-mouth communications, and complaint behavior. Thus, the marketing manager must balance enthusiasm for the product with a realistic view of the product's attributes.

Determinants of Satisfaction and Dissatisfaction   Because performance expectations and actual performance are major factors in the evaluation process, we need to understand the dimensions of product and service performance. A major study of the reasons customers switch service providers found competitor actions to be a relatively minor cause. Most customers did not switch from a satisfactory provider to a better provider. Instead, they switched because of perceived problems with their current service provider. The nature of these problems and the percentage listing each as a reason they changed providers follow (the percentages sum to more than 100 because many customers listed several reasons that caused them to switch):[30]

- *Core service failure* (44 percent)—mistakes (booking an aisle rather than the requested window seat), billing errors, and service catastrophes that harm the customer (the dry cleaners ruined my wedding dress).
- *Service encounter failures* (34 percent)—service employees were uncaring, impolite, unresponsive, or unknowledgeable.
- *Pricing* (30 percent)—high prices, price increases, unfair pricing practices, and deceptive pricing.
- *Inconvenience* (21 percent)—inconvenient location, hours of operation, waiting time for service or appointments.
- *Responses to service failures* (17 percent)—reluctant responses, failure to respond, and negative responses (it's your fault).
- *Attraction by competitors* (10 percent)—more personable, more reliable, higher quality, and better value.
- *Ethical problems* (7 percent)—dishonest behavior, intimidating behavior, unsafe or unhealthy practices, or conflicts of interest.
- *Involuntary switching* (6 percent)—service provider or customer moves, or a third-party payer such as an insurance company requires a change.

Other studies have found that waiting time has a major impact on evaluations of service.[31] Consumers have particularly negative reactions to delays over which they believe the service provider has control and during which they have little to occupy their time.[32] Obviously, firms should attempt to minimize the delays encountered by their customers. If delays are unavoidable, the cause should be clearly indicated, as well as accurate estimates of the duration.[33] To the extent possible, consumers should be provided with activities or entertainment during the delay.[34]

Other research has found that negative performance on a feature such as waiting time or ease of use has a stronger effect on satisfaction than does positive performance on that same feature.[35] This suggests that both products and services focus on meeting expectations across all relevant features before maximizing performance on a few.

Not surprisingly, the nature and extent of personal contact with customers in service encounters are of critical importance in determining customer satisfaction. Although extended, personalized customer contact is expensive, it is very effective at increasing satisfaction and repeat purchase intentions.[36] However, increasingly services are delivered by self-service technologies such as ATMs and online stores. A recent study found the following dissatisfaction-causing incidents:[37]

Incident Type	Example
Technology failure	The ATM broke down. Kept my card. I had to have the card reissued.
Service design flaw	I did not realize that some ATM machines limit how much you can get out. The machine did not tell me I went over my limit for the day. It just spit my card back out so I kept trying.
Process failure	After a month passed from placing my original order, I e-mailed the customer service center at Disney with my order confirmation number. They had lost my order.
Technology design flaw	I was trying to order books from a book club online. The system was confusing, and I ordered two copies of the same title without knowing it.
Customer failure	I was attempting to get money from an ATM and couldn't remember my number. I was leaving for Japan in an hour and it took my card.

Many firms now guarantee their services. These guarantees can range from inclusive and general—"Satisfaction guaranteed"—to specific in terms of coverage and pay out—"Delivery in 30 minutes or it's free." Such service guarantees can increase expected performance levels and patronage—but can also increase costs.[38]

For many products, there are two dimensions to performance: instrumental, and expressive or symbolic. **Instrumental performance** relates *to the physical functioning of the product*. **Symbolic performance** relates to *aesthetic or image-enhancement performance*. For example, the durability of a sport coat is an aspect of instrumental performance, whereas styling represents symbolic performance. Complete satisfaction requires adequate performance on both dimensions. However, for at least some product categories such as clothing "Dissatisfaction is caused by a failure of instrumental performance, while complete satisfaction also requires the symbolic functions to perform at or above the expected levels."[39]

In addition to symbolic and instrumental performance, products also provide affective performance. **Affective performance** is *the emotional response that owning or using the product or outlet provides*.[40] It may arise from the instrumental or symbolic performance or from the product itself; for example, a suit that produces admiring glances or compliments may produce a positive affective response. Or the affective performance may be the primary product benefit, such as for an emotional movie or novel.

We are just beginning to understand the factors that lead to satisfaction with online retailers. Initial research indicates that convenience, site design, and financial security are the dominant factors. These are illustrated by the following statements from focus groups:[41]

> It is easy to browse for books online. There is only a select group of authors that I read and I want to read everything they write . . . . I can give them the name of the author and a list will pop up (convenience, satisfaction).
>
> It seems to take forever to navigate down far enough into the site to find what I'm looking for. And frankly, I've gotten really tired of the advertising (site design, dissatisfaction).
>
> I don't like giving my credit card to someone online. They keep it on file. I don't like the thought of someone having my card number on file (financial security, dissatisfaction).

DISSATISFACTION RESPONSES

Figure 18–3 illustrates the major options available to a dissatisfied consumer.[42] The first decision is whether or not to take any external action. By taking no action, the consumer decides to live with the unsatisfactory situation. This decision is a function of the importance of the purchase to the consumer, the ease of taking action,[43] the consumer's existing level of overall satisfaction with the brand or outlet,[44] and the characteristics of the consumer involved.[45] It is important to note that even when no external action is taken, the consumer is likely to have a less favorable attitude toward the store or brand.

Consumers who take action in response to dissatisfaction generally pursue one or more of five alternatives. As Figure 18–3 indicates, most of these alternatives are damaging to the firm involved both directly in terms of lost sales and indirectly in terms of a customer with a less favorable attitude. Therefore, marketers should strive to minimize dissatisfaction *and* to effectively resolve dissatisfaction when it occurs.

Consumers are satisfied with the vast majority of their purchases. Still, because of the large number of purchases they make each year, most individuals experience dissatisfaction

FIGURE 18–3	Dissatisfaction Responses

with some of their purchases. For example, one study asked 540 consumers if they could recall a case in which one or more of the grocery products they normally purchase were defective. They recalled 1,307 separate unsatisfactory purchases.

These purchases produced the following actions (the study did not measure negative word-of-mouth actions such as warning friends):

- 25 percent of these unsatisfactory purchases resulted in brand switching.
- 19 percent caused the shopper to stop buying the products.
- 13 percent led to an in-store inspection of future purchases.
- 3 percent produced complaints to the manufacturer.
- 5 percent produced complaints to the retailer.
- 35 percent resulted in the item being returned.

In a similar study of durable goods, 54 percent of the dissatisfied customers said they would not purchase the brand again, and 45 percent warned their friends about the product.[46]

Marketing Strategy and Dissatisfied Consumers

> I feel mad. I put it in my Christmas letter to 62 people across the country. I mean, I told everybody don't buy one of these things because the transmission is bad.[47]

The above example is a marketer's nightmare. And the ease of communicating by e-mail and on websites makes such scenarios even more frightening:

> I'm the founder of this website and like everyone else, I got scammed by First USA. Of course, at the time I thought it was just me. After battling First USA and getting nowhere, I decided to throw up a quick web page. I was surprised when I got bombarded with e-mails from people saying the same thing happened to them. Since then, this site has grown tremendously.[48]

Firms need to satisfy consumer expectations by (1) creating reasonable expectations through promotional efforts and (2) maintaining consistent quality so the reasonable expectations are fulfilled. Since dissatisfied consumers tend to express their dissatisfaction to their friends, dissatisfaction may cause the firm to lose future sales to the consumer's friends as well as to the consumer.[49]

When a consumer is dissatisfied, the most favorable consequence is for the person to communicate this dissatisfaction to the firm but to no one else. This alerts the firm to problems, enables it to make amends where necessary, and minimizes negative word-of-mouth communications. Many firms have discovered that customers whose complaints are resolved to their satisfaction are sometimes even more satisfied than are those who did not experience a problem in the first place.[50] In addition, complaints generally work to the consumer's advantage as firms attempt to redress the problem.

Unfortunately, many individuals do not communicate their dissatisfaction to the firm involved. Those who do complain tend to have more education, income, self-confidence, and independence and are more confident in the business system than those who do not complain.[51] In U.S. society, and more so in many others, people are taught not to complain. Therefore, complaining takes emotional energy:

> I find it hard to say anything when I'm unhappy [with a purchase]. It takes talking to myself all the way to the store. I say, "how do I say that?" I practice it. If I can get my husband to do it, I will. I'm very uncomfortable, even afterwards. I don't want people to think that I'm such a crab or not be liked or not think, "That's not such a nice lady."[52]

Complaints about products frequently go to retailers and are not passed on to manufacturers. Many firms attempt to overcome this by establishing and promoting consumer hot lines—toll-free numbers that consumers can use to contact a representative of the firm when they have a complaint. General Electric spends $10 million a year on its 800-number Answer Center, which handles 3 million calls annually. GE feels that the payback is "multiple times" that.[53] Procter & Gamble provides the following examples of benefits received from its hot line:

- Duncan Hines brownie mix: "We learned that people in high-altitude areas need special instructions for baking, and these soon were added to the packages. We also found that one of the recipes on a box label was confusing, so we changed it."
- Toothpaste: "We spotted a pattern of people complaining that they couldn't get the last bit of toothpaste out of the tube without it breaking, so the tubes were strengthened."
- A sudden group of calls indicated that the plastic tops on Downy fabric softener bottles were splintering when twisted on and off, creating the danger of cut fingers. P&G identified the supplier of the fragile caps and learned that it had recently changed its formula. The new-formula caps were becoming brittle as they aged. Most of the bad caps had not left the factory, and P&G simply replaced them. Thus, a costly (financially and imagewise) product recall was avoided.
- P&G also receives calls with positive testimonials. These are forwarded to the appropriate advertising agency, where they are analyzed for insights into why people like the product. Several P&G campaigns have been based on these unsolicited consumer comments.[54]

Consumers increasingly expect to be able to express complaints via e-mail. Initial research shows firms that receive and respond quickly to such complaints can greatly increase customer satisfaction.[55]

Although hot lines and other procedures increase the ease with which consumers can express a complaint, they are not sufficient. Most consumers who complain want a tangible result. Further, the results desired vary by customer type and the nature of the problem, requiring customized response capabilities.[56] Failure to deal effectively with this expectation can produce increased dissatisfaction. Therefore, firms need to resolve the cause of consumer complaints, not just give the consumers the opportunity to complain.[57] For example, Burger King, which receives up to 4,000 calls a day on its 24-hour hot line (65 percent are complaints), resolves 95 percent of the problems on the initial call. To be certain the customers are truly satisfied, company representatives call back 25 percent within a month.

Firms need to be cautious in how they elicit customer evaluations of their products and services. Customers who are told in advance or who otherwise expect to provide an evaluation of a product tend to focus on any negative aspects that arise. This in turn reduces their satisfaction and their willingness to repurchase or recommend the product or service.[58]

Unfortunately, many corporations are not organized to effectively resolve and learn from consumer complaints. This area represents a major opportunity for many businesses.[59] In fact, for many firms, retaining customers by encouraging and responding effectively to complaints is more economical than attracting new customers through advertising or other promotional activities. It has been estimated that it costs only one-fifth as much to retain an old customer as to obtain a new one.[60] Training those employees who deal directly with customers to use appropriate communication styles and empowering them to resolve problems as they arise is one way firms can increase customer satisfaction and retention.[61]

Anticipating dissatisfaction and removing the potential cause before it occurs can pay substantial benefits to a firm. A few years ago, a problem was discovered with the Intel

Pentium chip. The problem was rare and would affect very few users under only limited applications. Intel was slow to acknowledge and respond to the problem. This in turn generated a significant amount of negative publicity, which harmed the company's image and sales.[62] Contrast Intel's response and results to those of LifeScan:

LifeScan makes meters that diabetics use to monitor their blood sugar levels. Several years ago, a single meter was found to be defective. In response, the company notified 600,000 customers virtually overnight and recalled the entire product line. Customers responded positively to this show of concern by LifeScan. Its market share has increased by 7 percent since the recall.

LifeScan has a full-time manager of customer loyalty who works closely with the marketing and customer service departments to measure and improve customer satisfaction and retention. Customer service representatives field 1.3 million calls per year and are trained and empowered to make decisions to satisfy each caller. These service reps also play a key role in new-product development activities.

LifeScan offers its customers a 24-hour toll-free hot line, telecommunications capability for the deaf (diabetes contributes to hearing impairment), 24-hour meter replacement (meters are stored at FedEx in Memphis to make this possible), educational information, a newsletter, and a five-year product warranty. Additional services are provided to distributors and health care professionals.[63]

LifeScan reacted before all but one of its customers had a chance to experience dissatisfaction. This quick action resulted in increased customer loyalty and sales. Whirlpool uses a sophisticated customer data system to proactively prevent consumer problems:

Whirlpool maintains records on 15 million customers and more than 20 million installed appliances, some dating back to the 1960s. It uses specialized database computers to scan volumes of records in parallel and seek out faint but significant patterns.

This system recently raised a warning. A few customers had reported a serious water leak after only a few loads had been washed. Engineers quickly located the problem—a faulty hose clamp. Production was halted and the clamp was replaced on all in-process machines, those in inventory, and those at dealers. More important, the few hundred consumers who had purchased the new model were identified by Whirlpool's customer database. These consumers were quickly notified and mechanics were sent to their homes to replace the clamp.[64]

CUSTOMER SATISFACTION, REPEAT PURCHASES, AND CUSTOMER COMMITMENT

Pizza Hut's customer satisfaction department conducts an aggressive customer satisfaction campaign at all of its company-owned outlets. A key part of the campaign is a major, ongoing survey of several thousand customers per week.

A percentage of all customers who have pizza delivered or who take it out are telephoned within 24 hours. The interview is limited to four minutes. A system is in place to ensure that at least 60 days elapse before a customer is interviewed again. In addition, one out of every 20 to 30 dine-in customers is given a coupon at the bottom of their receipt and a toll-free number to call to participate in a six-minute interview. Two-thirds of those who respond to this offer do so within 24 hours, so the dining experience is still fresh in their memory.

Half of the store manager's quarterly bonus is linked to the survey results. Thus, it serves as a motivational and control device for the managers. In addition, it identifies problems quickly and allows managers to solve them before the image of the outlet or of Pizza Hut is harmed.

The surveys have identified systemwide problems as well as issues at individual stores. When Pizza Hut launched its Stuffed Crust Pizza, initial sales were strong, but repeat sales did not materialize. The surveys revealed the nature of the problems associated with the new product and enabled the firm to take corrective action. It also provided insights that Pizza Hut can use in future new-product introductions.[65]

Pizza Hut is typical of the many American firms that have responded to increased competition by focusing their efforts on producing satisfied customers rather than on producing short-term sales. However, given increasingly sophisticated and value-conscious consumers and multiple brands that perform at satisfactory levels, producing satisfied customers is necessary but not sufficient for many marketers. Instead, the objective is to produce committed or brand-loyal customers.

Figure 18–4 illustrates the composition of the buyers of a particular brand at any point in time. Of the total buyers, some percentage will be satisfied with the purchase. As we have seen, marketers are spending considerable effort to make this percentage as high as possible. The reason is that, while many satisfied customers will switch brands,[66] satisfied customers are much more likely to become or remain repeat purchasers than are dissatisfied customers.[67] **Repeat purchasers** continue to buy the same brand though they do not have an emotional attachment to it.

As we saw earlier, some dissatisfied customers may also become or remain repeat purchasers. These individuals perceive the **switching costs**—*the costs of finding, evaluating, and adopting another solution*—to be too high. However, they may engage in negative word-of-mouth and are vulnerable to competitors' actions.

Repeat purchasers are desirable, but *mere* repeat purchasers are vulnerable to competitor actions. That is, they are buying the brand out of habit or because it is readily available where they shop, or because it has the lowest price, or for similar superficial reasons. These

---

FIGURE 18–4   Creating Committed Customers Is Increasingly the Focus of Marketing Strategy

customers have no commitment to the brand. They are not brand loyal. **Brand loyalty** is defined as

> a biased (i.e., nonrandom) behavioral response (i.e., purchase/recommend) expressed over time by a decision-making unit with respect to one or more alternative brands out of a set of such brands that is a function of psychological (decision-making, evaluative) processes.[68]

Service and store loyalty are generally defined in the same or a similar manner.[69] Thus, a consumer loyal to a brand (store or service), or a **committed customer,** has an emotional attachment to the brand or firm. The customer likes the brand in a manner somewhat similar to friendship. Consumers use expressions such as "I trust this brand," "I like this outlet," and "I believe in this firm" to describe their commitment:

> I tried it myself one time and eventually adopted a taste for it. Now I drink it all the time. I have it every morning after I come in from my run. I drink it after I clean the house. I always have a glass of it in my hand. That's me. I am very loyal to Gatorade. I would say that I am very loyal to that. I know they have other brands of that now, I see coupons all the time, but I have never even picked up a bottle of them. Never even tried them. Because I like Gatorade a lot. I really do.[70]

Brand loyalty can arise through identification, where a consumer believes the brand reflects and reinforces some aspect of his or her self-concept. This type of commitment is most common for symbolic products such as beer and automobiles. It is also likely in service situations that involve extended interpersonal encounters.[71] Brand loyalty may also arise through performance so far above expected that it delights the customer.[72] Such superior performance can be related to the product, the firm itself, or, as mentioned earlier, the manner in which the firm responds to a complaint or a customer problem.

Given the above, it is obvious that it is more difficult to develop brand-loyal consumers for some product categories than for others. Indeed, for low-involvement product categories with few opportunities for truly distinct performance or customer service, most firms should focus on creating satisfied repeat purchasers rather than loyal or committed customers.[73]

Committed customers are unlikely to consider additional information when making a purchase. They are also resistant to competitors' marketing efforts—for example, coupons. Even when loyal customers do buy a different brand to take advantage of a promotional deal, they generally return to their original brand for their next purchase.[74] Committed customers are more receptive to line extensions and other new products offered by the same firm. They are also more likely to forgive an occasional product or service failure.[75]

Finally, committed customers are likely to be a source of positive word-of-mouth communications. This is extremely valuable to a firm. Positive word-of-mouth communications from a committed customer increase the probability both of the recipient becoming a customer and of the recipient sharing the positive comments with a third person[76]— "I haven't eaten at Aron's yet, but Kim raves about the food and service."

It is for these reasons that many marketers have attempted to create committed customers as well as satisfied customers. Committed customers are much more profitable to the firm than mere repeat purchasers, who in turn are more profitable than occasional buyers.[77]

Repeat Purchasers, Committed Customers, and Profits

Churn is a term used to refer to *turnover in a firm's customer base*. If a firm has a base of 100 customers and 20 leave each year and 20 new ones become customers, it has a churn rate of 20 percent. Reducing churn is a major objective of many firms today. Why? It typically costs more to obtain a new customer than to retain an existing one, and new customers generally are not as profitable as longer-term customers. Consider the profits generated by one credit card firm's customers over time:[78]

Year	Profits
Acquisition cost	($51)
Year 1	30
Year 2	42
Year 3	44
Year 4	49
Year 5	55

Acquisition costs include such expenses as advertising, establishing the account, mailing the card, and so forth. First-year profits are low because many new customers are acquired as a result of a promotional deal of some type. In addition, their initial usage rate tends to be low and they don't use all the features. This is a common pattern for both consumer and industrial products. Auto service profits per customer increased from $25 the first year to $88 in the fifth year, and an industrial laundry found they went from $144 to $258.

Figure 18–5 shows the sources of the growth of profit per customer over time. *Price premium* refers to the fact that repeat and particularly committed customers tend to buy the

---

FIGURE 18–5   **Sources of Increased Customer Profitability over Time**

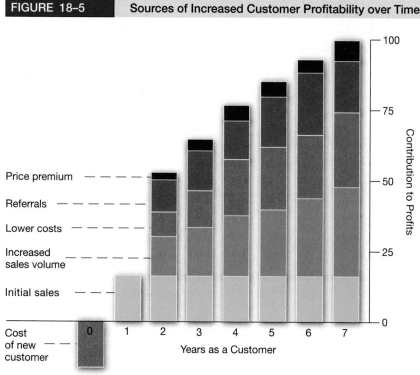

Source: © 1999 Time Inc. Reprinted by permission.

brand consistently rather than waiting for a sale or continually negotiating price. *Referrals* refers to profits generated by new customers acquired as a result of recommendations from existing customers. *Lower costs* occur because both the firm and the customer learn how to interact more efficiently over time. Finally, customers tend to use a wider array of a firm's products and services over time.

Although committed customers are most valuable to a firm, reducing churn can have a major impact on profit even if the retained customers are primarily repeat purchasers. Reducing the number of customers who leave a firm in a year increases the average life of the firm's customer base.[79] As we saw earlier, the longer a customer is with a firm, the more profits the firm derives from that customer. Thus, a stable customer base tends to be highly profitable per customer. Reducing the number of customers who leave various types of firms each year by 5 percent has been found to increase the average profits per customer as follows:[80]

Firm Type	Percent Increase in Average Profits per Customer
Auto service	30%
Branch banks	85
Credit card	75
Credit insurance	25
Insurance brokerage	50
Industrial laundry	45

The motivation for marketers to retain customers is obvious. Phil Bressler, the co-owner of five Domino's Pizza outlets in Maryland, found that a regular customer was worth more than $5,000 over the 10-year life of the franchise agreement. He makes sure that every employee in every store is constantly aware of that number. Poor service or a bad attitude may cost the outlet several thousands of dollars, not just the $10 or $15 that might be lost on the single transaction![81]

However, as Consumer Insight 18–2 indicates, retaining some customers is more profitable than retaining others.

Repeat Purchasers, Committed Customers, and Marketing Strategy

An important step in developing a marketing strategy for a particular segment is to specify the objectives being pursued. Several distinct possibilities exist:

1. Attract new users to the product category.
2. Capture competitors' current customers.
3. Encourage current customers to use more.
4. Encourage current customers to become repeat purchasers.
5. Encourage current customers to become committed customers.

Each of the objectives listed above will require different strategies and marketing mixes. The first two objectives require the marketer to convince potential customers that the marketer's brand will provide superior value to not using the product or to using another brand. Advertisements promising superior benefits, coupons, free trials, and similar strategies are common approaches. While some firms are content to consider the sale the last step, smart

Sophisticated data systems allow many firms to closely monitor the profitability as well as preferences of individual customers.[82] For example, every one of Continental Airlines' gate, reservation, and service agents can instantly access the history and economic value of every customer. This information includes very personal data such as past disagreements with gate agents. As a company vice president said, "We even know if they put their eyeshades on and go to sleep."

As you would expect, there are wide variations in profitability across customers. For example, at a typical commercial bank, the top 20 percent of customers generate six times more revenue than they cost. In contrast, the bottom 20 percent generate three to four times more costs than they do revenue.

In many industries, firms now utilize this individual profitability information to segment customers into service levels. Highly profitable customers receive excellent service, whereas those who generate low or negative profits receive little or no service.

At one electric utility, the top 350 business clients are served by 6 customer service representatives. The next 700 are served by 6 more, and the remaining 30,000 are served by 2. The 300,000 residential customers must deal with an automated 800 number.

Centura Banks of Raleigh, N.C., rates its 2 million customers on a profitability scale from one to five. "Ones" get substantial personal attention; "fives" do not.

First Union codes its credit card customers with colors that appear when their accounts appear on a service rep's screen. Green (profitable) customers are granted waivers and otherwise given white-glove treatment. Red (unprofitable) customers have no bargaining power. Yellow (marginal profit) customers are given a moderate level of accommodation.

Critical Thinking Questions

1. What ethic issues, if any, do you see from collecting and using individual data this way?
2. What risks, if any, do you see from this approach to providing service?

firms now realize the critical importance of retaining customers after the initial sale. This is true even for infrequently purchased items—rather than repeat sales, the marketer wants positive, or at least neutral, word-of-mouth communications.

The last three objectives listed earlier focus on marketing to the firm's current customers. All require customer satisfaction as a necessary precondition. As Figure 18–6 indicates, this requires that the firm deliver the value expected by the customer. Techniques for creating satisfied customers were described earlier. Marketing efforts focused on a firm's current customers are generally termed *relationship marketing*.

Relationship Marketing   *An attempt to develop an ongoing, expanding exchange relationship with a firm's customers* is called **relationship marketing.**[83] In many ways, it seeks to mimic the relationships that existed between neighborhood stores and their customers many years ago. In these relationships, the store owner knew the customers not only as customers but also as friends and neighbors. The owner could anticipate their needs and provide help and advice when needed. Relationship marketing attempts to accomplish the same results, but because of the large scale of most operations, the firm must use databases, customized mass communications, and advanced employee training and motivation.[84] Consider the following example:

Lees Supermarkets, a family-owned and -operated company, started a Shoppers Club that records the purchases of members. Frequent or heavy shoppers are offered special incentives and deals. These offers can be customized on the basis of past purchasing patterns. In addition, last Thanksgiving, 600 regular, high-volume members were rewarded with free turkeys. Such an unexpected reward can produce delight and loyalty among key customers.[85]

FIGURE 18–6   **Customer Satisfaction Outcomes**

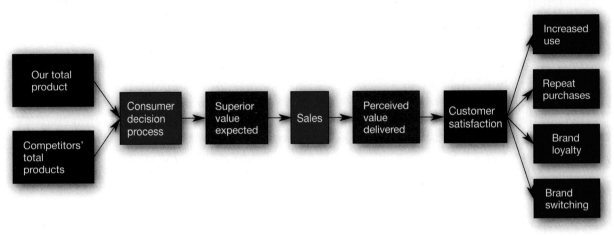

Relationship marketing has five key elements:[86]

1. Developing a core service or product around which to build a customer relationship.
2. Customizing the relationship to the individual customer.
3. Augmenting the core service or product with extra benefits.
4. Pricing in a manner to encourage loyalty.
5. Marketing to employees so that they will perform well for customers.

This list of elements makes it clear that relationship marketing is centered on understanding consumer needs at the individual consumer level.[87]

A substantial amount of effort is currently being focused on **customer loyalty programs.**[88] However, many of these programs are designed to generate repeat purchases rather than committed customers.[89] In addition to frequent-flier programs offered by most major airlines, programs designed to generate repeat purchases include the following:

- Saks-Fifth Avenue (Saks First) and Sears (Best Customer) identify frequent shoppers and make them members of their store "clubs." As members, they receive extra services, preshopping at sales, fashion newsletters, and so forth.
- Arby's Restaurants has Club Arby's that electronically tracks purchases and offers food prizes to repeat customers.
- Waldenbooks' Preferred Customer Program offers discounts and rebates to repeat purchasers. It also segments its membership according to the types of books each customer buys. This allows it to deliver customized direct-mail ads to its frequent shoppers.

Although programs such as those described above are often effective at generating repeat purchases, they do not necessarily create committed customers.[90] Committed customers have a reasonably strong emotional attachment to the product or firm. Generating committed customers requires that the firm consistently meet or exceed customer expectations. Further, customers must believe that the firm is treating them fairly and is, to some extent at least, concerned about their well-being. Thus, *generating committed customers requires a customer-focused attitude in the firm*. It also requires that this attitude be translated into actions that meet customers' needs.[91]

ILLUSTRATION 18–7

Successful customer loyalty programs are based on understanding the needs of key customers and providing benefits of value to them.

United Airlines attempts to create committed customers through the services it provides its passengers and an extensive frequent-flier program that gives increasing rewards the more one flies. For example, its Premier members get to board early, a privilege greatly appreciated by frequent fliers. The program has numerous affiliates that allow members to earn miles through credit card purchases, hotel stays, car rentals, phone calls, and a host of other activities (see Illustration 18–7). Miles can be redeemed for upgrades, tickets, cruises, vacations, and so forth.

Research is just beginning on creating site loyal customers for online marketers.[92] The appropriate strategy depends in part on the reason the site is being used—transactional versus experiential. A transactional site is visited primarily to make a purchase (buy a book); an experiential site is visited primarily for the pleasure the visit will provide (play fantasy baseball). However, for both types of sites customization to the individual level and building trust by protecting users' privacy are important means to developing loyal users.

SUMMARY

Following some purchases, consumers experience doubts or anxiety about the wisdom of the purchase. This is known as *postpurchase dissonance*. It is most likely to occur (1) among individuals with a tendency to experience anxiety, (2) after an irrevocable purchase, (3) when the purchase was important to the consumer, and (4) when it involved a difficult choice between two or more alternatives.

Whether or not the consumer experiences dissonance, most purchases are followed by product use. This use may be by the purchaser or by some other member of the purchasing unit. Monitoring product usage can indicate new uses for existing products, needed product modifications, appropriate advertising themes, and opportunities for new products. Product liability laws have made it increasingly important for marketing managers to be aware of all potential uses of their products.

Product nonuse is also a concern. Both marketers and consumers suffer when consumers buy products that they do not use or use less than they intended. Thus, marketers frequently attempt to influence the decision to use the product as well as the decision to purchase the product.

Disposition of the product or its package may occur before, during, or after product use. Understanding disposition behavior has become increasingly important to marketing managers because of the ecological concerns of many consumers, the costs and scarcity of raw materials, and the activities of federal and state legislatures and regulatory agencies.

Postpurchase dissonance, product usage, and disposition are potential influences on the purchase evaluation process. Consumers develop certain expectations about the ability of the product to fulfill instrumental and symbolic needs. To the extent that the product meets these needs, satisfaction is likely to result. When expectations are not met, dissatisfaction is the likely result.

Taking no action; switching brands, products, or stores; and warning friends are all common reactions to a negative purchase evaluation. A marketing manager generally should encourage dissatisfied consumers to complain directly to the firm and to no one else. Unfortunately, only a fairly small, unique set of consumers tends to complain. Developing such strategies as consumer hot lines can increase the percentage of dissatisfied consumers who complain to the firm.

After the evaluation process and, where applicable, the complaint process, consumers have some degree of repurchase motivation. There may be a strong motive to avoid the brand, a willingness to repurchase it some of the time, a willingness to repurchase it all of the time, or some level of brand loyalty or customer commitment, which is a willingness to repurchase coupled with a psychological commitment to the brand.

Marketing strategy does not always have the creation of brand loyalty as its objective. Rather, the manager must examine the makeup of the brand's current and potential consumers and select the specific objectives most likely to maximize the overall organizational goals.

Relationship marketing attempts to develop an ongoing, expanding exchange relationship with a firm's customers. It is used to increase brand usage, repeat sales, or customer commitment.

KEY TERMS

Affective performance 640
Brand loyalty 646
Churn 646
Committed customer 646
Consumer-to-consumer sales 636

Consumption guilt 628
Customer loyalty programs 650
Instrumental performance 640
Postpurchase dissonance 627
Product nonuse 632

Relationship marketing 650
Repeat purchasers 645
Switching costs 645
Symbolic performance 640
Use innovativeness 629

INTERNET EXERCISES

1. Monitor several product- or activity-related chat sites or interest groups for a week. Prepare a report on how a marketer could learn about the following by doing this.
   a. Customer satisfaction levels and customer commitment
   b. Product use
   c. Customer evaluation processes
2. Join Active.com. Evaluate its weekly e-mail newsletter.
3. Find a company site that helps the company in terms of relationship marketing. Describe and evaluate this effort.

4. Find an independent complaint website (go to Yahoo and search for "complaints about ____") for the following firms. What insights does it provide? How should the targeted company respond?
   a. United Airlines
   b. Disney
   c. Ford
5. How should marketers use eComplaints.com?
6. Find a product, company, or brand site that helps the consumer use a product properly or effectively. Describe and evaluate this effort.

DDB NEEDHAM LIFESTYLE DATA ANALYSES

1. What characterizes individuals who feel they have acquired too much debt? What are the marketing implications of this? What are the regulatory implications of this?

2. What characterizes people who become committed enough to favorite brands to resist other brands when they are on sale? What are the marketing implications of this?

REVIEW QUESTIONS

1. What are the major postpurchase processes engaged in by consumers?

2. How does the type of decision process affect the postpurchase processes?

3. What is *postpurchase dissonance?* What characteristics of a purchase situation are likely to contribute to postpurchase dissonance?

4. What actions do consumers take to avoid postpurchase dissonance before the purchase?

5. In what ways can a consumer reduce postpurchase dissonance?

6. What is *consumption guilt?*

7. What is *counterfactual thinking?*

8. What is *prefactual thinking?*

9. What is *use innovativeness?*

10. What is meant by *product nonuse,* and why is it a concern of marketers?

11. What is meant by the disposition of products and product packaging, and why does it interest governmental regulatory agencies and marketers?

12. What factors influence consumer satisfaction? In what way do they influence consumer satisfaction?

13. What is the difference between *instrumental* and *symbolic performance,* and how does each contribute to consumer satisfaction?

14. What is *affective performance?*

15. What courses of action can a consumer take in response to dissatisfaction? Which are used most often?

16. What determines satisfaction for online retailers?

17. What would marketers like consumers to do when dissatisfied? How can marketers encourage this?

18. What is *churn?* How does it affect profits?

19. What are the sources of increased profits from longer-term customers?

20. What is the relationship between *customer satisfaction, repeat purchases,* and *committed customers?*

21. What is the difference between *repeat purchasers* and *committed customers?*

22. What are *switching costs?*

23. Why are marketers interested in having committed customers?

24. What are five objectives that a marketing strategy for a particular segment might have? How will marketing strategies differ across the five objectives that a firm might have for a particular segment?

25. What is *relationship marketing?* What strategies are involved?

26. What are *loyalty programs?* What do most of them actually do?

DISCUSSION QUESTIONS

27. How should retailers deal with consumers immediately after purchase to reduce postpurchase dissonance? What specific action would you recommend, and what effect would you intend it to have on the recent purchaser of (gift of) the following?

   a. Automobile repair
   b. Cable TV
   c. Mouthwash
   d. Mountain bike
   e. United Way
   f. A dog

28. What ethical concerns are associated with maintaining and using a database like Whirlpool's?

29. What type of database should your university maintain on its students?

30. How should manufacturers deal with consumers immediately after purchase to reduce postpurchase dissonance? What specific action would you recommend, and what effect would you intend it to have on the recent purchaser of the following?
    a. Laptop computer
    b. Undergraduate college
    c. Athletic shoes
    d. Corrective eye surgery

31. Respond to the questions in Consumer Insight 18–1.

32. Discuss how you could determine how consumers actually use the following. How could this information be used to develop marketing strategy?
    a. Laptop computer
    b. Mouthwash
    c. Electric saw
    d. Amazon.com
    e. Bleach
    f. Bottled water

33. How would you go about measuring consumer satisfaction among purchasers of the following? What questions would you ask, what additional information would you collect, and why? How could this information be used for evaluating and planning marketing programs?
    a. Internet access
    b. Laptop computer
    c. Italian food restaurant
    d. Auto repairs
    e. Jewelry
    f. Buy.com

34. What level of product dissatisfaction should a marketer be content with in attempting to serve a particular target market? What characteristics contribute to dissatisfaction, regardless of the marketer's efforts?

35. Describe the last time you were dissatisfied with a purchase. What action did you take? Why?

36. Are you a *mere* repeat purchaser of any brand, service, or outlet? Why are you not a committed customer? What, if anything, would make you a committed customer?

37. Respond to the questions in Consumer Insight 18–2.

38. How could an automobile dealership use the service segmentation strategy described in Consumer Insight 18–2?

39. Are you a committed customer to any brand, service, or outlet? Why?

40. Design a customer loyalty program for the following.
    a. A Thai restaurant
    b. A ski resort
    c. Amazon.com
    d. A campus bookstore

APPLICATION ACTIVITIES

41. Develop a brief questionnaire to determine product nonuse among college students and the reasons for it. With four other classmates, interview 50 students. What do you conclude?

42. Develop a questionnaire designed to measure consumer satisfaction of a clothing purchase of $50 or more. Include in your questionnaire items that measure the product's instrumental, symbolic, and affective dimensions of performance, as well as what the consumer wanted on these dimensions. Then, interview several consumers to obtain information on actual performance, expected performance, and satisfaction. Using this information, determine if consumers received what they expected (i.e., evaluation of performance) and relate any difference to consumer expressions of satisfaction. What are the marketing implications of your results?

43. Develop a survey to measure student dissatisfaction with service purchases. For purchases they were dissatisfied with, determine what action they took to resolve this dissatisfaction and what the end result of their efforts was. What are the marketing implications of your findings?

44. Develop a questionnaire to measure repeat purchase behavior and brand loyalty. Measure the repeat purchase behavior and brand loyalty of 10 students with respect to the following. Determine why the brand loyal students are brand loyal.
    a. Fast-food restaurants
    b. Mouthwash
    c. Bottled water
    d. Coffee
    e. Clothing stores
    f. Online stores

45. With the cooperation of a durables retailer, assist the retailer in sending a postpurchase letter of thanks to every other customer immediately after purchase. Then, approximately two weeks after purchase, contact the same customers (both those who received the letter and those who did not) and measure their purchase satisfaction. Evaluate the results.

46. Interview a grocery store manager, a department store manager, and a restaurant manager. Determine the types of products their customers are most likely to complain about and the nature of those complaints.

47. Measure 10 students' disposition behaviors with respect to the following. Determine why they use the alternatives they do.
    a. Soft-drink containers
    b. Magazines
    c. Food cans
    d. Newspapers
    e. Plastic items
    f. Large items

48. Interview 20 students to determine which, if any, customer loyalty programs they belong to, what they like and dislike about them, and the impact they have on their attitudes and behaviors. What opportunities do your results suggest?

REFERENCES

1. E. O. Lawler, "Fine Line between Added Value, Spam," *Advertising Age,* October 29, 2001, p. 54.

2. G. J. Thompson, "Interpreting Consumers," *Journal Marketing Research,* November 1997, p. 444.

3. See J. C. Sweeney, D. Hausknecht, and G. N. Soutar, "Cognitive Dissonance after Purchase," *Psychology & Marketing,* May 2000, pp. 369–85.

4. M. F. Luce, "Choosing to Avoid," *Journal of Consumer Research,* March 1998, pp. 409–33.

5. See M. Tsiros and V. Mittal, "Regret," *Journal of Consumer Research,* March 2000, pp. 401–17; J. J. Hetts et al., "The Influence of Anticipated Counterfactual Regret on Behavior," *Psychology & Marketing,* April 2000, pp. 345–68; and A. D. J. Cooke, T. Meyvis, and A. Schwartz, "Avoiding Future Regret in Purchase-Timing Decisions," *Journal of Consumer Research,* March 2001, pp. 447–59.

6. See Thompson, "Interpreting Consumers."

7. S. J. Gould, "An Interpretative Study of Purposeful, Mood Self-Regulating Consumption," *Psychology & Marketing,* July 1997, pp. 395–426.

8. See S. Ram and H.-S. Jung, "Innovativeness in Product Usage"; and N. M. Ridgway and L. L. Price, "Exploration in Product Usage," both in *Psychology & Marketing,* January 1994, pp. 57–69 and 70–84; and K. Park and C. L. Dyer, "Consumer Use Innovative Behavior," in *Advances in Consumer Research,* vol. 22, eds. F. R. Kardes and M. Sujan (Provo, UT: Association for Consumer Research, 1995), pp. 566–72.

9. Based on N. J. Roese, "Counterfactual Thinking and Marketing"; A. R. McConnel et al., "What If I Find It Cheaper Someplace Else?"; and J. Landman and R. Petty, "It Could Have Been You," all in *Psychology & Marketing,* April 2000, pp. 277–80, 281–98, and 299–321.

10. S. Ram and H. J. Jung, "The Conceptualization and Measurement of Product Usage," *Journal of the Academy of Marketing Science,* Winter 1990, pp. 67–76.

11. G. Berstell and D. Nitterhouse, "Looking 'Outside the Box,'" *Marketing Research,* Summer 1997, pp. 5–11. See also K. Parker, "How Do You Like Your Beef?" *American Demographics,* January 2000, pp. 35–37.

12. A. B. Bower and D. E. Sprott, "The Case of the Dusty Stair-Climber," in *Advances in Consumer Research,* vol. 22, eds. F. R. Kardes and M. Sujan (Provo, UT: Association for Consumer Research, 1995), pp. 582–87. See also B. Wansink and R. Deshpande, *Marketing Letters* 5, no. 1 (1994), pp. 91–100.

13. Bower and Sprott, "The Case of the Dusty Stair-Climber," p. 585.

14. S. L. Wood, *Journal of Marketing Research,* May 2001, pp. 157–69.

15. E. M. Okada, "Trade-ins, Mental Accounting, and Product Replacement Decisions," *Journal of Consumer Research,* March 2001, pp. 433–66.

16. A. Biswas, "The Recycling Cycle," *Journal of Public Policy & Marketing,* Spring 2000, pp. 93–105.

17. See D. Halstead, D. Hartman, and S. L. Schmidt, "Multisource Effects on the Satisfaction Process," *Journal of the Academy of Marketing Science,* Spring 1994, pp. 114–29.

18. See K. A. Hunt and S. M. Keaveney, "A Process Model of the Effects of Price Promotions on Brand Image," *Psychology & Marketing,* November 1994, pp. 511–32.

19. V. Mittal, P. Kumar, and M. Tsiros, "Attribute-Level Performance, Satisfaction, and Behavioral Intentions over Time,"
Journal of Marketing, April 1999, pp. 88–101.

20. R. A. Spreng, S. B. MacKenzie, and R. W. Olshavsky, "A
Reexamination of the Determinants of Consumer Satisfaction,"
Journal of Marketing, July 1996, pp. 15–32.

21. See B. G. Goff, J. S. Boles, D. N. Bellenger, and C. Stojack,
"The Influence of Salesperson Selling Behaviors on Customer
Satisfaction with Products," *Journal of Retailing,* no. 2 (1997),
pp. 171–83.

22. See V. A. Zeithaml, L. L. Berry, and A. Parasuraman, "The
Nature and Determination of Customer Expectations of
Service," *Journal of the Academy of Marketing Science,*
Winter 1993, pp. 1–12; and K. E. Clow, D. L. Kurtz,
J. Ozment, and B. S. Ong, "The Antecedents of Consumer
Expectations of Services," *Journal of Services Marketing,* no. 4
(1997), pp. 230–48.

23. See J. Ozment and E. A. Morash, "The Augmented Service
Offering for Perceived and Actual Service Quality," *Journal of
the Academy of Marketing Science,* Fall 1994, pp. 352–63;
and G. B. Voss, A. Parasuraman, and D. Grewal, "The Roles
of Price, Performance, and Expectations in Determining
Satisfaction in Service Exchanges," *Journal of Marketing,*
October 1998, pp. 48–61.

24. For discussions of both conceptual and measurement issues,
see K. Gupta and D. Stewart, "Customer Satisfaction and
Customer Behavior," *Marketing Letters,* no. 3 (1996),
pp. 249–63; P. J. Danaher, "Using Conjoint Analysis to Determine the Relative Importance of Service Attributes," *Journal
of Retailing,* no. 2 (1997), pp. 235–60; R. N. Bolton and K. N.
Lemon, "A Dynamic Model of Customers' Usage of Services,"
Journal of Marketing Research, May 1999, pp. 171–86; C. P.
Bebko, "Service Intangibility and Its Impact on Customer
Expectations," *Journal of Services Marketing* 14, no. 1 (2000),
pp. 9–26; B. Bickart and N. Schwartz, "Service Experiences
and Satisfaction Judgments," *Journal of Consumer Psychology*
11, no. 1 (2001), pp. 29–41; D. M. Szymanski and D. H.
Henard, "Customer Satisfaction," *Journal of the Academy of
Marketing Science,* Winter 2001, pp. 16–35; J. C. Sweeney and
G. N. Soutar, "Consumer Perceived Value," *Journal of Retail-
ing* 77 (2001), pp. 203–20; P. K. Kopalle and D. R. Lehmann,
"Strategic Management of Expectations," *Journal of Marketing
Research,* August 2001, pp. 386–94; J. Wirtz and A. Mattila,
"Exploring the Role of Alternative Perceived Performance
Measures and Needs-Congruency in the Customer Satisfaction
Process," *Journal of Consumer Psychology* 11, no. 3 (2001),
pp. 181–92; and E. Garbarino and M. S. Johnson, "Effects of
Consumer Goals on Attribute Weighting, Overall Satisfaction,
and Product Usage," *Psychology & Marketing,* September
2001, pp. 929–49. A different view is S. Fournier and D. G.
Mick, "Rediscovering Satisfaction," *Journal of Marketing,*
October 1999, pp. 5–23.

25. See C. Droge, D. Halstead, and R. D. Mackoy, "The Role of
Competitive Alternatives in the Postchoice Satisfaction Forma-
tion Process," *Journal of the Academy of Marketing Science,*
Winter 1997, pp. 18–30; and K. A. Taylor, "A Regret Theory
Approach to Assessing Consumer Satisfaction," *Marketing
Letters,* no. 2 (1997), pp. 229–38.

26. A. Mattila, "An Examination of Consumers' Use of Heuristic
Cues in Making Satisfaction Judgments," *Psychology &
Marketing,* August 1998, pp. 477–500.

27. L. Dube and M. S. Morgan, "Trend Effects and Gender Differ-
ences in Retrospective Judgments of Consumption Emotions,"
Journal of Consumer Research, September 1996, pp. 156–62;
T. R. Shaffer and D. L. Sherrell, "Consumer Satisfaction with
Health-Care Services," *Psychology & Marketing,* May 1997,
pp. 261–85; T. A. Mooradian and J. M. Oliver, "I Can't Get No
Satisfaction," *Psychology & Marketing,* July 1997, pp. 379–92;
and R. A. Preng and T. J. Page, Jr., "The Impact of Confidence
in Expectations on Consumer Satisfaction," *Psychology &
Marketing,* November 2001, pp. 1187–1204.

28. M. Griffin, B. J. Babin, and D. Modianos, "Shopping Values of
Russian Consumers," *Journal of Retailing* 76, no. 31 (2000),
pp. 33–52.

29. See K. E. Clow and J. L. Beisel, "Managing Consumer Expectations of Low-Margin, High-Volume Services," *Journal of
Services Marketing* 9, no. 1 (1995), pp. 33–46.

30. S. M. Keaveney, "Customer Switching Behavior in Service
Industries," *Journal of Marketing,* April 1995, pp. 71–82.
See also D. Grace and A. O'Cass, "Attributions of Service
Switching," *Journal of Services Marketing* 14, no. 4 (2001),
pp. 300–21; and V. Mittal, J. M. Katrichis, and P. Kumar,
"Attribute Performance and Customer Satisfaction over Time,"
Journal of Services Marketing 15, no. 5 (2001), pp. 343–56.

31. S. Taylor, "Waiting for Service," *Journal of Marketing,* April
1994, pp. 56–69; S. Taylor and J. D. Claxton, "Delays and the
Dynamics of Service Encounters," *Journal of the Academy of
Marketing Science,* Summer 1994, pp. 254–64; and S. Taylor,
"The Effects of Filled Waiting Time and Service Provider
Control over the Delay on Evaluations of Service," *Journal of
the Academy of Marketing Science,* Winter 1995, pp. 38–48.

32. For related issues see P. Kumar, M. U. Kalwani, and M. Dada,
"The Impact of Waiting Time Guarantees on Customers'
Waiting Experiences," *Marketing Science,* no. 4 (1997),
pp. 295–314; and M. K. Hui, M. V. Thakor, and R. Gill,
"The Effect of Delay Type and Service Stage on Consumers'
Reactions to Waiting," *Journal of Consumer Research,*
March 1998, pp. 469–79.

33. See M. K. Hui and D. K. Tse, "What to Tell Consumers in
Waits of Different Lengths," *Journal of Marketing,* April 1996,
pp. 81–90; and B. G. C. Dellaert and B. E. Kahn, "How
Tolerable Is Delay?" *Journal of Interactive Marketing,* Winter
1999, pp. 41–54.

34. M. K. Hui, L. Dube, and J.-C. Chebat, "The Impact of Music
on Consumers' Reactions to Waiting for Services," *Journal of
Retailing,* no. 1 (1997), pp. 87–104; and G. Tom, M. Burns,
and Y. Zeng, "Your Life on Hold," *Journal of Direct
Marketing,* Summer 1997, pp. 25–31.

35. V. Mittal, W. T. Ross, Jr., and P. M. Baldsare, "The Asymmetric
Impact of Negative and Positive Attribute-Level Performance
on Overall Satisfaction and Repurchase Levels," *Journal of
Marketing,* January 1998, pp. 33–47. See also G. J. Gaeth
et al., "Consumers' Attitude Change across Sequences of Successful and Unsuccessful Product Usage," *Marketing Letters,*
no. 1 (1997), pp. 41–53.

36. See B. Mittal and W. M. Lassar, "The Role of Personalization in Service Encounters," *Journal of Retailing,* no. 1 (1996), pp. 95–109; R. A. Spreng and R. D. Mackoy, "An Empirical Examination of a Model of Perceived Service Quality and Satisfaction," *Journal of Retailing,* no. 2 (1996), pp. 210–14; N. Sirohi, E. W. McClaughlin, and D. R. Wittink, "A Model of Consumer Perceptions and Store Loyalty Intentions for a Supermarket Retailer," *Journal of Retailing,* no. 2 (1998), pp. 223–45; and W. O. Bearden, M. K. Malhotra, and K. H. Uscategui, "Customer Contact and the Evaluation of Service Experiences," *Psychology & Marketing,* December 1998, pp. 793–809.

37. M. L. Meuter et al., "Self-Service Technologies," *Journal of Marketing,* July 2000, pp. 50–64. See also M. J. Bitner and M. L. Meuter, "Technology Infusion in Service Encounters"; and A. Parasuraman and D. Grewal, "The Impact of Technology on the Quality-Value-Loyalty Chain," both in *Journal of the Academy of Marketing Science,* Winter 2000, pp. 138–49 and 168–74.

38. See G. H. G. McDougall, T. Levesque, and P. VanderPlaat, "Designing the Service Guarantee," *Journal of Services Marketing,* no. 4 (1998), pp. 278–93; and A. M. Ostrom and D. Iacobucci, "The Effect of Guarantees on Consumers' Evaluation of Services," *Journal of Services Marketing,* no. 5 (1998), pp. 362–78.

39. I. E. Swan and L. J. Combs, "Product Performance and Consumer Satisfaction: A New Concept," *Journal of Marketing,* April 1976, pp. 25–33.

40. See H. Mano and R. L. Oliver, "Assessing the Dimensionality and Structure of the Consumption Experience," *Journal of Consumer Research,* December 1993, pp. 451–66; and L. W. Turley and D. L. Bolton, "Measuring the Affective Evaluations of Retail Service Environments," *Journal of Professional Services Marketing* 19, no. 1 (1999), pp. 31–44.

41. D. M. Szymanski and R. T. Hise, "e-Satisfaction," *Journal of Retailing* 76, no. 3 (2000), pp. 309–22. See also Q. Chen and W. D. Wells, ".Com Satisfaction and .Com Dissatisfaction," *Advances in Consumer Research,* vol. 28, eds. M. C. Gilly and J. Meyers-Levy (Provo, UT: Association for Consumer Research, 2001), pp. 34–39.

42. See J. Singh, "A Typology of Consumer Dissatisfaction Response Styles," *Journal of Retailing,* Spring 1990, pp. 57–97; J. Singh, "Voice, Exit, and Negative Word-of-Mouth Behaviors," *Journal of the Academy of Marketing Science,* Winter 1990, pp. 1–15; K. Gronhaug and O. Kvitastein, "Purchases and Complaints," *Psychology & Marketing,* Spring 1991, pp. 21–35; S. W. Kelley and M. A. Davis, "Antecedents to Customer Expectations for Service Recovery," *Journal of the Academy of Marketing Science,* Winter 1994, pp. 52–61; and M. Davidow and P. A. Dacin, "Understanding and Influencing Consumer Complaint Behavior," *Advances in Consumer Research,* vol. 24, eds. M. Bruck and D. J. MacInnis (Provo, UT: Association for Consumer Research, 1997), pp. 450–56.

43. M. A. Jones, D. L. Motherbaugh, and S. E. Beatty, "Switching Barriers and Repurchase Intentions in Services," *Journal of Retailing* 76, no. 2 (2000), pp. 259–74; J. Lee, J. Lee, and L. Feick, "The Impact of Switching Costs on the Customer Satisfaction-Loyalty Link," *Journal of Services Marketing* 15, no. 1 (2001), pp. 35–48; and M. Lee and L. F. Cunningham, "A Cost/Benefit Approach to Understanding Service Loyalty," *Journal of Services Marketing* 15, no. 2 (2001), pp. 113–30.

44. M. A. Jones and J. Suh, "Tranaction-Specific Satisfaction and Overall Satisfaction," *Journal of Services Marketing* 14, no. 2 (2000), pp. 147–59.

45. J. Singh and R. E. Wilkes, "When Consumers Complain," *Journal of the Academy of Marketing Science,* Fall 1996, pp. 350–65; and K. P. N. Morel, T. B. C. Poiesz, and H. A. M. Wilkie, "Motivation, Capacity and Opportunity to Complain," *Advances in Consumer Research,* vol. 24, eds. M. Bruck and D. J. MacInnis (Provo, UT: Association for Consumer Research, 1997), pp. 464–69.

46. See also S. P. Brown and R. F. Beltramini, "Consumer Complaining and Word-of-Mouth Activities," in *Advances in Consumer Research,* vol. 16, ed. T. K. Srull (Provo, UT: Association for Consumer Research, 1989), pp. 9–11; and J. E. Swan and R. L. Oliver, "Postpurchase Communications by Consumers," *Journal of Retailing,* Winter 1989, pp. 516–33.

47. Thompson, "Interpreting Consumers."

48. L. J. Harrison-Walker, "E-Complaining," *Journal of Services Marketing* 15, no. 5 (2001), pp. 397–412.

49. M. L. Richins, "Negative Word-of-Mouth by Dissatisfied Consumers," *Journal of Marketing,* Winter 1983, pp. 68–78; M. L. Richins, "Word-of-Mouth as Negative Information," in *Advances in Consumer Research,* vol. 11, ed. T. C. Kinnear (Provo, UT: Association for Consumer Research, 1984), pp. 687–702; and M. T. Curren and V. S. Folkes, "Attributional Influences on Consumers' Desires to Communicate about Products," *Psychology & Marketing,* Spring 1987, pp. 31–45.

50. See R. A. Spreng, G. D. Harrell, and R. D. Mackoy, "Service Recovery," *Journal of Services Marketing* 9, no. 1 (1995), pp. 15–23; M. A. Hocutt, G. Chakraborty, and J. C. Mowen, "The Impact of Perceived Justice on Customer Satisfaction," *Advances in Consumer Research,* vol. 24, eds. M. Bruck and D. J. MacInnis (Provo, UT: Association for Consumer Research, 1997), pp. 457–63; and L. Dube and M. F. Maute, "Defensive Strategies for Managing Satisfaction and Loyalty in the Service Industry," *Psychology & Marketing,* December 1998, pp. 775–91.

51. A literature review and model is in N. Stephens and K. P. Gwinner, "Why Don't Some People Complain?" *Journal of the Academy of Marketing Science,* Summer 1998, pp. 172–89. See also A. L. Dolinsky et al., "The Role of Psychographic Characteristics as Determinants of Complaint Behavior," *Journal of Hospital Marketing,* no. 2 (1998), pp. 27–51.

52. Ibid.

53. B. Bowers, "For Firms, 800 Is a Hot Number," *The Wall Street Journal,* November 9, 1989, p. B–1.

54. J. A. Prestbo, "At Procter & Gamble, Success Is Largely Due to Heeding Consumer," *The Wall Street Journal,* April 29, 1980, p. 23.

55. J. Strauss and D. J. Hill, "Consumer Complaints by E-Mail," *Journal of Interactive Marketing,* Winter 2001, pp. 63–73.

56. See A. K. Smith, R. N. Bolton, and J. Wagner, "A Model of Customer Satisfaction with Service Encounters Involving

Failure and Recovery," *Journal of Marketing Research,* August 1999, pp. 356–72; A. Palmer, R. Beggs, and C. Keown-McMullan, "Equity and Repurchase Intention Following Service Failure," *Journal of Services Marketing* 14, no. 6 (2000), pp. 513–28; A. S. Mattila, "The Effectiveness of Service Recovery in a Multi-Industry Setting," *Journal of Services Marketing* 15, no. 7 (2001), pp. 583–96; and A. K. Smith and R. N. Bolton, "The Effect of Consumers' Emotional Responses to Service Failures on Their Recovery Effort Evaluations and Satisfaction Judgments," *Journal of the Academy of Marketing Science,* Winter 2002, pp. 5–23.

57. See C. Goodwin and I. Ross, "Consumer Evaluations of Response to Complaints," *Journal of Consumer Marketing,* Spring 1990, pp. 39–47; and J. G. Blodgett, D. J. Hill, and S. S. Tax, "The Effects of Distributive, Procedural, and Interactional Justice on Postcomplaint Behavior," *Journal of Retailing,* no. 2 (1997), pp. 185–210.

58. C. Ofir and I. Simonson, "In Search of Negative Customer Feedback," *Journal of Marketing Research,* May 2001, pp. 170–82.

59. See F. F. Reichheld, "Learning from Customer Defections," *Harvard Business Review,* March 1996, pp. 56–69. See also H. Estelami, "The Profit Impact of Consumer Complaint Solicitation across Market Conditions," *Journal of Professional Services Marketing* 20, no. 1 (1999), pp. 165–95.

60. P. Sellers, "What Customers Really Want," *Fortune,* June 4, 1990, pp. 58–62.

61. B. A. Sparks, G. L. Bradley, and V. J. Callan, "The Impact of Staff Empowerment and Communication Style on Customer Evaluations," *Psychology & Marketing,* August 1997, pp. 475–93.

62. See N. C. Smith, R. J. Thomas, and J. A. Quelch, "A Strategic Approach to Managing Product Recalls," *Harvard Business Review,* September 1996, pp. 102–12.

63. T. Tripett, "Product Recall Spurs Company to Improve Customer Satisfaction," *Marketing News,* April 11, 1994, p. 6.

64. J. W. Verity, "The Gold Mine of Data in Customer Service," *Business Week,* March 21, 1994, p. 113.

65. C. Rubel, "Pizza Hut Explores Customer Satisfaction," *Marketing News,* March 25, 1996, p. 15.

66. T. O. Jones and W. E. Sasser, Jr., "Why Satisfied Customers Defect," *Harvard Business Review,* November 1995, pp. 88–95; P. P. Leszczyc and H. J. P. Timmermans, "Store-Switching Behavior," *Marketing Letters,* no. 2 (1997), pp. 193–204; B. Mittal and W. M. Lassar, "Why Do Customer Switch?" *Journal of Services Marketing,* no. 3 (1998), pp. 177–94; and C. Homburg and A. Giering, "Personal Characteristics as Moderators of the Relationship between Customer Satisfaction and Loyalty," *Psychology & Marketing,* January 2001, pp. 43–66.

67. See V. Mittal and W. Kamakura, "Satisfaction, Repurchase Intent, and Repurchase Behavior," *Journal of Marketing Research,* February 2001, pp. 131–42.

68. J. Jacoby and D. B. Kyner, "Brand Loyalty versus Repeat Purchasing Behavior," *Journal of Marketing Research,* February 1973, pp. 1–9. See also M. P. Pritchard, F. W. Morgan, and D. R. Howard, "Analyzing the Commitment-Loyalty Link IN Service Contexts," *Journal of the Academy of*

Marketing Science, Summer 1999, pp. 333–48; M.-H. Huang and S. Yu, "Are Consumers Inherently or Situationally Brand Loyal," *Psychology & Marketing,* September 1999, pp. 523–44; C. Lin, W.-Y. Wu, and Z.-F. Wang, "A Study of Market Structure," *International Journal of Marketing Research,* Summer 2000, pp. 277–300; P. Warrington and S. Shim, "An Empirical Investigation of the Relationship between Product Involvement and Brand Commitment," *Psychology & Marketing*, September 2000, pp. 761–82; S. Rundle-Thiele and M. M. Mackay, "Assessing the Performance of Brand Loyalty Measures," *Journal of Services Marketing* 15, no. 7 (2001), pp. 529–46; and A. Chaudhuri and M. B. Holbrook, "The Chain of Effects from Brand Trust and Brand Affect to Brand Performance," *Journal of Marketing,* April 2001, pp. 81–93.

69. R. G. Javalgi and C. R. Moberg, "Service Loyalty," *Journal of Services Marketing,* no. 3 (1997), pp. 165–79; R. East et al., "Customer Defection from Supermarkets," *Advances in Consumer Research,* vol. 25, eds. J. W. Alba and J. W. Hutchinson (Provo, UT: Association for Consumer Research, 1998), pp. 507–12.

70. S. Fournier, "Consumers and Their Brands," *Journal of Consumer Research,* March 1998, p. 355.

71. See E. Garbarino and M. S. Johnson, "The Different Roles of Satisfaction, Trust, and Commitment in Customer Relationships," *Journal of Marketing,* April 1999, pp. 70–87; J. Singh and D. Sirdeshmukh, "Agency and Trust Mechanisms in Consumer Satisfaction and Loyalty Judgments," *Journal of the Academy of Marketing Science,* Winter 2000, pp. 150–67; and D. Sirdeshmukh, J. Singh, and B. Sabol, "Consumer Trust, Value, and Loyalty in Relational Exchanges," *Journal of Marketing,* January 2002, pp. 15–37.

72. R. L. Olvier, R. T. Rust, and S. Varki, "Customer Delight," *Journal of Retailing,* no. 3 (1997), pp. 311–36; and R. T. Rust and R. L. Oliver, "Should We Delight the Customer?" *Journal of the Academy of Marketing Science,* Winter 2000, pp. 86–94.

73. R. L. Oliver, "Whence Consumer Loyalty," *Journal of Marketing,* Special Issue 1999, pp. 33–44.

74. See J. Deighton, C. M. Henderson, and S. A. Neslin, "The Effects of Advertising on Brand Switching and Repeat Purchasing," *Journal of Marketing Research,* February 1994, pp. 28–43.

75. See D. Bejou and A. Palmer, "Service Failure and Loyalty," *Journal of Services Marketing,* no. 1 (1998), pp. 7–22.

76. M. Johnson, G. M. Zinkham, and G. S. Ayala, "The Impact of Outcome, Competency, and Affect on Service Referral," *Journal of Services Marketing,* no. 5 (1998), pp. 397–415.

77. E. W. Anderson, C. Fornell, R. T. Rust, "Customer Satisfaction, Productivity, and Profitability," *Marketing Science,* no. 2 (1997), pp. 129–45.

78. F. F. Reichheld and W. E. Sasser, Jr., "Zero Defections," *Harvard Business Review,* September 1990, pp. 105–11; and R. Jacob, "Why Some Customers Are More Equal Than Others," *Fortune,* September 19, 1994, pp. 215–24. See also V. A. Zeithaml, "Service Qualilty, Profitablity, and the Economic Worth of Customers," *Journal of the Academy of Marketing Science,* Winter 2000, pp. 67–85.

79. See S. Li, "Survival Analysis," *Marketing Research,* Fall 1995, pp. 17–23.

80. Reichheld and Sasser, "Zero Defections," p. 110.

81. See also S. Lingle "How Much Is a Customer Worth?" *Bank Marketing,* August 1995, pp. 13–16.

82. Based on D. Brady, "Why Service Sucks," *Business Week,* October 23, 2000, pp. 118–28. See also J. Ganesh, M. J. Arnold, and K. E. Reynolds "Understanding the Customer Base of Service Providers," *Journal of Marketing,* July 2000, pp. 65–87.

83. See G. S. Day, "Managing Market Relationships," *Journal of the Academy of Marketing Science,* Winter 2000, pp. 24–30.

84. See the special issue on relationship marketing, *Journal of the Academy of Marketing Science,* Fall 1995; and G. E. Gengler and P. P. Leszczyc, "Using Customer Satisfaction Research for Relationship Marketing," *Journal of Direct Marketing*, Winter 1997, pp. 23–29.

85. L. Freeman, "Marketing the Market," *Marketing News,* March 2, 1998, p. 1. Other examples are in G. B. Voss and Z. G. Voss, "Implementing a Relationship Marketing Program," *Journal of Services Marketing,* no. 11 (1997), pp. 278–98; B. G. Yovovich, "Scanners Reshape the Grocery Business," *Marketing News,* February 16, 1998, p. 1; and G. Brewer, "The Customer Stops Here," *Sales & Marketing Management,* March 1998, pp. 31–36.

86. L. L. Berry, "Relationship Marketing of Services," *Journal of the Academy of Marketing Science,* Fall 1995, pp. 236–45.

87. See N. Bendapudi and L. L. Berry, "Customers' Motivations for Maintaining Relationships with Service Providers," *Journal of Retailing,* no. 1 (1997), pp. 15–37.

88. See T. G. Vavra, "Rethinking the Marketing Mix to Maximize Customer Retention," in *Enhancing Knowledge Development in Marketing,* eds. D. W. Cravens and P. R. Dickson (Chicago: American Marketing Association, 1993), pp. 262–68.

89. See G. Levin, "Marketers Flock to Loyalty Offers," *Advertising Age,* May 24, 1993, p. 13; C. Miller, "Rewards for the Best Customers," *Marketing News,* July 5, 1993, p. 1; J. Fulkerson, "It's in the Cards," *American Demographics,* July 1996, pp. 38–43; and J. Passingham, "Grocery Retailing and the Loyalty Card," *Journal of the Market Research Society,* January 1998, pp. 55–63.

90. See G. T. Gundlach, R. S. Achrol, and J. T. Mentzer, "The Structure of Commitment in Exchange," *Journal of Marketing,* January 1995, pp. 78–92; L. O'Brien and C. Jones, "Do Rewards Really Create Loyalty?" *Harvard Business Review,* May 1995, pp. 75–82; and R. N. Bolton; P. K. Kannan, and M. D. Bramlett, "Implications of Loyalty Programs Membership and Service Experiences for Customer Retention and Value," *Journal of the Academy of Marketing Science,* Winter 2000, pp. 95–108.

91. See F. Rice, "The New Rules of Superlative Services"; and P. Sellers "Keeping the Buyers," both in *Fortune,* Autumn–Winter 1993, pp. 50–53 and 56–58; and G. A. Conrad, G. Brown, and H. A. Harmon, "Customer Satisfaction and Corporate Culture," *Psychology & Marketing,* October 1997, pp. 663–74.

92. See M. Abbott et al., "The Process of On-Line Store Loyalty Formation," *Advances in Consumer Research,* vol. 27, eds. S. J. Itoch and R. J. Meyer (Provo, UT: Association for Consumer Research, 2000), pp. 145–51; D. E. Schultz and S. Bailey, "Consumer/Brand Loyalty in an Interactive Marketplace," *Journal of Advertising Research,* May 2000, pp. 41–51; F. F. Reichheld and P. Schefter, "E-Loyalty," July 2000, pp. 105–13; and J. Holland and S. M. Baker, "Customer Participation in Creating Site Brand Loyalty," *Journal of Interactive Marketing,* Autumn 2001, pp. 34–45.

Cases

4–1 Supermarket Shopping in Europe

The Point-of-Purchase Advertising Institute (POPAI) conducted a major study of supermarket shopping in four European countries. Almost 3,000 consumers 16 or older were interviewed while shopping at a major supermarket. Respondents were first screened to ascertain that they were on a "major shopping trip" before the interview. Part of the results are shown in Table A.

Discussion Questions

1. What are the most significant shopping differences across these four countries?

2. What causes the most significant shopping differences across these four countries?

3. What are the strategy implications of the most significant shopping differences across these four countries for an EU-wide supermarket chain?

4. What, if any, are the strategy implications of the most significant shopping differences across these four countries for a manufacturer of products sold in supermarkets throughout the EU?

TABLE A		U.K.	Holland	Belgium	France
Cross-Country Variations in Major Shopping Trips to Supermarkets	Age (%)				
	55 and over	32%	32%	15%	22%
	35–54	49	48	50	43
	Under 35	20	20	34	35
	Female (%)	84	87	83	77
	Shop alone (%)	57	79	65	62
	How often do you use this store? (%)				
	Some of the time	18	32	47	27
	Most of the time	32	52	32	24
	All of the time	50	16	21	49
	Average time on a major trip (minutes)	48	23	38	53
	Number of items bought on major trip	30	15	14	26
	Number of major trips per week	1.1	1.2	1.1	1.0
	Total number of grocery trips per week	2.1	3.4	3.4	3.7
	Use a written shopping list (%)	61	70	74	76
	Store is over 5 km from home (%)	32	9	24	46
	Amount spent ($)	74	36	52	86
	Shopping patterns (%)				
	Visited aisles where intended purchases were	29	45	51	45
	Visited most aisles	35	28	34	38
	Visited all aisles	36	27	15	17
	In-store decision making (%)				
	Specifically planned	25	20	31	24
	Generally planned	8	24	9	12
	Substitute	4	4	4	6
	Unplanned	64	53	56	58

Source: The 1997/98 POPAI Europe Consumer Buying Habits Study (Paris, France: POPAI Europe, 1998).

4–2 General Motors' Electric Vehicle—EV1

The EV1 is a completely electric car developed and produced by General Motors and leased through select Saturn dealers in California and Arizona.

Saturn employs a group of EV specialists who work with the customer explaining how to get a charger installed in their home, how to use it, how to arrange the lease, secure state and federal tax credits, and so forth.

The EV1 has an electronically regulated top speed of 80 miles per hour. It comes with traction control, cruise control, antilock brakes, airbags, power windows, power door locks, power outside mirrors, AM/FM CD/cassette, tire inflation monitor system, and other features.

The EV1 has no engine, no tailpipe, no exhaust, no valves, no pistons, no timing belts, and no crankshaft. It does have a very aerodynamic body shape, low-rolling-resistance tires, lightweight wheels, a regenerative braking system (produces electricity during braking that is sent back to the batteries), a heat pump for efficient heating/cooling, and computer controls. And, of course, it has batteries and an electric motor.

High-capacity lead-acid batteries are standard with a higher-performance nickel-metal hydride battery pack available. Lessees of the EV1 need to install a special 220-volt inductive charging system at their home base. When not in use, the car is plugged into the charger and charges automatically. A full charge takes six hours for the lead batteries and eight for the nickel batteries. The lead batteries can also be recharged with portable charger that plugs into an ordinary 110-volt outlet. The batteries are maintenance free and are covered under the bumper-to-bumper warranty, so the lessee does not need to replace them.

The driving range with the lead batteries is 55 to 95 miles (75 to 130 with nickel), depending on driving style, terrain, temperature, and accessory usage. Saturn has worked with various utilities to establish 500 public charging stations at shopping malls, restaurants, beaches, airports, Saturn retail facilities, and key workplaces. Most do not charge a user fee.

An EV1 lease costs between $300 and $500 per month, depending on one's residence (which determines the government incentives available). Installing a home charger typically costs $2,500. At 10 cents per kilowatt hour and with a 100-mile trip, energy cost for the lead battery EV1 is 2.6 cents per mile. At $1.50 per gallon, a traditional car that gets 22 miles per gallon cost 6.83 cents per mile for gasoline. The EV1 does not require oil changes or tune-ups.

The EV1 is very environmentally friendly. It generates only 3 percent of the emissions of a typical car, including the emissions created in producing the recharging electricity. The lead batteries use 60 percent recycled lead and are 98 percent recyclable. The heat pump uses a CFC-free refrigerant. Charging the batteries at night uses off-peak electricity.

Discussion Questions

1. Describe the decision process a potential consumer would use in relation to the EV1.
2. What are the marketing strategy implications of the decision process a potential consumer would use in relation to the EV1?
3. Should Saturn attempt to trigger problem recognition for the EV1? Why? If so, how should it do it?
4. What information sources is a consumer likely to use regarding the purchase of an EV1?
5. What decision rule(s) is a consumer likely to use in the purchase of an EV1?
6. Is the purchase of an EV1 likely to be a family purchase decision? If so, what roles will each family member play?
7. What will determine customer satisfaction and commitment to the EV1?
8. How would you define the target market for the EV1?
9. Conduct a diffusion analysis for the EV1 and recommend appropriate strategy based on this analysis.

4–3   Is Sears on Target?

As a 1992 story on Sears in *Advertising Age* explained,

> The task facing Sears is very, very difficult. Sears has to set completely new strategies that are responsive to the new realities. For one thing, it has to make its stores attractive. Consumers have a myriad of retailing choices, and they are also conservative and frugal. Retailers first must make them want to spend and second induce them to spend at their store. Sears is not good at that; it doesn't stand out, and *it doesn't stand for anything* [italics added]. Do you know any woman who wants a Sears' cocktail dress? Its hard goods get in the way of its soft goods and vice versa.

Sears decided to tackle this challenge head-on. It closed 113 outdated stores, replaced its phone book–thick, all-inclusive catalog with 23 specialty catalogs; started carrying popular brands; accepted credit cards other than its own; moved its clothing lines to more fashionable items; and started a $4 billion renovation project for its remaining stores.

In 1993, it launched its "Softer Side of Sears" campaign to draw middle-income women shoppers to Sears' soft goods and fashion items. The campaign cleverly juxtaposed things such as hammers, batteries, and tires versus items such as satiny robes, stylish black dresses, and sexy shoes. The idea was to get women between the ages of 25 to 54 into the stores, a group that controls at least 70 percent of all dollars spent at Sears. In one ad a woman said, "I came in for a DieHard—and I left with something drop dead," showing a model in a sexy black dress. Sears' advertising agency was able to tweak the idea to cover dozens of categories. Eventually, it evolved the tag line into "Come See the Many Sides of Sears."

One reason for the strategy was research revealing that while women were the primary purchasers of Sears' major hard goods, Kenmore appliances, and Craftsman tools, they went elsewhere for fashion and personal items. Sears had few major brands of apparel to offer, and its store brands were not widely popular.

Sears' chairman Arthur Martinez described the goal of the campaign as follows:

> We've listened carefully to the women who shop at Sears for their families and homes and we know that they want affordable, fashionable apparel for themselves. We want the campaign to disarm the skeptics and pleasantly surprise our customers and feature the kind of merchandise that's on our sales floor right now.

Initial results were encouraging. Sales and profit increases were above the industry average for the next three years. Revenue per square foot of selling space increased from $289 at year-end 1992 to $353 at the end of 1995. However, by late 1999, Sears was announcing depressed earnings, a managerial shake-up, a 1,400 employee layoff at its headquarters, and a new marketing campaign.

The new campaign will be more value focused, with the theme "The Good Life at a Great Price. Guaranteed. Sears." Sears is expected to spend more than $600 million on advertising in the first year of the new campaign. Mark A. Cohen, Sears' executive vice president of marketing, said,

> Whether we like it or not, we're in a price game war, a value shootout with all our competition. With the "softer side" campaign, the customer feedback has been "We love the commercials, imagery and models, but we don't find those goods at Sears."

The campaign is the final piece in a series of changes the retailer announced in early 1999, including offering trendier brand-name clothing, reaching out to younger consumers with concert tours and teenage advisory panels, remodeling its stores, and selling merchandise on the Internet.

Cohen said the new campaign, which continues to target women, is intended to emphasize Sears' entire product line, positioning the chain as a one-stop-shopping destination for so-called lifestyle goods. One new TV ad, highlighting Sears' Fieldmaster private-label brand, depicts a man in a flannel-style shirt, sleeves rolled up, as he rock-climbs. The ad notes that the "rugged shirt" is $22.50, then adds, "For the man who fears nothing . . . except shopping." After one last view of the man, the scene cuts to the Fieldmaster logo and the new slogan.

In the summer of 2001, Sears changed its advertising theme again though its basic strategy was unaltered. The new advertising featured humor while emphasizing the wide variety of merchandise available at Sears. The new tag line was "Sears, where else." One ad shows

> A cranky little boy sitting on the floor in his Little Wonder overalls (Sears) as his mother frantically tries to pacify him with a Carter's blanket (Sears) and Euro Graco walker (Sears) to no avail. Dad comes down the stairs to record the scene on his Sony camcorder (Sears) but trips over the baby gate. The child laughs.

The Future?

Some experts say the rescue of the company from the brink of bankruptcy in 1992 only delayed the inevitable. Middle-priced stores such as Sears, JCPenney, and the late Montgomery Ward are being squeezed from both ends, by higher-priced competitors such as Macy's and Bloomingdale's and discount and specialty shops such as Wal-Mart, Target, and Abercrombie & Fitch. This is referred to as the *hourglass phenomenon,* and Sears appears to be in the middle where few customers are.

Sears' new CEO, Alan Lacy, has created a radical new strategy for Sears. He wants to move Sears sharply away from the traditional, everything-under-one-roof department store:

> We're trying to move away from that now. But we're also not trying to become a discounter. We feel we have the opportunity to be a really new Sears.

The "new" Sears will focus much more on appliances and tools and less on clothing and soft goods. As part of this, a "Tool Territory" will be featured in each outlet to display 72 brands with 18,000 tools.

Clothing will still be carried, but 570 brands will be dropped; and the introduction of a "megabrand" of classic clothes for women, men, and children is planned for the fall of 2002.

Sears will continue to face strong competition for its clothing and soft goods from powerful retailers such as Target and JCPenney, which is focusing exclusively in this area. Its new hard goods positioning will place it in much more direct competition with Lowe's and Home Depot.

"There's much more competition, and Sears, at its core, still has a cost structure that is quite a bit higher than their competition," one Chicago analyst said. "What happened was that companies like Wal-Mart came along. They were able to build a different model and grew up with a better cost structure from the get-go."

Table A provides demographic data on shoppers at different outlets.

Variable	Sears	JCPenney	Target	Gap
Percent of Adults Using	25%	33%	34%	13%
Gender				
Male	103	86	90	86
Female	98	113	109	113
Age				
18–24	70	84	103	154
25–34	87	88	110	139
35–44	106	104	117	121
45–54	111	113	105	101
55–64	116	109	89	38
> 64	108	102	64	24
Education				
College graduate	105	105	123	159
Some college	105	107	110	115
High school graduate	104	101	90	77
No degree	79	81	73	46
Occupation				
Professional	104	111	128	161
Managerial/administrative	100	110	128	155
Technical/clerical/sales	103	107	113	133
Precision/craft	107	79	96	84
Race/Ethnic Group				
White	102	100	102	99
Black	88	105	77	89
Spanish speaking	91	89	116	115
Region				
Northeast	117	92	38	138
North Central	107	116	135	99
South	90	93	83	81
West	94	102	146	97
Household Income				
< $10,000	57	70	58	61
$10,000–19,999	76	81	63	50
$20,000–29,999	93	99	82	59
$30,000–39,999	105	104	95	74
$40,000–49,999	111	104	108	91
$50,000–59,999	112	107	106	92
$60,000–74,999	115	115	121	124
$75,000+	109	105	127	167
Household Structure				
Single	76	85	99	131
Married	112	108	107	101

TABLE A

Demographics and Razor Use*

*100 = Average use or consumption, unless a percentage is indicated. Base = All adults.

Source: *Mediamark Reporter 2002—University* (New York: Mediamark Research Inc., March 2002).

Discussion Questions

1. What is Sears' store image and position? What should it be?

2. Evaluate the new positioning strategy compared to the old.

3. What criteria do the groups listed below use to select an outlet to purchase (*i*) dress clothes, (*ii*) casual clothes, (*iii*) power tools, and (*iv*) appliances?

   a. Teenagers

   b. Retired men

   c. Middle-aged professional men

   d. Young professional women

   e. Older working-class women

4. How should Sears determine the type of atmospherics it should have?

5. How would you encourage consumers who come to Sears for hard goods to purchase clothing items?

6. Develop a marketing strategy for Sears targeting the following groups.

   a. Hispanics

   b. African Americans

   c. Teenagers

   d. Middle-class women 25 to 50

   e. Middle-class men over 50

Source: S. Hume, "Sears' Next Struggle," *Advertising Age,* October 5, 1992, p. 4; "Sears Trades Its 'Softer Side' for Fresher Image," *Los Angeles Times,* August 18, 1999, p. C5; J. Mann, "Sears Unable to Deliver on Ad Campaign's Promises," *Kansas City Star,* August 24, 1999; B. Garfield, "Sears Abandons Softer Side," *Advertising Age,* August 27, 2001; and D. Eboghdady, "2 Chains Take Different Paths," *Register Guard,* April 24, 2002, p. 10D.

4–4 Vespa Boutiques

Vespa was a popular motor scooter in the United States until it withdrew from the market as a result of its inability to meet federal emission standards. In 2000 it returned. Its introduction included sponsoring the New York Marathon with new Vespas leading the race and the winners receiving a new 2001 Vespa. The Vespa ads appearing during the marathon showed a small red dot on a white screen. The dot moves closer, weaving to the tune "Flight of the Bumblebee." Soon it becomes clear that the dot is a Vespa. The tagline is "Vespa is back."

The opening of the first retail outlet for Vespa was celebrated a few weeks later at Paramount Studio's original *Roman Holiday* set with a fund raiser for Audrey Hepburn's children's charity. Ms. Hepburn helped make Vespas famous when she zipped around Rome on one in the popular movie *Roman Holiday*.

After the introductory period, Vespa launched a new tagline—"Vespa, the fun and only"—around a series of black-and-white pictures of twentyish models posing on the scooters. The ads ran in upscale magazines in cities where Vespa dealers were located or planned. In addition, teams of 12 models visited cafés and colleges in many of these cities. Their mission was described as "looking cool, sipping coffee, and tacitly pitching the Vespa."

In 2002, both Vespa and local dealer groups began to use sexually, hip-oriented advertising with the

tagline "Life is better with Vespa." A 30-second spot by the company is

Set in a backyard on a summer afternoon; a young man appears to heap praise on a woman reading in a nearby lawn chair. "You take me places I've never been before," he says in an Italian accent as he praises "her" curves and sleek figure. "Your petite but powerful body will purr with excitement when we are together." When he continues with "I must mount you now," the camera pans out to reveal a new Vespa, which he climbs aboard.

Vespa of Greater New York launched ads that showcase words ending in "issimo," such as "vroomisimo," and "sexissimo," and feature "barely clothed women sprawled over and around Vespas." In the San Francisco area, three billboards were developed that featured a woman's hands, arms, or legs grasping a male driver. A spokesman states, "Vespa is a passion brand that has been discovered by style leaders. Vespa is the sexiest way to get from A to B, and its Italian heritage allows us to own that."

While Vespa's general marketing and advertising strategy is certainly unique for a motor scooter, its distribution strategy is even more so. Vespa is distributed through a limited (64 in fall 2002) but growing number of Vespa boutiques. These outlets will sell only Vespas, Vespa merchandise, and espresso and pastries. Vespa merchandise will include product accessories, helmets, and such items as Vespa brand watches. The Vespa website describes the boutiques as follows:

> Since 1946, Vespa has been synonymous with entertainment, pleasure, freedom; feelings directly influencing the design of the new Vespa boutiques—unique retail environments created to showcase all the products which comprise the Vespa Lifestyle.

One expert on brand development has expressed surprise that Vespa, a utilitarian product in Europe, is positioning itself as a luxury brand in the United States: "To me, why would you want one? For prestige? Nah. It's the ultimate run-around machine."

Discussion Questions

1. What brand image is Vespa creating?
2. What outlet image is Vespa creating?
3. Are the outlet and brand images consistent?
4. If Vespa were to reposition as a utilitarian, fun, "run-around machine," how would the ads change?
5. If Vespa were to reposition as a utilitarian, fun, "run-around machine," would the existing distribution system be appropriate? How should it change?
6. What are the pros and cons of Vespa distributing through a mass merchant such as Sears or through multibrand retailers?
7. Evaluate Vespa's website (www.vespausa.com).
8. Vespa's current sexually themed ads appear to be male oriented. Do you agree? If so, is this wise given that young women are a significant portion of the scooter market?
9. Describe the decision process a typical consumer would use with respect to this product. What are the marketing implications of this?
10. Should management attempt to trigger problem recognition for the Vespa? Why? If they decided to, how should they do it?
11. What information sources is a consumer likely to use regarding the purchase of a Vespa?
12. What decision rule(s) is a consumer likely to use in the purchase of a Vespa?
13. Is the purchase of a Vespa likely to be a family purchase decision? If so, what roles will each family member play?
14. What will determine customer satisfaction and commitment to Vespa?
15. How would you define the target market for Vespas?

Source: J. Halliday, "Scooters and Pastry," *Advertising Age,* November 6, 2000, p. 4; K. Greenberg, "Reintroduced Vespa Takes a New Turn," *Brandweek,* May 28, 2001, p. 1; S. J. Heim, "Vespa's Sex Appeal Promoted in KBP Ads," *Adweek Western Edition,* April 22, 2002, p. 2; M. Anderson, "Vespa Gets Sexy in New Dealer Ads," *Adweek Eastern Edition,* May 13, 2002, p. 1; and K. Roundtree, "Viewpoint Studios Intros Racy TV Work for Vespa," *Adweek New England Edition,* July 2002, p. 1.

4–5   The Most Recognized and Respected Brand in the World?

What is the most recognized and respected brand in the world? Old, established brands such as Coca-Cola, McDonald's, and IBM could certainly make a case for this title. However, an upstart firm aims to topple these giants and claim this title for itself. Starbucks' stated company objective is "to establish Starbucks as the most recognized and respected brand in the world."

Starbucks was founded in 1971 by three academics. In Berkeley, California, the three friends met a Dutchman, Alfred Peet, who ran a coffee shop that was the focal point for the emerging food scene in the area. The three academics moved to Seattle and opened a coffee shop in Pike's Market featuring the fresh, high-quality beans used by Peet. They named the shop Starbucks after the coffee-loving first mate in Herman Melville's *Moby Dick.*

In 1982, Howard Schultz joined Starbucks as director of marketing and retail sales. In 1983, while visiting in Italy, he was struck by the enormous number of coffee shops where Italians started the day and later gathered to chat. "As soon as I saw it, I knew we should be doing this."

Schultz bought Starbucks from the three original owners in 1987. The firm lost money for three straight years while Schultz attempted to encourage consumption of darker, richer coffees. With a very limited budget, the firm began with billboards and transit ads with the headline "Familiarity breeds contempt" to encourage consumers to try the new product.

Schultz targeted 35- to 45-year-olds with higher-than-average incomes and educations. Women received slightly more emphasis than men. A manager described the basic strategy as follows: "We were trying to appeal to the top and have the market move to us."

Positive word-of-mouth communications, limited but effective advertising, a decision to provide brewing equipment and beans to restaurants, and consistent product quality led to eventual success in Seattle. By distributing the beans through mail order with ads in magazines such as *The New Yorker,* Starbucks began to develop national awareness.

Soon Washington State was saturated with Starbucks coffee shops (which sell coffee for on-premise consumption as well as to go, and also the coffee beans). California was targeted next, and outlets were opened in Washington, D.C., Denver, and Chicago. By early 2002, there were almost 5,000 Starbucks outlets, with nearly 900 of these located in 22 countries outside of North America. The firm plans to continue its rapid outlet growth both domestically and internationally.

Starbucks is considering launching a major television campaign but is concerned that its educational message doesn't translate well into a 30-second commercial. Therefore, it is considering an infomercial. Management is also concerned that standard advertising might destroy the unique mystique that surrounds Starbucks coffee.

Starbucks is facing challenges from numerous coffee bars that have appeared everywhere. Many of these are in portable stands and are set up in mall parking lots, gas station driveways, and virtually anywhere there is a high traffic flow. Also, machines now produce higher-quality coffee than in the past. Virtually all grocery stores now sell "gourmet" coffee beans, including Starbucks, which can be ground in the store or taken home whole.

In 1996, Starbucks and Dreyer's Grand Ice Cream Inc. formed a partnership. Dreyer's now distributes various flavors of Starbucks coffee ice cream such as Espresso Swirl and Javachip throughout the United States. Starbucks is also the flavor in Redhook Brewery's Double Black Stout beer.

Starbucks worked with Capitol Records to produce several Starbucks' jazz CDs that are sold through Starbucks outlets. It also sponsored, along with Beyond Music and the Sundance Channel, "Where Music Meets Film: Live from the Sundance Film Festival," a CD compilation of songs performed at the 1999 Sundance Music Studio. Starbucks had exclusive distribution rights through its retail outlets and website for the first eight weeks after the recording was released.

Starbucks' largest partnership is now with PepsiCo. This venture produces the cold, bottled coffee drink Frappuccino. The product carries the Starbucks label and is distributed by Pepsi.

Discussion Questions

1. What caused the major growth in the sales of gourmet coffee in the United States?
2. What caused Starbucks' success?
3. Should Starbucks conduct a major television advertising campaign? Justify your answer.
4. Should Starbucks prepare and use an infomercial? Justify your answer.
5. What types of situational factors could Starbucks use in its marketing strategy?
6. What risks are associated with using the Starbucks name on other products? What are the gains? Do you think it is a wise strategy?
7. Can Starbucks become one of the world's most recognized and respected brand names by 2010? What will it have to do to accomplish this goal?
8. Develop a strategy for Starbucks to use to expand into Mexico and South America.
9. Visit Starbucks' website (www.starbucks.com).
   a. Evaluate the site in terms of its communications effectiveness.
   b. Evaluate the site as a retail outlet.
10. Evaluate Starbucks' program for social responsibility. Does it receive proper recognition for its actions? If not, what, if anything, should it do about it?

4–6   A Product Failure at Saturn

Saturn, a division of General Motors, advertises around the following theme:

A different kind of company.
A different kind of car.

Though Saturn cars generally cost less than $20,000, the firm attempts to provide its customers with the same level of service and consideration typically associated with expensive luxury cars. Its stated objective is to be "the friendliest, best-liked car company in America." The manager of two dealerships in Maryland stated,

We're going to do more than what the customer expects, and in the long run, I think it will enhance our image.

Saturn's attempt to build an image of a high-quality car built by skilled, caring workers and sold in helpful, nonpressure dealerships received two small tests in its first two years. In one, it had to recall 1,836 cars that had received improper coolant. In another, it had to repair 1,480 cars with faulty seat-back recliners. In the second case, the firm made a TV commercial showing a Saturn representative flying to Alaska to fix the car of a resident who had purchased it in the lower 48.

However, in 1993, Saturn began receiving reports of a wire short-circuiting and causing a fire. Thirty-four fires (no injuries) were reported. Saturn faced a dilemma. A recall would involve 350,000 cars and a direct expense of as much as $35 million. Any negative publicity associated with the recall could seriously depress sales. Saturn had yet to break even, and General Motors was under serious financial pressure.

Saturn managers decided to deal with the problem in a manner consistent with its company objective described earlier. It quickly notified all purchasers of the affected cars and asked them to contact their dealers to have the defective wire replaced at no charge. The dealerships extended their operating hours, hired extra personnel, arranged door-to-door pickup and delivery, provided free car washes, and often provided barbecues or other festivities. All the repaired cars had a courtesy card placed inside that said,

> We'd like to thank you for allowing us to make this correction today. We know an event like this will test our relationship, so we want to repeat to you our basic promise—that everyone at Saturn is fully committed to making you as happy a Saturn owner as we can.

According to Steve Shannon, Saturn's director of consumer marketing, the decision to handle the recall in this manner was simple:

> The measure of whether we are a different kind of company is how we handle the bad times as well as the good. We're trying to minimize the inconvenience and show that we stand behind the cars, so that our owners don't lose faith in us or the cars.

How have consumers responded to the recall? Kim Timbers learned of the recall from friends who had heard of it on news reports before she received her letter from Saturn. She took her car to the dealer, who served her coffee and doughnuts during the 25-minute repair. Her response:

> I expected this would be my first bad experience with Saturn. But it was so positive, I trust them even more than when I purchased the car.

Discussion Questions

1. Describe the evaluative process and outcome that Timbers went through.
2. Saturn is attempting to create committed customers. Do you think it is succeeding? Why?
3. Evaluate the manner by which Saturn handled the recall. What options did it have?
4. How do you think publicity about the recall affected Saturn's image among nonowners?
5. How can Saturn determine if the direct cost of the recall is justified in terms of consumer response?
6. What should Saturn do after the recall is over?

4–7   Online Retailing to Ethnic Subcultures

Until recently, the Hispanic and African American subcultures lagged behind the general population in Internet use and online shopping. However, those differences are rapidly disappearing. All the various ethnic groups in the United States have at least some unique needs and desires. In many areas of the country there are relatively few members of any one group and therefore limited or no availability of specialized products targeting that group. This set of circumstances would seem to make online stores an optimal way to reach the various ethnic groups.

In fact, such stores are beginning to appear. One of the first successful ones targeted Asian Indians (who

were relatively early adopters of the Internet). Its site describes its operations as follows:

> Founded in 1998, Namaste.com is the premier retailer of Indian products in the United States. In the last three-and-a-half years we have had the privilege to reach and serve almost 50 percent of the Asian Indian households in North America, making us one of the most trusted Indian brands in North America. We have also served thousands of customers, in India and other parts of the world, with our various products and services.
>
> Whether it's a Haldiram snack, a tangy mango pickle, the latest Hindi movie DVD, money transfer to India, stunning

ethnic Indian outfits, all of your favorite treats are just a click away at Namaste.com. We offer an extensive variety of groceries from rice and dal to papads and pickles. You can also shop for a wide selection of music, from Bollywood hits to Hindustani and Carnatic classical, movies, books, ethnic Indian jewelry and clothes, multimedia, Indian games, as well as health and beauty products. Our popular services include safe and secure Money Transfer to India as well a Gifting to India.

A number of sites market products to the African American market. Most of these are currently small and specialized. One of the more diversified is UrbanStyleVillage.com:

Urban Style is a Black owned and operated company that is dedicated to developing and distributing products that reflect the lifestyles, traditions, humor and unique style of African American culture. We invite you to tour our site of Greeting Cards, Party Invitations, Stationery, African American Art, Journals, Calendars, Books, Games, Educational Activities, Greek Products, Collectibles, Figurines, Christmas and Kwanzaa Items, Toys, Dolls, Gifts and more.

At this time there are still few sites targeting Hispanics. Univision sells products on its site. MexiGrocer is perhaps the largest online retailer focusing on the group, as well as anyone wanting these products:

MexGrocer.com is a nationwide bilingual online grocery store for hard-to-find, nonperishable authentic Mexican food, household products, recipes, and cookbooks. We offer over 1,000 specialty items of imported and national leading food brands.

MexGrocer.com streamlines the shopping process by eliminating the difficulty of having to drive to multiple stores in search of authentic Mexican products not commonly in stock at conventional grocers. It also provides an expert solution to all amateur chefs looking for authentic Mexican recipes, as well as Mexican cookbooks in both English and Spanish. This exceptional concept is available at one user-friendly location, offering secure shopping, complemented by rapid and reliable delivery services.

We are the leading Mexican grocer on the Internet. Today, we have sold to over 3,700 cities in all 50 states of the United States and Canada. MexGrocer.com is a California Limited Liability company and was founded in early 2000 in San Diego, California.

Discussion Questions

1. Evaluate each of the three sites described above. Which is best? Why?
2. Are these sites active or passive?
3. Find and evaluate a leading online retailer focusing on the following subculture markets.
   a. Native American
   b. Korean
   c. Japanese
   d. Chinese
   e. Filipino
   f. Vietnamese
4. How should major retailers such as Target, Sears, or Macy's engage in online marketing to ethnic subcultures?

4–8   Increasing Egg Consumption

In 1945, per capita egg consumption was 402. By 1997, that figure had dropped to 236. Consumption rebounded somewhat to an estimated 254 in 1999. The sharp decline in per capita egg consumption has a number of causes. General changes in lifestyles and eating patterns have favored the use of cereals and other prepared foods over eggs. The massive advertising of cereal companies has caused consumers to shift their breakfast preferences away from eggs (the leading cereal brand often has an ad budget five times larger than the budget of the American Egg Board).

While the two factors described above hampered egg sales, the 1960's association of high cholesterol levels with heart disease had a devastating impact. Many mass media reports from 1960s through the 1990s emphasized the importance of cholesterol reduction as a means of reducing heart disease. Eggs have perhaps the highest concentration of cholesterol of any food product. The early reports recommended sharply reducing dietary cholesterol (cholesterol that one eats such as that found in eggs). This caused many consumers to recognize a problem with their current eating patterns (particularly egg consumption) and to seek and consume alternatives.

As research continued, it became increasingly clear that dietary cholesterol was not nearly the culprit it was initially thought to be. Instead, cholesterol produced by one's own body is the major problem. The consumption of fats, particularly saturated fats, tends to increase cholesterol, particularly the most harmful type, in many people. However, eggs and other cholesterol-containing foods continued to be shunned by consumers.

Starting in 1996, several fairly widely reported studies have shown that moderate amounts of dietary cholesterol (egg) consumption do not pose a risk of increased body cholesterol for most consumers. However, even these studies have produced only a modest resurgence in egg consumption—per capita consumption of shell eggs has increased less than an egg a month since 1996.

The American Egg Board (AEB)

The AEB is the industry association that promotes eggs. To provide information about consumers' attitudes and knowledge about eggs and to assess the effectiveness of its "I Love Eggs" campaign (its previous marketing effort), the AEB completed a three-part consumer research study in early 1998. More than one-third of consumers reported feeling better about eggs than they did just two years earlier, and most consumers in 1998 admit that they are no longer as concerned about consuming cholesterol as they were before.

Research also showed that convenience is still a major problem for eggs, particularly on weekdays when the time spent at breakfast is growing shorter. In addition, many consumers are not aware of the nutritional positives that eggs have to offer, particularly the quality of protein in an egg. Surprisingly, AEB research showed that another barrier to increased egg consumption is that consumers don't even think of eggs at breakfast.

In 1998, the AEB spent $20 million promoting eggs, with $11 million devoted to advertising. This was a sharp increase from prior years and was associated with a new theme: "If It Ain't Eggs, It Ain't Breakfast." The president of the AEB stated, "When consumers think about breakfast, we want them to think about eggs." The campaign will try to

reach consumers when they are thinking about breakfast by sponsoring NBC's "Today Show" concert series.

Launched in the spring, the new campaign shifted the American Egg Board's focus from combating negative publicity about eggs and cholesterol to celebrating the nutritional positives of eggs and protein. The ads will state that one large egg a day makes good nutritional sense as part of a balanced diet. The ads will continue to use the "Incredible egg" and the "I love eggs" slogans.

The 1998 AEB Annual Report describes the campaign as follows:

The "If It Ain't Eggs" campaign grew out of the idea that although a cold bowl of cereal or a bagel on the run might be fast, and they might fill you up, they just aren't breakfast. The television and radio campaign uses music to remind people about their favorite family meal in a fun, folksy way. It is a shift from changing attitudes about cholesterol to changing behavior and encouraging consumers to eat eggs more often.

The television commercial features three generations coming together to prepare a family breakfast with eggs as the centerpiece. It includes mouthwatering footage of a variety of egg dishes in order to "trigger the crave" for eggs. As permission to eat the eggs they love, the spot includes a protein message to educate consumers about the nutritional benefits of eggs.

The overall campaign goal to "Capture the Weekend Breakfast" remained intact. More breakfasts continue to be eaten on weekends, and most weekend breakfasts still don't include eggs. Thus, weekend breakfast remains AEB's greatest opportunity to increase consumption. Television and radio advertising was emphasized during three-day holiday weekends throughout the year to encourage consumers to include eggs in the additional breakfast occasion.

In addition to advertising, the AEB engages in consumer education and generates significant publicity. It describes some of its educational activities as follows:

For hard-to-reach young parents and their children, a new booklet, We Are Eggstra Special, was developed and distributed to over 163,000 chain and individually owned day care centers, Head Start facilities, and elementary schools with prekindergarten and kindergarten classes as well as to early childhood education district supervisors.

The booklet features hands-on activities for children not yet old enough to read—elementary math measurements, simple science and art projects, songs, poems, raps, and other language arts activities and, of course, cooking—all within a multicultural theme. Included in the mailing was a reproducible letter to parents announcing the program and providing both nutrition and food safety tips. With the completion of the preschool program, AEB has now provided accurate, up-to-date information to teachers at all levels of childhood education.

Seven years after its original release, *The Incredible Journey from Hen to Home* was given a facelift and an update. With jazzed-up colors and a new pocket folder, the material for fourth- through sixth-grade use was particularly revised in the areas of nutrition and food safety to include the Food Guide Pyramid and Fight BAC! campaign. More than 104,000 copies of the new *Journey* kit edition were sent to schools nationwide at the end of the year.

Following up on the previously released kit for active older adult programs, three new issues of a coordinating *Rediscover Eggs!* newsletter were sent to 4,000 retirement living communities, neighborhood senior centers, and nutrition sites. Each issue—bearing the seal of the American Academy of Family Physicians Foundation for credibility—contained articles on nutrition and food safety, recipes, egg craft instructions, and answers to common questions.

A video was produced to coordinate with *The Incredible Classroom Eggsperience* middle/high school print kit produced last year. The film was mailed to 25,000 family and consumer science department heads, media specialists, and classroom educators.

According to the AEB, in 1998 eggs were prominently featured 87 times in 25 magazines with a combined circulation of 204,439,472. Some of the articles included

- "Eggs for Supper," a five-page feature in *Good Housekeeping.*
- "The Case for Eggs," a six-page feature in *Cooking Light.*
- "Eggs Over Easy," three pages in *Parenting.*
- "The Good Egg," a four-page spread in *House Beautiful.*
- "The Truth about Eggs" in *Bon Appetit.*
- "Perfect Omelet" features in *Ladies Home Journal, Parents,* and *Woman's World.*

The AEB attempts to influence opinion leaders in a variety of ways. In 1998, a recipe contest was conducted among members of the International Association of Culinary Professionals (IACP) in conjunction with their Kids in the Kitchen Network section. IACP members in all sections—cookbook authors and food writers, cooking school owners, members of the food press, food media personalities, consultants, and entrepreneurs—were invited to submit recipes children could cook with or without help. Rather than prizes being awarded to the recipe developers, each selected a child/family charity or elementary, middle, or high school to receive a cash donation. The recipes are being compiled into a cook booklet to be publicized and distributed nationally.

In terms of general publicity, the AEB focused on generating widespread attention for a study published in the *Journal of the American College of Nutrition,* which showed that even people with moderately high cholesterol can eat two eggs a day. A multidimensional publicity campaign resulted in positive news stories in leading national magazines such as *Good Housekeeping* and *First for Women;* a syndicated story by the Gannett News Service reaching more than 500 newspapers across the country; and feature television segments on "Dr. Dean," a syndicated health program, and FOX's "Good Day New York."

In the winter, the AEB teamed up with the Pennsylvania State University's Center for Sports Medicine to launch a national nutrition/fitness campaign to showcase eggs as an ideal food for active people. Educational materials, including a consumer brochure, *Foods That Fuel: A Guide to Eating Your Way to Fitness,* emphasized the importance of consuming "fuel foods" such as eggs for optimal energy and maximum performance.

Table A provides demographic data relevant to egg consumption.

Discussion Questions

1. Consumers appear to have recognized a problem with egg consumption. Why is it so difficult to get them to "unrecognize" this problem?

2. Why don't consumers eat more eggs?

3. According to the research, eggs are not in the evoked set for breakfast for many consumers. What can the AEB do to change this?

4. What decision process do consumers use to decide what to have for breakfast during the week? During the weekend?

Variable	Heavy User[†]	Light User[‡]	Egg Substitute[§]	
Percent of Respondents	34%	28%	12%	**TABLE A**
Age				Demographics and
18–24	83	135	78	Egg Consumption*
25–34	101	95	82	
35–44	120	89	84	
45–54	106	89	81	
55–64	99	94	142	
>64	78	118	141	
Education				
College graduate	82	114	102	
Some college	101	97	80	
High school graduate	105	93	96	
No degree	110	101	137	
Occupation				
Professional	85	106	102	
Managerial/administrative	85	114	83	
Technical/clerical/sales	98	98	76	
Precision/craft	99	98	121	
Race/Ethnic Group				
White	101	100	96	
Black	92	104	126	
Spanish speaking	120	91	110	
Region				
Northeast	92	109	116	
North Central	97	106	88	
South	107	92	104	
West	99	98	91	
Household Income				
<$10,000	90	131	135	
$10,000–19,999	95	107	107	
$20,000–29,999	106	96	92	
$30,000–39,999	99	96	88	
$40,000–49,999	109	86	95	
$50,000–59,999	117	89	92	
$60,000–74,999	110	88	78	
$75,000+	89	103	108	
Household Structure				
Single	76	125	87	
Married	114	84	99	
Child <2	114	88	87	
Child 2–5	122	77	78	
Child 6–11	130	70	79	
Child 12–17	131	70	94	

*100 = Average use or consumption unless a percent is indicated. Base = Female homemakers.
[†]More than two dozen in last 30 days.
[‡]Less than two dozen in last 30 days.
[§]Any in last 30 days.

Source: *Mediamark Reporter 2002—University* (New York: Mediamark Research Inc., March 2002).

5. What evaluative criteria do consumers use in selecting a food for breakfast? Do these change from weekdays to weekends?

6. What insights do the demographic data offer the AEB?

7. How can the AEB use situations to increase egg consumption?

8. Evaluate the AEB's new campaign.

Sources: J. Pollack, "Egg Board Budgets $11 Mil," *Advertising Age,* May 25, 1998, p. 10; J. Neff, "The Great Egg Breakthrough," *Food Processing,* January 1998, p. 25; and the American Egg Board website (www.aeb.com).

4-9   Encouraging the Early Detection of Diseases

Public health officials and other concerned groups have struggled for years trying to persuade women to have breast cancer examinations and men to be checked for prostate cancer. The technical ability to detect disease or disease causing conditions has exploded in recent years. There are screening tests for high cholesterol (a heart attack risk factor), high blood pressure, osteoporosis, inherited breast cancer risk, HIV, and colon cancer, among others.

The advantages of early detection are great. Some diseases may be prevented entirely by early detection of potential causes (high cholesterol). Others are treated much more effectively and efficiently if detected and treated early. Thus, early detection can save lives, suffering, and money.

Despite such advantages, the use of early detection technology remains far below an optimal level. Some of this is due to the economics of the medical system. Lower-income individuals often lack adequate health insurance and are reluctant to spend scarce financial resources on tests for problems they may not have. However, even well-insured and prosperous individuals often forgo important tests. For example, it is estimated that 20 percent of American adults have dangerously high cholesterol, and many are unaware of this fact.

Why are consumers reluctant to take steps, often quite simple and inexpensive, that could literally save their lives. Some consumers believe that they are not susceptible to a particular health problem because of their age, genetics, or general condition. Given this belief, they do not see any value in taking a test that they are sure will merely confirm what they already "know." Marketers for Lipitor, a cholesterol-lowering drug, try to counter this by showing that apparently low-risk people such as figure-skater Peggy Fleming have cholesterol levels that need treatment.

Other consumers are in the opposite camp. They are fearful that the tests might reveal a problem. Even if such a problem is correctable if caught early, it is still bad news to have any type of disease or likelihood of a disease. Further, such a diagnosis generally involves at least short-term unpleasantness—a change in diet, physical or drug treatments, and anxiety. People are ambivalent at best about seeking out potentially bad news.

In light of the above, how does a firm or a nonprofit or public agency convince consumers to use appropriate early-detection technologies?

A number of opposing advertising approaches have been suggested. Should the ad use statistics or anecdotal evidence? Should the consequences be framed in terms of losses from not being tested or gains from being tested? Examples of each of these approaches are

- *Statistical, gain:* "Many women have no family history of breast cancer and have never felt any lump in their breast. But they follow the advice of the American Cancer Society and start having annual screening mammograms when they turn fifty. Because of this, doctors are able to detect their tumors at an early, treatable stage, and they are 30 percent less likely to die of breast cancer."
- *Statistical, loss:* "Many women have no family history of breast cancer and have never felt any lump in their breast. So they don't follow the advice of the American Cancer Society to start having annual screening mammograms when they turn fifty. Because of this, doctors are not able to detect tumors at an early, treatable stage, and they are 43 percent more likely to die of breast cancer."
- *Anecdotal, gain:* "No one in Sara Johnson's family had ever gotten breast cancer, and she had never felt any lump in her breast. But she followed the advice of the American Cancer Society and started having annual screening mammograms when she turned fifty. Because of this, doctors were able to detect her breast tumor at an early, treatable stage, and now Sara can look forward to a long life, watching her grandson, Jeffrey, grow up."
- *Anecdotal, loss:* "No one in Sara Johnson's family had ever gotten breast cancer, and she had never felt any lump in her breast. So she didn't follow the advice of the American Cancer Society to start having annual screening mammograms when she turned fifty. Because of this, doctors were not able to detect her breast tumor at an early, treatable stage, and now Sara may miss out on a long life, watching her grandson, Jeffrey, grow up."

Discussion Questions

1. Which of the four ads described above will work best? Why?
2. How would you trigger problem recognition for the early detection of disease among groups who have a relatively low risk for the disease?

3. How would you trigger problem recognition for the early detection of disease among groups who have a relatively high risk for the disease?

4. Describe the decision process a typical individual would go through in deciding to test for a disease?

5. What decision rule do consumers use in deciding to test for a disease?

6. What sources of information do consumers use in deciding to test for a disease?

7. Who influences the decision to test for a disease?

8. Develop a strategy to encourage people to test for a disease or health risk factor of your choice.

Source: D. Cox and A. D. Cox, "Communicating the Consequences of Early Detection," *Journal of Marketing,* July 2001, pp. 91–103; L. Sanders, "Aiming to Stay No. 1," *Advertising Age,* December 10, 2001, p. 4; and www.cdc.gov.

Organizations as Consumers

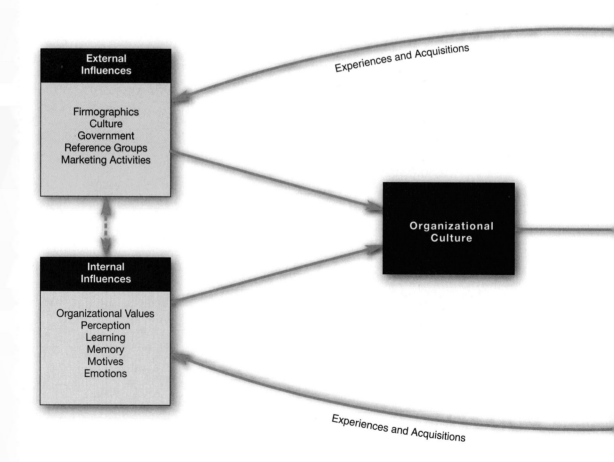

■ The stereotype of organizational buying behavior is one of a cold, efficient, economically rational process. Computers rather than humans could easily, and perhaps preferably, fulfill this function. In reality, nothing could be further from the truth. In fact, organizational consumer behavior is as human as individual and household consumer behavior.

Organizations pay price premiums for well-known brands and for prestige brands. They avoid risk and fail to properly evaluate products and brands both before and after purchase. Individual members of organizations use the purchasing and consumption process as a political arena and attempt to increase their personal, departmental, or functional power through purchasing. Marketing communications are perceived and misperceived by organization members. Likewise, organizations learn correct and incorrect information about the world in which they operate.

Organizational purchase decisions take place in situations with varying degrees of time pressure, importance, and newness. They typically involve more people and criteria than do individual or household decisions. Thus, the study of organizational buying behavior is a rich and fun-filled activity.

On this and the facing page is a version of our model of consumer behavior modified for organizational buying. Chapter 19 explains these modifications.

675

Decision Process

Situations

Problem Recognition
↓
Information Search
↓
Alternative Evaluation and Selection
↓
Outlet Selection and Purchase
↓
Postpurchase Processes

Needs/ Desires

"PATIENCE IS A VIRTUE."
–CHAUCER

"ENOUGH IS ENOUGH."
–WESTERN UNION

Haven't you spent enough time waiting to collect from your customers? Maybe that's why when they finally decide to pay, you should tell them to send their money by Western Union Quick Collect.® The Quick Collect service delivers guaranteed good funds in minutes. In fact, we're the fastest way to send good funds.

And the most convenient, with over 20,000 Western Union agent locations in the U.S.

For more information, ask your manager to call 1-800-525-6313. The sooner the better, because while patience may be a virtue, too much can ruin your business.

WESTERN UNION | QUICK COLLECT

The fastest way to collect good funds.℠

Organizational Buyer Behavior

chapter 19

☐ One of Western Union's important organizational market segments is collection agents. There are about 100,000 collection agents in 1,300 collection offices in the United States. Collection offices include collection agencies, credit card–issuing banks, mortgage companies, and finance companies.

Collectors request payment from debtors in a variety of ways—hand delivery, regular mail, or overnight mail of a check or money order are the most common. In 1989, Western Union introduced Quick Collect as an alternative means. With Quick Collect, the debtor pays at one of Western Union's 18,000 locations. The payment is then transferred to the collection agent within 15 minutes, eliminating the "check-is-in-the-mail"

story as well as eliminating earnings lost while payment is in transit.

According to Quick Collect's product manager,

We want the collectors to tell debtors to use Quick Collect every time. We needed to build awareness but more important, to establish relationships with individual collectors, which we felt we could do by rewarding them for being good at their job.

Western Union developed a revolving reward program that targets individual agents with a new one-month promotion every six months. The constant flow of new programs keeps the agents interested and participating.

A recent program used a scratch-and-win game. Collection managers received posters, game boards, and a one-month supply of scratch-off tickets. Every time a debtor paid using Quick Collect, the agent involved received a ticket. The agents had a 1-in-86 chance to win a prize such as a cellular phone or CD player. Another box on the ticket had a letter that agents could accumulate to try to spell "Quick Collect." Those who succeeded (about one per month) received a grand prize of air travel for two anywhere in the United States. The program is credited with increasing the use of Quick Collect by 30 percent.

To further develop its relationship with agents, Western Union publishes a quarterly magazine, the *Professional Collector,* which now has a circulation of 100,000. It contains lifestyle features and industry-specific articles on topics such as legal developments. It is designed to help the collectors see their jobs as a professional career. The reward program is incorporated into the magazine through a feature called the Champion Collector. Managers nominate their top agents. Winners' names are listed in this part of the magazine and they receive a plaque.

Western Union credits these programs as a major reason Quick Collect has experienced double-digit annual growth for the past seven years.[1]

Purchase decisions by businesses are often described as "rational" or "economic." However, businesses and other organizations are made up of individuals. These individuals, not "the organization," make the purchase decisions. Thus, as we saw in the opening example, they respond to contests and loyalty programs just as individual consumers do. Illustration 19–1 reflects the fact that communicating with organizational buyers involves many of the same principles of perception used to reach household buyers, such as color, contrast, and humor.

However, organizations are not just a collection of individuals. Organizations do develop unique rules and cultures that influence the behavior of their members. Thus, it is important that we understand the unique characteristics of organizations that relate to their purchasing behavior.

Understanding organizational purchasing requires many of the same concepts used to understand individual consumer or household needs. Although larger and often more complex than individual consumers and households, organizations too develop preferences, memories, and behaviors through perceptions, information processing, and experience. Likewise, organizations develop cultures that create relatively stable patterns of behaviors over time and across situations.

Like households, organizations make many buying decisions. In some instances, these buying decisions are routine replacement decisions for a frequently purchased, commodity product or service such as paper or pens. At the other end of the continuum, organizations face new, complex purchase decisions that require careful problem definition, extensive information search, a long and often technical evaluation process, perhaps a negotiated purchase, and a long period of use and postpurchase evaluation.

Because there are many similarities between analyzing consumer behavior and analyzing organizational buyer behavior, our basic conceptual model of buyer behavior still holds. Of course, some aspects of the model, such as social status, do not apply; but most others do, with some modification as shown in Figure 19–1. The purpose of this chapter is

Courtesy Computer Associates.

FIGURE 19–1   **Overall Model of Organizational Buyer Behavior**

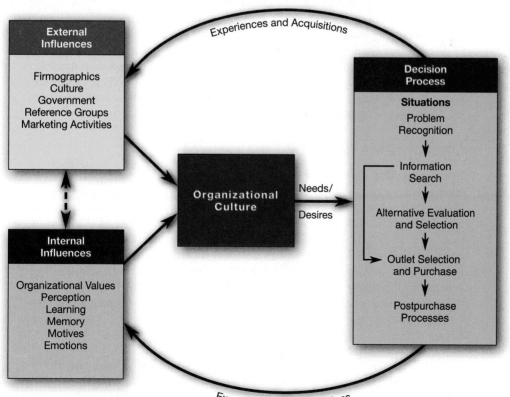

to discuss how this model of consumer behavior should be modified for application to organizational buying behavior and how the concepts of this model operate when marketing to organizations rather than to individual consumers or households.

We will begin our discussion by examining the organization decision process. Then we will examine the factors that determine organizational culture, the organizational equivalent of household lifestyle.

ORGANIZATIONAL PURCHASE PROCESS

Organizational buying decisions are often compared to family purchases. While this can produce useful insights, there are important distinctions between the two. Organizations generally have relatively objective and clearly articulated criteria, such as profit maximization, that guide purchases. Families lack such explicit, overarching goals. Most industrial purchases are made by individuals unknown to the other members of the organization, often including those who will use the product. This is not the case with families or households. Most organizational purchases have little effect on most other members of the organization, whereas most family purchases directly affect the other members of the family (by consuming scarce resources if in no other way).

Businesses often engage in reciprocal purchases (they buy from their customers when possible) and form strategic alliances with their suppliers. They may be proactive in helping suppliers develop products that meet their unique needs. These are not common options for households.

Most important, *many family purchases are inherently emotional and affect the relationships between the family members.*[2] The decision to buy a child a requested toy or new school clothes is more than simply an acquisition; it is a symbol of love and commitment to the child. The decision to take the family to a restaurant for a meal or to purchase a new television has emotional meaning to the other family members. Disagreements about how to spend money are a major cause of marital discord. The processes families use to make purchase decisions and the outcomes of those processes have important impacts on the well-being of the individual family members and the family itself. These factors are rarely operative in organizational buying decisions. Thus, while organizational decision making has some things in common with family decision making, it is not the same.

Decision-Making Unit

Decision-making units (DMUs) are *the individuals (representing functional areas and management) within an organization who participate in making a given purchase decision.* These often function as **buying centers** when they consist of individuals from various areas of the firm, such as accounting, engineering, manufacturing, and marketing, who meet specifically to make a purchase decision. They are often relatively permanent for recurring decisions and ad hoc for nonroutine ones. Large, highly structured organizations ordinarily involve more individuals in a purchase decision than do smaller, less formal organizations. Important decisions are likely to involve individuals from a wider variety of functional areas and organizational levels than are less important purchase decisions.

The following describes a Hewlett-Packard salesperson's view of the DMU and the buying process for very expensive imaging systems for large hospitals:

Selling in the hospital market is a two-stage process and the buying cycle ranges from 3 to 12 months. In the first stage, I deal with medical professionals. They are most concerned with image quality, product reliability, and service. I must establish relationships and awareness of our products' functionality and reliability with a number of people, and the product demonstration is critical.

Attribute*	Buyer Rating	Operations Rating
Ease of placing orders	**4.01**	3.71
Line-item availability	**4.55**	4.31
Packages clearly identified	4.46	**4.82**
Meets appointments	4.46	**4.73**
Delivers when requested	**4.87**	4.70
Delivered sorted and segregated	4.36	**4.75**
Palletizing/unitizing capability	3.72	**4.37**
Master carton packaging quality	3.81	**4.48**
Shelf unit packaging quality	3.97	**4.29**
Complete/accurate documentation	4.54	**4.81**
Well-documented deal/style codes	4.36	**4.60**
Length of order cycle	**4.14**	3.61
Consistency of order cycle	**4.38**	3.88

TABLE 19–1

Service Attribute Importance for Retail and Wholesale Buyers and Operations Personnel

*Measured on a 1 to 5 scale, with 5 being very important and 1 being not at all important. All are significantly different at the .05 level.

Source: Adapted from M. B. Cooper, C. Droge, and P. J. Daugherty, "How Buyers and Operations Personnel Evaluate Service," *Industrial Marketing Management,* no. 20 (1991), p. 83.

The second stage is negotiations with administrators, who are more driven by price and cost issues. But much depends on the hospital's situation. For example, if a hospital is renowned for cancer treatment, they want the best available systems in that area and are more price sensitive with other equipment.[3]

In Table 19–1, we see that buyers in retail and wholesale firms assign different priorities to the performance of suppliers than do the operations people in those same firms. Firms marketing to these firms must meet the needs of each group and communicate that to each group. Note that focusing only on the buyers, a common strategy, is not likely to be successful.

How the final purchase decision is made is in part determined by individual power, expertise, the degree of influence each functional area possesses in this type decision, how the organization resolves group decision conflicts, and the nature of the decision.[4]

Members of the decision-making unit play various roles, such as information gatherer, key influencer, decision maker, purchaser, or user. A plant manager could play all five roles, while corporate engineers may simply be sources of information.

Decision-making units are likely to vary over the product life cycle (new products versus older ones). Consider the changes in the decision-making unit that took place in the purchase of microprocessors by an original equipment manufacturer over the stages of the microprocessor's product life cycle. Early stages in the life of the new microprocessor presented a difficult, important decision that required a large DMU. As the product grew in its utilization, a simpler decision evolved, as did a change in the structure of the DMU. Finally, as the microprocessor moved into a mature stage, it became a routine low-priority decision involving primarily the purchasing function. These changes are illustrated below:

Stage of Product Life Cycle	Size of DMU	Key Functions Influencing the Purchase Decision
Introduction	Large	Engineering and R&D
Growth	Medium	Production and top management
Maturity	Small	Purchasing

Purchase Situation

The buying process is influenced by the importance of the purchase and the complexity and difficulty of the choice. Simple, low-risk, routine decisions are generally made by an individual or even an automated process without extensive effort. At the other extreme are decisions that are complex and have major organizational implications. A continuum of purchase situations lies between these two extremes. A useful categorization of organizational purchase situations is provided in Table 19–2 and described in the following paragraphs.[5]

Note that this is similar to the purchase involvement construct discussed in Chapter 14. For consumers, we divided the purchase involvement continuum into three categories—nominal, limited, and extended. These correspond closely to the straight rebuy, modified rebuy, and new task purchase situations shown in Table 19–2.

Straight Rebuy   This situation occurs when the purchase is of minor importance and is not complex. This is generally the case when reordering basic supplies and component parts. In such cases, the reordering process may be completely automated or done routinely by clerical personnel. Such purchases are often handled under a contract that is reviewed and perhaps rebid periodically. Price or reliability tend to be the dominant evaluative criteria. No consideration is given to strategic issues.

Modified Rebuy   This strategy is used when the purchase is moderately important to the firm or the choice is more complex. This typically involves a product or service that the organization is accustomed to purchasing but the product or the firm's needs have changed. Or, because the product is important to the firm (it is simple but the firm uses a lot of it or it is an important component of the firm's output), the firm may periodically reevaluate brands or suppliers. The DMU is likely to include several representatives, including some midlevel managers. More information is gathered and more evaluative criteria are analyzed. Strategic issues also begin to play a role.

New Task   This approach tends to occur when the buying decision is very important and the choice is quite complex. This would involve decisions on such things as an initial sales automation system or a new advertising agency. The buying organization will typically have had little experience with the decision and perhaps with the product or service. The DMU is likely to be large and evolve over time. Top management will be involved in the decision, and strategic issues will be of prime importance. The time involved is frequently quite long; for example, from problem recognition to implementation of a sales automation system typically takes 21 to 30 months.

TABLE 19–2		*Straight Rebuy*	*Modified Rebuy*	*New Task*
Organizational Purchase Situations and Buying Responses	**Situational Characteristics**			
	Purchase importance	Low	Moderate	High
	Choice complexity	Low	Moderate	High
	Purchasing Characteristics			
	Size of DMU	Very small	Medium	Large, evolving
	Level of DMU	Low	Mid-level	Top of organization
	Time to decision	Very brief	Moderate	Long
	Information search	None/very limited	Moderate	Extensive
	Analysis techniques	None/price comparisons	Several	Extensive, complex
	Strategic focus	None	Limited	Dominates

Clearly, the marketing strategy and tactics for one particular type of purchase situation would be inappropriate for others. Thus, marketers must understand the purchase task confronting their organizational consumers and develop appropriate marketing strategies.

Steps in the Organizational Decision Process

Because organizational decisions typically involve more individuals in more complex decision tasks than do individual or household decisions, marketing efforts to affect this process are much more complex.[6] Shown in Table 19–3 are stages in the decision process and sources of influence at each stage in a large insurance company's decision to add microcomputers to its office management function. Altogether there were 12 separate sources of influence, each with different levels of influence and affecting different stages of the purchase decision process.

To have a chance to win this large contract, a selling firm must provide relevant information to each source of influence. This is not a simple task, given that each source of influence has different motives and different criteria for evaluating alternative products, as well as different media habits.

Problem Recognition   In Table 19–3, the sales manager and office manager played the key role in recognizing the need to add microcomputers to their organization. In this instance, a continuing problem between field sales agents and internal administrative clerks led the office manager and sales manager to recognize the problem. Aiding their recognition of the problem were accounting personnel and microcomputer sales representatives who

Stages of the Purchase Decision Process	Key Influences within Decision-Making Unit	Influences Outside the Decision-Making Unit
Problem recognition	Office manager Sales manager	Field sales agents Administrative clerks Accounting manager Microcomputer sales representative
Information search	Data processing manager Office manager Purchasing manager	Operations personnel Microcomputer sales representative Other corporate users Office systems consultant
Alternative evaluation	General management Data processing manager Office manager Sales manager Purchasing manager	Office systems consultant Microcomputer sales representative
Purchase decision	General management Office manager Purchasing manager	
Product usage	Office manager Sales manager	Field sales agents Administrative clerks Accounting personnel Microcomputer sales representative
Evaluation	Office manager Sales manager General management	Field sales agents Administrative clerks Accounting personnel

TABLE 19–3

Decision Process in Purchasing Microcomputers for a Large Insurance Company

| TABLE 19–4 | Group Involvement in the Decision Process in High-Tech Organizations |

Stages of Decision Process	Percent Involved in Each Stage of Decision Process					
	Board of Directors	Top Management	Head of Department	Lab Technician or Operator	Purchasing Manager or Buyer	Finance Manager Accountant
Recognizing the need to purchase	7%	26%	70%	30%	0%	3%
Determining product specifications	0	33	74	33	3	0
Deciding which suppliers to consider	3	33	56	14	19	0
Obtaining quotations and proposals	0	26	52	19	14	3
Evaluating quotations and proposals	7	63	63	3	11	7
Final product or supplier selection	21	48	48	7	11	0

Source: R. Abratt, "Industrial Buying in Hi-Tech Markets," *Industrial Marketing Management* 15 (1986), p. 295. Copyright 1986; reprinted with permission from Elsevier Science.

called on the office manager. The combination of these sources of influence eventually led to an increased level of importance and the subsequent stage of information search.

Table 19–4 shows that in high-tech markets, the head of a department is most likely to recognize a problem or need to purchase. Perhaps more important is that purchasing managers are not a source of problem recognition. This points out the danger of salespeople calling on purchasing agents only. As shown in Table 19–4, problem recognition and determining specifications often occur without much involvement of purchasing personnel.

Information Search   Information search can be both formal and informal.[7] Site visits to evaluate a potential vendor, laboratory tests of a new product or prototype, and investigation of possible product specifications are part of formal information search. Informal information search can occur during discussions with sales representatives, while attending trade shows, or when reading industry-specific journals. Industrial buyers search for information both to help make the best decision and to support their actions and recommendations within the organization.[8]

For complex technology products, organizational buyers often hire consultants both to provide information and to help evaluate alternatives. Consider the role played by consultants in the purchase of sales automation systems:

The second step in the buying cycle was to evaluate the potential to automate existing processes . . . . Customers were usually not equipped to do this in-house. It was common for SA consultants to help them. Their deep understanding of the industry, and their skills and experience, made them the best option for this step.

In the third step, the customer decided how the different functions to be automated were related, and determined how data was to be collected, stored, and analyzed. This again was usually done by SA consultants with the support of the customer's information systems department.

The customer decided the type of SA software and hardware to be purchased . . . . Here again, the customer relied heavily on the consultant.[9]

Increasingly, organizational buyers are searching for product and price information on the Internet. Firms such as General Electric make such information readily available to potential buyers (see Illustration 19–2).

Evaluation and Selection   The evaluation of possible vendors and selection of a given vendor often follow a **two-stage decision process.**[10] The first stage is making the buyer's approved vendor list. A conjunctive decision process is very common. In this manner, the organization can screen out potential vendors that do not meet all its minimum criteria. In a government missile purchase, 41 potential manufacturers of a given missile electronics system were first identified. After site visits to inspect manufacturing capability and resources, the organization pared this list of 41 down to 11 that met the government's minimum criteria.

A second stage of organizational decision making could involve other decision rules, such as disjunctive, lexicographic, compensatory, or elimination-by-aspects. For the government purchase discussed above, a lexicographic decision process was next used, with the most important criterion being price. Using this decision rule, the organization selected two vendors.

The process of evaluation and selection is further complicated by the fact that different members of the decision-making unit have differing evaluative criteria. Recall the difference in criteria for imaging systems between hospital administrators and medical professionals described earlier. Table 19–5 shows that purchasing, management, engineering, and operations use differing sets of performance criteria. For example, purchasing is more concerned with pricing policies, terms and conditions, and order status; engineers are more concerned with product knowledge, product operations, and applications knowledge. A salesperson calling on these accounts would need to understand and respond to the unique as well as the shared criteria of these purchase influencers.

It is generally assumed that business purchases are strictly economic, with the goal of maximizing the profits of the purchasing organization.[11] However, power, prestige, security, and similar noneconomic criteria also play important roles in business purchase decisions. A recent study found that there are organizations that buy "green," similar to the "green consumers" described in Chapter 3. These organizations have policies or individual champions for socially responsible buying behavior by the organization.[12] Firms wishing to do business with these organizations must meet their requirements for products produced in an environmentally sound manner. The ad in Illustration 19–3 would appeal to these firms.

TABLE 19–5

Evaluative Criteria and Organizational Role

Evaluative Criteria Used in Purchase Decision	Functional Role in Organization			
	Purchasing	Management	Engineering	Operations
Vendor offers broad line	X	X		
Many product options available	X	X		
Ease of maintenance of equipment			X	X
Competence of service technicians		X	X	X
Overall quality of service		X	X	
Product warranty	X	X	X	X
Delivery (lead time)				X
Time needed to install equipment	X			X
Construction costs	X		X	X
Vendor has the lowest price	X	X	X	
Financial stability of vendor	X		X	X
Vendor willing to negotiate price	X			
Vendor reputation for quality	X	X	X	
Salesperson competence		X	X	X
Compatibility with equipment	X	X		
Available computer interface	X			

Source: Adapted from D. H. McQuiston and R. G. Walters, "The Evaluative Criteria of Industrial Buyers: Implications for Sales Training," *The Journal of Business and Industrial Marketing,* Summer–Fall 1989, p. 74.

ILLUSTRATION 19–3

Firms make decisions for more than economic reasons.

"There's a stretch along the Lower Roanoke River in North Carolina

21,008 magnificent acres,

that's been called one of America's last great places. It's where I grew up, and now I bring my

400 plant varieties,

kids here to teach them what nature's all about. My company, Georgia-Pacific, owns this land

214 species of birds

and we did something no forest products company has ever done before. We formed a partnership

and one partnership making sure

with The Nature Conservancy to co-manage and protect this place. We all want a better world

it all stays that way.

for our kids. It just feels good to be working for a company that's doing something about it."

Mason Lilley, Forester

Georgia-Pacific
The Forest Products Company

Courtesy Georgia Pacific.

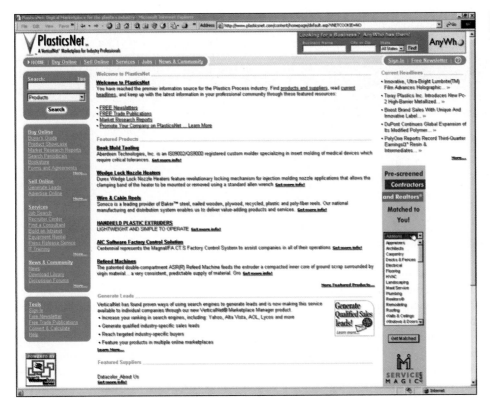

Purchase and Decision Implementation   Once the decision to buy from a particular organization has been made, the method of purchase must be determined. From the seller's point of view, this means how and when they will get paid. In many purchases, payment is not made until delivery. Others involve progress payments. For a firm working on the construction of a building or highway or developing a new military aircraft that will take several years, payment timing is critical.

On an international basis, purchase implementation and method of payment are even more critical. Some countries prohibit the removal of capital from their country without an offsetting purchase. This led Caterpillar Tractor Company to sell earthmoving equipment in South America in exchange for raw materials, such as copper, which it could sell or use in its manufacturing operations.

Terms and conditions—payments, warranties, delivery dates, and so forth—are both complex and critical in business-to-business markets. One U.S. manufacturer of steam turbines lost a large order to a foreign manufacturer because its warranty was written too much to the advantage of the seller.

Firms marketing to organizations increasingly use the Internet to sell their products directly to customers or through online wholesalers (see Illustration 19-4).[13] They also use it to generate leads for telephone or direct sales calls and to solicit orders either on the Internet or via an 800 number. Internet usage is becoming so common in organizational markets that firms without a strong Internet presence are increasingly at a disadvantage.

Usage and Postpurchase Evaluation   After-purchase evaluations of products are typically more formal for organizational purchases than are household evaluations of purchases. In mining applications, for example, a product's life is broken down into

TABLE 19-6   Customer and Management Perceptions of the Importance of After-Sale Services

After-Sales Service Item	Importance of Service Item			Ratings of Service		
	Customers	Managers	Gap	Customers	Managers	Gap
Attitude and behavior of technician	11.5	8.4	3.1	7.04	7.56	−0.52
Availability of technical service staff	16.1	12.9	3.2	7.64	8.12	−0.48
Repair time when service needed	15.4	17.4	−2.0	6.36	7.71	−1.35
Dispatch of breakdown call	15.5	9.8	5.7	6.92	7.57	−0.65
Availability of spare parts during call	10.0	10.1	−0.1	7.16	7.49	−0.33
Service contract options	5.2	6.8	−1.6	6.88	7.48	−0.60
Price–performance ratio for services rendered	8.1	14.5	−6.4	6.12	7.30	−1.18
Response time when service needed	18.2	20.1	−1.9	5.92	7.09	−1.17

Source: H. Kasper and J. Lemmink. "After-Sales Service Quality: Views between Industrial Customers and Service Managers," *Industrial Marketing Management* 18 (1989), p. 203.

different components such that total life-cycle cost can be assessed. Many mines will operate different brands of equipment side by side to determine the life-cycle costs of each before repurchasing one in larger quantities.

A major component of postpurchase evaluation is the service the seller provides during and after the sale.[14] Table 19–6 indicates the importance that one group of customers and managers assigned to different aspects of after-sales service. Notice that the managers did not have a very good understanding of what was important to their customers. Clearly, this firm needs a better understanding of its customers' needs.

Similar to households, dissatisfied organizational buyers may switch suppliers or engage in negative word-of-mouth communications. Firms marketing to organizations pursue strategies similar to those followed by consumer marketers in dealing with dissatisfied customers. They seek to minimize dissatisfaction and to encourage those who become dissatisfied to complain to them and to no one else.[15]

Otis Elevator uses customer problems and a sophisticated database not only to increase customer satisfaction but to improve the design and functioning of its elevators:

Otis Elevator's centralized service center, OtisLine, handles 1.2 million calls a year. Half are for unscheduled repairs. When answering such a call, the service rep punches in a code that identifies the customer's building. Immediately, a record of the equipment and its repair history appears. A series of canned questions elicits the essential new information. Within minutes, a radio message dispatches the appropriate Otis technician to the building.

This fast, efficient postproblem service is only a minor part of the picture. The technician completes a report on the problem and the needed repairs. A full-time 20-member engineering team reviews each case and has the computer scan for similar cases. The results may involve a design change in an elevator model or a change in the recommended maintenance schedule.[16]

Relationship marketing is at least as important in industrial marketing as it is in consumer marketing. The basic idea at the organizational level is for the seller to work closely with the buyer over time with the objective of enhancing the buyer's profits or operations while also making a profit.[17] Consumer Insight 19–1 describes a successful example of organizational relationship marketing.

Having examined organizational purchasing behavior in some detail, let us now apply the balance of our revised model to further our understanding of organizations as consumers.

W.W. Grainger distributes maintenance, repair, and operating (MRO) supplies to organizational buyers. To enhance its services to its customers, it formed Grainger Consulting Services (GCS), which helps customers understand and minimize the total cost of MRO supplies management.

Pharma Labs (a disguised name) is a pharmaceuticals manufacturer. GCS worked with Pharma on a fee basis to analyze its MRO supplies cost. It applied its models and research methods to four primary areas: processes (from how the need for items is identified to payment of invoices), products (product price, usage factors, brand standardization and application), inventory (on-hand value and carrying costs), and suppliers (performance, consolidation, and value-adding services provided).

Among other outcomes of the study, GCS recommended that Pharma consolidate its MRO supplies purchases. Pharma agreed and initiated a national account agreement with Grainger. Grainger placed a representative on site with Pharma to manage the purchase and inventory processes. This freed a Pharma maintenance technician who had been purchasing MRO supplies full-time to return to more value-adding activities in his department.

After six months, the various actions taken by Pharma based on the GCS report produced $387,000 in cost savings. Grainger's sales to Pharma increased from $50,000 to $350,000 per year! Thus, both companies benefited from their relationship.

Critical Thinking Questions

1. Is this truly relationship marketing? Why or why not?

2. What opportunities does Grainger's approach suggest for other types of firms marketing to organizations? To households?

Source: J. C. Anderson and J. A. Narus, "Business Marketing," *Harvard Business Review*, November 1998, pp. 53–65.

ORGANIZATIONAL CULTURE

At the hub of our consumer model of buyer behavior is self-concept and lifestyle. Organizations also have a type of self-concept in the beliefs and attitudes the organization members have about the organization and how it operates. Likewise, organizations have a type of lifestyle in that they have distinct ways of operating. We characterize these two aspects of an organization as its **organizational culture** (see Figure 19–1). Organizational culture is much like lifestyle in that organizations vary dramatically in how they make decisions and how they approach problems involving risk, innovation, and change.[18] The term **corporate culture** is often used to refer to the organizational culture of a business firm.

Organizational culture reflects and shapes organizational needs and desires, which in turn influence how organizations make decisions. For example, the Environmental Protection Agency, the Red Cross, and IBM are three large organizations. Each has a different organizational culture that influences how it gathers information, processes information, and makes decisions.

EXTERNAL FACTORS INFLUENCING ORGANIZATIONAL CULTURE

Firmographics

We discussed earlier the important role of consumer demographics in understanding consumer behavior. Firmographics are equally important. **Firmographics** involve both *organization characteristics*—for example, size, activities, objectives, location, and industry category—*and characteristics of the composition of the organization*—for example, gender, age, education, and income distribution of employees.

TABLE 19-7

Organizational Activities Based on Organizational Objective and Nature of Activity

General Organizational Objective	Nature of Organizational Activity		
	Routine	*Complex*	*Technical*
Commercial	Office management	Human resource management	New-product development
Governmental	Highway maintenance	Tax collection	Space exploration
Nonprofit	Fund-raising	Increase number of national parks	Organ donor program
Cooperative	Compile industry statistics	Establish industry standards	Applied research

Size   Large organizations are more likely to have a variety of specialists who attend to purchasing, finance, marketing, and general management; in smaller organizations, one or two individuals may have these same responsibilities. Larger organizations are generally more complex because more individuals participate in managing the organization's operations. That there are often multiple individuals involved in the purchase decision in a large organization means advertising and sales force efforts must be targeted at various functions in the firm. Each message might need to emphasize issues of concern only to that function. The same purchase decision in a smaller firm might involve only the owner or manager. Different media would be required to reach this person, and one message would need to address all the key purchase issues.

Activities and Objectives   The activities and objectives of organizations influence their style and behavior. For example, the Navy, in procuring an avionics system for a new fighter plane, operates differently than Boeing does in purchasing a similar system for a commercial aircraft. The Navy is a government organization carrying out a public objective, whereas Boeing seeks a commercial objective at a profit.

Table 19–7 is a matrix that provides examples of the interface between broad organizational objectives and activities. Organizational objectives can be categorized as commercial, governmental, nonprofit, and cooperative. The general nature of organizational activity is described as routine, complex, or technical. For example, a government organization purchasing highway maintenance services would operate differently from a government organization procuring missiles. Likewise, a cooperative wholesale organization set up as a buying cooperative for several retailers would have a different organizational culture from a cooperative research institute set up by firms in the semiconductor industry. And a nonprofit organization involved in organ donations is likely to differ from one organized to gather industry statistics.

Commercial firms can be usefully divided into public firms (stock is widely traded) and private firms (one or a few individuals own a controlling share of the firm). In public firms, management is generally expected to operate the firm in a manner that will maximize the economic gains of the shareholders. These organizations face consistent pressures to make economically sound, if not optimal, decisions.

However, about half of all business purchases involve privately held firms whose CEO is often the controlling shareholder. In this situation, the firm can and frequently does pursue objectives other than profit maximization. One study found that the following motives drive the management of such firms:[19]

- Building a place for the entire family to work and be involved.
- Having complete, autocratic control over an environment.
- Build a lasting "empire."
- Becoming wealthy.
- Doing what the family expects.

WHO DO YOU DO IT FOR?

Winner takes all.
New Rules. New Tools.

MICRON

Courtesy Micron Electronics Inc.

ILLUSTRATION 19–5

Industrial ads appeal to the values and personal concerns of managers, not just economic or product issues.

- Avoiding corporations or working for others.
- Obtaining status.
- Improving the world or the environment.

Segmenting these firms according to the motives of the owners is a useful approach for developing sales messages. For example, Micron Electronics is targeting the owners and managers of smaller, entrepreneurial firms. Its ads position it as understanding and caring about the needs and concerns of these individuals more than the larger firms do. One ad states, "They wouldn't give you the time of day. They said you weren't a player . . . . They're holding on line three." The ad in Illustration 19–5 recognizes that long hours these entrepreneurs work is not just for selfish reasons.

Location   As we saw in Chapter 5, there are a number of regional subcultures in the United States. These subcultures influence organizational cultures as well as individual lifestyles. For example, firms on the West Coast tend to be more informal in their operations than those on the East Coast. Dress is more casual, relationships are less formalized, and business is on more of a personal level in the West than elsewhere in the country. The Midwest and South also have unique business styles. Marketing communications and sales force training need to reflect these differences.

Location-based differences are magnified when doing business in foreign cultures. Firms that open branches outside their home countries frequently experience some difficulties managing the workforce and operating within the local community. Selling to organizations outside a firm's home culture poises as many challenges as selling to households in that culture (see Chapter 2). For example,

To get a bank in China's Sichuan province last year to buy more than 100 ATMs, Diebold had to offer the bank 23 units for free. Diebold's distributor was coerced into buying a floor in a building the bank had invested in. And the distributor, as well as Thorpe McConville, Diebold's general manager and CEO, and Kevin Wu, a deputy GM, needed to get approval from 10 people in a variety of the bank's departments. "You've always got to meet with 8 to 12 people, all of whom have a different agenda," Wu says. "And you've got to be prepared for political chaos."

The sales cycle took six months. McConville paid four visits to Sichuan, each time taking the prospects out for lunch, dinner, or karaoke.[20]

Industry Category   Two firms can be similar in terms of size (large), location (Illinois), activity (manufacturing), objective (profit), and ownership (public), and still have sharply differing cultures due in part to being in differing industries. If one of the two firms described above manufactured heavy equipment and the other computers, we would expect differing cultures to exist.

Organization Composition   Organization cultures influence the behaviors and values of those who work in the organizations. However, the types of individuals who work in the organization also heavily influence organization cultures. An organization composed primarily of young, highly educated, technically oriented people (say, a software engineering firm) will have a different culture from an organization composed primarily of older, highly educated, nontechnical individuals (say, an insurance firm). While the culture of most organizations is influenced more by the characteristics of the founder and top managers, the overall composition of the organizational membership is also important.[21]

Macrosegmentation   Organizations with distinguishing firmographics can be grouped into market segments through a process called **macrosegmentation.** These segments, based on differences in needs due to firmographics, are called *macrosegments.*[22] Micron Electronics' decision to focus on smaller firms, described earlier, is an example. First Chicago, one of America's largest banks, stated,

We've tried too long to be everything to everyone. We're in the process of rolling out a strategy in all our branches where we segment customers and tailor our marketing campaigns to those segments.

Two of the macrosegments the bank is targeting are midsized and small businesses. Each segment will have a marketing team that focuses on that segment.[23]

Culture/Government

Variations in values and behaviors across cultures affect organizations as well as individuals. For example, in most American firms shareholder or owner wealth is a dominant decision criterion. Corporate downsizing has resulted in hundreds of thousands of workers and managers losing their jobs in order to enhance profitability. These actions have been acceptable in American society. Similar corporate behavior would not be accepted in much of Europe or Japan. In these societies, worker welfare is often on a par with or above concern about corporate profit. Plant closure laws, layoff regulations, and worker benefits tend to be much higher than in America.

In America, Japan, and most of Europe, bribery and similar approaches for making sales are not acceptable, and these governments enforce a wide array of laws prohibiting such behaviors. In America, both the legal and social constraints against bribery are strong enough to make corporate gift giving from a supplier to a buyer difficult or impossible.[24] In other parts of the world, "bribes" are an expected part of many business transactions. This poses a difficult ethical dilemma for firms doing business in these regions. Ignoring any legal constraints imposed by the American government, *should an American firm provide an expensive "gift" to the purchasing agent in a foreign country where it is common knowledge that such gifts are essential to do business with the country's firms?*

In many parts of the world, businesses and governments are partners or at least work closely together. In the United States, an arm's-length or even adversarial relationship is more common. Consider the following description of IBM's relationship with the U.S. government and its consequences:

IBM's deal-making culture developed out of one of the greatest legal battles in history, the 13-year attempt by the U.S. Department of Justice to break IBM's monopoly on the market for mainframe computers. In the end, IBM settled the suit by consenting to some minor restrictions—such as not announcing in advance products that might chill competitors' sales—but at a cost as high as $100 million. A legal staff of hundreds was employed for the duration of the dispute. This ordeal left deep scars on the IBM psyche, resulting in a preoccupation with secrecy, an aversion to putting commitments in writing, and an elaborate system of legal reviews for even the most routine business transactions. At IBM, every press release, speech, and product disclosure is subject to legal approval, leading to interminable delays. This culture is unsuited to the fast-moving environment of the personal computer business.[25]

Will Microsoft's battle with the U.S. government have a similar effect on its culture?

Reference Groups

Reference groups influence organizational behavior and purchasing decisions. Perhaps the most powerful type of reference group in industrial markets is that of lead users. **Lead users** are *innovative organizations that derive a great deal of their success from leading change*. As a result, their adoption of a new product, service, technology, or manufacturing process is watched and often emulated by the majority.[26] This statement from a Hewlett-Packard salesperson illustrates their role:

Another aspect of hospital buying behavior is the role of key accounts. A pyramid of influence operates in this market, with smaller and medium-sized hospitals often relying on larger research and teaching hospitals for technology cues. Therefore, maintaining a strong position in influential hospitals is critical.[27]

Other reference groups such as trade associations, financial analysts, and dealer organizations also influence an organization's decision to buy or not buy a given product, or to buy or not buy from a given supplier. **Reference group infrastructure** refers to *the flow of purchase influence within an industry*. As an example, the success of new technology product depends on how the firm influences the reference groups located along the continuum separating it from its consumer market. The more the firm gains positive endorsement or use throughout this infrastructure, the greater its chances of customers treating it as a preferred source of supply.

If we combine the concept of lead users with reference group infrastructure, as shown in Figure 19–2, we have a more comprehensive picture of organizational reference group systems. Because the lead users play such a critical role, their adoption of a product, technology, or vendor can influence the overall infrastructure in two powerful ways. First, a lead-user decision to adopt a given supplier's innovative product adds credibility to the product and supplier. This in turn has a strong positive impact on the infrastructure that stands between the firm and its remaining target customers. Second, a lead-user decision to purchase will have a direct impact on firms inclined to follow market trends.

| FIGURE 19–2 | Combining Lead User and Infrastructure Reference Groups |

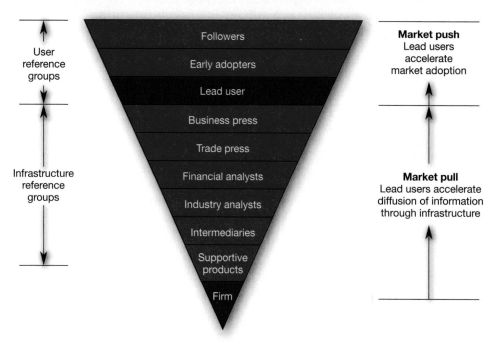

Source: Roger Best and Reinhard Angellhard, "Strategies for Leveraging a Technology Advantage," *Handbook of Business Strategy*, 1988.

The strategy implication of this is clear. Marketers of new industrial products, particularly technology products, should focus initial efforts on securing sales to visible lead users.

INTERNAL FACTORS INFLUENCING ORGANIZATIONAL CULTURE

Organizational Values

IBM and Apple Computer both manufacture and market computers. However, each organization has a distinct organizational culture. IBM is corporate, formal, and takes itself seriously. Apple is less formal, creative, and promotes a more open organizational culture. Marketing managers must understand these differences in order to best serve the respective organizational needs.

As you examine the eight common business values shown below, think of how IBM might differ from Apple, Macy's from Target, Amazon.com from Buy.com, or FedEx from the U.S. Postal Service. Each is a large organization, but each has a unique set of values that underlies its organizational culture. To the degree that organizations differ on these values, a firm marketing to them will have to adapt its marketing approach.

1. Risk taking is admired and rewarded.
2. Competition is more important than cooperation.
3. Hard work comes first, leisure second.

Courtesy BMC Software, Inc.

4. Individual efforts take precedence over collective efforts.
5. Any problem can be solved.
6. Active decision making is essential.
7. Change is positive and is actively sought.
8. Performance is more important than rank or status.

The values as stated above are representative of an innovative organization that seeks change, views problems as opportunities, and rewards individual efforts. It is hard to imagine the U.S. Postal Service or many other bureaucratic organizations encouraging such values. On the other hand, these values underlie many high-technology startup organizations.

The ad in Illustration 19–6 would appeal to organizations and individuals with a competitive orientation.

Perception

To process information, a firm must go through the same sequential stages of exposure, attention, and interpretation as consumers. Of course, given the more complex nature of organizations, the processes involved are also more complex.[28] A business customer develops certain images of seller organizations from their products, people, and organizational activities. Like people, organizations have memories and base their decisions on images or memories they have developed. Once an image is formed by an organization, it is very difficult

Well-done industrial advertising campaigns will often work across cultures to enhance the image of the firm.

Courtesy 3M.

to change. Therefore, it is important for an organization to develop a sound communications strategy to build and reinforce a desired image or brand position.[29]

Illustration 19–7 shows an ad from 3M's 1, 2, 3M campaign, which was very successful. The challenge was to unify 3M's 60,000 products and provide the organization with a meaningful image. It was important to show that not only are 3M products exciting technologically but they are useful and make a difference in peoples' lives. The campaign was highly successful in the United States, France, Latin America, and Australia. Research showed that perception of 3M as an innovative company with innovative products went from 10 to 51 percent, overall favorable impression of 3M increased from 65 to 85 percent, and the likelihood of recommending 3M and its products moved from 71 to 91 percent.[30]

Ad size and repetition have a positive effect on awareness and action. One major study found a 20 percent gain in awareness when two or more ads are placed in the same issue of a specialized business magazine compared with only one.[31] The size of the advertisement also affects action in the form of inquiries generated by the advertisement. A study of 500,000 inquiries to ads run in *Plastic World, Electronics Design News,* and *Design News* found that full-page ads were much more effective at generating inquiries than smaller ads (see Figure 19–3).

The potential power of industrial advertising can be seen in its impact on sales of an industrial safety product. Sales in the first year of the ad campaign increased almost fourfold, with advertising in one trade publication using an eight-page advertising schedule: six black-and-white ads and two color ads. When three color spreads were added to the schedule, sales continued to climb. When ad frequency was again increased, this time to six black-and-white single-page ads and 11 color spreads, product sales rose to 6.7 times precampaign sales.[32]

While advertising plays an important role in communicating to organizations, direct sales calls are the most important element of the communications mix in most industrial

FIGURE 19–3	Impact of Ad Size on Inquiries

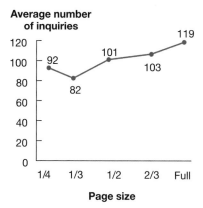

Source: *CARR Report No. 250.1* (Boston: Cahners Publishing Co., undated).

markets. This it the case despite the high cost of such calls:

Industry	Average Cost per Sales Call
Manufacturing	$159
Service	106
Retail	99
Wholesale distribution	81
All companies	113[33]

One reason for the significant role of salespeople is that businesses are not just economic entities. Business buyers prefer to do business with firms they know, like, and trust. Those relationships are most often formed between members of the firms involved, with sales personnel being the most common representative of the selling organization. As one successful salesperson stated,

You have to have a great product but you also have to make the customer like you as a salesperson.[34]

Learning

Like individuals, organizations learn through their experiences and perceptions.[35] Positive experiences with vendors are rewarding and tend to be repeated. Purchasing processes and procedures that prove effective tend to be institutionalized in rules and policies. Likewise, negative experiences with vendors produce learning and avoidance behavior, and purchasing procedures that don't work are generally discarded. Developing the capacity to learn efficiently is increasingly a key to organizational success.[36]

Motives and Emotions

Organizational decisions tend to be less emotional than many consumer purchase decisions. However, because humans with psychological needs and emotions influence these decisions, this aspect of marketing to an organizational customer cannot be overlooked or underestimated.

Quite often there is considerable personal or career risk in organizational purchase decisions. The risk of making a bad purchase decision can elicit feelings of self-doubt or psychological discomfort. These are personal emotions that will influence purchase decisions. FedEx appeals to risk avoidance with ads that ask, in essence,

> How do you explain to your boss that the important papers didn't arrive but you saved the company $5 by using a less expensive overnight mail service?

SUMMARY

Like households, organizations make many buying decisions. In some instances, these buying decisions are routine replacement decisions; at other times, they involve new, complex purchase decisions. Six purchase situations are common to organizational buying: *straight rebuy, modified rebuy,* and *new task.* Each of these purchase situations will elicit different organizational behaviors.

The organizational decision process involves problem recognition, information search, evaluation and selection, purchase implementation, and postpurchase evaluation. Quite often, a seller organization can influence the information search such that it establishes the choice criteria to be used in evaluation and selection. A conjunctive process is typical in establishing an evoked set, and other decision rules are used for selecting a specific vendor.

Purchase implementation is more complex and the terms and conditions more important than in household decisions. How payment is made is of major importance. Finally, use and postpurchase evaluation are often quite formal. Many organizations will conduct detailed in-use tests to determine the life-cycle costs of competing products or spend considerable time evaluating a new product before placing large orders. Satisfaction depends on a variety of criteria and on the opinions of many different people. To achieve customer satisfaction, each of these individuals has to be satisfied with the criteria important to him or her.

Organizations have a style or manner of operating that we characterize as organizational culture. *Firmographics* (organization characteristics such as size, activities, objectives, location, and industry category, and characteristics of the composition of the organization such as the gender, age, education, and income distribution of employees) have a major influence on organizational culture. The process of grouping buyer organizations into market segments on the basis of similar firmographics is called *macrosegmentation*.

Reference groups play a key role in business-to-business markets. *Reference group infrastructures* exist in most organizational markets. These reference groups often include third-party suppliers, distributors, industry experts, trade publications, financial analysts, and key customers. *Lead users* have been shown to be a key reference group that influences both the reference group infrastructure and other potential users.

Other external influences on organizational culture include the local culture in which the organization operates and the type of government it confronts. Internal factors affecting organizational culture include organizational values, perception, learning, memory, motives, and emotions.

Organizations hold values that influence the organization's style. Individuals in the organization also hold these values in varying degrees. When there is a high degree of shared values between the individuals and the organization, decision making occurs smoothly.

Organizations also develop images, have motives, and learn. Seller organizations can affect how they are perceived through a variety of communication alternatives. Print advertising, direct mail, and sales calls are the most common. Whereas organizations have rational motives, their decisions are influenced and made by people with emotions. A seller organization has to understand and satisfy both to be successful. Organizations learn through their experiences and information-processing activities.

KEY TERMS

Buying center 680
Corporate culture 689
Decision-making
units (DMUs) 680

Firmographics 689
Lead users 693
Macrosegmentation 692
Organizational culture 689

Reference group
infrastructure 693
Terms and conditions 687
Two-stage decision process 685

INTERNET EXERCISES

1. Evaluate the Detroit office of J. Walter Thompson's website (www.jwtdet.com).
2. Evaluate MCI's website (www.mci.com).
3. Evaluate *Advertising Age*'s website (adage.com).
4. Pick an industrial market and compare the websites of three firms. Which is best? Why?

REVIEW QUESTIONS

1. How can an organization have a culture? What factors contribute to different organizational cultures?
2. How would different organizational activities and objectives affect organizational culture?
3. What are *organizational values?* How do they differ from personal values?
4. What is meant by *shared values?*
5. What are *firmographics,* and how do they influence organizational culture?
6. Define *macrosegmentation,* and describe the variables used to create a macrosegmentation of an organizational market.
7. What types of reference groups exist in organizational markets?
8. What are *lead users,* and how do they influence word-of-mouth communication and the sales of a new product?
9. What is a *decision-making unit?* How does it vary by purchase situation?
10. How can a seller organization influence perceptions of a buyer organization?
11. What are *organizational motives?*
12. What is a *two-stage decision process?*
13. Why is purchase implementation a critical part of the organizational decision process?
14. What are the three purchase situations commonly encountered by organizations? How do organizations typically respond to each situation?

DISCUSSION QUESTIONS

15. Describe three organizations with distinctly different organizational cultures. Explain why they have different organizational cultures and the factors that have helped shape the style of each.
16. Respond to the questions in Consumer Insight 19–1.
17. Describe how IBM might vary in its organizational culture from the following. Justify your response.
    a. Dell Computer
    b. Compaq
    c. Apple
18. Discuss how the following pairs differ from each other in terms of organizational activities and objectives. Discuss how these differences influence organizational cultures.
    a. McDonald's, Target
    b. The Marines, the U.S. Post Office
    c. Buy.com, Banana Republic
    d. Honda, Procter & Gamble
19. What determines whether an individual's values or the organization's values will prevail in a purchase decision (given that they conflict)?

20. Discuss how Compaq might use a macrosegmentation strategy to sell computers to businesses.
21. Discuss how a small biotechnology firm could influence the reference group infrastructure and the lead users to accelerate adoption of its products in the market.
22. Discuss the marketing implications of the decision-making structure shown in Table 19–3. Then, using the information shown in Table 19–3, discuss how you would develop your marketing strategy for this purchase situation.

23. "Industrial purchases, unlike consumer purchases, do not have an emotional component." Comment.
24. For each of the three purchase situations described in the chapter (Table 19–2), describe a typical purchase for the following:
    a. Toyota
    b. A small advertising agency
    c. Starbucks
    d. Your university
    e. The U.S. Post Office

APPLICATION ACTIVITIES

25. Interview an appropriate person at a large and at a small organization and ask each to identify purchase situations that could be described as straight rebuy, modified rebuy, and new task. For each organization and purchase situation, determine the following:
    a. Size and functional representation of the decision-making unit
    b. The number of choice criteria considered
    c. Length of the decision process
    d. Number of vendors or suppliers considered
26. Review two issues of a magazine targeting organization buyers or purchase influencers. What percent of the ads contain emotional or other noneconomic appeals?
27. Interview a representative from a commercial, governmental, and nonprofit organization. For

each, determine its firmographics, activities, and objectives. Then relate these differences to differences in the organizational cultures of the organizations.
28. Interview a person responsible for purchasing for a business or government agency. Have that person describe and evaluate any attempts at relationship marketing by its suppliers. What do you conclude?
29. For a given organization, identify its reference groups. Create a hierarchical diagram, as shown in Figure 19–2, and discuss how this organization could influence groups that would in turn create favorable communication concerning this organization.

REFERENCES

1. G. Conlon, "True Romance," *Sales & Marketing Management,* May 1996, pp. 86–87.
2. See J. Park, P. Tansuhaj, and E. R. Spangenberg, "An Emotion-Based Perspective of Family Purchase Decisions," *Advances in Consumer Research,* vol. 22, eds. F. R. Kardes and M. Sujan (Provo, UT: Association for Consumer Research, 1995), pp. 723–28.
3. F. V. Cespedes, "Hewlett-Packard Imaging Systems Division," Harvard Business School case 9-593-080, September 6, 1994, p. 4.
4. R. Ventakesh, A. K. Kohli, and G. Zaltman, "Influence Strategies in Buying Centers," *Journal of Marketing,* October 1995, pp. 71–82; and M. A. Farrell and B. Schroder, "Influence Strategies in Organizational Buying Decisions," *Industrial Marketing Management* 25 (1996), pp. 393–403.
5. See W. J. Johnson and J. E. Lewin, "Organizational Buying Behavior," *Journal of Business Research,* January 1996, pp. 1–15; and E. J. Wilson, R. C. McMurrian, and A. G. Woodside, "How Buyers Frame Problems," *Psychology & Marketing,* June 2001, pp. 617–55.
6. S. J. Puri and C. M. Sashi, "Anatomy of a Complex Computer Purchase," *Industrial Marketing Management,* January 1994, pp. 17–27; and E. Day and J. C. Barksdale, Jr., "Organizational Purchasing of Professional Services," *Journal of Business and Industrial Marketing* 9, no. 3 (1994), pp. 44–51.
7. See A. M. Weiss and J. B. Heide, "The Nature of Organizational Search in High-Technology Markets," *Journal of Marketing Research,* May 1993, pp. 220–33.
8. P. M. Doney and G. M. Armstrong, "Effects of Accountability on Symbolic Information Search and Information Analysis by

Organizational Buyers," *Journal of the Academy of Marketing Science,* Winter 1996, pp. 57–65.

9. D. Narayandas, "SalesSoft, Inc.," Harvard Business School case 9-596-112, March 24, 1998.

10. J. B. Heide and W. M. Weiss, "Vendor Consideration and Switching Behavior for Buyers in High-Technology Markets," *Journal of Marketing,* July 1995, pp. 30–43.

11. See K. N. Thompson, B. J. Coe, and J. R. Lewis, "Gauging the Value of Suppliers' Products," *Journal of Business and Industrial Marketing* 9, no. 2 (1994), pp. 29–40.

12. M. E. Drumwright, "Socially Responsible Organizational Buying," *Journal of Marketing,* July 1994, pp. 1–19.

13. See E. D. Honeycut, Jr., T. B. Flaherty, and K. Benassi, "Marketing Industrial Products on the Internet," *Industrial Marketing Management* 27 (1998), pp. 63–72; S. Kaplan and M. Sawhney, "E-Hubs," *Harvard Business Review,* May 2000, pp. 97–103; D. James, "Play It Straight," *Marketing News,* May 21, 2001, p. 15; and G. S. Lynn et al., "Factors Impacting the Adoption and Effectiveness of the World Wide Web in Marketing," *Industrial Marketing Management* 31 (2002), pp. 35–49.

14. K. Smith, "Service Aspects of Industrial Products," *Industrial Marketing Management* 27 (1998), pp. 83–93.

15. S. W. Hansen, J. E. Swan, and T. L. Powers, "Encouraging 'Friendly' Complaint Behavior in Industrial Markets," *Industrial Marketing Management* 25 (1996), pp. 271–81.

16. J. W. Verity, "The Gold Mine of Data in Customer Service," *Business Week,* March 21, 1994, p. 113.

17. D. J. Flint, R. B. Woodruff, and S. F. Gardial, "Customer Value Change in Industrial Marketing Relationships," *Industrial Marketing Management* 26 (1997), pp. 163–75; and M. H. Morris, J. Brunyee, and M. Page, "Relationship Marketing in Practice," *Industrial Marketing Management* 27 (1998), pp. 359–71.

18. See S. Kitchell, "Corporate Culture, Environmental Adaptation, and Innovation Adoption," *Journal of the Academy of Marketing Science,* Summer 1995, pp. 195–205; and P. Berthon, L. F. Pitt, and M. T. Ewing, "Corollaries of the Collective," *Journal of the Academy of Marketing Science,* Spring 2001, pp. 135–50.

19. K. M. File and R. A. Prince, "A Psychographic Segmentation of Industrial Family Businesses," *Industrial Marketing Management,* May 1996, pp. 223–34.

20. G. Brewer, "An American in Shanghai," *Sales & Marketing Management,* November 1997, p. 42. See also N. D. Albers-Miller and B. Gelb, "Business Advertising Appeals as a Mirror of Cultural Dimensions," *Journal of Advertising,* Winter 1996, pp. 57–70.

21. See J. E. Stoddard and E. F. Fern, "Risk-Taking Propensity in Supplier Choice," *Psychology & Marketing,* October 1999, pp. 563–82.

22. See R. L. Griffith and L. G. Pol, "Segmenting Industrial Markets," *Industrial Marketing Management,* January 1994, pp. 39–46.

23. G. Brewer, "Selling an Intangible," *Sales & Marketing Management,* January 1998, pp. 52–58. See also S. P. Kalafatis and V. Cheston, "Normative Models and Practical Applications of Segmentation in Business Markets," *Industrial Marketing Management* 26 (1997), pp. 519–30.

24. See F. Gibb, "To Give or Not to Give," *Sales & Marketing Management,* September 1994, pp. 136–39.

25. J. Kaplan, *Startup* (New York: Houghton Mifflin Co., 1995), p. 120.

26. A. N. Link and J. Neufeld, "Innovation vs. Imitation: Investigating Alternative R&D Strategies," *Applied Economics,* no. 18 (1986), pp. 1359–63.

27. Cespedes, "Hewlett-Packard Imaging Systems Division."

28. D. I. Gilliland and W. J. Johnston, "Toward a Model of Business-to-Business Marketing Communications Effects," *Industrial Marketing Management* 26 (1997), pp. 15–29.

29. See S. M. Mudambi, P. Doyle, and V. Wong, "An Exploration of Branding in Industrial Markets," *Industrial Marketing Management* 26 (1997), pp. 433–46; and J. Lapierre, "The Role of Corporate Image in the Evaluation of Business-to-Business Professional Services," *Journal of Professional Services Marketing,* no. 1 (1998), pp. 21–41.

30. L. Hochwald, "It's the Sizzle That Sells," *Sales & Marketing Management,* April 1997, p. 51.

31. *CARR Report No. 120.3* (Boston: Cahners Publishing Co., undated).

32. "Study: Increase Business Ads to Increase Sales," *Marketing News,* March 14, 1988, p. 13.

33. M. Marchetti, "Hey Buddy, Can You Spare $113.25?" *Sales & Marketing Management,* August 1997, pp. 69–77.

34. G. Conlon, "A Day in the Life of Sales," *Sales & Marketing Management,* September 1997, pp. 42–63.

35. See J. M. Sinkula, "Market Information Processing and Organizational Learning," *Journal of Marketing,* January 1994, pp. 35–45; G. T. M. Hult and E. L. Nichols, Jr., "The Organizational Buyer Behavior Learning Organization," *Industrial Marketing Management,* May 1996, pp. 197–207; and S. J. Bell, G. J. Whitwell, and B. A. Lukas, "Schools of Thought in Organizational Learning," *Journal of the Academy of Marketing Science,* Winter 2002, pp. 70–86.

36. D. A. Garvin, "Building a Learning Organization," *Harvard Business Review,* July 1993, pp. 78–91; and S. F. Slater and J. C. Narver, "Market Orientation and the Learning Organization," *Journal of Marketing,* July 1995, pp. 63–74.

Cases

5–1   Mack Trucks' Integrated Communications Campaign

For 90 years Mack Trucks dominated the construction and refuse segments of the Class 8 (large) truck market. In fact, the expression "Built like a Mack truck" came to stand for solid, rugged construction. Unfortunately, 70 percent of the demand for large trucks is in the highway or over-the-road hauling segment, and this is also the segment with the highest growth rate.

Until the late 1980s, Mack did not compete effectively in the over-the-road segments. In 1990, Mack was purchased by the French automaker Renault. A plan to become a major competitor in the critical highway market segment was developed and implemented. The first stage involved the development and launch of two new over-the-road truck lines. According to Brian Taylor, Mack's vice president of marketing,

> We developed a product line that had good ergonomics. It was roomy and it had a smooth ride, but we faced a challenge with communicating those changes to our customers.

To meet this challenge, the firm initiated a series of research studies with the goal of developing an integrated communications campaign.

Research Studies

Four basic sources of information were used to guide the development of the integrated campaign.

1. Perceptual maps were derived that identified how Mack trucks were perceived relative to competing brands. The maps revealed that they were viewed as durable but not very comfortable.
2. Focus group sessions and one-on-one interviews with current and prospective Mack customers isolated additional driver and operator needs and concerns. This research helped identify the criteria the trucks would need to meet to be in the buyer's consideration set.
3. Industry trade publications frequently conduct surveys of fleet operators, truck owners, and truck drivers. These surveys cover a wide range of issues,

including desired truck features and shortcomings. These surveys were obtained and analyzed.
4. News clippings and other sources of data describing quality or service problems Mack had experienced in the past were also studied.

These studies indicated that Mack faced a significant communications challenge. According to Taylor, "'Built like a Mack truck' served us well in our core business, but it did not have a good connotation in the over-the-road segment. And that was a perception we had to change." A consultant on the project stated the challenge this way: "We had to create a campaign—an impression—in which customers would be willing to suspend their disbelief that Mack was more than they knew."

Objectives

Three primary objectives were developed for the campaign:

1. Change the perception of Mack trucks from "rugged, tough, and uncomfortable to drive," to "the most comfortable and driveable over-the-road trucks."
2. Change the perception of Mack engines from "heavy, expensive, and low tech," to "ideal for over-the-road applications, very economical and reliable."
3. Increase the number of over-the-road fleet buyers who have Mack in their consideration sets.

Accomplishing these objectives would require a change in Mack's current positioning from

> Mack is a great old brand. But they can't compete for my business because they don't have a package that meets my needs.

to

> Mack's turning things around. The CH model with the E7 engine is the right combination for my fleet. Plus, these guys really want my business.

This leads to the following positioning statement:

> The new Mack is the proud result of combining Mack tradition and unequaled driveability.

The Communications Strategy

The communications strategy integrated advertising, sales promotion, direct marketing, and public relations. For the advertising campaign, Mack's traditional bulldog was made hip in six new print ads with racing stripes, sunglasses, a champagne glass, or other symbols of change and uniqueness. The ads were colorful with limited text. Each focused on one key attribute such as fuel economy. The tagline for the campaign was "Drive one and you'll know."

The sales promotion program consisted of the "Bulldog National Test Drive Tour." This tour allowed truckers to test drive a new Mack truck at truck stops and trade shows throughout the country.

The direct marketing program included an 800 number in all print advertising that readers could use to get information about the nearest dealer, the test drive promotion, or to request specific model information. The "Fleet Focus" part of the campaign mailed materials to nearly 1,200 non-Mack fleet customers urging them to consider Mack in their next purchase and providing material to support that recommendation. Dealers were provided qualified lead cards generated from the 800 number, the test drives, and the direct-mail program.

Throughout the campaign, numerous news releases and articles were provided to trade publications. There was also an eight-city media tour in which Mack discussed its commitment to the public and the over-the-road segment. Mack redesigned the quarterly, 24-page *Bulldog* magazine to reflect the firm's customer service orientation.

Discussion Questions

1. Is this program likely to succeed? Why or why not? What, if anything, would you change?
2. Is a "hip" bulldog an appropriate symbol for a serious industrial product like a truck?
3. Why are Mack and its agencies so concerned with customer perception when its products are so good?
4. What criteria do you think fleet buyers have for including a brand in their consideration set? How do you think they choose from among the brands in the consideration set?
5. Why did the "built like a Mack truck" theme not work for the over-the-road segment.
6. How would you alter the campaign for use in these countries?

   a. Japan

   b. Germany

   c. China

   d. Brazil

5–2   Kenestic, Inc.

Kenestic, Inc., specializes in the manufacture and marketing of molded plastic products with unique durability, resistance to breakage, and long life. These products are used as components for other products such as automobiles, planes, and manufacturing equipment. Over time, Kenestic has developed an expertise in molded plastic that goes far beyond that of most of its competitors. In fact, most of Kenestic's products command a 15 to 25 percent price premium because of their unique performance capabilities.

Products and Customer Needs

Kenestic product development has focused on tough applications in which the wear life (how long the product lasts) and problems with breakage are important factors in buying decisions.

These are applications in which the ability to mold plastic into unique shapes and its light weight give it an advantage over metal products but for which strength and impact resistance requirements are higher than normal. In these applications, product failure often results in considerable repair expenses, lose of productivity, inconvenience, and occasionally physical danger.

Kenestic recently surveyed its customers' needs. Shown in Table A are customer importance ratings of purchase criteria and customer perceptions of Kenestic relative to competitors. On the top three most important purchase criteria, Kenestic is rated ahead of

TABLE A	Purchase Criteria	Importance	Competitive Position
Kenestic's Current Customers' Needs and Kenestic's Perceived Performance	Wear life of product	25%	Very good
	Breakage	20	Very good
	After-sale support	15	Very good
	Price of product	14	Poor
	Availability	10	Very poor
	Delivery	10	Poor
	Design productivity	6	Poor

TABLE B	Purchase Criteria	Importance	Competitive Position
Kenestic's Noncustomers' Needs and Kenestic's Perceived Performance	Availability	30%	Very poor
	Design productivity	25	Poor
	Price	20	Poor
	Delivery	15	Poor
	Wear life	5	Very good
	After-sale support	3	Very good
	Breakage	2	Very good

its competition. While Kenestic's prices are higher, customers are willing to buy its products because of its superior performance on the top three purchase criteria. For the three least important purchase criteria, Kenestic is rated behind its competitors.

Noncustomer Survey

The customer needs and perceptions shown in Table A are those of existing customers served by Kenestic. Because the noncustomer base was many times larger than its current customer base, Kenestic also conducted a noncustomer survey to find out more about non-customer needs and perceptions of Kenestic.

A portion of the noncustomer survey results are shown in Table B. While noncustomer perceptions of Kenestic relative to competition are similar to those of existing customers, their needs are very different. Noncustomers rated availability, price, and design productivity as their three most important purchase criteria. These are among the bottom four purchase criteria for existing customers.

Customer Decision Process

The wide difference in customer and noncustomer needs led to a recognition that the company did not adequately know how purchase decisions were made by either existing customers or noncustomers. While Tables A and B demonstrate differences in purchase criteria, these results do not provide sufficient insight into how these purchase criteria were used in a purchase decision. To find out, a purchase decision study was conducted, using a random sample of both customers and noncustomers.

The results of the purchase decision survey are shown in Figure A.

In making a decision to buy, customers first ask whether wear life or breakage is a serious issue. In 90 percent of user applications, it is not a problem. Thus, Kenestic's key benefits are not relevant for 90 percent of the applications encountered in mining, construction, and forestry.

If the application does warrant concern for wear life or breakage, availability is the next key concern. Kenestic products are not available when needed 30 percent of the time. If they are available, decision makers look at price in relationship to the product's economic value—the overall cost of the product including price, savings from increased wear life and potential damage from breakage, and added value derived from after-sale support. In 75 percent of the applications where wear life or breakage are a problem, Kenestic wins the business. However, this occurs in only roughly 5 percent of all user applications.

In applications where wear life or breakage is not a concern, the decision process focused on design productivity, where Kenestic was weak. Because of poor performance in this area, the company was not

FIGURE A   Customer Decision Process

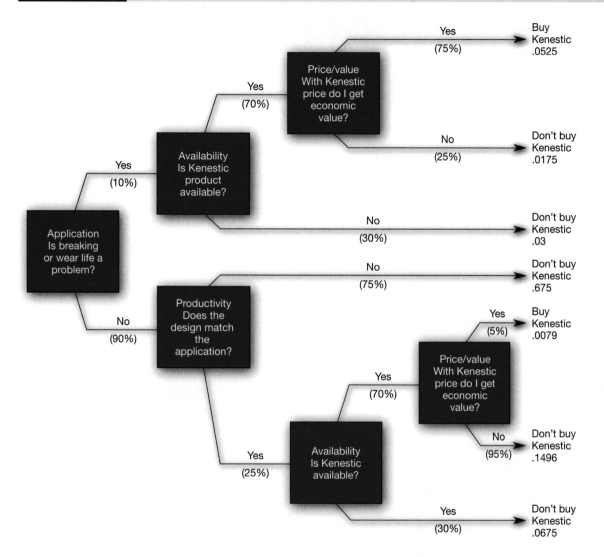

considered in 75 percent of these user applications. When the Kenestic product did fit the application, it was only available 70 percent of the time. And because higher price was not offset with savings due to wear life, breakage, or after-sales support, Kenestic only obtained 5 percent of these purchases. The net share is less than 1 percent of these applications.

Figure A demonstrates where and why Kenestic obtains its market share; but more important, it reveals where and why it loses market share. While its overall market share is around 6 percent, it has almost a 50 percent market share when wear life and breakage are important.

Discussion Questions

1. What are the limitations to looking at just customer or noncustomer ratings of purchase criteria?
2. What additional benefits can be obtained by understanding how purchase decisions are made?
3. Where should Kenestic focus its efforts, and what would be the impact of these efforts?
4. Explain how Kenestic's high price is offset in applications where wear life, breakage, and after-sale support are important. Also, explain why the economic value of the product is less attractive in applications where wear life and breakage are not a concern.

Consumer Behavior and Marketing Regulation

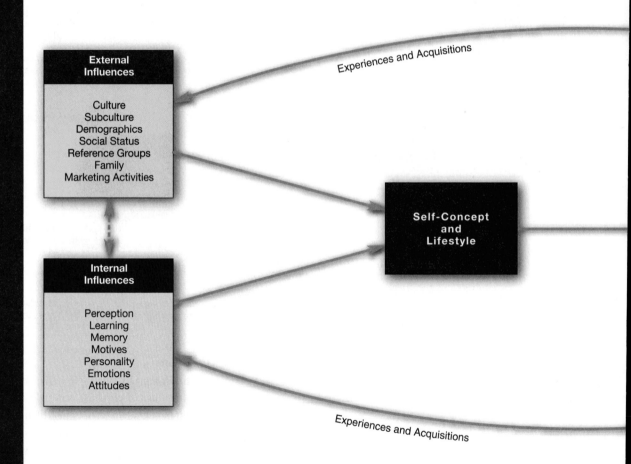

External Influences

Culture
Subculture
Demographics
Social Status
Reference Groups
Family
Marketing Activities

Internal Influences

Perception
Learning
Memory
Motives
Personality
Emotions
Attitudes

Self-Concept and Lifestyle

Experiences and Acquisitions

Experiences and Acquisitions

Throughout the text, we have emphasized that knowledge of consumer behavior is as important to those who would regulate consumer behavior as it is to those who engage in marketing activities. Government officials, consumer advocates, and citizens all need to understand consumer behavior to develop, enact, and enforce appropriate rules and regulations for marketing activities. Consumers in particular need to understand their own behaviors and how their purchase and consumption behaviors help determine the type of marketplace and society we have.

In this section, we will analyze the role of consumer behavior principles in regulating marketing practices.

We will pay particular attention to the regulation of marketing activities focused on children. We also discuss regulations covering advertising, product, and pricing practices aimed at adults.

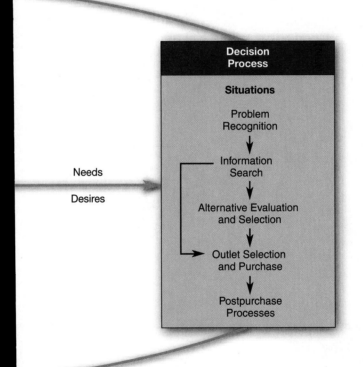

Needs

Desires

Decision Process

Situations

Problem Recognition

↓

Information Search

↓

Alternative Evaluation and Selection

↓

Outlet Selection and Purchase

↓

Postpurchase Processes

Marketing Regulation and Consumer Behavior

chapter 20

◻ Calvin Klein ignited a storm of controversy over "kiddie porn" in advertising. The firm denied any intention to portray children in a sexual or pornographic manner. According to the firm, the intent was to convey the idea that today's teens "have a real strength of character and independence."

The cause of the controversy was an advertising campaign that appeared in magazines, billboards, and on television featuring teenage models in provocative poses and, in some television ads, making suggestive comments. For example, one television commercial featured a slim young man with no shirt on standing next to a step ladder in an empty room:

MODEL: I'm not sure what to do.

VOICE: What do you do when you just stand around and you hear a good song on the radio or CD?

MODEL: I mosh, I like, run around the room.

VOICE: You march?

MODEL: Yeah, mosh.

VOICE: Go ahead:

The model dances around the ladder.

VOICE: That's a pretty good mosh.

MODEL: Thanks.

Other television ads had similar approaches. One of the print ads featured a young female in a foldout magazine insert in a very suggestive pose. Some reactions to these ads from adults included

- They gave me the willies! That purple shag carpet and the 70s-style wood paneling make me think of some dirty, sex-crazed old man with kids in the "playroom."

- The kids looked very unsure of themselves, and the man's voice sounded like a scummy animal.
- At first I must admit I was titillated by the centerfold shot, then disgusted when I saw how old she was.

A number of organizations, including the Catholic League, Morality in Media, and Agudah Israel of America, called for boycotts of Calvin Klein products. However, others, like the president of Gryo Advertising, defended the campaign:

> Young consumers see the campaign as twisted in a good way while older ones won't get it. They won't see the humor in it. It's kind of cheesy 80s to show some hot babe with her shirt coming undone. The Calvin Klein ads are cooler because they're kinda scary. There's nothing offensive in the ads. They're just disturbing and people don't know why. People say it's kiddie porn, and all Calvin Klein has to say is, "If you see that then you are seeing something that's not there," and he's right. The most offensive thing in there is the purple shag carpeting.

Another ad agency executive stated,

> It's almost tongue in cheek, but no one's getting the joke. It's way above a lot of kids' heads. This is almost too sophisticated for them to get the sexual element.

Indeed, interviews with some teenagers support this view:

- Amy (16)—It's just another commercial on TV. I've seen worse—have you ever watched "NYPD Blue"? Commercials matter to a certain extent. It really matters what's in fashion. I buy jeans that look good.
- Karen (15)—I thought they were funny. That guy behind the camera was asking some stupid questions. I didn't get why he was asking those questions. It's definitely a sexual thing, but to say child pornography is stupid.
- Libby (18)—I looked at the ads in the magazines and the models were skinny with long legs, and I figured, I'm skinny and I have pretty long legs. I just figured that was me, so I bought a pair. But I don't think it's in good taste to show young models who are so thin and unhealthy looking. Levi's is catering to the same age group, and the models are skateboarding and playing outside.[1]

As the opening example indicates, marketing practices are sometimes controversial. One ad agency executive concluded that "[in a] mass market, and that's where Calvin Klein is, you can't target one audience and eliminate the rest. Some people decided this campaign was very bad. But from a purely marketing standpoint, that doesn't matter. The real question is, do young people like these ads?"[2]

We believe that the last statement made by this executive is wrong for a variety of reasons. First, individual consumers or consumer groups may boycott brands that engage in marketing practices that they find offensive even if the primary target market likes them. In this case, if parents find the ads offensive, they may restrict their children's ability to purchase Calvin Klein products. If enough consumers become sufficiently upset with specific actions, they or consumer groups that represent them will demand regulatory action at the local, state, or federal level. More important, *marketing is not, or at least should not be, just about selling products*. It should enhance the lives of those affected by it. Ads that degrade or exploit individuals or groups do not, in the long run, meet the test of enhancing consumer welfare. Unfortunately, as the opening vignette indicates, it is not always easy to determine what constitutes exploitation.

Marketing is a highly visible, important activity. It affects the lives of individuals, the success of nonprofit groups, and the profits of businesses. As indicated throughout the text, there are many issues where the appropriate ethical action for marketers is not clear-cut. As a marketing manager, you will face many such situations in your career. However, society has declared that other marketing actions are clearly inappropriate. It has done so by enacting laws and regulations that prohibit or require specific marketing actions. In this chapter, we are going to examine the regulation of marketing practices. Regulating marketing activities requires the same level of understanding of consumer behavior as does managing marketing programs. Our consideration of the regulation of marketing practices will separate regulations designed to protect children from those designed to protect adults.

REGULATION AND MARKETING TO CHILDREN

The regulation of marketing activities aimed at children focuses primarily on product safety, advertising and promotions, and privacy protection. Product safety issues focus on appropriate product design and materials. We will concentrate on privacy protection and advertising and other promotional activities[3] targeting children as consumers. The regulation of these activities rests heavily on theories of children's consumer behavior, particularly their information-processing skills.

There are a variety of state, federal, and voluntary guidelines and rules governing marketing to children. Despite these rules, many feel that some marketers continue to take advantage of children and that the overall marketing system, particularly advertising, is socializing children to value things (products) rather than intangibles such as relationships and integrity.

One basis for the concern over marketing to children is based on *Piaget's stages of cognitive development* (Chapter 6, page 210), which indicate that children lack the ability to fully process and understand information, including marketing messages, until around 12 years of age.[4] This and related theories are the basis for most regulation of advertising aimed at children and, according to critics, for some marketing programs that deliberately exploit children.

Concerns about the Ability of Children to Comprehend Commercial Messages

The American advertising industry's primary self-regulatory body, the National Advertising Division of the Council of Better Business Bureaus, maintains a special unit to review advertising aimed at children—the **Children's Advertising Review Unit (CARU).** Two of the seven principles that underlie CARU's guidelines for advertising directed to children relate to their ability to comprehend commercial messages:

1. Advertisers should always take into account the level of knowledge, sophistication, and maturity of the audience to which their message is primarily directed. Younger children have a limited capacity for evaluating the credibility of information they receive. They also may lack the ability to understand the nature of the information they

provide. Advertisers, therefore, have a special responsibility to protect children from their own susceptibilities.

2. Realizing that children are imaginative and that make-believe play constitutes an important part of the growing-up process, advertisers should exercise care not to exploit unfairly the imaginative quality of children. Unreasonable expectations of product quality or performance should not be stimulated either directly or indirectly by advertising.

Some of the specific guidelines relating to information processing that guide CARU's policing of children's advertising are shown in Table 20–1.

CARU and others are interested in the impact that the *content* of children's advertising has, as well as the ability of children to process advertising messages. However, our current focus is limited to children's abilities to *comprehend* advertising messages. There are two main components to this concern: (1) Do children understand the selling intent of commercials? and (2) Can children understand specific aspects of commercials, such as comparisons?

Do Children Understand the Selling Intent of Commercials?   Research suggests that younger children have at least some difficulty understanding the selling intent of commercials.[5] Currently, the advertising industry strives to separate children's commercials from the programs by prohibiting overlapping characters and by using *separators* such as "We will return after these messages."

This problem is growing in intensity, as children's products are often the "stars" of animated children's films and television programs. Increasingly, product lines and television programs (and movies) are being designed jointly with the primary objective being sales of the toy line. Parents have expressed concerns ranging from the effects that toy-based programming has on their children's behaviors and emotional development to the fear that such programming may replace other more creative and child-oriented programs.[6]

This concern has led to a variety of proposals to restrict or eliminate such programs. These proposals have produced an ongoing debate about who controls the television set. One argument is that it is the parent's responsibility to monitor and regulate their children's viewing behaviors. If a sufficient number of parents find such programs inappropriate and refuse to let their children watch them, advertisers will quit sponsoring them and they will no longer be available. Another argument is that today's time-pressured parents do not have time to screen all the shows their children watch. Furthermore, tremendous peer pressure can develop for children to watch a particular show or own the products associated with it.

TABLE 20–1 Information-Processing–Related Guidelines of CARU	1. Care should be taken not to exploit a child's imagination. Fantasy, including animation, is appropriate for younger as well as older children. However, it should not create unattainable performance expectations nor exploit the younger child's difficulty in distinguishing between the real and the fanciful. 2. The performance and use of a product should be demonstrated in a way that can be duplicated by the child for whom the product is intended. 3. All price representations should be clearly and concisely set forth. Price minimizations such as "only" or "just" should not be used. 4. Program personalities or characters, live or animated, should not promote products, premiums, or services in or adjacent to programs primarily directed to children in which the same personality appears. 5. Children have difficulty distinguishing product from premium. If product advertising contains a premium message, care should be taken that the child's attention is focused primarily on the product. The premium message should be clearly secondary.

Source: *Self-Regulation Guidelines for Children's Advertising* (Council of Better Business Bureaus, Inc., Children's Advertising Review Unit, 2001).

Denying a child the right to watch such a show then causes arguments and resentments. Therefore, society should set appropriate standards within which broadcasters should operate. *Which, if either, of these views matches your own?*

Can Children Understand the Words and Phrases in Commercials?   The second aspect of comprehension involves specific words or types of commercials that children might misunderstand. For example, research indicates that disclaimers such as "Part of a nutritious breakfast," "Each sold separately," and "Batteries not included," are ineffective with preschool children.[7] Not only do young children have a difficult time understanding these phrases, but an analysis of Saturday morning advertising aimed at children revealed that most such disclaimers are presented in a manner that does not meet the Federal Trade Commission's "Clear and Conspicuous" requirements for such disclaimers.[8]

For example, one toy ad contained this disclaimer: "TV Teddy comes with one tape. Other tapes sold separately." However, it appeared near the bottom of the screen in lettering that measured only 3.5 percent of the screen height against a multicolor background. It was not repeated by an announcer and appeared for less than three seconds. A child would have to read at 200 words per minute to read the message! Unfortunately, this treatment of the disclaimer is more the rule than the exception.

CARU has special rules for comparison advertising and prohibits price minimizations such as "only" and "just." It also suggests specific phrasing for certain situations, such as "your mom or dad must say it's OK before you call" rather than "ask your parents' permission." Recent cases involving CARU and the information-processing skills of children include the following:

- Trendmasters' Rumble Robots advertising depicted the highest level of performance of the robot, which requires the purchase of upgrades, rather than the performance of the one available in the standard package. It changed this commercial at CARU's request.[9]
- Nabisco, Inc. agreed to change its advertising for KoolStuf Oreo Toaster Pastries after CARU brought a consumer complaint to its attention. The commercial showed Oreo cookies going into a toaster and popping up as KoolStuf toaster pastries. A four-year-old saw the commercial and tried to do the same thing by putting Oreos into a toaster. When they melted, he tried to remove them with a pair of metal tongs before being stopped by his mother.[10]
- Rose Art Industries agreed to alter its packaging after the CARU concluded that the size of the product relative to the size of the child shown in the package picture could lead a child to believe the Super Lite toy is larger than it is.[11]

The Federal Trade Commission (FTC) applied sanctions to Lewis Galoob Toys and its ad agency. The ads cited showed a doll dancing and a toy airplane flying, both of which require human assistance. The ads also failed to disclose that assembly was required for certain toy sets. Finally, the firm failed to "clearly and conspicuously" disclose that two toys shown together had to be purchased separately. An FTC spokesperson noted that the ads never appeared on network stations and speculated that the networks' internal review processes for children's ads would have precluded their being shown.[12]

Concerns about the Effects of the Content of Commercial Messages on Children

Even if children accurately comprehend television ads, there are concerns about the effects the content of these messages has on children. These concerns stem in part from the substantial amount of time American children spend viewing television. The large amount of time children devote to watching television, including commercials, gives rise to two major areas of concern:

- The impact of commercial messages on children's values.
- The impact of commercial messages on children's health and safety.

Five of the seven basic principles that underline the CARU's guidelines for advertising directed at children focus on these concerns (the other two are concerned with children's information-processing capabilities). They are

1. Recognizing that advertising may play an important role in educating the child, advertisers should communicate information in a truthful and accurate manner and in language understandable to young children with full recognition that the child may learn practices from advertising that can affect his or her health and well-being.
2. Advertisers are urged to capitalize on the potential of advertising to influence behavior by developing advertising that, wherever possible, addresses itself to positive and beneficial social behavior such as friendship, kindness, honesty, justice, generosity, and respect for others.
3. Care should be taken to incorporate minority and other groups in advertisements in order to present positive and prosocial roles and role models wherever possible. Social stereotyping and appeals to prejudice should be avoided.
4. Although many influences affect a child's personal and social development, it remains the prime responsibility of the parents to provide guidance for children. Advertisers should contribute to this parent–child relationship in a constructive manner.
5. Products and content that are inappropriate for use by children should not be advertised or promoted directly to children.

Several of the specific guidelines derived from these principles are provided in Table 20–2.

Health and Safety   CARU recently challenged a television commercial for 4Wheelers by Skechers, which ran during traditional children's viewing time. The ad featured teens skating and performing a stunt without the use of any safety gear such as helmets or pads.

TABLE 20–2	
Examples of Specific Guidelines of the Children's Advertising Review Unit	1. Representation of food products should be made so as to encourage sound use of the product with a view toward healthy development of the child and development of good nutritional practices. Advertisements representing mealtime should clearly and adequately depict the role of the product within the framework of a balanced diet. Snack foods should be clearly represented as such, and not as substitutes for meals.
	2. Children should not be encouraged to ask parents or others to buy products. Advertisements should not suggest that a parent or adult who purchases a product or service for a child is better, more intelligent, or more generous than one who does not. Advertising directed toward children should not create a sense of urgency or exclusivity, for example, by using words like "now" and "only."
	3. Benefits attributed to the product or service should be inherent in its use. Advertisements should not convey the impression that possession of a product will result in more acceptance of a child by his or her peers. Conversely, it should not be implied that lack of a product will cause a child to be less accepted by his or her peers. Advertisements should not imply that purchase and use of a product will confer upon the user the prestige, skills, or other special qualities of characters appearing in advertising.
	4. Advertisements should not portray adults or children in unsafe situations, or in acts harmful to themselves or others. For example, when athletic activities (such as bicycle riding or skateboarding) are shown, proper precautions and safety equipment should be depicted.

Source: *Self-Regulatory Guidelines for Children's Advertising* (Council of Better Business Bureaus, Inc., Children's Advertising Review Unit, 2001).

According to CARU, this violates the fourth guideline in Table 20–2. Skechers is appealing the ruling, stating that there are no children shown in the commercial; protective gear while skating or rollerblading is not required by law; it warns purchasers to "always" wear protective gear in the safety pamphlet that comes with the product; and the skates are not being portrayed in an athletic or sporting manner.[13] *What do you think? Is CARU correct or is Skechers?*

In many instances, children and teenagers are exposed to advertising directed at adults. For example, research indicates that tobacco ads routinely reach a high percentage of 12- to 17-year-olds when placed in popular consumer magazines (many doubt that this is unintended).[14]

Even ads clearly not targeting children can have potentially harmful consequences:

A television commercial for Calgonite automatic dishwasher detergent showed a woman inside an automatic dishwasher. The commercial was withdrawn voluntarily after CARU received a complaint that a three-year-old child had climbed into a dishwasher shortly after viewing the commercial.[15]

The problem caused by the Calgonite commercial illustrates the difficulty marketers face. This commercial was not aimed at children nor shown during a children's program. The fact that children watch prime-time television extensively places an additional responsibility on marketers.[16]

Ensuring that advertisements portray only safe uses of products is sometimes difficult, but it is not a controversial area. Advertising of health-related products, particularly snack foods and cereals, is much more controversial. The bulk of the controversy focuses on the heavy advertising emphasis placed on sugared and high-fat products. Advertising sugared products such as presweetened breakfast cereals does increase their consumption. However, this same advertising may also increase the consumption of related products, such as milk. What is not known, and probably cannot be determined, are the eating patterns that would exist in the absence of such advertising. That is, if children did not know about cereals such as Cap'n Crunch, would they eat a more nutritious breakfast, a less nutritious breakfast, or perhaps no breakfast at all?

Recently, children were attracted to nutellausa.com through a sweepstakes featuring Nutella's celebrity endorser, Kobe Bryant, that appeared in *Sports Illustrated for Kids,* as well as its website, sikids.com. This caused the following problem:

On the site, the firm made several claims comparing the dietary benefits of its product, Nutella, a hazelnut spread, with those of peanut butter. The website had been promoting the fact that, compared to leading peanut butter, Nutella has 37 percent less fat and 87 percent less sodium. However, the site omitted a comparison of a key nutritional concern for children—sugar content. Nutella has a sugar content of 21 grams in one serving as opposed to 2 grams or 3 grams in a serving of peanut butter. CARU's position was that, taking into consideration government guidelines and medical community recommendations on sugar consumption, children could get the wrong impression about the overall dietary benefits of Nutella as opposed to peanut butter. The firm altered the claims.[17]

Unfortunately, some marketers have not been very responsible in this area. For example, children's diets are higher in overall fat and saturated fat than health guidelines call for and obesity among children is increasing (see Case 2–10), as has advertising of high-fat and high-sugar foods during Saturday morning children's TV programs. Such advertising undoubtedly influences children's food choices and subsequent health.[18] It should be noted that some successful marketers of products consumed by children, such as Coca-Cola and PepsiCo, do not advertise on children's shows.[19]

Values Advertising is frequently criticized as fostering overly materialistic, self-focused, and short-term values in children:

> We cannot afford to raise a generation of children that measures its own value by the insignia on their clothes—not by the compassion in their hearts or the knowledge in their minds.[20]

One reason is the magnitude of advertising focused on kids under 12, estimated at almost $7 billion in 2000.[21] Kids are exposed to 30,000 commercial messages (from all sources) each year.[22] In one month, Nike ran 90 commercials for its shoes on MTV and only 21 on sports programs.[23] Many are concerned that this consistent pressure to buy and own things is producing negative values in children.

Numerous cosmetics companies are now targeting children as young as 8 with products and advertising. Most position the products in terms of fun rather than sensuality. For example, Disney's products are packaged in boxes with pictures of Tinkerbell, Winnie-the-Pooh, and similar characters.[24] According to an industry expert, girls 8 to 12 are now wearing platform heels and "low-rise jeans, tight miniskirts and midriff-baring T-shirts."[25] There is also an increase in concern about looking thin and eating disorders in children as young as 6.[26] Many find this apparent shortening of childhood and the related body image problems inappropriate. They assign a large part of the blame to the marketing of products such as cosmetics and personalities such as Britney Spears.

Summary of Advertising and Children CARU recently examined 604 hours of children's programming on ABC, NBC, CBS, USA Network, Nickelodeon, and two independent broadcasters. There were 10,329 commercials aired during the 604 hours. Of these 10,329 commercials, 385 were in violation of one of CARU's guidelines. Fast-food ads accounted for 109 of the violations, with Burger King having 83. The most common offense was to devote most of the commercial to describing a premium rather than the primary product. CARU guidelines require that ads aimed at children emphasize the product.

Advertiser compliance was highest on the three networks, which have their own review processes, with a 2 percent violation rate; independent stations were next at 3.7 percent; and 5 percent of the ads on cable violated the CARU guidelines.[27] Thus, the vast majority of ads meet CARU guidelines. However, given the enormous amount of time children spend watching television, most will see many ads that are in violation of these guidelines. In addition, these guidelines do not address such issues as advertising high-fat foods. Nor do they, nor could they, oppose generating desires for products that many families cannot afford. Nonetheless, CARU has greatly enhanced the level of responsibility in advertising aimed at children. Many consumer advocates would like it to expand the areas it covers and increase the stringency of its rules.

Controversial Marketing Activities Aimed at Children

There are a number of marketing activities targeted at children in addition to television advertising that are controversial and for which various regulatory proposals are being considered. For example, violent entertainment products (movies, videos, and music) labeled for those 17 and older were, until recently, routinely marketed to kids. Highly publicized acts of violence by teenagers produced threats of regulation and improved self-regulation by the industries.[28] However, it remains a problem. Three additional issues are described in this section.

Kids' Clubs   A popular way to market to children is through **kids' clubs.**[29] Firms such as Fox, Chuck E. Cheese, Toys "R" Us, Burger King, Disney, Hyatt, and Delta Airlines sponsor kids' clubs. The clubs typically provide membership certificates, a magazine, the chance to win prizes, and discounts or coupons for products offered by the sponsor. Kids' clubs vary widely in what they offer the members and how ethically they are run. Here is how Consumers Union characterized the majority of them:

> In a real club, kids are likely to find friends, shared interests and activities, and opportunities for fun and growth. In the promotional clubs common years ago, kids were likely to get membership cards, decoder rings, or other symbols that reinforced loyalty to the sponsoring radio or TV program, comic, or other product. In one of the new kids' clubs, kids are likely to get hard sell from many advertisers, a monthly magazine cum sales catalog, discount coupons, and other powerful incentives to buy.
>
> Clubs disguise commercial messages. Kids are invited to join something that promises to be "theirs," but turns out to be a way of manipulating them to buy things. The ad messages come disguised as "advice from your club," making them more difficult to resist.[30]

Table 20–3 describes the Nickelodeon Club and an advertisement that Nickelodeon used to attract advertisers to its club magazine. The selling intent of this club seems apparent.

Consumers Union has the following recommendation for regulating kids' clubs:

> The Federal Trade Commission should recognize that kids' clubs, whose purpose is to sell products, may mislead children, even if the commercial nature of the clubs is obvious to adults. The FTC should require kids' clubs to provide a substantial nonmerchandising service or activity for kids. Clubs intending to sell members' names in mailing lists should disclose that fact and give kids the opportunity to keep their names off the list.

TABLE 20–3

The Nickelodeon Club

The Characteristics of the Club
A one-year membership, which includes a subscription to *Nickelodeon Magazine,* costs $9.95. The magazine, with an insert promoting club membership, was launched through Pizza Hut. That insert promised special "kids-only" prices on club merchandise and "special offers or discounts" at Pizza Hut, Universal Studios in Florida, and TCBY yogurt. In addition to eight pages of ads, *Nickelodeon Magazine* devoted nine pages to the "Nick Store," where club merchandise is offered at two prices, a kid's price and a higher adult's price. One-third (17 of 52) of its pages sells things to kids. Other popular kid's magazines with no club affiliation tend to devote a smaller percent of their pages of advertising: One-fourth (22 of 80) pages of *Sports Illustrated for Kids* are ads, as is about one-sixth to one-tenth of *3-2-1 Contact.* Club members will also be sent product samples and coupons from Nick Club advertisers.

What the Nickelodeon Club Promises Advertisers
You (the advertiser) can capture all the excitement of the Nickelodeon name, the on-air attitude, and the off-air environment, by delivering your product message or coupon to the young consumers of today and the brand-loyal customers of tomorrow. With the Nick Nack Pack (product samples and coupons mailed to kids) and the *Nickelodeon Magazine,* Nick offers you home delivery of an entire generation—the Nickelodeon generation.

The preceding quote is from the packet Nickelodeon sends to prospective advertisers. It also quotes the Nickelodeon/Yankelovich Youth Monitor: "All kids tend to influence their parents across a number of categories—clothing, food, entertainment, nontraditional and larger ticket items." Among the data given: "60 percent of kids buy products because they have coupons for them."

While the kids are joining a fun club, Nickelodeon is building a large database of names. Along with the Sassy and MTV clubs, Nickelodeon offers to sell its kids' club membership list to direct-mail advertisers.

Source: *Selling America's Kids,* copyright 1990 by Consumers Union of U.S., Inc., Yonkers, NY 10103–1057. Reprinted by permission from *Consumer Reports,* 1990.

Would the Burger King Kids' Club described below meet the requirements recommended by Consumers Union?

> Kids (or their parents) can pick up a membership form at any Burger King for free. After it is sent in, they receive a kit containing a membership certificate, stickers, a membership card and iron-on transfers for T-shirts. On their birthdays, they receive a card good for a free meal at their local Burger King. Bimonthly Kids' Club newsletters are distributed through the restaurants. A quarterly 32-page, full-color magazine is sent to the members' homes. There are three different versions of the magazine geared to the age of the member. Each issue has six pages of outside advertising. Burger King does not sell its membership list.[31]

Advertising in the Classroom   Whittle Communications created a substantial controversy when it launched a closed-circuit television network (Channel One) that would provide 12 minutes of news to participating schools. If the schools' teachers agree to have their students watch the program most days, they receive the TV equipment free. However, the news program contains two minutes of commercials. Unlike home viewing, watching this news program is not voluntary and students cannot skip to other channels when the commercials are aired. It is now in thousands of middle and high schools. Research indicates that the commercials are having an impact on the students.[32]

Another major controversy arose when a teenager in Georgia was suspended from school for wearing a Pepsi T-shirt on "Coke day."[33] The school had an exclusive contract with Coca-Cola. While such events generate substantial publicity, numerous corporations place direct and indirect ads in schools every day:

- American Airlines sponsored a package of materials designed to teach children to read maps and globes. It was distributed to 9,500 teachers in communities served by the airline. A company spokesperson described American's motivation: "We thought it important to be a good corporate citizen and do things in schools that would benefit the learning experience. Today's students are tomorrow's workers. Of course, they're also tomorrow's airline passengers; we wanted them to learn the American name and to be familiar with the brand."
- Cover Concepts distributes book covers to schools for free. More than 60 million were distributed in a recent year. However, the covers contain ads for firms. Firms can target the schools and classes where their message will appear. Firms such as Nike, Nickelodeon, Procter & Gamble, and Quaker Oats are clients.[34]
- Many first-grade teachers use the AT&T Adventure Club, which includes student newsletters, classroom posters, and teaching guides. It is designed to develop an understanding of communications and to build AT&T brand awareness.
- Scholastic Inc., one of the nation's largest publishers of books and magazines for children, developed a program for Minute Maid to encourage 3.7 million elementary school kids to read a book a week over their summer vacation. Kids who sent away for a chart to keep track of their progress also received coupons for Minute Maid products. For each coupon redeemed, Minute Maid donated 10 cents to a nonprofit organization that promotes reading.
- Word of Mouse provides free mousepads to schools ranging from grade schools to colleges. Each colorful pad contains four age-appropriate ads for websites.
- Even school lunch menus now contain advertising. The Jefferson County Kentucky school district estimated that it saved $200,000 on menu costs in a test of the program.[35]

Table 20–4 describes a number of other "educational materials" programs offered by marketers for use in schools and Consumers Union's evaluation of the promotional content

Corporate Sponsor	Teaching Material	Promotional Content
Polaroid	Polaroid Education Program (lesson book, camera—"A visual approach to teaching basic skills")	*High*—Mentions "Polaroid" in every lesson and assignment, and requires 10 proofs of film purchase for the camera.
Kodak	Corkers (bulletin board ideas) and Teaching Tips from Kodak (tips from teachers on using photography to teach)	*Low*—Encourages taking photos but never mentions "Kodak."
Chef Boyardee	Teach . . . Good Nutrition (sets of reproducible masters)	*High*—Has its name and logo on every master; names its products in all recipes; and just encourages kids to eat pizza (no nutrition education).
McDonald's	Nutrient Pursuit (poster and activity to teach the four basic food groups)	*Low*—Its name isn't on the materials, but its logo is on the masters. Nutrition education is weak.
Tampax	Mysteries of Me (lesson plans and masters for three activities)	*High*—Pushes using Tampax by name, gives girls a coupon to order a $3 starter kit or a free sample, and has its name on the poster.
Procter & Gamble	Perspectives (case studies of P&G's past to teach economics and history) Food Preparation (booklet and worksheets)	*Moderate*—Builds P&G's image and talks about its products, but doesn't "sell." *Moderate*—Uses P&G brand name products in recipes, and includes coupons for free P&G products "for demonstrations/discussions."
Reynolds Wrap	"Preserve Freshness and Flavor with the Best Wrap Around" poster with teaching guide on back	*High*—Shows more than 30 foods wrapped in aluminum foil; says "Freeze in it! Cook in it! Store in it!" All information pushes using foil.
Almond Board of California	"Everybody's Nuts about Almonds" poster with teaching guide on back	*High*—Shows only almonds and package; "Nutrition" teaching guide shows why almonds are nutritionally superior to other nuts, including peanuts, and why they're so healthy— one-sided and misleading.

TABLE 20–4

"Educational" Materials Supplied to Schools

Source: *Selling America's Kids,* copyright 1990 by Consumers Union of U.S., Inc., Yonkers, NY 10103-1057. Reprinted by permission from *Consumer Reports,* 1990.

of these materials. Consumers Union and other groups want schools to be ad-free zones. They feel that all material provided to schools by organizations should be

- *Accurate:* Be consistent with established facts, appropriately referenced, and current.
- *Objective:* Present all relevant points of view, and clearly state the sponsor's bias.
- *Complete:* Not mislead by omission.
- *Nondiscriminatory:* Avoid ethnic, age, race, and gender stereotypes.
- *Noncommercial:* Not contain any of the sponsor's brand names, trademarks, related trade names, or corporate identification in the text or illustrations; avoid implied or explicit sales messages.
- *Evaluative:* Encourage cognitive evaluation of the subject taught.

Although many firms would agree with most of the above requirements, complete compliance with the noncommercial standard would greatly reduce the motivation of firms to provide valuable (sometimes) material to the schools.[36]

Internet Marketing and Children   Children are major users of the Internet. Not surprisingly, marketers use the Internet to communicate with kids. Two major concerns have emerged: invading children's privacy and exploitation of children through manipulative sales techniques.[37] We will consider the online privacy issue in the next section.

The Center for Media Education (CME) considers exploiting children to involve such techniques as building "playgrounds" that are primarily commercial in intent and blending advertising and content in sophisticated ways. For example the website for Kellogg is described by the CME as follows:

> [It] makes full use of Snap, Crackle, and Pop, Tony the Tiger, and Toucan Sam. The three elves are the hosts of the Clubhouse, welcoming children to explore the different rooms and encouraging them to participate in all the various activities. Youngsters can color pictures of the spokescharacters, download Rice Krispies Treats recipes, and do word-find puzzles. The Kellogg General Store sells licensed merchandise: Tony the Tiger watches, Toucan Sam sweatshirts, and Snap, Crackle & Pop T-shirts are just a few of the items that can be ordered online.

The Center for Media Education recommends the following principles to guide development of online commercial services:

1. Personal information should not be collected from children, nor should personal profiles of children be sold to third parties.
2. Advertising and promotions targeted at children should be clearly labeled and separated from content.
3. Children's content areas should not be directly linked to advertising sites.
4. There should be no direct interaction between children and product spokespersons.
5. There should be no online microtargeting of children (commercial or promotions developed for individual children), and no direct-response marketing.

Children's Online Privacy Issues

An example of invading children's privacy is the KidsCom communications playground (targeting kids 4 to 8), which required children to provide their name, age, sex, and e-mail address in order to enter the site. It also requested their favorite TV show, music groups, and the name of the child who referred them to KidsCom. Once in the playground, they can earn "KidsCash," which can be redeemed for prizes by supplying additional personal information.

An industry study found that almost 90 percent of children's sites on the Internet collect personal information from the children. Slightly more than half provided some disclosure about their information practices, but less than a fourth asked children to check with their parents before they provide information and less than 10 percent gave parents control over information collected from children.[38] Two studies by the Center for Media Education (CME), one of a random sample of children's websites and the second of the 80 most popular sites for children, found the following:[39]

	Random Sample	*Most Popular Sites*
Collect personal information	95%	88%
Post their privacy policies	27	75
Attempt to get parental consent	6	26
Get verifiable parental consent	3	13

The act requires that commercial websites that collect personal information from children under 13 obtain prior parental consent before they collect that information. The act only applies to websites, or portions thereof, directed to children or to websites that knowingly collect personal information from children under 13. The act does not apply to nonprofits.

Notice: Parents have the right to be notified about data collection and use practices. The parent must be informed about what information will be collected, how it will be used, and to whom and in what form the information will be disclosed to others. The notice must be prominently displayed and unavoidable.

Prior Parental Consent: With certain exceptions, information cannot be collected from children, used or disclosed unless the website operator has obtained verifiable parental consent through "reasonable effort."

Prevention of Further Use: Parents have the right to prevent further use of already collected personal identifying information and to prevent future collection of information from the child.

Collection of Personal Information Must Be Limited: The collection of personal identifying information for a child's participation in a game, prize, offer, or other activity on the website must be limited to what is reasonably necessary for the activity.

Access to Information: Parents of children under 13 have the right to access and review a description of the specific types of personal identifying information collected from the child and website operators must provide reasonable means to the parent to obtain the information itself that has been collected from the child.

Concern over the invasion of children's privacy prompted Congress to pass the **Children's Online Privacy Protection Act (COPPA)** in October 1998. It authorizes the FTC to develop specific rules to implement the provisions of the act as described in Table 20–5.

Rules based on these guidelines became effective in April 2000. A survey of children-oriented websites a year later reached the following conclusions:

1. Children's commercial websites have modified their data collection practices and limited the amount of data being collected.
2. More children's commercial websites that collect personally identifiable data are posting privacy policy notices informing parents of what they are collecting and how it will be used.
3. A few sites have developed creative solutions to adapt to COPPA and still allow children to have an interactive experience without revealing identifying information such as their e-mail address.
4. A majority of sites do not have a "clear and prominent" link to privacy policies.
5. Children's sites that have a link for feedback, such as e-mail, often overlook this as a data collection point.
6. A majority of sites did not obtain prior parental consent or provide parental notice as required by COPPA.
7. In attempting to restrict children under 13 from entering personal identifying information, some sites use methods that could encourage age falsification.[40]

Clearly COPPA had a positive impact in its first year. CARU recently adopted similar but more detailed rules. Privacy issues now dominate CARU cases:

*   The language "tipped off" children that they must be over 13 to use the interactive services offered on the site by stating: "U.S. law prohibits Alta Vista from registering anyone under the age of 13 without parental permission. Please verify your age below." It then asked prospective registrants if they were "less than 13 years old" or "13 or older." Those who registered could access all areas of the site, some of which were clearly inappropriate for children.[41]
*   Pinkspage, the fan site for the artist Pink, did not contain a privacy statement. In addition, CARU was concerned that a visitor of any age could submit personal identifying information such as an e-mail or street address at the "Fan Club" registration.[42]

- Scan-command.com features online games designed to be played by children ages 8 and up. It recently agreed to cease collecting parents' off-line contact information from children under 13 without prior parental consent. It also agreed to obtain parental consent before allowing children to sign up as a "scan-command.com agent," which, among other things, enables them to participate in a message board.[43]

REGULATION AND MARKETING TO ADULTS

Regulation of marketing activities aimed at adults focuses on marketing communications, product features, and pricing practices. There is increasing demand for regulation to protect the privacy of adults, particularly on the Internet. Consider the following:

> American Express announced plans to sell extensive information on its cardholders to merchants. These data would be combined with data on 175 million Americans compiled by KnowledgeBase. KnowledgeBase has information on age, marital status, family composition, household ownership, and so forth. By combining this demographic data with American Express purchase records, American Express plans to develop mailing lists of customers most likely to buy certain products. It will sell these lists to other firms. Cardholders can keep their names off the list by calling or writing American Express but the company has no plans to explicitly inform its customers of this use of their purchase records.

Many consumers find this use of information about their purchase histories and personal characteristics to be intrusive. Many magazines sell their subscription lists to various firms who use the information for direct marketing campaigns. Some charities sell or otherwise make available their donor lists. While the dissemination of credit card, subscription, and donation data is a concern, most attention is currently focused on the privacy of data collected on the Internet.[44]

One of the reasons the concern about Internet privacy is so strong is that data are often collected without the consumer explicitly providing it. A person visiting a website can have that fact recorded (his or her e-mail address at a minimum) as well as what parts of the site are visited, what information is requested, what links are accessed, and so forth without consent or even knowledge. Other information may be collected in a more direct manner. Information from various sites and sources can be pooled to develop individual profiles. Consumer Insight 20–1 provides the FTC's current approach to regulating Internet privacy practices.

The Better Business Bureau has a Code of Online Business Practices that is "designed to guide ethical business-to-consumer conduct in electronic commerce." It provides three broad requirements, each with substantial details and examples, with respect to information practices:

- Post and adhere to a privacy policy that is open, transparent, and meets generally accepted fair information principles.
- Provide adequate security for the type of information collected, maintained, or transferred to third parties.
- Respect customer's preferences regarding unsolicited e-mail.

Marketing Communications

There are three major concerns focused on the information that marketers provide to consumers, generally in the form of advertisements—the accuracy of the information provided, the adequacy of the information provided, and the cumulative impact of marketing

In May of 2000, the Federal Trade Commission issued its third report on online privacy issues to Congress.[45] This report concluded that self-regulation was not providing adequate privacy regulation and recommended national legislation. It recommended that consumer-oriented commercial websites that collect personal identifying information from or about consumers comply with four standards.

1. *Notice*—Websites would be required to provide consumers clear and conspicuous notice of their information practices, including what information they collect, how they collect it (e.g., directly or through nonobvious means such as cookies), how they use it, how they provide *choice, access,* and *security* to consumers, whether they disclose the information collected to other entities, and whether other entities are collecting information through the site.

2. *Choice*—Websites would be required to offer consumers choices as to how their personal identifying information is used beyond the use for which the information was provided (e.g., to consummate a transaction). Such choice would encompass both internal secondary uses (such as marketing back to consumers) and external secondary uses (such as disclosing data to other entities).

3. *Access*—Websites would be required to offer consumers reasonable access to the information a website has collected about them, including a reasonable opportunity to review information and to correct inaccuracies or delete information.

4. *Security*—Websites would be required to take reasonable steps to protect the security of the information they collect from consumers.

However, in 2001 the new chairman of the FTC concluded that "it is too soon to conclude that we can fashion workable legislation." At the same time, he did conclude that privacy protection in general and online privacy protection in particular are important issues. He indicated that the FTC was going to increase the resources it devotes to privacy protection by 50 percent.

Critical Thinking Questions

1. Should there be national legislation such as that proposed above? Why or why not?

2. In the absence of legislation, how should a firm collect and use data from those who visit its website?

information on society's values. We will briefly look at advertising's impact on society's values before focusing on the accuracy and adequacy of consumer information.

Advertising and Values   We discussed the impact of advertising on values in the previous section on advertising to children. The concern is the same for advertising directed at adults—the long-term effect of a constant flow of messages emphasizing materialistic or narcissistic values may be negative for both individuals and society. For example, an ad for Musk by Alyssa Ashley appeared in a magazine read by teenage females. It consisted of a picture of a teenage girl on the back of a motorcycle driven by a scruffy looking man with long hair, a beard, and a tattoo. The girl's dress is pulled up to the top of her thigh. The only other content was a picture of the product package and the headline—"Sometimes even good girls want to be bad." Many would argue that this ad promotes inappropriate values and behaviors.

Most ads for women's cosmetics and clothing, like the one in Illustration 20–1, emphasize beauty or sex appeal as major benefits. Each individual ad is probably harmless. However, critics charge that when people see such themes repeated thousands of times for hundreds of products, they learn to consider a person's looks to be more important than other attributes.[46] This can lead to injurious consumption patterns such as excessive tanning or inappropriate dieting despite knowledge of the associated health hazard.[47] These harmful effects may be most severe in younger women.[48] Further, those who cannot afford

Ads that emphasize beauty and attractiveness are often effective. Some critics charge that the cumulative effect of such ads over time results in too much value being placed on these attributes. Others note that beauty was deemed desirable and actively pursued long before the advent of advertising.

las flores no son las únicas que retoñan en primavera

Courtesy JCPenney Co.

such products or who are not "good-looking" suffer. Others argue that individuals have been concerned with their looks and possessions in virtually all cultures and times. They argue that advertising does not cause a society's values; it merely reflects them.

Portrayals of beauty and casual attitudes toward sex are not the only ways advertisements are argued to influence values. The portrayal of women in the mass media in general and in advertising in particular often has been limited to stereotypical roles or as decoration.[49] This in turn can influence the concepts girls develop of themselves and their role choices. Of course, many firms now portray females in a more positive, realistic fashion. The ad for Jane, shown in Illustration 20–2, emphasizes positive values while still promoting a beauty enhancement product. A Nike campaign has generated a positive response from many women as well as advertising critics. A television ad in the campaign combines quick camera takes and slow-motion shots of teenage girls on a playground, with images of girls playing on swing sets and monkey bars. The sound portion is a variety of girls' voices describing the long-term benefits of female participation in sports:

> I will like myself more; I will have more self-confidence if you let me play sports. If you let me play, I will be 60 percent less likely to get breast cancer. I will suffer less depression if you let me play sports.
> I will be more likely to leave a man who beats me. If you let me play, I will be less likely to get pregnant before I want to; I will learn what it means to be strong.[50]

The manner in which ethnic groups, the elderly, and other social groups are portrayed in ads and the mass media can affect the way members of these groups view themselves as

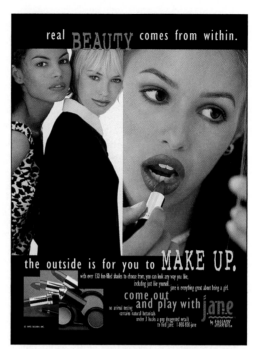

Courtesy Sassaby Cosmetics, Inc.

well as the way others see them.[51] Marketers need to ensure that their ads reflect the diversity of the American society in a manner that is realistic and positive for all the many groups involved. These portrayals should involve both the content of the ads and the shows sponsored by the ads.[52] For example, several Hispanic groups are considering a boycott of the major networks and some of their sponsors because of the virtually complete absence of Hispanic roles and actors on network television.

Consumer Information Accuracy   The salesperson tells you "My brand is the best there is." Does he or she need scientific proof to make such a statement? At what point does permissible puffery become misleading and illegal? Does it vary by the situation? The consumer group involved?[53]

An ad shows a pair of attractive female legs. The headline reads, "Her legs are insured for $1,000,000. Her policy came with one minor stipulation. Schick Silk Effects." Schick Silk Effects is a woman's razor. How do you interpret this ad? Many would assume that the insurance company insisted on her using only this brand as a condition of the policy. This suggests that the insurance company considers this razor to be very good at protecting women's legs while they shave.

However, in exceedingly fine print at the very bottom of the ad is this disclaimer: "Policy condition included by insurer at the request of Warner-Lambert Co." Warner-Lambert is the firm that markets Silk Effects. In other words, the firm that owns the razor had the requirement that this razor be used placed in the insurance policy. This leads to a very different interpretation of the ad. *Should this ad be illegal? Is it unethical?*

Suppose you saw a snorkel or swim fins with the National Association of Scuba Diving Schools' "Seal of Approval" on the package. What would this mean to you? Many of us would interpret it to mean that the product had been tested by the association or was manufactured to conform to a set of standards established by the association. However, the FTC charged that the seal was *sold* for use on diving products *without tests or standards.*[54]

ILLUSTRATION 20-3

Is imitation the sincerest form of flattery or a source of consumer confusion?

© 1994 Paul F. Kilmer.

Research shows that the more baking soda toothpaste contains, the more effective it is in cleaning away plaque and deep stains. How much baking soda should a brand of toothpaste contain before it can be called "baking soda" toothpaste? There is no rule. Arm & Hammer's contains 65 percent baking soda, but Crest Baking Soda Toothpaste has only 20 percent.[55] *Should there be rules for names such as this or is the required listing of the contents enough?*

Illustration 20–3 shows several major national brands and several competing brands with similar packages. *Are consumers misled by such packages? Or are these legitimate attempts to position competing products as being similar to the brand leaders?*[56]

Because of such problems, various businesses, consumer groups, and regulatory agencies are deeply concerned with the interpretation of marketing messages. However, determining the exact meaning of a marketing message is not a simple process. The National Advertising Division (NAD) of the Council of Better Business Bureaus recently asked Bayer to alter an *accurate* commercial for Aleve. The commercial accurately stated that Aleve provided longer-lasting relief with a smaller dosage than Tylenol ("Just 2 Aleve can stop the pain all day, it would take 8 Tylenol to do that"). The concern was that this would unintentionally convey a message of superior efficacy (it would stop more pain than Tylenol).[57]

Table 20–6 illustrates some of the areas where controversy over the interpretation of various marketing messages has existed.

Obtaining accurate assignments of meaning is made even more difficult by the variation in information-processing skills and motivations among different population groups.[58] For

TABLE 20–6

Regulation and the
Interpretation of
Marketing Messages

- The 4th U.S. Circuit Court of Appeals ruled that meat from a turkey thigh can be called a "turkey ham" even if it contains no pork. A lower court had reached the opposite conclusion. The ruling appeared to rely heavily on a technical definition of the term: *ham.*
- Maximum Strength Anacin's claim that it is "the maximum strength allowed" was ruled illegal because it "implies that an appropriate authority has authorized the sale of products like Maximum Strength Anacin." No such authorization exists.
- The Association of Petroleum Re-Refiners petitioned the FTC to reconsider requiring all re-refined oil products to "clearly and conspicuously" label the origin of the product. This has meant that "made from used oil" appears on all labels. The association feels that this disparages the quality of such lubricants, and they want to use the phrase "recycled oil product" instead.
- A court issued an injunction stopping the distribution of a new brand of gloves trademarked Blueberry because of potential confusion with an existing brand trademarked Cranberry. Each trademark contained a picture of the fruit with the name.
- Keebler Company's claim of "Baked not fried" for Wheatables and Munch'ems snack crackers was challenged before the NAD. While the crackers are baked, they are sprayed with vegetable oil after baking and have a fat content similar to fried products.
- Under the Federal Trademark Dilution Act (FTDA), Hasbro was able to stop the use of the Internet name candyland.com for a sexually explicit website because the site would injure the value of its registered trademark Candy Land (a line of children's games). Courts have generally held that only the owners of registered trademarks can use them as website addresses.

example, this warning was ruled inadequate in a product liability case involving a worker who was injured while inflating a truck tire:

Always inflate tire in safety cage or use a portable lock ring guard. Use a clip-on type air chuck with remote valve so that operator can stand clear during tire inflation.

The court held that (1) "there is a duty to warn *foreseeable* users of all hidden dangers" and (2) "in view of the unskilled or semiskilled nature of the work and the existence of many in the workforce who do not read English, warnings *in the form of symbols* might have been appropriate since the employee's ability to take care of himself was limited."[59] Thus, marketers must often go to considerable lengths to provide messages that the relevant audience will interpret correctly.

Fortunately, marketers are developing considerable knowledge on how to effectively present difficult messages about such issues as product risks, nutrition, and affirmative disclosures (see Chapter 8). In addition, consumer research is being used by both marketers and the courts to determine if an ad is misleading.[60]

Regulating the explicit verbal content of ads is difficult. Regulating the more subtle meanings implied by the visual content of ads is much more difficult.[61] For example, some are critical of beer advertisements that portray active young adults in groups having fun and consuming beer. These critics contend that the visual message of these ads is that alcohol consumption is the appropriate way for young adults to be popular and have fun. Recently, both government and business self-regulatory groups have begun regulating visual communications.

- The FTC recently challenged ads for Beck's beer that featured young adults drinking on a sailing ship. It charged that the ads promoted unsafe marine conduct.
- The NAD required Balance Bar to drop all claims referring to clinical studies and *visuals of physicians* in its advertising after ruling that its formula was not proved to be "clinically effective for the general population."

Corrective advertising is *advertising run by a firm to cause consumers to unlearn inaccurate information they acquired as a result of the firm's earlier advertising.* Three examples of corrective advertising messages follow:

- "Do you recall some of our past messages saying that Domino sugar gives you strength, energy, and stamina? Actually, Domino is not a special or unique source of strength, energy, and stamina. No sugar is, because what you need is a balanced diet and plenty of rest and exercise."
- "If you've wondered what some of our earlier advertising meant when we said Ocean Spray cranberry juice cocktail has more food energy than orange juice or tomato juice, let us make it clear: we didn't mean vitamins and minerals. Food energy means calories. Nothing more.

   "Food energy is important at breakfast since many of us may not get enough calories, or food energy, to get off to a good start. Ocean Spray cranberry juice cocktail helps because it contains more food energy than most other breakfast drinks.

   "And Ocean Spray cranberry juice cocktail gives you and your family vitamin C plus a great wake-up taste. It's . . . the other breakfast drink."
- Sugar Information, Inc.: "Do you recall the messages we brought you in the past about sugar? How something with sugar in it before meals could help you curb your appetite? We hope you didn't get the idea that our little diet tip was any magic formula for losing weight. Because there are no tricks or shortcuts; the whole diet subject is very complicated. Research hasn't established that consuming sugar before meals will contribute to weight reduction or even keep you from gaining weight."

Although the effectiveness of corrective advertising has been debated, the FTC considers it a useful tool in protecting the public. Likewise, firms injured by the false claims of competitors often request it as a remedy (Power Bar has requested the FTC to require Balance Bar to run corrective ads concerning the clinical claims described earlier). However, a recent court ruling has challenged the conditions under which the FTC can require corrective advertising. Significantly, the challenge centers on how strongly the false impression must be learned before corrective advertising is necessary to erase it.[62]

Adequacy of Consumer Information   It is important that consumers have not only accurate information but adequate information as well. To ensure information adequacy, a number of laws have been passed, such as the federal truth-in-lending legislation.

Nutritional labeling has been required for years and was significantly revised in 1990. Research findings on the impact of such labels are mixed, but the labels do provide valuable information to many consumers. A consistent stream of consumer behavior research since these rules were enacted has uncovered a number of potential improvements in the manner in which the information should be presented. Unfortunately, as with many such programs, those who are relatively disadvantaged in terms of education and income are least able to use this type of information.[63]

Marketers, consumer groups, and public officials would like consumers to have all the information they need to make sound choices. One approach is to provide all potentially relevant information. This approach is frequently recommended by regulatory agencies and is required for some product categories such as drugs. Problems with this approach can arise, however. For example, a relatively simple, one-page advertisement for Flonase nasal spray required the second full page of small type shown in Illustration 20–4 telling of dosage, precautions, and warnings in order to comply with federal full-disclosure regulations.

The assumption behind the full-disclosure approach is that each consumer will utilize those specific information items required for the particular decision. Unfortunately, consumers frequently do not react in this manner, particularly for low-involvement purchases.

ILLUSTRATION 20–4

Do consumers benefit from this level of required information, or does information overload set in?

Instead, they may experience *information overload* (see Chapter 8, page 288) and ignore all or most of the available data. For example,

A federal act required banks belonging to the Federal Reserve to explain to their customers the detailed protections built into money transfer systems available in electronic banking. Thus, Northwestern National Bank of Minneapolis was forced to create and mail a pamphlet explaining Amended Regulation E to its 120,000 customers. At a cost of $69,000 the bank created and mailed the 4,500-word pamphlet.

In 100 of the pamphlets, the bank placed a special paragraph that offered the reader $10 just for finding that paragraph. The pamphlets were mailed in May and June. As of August, not one person had claimed the money![64]

Examine Illustration 20–4 carefully. Would you read this ad? Many marketers claim that such ads add to the costs of advertising and therefore reduce the available consumer information without an offset in consumer benefit.[65] Many consumer advocates agree that the current approach is not meeting the needs of consumers.

A new issue confronting marketers and regulators is disclosure in Internet advertising. Disclosure involves providing relevant qualifiers to advertising claims such as "limited to stock on hand," or "available at participating outlets only." The FTC requires disclosures to be "clear and conspicuous" and this standard has been translated into clear guidelines for print, television, and radio ads. What constitutes "clear and conspicuous" on the Internet. Is it a banner? A pop-up? Does it need a frame around it? This is yet another area where knowledge of consumer information processing and consumer research can help produce effective regulatory guidelines.

Product Issues

Consumer groups have two major concerns with products—*Are they safe?* and *Are they environmentally sound?* A variety of federal and state agencies are involved in ensuring that products are safe to use. The most important are the Food and Drug Administration and the Consumer Product Safety Commission. Product safety is generally not a controversial issue. However, it is impossible to remove all risk from products.

Should tricycles be banned? Accidents involving tricycles are a major cause of injury to young children. Manufacturers, consumer groups, and individuals differ on where the line should be drawn and who should draw it. Some feel that tricycles should indeed be banned. Others feel that parents should decide if their children should ride tricycles. However, both would agree that information on both the risks of tricycle riding and ways of reducing the risk should be made available to purchasers, though there is disagreement on who should make the information available and how it should be made available. Of course, tricycles represent only one of many products subject to such a debate.

We examined consumers' desires for environmentally sound products in some detail in Chapter 3. As indicated there, many consumers want products whose production, use, and disposition produce minimal environmental harm. Many marketers are striving to produce such products. Nonetheless, many consumer groups want regulations requiring faster movement in this area and required, rather than voluntary, compliance with environmental standards.

Potentially injurious products such as guns, tobacco products, and alcoholic beverages are subject to a wide variety of regulations at the federal, state, and even city level. A recent controversy in this area is the introduction of "alcoholic lemonades." These beverages are bottled like beer or soft drinks, often have cartoon character labels, contain about the same amount of alcohol as beer, but are flavored like lemonade, which almost completely masks the alcohol taste (see Illustration 20–5).

Critics contend that the drinks are designed to hook teenagers on alcohol. According to one 16-year-old girl,

> They taste just like lemonade. That's why we drink them. You can drink them so fast. They just go right down.[66]

Should such products be banned? Attempts are being made to restrict the types of labels they can have as well as the way they can be advertised. *How would you deal with this issue?*

ILLUSTRATION 20–5

What regulations, if any, are appropriate for this controversial product category?

Pricing Issues

Consumer groups want prices that are fair (generally defined as competitively determined) and accurately stated (contain no hidden charges). The FTC is the primary federal agency involved in regulating pricing activities.

Perhaps the most controversial pricing area today is the use of reference prices. An **external reference price** is *a price provided by the manufacturer or retailer in addition to the actual current price of the product.* Such terms as "compare at $X," "usually $X," "suggested retail price $Y—our price only $X" are common ways of presenting reference prices (see Chapter 17, page 602). The concern arises when the reference price is one at which no or few sales actually occur. Most states and the federal government have regulations concerning the use of reference prices, but they are difficult to enforce. Given the history of abuse of reference prices, it is not surprising that many consumers are skeptical of them.

SUMMARY

Marketing to children is a major concern to regulators and consumer groups. A major reason for this concern is evidence based on Piaget's theory of cognitive development that children are not able to fully comprehend commercial messages. This had led to rules issued by both the Federal Trade Commission and the Children's Advertising Review Unit (CARU) of the National Advertising Division of the Council of Better Business Bureaus. These rules focus mainly on being sure that commercials are clearly separated from the program content and that the words and pictures in the commercials do not mislead children having limited cognitive skills.

In addition to concerns about children's comprehension of advertisements, there is concern about the effect of the content of commercials on children. The extensive advertising of high-fat and high-sugar products raises a concern about its effect on the health of children. Since children watch a substantial amount of prime-time television, there is also a danger that ads aimed at adults will inspire children to take inappropriate actions. In addition, there is concern that the enormous amount of advertising that children view will lead to values that are overly materialistic.

There are a number of marketing activities aimed at children other than television advertising that cause concerns. Kids' clubs with a strong emphasis on sales to children have been strongly criticized. Corporate programs that place strong sales messages in "educational" materials supplied to schools have also come under attack. Children's advocates are now particularly concerned about marketing to children on the Internet. The federal government has passed legislation to protect children's online privacy (Children's Online Privacy Protection Act). CARU also has guidelines on this topic.

Regulators and business alike are also concerned that adults receive accurate and adequate information about products. The cumulative impact of numerous ads focusing on narcissistic values and product ownership on society's values is a controversial issue.

The regulators and responsible marketers want consumers to have sufficient, adequate information to make sound purchase decisions. Attempts to regulate the amount of information provided sometimes overlook information overload and are not effective.

The focus of consumer concern and regulation of products is twofold: Are they safe? and Are they environmentally sound?

Concern with pricing is that prices be fair and accurately presented in a manner that allows comparison across brands.

KEY TERMS

Children's Advertising Review
 Unit (CARU) 711
Children's Online Privacy
 Protection Act (COPPA) 721

Corrective advertising 727
External reference price 731

Kids' clubs 717

INTERNET EXERCISES

1. Visit the Federal Trade Commission website (www.ftc.gov). Describe the issues and concerns the FTC is concerned with in terms of consumer protection and marketing.

2. Visit the CARU website (www.caru.org). Examine the past six months' news releases. Place each case in a category (such as privacy protection). What do you conclude?

3. Visit the Center for Media Education website (www.cme.org/cme). What are its current concerns with respect to marketing and the following?
 a. Children
 b. Adults

4. Visit the TrustE website (www.truste.com). Evaluate its approach to privacy. Will such a seal increase consumer confidence in a site? Justify your response.

5. Visit one of the sites listed below. Evaluate the effectiveness of the site in terms of marketing to children and the degree to which it meets the requirements of COPPA (Table 20–5).
 a. www.disney.com
 b. www.barbie.com
 c. www.oscar-mayer.com
 d. www.gijoe.com

6. Visit three companies' websites. Evaluate their privacy statements and policy.

7. Visit the Better Business Bureau website (www.bbb.org). Describe the issues the FTC is concerned with in terms of consumer protection and marketing to adults.

8. Visit an adult site such as Playboy.com. How hard would it be for a 10-year-old to access inappropriate content on this site?

DDB NEEDHAM LIFESTYLE DATA ANALYSES

1. What characterizes individuals who feel there is too much sex in advertising? What are the marketing implications of this? What are the regulatory implications of this?

2. What characterizes individuals who refuse to buy a brand whose advertising they dislike? What are the marketing implications of this? What are the regulatory implications of this?

3. What characterizes individuals who feel that big companies are just out for themselves? What are the marketing implications of this? What are the regulatory implications of this?

REVIEW QUESTIONS

1. What are the major concerns in marketing to children?

2. What are the two main issues concerning children's ability to comprehend advertising messages?

3. What is *CARU?* What does it do? What are some of its rules?

4. What are the major concerns about the *content* of commercial messages targeting children?

5. What are the issues concerning the impact of advertising on children's health and safety?

6. What are the issues concerning the impact of advertising on children's values?

7. What are the concerns associated with kids' clubs sponsored by commercial firms?

8. How do firms advertise in the classroom? What issues does this raise? What is Consumers Union's recommendation concerning advertising in the classroom?

9. Why are consumer advocates worried about marketing to kids on the Internet?

10. Describe the key provisions of *COPPA.*

11. How effective was COPPA in its first year?

12. What are the major concerns with marketing communications targeting adults?

13. What are the issues concerning the impact of advertising on adults' *values?*

14. What are the concerns with *consumer information accuracy?*

15. What are the concerns with *consumer information adequacy?*

16. What is *information overload?*

17. What is *corrective advertising?*

18. What are the major consumerism issues with respect to products?

19. What are the major consumerism issues with respect to prices?

20. What is *unit pricing?*

21. What is a *reference price?* What is the concern with reference prices?

DISCUSSION QUESTIONS

22. A television advertisement for General Mills' Total cereal made the following claim: "It would take 16 ounces of the leading natural cereal to equal the vitamins in 1 ounce of fortified Total." The Center for Science in the Public Interest filed a petition against General Mills claiming that the advertisement is deceptive. It was the center's position that the claim overstated Total's nutritional benefits because the cereal is not 16 times higher in other factors important to nutrition.

    a. Is the claim misleading? Justify your answer.

    b. How should the FTC proceed in cases such as this?

    c. What are the implications of cases such as this for marketing management?

23. Turkey ham looks like ham and tastes like ham but it contains no pork; it is all turkey. A nationwide survey of consumers showed that most believed the meat product contained both turkey and ham. The USDA approved this label based on a dictionary definition for the term *ham:* the thigh cut of meat from the hind leg of any animal. Discuss how consumers processed information

concerning this product and used this information in purchasing this product. (One court ruled the label to be misleading but was overruled by a higher court.)

a. Is the label misleading?

b. How should the FTC proceed in such cases?

24. How much and what type, if any, advertising should be allowed on television programs aimed at children of the following ages?

a. Under 6

b. 6 to 9

c. 10 to 12

25. Should there be special rules governing the advertising of food and snack products to children?

26. Does advertising influence children's values? What can the FTC or CARU do to ensure that positive values are promoted? Be precise in your response.

27. What rules, if any, should govern kids' clubs?

28. What rules, if any, should govern marketing to kids on the Internet?

29. What rules, if any, should govern advertising and promotional messages presented in the classroom?

30. Does advertising influence or reflect a society's values?

31. Do you agree that beer advertisements portraying groups of active young adults having fun while consuming beer teach people that the way to be popular and have fun is to consume alcohol?

32. Respond to the questions in Consumer Insight 20–1.

33. Do you think corrective advertising works? Evaluate the three corrective messages described in the text.

34. "Since riding tricycles is a major cause of accidental injury to young children, the product should be banned." State and defend your position on this issue (the first part of the statement is true).

35. How, if at all, would you regulate the new lemonade-flavored alcoholic beverages?

36. To what extent, if at all, do you use nutrition labels to guide your purchases? Why?

37. Do you believe reference prices generally reflect prices at which substantial amounts of the product are normally sold? Does this vary by store, season, or other circumstances?

APPLICATION ACTIVITIES

38. Watch two hours of Saturday morning children's programming on a commercial channel (not public broadcasting). Note how many commercials are run. What products are involved? What are the major themes? Would hundreds of hours of viewing these commercials over the course of several years have any impact on children's values or behaviors?

39. Interview a child 2 to 4 years of age, one between 5 and 7, and one between 8 and 10. Determine their understanding of the selling intent and techniques of television commercials.

40. Interview a child who belongs to one or more kids' clubs. Describe the club and the child's reactions to it. Determine the extent to which

the club is successful in selling things to the child.

41. Interview two grade school teachers and get their responses to material provided by corporations and Consumers Union's proposed rules for such materials.

42. Repeat Question 38 for prime-time television and adults.

43. Find and copy or describe an ad that you feel is misleading. Explain why.

44. Visit a large supermarket. Identify the best and worst breakfast cereal focused on children considering both cost and nutrition. What do you conclude?

REFERENCES

1. J. DeCoursey, "Klein's Apology Wearing Thin," *Advertising Age,* September 4, 1995, p. 35; J. Brady, "Fueling the Heat," *Advertising Age,* September 4, 1995, p. 1; P. Sloan and J. DeCoursey, "Gov't Hot on Trail of Calvin Klein Ads," *Adver-* *tising Age,* September 11, 1995, p. 1; A. Sachs, "Kiddie Porn or Bad Taste," *Advertising Age,* September 18, 1995, p. 52; and C. Miller, "Sexy Sizzle Backfires," *Marketing News,* September 25, 1996, pp. 1–2.

2. Miller, "Sexy Sizzle Backfires," p. 2.

3. For an overview of this area, see S. Bandyopadhyay, G. Kindra, and L. Sharp, "Is Television Advertising Good for Children," *International Journal of Advertising* 20, no. 1 (2001), pp. 89–116.

4. See D. R. John, "Consumer Socialization of Children," *Journal of Consumer Research,* December 1999, pp. 183–209.

5. See M. C. Martin, "Children's Understanding of the Intent of Advertising," *Journal of Public Policy & Marketing,* Fall 1997, pp. 205–16.

6. L. Carlson, R. N. Laczniak, and D. D. Muehling, "Understanding Parental Concern about Toy-Based Programming," *Journal of Current Issues and Research in Advertising,* Fall 1994, pp. 59–72.

7. M. A. Stutts and G. G. Hunnicutt, "Can Young Children Understand Disclaimers?" *Journal of Advertising,* no. 1 (1987), pp. 41–46.

8. R. H. Kolbe and D. D. Muehling, "An Investigation of the Fine Print in Children's Television Advertising," *Journal of Current Issues and Research in Advertising,* Fall 1995, pp. 77–95; and D. D. Muehling and R. H. Kolbe, "A Comparison of Children's and Prime-Time Fine-Print Advertising Disclosure Practices," *Journal of Advertising,* Fall 1998, pp. 37–47.

9. "Trendmasters Addresses CARU Concerns," CARU, Council of Better Business Bureaus, October 3, 2001.

10. "Nabisco Puts Safety First in TV Ads," CARU, Council of Better Business Bureaus, October 4, 2000.

11. "Rose Art Industries, Inc., and Hasbro Participate in CARU Self-Regulatory Forum," CARU, Council of Better Business Bureaus, February 22, 2000.

12. S. W. Colford, "FTC Hits Galoob, Agency for Ads," *Advertising Age,* December 10, 1990, p. 62.

13. "Skechers USA, Inc. Appeals CARU Decision," CARU, Council of Better Business Bureaus, April 10, 2002.

14. See J. B. Cohen, "Playing to Win"; D. M. Krugman and K. W. King, "Teenage Exposure to Cigarette Advertising in Popular Consumer Magazines"; and K. J. Kelly et al., "The Use of Human Models and Cartoon Characters in Magazine Advertisements for Cigarettes, Beer, and Nonalcoholic Beverages," all in *Journal of Public Policy & Marketing,* Fall 2000, pp. 155–67, 183–88, and 189–200.

15. "B-M Drops Spots after Query by NAD," *Advertising Age,* April 20, 1981, p. 10.

16. See C. Preston, "The Unintended Effects of Advertising upon Children," *International Journal of Advertising* 18, no. 3 (1999), pp. 363–76.

17. "Ferrero U.S.A. Cooperates with CARU on Comparative Claims," CARU, Council of Better Business Bureaus, December 20, 2001.

18. D. Halonen, "Group Seeks Curbs on Kids Advertising," *Advertising Age,* October 23, 2000, p. 93.

19. E. DeNitto, "Fast-Food Ads Come under Fire," *Advertising Age,* February 14, 1994, p. S-14.

20. H. Clinton, "FTC Action," *Advertising Age,* October 9, 2000, p. 58. For an opposing view, see R. Bergler, "The Effects of Commercial Advertising on Children," *International Journal of Advertising* 18, no. 4 (1999), pp. 411–25.

21. Clinto, "FTC Action."

22. R. Gardyn, "Mouse-Trapping the Student Market," *American Demographics,* May 2000, pp. 30–34.

23. See *Selling America's Kids* (Yonkers, NY: Consumers Union Educational Services, 1990), p. 14.

24. M. M. Cardonna, "Young Girls Targeted by Makeup Companies," *Advertising Age,* November 27, 2000, p. 15.

25. M. Scott, "Girls Clamoring for Grown-Up Shoe Styles," *Marketing News,* November 19, 2001, p. 25.

26. M. Irvine, "More Young Children Fret over Body Image," *Eugene Register Guard,* July 23, 2001, p. 1.

27. S. W. Colford, "Top Kid TV Offender: Premiums," *Advertising Age,* April 29, 1991, p. 52.

28. See K. Anders, "Marketing and Policy Considerations for Violent Video Games," *Journal of Public Policy & Marketing,* Fall 1999, pp. 270–3; I. Teinowitz, "FTC Report Refuels Debate on Violent Entertainment," April 30, 2001, p. 4; I. Teinowitz, "Violence Revisited," *Advertising Age,* December 3, 2001, p. 3; and I. Teinowitz, "Entertainment Gets a Pass," *Advertising Age,* December 10, 2001, p. 16.

29. C. Miller, "Marketers Hoping Kids Will Join Club," *Marketing News,* January 31, 1994, pp. 1–2.

30. See *Selling America's Kids,* p. 15.

31. See Miller, "Marketers Hoping Kids Will Join Club," p. 2.

32. See J. E. Brand and B. S. Greenberg, "Commercials in the Classroom," *Journal of Advertising Research,* January 1994, pp. 18–27.

33. J. Schwartz, "Schools for Sale?" *Marketing News,* August 17, 1998, p. 12.

34. C. Miller, "Marketers Find a Seat in the Classroom," *Marketing News,* June 20, 1994, p. 2.

35. B. Bosch, "What's for Lunch? Coupons," *Advertising Age,* November 27, 1995, p. 3.

36. See S. Thompson, "Pepsi Hits High Note with Students," *Advertising Age,* October 9, 2000, p. 30; and S. Jarvis, "Lesson Plans," *Marketing News,* June 18, 2001, p. 1.

37. This section is based on K. Montgomery and S. Pasnik, *Web of Deception* (Washington, DC: Center for Media Education, 1996).

38. I. Teinowitz, "FTC Chief Asks Congress to Ensure Privacy on Web," *Advertising Age,* June 8, 1998, p. 53.

39. "Many Kids' Web Sites Continuing to Collect Personal Information," Center for Media Education, July 19, 1999.

40. *Children's Online Privacy Protection Act—The First Year* (Washington, DC: Center for Media Education, April 2001), p. 4.

41. "Alta Vista Makes Changes," CARU, Council of Better Business Bureaus, February 14, 2001.

42. "CARU Refers Fansite of Singer Pink to Federal Trade Commission," CARU, Council of Better Business Bureaus, April 10, 2002.

43. "Scan-Command.Com Works with CARU," CARU, Council of Better Business Bureaus, April 17, 2002.

44. See K. B. Sheehan and M. G. Hoy, "Flaming, Complaining, and Abstaining," *Journal of Advertising,* Fall 1999, pp. 37–51;

K. B. Sheehan, "An Investigation of Gender Differences in On-Line Privacy Concerns," *Journal of Interactive Marketing,* Autumn 1999, pp. 24–38; E. M. Caudill and P. E. Murphy, "Consumer Online Privacy"; J. Phelps, G. Nowak, and E. Ferrell, "Privacy Concerns and Consumer Willingness to Provide Personal Information"; and K. B. Sheehan and M. G. Hoy, "Dimensions of Privacy Concern among Online Consumers," all in *Journal of Public Policy & Marketing,* Spring 2000, pp. 7–19, 27–41, and 62–73. See also *Journal of Public Policy & Marketing,* Spring 2000, pp. 27–41; and K. B. Sheehan and T. W. Gleason, "Online Privacy," *Journal of Current Issues and Research in Advertising,* Spring 2001, pp. 31–41; P. Paul, "Mixed Signals"; and R. Gardyn, "Swap Meet," both in *American Demographics,* July 2001, pp. 47 and 51–55; J. E. Phelps, G. D'Souza, and G. J. Nowak, "Antecedents and Consequences of Consumer Privacy Concerns," *Journal of Interactive Marketing,* Autumn 2001, pp. 2–17.

45. Based on R. Pitofsky, "Privacy Online," testimony before the U.S. Senate, May 25, 2000; and T. J. Muris, "Protecting Consumers' Privacy: 2002 and Beyond," speech at the Privacy 2001 Conference, both available at www.ftc.org.

46. See B. G. Englis, M. R. Solomon, and R. D. Ashmore, "Beauty *before* the Eyes of Beholders," *Journal of Advertising,* June 1994, pp. 49–64; C. R. Wiles, J. A. Wiles, and A. Tjernlund, "The Ideology of Advertising," *Journal of Advertising Research,* May, 1996, pp. 57–66; M. C. Martin and J. W. Gentry, "Stuck in the Model Trap," *Journal of Advertising,* Summer 1997, pp. 19–33; and M. K. Hogg, M. Bruce, and K. Hough, "Female Images in Advertising," *International Journal of Advertising* 18, no. 4 (1999), pp. 445–73.

47. S. Burton, R. G. Netemeyer, and D. R. Lichtenstein, "Gender Differences for Appearance-Related Attitudes and Behaviors," *Journal of Public Policy & Marketing,* Fall 1994, pp. 60–75.

48. R. Gustafson, M. Popovich, and S. Thompson, "Subtle Ad Images Threaten Girls More," *Marketing News,* June 4, 2001, p. 12.

49. For research in these areas, see R. W. Pollay and S. Lysonski, "In the Eye of the Beholder," *Journal of International Consumer Marketing* 6, no. 2 (1993), pp. 25–43; D. Walsh, "Safe Sex in Advertising," *American Demographics,* April 1994, pp. 24–30; and R. H. Kolbe and D. Muehling, "Gender Roles and Children's Television Advertising," *Journal of Current Issues and Research in Advertising,* Spring 1995, pp. 49–64.

50. C. Rubel, "Marketers Giving Better Treatment to Females," *Marketing News,* April 22, 1996, p. 10.

51. See L. Langmeyer, "Advertising Images of Mature Adults," *Journal of Current Issues and Research in Advertising,* Fall 1993, pp. 81–91; C. R. Taylor and J. Y. Lee, "Not in *Vogue,*" *Journal of Public Policy & Marketing,* Fall 1994, pp. 239–45; T. H. Stevenson and P. E. McIntyre, "A Comparison of the Portrayal and Frequency of Hispanics and Whites in English Language Television Advertising"; and M. T. Elliott, "Differences in the Portrayal of Blacks," both in *Journal of Current Issues and Research in Advertising,* Spring 1995, pp. 65–86; J. M. Bristor, R. G. Lee, and M. R. Hunt, "Race and Ideology,"

Journal of Public Policy & Marketing, Spring 1995, pp. 48–59; E. J. Wilson and A. Biswas, "The Use of Black Models in Specialty Catalogs," *Journal of Direct Marketing,* Autumn 1995, pp. 47–56; and K. Karande and A. Grbavac, "Acculturation and the Use of Asian Models in Print Advertisements," *Enhancing Knowledge Development in Marketing* (Chicago: American Marketing Association, 1996), pp. 347–52.

52. See L. J. Shrum, "Television and Persuasion," *Psychology & Marketing,* March 1999, pp. 119–40.

53. See A. Simonson and M. B. Holbrook, "Permissible Puffery versus Actionable Warranty in Advertising and Salestalk," *Journal of Public Policy & Marketing,* Fall 1993, pp. 216–33.

54. "Diving Association May Not Use 'Seal of Approval' Unless Based on Tests," *FTC New Summary,* May 21, 1982, p. 1. See R. F. Beltramini and E. R. Stafford, "Comprehension and Perceived Believability of Seals of Approval Information in Advertising," *Journal of Advertising,* September 1993, pp. 4–13.

55. J. Pollack, "Arm & Hammer Brand Fights Toothpaste Rivals," *Advertising Age,* July 27, 1998, p. 2.

56. See J.-N. Kapferer, "Brand Confusion," *Psychology & Marketing,* September 1995, pp. 551–68; and D. J. Howard, R. A. Kerin, and C. Gengler, "The Effects of Brand Name Similarity on Brand Source Confusion," *Journal of Public Policy & Marketing,* Fall 2000, pp. 250–64.

57. "Bayer & McNeil Participate in NAD Self-Regulatory Process," CARU, Council of Better Business Bureaus, July 8, 2002.

58. C. A. Cole and G. J. Gaeth, "Cognitive and Age-Related Differences in the Ability to Use Nutritional Information in a Complex Environment," *Journal of Marketing Research,* May 1990, pp. 175–84; and W. Mueller, "Who Reads the Label?" *American Demographics,* January 1991, pp. 36–40.

59. B. Reid, "Adequacy of Symbolic Warnings," *Marketing News,* October 25, 1985, p. 3.

60. M. L. Retsky, "Survey Research Is Useful in False Advertising Cases," *Marketing News,* April 27, 1998, p. 8; and M. L. Retsky, "Misleading Ads Could Be as Litigious as Outright Lies," *Marketing News,* August 3, 1998, p. 5.

61. See G. V. Johar, "Consumer Involvement and Deception from Implied Advertising Campaigns," *Journal of Marketing Research,* August 1995, pp. 267–79.

62. I. Teinowitz, "FTC Faces Test of Ad Power," *Advertising Age,* March 30, 1998, p. 26.

63. See A. L. Levy, S. B. Fein, and R. E. Shucker, "Performance Characteristics of Seven Nutrition Label Formats"; G. T. Ford, M. Hastak, A. Mitra, and D. J. Ringold, "Can Consumers Interpret Nutrition Information in the Presence of a Health Claim?"; C. Moorman, "A Quasi Experiment to Assess the Consumer and Informational Determinants of Nutrition Information Processing Activities"; and M. J. Barone, R. L. Rose, K. C. Manning, and P. W. Miniard, "Another Look at the Impact of Reference Information on Consumer Impressions of Nutrition Information," all in *Journal of Public Policy & Marketing,*

Spring 1996, pp. 1–62; A. Mitra et al., "Can the Educationally Disadvantaged Interpret the FDA-Mandated Nutrition Facts Panel," *Journal of Public Policy & Marketing,* Spring 1999, pp. 106–17; J. A. Garretson and S. Burton, "Effects of Nutrition Facts Panel Values, Nutrition Claims, and Health Claims," *Journal of Public Policy & Marketing,* Fall 2000, pp. 213–27; and G. Baltas, "The Effects of Nutrition Information on Consumer Choice," *Journal of Advertising Research,* March 2001, pp. 57–63.

64. "$10 Sure Thing," *Time,* August 4, 1980, p. 51. See also M. A. Eastlick, R. Feinberg, and C. Trappey, "Information Overload in Mail Catalog Shopping," *Journal of Direct Marketing,* Autumn 1993, pp. 14–19. For a different explanation, see Y. Ganzach and P. Ben-Or, "Information Overload, Decreasing Marginal Responsiveness, and the Estimation of Nonmonotonic Relationships in Direct Marketing," *Journal of Direct Marketing,* Spring 1996, pp. 7–12.

65. See M. Wilkie, "Rx Marketers 'Test' FDA Guides on Print DTC Ads," *Advertising Age,* April 6, 1998, p. 18.

66. D. Leonhardt, "A Little Booze for the Kiddies," *Business Week,* September 23, 1996, p. 158.

Cases

Below is Walt Disney Internet Group's (WDIG) privacy policy for children under 13 years old.

1. What types of information are WDIG sites collecting about kids who are 12 and younger?

Children can surf Disney.com or other WDIG sites, view content, and play some games without any personally identifiable information being collected. In addition, we occasionally do host some moderated chat rooms where no personally identifiable information is collected or posted. However, in some areas it is necessary to collect personally identifiable information from kids to allow participation in an activity (like entering a contest) or to communicate with our community (via e-mail or message boards).

WDIG believes it is good policy not to collect more personally identifiable information from kids 12 and younger than is necessary for them to participate in our online activities. In addition, be aware that all sites that are targeted to children 12 and younger are prohibited by law from collecting more information than they need.

The only personally identifiable information we collect from kids is first name, parent's e-mail address, and child's birth date. We collect birth date to validate a Guest's age. We may also collect personal information, like a pet's name, to help Guests remember their Log-in Name and Password if they forget them.

We also allow parents to request at any time that the information collected about their child be removed from our database. If you would like to deactivate your child's account, please send an e-mail message to ms_support@help.go.com with your child's Log-in Name and Password requesting that the account be cancelled.

2. How does WDIG use and share the personally identifiable information that has been collected?

No information collected from Guests 12 and younger is used for any marketing or promotional purposes whatsoever, either inside or outside Walt Disney Internet Group's family of sites.

The information collected about kids 12 and younger is used only by WDIG websites to provide services (such as calendars) or to conduct some games or contests. Although Guests 12 and younger may be allowed to participate in some contests where information is collected, notification and prizes are sent to the parents' or guardians' e-mail address provided during the initial registration process. Publication of contest winners' full names, ages, or images for individuals 12 and younger require parental or guardian consent. Sometimes a nonidentifiable version of a child's name will be published. In those circumstances, parents may not be contacted again for permission.

We do not allow kids 12 and younger to participate in unmoderated chat rooms.

We will give out personal information about kids if required by law, for example, to comply with a court order or subpoena; to enforce our Terms of Service, or site or game rules; or to protect the safety and security of Guests and our sites.

3. Does WDIG notify parents about the collection of information on kids 12 and younger?

Any time children 12 and younger register with us, we send an e-mail notification to their parent or guardian. In addition, we require parents to give express permission before we will allow their children to use e-mail, message boards, and other features where personally identifiable information can be made public to the Internet and shared with users of all ages.

We also give parents 48 hours to refuse any registrations kids make in order to play games and contests. If we don't hear back, we assume it's OK for a child to be registered with us. Once a child has registered, he or she will be allowed to enter any future registration-based games and contests, and parents aren't notified again. In this instance, we use the information collected only to notify parents when a child has won a game or contest. We don't use this information for any other purpose.

4. How do parents access information about their kids?
Here are three methods to review the information that has been collected about children who are 12 and younger.

1. When parents give their children access to interactive features like message boards, they are required to establish a family account. Once a family account is established, the primary account holder can review the personally identifiable information of all family member accounts including a child's. You can access this information by logging in to your family account at the Your Account home page.
2. If you are not already a member of any of the WDIG sites, you can review your child's personally identifiable information by logging in to your child's account at the Member Services home page. You will need to have your child's member name and password. There are instructions on the Your Account home page to help you recover your child's password if they've forgotten it.

You can also contact Customer Service to view the information that has been collected from or about your child by sending an e-mail to ms_support@help.go.com. If you have not yet established a family account, you will need to have your child's user name and password. Please include information (child's member name, parent e-mail address) in the e-mail that will help us identify your child's account so we can assist you with your inquiry or request.

5. What type of security does WDIG provide?
The importance of security for all personally identifiable information associated with our guests is of utmost concern to us. WDIG takes technical, contractual, administrative, and physical security steps to protect all visitors' information. When you provide credit card information, we use secure socket layer (SSL) encryption to protect it. There are some things that you can do to help protect the security of your information as well. For instance, never give out your Password, since this is what is used to access all of your account information. Also remember to sign out of your account and close your browser window when you finish surfing the Web so that other people using the same computer won't have access to your information.

6. How will WDIG notify parents if this privacy policy changes?
If WDIG changes this privacy policy, we will notify parents via e-mail.

7. Whom do I contact with questions or concerns about this privacy policy?
If you need further assistance, please send an e-mail with your questions or comments to ms_support@help.go.com
write us at:
Member Services
Walt Disney Internet Group
506 2nd Avenue
Suite 2100
Seattle, WA 98104
or call us at (509) 742-4698*
Walt Disney Internet Group is a licensee of the TRUSTe Privacy Program. If you believe that WDIG has not responded to your inquiry or your inquiry has not been satisfactorily addressed, please contact TRUSTe www.truste.org/users/users_watchdog.html.

Discussion Question
1. Evaluate this privacy policy.

*You must be 18 or have the permission of your parent or guardian to dial this number.

6-2 Safer Cigarettes?

In November 2001, Brown & Williamson Tobacco placed Advance cigarettes into Indianapolis stores for a sales test. Ads supporting the brand feature part of a man or woman's face focusing on one clear eye. The headline is "New ADVANCE . . . A step in the right direction." The tagline is "All of the taste . . . Less of the toxins." The text credits the toxin reduction to a "revolutionary new filter design," and a "patented new method for growing tobacco." The text again states "Less toxins and great taste." In addition to the required Surgeon General's warning, the ads contain a boxed statement: "There is no such thing as a safe cigarette, nor is there enough medical information to know if Advance with less toxins will lower health risks." This statement is also on the back of the package.

There are four views of the likely impact of this product and its message. Brown & Williamson obviously feels it meets a market need. It uses the "less toxins" claim because

> It seems to be the clearest and most impactful statement we could make of the facts that are behind Advance and the product itself. We did not want to get into polysyllabic chemical names.

One analyst feels that the tagline will backfire and remind smokers of the harmful effects of smoking:

> People are aware of the fact that when they purchase cigarettes, there are significant adverse health consequences, but it doesn't seem to be a winning proposition to remind them every time.

Mathew Myers, president of the Campaign for Tobacco-Free Kids, feels it is unethical and misleading:

> It's always a good thing to remove a known carcinogen from cigarettes, but it is irresponsible to make statements in marketing that will lead consumers to believe that the product is safer. And that's exactly what happens when a manufacturer touts a product as having fewer toxins, no matter how many disclaimers they put on it.

A final view is expressed by an analyst who sees very little demand for a safer or less toxic cigarette:

> Cigarette smokers are risk-takers. If they're truly concerned about health, they quit.

Discussion Questions

1. Which of the four positions described before is (are) most likely accurate? Why?
2. Why would consumers believe that Advance is safer if not a safe cigarette despite the disclaimer?
3. What are the ethical issues Brown & Williamson should have considered before launching this product?
4. What regulations, if any, should be applied to promoting toxin reduction in cigarettes?
5. Less educated individuals are much more likely to smoke and smoke heavily (if 100 equals an average rate of heavy smoking within a group; college graduates score 48, those who attended college are 86, those with high school degrees are 120, and those who did not graduate from high school are 151). Does this fact impose additional ethical or regulatory requirements concerning how Brown & Williamson communicates about Advance?

Source: C. B. DiPasquale, "B&W Smoke Boasts Fewer Toxins," *Advertising Age,* November 5, 2001, p. 3; "Blowing Smoke," *Advertising Age,* November 12, 2001, p. 26; B. Garfield, "Softly Lit or Blunt, 'Less Toxic' Cigarette Ads Hint at Health," *Advertising Age,* November 12, 2001; and C. B. DiPasquale, "B&W Leads Lower-Toxin Pitch," *Advertising Age,* June 24, 2002, p. S22.

Appendix A
Consumer Research Methods

In this appendix, we want to provide you with some general guidelines for conducting research on consumer behavior. While these guidelines will help you get started, a good marketing research text is indispensable if you need to conduct a consumer research project or evaluate a consumer research proposal.

SECONDARY DATA

Any research project should begin with a thorough search for existing information relevant to the project at hand. Internal data such as past studies, sales reports, and accounting records should be consulted. External data, including reports, magazines, government organizations, trade associations, marketing research firms, advertising agencies, academic journals, trade journals, and books, should be thoroughly researched.

Computer searches are fast, economical means of conducting such searches. Most university and large public libraries have computer search capabilities, as do most large firms. However, computer searches will often miss reports by trade associations and magazines. Therefore, magazines that deal with the product category or that are read by members of the relevant market should be contacted. The same is true for associations (for names and addresses, see *Encyclopedia of Associations,* Gale Research Inc.).

SAMPLING

If the specific information required is not available from secondary sources, we must gather primary data. This generally involves talking to or observing consumers. However, it could involve asking knowledgeable others, such as sales personnel, about the consumers. In either case, time and cost constraints generally preclude us from contacting every single potential consumer. Therefore, most consumer research projects require a sample—a deliberately selected portion of the larger group. This requires a number of critical decisions, as described below. Mistakes made at this point are difficult to correct later in the study. The key decisions are briefly described below.

Define the Population

The first step is to define the consumers in which we are interested. Do we want to talk to current brand users, current product-category users, or potential product-category users? Do we want to talk with the purchasers, the users, or everyone involved in the purchase process? The population as we define it must reflect the behavior on which our marketing decision will be based.

Specify the Sampling Frame

A sampling frame is a list or grouping of individuals or households that reflects the population of interest. A phone book and shoppers at a given shopping mall can each serve as a sampling frame. Perfect sampling frames contain every member of the population one time. Phone books do not have households with unlisted numbers; many people do not visit shopping malls, while others visit them frequently. This is an area in which we generally must do the best we can without expecting a perfect frame. However, we must be very alert for biases that may be introduced by imperfections in our sampling frame.

Select a Sampling Method

The major decision at this point is between a random (probability) sample and a nonrandom sample. Nonrandom samples, particularly judgment samples, can provide good results. A judgment sample involves the deliberate selection of knowledgeable consumers or individuals. For example, a firm might decide to interview the social activity officers of fraternities and sororities to estimate campus attitudes toward a carbonated wine drink aimed at the campus market. Such a sample might provide useful insights. However, it might also be biased, since such individuals are likely to have a higher level of income and be more socially active than the average student.

The most common nonrandom sample, the convenience sample, involves selecting sample members in the manner most convenient for the researcher. It is subject to many types of bias and should generally be avoided.

Random or probability samples allow some form of a random process to select members from a sample frame. It may be every third person who passes a point-of-purchase display, house addresses selected by using a table of random numbers, or telephone numbers generated randomly by a computer. If random procedures are used, we can calculate the likelihood that our sample is not representative within specified limits.

Determine Sample Size

Finally, we must determine how large a sample to talk to. If we are using random sampling, there are formulas that can help us make this decision. In general, the more diverse our population is and the more certain we want to be that we have the correct answer, the more people we will need to interview.

SURVEYS

Surveys are systematic ways of gathering information from a large number of people. They generally involve the use of a structured or semistructured questionnaire. Surveys can be administered by mail, telephone, or in person. Personal interviews generally take place in shopping malls and are referred to as mall intercept interviews.

Each approach has advantages and disadvantages. Personal interviews allow the use of complex questionnaires, product demonstrations, and the collection of large amounts of data. They can be completed in a relatively short period of time. However, they are very expensive and are subject to interviewer bias. Telephone surveys can be completed rapidly, provide good sample control (who answers the questions), and are relatively inexpensive. Substantial amounts of data can be collected, but it must be relatively simple. Interviewer bias is possible. Mail surveys take the longest to complete and must generally be rather short. They can be used to collect modestly complex data, and they are very economical. Interviewer bias is not a problem.

A major concern in survey research is nonresponse bias. In most surveys, fewer than 50 percent of those selected to participate in the study actually do participate. In telephone and personal interviews, many people are not at home or refuse to cooperate. In mail surveys, many people refuse or forget to respond.

We can increase the response rate by callbacks in telephone and home personal surveys. The callbacks should be made at different times and on different days. Monetary inducements (enclosing 25 cents or $1) increase the response rate to mail surveys, as do prenotification (a card saying that a questionnaire is coming) and reminder postcards.

If less than a 100 percent response rate is obtained, we must be concerned that those who did not respond differ from those who did. A variety of techniques are available to help us estimate the likelihood and nature of nonresponse error.

EXPERIMENTATION

Experimentation involves changing one or more variables (product features, package color, advertising theme) and observing the effect this change has on another variable (consumer attitude, repeat purchase behavior, learning). The variable(s) that is changed is called an *independent variable*. The variable(s) that may be affected is called a *dependent variable*. The objective in experimental design is to structure the situation so that any change in the dependent variable is very likely to have been caused by a change in the independent variable.

The basic tool in designing experimental studies is the use of control and treatment groups. A *treatment group* is one in which an independent variable is changed (or introduced) and the change (or lack of) in the dependent variable is noted. A *control group* is a group similar to the treatment group except that the independent variable is not altered. There are a variety of ways in which treatment and control groups can be combined to produce differing experimental designs.

In addition to selecting an appropriate experimental design, we must also develop an experimental environment. In a laboratory experiment, we carefully control for all outside influences. This generally means that we will get similar results every time we repeat a study. Thus, if we have people taste several versions of a salad dressing in our laboratory, we will probably get similar preference ratings each time the study is repeated with similar consumers (internal validity). However, this does not necessarily mean that consumers will prefer the same version at home or in a restaurant (external validity).

In a field experiment, we conduct our study in the most relevant environment possible. This often means that unusual outside influences will distort our results. However, if our results are not distorted, they should hold true in the actual market application. Thus, if we have consumers use several versions of our salad dressing in their homes, competitor actions, unusual weather, or product availability might influence their response (internal validity). However, in the absence of such unusual effects, the preferred version should be preferred if actually sold on the market.

QUESTIONNAIRE DESIGN

All surveys and many experiments use questionnaires as data collection devices. A questionnaire is simply a formalized set of questions for eliciting information. It can measure (1) behavior—past, present, or intended; (2) demographic characteristics—age, gender, income, education, occupation; (3) level of knowledge; and (4) attitudes and opinions. The process of questionnaire design is outlined in Table A–1.

TABLE A–1

Questionnaire Design Process

1. *Preliminary decisions*
   Exactly what information is required?
   Exactly who are the target respondents?
   What method of communication will be used to reach these respondents?
2. *Decisions about question content*
   Is this question really needed?
   Is this question sufficient to generate the needed information?
   Can the respondent answer the question correctly?
   Will the respondent answer the question correctly?
   Are there any external events that might bias the response to the question?
3. *Decisions about the response format*
   Can this question best be asked as an open-ended, multiple-choice, or dichotomous question?
4. *Decisions concerning question phrasing*
   Do the words used have but one meaning to all the respondents?
   Are any of the words or phrases loaded or leading in any way?
   Are there any implied alternatives in the question?
   Are there any unstated assumptions related to the question?
   Will the respondents approach the question from the frame of reference desired by the researcher?
5. *Decisions concerning the question sequence*
   Are the questions organized in a logical manner that avoids introducing errors?
6. *Decisions on the layout of the questionnaire*
   Is the questionnaire designed in a manner to avoid confusion and minimize recording errors?
7. *Pretest and revise*
   Has the final questionnaire been subjected to a thorough pretest, using respondents similar to those who will be included in the final survey?

ATTITUDE SCALES

Attitudes are frequently measured on specialized scales.

Noncomparative rating scales require the consumer to evaluate an object or an attribute of the object without directly comparing it to another object. Comparative rating scales provide a direct comparison point (a named competitor, "your favorite brand," "the ideal brand"). An example of each follows:

Noncomparative Rating Scale
How do you like the taste of Diet Pepsi?

Like it very much	Like it	Dislike it	Strongly dislike it
____	____	____	____

Comparative Rating Scale
How do you like the taste of Tom's of Maine compared to Ultra Bright?

Like it much more	Like it more	Like it about the same	Like it less	Like it much less
____	____	____	____	____

Paired comparisons involve presenting the consumer with two objects (brands, packages) at a time and requiring the selection of one of the two according to some criterion such as overall preference, taste, or color. Rank order scales require the consumer to rank a set of brands, advertisements, or features in terms of overall preference, taste, or importance. The constant sum scale is similar except it also requires the respondent to allocate 100 points among the objects. The allocation is to be done in a manner that reflects the relative preference or importance assigned each object. The semantic differential scale requires the consumer to rate an item on a number of scales bounded at each end by one of two bipolar adjectives. For example:

Honda Accord

Fast   _X_ ___ ____ ____ ____ ____ ____   Slow

Fancy   ____ ____ ____ ____ ____ _X_ ____   Plain

Large   ____ ____ ____ _X_ ____ ____ ____   Small

Inexpensive ____ ____ ____ ____ ____ _X_ ____   Expensive

The instructions indicate that the consumer is to mark the blank that best indicates how accurately one or the other term describes or fits the attitude object. The end positions indicate "extremely," the next pair in from the ends indicates "very," the middlemost pair indicates "somewhat," and the middle position indicates "neither/nor." Thus, the consumer in the example rates the Honda Accord as extremely fast, very plain, somewhat expensive, and neither large nor small.

Likert scales ask consumers to indicate a degree of agreement or disagreement with each of a series of statements related to the attitude object, such as the following:

---

1. *Macy's is one of the most attractive stores in town.*

Strongly agree	Agree	Neither agree nor disagree	Disagree	Strongly disagree
_____	_____	_____	_____	_____

2. *The service at Macy's is not satisfactory.*

Strongly agree	Agree	Neither agree nor disagree	Disagree	Strongly disagree
_____	_____	_____	_____	_____

3. *The service at a retail store is very important to me.*

Strongly agree	Agree	Neither agree nor disagree	Disagree	Strongly disagree
_____	_____	_____	_____	_____

To analyze responses to a Likert scale, each response category is assigned a numerical value. These examples could be assigned values such as Strongly agree = 1 through Strongly disagree = 5; the scoring could be reversed, or a +2 through −2 system could be used.

DEPTH INTERVIEWS

Depth interviews can involve one respondent and one interviewer, or they may involve a small group (8 to 15 respondents) and an interviewer. The latter are called focus group interviews, and the former are termed individual depth interviews or one-on-ones. Groups of four or five are often referred to as minigroup interviews. Depth interviews in general are commonly referred to as qualitative research. Individual depth interviews involve a one-to-one relationship between the interviewer and the respondent. The interviewer does not have a specific set of prespecified questions that must be asked according to the order imposed by a questionnaire. Instead, there is freedom to create questions, to probe those responses that appear relevant, and generally to try to develop the best set of data in any way practical. However, the interviewer must follow one rule: He or she must not consciously try to affect the content of the answers given by the respondent. The respondent must feel free to reply to the various questions, probes, and other, more subtle ways of encouraging responses in the manner deemed most appropriate.

Individual depth interviews are appropriate in six situations:

1. Detailed probing of an individual's behavior, attitudes, or needs is required.
2. The subject matter under discussion is likely to be of a highly confidential nature (e.g., personal investments).
3. The subject matter is of an emotionally charged or embarrassing nature.
4. Certain strong, socially acceptable norms exist (e.g., child-care) and the need to conform in a group discussion may influence responses.
5. A highly detailed (step-by-step) understanding of complicated behavior or decision-making patterns (e.g., planning the family holiday) is required.
6. The interviews are with professional people or with people on the subject of their jobs (e.g., finance directors).

Focus group interviews can be applied to (1) basic need studies for product ideas creation, (2) new-product ideas or concept exploration, (3) product-positioning studies, (4) advertising and communications research, (5) background studies on consumers' frames of reference, (6) establishment of consumer vocabulary as a preliminary step in questionnaire development, and (7) determination of attitudes and behaviors.

The standard focus group interview involves 8 to 12 individuals. Normally, the group is designed to reflect the characteristics of a particular market segment. The respondents are selected according to the relevant sampling plan and meet at a central location that generally has facilities for taping or filming the interviews. The discussion itself is led by a moderator. The competent moderator attempts to develop three clear stages in the one- to three-hour interview: (1) establish rapport with the group, structure the rules of group interaction, and set objectives; (2) attempt to provoke intense discussion in the relevant areas; and (3) attempt to summarize the group's responses to determine the extent of agreement. In general, either the moderator or a second person prepares a summary of each session after analyzing the session's transcript.

PROJECTIVE TECHNIQUES

Projective techniques are designed to measure feelings, attitudes, and motivations that consumers are unable or unwilling to reveal otherwise. They are based on the theory that the description of vague objects requires interpretation, and this interpretation can only be based on the individual's own attitudes, values, and motives.

Table 10–2 provides descriptions and examples of the more common projective techniques.

OBSERVATION

Observation can be used when (1) the behaviors of interest are public; (2) they are repetitive, frequent, or predictable; and (3) they cover a relatively brief time span. An observational study requires five decisions:

1. *Natural versus contrived situation.* Do we wait for a behavior to occur in its natural environment, or do we create an artificial situation in which it will occur?
2. *Open versus disguised observation.* To what extent are the consumers aware that we are observing their behavior?
3. *Structured versus unstructured observation.* Will we limit our observations to predetermined behaviors, or will we note whatever occurs?
4. *Direct or indirect observations.* Will we observe the behaviors themselves or merely the outcomes of the behaviors?
5. *Human or mechanical observations.* Will the observations be made mechanically or by people?

PHYSIOLOGICAL MEASURES

Physiological measures are direct observations of physical responses to a stimulus such as an advertisement. These responses may be controllable, such as eye movements, or uncontrollable, such as the galvanic skin response. Eye-tracking cameras allow researchers to determine how long a consumer looks at each element in a stimulus, such as a point-of-purchase display, ad, or package, and the sequence in which they are examined. Galvanic skin response can be measured (via a lie detector) to detect the intensity of emotional responses to ads or packages.

CONJOINT ANALYSIS

In conjoint analysis, the consumer is presented with a set of products or product descriptions in which the potential evaluative criteria vary. For example, they may be presented with the description of 24 different notebook computers that vary on four criteria. Two might be

---

Pentium 4 2.0 GHz   **Pentium 4 1.6 GHz**
Integrated modem   No modem
5.1 pounds   3.0 pounds
$2,500 $2,000

The consumer ranks all 24 such descriptions in terms of his or her preference for those combinations of features. Based on these preference ranks, sophisticated computer programs derive the relative importance consumers assign to each level of each attribute tested.

For example, in Figure A–1, a consumer was asked to rank in terms of overall preference 24 different computer designs featuring different levels of four key evaluative criteria. The preferences were then analyzed in light of the variations in the attributes. The result is a preference curve for each evaluative criterion that reflects the importance of that attribute. For example, processor is a particularly important evaluative criterion for this consumer while an integrated modem is of almost no importance.

Conjoint analysis is limited to the attributes listed by the researcher. Thus, a conjoint analysis of soft-drink attributes would not indicate anything about calorie content unless the researcher listed it as a feature. The Sunbeam study did not test such attributes as

FIGURE A–1	Using Conjoint Analysis to Determine the Importance of Evaluative Criteria for a Computer

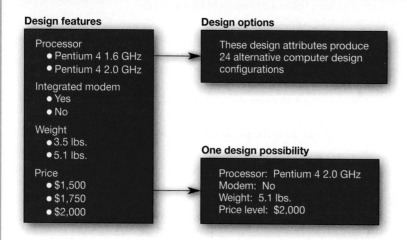

Design features

Processor
- Pentium 4 1.6 GHz
- Pentium 4 2.0 GHz

Integrated modem
- Yes
- No

Weight
- 3.5 lbs.
- 5.1 lbs.

Price
- $1,500
- $1,750
- $2,000

Design options

These design attributes produce 24 alternative computer design configurations

One design possibility

Processor: Pentium 4 2.0 GHz
Modem: No
Weight: 5.1 lbs.
Price level: $2,000

Consumer preferences

Price

Preference

Weight

Preference

Integrated modem

Preference

Processor

Preference

Relative importance

Evaluative criteria	Importance
Processor	45%
Modem	5
Weight	25
Price	25

■ Processor is the most important feature in this example, and Pentium 4 2.0 GHz is the preferred option.

■ While price and weight are also important, price becomes important only between $1,750 and $2,000.

brand name, color, weight, or safety features. If an important attribute is omitted, incorrect market share predictions are likely to result. In addition, conjoint analysis is not well suited for measuring the importance of emotional or feeling-based product choices. For example, what types of attributes would you use to perform a conjoint analysis of perfumes?

Appendix B
Consumer Behavior Audit*

In this appendix, we provide a list of key questions to guide you in developing marketing strategy from a consumer behavior perspective. This audit is no more than a checklist to minimize the chance of overlooking a critical behavioral dimension. It does not guarantee a successful strategy. However, thorough and insightful answers to these questions should greatly enhance the likelihood of a successful marketing program.

Our audit is organized around the key decisions that marketing managers must make. The first key decision is the selection of the target market(s) to be served. This is followed by the determination of a viable product position for each target market. Finally, the marketing mix elements—product, place, price, and promotion—must be structured in a manner consistent with the desired product position. This process is illustrated in Figure B–1.

MARKET SEGMENTATION

Market segmentation is the process of dividing all possible users of a product into groups that have similar needs the products might satisfy. Market segmentation should be done prior to the final development of a new product. In addition, a complete market segmentation analysis should be performed periodically for existing products. The reason for continuing segmentation analyses is the dynamic nature of consumer needs.

A. External influences
   1. Are there cultures or subcultures whose value system is particularly consistent (or inconsistent) with the consumption of our product?
   2. Is our product appropriate for male or female consumption? Will ongoing gender-role changes affect who consumes our product or how it is consumed?
   3. Do ethnic, social, regional, or religious subcultures have different consumption patterns relevant to our product?
   4. Do various demographic or social-strata groups (age, gender, urban/suburban/rural, occupation, income, education) differ in their consumption of our product?
   5. Is our product particularly appropriate for consumers with relatively high (or low) incomes compared to others in their occupational group (ROCI)?
   6. Can our product be particularly appropriate for specific roles, such as students or professional women?
   7. Would it be useful to focus on specific adopter categories?
   8. Do groups in different stages of the household life cycle have different consumption patterns for our product? Who in the household is involved in the purchase process?

*Revised by Richard Pomazal of Wheeling Jesuit College.

FIGURE B–1   Consumer Influences Drive Marketing Decisions

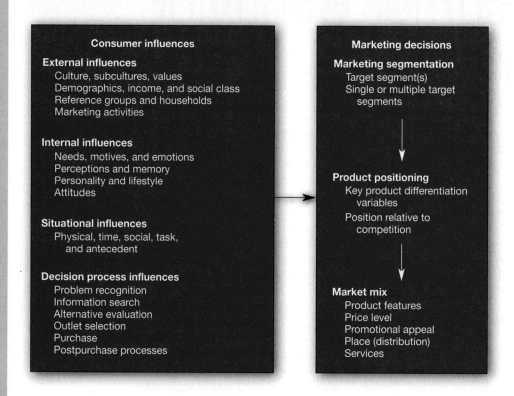

B. Internal influences
1. Can our product satisfy different needs or motives in different people? What needs are involved? What characterizes individuals with differing motives?
2. Is our product uniquely suited for particular personality types? Self-concepts?
3. What emotions, if any, are affected by the purchase and/or consumption of this product?
4. Is our product appropriate for one or more distinct lifestyles?
5. Do different groups have different attitudes about an ideal version of our product?
C. Situational influences
1. Can our product be appropriate for specific types of situations instead of (or in addition to) specific types of people?
D. Decision process influences
1. Do different individuals use different evaluative criteria in selecting the product?
2. Do potential customers differ in their loyalty to existing products/brands?

PRODUCT POSITION

A product position is the way the consumer thinks of a given product/brand relative to competing products/brands. A manager must determine what a desirable product position would be for each market segment of interest. This determination is generally based on the answers to the same questions used to segment a market, with the addition of the consumer's perceptions of competing products/brands. Of course, the capabilities and motivations of existing and potential competitors must also be considered.

A. Internal influences
    1. What is the general semantic memory structure for this product category in each market segment?
    2. What is the ideal version of this product in each market segment for the situations the firm wants to serve?
B. Decision process influences
    1. Which evaluative criteria are used in the purchase decision? Which decision rules and importance weights are used?

PRICING

The manager must set a pricing policy that is consistent with the desired product position. Price must be broadly conceived as everything a consumer must surrender to obtain a product. This includes time and psychological costs as well as monetary costs.

A. External influences
    1. Does the segment hold any values relating to any aspect of pricing, such as the use of credit or conspicuous consumption?
    2. Does the segment have sufficient income, after covering living expenses, to afford the product?
    3. Is it necessary to lower price to obtain a sufficient relative advantage to ensure diffusion? Will temporary price reductions induce product trial?
    4. Who in the household evaluates the price of the product?
B. Internal influences
    1. Will price be perceived as an indicator of status?
    2. Is economy in purchasing this type of product relevant to the lifestyle(s) of the segment?
    3. Is price an important aspect of the segment's attitude toward the brands in the product category?
    4. What is the segment's perception of a fair or reasonable price for this product?
C. Situational influences
    1. Does the role of price vary with the type of situation?
D. Decision process factors
    1. Can a low price be used to trigger problem recognition?
    2. Is price an important evaluative criterion? What decision rule is applied to the evaluative criteria used? Is price likely to serve as a surrogate indicator of quality?
    3. Are consumers likely to respond to in-store price reductions?

DISTRIBUTION STRATEGY

The manager must develop a distribution strategy that is consistent with the selected product position. This involves the selection of outlets if the item is a physical product, or the location of the outlets if the product is a service.
A. External influences
    1. What values do the segments have that relate to distribution?
    2. Do the male and female members of the segments have differing requirements of the distribution system? Do working couples, single individuals, or single parents within the segment have unique needs relating to product distribution?

3. Can the distribution system capitalize on reference groups by serving as a means for individuals with common interests to get together?
4. Is the product complex such that a high-service channel is required to ensure its diffusion?

B. Internal influences
1. Will the selected outlets be perceived in a manner that enhances the desired product position?
2. What type of distribution system is consistent with the lifestyle(s) of each segment?
3. What attitudes does each segment hold with respect to the various distribution alternatives?

C. Situational influences
1. Do the desired features of the distribution system vary with the situation?

D. Decision process factors
1. What outlets are in the segment's evoked set? Will consumers in this segment seek information in this type of outlet?
2. Which evaluative criteria does this segment use to evaluate outlets? Which decision rule?
3. Is the outlet selected before, after, or simultaneously with the product/brand? To what extent are product decisions made in the retail outlet?

PROMOTION STRATEGY

The manager must develop a promotion strategy, including advertising, nonfunctional package design features, publicity, promotions, and sales force activities that are consistent with the product position.

A. External factors
1. What values does the segment hold that can be used in our communications? Which should be avoided?
2. How can we communicate to our chosen segments in a manner consistent with the emerging gender-role perceptions of each segment?
3. What is the nonverbal communication system of each segment?
4. How, if at all, can we use reference groups in our advertisements?
5. Can our advertisements help make the product part of one or more role-related product clusters?
6. Can we reach and influence opinion leaders?
7. If our product is an innovation, are there diffusion inhibitors that can be overcome by promotion?
8. Who in the household should receive what types of information concerning our product?

B. Internal factors
1. Have we structured our promotional campaign such that each segment will be exposed to it, attend to it, and interpret it in the manner we desire?
2. Have we made use of the appropriate learning principles so that our meaning will be remembered?
3. Do our messages relate to the purchase motives held by the segment? Do they help reduce motivational conflict if necessary?
4. Are we considering the emotional implications of the ad and/or the use of our product?

5. Is the lifestyle portrayed in our advertisements consistent with the desired lifestyle of the selected segments?
6. If we need to change attitudes via our promotion mix, have we selected and properly used the most appropriate attitude-change techniques?

C. Situational influences
1. Does our campaign illustrate the full range of appropriate usage situations for the product?

D. Decision process influences
1. Will problem recognition occur naturally, or must it be activated by advertising? Should generic or selective problem recognition be generated?
2. Will the segment seek out or attend to information on the product prior to problem recognition, or must we reach them when they are not seeking our information? Can we use low-involvement learning processes effectively? What information sources are used?
3. After problem recognition, will the segment seek out information on the product/brand, or will we need to intervene in the purchase decision process? If they do seek information, what sources do they use?
4. What types of information are used to make a decision?
5. How much and what types of information are acquired at the point of purchase?
6. Is postpurchase dissonance likely? Can we reduce it through our promotional campaign?
7. Have we given sufficient information to ensure proper product use?
8. Are the expectations generated by our promotional campaign consistent with the product's performance?
9. Are our messages designed to encourage repeat purchases, brand loyal purchases, or neither?

PRODUCT

The marketing manager must be certain that the physical product, service, or idea has the characteristics required to achieve the desired product position in each market segment.

A. External influences
1. Is the product designed appropriately for all members of the segment under consideration, including males, females, and various age groups?
2. If the product is an innovation, does it have the required relative advantage and lack of complexity to diffuse rapidly?
3. Is the product designed to meet the varying needs of different household members?

B. Internal influences
1. Will the product be perceived in a manner consistent with the desired image?
2. Will the product satisfy the key purchase motives of the segment?
3. Is the product consistent with the segment's attitude toward an ideal product?

C. Situational influences
1. Is the product appropriate for the various potential usage situations?

D. Decision process influences
1. Does the product/brand perform better than the alternatives on the key set of evaluative criteria used by this segment?
2. Will the product perform effectively in the foreseeable uses to which this segment may subject it?
3. Will the product perform as well or better than expected by this segment?

CUSTOMER SATISFACTION AND COMMITMENT

Marketers must produce satisfied customers to be successful in the long run. It is often to a firm's advantage to go beyond satisfaction and create committed or loyal customers.

1. What factors lead to satisfaction with our product?
2. What factors could cause customer commitment to our brand or firm?

NAME INDEX

Stell, R., 622n
Stephens, N., 148n, 657n
Stern, B. B., 311n, 584n, 623n
Sternthal, B., 311n, 349n, 382n, 496n
Stevenson, J. S., 417n
Stevenson, T. H., 419n, 736n
Stewart, D. W., 313n, 349n, 351n, 656n
Stiving, M., 622n
Stoddard, J. E., 701n
Stojack, C., 656n
Stone, G., 553n
Strahilevitz, M. A., 108n, 450n
Strauss, J., 657n
Strauss, K., 310n
Street, P., 362, 403, 426
Stuart, E. W., 313n
Stuenkel, J. K., 496n
Stutts, M. A., 735n
Subharshan, D., 259n
Suh, J., 657n
Suh, Y., 584n
Sujan, M., 109n, 148n, 220n, 221n,
    260n, 309n, 349n, 350n, 382n,
    418n, 450n, 553n, 583n,
    655n, 700n
Sullivan, G. L., 419n
Sullivan, M. S., 351n
Sun, B., 621n
Sun, D., 51
Sundaram, D. S., 260n, 553n
Supphellen, M., 350n
Suri, R., 381n
Suro, R., 107n, 185n
Suter, T. A., 621n
Swait, J., 583n
Swan, I. E., 657n
Swan, J. E., 657n, 701n
Swayne, L. E., 419n, 622n
Sweeney, J. C., 621n, 655, 655n, 656n
Swinyard, W. R., 497n, 594
Swiss, D. J., 109n
Swoopes, S., 79, 242
Szmigin, I., 148n
Szymanski, D. M., 656n, 657n
Szymanski, K., 348n

T

Tagg, S., 418n
Tai, S. H. C., 75n, 451n
Talmadge, C., 620n
Talpade, S., 220n
Talukdar, D., 552n
Tam, D. D. C., 220n

Tam, J. L. M., 75n, 451n
Tan, C. T., 75n
Tan, J., 313n
Tang, C. S., 621n
Tansey, R., 107n
Tansuhaj, P., 220n, 700n
Tantillo, J., 313n
Tarn, D. D. C., 75n
Tax, S. S., 658n
Taylor, A., III, 620n
Taylor, C., 74n
Taylor, C. P., 185n, 186n
Taylor, C. R., 75n, 77n, 736n
Taylor, G. A., 185n
Taylor, K. A., 108n, 656n
Taylor, R. D., 553n
Taylor, S., 656n
Taylor, W., 380n, 382n
Teas, P. K., 350n
Teinowitz, I., 273, 735n, 736n
Tellis, G.-J., 621n
Tennis, B. M., 312n
Ter Hofstede, F., 75n, 76n, 77n
Thakor, M. V., 656n
Tham, L. L., 349n
Tharp, M. C., 186n, 310n
Thau, R., 187n
Theus, K. T., 311n
Thomas, E. G., 149n
Thomas, K. M., 185n
Thomas, R. J., 658n
Thomas, S., 450n
Thompson, A. M., 451n
Thompson, B., 418n
Thompson, C. J., 109n, 584n
Thompson, G. J., 220n, 623n,
    655n, 657n
Thompson, K. N., 701n
Thompson, S., 219n, 310n, 350n, 382n,
    584n, 735n, 736n
Thorson, E., 417n
Tian, K. T., 381n
Till, B. D., 349n, 350n, 417n, 418n
Timmermans, H. J. P., 381n, 658n
Tiong, T. C., 75n
Titus, P. A., 552n
Tjernlund, A., 107n, 108n, 736n
Tokinoya, H., 75n
Tom, G., 312n, 348n, 656n
Toncar, M. F., 76n
Tong, L., 77n
Touil, N., 380n
Touiol, N., 312n
Trapp, P. S., 143

Trappey, C. V., 310n, 311n,
    350n, 737n
Treise, D., 497n
Trifts, V., 584n
Tripett, T., 658n
Triplett, T., 108n, 382n
Tripp, C., 418n
Trivedi, M., 381n, 520n
Trocchia, P. J., 107n, 620n
Trosclair, C., 349n
Tse, A. C. B., 309n, 417n
Tse, D. K., 656n
Tsiros, M., 655n, 656n
Tucciarone, J. D., 377, 383n
Tucker, W. T., 35n
Tully, S., 77n
Turley, L. W., 349n, 621n, 657n
Tybout, A. M., 417n

U

Ulgado, F. M., 75n, 76n, 584n
Unnava, H. R., 312n, 349n, 382n, 496n
Urbany, J. E., 261n, 552n, 584n, 622n
Ursic, M. L., 584n, 585n
Uscategui, K. H., 657n

V

Vakratsas, D., 349n
van Dolen, W., 382n
Van Kenhove, P., 496n
Van Meurs, L., 309n
Van Osselaer, S. M. J., 348n,
    351n, 584n
Van Trijp, H. C. M., 380n, 521n
Van Waterschoot, W., 496n
van Witteloostuijn, A., 381n
Vanacker, B., 381n
VanderPlaat, P., 657n
Vanhuele, M., 350n
Vavra, T. G., 659n
Velliquette, A. M., 450n
Venkataramani, G., 350n
Venkatesh, R., 450n
Venkatraman, M. P., 553n
Ventakesh, R., 700n
Verity, J. W., 658n, 701n
Verlegh, P. W. J., 584n
Veryzer, R. W., 381n
Vincent, L., 623n
Viswanathan, M., 75n, 221n, 311n
Vladeck, D. C., 313n
von Gonten, M. F., 310n
Voss, G. B., 656n, 659n

CASE INDEX

SUBJECT INDEX